Microsoft® Office Communications Server 2007 R2 Resource Kit

Rui Maximo, Rick Kingslan, Rajesh Ramanathan, Nirav Kamdar
with the Microsoft Office Communications Server Team

PUBLISHED BY
Microsoft Press
A Division of Microsoft Corporation
One Microsoft Way
Redmond, Washington 98052-6399

Library of Congress Control Number: 2008940502

Printed and bound in the United States of America.

2 3 4 5 6 7 8 9 QWT 4 3 2 1 0 9

Distributed in Canada by H.B. Fenn and Company Ltd.

A CIP catalogue record for this book is available from the British Library.

Microsoft Press books are available through booksellers and distributors worldwide. For further information about international editions, contact your local Microsoft Corporation office or contact Microsoft Press International directly at fax (425) 936-7329. Visit our Web site at www.microsoft.com/mspress. Send comments to mspinput@microsoft.com.

Acquisitions Editor: Martin DelRe
Developmental Editor: Karen Szall
Project Editor: Victoria Thulman
Editorial Production: Custom Editorial Productions, Inc.
Technical Reviewer: Rick Kingslan, LJ Zacker; Technical Review services provided by Content Master, a member of CM Group, Ltd.
Cover: Tom Draper Design

Body Part No. X15-28142

Contents at a Glance

Contents

Foreword

Microsoft Office Communications Server simplifies the mechanics of communicating with others and broadens the potential for interactive collaboration. Our team's vision is to simplify and integrate the possible modes of communication into a seamless experience that centers on the person you want to interact with and the type of communication you want to have. This paradigm shift is the new world of Unified Communications.

Office Communications Server 2007 was a significant step forward in streamlined, integrated communications with unified presence, voice, instant messaging (IM), e-mail, and Web conferencing. Office Communications Server 2007 R2 delivers the next generation of Unified Communications with greater integration and richer features:

- **Call delegation** A user can manage calls on behalf of another user.
- **Team ring** Incoming calls can be forwarded to each member of a team.
- **Response Group Service** Administrators can create response groups for routing and queuing incoming phone calls to designated people.
- **Group Chat** Users can engage in persisted, ongoing IM conversations within chat rooms.
- **Dial-in Conferencing** Users can join an audio/video conference by dialing a number from any Public Switched Telephone Network (PSTN) phone.
- **Desktop Sharing** Windows users can share their computer desktops with other , including those running Apple and Linux operating systems.
- **SIP Trunking Support** Enterprises can connect their voice network to a PSTN via an Internet telephony service provider.
- **Mobility** Office Communicator Mobile users can communicate using presence, IM, and voice.
- **Enhanced Media** High Definition (HD) and VGA video support for peer-to-peer calls as well as improved resiliency and voice quality for all calls.
- **Enhanced Developer Platform** Richer application programming interfaces (APIs) to enable developers to do more with Office Communications Server and Visual Studio integration to enable faster/simpler development.

With this new edition of the *Office Communications Server Resource Kit*, Rui Maximo, Rick Kingslan, Rajesh Ramanathan, and Nirav Kamdar, along with 18 Microsoft insiders from the product, user assistance, and field teams, reveal the technical depth, scenarios, and diagnostic techniques specific to the Microsoft Office Communications Server 2007 R2 product. The *Microsoft Office Communications Server 2007 R2 Resource Kit* is the result of their efforts over the past year in pushing the first edition to a new higher standard. Rather than simply update the first edition, the project team rebuilt the book from the ground up, putting each chapter through extensive customer and peer review, removing extraneous content, adding important new content, ensuring that the information is readily understandable, and driving consistency and coherency across the 22 chapters. A special thanks to Susan Bradley for driving both editions of the Resource Kit to progressively high standards.

This book not only details the new features, it also adds five new chapters that delve into topics that are most important to customers, such as voice mail, Private Branch eXchange (PBX) integration (dual forking and Direct Session Initiation Protocol [SIP]), and client deployment. You'll also notice many new sidebars in this edition, with even more tips from the field and in-depth information from the product team. An updated troubleshooting chapter offers detailed examples and techniques. In addition, you'll find updated scripts that are easier to use and more easily customizable for your individual needs.

The first edition of the *Microsoft Office Communications Server 2007 Resource Kit* introduced Office Communications Server to those who were new to the product, and it provided a reference for experts who needed details about how the product works. The first edition of the Resource Kit was so successful that every new employee in the Microsoft Office Communications Server group now receives a copy. It has shown itself to be an important tool for customers, consultants, and our own developers. I hope that you will find this newest edition of the Resource Kit to be an indispensible tool that enables you to get the most out of Microsoft Office Communications Server 2007 R2. And as always, we look forward to your feedback for the next edition.

—Gurdeep Singh Pall
Corporate Vice President, Office Communications Group, Microsoft Corporation

Acknowledgments

The authors of *Microsoft Office Communications Server 2007 R2 Resource Kit* want to thank the numerous members of the Office Communications Server product team and other key contributors who helped make this second edition of the Resource Kit as comprehensive and accurate as possible. These people have contributed their time and effort to this project in several important ways, which include:

- Reviewing each chapter for technical accuracy and completeness.
- Providing sidebars that bring the product to life with descriptions of real world implementations or in-depth information on how certain features work.
- Providing auxiliary content and PowerShell functions for the CD, which enhances the usability of the book.
- Providing project management, technical management, lab management, and editorial support.
- Providing vision, leadership, advice, encouragement, resource support, and funding.

We acknowledge and thank the following product experts for their extensive and invaluable technical reviews. If we have forgotten anyone, please forgive us!

Albert Jee
Ali Rohani
Allen Brokken
Allen Sudbring
Amey Parandekar
Antenehe Temteme
Brian R, Ricks
Byron Spurlock
Chermaine Li
Daniel Glenn
Dhigha Sekaran
Drew Baldacci
Eric Wentz
Frédéric Dubut
Geoff Winslow
Grant Bolitho
Hao Yan
Huiwen Ru
Jason D. Richardson
Jean Ross
Jens Trier Rasmussen
John T. Young
Josh Jones
Keith Hanna
Lee Jarvie
Mahendra Sekaran

Maor Kashansky
Mark Corneglio
Matthew Fresoli
Mike Warren
Nick Smith
Nirav Kamdar
Patrick Kelley
Pauline Batthish
Peter Schmatz
Pradipta Kumar Basu
R. Lee Mackey Jr.
Radu Constantinescu
Rajesh Ramanathan
Rajmohan Rajagopalan
Ralph H. Elmerick
Rick Kingslan
Robert Cameron
Roger Keller
Rui Maximo
Sasa Juratovic
Satya Kondepudi
Scott Willis
Sean Olson
Stephane Cavin
Stephanie Pierce
Steven Van Houttum
Sunil Kasturi
Thomas Laciano
Thomas Theiner
Thomas Wenzl
Tina Fan
Venky Venkateshaiah
Vinit Deshpande
Vlad Eminovici
Wajih Yahyaoui
Wenbo Shi

We acknowledge and thank the following product experts for their informative real-world sidebars. If we have forgotten anyone, please forgive us!

Adam Dudsic
Byron Spurlock
CJ Vermette
Conal Walsh
Geoff Winslow
Greg Stemp
Jens Trier Rasmussen
John Lamb
Mike Warren
Nick Smith
Padu Padmanabhan
Paul Tidwell
Peter Schmatz
R. Lee Mackey Jr.
Radu Constantinescu
Roger Keller
Salman Khalid
Sonu Aggarwal
Stephanie Pierce
Thomas Laciano
Vassili Kaplan

We acknowledge and thank the following key contributors, without whom this book would be a dream, rather than a reality.

Rui Maximo for his role as lead author and technical lead on this project. Rui worked with dedication and passion, reviewing each chapter draft to ensure technical accuracy, logical presentation, consistent level and approach, cohesion, and coherence across 22 writers, 50+ technical reviewers, and 22 chapters. The enormity of this undertaking and its successful execution awes and humbles us.

Rick Kingslan for his role as tireless, optimistic champion and angel (in times of dire need). In addition, Rick was the book's technical reviewer and thus spent numerous hours testing procedures and identifying errors so that we can now ensure this book is an accurate and comprehensive resource for our customers.

James O'Neill for his role as developer of more than 100 Windows PowerShell functions for the CD, all of which he reviewed, tested, and updated to conform to the newest best practices. These functions demonstrate how an Office Communications Server environment can be administered using PowerShell commands. James completed this work while travelling extensively as an IT Pro Evangelist, making him our hero. Thank you, James, for being such a dedicated customer advocate.

James O'Neill, **Mitch Duncan,** and **Rick Kingslan** for their long hours and commitment in testing the PowerShell functions. Their goal was to ensure that the functions work perfectly for the many users who found them to be an invaluable aid in the first version of the Resource Kit and for those who have yet to discover how effective these functions really are.

Diane Forsyth for her role as glossary editor. Thanks to Diane's determined and effective efforts across the team, this version of the Resource Kit now has an extensive list of key terms and definitions.

Janet Lowen for her role as technical editor. Thanks to Janet, authors who needed assistance received an extra level of editorial support. In addition, Janet was instrumental in helping us complete the long list of tasks that went into finalizing the Resource Kit.

Mitch Duncan for his role in creating and managing the lab environment and art process. Mitch's efforts ensured that all screenshots in the book reflect the final product build.

Patricia Anderson, Office Communications Group User Assistance Senior Content Publishing Manager, for believing in the value of this book and for allocating writers from her team in our time of dire need.

Remco Stroeken, Senior Product Manager, for his belief in the importance of this book, and for providing the funding needed to create the second edition.

Susan S. Bradley, our tireless, fearless Project Manager, who managed this project from inception to delivery. Try convincing a large group of volunteers with full-time jobs to work for you during their personal time; then you will begin to understand the magnitude of the challenges Susan had to overcome. Without her leadership and perseverance, we would be trying to write this book still. Her humor and good will (and infectious laugh!) were instrumental in managing the stress of this project. On behalf of all the authors, thank you for leading us to the finish line!

Martin DelRe, Microsoft Learning Program Manager, who championed and supported this book and this project team from the first version. Without Martin's vision and continuing support, the *Office Communications Server 2007 R2 Resource Kit* would not exist.

Tim Toyoshima, Office Communications Group User Assistance Principal Group Manager, for his role as cross-team project sponsor and ever resourceful champion of providing customers with the product information they need. Without Tim's vision, leadership, and continuing support, the *Office Communications Server 2007 R2 Resource Kit* would not exist.

We also thank our outstanding and dedicated editorial team at Microsoft Learning, including **Karen Szall**, our Development Editor, and **Victoria Thulman**, our Project Editor. Their dedication and tireless effort were key to the successful delivery of this book. Thanks also to **Custom Editorial Productions, Inc.**, who handled the production aspects of this book and to **Sarah Wales-McGrath**, our copy editor.

—The Author Team

Personal Acknowledgements

Rui Maximo To my wife, Anne, and my kids, Marie, Mathew, Chloe, thank you for being by my side. As the lead author, I want to thank every author and sidebar contributor who had to endure my feedback through multiple rigorous reviews. Thank you for giving me the opportunity to shape and influence this book in more profound ways. To Susan Bradley, your enthusiasm and expertise in managing this project was indispensable in keeping this book on task. To Rick Kingslan, you've been a great partner working side-by-side. To Tim Toyoshima, Martin DelRe, and Remco Stroeken, thank you for believing in and sponsoring us. To the product group and our reviewers, without your collaboration this book wouldn't have been possible.

Rick Kingslan This has been an incredible journey. But not a journey alone. I want to thank my wife, Sue, who put up with long hours of writing, reviewing, and helping others on the team. Not to mention 3 years of local and international travel while I was in U.S. Services. Kristin, Amanda—yes, Dad still loves you! Also, to my son Mark, daughter-in-law Jessica, and grandson Andrew. You guys are awesome. Mark, Semper Fi! Keep your pilots and mates in the Black Knights fighter squadron safe. And Mom, thank you for everything over the past 49 years. To Nick Smith, best Unified Communications consultant I know. Thank you for the hard work on my behalf, showing me where I was wrong and being my constant second set of eyes. Rui my friend, my comrade in arms. You and I fought and argued, laughed, cried (you did . . .over my chapters), but in the end, I would not have traded this for anything. I am better for everyone that I have met since starting with Microsoft. This is *the* place to work.

Rajesh Ramanathan My contributions to this book would not have been possible without unstinting support from my family, especially my wife, Sudha, who made sure that Radha (5) and Varun (1) kept themselves busy with things other than my notebook computer while I wrote the chapters. Thanks Sudha and kids for making this happen. A couple of other people that deserve praise for their dedicated effort are Rui Maximo and Rick Kingslan, who painstakingly reviewed each and every word that I wrote, and Susan Bradley and Victoria Thulman, who had to put up with my tight schedules and schedule slips. And special thanks to all the peer reviewers from the product team. You folks have made writing this book a pleasure and have done a great job in motivating, reviewing, and coordinating this book.

Nirav Kamdar I would like to thank my reviewers Tina Fan, Byron Spurlock, and R. Lee Mackey Jr. for providing valuable feedback. Thanks to Adam Dudsic for compiling and providing content for the CD for my chapter. Thanks also to Rui Maximo and Susan Bradley for all the effort they put into this book and for making sure every chapter was delivered on time. And most important of all, I would like to thank my wonderful wife Rinki and sons Arnav and Arush for their understanding and support through the many weekday nights and weekends that I spent writing my chapters.

Introduction

Welcome to the *Microsoft Office Communications Server 2007 R2 Resource Kit!*

The *Microsoft Office Communications Server 2007 R2 Resource Kit* is the second edition of the most in-depth, comprehensive book ever written on Microsoft Office Communications Server: *Microsoft Office Communications Server 2007 Resource Kit*. This new edition builds on the deep technical information presented in the first edition, with an emphasis on planning, deploying, configuring, maintaining, and troubleshooting Microsoft Office Communications Server 2007 R2. The Microsoft author team not only updated the content with the latest insider information on Office Communications Server 2007 R2, but also reviewed a wealth of customer feedback and reviews from the first edition, which resulted in a focused effort to improve and add information on the topics customers need most. Each chapter of this new edition is substantially revised and updated. In addition, there are five new chapters. We hope you find this edition of the Resource Kit even more pertinent and usable than the first edition. Our commitment is to continue delivering the best content on future versions of Office Communications Server.

Although the target audience for this Resource Kit is experienced IT professionals who work in medium- and large-size organizations, anyone who wants to learn how to deploy, configure, support, and troubleshoot Office Communications Server 2007 R2 will find this Resource Kit invaluable. Within this Resource Kit, you will find in-depth information and task-based guidance on managing all aspects of Office Communications Server 2007 R2, including instant messaging (IM), Web conferencing with audio and video support, remote access, federation, public IM connectivity (PIC), Remote Call Control (RCC), dual forking, Enterprise Voice (using Voice over Internet Protocol, or VoIP), voice mail, and Enterprise Voice applications. You will encounter troubleshooting techniques and diagnostic tools to help you successfully deploy and monitor Office Communications Server. You will also find numerous sidebars contributed by members of the Unified Communications product team and Microsoft consultants, which provide deep insight into how Office Communications Server 2007 R2 works, plus best practices.

Finally, the companion CD includes additional tools, documentation, and a Windows PowerShell script that offers you a way to automate various aspects of managing Office Communications Server 2007 R2 from the command line.

Overview of the Book

The five parts of this book cover the following topics:

- **Part I: Overview and Architecture** Provides an overview of the new features in Office Communications Server 2007 R2, describes the usages for the different server roles, and considers the infrastructure and security required for an Office Communications Server 2007 R2 deployment.
- **Part II: Key Usage Scenarios** Describes in-depth the scenarios that the real-time features in Office Communications Server 2007 R2 offer and the technical details behind them.
- **Part III: Planning and Deployment** Provides guidance on how to plan an Office Communications Server 2007 R2 deployment through a specific example.
- **Part IV: Operations and Administration** Describes how to administer, monitor, back up, and restore Office Communications Server and manage the clients for Office Communications Server 2007 R2.
- **Part V: Technical Troubleshooting and Diagnostics** Provides in-depth information on diagnostics tools and how to troubleshoot Office Communications Server 2007 R2. To proficiently troubleshoot issues with Office Communications Server, it is helpful to understand the fundamentals of SIP routing and authentication.

The book also includes a reference glossary, as well as four appendices on various topics, all of which are included on the companion CD.

Document Conventions

The following conventions are used in this book to highlight special features or usage.

Reader Aids

The following reader aids are used throughout this book to point out useful details.

READER AID	MEANING
Note	Underscores the importance of a specific concept or highlights a special case that might not apply to every situation.
Important	Calls attention to essential information that should not be disregarded.
Caution	Warns you that failure to take or avoid a specified action can cause serious problems for users, systems, data integrity, and so on.
On the CD	Calls attention to a related script, tool, template, or job aid on the companion CD that helps you perform a task described in the text.

Sidebars

The following sidebars are used throughout this book to provide added insight, tips, and advice concerning different Office Communications Server features.

SIDEBAR	MEANING
Direct from the Source	Contributed by experts at Microsoft to provide "from-the-source" insight into how Office Communications Server works, best practices for managing Office Communications Server clients, and troubleshooting tips.
Real World	Contributed by experts to share best practices and lessons learned when deploying and supporting Office Communications Server.

IMPORTANT! **Sidebars are provided by individuals in the industry as examples for informational purposes only and may not represent the views of their employers. No warranties, express, implied, or statutory, are made as to the information provided in sidebars.**

Command-line Examples

The following style conventions are used in documenting command-line examples throughout this book.

STYLE	MEANING
Bold font	Used to indicate user input (characters that you type exactly as shown).
Italic font	Used to indicate variables for which you need to supply a specific value (for example, *file_name* can refer to any valid file name).
Monospace font	Used for code samples and command-line output.
%SystemRoot%	Used for environment variables.

Companion CD

The companion CD is a valuable addition to this book and includes the following:

- **Glossary**
- **Appendix A,** "Using the Windows Powershell Functions"
- **Appendix B,** "Numeric Ranges for Availability and Activity Levels in Office Communicator"
- **Appendix C,** "Direct SIP with IP-PBX in Office Communications Server 2007 R2"
- **Appendix D,** "Troubleshooting External Audio/Video Call Failures"
- **Windows PowerShell scripts** PowerShell functions for automating Office Communications Server 2007 R2 administrative tasks
- **eBook** An electronic version of the entire *Microsoft Office Communications Server 2007 R2 Resource Kit*
- **Links** Links to valuable resources referenced in the book chapters
- **Bonus Content** Sample chapters from more than 15 Windows Server 2008 titles from Microsoft Press as well as the full eBook of *Understanding Microsoft Virtualization Solutions*

Full documentation of the contents and structure of the companion CD can be found in the Readme.txt file on the CD.

Digital Content for Digital Book Readers: If you bought a digital-only edition of this book, you can enjoy select content from the print edition's companion CD.
Visit **http://go.microsoft.com/fwlink/?LinkId=139455** to get your downloadable content. This content is always up-to-date and available to all readers.

Find Additional Content Online

As new or updated material becomes available that complements this book, it will be posted online on the Microsoft Press Online Windows Server and Client Web site. The type of material you might find includes updates to book content, articles, links to companion content, errata, sample chapters, and more. This Web site is available at *www.microsoft.com/learning/books/online/serverclient*, and it is updated periodically.

Resource Kit Support Policy

Every effort has been made to ensure the accuracy of this book and the companion CD content. Microsoft Press provides corrections to this book through the Web at the following location:

http://www.microsoft.com/learning/support/search.asp

If you have comments, questions, or ideas regarding the book or companion CD content, or if you have questions that are not answered by querying the Knowledge Base, please send them to Microsoft Press by using either of the following methods:

E-mail: *rkinput@microsoft.com*

Postal Mail:

Microsoft Press
Attn: *Microsoft Office Communications Server 2007 R2 Resource Kit,* Editor
One Microsoft Way
Redmond, WA 98052-6399

Please note that product support is not offered through the preceding mail addresses. For product support information, please visit the Microsoft Product Support Web site at the following address:

http://support.microsoft.com

PART I

Overview and Architecture

CHAPTER 1

Overview of Office Communications Server 2007 R2

Microsoft Office Communications Server 2007 R2 is an enterprise server product that combines corporate instant messaging (IM), presence, federation, conferencing, group chat, group response, an attendant console, and telephony (Voice over IP, or VoIP) in a fully integrated Unified Communications (UC) solution. It can integrate with existing Private Branch eXchange (PBX) infrastructures to leverage the investment in communications that organizations have already made.

If the customer has invested in Microsoft Exchange Server 2007, integration with Exchange enhances the overall offering with the ability to enable Exchange to act as a voice mail solution—the Exchange user can receive voice mail anywhere that she can receive Exchange mail. Adding Speech Server 2007 further enhances the overall offering and provides a rich development platform for extending beyond the feature sets delivered in the box.

Office Communications Server and Exchange together are referred to as Unified Communications (UC) and present a compelling solution for the small, medium, and large customer to augment or even replace an existing legacy PBX.

Office Communications Server Editions and Components

Office Communications Server 2007 R2 is available in two editions: Standard Edition (SE) and Enterprise Edition (EE). The SE Server is a single-server configuration, whereas the EE pool is a multiserver configuration that provides the same functionality as the SE Server with higher scalability and reliability.

An Enterprise front-end pool scales by building servers that are load balanced and provide enough resources for the required load for each of the necessary roles. Determining how many front-end servers per Enterprise pool will be needed is a planning exercise and is covered in depth in Chapter 14, "Planning Example." Planning is also made much easier because of the planning tool that uses metrics defined by the Office Communications product group. This tool assists in defining the number and configuration of servers to achieve the desired technical goals. This tool is discussed in Chapter 14 as well.

Both the SE and EE contain a number of server roles. Some must be deployed, and others are available upon installation of an Enterprise pool or SE Server.

The server roles located on an Enterprise pool front-end server or SE Server are:

- IM Conferencing and Presence
- Telephony Conferencing Server
- Unified Communications Application Server (UCAS)
- Web Components Server (requires an installation of Internet Information Server 6.x or 7.x)
- Web Conferencing Server
- Audio/Video (A/V) Conferencing Server
- Application Sharing Conferencing Server

> ***NOTE*** **The list of server roles on the front end assume that you are using the Setup Wizard. There are options to deploy separate Web Component, Web Conferencing, A/V Conferencing, and Application Sharing Servers, but only through the LCSCmd.exe tool. This is what is known as an expanded topology.**

A dedicated SQL Server back end is required for the EE. For high availability, the SQL Server can be configured as an active/passive cluster. SE deploys Microsoft SQL Server Express 2005 as part of the SE installation and cannot be clustered.

Optional servers that can be deployed for further function, performance, and compliance reasons are:

- **Archiving** Enables IM message logging and includes the ability to collect Call Detail Records (CDRs)
- **Monitoring** Includes Quality of Experience (QoE)

- **Group Chat Server** Users can create and maintain a chat room where the discussions, files, and other collaboration that take place in the room are retained and are persistent, as well as secured to only the invited members of the room.

To enable Office Communications Server 2007 R2 for telephony, a Mediation Server is usually required to function as an intermediate between Office Communications Servers and the media gateway. Office Communications Server 2007 R2 also supports direct connectivity with a supported Internet Protocol (IP) PBX, called Direct Session Initiation Protocol (SIP). Office Communications Server 2007 R2 supports four different types of telephony configurations: Enterprise Voice (see Chapter 11, "VoIP Scenarios"), Remote Call Control (RCC; see Chapter 9, "Remote Call Control Scenarios"), dual forking (see Chapter 10, "Dual Forking Scenarios"), and RCC with dual forking (see Chapter 10).

Organizations can enable remote access for their users and federation with other organizations that have deployed Microsoft Live Communications Server 2005 Service Pack 1 (SP1), Microsoft Office Communications Server 2007, and Office Communications Server 2007 R2. To configure the Office Communications Server 2007 R2 Server for remote access and federation, an Edge Server is deployed in the perimeter network.

All roles will run on each of the consolidated Edge Servers, and more than one server is positioned behind hardware load balancers (HLBs). Multiple Edge Servers behind a hardware load balancer provide two direct benefits:

- **Scale** To provide more processing power to service more connections for the front-end pool servers
- **High availability** In the event a server should fail, more than one server provides for failover and recovery

The Evolution of Office Communications Server 2007 R2

Office Communications Server 2007 is the next iteration of a Microsoft product line that began with Microsoft Live Communications Server 2003 and 2005 and Office Communications Server 2007.

Live Communications Server 2003 introduced the availability of presence information that is updated automatically instead of requiring users to constantly update their status manually. This presence information was updated based on a variety of information, including user activity on the computer and calendar information from Microsoft Office Outlook. Live Communications Server 2003 also introduced corporate IM as a real-time means of communication. Presence and IM were incorporated into much of the Microsoft Office suite and servers, making them readily available to information workers. Specific examples of presence-aware Office applications and servers are Office Outlook and Microsoft Office SharePoint.

Live Communications Server 2005 SP1 expanded on the functionality offered by Live Communications Server 2003. Remote access, federation, and public IM connectivity (PIC) became available. Integration with PBXs enabled Microsoft Office Communicator 2005 to control the user's PBX phone by using the functionality of RCC, which is covered in Chapter 9. Phone activity was integrated into the user's presence so that it was possible to tell whether the user was on the phone.

Office Communications Server 2007 introduced a large set of new features since Live Communications Server 2005 SP1, where IM was the only mode of communication supported. In particular, Office Communications Server 2007 introduced support for IM conferencing where two or more people could partake in the conversation, Web Conferencing for the presentation and sharing of content or desktops, Audio/Video Conferencing for streaming video and audio, Enterprise Voice for internal VoIP calls and interoperability with IP PBX, and Public Switched Telephone Network (PSTN) for external calls.

New features of Office Communications Server 2007 R2 are discussed in Chapter 2, "New Features Overview," and in their respective content chapters.

Customizing the Platform

Office Communications Server 2007 R2 delivers Software Development Kits (SDKs) and application programming interfaces (APIs) that build on a successful history of enabling customers and third parties to enhance the platform. These SDKs and APIs enable a developer to build features and functions into the platform to deliver additional functionality, interoperability, and features over what Office Communications Server 2007 R2 delivers out of the box.

For optimal information for your development teams, please refer to the Microsoft Press book *Programming for Unified Communications*, forthcoming in Spring of 2009.

ON THE COMPANION MEDIA **Links to topics relevant to the information presented in this chapter are available on this book's companion media.**

Summary

Office Communications Server 2007 R2 is a significant upgrade that builds on the feature set of the previous release, Office Communications Server 2007. It provides a full set of real-time communications: IM, Web Conferencing, Audio/Video and VoIP, Group Chat, Group Response functionality, Attendant Console, Application Sharing, and an enhanced Microsoft Communicator Web Access. When Exchange 2007 integration is added, making the full ability for voice mail now just an e-mail away, Office Communications Server 2007 R2 is positioned to be a compelling end-to-end solution for all types of collaborative communications in the enterprise.

Additional Resources

- Office Communications Server 2007 R2 product home page, found at *http://go.microsoft.com/fwlink/?LinkID=133618*
- Office Communications Server 2007 R2 infrastructure requirements, found at *http://go.microsoft.com/fwlink/?LinkID=133602*
- Office Communications Server 2007 Release Notes, found at *http://go.microsoft.com/fwlink/?LinkID=133658*
- Office Communications Server 2007 Technical Library, found at *http://go.microsoft.com/fwlink/?LinkID=133654*
- Office Communications Server 2007 Documentation, found at *http://go.microsoft.com/fwlink/?LinkID=133654*
- Office Communications Server 2007 free evaluation download, found at *http://go.microsoft.com/fwlink/?LinkID=133620*
- Unified Communications Group Team Blog, found on Microsoft TechNet at *http://go.microsoft.com/fwlink/?LinkID=133659*

CHAPTER 2

New Features Overview

Microsoft Office Communications Server 2007 R2 introduces many new features, along with significant enhancements of existing functionality. This chapter provides an introduction to these new features and enhancements as well as a technical overview.

New Features

This first section of the chapter provides an overview of the new features and enhancements made to Office Communications Server 2007 R2 for voice, instant messaging (IM), and presence, as well as management and topology simplifications. The new features and enhancements include:

- Call Delegation
- Team Ring
- Group Chat
- Desktop sharing
- Server applications
- SIP trunking support
- Enhanced media
- Simplified firewall configuration for the A/V Edge Server
- Presence Enhancements
- Archiving, CDR, and Quality of Experience (QoE) Enhancements
- Simplified management

Call Delegation

The new Call Delegation feature in Office Communications Server 2007 R2 enables managers to delegate phone call handling to one or more administrative assistants or other delegates. When a delegate answers a call, the manager is notified that the call has been answered, along with the name of the delegate who answered.

Working in Microsoft Office Communicator 2007 R2, a manager selects a delegate from among the names in the manager's contact list and then selects Call-Forwarding Settings. The selected delegate uses the new Office Communicator 2007 R2 Attendant to handle calls for the manager.

Depending on the particular permissions that the manager delegates, the assistant can perform the following tasks:

- Screen person-to-person or conference calls on behalf of the manager. These calls can be audio only, audio and video, or audio and data.
- Join the voice portion of a conference on behalf of the manager.
- Listen to the manager's voice mail (if the manager has shared her Microsoft Office Outlook inbox).
- Place a person-to-person call on behalf of the manager.
- Initiate a conference call on the manager's behalf.
- Transfer calls to the manager.
- Modify the manager's call-forwarding settings.
- Search for contacts among the manager's shared Office Outlook contact list.
- Use a shortcut to transfer a call placed on behalf of another manager, such that the two managers speak directly to each other without having to first go through an assistant.
- Proxy remote user connections to the correct Standard Edition Server or Enterprise pool. This is necessary because remote user connections cannot be redirected.

These capabilities apply only to phone calls. The assistant cannot screen IM, IM conferences, or data-only calls.

The manager can also configure the following options from within the Communicator client:

- Designate a back-up assistant for times when the primary assistant is unavailable to handle his calls.
- Transfer a call to configured delegates, which are automatically placed on the Communicator 2007 R2 transfer menu.
- Share Outlook contacts with the assistant.

The following call delegation options are supported:

- One manager and one delegate
- One manager and multiple delegates
- Multiple managers and one delegate
- Multiple managers and multiple delegates

Team Ring

The new Team Ring feature in Office Communications Server 2007 R2 makes it possible to forward incoming calls to a defined team. When a team receives a forwarded call, each member's phone rings, and all members can see who forwarded the call. When a team member answers the call, the phones of all other members stop ringing.

The Team Ring feature is essentially a call-forwarding option that the team leader configures in Office Communicator 2007 R2. In the Call Forwarding Settings dialog box, the leader can set up a team, add members, and configure how calls are forwarded to other team members. Call team forwarding options include the following:

- **Ring Leader, Then Ring Team** A call forwarded to a team leader first rings the leader's phone for a specified number of seconds, and then it rings the phones of all team members. Each member can see who forwarded and accepted the call. After the call is answered, all team phones stop ringing.
- **Ring Leader And Team Simultaneously** A call forwarded to a team leader simultaneously rings the phones of all team members. After the call is answered, all team phones stop ringing.
- **Ring Team Only During Working Hours** A call forwarded to the team leader after working hours does not go to the team.
- **Ring Team When Leader Status Is Set To Do Not Disturb** If the leader's presence is set to Do Not Disturb, a call forwarded to the leader does not ring the leader's phone but automatically rings the phones of all other team members. After the call is answered, all team phones stop ringing. If the call is unanswered, it is forwarded to the leader's voice mail. If the caller has permission to break through to the leader, the leader's phone rings and the call is not forwarded to other team members.
- **Ring Team When Leader Status Is Set To Offline** If the leader's presence is set to Offline, a call forwarded to the leader does not ring the leader's phone but automatically rings the phones of all other team members. After the call is answered, all team phones stop ringing. If the call is unanswered, it is forwarded to the leader's voice mail.
- **Calls From Specific Callers Do Not Go To Team** Calls from contacts whom the leader has designated as Personal are never forwarded to team members.

Group Chat

Office Communications Server 2007 R2 Group Chat enables users to engage in persistent, ongoing IM conversations. Group Chat differs from Group IM in that the latter is not persistent. After a Group IM session has ended, its state is lost. With Office Communications Server 2007 R2 Group Chat, however, the conversation persists, along with all IM, files, Web links, and other associated data. This persistence makes it possible to maintain complete records of each session. It enables the instant exchange of business expertise across an organization and with external partners in a way that makes it possible to maintain a continuing flow of information among project members.

Group Chat requires deploying three components that are new with Office Communications Server 2007 R2:

- **Office Communications Server 2007 R2 Group Chat Server** Gives users access to Group Chat functionality.
- **The Office Communications Server 2007 R2 Group Chat Administration Tool** Enables an Office Communications Server administrator or delegate to manage chat rooms and users. An administrator can create categories and group channels, define their scope and membership, manage how users can use the group channels, and specify which users are administrators and managers.
- **Office Communicator 2007 R2 Group Chat** A desktop client application that makes chat room conversations and features available to end users and that enables users to send and receive IM, either in a chat room or singly with another user outside the chat room. To use chat rooms, this component must be installed in addition to Office Communicator.

With Office Communications Server 2007 R2 Group Chat, end users can perform the following tasks:

- Create a chat room, which is a persistent topic that users can join
- Restrict chat room access to selected users
- View all chat rooms in which the user is a member
- Join a chat room
- View and read messages posted to a chat room
- Post messages to a chat room
- Post Web links in a chat room
- Receive notifications when a user is added to a chat room or contact list
- Customize the chat room display
- Log chat room content
- Review chat room logs
- Create an auditorium chat room, where only certain members can post messages

- Send and receive IM without creating a chat room
- Save IM to a text file
- Choose whether to use Communicator or the chat room's client for IM; choosing one of the clients makes IM unavailable on the other client
- Archive chat room content and IM

Desktop Sharing

Desktop sharing enables users to transmit views of their desktops to others. Office Communications Server 2007 R2 introduces a Web-based client to enable users to initiate desktop sharing during any Web conference that the server hosts. The desktop sharing client is based on and integrated with the 2007 R2 release of the Microsoft Office Communicator Web Access client.

Desktop Sharing Requirements

The new desktop sharing client can be initiated by using the 2007 R2 version of the Communicator Web Access client, Office Communicator 2007 R2, Microsoft Office Live Meeting 2007 R2 (in meetings hosted by Office Communications Server instead of the Live Meeting service), and Microsoft Office SharedView. A desktop sharing session can also be initiated by using a Web browser to navigate to the desktop sharing Web site hosted by the Communicator Web Access server. Desktop sharing requires installation of the Microsoft Office Communicator Web Access plug-in.

Users running a supported client on a computer running the Windows operating system can initiate sharing, view, or take control of programs during a desktop sharing session. Users participating in a desktop sharing session using an Apple Macintosh or a computer running the Linux operating system can view or take control of programs but cannot initiate sharing.

Desktop Sharing Features

By using a supported client, users can initiate a desktop sharing session and invite other users, including users that are not enabled for Unified Communications (UC). Communicator Web Access and Office Communicator users can start desktop sharing during an existing IM conversation or audio/video conference. Communicator Web Access automatically generates a meeting URL for new participants at the time the desktop sharing session is initiated. Members of a distribution group can be added to a desktop sharing session. Users outside the organization's network can also join a desktop sharing session if Communicator Web Access is configured for external access.

At any time, the user currently hosting a session can give control to other participants (depending on the Office Communications Server meeting policy), deny control, retake control, or stop the session. While in a desktop sharing session, all users can send instant messages to other participants.

Audio Conferencing

Anyone in the session can add audio conferencing to a desktop sharing session if the Office Communications Server 2007 R2 environment has been configured with an Audio/Video (A/V) Conferencing Server and if the environment supports calls to the Public Switched Telephone Network (PSTN). When audio is added, Communicator Web Access initiates a call to the user's telephone, and then it calls the telephone numbers of other users in the session to add users to the audio conference. Conference Attendant Console users can participate in the audio conference portion of a desktop sharing session.

Server Applications

Office Communications Server 2007 R2 ships with four applications, which extend and enhance the server's existing voice and conferencing functionality. These applications run on the Office Communications Server 2007 R2 Application Server, which is installed on the same computer as the Enterprise Edition front-end server or Standard Edition Server. This topic summarizes the features and services these applications provide.

Dial-in Conferencing Feature

Dial-in conferencing enables anonymous users and enterprise users who want or need to use a PSTN phone to join the audio portion of an on-premise conference. Conferencing Attendant is an application that is run to enable this dial-in conferencing feature, and the Conferencing Announcement Service is an application that enhances this feature by providing announcements when users join or leave a conference.

Conferencing Attendant

Office Communications Server 2007 R2 Conferencing Attendant is an application that enables users to join an A/V conference by dialing in using a telephone on the PSTN. Conferencing Attendant can be installed to provide audio conferencing capabilities to phone users without requiring the services of a third-party Audio Conferencing provider. Conferencing Attendant also requires that the 2007 R2 release of Communicator Web Access be installed to provide the Dial-in Conferencing Web page, which users can access to manage their reservationless meeting information and personal identification number (PIN).

Conferencing Attendant provides the following features:

- User management of reservationless meeting information and PIN management through a Dial-In Conferencing Web page
- Support for multiple languages
- Music-on-hold
- Conference scheduling using an Outlook add-in
- Support for both anonymous and remote users

- Reservationless meetings
- Configurable access phone numbers

For a technical overview of Conferencing Attendant, see the section titled "Dial-in Conferencing Architecture" later in this chapter.

Conferencing Announcement Service

Conferencing Announcement Service uses a tone to announce when a phone user joins or leaves a conference. If the conference organizer dials out to a user with a request to join the conference, a tone plays when the user joins. Conferencing Announcement Service also announces when a phone user has been muted or unmuted. If you run Conferencing Attendant without also running Conference Announcement Service, there are no announcements for phone users.

For a technical overview of Conferencing Announcement Service, see the section titled "Dial-in Conferencing Architecture" later in this chapter.

Response Group Service

Office Communications Server 2007 R2 Response Group Service enables administrators to create and configure one or more small response groups for the purpose of routing and queuing incoming phone calls to one or more designated agents. These response groups can be deployed in departmental or workgroup environments and in entirely new telephony installations.

Typical usage scenarios include an internal help desk, customer service desk, or general external call handler. Response Group Service can increase response group usage and reduce the associated overhead by pushing the tasks of response group maintenance down to the users who directly benefit from them.

Response Group Service works with Office Communicator and the new Office Communications Server Attendant. Response Group Service also supports incoming calls from the local carrier network. Agents can use Communicator, Communicator Phone Edition, or Office Communications Server Attendant.

Response Group Service includes the following features:

- **Supported call routing algorithms** Response Group Service supports standard response group call-routing algorithms, including serial, longest-idle, parallel, and round robin. Routing algorithms are configured for each defined group of agents.
- **Interactive Voice Response (IVR)** Call navigation employs IVR, which detects and recognizes both speech and dual-tone multifrequency (DTMF) keypad input. Response Group Service IVR also supports text-to-speech and the WAV file format. The administrator can update IVR prompts.

- **Call queuing** Calls are queued pending the availability of an agent configured to accept the call.
- **Music-on-hold** Callers are put on music-on-hold until an agent becomes available.
- **Presence-based routing** Call routing takes agent presence status into account. The routing component would skip, for example, agents who are signed out or busy.
- **Response group templates** Predefined response group templates make it easy for an administrator to create a new response group. The administrator uses the response group template to define the usage experience of the call, including questions asked to the caller, options given to the caller, music-on-hold options, and configuration of business hours and holidays.
- **User management** Using a Web-based tool, administrators assign management responsibility for a response group (basic or enhanced hunt groups only) to any user. The user is thereby empowered to configure and manage the response group, including configuring music-on-hold and defining business hours. User management puts control over response groups in the hands of people who actually use them, while relieving administrators of much of the overhead associated with managing traditional response groups.
- **Agent types** Response Group Service supports both formal and informal agents. Formal agents are required to sign in or out of response groups. They might include someone who fills in when people are on vacation or lunch breaks or perhaps include separate groups of people who take calls at different times of the day. Informal agents are not required to sign in or out of response groups.
- **Simplified management** Response Group Service simplifies management of response groups by providing:
  - A Web-based response group deployment and configuration tool.
  - A standalone Microsoft Management Console (MMC) 3.0 snap-in, which can be opened from Office Communications Server 2007 R2.
  - Support for end users configuring and managing response groups.

Sample Scenarios

- John has a question about pay stub information he received in an e-mail. He calls human resources by clicking an alias in the e-mail. He navigates through an IVR and is put on music-on-hold until an agent becomes available.

  Mindy, the agent, gets an invitation alert in her Communicator or Office Communications Server Attendant client notifying her of John's call.
- John calls human resources as described in the previous scenario. The group of agents serving the queue in which John is waiting is configured for serial routing. With serial routing, Response Group Service rings each available agent for a designated

time before ringing the next agent. If no agent is located, the call is sent to a forward destination, such as a shared voice mail.

- Robin asks her assistant Paul to set up a response group for their organization. Paul asks the Office Communications Server administrator to create a response group and assign management responsibility to him. After the administrator has created the response group and assigned ownership to Paul, Paul can:
  - Define and update business hours and holidays.
  - Select which of the predefined holidays to support.
  - Upload different music-on-hold files.
  - Define Active Directory Distribution Groups as response groups.

Outside Voice Control

Outside Voice Control provides Enterprise Voice functionality and call control to mobile phones that are not otherwise enabled for Enterprise Voice. Microsoft Office Communicator Mobile clients can receive or make calls by using a single enterprise number or Session Initiation Protocol (SIP) Uniform Resource Identifier (URI). Unanswered calls are directed to the user's single Enterprise Voice mail repository. Users of devices that are running Office Communicator Mobile clients can use the voice functionality of that device as if it were part of the enterprise network, rather than the carrier network, by providing a callback number to the server.

SIP Trunking

Office Communications Server 2007 R2 simplifies and reduces the cost of deploying Enterprise Voice by enabling an enterprise to connect its voice network to a service provider offering PSTN origination, termination, and emergency services. This capability, a variety of what is known in the telecommunications industry as SIP trunking, enables enterprises to not deploy Internet Protocol (IP)-PSTN gateways, with or without Mediation Servers, to enable PSTN connectivity.

The Office Communications Server 2007 R2 SIP trunking capability enables the following scenarios:

- An enterprise user inside or outside the corporate firewall can make a local, long-distance, or emergency call specified by an E.164-compliant number that is terminated on the PSTN as a service of the corresponding service provider.
- Any PSTN subscriber can contact an enterprise user inside or outside the corporate firewall by dialing a Direct Inward Dialing (DID) number associated with that enterprise user.

Enhanced Media

Improved A/V collaboration is the centerpiece of Office Communications Server 2007 R2. Fundamental to this effort is an improvement in overall user experience both during phone calls and conferences. Among the media enhancements that have been implemented to achieve this goal are the following:

- **Improved media resiliency** End users can expect to have reliable voice communications that continue working even if transient network conditions cause signaling failure in an Office Communications Server component. If a user's attempt to establish a new media connection fails, such as during an attempt to add video to an existing voice connection, Office Communicator 2007 R2 automatically tries to restore this connection in the background without further user involvement.

> ***NOTE*** **If a signaling failure occurs for the duration of the call after it has initially been established, call control features such as hold, retrieve, and transfer will not work.**

- **Improved voice quality** Overall voice quality is significantly better for Office Communications Server 2007 R2. Improvements include:
  - Suppression of typing noise during calls.
  - Improved generation of "comfort noise," which reduces hissing and smoothes over the discontinuous flow of audio packets.
  - Improved echo detection and reduced echoing at the beginning of a call.
  - Better regulation of audio volume among peer-to-peer callers and conference participants.
  - Improved codec selection for calls to the PSTN over low-latency connections.
- **High-definition and VGA video** High-definition video (resolution 1270 x 720; aspect ratio 16:9) and VGA video (resolution 640 x 480; aspect ratio 4:3) are supported for peer-to-peer calls between users running Office Communicator 2007 R2 on high-end computers. For more information about infrastructure requirements for Office Communications Server 2007 R2, see *http://go.microsoft.com/fwlink/?LinkID=133602*. The resolution that each participant views in a single conversation may differ, depending on the video capabilities of their respective hardware.

  High-definition and VGA video are not supported for conferences.

  Administrators can set policies to restrict or disable high-definition or VGA video on clients, depending on computer capability, network bandwidth, and the presence of a camera able to deliver the required resolution. These policies are enforced through in-band provisioning.

Simplified Firewall Configuration for the A/V Edge Server

Office Communications Server 2007 R2 simplifies firewall configuration for the A/V Edge Server to support audio and video scenarios involving remote users and federated users. In Office Communications Server 2007, the perimeter network's external firewall needs to be configured to enable inbound and outbound connections with the public Internet to the A/V Edge Service on ports 3478 for User Datagram Protocol (UDP), 443 for Transmission Control Protocol (TCP), and 50,000–59,999 for both UDP and TCP. If application sharing does not need to be enabled for federated scenarios, then with Communications Server 2007 R2, the perimeter firewall can be configured to enable only inbound connections from the public Internet to the A/V Edge Server on ports 3478 for UDP and 443 for TCP. This reduced port range for inbound connections simplifies the configuration changes required on the external firewall. However, if application sharing needs to be enabled in federated scenarios, then ports 50,000–59,999 need to be opened for outbound TCP connections.

In Office Communications Server 2007, the external IP address of the A/V Edge Server has to be publicly routable and not located behind a Network Address Translation (NAT). In Communications Server 2007 R2, if a public IP address is not available, the A/V Edge Service can be deployed behind a NAT as part of a single Edge Server topology.

> ***NOTE*** **A publicly routable IP address is required if the topology contains multiple load-balanced A/V Edge Servers.**

Presence Enhancements

The ability to broadcast and view presence information is a fundamental requirement for effective real-time communications. Presence enhancements for Office Communications Server 2007 R2 primarily address the requirements of new voice scenarios. These requirements include:

- Increasing the number of subscribers to a contact object. For instance, the maximum number of category subscriptions is 3,000, which would enable 600 subscribers with one device each across five categories.
- Enabling the Response Group Service to subscribe to the presence of its agents.
- Creating Presence policies to set limits and restrictions for specific people.
- Implementing poll-based presence for newly created callers to the Response Group Service.
- Enabling an administrator to publish presence on behalf of a manager and to access all of the manager's published presence categories.

Archiving, CDR, and QoE Enhancements

Office Communications Server 2007 R2 delivers enhanced out-of-the-box monitoring and reporting capabilities for new features and scenarios while simplifying the deployment and administration of monitoring components. Archiving, Call Detail Records (CDR), and Quality of Experience (QoE) enhancements for Office Communications Server 2007 R2 include:

- CDR and archiving data for new scenarios and features, including Call Delegation, Team Calling, and Response Group Service.
- New CDR usage reports provide system usage details for conferencing, voice and video, and IM.
- New QoE metrics for audio quality, PSTN connections, and network connectivity. These new QoE metrics provide better-quality monitoring and diagnostics. QoE reports have been fully redesigned and enhanced with the new metrics.
- A new Office Communications Server role, the Monitoring Server, gathers both CDR and QoE data.
- The Office Communications Server 2007 R2 Archiving Server now performs only IM archiving–related functions.

Simplified Management

Office Communications Server 2007 R2 reduces management overhead and simplifies deployment and ongoing operations. These management improvements include the following.

Simplified Topologies

The recommended topology for Communications Server 2007 R2 is a consolidated configuration in which:

- All server roles in a pool are collocated on a single computer.
- Response Group Service, Conferencing Auto-Attendant, Conferencing Announcement Service, and Outside Voice Control are also collated on a single computer.
- All Edge Server roles in a perimeter network are collocated on a single computer.
- Both deployment and operational overhead are reduced, thus reducing cost of ownership. Scalability is achieved by adding computers to the pool or perimeter network and load balancing them.

  In addition, CDR and QoE monitoring and reporting have been combined in a single new server role, the Monitoring Server.

Enhanced Administrative Snap-In

The Administrative snap-in has been updated for Office Communications Server 2007 R2 to include the following:

- Application Server
- Response Group Distributor
- Conference Attendant
- Conference Announcement Service
- Call Control Service
- Application Sharing Conferencing Server

The new snap-in enables administrators to configure and manage each of these new components by using a familiar interface. In addition, these new components appear in the server-by-role view in the snap-in.

Conference Directories

Conference Directories are new entities that provide persistent identities to scheduled conferences. When a scheduled conference has to be moved to a new pool—for example, when its original pool is taken offline—the scheduled conference retains the identity that its Conference Directory provided. Conference Directories, including those that are as yet unassigned, are listed in the tree view of the administrative console.

Automatic Updates

Administrators can push updates to Office Communicator 2007 R2, Communicator Phone Edition, and the RoundTable without relying on the refresh cycles of other administrators and with little or no involvement from users.

Improved Certificate Wizard

An improved Certificate Wizard enables administrators to create multiple certificate requests offline for the same computer and then send them to an enterprise or public certificate authority (CA). After certificates are imported, the Certificate Wizard enables the administrator to specify the certificate assignments to specific services. The Certificate Wizard also warns when Subject Alternate Names (SANs) include spaces and special characters, which are not allowed.

In-Band Provisioning Enhancements

All clients (Communicator, Communicator Web Access, Communicator Mobile, and Communicator Phone Edition) are automatically provisioned at first sign-in, with the new settings introduced in Office Communications Server 2007 R2.

Optional Installation of Administrative Tools

Installation of the Office Communications Server 2007 R2 Administrative snap-in is now optional. The Communicator Web Access administrative snap-in and the deployment command line tool LcsCmd are also no longer installed by default.

Planning Tool

The Planning Tool for Office Communications Server 2007 R2 provides prescriptive guidance for planning and deployment. The Planning Tool is a wizard that asks a series of questions about features of interest, information about your organization, and anticipated capacity. Based on the answers you provide, the Planning Tool creates a recommended topology for each of your organization's main sites, specifies recommended hardware, and prescribes the planning and deployment steps to implement the topologies. The Planning Tool takes about 10 minutes to complete, depending on the complexity of your organization.

Technical Overview

This section of the chapter provides a technical overview of Office Communications Server 2007 R2 and its new features, which include:

- Reference topology
- Group Chat architecture
- Desktop sharing framework
- Server Application framework
- SIP trunking topology
- Media enhancements

Reference Topology

Figure 2-1 shows the Office Communications Server 2007 R2 consolidated topology.

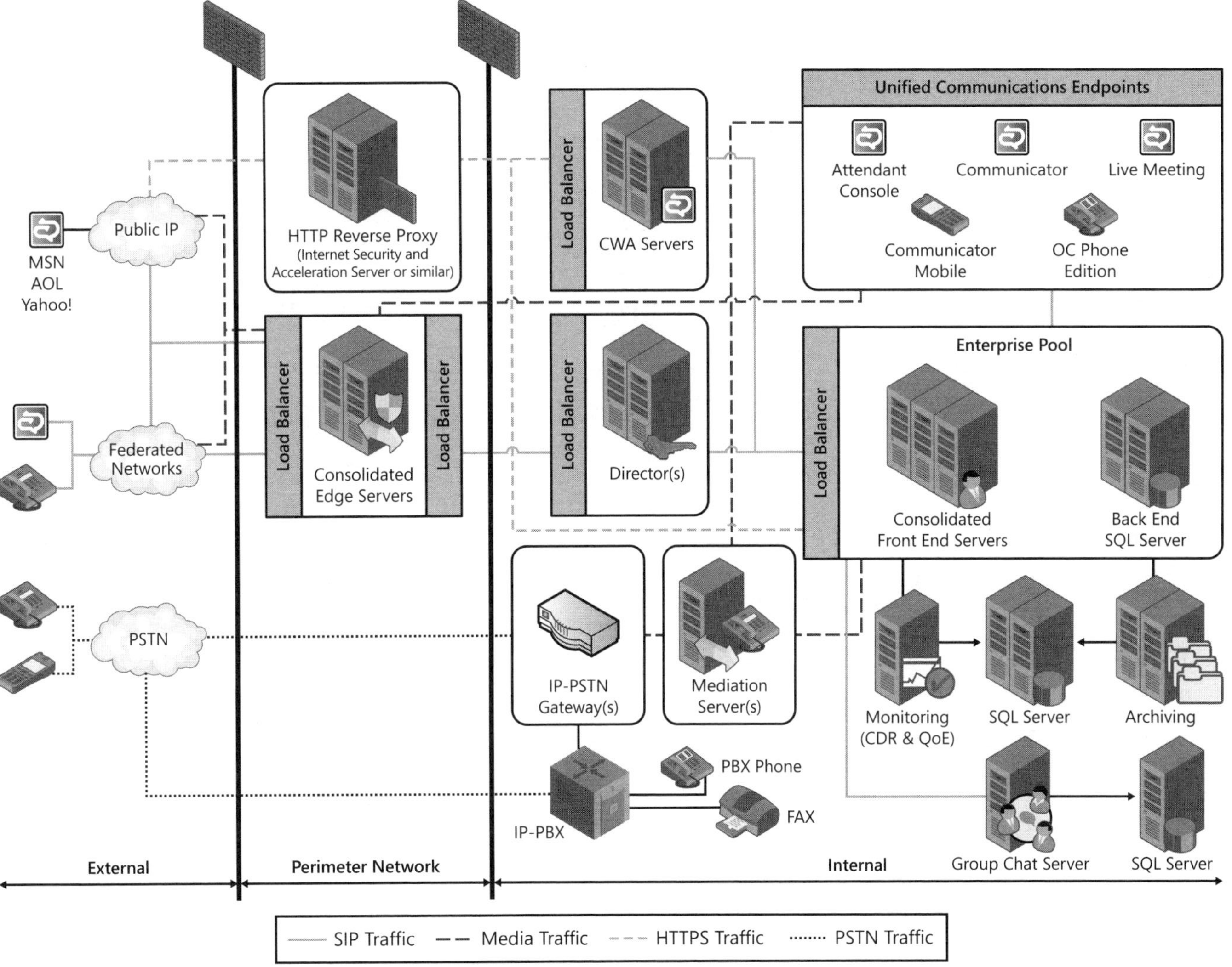

FIGURE 2-1 Reference topology

In the Office Communications Server 2007 R2 consolidated pool topology, the following server roles and services are collocated on the same computer as the front-end server:

- Address Book Service
- Application Server
- Application Sharing Conferencing Server
- A/V Conferencing Server
- Conference Announcement Service (optional)
- Conference Attendant (optional)
- Group Expansion Service
- IM Conferencing Server
- Outside Voice Control (optional)
- Response Group Service (optional)
- Telephony Conferencing Server
- Update Server
- Web Conferencing Server

In the Office Communications Server 2007 R2 consolidated Edge topology, the following server roles and services are collocated on the same computer as the Office Communications Server 2007 R2 Edge Server:

- Access Edge Server
- A/V Edge Server
- Web Conferencing Edge Server

For additional information on server roles, see Chapter 3, "Server Roles."

Group Chat

Office Communications Server 2007 R2 Group Chat enables users to engage in persistent IM conversations. For details about Group Chat features, see Group Chat Feature.

The minimum configuration and simplest deployment for Group Chat is a single-server topology, which includes the following computers:

- A single Group Chat Server running the following three server roles:
  - *Lookup Server* The Lookup Server provides the chat room address, distributes sessions to Channel Servers, and in multiple-server topologies manages load balancing.
  - *Channel Server* The Channel Server provides core functionality for chat rooms except for file posting, which is managed through the Web Service.
  - *Web Service* The Web Service is used to post files to group channels. Internet Information Services (IIS) version 6.0 hosts the Web Service.

  The Group Chat Server, like other Office Communications Server 2007 R2 servers, requires a 64-bit computer. This computer hosts the Microsoft SQL Server database for storing ongoing and archival chat data, as well as information about categories and channels that are created, user provisioning information from the Group Chat Administration Tool and initial sign-in, and basic configuration information about the Group Chat Servers.
- Group Chat client computers. These computers are not required to be 64 bit.

If compliance is required, the single-server topology must also include the following:

- **Compliance Server** If configured, the Group Chat compliance feature archives a comprehensive record of both logged and unlogged group chat activity. IM content is not archived unless archiving is configured in Office Communications Server. In this case, IM content is archived on the Archiving Server.
- **SQL Server Database** This database can be either the Group Chat database or a separate database on the Compliance Server.

Figure 2-2 shows all of the components of a topology with a single Group Chat Server and optional Compliance Server with a separate compliance database.

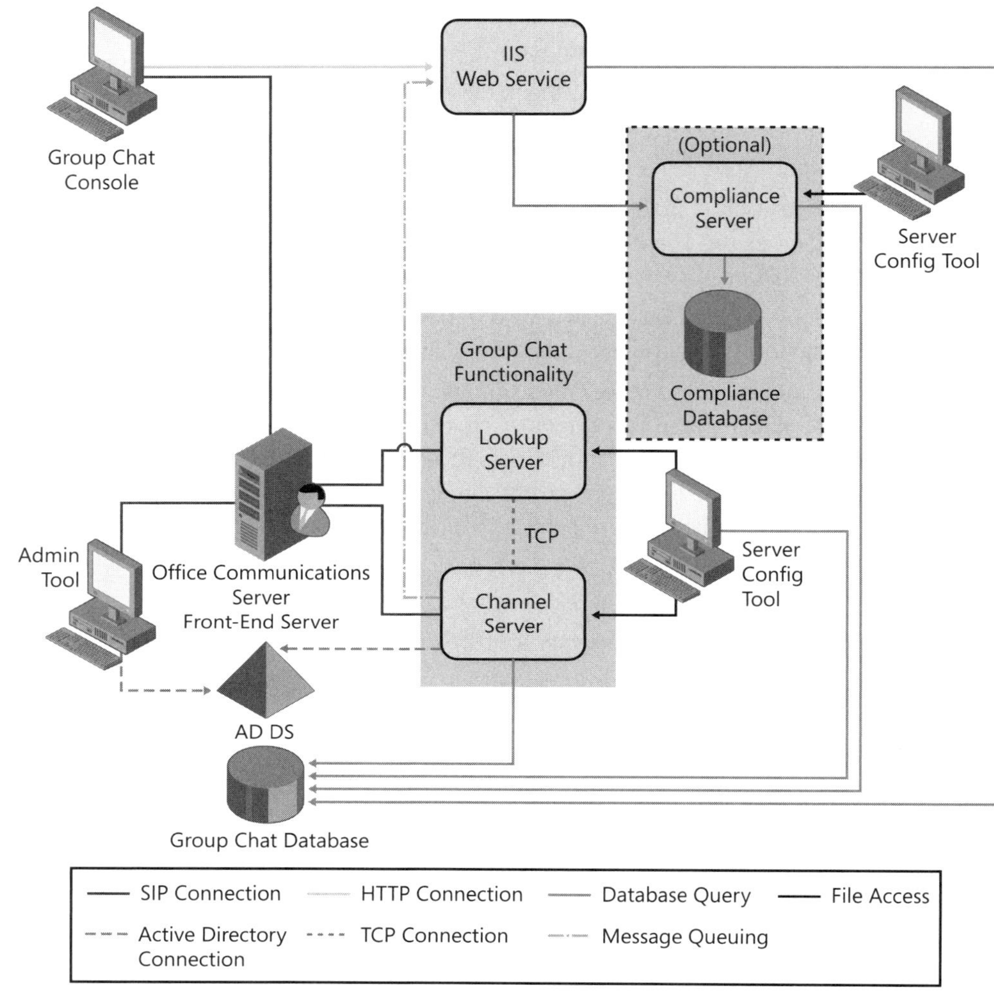

FIGURE 2-2 Single Group Chat topology

Figure 2-3 shows a multiple-server Group Chat topology.

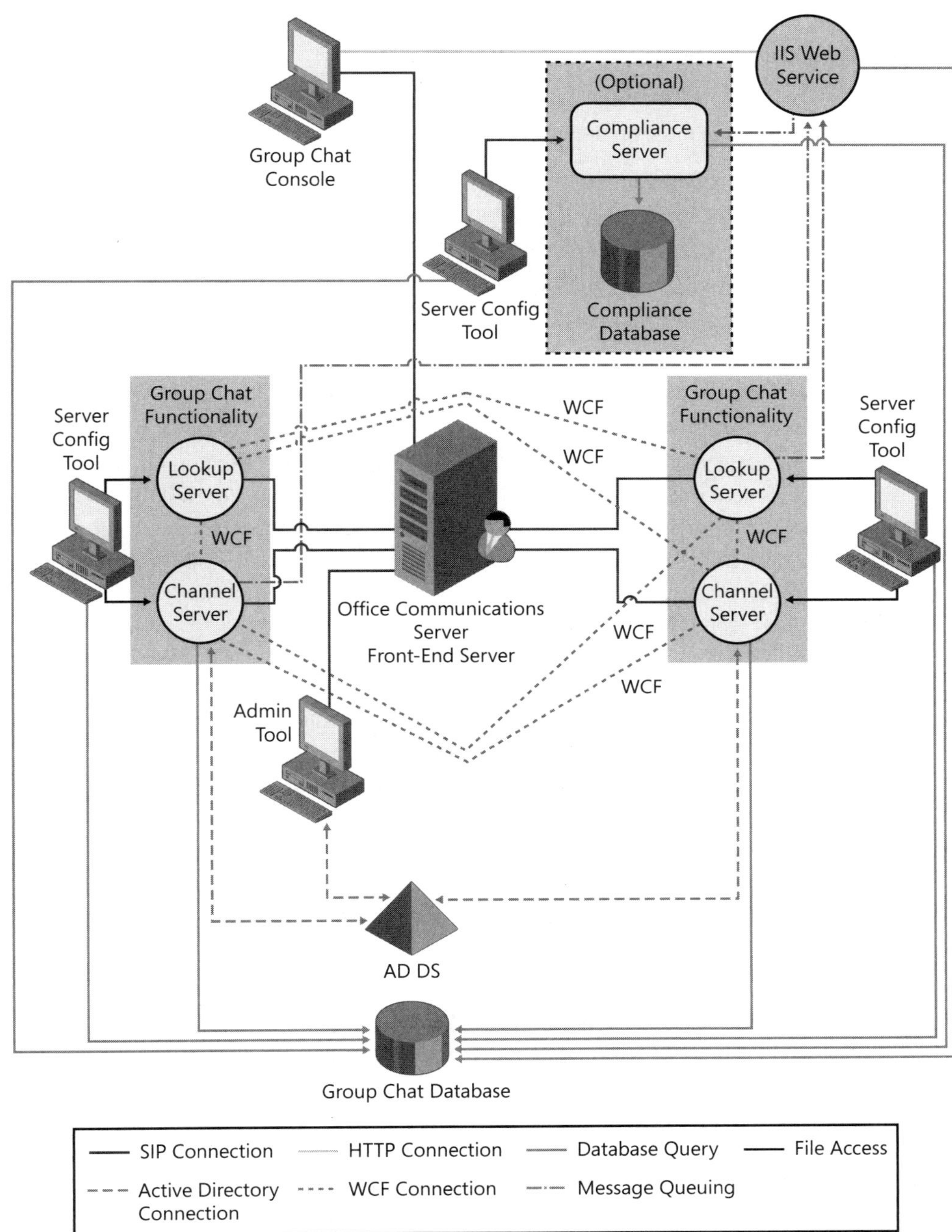

FIGURE 2-3 Multiple-server Group Chat topology

Administration of Group Chat from a separate computer (such as an administrative console) requires installation of the following on the computer:

- Group Chat Administration Tool

All of these computers must be deployed in the following ways:

- In an Active Directory domain, with at least one global catalog server in the forest root
- Outside the Office Communications Server 2007 R2 pool

Desktop Sharing Framework

Office Communications Server 2007 R2 supports desktop sharing in both peer-to-peer and conference scenarios. For details about supported functionality, see the section titled "Desktop Sharing" earlier in this chapter. The framework for sharing desktops includes the following principal components:

- **Communicator Web Access client** The 2007 R2 version of the Communicator Web Access client contains the hosting and viewing components for desktop sharing. The hosting component drives the desktop sharing session. This component sends graphical data to the Application Sharing Server or another client, such as Office Communicator 2007 R2, which is capable of understanding Remote Desktop Protocol (RDP). The viewing component displays the graphical data from the desktop sharing session to the user. Graphical data is obtained from the Communicator Web Access server. The viewer can also send keyboard and mouse data to the host by way of the Communicator Web Access server and the Application Sharing Conferencing Server.
- **Desktop-sharing client** The desktop sharing client is a Web-based viewer that is hosted on the Communicator Web Access client. When sharing is initiated, meeting participants are invited to view the sharer's desktop. If they accept, the desktop sharing client launches in a new viewing pane integrated with the Communicator Web Access client. Participants using Office Communicator 2007 R2 can launch the desktop sharing client directly from Communicator. Each participant's desktop sharing client receives graphical data from the Communicator Web Access server, which in turn receives it from the Application Sharing Conferencing Server.
- **Microsoft Office Communicator Web Access plug-in** Because the desktop sharing client is browser based, interaction with the underlying operating system has to be implemented through a native plug-in. The Microsoft Office Communicator Web Access plug-in is available as an option during installation of the Communicator Web Access client.
- **Communicator Web Access Server** The Communicator Web Access server is responsible for setting up, tearing down, and controlling the desktop sharing session for the Communicator Web Access client. The Communicator Web Access server also sends and receives sharing data both to and from the client. The Communicator Web Access server handles media only for Communicator Web Access viewers.

- **Application Sharing Conferencing Server** The Application Sharing Server is responsible for managing and streaming data for conferences that require desktop sharing. In multiparty conferences, the Communicator Web Access client, in the role of desktop sharing host, dials the conferencing server directly (or, in the case of external users, by way of an A/V Edge Server). The Communicator Web Access server connects to the conferencing server to receive desktop sharing data on behalf of the Web clients hosted on the Communicator Web Access server.

In Office Communications Server 2007 R2, desktop sharing components use RDP, which is also used by Terminal Services functionality in Microsoft Server 2003. Desktop sharing sessions that use RDP cannot support participants who are running earlier versions of Office Communications Server clients, nor can they include users of the office Live Meeting service. However, participants who are not running any Office Communications Server clients and do not have an Office Communications Server account can be invited to a desktop sharing session and join that session by navigating to a meeting URL hosted on the Communicator Web Access server, using a supported Internet browser.

Peer-to-Peer Application Sharing

In peer-to-peer scenarios, if either participant is running the Communicator Web Access client, starting a desktop sharing session escalates the conversation to a two-party conference involving the Application Sharing Conferencing Server. This escalation is necessary because the Communicator Web Access client relies on an RDP connection with the Application Sharing Conferencing Server. After a session escalates to a conference, it cannot revert to a peer-to-peer conversation.

Multiparty Conference Application Sharing

If the conference organizer initiates the conference with desktop sharing as the initial mode, the organizer's client first joins the Focus, and then it joins the Application Sharing Conferencing Server as a "sharer." Then, the organizer's client invites other parties to join the conference. They, in turn, join the Focus, and then they join the Application Sharing Conferencing Server.

If application sharing is introduced in an ongoing conference that began in a different mode, the sharer joins the Application Sharing Conferencing Server, which causes the Focus to send a roster update to other participants. This roster update includes an invitation to view the sharer's desktop.

Server Application Framework

This topic provides an overview of the new application infrastructure introduced with Office Communications Server 2007 R2.

The Office Communications Server 2007 R2 infrastructure includes the following components.

Application Server

NOTE **The Application Server does not support third-party applications.**

The Application Server is a new component on the Office Communications Server 2007 R2 front-end server. The Application Server provides a platform to deploy, host, and manage UC applications. By providing applications with essential services and a consistent model for installation, activation, provisioning, and upgrading, the Application Server simplifies application development, deployment, and administration.

Application

In this discussion, an *application* refers to a UC application that is hosted on the Application Server. Each Application Server in a pool hosts a separate instance of a given application. Each application instance is defined by a specific fully qualified domain name (FQDN).

Deployment and Topology

The Office Communications Server 2007 R2 Deployment Wizard installs the Application Server automatically as a separate process on the same computer as the front-end server. No administrator input is required. In addition, no settings are required to configure the Application Server, although the same pool name and pool certificate are used by all Application Server computers in a pool. The Application Server always runs as a separate process on the front-end server and cannot be deployed on a separate computer in the pool.

Once the Application Server is installed, the Deployment Wizard offers to activate four applications:

- Conferencing Attendant
- Conferencing Announcement Service
- Response Group Service
- Outside Voice Control

The administrator can choose to activate one or more of the applications or none at all.

Application deployment must be identical on all Application Servers in a pool. That is, if Conferencing Attendant, for example, is deployed on one Application Server, it must be deployed on all Application Servers in the pool.

The administrator can manage application-specific settings for all applications, except Response Group Service, using the Office Communications Server 2007 R2 Administrative snap-in. You can administer Response Group Service by using its separate Administrative snap-in.

For details about these applications, see the section titled "Server Applications" earlier in this chapter.

Activation

The Application Server does not start or stop independently from the applications it hosts. As each application instance is activated, it is added to the list of applications on the computer.

When an application is activated, the application is provisioned with contact objects and trusted service entries such that calls can be routed to it. This provisioning information includes the phone number or SIP URI associated with the application and the SIP port, as well as the FQDNs of the multiple instances of the application.

Call Routing

For purposes of call routing, each application is represented in the Office Communications Server 2007 R2 consolidated configuration by a contact object, which lists the Virtual IP (VIP) address and port of a hardware load balancer that has been configured with the IP addresses of all corresponding instances of the Application Server. The Application Server does not provide a single SIP listening port on behalf of all hosted applications. Instead, each application listens separately, using its own port. The hardware load balancer directs calls to different application instances according to its own proprietary algorithms.

Contact objects are required to enable applications to function as SIP endpoints, which can be provisioned with SIP URIs and can receive and send calls as if they were end users. Contact objects required for an application's internal use are created during activation if the required information is provided in the application manifest file.

Contact objects that function as SIP endpoints to make an application available to external users are created after deployment and activation by using the Office Communications Server 2007 R2 Administrative snap-in.

Response Group Topology

The Response Group Service enables users to create response groups that automatically distribute incoming calls to groups of agents. It also enables users to configure other settings, such as a welcome message, Interactive Voice Response, and music-on-hold.

The Response Group Service can be installed:

- On Office Communications Server 2007 R2 Standard Edition or Enterprise Edition.
- In a consolidated configuration or in an expanded configuration.

Response Group Service must be installed and identically configured on all front-end servers in a pool.

For best performance, it is recommended that you install the Response Group Service on Office Communications Server 2007 R2 servers at every location where response groups are required and an IP-PSTN gateway is deployed.

Topology

Figure 2-4 shows the Response Group Service deployed on Office Communications Server 2007 R2 Enterprise Edition servers in a consolidated configuration. In this example, calls from on-site and remote callers can be distributed to on-site and remote callees.

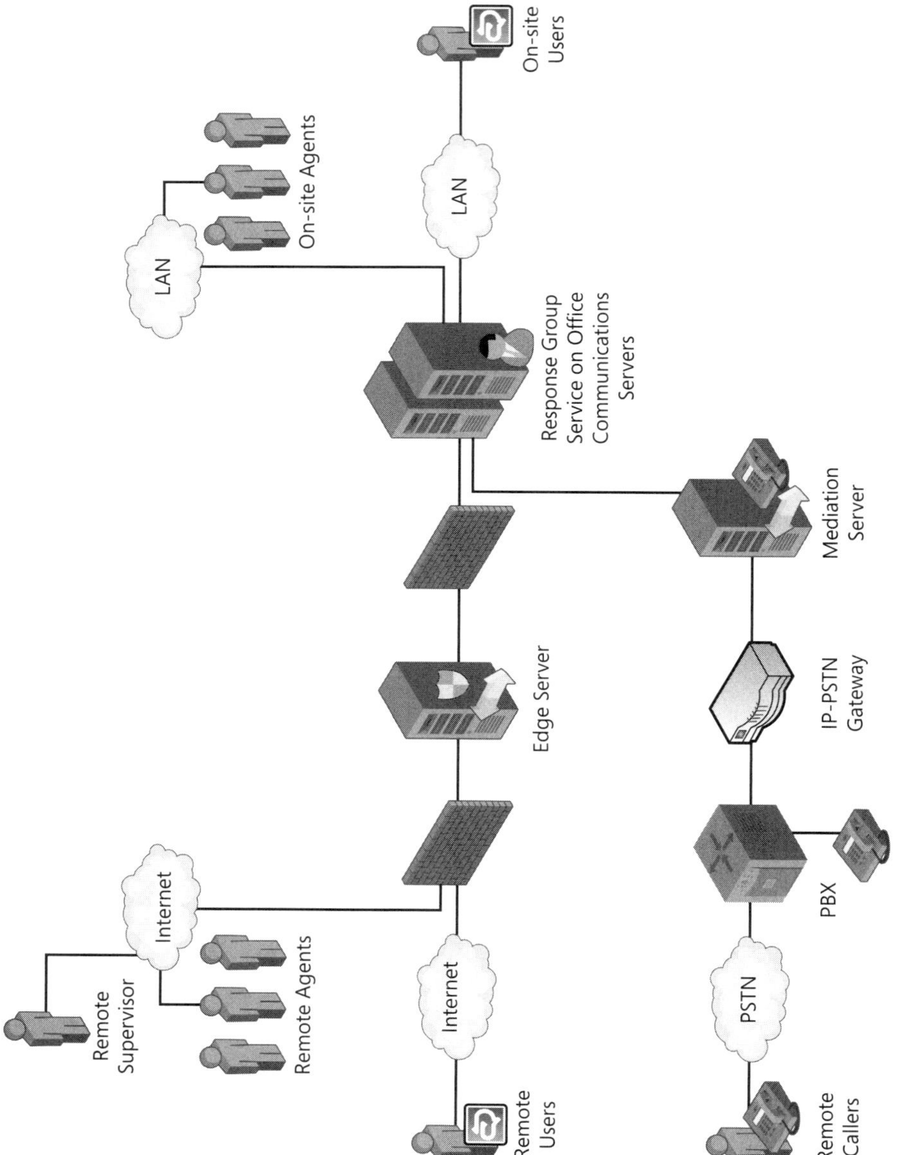

FIGURE 2-4 Response Group Service in an Office Communications Server 2007 R2 Enterprise Edition consolidated topology

Dial-in Conferencing Architecture

Dial-in conferencing enables anonymous users and enterprise users who want or need to use a PSTN phone to join the audio portion of an on-premises conference. Each conference that is enabled for PSTN dial-in includes the following information in the conference invitation:

- A numeric-only PSTN conference ID. The ID uniquely identifies the conference.
- One or more PSTN access numbers with associated language support.
- A link to an Office Communicator Web Access page containing a list of all other access numbers and instructions for how to set the user's PIN.

In addition, the conference invitation might include a numeric-only pass code for the conference that can be used by anonymous users.

Dial-in support is available to both enterprise and anonymous users. An enterprise user is one with Active Directory Domain Services credentials. An anonymous user does not have enterprise credentials but has been invited to the conference. A federated user who uses the PSTN to connect to a conference is considered to be an anonymous user in this context.

Enterprise users or conference leaders who join a PSTN conference dial one of the conference access numbers. Then, they enter their PSTN conference ID, followed by their UC extensions and PINs. The combination of extension and PIN enables the Conferencing Attendant to map enterprise users to their Active Directory credentials. As a result, enterprise users can be authenticated and identified by name in the conference. They can also assume a conference role predefined by the organizer.

Anonymous users who join a PSTN conference dial one of the conference access numbers, and then they enter a PSTN conference ID and a pass code for the conference if there is one. Anonymous users are not identified by name and cannot be assigned a predefined role.

ADDING A PSTN USER TO A CONFERENCE

A conference access number maps to the SIP URI of the Conferencing Attendant. When a PSTN user calls a conference access number, the meeting Focus initiates phone number lookup to obtain the SIP URI of the allocated Conferencing Attendant. The Mediation Server directs the call to the allocated Conferencing Attendant, which accepts the conference ID and passes it (in encrypted form) in a SIP SERVICE request to the front-end server.

The front-end server looks up the conference on the organizer's home server and returns the conference URL to the Conferencing Attendant in the response to the SERVICE request. The Conferencing Attendant uses the conference URL to join the Focus and send a dial-out command to the A/V Conferencing Server. The A/V Conferencing Server adds the caller to the conference, at which point the initial connection between the Mediation Server and the Conferencing Attendant is dropped.

ADDING CONFERENCING ANNOUNCEMENT SERVICE TO A CONFERENCE

Conferencing Announcement Service plays entry and exit tones to the PSTN participants in an audio conference. When a PSTN user calls into the conference, the A/V Conferencing Server adds an instance of Conferencing Announcement Service to the conference for the purpose of announcing the caller.

When a PSTN user dials in to a conference, the A/V Conferencing Server determines that the connection is from the PSTN and whether a Conferencing Announcement Service is already active for the conference. If not, the A/V Conferencing Server requests a new instance of Conferencing Announcement Service and invites it to join the conference. Conferencing Announcement Service plays the entry and exit tone for each PSTN participant. Conferencing Announcement Service also announces to PSTN callers whether they have been muted or unmuted.

Outside Voice Control

Outside Voice Control acts as an intermediary to connect mobile devices and UC endpoints. The mobile devices must be running 2007 R2 version of Microsoft Office Communicator Mobile for Windows Mobile.

Users with mobile devices running this client can send and receive voice calls as if their phones were part of the enterprise network instead of the cellular carrier network.

When a user makes a call from a supported mobile client to an enterprise peer, Outside Voice Control sets up the call as summarized in the following steps.

1. The mobile client uses a data-signaling channel to inform Outside Voice Control of the outbound call.
2. Outside Voice Control initiates a request to the Mediation Server and PSTN gateway to establish a call to the mobile client by using the mobile client's cellular network.
3. A cellular call is established with the mobile client. This is the first call leg.
4. Outside Voice Control establishes a second call leg with the home pool of the enterprise peer that is the recipient of the call.
5. A front-end Server in the recipient's home pool looks up the recipient's registered endpoints and then forks the call to all the recipient's endpoints, including mobile devices.
6. The second call leg is established with the endpoint that answers the call.
7. Outside Voice Control provides call management to bridge the two call legs between the mobile client and the enterprise peer. Media flows between the mobile client and the enterprise peer through the Mediation Server.

When an enterprise user or a phone user makes a call to a supported mobile client by using one-number calling, Outside Voice Control sets up the call as summarized in the following steps.

1. If the call originates from an enterprise peer, the call will connect directly to Office Communications Server. If the call originates from the PSTN, the call will connect to the Mediation Server.
2. A front-end server in the recipient's home pool looks up the recipient's registered endpoints and then forks the call to all the recipient's endpoints, including the user's cell phone that is running a supported mobile client.
3. When the request to establish a signaling channel reaches the supported mobile client, the mobile client is able to determine that the incoming session is an audio call.
4. The mobile client uses a data-signaling channel to inform Outside Voice Control of the incoming call.
5. The mobile client signals Office Communications Server to reroute the original signaling request to Outside Voice Control. Outside Voice Control initiates a request to a Mediation Server and PSTN gateway to establish a call to the mobile client's cellular network.
6. When the user answers the call on the mobile client device, Outside Voice Control and Office Communications Server connect the Mediation Server call leg with the originating call leg. Media flows directly between the Mediation Server and the caller.
7. Outside Voice Control remains in the signaling path to provide call management until the call is terminated.

SIP Trunking Topology

The term *SIP trunking* has various meanings within the telecommunications industry, including:

- A generic means to connect one vendor's IP Private Branch eXchange (PBX) with another vendor's equipment
- A generic means to connect multiple IP PBXs across a wide area network (WAN) within the same enterprise
- A generic means for an IP PBX to connect to a remote hosted service for the purpose of originating and terminating calls to the PSTN network

This final meaning is the sense in which the term *SIP trunking* is used in Office Communications Server 2007 R2.

The purpose of a SIP trunk in an Office Communications Server topology is to enable an enterprise to connect its on-premises voice network to a service provider offering PSTN origination and termination. Relying on an independent server provider for PSTN connectivity eliminates the need to deploy and maintain IP-PSTN gateways.

Figure 2-5 depicts the SIP trunking topology in Office Communications Server 2007 R2.

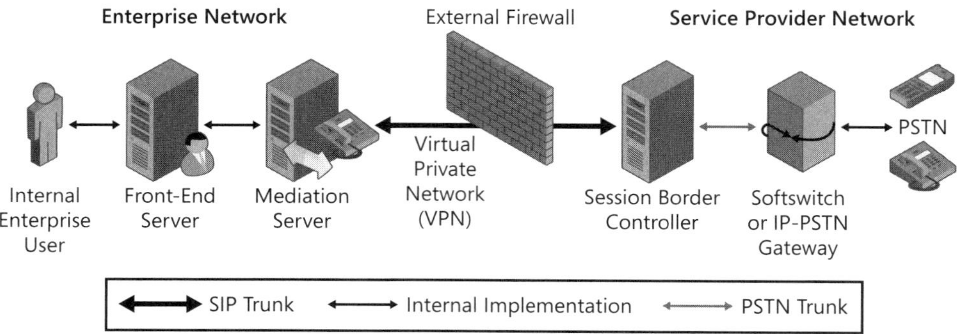

FIGURE 2-5 SIP trunking topology

As shown in the diagram, an IP virtual private network (VPN) is used for connectivity between the enterprise network and the PSTN service provider. The purpose of this private network is to provide IP connectivity, security, and (optionally) Quality of Service (QoS) guarantees. In such an environment, it is not required to additionally secure the SIP signaling traffic (with Transport Layer Security, or TLS) or the media traffic (with Secure Real-Time Protocol, or SRTP). Connections between the enterprise and the service provider therefore consist of plain TCP connections for SIP and plain RTP (over UDP) for media potentially tunneled through an IP VPN.

It is expected that the demarcation point in most service providers' networks will be a session border controller, although this is not required. Likewise, whether to use an IP-PSTN gateway or softswitch in the service provider network is up to the service provider.

In this SIP trunking topology, the Mediation Server performs media and signaling translation, just as it does when connected to an enterprise IP-PSTN gateway. All SIP traffic and media traffic between the enterprise network and the service provider network flows through the VPN and the Mediation Server.

The Mediation Server can discover the service provider proxy (the Session Border Controller in Figure 2-5) either through:

- Static provisioning, in which the Mediation Server is provisioned manually with a list of one or more FQDNs or IP addresses that represent the set of service provider proxies through which a connection should be tried.
- A Domain Name System (DNS) query against an FQDN published by the PSTN service provider.

The PSTN service provider can use either of these methods for discovering the list of enterprise proxies (Mediation Servers) to which it can connect.

Media Enhancements

Media enhancements for Office Communications Server 2007 R2 support new collaboration scenarios and improve the overall quality of experience in all A/V scenarios.

This section provides a technical overview of the following media enhancements:

- Early media support
- ICE protocol upgrade
- Video negotiation

Early Media Support

Early media refers to audio and video that is exchanged before the recipient accepts a call. Early media generated by the caller include voice commands or DTMF tones to activate Interactive Voice Response (IVR) systems. Early media generated by the call recipient include ringback tones, announcements, and requests for input.

Enhanced early media support in Office Communications Server 2007 R2 enables a caller to hear a ringback tone generated by the call recipient's mobile phone. This is also the case in team call scenarios, in which a call is routed to two team members, one of whom has configured simultaneous ringing for her mobile phone. Enhanced early media support also enables call connectivity checks while a call is ringing rather than only after it is connected, as is the case in Office Communications Server 2007.

ICE Protocol Upgrade

The Interactive Connectivity Establishment (ICE) implementation for Office Communications Server 2007 R2 complies with the latest ICE draft. This enhancement makes it possible for Office Communications Server 2007 R2 users to call users on Office Communications Server 2007 or on Voice over Internet Protocol (VoIP) UC phones supporting the latest ICE draft without requiring a PSTN gateway to connect the endpoints. Figure 2-6 illustrates the main scenarios.

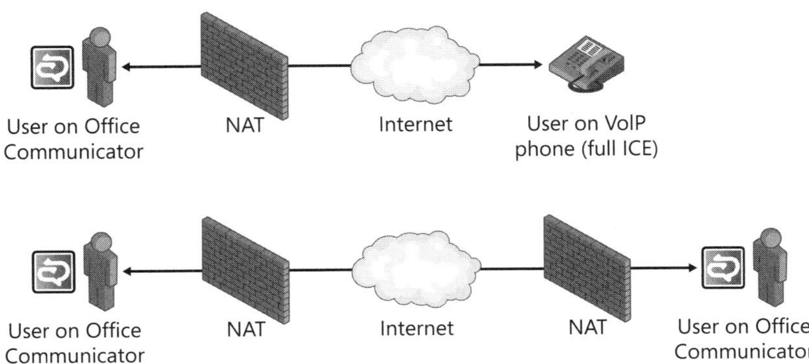

FIGURE 2-6 ICE scenarios

Video Negotiation

Video negotiation is a process whereby an endpoint proposing to send video can determine the video capabilities of the receiving endpoint prior to sending the video stream. The purpose of video negotiation is to make sure that the sending endpoint can produce and send a given resolution and that the receiving endpoint can receive and render that same resolution. The negotiation follows an offer/answer model until common agreement is found. The highest-quality video capability held in common is used in peer-to-peer calls unless the user at the receiving end prefers a lower resolution or frame rate.

An endpoint's video capability is based on several qualities, including central processing unit (CPU), available memory, attached devices, and network resources. For example, a user may have a camera that can send VGA video at 15 frames per second (fps) or Common Intermediate Format (CIF) video at 30 fps, but that cannot handle high-definition (HD) video. Video negotiation always resolves to CIF at 15 fps for multiparty video conferencing.

The video preference of the user at the receiving endpoint also helps to determine the final negotiated format. For example, a user may want to select a smaller video window even though the negotiated video settings enable a higher resolution. In such cases, the receiver instructs the sender to adopt a lower video format. The ability to specify video preferences in this way prevents inefficient use of bandwidth. Office Communicator offers three window sizes and therefore three preference settings: small, large, and full screen.

Summary

This chapter provided a description of the new features of and significant enhancements to the existing functionality introduced in Office Communications Server 2007 R2 as well as a technical overview. Now that you have read this chapter, you should have a better understanding of the new features that are offered as well as an overview of how they work and how they fit into the Office Communications Server 2007 R2 topologies. There are additional resources you can leverage to gain a deeper understanding of each of these areas, and this information is provided throughout the remainder of this book.

Additional Resources

- TechNet Technical Library, found at *http://go.microsoft.com/fwlink/?LinkID=133654.*
- The Communications Group Team Blog includes announcements by the Microsoft product team and is found at *http://go.microsoft.com/fwlink/?LinkID=133659.*

CHAPTER 3

Server Roles

Microsoft Office Communications Server 2007 R2 includes a number of specialized server roles. These server roles perform specific tasks that enable various usage scenarios. This chapter focuses on explaining the different server roles so that you can decide when to use them to fit your particular deployment needs. Most of these logical server roles can be collocated on the same physical servers. This chapter also discusses the supported configurations for collocating server roles.

Standard Edition Server

The basic building block of Office Communications Server 2007 R2 is the Standard Edition Server role. A Standard Edition Server includes all of the server roles that are required to provide presence, instant messaging (IM), and conferencing. The Standard Edition Server is both a Session Initiation Protocol (SIP) registrar and a SIP proxy, as defined in Request for Comment (RFC) 3261, in a single physical server. When installing a Standard Edition role, the Microsoft SQL Server Express database is automatically installed. This database stores data for all users who are enabled for SIP Communications. These users are "homed" on the Standard Edition Server.

The data that is stored for each user includes the following:

- Contact information (contact lists)
- Permissions (Allow/Block lists)
- Endpoints (devices on which the user is currently registered)
- Subscription information (pending subscriptions)
- Office Communications Server user settings published in Active Directory

Contact information refers to the list of contacts and groups created by the user.

Permissions refer to whether contacts are allowed or blocked from viewing the presence state of users. Office Communications Server 2007 R2 uses an extensible permission model referred to as enhanced presence, which is described in Chapter 1, "Overview of Office Communications Server 2007 R2."

Endpoints refer to each of the clients from which the same user is signed in to Office Communications Server. It is not uncommon for users to be signed in from multiple devices at the same time. Users might be simultaneously signed in to Office Communications Server from Microsoft Office Communicator on their desktop computers, from their laptops, from their smart phones running Microsoft Office Communicator Mobile, or from Microsoft Office Communicator Web Access running on Web browsers. The server tracks each of these endpoints to determine the most accurate presence state of the user. When an incoming invitation is sent to the user, Office Communications Server forks the invitation by sending the invitation to all of the user's endpoints. When the user responds from one of her devices, the server stops forking incoming messages from that contact, and it routes all subsequent messages for this session to the device from which the user accepted the original invite. After the session is terminated, any new messages from the same contact or any other contact are again forked to all endpoints to which the user is signed in.

DIRECT FROM THE SOURCE

What Is Forking and How Does It Conceptually Work?

Paul Tidwell
Software Development Lead

When a phone call "forks," all of your devices begin to ring at the same time. It is similar to what happens at your house: the phones in the kitchen, the living room, and the bedroom all ring when someone dials your home phone number. When you answer in the living room, for example, the phones in the bedroom and kitchen stop ringing. The experience with Office Communicator is the same except the locations are not necessarily in the same building or even the same city. Instead, you might be signed in at your office downtown, your home in the suburbs, and your laptop in an airport in Arizona. Whenever you receive a phone call, Office Communicator begins to ring in all of these locations so that you can answer wherever you happen to be. If you answer on your laptop, the phones at your office and at home stop ringing. Unlike your home phone, your conversation is private and cannot be overheard by picking up one of your far-flung extensions.

When an instant message forks, the message is sent to each place where you are signed in. If you reply to the message by using your laptop, each additional message you receive from the other person will go only to your laptop. The conversation continues this way until you close the conversation window, turn off the computer, or there is a long lull in the conversation.

Subscription information tracks all of the contacts for which the user wants to get presence updates. Presence updates occur when one of the user's contacts changes state, such as signing in to Office Communications Server, joining a phone call, and so on.

Figures 3-1 and 3-2 show the Office Communications Server user settings stored in Active Directory. User information and global Office Communications Server settings stored in Active Directory are synchronized to the database by a component of the Office Communications Server service called the user replicator (UR). The UR reads information from the closest Active Directory global catalog (GC). If a GC is unavailable, the Standard Edition Server cannot start; or if it is already running, it will fail to synchronize any updates.

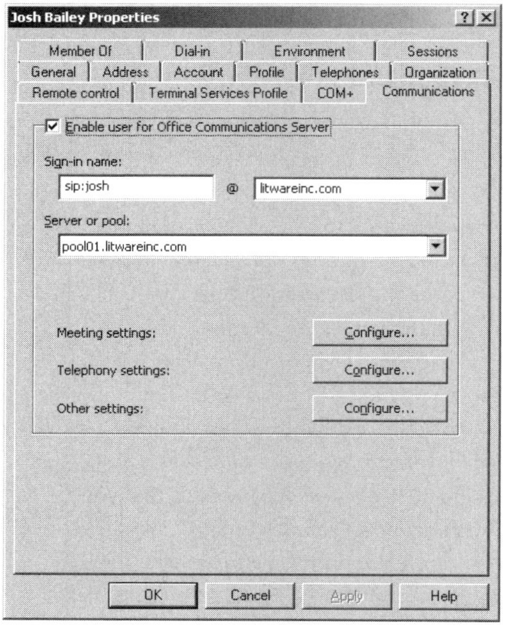

FIGURE 3-1 User settings

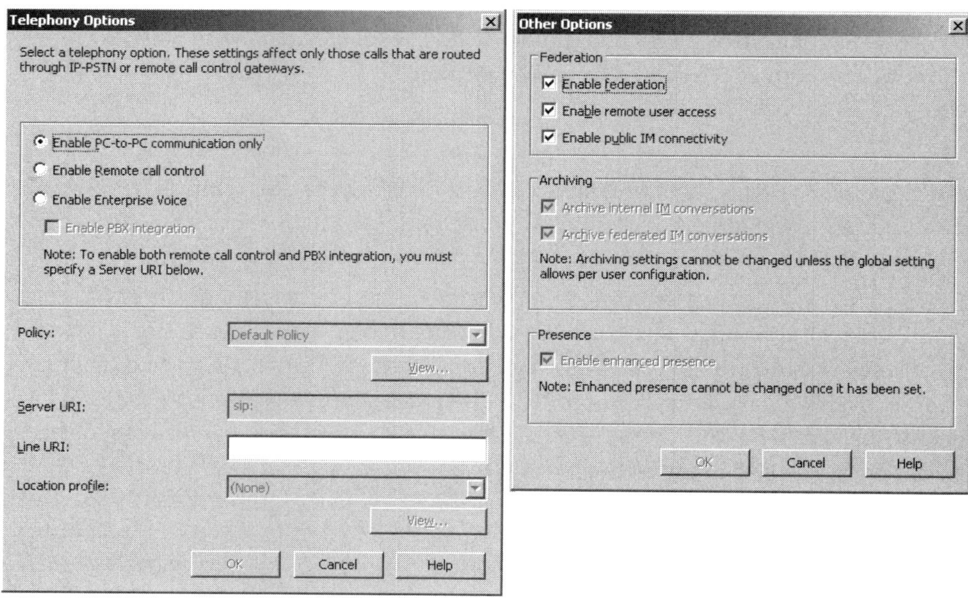

FIGURE 3-2 Advanced user settings

Because a Standard Edition Server maintains user information, it is important to periodically back up the database so that, in the event of a server failure, this data can be restored. Because of its scale, characteristics, and ease of deployment as a standalone server, the Standard Edition Server targets small- to medium-sized businesses or branch offices within large organizations. This topology is appropriate for organizations with fewer than 5,000 users or for pilot deployments where the main goals are simplicity and ease of management and where high availability is not a requirement.

Table 3-1 lists the system requirements for Office Communications Server 2007 R2, Standard Edition.

TABLE 3-1 Hardware and Software Requirements for Standard Edition Servers

COMPONENT	REQUIREMENT
Computer and processor	64-bit, 2.0-GHz or faster processor (two or more processors recommended)
Memory	512 MB of RAM (8 GB or more recommended)
Hard disk	Dual Ultra2 Small Computer System Interface (SCSI) hard drives with 36 GB of available hard disk space recommended
Operating system (all 64-bit editions)	Windows Server 2008 Standard Edition, Windows Server 2008 Enterprise Edition, Windows Server 2003 Standard Edition, Windows Server 2003 R2 Standard Edition, Windows Server 2003 Enterprise Edition, Windows Server 2003 R2 Enterprise Edition, Windows Server 2003 Datacenter Edition, or Windows Server 2003 R2 Datacenter Edition
Other	Public Key Certificates for Transport Layer Security (TLS), Active Directory directory service for Windows Server 2008, Windows Server 2003, or Windows 2000 with Service Pack 3 required

Enterprise Edition Pool

The Enterprise Edition deployment improves the scalability and availability of an Office Communications Server 2007 R2 deployment by separating the logical operations that a Standard Edition Server performs into individual servers. An Enterprise Edition deployment is referred to as an *Enterprise pool* because it involves multiple physical servers. An Enterprise pool decouples the back-end server running SQL Server and the SIP registrar and proxy service from the front-end servers. The front-end servers maintain transient information—such as logged-on state and control information for an IM, Web, or Audio/Video (A/V) conference—only for the duration of a user's session. This configuration is an advantage, because in the event of a system failure, a new front-end server can be quickly brought up to replace it. The front-end servers can further be expanded into specialized server roles by using a command-line option to separate the multipoint control units (MCUs) and Web Components onto separate physical servers. This results in the following two Enterprise pool models:

- **Enterprise pool, consolidated configuration** In this configuration, shown in Figure 3-3, all front-end servers are configured identically with the same set of server roles. The front-end servers, in addition to running the Instant Messaging (IM) Conferencing Server, can run any of the following additional server roles:
  - Web Conferencing Server
  - A/V Conferencing Server
  - Telephony Conferencing Server
  - Application Sharing Conferencing Server
  - Web Components Server
  - Communicator Web Access Server
  - Application Server

  Figure 3-3 shows both a single consolidated server deployment and a multiple consolidated server deployment. The multiple consolidated server configuration requires a physical hardware load balancer (HLB) to load balance client connections to the front-end servers and Web servers. (A hardware load balancer is not required in the single consolidated server deployment.) In the multiple consolidated server deployment, all front-end servers are configured with the same set of MCUs. These server roles must be configured uniformly on all front ends. All Internet Information Services (IIS) services must be configured in locked-down mode.

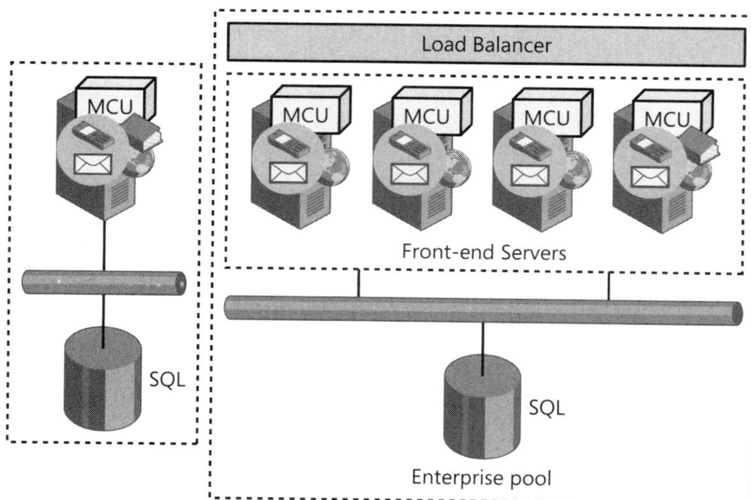

FIGURE 3-3 Consolidated configuration

- **Enterprise pool, expanded configuration** In this configuration, shown in Figure 3-4, each server member of the Enterprise pool runs a single server role per physical server. This arrangement enables this configuration to scale beyond the consolidated configuration. In this configuration, the MCUs must be individually addressable. IIS must not be installed on the front-end servers.

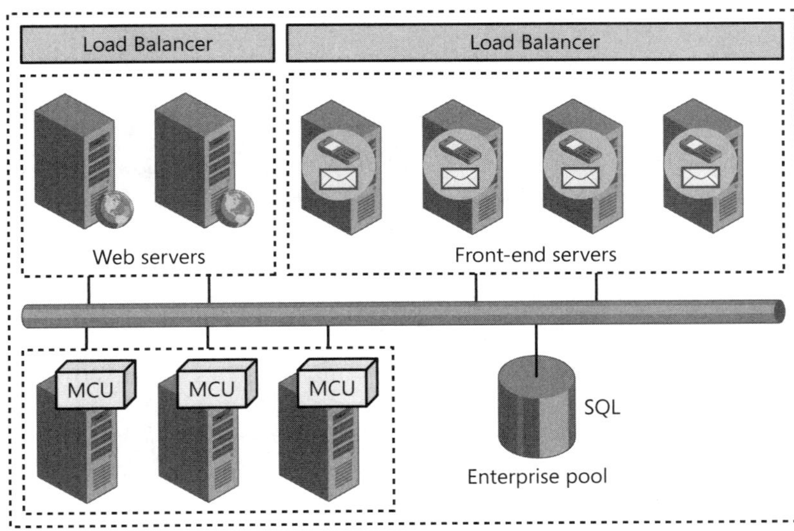

FIGURE 3-4 Expanded configuration

The expanded configuration requires a physical hardware load balancer (HLB) to load balance client connections to the front-end servers and Web servers. The HLB's virtual IP (VIP) address must be manually published in the Domain Name System (DNS). Clients connect to this VIP when signing in to the Enterprise pool. In both configurations, an Enterprise pool can scale up to four front-end servers.

For high availability on the back-end SQL Server, an Enterprise Edition pool deployment can be clustered by using Windows Server Clustering, which is a feature of the Enterprise Edition and Datacenter Edition of Windows Server 2003 and Windows Server 2003 R2, or Windows Server Failover Clustering, which is a feature of Windows Server 2008. Microsoft supports *only* active-passive SQL clustering for Office Communications Server 2007 R2 Enterprise pool deployments. Active-passive SQL clustering means one SQL node is active while the other SQL node is passive. The front-end servers in the pool are connected to the active node. The passive node takes over when the active node fails. The passive node must be an exact replica of the active node in the system configuration. The SQL Server can be shared with other applications as long as the Enterprise pool database is running on a separate SQL instance. Office Communications Server 2007 R2 supports running the back-end SQL Server on a 64-bit or 32-bit server.

All roles of Office Communications Server 2007 R2 Enterprise Edition require one of the following operating systems:

- The 64-bit edition of Windows Server 2008 Standard operating system, or the 64-bit edition of Windows Server 2008 Enterprise operating system
- The Windows Server 2003 R2 Standard x64 Edition operating system with Service Pack 2 (SP2), or the Windows Server 2003 R2 Enterprise x64 Edition operating system with SP2
- The Windows Server 2003 Standard x64 Edition operating system with SP2, or the Windows Server 2003 Enterprise x64 Edition operating system with SP2

All servers belonging to an Enterprise pool must be running on a Windows Server 2003 SP1 or Windows Server 2003 R2 computer joined to the same Active Directory domain. Thus, Microsoft does not support a scenario in which half of the front-end servers are deployed in domain A and half in domain B, while the back-end servers are deployed in domain C. Also, all servers in an Enterprise pool should be within geographic proximity with 1-gigabit connectivity between front-end servers and back-end servers.

Table 3-2 lists the system requirements for Office Communications Server 2007 R2 Enterprise Edition.

TABLE 3-2 Hardware and Software Requirements for Front-End Servers

COMPONENT	REQUIREMENT
Computer and processor	64-bit, dual processor, dual core with 3.0-GHz or faster processor
Memory	8 GB or more of RAM recommended
Cache	1 MB L2 per core recommended
Hard disk	2 SCSI hard drives with 72 GB of available hard disk space recommended
Network	1-gigabit network interface card (NIC) recommended
Operating system (all 64-bit editions and with the latest service pack)	Windows Server 2008 Standard Edition, Windows Server 2008 Enterprise Edition, Windows Server 2003 Standard Edition, Windows Server 2003 R2 Standard Edition, Windows Server 2003 Enterprise Edition, Windows Server 2003 R2 Enterprise Edition, Windows Server 2003 Datacenter Edition, or Windows Server 2003 R2 Datacenter Edition
Other	Public Key Certificates for Transport Layer Security (TLS), Active Directory domain/forest level Windows Server 2008, or Windows Server 2003

Director Role

When you are deploying a single Standard Edition Server or Enterprise pool, your topology remains simple. However, to handle a large number of users or users who are geographically dispersed, deploying multiple Standard Edition Servers or Enterprise pools might be necessary. In such situations, it is best to deploy a Director or array of Directors. The Director server role directs client traffic to the correct home server. Before explaining why it is important to deploy this role, some background information is necessary.

When users sign in to Office Communications Server, Office Communicator performs a DNS Service Record Locator (SRV) query to locate an Office Communications Server (Access Edge Server, Director, Standard Edition Server, or Enterprise pool) that is authoritative of the user's SIP domain, which is the right portion of the user's sign-in address. The client contacts the Internet Protocol (IP) address returned from the DNS query and attempts to sign in to this server. If this server is the user's home server, the server signs in the user. If not, this server redirects or proxies the connection to the user's home server or pool.

This will always be the case if your organization has only a single home server or pool. However, if you have deployed multiple Standard Edition Servers and Enterprise pools within your organization, which Standard Edition Servers and Enterprise pools do you advertise for this SRV record in DNS? Maybe you publish the fully qualified domain name (FQDN) of all your Standard Edition Servers and Enterprise pools. In that case, the DNS SRV query might or might not return the user's home server when Office Communicator queries DNS. If the DNS query returns the FQDN of a server that is not the user's home server, this server must redirect the client to the user's home server. This makes the initial sign-in traffic nondeterministic because clients signing in are not guaranteed to reach the user's home server in the first hop.

This nondeterministic configuration has several effects. First, each home server and pool must account for the performance load created from redirecting client requests attempting to sign in users not homed on that server or pool. In the worst-case scenario, every home server and pool must handle the load of redirecting sign-in traffic for all users in your organization. Second, if the DNS query returned directs the client to a server that is unavailable, the sign-in experience will be affected because the client must wait for the network timeout to expire before attempting to connect to another server.

To avoid home servers from having to redirect client traffic to the correct home server, you can elect to advertise a single Standard Edition Server or Enterprise pool in DNS for this SRV record. This server can be solely in charge of directing Office Communicator clients to their user's correct home server when signing in. This, in effect, specializes the role of a Standard Edition Server or Enterprise pool to that of a Director redirecting client traffic to the correct home server. Therefore, the server role name, Director, was designated. Although the Director can serve as a home server by assigning users to it, it is not recommended to assign users to a Director.

It is recommended to deploy a Director role when your organization hosts multiple Standard Edition Servers or Enterprise pools. The Director role forces the sign-in traffic into a deterministic path. Instead of publishing the FQDN of the Standard Edition Servers and Enterprise pools in DNS, the DNS SRV publishes the FQDN of the Director or bank of Directors. When Office Communicator attempts to sign in the user, its DNS SRV query returns the FQDN of the Director. The Director knows how to locate the user's home server and redirects the client to that server. The Director's role is to redirect internal clients to the correct Standard Edition Server or Enterprise pool where the user is homed on, as shown in Figure 3-5. This configuration allows Standard Edition Servers and Enterprise pools to handle SIP traffic only for their users.

DIRECT FROM THE SOURCE

Using a Pool of Directors to Boost Reliability

Byron Spurlock
Consulting Services (MCS) Consultant

As the Director role becomes more commonly used with remote user scenarios with Office Communications Server 2007 R2, there are some important planning considerations to keep in mind. The Director is the server that stands between your perimeter Edge Servers and your Office Communications Server 2007 R2 home server or pool. A few of the benefits of having a Director in place are to offload user authentication requests and to provide an extra layer of security between the Edge Servers in the perimeter network and your internal Office Communications Server 2007 R2 pool. For users in your organization to authenticate against a Director instead of the user's homed pool server, you need to point your SRV record for Automatic Configuration to your Director instead of your Standard Edition Server or Enterprise pool. Now, if you deploy a single Standard Edition or Enterprise Edition server as a Director server in this setup, you have introduced a single point of failure into your environment. To avoid this single point of failure, you can add one or more additional Enterprise Edition servers to the picture to create a pool. You would need to locate these pooled Enterrprise Edition Servers that function as Directors behind a physical hardware load balancer.

With Office Communications Server 2007, we supported an array of Standard Edition servers behind a load balancer, which was commonly referred to as a Director Array. From Office Communications Server 2007 R2 forward, an array of Standard Edition servers is no longer supported. However, a pool of enterprise edition servers configured as Directors is supported.

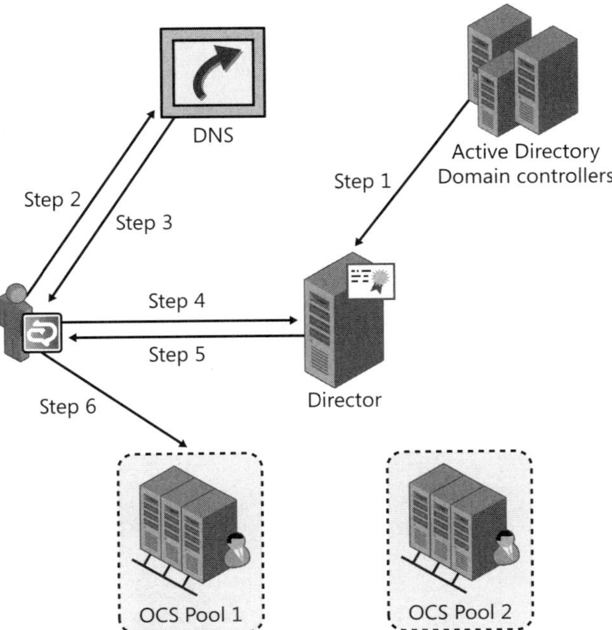

FIGURE 3-5 Director routing internal traffic

The process illustrated in Figure 3-5 is as follows:

1. The UR synchronizes user information with Active Directory domain controllers.
2. Communicator performs a DNS SRV query.
3. The DNS returns the FQDN of the Director.
4. Communicator connects to the Director.
5. The Director redirects Communicator to the user's home server or pool.
6. Communicator signs in to the user's home server or pool.

In addition to helping route traffic for internal deployments, a Director plays an important role for external topologies. When configuring federation, public IM connectivity, or remote access, deploying a Director as the Access Edge Server's next hop is required when remote access for users is needed. By using a Director or bank of Directors, the only IP address and port number that need to be opened on the internal firewall is access to the Director on port 5061 for SIP traffic.

By restricting the Access Edge Server to reach only the Director, you can limit access to your internal network if the Access Edge Server is ever compromised. None of the internal Standard Edition Servers and Enterprise pools are directly accessible by the Access Edge Server.

The Director provides the following benefits:

- Authenticates remote users. The Director prevents unauthorized users from entering the internal network.

- Proxy remote user connections to the correct Standard Edition Server or Enterprise pool. This is necessary because remote user connections cannot be redirected.
- Denial of Service (DoS) mitigation. Verifies the intended recipient of a message is a valid user. This protects internal servers from processing invalid messages from a public IM connectivity or federated partner.

For outgoing connections to the Access Edge Server, the Standard Edition Servers and Enterprise pools route traffic destined for external users (that is, federated contacts, public IM connectivity contacts, and remote users) to the Director. The Director then proxies the connection to the Access Edge Server. This is shown in Figure 3-6.

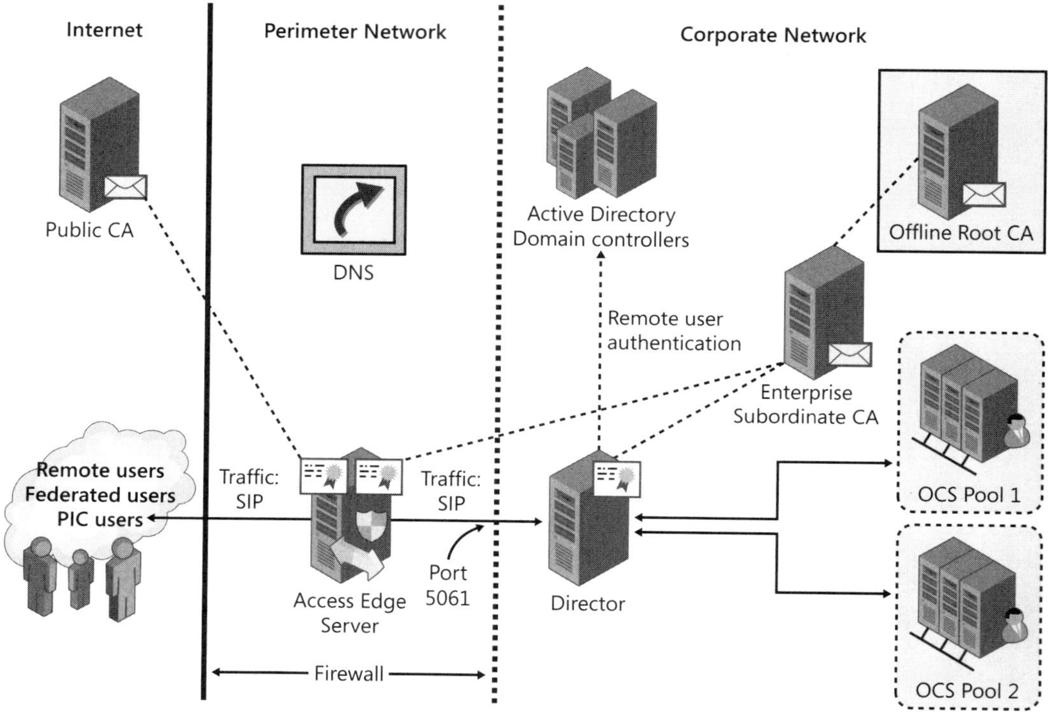

FIGURE 3-6 Director routing external traffic

Conferencing Servers

Conferencing Servers, also known as multipoint control units (MCUs), manage the content for Office Communications Server 2007 R2 conferences. Office Communications Server 2007 R2 provides the following MCUs:

- IM Conferencing Server
- Web Conferencing Server

- A/V Conferencing Server
- Telephony Conferencing Server
- Application Sharing Conferencing Server

Each of these server roles communicates directly with clients participating in a conferencing session. Each MCU uses its own protocol, which is optimized for the media it supports. These server roles also synchronize the state of the conference with a process called the *focus* that runs on the front-end server or Standard Edition Server. The protocol used to control the state of the conference session is called Centralized Conference Control Protocol (CCCP), also referred to as C3P. The focus sends state updates to the Conferencing Server using C3P, which the Conferencing Server listens for over an HTTPS channel.

Conferencing Servers host Web conferences only for organizers that are homed on the Standard Edition Server or Enterprise pool the server is a part of. Users homed on other Standard Edition Servers and Enterprise pools can join as participants to the conference, but they cannot schedule a meeting on a Conferencing Server that is not part of their home server. More details are covered in Chapter 6, "Conferencing Scenarios."

Each of these Conferencing Servers is described in more detail in the following sections. They share the same hardware and software requirements, which are detailed in Table 3-3.

> ***NOTE*** **To get the most up-to-date information about Conferencing Servers, refer to *http://www.microsoft.com/technet/prodtechnol/office/communicationsserver/evaluate/sysreqs/ocs-ee.mspx#EMD*.**

TABLE 3-3 Hardware and Software Requirements for Conferencing Servers

COMPONENT	REQUIREMENT
Computer and processor	64-bit, dual processor, dual core with 3.0-GHz or faster processor
Memory	8 GB or more of RAM recommended
Cache	1 MB L2 per core recommended
Hard disk	2 SCSI hard drives with 72 GB of available hard disk space recommended
Network	1-gigabit NIC recommended
Operating system (all 64-bit editions)	Windows Server 2008 Standard Edition, Windows Server 2003 Standard Edition, Windows Server 2003 R2 Standard Edition, or higher
Other	Public Key Certificates for Transport Layer Security (TLS), Active Directory domain/forest level Windows Server 2008, or Windows Server 2003

IM Conferencing Server

The IM Conferencing Server is automatically installed on every Standard Edition Server and every front-end server member of an Enterprise pool in both configurations (consolidated and expanded). It cannot be installed separately on a separate physical server. This service enables users to escalate a two-party IM session into a multiparty IM conference.

Escalating from a two-party IM session to a multiparty IM conference involves more than just adding new participants. New state information is involved in an IM conference, and this information must be synchronized across all the parties in an IM conference, such as tracking the roster (that is, a list of participants), determining which participants are conference leaders, displaying the participants' network of origin, and exposing a set of actions participants can perform (for example, mute, eject, and promote).

The focus controls the management of the conference session, and the IM Conferencing Server enforces it. The focus and the IM Conferencing Server communicate via the C3P protocol. Only port 5061 is required by the IM Conferencing Server.

If you use internal firewalls to compartmentalize your network, the IM Conferencing Server needs to have the same set of ports opened as the Standard Edition Server and Enterprise pool front-end server.

Web Conferencing Server

The Web Conferencing Server is responsible for multiplexing the Web conferencing data feed (for example, documents, application sharing, and whiteboard content) from the leader to all participants in the session. Persistent Shared Object Model (PSOM) is the protocol that the Web Conferencing Server uses to share documents and application content in real time to provide that collaborative experience. PSOM uses port number 8057.

The Web Conferencing Server is collocated with the Standard Edition Server and every front-end server in an Enterprise pool in a consolidated configuration. It can also be installed on its separate physical server for higher scalability. Installing a Web Conferencing Server on its own physical server is supported only in an Enterprise pool in an expanded configuration.

A/V Conferencing Server

Similar to the IM Conferencing Server and the Web Conferencing Server, the A/V Conferencing Server is an MCU for audio and video media. In the case of audio, the A/V Conferencing Server mixes the audio feeds from every participant before returning the mixed audio to each participant. This is computationally intensive. Therefore, it is recommended that you allocate a high-end server for this purpose.

The A/V Conferencing Server uses the Real-Time Audio (RTAudio) codecs for audio and Real-Time Video (RTVideo) codecs for video. Both of these protocols are designed to optimize performance in high-latency, low-bandwidth networks such as the Internet. Two-way communications are peer to peer. Therefore, for voice calls (which make up the large majority of audio communications), the A/V Conferencing Server is not involved.

Telephony Conferencing Server

The Telephony Conferencing Server provides the functionality of joining and controlling an audio conference hosted on a Public Switched Telephone Network (PSTN) bridge from a service provider such as AT&T, Verizon, BT, Intercall, or Premier. When users use the Microsoft Conferencing add-in for Microsoft Office Outlook to schedule a Live Meeting with audio or a conference call, at the time of the conference your desktop phone will be automatically set up to join the audio bridge hosted by your organization's carrier. The organizer will be able to control the audio from Communicator and perform activities such as muting everyone except the presenter, muting themselves, and removing participants.

The Telephony Conferencing Server is installed automatically as part of the Standard Edition Server and also on the front-end server in an Enterprise pool. It cannot be installed separately as its own service running on a separate physical server.

Application Sharing Conferencing Server

The Application Sharing Conferencing Server is a new server role in Office Communications Server 2007 R2. This server role provides the platform for desktop and application sharing in Office Communicator 2007 R2 and Office Communicator Web Access R2. The Application Sharing Conferencing Server installs with other conferencing components on the front-end server and manages the data exchange during desktop and application sharing sessions. The Application Sharing Conferencing Server is discussed in further detail in Chapter 6.

Application Server

Office Communications Server 2007 R2 introduces a component called the Application Server, which provides a platform for supplementary Unified Communications applications. The Application Server automatically installs on the front-end server. In Office Communications Server 2007 R2, the Application Server provides the following four applications:

- **Conferencing Attendant** The Conferencing Attendant application enables conference organizers to include a dial-in number when scheduling audio conferences so that users can join the audio by using a regular mobile, desk, or home phone.
- **Conference Announcement Service** This service provides announcement functionality so that a tone or message plays when a user joins or leaves a conference.

- **Response Group Service** This service emulates the "hunt group" functionality in traditional Private Branch eXchange (PBX) phone systems, whereby incoming calls to a specific phone number are queued and routed to designated agents based on predefined routing rules.
- **Outside Voice Control** The Outside Voice Control enables any mobile phone that is running Office Communicator Mobile to function as an Office Communications Server endpoint.

Depending on the organization's needs, any of these applications can be enabled or disabled. As is always the case, all front-end servers must be configured identically. Although the Application Server component installs on every front-end server, it is activated only when one of its applications starts.

Monitoring Server

If you need to track call detail records (for example, if you do want to collect statistical usage data without archiving the actual body of the IM conversation) or Quality of Experience (QoE) data, you should deploy the Monitoring Server.

To simplify data monitoring, Office Communications Server 2007 R2 consolidates the Call Detail Record (CDR) service with QoE data collection into a single server role, called the Monitoring Server. Because the CDR service is no longer hosted by the Archiving Server, organizations that require the CDR service are not required to deploy the Archiving Server. The Office Communications Server 2007 QoE Monitoring Server is deprecated in Office Communications Server 2007 R2.

Archiving Server

In Office Communications Server 2007 R2, the CDR service that was previously included in the Archiving and CDR Server is now part of the Monitoring Server. If your organization has a policy that requires the content of every communication to be logged for compliance purposes, you can find this functionality with the Archiving Server. This server role enables archiving of all messages at the server level. Because all IM conversations travel through the user's home server, it is possible to enforce archiving at the server level without requiring any cooperation from the client. This architecture offers the most control to the administrator.

The Archiving Server must be installed on a Windows Server 2003 or Windows Server 2003 R2 computer with Microsoft SQL Server 2000 SP3a (or higher) or Microsoft SQL Server 2005 SP1 (or higher) installed. See Table 3-4 for the hardware and software requirements for this role.

TABLE 3-4 Hardware and Software Requirements for Archiving Servers

COMPONENT	REQUIREMENT
Computer and processor	64-bit, dual processor, dual core with 2.6-GHz or faster processor
Memory	8 GB or more of RAM recommended
Cache	2 MB L2 per core recommended
Hard disk	2 × 72 GB, 15K or 10K RPM, RAID 0 (striped) or equivalent
Network	1-gigabit NIC recommended
Operating system (all 64-bit editions)	Windows Server 2008 Standard Edition, Windows Server 2003 Standard Edition, Windows Server 2003 R2 Standard Edition, or higher
Other	Public Key Certificates for Transport Layer Security (TLS), Microsoft SQL Server 2008 (32-bit or 64-bit), or SQL Server 2005 with Service Pack 2 (32-bit or 64-bit) Active Directory domain/forest level Windows Server 2008 or Windows Server 2003

Edge Servers

Office Communications Server 2007 R2 defines three Edge Server roles. These server roles are referred to as Edge Servers because they are deployed in the perimeter network of an organization's network. These server roles enable an organization to expose Office Communications functionality across the corporate network boundary to remote employees, federated partners, and public IM connectivity users. Office Communications Server 2007 R2 exposes the following Edge Server roles:

- Access Edge Server
- Web Conferencing Edge Server
- A/V Edge Server

These server roles are explained in more detail in the following sections. Hardware and software requirements for edge servers are shown in Table 3-5.

TABLE 3-5 Hardware and Software Requirements for Edge Servers

COMPONENT	REQUIREMENT
Computer and processor	64-bit, dual processor, dual core with 3.0-GHz or faster processor
Memory	8 GB or more of RAM recommended
Cache	1 MB L2 per core recommended
Hard disk	2 SCSI hard drives with 72 GB of available hard disk space recommended
Network	Two 1-gigabit NICs: one NIC for the external edge and the second NIC for the internal edge
Operating system (all 64-bit editions)	Windows Server 2008 Standard Edition, Windows Server 2003 Standard Edition, Windows Server 2003 R2 Standard Edition, or higher
Other	Public Key Certificates for Transport Layer Security (TLS), Active Directory domain/forest level Windows Server 2008, or Windows Server 2003

Access Edge Server

The Access Edge Server (formerly known as the Access Proxy in Live Communications Server 2005 SP1) must be deployed if you want to enable federation, public IM connectivity, or remote user access. The Access Edge Server handles the SIP traffic that is necessary to establish and validate connections. It does not transfer data or authenticate users. The Director, the internal Standard Edition Server, or the Enterprise pool authenticate users.

The Access Edge Server cannot be collocated with any other network perimeter service, such as Microsoft Internet Security and Acceleration (ISA) Server or the Microsoft Exchange 2007 Server Edge role; however, it can be collocated with the Web Conferencing Edge Server and the A/V Edge Server. In fact, the supported method of installing the Access Edge Server is along with the Web Conferencing and A/V Edge Server, all collocated on the same physical server known as the consolidated edge topology.

The Access Edge Server must be configured with two IP addresses, one that is visible to the Internet and one that is visible to the enterprise network. The recommended configuration (for performance and ease of securing the server) is to install two NICs, connecting the Internet to one and the enterprise network to the other. Access Edge Server configuration is discussed in further detail in Chapter 4, "Infrastructure and Security Considerations."

To provide high availability in Office Communicator Server R2, consolidated Edge Servers can be deployed in the perimeter network. A hardware load balancer must be configured on both sides of the consolidated Edge Servers, as shown in Figure 3-7.

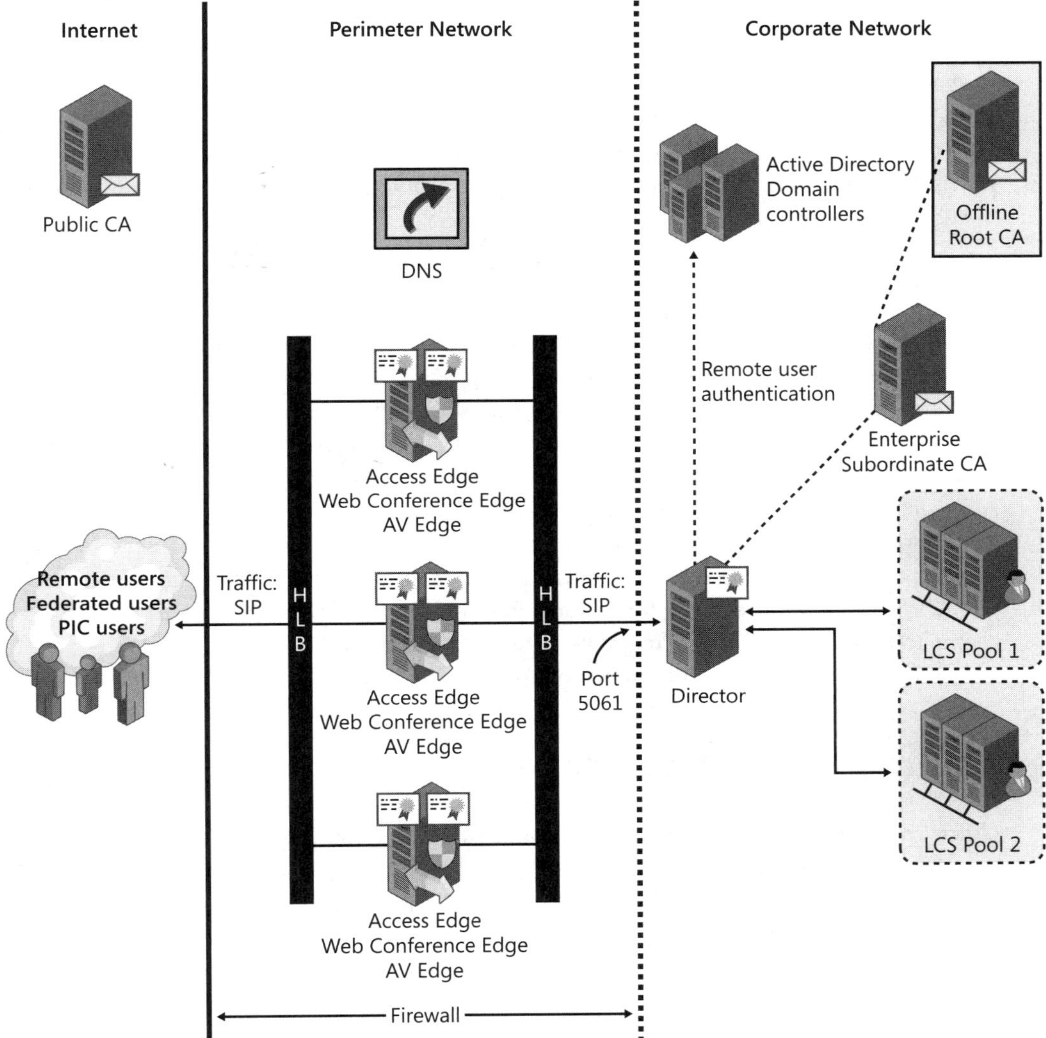

FIGURE 3-7 Array of Edge Servers

Web Conferencing Edge Server

The Web Conferencing Edge Server proxies PSOM Web conferencing media across the firewall between the Internet and the corporate network. The Web Conferencing Edge Server must be configured with two NICs: one network card connected to the Internet, and the other network card connected to the internal network. The network security administrator must open port 443 on the external NIC to allow users to connect from the Internet and port 8057 on the internal NIC so that Web Conferencing Servers can connect to it. Connections between the Web Conferencing Edge Server and the Web Conferencing Server are always initiated by the internal Web Conferencing Server. This design reduces the number of vectors into the corporate network.

If audio and video are not priorities for your edge deployment and high availability is still a concern, it is recommended that you combine the Access Edge Server role and the Web Conferencing Edge Server role on the same physical servers in an array with at least two physical servers. This configuration provides high availability while consolidating the number of Edge Servers required.

A/V Edge Server

The A/V Edge Server enables audio and video traffic to traverse the corporate perimeter network. The A/V Edge Server serves as a meeting point for bridging users connecting from the Internet to an A/V Conferencing Server associated with the user's home server. Users connect to the A/V Edge Server, and the A/V Conferencing Server connects to the A/V Edge Server. The A/V Edge Server relays the Real-Time Protocol (RTP) traffic between the users and A/V Conferencing Server. Similar to the other Edge Server roles, the A/V Edge Server must be configured with two NICs: one network card connected directly to the Internet and given a public routable IP address, and the other network card connected to the internal network. The A/V Edge Server uses the Information and Content Exchange (ICE) protocol to enable clients to traverse firewalls that might lie between the end user's client and the A/V Edge Server. A/V Edge Server configuration is discussed in further detail in Chapter 4.

Communicator Web Access

Office Communicator Web Access (CWA) enables users who have not installed the Office Communicator client to sign in to Office Communications Server by using a Web browser. Table 3-6 lists the platform and browser matrix that Communicator Web Access supports.

TABLE 3-6 Platform/Browser Support

PLATFORM	BROWSER
Windows	Internet Explorer Firefox
Mac OS X	Safari Firefox
Solaris	Firefox
Linux	Firefox

The CWA server role must be installed on a computer joined to your Active Directory forest, because it needs Active Directory connectivity to authenticate and authorize user access. CWA can be deployed for users inside and outside the organization's network.

CWA supports forms-based authentication, integrated Windows authentication (IWA), or custom authentication. Forms-based authentication can be used for external users. IWA refers to the native authentication protocols Kerberos and NT LAN Manager (NTLM) that are supported by Active Directory. IWA is supported only for internal usage. Custom authentication enables administrators to use a third-party authentication system to enable single sign-on or two-factor authentication. Custom authentication can be used for both internal and external users. After the user is authenticated, CWA determines the user's home server and registers the user. Because the home server trusts the CWA server, no further authentication is performed. CWA then proxies all traffic to and from the user's home server, as shown in Figure 3-8.

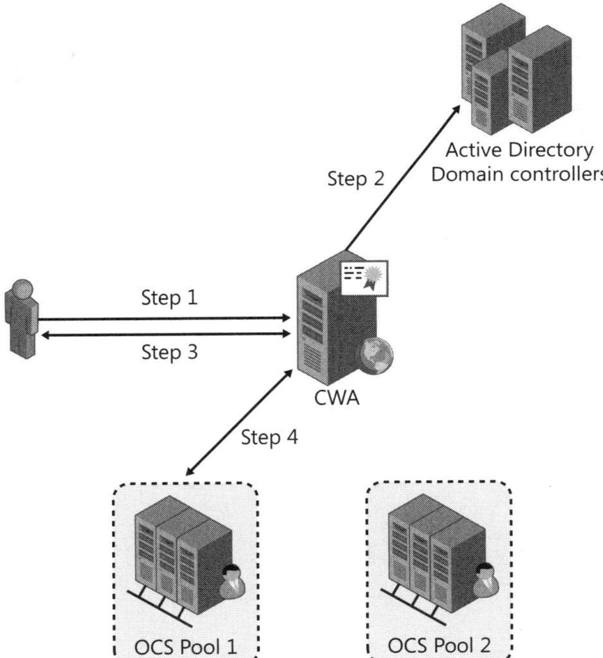

FIGURE 3-8 Internal deployment of CWA

The process illustrated in Figure 3-8 is as follows:

1. The user connects to the CWA URL to sign in.
2. CWA authenticates the user.
3. User requests are sent over HTTPS.
4. CWA proxies requests to the user's home server over SIP.

Collocating CWA on the same physical computer as another supported server role will diminish the overall performance of your server. Most customers in smaller deployments collocate CWA with a Director to avoid the cost and management of another physical server. If you have deployed Office Communicator to all your users, usage of CWA is likely to be light enough for a Director to handle because Office Communicator will be the primary client.

When making CWA accessible from outside your organization's firewall, it is strongly recommended that you secure your CWA server by using a reverse proxy such as Microsoft Internet Security and Acceleration (ISA) Server 2006 in your network perimeter. When configuring CWA for external access, you should use port 443. This topology is illustrated in Figure 3-9.

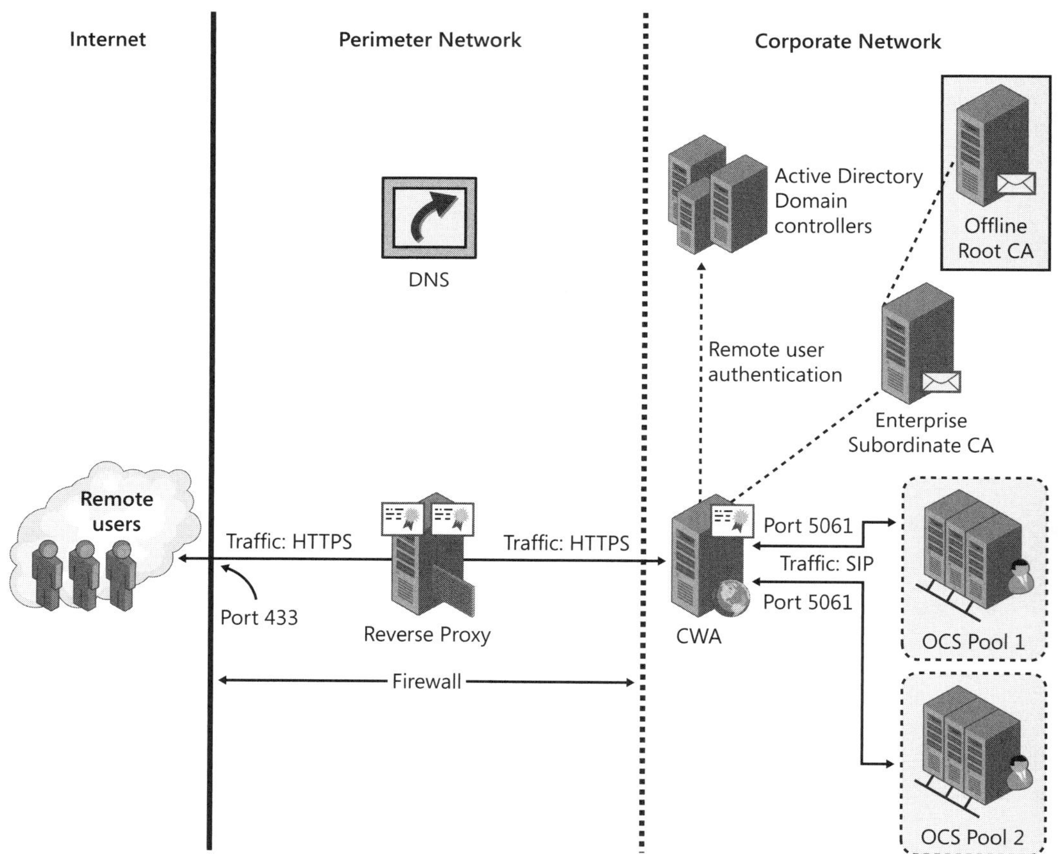

FIGURE 3-9 External deployment of CWA

Table 3-7 lists the system requirements for CWA, including supported browsers.

NOTE To get the most up-to-date information about Communicator Web Access, refer to *http://www.microsoft.com/technet/prodtechnol/office/communicationsserver/evaluate/sysreqs/cwa.mspx*.

TABLE 3-7 Hardware and Software Requirements for CWA

COMPONENT	REQUIREMENT
Computer and processor	64-bit, dual processor, dual core with 3.0-GHz or faster processor
Memory	4-GB DDR (double data rate), 266-MHz RAM
Hard disk	18 GB of available hard disk space
Network adapter	100-Mb or higher network adapter
Operating system (all 64-bit editions)	Windows Server 2008 Standard Edition, Windows Server 2008 Enterprise Edition, Windows Server 2003 Standard Edition, Windows Server 2003 R2 Standard Edition, Windows Server 2003 Enterprise Edition, or Windows Server 2003 R2 Enterprise Edition
Supported browsers	Internet Explorer 6.0 (SP1 recommended), Firefox 1.0, Safari 1.2.4, Netscape 7.2
Other	Office Communications Server 2007 R2, .NET Framework 2.0, ASP.NET 2.0, Public Key Certificates for Transport Layer Security (TLS), HTTPS, and IIS version 6.0 running on Windows Server 2003 or IIS version 7.0 running in IIS 6.0 compatibility mode on Windows Server 2008

Web Components Server

The Web Components Server is an ASP.NET Web service running on Internet Information Services (IIS). This virtual directory is used to perform distribution list (DL) expansions and join users to a Web conference when they click the URL in the meeting request. This server role is automatically installed on the Standard Edition Server and front-end servers of an Enterprise pool in a consolidated configuration. In an Enterprise pool, expanded configuration, the Web Components Server is installed on a separate physical server. This server role is well suited to be collocated with the Communicator Web Access server role in the Enterprise pool, expanded configuration, because both server roles are Web services and require IIS. See Table 3-8 for the hardware and software requirements for this role.

TABLE 3-8 Hardware and Software Requirements for the Web Components Server

COMPONENT	REQUIREMENT
Computer and processor	64-bit, dual processor, dual core with 2.6-GHz or faster processor
Memory	4 GB or more of RAM recommended
Cache	1-MB L2 per core recommended
Hard disk	2 SCSI hard drives with 18 GB of available hard disk space recommended
Network	1-gigabit NIC recommended
Operating system (all 64-bit editions)	Windows Server 2008 Standard Edition, Windows Server 2008 Enterprise Edition, Windows Server 2003 Standard Edition, Windows Server 2003 R2 Standard Edition, or higher
Other	Public Key Certificates for Transport Layer Security (TLS), Active Directory directory service for Windows Server 2008, Windows Server 2003, or Windows 2000 with Service Pack 3 required

Mediation Server

The Mediation Server is a server role necessary to bridge the PSTN traffic to and from the media gateway to the Office Communications Server network. Because some existing media gateways do not currently support the SIP protocol over Transmission Control Protocol (TCP) and optimized media codecs used by Office Communications Server 2007 R2, the Mediation Server is needed to translate the RTAudio and RTVideo codecs to the G.711 codec commonly used by media gateways. In addition to performing codec translation, the Mediation Server performs reverse number lookups (RNLs) to resolve phone numbers from incoming calls arriving from the media gateway to the corresponding SIP Uniform Resource Identifier (URI). After phone numbers are resolved into SIP URIs, the Mediation Server routes the call to the user's home server.

Table 3-9 lists the hardware and software requirements for the Mediation Server role.

> ***NOTE*** **To get the most up-to-date information about the Media Server role, refer to** ***http://www.microsoft.com/technet/prodtechnol/office/communicationsserver/evaluate/sysreqs/ocs-ee.mspx#EBG.***

TABLE 3-9 Hardware and Software Requirements for the Mediation Server

COMPONENT	REQUIREMENT
Computer and processor	64-bit, dual processor, dual core with 3.0-GHz or faster processor for up to 120 concurrent calls
Memory	2 GB or more of RAM recommended
Cache	1-MB L2 per core recommended
Hard disk	1 SCSI hard drive with 36 GB of available hard disk space recommended
Network	2 1-gigabit NICs: one NIC connected to the Office Communications Server network, and the second NIC connected to the media gateway
Operating system (all 64-bit editions)	Windows Server 2008, Windows Server 2003 Standard Edition, Windows Server 2003 R2 Standard Edition, or higher
Other	Public Key Certificates for Transport Layer Security (TLS), Active Directory Domain Services and Active Directory directory service for Windows Server 2008, Windows Server 2003, or Windows 2000 with Service Pack 3 required

Group Chat Server

Office Communications Server 2007 R2 Group Chat Server is a new server role in Office Communications Server 2007 R2. This server role provides the platform for group chat rooms, which allow for persistent, ongoing IM conversations. Chat rooms are particularly useful for ongoing collaboration among project team members because all data that is part of the IM conversation in a chat room persists. The Group Chat Server instantiates the chat room, manages its permissions, and maintains its state for the duration of the chat room.

Supported Collocation Server Roles

The list of supported collocation server roles for Office Communications Server 2007 R2 is shown in Table 3-10.

TABLE 3-10 Supported Collocation Server Roles for Office Communications Server 2007 R2

	STANDARD EDITION SERVER	FRONT-END SERVER	IM CONFERENCING SERVER	TELEPHONY CONFERENCING SERVER	WEB CONFERENCING SERVER	APPLICATION SHARING CONFERENCING SERVER	A/V CONFERENCING SERVER	WEB COMPONENTS SERVER	APPLICATION SERVER	DIRECTOR	COMMUNICATOR WEB ACCESS SERVER	EDGE SERVER	MEDIATION SERVER	ARCHIVING SERVER	MONITORING SERVER
Standard Edition Server		✓	✓	✓	✓	✓	✓	✓	✓		✓			✓	✓
Front-End Server	✓		✓	✓	✓	✓	✓	✓	✓		✓				
IM Conferencing Server	✓	✓		✓	✓	✓	✓	✓	✓		✓				
Telephony Conferencing Server	✓	✓	✓		✓	✓	✓	✓	✓		✓				
Web Conferencing Server	✓	✓	✓	✓		✓	✓	✓	✓		✓				
Application Sharing Conferencing Server	✓	✓	✓	✓	✓		✓	✓	✓		✓				
A/V Conferencing Server	✓	✓	✓	✓	✓	✓		✓	✓		✓				
Web Components Server	✓	✓	✓	✓	✓	✓	✓		✓		✓*			✓	✓
Application Server	✓	✓	✓	✓	✓	✓	✓	✓			✓				
Director											✓				
Communicator Web Access Server	✓	✓	✓	✓	✓	✓	✓	✓*	✓					✓	✓
Edge Server															
Mediation Server															
Archiving Server	✓							✓			✓				✓*
Monitoring Server	✓							✓			✓			✓*	

** These server roles are well suited to be collocated in the Enterprise pool, expanded configuration*

Summary

Office Communications Server 2007 R2 provides multiple server roles with specific purposes for building your enterprise instant messaging and conferencing infrastructure.

The Enterprise Edition scales the capacity of the Standard Edition Server to a larger magnitude by splitting the different logical functionality into separate physical servers. The Director redirects user connections to the user's home server or home pool. The Conferencing Servers, or MCUs, manage the content for Office Communications Server 2007 R2 conferences. The Application Server provides a platform for Conferencing Attendant, Conference Announcement Service, Response Group Service, and Outside Voice Control applications. The Edge Servers are deployed in the network perimeter to enable connectivity outside the organization's private network. The Archiving Server performs server-side recording of call details and archiving of all IM communications. The Monitoring Server performs CDR and QoE data gathering. Communicator Web Access provides a Communicator client experience from a Web browser for users without Office Communicator installed on their computers.

Additional Resources

- To get the most up-to-date information about OfficeCommunications Server 2007 R2 Standard Edition, refer to *http://www.microsoft.com/technet/prodtechnol/office/communicationsserver/evaluate/sysreqs/ocs-ee.mspx#EIB*. You can find this link on this book's companion media.
- To get the most up-to-date information about system requirements, refer to *http://www.microsoft.com/technet/prodtechnol/office/ communicationsserver/evaluate/sysreqs/ocs-ee.mspx*. You can find this link on this book's companion media.
- To get the most up-to-date information about Edge Servers, refer to *http://www.microsoft.com/technet/prodtechnol/office/ communicationsserver/evaluate/sysreqs/ocs-ee.mspx#EMD. You can find this link on this book's companion media.*
- TechNet resources, including webcasts, trial software, online course, and virtual labs, found at *http://technet.microsoft.com/en-us/office/bb267356.aspx*
- TechNet Technical Library, found at *http://technet.microsoft.com/en-us/library/bb676082.aspx*
- Communications Group Team Blog, including announcements by the Microsoft product team, found at *http://blogs.technet.com/uc/default.aspx*

CHAPTER 4

Infrastructure and Security Considerations

Microsoft Office Communications Server 2007 R2—similar to Microsoft Live Communications Server 2003, Microsoft Live Communications Server 2005, and Microsoft Office Communications Server 2007—takes advantage of other technologies to provide an integrated management experience and capitalize on existing technology investments customers might have already made. The primary technologies that Office Communications Server 2007 R2 relies on are as follows:

- Microsoft Active Directory Domain Services
- Microsoft Windows Server 2003 x64 or Microsoft Windows Server 2008 x64 operating systems
- Public key infrastructure (PKI) as used in Microsoft Windows Certificate Server and public certification authorities (CAs)
- Domain Name System (DNS)
- Microsoft SQL Server
- Hardware load balancers

- Media gateways
- Hypertext Transfer Protocol Secure (HTTPS) reverse proxy using Internet Security and Acceleration (ISA) Server

Infrastructure and Security Considerations

Office Communications Server 2007 R2 is the first version of Office Communications Server that runs on Windows Server 2008 and requires that the operating system be 64 bit. By itself, this is not a security issue, but it is an issue of reliability and stability.

Much like Microsoft Exchange Server 2007 before it, the forward progress of Office Communications Server is better served by the performance potential and the much larger memory available to the 64-bit hardware and operating system. This does mean that you will require 64-bit-capable hardware. Both Intel Corporation and Advanced Micro Devices (AMD) processors are supported under the x64 operating system. However, the Intel Itanium processor is not supported for installation of Office Communications Server. It is, however, supported to host the Microsoft SQL Server back end that is required by the Enterprise Edition of Office Communications Server.

Windows Server 2008 is inherently a more secure operating system because minimal services are deployed during the initial installation. For example, there are no roles installed, and if you need Web services, you must explicitly install Internet Information Services (IIS). File, print, Directory, and domain naming services are also not installed during the initial installation. And there is no .Net Framework except that which is required for the underlying operating system. All of these services must be installed as roles or features.

This provides for a system that is as secure as possible by default. As each role is installed, ports are opened on the mostly closed firewall, which has no inbound ports open by default. When a program or application is installed, it should make use of installation elements to open firewall ports and protocols. If it does not, the developer should provide the administrator with documentation about what ports and protocols should be open to enable proper communication. Part of this chapter deals directly with best and preferred practices for firewall ports and protocols that must be available for Office Communications Server to work correctly. Even though this work should be done for you at install time, knowing what is open through a firewall is critical information for any enterprise, for troubleshooting and compliance purposes.

Office Communications Server 2007 R2 is also supported on Windows Server 2003 x64. Windows Server 2003 does not have some of the more advanced features of Windows Server 2008, but it still has an efficient firewall that you will need to manage and support.

A recommendation for installing Office Communications Server 2007 R2 on either operating system is that you should not have any more services or features running than those that are required to allow Office Communications Server to run. This is even more important in the Edge services that sit in the perimeter of your firewall. The design of Office Communications Server is one of "defense in depth." The firewalls, routers, Edge Servers, Director, front-end servers, and pool servers all play a vital role, with certification services and Active Directory directory service providing specific and absolute authentication required by a complex system.

To date, it has been possible to locate separate Edge roles on dedicated servers. With the release of Office Communications Server 2007 R2, all roles are collocated on the same server. The security best practice for the new Edge Server configuration is that you should open only ports and protocols for the roles that you intend to use. If you are not planning to allow remote conference capability, the ports and protocols necessary for this role to run would not be opened in the firewall. Moreover, if you have no plans for any federation or remote access, there may be no reason to deploy any Edge Servers at all. This is part of your security planning and functional requirements steps. Obviously, if you do not need it, you do not implement it, and the security profile of your infrastructure is lowered because there are fewer factors to induce potential security problems.

Note that the key to safely implementing Office Communications Server is to always follow best security practices and thoroughly test all components that you implement. Knowing what is running and how it reacts to certain conditions is a mandatory step of securing your environment. The scope of this topic is much too large to cover here, and there are many books dedicated to the subject. Suffice it to say that implementing any server or service should receive a high degree of attention when it comes to security.

Understanding How Office Communications Server Takes Advantage of Active Directory

If your organization uses Active Directory as its primary directory service, you certainly understand the value of Active Directory. It is worthwhile, however, to understand how the integration of Office Communications Server 2007 R2 with Active Directory is beneficial to the organization and the IT administrator. This integration provides the following benefits:

- Global information that will be shared by all servers running Office Communications Server can be stored in Active Directory instead of replicating the information across servers.
- Server information can be published in Active Directory for easy discovery and asset management. This makes it possible to remotely manage servers running Office Communications Server from any computer joined to the Active Directory forest by using the administrator's tools that are installed as part of Office Communications Server.
- Users can sign in to Office Communications Server by using their Windows credentials, which provides a single sign-on experience. With single sign-on, users do not have to manage separate credentials.

One thing that has changed in Office Communications Server 2007 R2 is the location of global settings. Global settings provide information that every server in the forest needs. The default location for the settings is now the Configuration container instead of the System container of the forest's root domain.

If you decide to have the global settings in the System container, Active Directory replicates information stored in the System container among only the domain controllers and global catalog servers in the root domain. Domain controllers and global catalog servers in child domains will not have the Office Communications Server global settings replicated to them. Every Office Communications Server deployed in the forest must connect to a root domain global catalog to obtain this information. Because the best practice is to deploy servers running Office Communications Server in a child domain of the forest, servers will fail to activate if firewalls prevent them from accessing the domain controllers and global catalogs in the root domain. Or if already activated, they will fail to start. Figure 4-1 shows this root domain global catalog dependency.

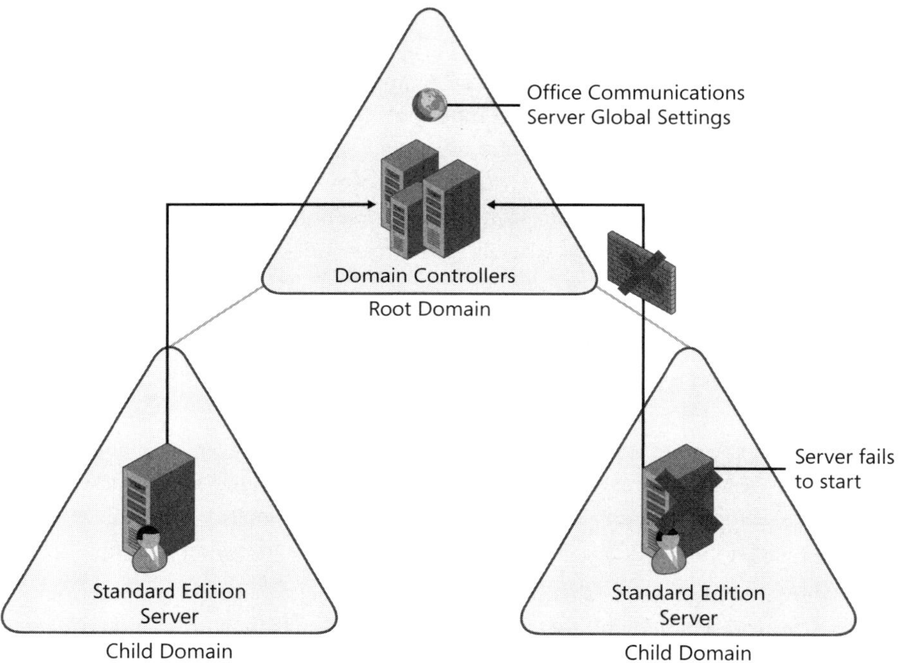

FIGURE 4-1 Global settings stored in the System container and the dependency on the root domain global catalog

The problem just described does not exist if you select the default option to use the Configuration container to store the global settings. Data defined in the Configuration container is replicated across all global catalogs in the forest. This implies that servers running Office Communications Server can also contact global catalogs in their domain for the global settings, as shown in Figure 4-2.

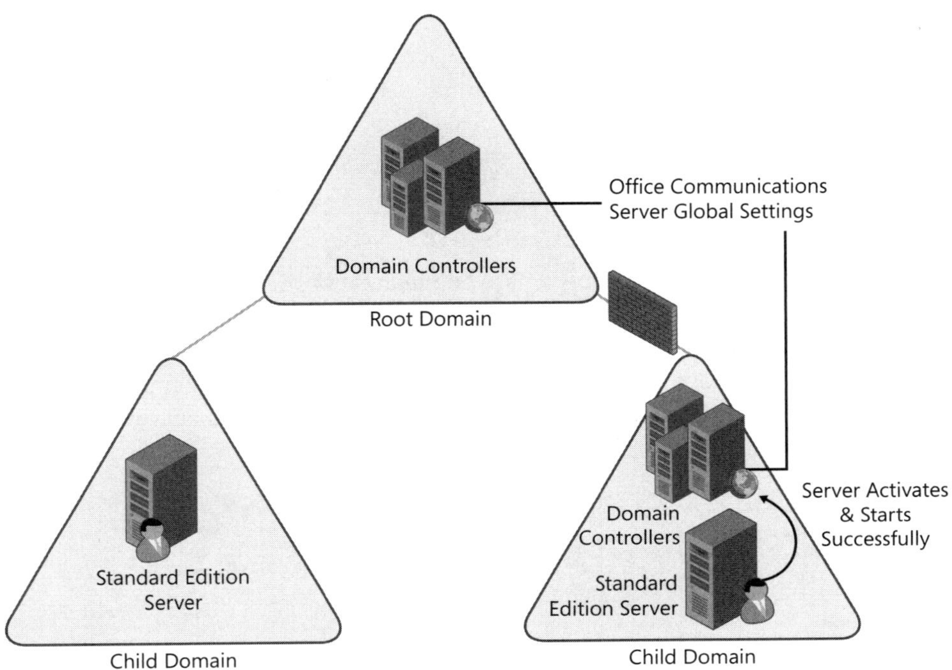

FIGURE 4-2 Global settings stored in the Configuration container allows contact with the global catalog in the local domain

Before Office Communications Server can add server- and service-specific settings to Active Directory, the Active Directory schema must be extended. This is the first step in preparing the Active Directory forest. Office Communications Server 2007 R2 requires the following three steps to prepare an organization's Active Directory forest.

1. Prep Schema**.** This step extends the Active Directory schema with new classes and attributes specific to Office Communications Server 2007 R2.
2. Prep Forest. This step creates the global settings in the System container in the root domain or the forest's Configuration container, which are used by all Office Communications Servers. Universal groups are also created during this step.
3. Prep current domain. This step must be run in every Active Directory domain where Office Communications Server 2007 R2 servers will be deployed or where users will be enabled for Office Communications. This step creates domain-level global security groups in the domain where it is carried out. These groups are used to manage Office Communications Servers deployed in the domain. Domain Prep gives permissions to the Universal groups created during Forest Prep to properties on user objects in the domain.

These steps are the same in the Standard Edition and the Enterprise Edition of Office Communications Server. It does not matter whether you complete them with the Standard Edition or Enterprise Edition. Setup automatically detects whether any required steps were not run, and it prevents the administrator from activating a Standard Edition Server or Enterprise Edition front-end server until these steps are completed successfully.

Performing the Prep Schema Step

To take full advantage of Active Directory, Office Communications Server extends the schema with requirements specific to its needs. This is similar to how Exchange Server extends the schema. Office Communications Server 2007 R2 extends the schema with 45 new classes and 106 new attributes. A root domain administrator who is a member of the Schema Administrators group must run this step once on a domain controller acting as the schema master in the root domain of the forest. This step is illustrated in Figure 4-3.

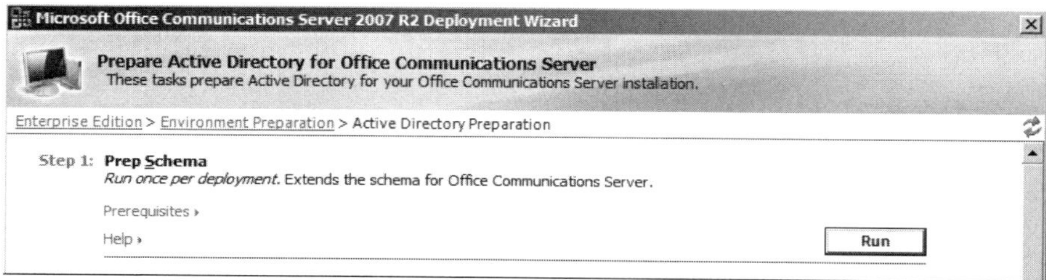

FIGURE 4-3 Prep Schema step

All schema extensions start with a unique namespace that is specific to Office Communications Server. This namespace is called *msRTCSIP-*"name", where *name* is the name of a class or attribute, *RTC* stands for Real-Time Communications, and *SIP* stands for Session Initiation Protocol (Request for Comment [RFC] 3261). Office Communications Server 2007 R2 is based on this protocol standard. By using a common namespace for all schema extensions, schema administrators can clearly identify which extensions are specific to Office Communications Server and know not to reuse them for other purposes. Setup provides a convenient way to verify that the schema extension has replicated throughout the forest before moving on to the next step, Prep Forest.

Performing the Prep Forest Step

After you extend the forest's Active Directory schema, you must perform the Prep Forest step, as shown in Figure 4-4. No objects are created in Active Directory during the Prep Schema step. The Prep Forest step must be run from the forest's root domain and is run only once. The Prep Forest step is unavailable until Prep Schema is completed successfully.

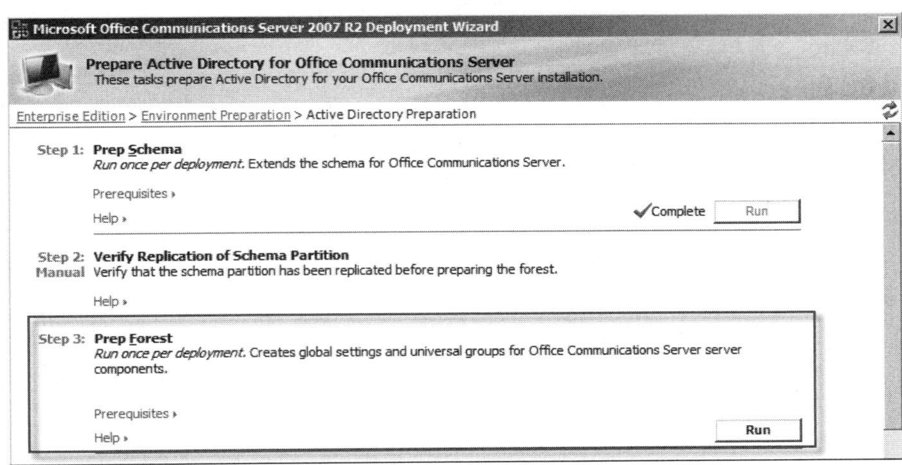

FIGURE 4-4 Prep Forest step

Running the Prep Forest step creates an instance of the *msRTCSIP-Service* class, called RTC Service. This container is the root where all global settings Office Communications Server uses are stored. Under this container are the following additional containers:

- **Global Settings** This container contains a set of attributes, plus the following three subcontainers:
  - GUID of class type *msRTCSIP-TrustedServer* This object defines the default SIP domain name for which this Active Directory forest is authoritative. By default, the SIP domain name is set to the forest's root domain fully qualified domain name (FQDN). Each SIP domain supported in your organization is represented by a different GUID of this class type. This setting is exposed on the General tab of the Office Communications Server Global Properties, as shown in Figure 4-5.

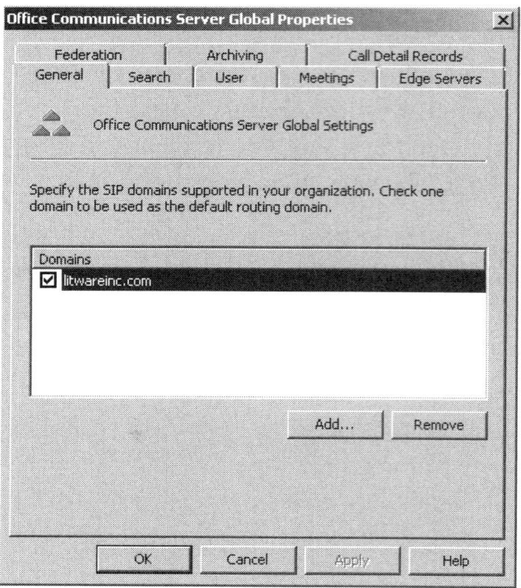

FIGURE 4-5 SIP domains in Global Properties at the forest level in Office Communications Server 2007 R2

- GUID of class type *msRTCSIP-TrustedServer* Each GUID represents a Standard Edition Server or an Enterprise pool front-end server that is trusted. This list of trusted servers is displayed in the tree view pane of the Admin Tools.
- GUID of class type *msRTCSIP-EdgeProxy* Each GUID represents the internal FQDN of an Edge Server deployed in your organization's network perimeter and trusted by your Office Communications Server infrastructure, as shown in Figure 4-6.

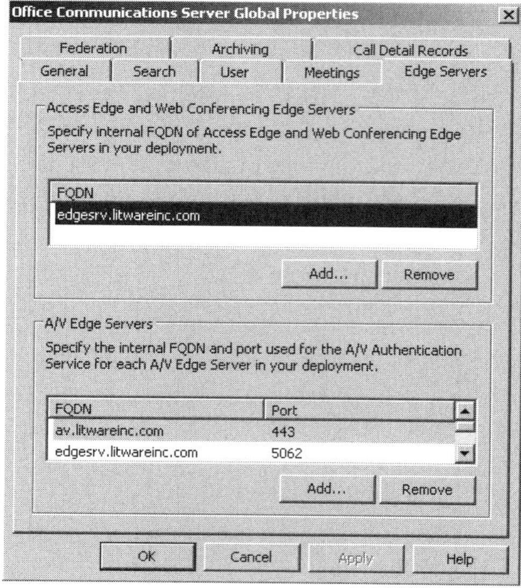

FIGURE 4-6 Edge Server configurations at the Global Properties level of Office Communications Server 2007 R2

- **Policies** This container lists all global policies defined by the administrator. Users the administrator has assigned to a policy are subject to the restrictions defined in the policy. Office Communications Server 2007 R2 exposes two types of policies: a Meeting type policy and a Unified Communications (UC) type policy. Each policy type contains a different set of configurable settings.
- **Location Normalization Rules** This container stores the set of rules the administrator has defined for how Office Communications Server clients should normalize phone numbers input by users to conform to the E.164 format. Each rule is composed of a pair of regular expressions (regex). The first regular expression is the match, and the second regular expression is the transform. For more information about normalization rules, see Chapter 11, "VoIP Scenarios."
- **Location Profiles** This container lists all the locations the administrator has defined. Each location is associated with a set of normalization rules that represent the dialing habits users for that region are accustomed to. For more information about normalization rules, see Chapter 11.
- **Phone Route Usages** This container stores all usages defined by the administrator. A usage is an arbitrary string that describes a set of routes. A phone route usage is associated with one or more phone routes. For more information about phone route usage, see Chapter 11.
- **Phone Routes** This container contains all the phone routes defined by the administrator. A phone route is a rule that defines which Mediation Servers should be routed to by phone calls that match a specific number pattern. For more information about phone routes, see Chapter 11.

> ***NOTE*** **All the aforementioned settings are available in Office Communications Server Admin Tools. To access them, open the Office Communications Server 2007 R2 link from the Administrative Tools folder. Right-click the forest node, select Properties, and then select Global Properties or Voice Properties.**

- **Application Contacts** This container contains special-use contact objects called application contacts. The *msRTCSIP-SourceObjectType* attribute specifies the purpose or type of the contact object. Server applications such as an Enterprise Voice application (see Chapter 13, "Enterprise Voice Application Scenarios") use these objects for routing. These types of server applications need to be addressable through SIP with a SIP Uniform Resource Identifier (URI) or a phone number, similar to a user. However, a user account would not be appropriate to assign to an application. Because a user cannot log in using a contact object, these objects are recommended for use by applications for security purposes. To uniquely represent these contact objects, their common name (CN) is a GUID. The attribute, *msRTCSIP-ApplicationDestination*, on the contact object specifies the server application this Application Contact points to. Chapter 13 provides more details on the use of these contact objects.

- **Location Contact Mappings** This container contains objects of type *msRTCSIP-LocationContactMapping*. These objects serve the purpose of associating an application contact to more than one location profile. In particular, the Enterprise Voice application Conference Auto-Attendant uses this facility.
- **Pools** This container stores all Standard Edition Servers and Enterprise pools.
- **Conference Directories** This container stores all instances of Conference Directory. A conference directory links all Public Switched Telephone Network (PSTN) dial-in conferences created on a specific pool to that specific pool. When users create a conference for PSTN dial-in, the meeting ID issued for the PSTN dial-in is based off of the conference directory. This makes it easy to move existing and recurring conferences to a different pool. A conference directory provides a level of indirection to make it possible to move conferences from one pool to another.
- **MCU Factories** This container stores all instances of an MCU Factory. An MCU Factory is created when the first instance of a specific vendor and type of multipoint control unit (MCU) (such as Conferencing Server) is activated. An MCU Factory manages the set of MCUs of a specific type that belongs to a Standard Edition Server or Enterprise pool.

  The MCU Factory is associated with one, and only one, Standard Edition Server or Enterprise pool.
- **Trusted MCUs** This container lists all trusted instances of the Conferencing Server. Office Communications Server creates an entry in this list when a Conferencing Server is activated. Office Communications Server blocks any communications with a Conferencing Server that are not listed in this container. It does this to prevent spoofing attacks (such as another server posing as a Conferencing Server). Office Communications Server validates that the FQDN listed in the Subject Name or Subject Alternate Name field of the certificate that is presented by the Conferencing Server is listed in this container. If the FQDN of the Conferencing Server is not present in this list, the server is not trusted.
- **Trusted Proxies** Similar to the Trusted MCUs container, this container lists all trusted instances of the proxy server. Instead of storing all server roles in the same container, Office Communications Server 2007 R2 creates separate containers for each server role.
- **Trusted Services** This container is meant to list trusted SIP servers, including third-party SIP servers, Microsoft Office Communicator Web Access Servers, and Mediation Servers.
- **Trusted Web Components Servers** This container lists all the trusted servers that have the Web Components Server role installed.

ON THE COMPANION MEDIA A complete list of all classes and attributes that are created can be found in the "Office Communications Server 2007 R2 Active Directory Classes and Attributes" document on the companion media in the Chapter 4 folder.

After creating the global objects, Prep Forest creates universal security groups. For administrators to manage the Office Communications Server infrastructure systems, they will have to be made members of the appropriate universal groups. These universal security groups are created in the Users organizational unit (OU) and can be found by using the Active Directory Users and Computers console. They are summarized in Table 4-1.

TABLE 4-1 Universal Groups Created by Office Communications Server

UNIVERSAL GROUP	DESCRIPTION
RTCUniversalUserAdmins	Members of this universal security group can manage users within the Active Directory forest who are enabled for Office Communications Server. Prep Domain grants this group read/write permissions to *RTCPropertySet*.
RTCUniversalReadOnlyAdmins	Members of this universal security group have read-only access to server and user settings in Active Directory.
RTCUniversalServerAdmins	Members of this universal security group can manage all aspects of Office Communications Server within the forest, including all server roles and users.
RTCUniversalGlobalReadOnlyGroup	Members of this universal security group have read-only access to Office Communications Server global settings in Active Directory.
RTCUniversalGlobalWriteGroup	Members of this universal security group have write access to Office Communications Server global settings in Active Directory.
RTCUniversalUserReadOnlyGroup	Members of this universal security group have read-only access to Office Communications Server global settings in Active Directory.
RTCUniversalGuestAccessGroup	Members of this universal security group have read-only access to certain Office Communications Server settings in Active Directory.
RTCUniversalServerReadOnlyGroup	Members of this universal security group can read server-related settings in Active Directory.

TABLE 4-1 Universal Groups Created by Office Communications Server

UNIVERSAL GROUP	DESCRIPTION
RTCHSUniversalServices	Members of this universal security group are service accounts used to run the Office Communications Server 2007 R2 Standard Edition Servers and Enterprise Edition front-end servers. This group enables servers to have read/write access to Office Communications Server global settings, as well as to user objects in Active Directory. This group has full access to *RTCPropertySet*. The *HS* in the name of the group refers to home server, which represents a Standard Edition Server or an Enterprise pool.
RTCArchivingUniversalServices	Members of this universal security group are service accounts used to run the Office Communications Server 2007 R2 Archiving Servers. This group provides permission to access the service's database.
RTCProxyUniversalServices	Members of this universal security group are service accounts used to run the Office Communications Server 2007 R2 proxy server.
RTCComponentsUniversalServices	Members of this universal security group are service accounts used to run the Office Communications Server 2007 R2 Conferencing Server, Web Components Server, and Mediation Server.

DIRECT FROM THE SOURCE

Infrastructure Groups

Nirav Kamdar
Senior Development Lead, Office Communications Server

The infrastructure groups that Office Communications Server 2007 R2 uses to build the other groups are as follows:

- **RTCUniversalGlobalWriteGroup**
- **RTCUniversalUserReadOnlyGroup**
- **RTCUniversalGuestAccessGroup**

Administrators should not modify permissions on these groups or add members directly to them.

Prep Forest defines two new property sets. With a *property set*, you can group a number of attributes into a set. You can apply security permissions to the property set, instead of to each individual attribute, through a single access control entry (ACE). These property sets are called RTCPropertySet and RTCUserSearchPropertySet and are of class type *controlAccess-Right*. They are defined under the *Extended-Rights* object in the Configuration container, as shown in Figure 4-7.

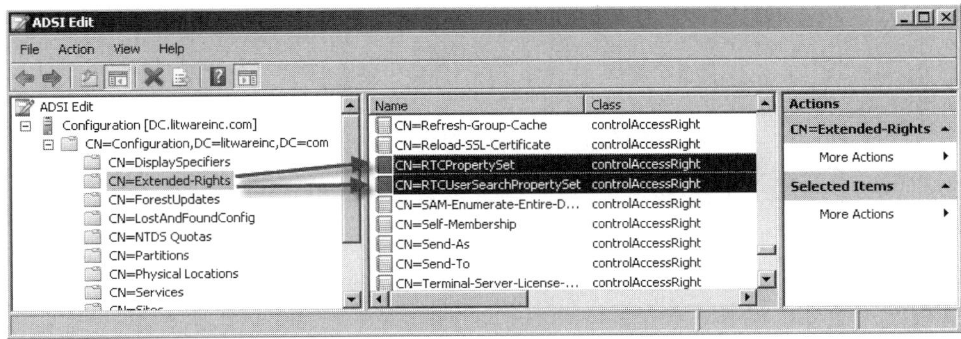

FIGURE 4-7 Office Communications Server property sets

The property set RTCPropertySet contains all the user attributes extended by Office Communications Server. To configure users for Office Communications Server, administrators must have read/write privileges to this property set. The RTCUniversalServerAdmins security group is given read permissions to this property set, so administrators of this group can view user configuration details but cannot configure users. The RTCUniversalUserAdmins security group is given read/write permissions to the property set, so administrators of this group are able to configure users for Office Communications Server. The RTCHSUniversalServices security group is given read/write permissions to this property set.

The RTCPropertySet property set is composed of the following attributes:

- *msRTCSIP-PrimaryUserAddress*
- *msRTCSIP-PrimaryHomeServer*
- *msRTCSIP-TargetHomeServer*
- *msRTCSIP-OptionFlags*
- *msRTCSIP-UserPolicy*
- *msRTCSIP-UserEnabled*
- *msRTCSIP-ArchivingEnabled*
- *msRTCSIP-FederationEnabled*
- *msRTCSIP-InternetAccessEnabled*
- *msRTCSIP-OriginatorSid*
- *msRTCSIP-Line*
- *msRTCSIP-LineServer*

- *msRTCSIP-UserExtension*
- *msRTCSIP-SourceObjectType*
- *msDS-SourceObjectDN*
- *msRTCSIP-ApplicationDestination*
- *msRTCSIP-ApplicationOptions*
- *msRTCSIP-UserLocationProfile*
- *msRTCSIP-ApplicationPrimaryLanguage*
- *msRTCSIP-ApplicationSecondaryLanguages*

The property set RTCUserSearchPropertySet is used to determine whether a user is authorized to search other users in the organization by using the Find functionality available in Office Communicator 2007 R2. By default, domain users are allowed to search each other without restriction, and only the RTCDomainUsersAdmins group has full permissions on this property set.

RTCUserSearchPropertySet is composed of a single attribute: *msRTCSIP-PrimaryUser-Address*.

Performing the Prep Domain Step

After Prep Forest is successfully completed, the Prep Domain step becomes available in the Setup program, as shown in Figure 4-8. Unlike Prep Schema and Prep Forest, Prep Domain remains available to run again in another child domain where Prep Domain has not been run yet.

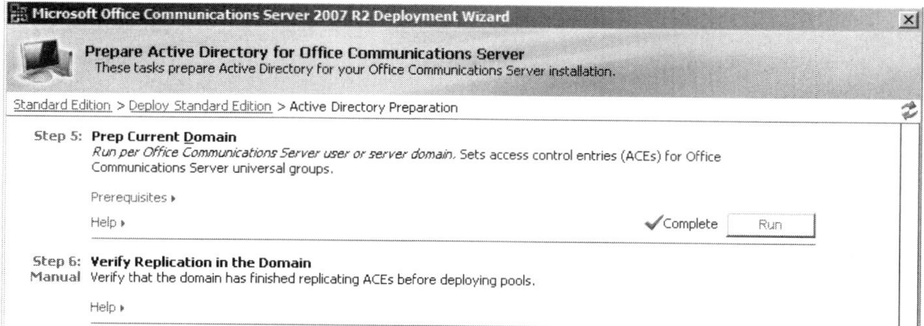

FIGURE 4-8 Prep Domain step

The general rule for knowing when to run Prep Domain is simple. This step must be run in every Active Directory domain in which Office Communications Server 2007 R2 will be deployed and in Active Directory domains in which users will be hosted on Office Communications Servers. It needs to be run only once per domain. If no servers running Office Communications Server will be deployed in the domain, running this step is not necessary. Domain administrator privileges are required to run Prep Domain.

Prep Domain adds permissions for the universal security groups created in the Prep Forest step to manage its domain users.

Changes in Active Directory to Support Operations

Office Communications Server takes advantage of Active Directory to publish service information. This means every Office Communications Server role is discoverable by querying Active Directory. A visible example of this feature is the automatic population of servers deployed in your Active Directory forest when you open the Office Communications Server Microsoft Management Console (MMC). Office Communications Server publishes this information in Active Directory during activation. This is why activation requires RTCUniversalServerAdmins or RTCUniversalGlobalWriteGroup privileges and membership in the Domain Admins group. The administrator needs sufficient permissions to write to Active Directory during activation.

During activation, the Setup program creates a service principal name (SPN) and registers this SPN with the service account used to run the service. By default, this service account is a user account called RTCService. The SPN is registered in the *servicePrincipalName* attribute of this object and is of the form *sip/<fqdn>*, as shown in Figure 4-9. For more information about how SPNs and service connection points (SCPs) work, see the related Microsoft TechNet article at *http://go.microsoft.com/fwlink/?LinkID=133666*.

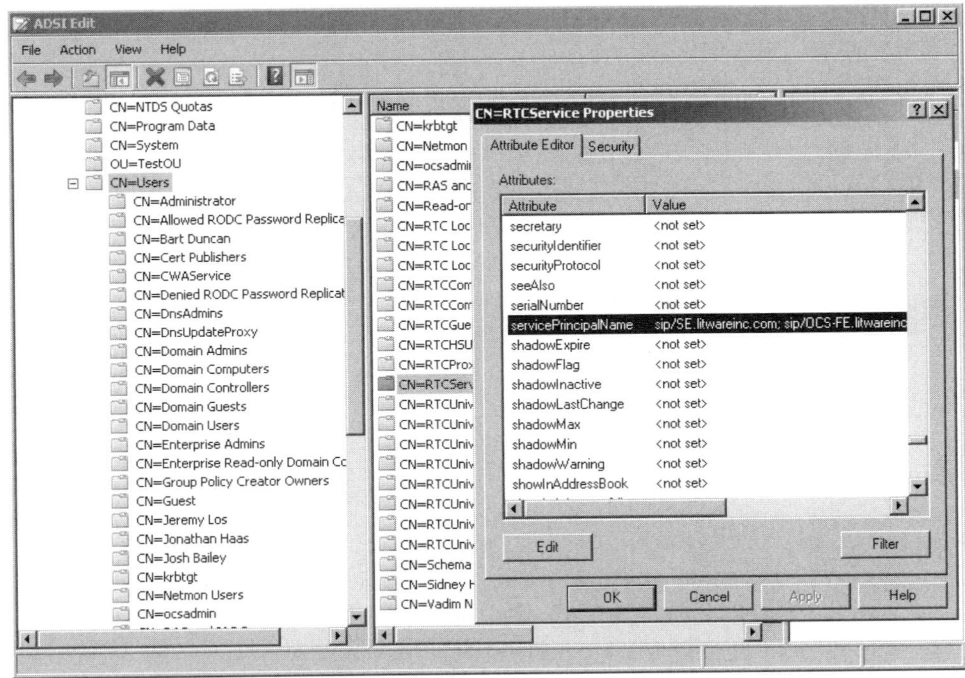

FIGURE 4-9 Service principal name

Activation publishes server information in three locations in Active Directory. Following Microsoft's best practices for Active Directory, Office Communications Server creates an SCP on the computer object that belongs to the physical server where Office Communications Server is installed. By creating an SCP on the computer object, third-party asset management applications can query the types of services running on each computer. This SCP related to Office Communications Server services installed by the administrator appears below the Microsoft node under the computer object. In the example shown in Figure 4-10, adsiedit.msc is used to view the SCPs on the computer object, OCS-FE. Eight services are installed:

- **LS ACP MCU** This service corresponds to the Telephony Conferencing Server.
- **LS AS MCU** This service corresponds to the Application Sharing Conferencing Server.
- **LS AV MCU** This service corresponds to the Audio/Video (A/V) Conferencing Server.
- **LS Data MCU** This service corresponds to the Web Conferencing Server.
- **LS IM MCU** This service corresponds to the IM Conferencing Server.
- **LS WebComponents Service** This service is a Web application running on IIS.
- **RTC Services** This service is the SIP server.
- **UC AppServer Services** This service hosts server applications such as Response Group Service and Conference Announcement Service, as well as third-party server applications.

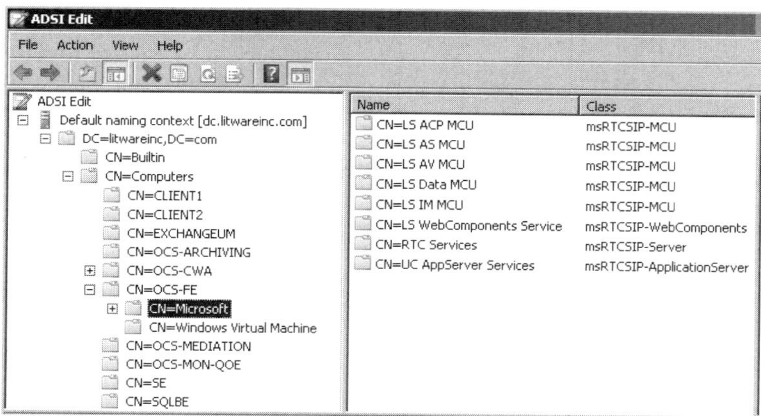

FIGURE 4-10 Active Directory global settings

Adsiedit.msc is a standard tool in Windows Server 2008 and is installed on any server on which you install the Active Directory Domain Services role. However, if you are using Windows Server 2003 x64, it is available as a Web download from Microsoft as part of the Windows Support Tools. You must register the dynamic-link library (DLL), adsiedit.dll, first by running the following command at a command prompt:

```
regsvr32 adsiedit.dll
```

It also is installed as one of the support tools that is on the Windows Server 2003 x64 media in the SUPPORT directory.

When a Standard Edition Server is activated or when an Enterprise pool is created, Office Communications Server creates a new entry under the Pools container of class type *msRTC-SIP-Pools* in Active Directory. Each entry represents a logical pool and is of class type *msRTC-SIP-Pool*. The *msRTCSIP-Pool* class defines the FQDN of the pool, as well as the association between front-end servers and the back-end server to a pool.

You can think of a Standard Edition Server as a pool with a single front-end server collocated on the same physical computer as the back-end server. Every time a new Standard Edition Server is installed and activated, a new pool entry is created. This is not the case for front-end servers in an Enterprise pool. When a new front-end server is installed and activated, it is linked to an existing entry that was previously established when the initial Enterprise pool was created. The CN of each object created under the msRTCSIP-Pools container is defined by the name of the pool. Each new pool entry contains a subnode called Microsoft. Under the Microsoft subnode, the following subnodes exist: LC Services, LS Web-Components Services, UC AppServer services, and four GUIDs representing an MCU Factory service for each type of media (Telephony, IM, Web Conferencing, A/V, and Application Sharing), as shown in Figure 4-11. The GUID in the CN of the MCU Factory service matches the CN of an MCU Factory listed under the MCU Factories container. Looking at the properties of the corresponding MCU Factory object will indicate which type of Conferencing Server it is.

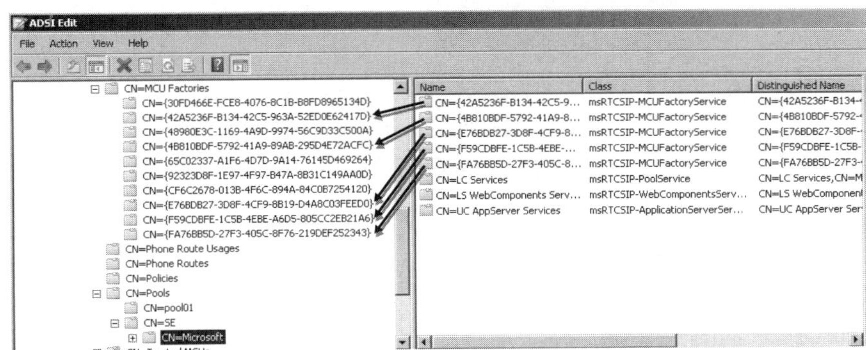

FIGURE 4-11 Pool representation in Active Directory

The LC Services subnode lists all the front-end servers as distinguished names (DNs) associated with the pool in the multivalued attribute *msRTCSIP-FrontEndServers*. The LS WebComponents Services subnode lists all the Web Components Servers as DNs that are associated with the pool in the multivalued attribute *msRTCSIP-WebComponentsService*. Each unique combination of vendor and type for the set of Conferencing Servers are represented as a GUID subnode of the *msRTCSIP-MCUFactoryService* type. Each GUID MCU Factory links to an entry in the MCU Factories container through the *msRTCSIP-MCUFactoryPath* attribute. The MCU Factory entry lists all the Conferencing Servers of the particular vendor and type associated with the pool. The logical representation of the relationship between pools, MCU Factories, and Conferencing Servers is illustrated in Figure 4-12.

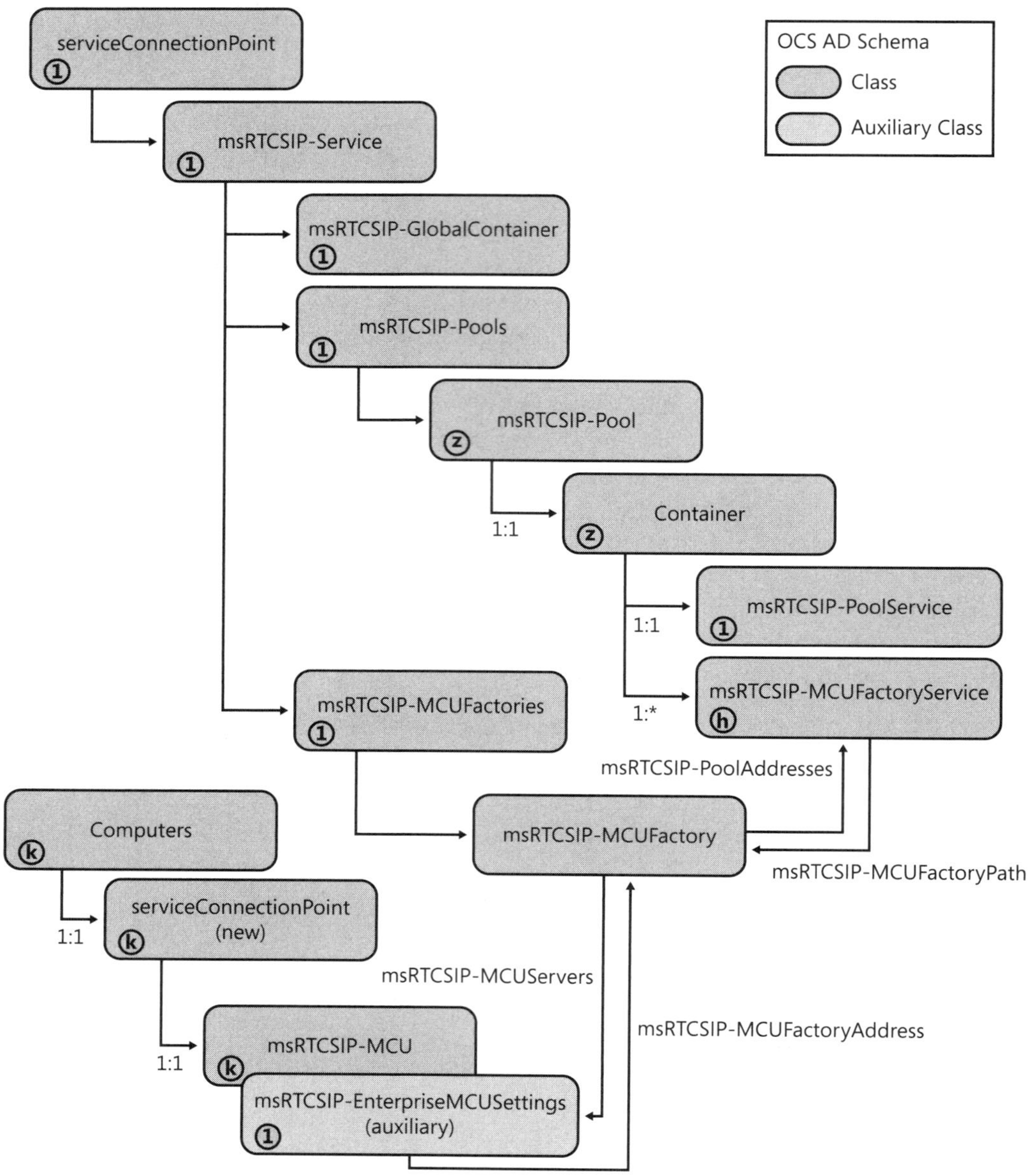

FIGURE 4-12 Logical representation of Conferencing Servers associated with a pool

The third location in which the server information is published in Active Directory is the Trusted Server list. The FQDN of every Office Communications Server is published. In addition to using server certificates to verify the authenticity of a server that claims to own a specific FQDN, the Trusted Server list is used to determine whether the server can be trusted. Without an entry containing its FQDN, a server is not trusted by other server roles and therefore cannot establish any communication with these other servers. If you find that users in a particular pool are not able to communicate with users in other pools, this could be the reason. Check that the pool's FQDN is listed in the Trusted Server list in Active Directory.

It might seem odd that every server's FQDN is defined again in the Trusted Server list when it is already available on the computer object. After all, you could determine the set of computers running Office Communications Server by querying all computer objects that have the RTC Services SCP. The primary reason that Office Communications Server does not use this approach is security. By default, Active Directory enables computer owners to modify the attributes on the corresponding computer objects. This permission privilege enables a malicious user to modify the computer object to appear as a server running Office Communications Server. Although this is not necessarily a concern in all organizations, administrators might lock down this privilege, reducing this threat dramatically. By using a Trusted Server list that only an administrator with RtcUniversalServerAdmin permission can modify, malicious users cannot spoof their computers to appear as trusted servers running Office Communications Server.

Performance of the Office Communications Server 2007 R2 management console is a secondary benefit. In most organizations, the number of computers tends to be at least as large as, if not larger than, the number of users. Querying all the computers in the organization to determine which ones are running Office Communications Server would be time-consuming. Such a query would have a substantial impact on the administrator's experience when loading the Office Communications Server 2007 R2 management console. Searching a smaller list makes it possible for the MMC to load faster.

In earlier versions of Live Communications Server, the Trusted Server list is represented in Active Directory in the System container under Microsoft/RTC Service/Global Settings as an *msRTCSIP-TrustedServer* class entry. Each trusted server entry is represented as a GUID under the Global Settings container. The GUID is generated during the activation step. To determine which GUID object matches a particular Standard Edition Server or Enterprise Edition front-end-server, you must look at the properties of the object in adsiedit.msc. The attribute *msRTCSIP-TrustedServerFQDN* contains the FQDN of the server that you can then recognize.

With the number of new server roles introduced in Office Communications Server 2007 R2, instead of storing all trusted servers under a single container (Global Settings), new containers are defined to separate trusted servers based on role. In Office Communications Server 2007 R2, these trusted server entries are located in the System container under Microsoft/RTC Service or in the Configuration container under Services/RTC Service. The various trusted server roles are defined in the following containers (and highlighted in Figure 4-13):

- Trusted Standard Edition Server and Enterprise pool front-end server entries are located in the RTC Service/Global Settings container. This location is the same as in Live Communications Server 2003 and 2005.
- Trusted Conferencing Server entries are located in the RTC Service/Trusted MCUs container.
- Trusted Web Components Server entries are located in the RTC Service/Trusted-WebComponentsServers container.

- Trusted Communicator Web Access Server, Mediation Server, and Enterprise Voice Application (Response Group Service, Conferencing Announcement Service, Conferencing Attendant, and so on) entries are located in the RTC Service/Trusted Services container. Third-party SIP servers should create a trusted server entry in this container as well; otherwise, Office Communications Servers will not trust their servers and any mutual transport layer security (MTLS) connections will be refused.
- Trusted proxy server entries are located in the RTC Service/Trusted Proxies container.

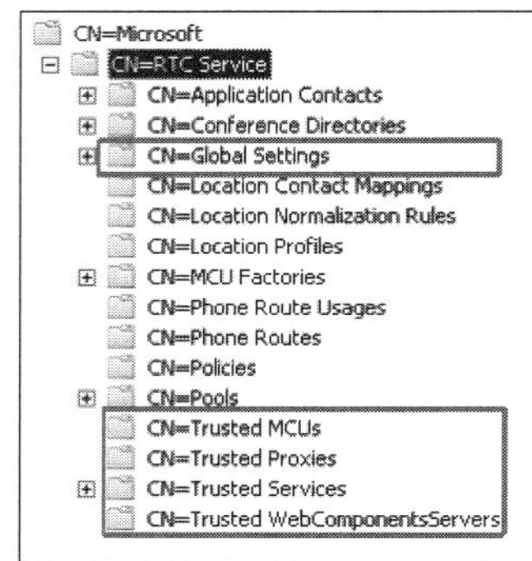

FIGURE 4-13 Trusted server representation in Active Directory

Note that not all GUIDs under the Global Settings container represent GUIDs of trusted servers. As the name indicates, the Global Settings container contains settings that are global to Office Communications Server.

In addition to storing global settings in Active Directory and publishing Office Communications Server information, all Standard Edition Servers and Enterprise Edition pools create an *msRTCSIP-Pools* object under the RTC Service/Pools container, as shown in Figure 4-14.

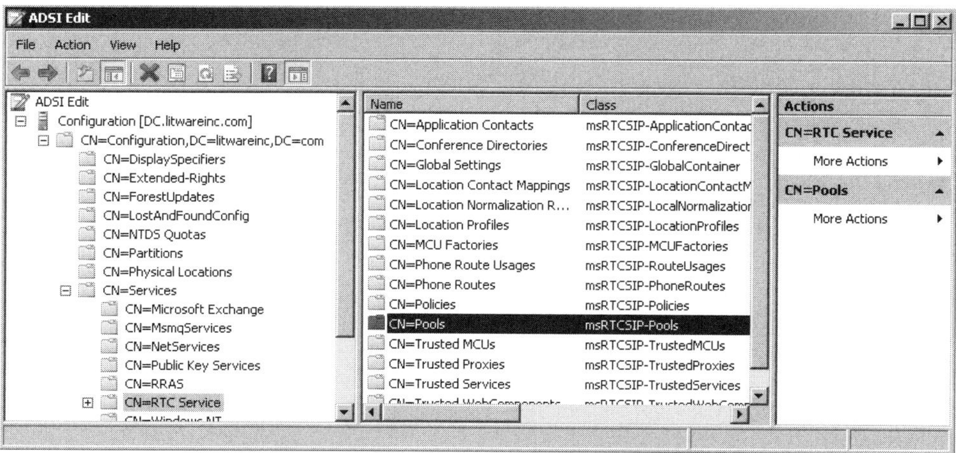

FIGURE 4-14 Pool settings

Each pool entry is associated with an MCU Factory. Every MCU Factory is defined in the RTC Service/MCU Factories container, as shown in Figure 4-15. An MCU Factory is created when the first instance of a unique media type (defined by the attribute *msRTCSIP-MCUType*) and vendor (defined by the attribute *msRTCSIP-MCUVendor*) of a Conferencing Server is activated.

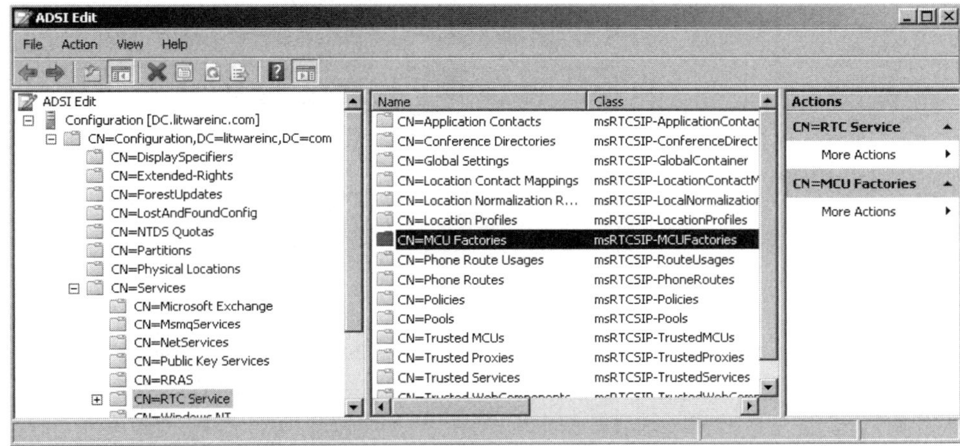

FIGURE 4-15 MCU Factories

The currently available media types are as follows:

- Meeting
- Instant messaging (IM)
- Phone-conference
- Audio/video

NOTE **For more information about media types, see Chapter 6, "Conferencing Scenarios."**

Office Communications Server 2007 R2 defines Voice over Internet Protocol (VoIP) settings used to normalize phone numbers and translate phone numbers to SIP URI where applicable before routing the call to its destination. Figure 4-16 shows the classes used for VoIP. For more information about VoIP, see Chapter 11.

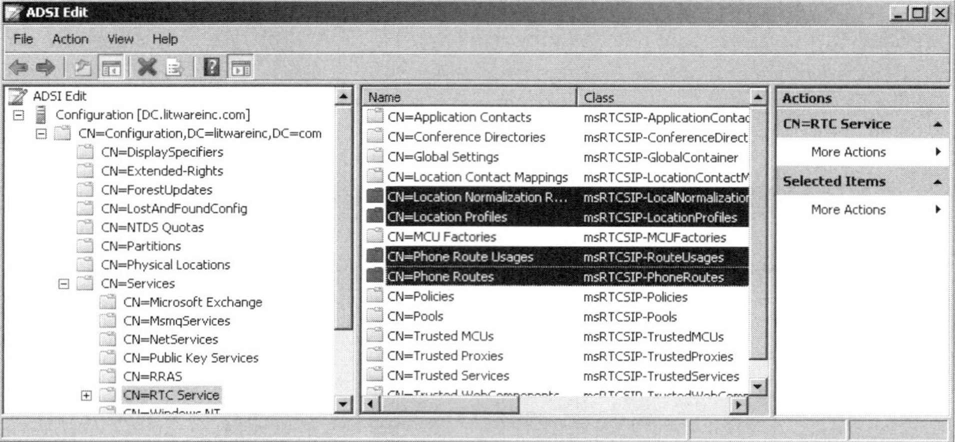

FIGURE 4-16 Global VoIP settings

The user class that represents a user account in Active Directory is also extended with attributes specific to Office Communications Server. Such attributes define settings that are configurable by an administrator member of the RTCDomainUserAdmins or RTCDomainServerAdmins group. For more information about user settings, see Chapter 18, "Administration."

Using DNS to Publish Office Communications Server

Office Communications Server uses DNS to publish Enterprise pools and Edge Servers so that they can be discoverable by other home servers and Edge Servers. Standard Edition Servers automatically publish their FQDN as A (Host) records in DNS; however, the FQDN of Enterprise pools need to be published in DNS manually by administrators. Administrators create an A record for the Enterprise pool's FQDN, mapped to the virtual IP (VIP) of the Enterprise pool's hardware load balancer (HLB). To federate with other partners and public IM connectivity (PIC) partners or allow remote users to connect to the internal Office Communications infrastructure, the external network interface card (NIC) of Edge Servers deployed in the network perimeter must be published in the public DNS.

Impact on Server Certificates

DNS and certificates work together to create a trust and the ability for server-to-server authentication and client-to-server authentication to occur.

For more information about certificates, see the section titled "Securing Office Communications Server with PKI" later in this chapter. The specific understanding from this section is that the clients and the servers involved in mutual authentication or simple authentication using a Transport Layer Security (TLS) certificate use DNS to find the name of a server and then compare the name retrieved from DNS to the name on the certificate that the server submits for authentication. If the name that DNS presents is different than the name on the certificate, the authentication fails.

Impact on FQDN Configurations

DNS is used to locate servers and to determine what interface of a server is to be used. If a server has two interfaces, which is common for all Edge Servers, DNS is referred to when needing to resolve the name to the IP address. The administrator needs to design a DNS system to resolve both the internal-facing interfaces as well as the external-facing interfaces. This can either be done with a split-brain DNS, a DNS structure that handles both internal queries and external queries with neither side knowing that the other exists. Or, a more common scenario is to have an internal DNS to handle all internal queries and an external DNS to handle all external queries.

SIP Namespaces

Office Communications Server introduces the concept of SIP namespaces or domains to route SIP requests internally and externally by using DNS. This is similar to how e-mail messages are routed.

When installing Office Communications Server 2007 R2, the default SIP domain server becomes authoritative for the Active Directory's forest (that is, root domain) name. For example, if your forest's FQDN is Litwareinc.com, Office Communications Server will be authoritative for the SIP domain @Litwareinc.com. In the case of a multitree Active Directory forest, Office Communications Server 2007 R2 picks up only the first tree's FQDN as its SIP domain. The other tree's FQDN must be defined manually. However, this default namespace is probably not the namespace you will want to expose externally. In most cases, you will want to make the user's SIP URI identical to the user's e-mail address for simplicity. This is not a requirement, but it keeps the user's corporate identity consistent. If your corporate e-mail namespace does not match your Active Directory root domain FQDN, you must change the default SIP namespace to match your Simple Mail Transfer Protocol (SMTP) namespace. Fortunately, you can modify the list of SIP domains.

You can easily modify the set of authoritative SIP domains through the Administrative Tools MMC. To open global settings, right-click the forest node and then select Properties. The General tab appears by default. Click Add and Remove to modify the list of authoritative SIP domains, as shown in Figure 4-17.

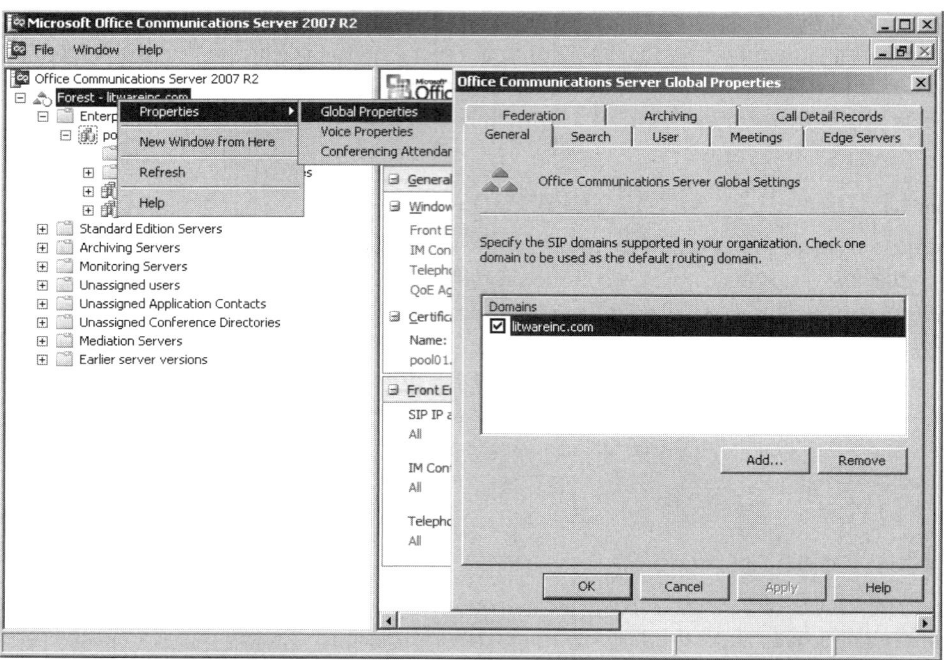

FIGURE 4-17 Configuring SIP domains for Office Communications Server

DIRECT FROM THE SOURCE

Default Domain

Nirav Kamdar
Senior Development Lead, Office Communications Server

One of the domains must be marked as the default domain. The default domain is used internally by Office Communications Servers to address each other using Globally Routable User Agent URIs (GRUUs).

Users in your organization must be enabled for Office Communications Server with a SIP URI that has a domain suffix supported by the Office Communications Servers in your organization.

After the initial configuration, there is little need to add or remove SIP domains; however, sometimes this need does arise. For example, if a company changes its public identity, the old SIP domain must be discontinued and the new SIP domain must be added. If a company with an existing deployment of Office Communications Server is merged with your organization and you want to support only a single SIP domain namespace, the acquired company's SIP domain name must be added to your Domain list until the migration is completed. For these and other reasons, simply adding the new SIP domain to the Domain list and removing the old SIP domain is not sufficient. In addition to this step, you must migrate all users whose SIP URI uses the acquired SIP domain to the existing SIP domain. To remain valid, each user's contacts also need to be updated from the acquired SIP domain to the new corporate SIP domain.

Migrate Users from One SIP Namespace to Another

A common administrative task is to move users from one SIP namespace to another. This could be done to move users from one company organization to another, such as a job or role change. It might also be done when a company decides to restructure the Office Communications Server environment to create more SIP domains to allow for a location-based organization of users.

The procedure to move users from one SIP domain to another is as follows.

1. Add the new SIP domain to the Domain list.
2. Update each user's SIP URI to the new SIP domain suffix.
3. Update each user's contact to the new SIP domain suffix.
4. Update all Access Edge Servers' public certificates to include the new SIP domain.

Performing step 1 is easy; however, steps 2 and 3 become more challenging because there are no tools to perform these steps. Fortunately, Office Communications Server 2007 R2 provides Windows Management Instrumentation (WMI) application programming interfaces (APIs) that can be leveraged via scripting (for example, VBScript and PowerShell) to automate these steps.

One approach is to query all users in Active Directory that are enabled for Office Communications Server, determine if any user matches the source SIP domain to change, and change the domain portion of the SIP URI (leaving the user name portion intact) to the target SIP domain desired. Because users could have added a contact with a SIP URI that you must change to match the new SIP domain name, this utility needs to "peek" into each user enabled for Office Communications Server, check whether any contact's SIP URI matches the same source SIP domain, and update the domain portion of the contact's SIP URI. Step 4 involves requesting a new server certificate from your preferred public CA provider. For additional details, see the section titled "Configuring the Subject Alternative Name" later in this chapter.

Securing Office Communications Server with PKI

Because Office Communications Server 2007 R2 leverages certificates to enforce the strong authentication of servers, it is important for administrators to understand how Office Communications Server uses certificates. Certificates are digital equivalents to a driver's license or a passport. Their purpose is to authoritatively identify an entity—in this case, a server. Similar to a driver's license and passport, which identify your height, weight, hair and eye color, and so on, the digital certificate provides specific properties that identify the server.

Every certificate is tied to a public key. Any information encrypted with this public key can be decrypted only by the holder of the corresponding private key. This is a public and private key pair and is unique. If you have a public key, it's important to know who the holder of the private key is, thus uniquely identifying the certificate owner. To determine whether I hold the private key, you generate a random piece of information that only you know (that is, the secret), encrypt it with the public key, and send it to me. If I am able to send back the plain text (that is, the secret) by decrypting the message you sent, you know that I hold the private key to the certificate.

Knowing that I hold the private key proves only that much: that I hold the private key to the certificate. The certificate could claim that I am Kim Akers, in the same way that a fake driver's license could identify me as Kim Akers. How then do you determine whether the information contained in the certificate can be trusted? Because you cannot trust me to tell the truth, you must find a more reliable source to validate that the information contained in the certificate is legal. In the case of a U.S. driver's license or passport, this source of authority is the government of the United States. In the case of digital certificates, the federal government is not in the business of issuing certificates to private businesses and citizens. So you must rely on a trusted public CA—such as VeriSign or eTrust—to issue certificates that other organizations are likely to trust. Certificates for Edge Servers must be requested and issued from public CAs. To reduce costs, certificates for internal Office Communications Servers that interact only with other servers and clients within your organizations can be issued from a private CA trusted within your organization.

Understanding how Office Communications Server uses the different properties of a certificate goes a long way toward helping you avoid pitfalls in configuring your servers. For more information about certificates, see the TechNet article "Certificates" at *http://go.microsoft.com/fwlink/?LinkID=133667*.

Configuring the Common Name or Subject Name

The CN of a certificate, also known as the *subject name* (SN) in the case of an Office Communications Server, identifies the server's FQDN, as defined in Active Directory. In the case of a front-end server member of an Enterprise pool, the CN must match the pool's FQDN. For a Standard Edition Server, the CN should match the computer's FQDN. You can find the CN of a certificate in the Subject field (on the Details tab) when viewing the properties of a certificate, as shown in Figure 4-18.

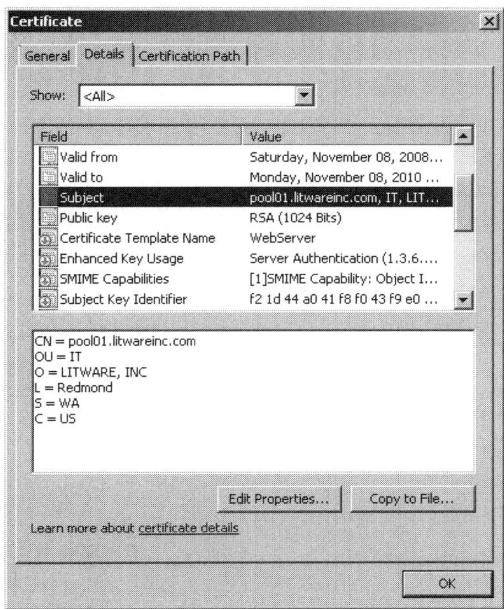

FIGURE 4-18 Certificate properties: Subject

Although an organization's internal DNS service is considered to be trustworthy, it is possible for a rogue server to do DNS cache poisoning and take over another server's FQDN. To prevent such possible attacks, the CN is used to authoritatively tie Office Communications Server to its FQDN. Office Communications Servers locate other Office Communications Servers through their FQDNs. After resolving the FQDN to an IP address, they validate that the server they reached is not a rogue server by verifying that the CN of the server's certificate lists the right FQDN. This enables any connecting server to authenticate the Office Communications Server. To verify that the server is an authorized Office Communications Server within your organization, the connecting server checks that the server's FQDN is listed on the Trusted Server list in Active Directory.

Configuring the Subject Alternative Name

The Subject Alternative Name (SAN) can be used to expose multiple SIP domains. An organization can have multiple SIP domains that it wants to publish to the public (that is, the Internet). Each SIP domain can represent a different business unit's brand of the organization. For example, the company Litware, Inc. has three brands: Datum, Fabrikam, and Litwareinc. It would be confusing for customers, partners, and vendors who are unaware of this brand's parent structure to reach Datum employees with a SIP URI of user@Litwareinc.com. It would be more intuitive for those employees to have a SIP URI of user@datum.com. Such an organization can expose multiple SIP domains to the Internet.

The certificate of an Access Edge Server can certify multiple SIP domains by placing additional SIP domains in the SAN field. If a SAN field is present, the SAN should contain the CN of the certificate (that is, the FQDN of the Access Edge Server or the FQDN of the HLB in the case of a bank of Access Edge Servers) as the first entry in the SAN to bind the original name into the SAN, followed by the complete list of SIP domains for which your organization is authoritative. The use of SAN allows a single Access Edge Server to be authoritative for multiple SIP domains. Without this approach, you could expose only one SIP domain per Access Edge Server. This limitation would require deploying multiple Access Edge Servers when an organization needs to expose multiple SIP domains, as in the case of Litware, Inc. Figure 4-19 illustrates an example of a certificate with a populated SAN.

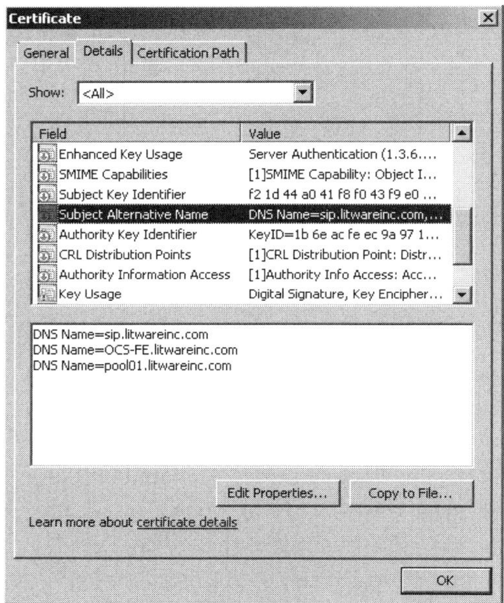

FIGURE 4-19 Certificate properties: Subject Alternative Name

Using a SAN can also be beneficial for your internal deployment of Office Communications Server, particularly when you do not want to deploy a Director. If the DNS Service Record Locator (SRV) record for Litware Inc., _sipinternaltls._tcp.Litwareinc.com, points to the A record, sip.Litwareinc.com, and if every home server's certificate contains sip.Litwareinc.com in the SAN field, then clients configured for automatic configuration will successfully authenticate these home servers. Because the A record, sip.Litwareinc.com, matches the server's certificate SAN field, users are able to sign in.

Configuring the CRL Distribution Points

The certificate distribution point (CDP) is a field used to publish the distribution point or points from where you can download certificate revocation lists (CRLs). The CRL is used to verify that the certificate has not been revoked since the time it was issued. You can download CRLs through a variety of methods indicated in the CDP. The most common CDPs are Hypertext Transfer Protocol (HTTP) and Lightweight Directory Access Protocol (LDAP) URLs. Edge Servers should be configured to download CRLs. Figure 4-20 illustrates an example of a CDP.

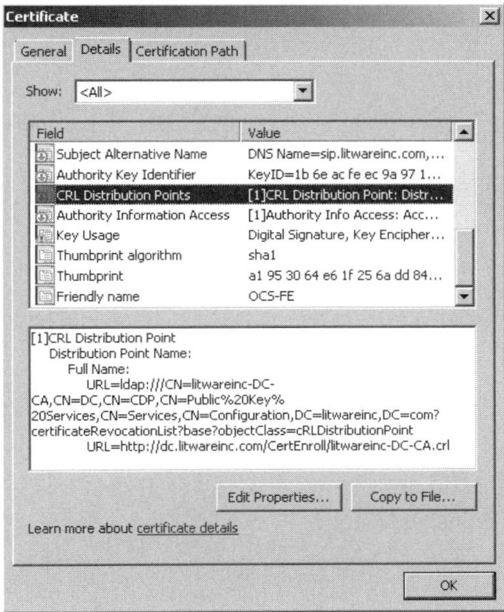

FIGURE 4-20 Certificate properties: CRL distribution points

Configuring for Enhanced Key Usage

The Enhanced Key Usage (EKU) field identifies the intended purpose of the certificate. If no EKU field is present in the certificate, the certificate is valid for all uses; however, the intended purpose of the certificate can be limited based on the EKU listed in the certificate of the CA's part of the certificate path. (Not having an EKU provides no limitations.) The EKU restrictions are inherited from the issuing parent CAs.

The two EKUs that Office Communications Server uses are:

- Server Authentication
- Client Authentication

Figure 4-21 illustrates these two EKUs.

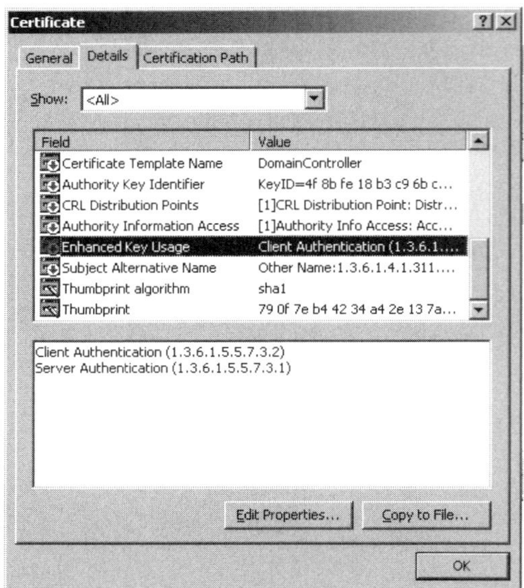

FIGURE 4-21 Certificate properties: Enhanced Key Usage

Server Authentication

This EKU must be present to grant the certificate the right to act as a server. This EKU is required for the host to be treated as a server when using MTLS.

Client Authentication

This EKU must be present to initiate outbound MTLS connections with the following server types:

- Live Communications Server 2003
- Live Communications Server 2005
- Public IM Connectivity (PIC) to AOL

Office Communications Server 2007 R2 removes the need for servers to have a client EKU when initiating outbound MTLS connections. However, AOL still requires this client EKU to be present in the certificate used by the Access Edge Server connecting to AOL through PIC.

Configuring the Certification Path

The certificate must be issued from a CA that your organization trusts. The CA represents the reliable source that can vouch for the trustworthiness of the certificate. To view the certificate chain leading to its root certificate, select the Certification Path tab when viewing the certificate, as illustrated in Figure 4-22. If the root certificate or any of its subordinate certificates are not trusted or have been revoked, the certificate will not be trusted. This is especially useful when validating properties of the issuing CAs to make sure that EKU usage rights of interest have been inherited, as well as granted locally.

FIGURE 4-22 Certificate properties: Certification Path

Scaling with SQL Server

Office Communications Server 2007 R2 uses SQL Server to store user and configuration data. The Standard Edition uses SQL Server 2005 Express, which Office Communications Server Setup automatically installs. However, it is possible to use the Standard or Enterprise version of SQL Server 2005 or 2008 as well for Standard Edition. The Enterprise Edition uses SQL Server 2005 Service Pack 1 (SP1) or SQL Server 2008, which must be installed separately on the back-end server. The back-end server computer must be installed with Windows Server 2003 or Windows Server 2008 and cannot be collocated with the front-end server. Encrypted File Systems (EFSs) should not be turned on in the %TEMP% directory; if it is, setup will fail.

> ***NOTE*** **An easy way to verify that encryption is not turned on is to start Windows Explorer, type %temp% in the Address field, and press Enter. Right-click anywhere in the empty space of the folder and select Properties. Click Advanced. Verify that the Encrypt Contents To Secure Data check box is not selected.**

For best results, two hard drives with fast access time should be installed on the back-end server. One hard drive is used for the SQL Server database and the other hard drive is used for the log files. A 4-processor server is the minimum requirement. For larger deployments, an 8-PROC server is recommended. A 1-gigabyte (GB) NIC for the back-end server is recommended. Office Communications Server 2007 R2 supports the use of 32-bit and 64-bit servers for the SQL Server back-end server.

You can build redundancy into the back-end server for the Enterprise Edition case. Office Communications Server 2007 R2 supports only single-instance failover, also commonly referred to as *active/passive clustering*. A two-node cluster is configured to fail over to the standby SQL Server if the primary SQL Server fails. SQL backup and restore remains the supported way for inter-pool disaster recovery.

> ***NOTE*** **Windows Server 2008 improves on overall server security by implementing a much more comprehensive firewall. One item of note is that, by default, all ports are closed until an application install or a server administrator creates a rule, in effect opening the ports to specific conditions defined by the rule. SQL Server 2008, as of this writing, warns you with a dialog box that you will need to open ports and refers you to the SQL Server 2008 technical information. SQL Server 2005 SP1 does not issue a warning at all.**
>
> **The minimum rule that you have to create is an inbound rule to allow Transmission Control Protocol (TCP) and port 1433 from the front-end servers. This can be done either using the Administrative Tool for managing the firewall or using the command-line tool netsh. For more information about management and rules for the Windows Server 2008 Advanced Firewall, see "Windows Firewall with Advanced Security and IPsec" at *http://go.microsoft.com/fwlink/?LinkID=133668l*.**

Building Redundancy with Hardware Load Balancing

An HLB is required for every Enterprise pool. The HLB is an important element of the redundancy story offered by Enterprise Edition. An Enterprise pool contains one or more front-end servers that perform the same function. Therefore, clients can connect to any of the available front-end servers. It is important that the client does not need to know which front-end server it should connect to. By using an HLB, clients connect to a single FQDN, and the HLB determines which front-end server should service the request based on availability and workload. After the HLB routes a client's connection to a particular front-end server, the HLB must be capable of routing all traffic from that client to the same front-end server for the duration of the user's session.

> ***NOTE*** **Only HLBs are supported for Office Communications Server 2007 R2. The Network Load Balancer component in Windows Server 2003 or Windows Server 2008 is not a supported option to meet this requirement.**

At the time of this writing, Microsoft has tested and supports Office Communications Server 2007 R2 with the following HLBs (see the section titled "Additional Resources" at the end of this chapter for the link):

- F5 Big-IP
- Nortel Application Switch (NAS)
- CAI Networks WebMux
- Foundry Networks ServerIron
- Cisco Application Control Engine (ACE)
- Citrix Netscaler

Destination NAT (DNAT) and Source NAT (SNAT) are two methods of applying the network address translation in devices such as HLBs. The difference between the two, like the name implies, is what the translation rewrites. In DNAT, the destination address (or target) is rewritten to comply with the rules of the translator. SNAT rewrites the source address (or sender). Both rewrites occur at the IP layer, ensuring that the sender can respond to the correct address.

However, DNAT is much more difficult to set up and configure properly. DNAT has been supported in Office Communications Server in the past but is no longer supported in Office Communications Server 2007 R2 due to the overall complexity of implementing DNAT. If your load balancer is currently using DNAT, you must convert the ports that the Office Communications Server systems are using to SNAT.

You must configure a static IP address for the VIP address of the HLB. The HLB must be configured with the static IP address of each front-end server of the Enterprise pool to load balance. For more information about how to configure the specific HLB of your choice, see the Partner Documentation section at *http://go.microsoft.com/fwlink/?LinkID=133669* and the upcoming section in this chapter, "Port and Protocol Configuration Considerations for Hardware Load Balancers."

Finally, you must publish the FQDN of the Enterprise pool in DNS. An A record must be defined for the pool FQDN, and the IP address to match to this FQDN should be the IP address of the HLB's VIP.

1. Select Start and select Administrative Tools.
2. Select DNS.
3. Right-click your domain's node under Forward Lookup Zones.
4. Select New Host (A).
5. Enter the Enterprise pool's FQDN in the Name field of the New Host dialog box, as shown in Figure 4-23.

This will result in a new Host (A) record being created in DNS for the FQDN of the VIP for the Enterprise pool.

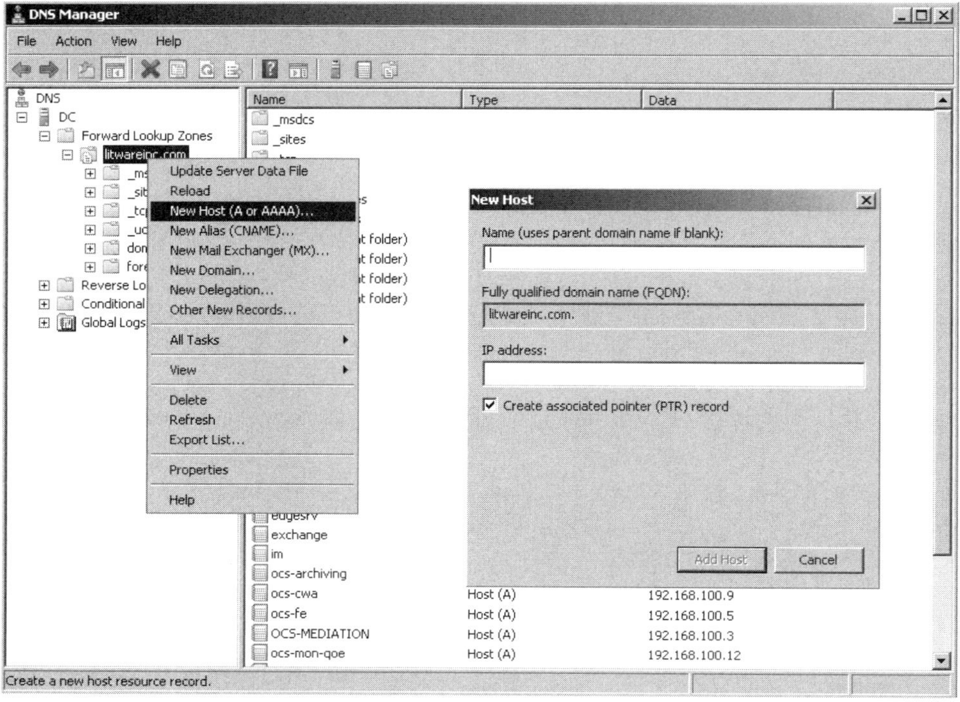

FIGURE 4-23 Publishing an Enterprise pool in DNS

Verify that you configured the HLB with this IP address and make sure you can resolve the pool's FQDN. You can easily do this by performing a ping command. To do this, open a command prompt window and type **ping *<pool fqdn>***.

The pool's FQDN is automatically defined once you specify the pool name. It is composed of the name specified in the Pool Name field and the domain's name shown in the Domain field in the Create Enterprise Pool Wizard. This is shown in Figure 4-24.

The pool name can be any value you select, as long as it does not conflict with the name of an existing pool. The pool name gets populated as the CN of the pool object and the value of the *msRTCSIP-PoolDisplayName* attribute.

The SQL Server instance is parsed, and the server name portion is stored in the *msRTCSIP-BackEndServer* attribute. By default, if no instance name is supplied, the instances created are called RTC, RTCDYN, and RTCCONFIG. It is recommended not to specify any instance name when creating a new pool. The RTC database contains user and pool information synchronized from Active Directory. The RTCDYN database stores transient information, such as subscriptions, endpoints, and publications. The RTCCONFIG database contains pool-level configuration settings specific to the Enterprise pool.

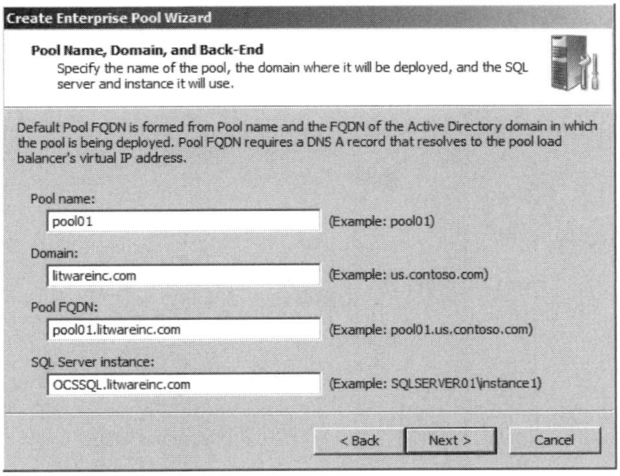

FIGURE 4-24 Create Enterprise Pool Wizard

Port and Protocol Configuration Considerations for Hardware Load Balancers

To properly configure your HLB for the Enterprise pool, it's helpful to understand the network traffic into the servers of an Enterprise pool. This background information makes it easier to optimize your HLB for Office Communications Server, Enterprise pool.

Understanding the network flow of servers is important as you begin to configure your HLB and any internal firewall that protects the servers within the Enterprise pool. The HLB primarily serves to distribute client SIP requests across all of the front-end servers. The HLB also serves to source NAT the network connections from the IM, Telephony, Web, and A/V Conferencing Servers (referred to as MCUs) to the Focus and MCU Factory. The Conferencing Servers can connect to any Focus running on each of the front-end servers because the conference information used by the Focus resides on the back-end server. Therefore, any Focus element can service the Conferencing Server request. Consequently the Conferencing Server must connect to the front-end servers, where the Focus runs, through the HLB to take advantage of the load-balancing functionality. This design provides more scalability and reliability.

In the case of an Enterprise pool in consolidated configuration, as shown in Figure 4-25, the Conferencing Server components reside on the front-end servers, and the load-balanced network connections need to appear as if they are originating from a server on a different subnet. This requires that the HLB support SNAT. SNAT provides the ability to translate the source IP address of the originating server to one that is owned by the HLB that supports the server-to-server network connections between different Office Communications Server 2007 R2 components residing on the same physical servers. Figure 4-26 illustrates information needed to resolve these same requirements for an expanded configuration.

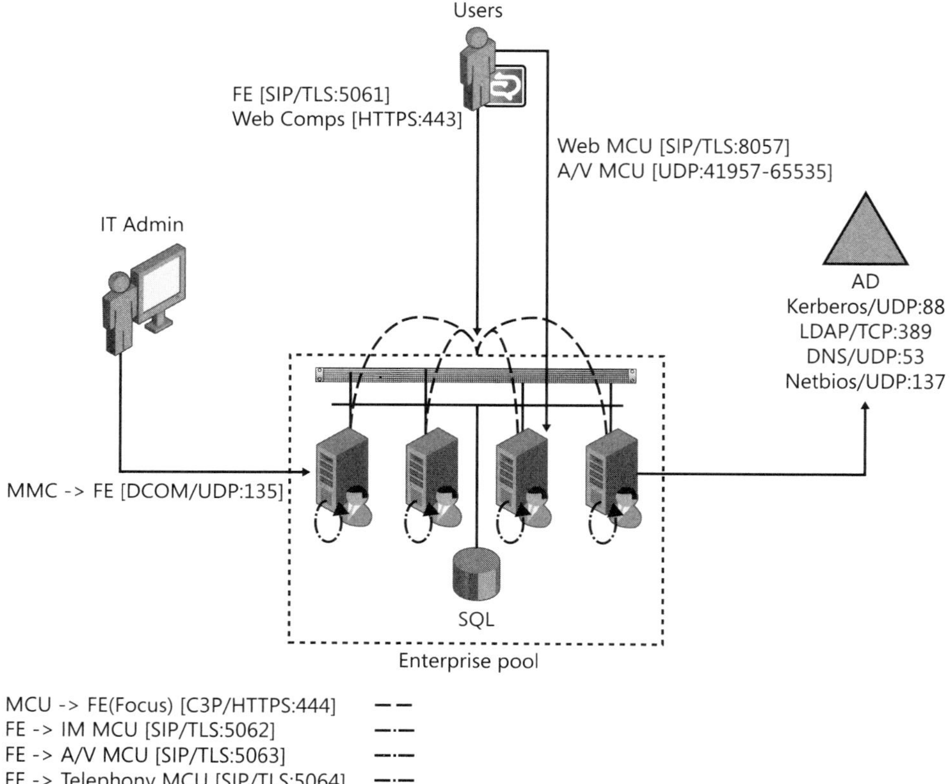

FIGURE 4-25 Network protocols and communication flows for an Enterprise pool in consolidated configuration

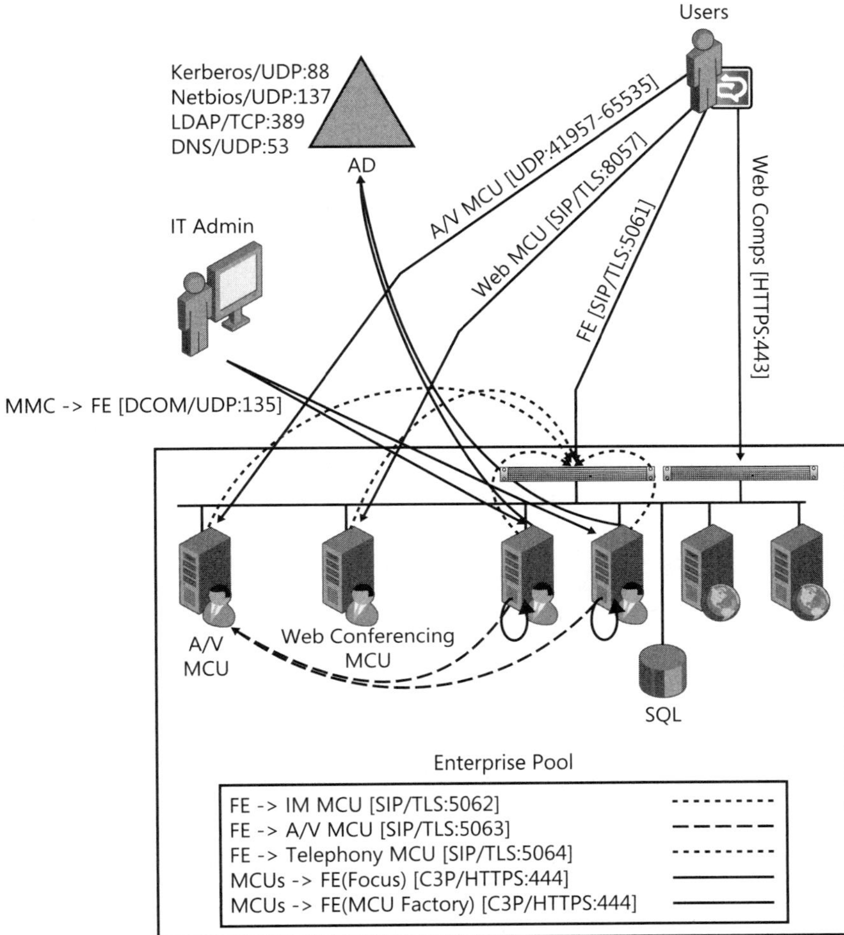

FIGURE 4–26 Network protocols and communication flows for an Enterprise pool in expanded configuration

Table 4-2 describes the ports and protocols that will need to be configured on the load balancers to allow for the traffic that will be sent to and from the servers and services that the load balancer is hosting. For example, a client's computer that needs to connect to a pool server behind the load balancer will need to connect on port 5061/TCP. Table 4-2 indicates this configuration in the first entry.

TABLE 4-2 Configuration Settings for Hardware Load-Balancer Ports

PORT REQUIRED	SOURCE	DESTINATION	DESCRIPTION
TCP 5061	Client PC	VIP for pool	Client IM traffic encrypted via SIP/TLS
TCP 4441	Front-end server actual IP	VIP for pool	Conference MCUs to Focus and MCU Factory to track health and schedule meetings
TCP 443	Client PC	VIP for pool	Web Components Server traffic (HTTPS) to download content for meetings
TCP 8057	Client PC	Web Conferencing Server	Web Conferencing MCU traffic (SIP/TLS) for meetings
User Datagram Protocol (UDP) 135	Admin PC	Front-end server actual IP	Distributed Component Object Model (DCOM) traffic for Office Communications Server 2007 R2 Admin tool
UDP 49152 – 65535	Client PC	A/V Conferencing Server	A/V Conferencing Server traffic

Bridging VoIP to the PSTN Network by Using a Media Gateway

For voice calls from Office Communications Server to reach the PSTN, a third-party media gateway is required to bridge the IP network and the PSTN network by translating the signaling and media to the protocols used by each network, as shown in Table 4-3.

TABLE 4-3 Protocol Translation That Media Gateway Performs

TECHNOLOGY	PSTN NETWORK	IP NETWORK
Signaling protocol	SS7 and others	SIP
Media codecs	G.711	RTAudio (Real-Time Audio)
Transport protocol	T-Carrier/E-Carrier	RTP (Real-Time Transport Protocol/SRTP (Secure RTP)
Network type	Circuit switched	Packet-based

Microsoft partners provide such a media gateway. (See the section titled "Additional Resources" at the end of this chapter for the link.) The three types of media gateways that Office Communications Server 2007 R2 supports are:

- **Basic media gateways** At the time of this writing, Microsoft has tested and supports media gateways from AudioCodes, Cisco, Dialogic, Ferrari Electronic AG, NEC, Net, Nuera Communications, Tango Networks, Quintum, and VegaStream.
- **Hybrid media gateways** At the time of this writing, Microsoft has tested and supports media gateways from Aculab, AudioCodes, Dialogic, Nortel, and Quintum.
- **Advanced media gateways** At the time of this writing, there are no Microsoft partners that currently offer advanced media gateways.

The third-party basic media gateways cannot translate media from RTAudio codecs to G.711 codecs or the other way around. Therefore, a Mediation Server role provided by Office Communications Server 2007 R2 is required to translate RTAudio to G.711, and it must be understood by the basic media gateway. If the media gateway does not support MTLS, the Mediation Server translates SIP from MTLS to TCP. There must be a one-to-one mapping of Mediation Server to media gateway. You cannot configure a Mediation Server to service multiple media gateways.

The third-party advanced media gateways do not require the assistance of a Mediation Server and are capable of directly translating RTAudio to and from G.711. Essentially, the advanced media gateway incorporates the functionality of the Mediation Server in the media gateway.

Alternatively, if the media gateway runs on Windows Server 2003 or Server 2008, it might be possible to co-locate the Mediation Server and the basic media gateway on the same server if supported by the media gateway vendor. Although not an advanced media gateway, this configuration improves overall return on investment (ROI) because it reduces the number of servers required to bridge to the PSTN network.

Firewall Scenarios and Configuration

Properly configured firewalls and reverse proxy servers provide a high level of first-line defense in your Office Communications Server infrastructure. The goal is to design a defense-in-depth strategy, of which the firewalls play an initial role. Regardless of how external communication is reaching your internal deployment, the traffic needs to be confined in such a way that only expected data flows of a predictable type are being allowed into your domain and enterprise. This is the express purpose of the firewalls and reverse proxies.

A number of firewall configurations can be implemented. Two of these implementations will be discussed and detailed in the following sections:

- Back-to-back firewall
- Three-legged firewall

Back-to-Back Firewall

The back-to-back firewall, shown in figure 4-27, is named for (at least) the two firewalls that make up the design. The outermost firewall provides a first level of security. It is configured to enable only traffic that will communicate with the servers that are placed in between the firewalls or in the network perimeter.

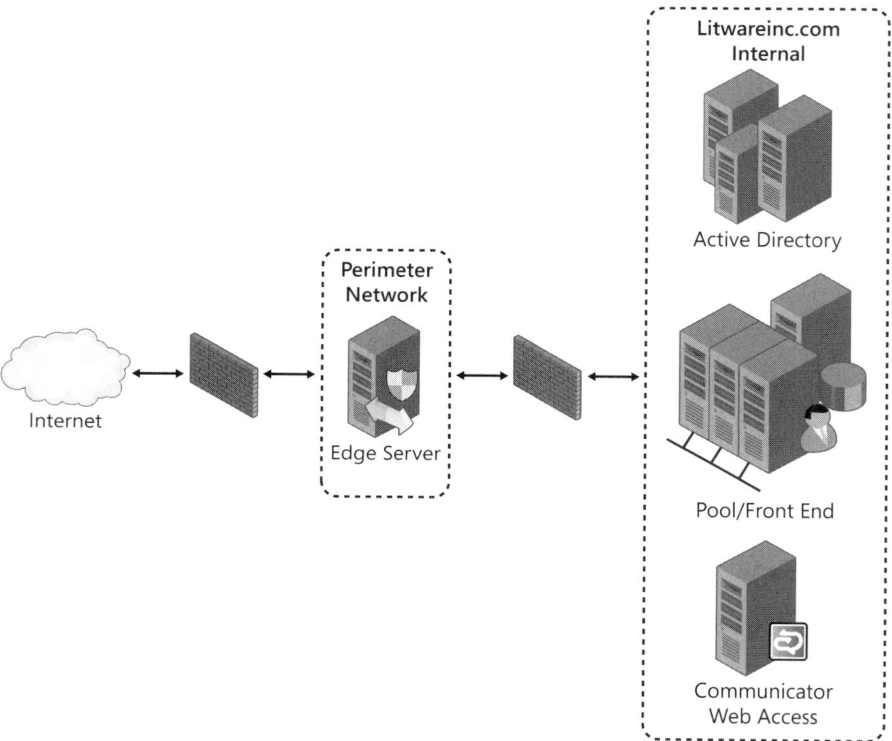

FIGURE 4-27 Back-to-back firewall design

For Office Communications Server, the Edge Servers and reverse proxies are placed in the network perimeter between the external and internal firewalls. Before you begin creating rules for the firewall, you should gather the specific ports, protocols, and direction of traffic for each server role that you intend to deploy. The set of rules that must be configured for the firewalls will vary based on the service that each component in a consolidated Edge Server will provide.

Three-Legged Firewall

The three-legged firewall is a configuration in which there is only one firewall, but there is still a need to create a port and protocol screened area to which data flow can be confined before being allowed into the internal network. Figure 4-28 shows a three-legged firewall configuration. The third interface in the firewall creates what is commonly referred to as a screened subnet.

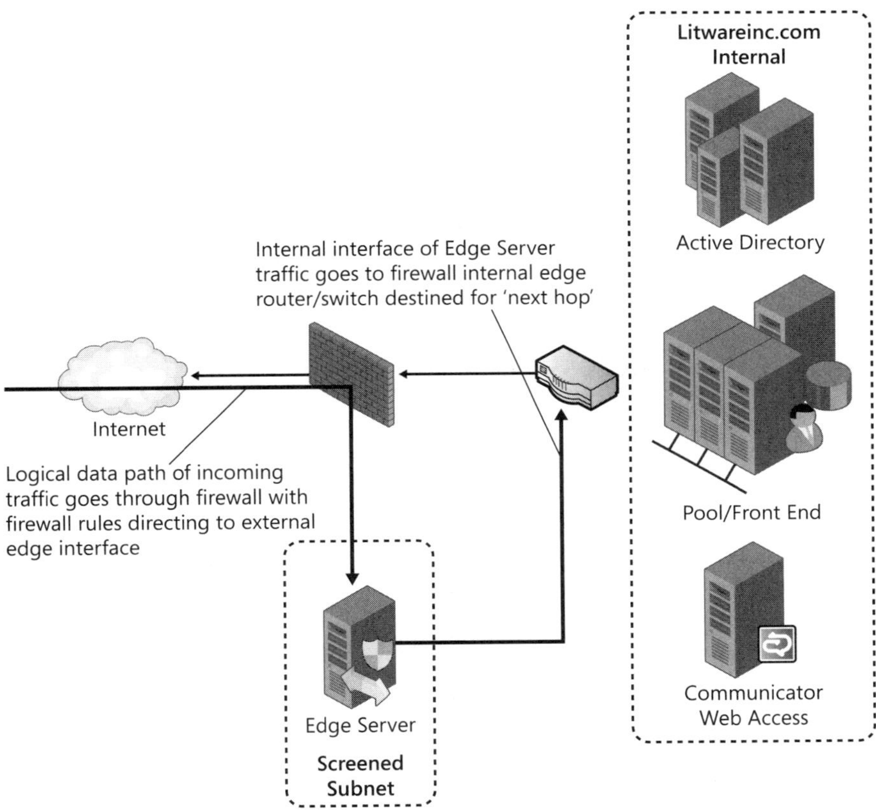

FIGURE 4-28 Screened subnet configuration using one firewall to manage inbound and outbound traffic

A screened subnet is a separate subnet that has its own IP network address. Servers are then configured to receive and send traffic on this screened subnet. The screening is the data flow control the firewall imposes based on the firewall's rule configuration. Traffic such as mail traffic over TCP port 25 would be sent to the IP address of the mail server on the internal network. Note that in the case of an Edge Server, only the external interface is screened. The internal interface is connected to the internal subnet side of the firewall.

In the following discussions of port and protocol configuration, the diagrams and firewall rules assume a back-to-back firewall configuration. If your enterprise is using a single firewall with a screened subnet, only the external rules will apply because router rules on the internal side of the single firewall would segment the Edge Server.

Port and Protocol Configuration for Edge Servers

Office Communications Server 2007 R2 supports only a consolidated Edge Server configuration. This does not mean that there is only one set of ports and protocols to configure. A consolidated Edge Server hosts the three server roles that make up the Access Edge Server, Web Conferencing Edge Server, and A/V Conferencing Server.

Because there are three roles on each Edge Server, you should assign three IP addresses to the external interface of the server or three virtual IPs to the HLB. This will enable specific and finite rules to be created to manage the data flow to a server role.

One configuration option to consider is to dedicate a subnet in your network perimeter for Office Communications Servers only. Set router rules to not enable any other traffic to the Office Communications Server subnet except traffic that is specifically destined for one of the servers or is destined for the internal servers. What this accomplishes is isolation, and it prevents any other traffic from outside your perimeter from affecting or attacking the Office Communications Servers.

Examining Rules for Access Edge Servers

The Access Edge Server initiates most of the communication for the other server roles. A client contacts the Access Edge Server and requests connection to a given set of services. This makes the Access Edge Server important in your environment.

The Access Edge Server handles SIP, a signaling protocol that carries messages requesting specific actions to be carried out. For example, the Access Edge Server handles IM without assistance from any of the other server roles. However, if a Web conference is requested, the Access Edge Server must be involved in the setup and management of the Web conferencing for the duration of the conference.

Access Edge Servers require MTLS certificates because they do mutual authentication with other servers that they communicate with. This communication is established over TCP/5061, as shown in Figure 4-29.

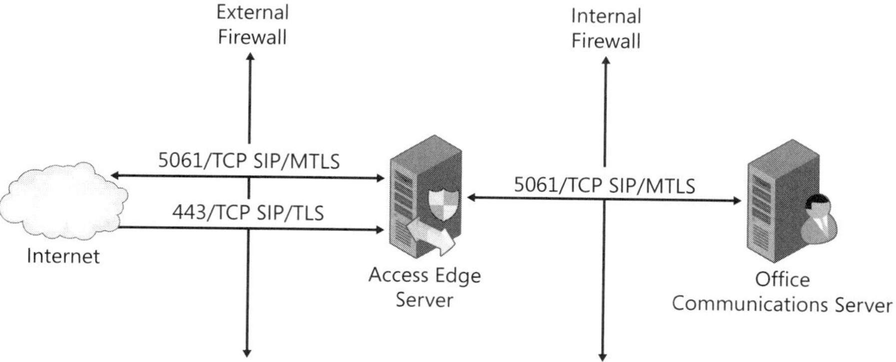

FIGURE 4-29 SIP traffic through an Access Edge Server

For the firewalls, the rules would be configured to allow the settings in Table 4-4.

TABLE 4-4 Firewall Rules for the Access Edge Server

ACCESS EDGE SERVER SERVICE: RTCSRV		
FIREWALL	**DIRECTION**	**PORT / PROTOCOL**
External	Inbound to external interface IP of Access Edge	5061/TCP SIP/MTLS
Internal	Inbound to interface of IP FE/Director[1]	5061/TCP SIP/MTLS
Internal	Outbound to internal interface IP of Access Edge	5061/TCP SIP/MTLS
External	Outbound from external interface IP of Access Edge	5061/TCP SIP/MTLS
External	Inbound to external interface IP of Access Edge	443/TCP SIP/TLS

[1] *A Director, although not required, is a recommended role that does pre-authentication of inbound SIP.*

Examining Rules for Web Conferencing Edge Servers

Web Conferencing Edge Servers handle traffic for users outside of your organization that are invited or conduct conferences using your internal Web Conferencing Servers. Specifically, this would be remote-access, federated or anonymous users. Internal users use the internal servers but can attend or conduct meetings with remote and federated users.

Persistent Shared Object Model (PSOM) traffic is used for Web conferences. The purpose of PSOM is to send data to and from Office Communicator/Live Meeting for the actual slide or multimedia information shown by the meeting presenter. PSOM uses port 8057 over TCP.

Authentication is performed between the server and clients by using TLS. Authentication between role servers is done using MTLS. A remote user who is a member of your domain will use NT LAN Manager (NTLM) and credentials will be authenticated by Active Directory. Users from a federated domain will be authenticated by their domain and allowed to interact with the Conferencing Server in your network because of the federation trust that is in place between your Office Communications Server infrastructure and the federated partner's. (For more on federations and how this trust is created and managed, refer to Chapter 8, "Public IM Connectivity Scenarios.") Anonymous attendees—people who are not members of your domain and are not members of a federated domain—authenticate by use of a digest authentication derived from the conference location and the unique conference key that is created for each Web conference.

An external Communicator client connects to the Edge Server by using PSOM over port TCP/443. A TLS connection is established between the Web Conferencing Edge Server and the client software. Figure 4-30 shows the data flow from client to Edge Server and the internal Web Conferencing Server to the Edge Server.

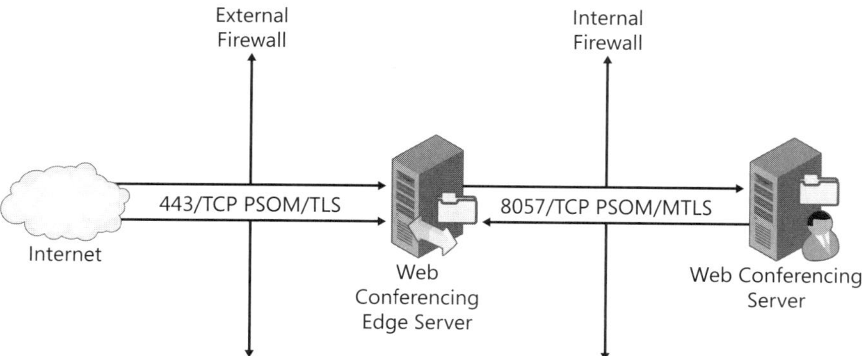

FIGURE 4-30 Traffic to the Web Conferencing Edge Server

The flow of traffic and the rules on firewalls in your environment are shown in Table 4-5.

TABLE 4-5 Firewall Rules for Web Conferencing Edge Servers

WEB CONFERENCING EDGE SERVER SERVICE: RTCDATAPROXY

FIREWALL	DIRECTION AND RULE	PORT/PROTOCOL
External	Inbound to external interface IP of Web Conferencing Edge Server	5061/TCP SIP/MTLS
Internal	Inbound to interface IP of Web Conferencing Server	5061/TCP SIP/MTLS
Internal	Outbound to internal interface IP of Web Conferencing Edge Server	8057/TCP PSOM/MTLS
External	Inbound to external interface IP of Web Conferencing Edge Server	443/TCP PSOM/TLS

Examining Rules for A/V Edge Servers

The A/V Edge Server is unique because the requirements for this role are complex and different from the other two roles. It requires a publicly addressable IP address.

The primary reason that the A/V Edge Server needs a publicly routable IP address is due to the nature of A/V streams. They are sensitive to latency and for that reason cannot handle the overhead of mechanisms such as Network Address Translator (NAT) that are found in nearly all firewalls.

NAT was never intended as a security mechanism. Although it does obfuscate the actual address of the internal client or server, the real purpose is to enable a single public IP address to be used to service thousands of users in a reserved IP address range (see Internet Engineering Task Force [IETF] RFC 1631). There is no NAT on the tunneled IP that directly exposes the A/V Edge Server. Internal clients communicating with external clients use their actual internal IP addresses. Initially, this might look like a security problem, but it is mitigated by the fact that the client and server establish a secure connection via TLS, and therefore the connection is encrypted.

The specific reason that NAT cannot be used is better explained by the operation of Interactive Connectivity Establishment (ICE) and Simple Traversal of UDP through NAT (STUN). ICE and STUN rely on a public IP address to work properly. IETF RFC 3489 explains this in much greater detail but essentially states that STUN assumes the server exists on the public Internet. If the server is on a private address, the user may or may not be able to use the discovered address and ports to communicate with other users. Worse, there is no reliable way to detect a condition in which communication will fail.

Another area of uniqueness for the A/V Edge Server is the number of TCP and UDP ports that optionally might be open to work correctly in a federation scenario. By default, TCP and UDP ports 50,000–59,999 must be open for federation.

The 10,000 ports are required only if you are using the A/V or Application Sharing Server role with a federated partner. Remote users accessing the A/V Edge Server will not use this port range. This range of 10,000 UDP ports is associated only with RTCMEDIARELAY, the service that hosts A/V on the Edge Server. The A/V Edge Server service allocates random ports only when they are assigned to incoming clients. These ports are then communicated to the client over SIP, notifying the client which ports to specifically connect to. Although the firewall may enable access to these ports on the A/V Edge Server, the ports are not opened by the services on the A/V Edge Server until allocated and communicated to the client.

UDP is preferred over TCP for A/V Edge Server use, and application sharing always uses TCP. UDP is prioritized over TCP is because UDP does not have the overhead that TCP does. UDP does not do a handshake; it merely sends the packet and, without waiting for a response, sends the next. This is a much more efficient method for A/V traffic, where the client at the receiving end can make up for packets that might be dropped, but it can't do anything about severe latency in the data stream that might be imposed by TCP overhead delays.

Figure 4–31 shows the port/protocol traffic associated with the A/V Edge Server.

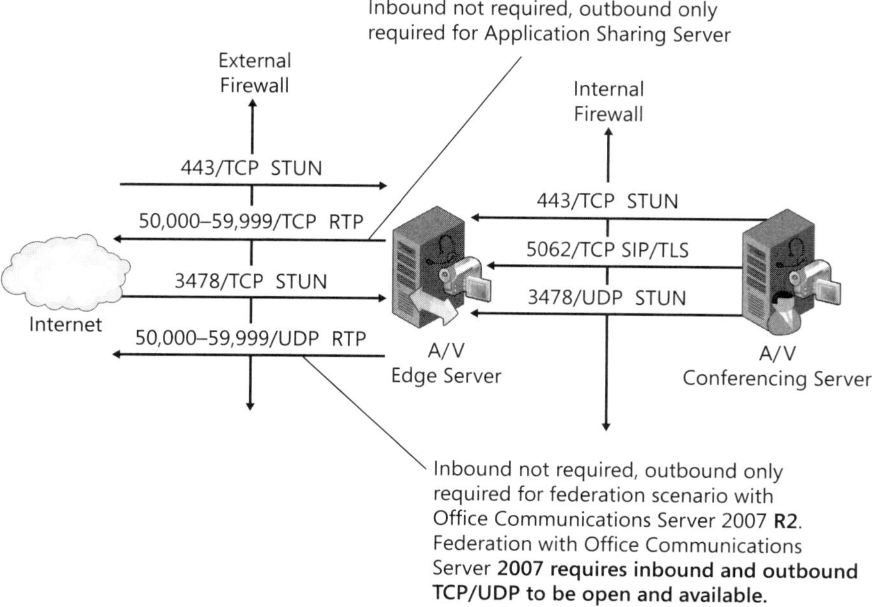

FIGURE 4-31 A/V Traffic in the typical Edge configuration

Table 4-6 defines the firewall rules that must be configured to ensure a properly operating A/V Edge Server.

TABLE 4-6 Firewall Rules for the A/V Edge Server

A/V EDGE SERVER SERVICES DATA: RTCMEDIARELAY

A/V EDGE SERVER SERVICES AUTHENTICATION: RTCMRAUTH

FIREWALL	DIRECTION AND RULE	PORT/PROTOCOL
Internal	Outbound to A/V Edge Server internal interface IP	443/TCP STUN/TCP
Internal	Outbound to A/V Edge Server internal interface IP	5062/TCP SIP/TLS
Internal	Outbound to A/V Edge Server internal interface IP	3478/UDP STUN/UDP
External	Inbound to A/V Edge Server external interface IP	443/TCP STUN/TCP
External	Inbound to A/V Edge Server external interface IP	50,000-59,999/TCP RTP/TCP
External	Inbound to A/V Edge Server external interface IP	3478/UDP STUN/UDP

TABLE 4-6 Firewall Rules for the A/V Edge Server

A/V EDGE SERVER SERVICES DATA: RTCMEDIARELAY			
A/V EDGE SERVER SERVICES AUTHENTICATION: RTCMRAUTH			
FIREWALL	**DIRECTION AND RULE**	**PORT/PROTOCOL**	
External	Inbound to A/V Edge Server external interface IP	50,000-59,999/UDP	RTP/UDP
External	Outbound from A/V Edge Server external interface IP	50,000-59,999/UDP	RTP/UDP
*External	Outbound/inbound to/from A/V Edge Server external interface IP	50,000-59,999/UDP	RTP/UDP
*External	Outbound/inbound to/from A/V Edge Server external interface IP	50,000-59,999/UDP	RTP/UDP

* Only needed when federating with a partner using Office Communications Server 2007. Rules should be reconfigured when all partners have upgraded to Office Communications Server 2007 R2. When initiating A/V communication, the client sends a series of SIP packets across the firewall to the Access Edge Server. This happens because of the way that ICE works. Each client allocates a port at the local endpoint (itself) and at the remote endpoint (the external edge of the A/V Edge Server). These allocated ports are called candidates. Because of the need to reduce latency as much as possible, each client needs both candidates. Once these candidates are acquired, they are sent to each of the other clients joining the same A/V conference. The candidates are communicated over the established SIP channel. When these candidates are received, each client builds a matrix of possible combinations. The clients each use the matrix of possible connections to send test packets to determine which port combination succeeds. ICE logic is used to accomplish this, and it prefers UDP over TCP. When the best path is determined, the clients proceed with the A/V conference.

Examining Rules for the Web Components Server

Office Communications Server 2007 R2 uses a Web service managed by the Web Components Server role to enable users to join a Web conference session, upload and download documents during a Web conference, expand distribution groups (DGs), and download the Address Book when connecting externally. Office Communications Server also offers another server role, called Communicator Web Access, for users to sign in to Office Communications Server by using a Web browser.

Internal users can connect to both of these server roles directly. For remote users and anonymous users, these server roles must be accessible externally from the Internet. The recommended way to securely expose your Web Components Server is through an HTTPS reverse proxy.

Users use a published URL to directly connect to the reverse proxy on a secure connection (HTTPS). The reverse proxy then proxies the client request over another HTTPS connection to the Web Components or Communicator Web Access server through a private URL. This is shown in Figure 4-32.

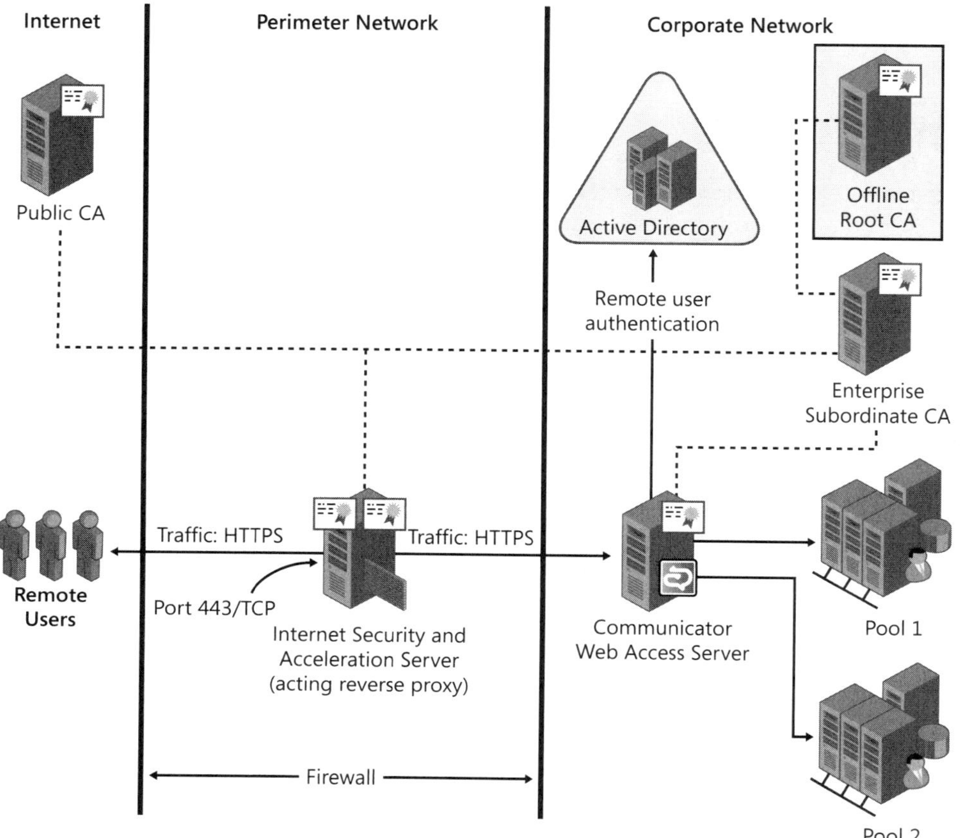

FIGURE 4-32 HTTPS reverse proxy

The reverse proxy is deployed in the perimeter network, whereas the Web Components and Communicator Web Access Servers are deployed on the internal network. Any reverse proxy can be used; however, Microsoft has tested only ISA Server 2006. For more information about how to securely publish Web applications to the Internet by using ISA Server, see the TechNet article at *http://go.microsoft.com/fwlink/?LinkID=133670*.

Summary

Office Communications Server 2007 R2 leverages existing technologies to best meet its needs. Technologies such as Active Directory, PKI, DNS Server, SQL Server, ISA Server (as a reverse proxy), HLBs, and media gateways support the deployment of Office Communications Server. It is important that you understand how these technologies are used so that your deployment of Office Communications Server is successful and as secure as possible.

Additional Resources

- Microsoft Unified Communications home page, found at *http://go.microsoft.com/fwlink/?LinkID=133630*
- Microsoft media gateway partners page, found at *http://go.microsoft.com/fwlink/?LinkID=133671*
- Microsoft load balancer partners page, found at *http://go.microsoft.com/fwlink/?LinkID=133624*
- Internet Engineering Task Force RFC1631, "The IP Network Address Translators (NAT)," found at *http://go.microsoft.com/fwlink/?LinkID=133672*
- Internet Engineering Task Force RFC3489, "Simple Traversal of User Datagram Protocol (UDP) Through Network Address Translators (NAT)," found at *http://go.microsoft.com/fwlink/?LinkID=133673*
- "Office Communications Server 2007 R2 Active Directory Classes and Attributes," a document describing all attributes and classes related to Office Communications Server, including those that are obsolete from previous versions of Live Communications Server and Office Communications Server

PART II

Key Usage Scenarios

CHAPTER 5

Basic IM and Presence Scenarios

This chapter describes the basic login, presence, and instant messaging (IM) scenarios by first providing a user-level view of actions taken in Microsoft Office Communicator 2007 R2 and then explaining in depth the protocols, algorithms, and systems that make these processes work. This chapter also provides background on basic server and client operations in terms of discovery, connectivity, and communications over Session Initiation Protocol (SIP) and as such is a useful reference when exploring other scenarios.

The login process seems simple from the user perspective because it involves only starting Office Communicator 2007 and typing a user name and credentials. However, a number of complex interactions between Microsoft Office Communications Server 2007 and Communicator 2007 help provide security and establish a reliable communications channel. Understanding these interactions is critical for troubleshooting user login failures, as well as client connectivity, authentication, and discovery issues.

Presence information can be managed and shared, allowing users to see if contacts are available, all available means to reach the contact, and how the contact might best be reached based on the contact's current activity level. This capability is critical for many enterprises, especially distributed or mobile organizations. Being able to receive notification when someone is back at his or her desk, contact someone for an immediate answer without having to initiate a phone conversation, and locate someone's contact information (including private information, if the contact allows it) all simplify communications in secure and productive ways. This section shows some of the user operations that control requesting presence information from others, publishing presence information, and managing and controlling how presence information is shared.

Instant messaging is a useful tool for getting quick answers from colleagues, reaching someone who is in a meeting without distracting others, or receiving and acting on a message while in a meeting (rather than stepping out to take a phone call). This section provides an overview of IM for individuals and groups, as well as pointers for sending hyperlinks and emoticons. Even though these are relatively simple user scenarios, technical details on how these are accomplished and how content-filtering works are provided to help with troubleshooting or configuration.

Understanding the Login Process

In this chapter, you first walk through the login process from the user perspective. Then you walk through the technical steps, decisions, and protocols that are going on in the background. Doing so provides a rich understanding that will aid in troubleshooting login problems and infrastructure problems.

Why Talk About the Login Process?

When looking at key usage scenarios for Office Communications Server 2007, logging in from Communicator 2007 is a critical step. When the system has problems, logging in is likely to be the first indication of an issue. Additionally, understanding the technology details behind the login process provides technical insight in becoming an expert administrator or consultant. The simple login process exercises many key aspects of the technology behind Communicator and the Office Communications Server infrastructure, so it is worth understanding in detail.

A Login Scenario

This scenario walks through a fictitious user, Jeremy Los, using Communicator 2007 R2 to log in to Office Communications Server 2007. This scenario assumes that Jeremy has just finished installation and is logging in for the first time. However, much of what will be shown applies to subsequent logins as well. The scenario shows what Jeremy sees during the login process and what steps he takes to complete the login.

Step 1: Signing In to an Account

Jeremy launches Communicator 2007 and clicks Sign In. Communicator asks for the sign-in address of his Communicator account, and he enters **jeremy@litwareinc.com**, which is the Session Initiation Protocol (SIP) Uniform Resource Identifier (URI). His administrator provisioned this URI. Most administrators use a SIP URI that matches the user's e-mail address so that it is easy for users to remember. Jeremy then clicks OK.

Step 2: Supplying Account Credentials (If Prompted)

If Jeremy is not currently logged in to the workstation with domain credentials, Communicator prompts him for sign-in information. Jeremy enters his Active Directory domain account user name and password, and then clicks Sign In, as shown in Figure 5-1. If Jeremy is logged in to his workstation with domain credentials, this step is not necessary.

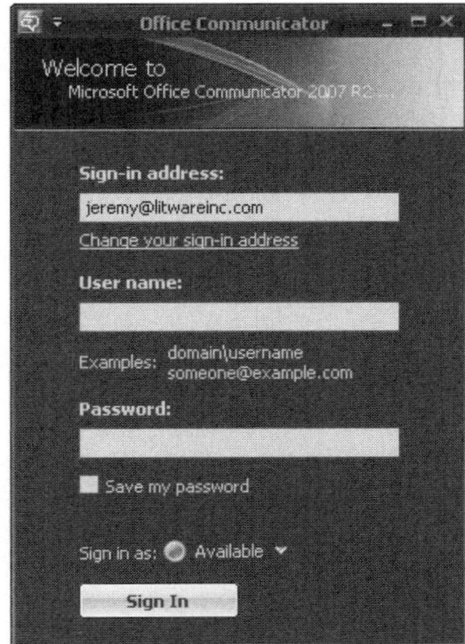

FIGURE 5-1 Communicator—Credentials

Step 3: The Login Process

After Jeremy enters his credentials, Communicator begins the login process to Office Communications Server.

Step 4: Login Complete

After the login process completes, Communicator shows Jeremy's presence information, call-forwarding details (if phone control is set up), and contact list, as shown in Figure 5-2.

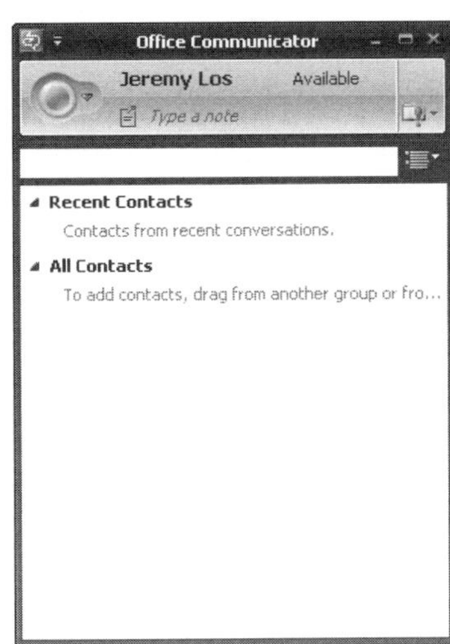

FIGURE 5-2 Communicator—Active

The Technical Details Behind the Login Process

Let's explore what is happening with Communicator 2007 and the Office Communications Server network in detail at the network level. Figure 5-3 provides an overview of the steps involved in the login process, which we will analyze.

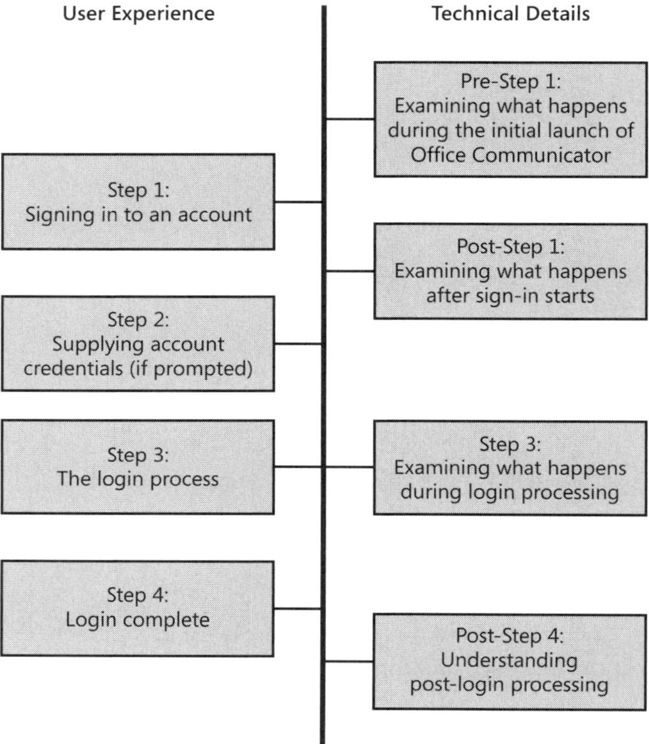

FIGURE 5-3 Login process steps

Pre-Step 1: What Happens During the Initial Launch of Communicator 2007

When Communicator is first launched, it determines if a log of its actions and activity needs to be written. Communicator logging can be controlled through the General menu when you select Options from the Tools menu. Two check boxes on the dialog box control logging and event log messages. All of the protocol messages for the remainder of this section were captured by enabling logging in Communicator and gathering protocol messages from the log.

NOTE Only the relevant portions of the protocol messages are shown in the figures. For full event log messages, enable logging and examine the output. Also important to note is that in Microsoft Windows Vista, a user must be a member of the Performance Log Users group to enable logging.

ENABLING THE COMMUNICATOR PROTOCOL LOGS

The logging options shown in the Communicator user interface (UI) are stored under the registry key HKEY_CURRENT_USER\Software\Microsoft\Tracing\Uccp\Communicator. The value *EnableFileTracing* can be turned on or off by setting it to 0 or 1, respectively. The valid range for *MaxFiles* is 1 or 2. It is set to 2 by default. This value specifies whether only one file should be created or multiple files should exist to maintain more history when the log file is recycled. *MaxFileSize* is set to 0x800000 (8.3MB) by default. It determines how large the log file can get before it is cleared and starts over. *FileDirectory* determines the directory where log files are stored. It is set to %USERPROFILE%\Tracing by default. When diagnosing problems, it can be valuable to increase the maximum file size. Note that manually changing these registry values requires a restart of Communicator for them to take effect.

The default settings create the login %USERPROFILE%\tracing\Communicator-uccapi-0.uccapilog. When this file reaches its maximum size, log data begins writing to the second file, Communicator-uccp-1.uccplog. New data continues to write to the second file until it becomes full, overwrites the first file, and clears itself. The second file continues to receive new log file data and the cycle repeats.

NOTE Enabling the Turn On Logging In Communicator check box also creates an ETL file, which is used only by Product Support Services (PSS) to troubleshoot issues.

WORKING WITH COMMUNICATOR APPLICATION EVENT LOGS

Enabling event logs in Communicator creates entries in the Application Event logs when there are failures. These entries are useful for diagnosing login problems. An example is shown next for reference. It clearly explains the problem, points to the data related to the problem, and explains the steps required to solve the issue.

The following event log error occurred because Communicator was configured to connect to an invalid port (9999) on the server instead of a valid port (5061, for example). The message explains that Communicator was unable to connect and by using a tool such as winerror.exe or lcserror.exe, the error code can be interpreted. Error 10065 is the Windows sockets error code for WSAEHOSTUNREACH, which means the host was unreachable.

```
Communicator failed to connect to server srv.litwareinc.com (192.168.3.1) on port 9999
due to error 10065. The server is not listening on the port in question, the service
is not running on this machine, the service is not responsive, or network connectivity
doesn't exist.

Resolution:
Please make sure that your workstation has network connectivity.  If you are
using manual configuration, please double-check the configuration.  The network
administrator should make sure that the service is running on port 9999 on server srv.
litwareinc.com (192.168.3.1).

For more information, see Help and Support Center at
http://go.microsoft.com/fwlink/events.asp.
```

NOTE **Winerror.exe is part of the Microsoft Windows Server 2003 Resource Kit Tools, and Lcserror.exe is part of the Office Communications Server 2007 Resource Kit Tools. Both of these can be found at *http://www.microsoft.com/downloads* with a search for either one of the Resource Kit Tools.**

Post-Step 1: What Happens After Sign-In Starts

At this point, Communicator must determine which server it should log in to by using the user's URI (jeremy@litwareinc.com) and any manual settings configured on the client. If manual settings were provided, the server to use is clear, but if the URI was the only thing provided, some discovery is necessary. The way in which Communicator does discovery varies based on configuration because Communicator can be instructed to allow only Transport Layer Security (TLS) over Transmission Control Protocol (TCP), to allow only strict server names, or both.

After the client discovers the server to connect to, it attempts to connect using TCP or TLS over TCP. If TLS is used, the server provides a certificate to authenticate itself to the client. The client must validate the certificate before proceeding. The client might negotiate compression (if using TLS over TCP), and then it initiates a SIP registration.

Next, the client sends a SIP REGISTER message to the server without any credentials. This prompts Office Communications Server to challenge for user credentials and specifies to the Communicator client the authentication protocols that it accepts. For additional details, see the section titled "Initial Registration" later in this chapter.

When it comes to providing credentials, Communicator has two options. Communicator can use the user's current Windows credentials to log in, or it can prompt the user for credentials.

NOTE The credentials manager in Windows can also be used to manage user names and passwords. More information about the credentials manager can be found in the Microsoft TechNet article "Windows XP Professional Resource Kit: Understanding Logon and Authentication" at *http://go.microsoft.com/fwlink/?LinkID=133674*, in the "Stored User Names and Passwords" section. For specific information about changes for Windows Vista and credential management, please see "New Authentication Functionality in Windows Vista" at *http://go.microsoft.com/fwlink/?LinkId=137130*.

If Communicator validates the server certificate, Communicator might request compression on the connection. Communicator enables compression only on encrypted links, and it determines whether to enable compression based on Group Policy settings (which defaults to enabling compression when there is less than or equal to a 128-Kb link speed). Communicator negotiates compression by using a NEGOTIATE request immediately after TLS is established. This message is only sent hop-to-hop for a given connection. The server can accept or reject this request based on its configuration. By default, the server accepts client compression requests.

The Initial Registration

After connectivity is established, the initial registration from the client is made to ensure that SIP is allowed on this port and to discover what authentication mechanism should be used with the server. A SIP REGISTER message is used for this purpose, and here is an example of that request:

```
REGISTER sip:litwareinc.com SIP/2.0
Via: SIP/2.0/TLS 192.168.3.100:2060
Max-Forwards: 70
From: <sip:jeremy@litwareinc.com>;tag=7ad9af1eb1;epid=aa6d968e18
To: <sip:jeremy@litwareinc.com>
Call-ID: 5d2ad5f9e7a24dacaf1075b97a04df91
CSeq: 1 REGISTER
Contact: <sip:192.168.3.100:2060;transport= tls;ms-opaque=aacb364544>;methods="INVITE,
MESSAGE, INFO, OPTIONS, BYE, CANCEL, NOTIFY, ACK, REFER, BENOTIFY";proxy=replace;+sip.
instance= "<urn:uuid:6BF396BA-A7D6-5247-89FB-C13B52F5840D>"
User-Agent: UCCP/2.0.6093.0 OC/2.0.6093.0 (Microsoft Office Communicator)
Supported: gruu-10, adhoclist, msrtc-event-categories
Supported: ms-forkingms-keep-alive: UAC;hop-hop=yes
Event: registrationContent-Length: 0
```

NOTE Access to raw protocol logs is available in Communicator with this release simply by selecting a check box in the configuration process.

The server's expected response is to challenge the client request for authentication. In the response shown next, the server is asking for Kerberos or NT LAN Manager (NTLM) authentication so that Communicator knows what authentication mechanisms can be used and also knows (for this connection) which server it needs to authenticate against (srv.litwareinc.com).

```
SIP/2.0 401 Unauthorized
Date: Fri, 04 May 2007 22:48:06 GMT
WWW-Authenticate: NTLM realm="SIP Communications Service",
targetname="srv.litwareinc.com", version=3
WWW-Authenticate: Kerberos realm="SIP Communications Service",
targetname="sip/srv.litwareinc.com", version=3
Via: SIP/2.0/TLS 192.168.3.100:2060;ms-received-port=2060;ms-received-cid=2600
From: <sip:jeremy@litwareinc.com>;tag=7ad9af1eb1;epid=aa6d968e18
To: <sip:jeremy@litwareinc.com>;tag=A1F542AB99D66616F9252CB6DF50257F
Call-ID: 5d2ad5f9e7a24dacaf1075b97a04df91
CSeq: 1 REGISTER
Content-Length: 0
```

The Authenticated Registration

After Communicator has the credentials, it is ready to start authenticating with the server. At this point, Communicator can simply use the credentials it has available to respond to the authentication challenge.

For NTLM, this takes three handshaking steps. Communicator must submit another anonymous REGISTER, specifying that it wants to use the NTLM authentication protocol in its next REGISTER so that the server will generate a true NTLM challenge (instead of just stating that NTLM authentication is required as it did in the previous 401 response). The server then provides an NTLM challenge to which Communicator can respond by using the user's credentials. As an aside, the server does not generate a true NTLM challenge unless the client prompts for one by asking for NTLM, because generating challenges is an expensive operation for the server. When the REGISTER message is sent this time, with the NTLM challenge response, the server can verify the user and will actually process the REGISTER request.

For Kerberos, this takes only two handshaking steps because Communicator always submits an anonymous REGISTER, identifies that Kerberos is challenged for, and then provides a Kerberos response in the REGISTER message that is sent next. The server can directly verify this response and process the REGISTER request. Kerberos has one less step because simply knowing the server name is enough for the client to request a Kerberos ticket to validate itself against the server.

> **NOTE** For more information about Kerberos and NTLM, see the Microsoft TechNet article "Kerberos Authentication Technical Reference" at *http://go.microsoft.com/fwlink/?LinkID=133675* or the Microsoft Developer Network (MSDN) article "NTLM Authentication" at *http://go.microsoft.com/fwlink/?LinkID=133676.*

Figure 5-4 shows the protocol messages exchanged by the client and the server during initial registration. An example using Kerberos authentication is shown in the upper half. The lower half shows the handshaking process when NTLM is used. This diagram also provides an overview to help in interpreting the actual protocol messages that are shown later.

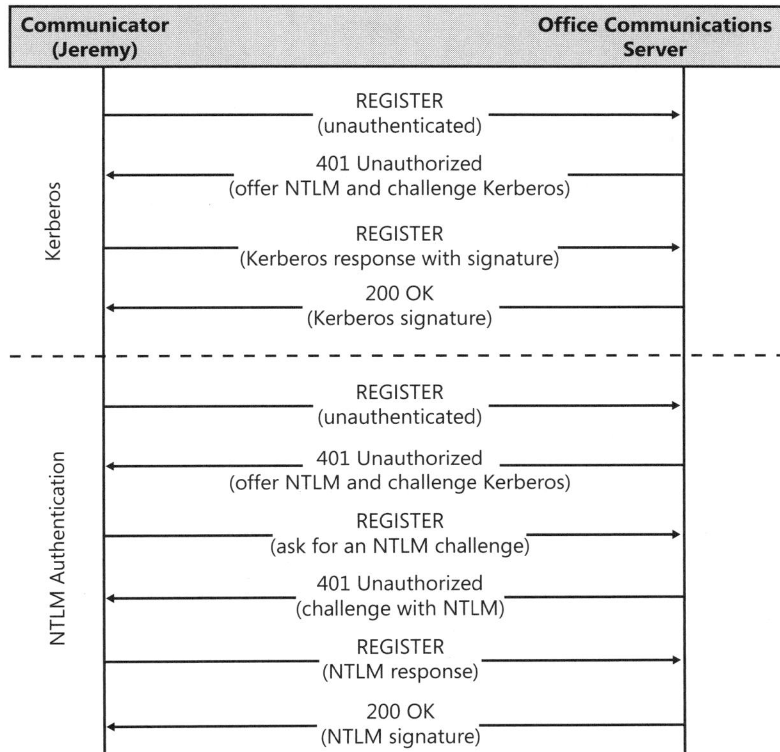

FIGURE 5-4 Initial registration—Authentication handshaking

In this example, the client provides its REGISTER request with a Kerberos ticket for the server that issued the original challenge, as follows:

```
REGISTER sip:litwareinc.com SIP/2.0
Via: SIP/2.0/TLS 192.168.3.100:2062
Max-Forwards: 70
From: <sip:jeremy@litwareinc.com>;tag=59e091cf1e;epid=aa6d968e18
To: <sip:jeremy@litwareinc.com>Call-ID: 2fd39df030554515a412e3aa2964489f
CSeq: 2 REGISTER
Contact: <sip:192.168.3.100:2062;transport= tls;ms-opaque=4d8a610d50>;methods="INVITE,
MESSAGE, INFO, OPTIONS, BYE, CANCEL, NOTIFY, ACK, REFER, BENOTIFY";proxy=replace;+sip.
instance=
"<urn:uuid:6BF396BA-A7D6-5247-89FB-C13B52F5840D>"
User-Agent: UCCP/2.0.6093.0 OC/2.0.6093.0 (Microsoft Office Communicator)
```

```
Authorization: Kerberos qop="auth", realm="SIP Communications Service",
targetname="sip/srv.litwareinc.com", gssapi-data="... (Kerberos ticket info)
Supported: gruu-10, adhoclist, msrtc-event-categories
Supported: ms-forking
ms-keep-alive: UAC;hop-hop=yes
Event: registration
Content-Length: 0
```

The Kerberos credentials can be a relatively large portion of the protocol message for the initial handshake, but it is a relatively minimal cost for the security provided for this and all future messages. Because subsequent messages will reference only the credentials and pass minimal data to validate the keys embedded in this exchange, this is a fairly minimal one-time, up-front cost.

For clarity and completeness, the authentication headers are shown as snippets for an exchange if NTLM were in use, as follows:

```
REGISTER sip:litwareinc.com SIP/2.0...
Call-ID: 2fd39df030554515a412e3aa2964489f
CSeq: 2 REGISTER...
Authorization: NTLM qop="auth", realm="SIP Communications Service",  targetname="srv.
litwareinc.com", gssapi-data=""...
```

The server responds by offering a true NTLM challenge that Communicator can respond to by using user credentials. This true challenge is easy to see because it is rather large (380 bytes) and starts with a standard header "TlRMTVN...", as follows:

```
SIP/2.0 401 Unauthorized...
WWW-Authenticate: NTLM opaque="33E7D13B", gssapi-data="...
"TlRMTVNTUAACAAAAAAAAADgAAADzgpjiFRIiVZ/HsigAAAAAAAAAAOQA5AA4AAAABQLODgAAAA8C
AA4AUgBFAEQATQBPAE4ARAABABgAUgBFAEQALQBMAEMAUwBEAFIALQAwADEABAA0AHIAZQBkAG0Ab
wBuAGQALgBjAG8AcgBwAC4AbQBpAGMAcgBvAHMAbwBmAHQALgBjAG8AbQADAE4AcgBlAGQALQBsAG
MAcwBkAHIALQAwADEALgByAGUAZABtAG8AbgBkAC4AYwBvAHIAcAAuAG0AaQBjAHIAbwBzAG8AZgB
0AC4AYwBvAG0ABQAkAGMAbwByAHAALgBtAGkAYwByAG8AcwBvAGYAdAAuAGMAbwBtAAAAAAA=",
targetname="srv.litwareinc.com", realm="SIP Communications Service"...
Call-ID: 2fd39df030554515a412e3aa2964489f
CSeq: 2 REGISTER...
```

Communicator can now use this NTLM challenge to generate an NTLM response, and it packages this in the next REGISTER message that it sends, as follows:

```
REGISTER sip:litwareinc.com SIP/2.0...
Call-ID: 2fd39df030554515a412e3aa2964489f
CSeq: 3 REGISTER...
Authorization: NTLM qop="auth", opaque="33E7D13B", realm="SIP Communications
```

```
Service", targetname="srv.litwareinc.com", gssapi-data="...
"TlRMTVNTUAADAAAAGAAYAHgAAAAYABgAkAAAAA4ADgBIAAAACgAKAFYAAAAYABgAYAAAABAAEACo
AAAAVYKQQgUBKAoAAAAPUgBFAEQATQBPAE4ARABqAGIAdQBjAGgARABFAEwATAAtAFgAUABTAC0AN
AAwADAARYHHoHZkV6SMRG47yl+zcIrUcTec6pSnLajtPCReLpIB6dFgYbOk9fWgnTl9Lg6N+wo5vP
ltIFyxOX6CU6kP3g=="...
```

Either way authentication was received, the server now has an authenticated REGISTER message and must respond to it. The server's response to the REGISTER message can fall into one of the following categories:

- **301 Redirect** In this case, the server tells Communicator what the user's home server is so that the user can directly connect and register most efficiently, as follows:
  - The existing connection will be closed, and the client will go through the connection process to connect to the server to which it was redirected.
  - The entire authentication and registration process will repeat with the new server to get back to this point, where a 200 OK message from the server (accepting the registration) would be expected.
- **200 OK** In this case, the server directly accepts the registration because it is the user's home server, or it is acting as a proxy because a redirect would fail as a result of Communicator not having direct connectivity to the home server. (Access Edge Servers will proxy registrations.)
- **403 Forbidden** In this case, the client is not allowed to log in because the SIP URI exists, but it is owned by a different user than the credentials that were supplied. The following are possible causes:
  - The user account is not enabled for Office Communications Server.
  - The user account is disabled, or the password is expired.
  - The credentials are invalid, or there was a typing error in the user name or password.
  - Communicator is logging in from the Internet, and the user is not enabled for remote access with Office Communications Server.
- **404 Not Found** In this case, the client is not allowed to log in because the user URI that was specified does not exist, even though valid user credentials were provided. (This failure could be because of a typing error in the URI.)
- **504 Server Time-Out** In this case, the server handling the request (probably an Access Edge Server) had difficulty routing the message, and there is either a configuration problem in the network or a service outage is occurring.

REAL WORLD

403 Forbidden

Thomas Laciano
Program Manager, RTC Customer Experience

Another possible cause of a 403 response is that the user is enabled but User Replicator has failed to synchronize changes from the domain to Microsoft SQL Server.

The most common problem caused by a customer is not allowing inheritable permissions on an organizational unit (OU). Beyond that, check the event log.

If Communicator receives a 504 or 403 error, it reports to the user that a general error has occurred and provides more details in the trace log. The event log should also provide a detailed description of the problem, along with hints to help understand how to resolve the problem. An example of one of the event log messages that can occur when an Access Edge Server is unable to route a message is shown next. This problem can be replicated easily on your own domain if your network has an Access Edge Server installed with Open Federation enabled. Simply try to send a message to a user in a domain that does not exist. (The example involves sending a message to unknownuser@cpandl.com, which is a fictitious domain that does not support SIP.) The nice thing about the log shown next is that it even tells you which server in the network failed. (The server sipfed.litwareinc.com identifies itself in the ms-diagnostics field from the 404 response and explains what failed: "Unable to resolve DNS SRV record.")

```
A SIP request made by Communicator failed in an unexpected manner (status
code404). More information is contained in the following technical data:

RequestUri:   sip:unknownuser@cpandl.com
From:         sip:jeremy@litwareinc.com;tag=a7e16ad66d
To:           sip:unknownuser@cpandl.com;tag=498ED6D80FE772442E7B51A625FB667E
Call-ID:      7ff2d267efa846778d741480d85fd522
Content-type: application/sdp

v=0
o=- 0 0 IN IP4 157.57.6.160
s=session
c=IN IP4 157.57.6.160
t=0 0
m=message 5060 sip null
a=accept-types:text/rtf application/x-ms-ink image/gif multipart/alternative
application/ms-imdn+xml

Response Data:
```

```
100  Trying
 404  Not Found
ms-diagnostics:  1008;reason="Unable to resolve DNS SRV  record";source="sipfed.
litwareinc.com"

Resolution:
If this error continues to occur, please contact your network administrator.
The network administrator can use a tool like winerror.exe from the Windows
Resource Kit or lcserror.exe from the Office Communications Server Resource
Kit in order to interpret any error codes listed above.

For more information, see Help and Support Center at
http://go.microsoft.com/fwlink/events.asp.
```

If Communicator receives a 301 response, the connection process starts again by resolving the host name it received in the Contact header and attempting to connect and register with this server.

> ***NOTE*** **Communicator has proof to allow it to trust the server it is registering against in the form of authentication signatures in the response and possibly even a validated certificate used by the first-hop server. Because of this, Communicator honors an authenticated redirect response from a server in its domain, even if the name does not line up with the SIP URI of the user. However, if Communicator receives a 200 response, the initial registration is complete and login processing continues from this point.**

In the example login, the server accepts the registration with a 200 OK response, as follows:

```
SIP/2.0 200 OK
ms-keep-alive: UAS; tcp=no; hop-hop=yes; end-end=no; timeout=300
Authentication-Info: Kerberos rspauth=
"602306092A864886F71201020201011100FFFFFFFF5C001B875485F1BC7E66F0006
6537A78", srand="40882645", snum="1", opaque="A7AB18E7", qop="auth",
targetname="sip/srv.litwareinc.com", realm="SIP Communications Service"
Via: SIP/2.0/TLS 192.168.3.100:2062;ms-received-port=2062;ms-received-cid=2700
From: "Jeremy Los"<sip:jeremy@litwareinc.com>;tag=59e091cf1e;epid=aa6d968e18
To: <sip:jeremy@litwareinc.com>;tag=A1F542AB99D66616F9252CB6DF50257F
Call-ID: 2fd39df030554515a412e3aa2964489f
CSeq: 2 REGISTER
Contact: <sip:192.168.3.100:2062;transport=tls;ms-opaque=4d8a610d50;
ms-received-cid=00002700>;expires=7200;+sip.instance="<urn:uuid:6bf396ba-
a7d6-5247-89fb-c13b52f5840d>";
gruu="sip:jeremy@litwareinc.com;opaque=user:epid:upbza9anR1KJ-8E7UvWEDQAA;gruu"
Expires: 7200
```

```
presence-state: register-action="added"
Allow-Events: vnd-microsoft-provisioning,vnd-microsoft-roaming-contacts,vnd-
microsoft-roaming-ACL,presence,presence.wpending,vnd-microsoft-roaming-self,
vnd-microsoft-provisioning-v2
Supported: adhoclistServer: RTC/3.0
Supported: msrtc-event-categories
Content-Length: 0
```

NOTE Because the same header information is repeated in each 200 OK response, the Authentication-Info, From, To, and Call-ID headers are left out in the remaining examples.

While we are looking at this example, the final 200 OK response has other interesting information to examine. First, the server provides credentials for itself that also prove to the client that the server can be trusted. This proof is especially important for TCP connections, where this is the only means of authentication the client has. The rspauth and targetname fields in the Authentication-Info header provide cryptographic proof that the authenticating server identifies itself with the name specified. Second, the single Contact header in the response tells Communicator that only the contact address that was just registered is currently logged on (that is, no other clients are active for Jeremy's account). Third, the ms-keep-alive and Allow-Events headers provide information to the client to help it understand how to stay connected and synchronized with the server, as well as what services are available. Finally, the Expires header tells Communicator how long the registration is valid. It must be refreshed within 7,200 seconds (2 hours), or it will automatically expire and be cleaned up by the server.

REAL WORLD

Troubleshooting Client Connections

Thomas Laciano
Program Manager, RTC Customer Experience

Troubleshooting the first client connection can be approached in a systematic way. Begin your troubleshooting with Active Directory Users and Computers and Office Communications Server 2007 Management Consoles. Is the user showing that she is enabled? If she is enabled here, you actually have one more place to check, because these views are showing what is configured but not necessarily what is in the database used by Office Communications Server.

Open a command prompt and navigate to the directory you installed the Office Communications Server Resource Kit Tools to. (You installed the Resource Kit Tools, right?) The default location is C:\Program Files\Microsoft Office Communications Server 2007\Reskit. Typing dbanalyze /? provides the available switches, as well as

sample syntax. For example, say you are interested in determining if the database includes the SIP URI of the user you are testing with. (Note that we are not covering the elements of the output here, merely referencing the tool for the purpose of validating the presence of a user in the database.) In this situation, you use the following command:

```
dbanalyze.exe /report:user /user:Jeremy@litwareinc.com
```

An example of output you might get from running this command follows:

```
Snooper Version: 3.0.6237.0

Report created at 5/30/2007 2:31:00 PM on sip.litwareinc.com.


User : jeremy@litwareinc.com
-----------------------------------------------
Resource Id        : 5
Home server        : sip.litwareinc.com
GUID               : 2e324a4b-c048-420f-9c8d-1d86bb9fc266
SID                : S-1-5-21-3158251299-35245958-1667159398-1173
Display Name       : Jeremy Los

OptionFlags        : 256
ArchivingFlags     : 0
Enabled            : True
MovingAway         : False
Unavailable        : False
RichMode           : True
Contact Version    : 2
Permission Version : 1
Email              : jeremy@litwareinc.com
Phone              :
Presence data      :

Contact Groups
--------------
1
Group Number : 1
Display Name : ~
External Uri :



Containers
----------
1
Container Number   : 0
```

```
Container Version  : 0
SameEnterprise     : False
Federated          : False
PublicCloud        : False
Everyone           : True
Member User        :
Member Domain      :
...
```

ON THE COMPANION MEDIA For a full example of command output from dbanalyze, see the file dbanalyze-jeremy.txt on the companion media, located in the \Appendixes,Scripts,Resources\Chapter 05 folder.

After you confirm that the user is enabled, also confirm that the global settings include the domain you selected for the SIP URI. This is a common issue for customers who have a SIP URI that does not match their Active Directory namespace or who have multiple SIP domains.

For example, the deployment for Litware might have used Litwareinc.local or Litwareinc.corp as the Active Directory namespace, which would require that we manually add Litwareinc.com to the list of domains supported by the configuration. If the server is listening with TCP, supported domains are no longer configured by default and therefore must be added. The benefit of adding TCP is that we can use the Internet Protocol (IP) address and a network analyzer in addition to the existing logs. Use the IP address first in the client configuration to eliminate any host name resolution problems. After confirmation, switch to the fully qualified domain name (FQDN) of the server to confirm host name resolution is working and, finally, configure for TLS over TCP with the FQDN of the server. After all of this has been verified, you can add the option of automatic configuration, which requires the Domain Name Service (DNS) Service Record Locator (SRV) records described later in Chapter 19, "Client and Device Administration."

Finally, new to Office Communications Server is diagnostics in the Office Communications Server Management Console. You can test connectivity and client sign-in, receiving a rather verbose output of the tests and status. If this still fails to provide you with a resolution to your problem, enable the client logs as described previously in this chapter and contact the support services team.

Step 3: What Happens During Login Processing

After registration is complete, a complex set of queries and notifications takes place between the client and the server as Communicator gathers information from the server and the rest of the network. Communicator gathers its own configuration information and then gathers presence information about users on the contact list. To speed things up, Communicator issues the first four subscriptions in parallel and receives the server responses as they come in. For simplicity, the requests and the responses are shown one by one, but keep in mind that this ordering is not precisely what is happening at the network level. Requests can be sent out in parallel by the client, and responses can come back in an unrelated order, based on network delays to and from each destination. Figure 5-5 provides an overview of the protocol messages exchanged between Communicator and the server infrastructure during this phase of the login process.

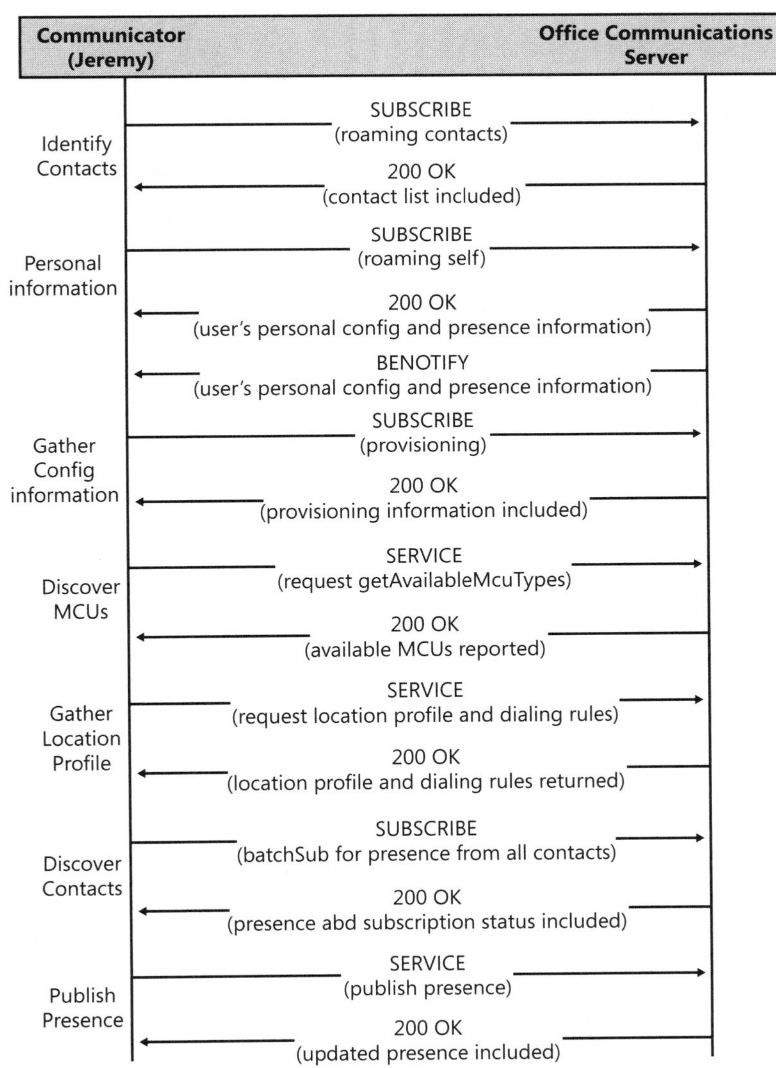

FIGURE 5-5 Login processing

This subscription enables Communicator to see the contact list, but it also enables it to identify whether contacts are added on other clients with which the user might be logged in. If the contact list changes, the server sends a notification containing the change. A SUBSCRIBE message is sent to the server to initiate the subscription to the contact list, as follows:

```
SUBSCRIBE sip:jeremy@litwareinc.com SIP/2.0
Via: SIP/2.0/TLS 192.168.3.100:2062
Max-Forwards: 70
From: <sip:jeremy@litwareinc.com>;tag=9099c0ba1d;epid=aa6d968e18
To: <sip:jeremy@litwareinc.com>
Call-ID: ecb20da4280142d1b69b920276785d2f
CSeq: 1 SUBSCRIBE
Contact: <sip:jeremy@litwareinc.com;opaque=user:epid:upbza9anR1KJ-8E7UvWEDQAA;gruu>
User-Agent: UCCP/2.0.6093.0 OC/2.0.6093.0 (Microsoft Office Communicator)
Event: vnd-microsoft-roaming-contactsAccept: application/vnd-microsoft-roaming-
contacts+xml
Supported: com.microsoft.autoextend
Supported: ms-benotify
Proxy-Require: ms-benotify
Supported: ms-piggyback-first-notify
Proxy-Authorization: Kerberos qop="auth", realm="SIP Communications Service",
opaque="A7AB18E7", crand="3b86002b", cnum="1",
targetname="sip/srv.litwareinc.com", response=
"602306092a864886f71201020201011100ffffffff6150d616a8e990a9b9971b4585bea994"
Content-Length: 0
```

The Event header identifies that the request is to get back the contact list (called roaming contacts). Other headers (such as the Supported and Proxy-Require headers) provide optional enhancements or specify capabilities to allow for more functionality to be put to use, specifically protocol optimizations. These optimizations include the use of *BENOTIFY* (which is a best-effort notification that does not require a response to confirm receipt), sending first notifications as part of the response to the subscription request, and automatic server extensions for subscriptions.

The response immediately includes information in the body because both the client and server support *ms-piggyback-first-notify*. This feature enables the information that typically needs to be sent in a subsequent NOTIFY message to simply be sent in the 200 response.

The server accepts the subscription to the contact list with a 200 response in which it also confirms protocol optimizations will be used and specifies that the subscription will be maintained for 41,472 seconds (11.5 hours), as follows:

```
SIP/2.0 200 OK
Contact: <sip:srv.litwareinc.com:5061;transport=tls> ... (header info)

CSeq: 1 SUBSCRIBE
```

```
Expires: 41472
Content-Type: application/vnd-microsoft-roaming-contacts+xml
Event: vnd-microsoft-roaming-contactssubscription-state: active;expires=41472ms-
piggyback-cseq: 1
Supported: ms-benotify, ms-piggyback-first-notify
<contactList deltaNum="17" >  <group id="1" name="~" externalURI=""  />
<contact uri="rui@litwareinc.com" name="" groups="1" subscribed="true" externalURI="" >
<contactExtension>   <contactSettings contactId="0a1d4375-32d1-42b1-be25-41a6720d2dde">
</contactSettings>   </contactExtension>
</contact></contactList>
```

The response contains the user's contact list (also called a buddy list). Because the *ms-piggyback-first-notify* extension was supported, the server provides the first notification in the body of the 200 response. Contacts and groups are identified, along with information about what groups they are in and whether they are maintained with an active subscription or just kept in the contact list.

Next, Communicator issues a subscription request for presence information about the user (Jeremy Los in this case), access-level settings that have already been configured by the user to control who has access to what information, and the list of contacts who currently have outstanding subscriptions.

```
SUBSCRIBE sip:jeremy@litwareinc.com SIP/2.0
Via: SIP/2.0/TLS 192.168.3.100:2062
Max-Forwards: 70
From: <sip:jeremy@litwareinc.com>;tag=64ecc96946;epid=aa6d968e18
To: <sip:jeremy@litwareinc.com>
Call-ID: bb8338fdba864da9bc9875dad6dbec7aCSeq: 1 SUBSCRIBE
Contact: <sip:jeremy@litwareinc.com;opaque=user:epid:upbza9anR1KJ-8E7UvWEDQAA;gruu>
User-Agent: UCCP/2.0.6093.0 OC/2.0.6093.0 (Microsoft Office Communicator)
Event: vnd-microsoft-roaming-selfAccept: application/vnd-microsoft-roaming-self+xml
Supported: com.microsoft.autoextend
Supported: ms-benotify
Proxy-Require: ms-benotify
Supported: ms-piggyback-first-notifyProxy-Authorization: Kerberos qop="auth",
realm="SIP Communications Service", opaque="A7AB18E7", crand="9c81fb7f",
cnum="2", targetname="sip/srv.litwareinc.com",
response="602306092a864886f71201020201011100ffffffffc33ae8f9e62252efa3320f9e3 99828e9"
Content-Type: application/vnd-microsoft-roaming-self+xml
Content-Length: 174
<roamingList xmlns="http://schemas.microsoft.com/2006/09/sip/roaming-self">
  <roaming type="categories"/>
  <roaming type="containers"/>
  <roaming type="subscribers"/>
</roamingList>
```

The Event header identifies the request as a subscription to information that pertains to the user (called roaming self). Again, Communicator identifies that it can support several protocol optimizations.

The server accepts the subscription with a 200 OK response. The body of the response contains a list of information about the user, established access levels that contacts have been granted, and users with current subscriptions. These messages are quite large and detailed, and this one does not contain much interesting content because not many contacts or access levels have been established yet. As the contact list grows and access control settings evolve, this XML document is expanded.

ON THE COMPANION MEDIA **All the protocol messages referenced in these examples are on the companion media, in the \Appendixes,Scripts,Resources\Chapter 05\CD Protocol Logs folder, and can be viewed in their entirety there.**

This user information is stored on the user's home server in the SQL (MSDE) database and is used by the client and server to determine whether subscriptions from other users are accepted and whether messages for the client will be delivered or rejected. This subscription also lets Communicator know if other clients the user might have running on other machines change authorization settings, because the server sends a notification of the changes. This subscription also enables Communicator to be notified when new subscriptions from other users come in so that the user can decide how to handle them.

After the subscription is initiated, a notification is eventually sent out by the server. An example of that best-effort notification is shown next for reference. (The majority of the XML body was removed for brevity, but it can be viewed from the protocol logs on the companion media.)

```
BENOTIFY sip:192.168.3.100:2062;transport=tls;ms-opaque=4d8a610d50;ms-
received-cid=00002700 SIP/2.0
Via: SIP/2.0/TLS
192.168.3.1:5061;branch=z9hG4bK0F226A22.4AC8062C;branched=FALSE
Authentication-Info: Kerberos rspauth=
"602306092A864886F71201020201011100FFFFFFFF85D8DA4A3CF277F582B4D4AF1AEBED6",
srand="88553BCA", snum="8", opaque="A7AB18E7", qop="auth",
targetname="sip/srv.litwareinc.com", realm="SIP Communications Service"
Max-Forwards: 70
To: <sip:jeremy@litwareinc.com>;tag=64ecc96946;epid=aa6d968e18Content-Length: 7638
From: <sip:jeremy@litwareinc.com>;tag=9A750080
Call-ID: bb8338fdba864da9bc9875dad6dbec7a
CSeq: 2 BENOTIFY
Require: eventlist
Content-Type: application/vnd-microsoft-roaming-self+xml
Event: vnd-microsoft-roaming-self
```

```
subscription-state: active;expires=51410
<roamingData
...
</roamingData>
```

Communicator next issues a subscription for provisioning information to help with initial configuration. This subscription is a one-time query (denoted by the Expires header, which asks for 0 seconds for the subscription lifetime). This subscription asks for server configuration, meeting policies, and policy settings that Communicator must enforce.

```
SUBSCRIBE sip:jeremy@litwareinc.com SIP/2.0
Via: SIP/2.0/TLS 192.168.3.100:2062
Max-Forwards: 70
From: <sip:jeremy@litwareinc.com>;tag=e7c43a41fd;epid=aa6d968e18
To: <sip:jeremy@litwareinc.com>
Call-ID: 7ea128a6ebe34481b5daa76132607e34
CSeq: 1 SUBSCRIBE
Contact: <sip:jeremy@litwareinc.com;opaque=
user:epid:upbza9anR1KJ-8E7UvWEDQAA;gruu>User-Agent: UCCP/2.0.6093.0 OC/
2.0.6093.0 (Microsoft Office Communicator)
Event: vnd-microsoft-provisioning-v2
Accept: application/vnd-microsoft-roaming-provisioning-v2+xml
Supported: com.microsoft.autoextend
Supported: ms-benotify
Proxy-Require: ms-benotify
Supported: ms-piggyback-first-notify
Expires: 0
Proxy-Authorization: Kerberos qop="auth", realm="SIP Communications Service",
 opaque="A7AB18E7", crand="e7e65db3", cnum="3", targetname=
"sip/srv.litwareinc.com", response=
"602306092a864886f71201020201011100ffffffff4dca80cf37e7ee6998209ab5923fc3cd"
Content-Type: application/vnd-microsoft-roaming-provisioning-v2+xml
Content-Length: 242
<provisioningGroupList xmlns=
"http://schemas.microsoft.com/2006/09/sip/provisioninggrouplist">
  <provisioningGroup name="ServerConfiguration"/>
  <provisioningGroup name="meetingPolicy"/>
  <provisioningGroup name="ucPolicy"/>
</provisioningGroupList>
```

The server accepts the one-time provisioning query with a 200 OK response, which contains a rich set of configuration and provisioning information for the client.

The provisioning information contains information about the Computer Telephony Integration (CTI) gateway for the user (one does not exist in this example) and the Address Book

Server (ABS) URL for the user: *http://srv.litwareinc.com/Abs/Int*. Additional information about phone integration and the CTI gateway can be found in Chapter 9, "Remote Call Control Scenarios." The Address Book Server URL offers Communicator a location where it can download basic information about enterprise users so that Communicator can search across these names to enable users to quickly add known contacts in the organization.

> ***NOTE*** **An example of using the Address Book Server information is shown in the section titled "Step 1: Looking Up a Contact" later in the chapter, which is part of the section titled "A Presence Sharing Scenario." Following that section, the section titled "Technical Details Behind the Presence Sharing Scenario" covers the related technical details.**

This response contains information about how to find the ABS, which enables fast and remote lookups of the corporate address book, provisioning information, and meeting and unified communications policy settings.

Next, Communicator issues a one-time query to identify which media types the server infrastructure can support for multiparty conferences. It sends a SERVICE request asking for the available multipoint control units (MCUs) to determine the media types that are available (IM, phone, and audio/video).

```
SERVICE sip:jeremy@litwareinc.com;gruu;opaque=app:conf:focusfactory SIP/2.0
Via: SIP/2.0/TLS 192.168.3.100:2062
Max-Forwards: 70
From: <sip:jeremy@litwareinc.com>;tag=43cae3a206;epid=aa6d968e18
To: <sip:jeremy@litwareinc.com;gruu;opaque=app:conf:focusfactory>
Call-ID: 2d7ca35fab1c45d1917bbdf754871b0c
CSeq: 1 SERVICE
Contact: <sip:jeremy@litwareinc.com;opaque=user:epid:upbza9anR1KJ-8E7UvWEDQAA;gruu>
User-Agent: UCCP/2.0.6093.0 OC/2.0.6093.0 (Microsoft Office Communicator)
Proxy-Authorization: Kerberos qop="auth", realm="SIP Communications Service",
opaque="A7AB18E7", crand="0ca09d1a", cnum="4",
targetname="sip/srv.litwareinc.com", response=
"602306092a864886f71201020201011100ffffffff4b8520aacbeee71780ccd31c1f2d1675"
Content-Type: application/cccp+xml
Content-Length: 302
<?xml version="1.0"?>
<request xmlns="urn:ietf:params:xml:ns:cccp"
xmlns:mscp="http://schemas.microsoft.com/rtc/2005/08/cccpextensions"
C3PVersion="1" to="sip:jeremy@litwareinc.com;gruu;opaque=app:conf:focusfactory"
from="sip:jeremy@litwareinc.com" requestId="17694972">
   <getAvailableMcuTypes/>
</request>
```

The server responds successfully and specifies that audio and video (audio-video), data conferencing and application sharing (meeting), instant messaging (chat), and phone conferencing (phone-conf) MCUs are available for use as shown in the body of the 200 OK response, as follows:

```
SIP/2.0 200 OK
... (header info)
CSeq: 1 SERVICE
Content-Type: application/cccp+xml
<response xmlns="urn:ietf:params:xml:ns:cccp"  ...
  <getAvailableMcuTypes>
   <mcu-types>
     <mcuType>audio-video</mcuType>
     <mcuType>meeting</mcuType>
     <mcuType>chat</mcuType>
     <mcuType>phone-conf</mcuType>
   </mcu-types>
  </getAvailableMcuTypes>
</response>
```

Communicator also queries for its location profile to get dialing rules. It issues another SERVICE request, as follows:

```
SERVICE sip:jeremy@litwareinc.com;gruu;opaque=app:locationprofile:get;default
SIP/2.0
Via: SIP/2.0/TLS 192.168.3.100:2062
Max-Forwards: 70
From: <sip:jeremy@litwareinc.com>;tag=43cae3a206;epid=aa6d968e18
To: sip:jeremy@litwareinc.com;gruu;opaque=app:locationprofile:get;default
Call-ID: 0842328998844bbe9602c6576997f359
CSeq: 1 SERVICE
Contact: sip:jeremy@litwareinc.com;opaque=user:epid:upbza9anR1KJ-8E7UvWEDQAA;gruu
User-Agent: UCCP/2.0.6249.0 OC/2.0.6249.0 (Microsoft Office Communicator)

Accept: application/ms-location-profile-definition+xml
Proxy-Authorization: NTLM qop="auth", realm="SIP Communications Service",
opaque="E8DC04B4", crand="d93f8137", cnum="4",
targetname="sip/srv.litwareinc.com", response="0100000033323839c87cccc75ec0b9fe"
Content-Type: application/ms-location-profile-definition+xml
Content-Length: 2
```

A 200 OK response from the server shows the dialing plan that is in place that the client should use, and it provides guidance on how extensions listed on a contact should be dialed in the last rule. This chapter simply points out these items. Additional information is provided in later chapters covering telephony and Voice over IP (VoIP).

Communicator now uses the contact list that was received during the query for roaming contacts and issues a batch subscription against all contacts. (There happens to be only one in this example, but there could be tens and even hundreds, depending on the user.) The subscription also lists the things that are of interest from the remote contacts (calendar information, notes, presence state, and so on). The batch subscription is sent in the body of a SUBSCRIBE message, as follows:

```
SUBSCRIBE sip:jeremy@litwareinc.com SIP/2.0
Via: SIP/2.0/TLS 192.168.3.100:2062
Max-Forwards: 70
From: <sip:jeremy@litwareinc.com>;tag=8024faf8af;epid=aa6d968e18
To: <sip:jeremy@litwareinc.com>
Call-ID: a1eeb9389b0b445d93eafcf531533371
CSeq: 1 SUBSCRIBE
Contact: <sip:jeremy@litwareinc.com;opaque=user:epid:upbza9anR1KJ-8E7UvWEDQAA;gruu>
User-Agent: UCCP/2.0.6093.0 OC/2.0.6093.0 (Microsoft Office Communicator)
Event: presence
Accept: application/msrtc-event-categories+xml, application/xpidf+xml,
text/xml+msrtc.pidf, application/pidf+xml, application/rlmi+xml,
multipart/related
Supported: com.microsoft.autoextend
Supported: ms-benotify
Proxy-Require: ms-benotify
Supported: ms-piggyback-first-notify
Require: adhoclist, categoryList
Supported: eventlist
Proxy-Authorization: Kerberos qop="auth", realm="SIP Communications Service",
opaque="A7AB18E7", crand="e396cb73", cnum="5",
targetname="sip/srv.litwareinc.com",
response=
"602306092a864886f71201020201011100ffffffff664a5be74c5546f938944757f539c2ed"
Content-Type: application/msrtc-adrl-categorylist+xml
Content-Length: 489
<batchSub xmlns="http://schemas.microsoft.com/2006/01/sip/
batch-subscribe" uri="sip:jeremy@litwareinc.com" name="">
 <action name="subscribe" id="18640544">
  <adhocList><resource uri="sip:rui@litwareinc.com"/></adhocList>
  <categoryList xmlns="http://schemas.microsoft.com/2006/09/sip/categorylist">
  <category name="calendarData"/><category name="contactCard"/>
  <category name="note"/>
  <category name="services"/>
  <category name="sourcenetwork"/>
  <category name="state"/>
  </categoryList>
 </action>
</batchSub>
```

The server responds with a successful response to the batch subscription in the form of a 200 OK response, as follows:

```
SIP/2.0 200 OK
Contact: <sip:srv.litwareinc.com:5061;transport=tls> ... (header info)

CSeq: 1 SUBSCRIBE
Expires: 27360
Require: eventlist
Content-Type: multipart/related; type="application/rlmi+xml";start=resourceList;
boundary=f018561c40be4d03b799bff0e31ca241
Event: presence
subscription-state: active;expires=27360
ms-piggyback-cseq: 1
Supported: ms-benotify, ms-piggyback-first-notify--
f018561c40be4d03b799bff0e31ca241Content-Transfer-Encoding: binary
Content-ID: resourceList
Content-Type: application/rlmi+xml
<list xmlns="urn:ietf:params:xml:ns:rlmi" uri="sip:jeremy@litwareinc.com"
version="0" fullState="false"/>--f018561c40be4d03b799bff0e31ca241Content-
Transfer-Encoding: binaryContent-Type: application/msrtc-event-categories+xml
<categories xmlns="http://schemas.microsoft.com/2006/09/sip/categories"
uri="sip:rui@litwareinc.com"> <category name="calendarData"/>
<category name="contactCard" instance="0" publishTime=
"2007-05-03T05:37:43.843">
<contactCard xmlns="http://schemas.microsoft.com/2006/09/sip/contactcard" >
<identity >    <name ><displayName >Rui Raposo</displayName></name>
</identity>  </contactCard> </category> <category name="note"/>
<category name="state" instance="1" publishTime="2007-05-04T22:46:17.583">
  <state xsi:type="aggregateState" xmlns:xsi=
"http://www.w3.org/2001/XMLSchema-instance"
xmlns="http://schemas.microsoft.com/2006/09/sip/state">
    <availability>3500</availability>
   </state>
  </category>
  <category name="services" instance="0" publishTime="2007-05-04T22:46:17.583">
   <services xmlns="http://schemas.microsoft.com/2006/09/sip/service">
    <service uri="sip:rui@litwareinc.com">
     <capabilities>
      <text render="true" capture="true" deviceAvailability="3500" />
      <gifInk render="true" capture="false" deviceAvailability="3500" />
      <isfInk render="true" capture="false" deviceAvailability="3500" />
     </capabilities>
    </service>
```

```
    </services>
  </category>
</categories>

--f018561c40be4d03b799bff0e31ca241--
```

The server is actually returning presence information for users that it maintains information for. In this example, the only existing contact, Rui, happened to be maintained on the same server, so his subscription is already confirmed (*subscribed="true"*). Because of this, Communicator itself does not need to issue any subscription requests directly. The server can accept all subscriptions locally. If some of the contacts are not maintained on the same server, Communicator manages to send a separate subscription directly to each contact (to which the remote contact's home server responds).

The rich presence schema shows the user's availability, activity, displayName, e-mail, phoneNumber, userInfo, and devices. The availability section identifies whether the user is busy either because his calendar currently has an appointment or because he manually set his availability. This information is combined, interpreted, and stored in an aggregate numeric value that determines availability. It is worth knowing that these number values are compared to known ranges that Communicator uses to aggregate activity and availability levels into states. The activity section is similar and combines information from all workstations to track whether the user is active, idle, or logged out. The userInfo section contains global information for the user that is used to compose the underlying data that contacts can view (depending on their level of access). The devices section contains a list of devices and the information that each of these devices publish. This information is merged by the server to give a singular view of the user and offer means for connectivity.

Finally, Communicator generates presence information for the client and publishes that information by sending a SERVICE request to the server with an embedded XML publish command, as follows:

```
SERVICE sip:jeremy@litwareinc.com SIP/2.0
Via: SIP/2.0/TLS 192.168.3.100:2062
Max-Forwards: 70
From: <sip:jeremy@litwareinc.com>;tag=7ae5f901b8;epid=aa6d968e18
To: <sip:jeremy@litwareinc.com>
Call-ID: d661a29ddb364c61ab1009edbe5e2b95
CSeq: 1 SERVICE
Contact: <sip:jeremy@litwareinc.com;opaque=user:epid:upbza9anR1KJ-8E7UvWEDQAA;gruu>
User-Agent: UCCP/2.0.6093.0 OC/2.0.6093.0 (Microsoft Office Communicator)
Proxy-Authorization: Kerberos qop="auth", realm="SIP Communications Service",
opaque="A7AB18E7", crand="8ddc94ae", cnum="6", targetname="sip/srv.litwareinc.com",
response="602306092a864886f71201020201011100ffffffff2a567bb3a6d1ce598e39074
cf9e13419"Content-Type: application/msrtc-category-publish+xml
```

```
Content-Length: 1392
<publish xmlns="http://schemas.microsoft.com/2006/09/sip/rich-presence">
<publications uri="sip:jeremy@litwareinc.com">
  <publication categoryName="device" instance="198826231" container="2"
version="0" expireType="endpoint">
   <device xmlns="http://schemas.microsoft.com/2006/09/sip/device"
endpointId="6BF396BA-A7D6-5247-89FB-C13B52F5840D">
    <capabilities preferred="false" uri="sip:jeremy@litwareinc.com">
     <text capture="true" render="true" publish="false"/>
     <gifInk capture="false" render="true" publish="false"/>
     <isfInk capture="false" render="true" publish="false"/>
    </capabilities>
    <timezone>00:00:00-06:00</timezone>
    <machineName>OC-CLIENT</machineName>
   </device>
  </publication>
  <publication categoryName="state" instance="817733007" container="3"  version="0"

expireType="endpoint">  <state xmlns="http://schemas.microsoft.com/2006/09/sip/state"
manual="false" xmlns:xsi="http://www.w3.org/2001/XMLSchema-instance"
xsi:type="machineState">
    <availability>3500</availability>
    <endpointLocation></endpointLocation>
   </state>
  </publication>
  <publication categoryName="state" instance="817733007" container="2" version="0"
expireType="endpoint">
   <state xmlns="http://schemas.microsoft.com/2006/09/sip/state" manual="false"
xmlns:xsi="http://www.w3.org/2001/XMLSchema-instance" xsi:type="machineState">
    <availability>3500</availability>
    <endpointLocation></endpointLocation>
   </state>
  </publication>
 </publications>
</publish>
```

The server accepts this presence publication with a 200 OK response that contains the complete presence document for the user across all devices, after the published presence information for this workstation is taken into account, as follows:

```
SIP/2.0 200 OK
... (header info)
CSeq: 1 SERVICE
Content-Type: application/vnd-microsoft-roaming-self+xml
<roamingData xmlns="http://schemas.microsoft.com/2006/09/sip/roaming-self"
```

```
xmlns:cat="http://schemas.microsoft.com/2006/09/sip/categories"
xmlns:con="http://schemas.microsoft.com/2006/09/sip/containers"
xmlns:sub="http://schemas.microsoft.com/2006/09/sip/presence-subscribers">
<categories xmlns="http://schemas.microsoft.com/2006/09/sip/categories"
uri="sip:jeremy@litwareinc.com">  <category name="state" instance="1"
publishTime="2007-05-04T22:48:10.357" container="2" version="1"
expireType="user">    <state xsi:type="aggregateState"
xmlns:xsi="http://www.w3.org/2001/XMLSchema-instance"
xmlns="http://schemas.microsoft.com/2006/09/sip/state">
    <availability>3500</availability>
   </state>  </category>  <category name="state" instance="268435456"
publishTime="2007-05-04T22:48:10.357" container="2" version="1"
expireType="user">    <state xsi:type="aggregateMachineState"
endpointId="6bf396ba-a7d6-5247-89fb-c13b52f5840d"
xmlns:xsi="http://www.w3.org/2001/XMLSchema-instance"
xmlns="http://schemas.microsoft.com/2006/09/sip/state">
    <availability>3500</availability>

   </state>  </category>  <category name="state" instance="817733007"
publishTime="2007-05-04T22:48:10.357" container="2" version="1"
expireType="endpoint" endpointId="6BF396BA-A7D6-5247-89FB-C13B52F5840D">
<state xmlns="http://schemas.microsoft.com/2006/09/sip/state"
xmlns:xsi="http://www.w3.org/2001/XMLSchema-instance" manual="false"
xsi:type="machineState" >
    <availability >3500</availability>
    <endpointLocation ></endpointLocation>
   </state>  </category>  <category name="device" instance="198826231"
publishTime="2007-05-04T22:48:10.357" container="2" version="1"
expireType="endpoint" endpointId="6BF396BA-A7D6-5247-89FB-C13B52F5840D">
<device xmlns="http://schemas.microsoft.com/2006/09/sip/device"
endpointId="6BF396BA-A7D6-5247-89FB-C13B52F5840D" >
    <capabilities preferred="false" uri="sip:jeremy@litwareinc.com" >
     <text capture="true" render="true" publish="false" ></text>
     <gifInk capture="false" render="true" publish="false" ></gifInk>
     <isfInk capture="false" render="true" publish="false" ></isfInk>
    </capabilities>
    <timezone >00:00:00-06:00</timezone>
    <machineName >OC-CLIENT</machineName>
   </device>  </category>
... (additional presence information for each category)
</categories></roamingData>
```

For all users who are not maintained on the same server that the user is, the bulk subscription response tells Communicator to resubscribe. After Communicator finishes registering and establishing subscriptions for basic user settings and local contacts on its server, it moves into the logged-in state and enables the user to start issuing commands and viewing presence information.

Post-Step 4: Post-Login Processing

To prevent delays because of slower links, Communicator waits to gather presence information for users who are not maintained on the same server until after the client UI is presented and the user is logged in. Communicator then issues individual subscriptions for all the remaining users by issuing a small set of subscriptions and issuing the next subscriptions as the previous subscriptions complete. The scenarios described do not have additional contacts that are not homed on the same server, so this is not presented in detail. However, a simple subscription dialog is established for each contact, and notifications of presence changes occur directly with the server where the contact is maintained.

At this point, the login process is complete. It is worth understanding that this login section simply establishes connectivity and an authenticated relationship with the infrastructure, gathers information about the user and the Office Communications Server infrastructure, and establishes the subscriptions used to get real-time updates. Additional work is required of Communicator to maintain these subscriptions to prevent them from expiring over time and to refresh the authenticated registration established with the infrastructure. The following sections discuss features and functionality provided by Communicator 2007 after it is logged in.

How Presence Information Is Shared

To explain how presence information is shared, in this section we first need to define and explain presence. Then we can explain usage examples that involve presence information as the user sees it, based on the steps taken and the feedback Communicator 2007 provides. Finally, the technical steps, decisions, and protocols that are going on in the background are explained to provide a rich experiential understanding that will aid in troubleshooting presence problems and setting presence authorization properly based on your needs.

What Is Presence?

Virtual communication systems must provide the same information that people typically have if they are sitting next to each other or working in the same office. Is the other person there, is she busy, and is she able to talk? Presence information attempts to capture and identify whether a remote user is willing to communicate and what means that user has to communicate. Office Communicator 2007 R2 and Office Communications Server 2007 R2 provide much more than these basics, however. Communicator enables publishing of location on a per-client basis (home, office, or custom location) and publishing of custom informational notes (which can be kept in sync with "out of office" e-mail auto-responses from Microsoft Office Outlook). It even ties this in with scheduling information to enable authorized partners to view calendar details. In this way, presence in Office Communications Server 2007 R2 is about the ability and willingness to communicate, but it also contains information about the partner that goes beyond communication with the partner.

A Presence Sharing Scenario

This scenario walks Jeremy Los through using Office Communicator 2007 to gather presence information from Office Communications Server and control the level of access another person has to his presence information. Office Communications Server must have already been installed on the enterprise network, and Jeremy must have already installed Communicator on his workstation and have completed a successful login. The overview will show what Jeremy (and his remote contact, Vadim N. Korepin) sees from the Communicator user interface and what steps he and his remote contact take.

Step 1: Looking Up a Contact

Jeremy clicks the contact search box at the top of the Communicator 2007 window and types the name of a local colleague he wants to contact, Vadim N. Korepin. Information on Vadim is retrieved and displayed. (See Figure 5-6.) Note that a contact card with information can be shown by clicking the small arrow that appears to the left of the presence icon when you hover over this area with the mouse. From this list, contacts can be called (using a phone or computer on either end, if support is provided) by clicking on the phone icon to the right of the contact name, or an instant message can be sent by simply double-clicking the name.

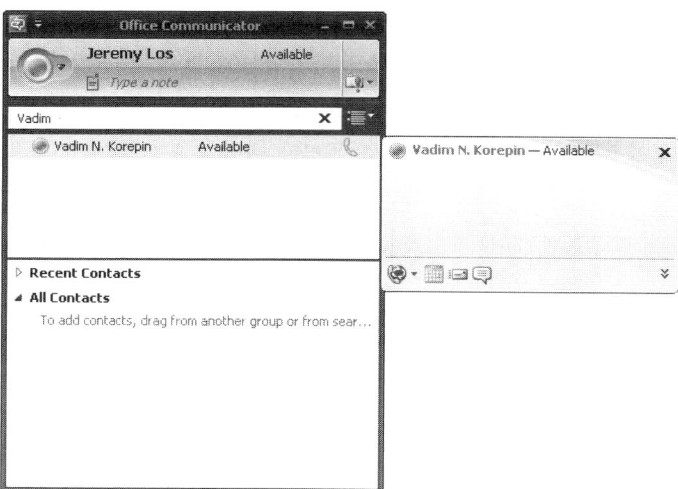

FIGURE 5-6 Communicator—Contact lookup and contact card

Step 2: Adding a Contact

Because Jeremy works regularly with Vadim, he wants to make Vadim's contact information readily available. He right-clicks the contact listing and selects Add To Contact List, which brings up a menu of contact groups he has set up. Jeremy selects All Contacts to add Vadim to the list of contacts that are readily available on the main Communicator window, as shown in Figure 5-7.

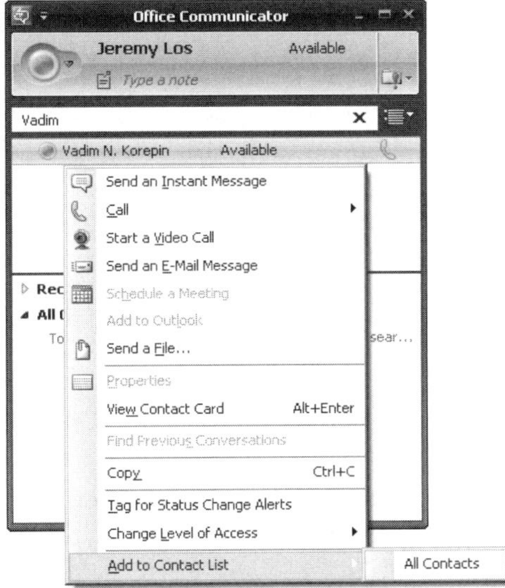

FIGURE 5-7 Adding a contact in Office Communicator 2007 R2

Step 3: Receiving an Offline Indication

Jeremy looks in the main Communicator 2007 window and sees that Vadim is currently offline, as shown in Figure 5-8. Jeremy proceeds with other work while waiting for Vadim to become available.

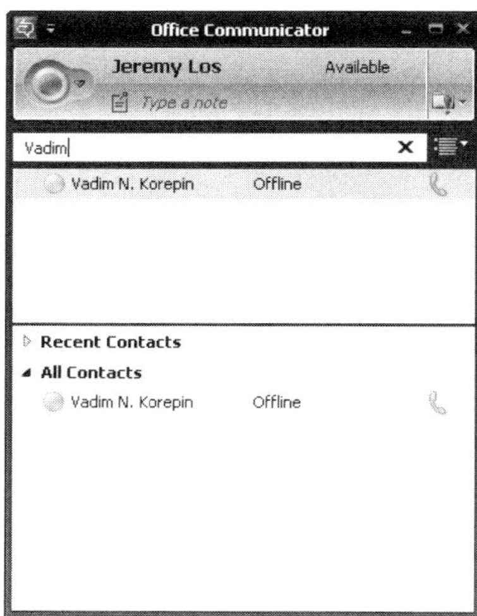

FIGURE 5-8 Communicator—Contact offline

Step 4: Logging In the Contact and Receiving Updated Presence Information

Vadim logs in to his office workstation when he arrives at work. Vadim receives an alert telling him that Jeremy added him as a contact, as shown in Figure 5-9. Vadim decides to add Jeremy as a contact during authorization and clicks OK.

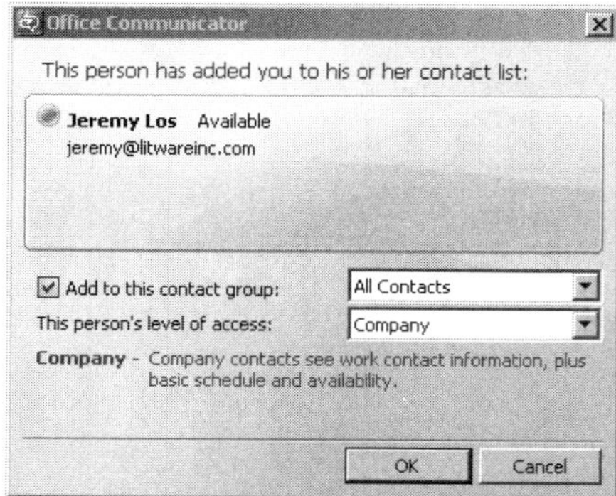

FIGURE 5-9 Communicator—Added to contact list

Meanwhile, Jeremy receives a notification from Communicator that Vadim has come online, as shown in Figure 5-10.

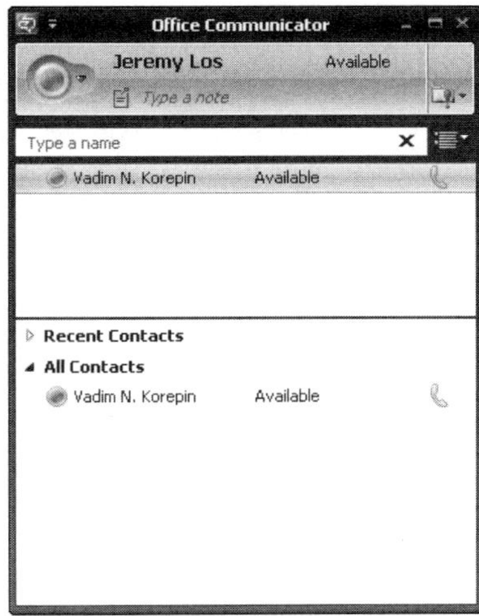

FIGURE 5-10 Communicator—Presence update

Step 5: Controlling the Access Level of a Contact

Jeremy has worked previously with Vadim and trusts him with more detailed contact information about himself. He wants to share details from his calendar with Vadim to make sure they stay in sync. Jeremy right-clicks Vadim's contact listing and Change Level Of Access, and he switches it to Team, as shown in Figure 5-11. This change grants Vadim rights to see details about Jeremy's schedule and availability.

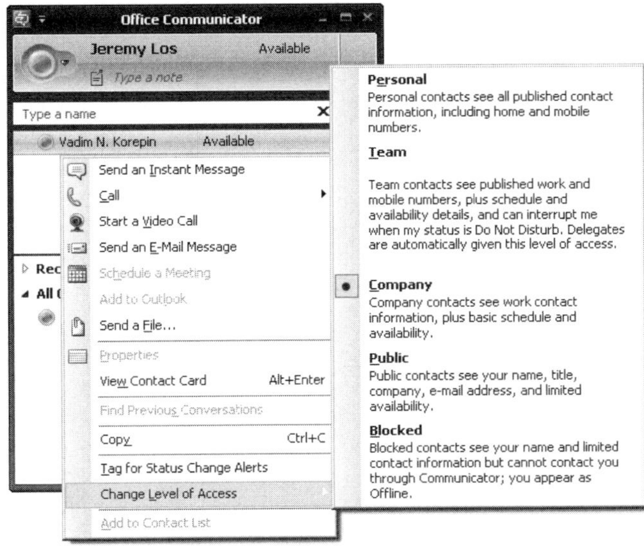

FIGURE 5-11 Communicator—Control access level

Technical Details Behind the Presence Sharing Scenario

This section provides technical background on what is happening with Communicator 2007 and the network of Office Communications Servers. Reviewing this section should aid you in understanding the product and thinking through troubleshooting presence-related scenarios later, if the need arises. Presence queries, presence notifications, contact lists, authorization, routing, and the SIP are covered as they relate to these presence scenarios. Figure 5-12 provides an overview of the steps involved in the presence sharing scenario that we will analyze.

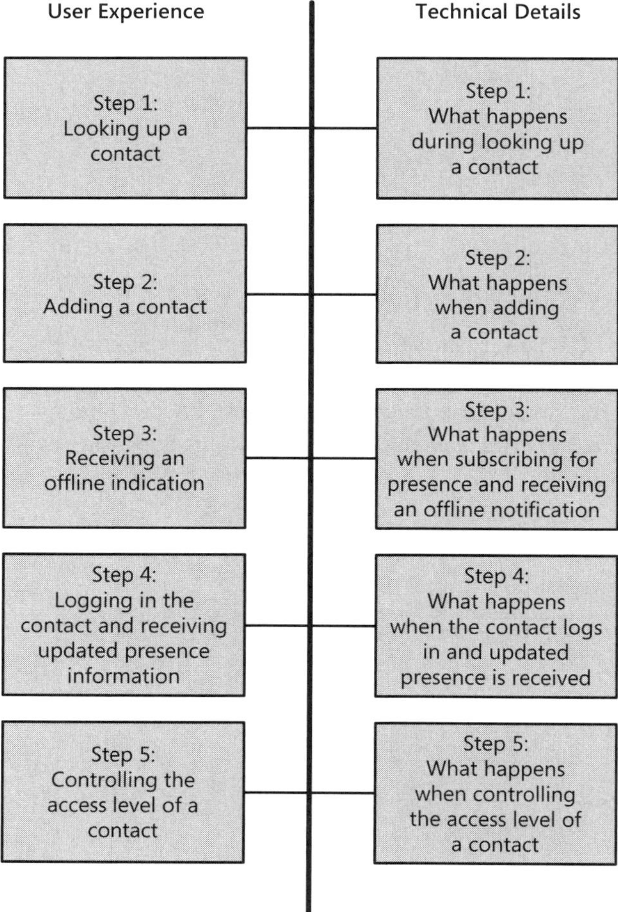

FIGURE 5-12 Presence sharing steps

Step 1: What Happens During Looking Up a Contact

When Communicator is asked to look up a contact, it leverages the contact list it synchronizes with Office Communications Server and the address book that it synchronizes from Office Outlook on the local machine or the address book that it downloads from the Address Book Server–publishing URL. The Address Book Server–publishing URL is handed to the client as a result of the subscription step for provisioning and configuration information during login. Step 3 from the section titled "The Technical Details Behind the Login Process" earlier in this chapter shows the Address Book Server–publishing URL received, as follows:

```
<absInternalServerUrl>http://srv.litwareinc.com/Abs/Int</absInternalServerUrl>
```

With these contact lists combined, Communicator simply indexes the list and is ready to quickly provide search results. As a user types in a contact name, the list is searched by e-mail address, SIP URI, and first/last name. If the name is not recognized and typing pauses, an entry is created (which might or might not be a valid contact at the moment). If an entry exists that is not already in Communicator's list of subscriptions, there is no existing knowledge of the presence information for the new contact entry. This unknown entry results in a presence query in an attempt to determine if this account exists and, if it does, the contact's presence status.

The presence query that would have been made in the example while looking up Vadim's information is shown next. It involves making a SERVICE request with an XML body that issues a *getPresence* query, as follows:

```
SERVICE sip:vadim@litwareinc.com SIP/2.0
Via: SIP/2.0/TLS 192.168.3.100:1467
Max-Forwards: 70
From: <sip:jeremy@litwareinc.com>;tag=81b8232d08;epid=aa6d968e18
To: <sip:vadim@litwareinc.com>
Call-ID: c31cb9c85d564f15b96a7faf253bd8f0
CSeq: 1 SERVICE
Contact: <sip:jeremy@litwareinc.com;opaque=user:epid:upbza9anR1KJ-8E7UvWEDQAA;gruu>
User-Agent: UCCP/2.0.6093.0 OC/2.0.6093.0 (Microsoft Office Communicator)
Proxy-Authorization: Kerberos qop="auth", realm="SIP Communications Service",
opaque="E8EA7EDD", crand="fccc07aa", cnum="8",
targetname="sip/srv.litwareinc.com", response=
"602306092a864886f71201020201011100ffffffff7be3d5766e71b585c2b165da61edf9ee"
Content-Type: application/SOAP+xml
Content-Length: 261

<SOAP-ENV:Envelope xmlns:SOAP-ENV="http://schemas.xmlsoap.org/soap/envelope/">
 <SOAP-ENV:Body>
  <m:getPresence xmlns:m="http://schemas.microsoft.com/winrtc/2002/11/sip">
```

```
    <presentity uri="sip:vadim@litwareinc.com"/>
  </m:getPresence>
 </SOAP-ENV:Body>
</SOAP-ENV:Envelope>
```

The server could respond in several ways to this SERVICE request, as follows:

- **200 OK** In this case, the server network responds with whatever contact and presence information is available for the user. Most enterprises enable presence within the company automatically, but if you go outside of the corporate network to get presence for a remote contact, this is not always the case.
- **404 Not Found** In this case, the server network identifies that the contact does not exist (either locally, remotely, or because the domain could not be routed to).
- **504 Server Time-Out** In this case, a server (if the user is external, the Access Edge Server is most likely; if internal, the front-end server) was unable to forward the message, or a valid remote domain could not be found. This could be because of a network configuration problem, because of a network outage, or simply because of a mistyped domain name or because the domain does not exist currently.

For any failure cases, the ms-diagnostics header should have information about the failure to help you understand whether there is a problem with the URI specified by the user or whether the network has an unexpected issue.

In this example, the server sends a 200 OK response. The response shows that Vadim is offline and it also shares some of his contact information, as follows:

```
SIP/2.0 200 OK
... (header info)
CSeq: 1 SERVICE
Content-Type: application/SOAP+xml
<SOAP-ENV:Envelope xmlns:SOAP-ENV="http://schemas.xmlsoap.org/soap/envelope/">
 <SOAP-ENV:Body>
  <m:getPresence xmlns:m="http://schemas.microsoft.com/winrtc/2002/11/sip">
   <presentity uri="vadim@litwareinc.com"
xmlns="http://schemas.microsoft.com/2002/09/sip/presence"
xmlns:xsi="http://www.w3.org/2001/XMLSchema-instance" >
    <availability aggregate="0" description=""  />
    <activity aggregate="0" description=""  />
    <displayName displayName="Vadim N. Korepin"  />
   </presentity>
  </m:getPresence>
 </SOAP-ENV:Body>
</SOAP-ENV:Envelope>
```

This response not only shows us that the user exists (because the response did not fail), but it provides information about the user's *availability* (how he specified his presence state) and his *activity* (which is programmatically determined). Together, this activity information helps other clients understand whether an online client is really away even though the client indicates that he is "available." The *availability aggregate* and *activity aggregate* values present this information numerically: a 0 means that the user is unavailable and has no activity information. Additionally, e-mail, phone number, and calendar availability can be provided, but they were not offered in this initial response.

Step 2: What Happens When Adding a Contact

When Communicator is asked to add a contact, it has two things to do. First, it must update the contact list that is stored on the server. This ensures that other (presumably idle) logged-in clients for this user know to update their contact lists, and it also ensures that future client logins remember that this contact is added. The second thing Communicator must do is set up a subscription with that contact so that she can receive presence information and notifications of presence changes in the future. All subscription requests are time limited. Communicator does the bookkeeping to keep the subscription continually renewed before it expires each time.

An example of the SERVICE request to update the contact list follows.

```
SERVICE sip:jeremy@litwareinc.com SIP/2.0
Via: SIP/2.0/TLS 192.168.3.100:1467
Max-Forwards: 70
From: <sip:jeremy@litwareinc.com>;tag=adb5417230;epid=aa6d968e18
To: <sip:jeremy@litwareinc.com>;tag=D1972B5B
Call-ID: 46670f6cf7854110888a68bf9d4fef8c
CSeq: 2 SERVICE
Contact: <sip:jeremy@litwareinc.com;opaque=user:epid:upbza9anR1KJ-8E7UvWEDQAA;gruu>
User-Agent: UCCP/2.0.6093.0 OC/2.0.6093.0 (Microsoft Office Communicator)
Proxy-Authorization: Kerberos qop="auth", realm="SIP Communications Service",
opaque="E8EA7EDD", crand="49aff62c", cnum="13",
targetname="sip/srv.litwareinc.com", response=
"602306092a864886f71201020201011100ffffffff22e9b5b8a4d8711e7d02c5ffe0af30d7"
Content-Type: application/SOAP+xml
Content-Length: 483
<SOAP-ENV:Envelope xmlns:SOAP-ENV="http://schemas.xmlsoap.org/soap/envelope/">
 <SOAP-ENV:Body>
  <m:setContact xmlns:m="http://schemas.microsoft.com/winrtc/2002/11/sip">
   <m:displayName/>
   <m:groups>1 </m:groups>
   <m:subscribed>true</m:subscribed>
   <m:URI>vadim@litwareinc.com</m:URI>
```

```
    <contactExtension>
     <contactSettings contactId="db48d962-7878-44d6-a469-2f976b7aace3"/>
    </contactExtension>
    <m:externalURI></m:externalURI>
    <m:deltaNum>2</m:deltaNum>
   </m:setContact>
  </SOAP-ENV:Body>
</SOAP-ENV:Envelope>
```

The SERVICE request sends a SETCONTACT request (in XML) to the server to add the URI, vadim@litwareinc.com, to the contact list. It also labels this contact with a contactId to reference it specifically in future change notifications. The server confirms the change with a 200 OK response, as follows:

```
SIP/2.0 200 OK
... (header info)
CSeq: 2 SERVICE
Content-Length: 0
```

Next, the server must notify all watchers for the contact list that the contact list has changed. Because Communicator subscribed to the user's contact list during login, it receives a notification of the change that it just made, as follows:

```
BENOTIFY sip:192.168.3.100:1467;transport=tls;
ms-opaque=7c11559fb8;ms-received-cid=00000A00 SIP/2.0
Via: SIP/2.0/TLS
192.168.3.1:5061;branch=z9hG4bK50F66FF8.FD5CCE8F;branched=FALSE
Authentication-Info: Kerberos rspauth=
"602306092A864886F71201020201011100FFFFFFFF010DB5FD2506B119E77AEBF785DD1084",
srand="D5844BEE", snum="18", opaque="E8EA7EDD", qop="auth",
targetname="sip/srv.litwareinc.com", realm="SIP Communications Service"
Max-Forwards: 70
To: <sip:jeremy@litwareinc.com>;tag=adb5417230;epid=aa6d968e18Content-Length: 305
From: <sip:jeremy@litwareinc.com>;tag=D1972B5B
Call-ID: 46670f6cf7854110888a68bf9d4fef8c
CSeq: 3 BENOTIFY
Content-Type: application/vnd-microsoft-roaming-contacts+xml
Event: vnd-microsoft-roaming-contacts
subscription-state: active;expires=48415
<contactDelta deltaNum="3" prevDeltaNum="2" >
 <addedContact uri="sip:vadim@litwareinc.com" name="" groups="1 "
subscribed="true" externalURI="" >
```

```
    <contactExtension>
      <contactSettings contactId="db48d962-7878-44d6-a469-2f976b7aace3" >
      </contactSettings>
    </contactExtension>
  </addedContact>
</contactDelta>
```

As an aside, this notification is only a change notification, which means that it shows only what has changed—not the whole contact list. This efficient means of notification avoids extra parsing and data passing on the network, but it can also run into problems when updates occur from multiple sources at the same time. To avoid this, the *deltaNum* and *prevDeltaNum* fields are used to denote which version of the document this notification was built from. When Communicator sent the original request to add a contact, it specified a *deltaNum* of *2*, and this request is indicating that the latest update was built off of this change. If Communicator sent another update that is not processed yet, Communicator can still interpret this notification.

At this point, Communicator has successfully added the contact, has received confirmation of the change, and is ready to subscribe to the new contact.

Step 3: What Happens When Subscribing for Presence and Receiving an Offline Notification

A presence subscription is sent out to the contact of interest (Vadim), as follows:

```
SUBSCRIBE sip:vadim@litwareinc.com SIP/2.0
Via: SIP/2.0/TLS 192.168.3.100:1467
Max-Forwards: 70
From: <sip:jeremy@litwareinc.com>;tag=944c2873c1;epid=aa6d968e18
To: <sip:vadim@litwareinc.com>Call-ID: 85b56acd9b374c70baa50bf89a09b867
CSeq: 1 SUBSCRIBE
Contact: <sip:jeremy@litwareinc.com;opaque=user:epid:upbza9anR1KJ-8E7UvWEDQAA;gruu>
User-Agent: UCCP/2.0.6093.0 OC/2.0.6093.0 (Microsoft Office Communicator)
Event: presence
Accept: application/msrtc-event-categories+xml, application/xpidf+xml,
text/xml+msrtc.pidf, application/pidf+xml, application/rlmi+xml,
multipart/related
Supported: com.microsoft.autoextend
Supported: ms-benotify
Proxy-Require: ms-benotify
Supported: ms-piggyback-first-notify
Proxy-Authorization: Kerberos qop="auth", realm="SIP Communications Service",
opaque="E8EA7EDD", crand="dc7167ba", cnum="15",
targetname="sip/srv.litwareinc.com", response=
```

```
"602306092a864886f71201020201011100ffffffff6f653032d2c6d18a6b15cf4edf3dfc33"
Content-Type: application/msrtc-adrl-categorylist+xml
Content-Length: 519
<batchSub xmlns="http://schemas.microsoft.com/2006/01/sip/batch-subscribe"
uri="sip:jeremy@litwareinc.com" name="">
  <action name="subscribe" id="1170624">
   <adhocList>
    <resource uri="sip:vadim@litwareinc.com">
    <context></context>
   </resource>
  </adhocList>
  <categoryList xmlns="http://schemas.microsoft.com/2006/09/sip/categorylist">
   <category name="calendarData"/>
   <category name="contactCard"/>
   <category name="note"/>
   <category name="services"/>
   <category name="sourcenetwork"/>
   <category name="state"/>
  </categoryList>
 </action>
</batchSub>
```

This request uses the XML body to query for presence information. It is asking for all the presence information on vadim@litwareinc.com that is available—calendaring information, contact card information, notes, services available, network location (enterprise network, federated network, and so on), and current presence state. The remote contact's home server responds to the request (based on presence authorization).

WHAT HAPPENS DURING PRESENCE AUTHORIZATION

For our example, the server responds with a 200 OK response containing presence details, as follows:

```
SIP/2.0 200 OK
Contact: <sip:srv.litwareinc.com:5061;transport=tls> ... (header info)

CSeq: 1 SUBSCRIBE
Expires: 30384
Content-Type: text/xml+msrtc.pidf
Event: presence
subscription-state: active;expires=30384
ms-piggyback-cseq: 1
Supported: ms-benotify, ms-piggyback-first-notify
<presentity uri="vadim@litwareinc.com"
xmlns="http://schemas.microsoft.com/2002/09/sip/presence"
```

```
xmlns:xsi="http://www.w3.org/2001/XMLSchema-instance" >
  <availability aggregate="0" description=""  />
  <activity aggregate="0" description=""  />
  <displayName displayName="Vadim N. Korepin"  />
</presentity>
```

This response from the remote contact's home server tells us only that the contact is offline. An availability and activity aggregate of 0 means that the contact is unreachable. Because Vadim has not authorized Jeremy Los to see presence information, minimal information is shared. (This information is ambiguous; it could be because Jeremy is actually denied access or because Vadim has not authorized him yet.)

Step 4: What Happens When the Contact Logs In and Updated Presence Is Received

When Vadim logs in, he receives a notification from the server that Jeremy is waiting for presence authorization, because his list of pending watchers includes Jeremy. This was shown in the section titled "Step 3: What Happens During Login Processing" within the section titled "The Technical Details Behind the Login Process" earlier in this chapter. In Vadim's case, the list the server sends is not empty and instead contacts Jeremy's URI, as follows:

```
SIP/2.0 200 OK...
From: "Vadim N. Korepin"<sip:vadim@litwareinc.com>;tag=e32b927182;epid=6fe87e039b
To: <sip:vadim@litwareinc.com>;tag=6C3D0080
Call-ID: 5bf9529db3b14cc08a3bdeeb166f0615
CSeq: 1 SUBSCRIBE
Expires: 47303...
Event: vnd-microsoft-roaming-self...
 ...
<subscribers xmlns="http://schemas.microsoft.com/2006/09/sip/presence-
subscribers"> <subscriber user="jeremy@litwareinc.com" displayName="Jeremy Los"
acknowledged="false" type="sameEnterprise"/></subscribers>...
```

When Vadim allows Jeremy to see his presence information (and asks to add him as a contact as well), a SERVICE request is sent to the server to acknowledge Jeremy as a subscriber and to change the authorization list. Vadim's clients are all notified that the authorization list changed (to alert inactive clients that might still be logged in).

```
SERVICE sip:vadim@litwareinc.com SIP/2.0
Via: SIP/2.0/TLS 192.168.3.101:1073
Max-Forwards: 70
From: <sip:vadim@litwareinc.com>;tag=6e3dba1e93;epid=6fe87e039b
```

```
To: <sip:vadim@litwareinc.com>
Call-ID: 0ea64766096741cd92dd4296d3703988
CSeq: 1 SERVICE
Contact: <sip:vadim@litwareinc.com;opaque=user:epid:EfpLp1FJKl6EFEzM2Ml2OQAA;gruu>
User-Agent: UCCP/2.0.6093.0 OC/2.0.6093.0 (Microsoft Office Communicator)
Proxy-Authorization: Kerberos qop="auth", realm="SIP Communications Service",
opaque="8FFADC36", crand="d723fdf4", cnum="12",
targetname="sip/srv.litwareinc.com", response=
"602306092a864886f71201020201011100ffffffff8819cae15eaa9fd62e5730ad9d757ebf"
Content-Type: application/msrtc-presence-setsubscriber+xml
Content-Length: 164
<setSubscribers xmlns=
"http://schemas.microsoft.com/2006/09/sip/presence-subscribers">
 <subscriber user="jeremy@litwareinc.com" acknowledged="true"/>
</setSubscribers>
```

The request is accepted by Vadim's home server, as follows:

```
SIP/2.0 200 OK
... (header info)
CSeq: 1 SERVICE
Content-Length: 0
```

The server sends notification that the list changed and indicates that there was a *contact-Delta* event because of an *addedContact* event for jeremy@litwareinc.com, who is now being subscribed to, as follows:

```
BENOTIFY sip:192.168.3.101:1073;transport=tls;
ms-opaque=3f6ee3c2ab;ms-received-cid=00000C00 SIP/2.0
Via: SIP/2.0/TLS
192.168.3.1:5061;branch=z9hG4bK3038528D.91797EAB;branched=FALSE
Authentication-Info: Kerberos rspauth=
"602306092A864886F71201020201011100FFFFFFFF0E7982BDD363E7034027E38D915280AC",
srand="ACCB75D8", snum="17", opaque="8FFADC36", qop="auth",
targetname="sip/srv.litwareinc.com", realm="SIP Communications Service"
Max-Forwards: 70
To: <sip:vadim@litwareinc.com>;tag=f64cbe4fb6;epid=6fe87e039b
Content-Length: 165
From: <sip:vadim@litwareinc.com>;tag=BE9E675E
Call-ID: c1737cc0857a4be4b6fb40aead466060
CSeq: 3 BENOTIFY
Content-Type: application/vnd-microsoft-roaming-contacts+xml
Event: vnd-microsoft-roaming-contacts
subscription-state: active;expires=32134
```

```
<contactDelta deltaNum="3" prevDeltaNum="2" >
 <addedContact uri="sip:jeremy@litwareinc.com" name="" groups="1 "  subscribed="true"
externalURI=""  />
</contactDelta>
```

After authorization is allowed, a more complete view of Vadim's presence is sent to Jeremy through BENOTIFY messages. For brevity, only the content of the message is shown, simply to highlight the availability and capability information that was made available, as follows:

```
<categories xmlns="http://schemas.microsoft.com/2006/09/sip/categories"
uri="sip:vadim@litwareinc.com">
<category xmlns="http://schemas.microsoft.com/2006/09/sip/categories"
name="contactCard" instance="0" publishTime="2007-05-03T05:37:43.113">
  <contactCard xmlns="http://schemas.microsoft.com/2006/09/sip/contactcard" >
   <identity >
    <name ><displayName >Vadim N. Korepin</displayName></name>
   </identity>
  </contactCard>
 </category>
 <category xmlns="http://schemas.microsoft.com/2006/09/sip/categories"
name="state" instance="1" publishTime="2007-05-04T19:30:25.930">
  <state xsi:type="aggregateState"
xmlns:xsi="http://www.w3.org/2001/XMLSchema-instance"
xmlns="http://schemas.microsoft.com/2006/09/sip/state">
   <availability>3500</availability>
  </state>
 </category>
 <category xmlns="http://schemas.microsoft.com/2006/09/sip/categories"
name="services" instance="0" publishTime="2007-05-04T19:30:25.930">
  <services xmlns="http://schemas.microsoft.com/2006/09/sip/service">

   <service uri="sip:vadim@litwareinc.com">
   <capabilities>
    <text render="true" capture="true" deviceAvailability="3500" />
    <gifInk render="true" capture="false" deviceAvailability="3500" />
    <isfInk render="true" capture="false" deviceAvailability="3500" />
   </capabilities>
   </service>
  </services>
 </category>
</categories>
```

The presence information shown here is still simplistic, because it does not integrate with Outlook for calendar details, nor has any Note field been set. The device availability is presented as a numeric value that Communicator calculates and interprets to present a textual or graphical indication of a user's presence.

ON THE COMPANION MEDIA **These protocol messages are part of the complete set of protocol messages on the companion media for this chapter, in the \Appendixes,Scripts,Resources\Chapter 05\CD Protocol Logs folder, and you can view them in their entirety there.**

Step 5: What Happens When Controlling the Access Level of a Contact

When the level of access is changed for a given contact, a SERVICE request is sent to tell the server to change the authorization container in which the contact is maintained. These containers receive varying levels of detail about presence changes, and all contacts in each container are given the details available for their authorization level. The response and subsequent notification from the server identifying that the list changed are left out here for brevity's sake. These are available on the companion media for reference, but an example of the SERVICE request follows.

```
SERVICE sip:jeremy@litwareinc.com SIP/2.0
Via: SIP/2.0/TLS 192.168.3.100:1467
Max-Forwards: 70
From: <sip:jeremy@litwareinc.com>;tag=0b8629457f;epid=aa6d968e18
To: <sip:jeremy@litwareinc.com>
Call-ID: 045284d5f9d7439c8df7fb629be00dca
CSeq: 1 SERVICE
Contact: <sip:jeremy@litwareinc.com;opaque=user:epid:upbza9anR1KJ-8E7UvWEDQAA;gruu>
User-Agent: UCCP/2.0.6093.0 OC/2.0.6093.0 (Microsoft Office Communicator)
Proxy-Authorization: Kerberos qop="auth", realm="SIP Communications Service",
opaque="E8EA7EDD", crand="f4595ce8", cnum="18",
targetname="sip/srv.litwareinc.com", response=
"602306092a864886f71201020201011100ffffffff2a3751d364162d072028848f060005a5"
Content-Type: application/msrtc-setcontainermembers+xml
Content-Length: 219
<setContainerMembers xmlns=

"http://schemas.microsoft.com/2006/09/sip/container-management">
 <container id="300" version="0">
  <member action="add" type="user" value="vadim@litwareinc.com"/>
 </container>
</setContainerMembers>
```

Various access levels are defined by the containers. Each container has a predefined level of access to presence information, and contacts can simply be added to or removed from these containers to easily manage the level of information a contact receives. Containers increase complexity for the protocol messages and make it more difficult to understand what the system is doing. However, they simplify managing and authorizing contacts, eliminating authorization as a customization step for each contact.

All the presence information is maintained through subscriptions, which send updates when things change and eventually expire over time if they are not regularly renewed. (Communicator handles this automatically for the user.) The next section shows examples for instant messaging scenarios and talks about the technical details involved.

Instant Messaging

Instant messaging (IM) is already widely in use and fairly well understood. It involves two or more individuals communicating with each other using text messages. However, the point of this section is to explain how IM works and to identify the pieces of the system that enable it. Knowing this should help with troubleshooting messaging problems and make it easier to understand how to build applications and integrate systems that work alongside IM.

An Instant Messaging Scenario

This scenario walks Jeremy Los through using his Communicator 2007 client from his office to communicate and interact with coworkers. Instant messaging, sending hyperlinks and emoticons, sharing files, sharing video and audio, and setting up multiple people in a messaging conference are all shown. The scenario shows Jeremy Los interacting with two coworkers, Vadim N. Korepin and Rui Raposo.

Step 1: Opening a Messaging Window

Jeremy double-clicks Vadim N. Korepin, who is in his contact list, to open a messaging window, as shown in Figure 5-13.

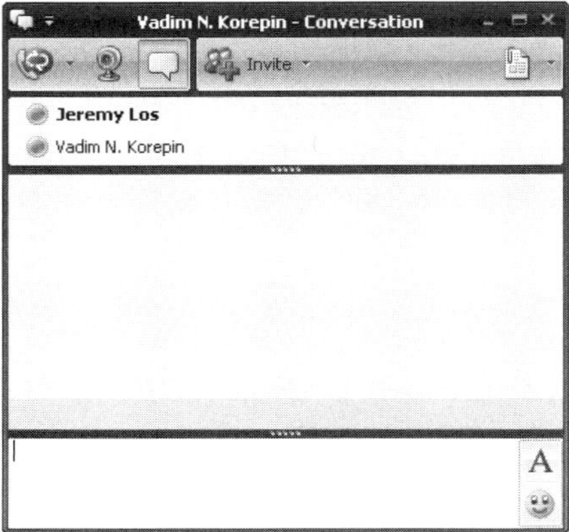

FIGURE 5-13 Communicator—Messaging window

Step 2: Typing and Sending a Message

Jeremy types the message **Sorry to hear about the coffee cup :)** into the text box at the bottom of the messaging window, and the message is sent when he hits Enter on the keyboard. This sends a message to Vadim, and Jeremy's message is shown in the current message history window to make tracking the conversation easier, as shown in Figure 5-14.

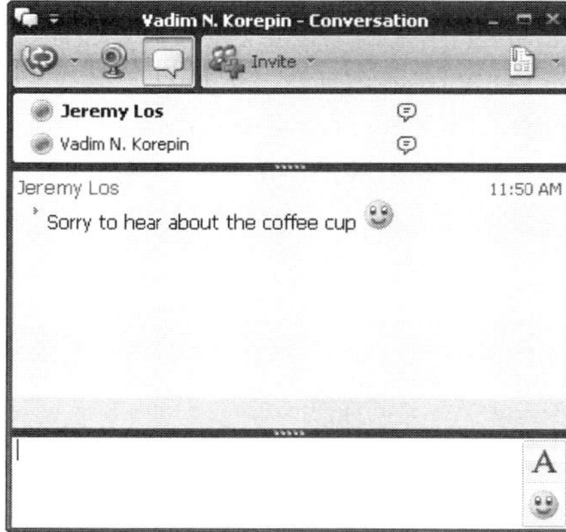

FIGURE 5-14 Communicator—Message sent

Vadim receives a notification on his desktop, as shown in Figure 5-15, alerting him that Jeremy sent him a message to initiate a new conversation. This notification can be clicked to open the messaging window, or Vadim can open the window directly from the task bar. (It will be blinking to show that an unread message has been received.)

FIGURE 5-15 Communicator—Message notification

Step 3: Receiving the Message

Jeremy receives the message from his coworker, and it shows up in the message history window, as shown in Figure 5-16.

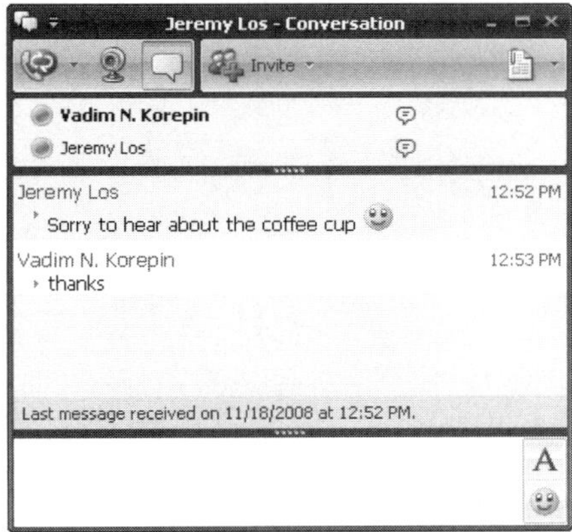

FIGURE 5-16 Communicator—Receiving a message

Step 4: Sending a Hyperlink

Jeremy sends a hyperlink to an interesting article by pasting the URL into the text box and sending it, as shown in Figure 5-17.

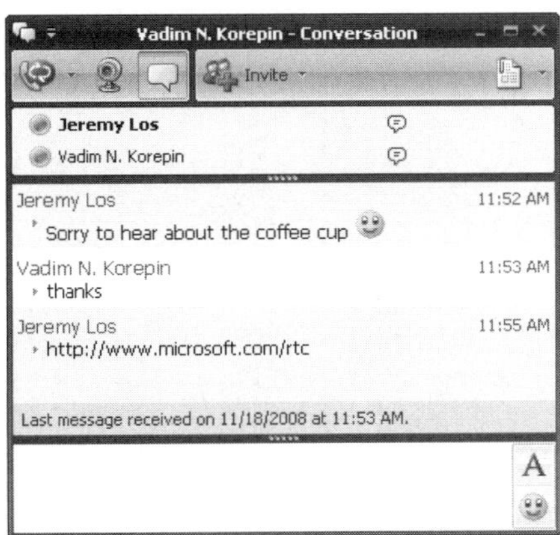

FIGURE 5-17 Communicator—Sending a hyperlink

Vadim receives the hyperlink, but it has a leading "_" inserted, which prevents it from showing up properly as a hyperlink, as shown in Figure 5-18. More information about what is happening here with content filtering is provided in the next section, titled "The Technical Details Behind the Instant Messaging Scenario."

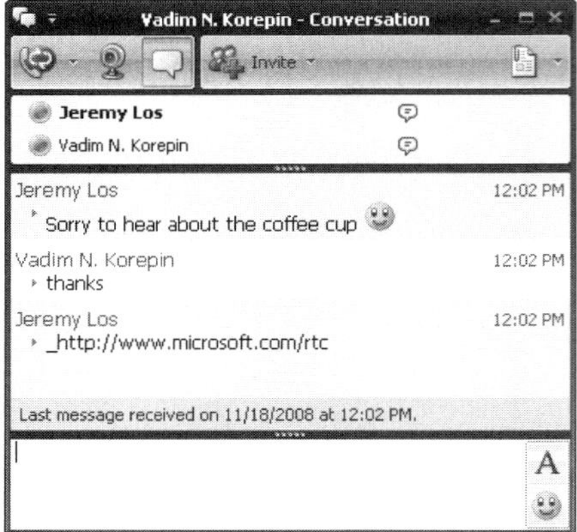

FIGURE 5-18 Communicator—Receiving a hyperlink

Step 5: Sending a File

Jeremy sends a file by using the File icon button on the top-right of the messaging window and waits for Vadim to accept the file, as shown in Figure 5-19. Vadim receives a similar view where he can accept the transfer and view the file by clicking the File icon shown in the messaging history after the download completes.

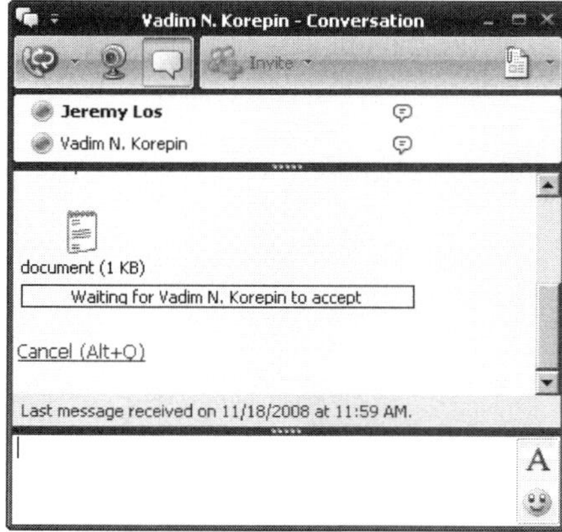

FIGURE 5-19 Communicator—Sending a file

Step 6: Sharing Video

Jeremy decides to share video, because both he and Vadim have a camera. After they talk briefly, they stop sharing the video session, as shown in Figure 5-20.

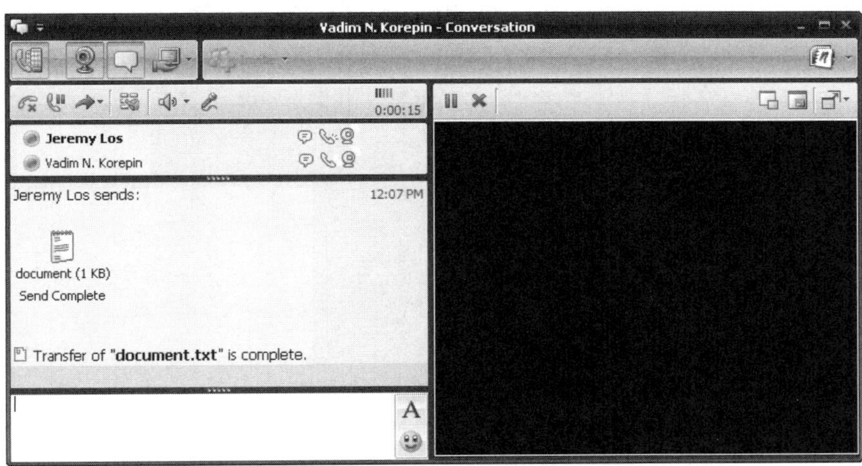

FIGURE 5-20 Communicator—Sharing video

Step 7: Ending the Conversation

At some point the conversation is complete, so Jeremy closes the window, effectively ending the conversation.

The Technical Details Behind the Instant Messaging Scenario

This section illustrates what is happening with Communicator 2007 and the network of Office Communications Servers at a level of technical detail that should aid in understanding the product and in thinking through how to troubleshoot message scenarios later, if the need arises. We will explore messaging, sending hyperlinks, and message routing in detail. Figure 5-21 provides an overview of the steps involved in the instant messaging scenario that we are analyzing.

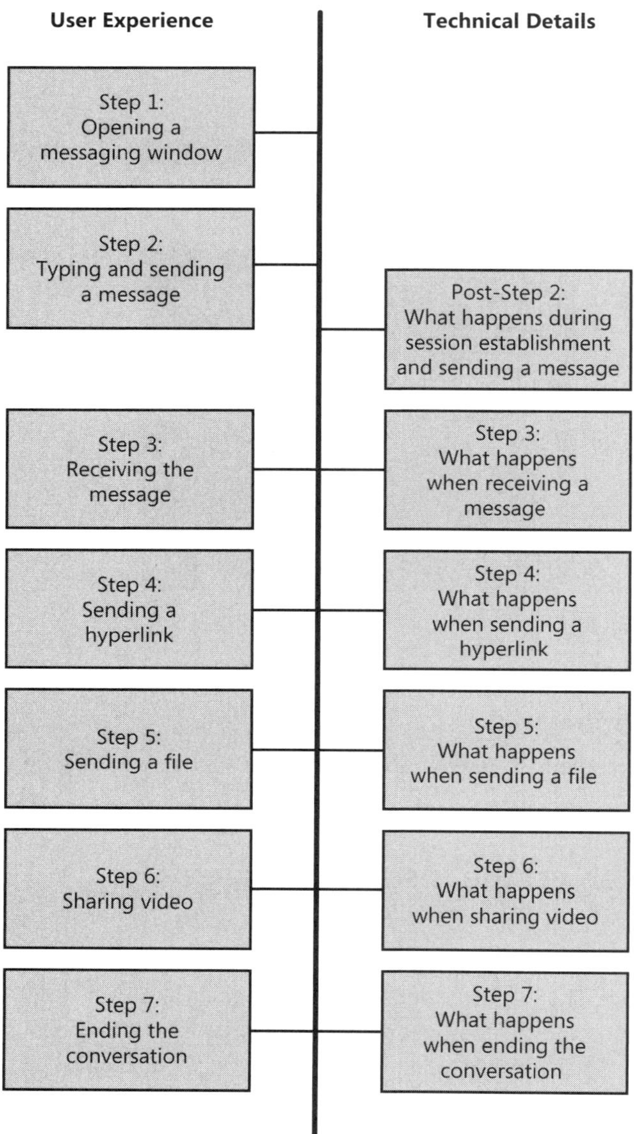

FIGURE 5-21 Instant messaging steps

Post-Step 2: What Happens During Session Establishment and Sending a Message

Setting up a conversation at a protocol level is much more involved than it would seem from the user interface. A summary of the protocol messages involved is shown in Figure 5-22, which also serves as a visual overview of the protocol message flow involved in establishing a messaging session and in sending the first message.

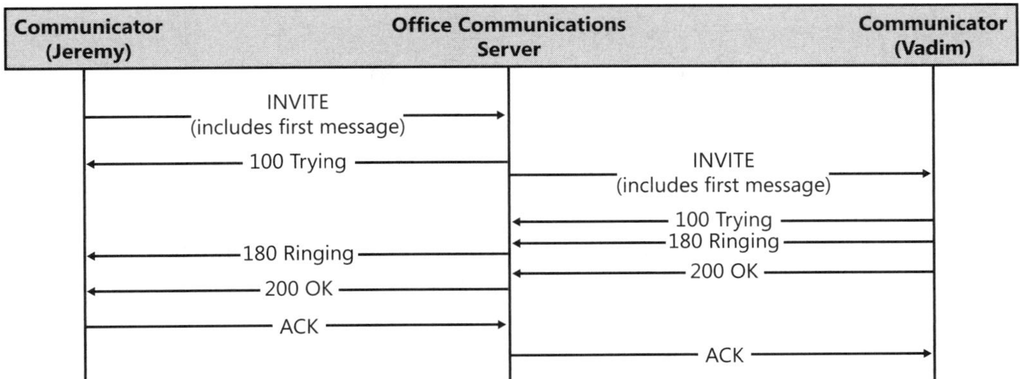

FIGURE 5-22 Session establishment and sending a message

> ***NOTE*** **Session establishment using Communicator 2007 works in much the same way that making a phone call through an operator does. The caller (Communicator) first rings the operator (the Office Communications Server home server) and asks to be connected to a user. The operator generally tells the caller to hold the line (which is similar to the 100 Trying message from the server) while he looks up the line associated with the person called (which is similar to the server querying its database). Next the operator makes the connection, and the phone of the person called rings (180 Ringing message comes back). Finally, the person called picks up the phone (the 200 OK message sent from the remote contact) and the call is established.**

When the first message is sent—Sorry to hear about the coffee cup :)—a messaging session is established at a protocol level. This is initiated by an INVITE message to establish the session. The INVITE actually carries the first message in the session and is base64-encoded into the *ms-body* parameter of the Ms-Text-Format header so that it can be presented with the request to start a messaging session.

> ***NOTE*** **Emoticons are icons that represent sequences of underlying text. For example, the colon and right-parenthesis characters can be typed together as :) to make a smile, and this is interpreted and shown as an icon in Communicator. You can select icons within Communicator, but they all are simply represented by text underneath. Sometimes this can result in unintended emoticons, which is something you should be aware of. A text sequence like "Answer:Probably" will actually have the ":P" converted into a smiling face with its tongue sticking out. One unfortunate aspect is that users see this only after they send the message, not while they are typing it.**

```
INVITE sip:vadim@litwareinc.com SIP/2.0
Via: SIP/2.0/TLS 192.168.3.100:1467
Max-Forwards: 70
From: <sip:jeremy@litwareinc.com>;tag=e57383c75b;epid=aa6d968e18
To: <sip:vadim@litwareinc.com>
Call-ID: d1a1cdc2192048f7a8e9703774cfebcc
CSeq: 1 INVITE
Contact: <sip:jeremy@litwareinc.com;opaque=user:epid:upbza9anR1KJ-8E7UvWEDQAA;gruu>
User-Agent: UCCP/2.0.6093.0 OC/2.0.6093.0 (Microsoft Office Communicator)
Ms-Text-Format: text/plain; charset=UTF-8;
msgr=WAAtAE0ATQBTAC0ASQBNAC0ARgBvAHIAbQBhAHQAOgAgAEYATgA9AE0AUwA1ADIAMABTAGgAZ
QBsAGwAJQAyADAARABsAGcAJQAyADAAMgA7ACAARQBGAD0AOwAgAEMATwA9ADAAOwAgAEMAUwA9ADA
AOwAgAFAARgA9ADAACgANAAoADQA;  ms-body=U29ycnkgdG8gaGVhciBhYm91dCB0aGUgY29mZmVlIGN1cCA
6KQ== Supported: ms-delayed-accept
Supported: ms-renders-isf
Supported: ms-renders-gif
Supported: ms-renders-mime-alternative
Ms-Conversation-ID: AceOhaxSC0KoxENJSUqzhraNmoHCew==
Supported: timerSupported: ms-sender
Roster-Manager: sip:jeremy@litwareinc.com
EndPoints: <sip:jeremy@litwareinc.com>, <sip:vadim@litwareinc.com>
Supported: com.microsoft.rtc-multiparty
Supported: ms-mspms-keep-alive: UAC;hop-hop=yesSupported: ms-conf-invite
Proxy-Authorization: Kerberos qop="auth", realm="SIP Communications Service",
opaque="E8EA7EDD", crand="e870674a", cnum="19",
targetname="sip/srv.litwareinc.com", response=
"602306092a864886f71201020201011100ffffffff3ee9fabb267878a043ed3695933d69f8"
Content-Type: application/sdp
Content-Length: 205
v=0o=- 0 0 IN IP4 192.168.3.100s=sessionc=IN IP4 192.168.3.100t=0 0
m=message 5060 sip nulla=accept-types:text/rtf application/x-ms-ink image/gif
multipart/alternative application/ms-imdn+xml
```

The body of the message describes more about what capabilities the initiator has, and this is talked about in the SIP RFC 3261 standard.

The first server that receives the message responds with a 100 response, and then the remote client responds immediately to provide a temporary response. However, it does not send a final receipt of confirmation until a user accepts the invitation. This three-way handshake establishes the session and allows for a negotiation of session information between both clients, as follows:

```
SIP/2.0 100 Trying
Authentication-Info: Kerberos rspauth=
"602306092A864886F71201020201011100FFFFFFFF4CC448BBF8DD25781477D1A85E1D3DBC",
srand="EAE80D89", snum="31", opaque="E8EA7EDD", qop="auth",
targetname="sip/srv.litwareinc.com", realm="SIP Communications Service"
```

```
Via: SIP/2.0/TLS 192.168.3.100:1467;ms-received-port=1467;ms-received-cid=A00
From: <sip:jeremy@litwareinc.com>;tag=e57383c75b;epid=aa6d968e18
To: <sip:vadim@litwareinc.com>
Call-ID: d1a1cdc2192048f7a8e9703774cfebcc
CSeq: 1 INVITE
Content-Length: 0
```

The remote client sends a temporary response to confirm that it is waiting for the user to respond to the request, as follows:

```
SIP/2.0 180 Ringing
Authentication-Info: Kerberos rspauth=
"602306092A864886F71201020201011100FFFFFFFF69BE23EA5A0169F00998D21963CEABF6",
srand="44C23DFA", snum="32", opaque="E8EA7EDD", qop="auth",
targetname="sip/srv.litwareinc.com", realm="SIP Communications Service"
Via: SIP/2.0/TLS 192.168.3.100:1467;ms-received-port=1467;ms-received-cid=A00
From: "Jeremy Los"<sip:jeremy@litwareinc.com>;tag=e57383c75b;epid=aa6d968e18
To: "" <sip:vadim@litwareinc.com>;epid=6fe87e039b;tag=5c939f2392
Call-ID: d1a1cdc2192048f7a8e9703774cfebcc
CSeq: 1 INVITE
User-Agent: UCCP/2.0.6093.0 OC/2.0.6093.0 (Microsoft Office Communicator)
Content-Length: 0
```

The remote client confirms that the invitation is accepted and provides session capability information in the body of the message, as follows:

```
SIP/2.0 200 OK
... (header info)
CSeq: 1 INVITE
Record-Route: <sip:srv.litwareinc.com:5061;transport=tls;ms-role-rs-from;
ms-role-rs-to;ms-opaque=aaB_D3-f9AM9QxeVkHOWddzAAA;lr; ms-route-sig=aasNJOIb7XhGlfWKA4
UvKlDEpMRMM2Fwj8K3gtHgAA>
Contact:
<sip:vadim@litwareinc.com;opaque=user:epid:EfpLp1FJKl6EFEzM2Ml2OQAA;gruu>
User-Agent: UCCP/2.0.6093.0 OC/2.0.6093.0 (Microsoft Office Communicator)
Require: com.microsoft.rtc-multiparty
Supported: com.microsoft.rtc-multiparty
Supported: ms-sender
Supported: ms-renders-isf
Supported: ms-renders-gif
Supported: ms-renders-mime-alternative
Supported: ms-conf-invite
Content-Type: application/sdp
Content-Length: 222
v=0o=- 0 0 IN IP4 192.168.3.101s=sessionc=IN IP4 192.168.3.101t=0 0
m=message 5060 sip sip:vadim@litwareinc.coma=accept-types:text/rtf application/
x-ms-ink image/gif multipart/alternative application/ms-imdn+xml
```

This response establishes a few things for the dialog so that communications can begin. First, it establishes that both parties are interested in communicating and that they are able to reach each other. Second, it establishes routes and contact points for each user. This tells Communicator how to route messages. Communicator uses the Record-Route and the Contact headers to directly send messages to the endpoint with which it has established the dialog. The Record-Route header contains a signed route that can easily be validated by the server and used to directly route the request. The Contact header has a unique identifier (the epid, or endpoint identifier) that the home server can use to route the request to the specific Communicator instance of interest (if multiple instances are logged in). Third, it provides capabilities information through the body to both parties so that the means of communication are known and the interaction can be extended or upgraded as desired.

The initiating client acknowledges the session capabilities and completes the three-way handshake to establish the session, as follows:

```
ACK sip:srv.litwareinc.com:5061;transport=tls;ms-role-rs-from;ms-role-rs-to;
ms-opaque=aaB_D3-f9AM9QxeVkHOWddzAAA;lr; ms-route-sig=aasNJOIb7XhGlfWKA4UvKlDEpMRMM2Fw
j8K3gtHgAA SIP/2.0
Via: SIP/2.0/TLS 192.168.3.100:1467
Max-Forwards: 70
From: <sip:jeremy@litwareinc.com>;tag=e57383c75b;epid=aa6d968e18
To: "" <sip:vadim@litwareinc.com>;epid=6fe87e039b;tag=5c939f2392
Call-ID: d1a1cdc2192048f7a8e9703774cfebcc
CSeq: 1 ACK
Route: <sip:vadim@litwareinc.com;opaque=user:epid:EfpLp1FJKl6EFEzM2Ml2OQAA;gruu>
User-Agent: UCCP/2.0.6093.0 OC/2.0.6093.0 (Microsoft Office Communicator)
Proxy-Authorization: Kerberos qop="auth", realm="SIP Communications Service",
opaque="E8EA7EDD", crand="e4f67482", cnum="20",
targetname="sip/srv.litwareinc.com", response=
"602306092a864886f71201020201011100ffffffffc78b87bfa700f1757a4e60fed1847916"
Content-Length: 0
```

This ACK request finalizes the dialog by using the route set provided to test that it works properly. From this point on, the initiating client expects that the dialog is available and the recipient expects that the dialog is established after the ACK arrives as a confirmation that the route set worked in at least one direction. The first line of the request contains the request URI, which is the information used to route the request. This line contains the information that was sent back in the Record-Route header from the 200 OK response (including the signature). Additionally, the next routing target (gathered from the Contact header in the 200 OK response) is placed in the Route header.

> ***NOTE*** **This section does not discuss messaging sessions with multiple recipients. This is because after more than two people are involved in a session, a conference is created with which all clients interact. Detailed information on conferencing is covered in Chapter 6, "Conferencing Scenarios."**

Step 3: What Happens When Receiving a Message

Another message type that you see during interactions is the INFO message. This message is used to send little notifications within an INVITE dialog—to alert the other party when a user is typing a message (before it is sent), for example. Here is an example of the INFO message received by Jeremy from Vadim before his response was sent to signal that he was typing a response. The KeyboardActivity data in the body is the key information being passed by this message, as follows:

```
INFO sip:192.168.3.100:1467;transport=tls;ms-opaque=7c11559fb8; ms-received-
cid=00000A00;grid SIP/2.0
Via: SIP/2.0/TLS 192.168.3.1:5061;
branch=z9hG4bKEC902A23.8CE260FA;branched=
FALSE;ms-internal-info="ba9qTQQ5XMtq_uYWsHUg3gqjoqThSM4mD6sl50CgAA"
Authentication-Info: Kerberos rspauth=
"602306092A864886F71201020201011100FFFFFFFFC03B6B0D6388E4EE53C6ABA080FFAC55",
srand="53D1DBCD", snum="35", opaque="E8EA7EDD", qop="auth",
targetname="sip/srv.litwareinc.com", realm="SIP Communications Service"
Max-Forwards: 69
Via: SIP/2.0/TLS 192.168.3.101:1073;ms-received-port=1073;ms-received-cid=C00
From: "" <sip:vadim@litwareinc.com>;epid=6fe87e039b;tag=5c939f2392
To: "Jeremy Los"<sip:jeremy@litwareinc.com>;tag=e57383c75b;epid=aa6d968e18
Call-ID: d1a1cdc2192048f7a8e9703774cfebcc
CSeq: 1 INFO
Contact: <sip:vadim@litwareinc.com;opaque=user:epid:EfpLp1FJKl6EFEzM2Ml2OQAA;gruu>
User-Agent: UCCP/2.0.6093.0 OC/2.0.6093.0 (Microsoft Office Communicator)
Supported: timer
Content-Type: application/xml
Content-Length: 87
<?xml version="1.0"?>
<KeyboardActivity>
  <status status="type" />
</KeyboardActivity>
```

When a message is received (or sent) within a messaging session, a MESSAGE message is used. An example of the MESSAGE received by Jeremy from his coworker (transmitted within the INVITE session by using the same Call-ID) is shown here:

```
MESSAGE sip:192.168.3.100:1467;transport=tls;ms-opaque=7c11559fb8;ms-received-
cid=00000A00;grid SIP/2.0
Via: SIP/2.0/TLS 192.168.3.1:5061;branch=z9hG4bK06E6DAB4.5A2D0AB6;
branched=FALSE;ms-internal-info="baj3AsctgNBuSN4A27AfVbksRFndBaLQq2sl50CgAA"
Authentication-Info: Kerberos rspauth=
"602306092A864886F71201020201011100FFFFFFFF3D2E62CC853438235B3E6E21C525BA76",
srand="A7C06D90", snum="37", opaque="E8EA7EDD", qop="auth",
targetname="sip/srv.litwareinc.com", realm="SIP Communications Service"
```

```
Max-Forwards: 69
Via: SIP/2.0/TLS 192.168.3.101:1073;ms-received-port=1073;ms-received-cid=C00
From: "" <sip:vadim@litwareinc.com>;epid=6fe87e039b;tag=5c939f2392
To: "Jeremy Los"<sip:jeremy@litwareinc.com>;tag=e57383c75b;epid=aa6d968e18

Call-ID: d1a1cdc2192048f7a8e9703774cfebcc
CSeq: 3 MESSAGE
Contact: <sip:vadim@litwareinc.com;opaque=user:epid:EfpLp1FJKl6EFEzM2Ml2OQAA;gruu>
User-Agent: UCCP/2.0.6093.0 OC/2.0.6093.0 (Microsoft Office Communicator)
Supported: timer
Content-Type: text/rtf
Content-Length: 242

{\rtf1\ansi\ansicpg1252\deff0\deflang1033{\fonttbl{\f0\fnil\fcharset0 MS Shell
Dlg 2;}{\f1\fnil MS Shell Dlg 2;}}
{\colortbl ;\red0\green0\blue0;}
{\*\generator Msftedit 5.41.15.1507;}\viewkind4\uc1\pard\tx720\cf1\f0\fs20
thanks\f1\par
}
```

NOTE For privacy purposes, the body of MESSAGE messages is not logged by default, so you usually never see this information in your client or server logs. This option can be enabled only on server logs (not client logs). The registry key to enable this is HKLM\SYSTEM\CurrentControlSet\Services\RtcSrv\Parameters, where the *DWORD* value of *EnableLogging-AllMessageBodies* must be set to 1. This registry key causes the server logs to show message bodies after the server is restarted, but it is important to note that this is a *big* security and privacy risk and should be used only for educational purposes on test systems.

In MESSAGE messages, the body contains the textual message (*thanks* in this example) to be transmitted, with formatting information wrapping it to describe the font, color, and so on.

Step 4: What Happens When Sending a Hyperlink

When a hyperlink or Web link (such as *http://www.microsoft.com/rtc*) is sent as text to another user, many things are happening in the background. First, the message is sent as raw text along with the rest of the message in a MESSAGE message, just as any other text a user might have typed. However, intermediate internal servers, intermediate Access Edge Servers, and the remote client might interpret, alter, or display the message differently based on policy. Office Communications Server 2007 installs with the Intelligent IM Filter active and enables local intranet URLs. However, it inserts a "_" character in front of Internet URLs to prevent it from showing up as an active hyperlink.

An example that shows the IMFilter server log processing this request is shown next (in place of the protocol message, which would just contain the content shown in the log). This log can be gathered on the server using the Logging Tool. Additional details on the Logging Tool are described in Part V of this book, "Technical Troubleshooting and Diagnostics." The log shown next is summarized where you see ellipses (...) to make it easier to read and to remove information that is not of interest to our example. The log basically tracks the filter, watching message content for clickable URLs and then adding an underscore (_) character to the beginning, as follows:

```
TL_INFO ... ContentType: text/rtf
TL_INFO ... ReadonlyPrefixLength: 0
TL_INFO ... Content:
'{\rtf1\ansi\ansicpg1252\deff0\deflang1033{\fonttbl{\f0\fnil\fcharset0 MS
Shell Dlg 2;}}
{\colortbl ;\red0\green0\blue0;}
{\*\generator Msftedit 5.41.15.1507;}\viewkind4\uc1\pard\tx720\cf1\f0\fs20
http://www.microsoft.com/rtc\par
}'
TL_INFO ... (IIMFilter,IIMFilter.CheckForClickableURL:462.idx(775))( 028F1359 )
http://www.microsoft.com/rtc - URL NOT ignored - SecurityZone = Internet
TL_INFO ... Request modified to convert one or more clickable URLs to unclickable URLs
TL_INFO ... Updated content with ContentType: text/rtf
TL_INFO ... Content:
'{\rtf1\ansi\ansicpg1252\deff0\deflang1033{\fonttbl{\f0\fnil\fcharset0 MS
Shell Dlg 2;}}
{\colortbl ;\red0\green0\blue0;}
{\*\generator Msftedit 5.41.15.1507;}\viewkind4\uc1\pard\tx720\cf1\f0\fs20
_http://www.microsoft.com/rtc\par
}'
TL_INFO ... Proxy request
```

Communicator also has a group policy setting (EnableURL) that it enforces to either display hyperlinks as clickable text or as raw text that requires the user to manually copy the text into a browser. All of this is happening simply to enable more control from the network and to prevent bad links from being circulated or accidentally clicked by unsuspecting users.

Step 5: What Happens When Sending a File

Sending a file to another user involves a few SIP transactions and then a direct connection between Communicator clients to transfer the file. The file transfer does not go through any of the server infrastructure at all other than the negotiation transactions. Figure 5-23 provides an overview of the protocol interactions and the establishment of the direct connection between Communicator clients (for the purpose of transferring the file).

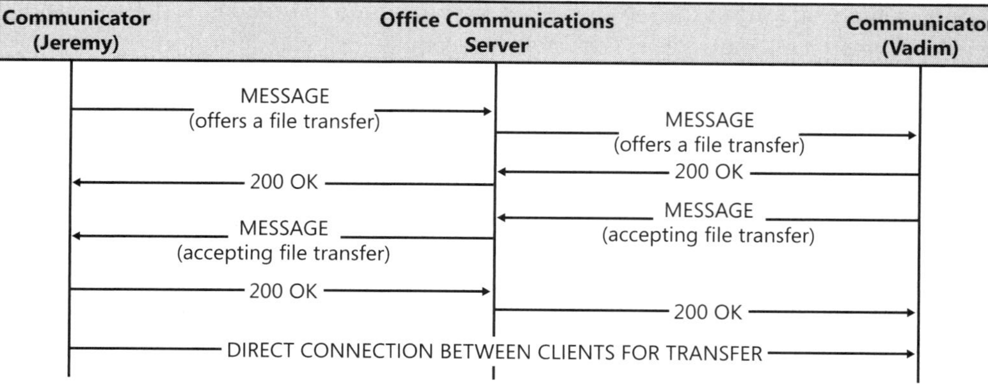

FIGURE 5-23 File transfer handshaking

When Jeremy initiates a file transfer request, the existing session is used and a MESSAGE is sent where the body identifies that a file is available for transfer, as follows:

```
MESSAGE sip:srv.litwareinc.com:5061;transport=tls;ms-role-rs-from;ms-role-rs-to;
ms-opaque=aaB_D3-f9AM9QxeVkHOWddzAAA;lr;ms-route-sig=
aasNJ0Ib7XhG1fWKA4UvKlDEpMRMM2Fwj8K3gtHgAA SIP/2.0
Via: SIP/2.0/TLS 192.168.3.100:1467
Max-Forwards: 70
From: <sip:jeremy@litwareinc.com>;tag=e57383c75b;epid=aa6d968e18
To: "" <sip:vadim@litwareinc.com>;epid=6fe87e039b;tag=5c939f2392
Call-ID: d1a1cdc2192048f7a8e9703774cfebcc
CSeq: 6 MESSAGE
Route: <sip:vadim@litwareinc.com;opaque=user:epid:EfpLp1FJKl6EFEzM2Ml2OQAA;gruu>
Contact: <sip:jeremy@litwareinc.com;opaque=user:epid:upbza9anR1KJ-8E7UvWEDQAA;gruu>
User-Agent: UCCP/2.0.6093.0 OC/2.0.6093.0 (Microsoft Office Communicator)
Supported: timer
Proxy-Authorization: Kerberos qop="auth", realm="SIP Communications Service",
opaque="E8EA7EDD", crand="760faa07", cnum="28",
targetname="sip/srv.litwareinc.com",
response= "602306092a864886f71201020201011100ffffffff2a46ed40d0acdeacd7bbf79110ea5214"
Content-Type: text/x-msmsgsinvite; charset=UTF-8
Content-Length: 234

Application-Name: File TransferApplication-GUID: {5D3E02AB-6190-11d3-BBBB-
00C04F795683}Invitation-Command: INVITEInvitation-Cookie: 625392Application-
File: doc.txtApplication-FileSize: 28Connectivity: NEncryption: R
```

The body of the message identifies that this is a file transfer request and not a messaging request. The *Application-Name* parameter specifies that a file transfer is offered, and the *Application-File* parameter specifies the name of the file. The file size is also specified so that the recipient knows how much it must transfer. The *Connectivity* parameter identifies whether the client is behind a Network Address Translation (NAT) device, and an "N" indicates that it is. The *Encryption* parameter identifies whether the sender supports (S) or requires (R) encryption of the transferred file. This information begins the handshake for the file transfer and provides the Invitation-Cookie for reference in responding to this offer in a later MESSAGE from the recipient.

> **NOTE** Office Communications Server 2007 installs with the Intelligent IM Filter active, and it blocks all directly executable binaries and scripts from being transferred. Files with extensions such as .zip, .doc, and .xml are all enabled and allowed by default. To see which extensions are blocked, you can look at the Office Communications Server 2007 Microsoft Management Console (MMC) snap-in, right-click the server to select Application Properties, select Intelligent IM Filter, and then move to the File Transfer Filter tab.

For our example, Vadim's Communicator confirms receipt of the MESSAGE offering a file transfer, as follows:

```
SIP/2.0 200 OK
... (header info)
CSeq: 6 MESSAGE
Contact: <sip:vadim@litwareinc.com;opaque=user:epid:EfpLp1FJKl6EFEzM2Ml2OQAA;gruu>
User-Agent: UCCP/2.0.6093.0 OC/2.0.6093.0 (Microsoft Office Communicator)
Content-Length: 0
```

Next, Vadim's Communicator sends a MESSAGE back when Vadim accepts the file transfer to identify where the file should be sent, as follows:

```
MESSAGE sip:192.168.3.100:1467;transport=tls;ms-opaque=7c11559fb8;ms-received-
cid=00000A00;grid SIP/2.0
Via: SIP/2.0/TLS 192.168.3.1:5061;branch=z9hG4bK9310B3FD.583AF9C8;
branched=FALSE;ms-internal-info="bamr7aJF7hHA-WG_mThfb47YQEsOtYOvnIsl50CgAA"
Authentication-Info: Kerberos rspauth=
"602306092A864886F71201020201011100FFFFFFFFE00D15EEBF15E83C6D8C14A42A949B80",
srand="3B024C50", snum="42", opaque="E8EA7EDD", qop="auth",
targetname="sip/srv.litwareinc.com", realm="SIP Communications Service"
Max-Forwards: 69
Via: SIP/2.0/TLS 192.168.3.101:1073;ms-received-port=1073;ms-received-cid=C00
From: "" <sip:vadim@litwareinc.com>;epid=6fe87e039b;tag=5c939f2392
To: "Jeremy Los"<sip:jeremy@litwareinc.com>;tag=e57383c75b;epid=aa6d968e18
Call-ID: d1a1cdc2192048f7a8e9703774cfebcc
CSeq: 4 MESSAGE
Contact: <sip:vadim@litwareinc.com;opaque=user:epid:EfpLp1FJKl6EFEzM2Ml2OQAA;gruu>
User-Agent: UCCP/2.0.6093.0 OC/2.0.6093.0 (Microsoft Office Communicator)
Supported: timer
Content-Type: text/x-msmsgsinvite; charset=UTF-8
```

```
Content-Length: 302

Invitation-Command: ACCEPTInvitation-Cookie: 625392Request-Data:
IP-Address:Encryption-Key: jdQO/KXdOgzT6pxHI3pG9qc/+HECOZchHash-Key:
bKJQfXeSgWBpFI2LGOHZ/0QveOJwoBwDIP-Address: 192.168.3.101Port: 6891PortX:
11178AuthCookie: 27079318Request-Data: IP-Address:Sender-Connect: TRUE
```

This information tells Jeremy's Communicator that it should connect to the IP address and port specified to send the encrypted file with the key specified. The AuthCookie specified is also used on the simple FTP connection between the clients as a handshaking device to disambiguate the session.

Jeremy's Communicator client confirms receipt of the MESSAGE accepting the file transfer, as follows:

```
SIP/2.0 200 OK
... (header info)
CSeq: 4 MESSAGE
Contact: <sip:jeremy@litwareinc.com;opaque=user:epid:upbza9anR1KJ-8E7UvWEDQAA;gruu>
User-Agent: UCCP/2.0.6093.0 OC/2.0.6093.0 (Microsoft Office Communicator)
Proxy-Authorization: Kerberos qop="auth", realm="SIP Communications Service",
opaque="E8EA7EDD", crand="bebf384d", cnum="29",
targetname="sip/srv.litwareinc.com",
response= "602306092a864886f71201020201011100ffffffff4c249327d5a9c2195e194c3235e84318"
Content-Length: 0
```

At this point, Jeremy's Communicator connects directly to Vadim's Communicator (at the IP address and port specified) and begins a simple FTP session where the encrypted file is transferred. The wire protocol is not explained in detail here, but a quick view of what is happening is laid out simply for completeness in the following code sample. (The use of Jeremy and Vadim in the example actually refers to the Communicator client each is using.)

```
[Jeremy connects to Vadim]
Vadim sends: VER MSN_SECURE_FTP
Jeremy sends: VER MSN_SECURE_FTP
Vadim sends: USR vadim@litwareinc.com 27079318
Jeremy sends: FIL 28
Vadim sends: TFR
[Jeremy sends binary encrypted data]
Vadim sends: BYE 16777989
Jeremy sends: MAC [signature using hash]
[Jeremy closes the connection]
```

The preceding interaction is simply a minimal handshake on a raw socket to transfer the encrypted file with a signature. After this interaction, the file transfer is complete.

Step 6: What Happens When Sharing Video

Negotiating an audio and video session can involve a lot of handshaking. The protocol messages that were involved are shown in Figure 5-24, which serves as an overview for the remainder of this section. However, only the bodies of the INVITE and 200 OK messages are discussed in detail in this section.

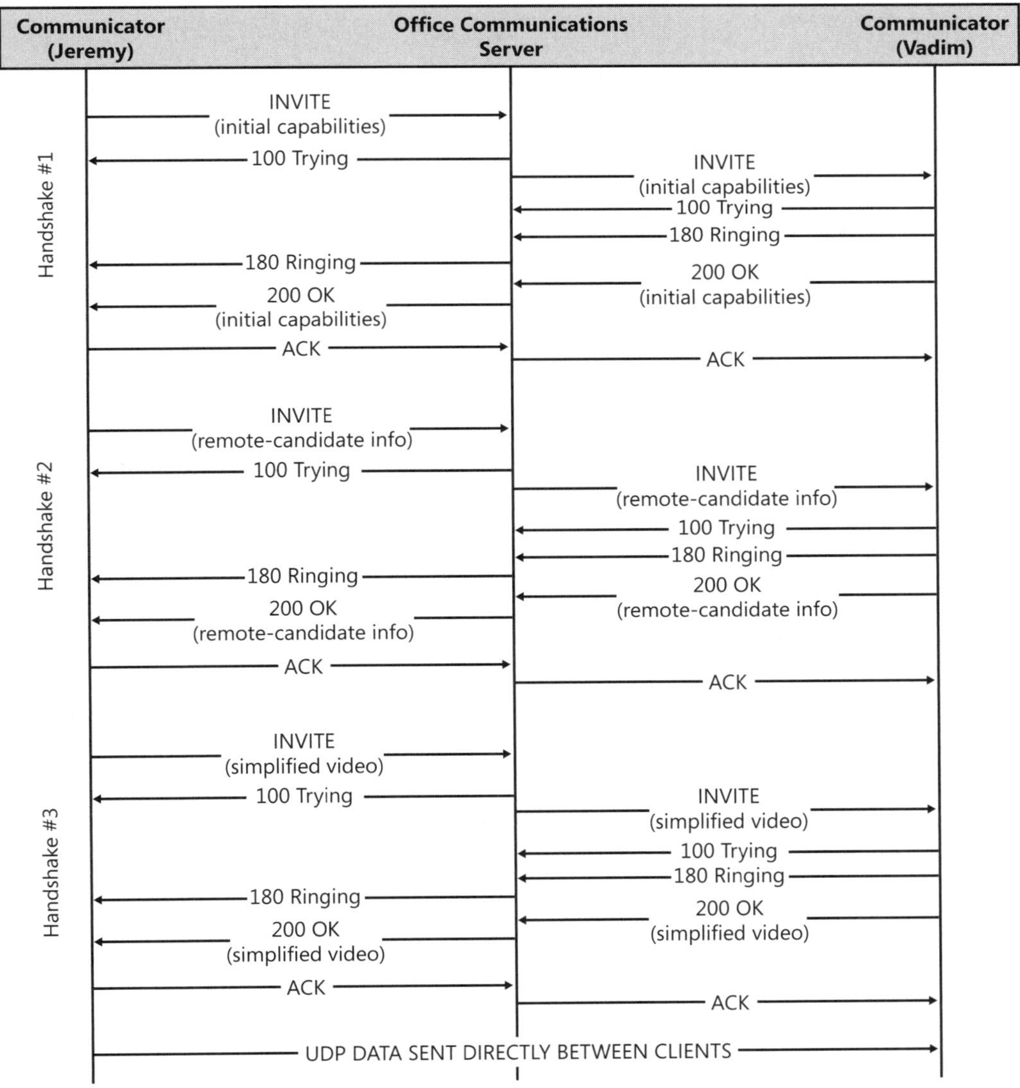

FIGURE 5-24 Audio and video session handshaking

When video is added to the session, Jeremy's Communicator client negotiates a new session including video and audio by sending an INVITE message for a new session. For brevity, only the protocol message bodies are shown and irrelevant protocol messages are skipped entirely. The body of the INVITE message from Jeremy's Communicator client follows:

```
v=0o=- 0 0 IN IP4 192.168.3.100s=sessionc=IN IP4 192.168.3.100b=CT:99980t=0 0
m=audio 60160 RTP/AVP 114 111 112 115 116 4 8 0 97
101k=base64:WYvabwXemv2PqGEj52+xHzXlpUN+MKRUJ2j2Rra/o/7JGjPiQBJHLM/Gr+xya=
candidate:XAP7A3WqUxk5m9zYTfROszesQz9Jdgvoqu5B5zzqwFw 1 7c99RFukBeRXvntIUMo4CA
UDP 0.830 192.168.3.100 60160 a=
candidate:XAP7A3WqUxk5m9zYTfROszesQz9Jdgvoqu5B5zzqwFw 2 7c99RFukBeRXvntIUMo4CA
UDP 0.830 192.168.3.100 21120 a=cryptoscale:1 client AES_CM_128_HMAC_SHA1_80
inline:OC8ZUW5hfFMjxwMk5GwUARUcuevPVTDjuLAvr93K|2^31|1:1a=
crypto:2 AES_CM_128_HMAC_SHA1_80
inline:UrEdZ6/u+pj+MABtYK7y/3/ZL/JSRjHe3tEjNEGn|2^31|1:1a=maxptime:200a=rtcp:2
1120a=rtpmap:114 x-msrta/16000a=fmtp:114 bitrate=12000a=rtpmap:111
SIREN/16000a=fmtp:111 bitrate=16000a=rtpmap:112 G7221/16000a=fmtp:112
bitrate=24000a=rtpmap:115 x-msrta/8000a=fmtp:115 bitrate=12000a=rtpmap:116
AAL2-G726-32/8000a=rtpmap:4 G723/8000a=rtpmap:8 PCMA/8000a=rtpmap:0
PCMU/8000a=rtpmap:97 RED/8000a=rtpmap:101 telephone-event/8000a=
fmtp:101 0-16a=encryption:optional
m=video 13952 RTP/AVP 121 34 31k=
base64:3QA+RtpnuOd4cCaj/rWBfeW+Hn9AvxcLhLDkB9yVzwJVftCkEcBSL+lBAmOua=
candidate:PVpOw5+rY86zX6Emqm+9zIGUlfTTOU9iEeBBKRfsvks 1 gt+GQX3LSYECKrIM9skhWg
UDP 0.840 192.168.3.100 13952 a=
candidate:PVpOw5+rY86zX6Emqm+9zIGUlfTTOU9iEeBBKRfsvks 2 gt+GQX3LSYECKrIM9skhWg
UDP 0.840 192.168.3.100 50944 a=cryptoscale:1 client AES_CM_128_HMAC_SHA1_80
inline:BsqZIvEl3PQRq4kwE8lRxSeSeDRriKAyS6uPIRBY|2^31|1:1a=crypto:2
AES_CM_128_HMAC_SHA1_80 inline:E3eOmRQAY7c2fSrzR3zrGX8Z1WUI1lGBRxk7GiH2|2^31|1:1a=
maxptime:200a=rtcp:50944a=rtpmap:121 x-rtvc1/90000a=rtpmap:34 H263/90000a=
rtpmap:31 H261/90000a=encryption:optional
```

This INVITE message body asks for an audio/video peer-to-peer conference and offers the media parameters and capabilities for the initiating Communicator client.

The 100 and 180 temporary responses are not shown here for the sake of brevity and because they do not really provide any interesting information. However, the 200 response provides capability information from the recipient, as follows:

```
v=0o=- 0 0 IN IP4 192.168.3.101s=sessionc=IN IP4 192.168.3.101b=CT:99980t=0 0
m=audio 10496 RTP/AVP 114 111 112 115 116 4 8 0 97
101a=candidate:jUpPjJEHNyN3RNHn+LlReOz7YZbWN3BpqnNqJw9KSrA 1
9VE2N1fM/Ug4DHk/KSO/xw UDP 0.830 192.168.3.101 10496 a=
candidate:jUpPjJEHNyN3RNHn+LlReOz7YZbWN3BpqnNqJw9KSrA 2 9VE2N1fM/Ug4DHk/KSO/xw
UDP 0.830 192.168.3.101 53120 a=crypto:2 AES_CM_128_HMAC_SHA1_80
inline:FxTfuRY3zYOR7EPAvnkKjOlOSm4Dwbc/ov1v1qkB|2^31|1:1a=maxptime:200a=
```

```
rtcp:53120a=rtpmap:114 x-msrta/16000a=fmtp:114 bitrate=12000a=rtpmap:111
SIREN/16000a=fmtp:111 bitrate=16000a=rtpmap:112 G7221/16000a=fmtp:112
bitrate=24000a=rtpmap:115 x-msrta/8000a=fmtp:115 bitrate=12000a=rtpmap:116
AAL2-G726-32/8000a=rtpmap:4 G723/8000a=rtpmap:8 PCMA/8000a=rtpmap:0

PCMU/8000a=rtpmap:97 RED/8000a=rtpmap:101 telephone-event/8000a=fmtp:101
0-16a=encryption:optional
m=video 14976 RTP/AVP 121 34 31a=
candidate:1t+HmBqSsE7M8/xGXLbb4U0SG1drKqrEi/RhuqWA5Eo 1 87LtCGRXUnVdv8WaYO+85Q
UDP 0.840 192.168.3.101 14976 a=
candidate:1t+HmBqSsE7M8/xGXLbb4U0SG1drKqrEi/RhuqWA5Eo 2 87LtCGRXUnVdv8WaYO+85Q
UDP 0.840 192.168.3.101 2304 a=crypto:2 AES_CM_128_HMAC_SHA1_80
inline:foe41lE6qfhFItmaGWs13hIJXiAzq98kCZKSJDpB|2^31|1:1a=maxptime:200a=rtcp:2
304a=rtpmap:121 x-rtvc1/90000a=rtpmap:34 H263/90000a=rtpmap:31
H261/90000a=encryption:optional
```

This response confirms that audio and video are available, as well as identifies the media parameters and capabilities for the client.

An ACK message is sent from Jeremy's Communicator client to finish the handshake, but this is not shown because it does not provide any useful additional information.

A second-round INVITE is sent next, with the only change being an additional field (a=remote-candidate) that is added in the body as shown in the following code sample. (The same is true of the 200 OK response.)

```
...
m=audio 60160 RTP/AVP 114 111 112 115 116 4 8 0 97 101a=
remote-candidate:jUpPjJEHNyN3RNHn+LlReOz7YZbWN3BpqnNqJw9KSrA...
m=video 13952 RTP/AVP 121 34 31
a=remote-candidate:1t+HmBqSsE7M8/xGXLbb4U0SG1drKqrEi/RhuqWA5Eo...
```

Finally, a third-round INVITE is sent where the video media is simplified down (the same is true of the 200 OK response) to a single line descriptor, as follows:

```
...
m=video 0 RTP/AVP 34
```

This whole process is a way for the two Communicator clients to exchange information about each other that relates to preferences and capabilities. After this session is finally negotiated and created, User Datagram Protocol (UDP) messages are exchanged between the published IPs and ports for each Communicator client as video and audio are shared. This continues until the conference ends based on a user's request.

Step 7: What Happens When Ending the Conversation

When Jeremy closes the messaging window, Communicator sends a BYE message within the dialog that was established to alert Vadim's client that the communication dialog is being closed. An example of the BYE message and the response from Vadim's client are shown here for reference:

```
BYE sip:srv.litwareinc.com:5061;transport=tls;ms-role-rs-from;ms-role-rs-to;
ms-opaque=aaB_D3-f9AM9QxeVkHOWddzAAA;lr;
ms-route-sig=aasNJOIb7XhG1fWKA4UvKlDEpMRMM2Fwj8K3gtHgAA SIP/2.0
Via: SIP/2.0/TLS 192.168.3.100:1467
Max-Forwards: 70
From: <sip:jeremy@litwareinc.com>;tag=e57383c75b;epid=aa6d968e18
To: "" <sip:vadim@litwareinc.com>;epid=6fe87e039b;tag=5c939f2392
Call-ID: d1a1cdc2192048f7a8e9703774cfebcc
CSeq: 8 BYE
Route: <sip:vadim@litwareinc.com;opaque=user:epid:EfpLp1FJKl6EFEzM2Ml2OQAA;gruu>
User-Agent: UCCP/2.0.6093.0 OC/2.0.6093.0 (Microsoft Office Communicator)
Proxy-Authorization: Kerberos qop="auth", realm="SIP Communications Service",
opaque="E8EA7EDD", crand="58dad80d", cnum="51",
targetname="sip/srv.litwareinc.com", response=
"602306092a864886f71201020201011100ffffffffec97e0568a70bf53982604eb4d04ebe5"
Content-Length: 0
```

Vadim's Communicator responds to acknowledge that it received the dialog close event, as follows:

```
SIP/2.0 200 OK
... (header info)
CSeq: 8 BYE
User-Agent: UCCP/2.0.6093.0 OC/2.0.6093.0 (Microsoft Office Communicator)
Content-Length: 0
```

However, at this point, both clients have cleared any remaining state about the communication dialog and if another message is sent by either of them, a new dialog is established.

NOTE **For reference, if Jeremy ends the messaging session before Vadim accepts it, a CANCEL message is sent instead. A BYE is sent on an established session, and a CANCEL is sent if the session is not fully established (that is, the 200 OK and ACK are not completed).**

Summary

This chapter shows examples of usage scenarios, including a basic login, some use and control of presence information, and instant messaging. The technical details behind these usage scenarios are discussed, providing insight into how Office Communications Server and Communicator work together to provide useful functionality. Such technical understanding is essential for administrators who need to implement, configure, and troubleshoot Office Communications Server in their enterprises. This chapter also provides the core background on basic server and client operations in terms of discovery, connectivity, and communications over the Session Initiation Protocol (SIP) and as such is useful to refer back to as reference material when exploring the other scenario chapters.

Additional Resources

- The return code ranges for Office Communicator availability and the activity ranges, based on presence status, are detailed in Appendix B, "Numeric Ranges for Availability and Activity Levels in Office Communicator." This appendix is on the companion media in the \Appendixes,Scripts,Resources\Appendix B folder.
- For product documentation, community tools, frequently asked questions (FAQs), discussion groups, and pointers to up-to-date information on the product and community events, see the Office Communications Server home page at *http://go.microsoft.com/fwlink/?LinkID=133615*. Pointers that are mentioned in the chapter are listed here.
- Winerror.exe is part of the Windows Server 2003 Resource Kit Tools, and lcserror.exe is part of the Office Communications Server 2007 Resource Kit Tools. Both of these can be found at *http://www.microsoft.com/downloads* with a search for either one of the Resource Kit Tools.
- More information about the credentials manager can be found in the Microsoft TechNet article "Windows XP Professional Resource Kit: Understanding Logon and Authentication" at *http://go.microsoft.com/fwlink/?LinkID=133674*, in the "Stored User Names and Passwords" section.
- A technical reference for Transport Layer Security (TLS) can be found by searching for the Microsoft TechNet article "TLS/SSL Technical Reference" at *http://go.microsoft.com/fwlink/?LinkID=133677*.
- For more information about Kerberos and NTLM, see the Microsoft TechNet article "Kerberos Authentication Technical Reference" at *http://go.microsoft.com/fwlink/?LinkID=133675* or the Microsoft Developer Network (MSDN) article "NTLM Authentication" at *http://go.microsoft.com/fwlink/?LinkID=133676*.

- For information about NTLM, Kerberos, and TLS/SSL, see the Windows Security Collection of the Windows Server 2003 Technical Reference at *http://go.microsoft.com/fwlink/?LinkID=133678*.
- For information about SIP, see "Session Initiation Protocol [RFC 3261]" at *http://go.microsoft.com/fwlink/?LinkID=133679*. In addition, two useful books about SIP are the following:
  - *SIP: Understanding the Session Initiation Protocol*, Second Edition by Alan B. Johnston (Artech House Publishers, 2003)
  - *SIP Demystified* by Gonzalo Camarillo (McGraw-Hill Professional, 2001)
- There are many useful community-driven Web sites that support Office Communications Server. One that stands out is the LCS Guides site at *http://go.microsoft.com/fwlink/?LinkID=133680*.
- A full collection of protocol logs is on the companion media, in the \Appendixes, Scripts,Resources\Chapter 05\CD Protocol Logs folder, for reference. These are useful for seeing example protocol messages and complete message flow. Many of the messages are not discussed here in the book to avoid repeating content and to skip some of the less interesting transactions, but these are all available in a complete form in the sample logs on the companion media. You might also find these useful when troubleshooting for comparison purposes.
- The text file dbanalyze-jeremy.txt on the companion media, in the \Appendixes,Scripts,Resources\Chapter 05 folder, shows full sample output from the dbanalyze command, as explained in the sidebar titled "Real World: Troubleshooting Client Connections" earlier in this chapter.

CHAPTER 6

Conferencing Scenarios

Microsoft Office Communications Server 2007 R2 enables enterprise users inside and outside the corporate firewall to create and join real-time Web conferences that are hosted on internal corporate servers. These conferences or meetings (which are referred to as *on-premise* conferences) can be scheduled or spontaneous. Attendees of these conferences can communicate by using instant messaging (IM), audio, video, application sharing, slide presentations, and other forms of data collaboration. Enterprise users can invite external users that do not have Active Directory Domain Services accounts to participate. Users who are employed by federated partners and who have a secure and authenticated identity can also join conferences and, if invited to do so, can act as presenters. Conference organizers control access to the conferences they organize by defining access types.

For administrators, Office Communications Server 2007 R2 provides meeting policies, global-level settings, pool-level settings, and user-level settings to enable administrators to control almost every aspect of on-premise conferencing capabilities, such as access control, resource management, conference life cycle management, and so on. The scalable conferencing architecture that is based on pools ensures high availability of conferences. If a server supporting a conference fails, the conference automatically rolls over to another server that has the same server role. Moreover, Office Communications Server also supports features that meet common compliance requirements. Basic conference information, such as creation time, activation time, users who join, and users who leave, is logged in the Call Detail Record (CDR) database. Most data collaboration contents are also recorded in a specific compliance file share. Both CDR and the compliance functions are discussed in Chapter 16, "Monitoring."

This unified, server-based conferencing solution provides an alternative to hosted Web conferencing for organizations that require a more secure and controlled collaboration experience.

In Office Communications Server 2007 R2, new features and functions are available that will also enhance the overall usability and user experience for the product. This chapter will highlight these new features.

This chapter introduces the conferencing scenarios and capabilities that Office Communications Server 2007 R2 supports. The chapter also describes the technical details behind these scenarios, including the conferencing architecture, conference life cycle, and call flow. Finally, the chapter concludes with a discussion of Meeting policy and policy enforcement.

ON THE COMPANION MEDIA **You can find information related to the topics addressed in this chapter via links available to you on this book's companion CD.**

Understanding Conferencing User Types

In an Office Communications Server conference, all users are authenticated. Authentication is performed either by the front end of an Office Communications Server pool, by a Director server if a Director is deployed, or by a federated server. Depending on the type of credentials used for authentication, Office Communications Server supports three types of users: authenticated enterprise users, federated users, and anonymous users.

Authenticated Enterprise Users

An authenticated enterprise user is an employee of the enterprise who hosts the Office Communications Server conference and who meets the following requirements:

- Has a persistent Active Directory identity
- Is enabled for communications in Active Directory and in Office Communications Server management console, and is assigned a valid Session Initiation Protocol (SIP) Uniform Resource Identifier (URI)
- Is assigned to either a valid Office Communications Server 2007 R2, Microsoft Office Communications Server 2007 or a Microsoft Office Live Communications Server 2005 Service Pack 1 (SP1) pool

Authenticated enterprise users who are hosted on an Office Communications Server pool can create and participate in an Office Communications Server conference. However, authenticated enterprise users that are hosted on an Office Live Communications Server 2005 SP1 pool cannot create a conference, but they can participate in an Office Communications Server 2007 R2 conference.

Authenticated enterprise users can be further classified into two categories according to the location from which they access Office Communications Server:

- **Internal user** Internal users connect to Office Communications Server from a location behind the corporate firewall.
- **Remote user** Remote users connect to Office Communications Server from a location outside the corporate firewall. They include employees working at home; those who are traveling; and other remote workers, such as trusted vendors, who have been granted enterprise Active Directory credentials for their terms of service.

Office Communications Server employs two Integrated Windows authentication methods to authenticate enterprise users. Internal users are authenticated by using either NT LAN Manager (NTLM) or Kerberos, depending on the server setting. For remote users, only NTLM is supported because Kerberos requires that the client have a direct connection to Active Directory, which is generally not the case for users connecting from outside the corporate firewall.

Federated Users

A federated user is not an employee of the enterprise that is hosting the Office Communications Server conference. Instead, a federated user is an employee of a federated partner who meets the following requirements:

- Has a persistent identity in the federated partner's Active Directory
- Is enabled for communications in the federated partner's Active Directory and in Office Communications Server management console, and is assigned a valid SIP URI
- Is assigned to either a valid Office Communications Server 2007 R2, Office Communications Server 2007, or a Live Communications Server 2005 SP1 pool that is hosted in the federated partner domain

Federated users are authenticated by the Office Communications Server 2007 R2, Office Communications Server 2007, or Live Communications Server 2005 SP1 that is hosted in the trusted federated partner domain. Therefore, they are trusted as authenticated users by the Office Communications Server 2007 R2 server that hosts the conference. Federated users can join conferences, but they cannot create conferences in federated enterprises.

For more information about federated users, see Chapter 7, "Remote Access and Federation Scenarios."

Anonymous Users

An anonymous user is not an employee of the enterprise that is hosting the Office Communications Server conference or an employee of a federated partner. Instead, an anonymous user is any user who does not have a persistent Active Directory identity in the enterprise that is hosting the Office Communications Server or federated partner enterprise.

Anonymous users can connect from the following three locations outside the corporate firewall:

- An enterprise that deploys Office Communications Server 2007 R2, Office Communications Server 2007, or Live Communications Server 2005 SP1. However, the enterprise domain is not federated with the enterprise hosting the conference.
- An enterprise that deploys neither Office Communications Server 2007 R2, Office Communications Server 2007, nor Live Communications Server 2005 SP1.
- The Internet.

Anonymous users are authenticated by using Digest authentication. For conferences that allow anonymous users to participate, Office Communications Server generates a conference key. Anonymous users must present the conference key when they join the conference.

> ***NOTE*** **Anonymous users can join Office Communications Server conferences, but they cannot create conferences on the server.**

Understanding Conferencing User Roles

Regardless of authentication types, conference participants fall into one of two user role groups during a conference: presenters or attendees. Office Communications Server 2007 R2 keeps track of user roles for each conference participant. These user roles are used to authorize users to have access to different in-conference functionalities, which are summarized in the following list.

- **Presenter** A user who is authorized to present information at a conference by using whatever media is supported. A presenter is also granted rights to manage a conference, such as locking a conference, ending a conference, promoting other participants to the presenter role, removing a user from a conference, changing the list of in-conference features nonpresenter participants can access, and other conference management tasks.
- **Attendee** A user who has been invited to attend a meeting but who is not authorized to act as a presenter. An attendee can be promoted to presenter by other presenters during a conference.

> ***NOTE*** **Promotion of user roles is not persistent across different instances of the same conference. If an attendee is promoted to the presenter role during a conference, she has the presenter role until she leaves the conference. The next time the attendee joins the same conference, she will again be assigned the attendee role. Only participants who are designated as presenters by the organizer at the time the conference is created—meaning that they are pre-set presenters—can join a conference with the automatic presenter role. In addition, currently, Office Communications Server does not support demoting a presenter to attendee.**

All authenticated enterprise users and federated users can join a conference as pre-set presenters. Anonymous users can join a conference only as attendees. However, once they have joined, anonymous users can be promoted to presenter by any existing presenter in a conference. In addition, there is an implicit role of organizer who creates a conference, whether impromptu or by scheduling.

Every Office Communications Server 2007 R2 conference is associated with an organizer. An organizer must be an authenticated enterprise user. If a user is deleted from the enterprise Active Directory, all Office Communications Server 2007 R2 conferences the user organizes are also removed from the conferencing database on the back-end database. The content that was created in conferences that were organized by such an organizer is also removed through a content expiration feature. An organizer is by definition also a presenter and determines who else can be a presenter. An organizer can make this determination either at the time a meeting is scheduled or after the meeting is started.

Understanding Conference Security and Access Types

Security is a top priority for on-premise conferencing. In Office Communications Server 2007 R2, all messaging and media in conferencing are encrypted, using the same security infrastructure as Live Communications Server 2005 SP1. Office Communications Server 2007 R2 also provides additional safeguards for conferencing. These safeguards include the following features:

- Strong authentication using Integrated Windows authentication and Digest authentication. For users who are members of the hosting domain, their domain credentials would be required using Integrated Windows authentication. For nondomain members, Digest authentication is used through the input of the conference ID and the meeting password making up the authentication digest.
- Role-based authorization for conference control. Role-based authorization allows for control over who can access what resources. Typically, a presenter would have read and write permissions, while an attendee would have read-only permissions.
- Control over the level of access through three predefined access types. The defined types are organizer, presenter, and attendee. The organizer can set up and schedule the meeting and send out invites, as well as promote attendees to presenter status. The presenter can manage the content of the conference, present it, and promote others to presenter status. An attendee can attend and view the materials, as well as optionally download a copy. They can also be promoted by either the organizer or the presenter to presenter status.
- Policy-based administration to allow administrators to control resource use and security. Meeting features are grouped and managed by using Meeting policies. Administrators control which meeting features a meeting organizer can use during a meeting by configuring and applying specific policies. For more information about

Meeting policy, see the section titled "Meeting Policy and Policy Enforcement" later in this chapter.

- Conference access types for organizers to use when they create a conference. Organizers can set the conference to have one of three access types: "Invite Within Network" (Open authenticated in Office Communications Server 2007); "Invite Within Network (Restricted)" (Closed authenticated in Office Communications Server 2007); "Invite Anyone" (Allow anonymous in Office Communications Server 2007).

Invite Within Network Conferences

All authenticated enterprise users can join a conference designated as "Invite Within Network". They join as attendees unless the meeting organizer has designated them presenters.

An Invite Within Network conference is suitable in situations where the participant list is dynamic or unknown, such as an open forum meeting that takes place during the lunch hour. Authenticated enterprise users can join any Invite Within Network meeting that is hosted on any Office Communications Server pool, even if the conference organizer does not specifically invite them. This is usually achieved by one user forwarding a conference invitation to another user.

Federated users can join the meeting as attendees if the organizer invites them. Federated users are not able to join the meeting as presenters, but they can be promoted to presenter during the meeting. However, Office Communications Server does not support creating an Invite Within Network conference with federated users as pre-set presenters. If you want to prevent federated users from participating in an Invite Within Network meeting, you can do so by not configuring the Access Edge Server for federation or by disabling the organizer for federation.

Invite Within Network (Restricted) Conferences

Only authenticated enterprise users who are specifically invited by the conference organizer can join a Invite Within Network (Restricted) conference.

Invite Within Network (Restricted) conferences are suitable in situations where tight control of the conference content is required, such as a meeting that discusses confidential company financial information. An authenticated user who is not explicitly invited cannot join a Invite Within Network (Restricted) conference, even if the user has conference join information from forwarded invitations.

Federated users can join a Invite Within Network (Restricted) conference if explicitly invited. They can join either as attendees or as pre-set presenters. Currently, client implementation prevents a user from scheduling a Invite Within Network (Restricted) conference with federated users.

Invite Anyone Conferences

Invite Anyone conferences have the most relaxed access control. Invite Anyone conferences can be joined by authenticated enterprise users and federated users, as well as anonymous users, as long as those users have conference join information.

Invite Anyone conferences are suitable in situations where collaboration between enterprise users and outside users is required, such as a sales meeting that invites potential outside customers.

To create a meeting of this type, the meeting organizer must be authorized to invite anonymous users. Enterprise users and federated users join as attendees unless they have been designated as presenters by the meeting organizer. Anonymous users join only as attendees, although they can be promoted to the presenter role by presenters after they have entered the meeting. To enter a meeting, anonymous users must present a conference key, which they receive in an e-mail meeting invitation, and they must pass Digest authentication.

Table 6-1 summarizes different situations in which users can be allowed into Office Communications Server conferences.

TABLE 6-1 Conference Access Types

CONFERENCE TYPE	AUTHENTICATED ENTERPRISE USER		FEDERATED USER		ANONYMOUS USER	
	DIRECTLY INVITED	FORWARDED	DIRECTLY INVITED	FORWARDED	DIRECTLY INVITED	FORWARDED
Invite Within Network	√	√	√	√	×	×
Invite Within Network (Restricted)	√	×	√	×	×	×
Invite Anyone	√	√	√	√	√	√

* √ *means the user can join;* × *means the user cannot join*

Understanding Conferencing Media Types

Office Communications Server 2007 R2 conferences provide rich multimedia experiences. The following sections discuss the four main types of multimedia conferencing: multiparty instant messaging, data collaboration, audio/video (A/V), and audio conferencing provider support.

Multiparty Instant Messaging

Multiparty instant messaging, or Group IM, refers to an IM conversation among three or more parties. The Microsoft Windows Messenger 5.x and Microsoft Office Communicator 2005 clients, along with Live Communications Server 2005 SP1, already support Group IM based on establishing a separate connection between each two-user pair engaged in the conversation. In Office Communications Server 2007 R2, a Group IM session is implemented as a server-hosted conference with IM modality. This approach is more scalable and offers greater flexibility to participants than a group conversation that is based on a large number of linked peer-to-peer conversations.

The main client for multiparty IM conferences is Microsoft Office Communicator 2007 R2. A Group IM session can be created in one of the following ways:

- By sending an instant message to multiple parties
- By inviting additional parties to a two-person IM conversation
- By sending an instant message to a Microsoft Exchange Server distribution list

DIRECT FROM THE SOURCE

Group Expansion Web Service

Hao Yan
Senior Program Manager

Office Communications Server 2007 R2 provides a group expansion Web service that expands an Active Directory distribution group into a list of users. This expansion enables users to invite one or more individual members of the group to an IM session. Distribution groups of up to 1,000 users can be expanded, and an IM session can include as many as 100 members.

The expansion of the following four types of Active Directory distribution groups is supported by the Web service:

- **Universal distribution groups that are e-mail enabled**
- **Global distribution groups that are e-mail enabled**
- **Universal security groups that are e-mail enabled**
- **Global security groups that are e-mail enabled**

Data Collaboration

Data collaboration conferences are often referred to as Web conferences. Office Communications Server 2007 R2 supports a rich mix of data collaboration possibilities, including the following:

- **PowerPoint presentations** Office Communications Server 2007 R2 provides native Microsoft Office PowerPoint support, which includes uploading and sharing slide decks that are created by using Office PowerPoint and that include animations and other rich features.
- **Application and desktop sharing** Office Communications Server 2007 R2 enables sharing of applications among multiple participants and giving other participants control of the desktop or application. Administrators can customize the level of sharing or

control that is allowed in their organization or disable this feature completely through Meeting policy.

- **Microsoft Office Document Imaging (MODI) support** Office Communications Server 2007 R2 also supports uploading and sharing of any document format that supports the MODI print driver. This support provides conference users the ability to share in read-only mode virtually any kind of documents that can be printed to MODI file format, including all Microsoft Office document formats, Adobe PDF format, and HTML file format.
- **Web slides** Sharing URLs to Web pages that can be viewed and navigated independently by all meeting participants.
- **Multimedia content** Office Communications Server supports uploading and sharing media files (such as Flash or Microsoft Windows Media technology files). The viewing of the media files by all meeting participants can be synchronous (controlled by the presenter) or asynchronous (participants view files independently).
- **Handouts** Exchanging files in their native formats among meeting participants.
- **Snapshot slides** Capturing and displaying a static view of (an area of) the user's desktop.
- **Whiteboards** Free-form drawing and writing in a common shared space.
- **Text slides** Writing and sharing text on a virtual whiteboard (separate from the graphical whiteboard features).
- **Annotations** Annotating many types of slides, including PowerPoint slides and MODI document slides.
- **Polling** The ability to create questions and answers and compile and share responses from participants.
- **Q&A** Asking and answering questions during a meeting.
- **In-meeting chat** Peer-to-peer IM within the context of a meeting.
- **Shared notes** The ability to edit and share meeting notes with other participants.

The main client for data collaboration conferences is Office Communicator 2007 R2. Microsoft Live Meeting 2007 is deprecated with the functionality built into the Office Communicator client. A data collaboration session can be created in one of the following ways:

- By scheduling a data collaboration conference in Microsoft Office Outlook with the Outlook Conferencing Add-in
- By selecting Meet Now in Office Live Meeting 2007
- By adding data collaboration to an existing IM and A/V session in Office Communicator 2007 R2

Audio and Video Conferencing

Office Communications Server 2007 R2 supports multiparty A/V conferencing. Through advanced wideband codecs such as Real-Time Audio (RTAudio) and Real-Time Video (RTVideo), Office Communications Server (through the A/V Conferencing Server role) delivers high-quality audio and video in a conference.

The audio streams from all participants are mixed at the server and broadcasted to all participants. For video, the video stream of the most active speaker is sent to all participants. When deployed on a separate computer, the A/V Conferencing Server can support up to 250 participants within a single session.

The main clients for A/V conferences are Office Communicator 2007 R2 and Office Live Meeting 2007. An A/V conference session can be initiated in the following ways:

- By scheduling a data collaboration conference with audio and video in Office Outlook with the Outlook Conferencing Add-in
- By scheduling a conference call with audio and video in Outlook with the Outlook Conferencing Add-in
- By starting an A/V conversation with two or more other participants in Office Communicator

Audio Conferencing Provider Support

External audio conference participants who have not deployed Office Communications Server can participate through the services of a third-party Audio Conferencing Provider (ACP). The provider enables conferencing over an external Public Switched Telephone Network (PSTN) bridge.

Office Live Meeting 2007 is the main client that supports ACP conferences. It provides user interfaces to control various aspects of the audio conference hosted on an external PSTN bridge, such as mute self, unmute self, mute all, and so on.

ACP integration is managed by the Telephony Conferencing Server, which always runs as a separate process on either an Office Communications Server 2007 R2 Standard Edition Server or Enterprise Edition front-end server. Integration with the ACP occurs by configuring a federated connection with the external service provider, as you would with any other federated partner.

Understanding Communicator Web Access Server R2

There are several new and enhanced features in Communicator Web Access Server R2. The features that have a direct effect on conferencing include the following:

- **Support for distribution groups** The client can add distribution groups to contact lists and use these distribution groups for exchanging instant messages with groups rather than individual contacts.

- **Audio conferencing** Communicator Web Access can receive, initiate, and manage audio conference calls.
- **Desktop sharing** A client can initiate desktop sharing with another user by using the Communicator Web Access browser interface.
- **Hosting for dial-in audio conferencing Web page** Office Communications Server R2 functionality for dial-in conferencing is extended by means of a Web page that is hosted by Communicator Web Access R2.

Support for Distribution Groups

The Communicator Web Access Server enables users to add distribution lists to their contact lists. A distribution group in the contact list enables a Web client to initiate an instant message session with multiple users by using the distribution group membership.

Administratively, this is an easy feature to implement and manage because the functionality is built in and is active when the Conferencing Web Access Server is brought up. The main dependency is Active Directory, which will already be in place in your environment.

Audio Conferencing

Audio conferencing in Communicator Web Access R2 is a multiparty audio conference in which there are at least two other participants. The user provides Communicator Web Access Web with his local telephone number, such as a cell phone or home phone, as shown in Figure 6-1. Communicator Web Access will then connect the user's phone to the PSTN and initiate calls to the other attendees by using the A/V Conferencing Server.

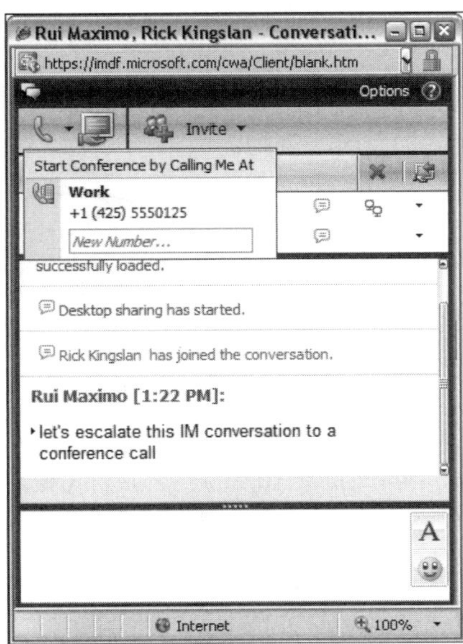

FIGURE 6-1 Start an audio conference by requesting that Communicator Web Access Server contact you at the phone number you want.

Communicator Web Access Servers can also control and manage incoming calls. The requirement for managing incoming calls is that you already have a deployed voice environment with Office Communications Server 2007 R2 that is prepared to receive calls from the PSTN. No additional configuration is necessary to implement audio conferencing with Communicator Web Access R2.

Desktop Sharing

Ad hoc desktop sharing (the ability to share a desktop with another user) has been a consistent feature of Communicator Web Access. With Communicator Web Access R2, users can share their desktops through Web browsers when connected through a Communicator Web Access R2 server. There are additional requirements to enable this functionality at the client side. Users must install plug-ins for their browsers, as shown in Figure 6-2.

After this plug-in is installed, a Windows user can initiate sharing, view, or take control of a desktop sharing session. Users that have computers based on Apple Macintosh or Linux can view or take control, but will not be able to initiate a desktop sharing session.

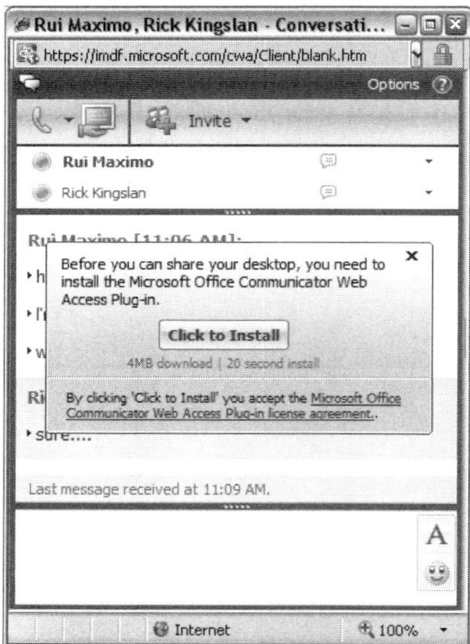

FIGURE 6-2 Desktop sharing requires a plug-in to initiate a session

When the new desktop sharing session is initiated, a meeting URL is created for new participants, as shown in Figure 6-3. When you use Distribution Group support, you can use a group contact to invite all members of the group. If a user is configured and enabled for outside access (remote access), they can join the sharing session. IM to any other user in the session is available to all participants.

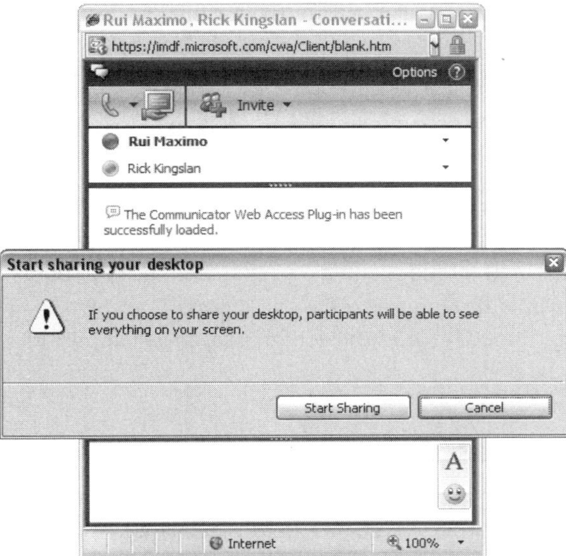

FIGURE 6-3 Initiation of the desktop sharing session through a Web browser

After the session is started, all participants will be able to see everything on the presenter's screen as shown in Figure 6-4. Caution the presenter that items and information that should not be disclosed to participants should be minimized or ended before sharing the desktop,

FIGURE 6-4 Desktop sharing with IM window on left and shared desktop in middle.

Audio conferencing, discussed previously, is also available with desktop sharing by using the call feature described.

Hosting for Dial-in Audio Conferencing Web Page

Users who are not able to get to a computer to use Office Communicator, but who still want to attend a conference, can call in to the call by using a mobile, desk, or home phone. When arranging the conference call, the conference organizer adds a conference call-in number. The caller then enters a conference identification number and a personal identification number (PIN) when prompted. The attendee would have received the conference ID and PIN in an e-mail inviting him to the conference. After the caller joins the conference, he will appear in the conference roster.

Configuring Communicator Web Access Server R2

The Communicator Web Access Server enables remote users to participate in IM, conferencing, application sharing, audio conferences, and more. Of course, before being able to allow users to access the server, it has to be implemented and configured.

Installing Communicator Web Access by using the deployment tools As you might expect, Communicator Web Access R2 can be deployed only after you have installed Office Communications Server 2007 R2. As soon as Office Communications Server 2007 R2 is running, you can install Communicator Web Access on any server that is a member of a domain within the Office Communications Server forest. Note that you must either be a member of the Domain Admins group or have been delegated the required permissions to install Communicator Web Access. Refer to Figure 6-5 for an architectural overview of a deployed Communicator Web Access R2 installation.

Installing and Activating Communicator Web Access

The installation of Communicator Web Access is a straightforward process once you have the base server set up and configured. There are four main steps to follow to successfully set up the server.

1. Install Communicator Web Access.
2. Activate the Communicator Web Access server.
3. Create the virtual server.
4. Publish the Communicator Web Access URLs to Active Directory.

Each of the main procedures in the preceding list is detailed in the following sections. Completing the four main steps will result in a functional Communicator Web Access server for your Office Communications Server infrastructure.

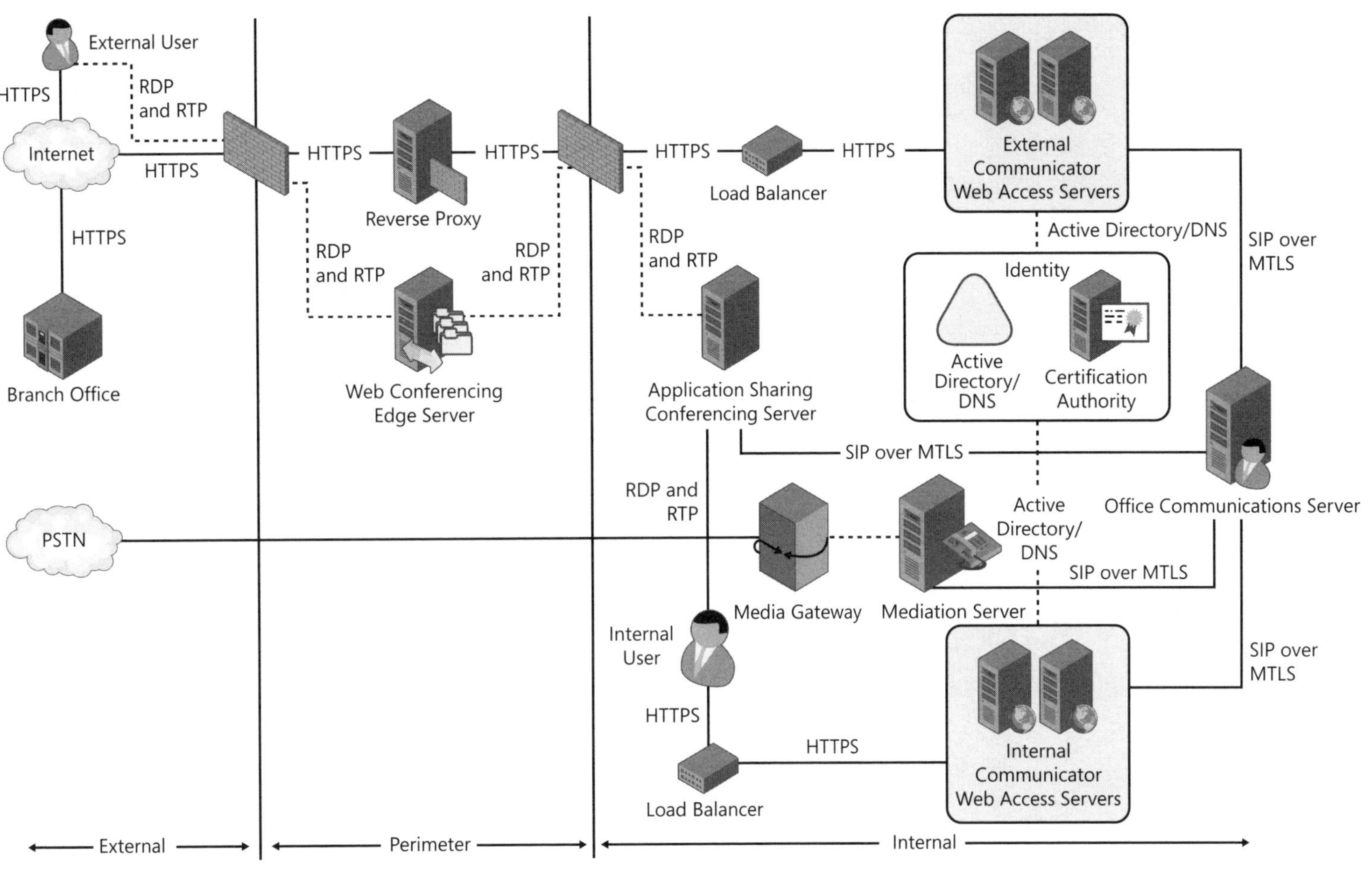

FIGURE 6-5 Reference architecture of Communicator Web Access as deployed for both internal and external access

Installing Communicator Web Access

To install Communicator Web Access, follow these steps.

1. Log on to the computer where Communicator Web Access is to be installed.
2. From the Office Communications Server 2007 installation media, double-click the appropriate setup file. This will be SetupEE.exe if you are running the Enterprise Edition of Office Communications Server, or SetupSE.exe if you are running the Standard Edition. This will start the Office Communications Server 2007 R2 Deployment Wizard.
3. On the wizard's home page, click Deploy Other Server Roles.
4. On the Deploy Other Server Roles page, click Deploy Communicator Web Access.
5. On the Deploy Office Communications Server 2007, Communicator Web Access page, under Step 1: Install Communicator Web Access, click Install.
6. On the Welcome page, click Next.
7. On the License Agreement page, click I Accept The Terms Of This License Agreement and then click Next. If you do not accept these terms, setup will terminate.
8. On the Install Location page, type in the local path where you want Communicator Web Access to be installed (or accept the default location) and then click Next.
9. On the Confirm Installation page, click Next. Setup will proceed to copy the files and install Communicator Web Access.
10. On the Installation Complete page, click Finish.

Do not close the Deployment Wizard window. Instead, continue directly with the next procedure, activating the Communicator Web Access Server.

Activating the Communicator Web Access Server

To activate the Communicator Web Access Server, follow these steps in the Deployment Wizard.

1. Under Step 2: Activate Communicator Web Access, click Run.
2. On the Welcome page, click Next.
3. On the Select Domain Service Account page, in the Account Name text box, either type a name for the service account under which Communicator Web Access will run or accept the default service name (CWAService). In the Password text box, type a password to be used for the account. (Passwords must meet the password strength and complexity requirements used in your domain.) In the Confirm Password text box, retype the password and then click Next.
4. On the Select Server Certificate page, click Select Certificate.
5. In the Select Certificate dialog box, in the Issued To column, click the certificate issued to the Communicator Web Access server. Note that servers will be listed by their fully qualified domain name (FQDN). For example, the server cwaserver1 in the domain litwareinc.com would be listed by using the following FQDN: cwaserver1.litwareinc.com. After selecting the proper certificate, click OK.

6. On the Select Server Certificate page, verify that the Issued To text box contains the value CN= followed by the FQDN of the server (for example, CN=cwaserver1.litwareinc.com). Click Next.
7. On the Confirm Installation page, click Next.
8. On the Activation Complete page, click Close. If you want to review the tasks the Activation Wizard completed, click View Log before clicking Close.

Do not close the Deployment Wizard window. Instead, continue directly to the next procedure, creating the virtual server.

Creating the Virtual Server

To create the virtual server, follow these steps in the Deployment Wizard.

1. Under Step 3: Create Virtual Server, click Run.
2. On the Welcome page, click Next.
3. On the Select Virtual Server Type page, select the server type that you want to use, either internal or external. An internal server is designed for users who log on to Communicator Web Access from within an organization's firewall. An external server is designed for users who log on to Communicator Web Access from outside the firewall. Make the selection and then click Next.
4. On the Select Authentication Type page, select either Use Built-in Authentication (the default) or Use Custom Authentication and then click Next. Support for Integrated Windows authentication and for forms-based authentication are included in Communicator Web Access; if you plan to use either of these authentication methods, you should choose built-in authentication. If you will be using a third-party authentication method (such as two-factor authentication or single sign-on), select the custom authentication option. (Note that custom authentication methods typically require a reverse proxy server or other authentication server located somewhere in the perimeter network.) If you select custom authentication, you will also have the option of specifying the URL of a Web page that users will be directed to when they sign out. Simply type that address in the Sign-Out URL (Optional) text box.
5. If you are configuring the Communicator Web Access Server for internal users, on the Select Authentication page, select one or both of the check boxes to indicate whether you will use forms-based authentication, Integrated Windows authentication (NTLM and Kerberos), or both. Integrated Windows authentication is the most secure authentication method and is also the simplest for users. After making the required configuration changes to Internet Explorer, a user logged on to a computer with domain credentials can be connected to Communicator Web Access without having to log on to the service as well. However, integrated Windows authentication can be used only by users running Microsoft Windows and a browser that supports Kerberos Version 5 network authentication. In addition, this type of authentication is accessible only behind the organization's firewall.

Forms-based authentication is less secure than Integrated Windows authentication because user credentials (user name, domain, and password) are entered using plain text. (To ensure that credentials are passed to the server in encrypted format, configure your server to use HTTPS.) With forms-based authentication, users trying to connect to Communicator Web Access will be presented with a dialog box requiring them to enter their domain credentials. These credentials must be validated before the user can access the service.

This page appears only if you are configuring the server for internal users. If you are configuring the server for external users, you will not see the Select Authentication page because only forms-based authentication (or a custom authentication method) is supported for users outside the firewall.

Note that it *is* possible to change the authentication type after the virtual server has been created. To do this, open the Microsoft Office Communications Server 2007 R2 Communicator Web Access snap-in, right-click the virtual server name, and then click Properties. In the Communicator Web Access Properties dialog box, on the Authentication tab, change the authentication type as needed. If you are using forms-based authentication, this dialog box also enables you to specify timeout values (in minutes) for both public and private computer access.

6. On the Select Browser Connection Type page, accept the default of HTTPS (recommended) and then click Select Certificate. For security reasons, it is highly recommended that you use HTTPS, even if your deployment does not require it. If you *do* select HTTP, the option for selecting a certificate will be unavailable to you. In that case, simply click Next. The following message will appear:

   You have selected HTTP connectivity. This is an insecure form of connectivity. Without proper network safeguards, you may incur security risks.

   If you click Yes, the connection type will be set to HTTP. If you click No, you will have the opportunity to select HTTPS as the connection type.

   If, as recommended, you select HTTPS (and click Select Certificate) in the Select Certificate dialog box, select a certificate with the FQDN of your Communicator Web Access Server (or load balancer, as appropriate) and then click OK. On the Select Browser Connection Type page, click Next.

   Note that it is possible to change the connection type after the virtual server has been created. To do this, open the Microsoft Office Communications Server 2007 R2 Communicator Web Access snap-in, right-click the virtual server name, and then click Properties. In the Communicator Web Access Properties dialog box, on the Connectivity tab, change the connection type as needed. This dialog box also enables you to change the virtual server IP address and port number.

7. On the Select IP Address and Port Aetting page, select an IP address from the drop-down list or keep the default value (All Unassigned). In the Port box, type the port setting for Communicator Web Access or accept the default value (443 for HTTPS and

80 for HTTP). Click Next. If the selected port is already in use, the following message will appear:

A port conflict has been detected. If you continue without changing the port number the virtual server will be created in stopped mode.

If you click Yes, the port value will be retained and the virtual server will be created but will not be started. If you click No, you will have the opportunity to enter a new port number. Keep in mind that virtual servers cannot be used until they have been started.

8. On the Name The Virtual Server page, type a name to be given to the virtual server or accept the default name Communicator Web Access. (This is the name used to identify the virtual server in the Communicator Web Access snap-in and in the Internet Information Services Manager snap-in.) Click Next.
9. On the Specify A Listening Port page, type in a port number and then click Next. The virtual server will use this port to monitor for SIP messages.
10. On the Select A Pool page, type the FQDN of the server to be used as the "next hop" server. Enter a port number in the Port text box and then click Next.

    In Communicator Web Access R2, anonymous users are allowed to take part in audio conferences or desktop sharing sessions. However, that presents Communicator Web Access with a challenge. When an authenticated users joins a conference or desktop sharing session, Communicator Web Access automatically proxies messages to the user's home server. By definition, anonymous users do not have a home server. Therefore, you must designate a server to function as a home server so that Communicator Web Access has a location to which to proxy messages.

    Note that it is possible to change the next hop server after the virtual server has been created. To do this, open the Microsoft Office Communications Server 2007 R2 Communicator Web Access snap-in, locate the virtual server, right-click it, and then click Properties. In the Communicator Web Access Properties dialog box, on the Next Hop tab, change the server name and port as needed.
11. On the Automatically Start Virtual Server page, select the default Start The Virtual Server After The Create Virtual Server Finishes and then click Next. If you clear this value, the virtual server will be created but not started. If you choose not to start the virtual server right away, you can manually start the server by right-clicking the server name in the Communicator Web Access snap-in and clicking Start.
12. On the Review Virtual Server Settings page, click Next.
13. On the Create Virtual Server Complete page, click Close. If you want to review the tasks the Activation Wizard has completed, click View Log before clicking Close.

    Note that virtual servers can also be created by using the Communicator Web Access snap-in. To do this, right-click the Communicator Web Access Server in the snap-in and then click Create Virtual Web Server. Doing so will start the virtual server Setup Wizard.

Do not close the Deployment Wizard window. Instead, continue with the next procedure, publishing the Communicator Web Access URLs in Active Directory.

Publishing the Communicator Web Access URLs in Active Directory

1. Under Step 4 in the Deployment Wizard: Publish Communicator Web Access URLs, click Run.
2. In the Publish Web Addresses dialog box, enter the URL for the new server in the appropriate box (Internal Web Address for an internal server; External Web Address for an external server) and then click Publish. Make sure you reference the correct protocol when entering the URL. For example, if you selected HTTPS as the connection type, the URL might look like this: https://im.litwareinc.com. If you chose HTTP as the connection type, the URL might look like this: http://im.litwareinc.com.
3. In the subsequent message box, click OK. Note that you can also publish URLs by using the Communicator Web Access snap-in. To do so, right-click the Microsoft Office Communications Server 2007 R2, Communicator Web Access node and then click Publish Web Addresses.
4. Close the Deployment Wizard window.

Examining the Technical Details Behind Conferencing Scenarios

This section describes the technical details behind Office Communications Server 2007 R2 conferencing scenarios. The conferencing component architecture is discussed first. Then the life cycle of a conference is discussed. Finally, this section will explore more technical details about data collaboration conferences.

Understanding the Conferencing Architecture

Many components participate in an Office Communications Server on-premise conference. They handle functionalities such as authentication, authorization, signaling, conference control, storage, and media mixing and processing. Figure 6-6 shows the logical component architecture for conferencing.

Conferencing Clients

There are two types of client conferencing applications: scheduling clients and conferencing clients.

- **Scheduling client** A scheduling client is a client application that handles the creation, modification, or deletion of a conference. This client can also handle scheduling the details of a conference, such as start and end time, participant list, and recurrence. Optionally, the client can send invitation notifications for conference participants.

- **Conferencing client** A conferencing client is a client application that can join and participate in an Office Communications Server conference. The main functionalities of a conferencing client include joining a conference, showing a list of conference participants and their status, and providing a user interface for the user to control different aspects of the conference.

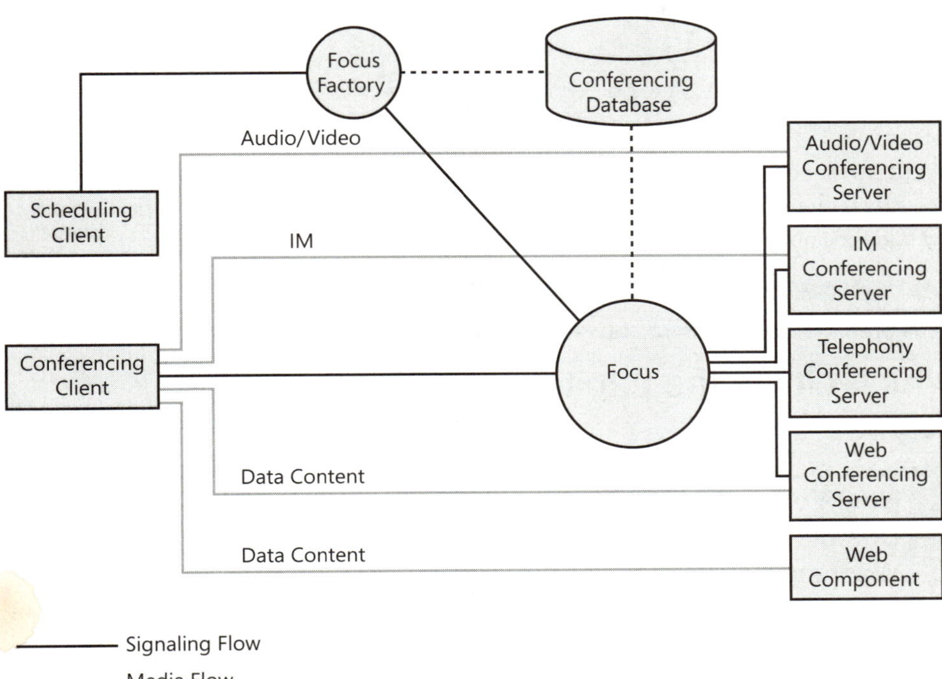

FIGURE 6-6 Conferencing component architecture

The separation between a scheduling client and a conferencing client is only logical, based on the set of conferencing-related functionalities that each performs. In reality, client applications can have both scheduling and conferencing capabilities.

MICROSOFT OFFICE LIVE MEETING CONSOLE 2007 R2

Microsoft Live Meeting Console 2007 R2 is the primary conferencing client for scheduled Web conferences. It provides support for a full range of features that enable participants to have an effective collaborative meeting. These features include the following:

- Data collaboration, such as with PowerPoint presentations, using the integrated whiteboard polling, shared notes, and other collaboration tools. Live Meeting Console is the only client that supports application sharing.

- Audio and video. Live Meeting Console supports real-time multiparty audio and video, complete with active speaker detection and display.
- Audio Conferencing Provider integration. Live Meeting Console is the only client that supports integration between an Office Communications Server conference and a phone-based audio conference hosted by an outside ACP. The console provides user interfaces for users to control the audio conference, such as mute self, mute all, and so on.
- In-meeting chat. Live Meeting Console supports peer-to-peer text chat between two conference participants.

Office Live Meeting Console 2007 R2 is also a scheduling client. It provides a Meet Now functionality that enables users to create an instant conference and invite other participants from within the conference. Figure 6-7 shows a Poll question in Live Meeting.

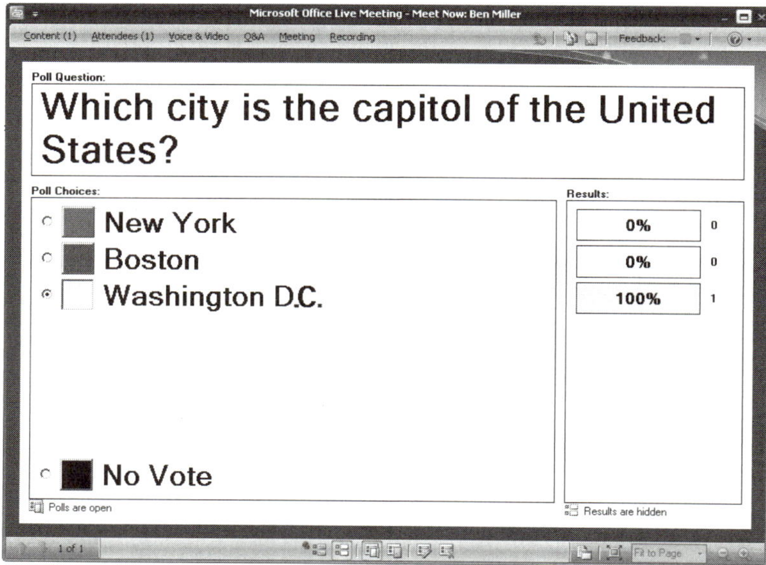

FIGURE 6-7 Poll question in Office Live Meeting

MICROSOFT OFFICE COMMUNICATOR 2007 R2

Microsoft Office Communicator 2007 R2 is the primary client application for instant communications and spontaneous collaboration. It provides the following capabilities:

- Multiparty IM conference, based on multiple contacts in a contact list or an Active Directory distribution group
- Multiparty A/V conference
- Seamless escalation from IM or A/V conferences to data collaboration conference in Office Live Meeting Console

Figure 6-8 shows a Group IM session in the Office Communicator 2007 R2 client.

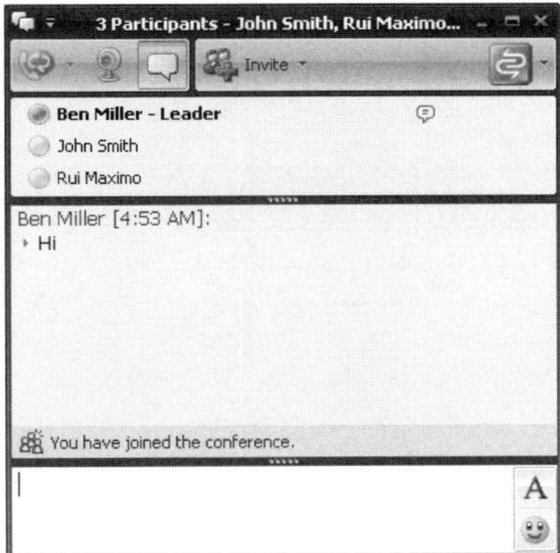

FIGURE 6-8 IM session in the Office Communicator client

MICROSOFT CONFERENCING ADD-IN FOR MICROSOFT OFFICE OUTLOOK

The Microsoft Conferencing add-in for Outlook is the primary scheduling client. The add-in enables users to use the familiar Outlook interface for scheduling an Office Communications Server conference. In addition to the usual conference information that Outlook handles, such as meeting start and end times and recurrence, the add-in enables users to apply meeting settings that are specific to an Office Communications Server conference, such as meeting access type, presenter list, and audio information. It also generates a preformatted meeting invitation that contains all the necessary information for joining the conference. The meeting invitation is sent to all the invited participants via e-mail.

Users can choose from two options to schedule their conferences:

- **Schedule a Live Meeting** This option schedules a conference that will happen in the Office Live Meeting Console 2007 R2 client. All modalities will be provisioned for the conference.
- **Schedule a Conference Call** This option schedules a conference that will happen in the Office Communicator 2007 R2 client. Only the computer-based audio modality is provisioned at the start of the conference. (Conference participants can add other modalities later.)

Figure 6-9 shows the Conferencing add-in for an Outlook client.

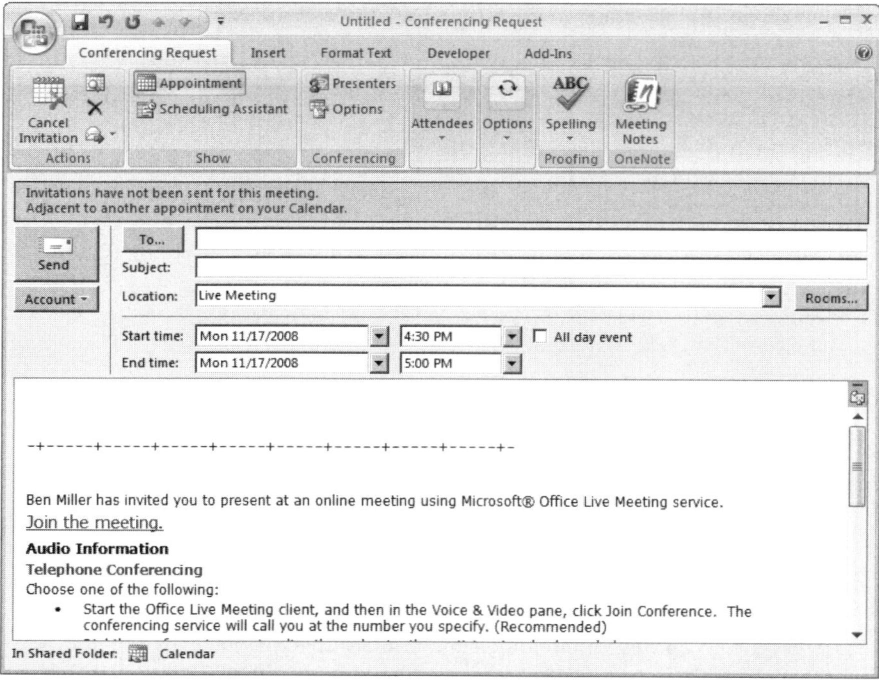

FIGURE 6-9 Conferencing add-in for Outlook

The Conferencing Database

In the Office Communications Server conferencing architecture, two databases (RTC and RTCDyn) provide storage for conference properties and conference state, respectively. Those databases are hosted on the Microsoft SQL Server back-end server.

The RTC database stores persistent user data, including the contact list, access control information, and static conferencing information. Static conference properties are stored in this database from the time the conference is created until the time the conference is deleted from the server. The data will be persisted here until either the data is explicitly removed or the configured time (by default 90 days and set by the Conference Content Retention policy) is reached. Following is a list of conference properties that are included in the RTC database:

- Conference identifier. The conference ID along with the SIP URI of the organizer uniquely identifies a conference.
- Conference expiration date. This setting indicates when it is safe for the server to delete the conference automatically.
- Conference access type. For example, Invite Within Network.
- Conference access key. The key that is sent to anonymous users.
- Supported media types.
- A list of meeting participants and their roles.

The RTCDyn database stores transient conference state information, such as the up-to-date participant list and the roles of participants, subscription information, conference lock, and other state information. That information is specific to each instance of a conference and is removed when a conference ends. It is, however, important to persist that information in a database during the conference. Doing this ensures high availability for the conference. If one server component fails or stops responding, another server with the same role can easily take over and continue to serve the same conference by using information from the database.

DIRECT FROM THE SOURCE

Where Conference Scheduling Information Is Stored

Hao Yan
Senior Program Manager, Office Communications Server

The RTC database does not contain conference scheduling information. Supporting a meeting start time and end time, recurrence schedule, and exceptions to recurrence are all important for a prescheduled conference. However, that information is maintained outside of the conferencing database and Office Communications Server. Instead, conference calendar information is maintained by scheduling clients as appropriate. For example, the Microsoft Conferencing add-in for the Outlook client saves the time information as part of a Microsoft Exchange Server calendar item.

Focus

The Focus Server is a conference state server that acts as the coordinator for all aspects of a conference. It is implemented as a SIP user agent that is addressable by using a conference URI. The Focus runs in the User Services module of all front-end servers. A separate instance of the Focus exists for each active conference.

The Focus is responsible for the following tasks:

- Activating conferences
- Enlisting required conferencing servers
- Authenticating participants before allowing them to enter a conference
- Managing conference participant roles and privileges
- Authorizing conferencing control commands from participants based on the conference organizer's Meeting policy
- Managing conference state

- Maintaining SIP signaling relationships between conference participants and conferencing servers, providing a conduit for control commands to flow between clients and the conferencing servers
- Accepting subscriptions to conferences and notifying clients of changes in conference state, such as the arrival and departure of participants and the addition or removal of media

When a new media type needs to be activated for a conference, the Focus also instantiates the conference on the appropriate conferencing server, communicates with the conferencing server about adding a new user, gets the authorization credentials so that the client can connect to that conference, and then sends the media information to the client. The same sequence is repeated for all clients who want to add this media. When a new media type is added to the conference, the sequence is repeated with the new conferencing server for that media type. By centralizing security enforcement and roster management, the Focus relieves each of the conferencing servers of this duty.

The Focus Factory

The Focus Factory is an entity that creates, deletes, and modifies meetings in the conferencing database. It is also implemented as a SIP user agent that is addressable by using a Focus Factory URI and runs in the same process as the Focus. When a client application creates a new conference, the client sends a SIP SERVICE message, which carries Centralized Conferencing Control Protocol (C3P) commands as the message payload, to the Focus Factory. For more information about C3P commands, see the section titled "The Conferencing Protocols" later in this chapter. The Focus Factory creates a new instance of the meeting in the conference database and returns information, including the conference URI, about the newly created conference to the client.

Conferencing Servers and the Conferencing Server Factory

Supporting multiparty conferences requires using the Conferencing Server role, which is also known as a multipoint control unit (MCU). Each type of conferencing server is responsible for managing one or more media types. Office Communications Server 2007 R2 includes four conferencing servers:

- **Web Conferencing Server** Manages conference data collaboration, including native support for PowerPoint presentations, Microsoft Office document sharing, use of the integrated whiteboard, application sharing, polling, questions and answers, compliance logging, annotations, meeting summaries, handouts, and various multimedia formats. The Web Conferencing Server uses the Persistent Shared Object Model (PSOM), a Live Meeting protocol, for uploading slides to a meeting.
- **A/V Conferencing Server** Provides multiparty IP audio and video mixing and relaying by using industry standard Real-Time Transport Protocol (RTP) and Real-Time Control Protocol (RTCP).

- **IM Conferencing Server** Enables Group IM by relaying IM traffic among all participants. All messages among the participants are routed through the IM Conferencing Server.
- **Telephony Conferencing Server** Responsible for ACP integration. Supports dial-out and dial-in, as well as standard third-party call control features such as mute and eject.

A conferencing server consists of two logical pieces: a media controller (MC) and a media processor (MP). The MC on a conferencing server is responsible for managing the control commands between the Focus and a conferencing server. In the Office Communications Server architecture, all conference control commands are sent by clients to the Focus, which then relays these commands to the appropriate conferencing server or servers after verifying that the client that sent the request has the privileges to perform that operation.

Media is exchanged directly between clients and the conferencing server or servers. The MP is responsible for media management, such as mixing, relaying, and transcoding. Transcoding is direct digital-to-digital translation from one signal-encoding format to another. On a Web Conferencing Server, the MP is a software component that is responsible for managing data collaboration. On an A/V Conferencing Server, the MP mixes audio streams, switches video streams, and converts the media for clients who are on slow links. Of all the conferencing components, the MP can use the most central processing unit (CPU) and network resources. In the Office Communications Server conferencing architecture, an MC and an MP are co-located on the same server to simplify deployment.

In a conference, when a media type needs to be added, the Focus requests a conferencing server for that media type through the Conferencing Server Factory. The Conferencing Server Factory is a lightweight logical component responsible for provisioning a conference for a particular media type on a conferencing server. The MCU Factory takes into account the current load on the conferencing servers before assigning a conferencing server to a conference. There is one MCU Factory instance on each front-end server that handles all media types.

DIRECT FROM THE SOURCE

Office Communications Server 2007 R2 Conferencing Scale

Sean Olson
Principal Group Program Manager, Office Communications Server

Early in the planning phase of Office Communications Server 2007 R2, a critical decision point became the size of meetings that would be supported on the server. After reviewing competitive products, speaking with customers, and mining the experience from our own Live Meeting service, it became clear that the majority of meetings were actually small (4 to 6 participants). More research revealed that 80 percent of meetings had fewer than 20 participants, and 99.98 percent of meetings

had fewer than 100 participants. We then polled customers to see if 200 to 250 participants would meet their needs. Customers said that it would but that there were occasionally larger meetings that would exceed this limit. The decision was made to focus on the typical information worker meeting (4 to 6 users) and allow room for growth up to 200 to 250 participants. Meetings larger than that would need to take advantage of the Live Meeting hosted service, which can scale beyond 1,000 participants in a meeting. Apart from the raw server scaling characteristics of such meetings, it was clear from our own operational experience that it takes dedicated staff and processes to make such large meetings effective. In essence, running such large meetings requires a different solution altogether if done properly.

How the Goal Was Tested

The user model for performance testing of conferencing takes into account a number of factors:

- The number of users on the pool
- The effective concurrency rate for meetings
- The media types (mixes) that are available for each meeting
- The location from which users come: inside the enterprise, outside the enterprise, federated, or anonymous

To determine the number of meetings to test with, the total number of users (for example, 50,000) was multiplied by a concurrency rate (for example, 5 percent). The result is the number of users expected to be in a meeting at any given time (in this example, 2,500 users). The number of expected users was then divided by the number of conferencing servers in the deployment (for example, 2), and that results in the number of participants per conferencing server (in this case, 1,250). That number can then be divided by the average meeting size (for example, 6), which results in the average number of meetings per conferencing server (in this example, approximately 210). We tested a variety of meeting sizes to ensure that the server will scale appropriately. This calculation represents an average test load.

One specific test that we performed ensured that Office Communications Server 2007 R2 can support a meeting with up to 250 participants. This includes audio, video, and data. In that test, a large meeting is run on a conferencing server. However, we do not attempt to run multiple large meetings on a single conferencing server because the data previously collected indicated that these types of meetings are relatively rare.

No Magic Numbers

When you see numbers like 250 (the largest meeting size) and 1,250 (the number of users on a single conferencing server), it can be easy to think that these are hard-coded values. But there are no hard-coded numbers in the software. These numbers represent the tested capacities for a particular user model and a particular set of hardware. For more information about planning for capacity, see *the Planning Guide for Office Communications Server 2007 R2* at http://go.microsoft.com/fwlink/?LinkID=133603.

It is important to remember that you will not find the number 250 hard-coded into Office Communications Server 2007 R2. The maximum number of participants in a meeting is controlled by the administrator through Meeting policy. This is an administrator policy that can be set either through the Microsoft Management Console (MMC) or Windows Management Instrumentation (WMI). For more information about Meeting policy, see the deployment documentation at http://go.microsoft.com/fwlink/?LinkID=133654.

If you look at these policies in the MMC, note that the default is actually much lower than 250. This is because it is assumed that users who are allowed to create large meetings are privileged users and therefore have a nondefault policy. Meeting policies apply to the organizer of the meeting. Some organizers might be allowed to have 200-person meetings; others might be allowed to have only 10 people in a meeting. This is an administrator decision that is enforced by Office Communications Server.

Pushing the Limits

To understand what happens when the default number of participants is exceeded, it is helpful to first understand how a conferencing server manages its load dynamically. When the first user joins a meeting, a conferencing server for the appropriate media type or types is allocated. The conferencing server that is allocated comes from a set of conferencing servers associated with the pool.

In the preceding example, "How the Goal Was Tested," there are two Web Conferencing Servers in a pool for 50,000 users. Each conferencing server is responsible for managing its load and reporting its ability to host additional meetings. If a conferencing server has exceeded its capacity, it can report this, and the pool will allocate a different conferencing server. This is all done in real time at the time of the meeting; a user cannot reserve resources in advance, and certain meetings cannot be made a priority over other meetings when allocating resources. A 250-person meeting is likely to require the resources of a single conferencing server, and other meetings will be allocated on other conferencing servers in that pool. For example, you have a large meeting with 250 people on a single conferencing server and the 251st user tries to join that meeting. If the Meeting policy allows this and the conferencing server has spare capacity, the user will be allowed to join. This test is performed for each user that joins, and it is possible for two large meetings to compete for resources on the same conferencing server. Smaller meetings are easier to host on the same server because each requires fewer resources.

The capacity of the conferencing servers is mainly measured by CPU and memory. Dual-processor or dual-core servers that have 4 gigabytes (GB) of memory have been tested and are recommended. If you use more powerful hardware, you will have more capacity and be able to host larger meetings. The recommended hardware is based on a reasonable balance between cost and typical usage (as stated earlier, 99.98 percent of meetings have fewer than 100 users). Achieving as many as 1,000 participants in a meeting is theoretically possible by using the right hardware; however, it has not been a goal of the Office Communications Server 2007 R2 release and is not directly supported at this time.

For large meetings, it is important to consider more than server scale. You will need the right support and processes in place to make a 1,000-user meeting successful. Supporting a meeting of this size typically means having dedicated IT staff on hand to deal with support calls or "operator assistance" needs, as well as having the infrastructure to manage invitations, follow up on problems, distribute handouts, and other meeting tasks. You also need to ensure that you have the appropriate network infrastructure in place with the required bandwidth to host such a large meeting.

Proper monitoring and capacity planning will ensure that you have the right hardware to scale to your needs. As your needs change, you can add more conferencing servers (or front-end servers in the consolidated topology) to meet your growing needs.

Recommendations for Larger Meeting Sizes

Here are a few recommendations if you want to push the limit on the meeting size:

- Create a dedicated Meeting policy for those organizers who are authorized to host such large meetings.
- Ideally, create a dedicated pool for those organizers so that you can dedicate hardware resources particularly for these meetings. This is one form of resource reservation.
- Invest in the support infrastructure that is required to make these meetings run smoothly (people, processes, network, and hardware).

Web Components

Web Components are the set of ASP.NET applications and virtual directories that are created on Internet Information Services (IIS) during the deployment of Office Communications Server 2007 R2. The Web components support the following functionalities:

- The data collaboration content of a conference is hosted using the *conf* Web component in encrypted format. The Web Conferencing Server instructs clients to download the content through HTTPS and provide an encryption key to the client for decryption.
- The Office Communicator client uses IIS to download Address Book Server files when the client is outside the corporate firewall.
- An ASP.NET application running on top of IIS is used for the Group Expansion Web Service.
- An ASP.NET application running on top of IIS is used for the Web Scheduler tool in the Office Communications Server 2007 R2 Resource Kit, which is a Web-based scheduling solution.

Process and Machine Boundaries for Conferencing Components

Figure 6-10 shows the computer and process boundaries for all the conferencing components that we discussed in the previous sections.

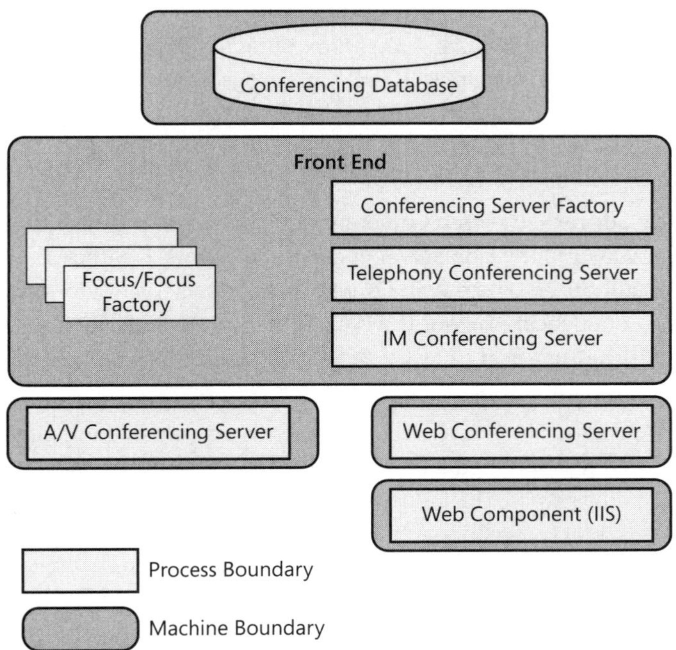

FIGURE 6-10 Conferencing component process and computer boundary

The Focus, Focus Factory, Conferencing Server Factory, IM Conferencing Server, and Telephony Conferencing Server all run as part of the front-end server. They cannot be separated and installed on different computers.

The Web Conferencing Server and the A/V Conferencing Server can be run on the same computer as the front-end server (in an Office Communications Server 2007 R2 Standard

Edition or Enterprise Edition consolidated topology). However, they can also be a separate server role and installed on their own hardware as in an Office Communications Server 2007 R2 Enterprise Edition expanded topology. This configuration enables enterprises to scale out their Office Communications Server 2007 R2 deployments by deploying as many conferencing servers as necessary to meet their usage models. The host for Web Components (IIS) can be installed as part of every Office Communications Server 2007 R2 Standard Edition server or Enterprise Edition consolidated topology server, or as a separate Web farm behind a hardware load balancer in the Enterprise Edition expanded topology.

Edge Servers

Office Communications Server 2007 R2 enables enterprise users that are working outside the enterprise network to participate in on-premise conferences. In addition, it also enables enterprise users to invite federated users and anonymous users to participate in on-premise conferences. Enabling conferencing and the ability to share data and media with users outside the corporate firewall requires the following four server roles in the perimeter network:

- **Access Edge Server** Formerly known as the Access Proxy, the Access Edge Server handles all SIP traffic across the corporate firewall. The Access Edge Server handles only the SIP traffic that is necessary to establish and validate connections. It does not handle data transfer, nor does it authenticate users. Authentication of incoming traffic is performed by the Director or the front-end server.
- **Web Conferencing Edge Server** The Web Conferencing Edge Server proxies PSOM traffic between the Web Conferencing Server and external clients. External conference traffic must be authorized by the Web Conferencing Edge Server before it is forwarded to the Web Conferencing Server. The Web Conferencing Edge Server requires that external clients use Transport Layer Security (TLS) connections and obtain a conference session key.
- **A/V Edge Server** The A/V Edge Server provides a single trusted connection point through which incoming and outgoing media traffic can securely traverse Network Address Translation (NAT) and firewalls. The industry-standard solution for multimedia traversal of firewalls is Interactive Connectivity Establishment (ICE), which is based on the Simple Traversal of User Datagram Protocol (UDP) through NAT (STUN) and Traversal Using Relay NAT (TURN) protocols. The A/V Edge Server is a STUN server. All users are authenticated to secure both access to the enterprise and use of the firewall traversal service that is provided by the A/V Edge Server. To send media inside the enterprise, an external user must be authenticated and must have an authenticated internal user agree to communicate with them through the A/V Edge Server. The media streams themselves are exchanged by using Secure Real-Time Protocol (SRTP), which is an industry standard for real-time media transmission and reception over IP.

- **HTTP Reverse Proxy** Office Communications Server 2007 R2 conferencing support for external users also requires deploying an HTTP reverse proxy in the perimeter network for the purpose of carrying HTTP and HTTPS traffic to the Web Components (IIS) for external users.

Figure 6-11 shows the conferencing component architecture with Edge Servers.

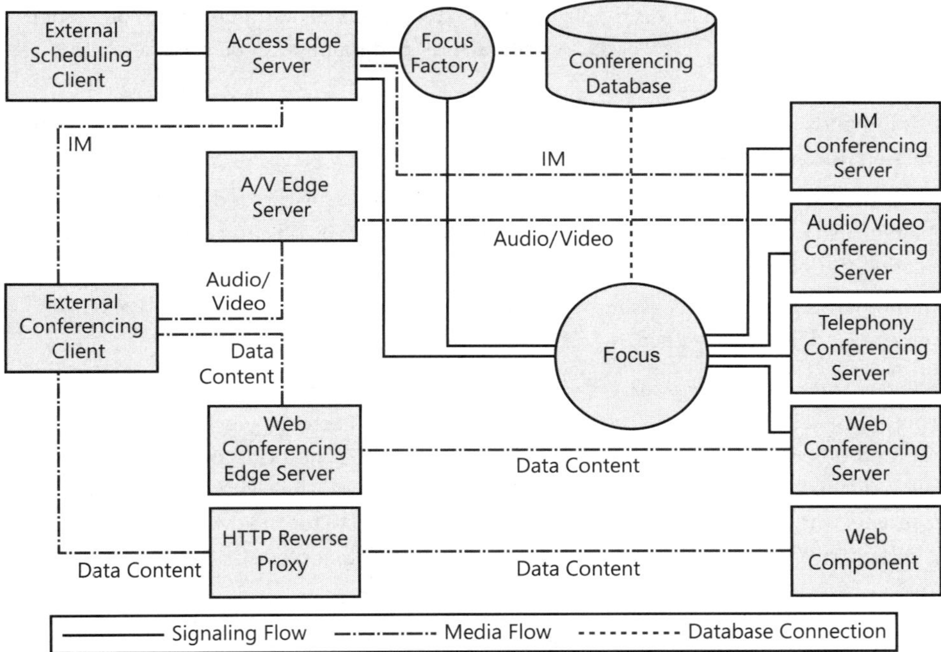

FIGURE 6-11 Conferencing component architecture with Edge Servers

The Conferencing Protocols

This section discusses various protocols for the communication between different components in the conferencing architecture. On a high level, there are two classes of protocols involved in an on-premise conference: signaling and media.

SIGNALING PROTOCOLS

Signaling protocol refers to protocols that facilitate session establishment, capability exchange, state exchange, and conference control.

SIP is the primary signaling protocol that Office Communications Server uses. SIP is the industry-standard protocol described in Internet Engineering Task Force (IETF) Request for Comment (RFC) 3261, which defines a standard way to perform session setup, termination, and media negotiation between two parties.

The SIP *NOTIFY/BENOTIFY* methods are used to convey changes in conference state. *Conference state* describes the various entities that are associated with a conference. It is described by using the IETF RFC conference event (http://go.microsoft.com/fwlink/?LinkID=133681) package.

Various conference control and state modification tasks are achieved by using C3P protocol. C3P is an XML-based protocol that provides a thin wrapper around the conference event package and also provides various media-specific extensions. C3P commands can be carried through SIP *INFO* or *SERVICE* methods. In general, C3P commands can be classified into three categories:

- Commands that terminate on the Focus and do not involve conferencing server interaction (for example, renameUser)
- Commands that are authorized by the Focus but are simply proxied to conferencing servers, so no Focus state is modified unless the conferencing server generates a notification (for example, modifyEndpointMedia)
- Commands that are processed by the Focus as well as by conferencing servers (for example, deleteConference, modifyConferenceLock)

The Focus and conferencing servers communicate using C3P and use HTTPS as the carrier protocol for C3P. Clients communicate with Focus and Focus Factory by using SIP *INFO* or *SERVICE* methods. SIP *INVITE, ACK, BYE, UPDATE*, and *CANCEL* methods are used to establish a signaling dialog between a conferencing client and the Focus. The client signals conferencing servers with the corresponding supported protocols: SIP for the IM Conferencing Server, Telephony Conferencing Server, and A/V Conferencing Server and PSOM for the Web Conferencing Server.

MEDIA PROTOCOLS

The term *media protocols* refers to protocols that facilitate the exchange of specific types of media between clients and a conferencing server.

The Web Conferencing Server uses PSOM, a Live Meeting protocol, for exchanging data collaboration content and control with conferencing clients. The concept of a distributed object is central to PSOM operations. A distributed object is a set of two interfaces: one interface for the object's client side, and one interface for the object's server side. Protocol messages are mapped to methods of these interfaces. The client interface contains messages sent to the client side of a connection. The server interface contains messages sent to the server side of a connection.

The IM Conferencing Server uses the Session Initiation Protocol for Instant Messaging and Presence Leveraging Extensions (SIMPLE) to communicate with IM conferencing clients. SIMPLE is an open standard defined by IETF RFC 3428 (http://go.microsoft.com/fwlink/?LinkID=133682).

RTP/RTCP is a standard protocol employed by the A/V Conferencing Server to exchange audio and video streams with conferencing clients. RTP defines a standardized packet format for delivering audio and video over the Internet. RTCP provides out-of-band control information for an RTP flow. In Office Communications Server, all communications are encrypted. The A/V Conferencing Server actually uses the SRTP/SRTCP (Secure Real-Time Control Protocol) protocol, which provides encryption over RTP/RTCP.

Figure 6-12 provides an overview of how the various conferencing protocols interact with different Office Communications Server components.

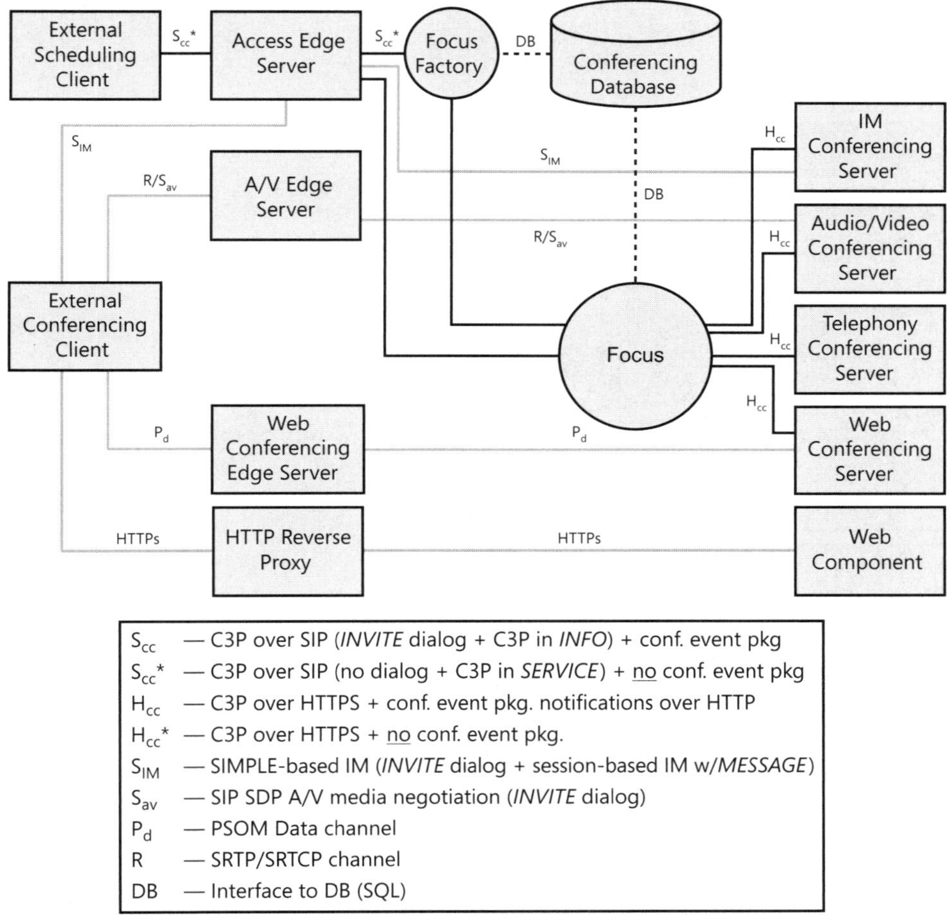

FIGURE 6-12 Conferencing protocols

Understanding the Conference Life Cycle

Each Office Communications Server conference has the life cycle shown in Figure 6-13. A scheduling client creates a conference via the Focus Factory. The conference can be activated/joined and deactivated at any time after it is created and after it is cleaned up (has expired) from the server. The conference expires only after the specified expiration date has passed.

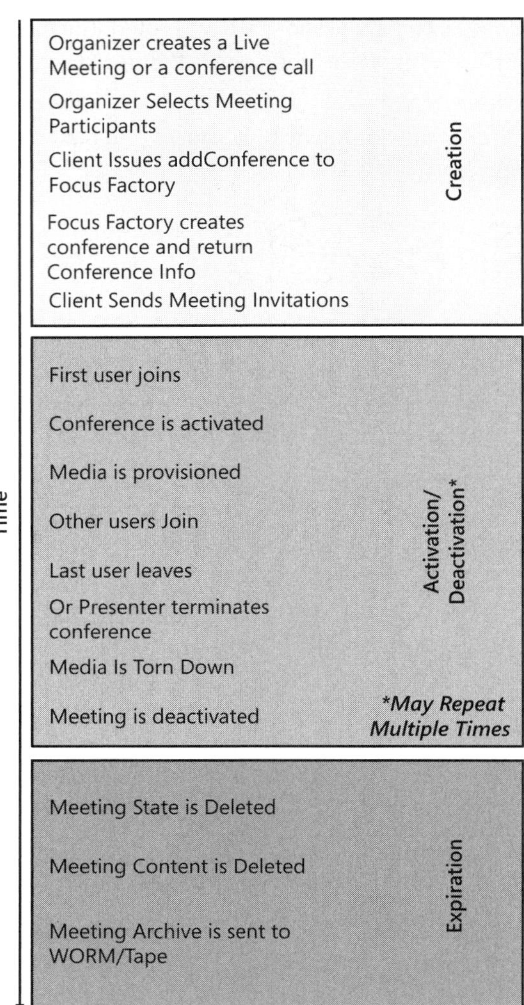

FIGURE 6-13 Conference life cycle

Conference Creation

An Office Communications Server 2007 R2 conference can be created in one of the following ways:

- By scheduling a Web conference or conference call from the Microsoft Conferencing add-in for Outlook
- By creating a multiparty IM or A/V conferencing session from the Office Communicator 2007 R2 client

- By using the Share Information Using Live Meeting option in the Office Communicator 2007 R2 client
- By creating an ad hoc meeting by using the Meet Now functionality of the Office Live Meeting 2007 client
- By scheduling a Web conference or audio conference by using the Web Scheduler Resource Kit Tool

In all the preceding scenarios, the scheduling client communicates with the Focus Factory, which actually creates records in the conferencing database. Only authenticated enterprise users who are home on an Office Communications Server 2007 R2 pool can create conferences. The key inputs to the Focus Factory include the following:

- Organizer SIP URI, which is the SIP URI that identifies the organizer of the conference.
- Conference ID, which is an alphanumeric string that identifies the conference. The Conference ID has to be unique for the same organizer.
- Subject, which is the subject of the conference. This is used for display in the conferencing client.
- Conference access type, which can be Invite Within Network, Invite Within Network (Restricted), or Invite Anyone.
- Conference key, which is an alphanumeric string that is used to authenticate anonymous users.
- Participant list and roles.
- Expiration time. The scheduling client can specify an optional expiration time at which it is safe to delete the conference completely from Office Communications Server.
- Provisioned conferencing servers. This specifies the type of media that is required in the conference.
- Conferencing server–specific information, such as numbers to dial in for the Telephony Conferencing Server.

The key output from the Focus Factory is the conference URI. A conference URI is a globally unique identifier that represents the conference. A sample conference URI is shown here:

```
sip:ben@litwareinc.com;gruu;opaque=app:conf:focus:id:5D3747C1DEEB684B8962F4078723A65A
```

The *opaque* parameter identifies the type of the resource that has generated or owns this URI. For a conference URI, this is always the Focus component, and hence the *opaque* parameter of the URI always contains the *app:conf:focus* prefix. The conference URI also contains the organizer SIP URI and the conference ID, which together uniquely identify the conference.

The conference URI is used by the scheduling clients to construct a conference join URL. For Office Live Meeting Console–based conferences, a *meet:* URL is used. For example:

```
meet:sip:ben@litwareinc.com;gruu;opaque=app:conf:focus:id:5D3747C1DEEB684B8962F4078723A65A
```

For Office Communicator–based audio-only conferences, a *conf:* URL is used. For example:

```
conf:sip:ben@litwareinc.com;gruu;opaque=app:conf:focus:id:
a291a144d9764f38973835f816e52db1 %3Fconversation-id=b2796a94efe040cb9afadc49157557e6
```

Conference Activation

A conference is activated when the first participant successfully joins the meeting. The first user who joins the meeting can be an enterprise user, a federated user, or an anonymous user. Users are allowed to join the meeting regardless of their presenter or attendee role. A conference can be activated any time after it is created and before it is permanently deleted from the conferencing database.

The following happens when a conference is activated.

1. An instance of the meeting, called the Focus, is created on the Office Communications Server front-end server. This conference instance maintains the following instance-specific pieces of information:
   - A list of participants in the conference that includes the following:
   - Participants connected to the Focus
   - Participants connected to each conferencing server
   - State for each server
2. A SIP dialog between the client and the Focus is established. The conference event subscription/publication is established.
3. The Focus provisions a conferencing server of each required media type in the conference. This information is specified when the conference is created.
4. An addConference C3P command is sent to all provisioned conferencing servers. Each conferencing server allocates resources for the conference and becomes ready for the conference.
5. The client establishes a direct connection with each provisioned conferencing server.

Conference Deactivation

A meeting is deactivated when the Focus instance of the conference is removed from the front-end servers. A conference can be deactivated any time after it is activated in the following ways:

- The organizer or a presenter manually ends the meeting.
- All participants leave the meeting.
- Twenty-four hours (the default) pass since the last participant joined the meeting.

- Ten minutes (the default) pass without an authenticated enterprise user being in the meeting.
- An administrator disables the meeting organizer for Office Communications Server or deletes the meeting organizer's user account from Active Directory.

The following happens when a conference is deactivated.

1. The instance of the conference, the Focus, is removed. All associated instance-specific information is removed from memory and from the RTCDyn conferencing database.
2. All client-Focus dialogs are ended.
3. All conferencing servers involved in the conference receive a deleteConference C3P command from the Focus.
4. All client–conferencing server dialogs are ended. All remaining attendees are disconnected. All resources that are allocated for the conference from all conferencing servers are released.

A deactivated conference still exists in the RTC conferencing database and can be reactivated at any time until the meeting expires as described in the following section.

Conference Expiration

To save disk space and improve performance, Office Communications Server does not store conferences and their content indefinitely. When a conference is created, the conference is given an expiration time. When a conference expires, the conference data record is deleted from the back-end conferencing database and all content data associated with the meeting is deleted. After a meeting expires, no participants, including the organizer, can join the meeting.

The front-end server runs a low-priority expiration thread for the RTC database. When woken up, the thread searches for conferences that meet all of the following criteria:

- There is an expiration time associated with the conference, and the expiration time has passed; or there is no expiration time associated with the conference, and six months have passed since the last recorded conference activation.
- The conference is not currently active.

Any meetings that satisfy the preceding criteria are deleted from the RTC database.

When creating a conference on the server, it is up to the scheduling client to specify the expiration time. The expiration time is communicated to each conferencing server that is involved when the conference is activated. Here are some recommendations based on the conference type:

- For one-time scheduled conferences, set the expiration time to be the scheduled end time plus 14 days.

- For recurring scheduled conferences with an end date, set the expiration time to be the scheduled end time of the last occurrence plus 14 days.
- For recurring scheduled conferences without specified end dates, do not set an expiration time or set null as the expiration time.
- For ad hoc IM or A/V conferences, set the expiration time to be eight hours.

NOTE **If no expiration time is specified by the client, the maximum grace period (six months) allowed by the server is used as the expiration time. This maximum allowed grace period is reset whenever a conference is activated. For example, after a conference is activated and deactivated, it will expire in six months. If, after three months, the meeting is activated again then the conference will expire in another six months, not three months.**

Similarly, the Web Conferencing Server also runs a low-priority expiration thread similar to the one that runs on the front-end server. When woken up, the thread scans the conference content metadata file share and checks for the expiration time for each conference. The Web Conferencing Server adds a grace period (by default 14 days) on top of the expiration time. It deletes the content folder associated with a conference only if the conference expiration time plus the grace period has passed.

Examining the Technical Details Behind Web Conferencing

In this section, we discuss some technical details of data collaboration conferences and Web conferences. In particular, this section covers technical details of the following scenarios:

- Conferencing client joining the Focus
- Conferencing client joining the Web Conferencing Server
- Conferencing client uploading data content to the Web Conferencing Server
- Conferencing client receiving data content from the Web Conferencing Server and displaying it

The Client Conference Joining Sequence

A user can join a conference primarily in two ways:

- By clicking the Join link inside the conference invitation e-mail message or the Join link in the IM window in Office Communicator 2007 R2
- By launching Office Live Meeting Console and entering the conference join information

Figure 6-14 illustrates the client conference join process.

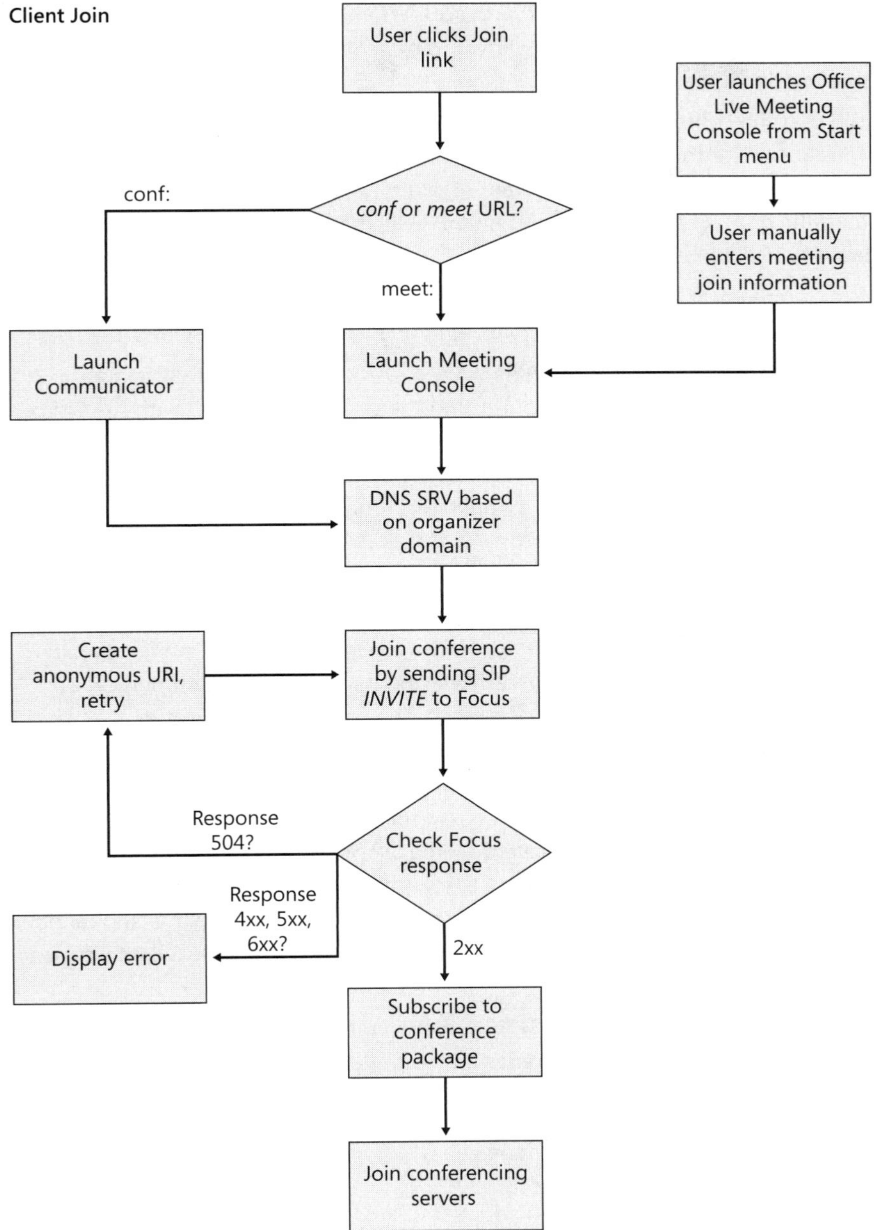

FIGURE 6-14 Client conference join sequence

Both Office Communicator 2007 R2 and Office Live Meeting Console 2007 R2 clients register an operating system protocol handler when they are installed. Office Communicator 2007 R2 registers a protocol handler for the *conf:* protocol. Office Live Meeting Console 2007

R2 registers a protocol handler for the *meet:* protocol. When users click the Join link in an invitation e-mail or in the IM conversation window, the client that will launch depends on the *conf:* or *meet:* prefix of the join URL.

The first step that the conferencing client performs after launch is to discover Office Communications Server for the user, based on the configured user SIP URI in the client. This discovery logic performs a series of Domain Name System (DNS) Service Record Locator (SRV) queries based on the domain portion of the user's SIP URI. The following four cases could result from the DNS SRV queries:

- An Office Communications Server is found, and it is the server that hosts the conference. In this case, the client sends the join SIP *INVITE* targeted at the server. The user joins as an enterprise authenticated user.
- An Office Communications Server is found, and the server is federated with the Office Communications Server that hosts the conference. In this case, the client sends the join SIP *INVITE* targeted at the Office Communications Server 2007 R2 server that hosts the conference. The user is authenticated by the Office Communications Server 2007 R2 server in her own domain, and the SIP *INVITE* is successfully routed to the Office Communications Server pool that hosts the conference. The user joins as a federated user.
- An Office Communications Server 2007 R2 server is found, and the server is federated with the Office Communications Server 2007 R2 server that hosts the conference. In this case, the client sends the join SIP *INVITE* targeted at the Office Communications Server 2007 R2 server that hosts the conference. The Office Communications Server 2007 R2 server authenticates the user in her own domain. However, the SIP *INVITE* cannot be successfully routed because there is no federated link between the user's own Office Communications Server domain and the conference organizer's Office Communications Server domain (indicated by the SIP 504 response to the SIP *INVITE*). In this case, the conferencing client will try to join the conference as an anonymous user. The conferencing client must be able to generate a sufficiently unique and random anonymous SIP URI of the form *<ID>@anonymous.invalid* when joining a conference as an anonymous participant.
- An Office Communications Server 2007 R2 server is not found. In this case, the conferencing client will try to join the conference as an anonymous user. The conferencing client must be able to generate a sufficiently unique and random anonymous SIP URI of the form *<ID>@anonymous.invalid* when joining a conference as an anonymous participant.

The SIP *INVITE* that the client sends has an addUser C3P command as the body of the SIP message. The following is an example:

```
INVITE sip:ben@litwareinc.com;gruu;opaque=app:conf:focus:id:
5D3747C1DEEB684B8962F4078723A65A SIP/2.0
From: <sip:ben@litwareinc.com>;tag=958d8a3fbc;epid=c5574cd6b6
To: <sip:ben@litwareinc.com;gruu;opaque=app:conf:focus:id:
5D3747C1DEEB684B8962F4078723A65A>
```

```
Content-Type: application/cccp+xml
Content-Length: 736

<request C3PVersion="1" to="sip:ben@litwareinc.com;gruu;opaque=app:conf:focus:id:
5D3747C1DEEB684B8962F4078723A65A" from="sip:ben@litwareinc.com" requestId="0">
<addUser> <conferenceKeys confEntity="sip:Ben@litwareinc.com;gruu;opaque=app:conf:
focus:id:
5D3747C1DEEB684B8962F4078723A65A"/>
<ci:user entity="sip:Ben@litwareinc.com">
<ci:roles>
<ci:entry>attendee</ci:entry>
</ci:roles>
<ci:endpoint entity="{339F927D-6AD4-4090-9104-8414B99EE045}" />
</ci:user> </addUser> </request>
```

The addUser request contains the conference URI and the user SIP URI, which must be the same as the SIP To and From URIs, respectively. In addition, it can contain a requested role. The endpoint entity is optional, and the Focus ignores the body of the endpoint entity and uses just the entity URI that the client supplied.

Figure 6-15 shows the server handling logic for such an SIP join *INVITE*.

When the addUser C3P command is accepted, the Focus responds with the granted role in the 200 response:

```
SIP/2.0 200 Invite dialog created
Contact: <sip:sip.litwareinc.com:5061;transport=tls>;isfocus
Content-Length: 1095
From: "Ben Miller"<sip:Ben@litwareinc.com>;tag=958d8a3fbc;epid=c5574cd6b6
To: <sip:Ben@litwareinc.com;gruu;opaque=app:conf:focus:id:
   5D3747C1DEEB684B8962F4078723A65A>;tag=CC020080
Allow: INVITE, BYE, ACK, CANCEL, INFO, UPDATE
Content-Type: application/cccp+xml

<response requestId="0" C3PVersion="1" from="sip:Ben@litwareinc.com;gruu;opaque=app:
conf:focus:id:
   5D3747C1DEEB684B8962F4078723A65A" to="sip:Ben@litwareinc.com" code="success">
<addUser> <conferenceKeys confEntity="sip:Ben@litwareinc.com;gruu;opaque=app:conf:
focus:id:
   5D3747C1DEEB684B8962F4078723A65A"/>
<ci:user entity="sip:Ben@litwareinc.com">
<ci:roles>
<ci:entry>presenter</ci:entry>
</ci:roles>
</ci:user> </addUser> </response>
```

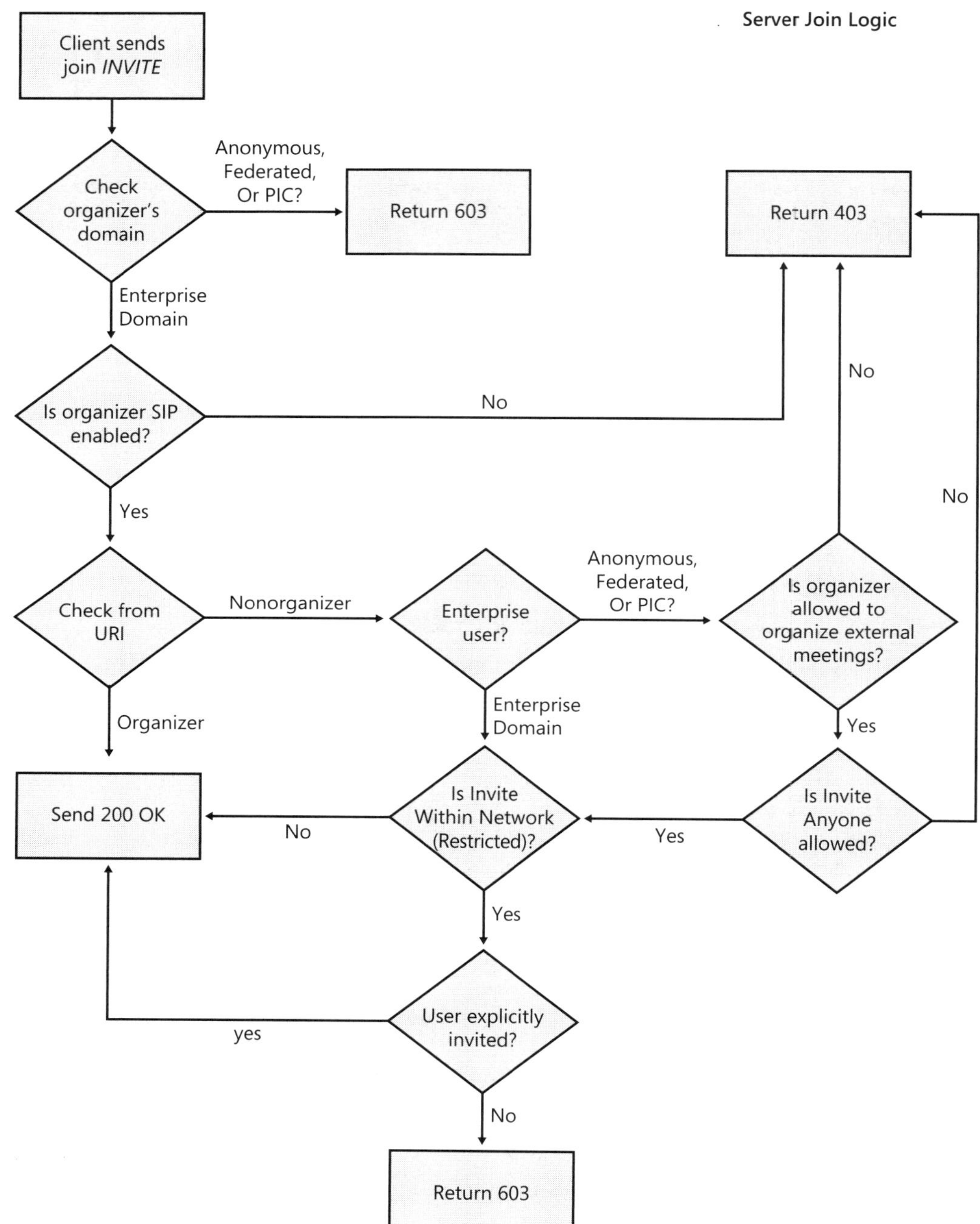

FIGURE 6-15 Client join sequence, server view

At this point, the signaling dialog is successfully established between the joining client and the Focus. The Focus then notifies existing conference participants that the user has joined the conference.

```
NOTIFY sip:157.56.67.50:2383;transport=tls;ms-opaque=02e9ae1f28;
   ms-received-cid=00031600;grid SIP/2.0
To: <sip:Ben@litwareinc.com>;tag=ccb81c3509;epid=c5574cd6b6
Content-Length: 2373
From: <sip:Ben@litwareinc.com;gruu;opaque=app:conf:focus:id:5D3747C1DEEB684B8962F40787
23A65A>;tag=183C0080
Content-Type: application/conference-info+xml
Event: conference
subscription-state: active;expires=3600

<conference-info entity="sip:Ben@litwareinc.com;gruu;opaque=app:conf:focus:id:
   5D3747C1DEEB684B8962F4078723A65A" state="partial" version="2">
<users state="partial">
<user entity="sip:Ben@litwareinc.com" state="full">
<display-text>Ben Miller</display-text>
<roles>
<entry>presenter</entry>
</roles>
<endpoint entity="{339F927D-6AD4-4090-9104-8414B99EE045}" msci:session-type="focus"
msci:endpoint-uri="sip:Ben@litwareinc.com;opaque=user:epid:AD0UTS5Dcl0h9zyK1XWK2AAA;
gruu">
<status>connected</status>
</endpoint>
```

After a SIP signaling dialog is successfully established, the conferencing client and the Focus establish a subscription dialog. The client first sends a SIP *SUBSCRIBE*:

```
SUBSCRIBE sip:Ben@litwareinc.com;gruu;opaque=app:conf:focus:id:
   5D3747C1DEEB684B8962F4078723A65A SIP/2.0
From: <sip:Ben@litwareinc.com>;tag=958d8a3fbc;epid=c5574cd6b6
To: <sip:Ben@litwareinc.com;gruu;opaque=app:conf:focus:id:5D3747C1DEEB684B8962F407872
3A65A>
Event: conference
Accept: application/conference-info+xml
Supported: com.cotoso.autoextend
Supported: ms-benotify
Proxy-Require: ms-benotify
Supported: ms-piggyback-first-notify
Content-Length: 0
```

The Focus then processes the subscription. If no corresponding active signaling dialog is found, the Focus fails the subscription. Once the subscription is accepted, the Focus responds to it and then generates a notification.

```
SIP/2.0 200 OK
Content-Length: 3611
From: "Ben Miller"<sip:Ben@litwareinc.com>;tag=0dc4a6c3d2;epid=c5574cd6b6
To: <sip:Ben@litwareinc.com;gruu;opaque=app:conf:focus:id:
   A24F0AA5223B4B478801FA8F60D2191D>;tag=31740080
Expires: 3546
Content-Type: application/conference-info+xml
Event: conference
subscription-state: active;expires=3546
ms-piggyback-cseq: 1
Supported: ms-benotify, ms-piggyback-first-notify
...
```

The subscription dialog is periodically refreshed. The lifetime of the subscription dialog is the same as the lifetime of the signaling dialog. Even though these are two independent dialogs, the Focus terminates the subscription dialog when the signaling dialog is terminated.

After both the signaling and subscription dialogs are established, the conferencing client can receive conference state change notifications, such as another user join, from the Focus. Figure 6-16 illustrates the client focus join sequence.

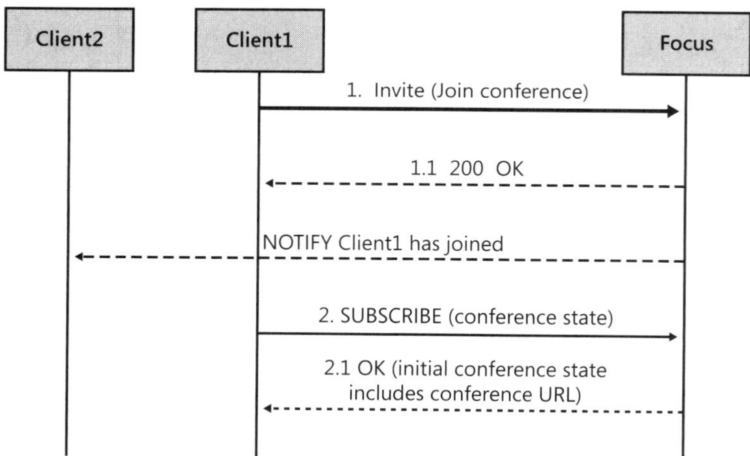

FIGURE 6-16 Focus join sequence

The Client Join Sequence to the Web Conferencing Server

Conferencing clients use the addUser C3P command to join themselves to the conferencing servers involved in the conference. The addUser command works in two modes: dial-in and dial-out. In dial-in mode, the client sends addUser to the conferencing server (with the message being proxied by the Focus) to request permission to create a session with it. In the addUser response, the conferencing server responds with connection information that the client uses to establish signaling and media sessions. In addUser dial-out mode, the client requests that the conferencing server initiate the signaling/media session establishment, and hence, the addUser command completes only after the session is established.

Conferencing clients use the addUser dial-in mode to join the Web Conferencing Server. Figure 6-17 shows the flow for a client to join the Web Conferencing Server.

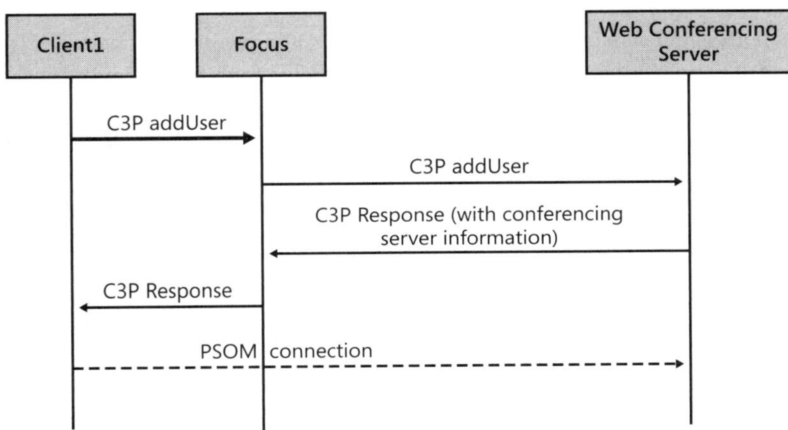

FIGURE 6-17 Web Conferencing Server join sequence

Some of the notifications that conferencing clients receive from the Focus after they join a conference are about conferencing server URIs. For example:

```
NOTIFY sip:ben@litwareinc.com SIP/2.0
...
<conference-info xmlns="urn:ietf:params:xml:ns:conference-info"
entity="sip:ben@litwareinc.com;gruu; opaque=app:conf:focus:id:
5D3747C1DEEB684B8962F4078723A65A"
       state="full" version="5" >
       <conference-description>
        <display-text>Weekly Sales Meeting</display-text>
        <subject>Agenda: This month's goals</subject>
        <conf-uris>
              <entry>
                 <uri>sip:ben@litwareinc.com;opaque=conf:meeting: id:
5D3747C1DEEB684B8962F4078723A65A</uri>
                 <display-text>meeting</display-text>
                 <purpose>meeting</purpose>
              </entry>
              <entry>
```

```
                <uri>sip:ben@litwareinc.com;opaque=conf:audio-video: id:
5D3747C1DEEB684B8962F4078723A65A</uri>
                <display-text>audio video mcu</display-text>
                <purpose>audio-video</purpose>
             </entry>
         </conf-uris>
       </conference-description>
...
</conference-info>
```

To join the Web Conferencing Server, the client then constructs an addUser C3P request and sends it to the Focus requesting to dial in to the Web Conferencing Server. The request contains a role that matches the current role of the user in the conference, specifies a joining-method value of *dialed-in*, and also supplies an endpoint that is usually a globally unique identifier (GUID) for the session. The From URI of the SIP request must match the *from* attribute of the C3P request. An *mcuUri* attribute must be present in the *addUser* element, and it specifies the MCU (conferencing server) to which this request should be routed. In the case just shown, the Web Conferencing Server URI is as follows:

```
sip:ben@litwareinc.com;opaque=conf:meeting:conf-id
```

Here is an example of this addUser C3P request:

```
INFO ConfURI
To: ConfURI
From: sip:ben@litwareinc.com;tag=f7588dc66124429ab736;epid=1
...SIP headers..

<request xmlns="urn:ietf:params:xml:ns:cccp" requestId="2"
    from="sip:ben@litwareinc.com"
    to="sip:ben@litwareinc.com;gruu; opaque=app:conf:focus:id:
5D3747C1DEEB684B8962F4078723A65A">
 <addUser mscp:mcuUri="sip:ben@litwareinc.com;opaque=conf:meeting: id:
5D3747C1DEEB684B8962F4078723A65A">
    <conferenceKeys confEntity=" sip:ben@litwareinc.com;gruu; opaque=app:conf:
focus:id:5D3747C1DEEB684B8962F4078723A65A">
    <user entity="sip:ben@litwareinc.com">
        <roles>
            <entry>presenter</entry>
            </roles>
            <!-Exactly one endpoint node may be present -->
            < endpoint entity="
               {F43E937E-6C66-4649-9481-13133FCF64FE}">
          <!-Exactly one joining-method and it must be equal
               to dialed-in -->
```

```
            <joining-method>dialed-in</joining-method>
            <!-- Optional MCU specific parameters -->
         </endpoint>
      </user>
   </addUser>
</request>
```

The Focus forwards the dial-in request to the Web Conferencing Server after stamping the request with the originator URI and proper authorization. If the Web Conferencing Server decides to accept the C3P request, it should construct a standard addUser response and return it to the Focus, which will then proxy the response to the client.

All conferencing servers must supply contact information that the client can use to connect. For conferencing servers that use SIP as a signaling protocol (such as the A/V Conferencing Server), this takes the form of supplying a SIP Contact URI and SIP To URI. The SIP To URI must always be equal to the *mcuUri* supplied in the addUser call. The SIP Contact URI refers to the Conferencing Server URI (a listening address/port/transport on which the conferencing server is listening and can receive SIP requests). For a Web Conferencing Server that uses PSOM instead of SIP, this takes the form of supplying a suitable URL that the client understands.

Some conferencing servers might supply an authorization token or some other parameter to the client. The semantics of such parameters are a contract between the conferencing server and the client. The following is a sample response to the addUser request to join a Web Conferencing Server:

```
From: < sip:ben@litwareinc.com;gruu; opaque=app:conf:focus:id:5D3747C1DEEB684B8962F40
78723A65A>;
   tag=052B0080
To: <ben:ben@litwareinc.com>;tag=d1991b44ef;epid=10caaf88e2
...
<response from=" sip:ben@litwareinc.com;gruu; opaque=app:conf:focus:id:5D3747C1DEEB684
B8962F4078723A65A" to="sip:ben@litwareinc.com" responder=" sip:ben@litwareinc.com;
   opaque=conf:meeting: id:5D3747C1DEEB684B8962F4078723A65A"
   code="success">
<addUser><conferenceKeys confEntity=" ben@litwareinc.com;gruu; opaque=app:conf:focus:
id:5D3747C1DEEB684B8962F4078723A65A"/>
<user xmlns="urn:ietf:params:xml:ns:conference-info" entity="sip:ben@litwareinc.
com"><display-text>Hao Yan</display-text><roles><entry>presenter</entry>
</roles><endpoint entity="{1D3F15F1-68CA-4EF0-9805-704EB5795F60}">
<joining-method>dialed-in</joining-method><media id="1"><type>meeting
</type><label>meeting</label></media><authMethod xmlns="http://schemas.microsoft.com/
rtc/2005/08/confinfoextensions">
   enterprise</authMethod><accessMethod xmlns="http://schemas.microsoft.com/
rtc/2005/08/confinfoextensions">
```

```
   internal</accessMethod>
</endpoint></user><info xmlns="http://schemas.microsoft.com/rtc/2005/08/
cccpextensions"><contact>pod/ben/check/check1.html</contact></info>
<connection-info xmlns="http://schemas.microsoft.com/rtc/2005/08/cccpextensions">
<entry><key>serverURL</key><value>https://conference.litwareinc.com/etc/place/null
</value></entry><entry><key>pw.eName</key><value>sip:ben@litwareinc.com;gruu;
opaque=app:conf:focus:id:5D3747C1DEEB684B8962F4078723A65A </value>
</entry><entry><key>PodName</key><value> ben@litwareinc.com;gruu; opaque=app:conf:
focus:id:5D3747C1DEEB684B8962F4078723A65A</value></entry><entry><key>pwuid
</key><value>sip:ben@litwareinc.com</value></entry><entry><key>sAuthId</key>
<value>71C000000000000001A36B1629961D219</value></entry><entry><key>pwrpc.modes
</key><value>tls</value></entry><entry><key>pwrpc.port</key><value>8057</value>
</entry><entry><key>pwrpc.authPattern</key><value>&lt;sAuthId&gt;</value>
</entry><entry><key>pw.rtcp.enabled</key><value>false</value>
</entry><entry><key>pwrpc.tcpEnableSig</key><value>false</value>
</entry><entry><key>locale</key><value>en_US</value></entry><entry><key>directURL
</key><value>https://conference.litwareinc.com:8057</value></entry><entry>
<key>pwrpc.pwsURI</key><value>https://conference.litwareinc.com:8057</value>
</entry><entry><key>uType</key><value>pre</value></entry><entry>
<key>alternativeName</key><value>conference.litwareinc.com</value></entry>
</connection-info></addUser></response>
```


The information included in the C3P response includes the following:

- The FQDN or IP address of the Web Conferencing Server and port number.
- The URL for HTTPs content download.
- Access information (FQDN and port) for zero, one, or more Web Conferencing Edge Servers if the client connects from outside of the corporate firewall.
- An authorization cookie for the Web Conferencing Edge Server if the client connects from outside of the corporate firewall. The cookie is base64 encoded. The client needs to present this cookie when establishing a connection with the Web Conferencing Edge Server.
- An authorization cookie for the Web Conferencing Server. This cookie is also encoded in base64. The client needs to present this cookie when establishing a connection with the Web Conferencing Server.
- A unique identifier for the meeting (for example, the Conference URI). This is necessary for the client to identify which conference it is joining when making a connection to the Web Conferencing Server.

Conference Control

Once a signaling dialog is established with the Focus, clients can send conference control CP commands on the dialog. In general, conference control commands can be classified into three categories:

- Commands that terminate on the Focus and do not involve MCU interaction (for example, renameUser)
- Commands that are authorized by the Focus but are simply proxied to MCU, so no Focus state is modified unless the MCU generates a notification (for example, modify-EndpointMedia)
- Commands that are processed by the Focus as well as by MCUs (for example, delete-Conference and modifyConferenceLock)

A typical conference control command operates as follows:

1. The client sends a SIP *INFO* request to the Focus, with the body containing a C3P command.
2. The Focus validates and authorizes the C3P request.
3. The Focus operates on the C3P request and generates one or more SIP responses back to the client, containing a C3P pending or a final response.
4. The Focus might proxy or fork the request to one or more conferencing servers as necessary. Responses from the conferencing servers are proxied back to the client except in the forking-command case, where they are consumed by the Focus.
5. All entities maintain C3P transaction timers to control the lifetime of the request.

When the Focus accepts the command from the sender, it usually generates a C3P request to the conferencing servers in the conference and also responds with a SIP 202 Accepted message to the *INFO* request. When the C3P result is available, the Focus generates another *INFO* request and sends it to the client. The C3P request might succeed or fail or might succeed/fail after an interim response has been generated. Moreover, a successful C3P request is usually followed by the conferencing servers sending a C3P notification containing the updated conference state. On receipt of this notification, the Focus updates the conference state and generates a notification to all clients.

Figure 6-18 shows the call flow of the C3P modifyConferenceLock command. This command is issued when a presenter in the conference tries to lock or unlock a conference in the client. In this case, the command is forked by the Focus and sent to both the A/V Conferencing Server and the Web Conferencing Server.

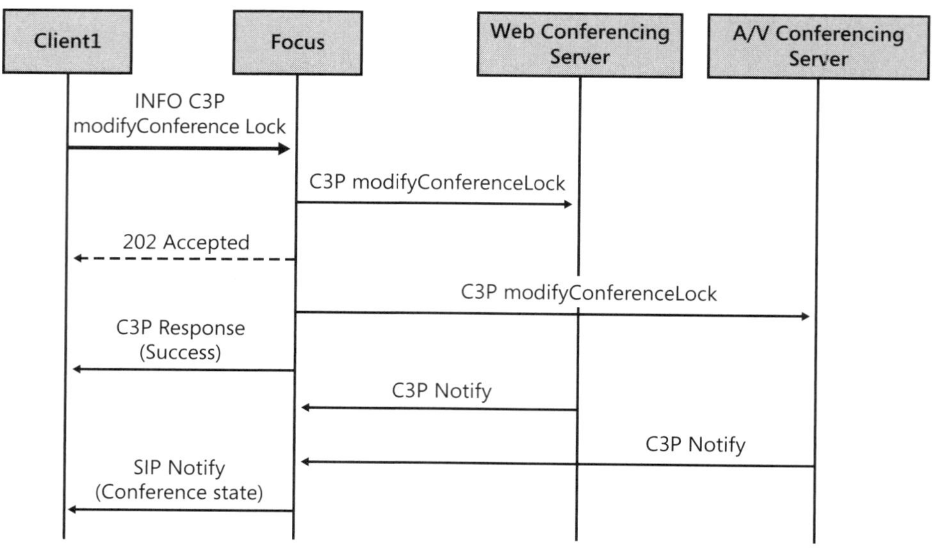

FIGURE 6-18 Web Conferencing Server join sequence

Web Conferencing Server Content Management

In Office Communications Server 2007 R2, the Web Conferencing Server stores in-conference data contents and its state information in files. For each Office Communications Server pool, two file shares are configured:

- Metadata file share, used for storing conference state information and metadata that describes data content.
- Content file share, used for storing user uploaded data content, such as a PowerPoint file. The uploaded contents are encrypted when stored into the content file share.

All Web Conferencing Servers in the pool use these file shares. The file shares are identified using Universal Naming Convention (UNC) paths. They can reside on the same machine as the Web Conferencing Server (as is the case for Office Communications Server 2007 R2 Standard Edition) or on different (dedicated) file servers (as is recommended for Office Communications Server 2007 R2 Enterprise Edition).

The file shares are access controlled so that no conferencing client has direct access to them. The metadata share is for Web Conferencing Server internal use only. The Web Conferencing Server needs to have both read and write privileges to the share. The content file share, on the other hand, can be accessed by the conferencing client indirectly via IIS. An IIS virtual directory is created and linked to the content file share when the Office Communications Server Web Component is installed so that the client can access the files in the content file share via HTTPs. The Web Conferencing Server requires write privileges to the content file share, whereas IIS requires only read rights to the share.

Figure 6-19 shows the Web Conferencing Server that manages the two file shares.

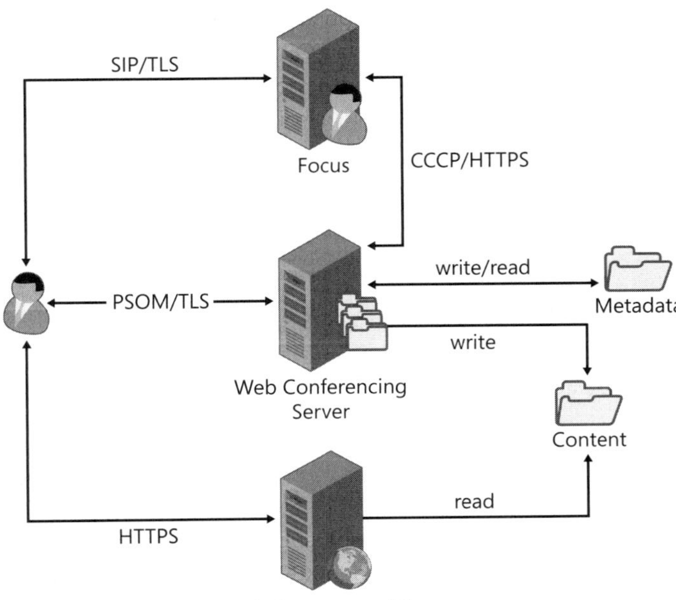

FIGURE 6-19 Web Conferencing Server content management

When the Web Conferencing Server starts a conference—that is, when it receives an addConference command from the Focus—a metadata folder is created for the particular conference under the folder specified by the metadata file share UNC. The metadata file share is structured in the following ways:

- For each organizer, the Web Conferencing Server creates a separate folder under the metadata root folder. The organizer folder name is a computed hash value from the organizer SIP URI.
- For each conference, the Web Conferencing Server creates a separate folder under the organizer subfolder. The conference folder name is the same as the conference ID.
- Metadata files for a conference are stored under the conference folder. All files except the conference.xml file under the conference folder are encrypted. The conference.xml file contains a randomly generated encryption key for the conference. The key is used to encrypt all other metadata files in the conference. Because sensitive information such as the encryption key is stored in this folder, the administrator should give read and write permissions to this folder just to the users group that runs the Web Conferencing Server.

Figure 6-20 shows the metadata folder structure.

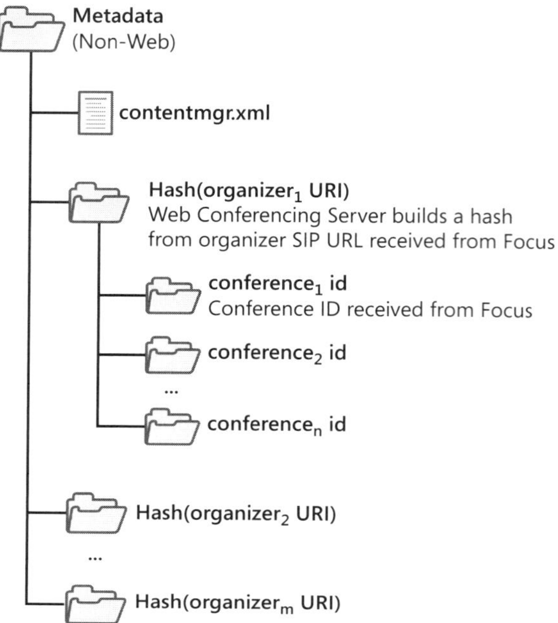

FIGURE 6-20 Metadata folder structure

> ***NOTE*** **The contentmgr.xml file is used to coordinate content expiration processes running in multiple Web Conferencing Servers. The expiration process uses a lock/unlock mechanism to ensure that only one server can delete a specific conference folder at any given time.**

The content file share is structured the same way as the metadata file share. Figure 6-21 shows the content folder structure.

This Slide Files folder contains all the user uploaded slide content shared over HTTPS. All files are encrypted using Advanced Encryption Standard (AES) and a randomly generated key (one for each content file). The key is stored in a corresponding metadata file in the corresponding metadata folder. The names of the files are randomly generated to hide the original file name. The generated file name, along with the original file name, are both stored in the corresponding metadata file. The ft folder stores all the handouts—the files that are natively transferred without any conversion—in encrypted form.

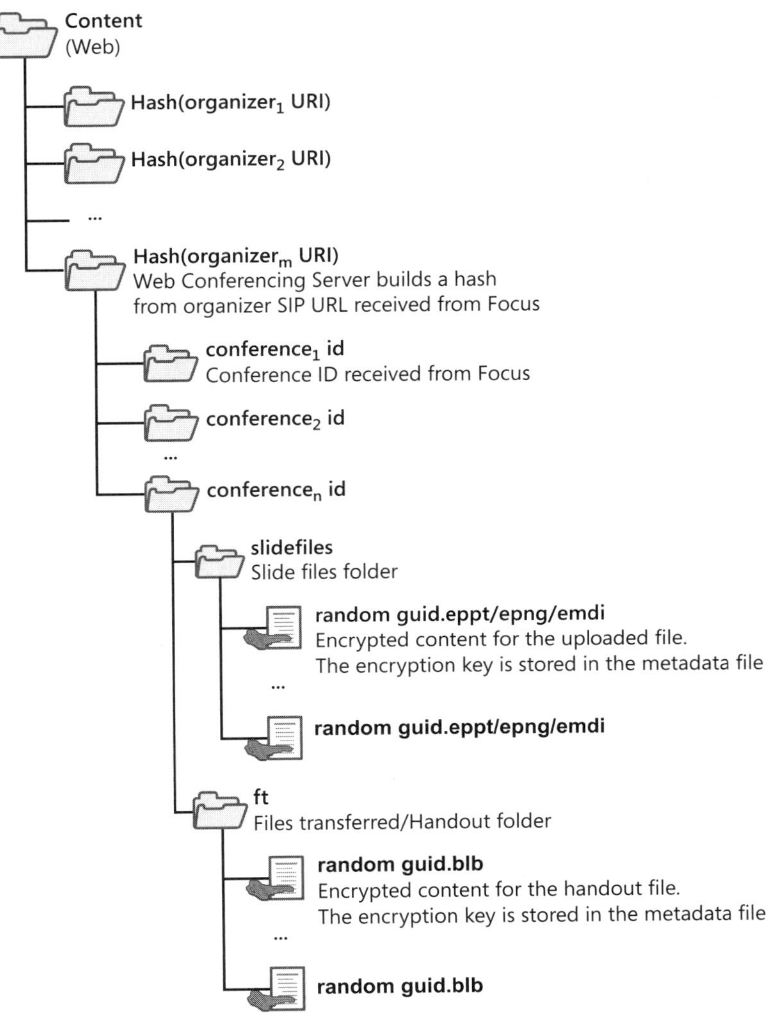

FIGURE 6-21 Content folder structure

Web Conferencing Server Content Upload and Download

There are two types of data content in a Web conference: user uploaded and user generated. User uploaded content is content that has an origin (either a file or a picture) on the client side and that is uploaded to the Web Conferencing Server by using the PSOM protocol. User uploaded content includes PowerPoint presentation files, MODI documents, handouts, and snapshot slides. User generated content is content that does not come from an original file but instead is created in the conference. This content includes annotations, Poll content, question-and-answer content, shared notes, text slides, Web slides, and so on.

The upload process is the same for both types of contents. The download process differs, however. The IIS hosts the uploaded content; the Web Conferencing Server sends a URL to the content and an encryption key to clients so that clients can download and decrypt the content. The generated content is downloaded over PSOM.

Figure 6-22 illustrates the flow for uploading and downloading generated content.

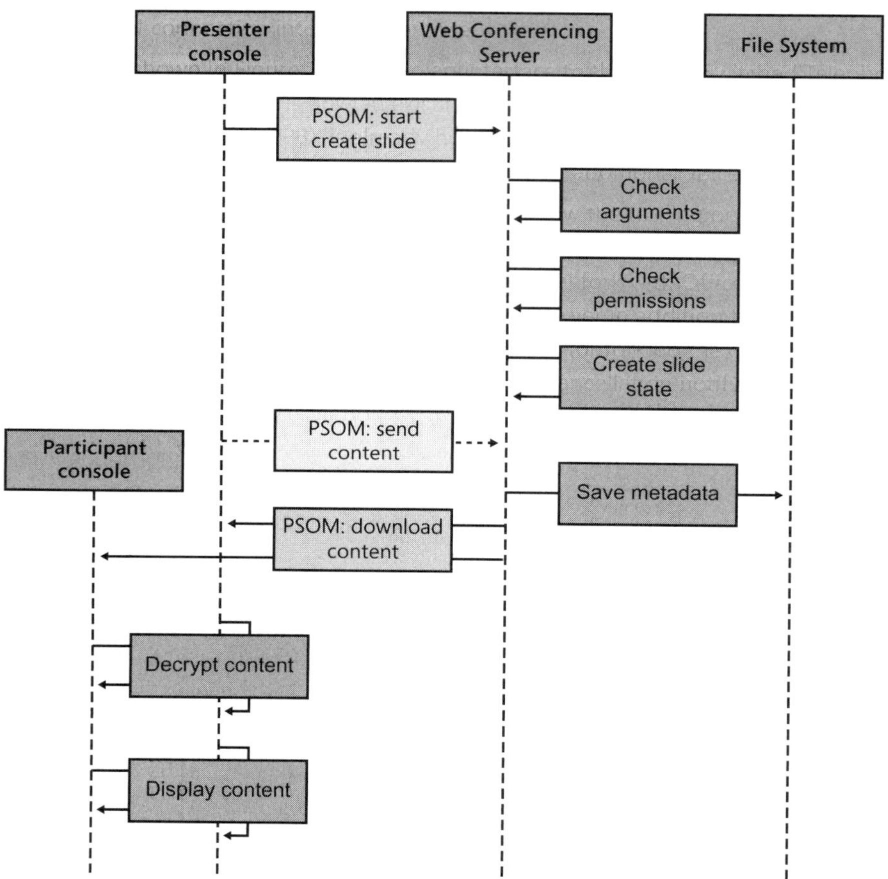

FIGURE 6-22 Upload and download of generated content

The following happens in sequence in the flow shown in Figure 6-22.

1. Over PSOM, the user creates a slide and its content.
2. The Web Conferencing Server checks the permission for the user (that is, whether the user is allowed to create that particular type of content).
3. The Web Conferencing Server creates the state for the new slide and saves the state on the file system (in the metadata folder for the conference) in encrypted format.
4. The Web Conferencing Server shares back to all clients in the conference the new slide state.

For all generated content except for Poll slides, the content is sent with the first PSOM message that creates the slide. For Poll slides, the content (questions and choices) is sent in a new PSOM message after the initial Create Slide message has been sent. The generated content is saved in the metadata folder as encrypted XML files only. It is not saved in the Content folder of the conference. Following is sample XML metadata for Poll slides (before encryption):

```
<?xml version="1.0" encoding="UTF-8"?>
<POLL>
   <POLLENTITY ID="0AA61051-12BC-A1FF-A98F-A240BCB8ABDB"
         TYPE="QUESTION" TIMESTAMP="5/21/2007 11:39 AM">
   <POLLUSER VALUE="sip:ben@litwareinc.com"/>
   <POLLCHOICE VALUE="MON"/>
   <POLLCHOICE VALUE="TUE"/>
   <POLLCHOICE VALUE="WED"/>
   <POLLCHOICE VALUE="THU"/>
   <POLLCHOICE VALUE="FRI"/>
   <POLLCHOICE VALUE="SAT"/>
   <POLLCHOICE VALUE="SUN"/>
   </POLLENTITY>
</POLL>
```

Figure 6-23 illustrates the flow for uploading and downloading uploaded content.

The following happens in sequence in Figure 6-23.

1. The user starts uploading existing content. A PSOM message is sent from the user's client to the Web Conferencing Server.
2. The Web Conferencing Server checks the permission for the user (that is, whether the user is allowed to create that particular type of content).
3. The user's client prepares the content for upload. The kind of preparation depends on the type of content being uploaded:
   - For PowerPoint presentation files, the client converts each slide into a picture PNG file and then packages and compresses both the original PPT(x) file and all the PNG files into one LMP file.
   - For Microsoft Office files, the client converts the files into MODI files and then converts each page of the MODI files into a picture PNG file. The client then packages and compresses both the MODI MDI file and all the PNG files into one LMP file.
   - For handouts, the client just compresses and packages the file into one LMP file.

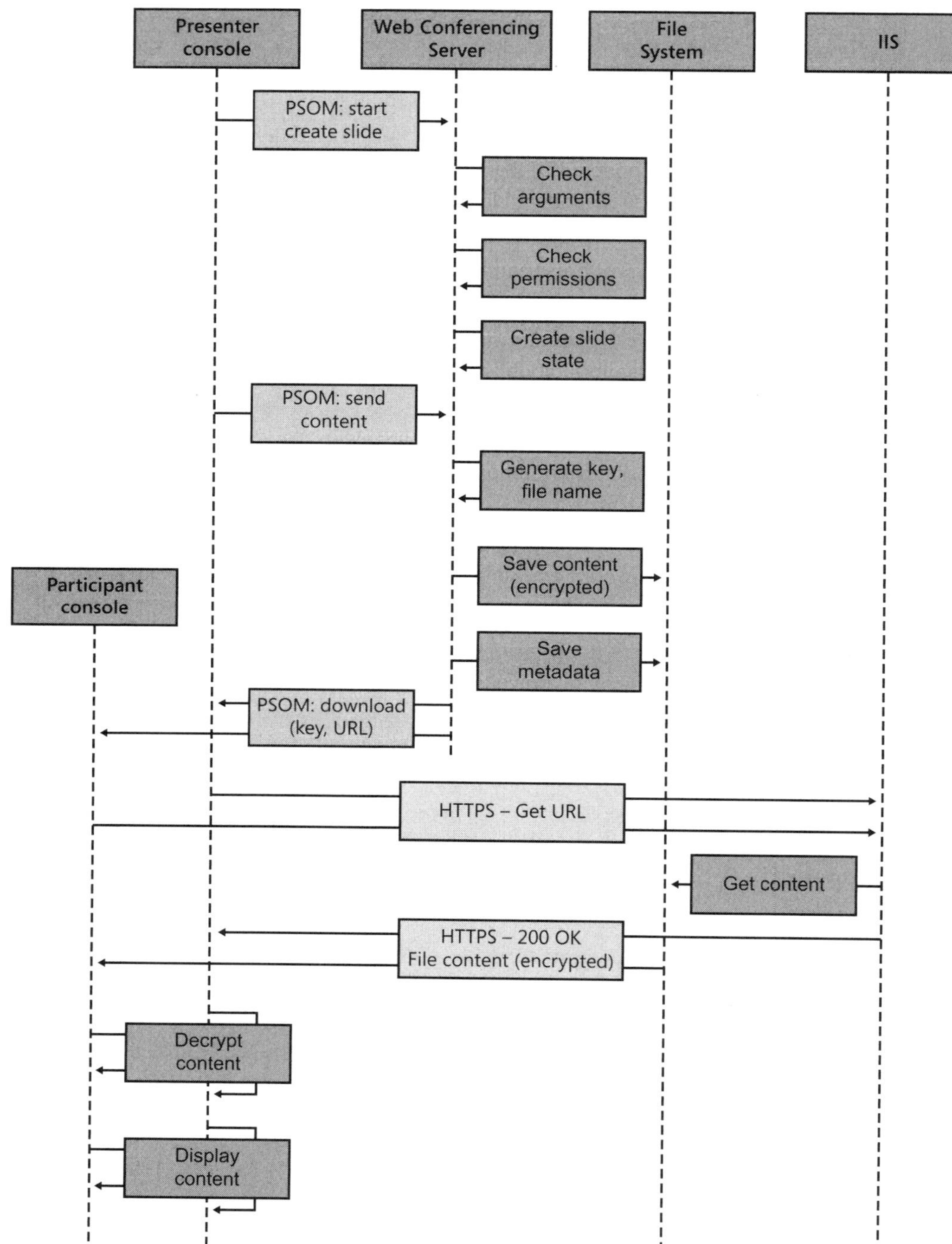

FIGURE 6-23 Upload and download of uploaded content

4. The client starts sending the LMP file over a stream to the Web Conferencing Server.
   - The Web Conferencing Server unpacks the LMP file. For each file that is unpacked, the Web Conferencing Server generates an encryption key and uses it to encrypt the file. The encrypted content file is saved in the content file folder for the conference. The encryption key and metadata information, such as the user SIP URI, are saved in an encrypted metadata XML file under the metadata folder for the conference.
   - The Web Conferencing Server computes the URLs from which the saved encrypted contents can be accessed via HTTPS. This is possible because the Web Component sets up a virtual directory that points to the same content file share that the Web Conferencing Server writes to.
   - The Web Conferencing Server sends back to the clients, via PSOM, the URL and the encryption key for the content files.
   - Each client participating in the conference uses the URL to download the encrypted content from IIS.
   - Using the encryption key, each client decrypts the content and displays it.

Meeting Compliance

Compliance with regulatory requirements was the motivation for adding IM archiving capabilities to Live Communications Server. Those same requirements apply to certain aspects of an Office Communications Server conference as well. When combined, two features in Office Communications Server provide compliance for on-premise conferencing.

First, the CDR feature records meeting participation information, including the following:

- The actual start and end time of the Live Server meeting
- The list of participants who attended the meeting

Second, the Meeting Compliance feature running on the Web Conferencing Server, if enabled, records content activities, including:

- A log of any content upload activity, including who uploaded content into the conference and at what time
- The original uploaded content, whether or not it was subsequently deleted and prior to annotation
- Any annotation on any content, or any whiteboard content
- A log of any questions and answers
- A log of any polling activity
- A log of any chat activity
- A log of any native file transfer upload activity

The logs of activities are stored in XML files, and the uploaded contents are saved in the content's original format. Those compliance XML logs and content files are stored in a configurable file share identified by a UNC path. Unlike the metadata and content file shares, the compliance file share stores compliance logs and contents unencrypted. Administrators must be careful when granting permissions to this file share. The Web Conferencing Server needs write permissions, and only authorized users should have read or write permissions.

Figure 6-24 shows the folder structure for the meeting compliance file share. The folder structure is similar to that of the metadata and content file shares. Under each conference ID folder, the content folder stores all content upload activities for uploaded contents, with the original uploaded files going to the content-upload directory. The Chat, Poll, and QnA folders store XML logs for Chat, Poll, and Q&A activities, respectively.

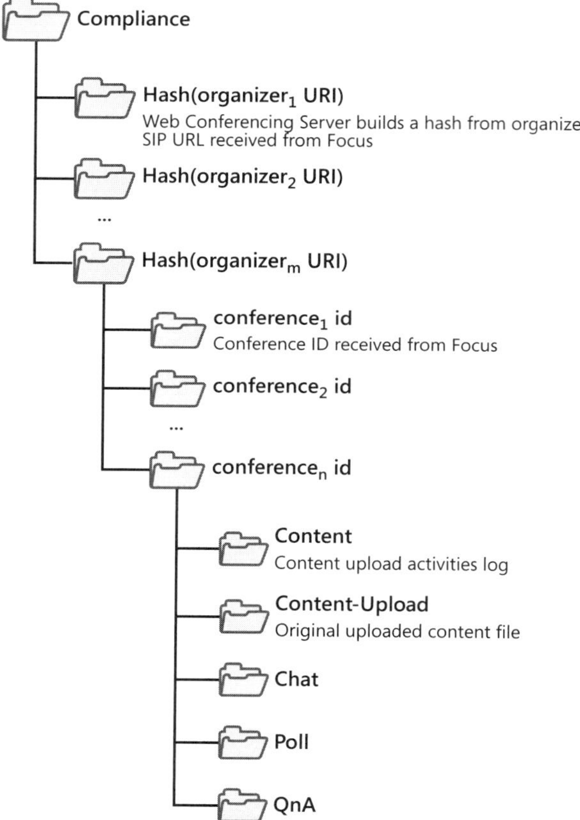

FIGURE 6-24 Compliance file share folder structure

The following is a sample XML log file for a poll that takes place in a meeting:


```
<?xml version="1.0" encoding="UTF-8"?>
<POLLLOG>
  <POLLENTITY ID="0AA61051-12BC-A1FF-A98F-A240BCB8ABDB"
         TYPE="QUESTION" TIMESTAMP="5/21/2007 11:39 AM">
    <POLLUSER VALUE="sip:ben@litwareinc.com [Ben]" />
    <POLLQUESTION VALUE="What day is today?" />
    <POLLCHOICE VALUE="MON" />
    <POLLCHOICE VALUE="TUE" />
    <POLLCHOICE VALUE="WED" />
    <POLLCHOICE VALUE="THU" />
    <POLLCHOICE VALUE="FRI" />
    <POLLCHOICE VALUE="SAT" />
    <POLLCHOICE VALUE="SUN" />
  </POLLENTITY>
  <POLLENTITY ID="0AA61051-12BC-A1FF-A98F-A240BCB8ABDB"
         TYPE="CHOICE" TIMESTAMP="5/21/2007 11:39 AM">
    <POLLUSER VALUE="sip:ben@litwareinc.com [Ben]" />
    <POLLSEQ VALUE="1" />
    <POLLCHOICE VALUE="1" />
  </POLLENTITY>
  <POLLENTITY ID="0AA61051-12BC-A1FF-A98F-A240BCB8ABDB"
         TYPE="CHOICE" TIMESTAMP="5/21/2007 11:39 AM">
    <POLLUSER VALUE="sip:john@litwareinc.com [John]" />
    <POLLSEQ VALUE="2" />
    <POLLCHOICE VALUE="0" />
  </POLLENTITY>
  <POLLENTITY ID="0AA61051-12BC-A1FF-A98F-A240BCB8ABDB"
         TYPE="CHOICE" TIMESTAMP="5/21/2007 11:39 AM">
    <POLLUSER VALUE="sip:ben@litwareinc.com [Ben]" />
    <POLLSEQ VALUE="3" />
    <POLLCHOICE VALUE="0" />
  </POLLENTITY>
  <POLLENTITY ID="0AA61051-12BC-A1FF-A98F-A240BCB8ABDB"
         TYPE="CHOICE" TIMESTAMP="5/21/2007 11:39 AM">
    <POLLUSER VALUE="sip:john@litwareinc.com [John]" />
    <POLLSEQ VALUE="4" />
    <POLLCHOICE VALUE="-1" />
  </POLLENTITY>
  <POLLENTITY ID="0AA61051-12BC-A1FF-A98F-A240BCB8ABDB"
         TYPE="CHOICE" TIMESTAMP="5/21/2007 11:39 AM">
    <POLLUSER VALUE="sip:john@litwareinc.com [John]" />
    <POLLSEQ VALUE="5" />
    <POLLCHOICE VALUE="0" />
  </POLLENTITY>
```

The administrator can enable and disable the Meeting Compliance feature on each Office Communications Server pool. The administrator can also set the compliance logging to operate in a *critical* mode. In this mode, new conferences are blocked from starting. Existing conferences are immediately terminated if at any point in time the Web Conferencing Server must access the compliance file share for any reason.

Web Conferencing Content Tools

The Web Conferencing Server organizes the three content-related file shares for fast, efficient storage and retrieval of content. In addition, metadata and the contents of the content file share are stored using strong encryption. These two factors make it difficult for administrators to examine or move the content of a particular conference.

The Resource Kit for Office Communications Server 2007 R2 provides three tools that help administrators manage the content in the file shares. For more information about installing and using these tools, see the Resource Kit Tools documentation.

DMINSIDER.EXE

For security reasons, a Web Conferencing Server saves conference contents in encrypted format in the content file share. Therefore, even if the user has access to the content file share, the administrator cannot view the actual content. The DMInsider.exe tool helps Office Communications Server 2007 R2 administrators find and view conference content managed by the Web Conferencing Server. The tool provides the following main functionalities:

- Ability to list and view content by organizers and by conferences. The content is rendered in the same way as it is rendered in the Office Live Meeting Console.
- Ability to list and view XML-based conference compliances logs. The tool can render the compliance content in the same way as it is rendered in the Office Live Meeting Console.
- Ability to view statistics about the content file share. The statistics information includes the number of organizers, the number of conferences hosted on a particular file share, and so on.

DMHASH.EXE

The Web Conferencing Server stores the content of conferences by organizers. The content of all conferences organized by one user is stored in the same directory. The directory name is a hash string that is computed based on the organizer's SIP URI. This makes it difficult for administrators to locate the conference content folders for a particular organizer.

The DMHash.exe tool helps an Office Communications Server 2007 R2 administrator generate the hash value for a user URI. The hash value is used to create content folders for each organizer. It is useful for administrators to move a user's conference content when the user's SIP URI is changed.

DMDEL.EXE

The DMDel.exe tool helps an Office Communications Server 2007 R2 administrator find conference content that is older than a specified date and then delete that content.

The Web Conferencing Server, by default, deletes conference content that has not been activated for roughly 28 days. This tool enables administrators to manually delete inactive conference content on their own time.

Meeting Policy and Policy Enforcement

Conference features, except for anonymous participation, are grouped and managed using Meeting policies. You control which features a conference organizer can use during a conference by configuring and applying specific policies. The conference organizer's Meeting policy controls the conference and applies to all Meeting participants. The Meeting policy of other participants does not affect what the participants can or cannot do in the conference. For example, Ben is configured with a Meeting policy that has IP audio enabled and John is configured with a default Meeting policy that has IP audio disabled. As an attendee of Ben's Meeting, John can use IP audio because the Meeting uses Ben's Meeting policy. However, when John organizes a conference, none of the participants in the conference can use IP audio because John's Meeting policy applies in that case.

By default, Office Communications Server 2007 R2 has five Meeting policy definitions. All Meeting policies include the same features, but any or all of the features can be configured differently for each Meeting policy. Administrators can assign Meeting policy globally—that is, assign one Meeting policy for all users hosted on all pools in the same Active Directory forest. Administrators can also assign Meeting policy on a per-user basis. In the case of assigning Meeting policy on a per-user basis, administrators select a Meeting policy for each user as part of the user options. The list below shows the policy settings that you configure for each policy to manage features.

Conference Access Type Settings

- **Policy Name** A name that you specify. We recommend that the name describe the purpose of the policy. The name cannot exceed 256 Unicode characters
- **Maximum Meeting Size** The maximum number of participants that an organizer's meeting can admit. An organization can invite more participants than the maximum meeting size, but once attendance reaches the maximum meeting size, no one else can join the meeting. The maximum number is 1,000.
- **Enable Web Conferencing** Enables Web conferencing for users of the policy. If you select this option, you also need to configure the following options:
  - Whether to use native format for PowerPoint presentation graphics program files
  - Support for program and desktop sharing
  - Support for recording meetings

  These options are covered in detail later in this list.

- **Use Native Format For PowerPoint Files** When a user uploads PowerPoint content, it is converted to PNG files that the server renders. PNG files are similar to screen shots.

  If this option is enabled in a policy (the default), when a presenter makes a slide deck active, each attendee's Live Meeting 2007 client automatically downloads the PowerPoint presentation in its native format (PPT file) as well as the converted PNG files. The PowerPoint data is available only for the duration of the meeting.

  Conversely, if the policy does not enable this option, when a presenter makes a slide deck active, each Live Meeting 2007 client automatically downloads only the converted PNG files. If you do not use native PowerPoint format, the original source is unavailable and cannot be changed. Attendees also cannot see any active content or animation. Preventing native format increases security because the original source is unavailable and cannot be modified.

  This option is generally not selected if there are concerns about the bandwidth required to download slides in native mode or if original files should not be shared with participants. If this option is not selected, PowerPoint slides are downloaded as *.png images, which are equivalent to screen shots.

- **Enable Program And Desktop Sharing** This setting enables presenters in a meeting to share applications or an entire desktop with other participants.

  If it is selected in a Meeting policy, the presenter can allow all participants with Active Directory accounts to take control of the organizer's desktop or a program that is running on the desktop.

  You can specify the range of colors (color depth) used to display slides and other meeting content, as follows:

  - Gray scale (16 shades)
  - Gray scale (256 shades)
  - 256 colors
  - High color (16 bit)
  - True color (24 bit)

  The default color depth for displaying slides and other meeting content in the Default Policy and Policy 5 (Low) Meeting policies is High Color (16 Bit). For Office Communications Server 2007 R2 and earlier versions, the default for these two meeting profiles is 256 Colors. If you install Office Communications Server 2007 R2 in an environment in which a pre-release version of Office Communications Server 2007 R2 was installed, the default will continue to be 256 Colors for all servers in the environment. You should change the setting for these two policies on all servers in your environment to either True Color (24 Bit), which is recommended for the best meeting experience, or High Color (16 Bit). Original documents are not affected by the color definition settings when viewed outside of a meeting.

- **Allow Presenter To Record Meetings** This setting enables internal presenters to record meetings and to make them available for consumption later by others using the LiveMeeting console.
- **Presenter Can Allow Attendees To Record Meetings** If you select the Allow Presenter To Record Meetings option, you can also allow the presenter to allow attendees to record meetings. The option gives the attendee the ability to have the presentation available immediately.
- **Enable IP Audio** This setting enables audio conferencing (Enterprise Voice) over TCP. This option controls whether a streaming of audio over the Internet connection is allowed in meetings organized by users who have been assigned this meeting policy. This option is generally not selected if there are concerns about the bandwidth required for IP audio.

  Enabling IP audio for meetings requires deployment of the appropriate audio hardware, including headsets, microphones, or speakers.

  Enabling IP audio can negatively impact performance and the Office Communications Server infrastructure because of the additional server resources that are required to process and send IP audio
- **Enable IP Video** If you select the Enable IP Audio option, you can also enable support for IP video.

  This option controls whether a streaming of video over the Internet connection is allowed in meetings organized by users in this forest who have been assigned this Meeting policy. This option is generally not selected if there are concerns about the bandwidth required for video.

  Enabling IP video for meetings requires deployment of the appropriate video hardware, including webcams or Microsoft Office RoundTable.

  Enabling IP video can negatively impact performance and the Office Communications Server infrastructure because of the additional server resources that are needed to produce and output the video stream.

Whether a user can invite anonymous users into her conferences is configured outside of the Meeting policy. This is because in an enterprise, only a small percentage of users (such as people in the sales department) need to invite external partners or customers into their conferences. Enabling anonymous conferences separately from the Meeting policy enables customers to specify a global Meeting policy for all users in the enterprise, but it gives only selected users the privilege to invite anonymous users. The following configuration options are available for anonymous participation:

- Give permission at the global level to invite anonymous participants to meetings, in which case all users in an Active Directory forest can invite anonymous participants to meetings.

- Deny permission to all users at the global level, in which case no users in the forest can invite anonymous participants to meetings.
- Enforce a Meeting policy per user, in which case only individual user accounts configured to allow anonymous participation can invite anonymous participants.

Summary

This chapter introduced basic concepts and scenarios for Microsoft Office Communications Server on-premise conferences. It also described the architecture that supports those conferencing scenarios. The technical details behind Web conferencing show you the life cycle of a typical conference and also explain the client joining process and content management by the Web Conferencing Server. Such technical understanding is essential for administrators who need to implement, configure, and troubleshoot on-premise conferencing in Office Communications Server.

Additional Resources

The following three Web conferencing content tools mentioned in this chapter are included as part of the Office Communications Server 2007 R2 Resource Kit Tools:

- DMInsider.exe
- DMHash.exe
- DMDel.exe

You can install the Office Communications Server 2007 R2 Resource Kit Tools from the Office Communications Server 2007 Resource Kit Tools folder on the companion media.

CHAPTER 7

Remote Access and Federation Scenarios

This chapter describes remote access and federation for common scenarios in Microsoft Office Communications Server 2007 R2. This chapter does not cover all of the possible scenarios or configurations; it covers the configurations that are most widely deployed.

Basic remote access topologies are identified, and then each of the primary and extended remote access scenarios is explained. An overview of each remote access scenario is shown from the user's perspective, and then the technical details that make the scenario possible are presented.

If your organization has remote users, remote access enables them to have the same technologies that they would if they were inside your enterprise. Because the workplace is always changing and more users are located where they can work most effectively, IT professionals can no longer assume that users will be at a desk at the office logged into a machine that is safely inside the corporate firewall. Remote access enables users to use the familiar Microsoft Office Communicator 2007 R2 or Microsoft Office Live Meeting 2007 R2 tools and collaborate with their team members wherever they are located. Whether the user is at home, at the coffee shop down the street, or at a remote location in another country, the experience and the tools should be the same.

Federation enables users in partnering businesses to collaborate and communicate in real time to provide better and faster service to customers. For example, federation enables users in Litware, Inc. to add contacts for their colleagues at Fabrikam. This allows for real-time collaboration through instant messaging (IM) and other communication tools. Similar to remote access, use of the familiar Office Communicator 2007 R2 and Office Live Meeting 2007 R2 provides for a rich toolset and easy access to information workers. This chapter also discusses the roles that the Edge Servers play in remote access and federation.

> ***NOTE*** **The collocation of server roles has changed since Microsoft Office Communications Server 2007. What is presented in this chapter is the supported server role collocation strategy. As of this writing, no supported scenario allows for the Access Edge, Web Conferencing Edge, or Audio/Video Edge Servers to exist as standalone components or in load-balanced arrays. Also, note that it is now supported to locate Access Edge Servers in any or all locations and not just in the primary data center, which is the only possible location in Office Communications Server 2007.**

Considerations for enterprises that have multiple locations are also discussed. The following list contains the three main server roles, which have been discussed in earlier chapters, as well as some special roles that are involved in remote access and federation.

- **Access Edge Server role** Handles Session Initiation Protocol (SIP) for signaling purposes and is the basis of instant messaging (IM)
  - Uses Office Communicator to log on to the enterprise network
  - Requires that the enterprise deploys the Access Edge Server role
- **Web Conferencing Edge Server role** Provides services that are necessary for Live Meeting conferences
  - Uses the Live Meeting 2007 R2 client remotely to connect to a data conference
  - Requires that the Access Edge Server role and Web Conferencing Edge Server role are deployed by the enterprise
- **Audio/Video (A/V) Edge Server role** Provides services for audio as well as streaming video
  - Uses Office Communicator remotely for A/V conferences
  - Requires that the Access Edge Server role and the A/V Edge Server role are deployed by the enterprise
- **Microsoft Office Communicator Web Access Server** A special-purpose server that enables users to access some functions (for example, presence, conferences, application sharing, and IM) from any compliant browser

- Uses Office Communicator Web Access (2007 R2 release) to log on to the enterprise network
- Requires that the Office Communicator Web Access Server is deployed by the enterprise

Understanding Basic Remote Access Topologies

Office Communications Server 2007 R2 offers the following three topologies in which remote access can be deployed:

- Single Edge Server topology
- Scaled single-site Edge Server topology
- Multisite Edge Server topology

Choosing a topology for your organization is based mainly on cost and the number of users in your organization. The single Edge Server topology is simple and easy to manage, but it does not handle a large number of users or offer high availability. The multisite Edge Server topology can be scaled to suit a worldwide enterprise with multiple locations, can provide a high-availability strategy, and will support thousands of users, but it is more complex to administer. One of the four topologies described in this chapter will work for most organizations.

In each topology, firewalls protect the edge network from the Internet and protect the enterprise network from malicious traffic from the edge network. The consolidated Edge Server validates traffic and connects to the internal servers in the organization server.

> ***NOTE*** **Previous versions of Live Communications Server and Office Communications Server support load-balanced Standard Edition Servers as Directors. Office Communications Server 2007 R2 does not support load-balanced Standard Edition Servers. You will need to use load-balanced Enterprise Edition front-end servers to accomplish this requirement.**

Single Edge Server Topology

The single Edge Server topology is a single server that hosts three server roles, as shown in Figure 7-1. The roles with their associated primary protocols are as follows:

- **Access Edge Server** Session Initiation Protocol (SIP).
- **Web Conference Edge Server** Persistent Shared Object Model (PSOM).
- **A/V Edge Server** Real-Time Protocol (RTP) and Simple Traversal of User Datagram Protocol (UDP) through the Network Address Translation (NAT) protocol. The simplified name for this protocol is STUN and is defined by the Internet Engineering Task Force (IETF) under Request for Comment (RFC) 3489.

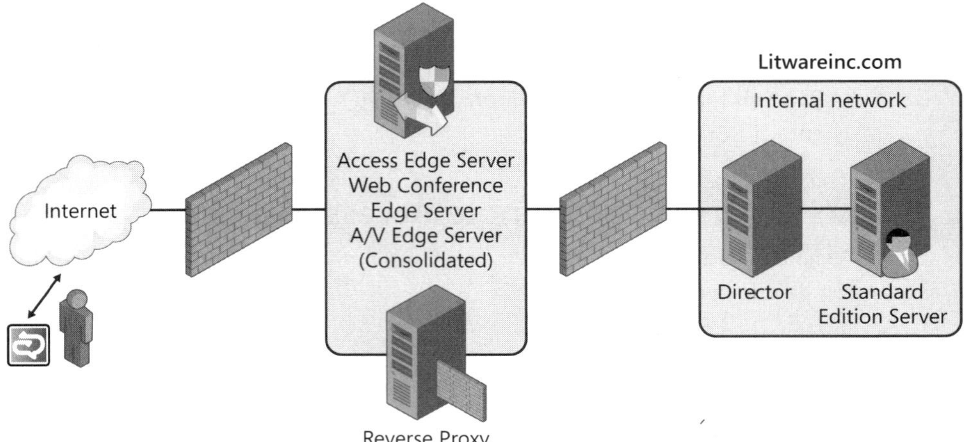

FIGURE 7-1 Single Edge Server topology

The simplest installation involves minimizing the hardware required to provide access by consolidating the installation of the Access, Web Conferencing, and A/V Edge Servers on the same physical server in the edge network. Firewalls protect the edge network from the external network and protect the enterprise network from irregular access from the edge network. The consolidated Edge Server validates traffic from the edge network and connects to the internal servers in the organization, which could be a pool of servers or a single Office Communications Server Standard Edition Server.

> ***NOTE*** **Starting with Office Communications Server 2007 R2, the consolidated Edge Server deployment is the only configuration supported by Microsoft, regardless of whether you are using Standard Edition or Enterprise Edition.**

For a single Edge Server topology, remote access Office Communicator clients use Transport Layer Security (TLS) to securely connect to the Access Edge Server from the Internet. This scenario may require multiple Internet Protocol (IP) addresses to be bound to the network interface to handle calls to the collocated roles. Office Communicator discovers the enterprise Access Edge Server through Domain Name System (DNS) Service Record Locators (SRVs). This interaction is similar to how internal clients connect. For more information about internal logon and DNS SRV records, see Chapter 5, "Basic IM and Presence Scenarios."

To prevent spoof and "man-in-the-middle" (a widely used security term, also known as the bucket brigade) attacks, Transmission Control Protocol (TCP) is not offered for clients that connect from external networks. The Access Edge Server has a certificate issued by a well-known certification authority (CA) that Microsoft Windows trusts. This enables computers outside the network that are not members of the domain to connect, validate, and trust the Access Edge Server certificate. This trust is necessary to prevent DNS spoofing attacks that could enable the connecting Office Communicator client to negotiate authentication and pass communications through an undesired intermediary. The Access Edge Server then uses another certificate (issued by a public or private CA) to connect securely to the Director server inside the enterprise network. Note that the Access Edge Server helps protect the internal servers against network-level attacks, validates the SIP network protocol messages that it receives, validates the domain that the client uses to log on, and then forwards requests to the internal Director.

NOTE **For more information about how Office Communicator uses DNS SRV records during remote access and local enterprise logon, see Chapter 5. The section titled "The Technical Details Behind the Login Process" explains which DNS SRV records are queried and how the result is interpreted. Remote access mainly involves the sipexternal.<domain> host (A) record and the _sip._tls.<domain> record.**

The single Edge Server topology can support concurrent IM, Web conference, and A/V traffic. Although this is the simplest topology to administer, there are limits to what a single server can handle. You may find that as the needs and user requirements of your organization grow, one of the other topologies discussed in this chapter will be more applicable. For more information about capacity planning, see Chapter 14, "Planning Example."

Scaled Single-Site Edge Server Topology

The scaled single-site Edge Server topology enables you to quickly add new servers to the edge network as your environment grows and more users begin to consume services. This topology also provides for increased availability. If, for example, a Web Conferencing Server fails, other Web Conferencing Servers can take over the workload.

In this topology, hardware load balancers are required on the external and the internal sides of the edge network. Hardware load balancers are required because the potential for latency over software solutions is lower. Software-based load balancers are not supported. For more information, see the Microsoft Knowledge Base article titled "The Windows Server 2003-Based Network Load Balancing Service Is Not Supported by Communications Server 2007 in Production or Lab Deployments," found at *http://support.microsoft.com/kb/939800*.

It is important to remember that whether the load balancer is serving one server or ten, the servers are all referenced by the virtual IP (VIP) of the load balancer. In the case of the DNS, the only IP address that needs to be registered is the VIP of the load balancer. In fact, it is better not to register the servers separately. Also, when you configure certificates in a scaled single-site Edge Server topology, the subject name should be the DNS name of the VIP address of the load balancer, not the host name of any server in the array.

NOTE A set of servers that sits behind a load balancer and that shares common functions, such as four consolidated Edge Servers, is commonly referred to as an array.

Figure 7-2 shows four consolidated Edge Servers. Each of the servers provides the Access Edge role, the Web Conference Edge role, and the A/V Edge role.

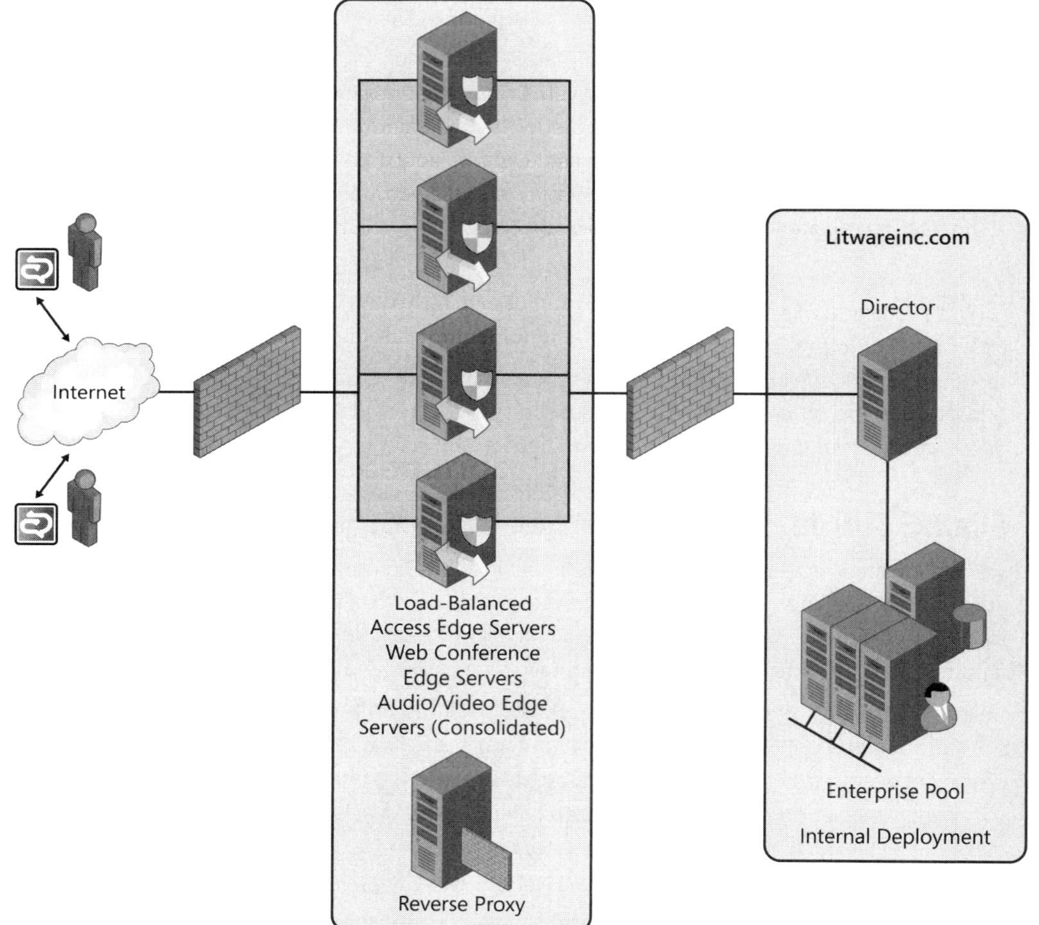

FIGURE 7-2 Scaled single-site Edge Server topology

Hardware load balancers provide a distinct advantage in scaling your edge architecture—you can add servers to provide for greater availability and greater load handling. In other topologies, the only way to scale your consolidated Edge Servers is to scale up, meaning a server that has more processing power and memory. The scaled single-site topology also enables you to scale out. Instead of using fewer, more powerful servers, you can use more but less powerful servers that are typically more cost effective. The other benefit, as mentioned earlier, is the ability to realize availability as an enhancement. In the topologies that we have discussed to this point, if an Access Edge Server fails, your enterprise will not be able to communicate until it is recovered. With the scaled single-site Edge Server topology, you have more than one consolidated Edge Server in place so that your enterprise will continue to operate if one of those servers fails. Being down during recovery is no longer a production threat because the other servers will continue to provide service.

Multisite Edge Server Topology

The recommended multisite Edge Server topology is similar to the single-site Edge Server topology for the primary site; however, for greater scalability, it has a set of load-balanced consolidated Edge Servers. The remote site has consolidated Edge Servers installed to prevent the introduction of media session delays by routing media through the local site, as shown in Figure 7-3. Because the domain DNS SRV records publish only the primary site (for federation and remote access purposes), the SIP traffic from remote Office Communicator clients always travels through the primary site in this topology. Because SIP traffic does not use as much bandwidth as media traffic, the Access Edge Servers can be managed at the primary site.

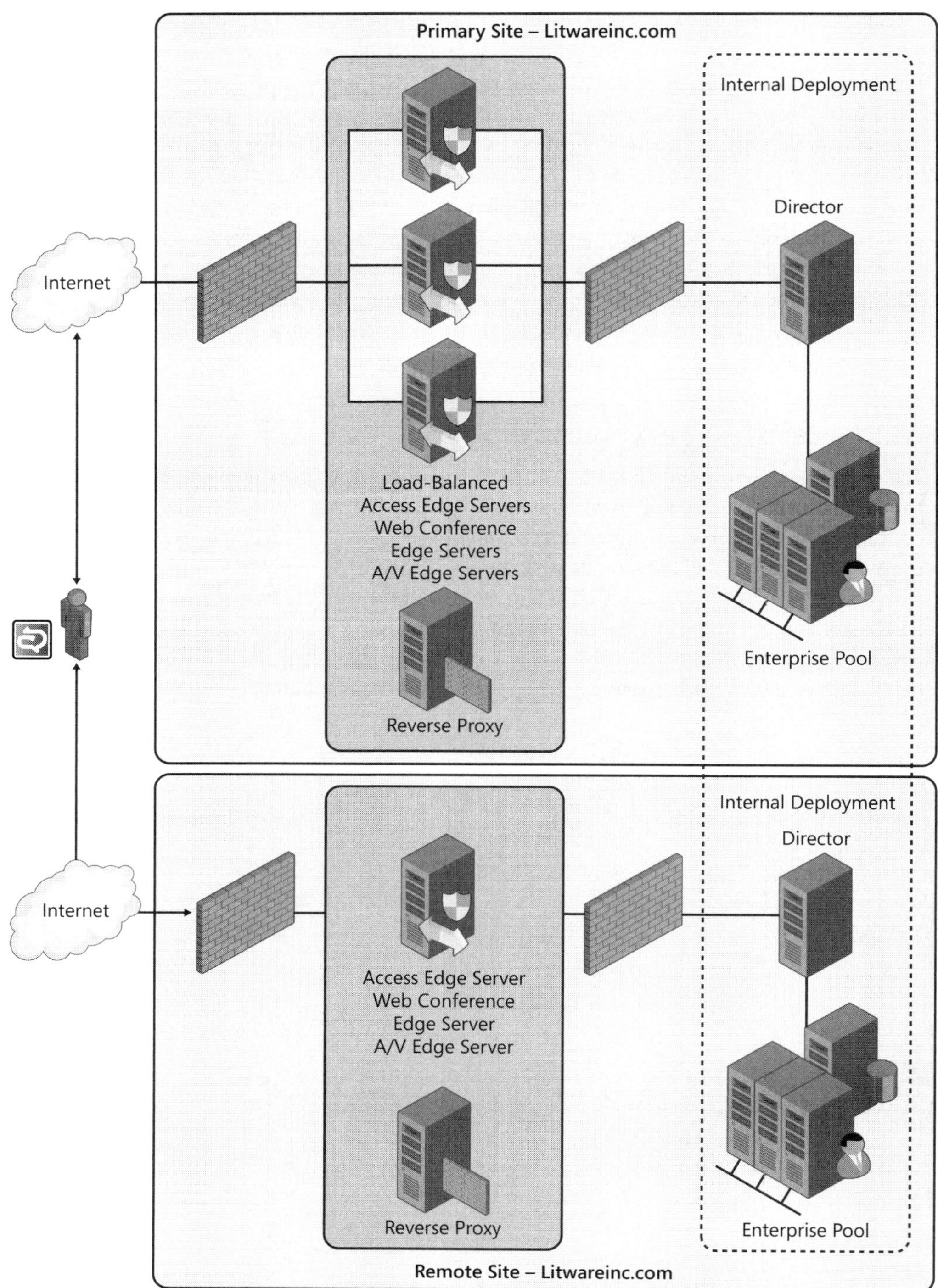

FIGURE 7-3 Multisite Edge Server topology

Understanding Basic Remote Access Scenarios

The following sections describe the three basic remote access scenarios:

- **Basic remote access (for IM and presence information)** Uses Office Communicator to log on to the enterprise network
- **Web Conferencing remote access** Uses the Live Meeting 2007 client to connect to a data conference
- **A/V Conferencing remote access** Uses Office Communicator for audio/video conferencing

Understanding Basic Remote Access for IM and Presence Information

Basic remote access uses Office Communicator to log on from an external network to connect to the Access Edge Server in the enterprise edge network. This scenario does not require the use of a virtual private network (VPN) and is an easy way for enterprise users to connect from home or external sites. The basic remote access scenario involves a user experience that is identical to that described in the internal access scenario in Chapter 5, in the section titled "Understanding the Login Process." The scenario, shown in Figure 7-4, uses the Office Communicator client to connect via the Access Edge Server to a Director that passes the traffic (after authentication and authorization) to the internal home server (or pool) for the user.

Office Communicator uses the same logic during a remote access logon as it does during a logon procedure on an internal network. The client does not know what network it is on until some exploration is done through discovery of DNS SRV and host (A) records. These records are used to discover internal and external Office Communications Server contact points. For basic remote access, three main records are used, shown here for the example domain Litwareinc.com.

- _sip._tls.litwareinc.com (SRV record)
- sipexternal.litwareinc.com (a record for single-server use)
- vipexternal.litwareinc.com (a record if a load balancer is used)

After the connection point for basic remote access is identified, Office Communicator always negotiates TLS over a TCP connection. This is mandated by the clients and servers to maintain data privacy and to prevent man-in-the-middle intrusions on the external network. Note that certificate problems are the primary cause of connection failures with the front-end server. It is highly recommended that you use a certificate from a public CA. Your clients must trust the certificate on the external interface of the Access Edge Server. A root CA certificate from the issuing CA of the certificate installed on the Access Edge Server establishes this trust. If the client cannot trust the certificate on the Access Edge Server, Office Communicator clearly identifies this problem with an alert and with entries in the event log. If trace logs are enabled on the client, the error information is written in the trace log for additional troubleshooting.

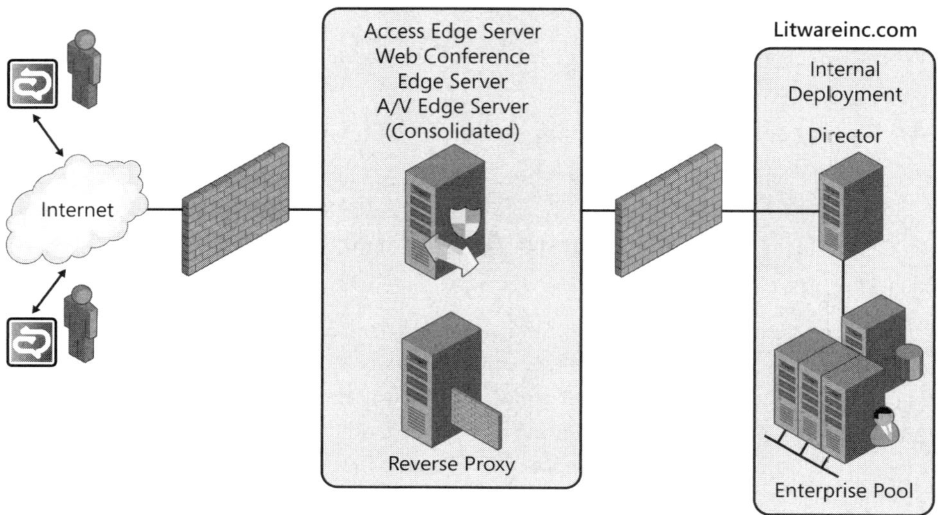

FIGURE 7-4 Basic remote access scenario example

The connection point will always be an Access Edge Server for supported topologies, and this server is responsible for performing simple message validation based on the supported enterprise domains and for protecting the enterprise network against network-level and protocol-level attacks. The Access Edge Server also has the ability to filter messages to provide additional functionality or protection. The Access Edge Server tags the messages as remote access requests and passes them to the next internal server (usually a Director server). The following header is added to the request to identify it as being from an external user and to track the name of the Access Edge Server that handled the request.

```
ms-edge-proxy-message-trust: ms-source-type=InternetUser;
ms-ep-fqdn=server22.litwareinc.local;
ms-source-verified-user=verified
```

The Director, which is an Office Communications Server Standard Edition Server or an Office Communications Server Enterprise Edition pool server, enforces authentication against Active Directory by the NT LAN Manager (NTLM), validates the user's right to log on to the Office Communications Server infrastructure, and determines whether the user has a right to use remote access. This server supports the rest of the network infrastructure by pre-authenticating the incoming requests against Active Directory. The Director then uses its knowledge of the other Office Communications Server R2 servers to forward requests to the user's home server or pool. From this point, the logon process is identical to a standard internal network logon process. However, an additional header is placed in responses to help Office Communicator identify that it is in a remote access scenario.

```
ms-user-logon-data: RemoteUser
```

The reverse proxy has a distinction in that it tracks *edges* during protocol operations so that it can differentiate messages that are proxied from the outside in and from the inside out. This tracking shows up in the trace logs and can be confusing when an *incoming* message comes from the internal network or an *outgoing* message is being routed to the internal network. Messages are logged as they come in and as they are forwarded, both to and from the internal and external networks.

Understanding Remote Access for Web Conferencing

Web conferencing remote access uses the Live Meeting 2007 R2 client from a remote network to conduct a meeting or share information with other enterprise or federated users. This section contains an example of a simple conference and presents the technical details that make it possible. Conducting a Web conference is similar to basic remote access for the SIP communications channel, but it also involves the Web Conferencing Edge Server to bridge application-sharing sessions to internal Web Conferencing Servers that form the conference hub. Additionally, a reverse proxy in the edge network provides access to the internal Web server where conference content is available. Figure 7-5 provides a functional diagram of this topology.

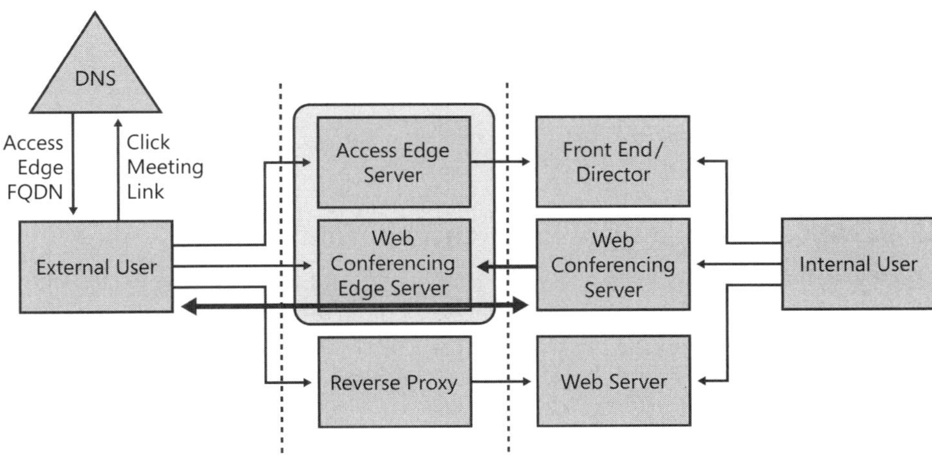

FIGURE 7-5 Topology of the conferencing remote access scenario

The following scenario involves two external users, Vadim N. Korepin and Jeremy Los, who are active contacts with each other. The scenario assumes that Office Communicator 2007 R2 and Office Live Meeting 2007 R2 clients are installed on each user's workstation. This scenario also assumes that the users are logged on remotely and are enabled for remote access. The users have the ability to schedule conferences and to access Web conferencing. Vadim wants to share a game of FreeCell that he is working on so that he can get Jeremy's advice about what to do next in a timely manner. This scenario uses Office Communicator 2007 R2 to establish and connect to the conference, but these two users can also use the Live Meeting 2007 R2 client to join a scheduled conference either directly or by clicking a conference URL.

Step 1: Use Office Communicator to Start a Conference

Vadim N. Korepin opens a session in Office Communicator with Jeremy Los, clicks the sharing button, and selects Share Information Using Live Meeting, as shown in Figure 7-6. Vadim's Office Communicator launches the Live Meeting 2007 client, which creates the conference and joins it directly.

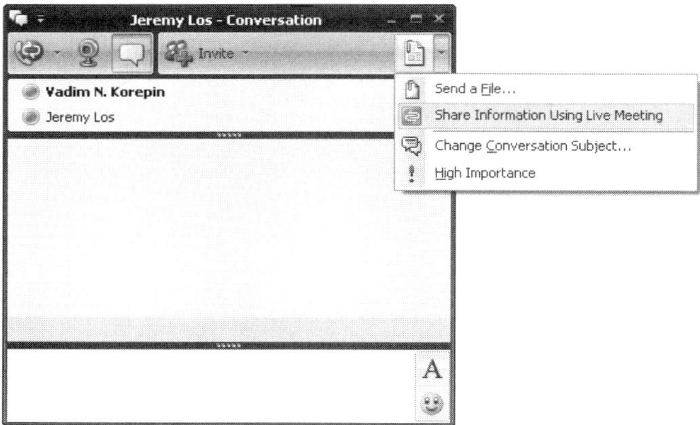

FIGURE 7-6 Initiating a data conference from Office Communicator

Step 2: Accept and Join a Web Conferencing Invitation

At this point, Jeremy receives a message that informs him that Vadim would like to start an application-sharing session. If he accepts the invitation that he received in Office Communicator, both his and Vadim's workstations will open the Live Meeting 2007 R2 client to begin a Web conference.

Step 3: Begin Sharing an Application

After Vadim and Jeremy connect to the session, Vadim shares his application by using the Content menu to select Share and then Share A Program, which shows a list of running programs. From this list, Vadim selects FreeCell.exe. This enables him to share the application for

Jeremy to view so that their analysis can begin, as shown in Figure 7-7. From here, Vadim can delegate application control to Jeremy or make other applications, tools, and data available.

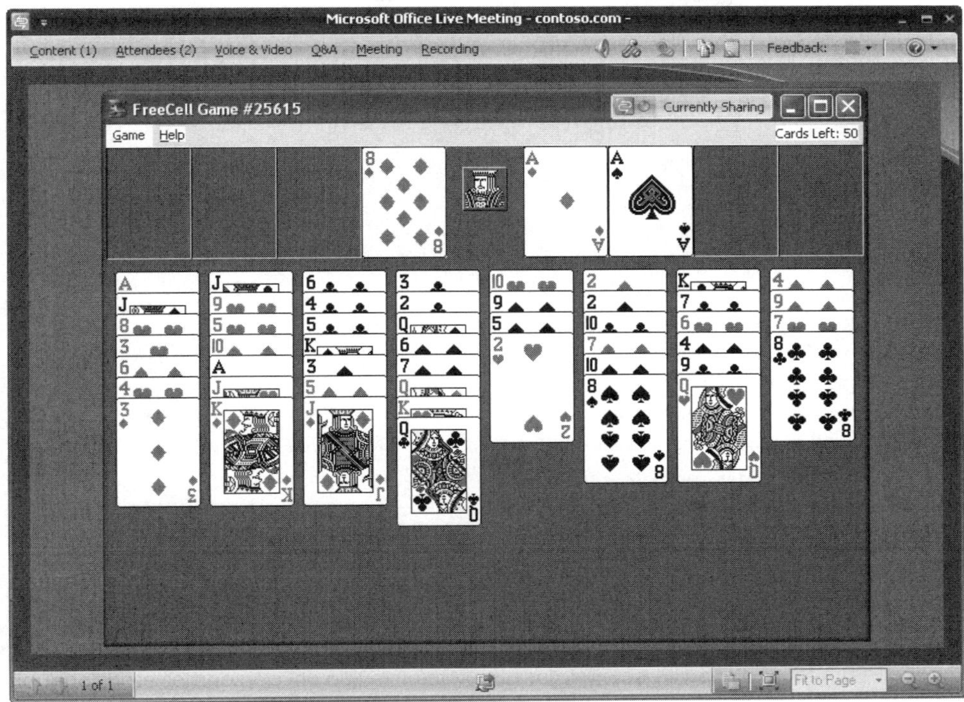

FIGURE 7-7 Web conferencing session with application sharing

Examining the Web Conferencing Remote Access Scenario

When a user connects remotely, he uses Office Communicator to log on through an Access Edge Server role, which uses SIP signaling to establish the session. He is then connected to the Web Conferencing edge role as a data conferencing connection point, which was reserved by the SIP session and will receive the HTTP reverse proxy as the URL for establishing a Web-based session. In an internal scenario, a local Web Conferencing Server and URL are used to access data conferencing services directly.

When Vadim creates an unscheduled conference and invites Jeremy, Vadim's instance of Office Communicator makes a SIP SERVICE request asking that a conference be created, as shown in the following example:

```
SERVICE
sip:vadim@litwareinc.com;gruu;opaque=app:conf:focusfactory SIP/2.0
From: <sip:vadim@litwareinc.com>;tag=54268ccbd8;epid=0b28f0b0b5 To:
sip:vadim@litwareinc.com;gruu;opaque=app:conf:focusfactory
CSeq: 1 SERVICE
...
```

```
Content-Type: application/cccp+xml
Content-Length: 1233

<?xml version="1.0"?>
<request xmlns="urn:ietf:params:xml:ns:cccp"
xmlns:mscp=http://schemas.microsoft.com/rtc/2005/08/cccpextensions C3PVersion="1"
to=sip:vadim@litwareinc.com;gruu;opaque=app:conf:focusfactory from="sip:vadim@
litwareinc.com" requestId="26587488">
  <addConference>
     <ci:conference-info xmlns:ci="urn:ietf:params:xml:ns:conference-info" entity=""
xmlns:msci="http://schemas.microsoft.com/rtc/2005/08/confinfoextensions">
    <ci:conference-description>
      <ci:subject></ci:subject>
      <msci:conference-id>6CD0FA33C0F133499647246DA968BF6B
          </msci:conference-id>
      <msci:expiry-time>2007-09-25T13:44:34Z</msci:expiry-time>
      <msci:admission-policy>openAuthenticated</msci:admission-policy>
    </ci:conference-description>
    <msci:conference-view>
      <msci:entity-view entity="chat"/>
      <msci:entity-view entity="audio-video"/>
      <msci:entity-view entity="meeting">
      <msci:entity-settings>
        <msdata:settings xmlns:msdata="http://schemas.microsoft.com/rtc/2005/08/
dataconfinfoextensions">
          <msdata:app-viewing-behavior>enableWithFullSharing
              </msdata:app-viewing-behavior>
          <msdata:conferencing-type>collaboration
              </msdata:conferencing-type>
        </msdata:settings>
      </msci:entity-settings>
      </msci:entity-view>
    </msci:conference-view>
    </ci:conference-info>
  </addConference>
</request>
```

This message is sent to the user's Uniform Resource Identifier (URI), but with an additional parameter, *;opaque=app:conf:focusfactory*, which specifies that the request is destined for the conference Focus Factory that is responsible for creating the meeting. In the body of the message, the request also specifies information about the conference to be created. Examples of data in the body of the message include the *msci:conference-id* attribute, which specifies the conference ID that should be used, and the *msci:admission-policy* attribute, which specifies the security level for the meeting (in this case, *openAuthenticated* means that all authenticated users can join, but anonymous Internet users cannot). It is also important to note that even though the conference type terminology has changed (as mentioned earlier in the section "Understanding On-Premises Conferencing Rules for Federated and Nonfederated Users"), the wire protocol has not, as shown in the *msci:admission-policy* which is still communicated as **openAuthentication**. In the following example, the SERVICE request receives a 200 OK response that passes back some basic information about the conference that was just created.

```
SIP/2.0 200 OK
From: "Vadim N. Korepin"<sip:vadim@litwareinc.com>;tag=54268ccbd8;epid=0b28f0b0b5
To: <sip:vadim@litwareinc.com;gruu;opaque=app:conf:focusfactory>;tag=38971651
CSeq: 1 SERVICE
...
Content-Type: application/cccp+xml

<response xmlns="urn:ietf:params:xml:ns:cccp" xmlns:msacp=
   "http://schemas.microsoft.com/rtc/2005/08/acpconfinfoextensions"
xmlns:msav="http://schemas.microsoft.com/rtc/2005/08/avconfinfoextensions"
xmlns:mscp="http://schemas.microsoft.com/rtc/2005/08/cccpextensions"
xmlns:msci="http://schemas.microsoft.com/rtc/2005/08/confinfoextensions"
xmlns:msdata="http://schemas.microsoft.com/rtc/2005/08/dataconfinfoextensions"
xmlns:msim="http://schemas.microsoft.com/rtc/2005/08/imconfinfoextensions"
xmlns:ci="urn:ietf:params:xml:ns:conference-info"
xmlns:cis="urn:ietf:params:xml:ns:conference-info-separator"
xmlns:msls="urn:ietf:params:xml:ns:msls" requestId="26587488"
    C3PVersion="1"
from="sip:vadim@litwareinc.com;gruu;opaque=app:conf:focusfactory"
to="sip:vadim@litwareinc.com" code="success">
  <addConference>
<conference-info xmlns="urn:ietf:params:xml:ns:conference-info"
entity="sip:vadim@litwareinc.com;gruu;opaque=app:conf:focus:id:6CD0FA33C0F13349964724
6DA968BF6B"
 state="partial" version="1"/>
  </addConference>
</response>
```

Next, Vadim's Office Communicator sends a SIP INVITE message to the conference that was just created to establish a session and add Vadim as an attendee for the conference, as shown in the following example:

```
INVITE
sip:vadim@litwareinc.com;gruu;opaque=app:conf:focus:id:
6CD0FA33C0F133499647246DA968BF6B SIP/2.0
From: <sip:vadim@litwareinc.com>;tag=80fd98dd31;epid=0b28f0b0b5 To:
<sip:vadim@litwareinc.com;gruu;opaque=app:conf:focus:id:
6CD0FA33C0F133499647246DA968BF6B>
CSeq: 1 INVITE
...
```

```
Content-Type: application/cccp+xml
Content-Length: 716

<?xml version="1.0"?>
<request xmlns="urn:ietf:params:xml:ns:cccp"
    xmlns:mscp="http://schemas.microsoft.com/rtc/2005/08/cccpextensions"
    C3PVersion="1"
    to="sip:vadim@litwareinc.com;gruu;opaque=app:conf:focus:id:6CD0FA33C0F13349964724
6DA968BF6B"
     from="sip:vadim@litwareinc.com" requestId="0">   <addUser>
<conferenceKeys
confEntity=
"sip:vadim@litwareinc.com;gruu;opaque=app:conf:focus:id:6CD0FA33C0F133499647246DA968B
F6B"/>
<ci:user xmlns:ci="urn:ietf:params:xml:ns:conference-info"entity="sip:vadim@
litwareinc.com">
      <ci:roles>
        <ci:entry>attendee</ci:entry>
      </ci:roles>
      <ci:endpoint entity="{4BB86066-3927-424B-A7DD-2E07FD6B611C}" xmlns:msci="http://
schemas.microsoft.com/rtc/2005/08/confinfoextensions"/>
    </ci:user>
  </addUser>
</request>
```

The conference Focus responds with a 200 Invite dialog created message, confirming that Vadim is added as a presenter for the conference, as shown in the following example. Vadim's client sends back an acknowledge (ACK) to confirm the invitation (which is not shown for this example).

```
SIP/2.0 200 Invite dialog created
From: "Vadim N. Korepin"<sip:vadim@litwareinc.com>;tag=80fd98dd31;
    epid=0b28f0b0b5 To:<sip:vadim@litwareinc.com;gruu;opaque=app:conf:focus:id:
    6CD0FA33C0F133499647246DA968BF6B>;tag=84670080
CSeq: 1 INVITE
...
Content-Type: application/cccp+xml

<response xmlns="urn:ietf:params:xml:ns:cccp" xmlns:msacp="http://schemas.microsoft.com/
   rtc/2005/08/acpconfinfoextensions"
xmlns:msav="http://schemas.microsoft.com/rtc/2005/08/
avconfinfoextensions"
xmlns:mscp="http://schemas.microsoft.com/rtc/2005/08/cccpextensions"
xmlns:msci="http://schemas.microsoft.com/rtc/2005/08/confinfoextensions"
xmlns:msdata="http://schemas.microsoft.com/rtc/2005/08/dataconfinfoextensions"
```

```
xmlns:msim="http://schemas.microsoft.com/rtc/2005/08/imconfinfoextensions"
xmlns:ci="urn:ietf:params:xml:ns:conference-info"
xmlns:cis="urn:ietf:params:xml:ns:conference-info-separator"
xmlns:msls="urn:ietf:params:xml:ns:msls" requestId="0" C3PVersion="1"
from="sip:vadim@litwareinc.com;gruu;opaque=app:conf:focus:id:
    6CD0FA33C0F133499647246DA968BF6B"
    to="sip:vadim@litwareinc.com" code="success">
  <addUser>
<conferenceKeys confEntity="sip:vadim@litwareinc.com;gruu;opaque=app:conf:focus:id:
    6CD0FA33C0F133499647246DA968BF6B"/>
    <ci:user entity="sip:vadim@litwareinc.com">
      <ci:roles>
        <ci:entry>presenter</ci:entry>
      </ci:roles>
    </ci:user>
  </addUser>
</response>
```

Next, Vadim's Office Communicator client sends a SUBSCRIBE message to the conference to receive notifications from the conference as events occur (such as when other users join), as shown in the following example:

```
SUBSCRIBE
sip:vadim@litwareinc.com;gruu;opaque=app:conf:focus:id:
    6CD0FA33C0F133499647246DA968BF6B SIP/2.0
From: <sip:vadim@litwareinc.com>;tag=694f84821b;epid=0b28f0b0b5 To:
  <sip:vadim@litwareinc.com;gruu;opaque=app:conf:focus:id:
    6CD0FA33C0F133499647246DA968BF6B>
CSeq: 1 SUBSCRIBE
...
Event: conference
Accept: application/conference-info+xml
Content-Length: 0
```

Vadim's Live Meeting client then connects to the Web Conferencing Edge Server after connecting through the HTTP reverse proxy with which it was provisioned during logon. His Office Communicator client sends the following invitation, which provides information about the conference that has been established, to Jeremy.

```
INVITE sip:jeremy@litwareinc.com SIP/2.0 From: <sip:vadim@litwareinc.com>;
tag=7bf3e5f500;epid=0b28f0b0b5 To: <sip:jeremy@litwareinc.com>
CSeq: 1 INVITE
...
Content-Type: application/ms-conf-invite+xml
Content-Length: 193
```

```
<Conferencing version="2.0">
<focus-uri>sip:vadim@litwareinc.com;gruu;opaque=app:conf:focus:id:
     6CD0FA33C0F133499647246DA968BF6B</focus-uri>
  <subject></subject>
  <data available="true"/>
</Conferencing>
```

This invitation is accepted, and then Jeremy's Office Communicator and Live Meeting clients will process the same interactions that Vadim's Office Communicator and Live Meeting client did.

Note that if a user joined anonymously by using the Live Meeting client, he would have to authenticate by using Digest authentication to pass a hash of the meeting password. This authentication ensures that all servers the user connects to in the edge network can validate the user. This first-level authentication hands back meeting keys that are passed to the Web Conferencing Edge Server to prevent unauthorized access.

> ***NOTE*** **Digest authentication for anonymous users uses the conference password and creates a Digest hash, which is used for authentication. Enterprise users using remote access authenticate via NTLM.**

Understanding Remote Access for Audio and Video Conferencing

Audio and video conferencing remote access enables enterprise users in the external network to share video and audio sessions with internal and other external users. Figure 7-8 shows an example of the topology, with the SIP connections (TLS over TCP) shown as gray lines and the media sessions shown as black lines.

The A/V Edge Server provides a single, trusted connection point through which inbound and outbound media traffic can securely traverse NATs and firewalls. The industry-standard solution for multimedia traversal of firewalls is Interactive Connectivity Establishment (ICE), which is based on STUN and Traversal Using Relay NAT (TURN) protocols. The A/V Edge Server is a STUN server. All users are authenticated to secure access to the enterprise and use the firewall traversal service that the A/V Edge Server provides. Authenticated users receive a token from the authenticating server, and this token can be used to validate the user's requests of the A/V Edge Server. To send media inside the enterprise, an external user must be authenticated and must have an authenticated internal user agree to communicate with them through the A/V Edge Server. The media streams themselves are exchanged using Secure Real-Time Protocol (SRTP) and Secure Real-Time Control Protocol (SRTCP), which is an industry standard for real-time media transmission and reception over IP.

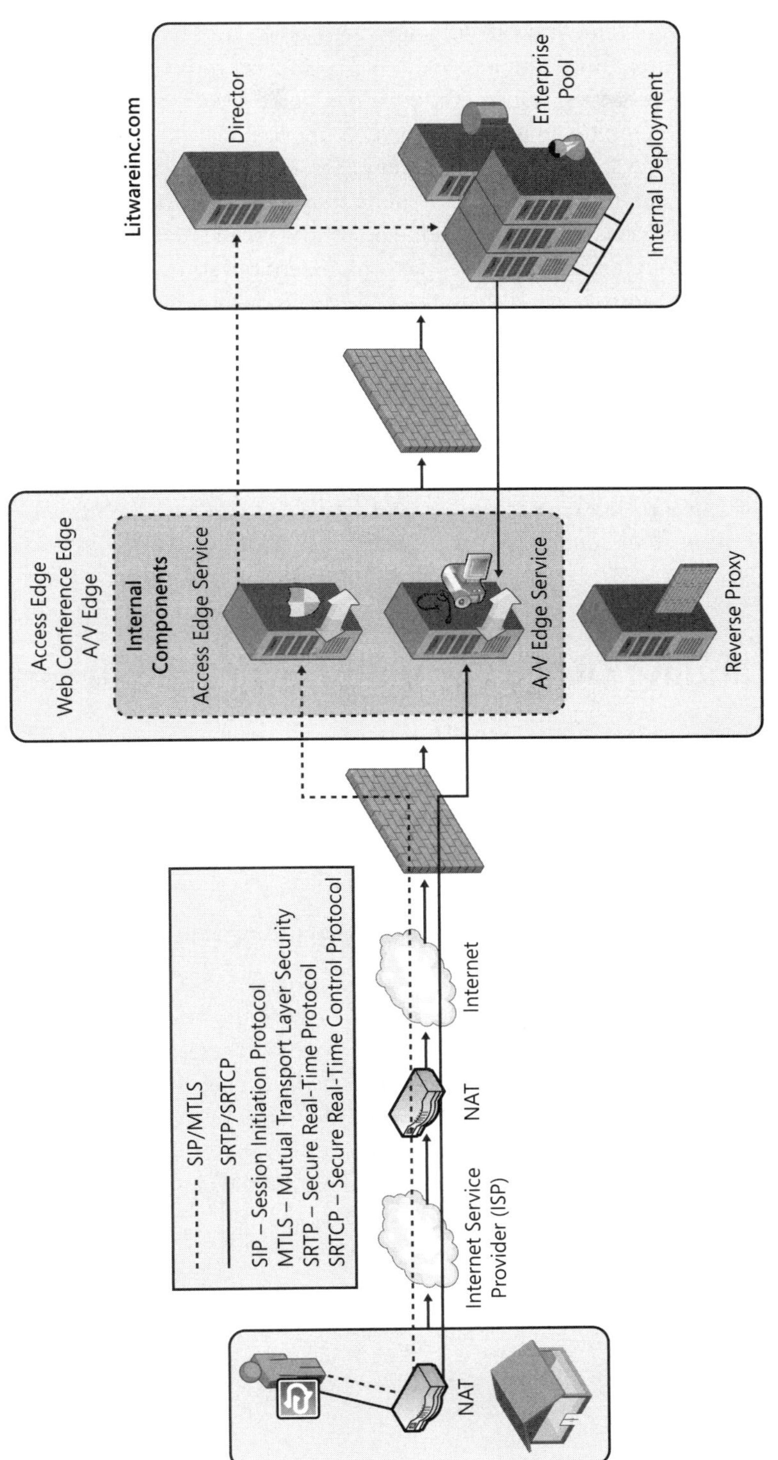

FIGURE 7-8 Topology of the A/V conferencing remote access scenario

Office Communicator remote access forces authentication over the SIP session with the Access Edge Server. After Office Communicator has logged on and authenticated, it can contact the A/V Edge Server on the public IP address by using a secure token that it can retrieve from the MS-AVEDGEA server—this is what prevents anonymous and unauthenticated users from using the A/V Edge Server for malicious purposes. The A/V Edge service allocates the user a port to use for the session. Office Communicator can then invite (through SIP) another user by using the internal A/V MCU as a bridge point. The recipient of the invitation can use a secure token (after authenticating to the Microsoft extensions to Traversal Using Relay NAT [MSTURN] service) to register directly with the A/V Edge Server or internal A/V MCU based on the recipient's network location. Finally, media is exchanged over the negotiated ports, using the servers to bridge traffic.

> ***NOTE*** **The A/V Authentication Service is consolidated with, and provides authentication services for, the A/V Edge Server. Outside users attempting to connect to the A/V Edge Server require an authentication token provided by the A/V Authentication Service before their requests can go through.**

Understanding Office Communicator Web Access 2007 R2

This section provides basic information about how to enable Office Communicator Web Access 2007 R2. An introduction to the basic topology requirements is provided along with some overview information.

Enabling Office Communicator Web Access 2007 R2

Office Communicator Web Access is a Web-based version of the Office Communicator client and provides a great way to enable alternate operating systems and nondomain workstations without an installation process. Communicator Web Access provides internal and remote access to the Office Communications Server infrastructure by enabling IM, presence, ad hoc application sharing capabilities, and more. However, file transfer, A/V conferencing, and whiteboard sessions are not available with Communicator Web Access. The Web browsers that are supported by Office Communicator Web Access are shown in Table 7-1.

TABLE 7-1 Supported Browsers for Office Communicator Web Access 2007 R2

OPERATING SYSTEM	BROWSER	AUTHENTICATION MECHANISM
Windows 2000 Service Pack4 (SP4)	Microsoft Internet Explorer 6 SP1	NTLM Kerberos Forms-based Custom
Windows XP SP2	Internet Explorer 6 SP2 Windows Internet Explorer 7	NTLM Kerberos Forms-based Custom
	Mozilla Firefox 2.0 and later	Forms-based Custom
Windows Vista	Internet Explorer 7	NTLM Kerberos Forms-based Custom
	Mozilla Firefox 2.0.0.3 and later	Forms-based Custom
Mac OS X 10.4.9	Apple Safari 2.0.4 Mozilla Firefox 2.0 and later	Forms-based Custom

Communicator Web Access 2007 R2 has several new enhancements that are not present in Communicator Web Access 2007, including the following:

- Automatic discovery of local servers in the Microsoft Management Console (MMC)
- Richer Communicator Web Access user interface
- Custom authentication, such as single sign-on and two-factor authentication support
- Incoming Voice over Internet Protocol (VoIP) call routing and management
- Web conference attendance
- Ad hoc application sharing
- Distribution group access

A Communicator Web Access topology can provide support for Web-based access internally and remotely by using load-balanced Web servers to host Communicator Web Access, as shown in Figure 7-9. Communicator Web Access can be deployed in several different topologies, including the following:

- A single Communicator Web Access server for both internal and external users

- Load-balanced Communications Web Access servers for both internal and external users
- Separate Communicator Web Access servers for internal and external users
- Separate Communicator Web Access server arrays for internal and external users

The following topologies *are not supported* for deploying Communicator Web Access:

- Communicator Web Access should not be deployed in the perimeter network.
- Communicator Web Access should not be installed on a domain controller.

Remote access logons that use Communicator Web Access go through the following process when logging on to the topology, as shown in Figure 7-9:

1. The remote user on the public Internet uses her Web browser to connect to the Office Communicator Web Access URL (for example, *https://im.litwareinc.com*). This request securely connects through the reverse proxy in the edge network, which routes the connection to the load balancer for the external Communicator Web Access Web farm.
2. The Web browser verifies that the server certificate on the external interface of the reverse proxy comes from a trusted CA, and it validates that the Subject Name (SN) or Subject Alternate Name (SAN) field is represented in the certificate (for example, im.litwareinc.com).
3. Communicator Web Access authenticates the user, validates the SIP URI, and ensures the user is allowed to log on using remote access. Communicator Web Access can use integrated Windows authentication or forms-based authentication to authenticate the user. Internal users can use Kerberos or NTLM. External users and browsers that do not support Integrated Windows can use NTLM.

> ***NOTE*** **Forms-based authentication passes the password in clear text, so it should always be used with HTTPS to encrypt the communications channel. This is important for internal users and should be required for external users.**

4. The mutual transport layer security (MTLS) server certificate configured for Communicator Web Access is used to authenticate and encrypt connections between the Communicator Web Access server and the Office Communications Server 2007 R2 server. This connection will be used to transport the user's SIP-based communications to and from the rest of the Office Communications Server infrastructure.

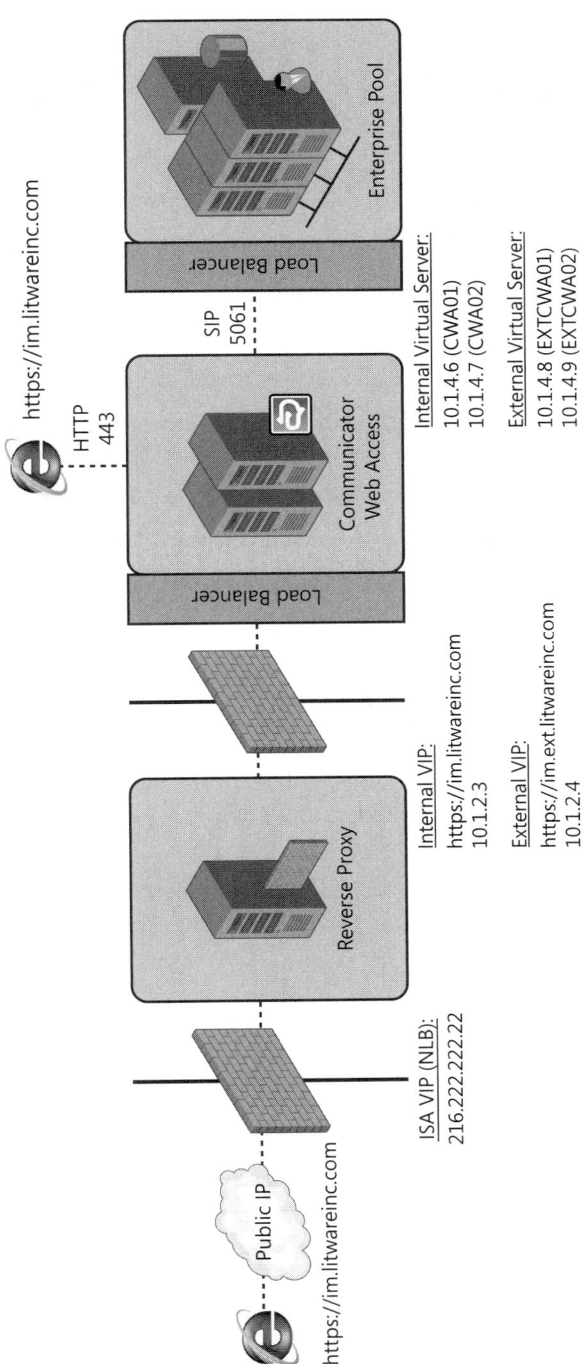

FIGURE 7-9 Communicator Web Access topology

DIRECT FROM THE SOURCE

Communicator Web Access Port Usage

Byron Spurlock
Consulting Services Consultant

Communicator Web Access communicates over the following incoming port:

- TCP port 80 (HTTP) or TCP port 443 (HTTPS)

HTTPS is recommended for security.

Communicator Web Access communicates over the following outgoing ports:

- TCP port 3268 Lightweight Directory Access Protocol (LDAP) to the Global Catalog (GC) server
- TCP port 389 (LDAP) to the Active Directory Domain Controller
- TCP port 5061 (MTLS) to the Office Communication Server 2007 Server or pool

Understanding Federation

Federation is a trust relationship between two entities. If two companies that are separate enterprises need to communicate, they federate to enable easy access to common data.

NOTE Federation is not the same as Active Directory Federation Services, but it serves the same purpose: enabling two enterprises that do not share a common authentication base to interact with each other.

For example, a manufacturing company and a supply chain partner that sells raw goods to that company might federate their enterprises to enable collaboration and access to common applications. Access can be managed in much the same way that access is managed in separate organizations, within a single entity, because users and groups can be populated with IM contacts from either enterprise. The difference is that there is no common address book that contains all the names from both enterprises. Similar to e-mail, you have to find and enter the name of the target person you are trying to contact into Office Communicator 2007 R2. The difference between e-mail and federated contacts is that you have control over who can contact you, whereas e-mail does not offer such specific controls (short of spam filters).

In Office Communications Server 2007 R2, the purpose of federation is to enable collaboration between users in completely separate enterprises. Using our example of the manufacturing and the raw materials companies, suppose Bob (an employee of the manufacturing company) needs to confirm details with Alice (an employee of the supply company) of an upcoming contract. Both have Office Communicator, so Bob can check Alice's presence. When he sees that her presence indicates that she is available, Bob initiates an IM session with Alice. In addition, they both need to review the details in the contract, so Bob starts a Live Meeting session to share the contract where they can both work on the document and the final details. Both companies have used federation to enable Bob and Alice to be more productive in their jobs.

A user does not need to belong to any of the companies in a federation to be able to communicate within a federation. Instead, they can access these resources as a *federated user*, that is, an external user (not a member of your enterprise) who possesses valid credentials and can authenticate to his enterprise. Once federated users authenticate, they are treated as if they are a part of your enterprise as far as Office Communications Server 2007 R2 services are concerned. Policies and configuration settings in Office Communications Server 2007 R2 can manage and modify the access that each user has.

Now that we've provided a short explanation of what a federation is and how it can help users within different enterprises, we can talk about the various federation topologies. In the sections that follow, we will discuss these federation topologies:

- **Direct federation** Direct federation refers to the one-to-one agreement, or trust, that is established between two entities. Direct federation requires specific entries on the Access Edge Server and the DNS Server.
- **Enhanced federation** Federated partner discovery (the process by which enhanced federation is accomplished) is similar to direct federation, but it requires much less administrative effort to establish and maintain. SRV records are used in the DNS to identify the federation. For more information about which SRV records are required, see the section titled "Understanding Federated Partner Discovery" later in this chapter.
- **Federation with public IM providers** Federation with public IM providers, such as Yahoo!, MSN, and AOL, is briefly discussed in this section. For more information about how public IM works, how to establish it, and how to administer it, see Chapter 8, "Public IM Connectivity Scenarios."

This chapter will also discuss user and administrator scenarios and the steps that must be taken to accomplish those scenarios.

Administration of federation requires the following prerequisites:

- Use public CA certificates.
- Enable users for federation.
- Apply settings on Access Edge Servers to allow the SIP domain of the partner organization.
- Obtain the fully qualified domain name (FQDN) of the federated partner's Access Edge Server.

Understanding Direct Federation

Direct federation implies that two enterprises are establishing an explicit trust between each other, as shown in Figure 7-10. This trust says that the enterprises have entered into an agreement in which they will directly share contacts and presence information that is related to those contacts. This makes it easier for users within each enterprise to communicate and to determine when a person is available. Presence information is reflected in applications that are *presence aware*, that comply with the requirements of Office Communications Server 2007 R2, and that are installed on a federation-enabled user's computer. Examples of these are Microsoft Office Communicator 1.0 (and later), Microsoft Office Outlook 2003 (and later), and Microsoft Office SharePoint 2003 (and later).

The trust element is established by certificates that ensure that either partner can absolutely confirm that person on the other end of the established trust is who they say they are, as well as ensure that the trusted partner domain name is entered on the Allowed tab of the Access Edge Server. We will discuss certificate types that can be used to accomplish this task in the section titled "Understanding the Requirements for and Use of Certificates in Federation" later in this chapter. Options for federation settings will be defined as well.

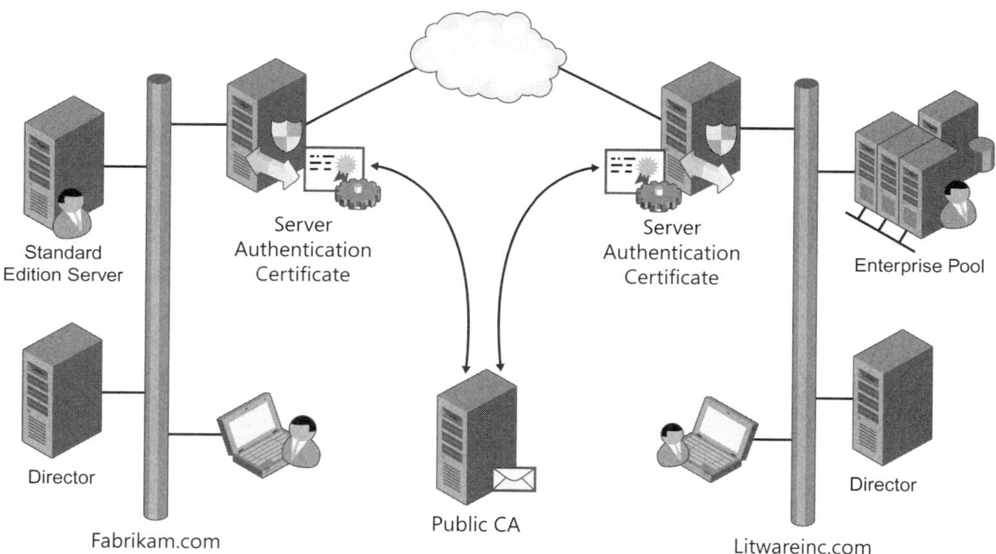

FIGURE 7-10 Direct federation that is defined by the FQDN and IP to specific Office Communications Server 2007 R2 enterprises

DIRECT FROM THE SOURCE

A Certificate and DNS Name Anomaly to Note

Thomas Laciano
Program Manager, Office Communications Server Customer Experience

Direct federation requires that changes be communicated to all peers with whom you are federating. This creates additional administrative work. However, direct federation allows for one name in the certificate for companies with multiple domains. The Allow tab creates a defined relationship between the domain name and the SIP FQDN of the Access Edge Server that is responsible for the SIP conversations as shown in the following example:

```
Litwareinc.com     sip.litwareinc.com
Litwareinc.au      sip.litwareinc.com
```

Enhanced federation eliminates this administrative overhead and uses the DNS to determine the SIP FQDN for the requested domain. The DNS is treated with tighter rules of logic because it can easily be compromised. So, for example, litwareinc.au for enhanced presence will require a SIP FQDN of <*host*>.litwareinc.au.

You can exaggerate the example for illustrative purposes. If you query the DNS for an SRV record for the litwareinc.au domain, you might be tempted to accept <*host*>. litwareinc.com because you recognize the company. However, when you compare your request to the result, litwareinc.com is not the same as litwareinc.au. You queried for a host that handles the litwareinc.au domain, and thus only a host record for that namespace will suffice. You will expect a certificate for litwareinc.au also.

Of the three types of federation, direct federation is the simplest to implement. However, it requires more administrative resources.

Most of the work in a direct federation model takes place on the Access Edge Server. It provides a separate, distinct role for incoming communications to be received, and it is an outgoing portal for communications that are bound for external destinations. As with all roles in Office Communications Server 2007 R2, certificates play an important role in establishing a level of security, trust, and confidentiality. Certificates and DNS record-naming inconsistencies between the host name and the certificate subject name or subject alternate name are a common cause of error in the configuration and setup of Office Communications Server 2007 R2.

A Director server is a recommended, but not mandatory, server role that sits logically between your Edge Servers and the pool. The role of the Director is to pre-authenticate and pre-authorize incoming traffic that is destined for your internal SIP domains. In the case of the

Director process, pre-authentication determines whether the SIP domain, the user, or both are known to the Director. Earlier, in Figure 7-10, you saw that users in the Litwareinc.com domain can be pre-authenticated by the Director, but users of Fabrikam.com cannot. There is a one-way replication from Active Directory to the Director, and only mandatory attributes are necessary to pre-authenticate and pre-authorize. The director is authenticating only that the Fabrikam domain is allowed and that the users are recognized and belong to the Fabrikam domain. The role of the internal servers is a minor part in federation. The internal servers, along with the way that they operate and support users, are no different than they would be if the federation did not exist.

Direct federation becomes administratively more complex as additional partners are added. Ten is manageable. The administrative overhead involves defining the Access Edge Servers and managing certificates for each partner. The administrative effort in managing additional partner federations becomes increasingly difficult and potentially error prone as the administrator manages the addition or removal of entries on the Allow tab of the Access Edge Server as well as the attainment or removal of certificates from federated partners.

To maintain a reasonable level of administrative overhead, the recommended maximum number of partners is 10.

You can enable discovery of federation partners and add federated partners to the Allow list. Adding specific partners to the Allow list gives them a higher level of trust. The Access Edge Server can still discover federated partners other than the ones on the Allow list, but specific rules are applied to those partners who are *not* on the Allow list. To enable federation in an enterprise, perform the following steps in the Office Communications Server 2007 R2 administrative tool on a Standard Edition Server or Enterprise pool front-end server:

1. Click Start, click Administrative Tools, and then click Open Office Communications Server 2007 R2 MMC.
2. Select the Forest,<*domain name*> node.
3. Right click Global Policy Properties.
4. A dialog box will open (as shown in Figure 7-11).
5. Click the Federation tab.
6. Select the Enable Federation And Public IM Connectivity check box.
7. Specify the FQDN of the next-hop server Director, load balancer, or Access Edge Server.

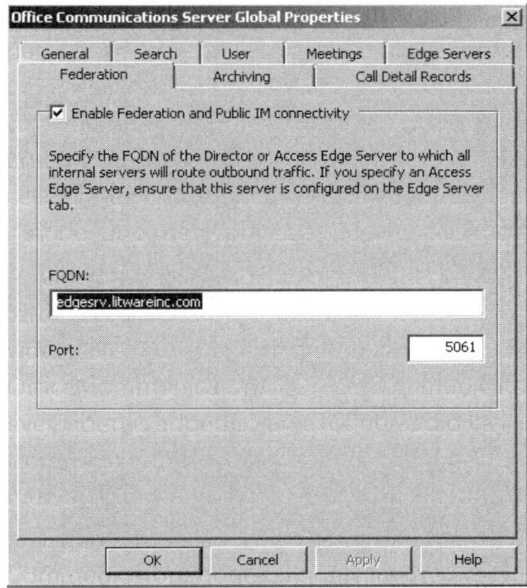

FIGURE 7-11 To enable federation, check the box and insert the FQDN of your Access Edge Server.

Adding a Trusted Federated Partner Domain

To add a trusted federated partner domain and the FQDN of its Access Edge Server, do the following:

1. Log on to each of the Access Edge Servers as a member of the Administrators group or a group that has equivalent user rights.
2. Click Start, click All Programs, click Administrative Tools, and then click Computer Management.
3. In the console tree, expand Services And Applications, right-click Microsoft Office Communications Server 2007 R2, and then click Properties.
4. On the Allow tab, click Add, as shown in Figure 7-12.

   The benefit of defining global properties is that doing so is much easier to manage than defining multiple separate options. This configuration affects all default routes for all pools. If you need an exception, you can define it locally.

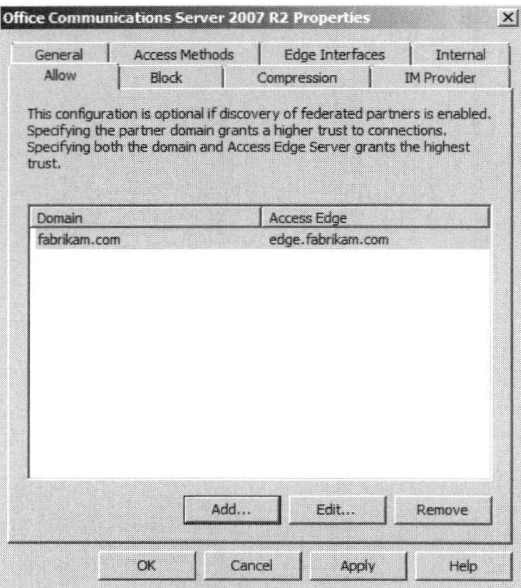

FIGURE 7-12 Define the Allow property for a federated SIP domain and the Access Edge Server of the partner.

5. In the Add Federated Partner dialog box, do the following:
   a. In the Federated Partner Domain Name text box, type the domain of the federated partner domain.
   b. In the Federated Partner Access Edge Server (Optional) text box, type the FQDN of each Access Edge Server that you want to add to your Allow list. If the FQDN of a partner's Access Edge Server changes, you must manually update your configuration for this partner, as shown in Figure 7-13.
   c. Click OK.

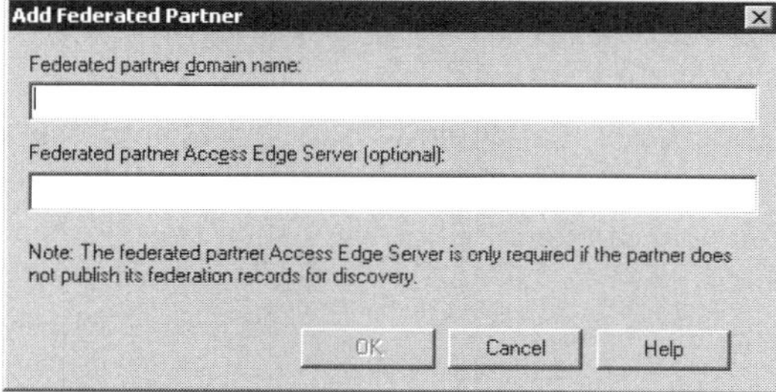

FIGURE 7-13 Input dialog box for defining the federated partner domain and FQDN of the Access Edge Server

Repeat this procedure for each federated partner that you want to add to your Allow list and then click OK.

Understanding Federated Partner Discovery

SRV records play an important role in federated partner discovery. Unlike direct federation, where the path and FQDN of the destination federated partner is defined, the Access Edge Server parses the DNS server for any existing SRV records that define potential federated locations, as shown in Figure 7-14.

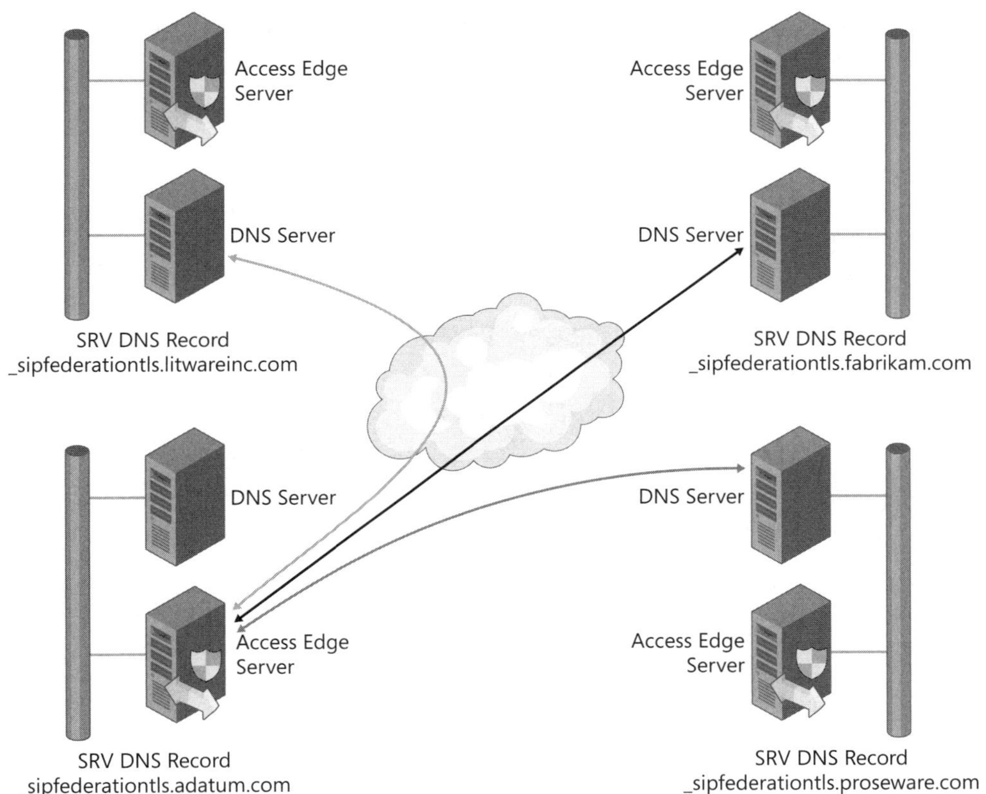

FIGURE 7-14 Federated partner discovery in which the Access Edge Server queries DNS for SRV records.

SRV records are a special type of DNS record that defines a service that a server offers. The SRV record defines the name of the server, the protocol, and a port that can be used. For those familiar with Active Directory, SRV records are used to define which domain controllers offer LDAP, Kerberos, GC, and other services. For Office Communications Server 2007

R2 federation, SRV records define what servers are available to offer federated services. The format of the record is as follows:

```
Service :  _sipfederationtls
Protocol:  _tcp
Priority:  <variable>
Weight:  <variable>
Port:  5061
Target:  access.fabrikam.com
```

> **NOTE** For more information about how SRV records are defined, see the IETF RFC Document 2782 at *http://go.microsoft.com/fwlink/?LinkID=133684.*

There is also an A, or host, record that connects the SRV record's entry to the actual Access Edge Server. In this example, consider the host access.fabrikam.com, shown in Figure 7-15. Recall that this is the external interface of the Edge Server, which should have two interfaces. One interface is for the internal communication, and the other is for the perimeter communication.

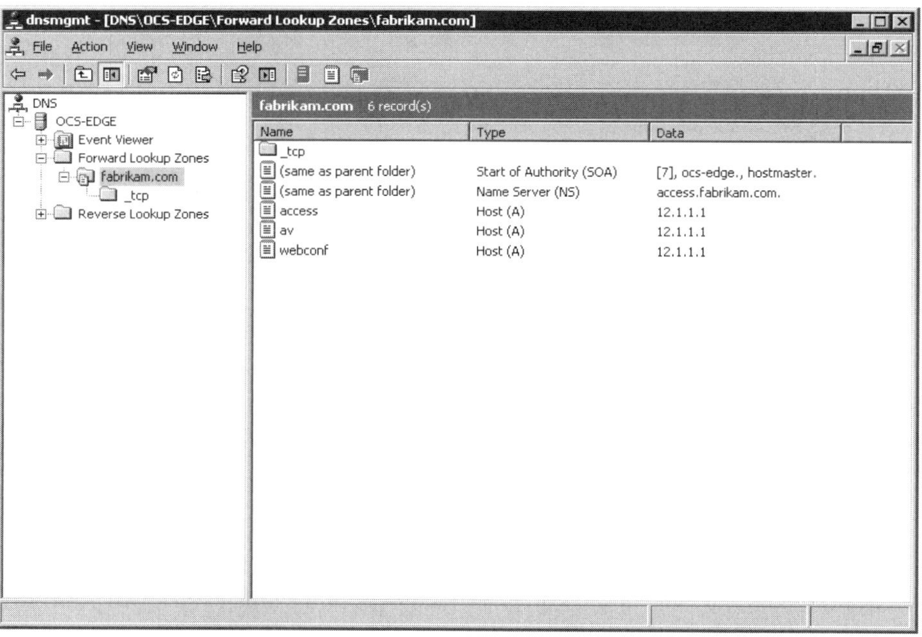

FIGURE 7-15 In these DNS SRV records, the A records that SRV points to define names for Office Communications Server R2 services.

The important thing to remember is that if you ask the DNS for SRV records, it returns records that can provide the services of Office Communications Server 2007 R2 federation. (These are the results of the query for SRV records and then the subsequent query for the A record of the server named in the SRV record.) This is a critical step in the process to determine which servers can provide the necessary services to establish a federated partnership. Access Edge Servers can query the DNS for SRV records that meet the correct criteria and return results for any other Access Edge Server that offers federation.

The Access Edge Server queries for all the SRV records that meet the federation SRV record criteria, and the DNS server complies with a list of A records for other Edge Servers that advertise the federation SIP service, as shown in Figure 7-16. It is the Access Edge Servers that negotiate a partnership, which will be discussed later in this chapter. The final setup involves the use of certificates, allow and deny settings, and DNS configuration. Any of these can complicate the process of troubleshooting; therefore, creating documentation as you go is highly recommended.

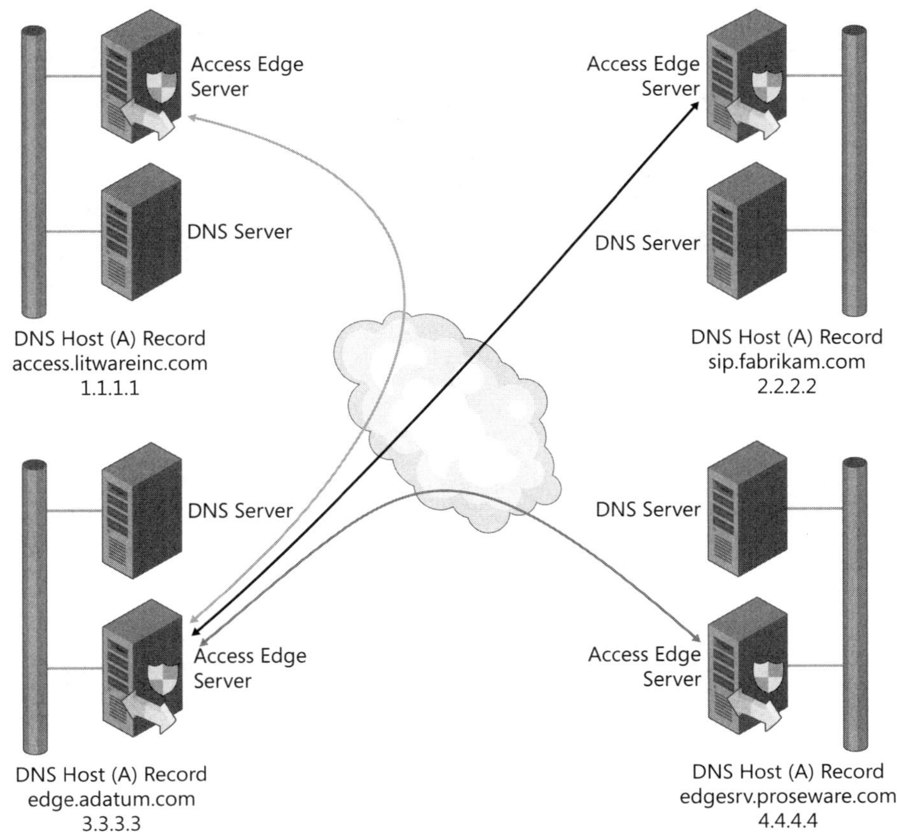

FIGURE 7-16 Access Edge Server finds other Office Communications Server R2–capable servers through a query to the DNS and A record resolution.

Note that federated partner discovery is evaluated and controlled in three ways:

- Allow automatic discovery of all federated partners.
- Allow discovery of partners, but assign trust levels by using the Allow tab.
- Do not allow partner discovery; instead, allow access only to partners or Edge Servers that are specifically defined. (This is the direct federation method discussed earlier in this chapter.)

To enable discovery of federated partners, do the following:

1. Log on to the Access Edge Server as a member of the Administrators group or a group that has equivalent user rights.
2. Click Start, click All Programs, click Administrative Tools, and then click Computer Management.
3. In the console tree, expand Services And Applications, right-click Microsoft Office Communications Server 2007 R2, and then click Properties.
4. On the Access Methods tab, select the Allow Discovery Of Federation Partners check box, as shown in figure 7-17.

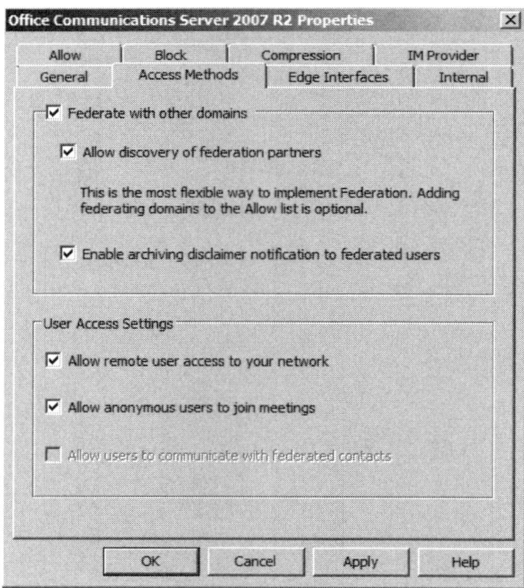

FIGURE 7-17 Select appropriate check boxes to define methods for federated discovery, archiving disclaimer, and types of remote access.

DIRECT FROM THE SOURCE

How Federated Traffic Is Evaluated When Using Automatic Discovery

Byron Spurlock
Consulting Services Consultant

If you choose to use automatic discovery of federated partners, the Access Edge Server automatically evaluates incoming federated traffic in the following way: If a federated party has sent more than 1,000 URIs in one second (valid or invalid) in the local domain, the Access Edge Server places the connection on the Watch list. The Access Edge Server then blocks any additional requests. If the Access Edge Server detects suspicious traffic on a connection, it limits the federation partner to a low message rate of 1 message per second. The Access Edge Server detects suspicious traffic by calculating the ratio of #successful to #failed responses.

The Access Edge Server also limits legitimate federated partner connections (unless added to the Allow list) to 20 messages per second. If you want to allow more than 1,000 URI requests sent by a legitimate federated partner or a volume of more than 20 messages per second sent to your organization, you must add the federated partner to the Allow tab. After configuring federation, you can use Office Communications Server 2007 R2 administrative tools to monitor and manage federated partner access on an ongoing basis. For more information, see the "Microsoft Office Communications Server 2007 Document: Administration Guide" at *http://www.microsoft.com/downloads/details.aspx?FamilyID=cb7dc2de-4504-484e-9229-bd8614be0633&DisplayLang=en.*

Understanding Federation with Public IM Providers

Establishing an IM relationship with another enterprise might sound familiar. If you have used the MSN, AOL, or Yahoo! IM clients, you have done this. Office Communications Server 2007 R2 enables you to establish a federation relationship between your enterprise environment and one, two, or all three of these IM providers.

Chapter 8 deals specifically with the process and technology of how Office Communications Server 2007 R2 enables you to do this. However, it is important to understand that this chapter is the foundation of how the relationship with public IM providers is established.

Understanding the Requirements for and Use of Certificates in Federation

Certificates play an important role in federation scenarios. The Access Edge Server of each federated enterprise must have an MTLS certificate. The MTLS certificate requires that the Edge Servers mutually authenticate. If MTLS authentication cannot be established, there is no communication.

As discussed in Chapter 4, "Infrastructure and Security Considerations," the DNS and certificates provide a strong authentication and encryption channel for data flow between the federated partners. Users will still use TLS, but servers must use MTLS for maximum security.

> ***NOTE*** **If your IM servers do not communicate after you put your plan in place, this problem is likely to be caused by a DNS or certificate naming conflict or mismatch. You should also ensure that all switch ports are on and configured correctly, check the server services for proper state of operation, and verify your IP configuration.**

Understanding On-Premises Conferencing Rules for Federated and Nonfederated Users

There is more to federation than just allowing partner enterprises to exchange instant messages. There are also conferencing services that enable partnering organizations to host a meeting on one or the other's infrastructure where they can present content, such as Office PowerPoint presentations. Externally, this is the Live Meeting service that Microsoft hosts for customers that includes the ability to host audio and video, such as real-time discussions using microphones, Web cams, or the Microsoft RoundTable device.

For meetings of this type, an allowance is made for anonymous users. Each must have a conference invitation (made up of a URL or URI that has session information, location information, and an invite key) to successfully join the conference.

Although the requirements for federated users with verifiable credentials are not too different, they have the following characteristics:

- Can attend Invite Within Network meetings
- Can be promoted to the role of presenter in Invite Within Network meetings
- Cannot participate in Invite Within Network (Restricted) meetings.

As mentioned in more detail in Chapter 6, "Conferencing Scenarios," terminology has changed from Office Communications Server 2007 as it relates to conference types. Open authenticated is now known as Invite Within Network, closed authenticated is now Invite Within Network (Restricted), and allow anonymous is now Invite Anyone.

Verifiable credentials means that you are an authenticated member of the domain in which the meeting is hosted or you are an authenticated member of a partner domain. The fact that you must be authenticated to your home domain prevents you from being an authenticated member from a nondomain location (such as a kiosk or another computer that is not in your company domain).

Configuring and Administering Federation

This section covers how to configure Edge Servers and user accounts for federation and how to manage federated partner access in an Office Communications Server 2007 R2 environment. This section will also look briefly at how to manage multiple accounts and how to block external domains.

Configuring User Accounts for Federation

You can explicitly manage users by overriding the global settings (in the Office Communications Server snap-in at the forest node level), or you can manage users as individuals. To configure a user object for federation, do the following:

1. Open the Office Communications Server 2007 R2 management console.
2. Expand the Pools node (Enterprise or Standard).
3. Expand the Users node and then locate the user that you want to configure.
4. Right-click the user, click Properties, and then click Configure.
5. Select the Enable Federation check box.

Administering Federated Partner Access

If you have configured support for federated partners, including an Audio Conferencing Provider (ACP) that is providing telephony integration, it is required that you actively manage the lists of external domains that can communicate with the servers in your organization.

The administrator can view a list of the federated domains that have most recently made at least one connection to your Access Edge Server. This list is not all-inclusive, and if numerous domains are trying to access your Access Edge Servers, domains that have not made an attempt for a while will roll off the list. To best use this feature, it is highly recommended that DNS-based discovery (via the SRV records) of Access Edge Servers be implemented as the federation configuration method of choice. You can also use federated partner discovery in conjunction with the Allow tab to control domains that you specifically will accept; all others will be blocked. For increased security, explicitly specify the FQDN of a federated partner's Access Edge Server.

When a domain is configured on the Allow list, communications with this domain are assumed to be legitimate. The Access Edge Server does not provide any means of traffic control over connections for these domains. In the case of DNS-based discovery of federated domains that are not on the Allow tab, connections are not fully trusted, and the Access Edge Server actively monitors these connections and limits the allowed throughput.

Two situations may cause the limit of 1,000 URIs to be met: one situation is problematic, and one is probable and expected.

- **Problematic** The remote party is attempting a directory attack on the local domains. If the traffic from this partner is deemed to be legitimate, the sending domain must be added to the Allow tab because the Access Edge Server will have already blocked further connections.
- **Probable and expected** Valid traffic between the local and federated domains exceeds the limit of 1,000 URIs in a second.

Further traffic from this domain will be dropped. If an administrator knows that the message rate from a given domain will exceed the 1,000 URI limit, the sending domain should be added to the Allow list; otherwise, messages beyond the 1,000 URI limit will not be accepted.

The information that the Access Edge Server acts on can be viewed by an administrator in the Office Communications Server 2007 R2 MMC on the Access Edge Server. Clicking the Open Federation tab reveals information about Allowed and Open Federated partners, as shown in Figure 7-18.

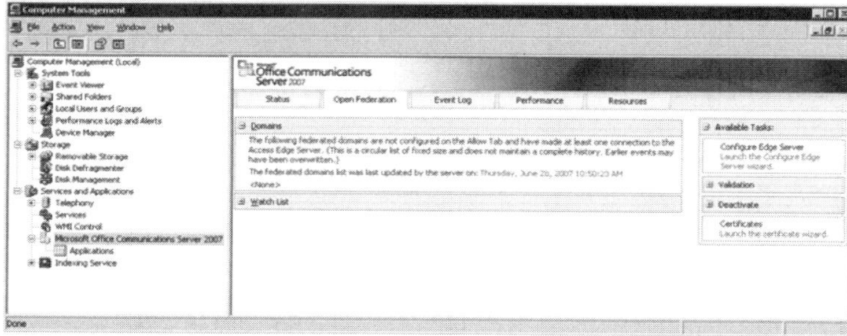

FIGURE 7-18 Open Federation tab, from which you can view and monitor usage for federated domains on the Access Edge Server.

Managing Multiple User Accounts

It is also possible to manage a large number of accounts by doing the following:

1. Open Active Directory Users and Computers.
2. Select an organizational unit, group, or collection of users.
3. Right-click and then select Configure Users.
4. Click Next on the first page of the Configure Office Communications Server Users Wizard.
5. On the Configure User Settings page, select Federation, ensure that the Enable radio button is set, and then click Next, as shown in Figure 7-19.

Note also in Figure 7-19 that there are six sections to this dialog box. Two of them refer to archiving, which is discussed in Chapter 3, "Server Roles," and in Chapter 16, "Monitoring."

Discussion of the functions that a user gains when Public IM Connectivity is checked and enabled is located in Chapter 8. The features that a user gains when Enhanced Presence is checked and enabled are located in 22, "Routing and Authentication." Two of these are germane to our topic of remote access Place Figure 7-19 after this paragraph.

In the previous procedure, Office Communications Server–enabled users were given the permission (that is, they were enabled) to communicate with federated partner users. The Remote User Access check box allows the same control over enabled users, yet they need to access the infrastructure remotely using Office Communicator. Selecting Enable allows Remote User Access action, and selecting Disable denies the remote access privilege to the currently selected collection of users, groups, or organizational units.

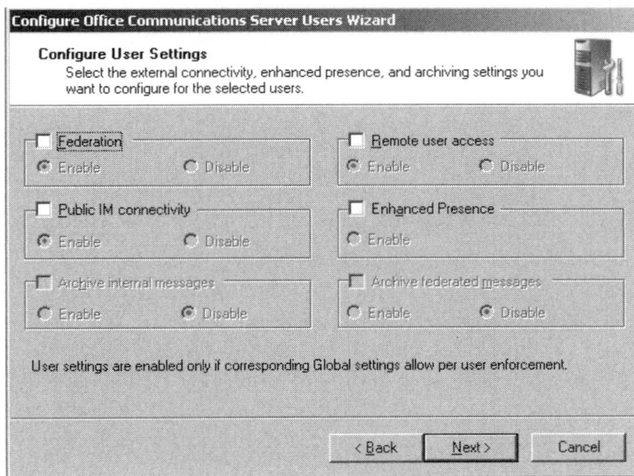

FIGURE 7-19 Configuration of user settings through the Configure Office Communications Server Users Wizard

However, these settings cannot take effect unless the global policy settings defined under the Forest - <*domain name*> node are set at the Federation tab. It is necessary to access the global properties OR the Global Properties dialog box by using the Office Communications Server 2007 R2 MMC on the front-end server or the Standard Edition Server.

You can access these global policies by doing the following (refer to Figure 7-22):

1. Click Start, click Administrative Tools, and then click Open Office Communications Server 2007 R2 MMC.
2. Click the Forest - <*domain name*> node.
3. Right-click, select Properties, and select Global Properties.
4. Select the Federation tab.

Note the Enable Federation And Public IM Connectivity check box. Once this check box is selected, the FQDN and Port text boxes will also be available. The FQDN of the server that you should input here is the server that will provide your outbound route for all SIP traffic destined for outside your infrastructure. The FQDN could be one of the following:

- Single Director
- Internal interface of load-balanced array of Directors
- Internal-facing interface of the single Access Edge Server
- Internal-facing interface of the hardware load balancer for an array of Access Edge Servers

When managing user accounts, you also need to keep anonymous users in mind. Anonymous (nonauthenticated) users are a reality that you must consider in an environment where you are accommodating users from domains with which there might be a casual relationship. You will need to decide whether to allow anonymous users into your environment and then decide whether they can access Live Meetings or A/V conferences. Anonymous users can be unsettling to some administrators and IT security staff, but Office Communications Server 2007 R2 has a number of safeguards for anonymous users.

First, users are not completely anonymous. You have to send them an invitation before they can access the conference or meeting. Second, they are accessing the Edge Servers, not your internal environment. Third, they have authenticated to their environment and their Active Directory in the case of a federated relationship. This is similar to allowing a user to access your Web server, except that these services are using streaming protocols instead of HTTP. Administrative control determines the options that dictate which anonymous users can be invited and in what manner.

Global properties enable you to set a policy that defines whether the Anonymous User settings are global or per user. Access the global properties by opening the Office Communications Server 2007 R2 management console and right-clicking the Forest node. As shown in Figure 7-20, a menu enables you to select Properties and then Global Properties.

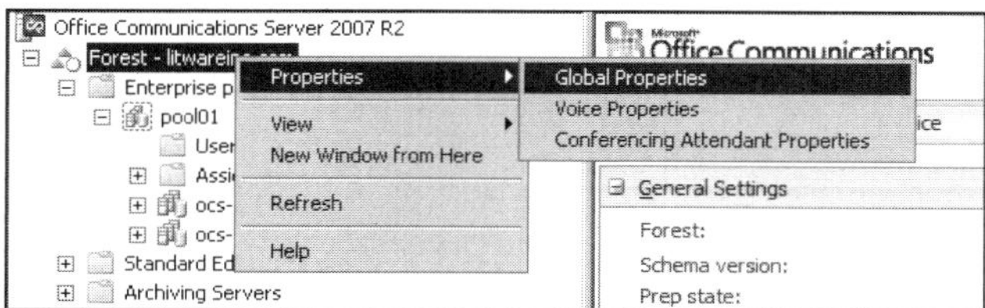

FIGURE 7-20 By selecting Global Properties, you can set properties that will be applied to the entire forest.

After you open the Global Properties dialog box, select the Meetings tab, as shown in Figure 7-21. You can select from three settings:

- **Allow users to invite anonymous participants** This option enables your users to invite users who are not members of your domain to attend anonymous meetings. Your users will be able to schedule and send invitations on behalf of nonmembers, and they can create ad hoc meetings. Of course, some of the abilities and settings are dependent on the Office Communicator client, and this can be controlled administratively as well. Just because users have the ability to send invitations does not necessarily mean that they are allowed to do so.

- **Disallow users from inviting anonymous participants** This option prevents users from inviting users who are not members of your domain (that is, who do not have authentication credentials to your domain—and this includes federated users) to meetings.
- **Enforce per user** This option leaves the administrative capacity to set whether a user can allow an anonymous user on a per-user basis. Although it might seem overly intensive, you can set this option if you intend to grant this ability to only a few people. For example, you can grant this ability to administrative assistants who are responsible for setting up meetings and are generally accountable for sending out external meeting notices—whether they are notices for meetings in your department or notices that the CEO is holding a shareholders' meeting.

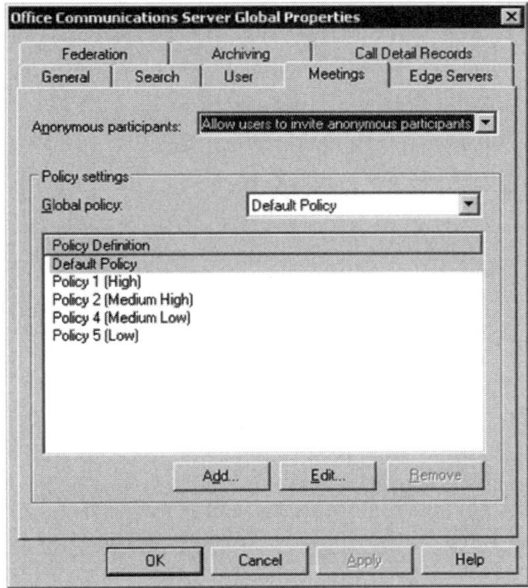

FIGURE 7-21 Selection of policies available to edit and apply to address administrative requirements

To re-emphasize, anonymous access still requires specific meeting keys, a URL/URI, and other identifying elements. Anonymous users are anonymous *only* because they do not have authentication credentials for your domain.

Blocking External Domains

It is sometimes necessary to explicitly block a specific domain because of continued unsolicited instant messages (SPIM) or attempts to compromise security. This is accomplished much like an Allow. Use the same beginning dialog box, but click the Block tab instead of the Allow tab.

1. Log on to the Access Edge Server as a member of the Administrators group or a group with equivalent user rights.
2. On the Access Edge Server, open Computer Management.

3. In the console tree, expand Services And Applications, right-click Office Communications Server 2007 R2, and then click Properties.
4. On the Block tab, click Add.
5. In the Add Blocked SIP Domain dialog box, in the SIP Domain text box, type the name of the domain to be added to the list of blocked SIP domains as shown in Figure 7-22. This name should be unique and should not already exist on the Block list for this Access Edge Server. The name cannot exceed 256 characters in length. Click OK.

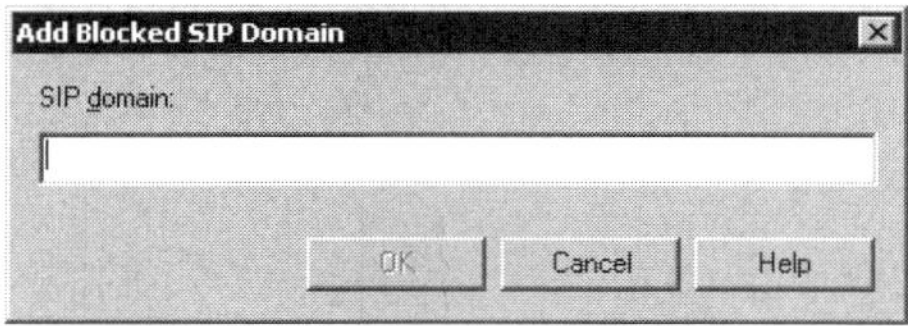

FIGURE 7-22 Enter domains that you want to block from access through this dialog box.

Examining the Technical Details Behind the Federation Scenario

A discussion of how federation is accomplished isn't complete without an in-depth look at the flow of messages and the protocols that accomplish it.

How Clients from Two Federated Domains Get Online and Register Presence

SIP is a signaling protocol—it uses verbs, or methods, much like Simple Mail Transfer Protocol (SMTP) does to talk to server processes. Many of these methods are clear as to what they are doing when presented to the server process.

The scenario we will examine is one in which two federated domains each have a user who wants to use IM with the user on the other domain. The domains we will use are Litwareinc.com and Fabrikam.com. Our users, Kim Akers (kakers@litwareinc.com) and John Peoples (jpeoples@fabrikam.com) communicate frequently by Office Communicator. They need to enter each other's SIP contact address in Communicator. Because there is no address book service between two federated enterprises, you need to know the contact information for the other person, similar to using SMTP.

John Peoples has entered kakers@litwareinc.com into his Communicator client, and Kim Akers has entered jpeoples@fabrikam.com into hers. John and Kim are now ready to initiate their communication, as shown in Figure 7-23.

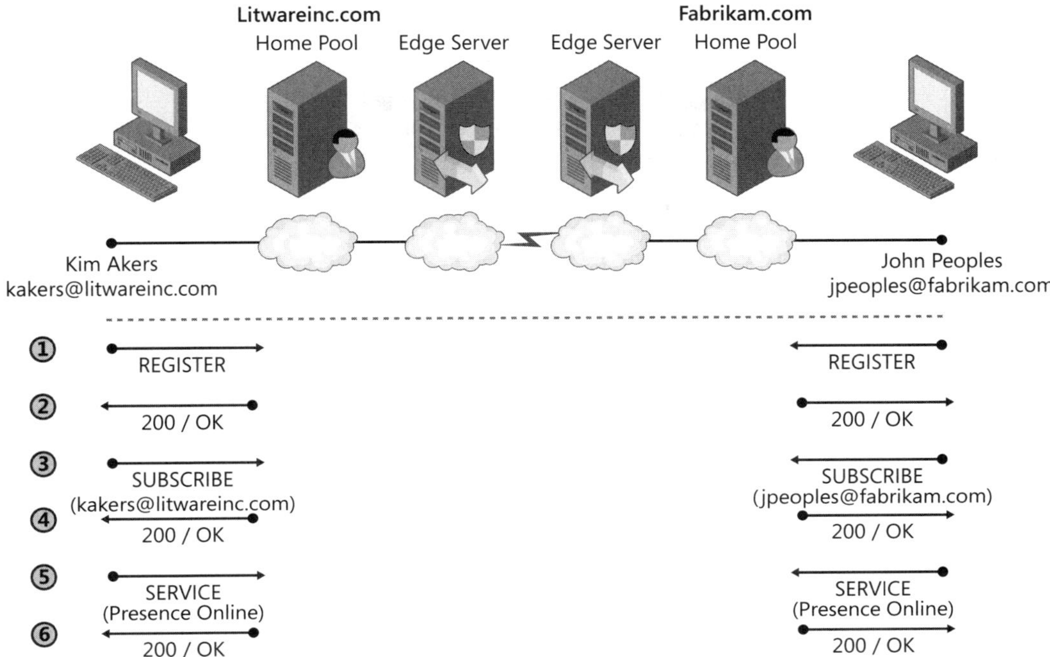

FIGURE 7-23 Client-to-home server conversation

If you use logging from the pool server (decoded by the snooper.exe tool in the Office Communications Server 2007 R2 Resource Kit tools [see Chapter 20, "Diagnostic Tools and Resources," for more information about using the Snooper tool]) and the Access Edge Server, what you see is a great deal more than the required message elements. Numerous DIAGNOSTIC messages and other messages ensure that the flow is correct and that the messages are arriving properly. The continued communication between the pool server and the Edge Server has nothing to do with maintaining communication for Kim and John.

NOTE The following discussion tracks the most important steps and is not a full step-by-step look at each and every message. The missing steps are typically OK or DIAGNOSTIC messages that don't provide anything more than a simple "I heard you." To avoid redundancy, the analysis of each type of message is limited unless something was new to learn or observe in a subsequent message. The outlined steps depend on the diagram presented in Figure 7-23.

IMPORTANT The steps in the following traces depend on the diagram presented in Figure 7-23. Steps are missing because we are not following each step, only those that are not redundant.

Step 1: REGISTER sip:litwareinc.com SIP/2.0

The first part of the message flow begins with the initial discussion of the Communicator client with the home pool server. The client who is logging in must register with the pool to which she is a member. This tells the server where the client can be reached. Finally, note that the certificates that were prepared are being used to establish TLS.

```
TL_INFO(TF_PROTOCOL) [0]06F4.0CDC::08/22/2007-19:09:27.536.
    00000440 (SIPStack,SIPAdminLog::TraceProtocolRecord:
    SIPAdminLog.cpp(122))
$$begin_record
Instance-Id: 00000280
Direction: incoming
Peer: 10.0.0.24:2065
Message-Type: request
Start-Line: REGISTER sip:vdomain1.com SIP/2.0
From: <sip:kakers@litwareinc.com>;tag=b801f3431d;epid=5d3080be61
To: <sip: kakers@litwareinc.com>
CSeq: 2 REGISTER
Call-ID: 091eeac004fb4d94bee8845581203051
Via: SIP/2.0/TLS 10.0.0.24:2065
Max-Forwards: 70
Contact: <sip:10.0.0.24:2065;transport=tls;ms-opaque=57561cdbc3>;methods="INVITE,
MESSAGE, INFO, OPTIONS, BYE,
    CANCEL, NOTIFY, ACK, REFER, BENOTIFY";proxy=replace;
    +sip.instance=
    "<urn:uuid:20C60920-2E75-5AB3-9252-DF040FAD120E>"
User-Agent: UCCP/2.0.6502.502 OC/2.0.6502.502 (Microsoft Office Communicator)
Authorization: Kerberos qop="auth", realm=
    "SIP Communications Service", targetname=
    "sip/pool.litwareinc.com", gssapi-data=
    "YIIEmQYJKoZIhvcSAQICAQBuggSIMII
<snip of gssapi data>
1y5947WB1ux7FUNWDi6hzm44H9DHWrnglDmYG4jDxmW+razdEP1l1MUXvuAbE=",
    version=3
Supported: gruu-10, adhoclist, msrtc-event-categories
Supported: ms-forking
ms-keep-alive: UAC;hop-hop=yes
Event: registration
Content-Length: 0
Message-Body:
```

Step 3: SUBSCRIBE sip:kakers@litwareinc.com SIP/2.0

The registered user agent uses a SUBSCRIBE method to receive notifications on the change of state or other elements. Specifically, the user agent needs to know about events that occur that are of interest, and it establishes event handlers that the client is interested in so that the proper notification is sent when that event is triggered. There is no corresponding UNSUBSCRIBE method to terminate a SUBSCRIBE method. However, a SUBSCRIBE message is sent with the Expires header field set to 0. Following the conversation in the message flow is simplified by following the tag and epid fields. Also, note the user agent. The SUBSCRIBE request occurs mostly in the last couple of lines.

```
TL_INFO(TF_PROTOCOL) [0]06F4.0CDC::08/22/2007-19:09:27.586.
    00000473 (SIPStack,SIPAdminLog::TraceProtocolRecord:
    SIPAdminLog.cpp(122))
$$begin_record
Instance-Id: 00000284
Direction: incoming
Peer: 10.0.0.24:2065
Message-Type: request
Start-Line: SUBSCRIBE sip:kakers@litwareinc.com SIP/2.0
From: <sip:kakers@litwareinc.com>;tag=76293b8509;epid=5d3080be61
To: <sip:kakers@litwareinc.com>
CSeq: 1 SUBSCRIBE
Call-ID: b6076edf0ea146e594624fe3ae1ba0f7
Via: SIP/2.0/TLS 10.0.0.24:2065
Max-Forwards: 70
Contact: <sip:kakers@litwareinc.com;opaque=user:epid:
    IAnGIHUus1qSUt8ED60SDgAA;gruu>
User-Agent: UCCP/2.0.6502.502 OC/2.0.6502.502 (Microsoft Office
    Communicator)
Event: vnd-microsoft-roaming-self
Accept: application/vnd-microsoft-roaming-self+xml
Supported: com.microsoft.autoextend
Supported: ms-benotify
Proxy-Require: ms-benotify
Supported: ms-piggyback-first-notify
Proxy-Authorization: Kerberos qop="auth", realm=
"SIP Communications Service", opaque="3A852553",
    crand="c458b6ff", cnum="2", targetname="sip/pool.litwareinc.com",
    response="602306092a864886f71201020201011100ffffffffc098b3
    7c7b9497ccca0f8eb3b407cd5c"
Content-Type: application/vnd-microsoft-roaming-self+xml
Content-Length: 174
Message-Body: <roamingList xmlns="http://schemas.microsoft.com/2006/09/sip/roaming-self">
    <roaming type="categories"/><roaming type="containers"/>
    <roaming type="subscribers"/></roamingList>
$$end_record
```

The response to this message is a pair of verbose 200 OK messages that informs the client what they are now subscribed for and confirms the events. A snippet of one of those messages is shown next. Note that there is no defined expire time because the server expects to see a SUBSCRIBE with the Expires: 0 field to terminate the SUBSCRIBE.

```
<category name="contactCard" instance="0" publishTime="2007-08-22T18:57:41.610"
container="0" version="2" expireType="static">
<contactCard xmlns="http://schemas.microsoft.com/2006/09/sip/
    contactcard" >
<identity >
<name >
<displayName >
Kim Akers</displayName>
</name>
<email >
kakers@litwareinc.com</email>
</identity>
</contactCard>
</category>
<category name="note" instance="0" publishTime=
    "2007-08-22T19:01:00.317" container="32000" version="1"
    expireType="static"/>
<category name="note" instance="0" publishTime=
    "2007-08-22T19:01:00.317" container="100" version="1"
     expireType="static"/>
<category name="state" instance="0" publishTime=
    "2007-08-22T19:01:00.317" container="32000" version="1"
    expireType="static">
<state xmlns="http://schemas.microsoft.com/2006/09/sip/state" xmlns:xsi="http://www.
w3.org/2001/XMLSchema-instance" manual=
    "false" xsi:type="aggregateState" ><availability >
    18500</availability><endpointLocation ></endpointLocation>
</state>
</category>
<category name="state" instance="0" publishTime=
    "2007-08-22T19:09:05.720" container="400" version="1"
    expireType="static">
```

Step 5: SERVICE sip:kakers@litwareinc.com SIP/2.0

The SERVICE method is used in this case to turn the presence on for Kim Akers. At this point, Kim can now be seen online and anyone who has her in his contact list will be able to see that she is online (assuming, of course, that she hasn't specifically set her presence as Offline) and what her current status is.

```
TL_INFO(TF_PROTOCOL)
[0]06F4.0CDC::08/22/2007-19:10:04.517.0000055d
(SIPStack,SIPAdminLog::TraceProtocolRecord:
    SIPAdminLog.cpp(122))$$begin_record
Instance-Id: 0000029B
Direction: incoming
Peer: 10.0.0.24:2065
Message-Type: request
Start-Line: SERVICE sip:kakers@litwareinc.com SIP/2.0
From: <sip:kakers@litwareinc.com >;tag=446e225cd5;epid=5d3080be61
To: <sip:kakers@litwareinc.com >
CSeq: 1 SERVICE
Call-ID: a613e9b91a774db4bf65ba293814ad92
Via: SIP/2.0/TLS 10.0.0.24:2065
Max-Forwards: 70
Contact: <sip:kakers@litwareinc.com;opaque=user:epid:
    IAnGIHUus1qSUt8ED60SDgAA;gruu>
User-Agent: UCCP/2.0.6502.502 OC/2.0.6502.502 (Microsoft Office
    Communicator)
Proxy-Authorization: Kerberos qop="auth", realm=
    "SIP Communications Service", opaque="3A852553",
    crand="87e1e7a1", cnum="11",
    targetname="sip/pool.litwareinc.com",
    response="602306092a864886f71201020201011100ffffffffdf
    2ec24a2d6d546878a3ddc6ade6690d"
Content-Type: application/msrtc-presence-setsubscriber+xml
Content-Length: 162
Message-Body: <publish
    xmlns="http://schemas.microsoft.com/2006/09/sip/rich-
    presence"><publications uri="sip:kakers@litwareinc.com">
    <publication categoryName="device" instance="722818101"
     container="2" version="0" expireType="endpoint"><device
xmlns="http://schemas.microsoft.com/2006/09/sip/device"
    endpointId="87AAC0AD-3A90-5901-A799-B4672392F3BF">
    <capabilities preferred="false" uri="sip:kakers@litwareinc.com">
    <text capture="true" render="true" publish="false"/><gifInk
    capture="false" render="true" publish="false"/><isfInk
    capture="false" render="true" publish="false"/></capabilities>
    <timezone>00:00:00+01:00
```

```
    </timezone><machineName>CLIENT</machineName></device>
    </publication><publication categoryName="state"
instance="850482499" container="3" version="0" expireType=
    "endpoint"><state xmlns="http://schemas.microsoft.com
    /2006/09/sip
    /state" manual="false" xmlns:xsi="http://www.w3.org/2001
    /XMLSchema-instance" xsi:type="machineState"><availability>3500</availability>
    <endpointLocation></endpointLocation></state></publication>
    <publication categoryName="state" instance="850482499"
    container="2" version="0" expireType="endpoint"><state>
    xmlns="http://schemas.microsoft.com/2006/09/sip/state"
    manual="false"
    xmlns:xsi="http://www.w3.org/2001/XMLSchema-instance"
    xsi:type="machineState"><availability>3500</availability>
    <endpointLocation></endpointLocation></state></publication>
</publications></publish>
$$end_record
```

This completes the initial "getting online" sequence—Kim Akers is online, and John Peoples is online as well. If John and Kim have each other in their Contacts list, they should be able to see that the other person is online by use of the presence indicator. We've initiated and opened the Office Communicator client, signed in to our pool (home) server, and set our current presence status.

Communication from One Federated Enterprise to Another

Now that Kim and John are ready to start a conversation, let's examine the details of adding users to the remote user's pool via the SUBSCRIBE and NOTIFY messages from one enterprise to another across the federated connection, as shown in Figure 7-24.

> ***NOTE*** **The following discussion tracks the most important steps and is not a full step-by-step look at each and every message. Also, to avoid redundancy, the analysis of each type of message is limited unless there was something new to learn or observe in a subsequent message.**

> ***IMPORTANT*** **As in the previous example, this set of traces depends on the steps outlined in Figure 7-24. We are not following every step, just those that would be important to understand the flow of traffic and data. This information is useful for troubleshooting purposes.**

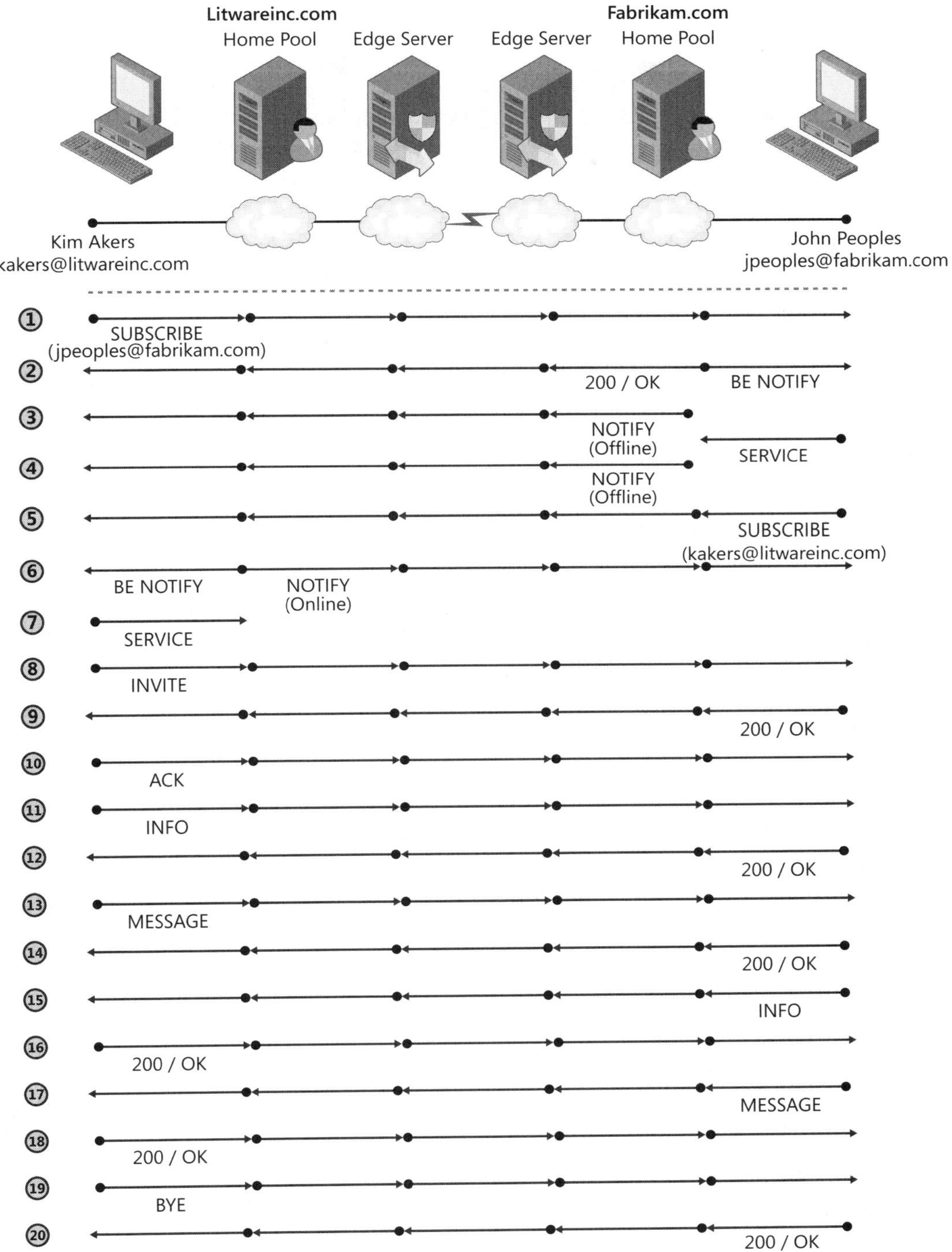

FIGURE 7-24 Full federation conversation with user-to-user instant messaging

Step 1: SUBSCRIBE sip:jpeoples@fabrikam.com SIP/2.0

John and Kim are now logged in and signed in to their respective enterprises. Now, the respective users have to be able to get enough information to be able to receive event notifications about their contact records. Because Kim and John have each other's records, the client knows that it has to subscribe to the home pool of the other user. The flow begins with a SUBSCRIBE to Fabrikam.com via Kim's home pool and Access Edge Servers.

```
TL_INFO(TF_PROTOCOL)
[0]05F8.0944::08/22/2007-19:10:01.170.000007fe
    (SIPStack,SIPAdminLog::TraceProtocolRecord:
SIPAdminLog.cpp(122))$$begin_record
Instance-Id: 000000B6
Direction: outgoing;source="internal edge";destination=
   "external edge"
Peer:accessproxy.litwareinc.com:5061
Message-Type: request
Start-Line: SUBSCRIBE sip:jpeoples@fabrikam.com SIP/2.0
From: "Kim Akers"<sip:kakers@litwareinc.com>;tag=b5942d9dd9;
    epid=7469ade8c2
To: <sip:jpeoples@fabrikam.com>
CSeq: 1 SUBSCRIBE
Call-ID: f6c1d48ef2084b82b080aedeb3f31707
Record-Route: <sip:accessedge.litwareinc.com:5061;transport=tls;
    epid=7469ade8c2;lr>;tag=CC4625642D8B2D9A579AD58F130DD603
Via: SIP/2.0/TLS 11.0.0.25:1061;branch=z9hG4bKEEEBA844.0226596C;branched=FALSE;
ms-internal-info="abnlJuPbnBNx-r4dTTJSZtvBOOuVACJlls2H2kKQAA"
ms-asserted-verification-level: ms-source-verified-user=verified
Max-Forwards: 68
Via: SIP/2.0/TLS 10.0.0.20:1504;branch=z9hG4bK27C8ADD2.3872BC78;branched=FALSE;
ms-received-port=1504;ms-received-cid=1600
Via: SIP/2.0/TLS 10.0.0.24:1251;ms-received-port=1251;
ms-received-cid=1F00
  <SNIP>
```

On the Fabrikam.com Access Edge Server, we can find the SUBSCRIBE message as it comes into the server:

```
TL_INFO(TF_PROTOCOL)
[0]09B4.0CAC::08/22/2007-19:10:01.537.00000009
    (SIPStack,SIPAdminLog::TraceProtocolRecord:
SIPAdminLog.cpp(122))$$begin_record
Instance-Id: 0000022B
Direction: incoming;source="external edge";destination=
    "internal edge"
Peer: accessedge.litwareinc.com:1061
Message-Type: request
```

```
Start-Line: SUBSCRIBE sip:jpeoples@fabrikam.com SIP/2.0
From: "Kim Akers"<sip:kakers@litwareinc.com>;tag=b5942d9dd9;
    epid=7469ade8c2
To: <sip:jpeoples@fabrikam.com.com>
CSeq: 1 SUBSCRIBE
Call-ID: f6c1d48ef2084b82b080aedeb3f31707
Record-Route: sip:edgeserver.fabrikam.com:5061;transport=tls;
    epid=7469ade8c2;lr;tag=CC4625642D8B2D9A579AD58F130DD603
<snip>
```

The DIAGNOSTIC message that is seen right after the preceding message shows that our federation is recognized and the SIP domain has been recognized:

```
TL_INFO(TF_DIAG) [0]09B4.0CAC::08/22/2007-19:10:01.577.0000000d
     (SIPStack,SIPAdminLog::TraceDiagRecord:
SIPAdminLog.cpp(144))$$begin_record
LogType: diagnostic
Severity: information
Text: The message has an Allowed Partner Server domain
SIP-Start-Line: SUBSCRIBE sip:jpeoples@fabrikam.com SIP/2.0
SIP-Call-ID: f6c1d48ef2084b82b080aedeb3f31707
SIP-CSeq: 1 SUBSCRIBE
Peer: accessedge.litwareinc.com:1061
Data: domain="litwareinc.com"
$$end_record
```

Step 2: BENOTIFY and OK 200

In this set of actions, several things happen in a quick sequence. If you look at the message flow, you'll see that the home server sends a BENOTIFY message to John Peoples's client, and it also sends a 200 OK message back to Kim Akers. The 200 OK tells her client that it is now subscribed successfully on the Fabrikam.com domain and, much like the preceding SUBSCRIBE message, it also indicates what the SUBSCRIBE contained.

The BENOTIFY is a bit different. When a SUBSCRIBE comes in, we're subscribing to the pool on which a user is a member. The home server has to tell the client that the SUBSCRIBE is taking place, and the client now has some things to do. The BENOTIFY to John's client looks like this:

```
TL_INFO(TF_PROTOCOL) [0]06F4.0AF8::08/22/2007-19:10:04.507.0000055a
     (SIPStack,SIPAdminLog::TraceProtocolRecord:
SIPAdminLog.cpp(122))$$begin_record
Instance-Id: 0000029A
Direction: outgoing;source="local"
```

```
Peer: 11.0.0.25:2065
Message-Type: request
Start-Line: BENOTIFY sip:11.0.0.25:2065;transport=tls;
    ms-opaque=57561cdbc3;ms-received-cid=2D00 SIP/2.0
From: <sip:jpeoples@fabrikam.com>;tag=55D24D67
To: <sip: jpeoples@fabrikam.com >;tag=50d3171d57;epid=5d3080be61
CSeq: 2 BENOTIFY
Call-ID: 63dab314323b44a08637aa1775518841
Via: SIP/2.0/TLS 11.0.0.35:5061;branch=z9hG4bKA56C7273.03AB7EC2;branched=FALSE
    Authentication-Info: Kerberos rspauth="602306092A864886F712010
    20201011100FFFFFFFFC64C8A2A6175A0639CA680B771C00C1F",
    srand="911862A4", snum="14", opaque="3A852553", qop="auth",
    targetname="sip/pool.fabrikam.com", realm="SIP Communications
    Service"
Max-Forwards: 70
Content-Length: 163
Content-Type: application/vnd-microsoft-roaming-contacts+xml
Event: vnd-microsoft-roaming-contacts
subscription-state: active;expires=52019
Message-Body: ----****MESSAGE BODY DELETED****----
$$end_record
```

Steps 3 and 4 are going to respond to the BENOTIFY and initiate a SERVICE method. But just before that, John's home server ensures that his presence is in an offline state. The SERVICE method fires, and John's client notifies the home pool server that he has received the BENOTIFY and that he's ready to communicate. The home pool responds by sending John's presence to Litwareinc.com, which will be reflected in Kim's client, and to the state that John indicated when he first signed on.

In step 5, John initiates a SUBSCRIBE that is destined for the Litwareinc.com domain and that will accomplish the same set of processes that occurred in Fabrikam when Kim initiated her SUBSCRIBE. Also, the BENOTIFY is sent to Kim and the SERVICE method fires, just as it did for John.

John and Kim are both online, can see each other's presence, and are on the verge of starting the conversation.

Step 8: INVITE sip:jpeoples@fabrikam.com SIP/2.0

Step 8 is the initial INVITE message from Kim Akers to John Peoples—the method used to initiate the actual IM conversation. Note that this is the first message that indicates there is full awareness on the part of both parties, and endpoints:

```
TL_INFO(TF_PROTOCOL) [0]05F8.0944::08/22/2007-19:10:12.876.00000835
    (SIPStack,SIPAdminLog::TraceProtocolRecord:
SIPAdminLog.cpp(122))$$begin_record
```

```
Instance-Id: 000000BA
Direction: incoming;source="internal edge";destination=
    "external edge"
Peer: pool.litwareinc.com:1504
Message-Type: request
Start-Line: INVITE sip:jpeoples@fabrikam.com SIP/2.0
From: "Kim Akers"<sip:kakers@litwareinc.com>;tag=af89c73ee3;
    epid=7469ade8c2
To: <sip: jpeoples@fabrikam.com >
CSeq: 1 INVITE
<snip>
EndPoints: <sip:kakers@litwareinc.com>, <sip:jpeoples@fabrikam.com>
Supported: com.microsoft.rtc-multiparty
<snip>
```

Following the INVITE (in steps 9 and 10) is an OK that John's client received the INVITE and an ACK back to John that Kim has received the OK to the messaging session. At this point, things are pretty much established.

Remember that SIP is a signaling protocol. There is no way to know for sure that the other party received the message unless we respond. Almost everything has an OK associated with it. However, the ACK is unique to the INVITE request because this is a three-way handshake process. Also, you should remember that SIP is generally a one-sided conversation. It is two clients that have established their *own* message flow. That one responds is merely courtesy and part of the protocol.

Step 12: INFO

In Office Communications Server 2007 R2 instant messaging, it's the INFO message (step 12) that tells John's client that Kim is typing and also displays the text "Kim is typing a message" in his client.

```
<snip>
Route: <sip:pool.fabrikam.com:5061;transport=tls;ms-role-rs-to;lr>
User-Agent: UCCP/2.0.6502.502 OC/2.0.6502.502 (Microsoft Office Communicator)
Supported: timer
Content-Type: application/xml
Content-Length: 87
Message-Body: <?xml version="1.0"?>
<KeyboardActivity>
 <status status="type" />
</KeyboardActivity>
$$end_record
```

Step 13: MESSAGE

Kim has completed typing and is sending her initial message to John. The message text is not seen in the Snooper tool, which shows the following: Message-Body: ----****MESSAGE BODY DELETED****----.

```
TL_INFO(TF_PROTOCOL) [0]05F8.0944::08/22/2007-19:10:13.217.000008ba
    (SIPStack,SIPAdminLog::TraceProtocolRecord:
SIPAdminLog.cpp(122))$$begin_record
Instance-Id: 000000C4
Direction: outgoing;source="internal edge";destination=
"external edge"
Peer: accessedge.litwareinc.com:5061
Message-Type: request
Start-Line: MESSAGE sip:jpeoples@fabrikam.com;opaque=user:epid:
IAnGIHUus1qSUt8ED60SDgAA;gruu SIP/2.0
From: <sip:kakers@litwareinc.com>;tag=af89c73ee3;epid=7469ade8c2
To: "" <sip:jpeoples@fabrikam.com>;epid=5d3080be61;
tag=4c8535fa6e
CSeq: 2 MESSAGE
Call-ID: 5c2aad6c090241c9bb3b86753b53cee1
Via: SIP/2.0/TLS 11.0.0.25:1061;branch=z9hG4bK75B30E9F.92A6F7E6;branched=FALSE;
ms-internal-info="abEScJu0wN6e6exY40NhVTSh_aIGKSpvfm2H2kKQAA"
ms-asserted-verification-level: ms-source-verified-user=verified
ms-archiving: TRUE
Max-Forwards: 68
Via: SIP/2.0/TLS 10.0.0.20:1504;branch=z9hG4bK58136098.0DBECCED;branched=FALSE;
ms-received-port=1504;ms-received-cid=1600
<snip>
```

The remainder of the message flow involves a series of back-and-forth MESSAGE, 200 OK, and INFO messages. At the end of the session, they end their conversation—or one person decides to end the session. With the final message that we're going to look at, one person sends the BYE method and the session is terminated. (Obviously, the other person can re-establish the communication, which involves most of the steps that we've reviewed in this section.)

Step 19: BYE

Oddly, not much is interesting about this message. We just simply say BYE.

```
TL_INFO(TF_PROTOCOL)
[0]05F8.0944::08/22/2007-19:10:31.754.00000923
(SIPStack,SIPAdminLog::TraceProtocolRecord:
SIPAdminLog.cpp(122))$$begin_record
Instance-Id: 000000CA
```

```
Direction: outgoing;source="internal edge";destination=
    "external edge"
Peer: edgeserver.fabrikam.com:5061
Message-Type: request
Start-Line: BYE sip:jpeoples@fabrikam.com;opaque=user:epid:
    IAnGIHUus1qSUt8ED60SDgAA;
gruu SIP/2.0
From: <sip:kakers@litwareinc.com>;tag=af89c73ee3;epid=7469ade8c2
To: "" <sip:jpeoples@fabrikam.com>;epid=5d3080be61;
    tag=4c8535fa6e
CSeq: 3 BYE
Call-ID: 5c2aad6c090241c9bb3b86753b53cee1
Via: SIP/2.0/TLS 11.0.0.25:1061;branch=z9hG4bKD2EEC434.230ACDF5;branched=FALSE;
ms-internal-info="abBF-BCHJPotZZ4WauGOrWULVm-qEjCs312H2kKQAA"
ms-asserted-verification-level: ms-source-verified-user=verified
Max-Forwards: 68
Via: SIP/2.0/TLS 10.0.0.20:1504;branch=z9hG4bKB5A56090.D7906399;branched=FALSE;
ms-received-port=1504;ms-received-cid=1600
Via: SIP/2.0/TLS 10.0.0.24:1251;ms-received-port=1251;
ms-received-cid=1F00
Route: <sip:assessedge.litwareinc.com:5061;transport=tls;
    epid=5d3080be61;lr;ms-key-info=jACAANllrITgfVcd4OTHAQEC
    AAADZgAAAKQAAErVfkqSMT4KWRwNZJ9pTueIXj9JstdoDPUx9993-kqbW
    A6eDmg7tjwUXo9W_VhTmuPGcxExiybWGAshIi4C9dNRNXYQEkyEv7V1OY
    J1-gEH2ezJXyEclUq3o4RXL5WXqzulCMYmXTt_OwA8gQIeCILVPQY5ty
    ZvZMlqg8pQJ4lkFjqA1Nq1R4LKfdXA4s0lf0M7K2cX-iqosQf6sK-or2G
    Ice7zj2qhcibEOReEXe6YoIWk-nvDeSTmrDMMzR6TKkEltjA6I5BYkU_Cx
    oJ8H9xdLEEjtTWH3Fqn7javve1OVaRNywoCNVc_BQOZ8frx5hKv07frixn
    jOuO8FzjthnQA;ms-route-sig=cavUCK1BG4udtUgjn2qUfRLCzTjFdx7R
    j28P9FsQAA>
Route: <sip:pool.fabrikam.com:5061;transport=tls;ms-role-rs-to;lr>
User-Agent: UCCP/2.0.6502.502 OC/2.0.6502.502 (Microsoft Office
    Communicator)
Content-Length: 0
Message-Body:
```

The subsequent and final 200 OK from jpeoples@fabrikam.com is step 20:

```
TL_INFO(TF_PROTOCOL)
[0]05F8.0944::08/22/2007-19:10:31.764.00000926
(SIPStack,SIPAdminLog::TraceProtocolRecord:
SIPAdminLog.cpp(122))$$begin_record
Instance-Id: 000000CB
Direction: incoming;source="external edge";destination=
    "internal edge"
```

```
Peer: edgeserver.fabrikam.com:5061
Message-Type: response
Start-Line: SIP/2.0 200 OK
From: "John Peoples"<sip:jpeoples@fabrikam.com>;tag=af89c73ee3;
    epid=7469ade8c2
To: "" <sip:kakers@litwareinc.com>;epid=5d3080be61;tag=4c8535fa6e
CSeq: 3 BYE
<snip>
```

Summary

This chapter highlighted remote access, federation, and some of the topologies used in the edge network. The consolidated, scaled single-site, and multisite topologies were all identified and briefly explained. In addition, each of the three Edge Server roles (Access, Web Conferencing, and A/V Edge Server) were identified along with how they are involved in enabling conferencing, federation, and basic remote access capabilities. Office Communicator Web Access 2007 R2 was identified as an extended remote access tool that provides easier access for many uses.

Federation is an important part of the capabilities in Office Communications Server 2007 R2. The feature set has been refined and streamlined for a much more configurable and secure solution. In addition, the Audio/Video feature set and the Live Conferencing capabilities all can be launched from the Office Communicator client, enabling local, federated, and anonymous parties to take part in a variety of communications and collaboration methods. With all of these capabilities, Office Communications Server 2007 R2 delivers a rich and compelling solution for intra-enterprise and extra-enterprise solutions.

Finally, as Chapter 8 details, federation sets the stage for a manageable and controllable public IM solution. The ability to manage which providers (Yahoo!, AOL, or MSN) your users have access to is a powerful tool. All of this is available from Office Communicator 2007 R2, Web browser, Live Meeting 2007 R2, and Office Communications Server 2007 R2.

Additional Resources

- Office Communications Server R2 Edge Server Deployment Guide, found at *http://go.microsoft.com/fwlink/?LinkID=133685*
- Office Communication Server 2007 R2 Resource Kit Tools (snooper.exe used in this section), found at *http://go.microsoft.com/fwlink/?LinkID=133686*

- The article "You Cannot Start the Communications Server 2007 Logging and Tracing Tool from an Access Edge Server or from a Front-End Server," found at *http://go.microsoft.com/fwlink/?LinkID=133687*
- [MS-AVEDGEA]: Audio Video Edge Authentication Protocol Specification, found at *http://go.microsoft.com/fwlink/?LinkID=133688*
- *Windows Server 2008 PKI and Certificate Security* by Brian Komar (Microsoft Press, 2008)
- Edge Planning Tool for Office Communications Server 2007, found at *http://go.microsoft.com/fwlink/?LinkID=133690*

CHAPTER 8

Public IM Connectivity Scenarios

Expanding on its popularity in the business arena, a large segment of the population now uses instant messaging (IM) for casual communication outside the workplace. Today, IM is a communication means of choice, whether to communicate to business colleagues around the world or friends across the street. Instant messaging is defined as a one-to-one or many-to-many conversation carried out through a software tool. For Microsoft Office Communications Server 2007 and Microsoft Office Communications Server 2007 R2, this is the Office Communicator tool. Instant messaging enables people who are either close in proximity to each other or far away to communicate in real time by establishing communication and then typing their conversation in the Office Communicator tool.

IM is based on the Internet Engineering Task Force (IETF) standards discussed in Chapter 4, "Infrastructure and Security Considerations." Because Office Communications Server 2007 R2 is also based on the IETF standards, it integrates easily with IM.

What Is Public IM Connectivity?

Public IM connectivity extends basic IM capabilities and enables Office Communications Server 2007 R2 to consolidate three of the major IM providers—AOL, Yahoo!, and MSN—into the Office Communicator client. This enables users to collect their contacts in one place and communicate with them from one consistent interface. This ability to work from one interface simplifies small tasks, such as confirming an order with a supplier, as well as complex tasks, such as handling an issue with a large partner.

For the enterprise, public IM connectivity also enables you to manage a set of communication policies by using the Office Communications Server 2007 R2 console. IM can be a difficult form of communication to manage, because users can unknowingly divulge information that they might not in other forms of communication, possibly resulting in disclosures that would violate the Sarbanes-Oxley Act (SOX), the Health Information Portability and Accountability Act (HIPAA), or other regulations regarding communications. A common set of policies can help an organization comply with these regulations, as well as reduce the likelihood of problems that can arise from simple mischief.

NOTE **Sarbanes-Oxley (SOX) and the Health Information Portability and Accountability Act (HIPAA) are two regulations that define how information is handled and protected. SOX pertains mostly to financial organizations and their providers. Most businesses are affected to some degree by SOX, because all companies handle some type of information that is ultimately governed by SOX. The act imposes specific rules on protection mechanisms for data in the company and requires that upper management (chief executive officer and chief financial officer) sign off on an annual audit performed by a certified firm or process. This audit ensures that the proper controls are in place to manage data and information and that they are properly applied.**

HIPAA directly affects the health care industry but is far reaching because it also affects any entity that might have access to customer or client records. The basis of HIPAA is that patient and physician records are protected so that the information is not disclosed to someone who has no need to use that information. Specifically, data must be encrypted at rest and in motion (for example, held in a database when at rest).

This chapter explains public IM setup, configuration, management, and compliance tools that are built into Office Communications Server 2007 R2 and how those tools can maximize the features that your users are already using.

Public IM Connectivity Scenarios

Office Communications Server 2007 R2 provides the means to communicate with other users on the public IM services that are managed and maintained by AOL, Yahoo!, and MSN. After the communication is established, users can share contacts and presence information, as well as communicate in real time across these networks. However, file transfers, games, formatted text, multimedia, and conferencing will be unavailable between Microsoft Office Communications users and public IM providers.

Enterprises that want to use public IM connectivity for their infrastructure need to:

- Obtain licensing for public IM connectivity, in addition to the license for Office Communications Server 2007 R2 and the Office Communications client.

- Set up and provision the site domain identification and presence by using a Microsoft Web site that is dedicated to the purpose of managing registration and provisioning for public IM connectivity.

The license purchased includes all three IM providers (MSN, Yahoo!, and AOL). However, the administrator controls whether users have access to one, two, or all three of the providers.

By default, none of the three providers are accessible. You must complete a two-step process to enable your users to access the IM providers. First, you must provision the providers for your enterprise. Then, you can enable your users for one, two, or all three providers by configuring the options under Federation in the Office Communications Server management tool. If you need to enable or disable a provider at a later time, you can run the provisioning process again.

As in other federation scenarios, users in your organization can add users of the public IM networks to their Allow and Block lists in the Office Communicator client. To allow or block these lists in Office Communicator, users should do the following:

1. Open Office Communicator.
2. Select the drop-down list in the upper left of Office Communicator .
3. Select Tools and then Add A Contact.
4. Select either Use An Email Address Or Sign-In Address or Search For A Contact.
5. Fill in the required e-mail or contact information, or select from Search for the contact you need to add.

The following three scenarios are possible:

- An external user of one of the public IM networks who is added to an Allow list can exchange IM with and see presence information for the owner of the list.
- An external public IM user who is not on either an Allow list or a Block list can exchange IM and presence information with an internal user, but the internal user can block all such requests.
- An external public IM user who is added to a Block list can neither exchange IM with, nor see presence information for, the owner of the list.

Administrators have full control over who in their organization is authorized for public IM connectivity. After authorization, a user can communicate with all public IM service providers that are enabled for the organization. If MSN and Yahoo! are both enabled, you cannot prevent a user from using MSN and allow only Yahoo! to be used.

Administrators can authorize public IM connectivity for individual users or for groups and can change these authorizations as needed. Administrators can exercise additional control over unsolicited commercial IM or spam over IM (SPIM) by configuring message filters that restrict access from unverified users. For more information about message filtering, see the section titled "Security Considerations" later in this chapter or the section titled "Configuring Intelligent IM Filtering" in the Office Communications Server 2007 R2 Administration Guide, found at *http://go.microsoft.com/fwlink/?LinkId=137125*.

NOTE Intelligent message filtering is a feature of the IM process that can be configured to look for file attachments and hyperlinks. It enables you to block all URLs, allow only local URLs, warn the user that the IM might not be safe, or convert the URLs to plain text. You can also configure URL prefixes that you want to block, for example, ftp: or gopher:

You can either enable file transfers, block all file transfers, or block only file transfers of the type that you specify. If you choose the latter, there is a black list of file extensions that you must input to not allow.

IM traffic between an organization and a public IM service provider uses an encrypted mutual transport layer security (MTLS) connection. For the purpose of connecting to MSN, AOL, and Yahoo!, an organization must use a certificate from a public certification authority (CA) chosen from the list of trusted CAs in Microsoft Windows Server 2003.

As shown in Figure 8-1, corporate IM users typically connect to the home server by using Office Communicator as a client. External IM users connect to the Access Edge Server through perimeter firewalls.

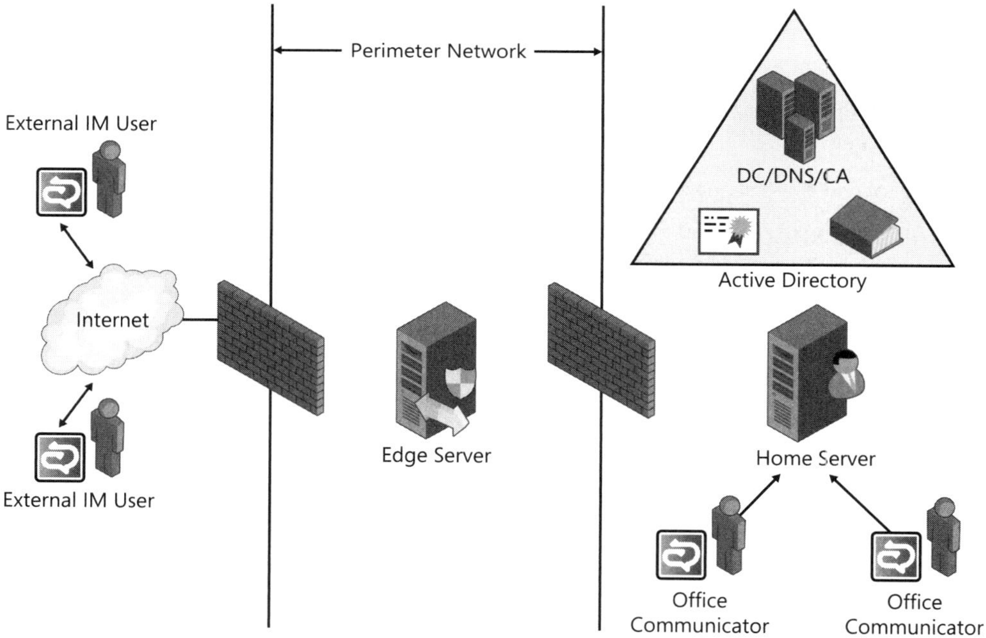

FIGURE 8-1 Public IM connectivity topology

Configuring Public IM Connectivity

The following are some items to take into account before implementing public IM connectivity in your enterprise.

- **Acquiring a certificate** Public IM connectivity requires mutual transport layer security (MTLS), using a certificate obtained from a public certification authority. For AOL, client and server Enhanced Key Usage (EKU) is required. Chapter 4 explains certificates, their types, and how to acquire them. Refer to that chapter for information about what is necessary to obtain the proper certificate types for your requirements.
- **Acquiring service licenses** Before completing the provisioning form and initiating the request to connect with the public IM service providers, you must purchase service licenses. You cannot complete the provisioning process without first buying the service licenses.
- **Enabling connections to public IM service providers** Each IM service provider with which you want to federate must be enabled and configured on the Access Edge Server. For more information, see the section titled "Enabling Federation with Public IM Service Providers" later in this chapter.
- **Authorizing users for public IM connectivity** You can authorize all your enterprise users, certain groups of users, or particular individuals. Users who are not authorized for public IM connectivity can be authorized for other types of federation and remote user access.
- **Submitting a PROVISIONING request** Your organization and the public IM service provider must exchange network connectivity information to activate federation for IM connectivity to the external provider sites. To perform this exchange, connect and sign into the Microsoft Volume License Services (MVLS) management site at *http://go.microsoft.com/fwlink/?LinkID=133691* and then select Online Offerings. Completing and submitting the Web form will initiate a PROVISIONING request. It may take up to 30 days to process the request because Microsoft and each of the providers have work that must be accomplished to complete the request.
- **Configuring DNS** If you configure a public provider as described in the section titled "Enabling Federation with Public IM Service Providers" later in this chapter, the Domain Name System (DNS) Service Record Locator (SRV) record must be published by your partners for you to locate them as allowed partners or discovered partners. For information about the other federation scenarios, see Chapter 7, "Remote Access and Federation Scenarios."

Enabling Federation with Public IM Service Providers

Chapter 7 defines how federation works in Office Communications Server 2007 R2. Public IM connectivity is a special case of federation. For specifics on federation, please refer to Chapter 7. This section only defines the specifics of how to configure public IM connectivity and does not go into any detail of federation, which is required for public IM connectivity.

Enabling federation with the public IM service providers requires completion of the steps outlined in this section.

Step 1: Provision of Federation with the Public IM Service Providers

Your organization and the public IM service provider must exchange network information to activate the federation that will result in public IM connectivity. This is done by using the provisioning site discussed in the section titled "Configuring Public IM Connectivity" earlier in this chapter.

> ***NOTE*** **Before you complete the provisioning form and initiate the request to connect with the public IM service providers, you must purchase service licenses for Office Communications connectivity and install Office Communications Server according to the terms and conditions of your Microsoft Volume Licensing agreement. If you do not first purchase the appropriate licenses, the provisioning process cannot be completed.**

Step 2: Configure DNS for the Access Edge Server

If you enable enhanced federation or configure a public or private provider in the IM service providers table, you must configure the correct DNS Host (A) record and Service (SRV) record to allow external parties to locate and identify your Access Edge Server.

Step 3: Obtain a Public Certificate

Public IM connectivity requires MTLS using a certificate with Server EKU obtained from a public certification authority. For more information, see Chapter 4.

Step 4: Configure the Access Edge Server for Federation

Public IM connectivity requires federation to be enabled on the Edge Server. For more information on configuring federation in your environment, see Chapter 7.

Step 5: Enable Connections to Public IM Service Providers

Each IM service provider with whom you want to federate must be enabled and configured on the Access Edge Server. If you do not enable and configure a provider, users will not have access to this provider. As mentioned earlier, public IM is a special case of federation and should be treated like a federated partner. More information is contained in the section titled "Enabling Connections to Public IM Service Providers" later in this chapter.

Step 6: Authorize Users for Public IM Connectivity

You can authorize all your internal users, certain groups of users, or particular individuals. Users who are not authorized for public IM connectivity can be authorized for other types of federation and remote access. Remote access and federation are discussed in Chapter 7. For specific public IM connectivity user configuration, see the section titled "Authorizing Users for Public IM Connectivity" later in this chapter.

Provisioning Federation with the Public IM Service Providers

The first step in enabling public IM connectivity is to initiate provisioning with one or more of the public IM service providers (MSN, AOL, and Yahoo!). You must purchase the required number of licenses for public IM connectivity. After you purchase separate service licenses for public IM connectivity, to prepare and initiate PROVISIONING, complete the Web form at *http://go.microsoft.com/fwlink/?LinkID=133691*.

The following information is required to complete the form:

- The Master Agreement Number, which identifies your organization's Microsoft Business Agreement and establishes the general terms and conditions of its relationship with Microsoft. Contact your software benefits administrator for this information.
- The Enrollment Agreement Number, which identifies your company's purchase of licenses for public IM connectivity. Contact your software benefits administrator for this information.
- The names of your organization's Session Initiation Protocol (SIP) domains.
- The fully qualified domain name (FQDN) of your organization's Access Edge Server.
- The network administrator's contact information.
- The names of the public IM service providers with which you want to federate.

Microsoft will send you an e-mail message confirming that it has received your provisioning information and is in the process of validating the request. Upon validation, Microsoft will send you a second e-mail message verifying that your information has been forwarded to the appropriate public IM service providers and providing an estimate of how long the process is likely to take. If the OFFERING request is not validated, you will receive an e-mail message explaining how to resolve the issues.

After validating your Edge Server and SIP domains, Microsoft will forward the information to the public IM service providers with which you want to connect. The public IM service providers will then provision their routing tables to direct instant messages targeting your SIP domains to the Access Edge Server specified in the form. After provisioning is complete, each public IM service provider informs Microsoft, which sends you a final e-mail message confirming that the process is complete. After you receive this final message, you can establish a connection from your Access Edge Server to the public IM service providers to which you want to connect.

After you provision federation with one or more public IM service providers, the next step is to configure the external interface of your Edge Server for MTLS. This step requires obtaining the necessary certificate from a public certification authority.

NOTE **A certificate from a public certification authority is mandatory. The certificate must be trusted by the public IM providers. The public IM providers have root certificates from all major commercial public certification authorities and will not recognize a certificate obtained from your internal, public key infrastructure (PKI).**

The final step is to test and confirm connectivity with each of the providers and then provide detailed instructions to your end users about how to connect with external users at each of the public IM providers.

CAUTION **Provisioning is complex and involves routing changes to the networks of Microsoft's partners. As a result, provisioning is optimized to work as a single-threaded process. If you want to change provisioning data—specifically, Access Edge Server, your FQDN, SIP domains, and the partners to which you want to connect—you must wait until the PROVISIONING request is complete before you submit the changes.**

If you want to change provisioning data after provisioning has been completed, you need to enter data for all of your existing providers, as well as for any new ones that you want to add. For this reason, please print and save the Thank You page that is displayed upon successful submission of your data. This page has the tracking number and a copy of the data that you submitted, which will make your CHANGE request much simpler and reduce the time required and the potential for mistakes.

DIRECT FROM THE SOURCE

End-User Licensing and Auditing

Anjali Verma
Senior Test Lead

Licensing for public IM on Office Communications Server is monitored through a combination of honor system and auditing. The public providers get paid based on the number of people using the system, so you should assume they each have their own auditing systems and will identify rampant licensing violations. There is a lot involved in how Microsoft and the public providers monitor, but the basic mechanism is that user counts for every Uniform Resource Identifier (URI) that is using public IM are auditable by the public providers. This sidebar describes a query tool that administrators can use to view IM usage data within their organizations.

> ***NOTE*** Because of the lead time that is required for licensing, we recommend that customers purchase lot sizes and then deploy users against those lots.

Querying for Public IM Usage Statistics

Use the public Internet connectivity usage query script Picstats.sql to report statistics related to public IM use. For example, you can use the script to determine the average number of public IM users that are in the contact lists of your deployed users. This tool is part of the Office Communications Server Resource Kit Tools installation, and you can see a schematic presentation of the data provided by this tool in the section titled "Sample Query Output" later in this sidebar.

ON THE COMPANION MEDIA Note that you must be logged on to an account that is in a role that is allowed to run the query script Picstats.sql. For more information, refer to the Readme file in the Office Communications Server Resource Kit Tools installation folder \OCS 2007 Resource Kit Tools on the companion media.

To start the public Internet connectivity usage query script Picstats.sql, do the following:

1. On the Windows taskbar, click Start, click Run, type **cmd**, and then click OK. (If doing this from a server other than the SQL server, you will need to install the SQL tools and connect to the SQL server.)
2. At the command prompt, type **cd %Program Files%\Microsoft SQL Server\90\Tools\Binn** and then press Enter.
3. Enter the appropriate query script, Picstats.sql syntax, and then press Enter.

The syntax for this query script is as follows:

```
osql.exe -E -S <sqlserver>\rtc -d rtc -i picstats.sql
```

Here <*sqlserver*> represents the Microsoft SQL Server instance to which you want to connect. The *-E* flag instructs object-structured query language (OSQL) to attempt to connect by using Windows Authentication. The default value is to the *rtc* instance on the local computer.

Sample Query Output

The following is an example of a valid query script Picstats.sql command:

```
osql.exe -E -S pool-be.contoso.com\rtc -d rtc -i picstats.sql
```

The query script Picstats.sql returns three rows of data based on the contact list information stored within the SQL server that is associated with your Office Communications Server pool. For more information, see the following sample output and the description following it.

PIC Domain	Min Contacts/User	Max Contacts/User	Avg Contacts/User	StDev Contacts/User
AOL	1.00	102.00	17.07	13.73
Yahoo!	1.00	4.00	1.80	1.30
MSN	1.00	96.00	16.79	13.56

Users with at Least One PIC Contact	Total Enterprise Users	% with atLeast One PIC Contact
1000.00	2674.00	37.40

Min PIC %/User	Max PIC %/User	Avg PIC %/User	StDev PIC %/User
0.00	100.00	33.52	34.27

The first row in the output shows the minimum, maximum, average, and standard deviation in contacts per user for each of the three providers.

The second row shows the number of users that have at least one public IM connectivity contact, the total number of enterprise users, and the percentage and count of users that have at least one public IM connectivity contact.

The third row is similar to the first row, but it provides a summary number rather than a breakout per provider. This row provides the minimum, maximum, average, and standard deviation in total contacts per user.

Public IM Connectivity Monthly Subscription Licenses

Public IM connectivity monthly subscription licenses are available on a per-user, per-month subscription and are an addition to the Client Access license (CAL). Similar to all online services models, public IM connectivity has two licensing components associated with its use: a Services Subscription license (SSL) and a User Subscription license (USL). One public IM connectivity SSL is required for each company agreement, and one public IM connectivity USL is required for each user that is accessing any or all of the public IM service providers.

Pricing for public IM connectivity includes access to all three public IM service providers: Microsoft Network (MSN), America Online (AOL), and Yahoo!.

There is no public IM service provider license available for only one or only two providers. Public IM connectivity is sold as a per-user, per-month service agreement; however, public IM connectivity service licenses can be added to a current customer's select, enterprise, or government agreements.

There is no minimum license requirement. Customers can also add licenses at any time. There is no refund or reimbursement for public IM connectivity licenses that are not used. Public IM connectivity service licenses can be added to a current customer's select, enterprise, or government agreements. Customers can prorate the months left on their agreements by adding public IM connectivity service licenses, but the termination of public IM connectivity service must end in conjunction with the customer's agreement. For example, if a customer has 17 months left on its current agreement, it has the option to buy 17 months of public IM connectivity service.

Microsoft offers volume licensing solutions that scale to meet the needs of small, medium, and enterprise businesses and organizations. Licensing programs provide volume pricing and are designed to save organizations time and money by making the purchase and management of multiple software licenses easier. To view licensing terms, conditions, and supplemental information that is relevant to the use of products licensed through Microsoft Volume Licensing Programs, visit the Microsoft Volume License Services Web site at *http://go.microsoft.com/fwlink/?LinkID=133691*.

Enabling Connections to Public IM Service Providers

IM service providers typically, though not necessarily, host multiple SIP domains. Before Office Communications Server, federating with an organization's multiple domains required that you enter each domain explicitly in the direct partner table. The following two mechanisms in Office Communications Server simplify federating with organizations that host multiple domains:

- The IM service providers table, which requires you to specify an Edge Server but not every domain that it might serve
- The hosting of multiple domains by including multiple FQDNs in a certificate on the Access Edge Server

> ***NOTE*** **Public IM connectivity enables users in your organization to use IM to communicate with users of instant messaging services that are provided by public IM service providers, including MSN, Yahoo!, and AOL. Use the IM Provider tab in the Office Communications Server 2007 Properties dialog box, found in the Services and Applications node in Computer Management on the Access Edge Server, to control the IM service providers that are allowed to federate with your organization. You can add or remove an IM service provider, as well change other settings for any IM service provider (including temporarily blocking the IM service provider). For more information about configuring IM providers, see the section titled "Configuring IM Provider Support on Edge Servers" in the Office Communications Server 2007 R2 Administration Guide, found at** ***http://go.microsoft.com/fwlink/?LinkId=137126.***

> ***IMPORTANT*** **You cannot configure any routing method that requires DNS SRV. If your Edge Server is configured with a default route, or if you want to configure it with a default route, you must first remove the three public IM service providers that populated the IM service providers table when you installed Office Communications Server.**

Considerations Involving Public IM Providers

Basic IM and presence work with all public IM providers. Note the following exceptions:

- When an Office Communications Server user sets his presence to Do Not Disturb in Office Communicator, users on the Yahoo! public IM networks can still send instant messages without knowing that the Office Communications Server user cannot see the messages.
- The public IM networks do not support group IM. As a result, users hosted on the public IM networks (MSN, AOL, and Yahoo!) cannot join IM conferences hosted by Office Communications Server.

Administrators also need to consider how to handle existing accounts on provider networks, public IM connectivity capacity questions, and security issues. These issues are discussed in the following sections of this chapter.

Existing Accounts on Provider Networks

Users who have existing e-mail accounts will receive an e-mail message notifying them that to continue using IM, they must change their e-mail address. Users that do not have IM accounts on a public provider will receive new e-mail accounts. Users' existing public IM contact lists and e-mail messages will be transferred to the new sign-in ID and e-mail address. A user's IM and e-mail contacts will be updated with the user's new sign-in ID. The message will provide a link to a Web page for help with making the change.

Table 8-1 provides examples of how AOL and Yahoo! screen names are added to contact lists of Office Communications Server users.

TABLE 8-1 Adding AOL and Yahoo! Screen Names to Contact Lists

EXAMPLE	USER NAME TO BE ADDED TO OFFICE COMMUNICATIONS SERVER CONTACT LIST
An Office Communications Server user wants to add AOL user kim.akers@corp.aol.com to the Office Communicator client's contact list.	kim.akers@aol.com
An Office Communications Server user wants to add AOL user kim970 to the Office Communicator client's contact list.	kim970@aol.com
An Office Communications Server user wants to add Yahoo! user kimakers@yahoo.com to the Office Communicator client's contact list.	kimakers@yahoo.com

HOW IT WORKS

How the Provider Migrates Existing MSN Accounts

For information about how MSN migrates accounts, see Figure 8-2, which describes the change process.

MSN users who are already using MSN Connect must change their e-mail IDs. Users' existing MSN contact lists and e-mail messages will be transferred to the new sign-in ID and e-mail address. Users' IM and e-mail contacts will be updated with each user's new sign-in ID. Windows Live Messenger Service will work unless the organization's administrator has blocked access.

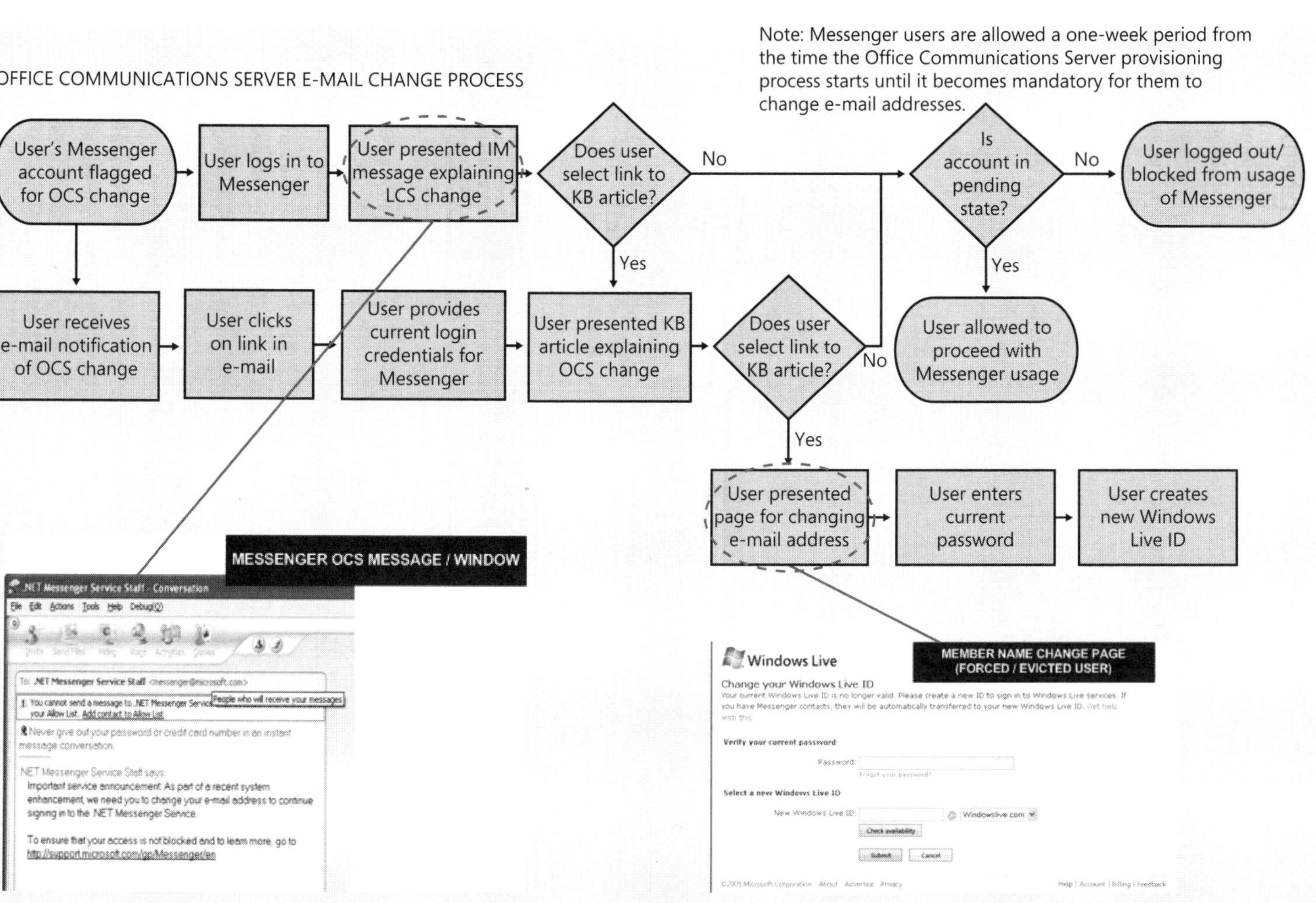

FIGURE 8-2 Migrating MSN accounts

Capacity Planning Considerations

Public IM capacity in Office Communications Server is determined by the bandwidth of the organization's Internet connection. A T-1 connection to public providers offers greater IM access than a 256-kilobyte (k) connection. Note that SIP, when used for IM communication, is capable of supporting large numbers of users. For information about capacity planning, see Chapter 14, "Planning Example."

Security Considerations

The main security issue with public IM is controlling spam over instant messaging (SPIM). SPIM occurs when electronic junk e-mail (spam) shows up as unwanted messages in a user's IM. There are two mechanisms through which to help control SPIM: limiting public contacts and limiting message content.

> ***NOTE*** **All SIP traffic must be carried over the Transport Layer Security (TLS) protocol. Internet Protocol (IP) security (IPsec) is not supported. User Datagram Protocol (UDP) is not supported. Compression is done only by TLS negotiation (RFC 2246).**

Controlling SPIM by Limiting Public Contacts

There are several techniques that you can use to control SPIM by limiting contacts, as explained in this section.

- When you enable users for public IM connectivity
- When you enable IM service providers
- When enabling users that are on a recipient's contact list

> ***NOTE*** **SPIM can come from sources that users do not recognize because of the nefarious ways that valid contacts are gathered (for example, stealing contact lists from users and providers, or monitoring unsecured channels of communication).**

LIMITING SPIM WHEN YOU ENABLE USERS IN ACTIVE DIRECTORY USERS AND COMPUTERS

To limit the potential for SPIM, enable individual users for public IM connectivity by using Active Directory Users and Computers as follows.

1. Log on as a member of the DomainAdmins RTCUniversalServerAdmins group to an Enterprise Edition Server, a Standard Edition Server, or a server that is a member of an Active Directory domain and that has the Office Communications Server administration tools installed.
2. Open Active Directory Users and Computers.

3. Click Start, click All Programs, click Administrative Tools, and then click Active Directory Users And Computers.
4. In the console tree, expand the Users container or the other organizational unit (OU) that contains the user account for which you want to enable federation, public IM connectivity, or remote user access.
5. Right-click the user account name and then click Properties.
6. On the Communications tab, click the Configure button next to Additional Options.
7. In User Options, under Federation, do the following:
   a. To enable the user account for federation, select the Enable Federation check box.
   b. To enable the user account for public IM connectivity, select the Enable Public IM Connectivity check box.
   c. To enable the user account for remote access, select the Enable Remote User Access check box.
8. Click OK twice.

LIMITING SPIM WHEN YOU ENABLE IM SERVICE PROVIDERS

To limit SPIM when configuring IM provider support on an Access Edge Server, use the Access Edge Server Properties dialog box, as follows.

1. On the Access Edge Server, open Computer Management.
2. In the console tree, expand Services And Applications, right-click Office Communications Server 2007 R2, and then click Properties. (See Figure 8-3.)

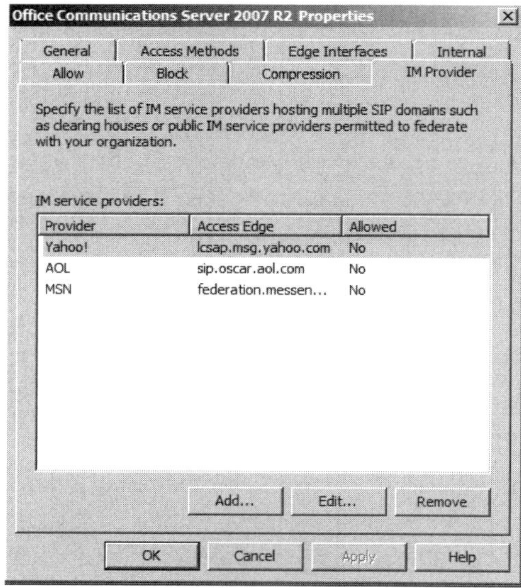

FIGURE 8-3 IM Provider tab

3. On the IM Provider tab, do one of the following:
   - To view or edit the settings for an IM service provider, in the Microsoft Office Communications Server 2007 R2 Properties dialog box, select the IM Provider tab, click the name of the IM service provider, and then click Edit.
   - In the IM Service Provider dialog box, view or change settings as appropriate and then click OK.
4. To temporarily block any IM service provider in the list, you can temporarily disable support. Follow these steps to do so.
   a. Click the name of the IM service provider and then click Edit.
   b. In the Edit IM Service Provider dialog box, clear the Allow This IM Service Provider check box and then click OK.

   This blocks the IM service provider until you later select the check box, but it does not delete the configuration information. Temporarily blocking a service provider prevents having to repeat the provisioning steps.
5. To permanently remove an IM service provider from the list, click the name of the server and then click Remove.

   If you later want to add the IM service provider again, you must use the procedure described in the section titled "Provisioning Federation with the Public IM Service Providers" earlier in the chapter to add the provider and specify all settings.
6. To add an IM provider, click Add.
7. In the Add IM Service Provider dialog box, specify the appropriate options shown in Figure 8-4. Then click OK.

LIMITING SPIM WHEN ENABLING USERS THAT ARE ON A RECIPIENT'S CONTACT LIST

To limit SPIM when enabling users that are on a recipient's contact list, use the Add IM Service Provider dialog box to permit IM traffic with only contact list items, as shown in Figure 8-4, as follows.

1. On the Access Edge Server, click Start, point to All Programs, point to Administrative Tools, and then click Computer Management.
2. If necessary, expand Services And Applications.
3. Right-click Microsoft Office Communications Server 2007 R2 and then click Properties.
4. On the IM Provider tab, click Add.
5. In the Add IM Service Provider dialog box, select the Allow This IM Service Provider check box to enable the new provider.
6. In the IM Service Provider Name text box, type the name of the IM service provider. This name will appear in the Provider column of the IM service providers, as in Figure 8-3.

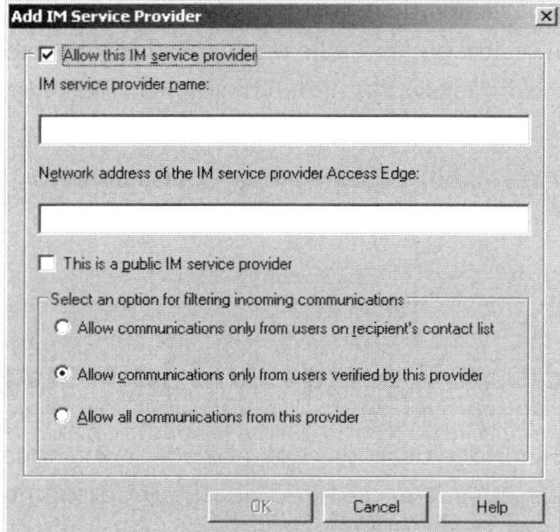

FIGURE 8-4 Add IM Service Provider dialog box

7. In the Network Address Of The IM Service Provider Access Edge text box, type the FQDN of the provider's Access Edge Server.
8. Select the This Is A Public IM Service Provider check box only if the provider is MSN, AOL, or Yahoo!
9. Select an option for filtering incoming communications. To limit IM to users on contact lists, select the option Allow Communications Only From Users On Recipient's Contact List.
10. Click OK.
11. To continue, click OK again or Apply.

Controlling SPIM by Limiting Message Content

You can use the Intelligent IM Filter application to protect your Office Communications Server 2007 R2 deployment against harmful instant messages from unknown endpoints outside the corporate firewall. The Intelligent IM Filter provides the following filtering features:

- Enhanced URL filtering
- Enhanced file transfer filtering

To configure URL filtering, do the following.

1. On the Access Edge Server, open Computer Management.
2. In the console tree, expand Services And Applications, right-click Office Communications Server 2007 R2, point to Application Properties, and then click Intelligent IM Filter. (See Figure 8-5.)

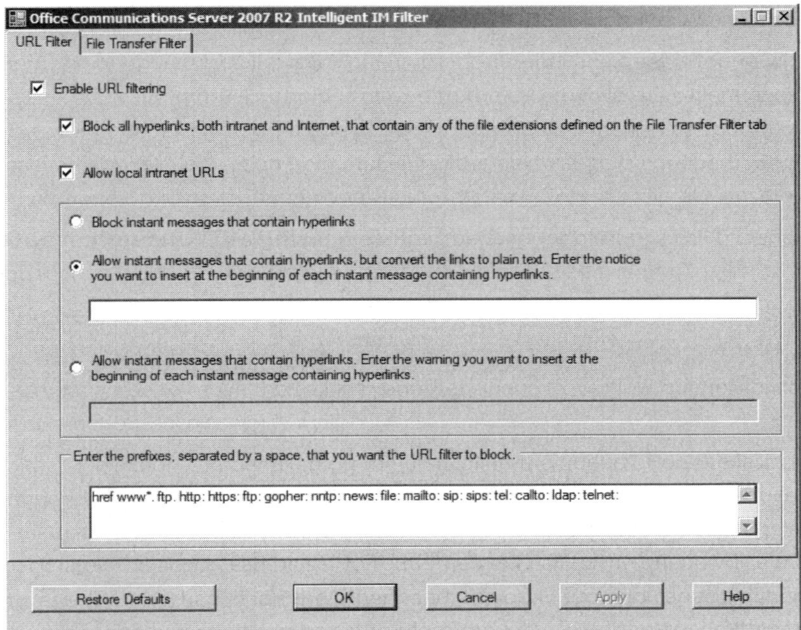

FIGURE 8-5 Intelligent IM Filter

3. On the URL Filter tab:
   - Choose to enable URL filtering by selecting Enable URL Filtering.
   - Block All Hyperlinks, Both Intranet And Internet, That Contain Any Of The File Extensions Defined On The File Transfer Filter Tab relies on the input box on the File Transfer tab being filled out with extensions you do not want to allow.
   - Allow Local Intranet URLs will allow URLs only from your local intranet in IM.
   - Block Instant Messages That Contain Hyperlinks is a blanket denial of all IM containing hyperlinks.
   - The Allow Instant Messages That Contain Hyperlinks, But Convert The Links To Plain Text. Enter The Notice You Want To Insert At The Beginning Of Each Instant Message Containing Hyperlinks option also enables you to send a notice to your user as to why the link is in plain text.
   - The Allow Instant Messages That Contain Hyperlinks. Enter The Warning You Want To Insert At The Beginning Of Each Instant Message Containing Hyperlinks option enables unmodified hyperlinks but enables a warning message to be sent to the IM recipient in advance of the hyperlink.
   - Enter The Prefixes, Separated By A Space, That You Want The URL Filter To Block. These are URL types that you do not want to allow. Examples would be nntp, news, and gopher.

NOTE It is also possible to access the Intelligent IM Filter by right-clicking either the Enterprise pool or the Standard Edition Server.

To configure a file transfer filter, do the following.

1. On the Access Edge Server, open Computer Management.
2. In the console tree, expand Services And Applications, right-click Office Communications Server 2007 R2, point to Application Properties, and then click Intelligent IM Filter, as shown in Figure 8-6.

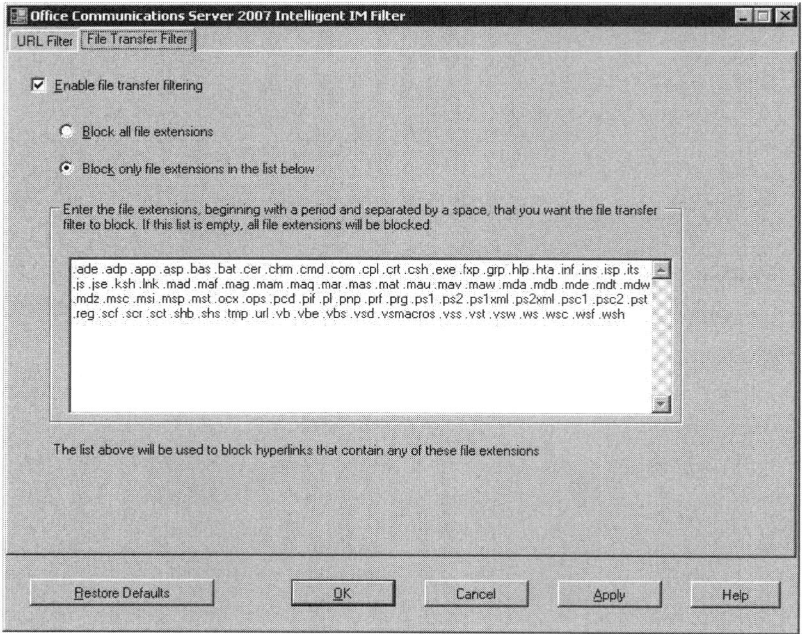

FIGURE 8-6 File Transfer Intelligent Filtering Options

3. On the File Transfer Filter tab, configure the appropriate settings.
   - Checking Enable File Transfer Filtering turns on the filtering engine on instant messages received.
   - The Block All File Extensions option disables the ability to receive files with any extension.
   - Block Only File Extensions In The List Below uses the black list that you create and maintain of all file extensions that you do not want to allow. The Enter The File Extensions, Beginning With A Period And Separated By A Space, That You Want The File Transfer Filter To Block. If This List Is Empty, All File Extensions Will Be Blocked input box works in conjunction with the Block Only File Extensions In The List Below and the URL filter option Block All Hyperlinks, Both Intranet And Internet, That Contain Any Of The File Extensions Defined On The File Transfer Filter Tab.

NOTE It is also possible to access the Intelligent IM Filter by right-clicking either the Enterprise pool or the Standard Edition Server.

Also, you can consider using the advanced protection features of Forefront for Office Communications Server, a product from the Microsoft Forefront product group that isespecially suited to these tasks and much more. For more information, see *http://go.microsoft.com/fwlink/?LinkID=133692*.

For more information about the Intelligent IM Filter application, see the section titled "Configuring Intelligent IM Filtering" in the Office Communications Server 2007 R2 Administration Guide, found at *http://go.microsoft.com/fwlink/?LinkId=137125*.

Considerations Involving Media Sharing

Media sharing over a public IM connection is not an issue administrators need to worry about. Users cannot share audio-visual or binary files over a connection to a public IM provider. Keep the following considerations in mind in case users ask:

- Between a public IM provider and Office Communications Server, only text and presence information can be exposed.
- Between two Office Communications Servers, sharing of audio-visual or binary files in an IM session is supported.

Authorizing Users for Public IM Connectivity

The easiest way to configure multiple users for public IM connectivity is to use the Configure Office Communications Server Users Wizard, as shown in Figure 8-7. You can access the wizard by using the Active Directory Users and Computers snap-in or the Office Communications Server administrative snap-in on an Office Communications Server that is attached to your SIP domain.

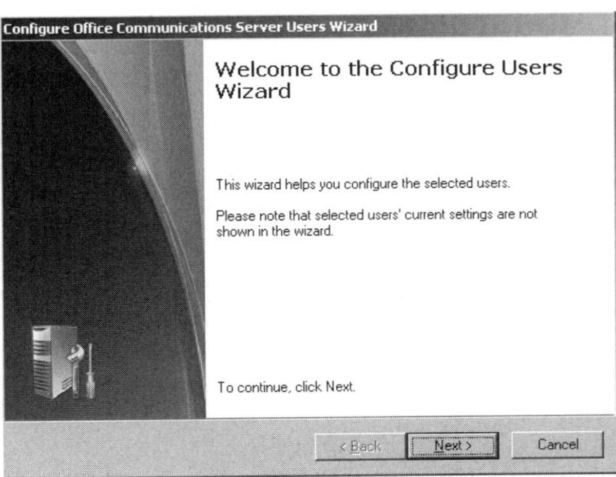

FIGURE 8-7 Configure Office Communications Server Users Wizard

Using the Active Directory Users and Computers Snap-In

To enable multiple users for public IM connectivity by using the Active Directory Users and Computers snap-in, do the following.

1. If the computer is a domain controller, click Start, point to All Programs, point to Administrative Tools, and then click Active Directory Users And Computers. Otherwise, you will need to install the Active Directory management tools.
2. Go to the folder where your user accounts reside.
3. Do one of the following:
   - Right-click the Users folder or the folder where your user accounts reside and then click Configure Users to configure all user accounts in this folder.
   - Click the Users folder. In the details pane, select the user or users that you want to configure and then click Configure Users.
4. On the Welcome To The Configure Users Wizard page, click Next.
5. Under Configure User Settings, select Public IM Connectivity.
6. On the Configure Operation Status page, if you want to export the log, click Export to save the XML file.
7. Click Finish.

Using the Office Communications Server Administrative Snap-In

To enable multiple users for public IM connectivity by using the Office Communications Server administrative snap-in, do the following.

1. Click Start, point to All Programs, point to Administrative Tools, and then click Office Communications Server 2007 R2.
2. In the console tree, expand the forest node.
3. Expand subsequent nodes under the Domains node until you reach the domain that the server or pool resides in.
4. Expand the Standard Edition Servers or Enterprise Pools node.
5. Expand the server or pool.
6. Do one of the following:
   - Right-click the Users folder and then click Configure Users to configure all user accounts on this server or pool.
   - Select the user or users that you want to configure and then click Configure Users.
7. On the Welcome To The Configure Users Wizard page, click Next.
8. Under Configure User Settings, select Public IM Connectivity.
9. On the Configure Operation Status page, if you want to export the log, click Export to save the XML file.
10. Click Finish.

NOTE To perform this task, you must be logged on as a member of the RTCDomain-UserAdmins group.

You can also enable or disable public IM connectivity for individual users. To configure an individual user for public IM connectivity by using the Active Directory Users and Computers snap-in, do the following.

1. If the computer is a domain controller, click Start, point to All Programs, point to Administrative Tools, and then click Active Directory Users And Computers. If the computer is not a domain controller, you will need to install the Active Directory management tools.
2. Go to the folder where your user accounts reside.
3. Expand the folder.
4. Right-click the user account that you want to configure and then select Properties. The Administrator Properties dialog box appears.
5. On the Communications tab, make sure that the Enable User For Office Communications Server check box is selected. If it is not, select it now.
6. Enter a sign-in name and then select a server or pool for the user to sign in to, as shown in Figure 8-8.
7. Click Configure.
8. Under User Options, select the Enable Public IM Connectivity check box and then click OK.
9. Click OK.

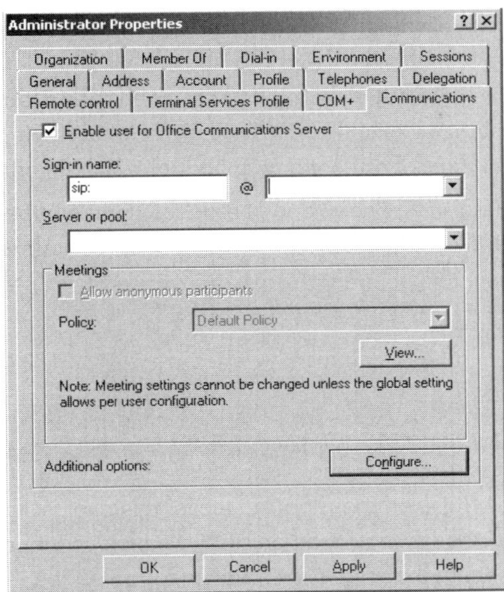

FIGURE 8-8 Enable User For Office Communications Server

IMPORTANT An individual user can be authorized for federation, public IM connectivity, remote access, or any combination of the three. Enabling public connectivity for a user does not require disabling federation or remote access.

Disabling Public IM Connectivity

You can also disable public IM connectivity for one or more users at any time. To do so, follow the procedure for enabling public IM connectivity for one or more users in the section titled "Using the Active Directory Users and Computers Snap-In" earlier in this chapter, but clear the Enable Public IM Connectivity check box instead of selecting it.

Configuring Per-User and Global Settings

When you enable individual user accounts for Office Communications Server 2007 R2 in Active Directory Users and Computers, you can change user account settings to specify the functionality available to each user. For information about the impact of global, group, and individual settings, see the section titled "Managing User Accounts" in the Office Communications Server 2007 R2 Administration Guide, found at *http://go.microsoft.com/fwlink/?LinkId=137128*.

As shown in the previous sections, settings for user accounts can be configured in different ways. In general, settings can be configured by using the following methods:

- Globally for all users in the forest by using the Office Communications Server 2007 R2 administrative snap-in.
- Individually or in groups by using the Configure Office Communications Server Users Wizard in the Office Communications Server 2007 R2 administrative snap-in or the Active Directory Users and Computers snap-in. After you enable user accounts in Active Directory Users and Computers, it is recommended that you use the Configure Users Wizard to configure user accounts—especially for newly enabled user accounts—because it enables you to configure multiple users at a time.
- Individually by using the Communications tab of the user account Properties tab in Office Communications Server 2007 R2 or Active Directory Users and Computers. This approach is useful if you want to change a small number of settings for a small number of user accounts, or for configuring settings that cannot be configured by using the Configure Users Wizard.

All methods are not available for configuration of all settings. Additionally, some of the user account settings that have global settings require that the global setting be configured prior to configuring settings on specific user accounts. Table 8-2 describes which of the methods can be used to configure each of the specific user settings, as well as the global configuration requirements.

TABLE 8-2 Configuring Per-User and Global Settings for User Accounts

USER SETTING	DESCRIPTION	GLOBAL CONFIGURATION	CONFIGURABLE IN THE CONFIGURE OFFICE COMMUNICATIONS SERVER USERS WIZARD?	CONFIGURABLE FROM THE PROPERTIES, COMMUNICATIONS TAB?
Federation	Enables or disables an Office Communications Server 2007 R2 user's ability to communicate with users from other organizations that have an Office Communications Server 2007 R2 deployment and a federated link.	Users cannot be enabled for federation unless federation is enabled at the global level.	Yes, but it takes effect only when federation is enabled at the global level.	Yes, but it takes effect only when federation is enabled at the global level.
Public IM connectivity	Enables or disables an Office Communications Server 2007 R2 user's ability to communicate with users hosted on AOL, Yahoo!, or MSN Internet services.	Users cannot be enabled for public IM connectivity unless federation is enabled at the global level.	Yes, but it takes effect only when public IM connectivity is enabled at the global level.	Yes, but it takes effect only when public IM connectivity is enabled at the global level.
Archiving	Enables or disables archiving of IM conversations of the Office Communications Server 2007 R2 user. This control can be enabled independently for internal conversations and for conversations with users outside your organization.	Yes. At the global level, you can choose to enable archiving for all users, disable archiving for all users, or enable and disable archiving on a per-user basis.	Yes, but only if the global setting is configured to enable and disable archiving on a per-user basis.	Yes, but only if the global setting is configured to enable and disable archiving on a per-user basis.
Invite anonymous participants to meetings	Enables or disables the ability for Office Communications Server 2007 R2 users in your organization who are allowed to organize meetings to invite participants outside your organization.	Yes. At the global level, you can choose to allow users to invite anonymous participants, disallow users from inviting anonymous participants, or enforce settings at a per-user level.	Yes, but only if the global setting is configured to allow configuration of anonymous participation on a per-user basis.	Yes, but only if the global setting is configured to allow configuration of anonymous participation on a per-user basis.

TABLE 8-2 Configuring Per-User and Global Settings for User Accounts

USER SETTING	DESCRIPTION	GLOBAL CONFIGURATION	CONFIGURABLE IN THE CONFIGURE OFFICE COMMUNICATIONS SERVER USERS WIZARD?	CONFIGURABLE FROM THE PROPERTIES, COMMUNICATIONS TAB?
Meeting policy	Enforces a meeting policy for an Office Communications Server 2007 R2 user who is allowed to organize meetings. The policy specifies aspects of meetings that the organizer can create. The policy name is used to specify which meeting policy to apply.	Yes. At the global level, you can set up one or more meeting policies for specific uses and either select a single global meeting policy to be applied to all users in the forest or specify that the meeting policy is to be applied on a per-user basis.	Yes, if you specify at the global level to apply the meeting policy on a per-user basis.	Yes, if you specify at the global level to apply the meeting policy on a per-user basis.
Enterprise Voice policy	A Voice policy associates telephone usage records with users.	Yes. At the global level, you can set up one or more Voice policies for specific uses and either select a single global Voice policy to be applied to all users in the forest or specify that the Voice policy is to be applied on a per-user basis.	Yes, but only if the global policy is configured to specify Voice policy on a per-user basis.	Yes, but only if the global policy is configured to specify Voice policy on a per-user basis.

The user settings that do not have global settings are configured only at the user level. Table 8-3 shows the configurable user settings that do not use global settings and the configuration methods available for each setting.

TABLE 8-3 User Settings that Do Not Use Global Settings

USER SETTING	DESCRIPTION	CONFIGURABLE IN THE CONFIGURE OFFICE COMMUNICATIONS SERVER USERS WIZARD?	CONFIGURABLE FROM THE PROPERTIES, COMMUNICATIONS TAB?
Enable user for Office Communications Server	Enables an Active Directory user for Office Communications Server 2007 R2.	No.	Yes, if an account has been initially enabled in Active Directory Users and Computers and then disabled, it can be re-enabled on the Properties, Communications tab.
Sign-in name	Similar to a user's e-mail address, the sign-in name uniquely defines the user's SIP address as a SIP URI.	No.	Yes.
Server or pool	FQDN of the Standard Edition Server or Enterprise pool where a user's data is stored.	No.	Yes.
Enhanced presence	Enables or disables enhanced presence, which enables users to control their presence with more detail. This enables users to create different presence categories and assign data items to the categories. Different views of the categories can be created. With enhanced presence, users can expose different presence states for different categories of contacts.	Yes, but once it is enabled, it cannot be disabled for a user.	Yes, but once it is enabled, it cannot be disabled for a user.
Remote user access	Enables or disables a Live Communications user to sign in to Office Communications Server 2007 R2 services from outside the perimeter network of the user's organization without requiring a virtual private network (VPN).	Yes.	Yes, as an additional option.
PC-to-PC communications only	Enables or disables only PC-to-PC audio communications for the user, but not Remote Call Control or Enterprise Voice. This option does not require deployment of a Remote Call Control server or Unified Messaging.	No.	Yes, as an additional option.

TABLE 8-3 User Settings that Do Not Use Global Settings

USER SETTING	DESCRIPTION	CONFIGURABLE IN THE CONFIGURE OFFICE COMMUNICATIONS SERVER USERS WIZARD?	CONFIGURABLE FROM THE PROPERTIES, COMMUNICATIONS TAB?
Remote Call Control	Enables or disables Office Communications Server 2007 R2 user control of a Private Branch eXchange (PBX) desktop telephone by using Office Communicator 2007. This option also enables PC-to-PC audio communications.	No.	Yes, as an additional option.
Enterprise Voice	Enables or disables Enterprise Voice for the user. This option also enables PC-to-PC audio communications.	Yes.	Yes, as an additional option.
Enable PBX integration	Enables or disables PBX integration for an Enterprise Voice user. This option requires first enabling Enterprise Voice for the user.	No.	Yes, as an additional option.
Line URI (user's phone/device)	URI that uniquely identifies the user's telephone line. This URI can be in the form of a SIP URI or a TEL URI.	No.	Yes, as an additional option.
Remote Call Control server URI	SIP URI that uniquely identifies the Remote Call Control gateway that controls the telephone line.	No.	Yes, as an additional option.

Technical Details Behind the Public IM Connectivity Scenarios

To understand network message flow in the Public IM Connectivity scenarios, the following sections will look at two scenarios and the accompanying illustrations of the resulting message flows.

Scenario One: Adding a Contact in Office Communicator 2007

In this scenario, the user enters an account name for a recipient that they want to send instant messages to, performs a search, and adds the recipient account name as a contact. This process has seven steps that are numerically keyed to Figure 8-9. Where possible, each step is illustrated by using a corresponding sample SIP message. The illustrative SIP output following the steps is what an administrator might see when using logging to trace the messages.

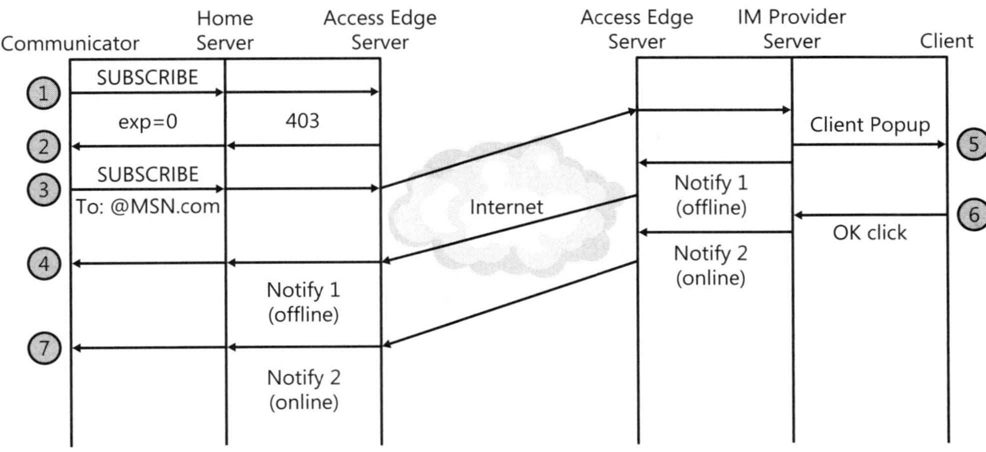

FIGURE 8-9 Communicator Startup

Step 1: Specify Recipient's Account

The user types **kim970@msn.com** for a user search. The message body shows that the information was sent to the recipient's public IM servers:

```
Start-Line: SUBSCRIBE sip:kim970@msn.com SIP/2.0
From: "PIC Test (pic1) lcsent01"<sip:pic1@ocs-edge.litwareinc.com>;tag=dfac414f0f;epid
=ce4ccd49ad
To: <sip:kim970@msn.com>
CSeq: 1 SUBSCRIBE


<snip>
```

Step 2: Recipient's Presence Displayed as Unknown

The account comes up, presence shows as unknown after a short delay, and the information relating to the reason is reflected in the ms-diagnostics message that says "SIPPROXY_E_EPROUTING_MSG_INT_GET_RICH_PRESENCE_FILTERED". This indicates that the presence information was filtered.

```
Start-Line: SIP/2.0 403 Forbidden
From: "PIC Test (pic1) lcsent01"<sip:pic1@ocs-edge.litwareinc.com>;tag=dfac414f0f;epid
=ce4ccd49ad
To: <sip:kim970@msn.com>;tag=C122BE2A56CD774DA0AC6DEC165DB900
CSeq: 1 SUBSCRIBE
```

```
<snip>

HRESULT="C3E93D80(SIPPROXY_E_EPROUTING_MSG_INT_GET_RICH_PRESENCE_FILTERED)"
```

Step 3: Recipient's Account Added as a Contact

The user adds the account as a contact, which allows Rich Presence information to be acknowledged and displayed in the client.

```
Start-Line: SUBSCRIBE sip:kim970@msn.com SIP/2.0
From: "PIC Test (pic1) lcsent01"<sip:pic1@ocs-edge.litwareinc.com>;tag=f14fbece50;epid
=ce4ccd49ad
To: <sip:kim970@msn.com>
CSeq: 1 SUBSCRIBE

<snip>

User-Agent: UCCP/2.0.6362.0 OC/2.0.6362.0 (Microsoft Office Communicator)
Event: presence
Accept: application/msrtc-event-categories+xml, application/xpidf+xml, text/xml+msrtc.
pidf,
     application/pidf+xml, application/rlmi+xml, multipart/related
Supported: com.microsoft.autoextend
Supported: ms-piggyback-first-notify
Content-Type: application/msrtc-adrl-categorylist+xml
Content-Length: 501
Message-Body: <batchSub xmlns="http://schemas.microsoft.com/2006/01/sip/batch-
subscribe" uri=
"sip:pic1@ocs-edge.litwareinc.com" name=""><action name="subscribe" id="1008912">
<adhocList><resource uri="sip:kim970@msn.com"><context></context></resource>
</adhocList><categoryList xmlns="http://schemas.microsoft.com/2006/09/sip/
categorylist"><category name="calendarData"/>
    <category name="contactCard"/><category name="note"/><category
name="services"/><category name="state"/></categoryList></action></batchSub>
```

Step 4: Recipient's Presence Displayed as Offline

Account presence shows as offline, which indicates that the Rich Presence is now working as expected and that the contact is offline at the current time.

```
Start-Line: NOTIFY sip:pic1@ocs-edge.litwareinc.com;opaque=user:epid:XHiWcZA4TlaDkwMgk
svyrQAA;gruu SIP/2.0
From: <sip:kim970@msn.com>;tag=65d68a1bc4
```

```
To: <sip:pic1@ocs-edge.litwareinc.com>;epid=ce4ccd49ad;tag=f14fbece50
CSeq: 1 NOTIFY


<snip>
EVENT: presence
SUBSCRIPTION-STATE: active
<snip>


    <status>
      <basic>closed</basic>
    </status>
```

Step 5: Recipient Receives Notification

User kim970@msn.com gets a pop-up window that indicates that Office Communicator user pic1 has added Kim to her contacts.

Step 6: Recipient Adds a User to the Buddy List

User kim970@msn.com adds the Office Communicator user to her buddy list.

Step 7: Recipient's Presence Displayed as Online

Presence shows as online in Office Communicator for kim970@msn.com because a series of SIP messages from sender to recipient are now being sent and received.

```
From: <sip:kim970@msn.com>;tag=65d68a1bc4
To: <sip:pic1@ocs-edge.litwareinc.com>;epid=ce4ccd49ad;tag=f14fbece50
Start-Line: NOTIFY sip:pic1@ocs-edge.litwareinc.com;opaque=user:epid:XHiWcZA4TlaDkwMgk
svyrQAA;gruu SIP/2.0
From: <sip:kim970@msn.com>;tag=65d68a1bc4
To: <sip:pic1@ocs-edge.litwareinc.com>;epid=ce4ccd49ad;tag=f14fbece50
CSeq: 1 NOTIFY
<snip>CONTACT: <sip:kim970@msn.com:5061;transport=tls;maddr=BAYM-TG399.tgw.messenger.
msn.com>
CONTENT-LENGTH: 489
EVENT: presence
SUBSCRIPTION-STATE: active


<snip>
    <status>
      <basic>open</basic>
    </status>
```

Scenario Two: Sending a Single Message

In this scenario, the user sends a single message to the recipient. This process has six steps that are numerically keyed to Figure 8-10. When possible, each step is illustrated by using a corresponding sample SIP message.

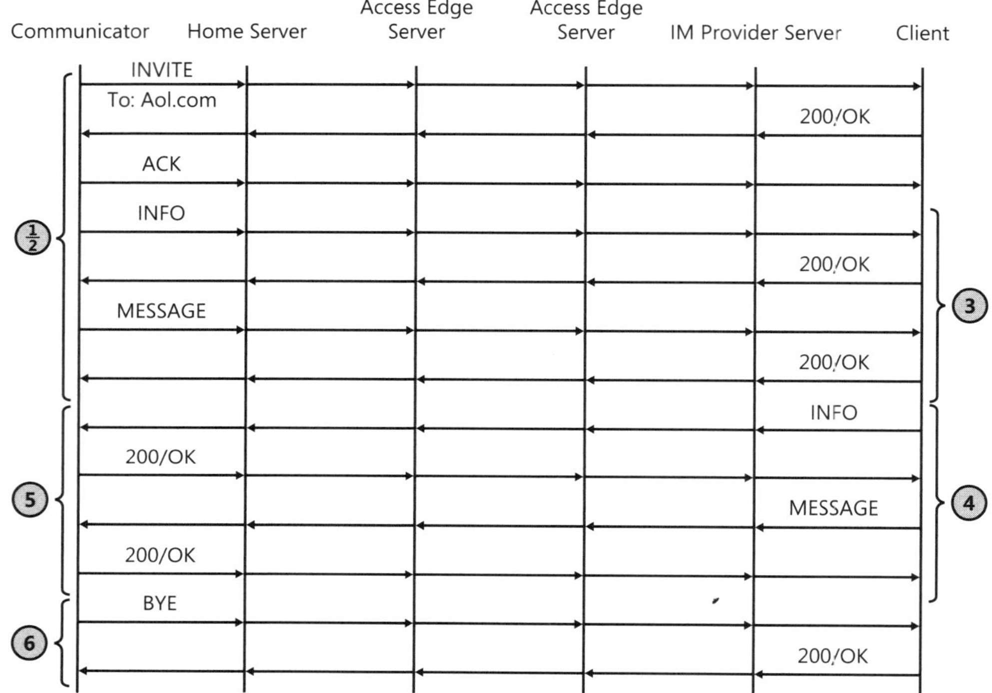

FIGURE 8-10 Communicator Startup; partner Access Edge Server to partner Access Edge Server communication

Step 1: User Selects a Recipient from the Buddy List in Office Communicator

A user double-clicks kim970@aol.com in Office Communicator to initiate communication.

Step 2: User Types a Message to a Recipient

A messaging window opens, and the Office Communicator user types a message to kim970@aol.com.

```
Start-Line: INVITE sip:kim970@aol.com SIP/2.0
From: "PIC Test (pic1) lcsent01"<sip:pic1@ocs-edge.litwareinc.com>;tag=d277e1abbb;epid
=ce4ccd49ad
To: <sip:kim970@aol.com>
```

```
CSeq: 1 INVITE


<snip>


From: <sip:pic1@ocs-edge.litwareinc.com>;tag=d277e1abbb;epid=ce4ccd49ad
To: <sip:kim970@aol.com>;tag=1187999459aol
<snip>
```

Step 3: Recipient Receives a Message from a User

The AOL user sees message text in the pop-up window and status information that says the Office Communicator user is typing.

```
Start-Line: MESSAGE sip:sip.oscar.aol.com:5061;maddr=64.12.162.248;transport=tls
SIP/2.0
From: <sip:pic1@ocs-edge.litwareinc.com>;tag=d277e1abbb;epid=ce4ccd49ad
To: <sip:kim970@aol.com>;tag=1187999459aol
CSeq: 2 MESSAGE


<snip>
<KeyboardActivity>
 <status status="type" />
</KeyboardActivity>


<snip>
Start-Line: SIP/2.0 200 OK
From: <sip:pic1@ocs-edge.litwareinc.com>;tag=d277e1abbb;epid=ce4ccd49ad
To: <sip:kim970@aol.com>;tag=1187999459aol
CSeq: 2 MESSAGE


<snip>


Content-Length: 2
Message-Body: hi
<snip>
```

Step 4: Recipient Types a Reply to the User

The AOL user types a message to the Office Communicator user in return.

```
Start-Line: INFO sip:pic1@ocs-edge.litwareinc.com SIP/2.0
From: <sip:kim970@aol.com>;tag=1187999459aol
To: <sip:pic1@ocs-edge.litwareinc.com>;tag=d277e1abbb;epid=ce4ccd49ad
CSeq: 2 INFO


<snip>
<KeyboardActivity>
 <status status="type" />
</KeyboardActivity>
<snip>
Start-Line: SIP/2.0 200 OK
From: <sip:kim970@aol.com>;tag=1187999459aol
To: <sip:pic1@ocs-edge.litwareinc.com>;tag=d277e1abbb;epid=ce4ccd49ad


<snip>
Start-Line: MESSAGE sip:pic1@ocs-edge.litwareinc.com SIP/2.0
From: <sip:kim970@aol.com>;tag=1187999459aol
To: <sip:pic1@ocs-edge.litwareinc.com>;tag=d277e1abbb;epid=ce4ccd49ad
CSeq: 3 MESSAGE


<snip>
Message-Body: hi
<snip>
Start-Line: SIP/2.0 200 OK
From: <sip:kim970@aol.com>;tag=1187999459aol
To: <sip:pic1@ocs-edge.litwareinc.com>;tag=d277e1abbb;epid=ce4ccd49ad


<snip>
```

Step 5: User Receives a Message from the Recipient

The Office Communicator user receives a message and status information that says the AOL user is typing.

Step 6: Conversation Finished

The Office Communicator user closes the IM window, which ends the conversation and which is indicated by the "BYE" message.

```
Start-Line: BYE sip:sip.oscar.aol.com:5061;maddr=64.12.162.248;transport=tls SIP/2.0
From: <sip:pic1@lcsent01.directtaps.net>;tag=d277e1abbb;epid=ce4ccd49ad
To: <sip:kim970@aol.com>;tag=1187999459aol
CSeq: 3 BYE


<snip>
Start-Line: SIP/2.0 200 OK
From: <sip:pic1@lcsent01.directtaps.net>;tag=d277e1abbb;epid=ce4ccd49ad
To: <sip:kim970@aol.com>;tag=1187999459aol
CSeq: 3 BYE


<snip>
```

Summary

This chapter examined how Office Communications Server 2007 R2 provides the means for communicating with users of instant messaging services that are provided by MSN, AOL, and Yahoo!. This enables authorized Office Communications Server users to add contacts, share presence information, and communicate in real time with IM users in these public networks. Office Communications Server enables administrators to authorize public IM connectivity on a per-user or group basis and change settings for individual and group authorizations as needed. Office Communications Server also helps administrators control SPIM by configuring message filters to restrict access from unverified users.

Additional Resources

- "Configuring Intelligent IM Filtering" in the Office Communications Server 2007 R2 Administration Guide, at *http://go.microsoft.com/fwlink/?LinkId=137125*
- "Enabling User Accounts for Office Communications Server" in the Office Communications Server 2007 R2 Administration Guide, at *http://go.microsoft.com/fwlink/?LinkId=137129*
- "Configuring IM Provider Support on Edge servers" in the Office Communications Server 2007 R2 Administration Guide, at *http://go.microsoft.com/fwlink/?LinkId=137126*

- "Managing User Accounts" in the Office Communications Server 2007 R2 Administration Guide, at *http://go.microsoft.com/fwlink/?LinkId=137129*
- "Step 2.2. Configure DNS" in the Office Communications Server 2007 R2 Edge Server Deployment Guide, at *http://go.microsoft.com/fwlink/?LinkID=133685*
- "Capacity Planning" in the Office Communications Server 2007 R2 Planning Guide, at *http://go.microsoft.com/fwlink/?LinkID=133725*

CHAPTER 9

Remote Call Control Scenarios

Many standard office environments have workspaces that contain a computer running a Microsoft operating system with Microsoft Office, and a Private Branch eXchange (PBX) phone. Typical information workers perform their daily work using this standard technology. In daily workflow, calls are placed to phone numbers of contacts whose contact information is located in Microsoft Office Outlook or the Global Address List, based on data stored by Microsoft Active Directory Domain Services. Without the ability to place a phone call directly from the desktop computer, the user must manually enter a phone number on the desktop phone while looking at the screen and typing the digits. This is not only inconvenient but also can result in calls placed to the wrong destination.

The Remote Call Control (RCC) scenario for Microsoft Office Communications Server 2007 R2 eliminates the necessity of manually entering phone numbers stored on the computer into a PBX phone. Furthermore, a user's Microsoft Office Communicator presence state will reflect the fact that she is in a call by changing the presence state to "in a call" status. This scenario is supported by Microsoft Office Live Communications Server 2005 Service Pack 1 (SP1) and by Office Communications Server 2007 R2 with Office Communicator 2007 R2. Integration between Office Communicator 2007 R2 and Office Communicator Phone Edition 2007 R2 also provides RCC-like features. This aspect is covered later on in Chapter 11, "VoIP Scenarios."

The user enabled for RCC can control her PBX phone through the Office Communicator 2007 R2 graphical user interface (GUI). If the company has the Office Communications Server 2007 R2 Edge Server deployed to allow Remote Access scenarios, it is even possible for the user to control her office desktop phone while she is connected remotely from the Internet. For example, a user can receive an incoming call on her PBX extension in the office and deflect the incoming call to her mobile phone by clicking the pop-up alert toast that indicates the incoming call on Office Communicator 2007 R2.

In the RCC scenario, the voice media stream of a phone call stays on the existing PBX phone and is not handled by Office Communicator 2007 R2. This is one of the major differences between the RCC scenario and the Enterprise Voice scenarios, as described in Chapter 11.

ON THE COMPANION MEDIA **See this book's companion CD for resources related to this chapter.**

A Remote Call Control Scenario

As shown in Figure 9-1, a user using the RCC scenario has a PBX phone with a desktop computer running Office Communicator 2007 enabled for RCC.

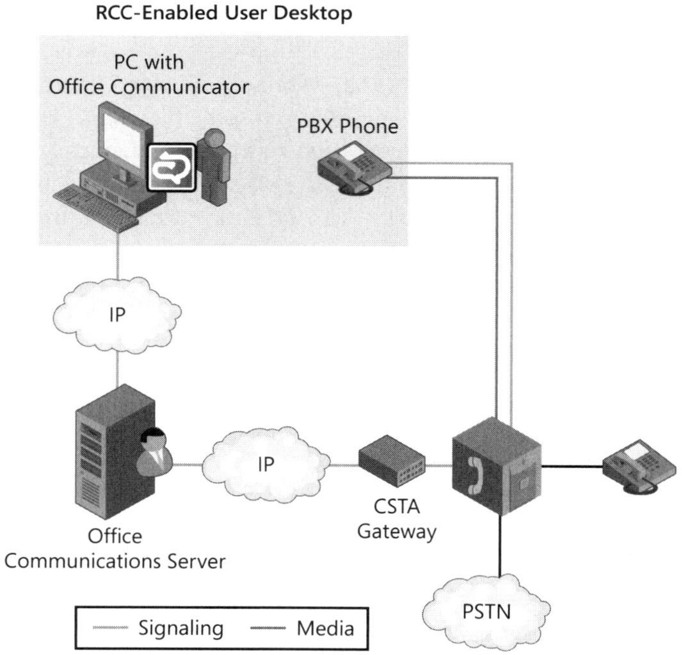

FIGURE 9-1 System architecture diagram for RCC scenario

Apart from enabling the user's Office Communicator 2007 R2 for RCC, it is necessary to install at least one Session Initiation Protocol/Computer-Supported Telephony Applications (SIP/CSTA) gateway connected on the existing PBX that hosts the user's PBX phone. CSTA is an international standard set by the European Computer Manufacturers Association (ECMA) to combine network servers with PBX environments.

There are PBX-specific SIP/CSTA gateways and vendor-neutral SIP/CSTA gateways, such as Genesys Enterprise Telephony Software (GETS) from Genesys, and it is the task of these gateways to transmit call-related signaling information from the PBX to Office Communicator 2007 R2 and vice versa. The SIP/CSTA gateway does this by establishing and terminating SIP sessions on the IP network site and converting CSTA commands received on the SIP network to these signaling messages understood by the PBX. CSTA does not handle the voice media stream of the call, only the signaling aspects of the call.

What Functionalities Are Available?

The following functionalities are available in Office Communicator 2007 R2 when a user is enabled for RCC. Note that each of these features is available in the Office Communicator user interface (UI) only when the PBX advertises these capabilities as part of the GetCSTA-CapabilitiesResponse message.

- **Make call** The RCC-enabled user can initiate a phone call by clicking a call menu provided in Office Communicator 2007 R2 or Microsoft Office Outlook 2007.
- **Receive call** The RCC-enabled user can accept an incoming call that is presented to her in the form of a pop-up window by clicking on the pop-up window. The existing PBX phone will go off-hook, and the speaker phone will be activated.
- **Caller identification** If the RCC-enabled user receives an incoming call, Office Communicator 2007 R2 will try to resolve the calling party number to a more user-friendly format by presenting the calling party's name. This will be successful only if the phone number can be matched against an entry in Office Outlook's contact list, an Office Communicator 2007 R2 contact, or the Global Address List.
- **Call waiting** If the RCC-enabled user is already in a call and receives a second call, Office Communicator 2007 R2 displays a pop-up notification toast to inform the user about this second call waiting.
- **Call hold and retrieve** The RCC-enabled user is able to use the conversation window of Office Communicator 2007 R2 to place an existing connection on hold and to retrieve it later. By placing the call on hold, the call is held on the PBX and—if available—the existing PBX plays music to the caller on hold.
- **Alternate call** The RCC-enabled user can manage multiple calls at one time. Each call is represented by a separate communication window. The user can switch between the calls but can have only one active call at a time. All other calls are automatically placed on hold. Note that the other calls could be RCC calls, Voice over Internet

Protocol (VoIP) calls, or VoIP conferences. The number of concurrent calls depends on the capabilities of the PBX.

- **Single-step transfer** Unannounced to the caller, the RCC-enabled user can forward an incoming call to another phone number by clicking the appropriate transfer button in Office Communicator 2007 R2. This is one of the Office Communicator 2007 R2 functionalities that is significantly easier to use than on a regular PBX phone.
- **Consultative transfer** The RCC-enabled user can place an existing call on hold, establish another call, and later connect the former call with the latter call. And the user herself drops out of the call. This is another one of the Office Communicator 2007 R2 functionalities that is significantly easier to use than on a regular PBX phone. Note that in Office Communicator 2007 R2, consultative transfer is available only if single-step transfer is already supported by the PBX.
- **DTMF (dual-tone multifrequency) digits** The RCC-enabled user can initiate the sending of DTMF digits through the PBX system by using the Office Communicator 2007 R2 conversation window DTMF dial pad during an active call.
- **Call forwarding** The RCC-enabled user can set the calls to be forwarded to another user or phone number. This feature will turn on Call Forwarding in the PBX system.
- **Conversation history** The RCC-enabled user can see all of her incoming and outgoing calls in the Conversation History folder in Outlook.
- **Missed call** The RCC-enabled user receives Missed Call Notifications in her Outlook Inbox for calls that the user did not answer when Office Communicator 2007 R2 is running. Note that Office Communicator 2007 R2 generates the missed call locally, and the functionality is not available when Office Communicator 2007 R2 is not running.
- **Reply with IM** The RCC-enabled user can reply to an incoming call with an instant message. The instant message is sent to the instant message address associated with the calling party. This works only if the calling party number can be resolved to a contact in the recipient's Office Communicator 2007 R2 contact list or if the calling party is present in the address book.
- **Call notes** The RCC-enabled user can type notes in Microsoft Office OneNote directly from the Conversation window in Office Communicator 2007 R2.

NOTE **The following functionalities are provided with Office Live Communications Server 2005 SP1 but are not provided with Office Communications Server 2007 R2:**

- **Conference calling using the PBX's conferencing feature**
- **Location-based forwarding**
- **Setting the Do Not Disturb presence state on a PBX phone**
- **Showing display names that are provided by PBX via CSTA gateway**

Even if a user is enabled for RCC and the telephone functionalities are limited to a set of call control functionalities of the existing PBX phone, the following VoIP-related features are also available to an RCC-enabled user:

- Make and receive Communicator-to-Communicator audio calls
- Make and receive Communicator-to-Communicator audio/video calls
- Establish a video conversation between two Office Communicator 2007 R2 clients while audio is handled by the PBX.

In addition, an RCC-enabled user can be invited to a VoIP conference created by an Enterprise Voice user and will be able to join to the audio and video using Office Communicator 2007 R2. This requires the user to use VoIP audio with Communicator and a headset attached to the computer running Office Communicator 2007 R2.

> ***NOTE*** **With Office Communicator 2007 R2 and Office Communications Server 2007 R2, it is not possible to place computer-to-phone calls and phone-to-computer calls when the user is enabled for RCC, even if a SIP/PSTN (Public Switched Telephone Network) gateway is deployed. Instead, the Enterprise Voice scenario provides this exact functionality. There is one exception where RCC and Enterprise Voice can be configured for a single user. It is explained in Chapter 10, "Dual Forking Scenarios."**

Setting Up the Remote Call Control Scenario

To set up the RCC scenario, you need to perform this series of steps. Steps 1 through 4 are described in more detail in the sections that follow.

1. Install the SIP/CSTA gateway and configure the CSTA interface on the PBX.
2. Configure a user for RCC by doing the following:
   a. Enable the user for RCC in Active Directory.
   b. Configure a Server Uniform Resource Identifier (URI) that identifies the CSTA gateway.
   c. Configure a Line URI for the user that identifies the phone number in the CSTA gateway.
3. Configure a route on the Office Communications Server pool for the Server URI.
4. Normalize phone numbers in Active Directory so that these are dialable from Communicator.
5. Start Communicator.

Step 1: Installing the SIP/CSTA Gateway and Configuring the SIP/CSTA Interface

For integration with the existing telephone environment, a SIP/CSTA gateway is needed. This gateway is connected to the SIP/CSTA interface provided by the existing PBX. It is possible to have multiple SIP/CSTA gateways connected to Office Communications Server 2007 R2, but a user can be configured to a single SIP/CSTA gateway or PBX. Only one SIP/CSTA gateway per PBX node is recommended to avoid numbering-plan conflicts.

PBX-specific SIP/CSTA gateways and vendor-neutral SIP/CSTA gateways are available on the market. You need to select a SIP/CSTA gateway that supports your existing PBX if the PBX doesn't offer a SIP/CSTA interface. Refer to your vendor's SIP/CSTA gateway documentation for configuration.

Step 2: Configuring a User for RCC

To configure a user for RCC, you first need to enable the user for RCC in Active Directory by using the Active Directory Users and Computers Management Console. In the Office Communications Server 2007 R2 Active Directory snap-in under Advanced Settings, select the configuration option Enable Remote Call Control, as shown in Figure 9-2.

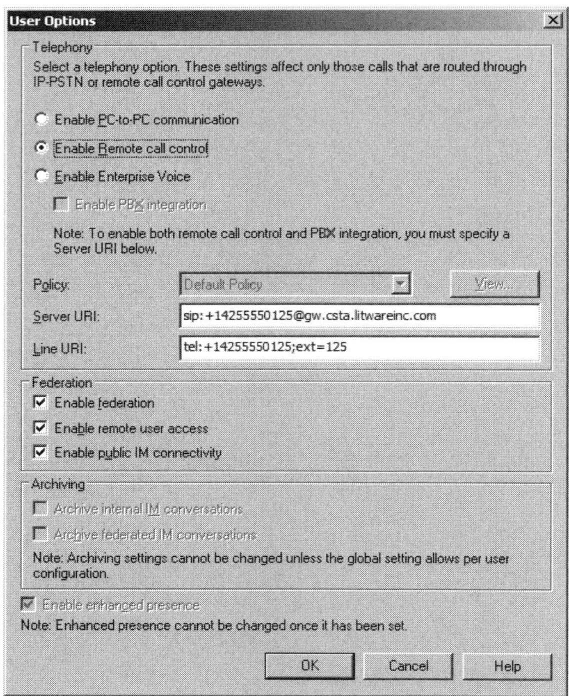

FIGURE 9-2 Enabling and configuring a user for RCC

You then configure a Server URI for the user. This Server URI points to the SIP/CSTA gateway. Office Communicator 2007 R2 sends its SIP call control messages to the SIP/CSTA gateway defined in the Server URI field. The syntax of the Server URI entered here must match the requirements of the SIP/CSTA gateway. (Please refer to the documentation provided by your SIP/CSTA gateway vendor.) Here are some examples of Server URIs:

- Sip:+14255550125@gw.csta.litwareinc.com

  (sip:<E.164 number>@<SIP/CSTA gateway FQDN>)
- Sip:cstagw@gw.csta.litwareinc.com

  sip:<user>@<SIP/CSTA gateway FQDN>)

The E.164 number is the phone number of the user in E.164 format (+<Country Access Code><Area Code><local number>, such as +14255550125), and the SIP/CSTA gateway fully qualified domain name (FQDN) is the FQDN of the SIP/CSTA gateway.

Finally, you configure a Line URI for the user. This URI is used to send call control information to and receive it from the SIP/CSTA gateway. The syntax must match the requirements of the SIP/CSTA gateway. (For more information, refer to the SIP/CSTA gateway documentation provided by the SIP/CSTA gateway vendor.) For example, the following syntaxes are common:

- tel:+14255550125;ext=125

  tel:<E.164 number>;ext=<extension>)
- tel:+14255550125;phone-context=litware.com

  The E.164 number and the number string following *ext=* must match the number and extension the user has on the existing telephone environment.

Step 3: Configuring a Route on the Office Communications Server Pool for the Server URI

All SIP traffic from Office Communicator 2007 R2 goes through Office Communications Server 2007 R2 and is proxied by the server to the SIP/CSTA gateway. Office Communicator 2007 R2 sends its SIP *INVITE* and SIP *INFO* call control messages to this SIP/CSTA gateway, which is configured in the Server URI field. This must be the FQDN of the SIP/CSTA gateway. On Office Communications Server 2007 R2, for every Server URI, a route must be configured with the destination address to which Office Communications Server 2007 R2 must proxy SIP call control messages. You can configure this under pool-level settings on the Routing tab, as shown in Figure 9-3.

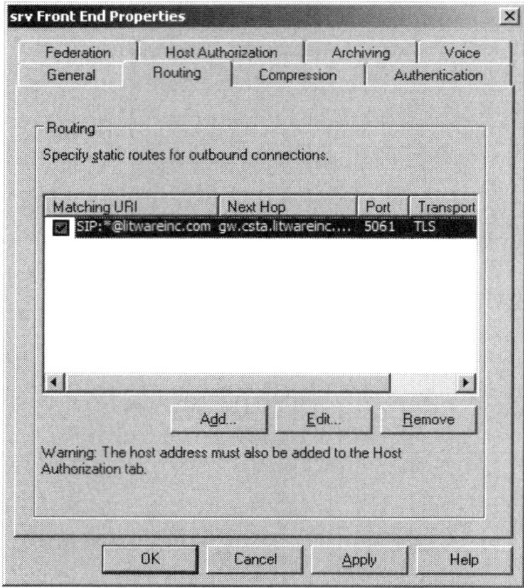

FIGURE 9-3 Configuring routes for Server URIs

For each route to a SIP/CSTA gateway, the following settings must be configured:

- **Matching URIThe syntax, sip:** *@[SIP/*CSTA gateway FQDN*] means that this route will be used for any number (*) configured in the Server URI field of the Active Directory user properties page where the FQDN of the SIP/CSTA gateway matches the value entered here.
- **Next Hop** The FQDN or IP address of your SIP/CSTA gateway.
- **Port** The port the SIP/CSTA gateway is configured to listen for SIP traffic.
- **Transport Protocol** The transport protocol that the SIP/CSTA gateway is configured to use.

NOTE **If Transport Layer Security (TLS) is configured as the transport protocol, the FQDN must be entered in the Next Hop field. If Transmission Control Protocol (TCP) is selected, the IP Address of the SIP/CSTA gateway must be entered in the Next Hop field. The FQDN is needed in the TLS mode to allow certificate verification for secure communication. If TLS is not used, a host authorization entry must also be added so that the Office Communications Server treats the CSTA gateway as authenticated.**

NOTE **It is possible to have multiple SIP/CSTA gateways configured in the same Office Communications Server 2007 R2 pool.**

Step 4: Normalizing Phone Numbers

Phone numbers need to be normalized before they are presented to the client so that they can be used for resolving calling party information to a user name. The process of normalization converts the number into a global E.164 format that can then uniquely map to a single user in the directory. Because normalized numbers are globally unique and routable, they can also be shared with other Communicator users through presence and will work correctly when the Click to Call feature is used in Communicator to call these numbers.

The functionality of matching an incoming E.164 number to an entry in the Global Address List or local Outlook Contacts is called reverse number lookup (RNL). If Office Communicator 2007 R2 successfully applies RNL and finds a name that matches a calling party number, this name is presented to the user in the pop-up window and the Conversation window instead of the calling party number.

For the RCC scenario, Office Communicator 2007 R2 downloads these normalization rules as part of the Address Book Service (ABS) download. These rules are in the form of regular expressions. The normalization rules are applied to phone numbers in Outlook contacts so that these numbers can be dialed, and they are also used for RNL. Office Communicator also applies the normalization rules when a phone number is dialed manually from Office Communicator. The same regular expressions that Office Communicator downloads and applies are also used by Office Communications Server 2007 R2 for normalizing phone numbers that are stored in the ABS.

> ***NOTE*** **Regular expressions for number normalization can be configured as described in the following file on Office Communications Server 2007 R2 Standard Edition or Enterprise Edition:**
>
> **installation path OCS%\Microsoft Office Communications Server 2007\Web Components\Address Book Files\Sample_Company_Phone_Normalization_Rules.txt**
>
> **This file also contains examples and an explanation of how to test the phone number normalization rules.**

Some CSTA implementations on PBX provide these RNL functionalities. Thus, instead of or in addition to the calling party number, a display name is transmitted to Office Communicator on an incoming call. Office Communicator 2007 R2 ignores this display name because it is not possible for Office Communicator 2007 R2 to verify the authenticity of the name.

Depending on the implementation in the PBX, the calling party number can have the following formats:

- E.164 format (for example, +14255550125)
- E.164 Switchboard with extension (+14255550125;ext=1212; recommended)
- Local number (1212;phone-context=litware.com)

NOTE The format of the calling party number entered in the PBX must match the requirements of the SIP/PSTN gateway. Sometimes this is in the E.164 format and sometimes it is not. It is recommended that you use E.164 or E.164 Switchboard with extension formats because numbers in the local formats are not dialable across federated links when they are shared using presence.

If the calling party number string does not contain a number on an incoming call, Office Communicator 2007 R2 will not apply RNL.

Understanding the Technical Details Behind the RCC Scenario

Office Communicator 2007 R2 has to send call-related information to and receive call-related information from the SIP/CSTA gateway. When Office Communicator 2007 R2 starts, it establishes a long-term SIP dialog with the SIP/CSTA gateway to transmit call control–related information on incoming calls, on outgoing calls, or in call commands, and it keeps this dialog established until Office Communicator 2007 R2 is shut down. SIP *INFO* messages are used to send call-related information to and from the SIP/CSTA gateway. The call-related information is encoded as XML, which is the payload of these SIP *INFO* messages.

In Office Communicator 2007 R2, the SIP implementation follows ECMA Technical Report TR/87. The aforementioned XML encoding of call-related information follows the ECMA-323 standard.

NOTE Office Communications Server 2007 R2 is not aware that a long-term SIP dialog is created between Office Communicator 2007 and the SIP/CSTA gateway. Office Communications Server 2007 R2 can terminate the SIP dialog between 12 to 24 hours because of route expiration. Therefore, Communicator 2007 R2 periodically checks the status of the dialog and re-establishes the SIP dialog with the SIP/CSTA gateway if it is broken. This mechanism also helps recover the connection from failures in the SIP/CSTA gateway side.

The following is an example of the SIP INFO message between Office Communicator 2007 R2 and the SIP/CSTA gateway:

```
INFO sip:+14255550125@gw.csta.litwareinc.com:5061;transport=tls;ms-role-rs-from;lr;ms-
route-sig=fsw3ylQ4X4vWNp2izAEQzWGw7NpJnQ1WDx_Z8POwAA SIP/2.0
Via: SIP/2.0/TLS 172.24.32.119:51063
Max-Forwards: 70
From: <sip:bob1@ocs.litwareinc.com>;tag=9708e2df90;epid=bd23d94254
To: <sip:+14255550125@gw.csta.litwareinc.com>;tag=1fa3a090-e86b1dac-13c4-40030-647a3-
edaf1a3-647a3
```

```
Call-ID: a3f0077597a645ed91dfed3bf7e88d93
CSeq: 2 INFO
User-Agent: UCCP/2.0.6362.0 OC/2.0.6362.0 (Microsoft Office Communicator)
Content-Disposition: signal;handling=required
Supported: timer
Proxy-Authorization: Kerberos qop="auth", realm="SIP Communications Service",
opaque="F6103640", crand="d4eeb47a", cnum="11", targetname="sip:+14255550125@gw.csta.
litwareinc.com", response="602306092a864886f71201020201011100ffffffff54c977329332842b8
245d15438797106"
Content-Type: application/csta+xml
Content-Length: 313

<?xml version="1.0"?>
<GetCSTAFeatures xmlns="http://www.ecma-international.org/standards/ecma-323/csta/ed3">
  <extensions>
    <privateData>
      <private>
        <lcs:line xmlns:lcs="http://schemas.microsoft.com/Lcs/2005/04/RCCExtension">te
l:+14255550125;ext=125</lcs:line>
      </private>
    </privateData>
  </extensions>
</GetCSTAFeatures>


SIP/2.0 200 OK
Authentication-Info: Kerberos rspauth="602306092A864886F71201020201011100FFFFFFFF8
4471479F62D94AC3307F0F1CA27DA36", srand="EFB30DB0", snum="13", opaque="F6103640",
qop="auth", targetname="sip:+14255550125@gw.csta.litwareinc.com", realm="SIP
Communications Service"
From: <sip:bob1@ocs.litwareinc.com>;tag=9708e2df90;epid=bd23d94254
To: <sip:+14255550125@gw.csta.litwareinc.com>;tag=1fa3a090-e86b1dac-13c4-40030-647a3-
edaf1a3-647a3
Call-ID: a3f0077597a645ed91dfed3bf7e88d93
CSeq: 2 INFO
Content-Disposition: signal;handling=required
Via: SIP/2.0/TLS 17.1.19:51063;ms-received-port=51063;ms-received-cid=185D300
Supported: 100rel,replaces,timer
User-Agent: Example Gateway Release 1.0 version 4.2.3
Contact: <sip:+14255550125@gw.csta.litwareinc.com>
Content-Type: application/csta+xml
Content-Length: 985
<?xml version="1.0" encoding="UTF-8"?>
```

```
<GetCSTAFeaturesResponse xmlns="http://www.ecma-international.org/standards/ecma-323/
csta/ed3" xmlns:xsi="http://www.w3.org/2001/XMLSchema-instance">
  <supportedServices>
    <systemStatServList>
      <requestSystemStatus />
    </systemStatServList>
    <monitoringServList>
      <monitorStart />
      <monitorStop />
    </monitoringServList>
    <callControlServList>
      <answerCall />
      <clearConnection />
      <consultationCall />
      <deflectCall />
      <holdCall />
      <makeCall />
      <retrieveCall />
      <singleStepTransfer />
      <transferCall />
    </callControlServList>
    <callAssociatedServList>
      <generateDigits />
    </callAssociatedServList>
    <logicalServList>
      <setForwarding />
    </logicalServList>
  </supportedServices>
  <supportedEvents>
    <callControlEvtsList>
      <connectionCleared />
      <delivered />
      <diverted />
      <established />
      <failed />
      <held />
      <originated />
      <retrieved />
      <transferred />
    </callControlEvtsList>
    <logicalEvtsList>
      <forwarding />
    </logicalEvtsList>
  </supportedEvents>
</GetCSTAFeaturesResponse>
```

In the preceding SIP *INFO* message, Office Communicator 2007 R2 is requesting the list of supported PBX features. The PBX advertises its supported feature set with the GetCSTA-FeaturesResponse message. This is an important transaction to note because it impacts features lighting up in the Office Communicator user interface. For example, the PBX in the previous response supports the Call Transfer function because the <TransferCall/> primitive is present in the <CallControlServList> node. Therefore, Office Communicator will enable the Transfer button. Further examples in later sections of this chapter highlight how Office Communicator 2007 R2 interacts with the SIP/CSTA gateway.

Bootstrapping

Bootstrapping sequence establishes the communication path between Office Communicator and the SIP/CSTA gateway. The first part of bootstrapping is downloading the Line URI and Server URI parameters from Office Communications Server by using the in-band provisioning mechanism. Office Communicator then establishes a long-term *INVITE* dialog with the SIP/CSTA gateway specified in the Server URI. Office Communicator sends the RequestSystem-Status CSTA command, to which the PBX responds with a RequestSystemStatusResponse message. Once this exchange is completed, the SIP *INVITE* dialog is set up, and *INFO* messages can be sent in this dialog.

The first *INFO* message is the GetCSTAFeatures message that you have seen before, which Office Communicator sends to the SIP/CSTA gateway to discover the call related features supported by the PBX. The second *INFO* message with the CSTA command, MonitorStart, indicates that Office Communicator should start monitoring the user's PBX phone line. This is required so that the PBX starts sending events about the line state to Office Communicator via the SIP/CSTA gateway. Once these events are exchanged, Office Communicator is ready to make and receive RCC calls. Figure 9-4 illustrates the bootstrapping procedure.

> ***NOTE*** **Communicator periodically sends a RE-INVITE with RequestSystemStatus approximately every 10 minutes to ensure that the SIP/CSTA gateway is up and running and that the long-lasting SIP dialog is maintained. This is a heartbeat mechanism that is maintained from Office Communicator 2007 R2 to the SIP/CSTA gateway.**

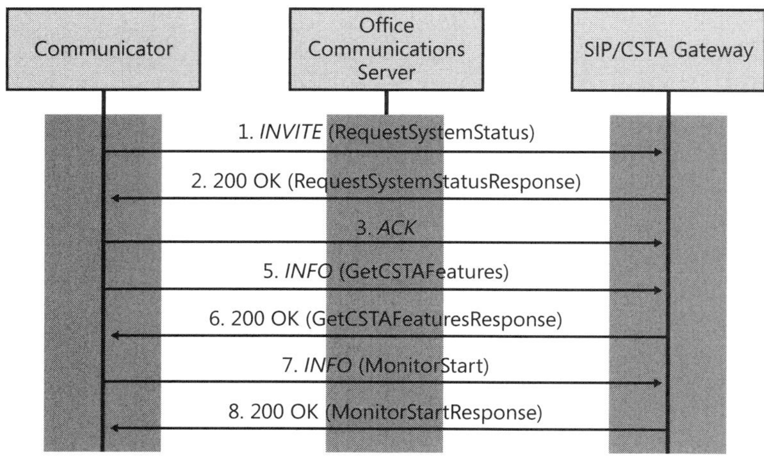

FIGURE 9-4 Bootstrapping RCC

Receiving a Call

On an incoming call, the PBX rings the user's existing PBX phone and also sends out an incoming call notification to Office Communicator through the SIP/CSTA gateway using a SIP *INFO* message sent from the SIP/CSTA gateway to Office Communicator 2007 R2. The user can either answer the incoming call on his PBX phone by picking up the receiver or accept the incoming call from Office Communicator, which activates the speaker phone functionality on the PBX phone.

Received calls are always indicated to Office Communicator using a DeliveredEvent *INFO* message that originates from the SIP/CSTA gateway. Once the user picks up the call, an AnswerCall message is sent to the PBX, which responds with an EstablishedEvent message to indicate the successful call set-up. Figure 9-5 illustrates how a call is received.

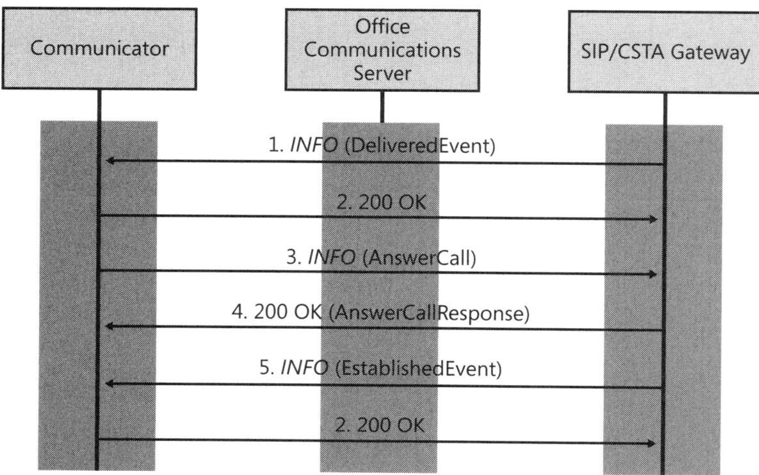

FIGURE 9-5 Receiving a call

REAL WORLD

Troubleshooting Remote Call Control Scenarios

John Lamb
Director, Modality Systems Limited

Setting up Remote Call Control (RCC) integration between Office Communications Server 2007 R2 and a PBX is usually a straightforward process. It involves configuring your Office Communications Server environment to exchange RCC messages with your PBX. Many new PBXs support native integration with Office Communications Server, and for those that do not, a third-party RCC gateway can be used to facilitate the integration.

However, one of the more problematic RCC scenarios is the Reverse Number Lookup (RNL) aspect of matching an incoming call number to a name in the directory. When an RCC-enabled user receives a call on her desk phone, the RCC message exchange causes Office Communicator to alert the user that her phone is ringing. This notification message displays information about the caller's phone number. If RNL is working properly, the notification will also display the caller's name.

The challenge with RNL lies with getting the caller's phone number as sent by the PBX (or gateway) to be in the same format as the phone number stored in the Office Communicator address book. Because the phone numbers in the address book are stored in E.164 format, for example, +442071234567, this is what the PBX must send in the RCC message.

The quickest way to determine what the PBX is sending is to enable logging in Office Communicator. This is enabled on the General tab within the Options user interface. When logging is enabled, a text file is created in the %USERPROFILE%\Tracing directory that contains debugging information, including the SIP messages that are exchanged. This log file will have a .uccapilog extension (Office Communicator 2007 R2), or a .uccplog extension (Office Communicator 2007).

Once logging is enabled, reproduce the incoming call and then open the text file and look for the SIP *INFO* message containing the CSTA XML body containing the incoming call notification. The SIP *INFO* message should contain something that looks like this:

```
<OriginatedEvent xmlns="http://www.ecma-international.org/standards/ecma-
323/csta/ed3">
     <monitorCrossRefID>1253</monitorCrossRefID>
     <originatedConnection>
          <callID>4067933</callID>
          <deviceID typeOfNumber="dialingNumber">tel:12345;phone-
context=dialstring</deviceID>
```

```
      </originatedConnection>
      <callingDevice>
           <deviceIdentifier>tel:12345;phone-context=dialstring</
deviceIdentifier>
      </callingDevice>
      <calledDevice>
           <deviceIdentifier>tel:+442079876543;phone-context=dialstring</
deviceIdentifier>
      </calledDevice>
      <localConnectionInfo>connected</localConnectionInfo>
      <cause>normal</cause>
      <callLinkageData>
<globallyUniqueCallLinkageID>2E2600000000003E125D</
globallyUniqueCallLinkageID>
      </callLinkageData>
</OriginatedEvent>
```

In this case, look for the <callingDevice><deviceIdentifier> node in the XML body of the CSTA message. In the previous example, you can see that the PBX (or gateway) is sending the following calling device ID:

```
tel:12345;phone-context=dialstring
```

Because this is not in E.164 format, Office Communicator will not be able to match this number with anything in its address book. The simplest solution is to configure the PBX or RCC gateway to perform digit manipulation so that the number will be in the correct format. In this case, the number should be:

```
tel:+442070012345;phone-context=dialstring
```

Consult the PBX or gateway vendor's documentation to see if this type of number manipulation is supported.

Making a Call

When a call is made, Office Communicator sends a MakeCall message to the SIP/CSTA gateway with the normalized phone number to connect to. When the user types a phone number manually, Office Communicator will apply the normalization rules to generate an E.164 number before sending it to the SIP/CSTA gateway.

> ***NOTE*** **Phone numbers from the Click To Call list are already normalized.**

Once the MakeCall request is made, the SIP/CSTA gateway responds with several events. OriginatedEvent indicates that the PBX has initiated a call, DeliveredEvent indicates the call has been delivered to the other end, and EstablishedEvent indicates an answer. Figure 9-6 illustrates how a call is made.

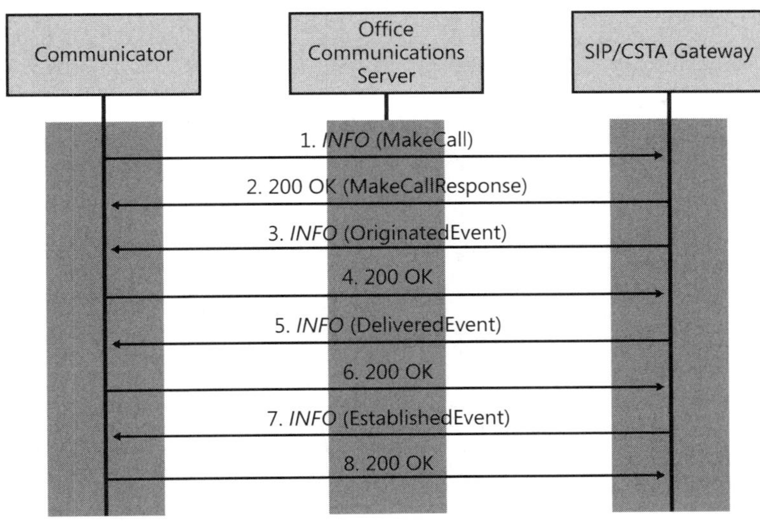

FIGURE 9-6 Making a call

Summary

The RCC scenario is a lightweight telephone integration scenario that provides Office Communicator 2007 R2 users the ability to integrate their PBX phone with the ease of use of their other business applications, such as Outlook. It is not necessary to migrate the existing PBX system to a VoIP-based IP telephony solution to enable these scenarios. This chapter provides information on the functionalities of RCC, background information on how the scenario works, the infrastructure that must be set up, and what must be configured on Office Communications Server 2007 R2 to implement the RCC scenario.

Additional Resources

- A description of the Genesys GETS SIP/CSTA gateway can be found at *http://www.genesyslab.com/products/enterprise_collaboration.asp*.
- ECMA-269 information can be found at *http://www.ecma-international.org/publications/standards/Ecma-269.htm*.
- ECMA-323 information can be found at *http://www.ecma-international.org/publications/standards/Ecma-323.htm*.
- ECMA TR/87 information can be found at *http://www.ecma-international.org/publications/techreports/E-TR-087.htm*.

CHAPTER 10

Dual Forking Scenarios

This chapter covers the voice features in Microsoft Office Communications Server 2007 R2 when Microsoft Office Communicator 2007 R2 is coupled with the user's Private Branch eXchange (PBX) phone. This configuration in which Office Communications Server operates in coexistence with the PBX is called dual forking. This chapter examines the user experience in a dual forking environment, goes into the technical details of Office Communications Server's dual forking design, and finally covers the configuration aspects of dual forking.

What Is Dual Forking?

Dual forking (or PBX integration) is a Voice over Internet Protocol (VoIP) scenario that enables the user to use both the PBX phone as well as Office Communicator softphone at the same time. The organization is not required to rip and replace the existing PBX system. Users can keep the same PBX phone number as before. Incoming calls to the PBX phone ring both the PBX phone as well as Office Communicator. The user has the option to answer the call from either endpoint. Outgoing calls can be placed using the PBX phone or using Office Communicator. The experience for end users is similar to providing an additional phone line from anywhere Office Communicator is available.

Dual forking enables administrators to leverage existing investments in the PBX architecture and at the same time deploy new telephony capabilities that Office Communications Server supports. Users get the benefit of outside voice without having virtual private network (VPN), click to call from Microsoft Office (Outlook, SharePoint, Word, and so on), conferencing features, and various other benefits provided by Office Communications Server's VoIP capabilities, as described in Chapter 11, "VoIP Scenarios."

Although dual forking leverages the existing PBX infrastructure investments, it does not provide the full capabilities of Office Communications Server that an Enterprise Voice user has, as described in Chapter 11. Some scenarios, such as call forwarding or conferencing, will not provide optimal experiences. These differences are highlighted in the rest of the chapter.

> ***NOTE*** **Dual forking works with PBXs that have been certified to support this scenario. The list of PBXs is available at the following location:** ***http://go.microsoft.com/fwlink/?LinkID=133697.***

Overview of Dual Forking Scenarios

Users configured for dual forking will have an experience similar to that of users configured for Enterprise Voice (see Chapter 11) from click to call in Office Communicator to calling Response Groups. Dual forking can be set up in two different configurations. The first configuration is dual forking without Remote Call Control (RCC) to the PBX. The second configuration is dual forking coupled with RCC to the PBX. This section explores where the user experience differs in dual forking and dual forking with RCC.

> ***NOTE*** **Office Communicator Phone Edition does not support the dual forking scenario. The only audio-capable client that supports dual forking is Office Communicator.**

The section titled "Examining Technical Details Behind Dual Forking Scenarios" later in this chapter offers more detail on how these scenarios work.

Originating a Two-Party Call

Making a call in a dual forking environment is similar to making a call in an Enterprise Voice environment. When RCC is available, the user can choose whether to place the call from the PBX phone or Office Communicator. This is shown in Figure 10-1.

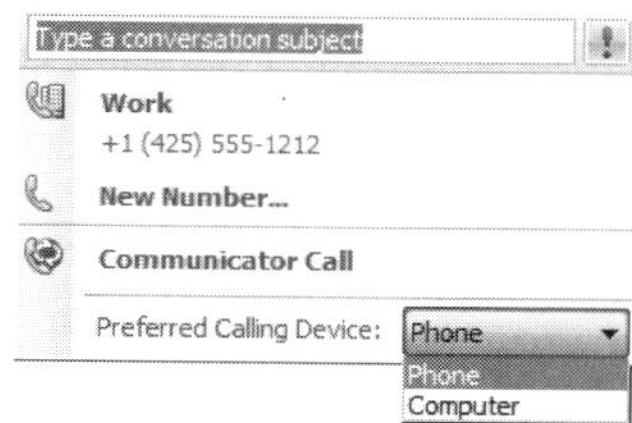

FIGURE 10-1 Click to call

> ***NOTE*** **This experience is also available in the RCC-only configuration.**

Answering a Two-Party Call

Answering a call in a dual forking environment is similar to answering a call in an Enterprise Voice environment. When RCC is available, dual forking enables the call to be answered on either Office Communicator or the PBX phone. Clicking the incoming call notification answers the call on the default device (which can be set to Computer or Phone from Call Forwarding Settings). The redirect option enables the user to select a different device. This is shown in Figure 10-2.

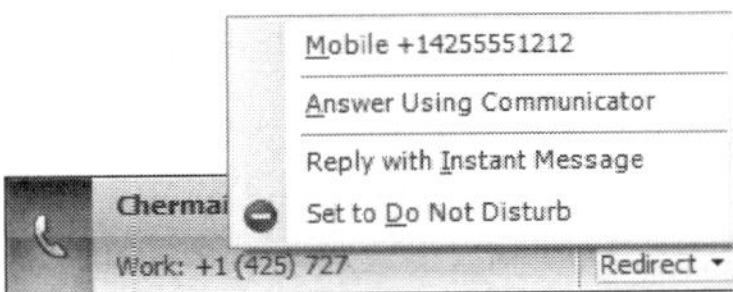

FIGURE 10-2 Receiving a call and answering from an alternate device when RCC is enabled

In Call Experience

The in call experience for dual forking is similar to the in call experience for an Enterprise Voice environment. If the PBX phone is used for calling (RCC scenario), then the user experience differs from using Communicator because the call controls that are available to an RCC-enabled user depend on what features are supported by the PBX (see Chapter 9, "Remote Call Control Scenarios"). Another notable difference is that the RCC conversation window does not have speaker or microphone controls. Call controls when RCC is used to make or answer calls are shown in Figure 10-3.

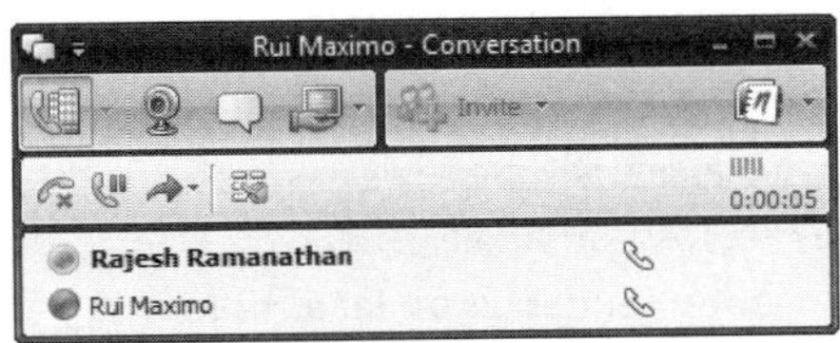

FIGURE 10-3 Call Controls for an RCC user

Conferencing Experience

Dual forking scenarios enable the user to use the conferencing capabilities of either the PBX system or Office Communications Server. A multiparty audio conference can be started on either the PBX side or the Office Communications Server side. The multiparty audio conference can be started by adding another user to a two-party call or when a call with three or more people is started directly. The Office Communications Server and PBX systems will maintain the roster for the conferences independently.

For example, user A starts a call with user B, who is also a dual forking user. User A uses Office Communicator as the endpoint. User B selects to answer the call on the PBX phone. User A now adds user C to the two-party call to create a conference. Office Communicator creates the audio conference on the Office Communications Server's A/V Conference Server. User A sees a conference roster and is able to view user B and user C joined to the conference. However, user B continues to see user A as the only person in the call because the PBX system does not have access to the conference roster in Office Communications Server.

Conference calls hosted on the Office Communications Server infrastructure give Office Communicator users information about participants in the call and access to conference controls. Therefore, in the preceding example, if user B had picked up the call from Office Communicator instead of her PBX phone, the conference roster information would be available to user B from Office Communicator.

> ***NOTE*** **When RCC is used in conjunction with dual forking to make calls or answer two-party calls, such calls cannot be escalated to an audio conference from that endpoint. This is because Office Communicator is using the Computer Supported Telephony Applications (CSTA) protocol to control the PBX phone, and conferencing using CSTA is not supported from Office Communicator.**

Configuring Call Forwarding

The user can configure call forwarding on Office Communications Server from a client such as Office Communicator. This is similar to the capabilities that the user has when enabled for Enterprise Voice, as described in Chapter 11.

> ***NOTE*** **Certain call forwarding features for Enterprise Voice users, which are described in Chapter 11, are not available to dual forking users. See the section titled "Understanding Routing Rules in Dual Forking Scenarios" later in this chapter for details on features that are available.**

One of the features likely not to be available to the user from Office Communicator, but which can be available on the PBX phone, is voice mail. The reason voice mail is not available in Office Communicator to dual forking users is because the administrator would likely use the existing PBX's voice mail system instead of Exchange Unified Messaging, which is the only voice mail system supported by Office Communicator.

When optional RCC is enabled for dual forking users, the user is enabled to set call forwarding rules from the PBX. The capability to control forwarding in Office Communications Server is no longer available. The call forwarding user interface (UI) in that configuration is the same as the user would get when RCC is enabled. This is shown in Figure 10-4.

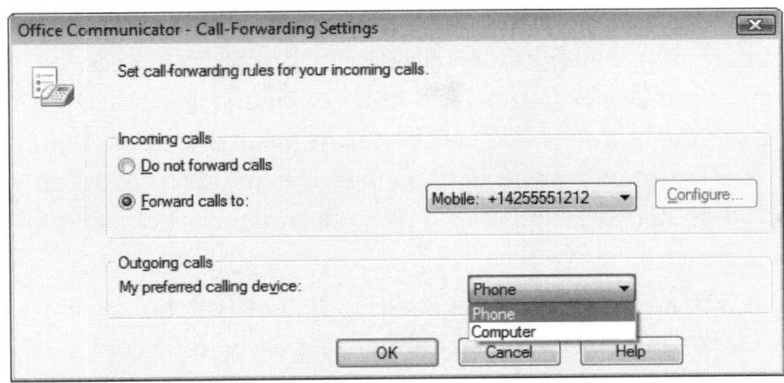

FIGURE 10-4 Call Forwarding options for the dual forking user when RCC is enabled

Examining Technical Details Behind Dual Forking Scenarios

Dual forking takes its name from the concept of forking; an incoming call is routed simultaneously to multiple destinations. The *dual* in this term refers to the fact that for each incoming call, both Office Communications Server and the PBX fork the call not only to their own endpoints but also send the call to each other. This is shown in Figure 10-5.

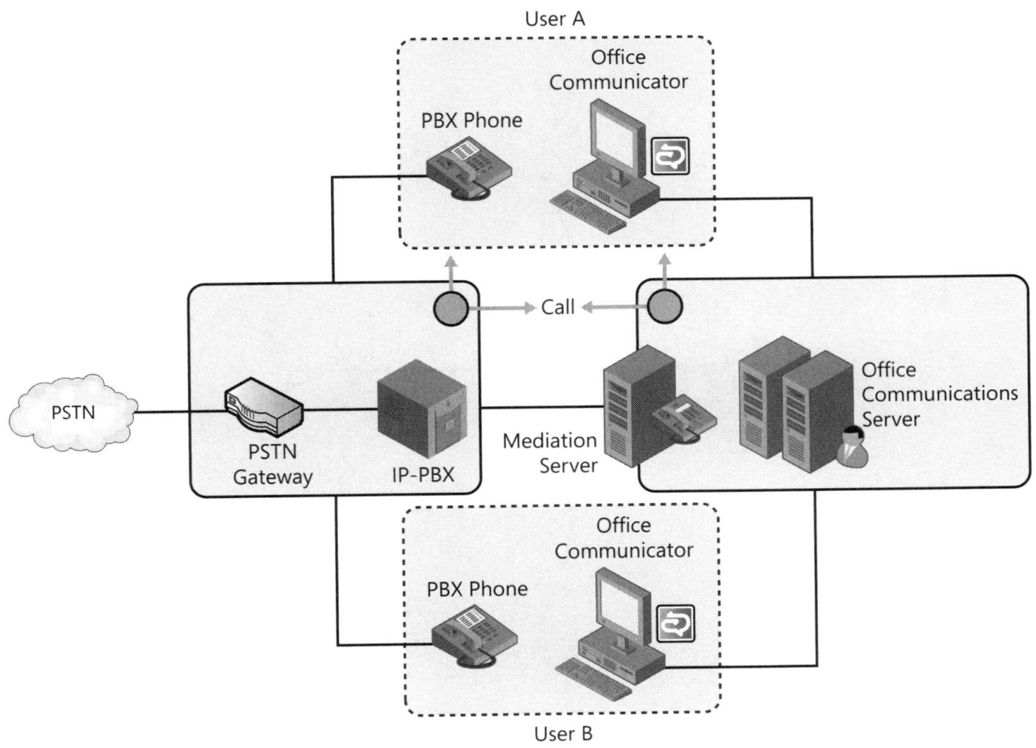

FIGURE 10-5 Dual forking topology

In Figure 10-5, two users—user A and user B—are configured for dual forking. Each user has a PBX phone and Office Communicator. When user A calls user B, the call is "forked" to both the PBX and Office Communications Server systems. User B's PBX phone as well as his Office Communicator ring. User B has the option to answer the call from either device. This capability is particularly useful if user B is roaming outside the enterprise. In this case, user B can answer the call from a laptop computer running Office Communicator without having to set up a VPN connection into the enterprise.

The PBX shown in Figure 10-5 is also an interface to the Public Switched Telephone Network (PSTN) because that is how an existing PBX within an enterprise is likely to be configured. In all likelihood, the PBX is already hooked up to a voice mail system; therefore, Office Communications Server does not need to provide an additional voice mail solution.

Figure 10-6 shows a more detailed example of how the forking occurs when a call originates from the PBX or the PSTN side. In this case, the PBX is the first entity in the chain to receive the call. Because the PBX is configured to dual fork with Office Communications Server, it sends the call to Office Communications Server in addition to ringing the callee's PBX phone. The PBX in this case acts like an "anchor" for forking the call. The anchor ensures that when the call is answered at any one device, a cancellation notification is sent to the callee's other ringing devices in both systems.

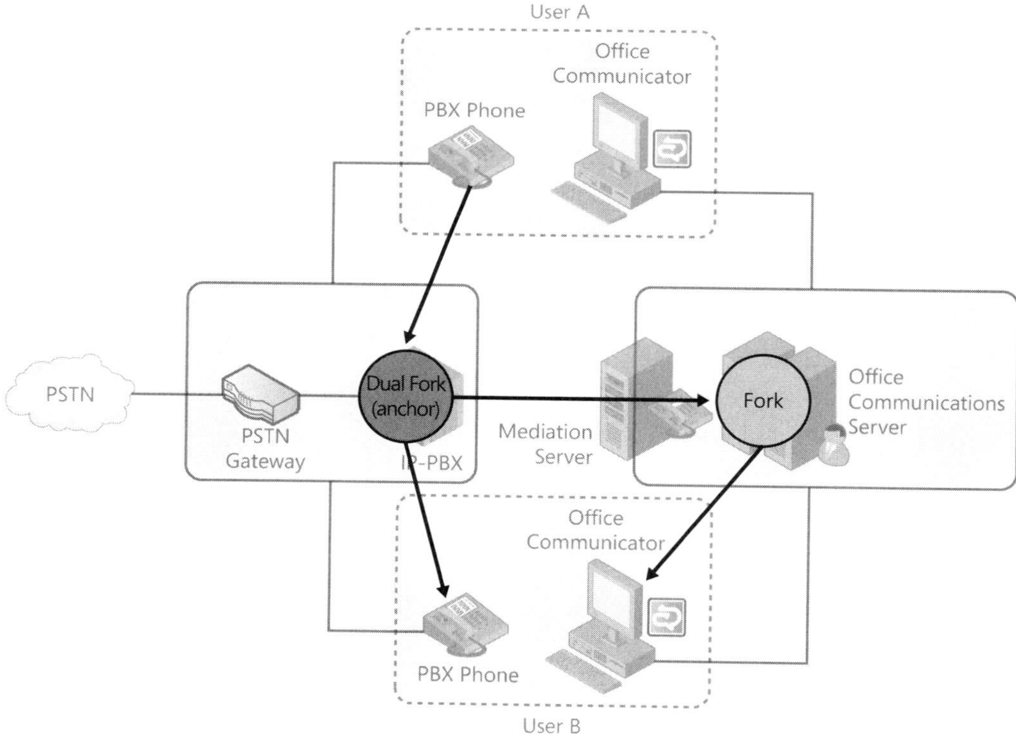

FIGURE 10-6 Incoming call, dual forked at PBX

Figure 10-7 shows another scenario in which the call originates from the Office Communications Server network instead of the PBX network. In this scenario, the call originating from user A's Office Communicator is forked by Office Communications Server to user B's Office Communicator endpoints and to the PBX, which then rings user B's PBX phone. In this case, Office Communications Server acts as the "anchor" and ensures that when the call is answered, all other ringing endpoints receive a cancel notification. User B can receive the call from either device, similar to the previous scenario.

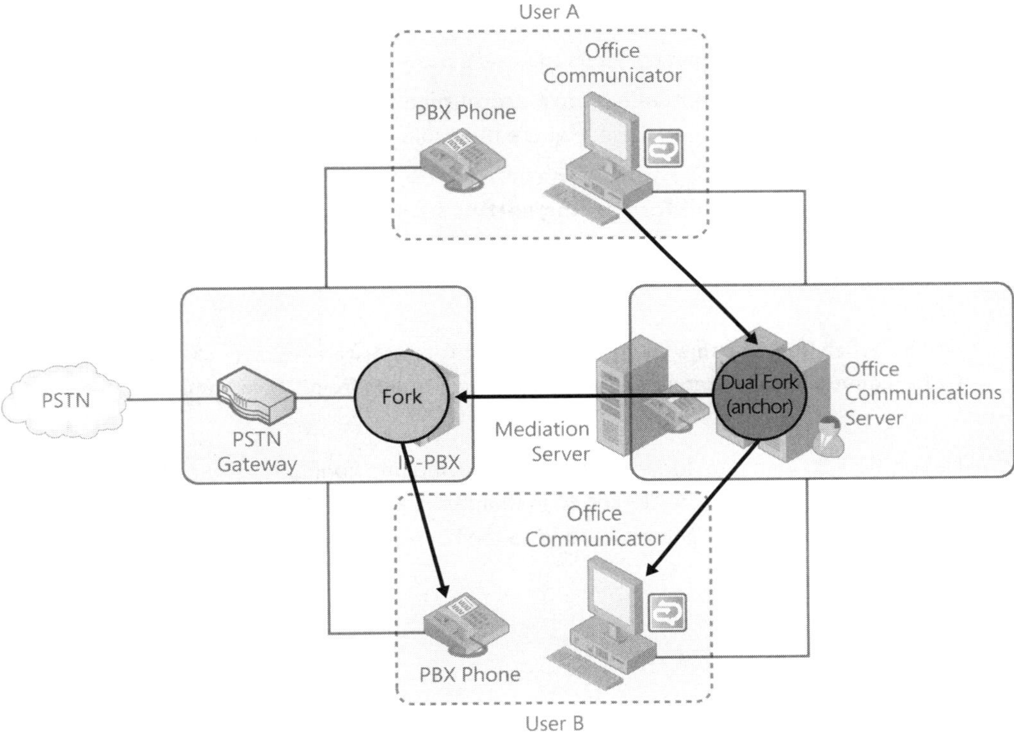

FIGURE 10-7 Incoming call, dual forked at Office Communications Server

> ***NOTE*** **In a dual forking configuration, the Mediation Server must perform the task of interworking the codecs on both ends. This could lead to some impact on quality. For example, Real-Time Audio (RTAudio) is a wideband (16 bit) codec, and when the call is answered on the PBX phone, the Mediation Server must convert to a G-711 (8-bit narrowband) codec, which is a lower-quality codec. Therefore, the audio quality depends on the type of codecs the PBX system natively supports.**

Understanding RCC in Dual Forking Scenarios

So far we have seen how the dual forking scenario enables the user's Office Communicator and PBX phones to work together as endpoints. Chapter 9 explained how the RCC scenario enables Office Communicator to remotely control calls in the PBX system.

The dual forking scenario can also leverage the RCC functionality to provide a more integrated experience with the PBX. This optional functionality adds the following capabilities to the dual forking deployment:

- **Presence integration** When the call is answered from the PBX phone, Office Communicator automatically sets the user's presence to the In a Call state.
- **Flexibility to answer calls from Communicator** Users can answer calls from Office Communicator and select where the audio is directed—either to the computer or to the PBX phone.
- **Controlling PBX call forwarding settings from Communicator** Office Communicator uses the call forwarding configuration from the PBX. It also can set call forwarding rules on the PBX directly.

> ***NOTE*** **When RCC is enabled with dual forking, the call forwarding settings configured in Office Communications Server can no longer be controlled from Office Communicator.**

Deploying RCC with dual forking requires deploying and configuring a Session Initiation Protocol (SIP)/CSTA gateway, as described in Chapter 9. Figure 10-8 shows the dual forking topology with the SIP/CSTA gateway added to the configuration.

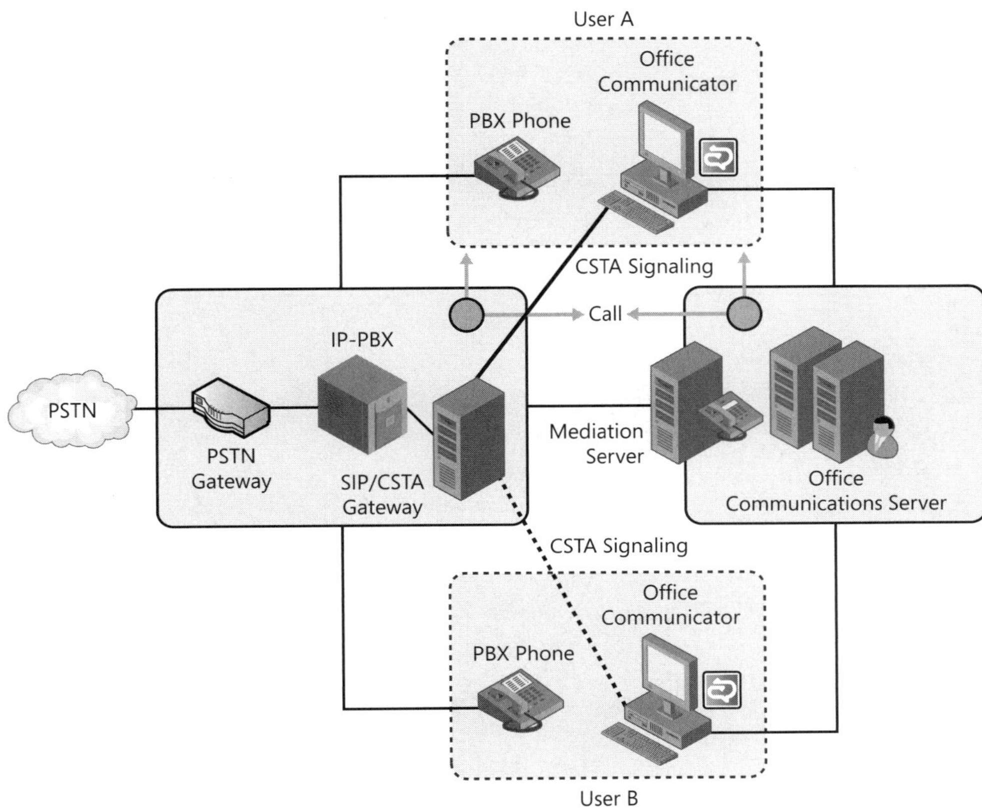

FIGURE 10-8 SIP/CSTA gateway in the dual forking topology

In this configuration, dual forking with RCC, Office Communicator gets notified twice of incoming calls: once by the SIP/CSTA gateway and again by the Office Communications Server that the PBX signaled to route the call. This is illustrated in Figure 10-9.

If user B answers the call from path 1, RCC is used to answer the call, and the call is terminated on the PBX phone. If user B answers the call from path 2, dual forking is used to answer the call, and the call is terminated on Office Communicator.

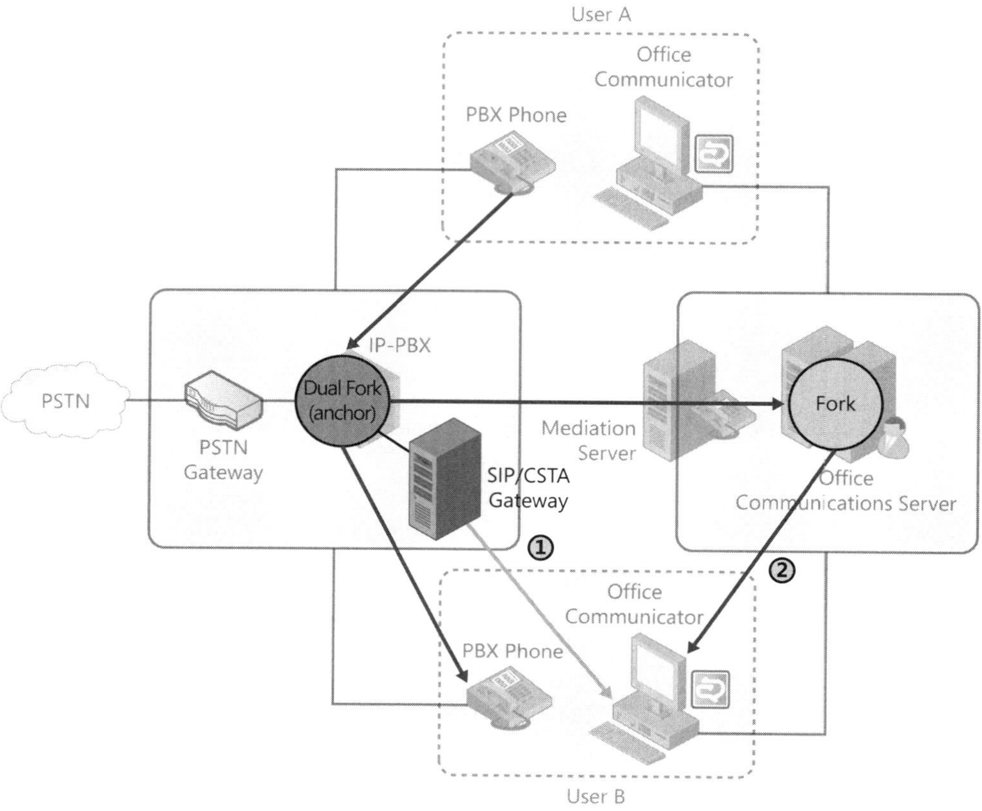

FIGURE 10-9 Two calls in Communicator with dual forking and RCCs

> ***NOTE*** **Some functionality, such as escalating a two-party call to a conference, is not supported when RCC is used to answer the call. Therefore, users get a much richer experience with the calls when they answer on Office Communicator than they would if they used RCC to answer the call.**

Understanding Loop Detection

Because dual forking requires sending calls from Office Communications Server to the PBX, and in the reverse, calls could potentially bounce from one system to another. Office Communications Server provides the following mechanisms to prevent looped calls:

- Office Communications Server does not fork calls that it receives from the PBX back to the PBX.

- Office Communications Server inserts a proprietary SIP header, named ms-call-source, in every INVITE message that is forked to the PBX. The ms-call-source header notifies the PBX that it should suppress forking of the call back to Office Communications Server.
- Office Communicator 2007 clients have built-in logic to reject a suspected loop call from the PBX. They specifically check for whether a new call is coming in when an existing call is ringing and what the source header in those calls specifies. This loop detection mechanism serves as a fail-safe mechanism for situations in which a PBX does not support loop detection logic that is based on the ms-call-source header mentioned in the previous bullet point.

A PBX without the logic to suppress forking based on the ms-call-source header is shown in Figure 10-10, which illustrates the loop detection mechanism and the various points where a loop could occur. In this example, a call originates from user A's Office Communicator, and the Office Communications Server dual forks the call to the PBX as well as to the callee's Office Communicator. Both the callee's PBX phone and Office Communicator ring. The callee selects to answer the call from Office Communicator. The Office Communications Server, which performed the dual forking for the call, also sends out a CANCEL message to the PBX so that the other PBX phones stop ringing.

"1: loop detect" in Figure 10-10 illustrates how the PBX sends the call back to Office Communications Server, which originated the call. Because the PBX does not understand the ms-call-source header, it fails to suppress the loop back. A PBX certified for dual forking support should have suppressed the call at this point.

Next, the call returns to the Office Communications Server, which is unable to prevent the loop because there isn't a way Office Communications Server can correlate that the incoming call from the PBX is the same call it sent. It appears as a new call originating from the PBX. This is highlighted as "2: loop detect". Had the call originated from the PBX instead of Office Communications Server, then Office Communications Server would not have sent the call back to the PBX from this loop detection point.

Finally, the call reaches user B's Office Communicator, which detects that this call is originating from the PBX based on ms-call-source header. It declines the duplicate call because there is already another call in the ringing state from the same user. Office Communicator rejects the call with a 605 reason code. This is highlighted as "3: loop detect". This causes Office Communications Server to suppress ringing any other clients the user is signed in to. Office Communications Server then sends back a 480 temporarily available response to the PBX.

> ***NOTE*** **The dual forking loop detection fallback behavior is based on PBXs treating the 480 temporarily unavailable response correctly. That is, when this response code is received from one endpoint, only that endpoint is "temporarily available," and other endpoints continue to ring.**

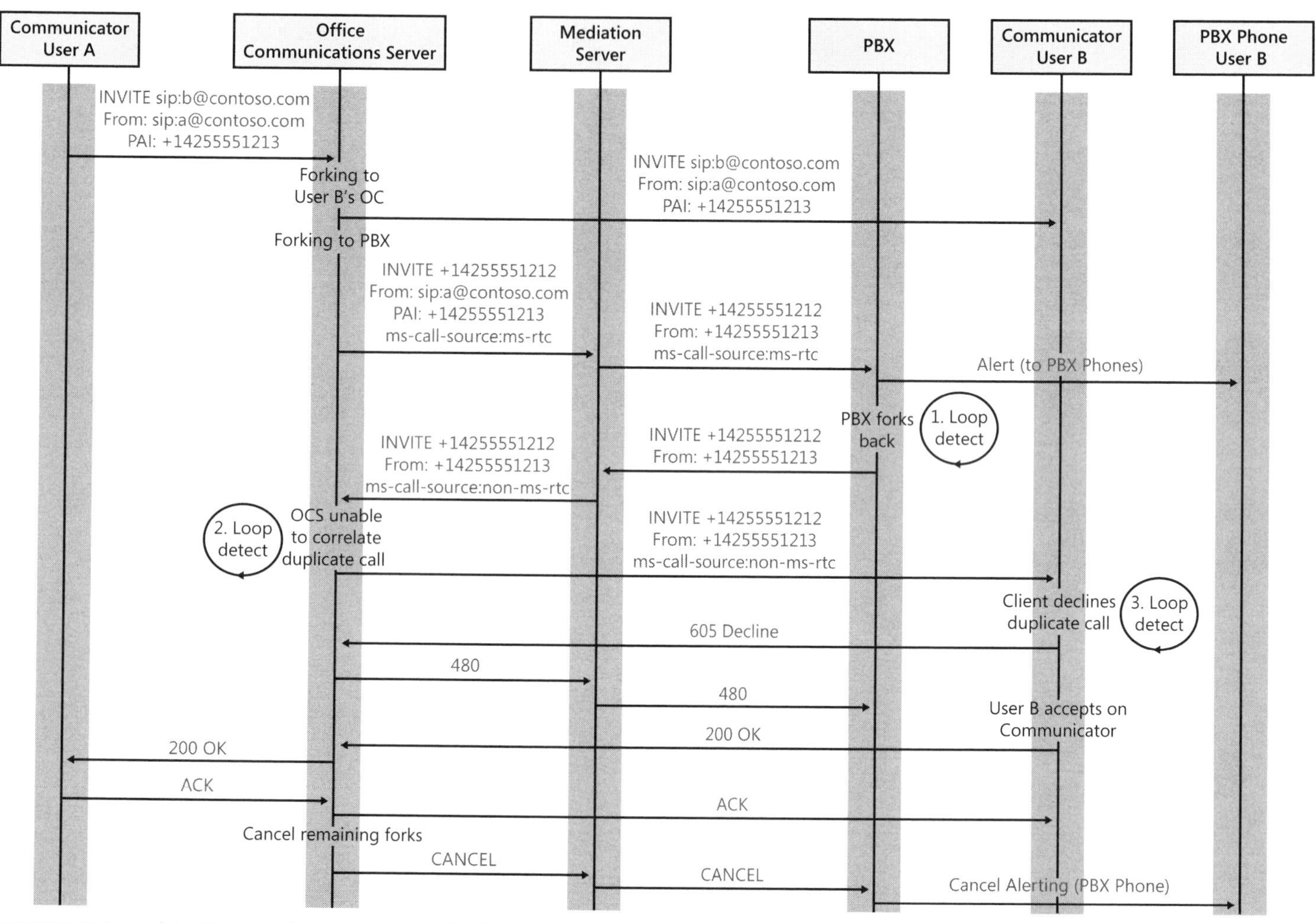

FIGURE 10-10 Loop detection at various points for a call originated by Communicator

Understanding Routing Rules in Dual Forking Scenarios

Both the Office Communications Server and PBX systems provide separate call forwarding rules. When RCC is not configured with dual forking, these rules can be set independently and could potentially conflict with each other.

To illustrate, suppose user A sets call forwarding to direct calls to user B from Office Communicator. When an incoming call is addressed to user A, Office Communications Server will forward the call to user B per user A's call forwarding rule. However, the PBX is unaware of this forwarding behavior. The PBX continues to ring user A's PBX phone, whereas Office Communications Server will ring user B's Office Communicator. The dual forking design mitigates this erroneous behavior by using an intermediate call progress SIP signal (181 Call Is Forwarded) that alerts the other system that a forwarding is activated. Once such an alerting signal is received, the PBX stops alerting user A's phone and keeps the call leg with Office Communications Server up.

> ***NOTE*** **PBX systems that do not support the intermediate call progress SIP signal will exhibit the undesirable behavior of the two systems ringing different destinations. A PBX certified for dual forking will support the call progress signal specified above.**

From the perspective of the end user, most of the Office Communications Server forwarding rules are similar to a pure Enterprise Voice–enabled user (see Chapter 11), with the following exceptions:

- Users cannot be added as delegates or team members.
- Voice mail options will not be available for forwarding.
- When Do Not Disturb is set on Office Communications Server, calls will still ring on the PBX phone instead of being suppressed. Office Communications Server enables calls to ring on the PBX phone because routing the calls to the voice mail system is handled by the PBX system. For Do Not Disturb to work consistently, the dual forking user must manually set the PBX phone to Do Not Disturb as well.

Table 10-1 summarizes the differences in call forwarding behavior between these configurations. The table indicates whether these features can be accessed from Office Communicator. An entry in the table marked *Office Communications Server* indicates the feature is available and Office Communications Server provides the feature. An entry marked *PBX* indicates the feature is available in Office Communicator and the PBX provides the feature. Features marked *Not Supported* cannot be configured for a user in this configuration from Office Communicator. An entry marked *Optional* indicates the feature can be optionally turned ON.

TABLE 10-1 Call Forwarding Features in Communicator Forwarding UI

FORWARDING FEATURE	ENTERPRISE VOICE (OFFICE COMMUNICATIONS SERVER, VOIP)	ENTERPRISE VOICE WITH PBX INTEGRATION (DUAL FORKING)	ENTERPRISE VOICE WITH PBX INTEGRATION AND RCC (DUAL FORKING WITH RCC)
Call Forwarding Immediate	Office Communications Server	Office Communications Server	PBX
Call Forwarding Unanswered	Office Communications Server	Office Communications Server	Not Supported
Ring Duration	Office Communications Server	Office Communications Server	Not Supported
Simultaneous Ring PSTN Phone	Office Communications Server	Not Supported	Not Supported
Delegate Configuration	Office Communications Server Delegates use Attendant Console	Not Supported	Not Supported
Team Call	Office Communications Server	Not Supported	Not Supported
Forward to Voice Mail	Optional	Not Supported	Not Supported
Presence-Based Forwarding (Do Not Disturb)	Office Communications Server	Office Communications Server only (PBX phone will ring)	Office Communications Server only (PBX phone will ring) Note: Do Not Disturb integration with RCC is not supported
Working Hours Only Forwarding	Office Communications Server	Office Communications Server	Not Supported

NOTE **Any other call forwarding feature that is activated in the PBX will not be reflected in Office Communicator.**

Understanding Phone Numbers in Dual Forking Scenarios

Dual forking scenarios leverage calls being routed across Office Communications Server and the PBX by using phone numbers. Office Communications Server forks the call to the PBX addressed to the user's phone number. Similarly, the PBX system sends the forked call to the Office Communications Server addressed to a phone number. Therefore, for dual forking to work properly, phone numbers specified in Active Directory and in the PBX system must be mapped to the same user.

When the user is configured for dual forking, Office Communications Server uses the user's *Line URI* attribute defined in Active Directory to route calls to the PBX. The *Line URI* should contain a phone number defined according to the Request for Comment (RFC) 3966 TEL URI format. The PBX should be able to accept calls destined for the phone number specified in the *Line URI* and ring the appropriate phone line associated with that *Line URI*. When sending calls to Office Communications Server, the PBX inserts the destination phone number in the To URI of the SIP request. Office Communications Server matches the phone number in the To URI to the *Line URI* of the callee and routes the call to the correct user. Therefore, incoming calls from the PBX should have phone numbers in the To URI that match the phone number in Active Directory.

In addition to routing calls to the correct destination, Office Communicator clients use the phone number in the From URI (if properly formatted by the PBX) to perform reverse name lookup and match the phone number to the caller's *Line URI*, which provides caller ID information to the callee.

When configuring dual forking with RCC, it is important that phone numbers in the From URI that is being sent in the VoIP INVITE from the PBX match the phone number in the calling party information in the incoming CSTA message. Office Communicator uses the calling party information to suppress the other incoming call notification and provide the redirect option to the alternate device (as seen in Figure 10-2).

The following phone number formats are supported:

- E.164, such as +14255551212
- E.164 with extension, such as +14255551212;ext=1212

The second format is recommended for PBXs that do not support Direct Inward Dialing (DID) numbers but do have a switchboard number available. In this situation, the number +14255551212 is the switchboard number and ext=1212 is the local extension.

> ***NOTE*** **When the user is configured for dual forking with RCC, and there is a mismatch in the From phone numbers between the VoIP INVITE and the RCC call or if the phone number is anonymous, then Office Communicator will not be able to match the two calls to merge the call notification. In this case, the user will see two incoming call notifications for the same call, with one corresponding to the RCC call and one corresponding to the VoIP call.**

Understanding Normalization in Dual Forking Scenarios

Phone number normalization in a dual forking scenario uses normalization rules closer to VoIP scenarios (Enterprise Voice) than to RCC. In dual forking, the user must be able to use Office Communicator as a softphone to dial a number, and this requires support for location-based normalization rules. For more details on normalization, see Chapter 11.

Table 10-2 outlines the normalization rules used in different scenarios. Note that Address Book Server (ABS) rules are used for normalizing the phone numbers across the directory, whereas the per-location normalization on the clients depends on the specific configurations.

TABLE 10-2 Normalization Rules for Office Communications Server 2007 R2

CONFIGURATION	NORMALIZING PHONE NUMBERS IN GLOBAL ACCESS LIST	NORMALIZING USER-DIALED NUMBERS BY CLIENT	ROUTING CALLS BY SERVER
Enterprise Voice	ABS rules	Location Profile rules	Location Profile rules
Enterprise Voice with PBX Integration	ABS rules	Location Profile rules	Location Profile rules (on Office Communications Server only)
Enterprise Voice with PBX Integration and RCC	ABS rules	Location Profile rules	Location Profile rules (on Office Communications Server only)
RCC	ABS rules	ABS rules	Not used

Configuring Dual Forking

Configuring a user for dual forking requires the following steps.

1. Configuring Office Communications Server. This requires configuring Enterprise Voice first, which involves configuring phone routes, policies, location profiles, and normalization rules. Details on how to configure these settings are covered in Chapter 11.

> ***NOTE*** **When configuring a policy for the user, ensure that the policy has Simultaneous Ring to PSTN Phone turned off. This is a check box in the Policy dialog box, as shown in Figure 10-11. (For detailed configuration of Voice policies, see Chapter 11.) This is a recommended step so that forking the call to the PSTN phone does not interact with forking to the PBX. If this policy is not configured and the user enables Simultaneous Ring from PSTN Phone, the PSTN phone can receive two incoming call notifications for the same call in certain scenarios. If the PSTN system has voice mail, the adverse side effect could be that some calls are always answered by voice mail directly.**

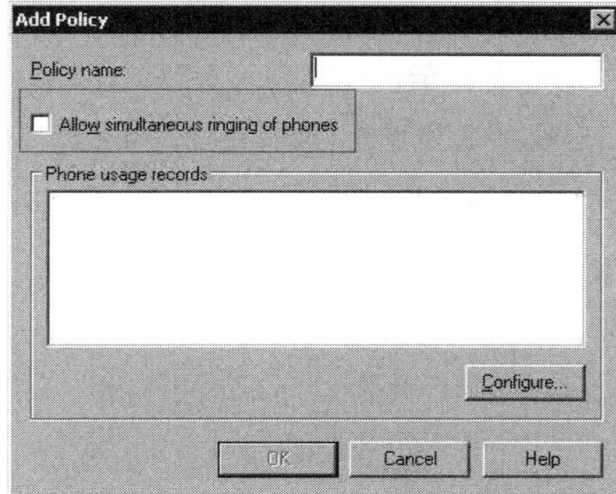

FIGURE 10-11 Simultaneous Ringing Phone policy

Once these configurations are done, users can be configured for dual forking. This step is covered in this section.

2. Configuring the PBX. This step varies based on the PBX vendor. This configuration is not covered in this chapter. Consult your PBX vendor's documentation for more details. Also check if the PBX is certified for dual forking. (For more information, see the section titled "Additional Resources" later in this chapter for Qualified IP PBX's for Office Communicator.)

   To configure a single user for Enterprise Voice with dual forking, select the user's Properties from the right-click menu in DSA.MSC or the Admin Tools Microsoft Management Console (MMC). On the Communications tab, select Configure to view additional options. In the Telephony section, select Enable Enterprise Voice Routing and configure the user's phone number. Check Enable PBX Integration to enable dual forking to the PBX. Specify a valid TEL URI assigned to the user in the *Line URI* field. This TEL URI is the same as the user's existing phone number in RFC 3966 format. For example, if a user has the phone number 4255551212, the TEL URI should be set to tel:+14255551212. These settings are shown in Figure 10-12.

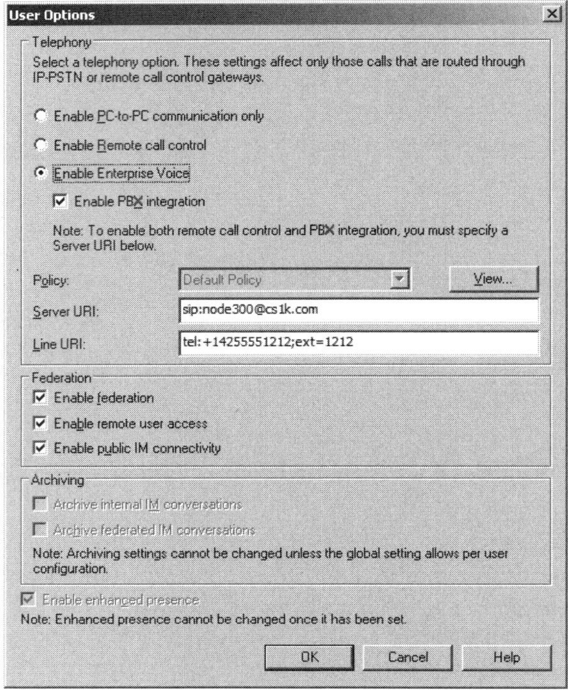

FIGURE 10-12 Configuring users for dual forking

To enable dual forking with RCC, all that is necessary is to specify the SIP URI of the SIP/CSTA gateway in the *Server URI* field. This field is sufficient for Office Communicator to connect to the SIP/CSTA gateway for enabling RCC functionality.

REAL WORLD

Deploying Dual Forking with RCC with Nortel CS 1000

Sonu Aggarwal
CEO, UnifySquare, Inc.

Duncan Blake
Enterprise Voice Architect, UnifySquare, Inc.

Implementing dual forking with RCC between Office Communications Server 2007 R2 and Nortel CS 1000 requires some planning and preparation. Plan on at least an eight-week project time frame for a production implementation in the field. Check with the Nortel channel stipulations regarding whether you need to involve a Nortel certified technician and a technician from Nortel Services.

A few areas you need to watch out for while configuring dual forking with RCC include:

Patching It is important that the CS1K PBX be patched with the right PIPs, and that the Mediation Server, front-end server, Office Communications Server proxy, and Communicator itself be patched appropriately for dual forking with RCC.

Versioning The requirements for configuring the Nortel CS1K change significantly between Nortel CS1K version 5.0 and 5.5. For example, in the CS1K 5.0 configuration, forking is enabled by creating a Personal Call Assistant (PCA) to a dummy number, which is then routed to the Nortel MCM server. In CS1K 5.5, PCAs have been replaced by universal extensions (UEXTs), although the underlying PCA service still needs to be running on the CS1K.

Normalization Ensuring that converged system alerts work correctly requires that two separate sets of normalization rules are set correctly—for dual forking calls (SIP INVITEs) as well as RCC calls (SIP INFOs). It also requires that the clients download updated Address Book information from the ABS with phone numbers in the prescribed format. This is accomplished through correctly formatting the correct *AD Phone Number* field or the correct *Proxy* field in Active Directory and then regenerating Address Book information.

Routing Routing is complicated by the fact that the MCM Server has two roles, acting both as a CSTA gateway (for RCC signaling traffic) and as a SIP proxy (for the SIP signaling and media traffic through the Mediation Server). Both the MCM and the Office Communications Server Mediation Server typically have two separate networks or subnets with which they need to communicate: the Office Communications Server network and the PBX network (or, in CS1K-specific terms, the TLAN). The Office Communications Server network can be viewed as "internal" to the Office Communications Server cloud, and the TLAN be viewed as "external" (again, to the Office Communications Server cloud). The Office Communications front-end server has a static route for RCC SIP traffic that points to the "internal" edge of the MCM Server. However, the Mediation Server is configured to point to the *external* edge of the MCM Server as the Mediation Server gateway. In certain call flows in the dual forking/RCC scenario, the Mediation Server will use the Via: header of incoming traffic (which is based on the fully qualified domain name [FQDN]) to route responses. If the Mediation Server can resolve the internal edge of the MCM Server using the Domain Name System (DNS), this may result in a condition in which the networking stack will erroneously send traffic to the inner edge of the MCM Server. The MCM will correctly send a SIP ACK to the internal edge of the Mediation Server (the IP address from which the traffic came). However, the Mediation Server will ignore this ACK because it is received on the wrong interface for SIP traffic from the gateway.

Although the root cause is a dropped ACK, the symptom manifests itself as an established call "mysteriously" getting dropped at the 32-second mark. The easiest solution for this problem is to add an entry to the Mediation server "hosts" file, ensuring that the Mediation Server will always resolve the MCM Server FQDN to the MCM Server's external IP address. Not being particularly intuitive, though, this is an easily overlooked step.

Summary

Dual forking is a way to leverage an existing investment in PBX infrastructure and deploy additional VoIP capabilities powered by Office Communications Server. Adding RCC to the dual forking configuration allows the administrator to offer more integration with the PBX. Users configured for dual forking have access to Office Communications Server's functionality (such as outside user support, conferencing support, and click to call) along with the telephony capabilities provided by the PBX. This chapter covered the functionalities of dual forking, information on how the scenario works, the infrastructure needed, and how to configure dual forking. It also covered details about various scenarios in which the user experience differs from the Enterprise Voice experience.

Additional Resources

- Qualified IP/PBXs for Microsoft Office Communicator 2007 R2, found at *http://go.microsoft.com/fwlink/?LinkID=133697.*
- Office Communications Server 2007 partners, found at *http://go.microsoft.com/fwlink/?LinkID=133699.*
- Office Communications Server Open Interoperability Program, found at *http://go.microsoft.com/fwlink/?LinkID=133622.*
- TEL URI RFC 3966, found at *http://go.microsoft.com/fwlink/?LinkID=133700.*
- Selecting a deployment option for Office Communications Server, found at *http://go.microsoft.com/fwlink/?LinkID=133701.*
- Office Communications Server 2007 user documentation, including the "Enterprise Voice Planning and Deployment Guide," can be found on the companion media in the \Additional Reading folder. The "Enterprise Voice Planning and Deployment Guide" file is named Office Communications Server_VoIP_Guide.doc.

CHAPTER 11

VoIP Scenarios

This chapter covers the voice features available in Microsoft Office Communications Server 2007 R2 and describes how the user experience is seamlessly integrated into the productivity tools of the information worker. The chapter then goes into the technical details of Enterprise Voice design in Office Communications Server. Finally, the server components that are involved to make an Enterprise Voice deployment possible are discussed in detail.

What Is VoIP?

Voice over Internet Protocol (VoIP) enables placing and receiving voice calls over the Internet Protocol (IP) network. The call might or might not traverse the Public Switched Telephone Network (PSTN). VoIP is different from Remote Call Control (RCC). RCC is related to controlling the Private Branch eXchange (PBX) phone from a computer running Office Communicator, whereas in VoIP the audio traffic is carried over the IP network. VoIP has the potential of eliminating the need for a PBX network, which most large organizations must deploy and maintain in addition to their IP network. Managing these two independent networks, each with its own idiosyncrasies, requires administrators with various backgrounds and skills.

VoIP technology promises to deliver many improvements, such as infrastructure and network consolidation, lower management and toll costs, and better interoperability between systems from different vendors. The VoIP functionality of Office Communications Server 2007 R2 can replace PBX functionality in many cases and interoperate with existing PBXs in other cases.

Microsoft's VoIP offering, Office Communications Server 2007 R2, provides an integrated user experience where voice communication is integrated into the same applications used by information workers to communicate electronically, such as Microsoft Office 2007, Microsoft Office SharePoint 2007, and Exchange 2007 SP1. With Office Communications Server 2007 R2, voice becomes one of many communications modes—e-mail, instant messaging (IM), desktop sharing, Web conferencing, file transfer, video—that are accessible from a single consistent user interface (UI). This ease of use encourages user adoption of more advanced features such as call forwarding, call redirection, and multiparty calls.

Another important advantage is portability. With Office Communicator 2007 R2 installed on their laptops and an Edge Server deployed in their organizations' peripheral networks, users have access to their work numbers from anywhere in the world where Internet connectivity is available. This is a powerful proposition given a global economy where more and more workers telecommute. Office Communications Server 2007 R2 makes it possible for information workers to free themselves from the constraints of the office or cubicle.

ON THE COMPANION MEDIA **Links to information related to the topics in this chapter are provided on the companion media.**

Overview of VoIP Scenarios

The topics in this section include general VoIP features of Office Communications Server 2007 R2. The next section, "Examining the Technical Details Behind VoIP Scenarios," describes the technical aspects of using these features.

Using Two-Party Calling

With basic two-party calling, one party can dial a number and establish an audio conversation with another party. The user can select a contact from his contact list and click the call icon. A conversation subject can be set so that the called party knows what the call is about. Alternatively, the user can right-click the contact and select a number from the drop-down menu, as shown in Figure 11-1. After the user installs Office Communicator, this right-click menu is also available in every Microsoft Office program (Word, Outlook, and so on) including Office SharePoint, as shown in Figure 11-2. This consistent user experience reinforces users' familiarity with making a call.

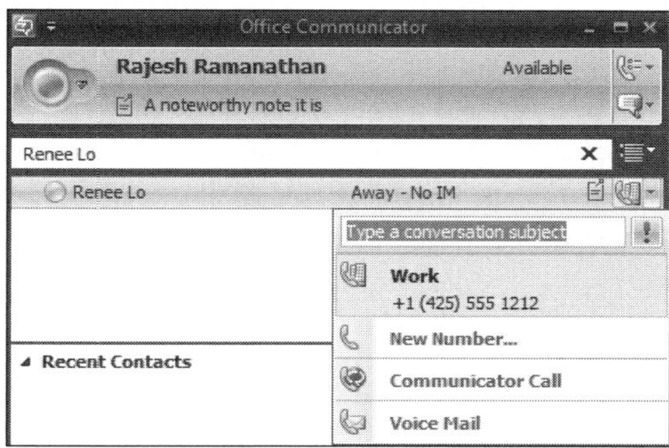

FIGURE 11-1 Calling from Office Communicator

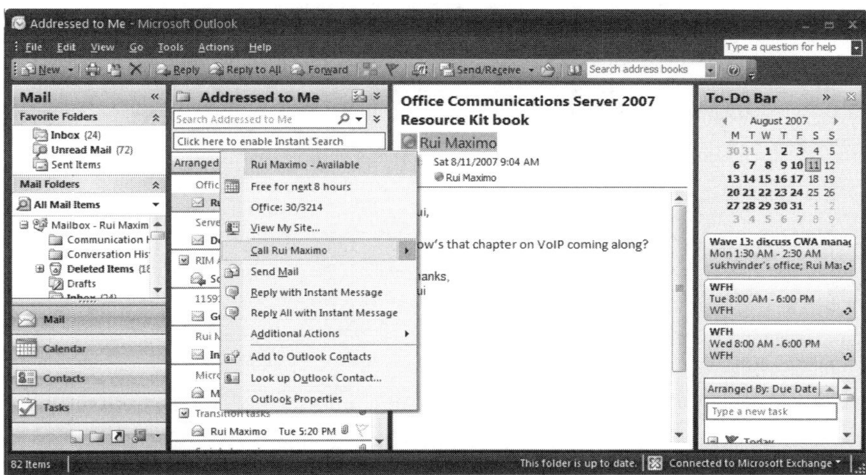

FIGURE 11-2 Calling from Office Outlook

Calling an internal user is one click away because the caller can dial based on user name by locating the called party in the contact list or performing a search. But what about external users? In the case of external users, the caller will not be able to locate the party to be called by name unless the user adds this external party to the Outlook address book. Instead, a phone number must be dialed. Dialing from Communicator is as simple as typing the phone number in the Search field and pressing the Enter key or clicking the phone icon, as shown in Figure 11-3.

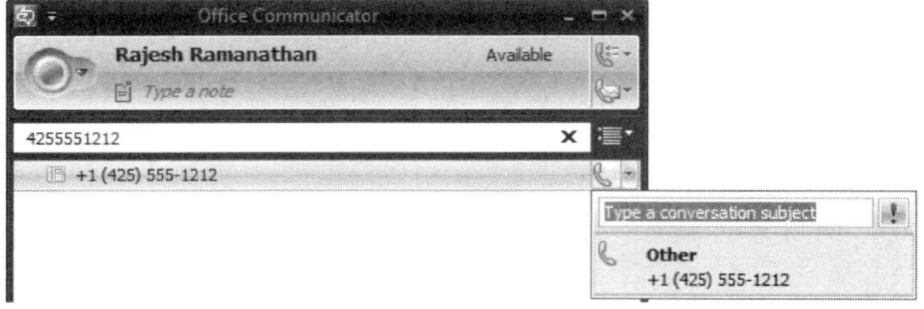

FIGURE 11-3 Calling external phone numbers

When an internal or external call is placed, Communicator displays an unobtrusive conversation window with visual controls that replace the obscure dial codes of PBX phones, making it much easier for users to discover these features and use them, as shown in Figure 11-4.

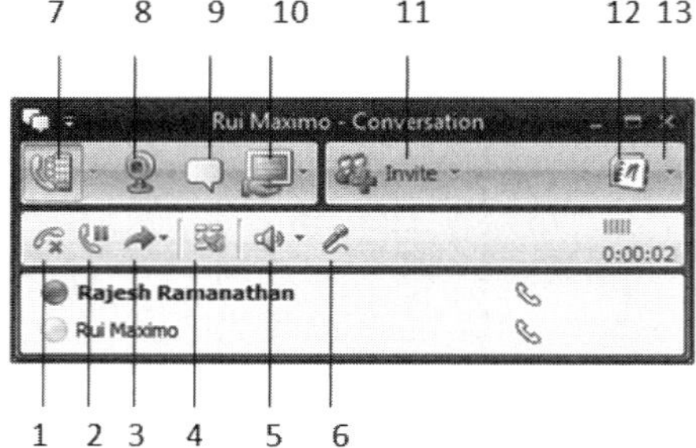

FIGURE 11-4 Communicator conversation window

The controls shown in Figure 11-4 are numbered to match the following descriptions:

1. End the call.
2. Hold the call.
3. Transfer the call.
4. Expand the standard 3 x 4 dial pad.

5. Change the volume.

6. Mute the microphone.
7. Click to call.
8. Add video to the call.

   Once video is added to a call, the video controls are displayed. These controls enable the user to change video size, change picture in picture, pause, or hold video. Note that changing to Large Size will cause the quality of the video to switch to VGA resolution (640 x 480) automatically. Selecting Full Screen can enable full-screen, high definition (HD)-quality–video for the call, provided the administrator has enabled this functionality for the user. See Chapter 19, "Client and Device Administration," for details.

9. Add IM to the call.
10. Add a Desktop Sharing session to the call.

    Once Desktop Sharing is added to the call, the desktop sharing controls are displayed to the sharer on top of the screen. The sharer's screen also displays a border highlighting the content that is shared.

11. Invite additional participants to the call.
12. Take notes associated with the call, using Microsoft OneNote.
13. The down-arrow caret displays a drop-down menu with additional options, such as taking notes, sending a file to the other person the user is talking to, and setting and changing the conversation subject so that the called party gets an indication of the topic the calling party wants to discuss before answering the call. Also, similar to e-mail messages, the caller has the option to set a high-priority importance indicator for the called party to see.

NOTE **The option for sending a file is available only during two-party conversations.**

Once the call is established, the audio comes through the computer speakers and microphone. For optimal audio quality, use a Universal Serial Bus (USB) phone or headset that is certified to work with Microsoft Office Communicator.

Configuring Call Deflection

Call deflection refers to the ability of the called party to redirect the calling party to a different phone number before picking up the call. This capability is valuable if you're about to step out for a meeting but need to answer a call, which perhaps is a call you've been expecting. Ideally, the called party is able to redirect the call to her cell phone to take the call while commuting to her next appointment. Redirecting the call from your office phone to your mobile phone is a valuable feature that's possible with Office Communicator 2007 R2. When a call comes in, a small window containing a system alert appears by default in the bottom right corner of the computer screen with an accompanying ringing sound. Deflecting the call is as simple as clicking the Redirect caret and selecting a phone number to forward the call to, as shown in Figure 11-5. This is essentially call forwarding on the fly.

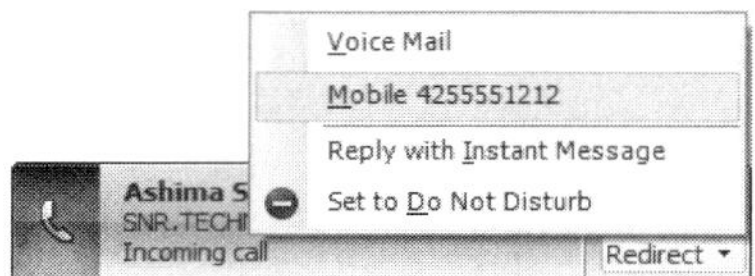

FIGURE 11-5 Communicator incoming call deflection

Users have the flexibility to receive calls directed to their work numbers from home. For example, if your home computer doesn't have Communicator 2007 R2 installed, you can sign in to Office Communications Server by using Microsoft Office Communicator Web Access (2007 R2 release) from a Web browser. Like Communicator 2007 R2, Office Communicator Web Access (2007 R2 release) also supports call deflection. Similar to Office Communicator, a system alert appears on the screen indicating a call is incoming, as shown in Figure 11-6. To deflect the incoming call from your work number to your home number, click the Redirect caret and select one of the published phone numbers to forward the call to. The caller thinks the call was answered at the office even though the call was forwarded seamlessly to a different number.

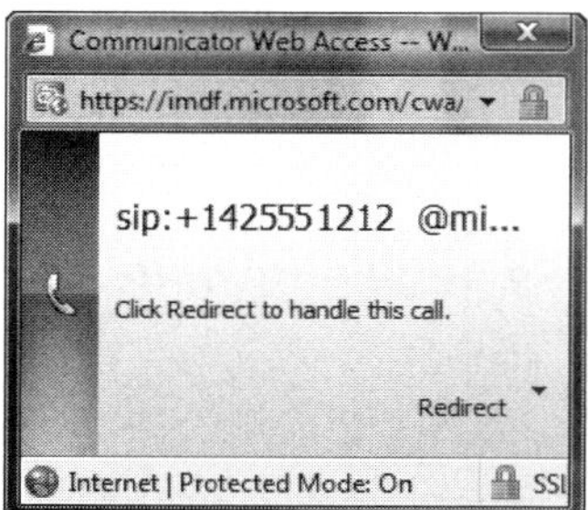

FIGURE 11-6 Communicator Web Access (2007 R2 release) incoming call

Before an incoming call can be redirected to a predefined phone number, the phone number must be published in the user's settings. Once published, these phone numbers are available for selection in the Redirect drop-down menu. To publish these phone numbers, navigate to the Options dialog box under Tools and select the Phones menu, as shown in Figure 11-7.

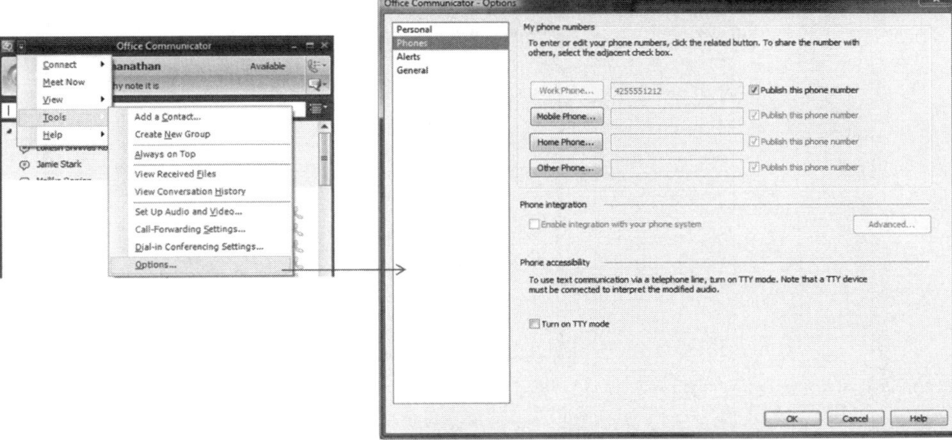

FIGURE 11-7 Phone options

> ***NOTE*** **Published phone numbers are visible only to contacts in the Personal and Team access levels.**

Configuring Call Forwarding

Call forwarding enables you to configure your phone to automatically forward incoming calls directly to voice mail, to a contact, or to another phone number published in your Phones menu, as shown in Figure 11-7. Alternatively, the option to simultaneously ring a PSTN phone number or to forward the call is available. Figure 11-8 shows how to locate these settings and configure them from Office Communicator 2007 R2.

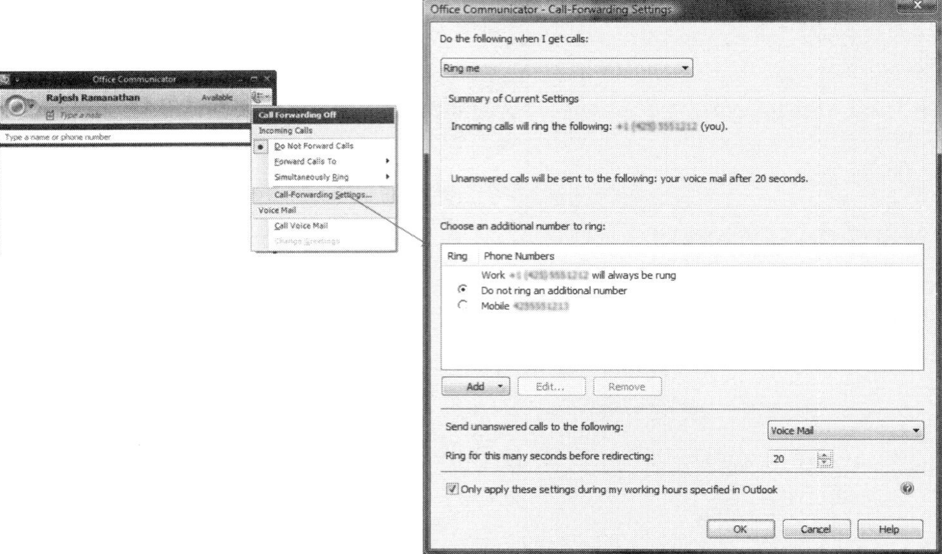

FIGURE 11-8 Call-forwarding settings

The Call-Forwarding Settings dialog box provides a quick way for users to share their own phone line with their delegates, similar to how they manage calendar delegates by using Outlook.

Office Communicator 2007 R2 provides two methods to share the phone line with other users or delegates. The first is a simple lightweight delegation option that enables users to configure Team Call. With Team Call, a user can let his colleagues pick up incoming calls on his behalf. All the user needs to do is to configure a Team-Call Group list in the call-forwarding settings (see Figure 11-8) with appropriate colleagues. If the user doesn't answer an incoming call, the call is forwarded to the Team-Call Group members. Team Call works with the user and his colleagues, who are all using Office Communicator 2007 R2.

The second method is for users who have dedicated assistants to pick up their calls. Users can easily configure one or more assistants (who are using Office Communications Server 2007 Attendant Console R2) as their delegates. When using the delegation feature, Office Communications Server 2007 Attendant Console R2 (Attendant Console) is the recommended client for the delegate to obtain the best experience. This client enables the delegate not only to receive incoming calls on behalf of the user, but also to place outgoing calls on behalf of the user. There are several interesting scenarios for delegation that are solved by the Attendant Console. For example, setting up recurring conference calls by using templates is possible, as is taking notes during a call. Figure 11-9 shows the Attendant Console.

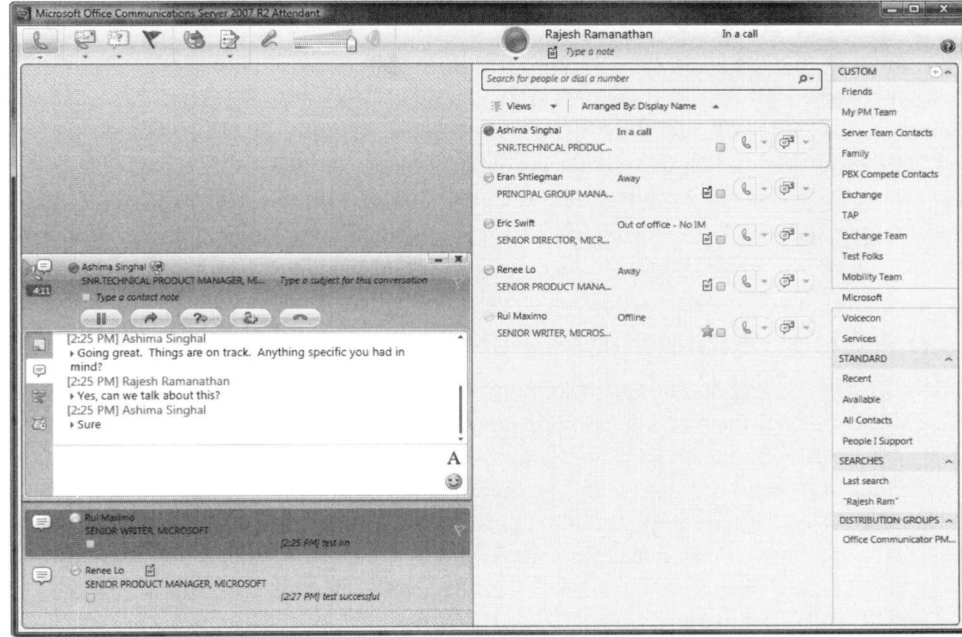

FIGURE 11-9 Office Communications Server 2007 R2 Attendant Console

Communicator Web Access (2007 R2 release) provides a nearly identical interface for configuring these settings. So, if you've already left the office and forgot to configure your call-forwarding settings, it's not too late to do it as soon as you are within reach of any computer with an Internet connection, as shown in Figure 11-10.

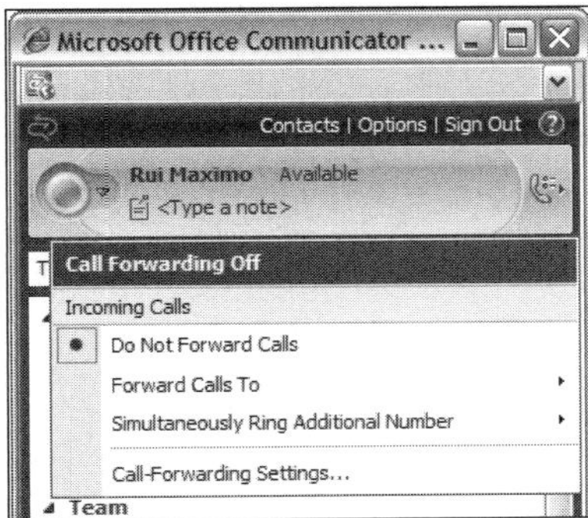

FIGURE 11-10 Communicator Web Access call-forwarding settings

> ***NOTE*** **Office Communicator 2007 R2 enables users to add delegates or team members to distribute incoming calls. These members must be configured for Enterprise Voice as well.**

Using Voice Mail

Office Communications Server 2007 R2 supports voice mail with Exchange Server 2007 Unified Messaging (UM) as the voice mail storage application—or in the case where Office Communications Server 2007 R2 is integrated with a supported PBX, Office Communications Server 2007 R2 enables the PBX to handle voice mail. Even if Communicator is not running, calls are routed to the user's voice mail, and the user can later call her voice mail to listen to her messages or retrieve them directly from within her Outlook inbox. Chapter 12, "Voice Mail Scenarios," covers voice mail in more detail.

Using Ad Hoc Conference Calling

A conference call occurs when three or more parties participate in the same call. There are multiple ways to establish an ad hoc conference call. A conference call can be started by adding all the parties at once—such as calling everyone on an e-mail thread from Microsoft Office Outlook 2007 or selecting the participants from the contact list in Office Communicator and initiating the call—or adding additional participants to a two-party call in progress. Figure 11-11 shows how to add participants to a two-party call. The peer-to-peer two-party call is changed on the server into a conference call. A focus is started. The focus is directed to one of the available conferencing servers associated with the pool, where the leader is homed to create a conferencing session. The session mixes all the audio feeds before sending the audio back to all the participants.

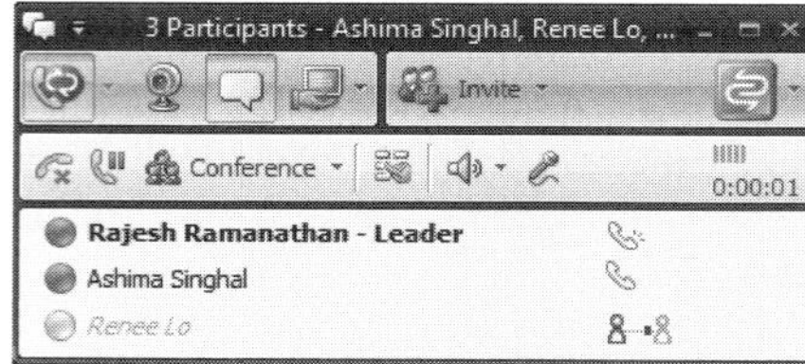

FIGURE 11-11 Add participants to an existing conversation

Another way of conducting an ad hoc conference call is to select all the participants before beginning the conversation. Instead of escalating from a two-party call, this approach immediately establishes a conference call, as shown in Figure 11-12.

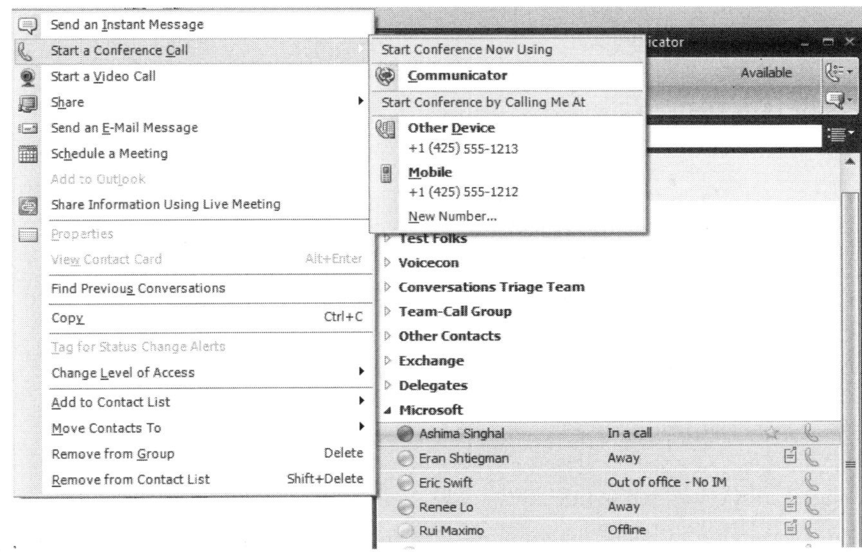

FIGURE 11-12 Start a conversation with multiple participants

Using Office Communicator and Phone Edition Integration

Office Communicator 2007 R2 provides seamless pairing and integrated operation with Office Communicator Phone Edition R2. Using this capability, users can accept an incoming call from Office Communicator, and the audio will be handled by Office Communicator Phone Edition. Office Communicator Phone Edition will automatically answer the call and go into speaker mode. Office Communicator Phone Edition acts as an independent deskphone that terminates audio and yet can be controlled by Office Communicator from the desktop computer so that operations such as calling from Microsoft Outlook can be supported. Other capabilities such as making calls, escalating to conferences, and adding video are also supported. Advanced scenarios such as conferencing become easy because users can drag other users from Office Communicator's user interface instead of using the keypad or the touch screen on Office Communicator Phone Edition. This experience is similar to Remote Call Control (RCC), as described in Chapter 9, "Remote Call Control Scenarios." The main difference is that no additional hardware equipment or configuration is needed to support this scenario.

To get the integration experience, Office Communicator Phone Edition must be connected to the desktop computer by using a USB cable. Office Communicator automatically detects and pairs with the Office Communicator Phone Edition (deskphone) if the USB connection is available. Figure 11-13 shows Office Communicator 2007 R2 paired with the deskphone. The USB interface has several uses. First, it enables Office Communicator to detect and connect to the deskphone. Users who are using laptop computers can simply dock their computers or connect the USB cable to get integration with their deskphone. Second, it enables Microsoft Office Live Meeting to stream audio to the deskphone, thus reducing the need to deploy a separate audio device for meetings.

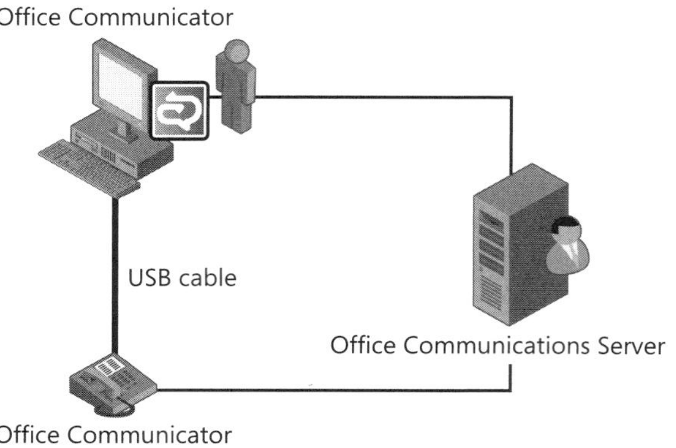

FIGURE 11-13 Office Communicator with Office Communicator Phone Edition integration

Several other scenarios are possible from this integrated configuration:

- Locking and unlocking the desktop computer will automatically lock or unlock Office Communicator Phone.
- Signing on and performing password updates are simpler because the user no longer needs to enter the password in the Office Communicator Phone by using the touchpad.
- Office Live Meeting 2007 R2 can now use Office Communicator Phone's speaker and microphone capabilities to play Live Meeting audio.

The calling experience on Office Communicator is similar between the paired and unpaired modes. However, Office Communicator Phone Edition supports only a single audio source, which can be the USB interface to the desktop (for scenarios involving Live Meeting or video), an audio call, an ongoing audio, or an audio conference call on the phone. Users can choose what audio stream they would like to hear and can select the appropriate one from the Phone's user interface. This is illustrated in Figure 11-14.

FIGURE 11-14 Office Communicator Phone with audio call and USB streaming

Using Response Group Service

Response Group Service for Office Communications Server 2007 R2 provides the equivalent of hunt groups for Automated Call Distribution (ACD) services. Using Office Communicator, a user can search for hunt groups and easily differentiate them from other users or distribution groups in Office Communicator. Chapter 13, "Enterprise Voice Application Scenarios," provides more details about Response Group Service.

Examining the Technical Details Behind VoIP Scenarios

The components that compose a VoIP topology are illustrated in Figure 11-15. This topology supports the following scenarios: calling and receiving calls outside your organization's network (PSTN), providing external access for users, and receiving voice mail. New server roles come into play when deploying an Enterprise Voice infrastructure. In addition to the basic Office Communications Server home pool, which is either an Office Communications Server 2007 R2 Standard Edition Server or an Enterprise Edition pool, the following server roles are required or recommended.

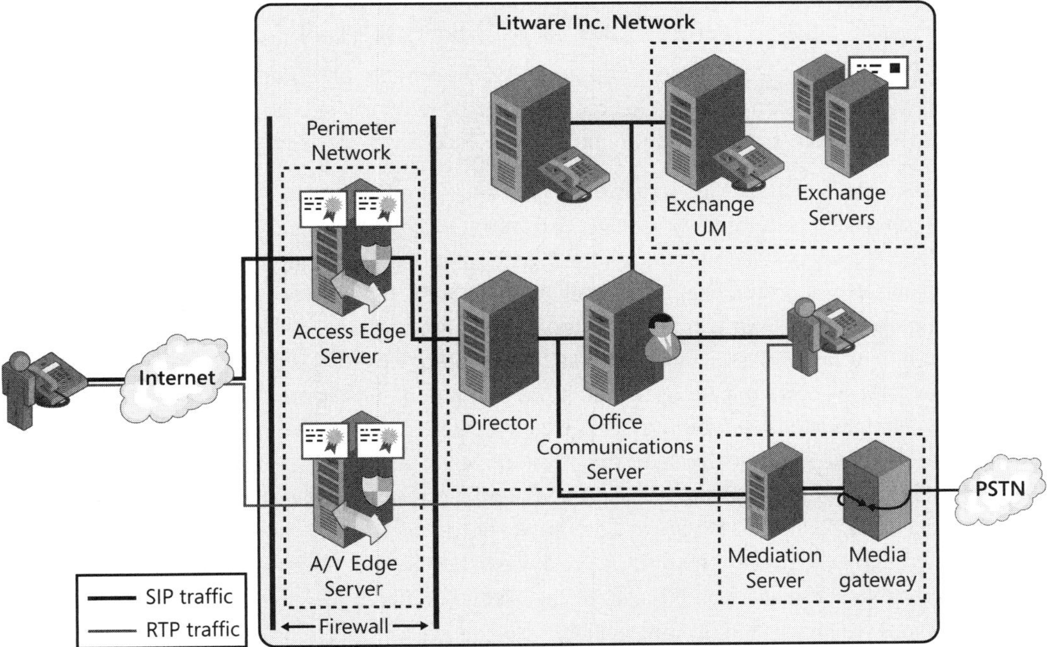

FIGURE 11-15 Enterprise Voice topology. Note that the lines connecting the different server roles represent protocol traffic and do not necessarily represent the number of NICs the server must be configured with.

The elements specific to the VoIP topology that are in addition to a deployment of Office Communications Server for IM, presence, and conferencing are described in the following list.

- **Media gateway** This is a third-party server solution offered by Microsoft partners.
- **Mediation Server** Depending on the type of media gateway used, this Office Communications Server role is required.
- **A/V Edge Server** This Office Communications Server role is required to enable audio traffic to traverse the corporate firewall for users who are connecting from the Internet.
- **Access Edge Server** If you are giving users remote access to place and receive calls from outside the corporate firewall, the Access Edge Server must be deployed in addition to deploying an A/V Edge Server. Depending on capacity requirements, it is possible to collocate both the Access Edge Server role and the A/V Edge Server role on the same physical server.
- **Exchange Unified Messaging (UM)** This Exchange Server role is required to enable Exchange Server to serve as the voice mail system for Office Communications Server. Exchange UM is also used to provide auto-attendant and call notification service.
- **Monitoring Server** This Office Communications Server role is recommended to collect Call Detail Records (CDRs) for monitoring Quality of Experience (QoE) of calls.
- **Devices** These are VoIP endpoints that are capable of terminating a voice call. This includes Session Initiation Protocol (SIP)–enabled hardware phones as well as soft-phones such as Office Communicator 2007 R2.

To place calls to and receive calls from outside your organization's network, a third-party media gateway is required. The gateway's purpose is to bridge the PSTN network and your corporate IP network. Depending on the type of media gateway used, you might need to deploy an Office Communications Server 2007 R2 Mediation Server to interoperate with the media gateway that your vendor provides. The Mediation Server performs codec translation between RTAudio and legacy codecs. Real-Time Audio (RTAudio) is an advanced audio codec used by Office Communications Server. It has been tried and tested in Microsoft Windows Live Messenger, which serves in excess of 1 billion voice minutes per month using RTAudio, to provide optimal audio quality over the Internet. Because most media gateways support only SIP over User Datagram Protocol (UDP), the Mediation Server converts SIP over the Transport Layer Security (TLS) used by Office Communications Server to SIP over UDP. There is a one-to-one mapping between the gateway and Mediation Server, because the gateway must be configured to route all incoming calls to the Mediation Server. The Mediation Server also acts like a client for Interactive Connectivity Establishment (ICE), which enables users connected from outside the enterprise firewall to make calls to and receive calls from the PSTN network.

To provide users external access, enabling them to dial and receive calls when connected from outside their corporate network, the following server roles are necessary: Access Edge Server and A/V Edge Server. These server roles must be deployed in the perimeter network.

For voice mail capability, the Exchange Server 2007 Unified Messaging (UM) server role is required. In addition to Exchange UM Servers, Exchange Mailbox Servers are required as well to store the voice mail. More details about voice mail connectivity with Exchange UM are presented in Chapter 12.

Finally, VoIP-enabled devices that support the SIP protocol with Microsoft's extensions for signaling and the Real-Time Protocol (RTP) for audio media are needed to terminate the calls. Microsoft's primary softphone client is Office Communicator 2007 R2; however, Microsoft as well as third-party partners provide a variety of hardphone and softphone options.

As with any telecommunication solution, Office Communications Server 2007 R2 Enterprise Voice must perform the following activities:

- **Outbound routing** Route calls from the organization running Office Communications Server Enterprise Voice to the PSTN
- **Inbound routing** Route calls from the PSTN to the organization's Office Communications Server Enterprise Voice system

These routing activities are enforced by the front-end service in both the Standard Edition Server and Enterprise Edition pool as an integral part of Office Communications Server.

Understanding How Outbound Calls Are Routed

Outbound routing of VoIP traffic in Office Communications Server 2007 R2 is managed by the Outbound Routing component on the front-end server. When a user places a call, the client first attempts to normalize the dialed phone number. It then sends the request to the user's home pool. Based on the permissions allowed in the Voice policy that is assigned to the user, the home pool determines where to route the call. The call (SIP INVITE) is routed to a Mediation Server. The audio media for the call is routed directly from the client to the Mediation Server. The Mediation Server forwards the call to the media gateway. The media gateway bridges the call to the PSTN. Figure 11-16 illustrates this process. Each of the elements—users, policies, usages, routes, and gateways—is represented as an object in Active Directory and is exposed as a Windows Management Instrumentation (WMI) class at the management Application Programming Interface (API) layer.

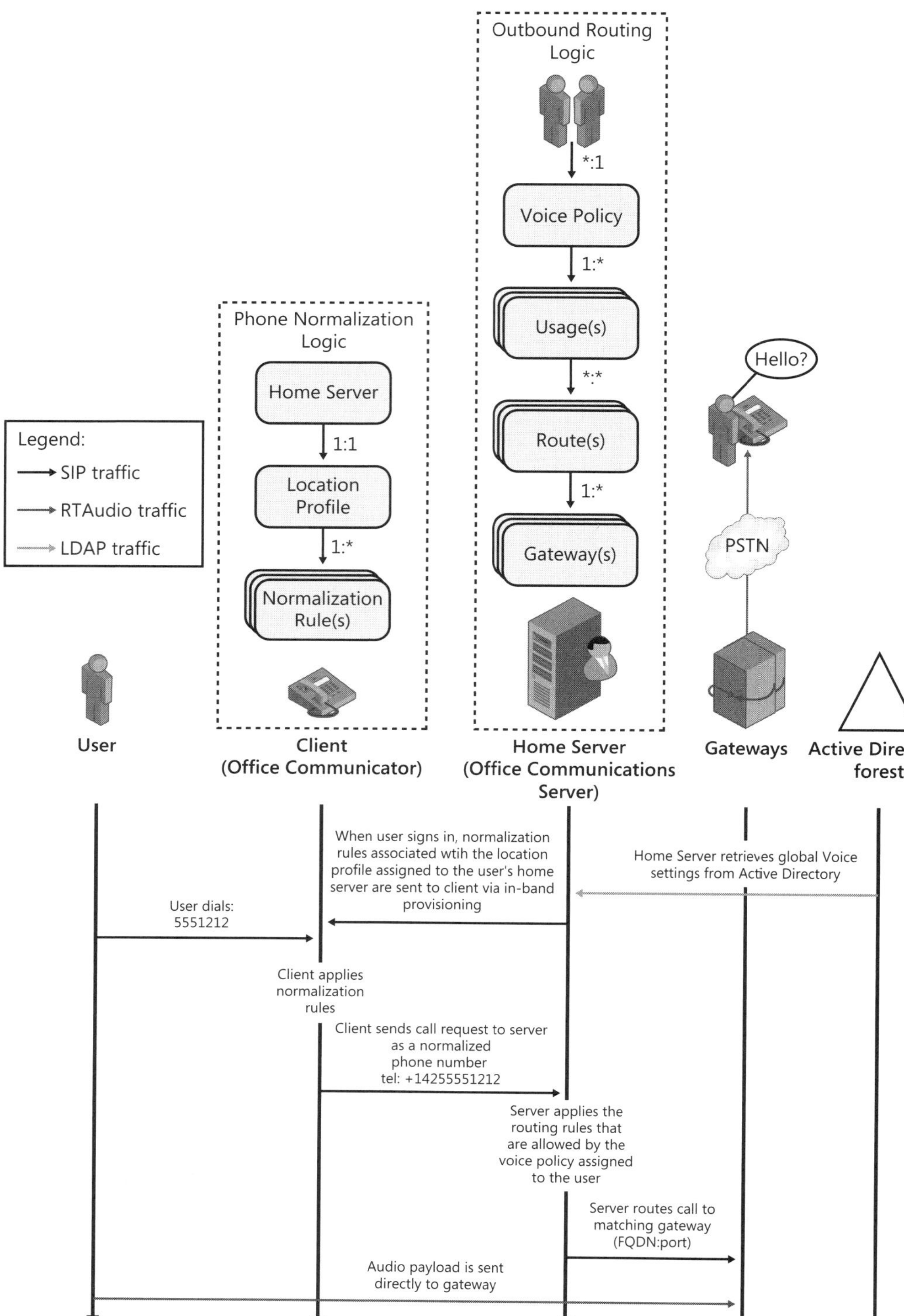

FIGURE 11-16 Outbound routing logic

Figure 11-17 illustrates the logic flow performed by the user's home server.

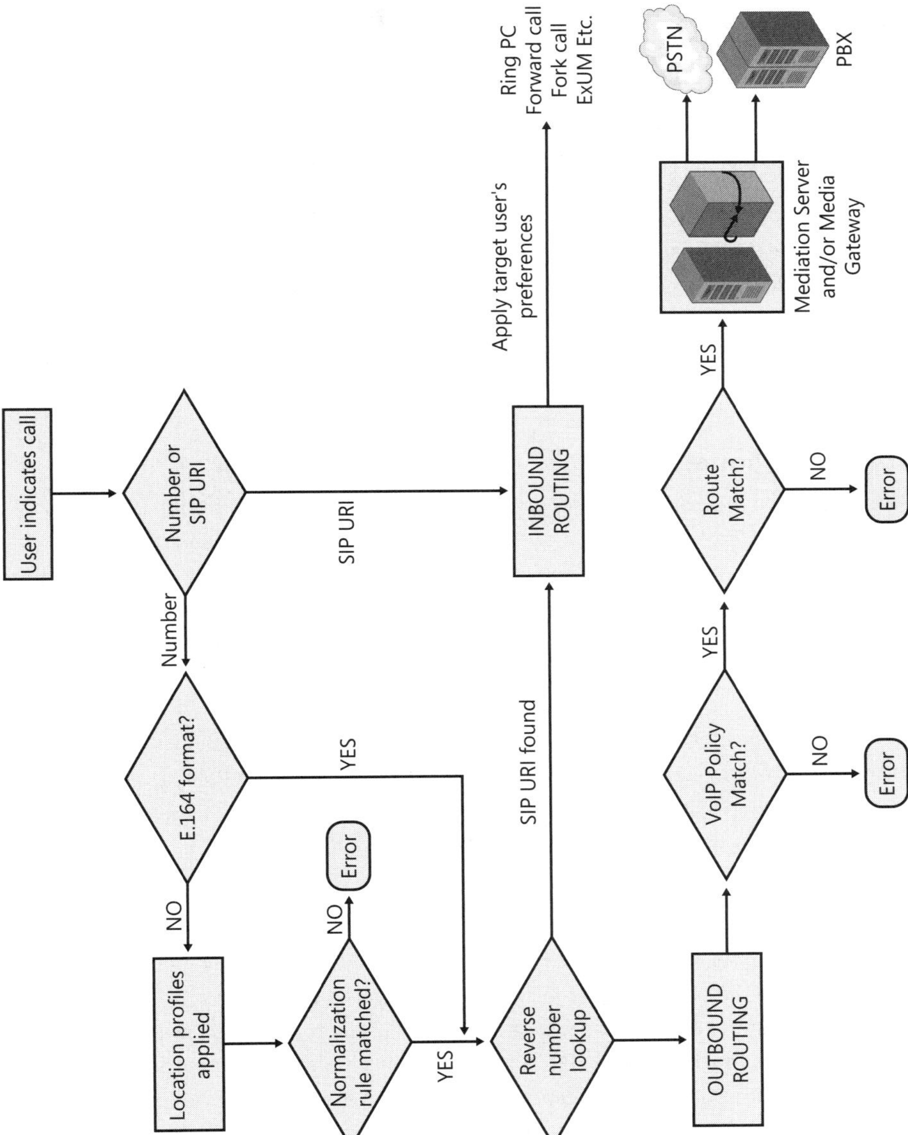

FIGURE 11-17 Call flow logic in the home server

Understanding Voice Policies

Every user enabled for Enterprise Voice is associated by the administrator to a Voice policy. A Voice policy defines the call privileges assigned to a user. The call privileges determine which routes the user is allowed to use. Each user must be associated to a single Voice policy. The administrator creates the number of available policies.

Each Voice policy contains a setting to allow or disallow users to enable simultaneous ringing and a collection of ordered phone usages. The Voice policy, similar to the Meeting policy, is a logical container of settings defined as an XML document stored in Active Directory. The value of this design is that it can be extended in future versions of Office Communications Server to support additional policy settings without requiring an Active Directory schema extension. For example, a Voice policy not associated with any phone usages has the effect of preventing users assigned to that policy from making any outbound calls to the PSTN. Such users would be able to dial only internal numbers.

Understanding Phone Usage

A phone usage defines the phone routing privileges users are allowed. A phone usage is a collection of phone routes. It is a string that must be a unique keyword, meaning no other phone usage can have the same name. The administrator can create as many usages as she wants. Although a Voice policy can be directly associated with a route or a set of routes instead of phone usages, the phone usage keyword is an abstraction used to maintain the association between policies and routes. If policies were directly associated to routes (effectively removing the concept of phone usages) and the administrator modified the name of a route, every policy associated with that route would need to be updated. By using a phone usage, which is an attribute of both a policy and a route, to create the association between the policy and the route, the relationship between the policy and route is preserved even if the route's name is changed.

Understanding Phone Routes

A phone route defines how to route a call specified by a phone number to one or more Mediation Servers. The Mediation Server must be configured to route to a specific media gateway. The media gateway then either routes the call directly to the PSTN or it routes the call to an IP-PBX before reaching the PSTN. A route contains a phone number pattern and a list of gateways. This list of gateways includes Mediation Servers if using either basic media gateways or advanced and hybrid media gateways. A route must be assigned to at least one phone usage. This association between the pattern and gateways specifies how to route phone numbers that match that particular pattern.

The pattern specifies a range of phone numbers that it can match. It is defined as a regular expression (regex) that can include and exclude phone numbers. To help build these regular expressions more easily, use the Enterprise Voice Route Helper tool. If the phone number dialed matches the route's regex pattern, the call is routed to one of the gateways defined in the route.

More than one gateway can be listed in the phone route. Office Communications Server routes calls to the gateways in a round-robin fashion as a way to balance the traffic across the gateways. If a gateway fails or is taken out of service for maintenance, Office Communications Server immediately attempts to route the call to another gateway in the route's list. After 10 attempts to route calls to a failed gateway, Office Communications Server subsequently throttles traffic to that gateway until it becomes responsive again. If the gateway continues to fail to respond after an additional 10 attempts, Office Communications Server stops routing calls to that gateway entirely until it becomes responsive.

The list of gateways defined in the route is described by the gateway's fully qualified domain name (FQDN) and the port number that the gateway is listening on. If the phone number does not match the regex pattern, the next route associated with the policy assigned to the user is checked until a match is found. If no match is found, the call cannot be routed and fails to reach its destination. The user receives a notification that the call could not be completed.

Understanding How Inbound Calls Are Routed

Let's examine how Office Communications Server 2007 R2 routes a call originating from the PSTN network to a user in your corporate network. Figure 11-18 illustrates this logic.

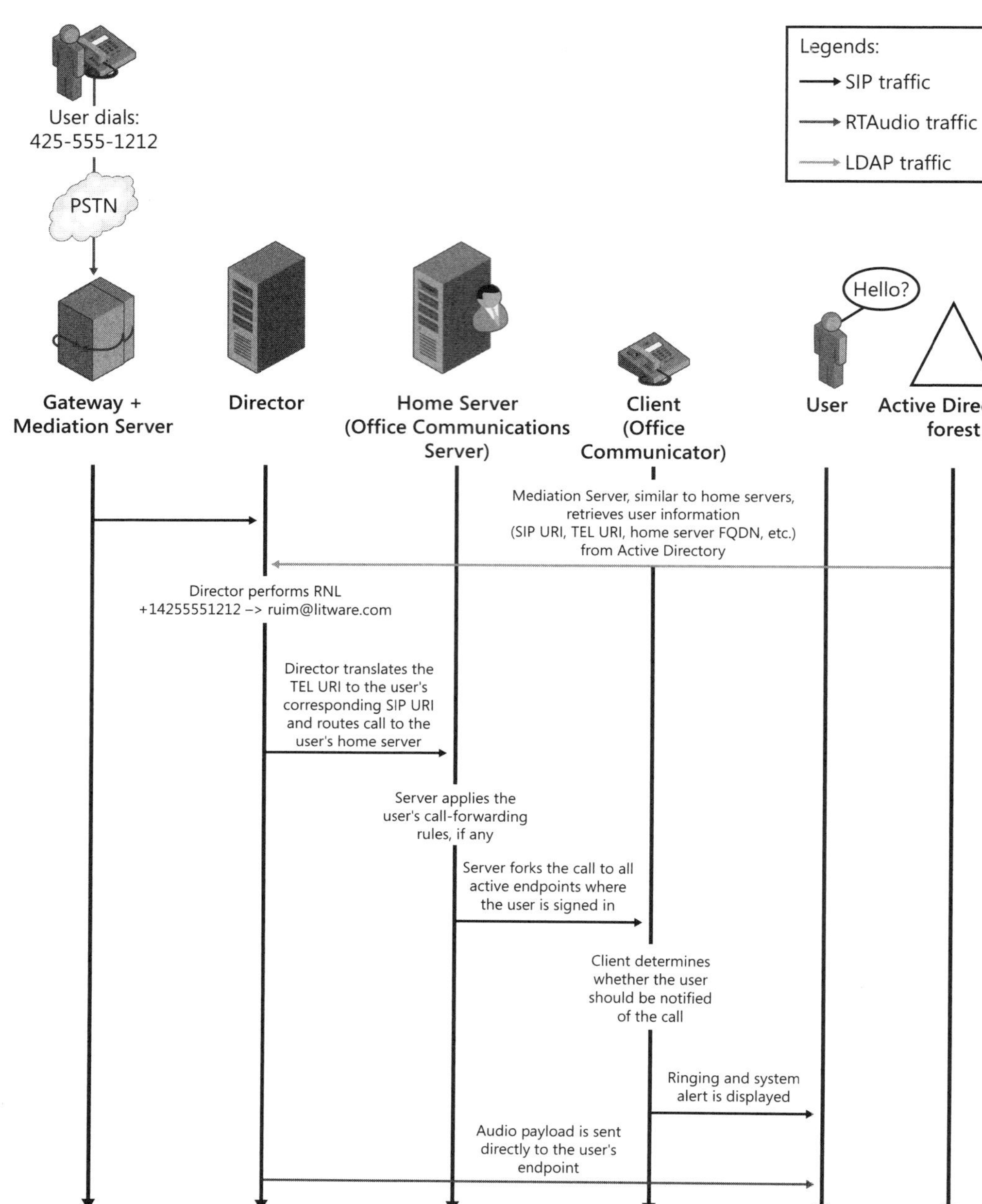

FIGURE 11-18 Inbound routing llogic

NOTE **Inbound calls can originate from another internal user or from a federated partner over a federated link. Before routing the call to a media gateway, Office Communications Server checks whether the phone number matches an internal user's number. If the phone number matches an internal user's number, the TEL URI (Uniform Resource Identifier) is replaced by the internal user's SIP URI and routed to that user.**

When an outside call originating from the PSTN arrives for a user within your organization, the handoff between the two networks occurs at one of the organization's media gateways. If a basic media gateway or basic hybrid media gateway is used, the gateway sends the call to the Mediation Server to which it is configured to route. The Mediation Server routes the signal to the Director it is configured to route to. The Director performs a reverse number lookup (RNL) to determine which user owns the called phone number, referred to as the TEL URI.

NOTE **Although highly recommended in a multipool deployment, a Director is not required.**

The assignment of the phone number to the user is configured in the *msRTCSIP-Line* attribute of the user's object in Active Directory. If a match is not found, the Director cannot route the request and the call fails. Once a match is found, the TEL URI (for example, +14255551212) is translated into the user's SIP URI (for example, sip:ruim@litware.com). The Mediation Server then determines the FQDN of the user's home pool and routes the SIP request. The SIP INVITE request is sent to the user's home pool. The home pool performs additional logic. It applies any call-forwarding rules the user might have set. For example, if the called party is set to simultaneously ring another phone number, Office Communications Server routes the call to the new number in addition to forking the call to all the registered endpoints the called party is signed in to. It drops the call if the user sets his presence to Do Not Disturb. The only exception to this rule is if the caller is a contact in the called party's Personal or Team access level. Then the call notification will be displayed. If the called party answers the call, the audio is routed directly from the Mediation Server to the user's client.

If the called party is not signed in to Office Communications Server, the home pool determines that there are no active endpoints and instead of forking the incoming call to the user's endpoints, it directly routes the call to the user's voice mail server, Exchange Server 2007 Unified Messaging (UM). The user does not need to be signed in to Office Communications Server for voice mail to work. The called party can retrieve his messages once he opens Outlook and connects to his Exchange mailbox.

Understanding Normalization

Although the concepts described so far make inbound and outbound calling possible, there are two limitations that must be addressed. First, this routing design works well if there is only a single way to represent a phone number. However, this is not always the case. Because the phone number is represented as a string, there are multiple ways to specify the same phone number. For example, the phone number (425) 555-1212 can be represented in the following ways:

- (425) 555-1212
- 425-555-1212
- +14255551212
- 0014255551212
- 425.555.1212
- 555-1212 (this assumes the area code 425)
- 5551212
- 555.1212
- 51212 (if the number is an internal extension)
- (425) 555-1212 x51212

Although this list is not comprehensive, it demonstrates that the same phone number can be represented as a string in a variety of ways. It's unlikely that the regex pattern defined in the route will be able to match all these variations. For the pattern-matching of the route to work, some form of normalization is necessary. This is the first problem.

Because there are multiple ways to address this issue, the International Telecommunication Union-Telecom (ITU-T) Standardization Committee created the E.164 recommendation. The E.164 recommendation defines the international public telecommunication numbering plan, which specifies a methodology that provides a standardized method for presenting the domestic numbering plans of all countries.

A second problem is that some of the phone number variations are ambiguous. For example, the 555-1212 string assumes a local area. If the user were to dial this number in Redmond, Washington, the area code that should be assumed is 425; however, if the user were to dial this same number in Seattle, Washington, the area code that should be used is 206. To correctly normalize a phone number into E.164 format, a context is necessary to correctly interpret it based on the user's locale.

To address these two problems, Office Communications Server 2007 R2 exposes the following concepts:

- **Normalization rules** Normalization rules define a match pattern and a translation pattern. Both patterns are represented as regex rules that describe how to translate a given phone number into a well-formatted number in E.164 format. Translating all numbers to E.164 format simplifies the regex defined in the route to match only phone numbers that have already been normalized by the normalization rules.

- **Location profiles** A location profile is a collection of normalization rules. The location profile defines the collection of rules to apply for a particular region. A region can be a state, province, country, or city that has specific dialing rules. For example, if the user is dialing from Redmond, Washington, the normalization rules for that area code are applied to any phone number the user dials. So if the Redmond user enters, say, an eight-digit number, Office Communications Server 2007 R2, following a rule in the Redmond location profile, adds the area code 425 when the number is dialed.

The roles these components play in the routing logic of voice communications is illustrated in the Phone Normalization Logic dotted-line box in Figure 11-16. Location profiles and normalization rules are both defined by the administrator in charge of an organization's telephony infrastructure.

Each user is assigned a location profile, and upon dialing a phone number, the ordered list of normalization rules associated with the user's location profile is applied. If a first match to a normalization rule is found, the client translates the phone number into E.164 format before the SIP request is sent to the user's home pool. If a match is not found, the phone number is still sent to the user's home pool, but it is tagged as a dial string because it could not be normalized. The dial string that the client sends to Office Communications Server includes a *phone-context* attribute that specifies the name of the user's location profile. The server attempts to resolve the phone number by using the specified location profile normalization rules.

> ***NOTE*** **Office Communications Server 2007 R2 enables administrators to assign specific location profiles to users. Thus, users located in different regions can be homed on the same pool without having to share the same location profile. This is a new feature in Office Communications Server 2007 R2.**

For example, *INVITE SIP:5551212;phone-context=redmond@litwareinc.com* is an example of a dial string. The non-normalized phone number is 5551212, and the specified location profile is Redmond.

Office Communications Server 2007 R2 Enterprise Voice enables users to make and receive calls anywhere Internet access is available. They simply sign in to Office Communications Server and place calls as usual. Regardless of their geographic location, users' dialing patterns can remain the same as long as they are using the same location profile. If the administrator changes the location profile to a different profile, the dialing patterns might change. Office Communications Server uses in-band provisioning to push the normalization rules associated with the location profile assigned to the user. If the user is not assigned a location profile by the administrator, the user is assigned a default location profile. This is the default location profile assigned to the user's home pool configured by the administrator.

Office Communicator caches these normalization rules and is responsible for applying them when a user dials phone numbers. Office Communicator also applies the normalization rules to Outlook contact phone numbers when Office Communicator starts and adds these numbers to its local search cache. This allows Office Communicator to perform fast reverse name lookup on Outlook contacts when a call comes in. As a result, no matter what their locations might be, Enterprise Voice users are always calling from home.

For example, if the user dials the number 555-1212, the client runs through the normalization rules it got from the user's home pool. If one of the rules matches, the phone number is normalized. The request is sent to the user's home pool with the normalized phone number. The home pool checks whether the phone number matches any internal user's phone number. If it matches an internal user, the phone number is replaced by the user's SIP URI and is routed to that user's home pool. If a match to an internal user is not found, the home pool performs a route-matching analysis. Once a match is found, the request is routed to one of the gateways listed in the route. The client then sends the audio media directly to the gateway.

So far we have discussed normalization rules associated with location profiles, which are used dynamically at runtime when calls are placed. Office Communications Server also has Address Book Service (ABS)–based normalization rules, which are used to clean up the phone number entries in the Global Address List (GAL) before calls are made. The purpose of these rules is to ensure that existing phone numbers in Active Directory are normalized to an E.164 format so that these numbers can be added to the translation database for inbound routing.

Numbers normalized using the ABS normalization rules are also present in the Global Address Book (GAL) database that clients download from the Address Book Service. The client uses this information to perform reverse name lookup for calls coming in from contacts within the same enterprise. This provides the Caller ID feature in Office Communicator.

Understanding Office Communicator to Office Communicator Phone Edition Integration

Before we go into more detail about VoIP configuration, let us take a brief look at how Office Communicator 2007 R2 and Office Communicator 2007 R2 Phone Edition can work together to provide an even richer experience. Both Office Communicator and Office Communicator Phone Edition communicate with each other through a persistent SIP session they establish through Office Communications Server.

To enable Office Communicator to Office Communicator Phone Edition integration, a USB cable connection is required. When Office Communicator starts, it detects whether there is an Office Communicator Phone Edition device attached to the USB channel. It initiates a persistent SIP INVITE session over the IP network through Office Communications Server. Similar to the Computer-Supported Telepathy Applications (CSTA) protocol that is used for Remote Call Control to a PBX phone (see Chapter 9), Office Communicator uses the persistent INVITE session to send SIP INFO messages containing a payload of Third-Party Control Protocol (TPCP) commands to Office Communicator Phone Edition such as placing a call, answering a call, and so on. In the reverse direction, Office Communicator Phone Edition sends notifications using INFO messages that contain the TPCP protocol payload.

TPCP is a Microsoft protocol that is used in other scenarios as well, such as when a third-party server is required to make connections between two endpoints. An example of the use of TPCP is with Communicator Mobile. Whenever a user selects to call from Communicator Mobile, a TPCP message is sent to the Office Communications Server within the user's enterprise. The Office Communications Server originates an outgoing PSTN call through the cellular network to the user's cell phone. It also sends an INVITE to the destination phone number and then connects the two calls together.

One of the key aspects of this integration design is how the audio and video media are terminated. Because Office Communicator Phone Edition does not support video media, any video calls must be terminated on Office Communicator, and the audio is streamed from Office Communicator to Office Communicator Phone Edition over the USB channel. Whenever video is added to an existing audio call, Office Communicator will become the endpoint from which both the audio and video media channels flow and will stream the received audio media of the call to Office Communicator Phone Edition over the USB link.

Figures 11-19 and 11-20 illustrate the two modes in which Office Communicator and Office Communicator Phone Edition can interact when connected over a USB cable.

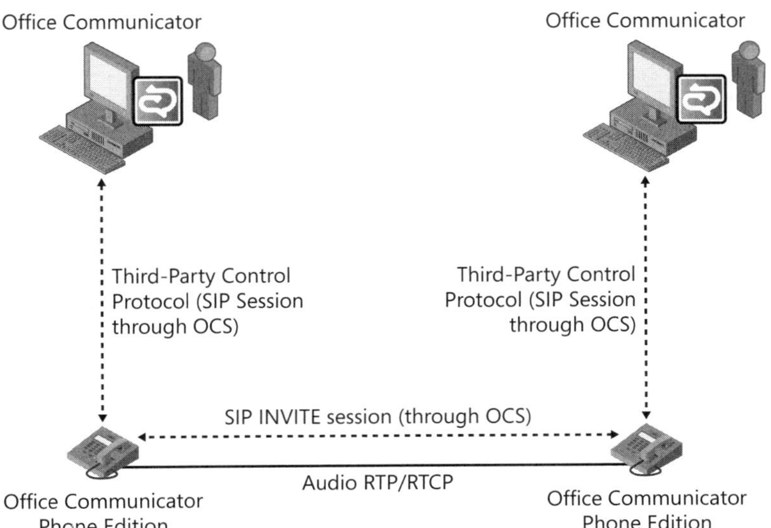

FIGURE 11-19 Audio interaction between Communicator and Phone

In Figure 11-19, an audio call is made from the Office Communicator desktop client. Office Communicator sends the command to set up the audio call to Office Communicator Phone Edition over the TPCP protocol. Communicator Phone Edition originates an INVITE to the remote party, which in this case also has a paired configuration. When the callee's Office Communicator Phone Edition receives the INVITE, it informs Office Communicator about the incoming call through the TPCP protocol. When the callee answers the call from Office

Communicator, a TPCP command is sent to Office Communicator Phone Edition to answer the INVITE with a 200 OK.

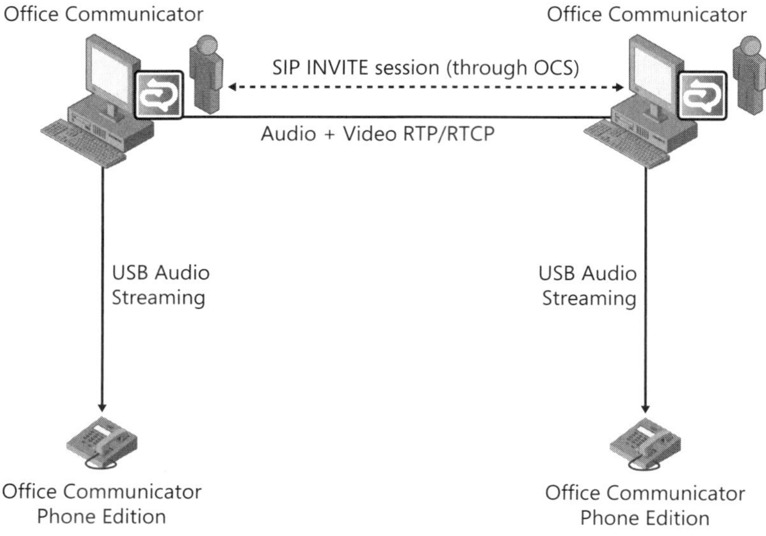

FIGURE 11-20 Video interaction between Communicator and Phone

In Figure 11-20, a video call was made from the Office Communicator client. In this case, Office Communicator sends the audio/video INVITE directly to the callee because only Office Communicator has the ability to consume video RTP media. The audio portion of the call is now streamed to Office Communicator Phone Edition through the USB interface. This enables using the speakerphone capabilities of Office Communicator Phone Edition. On the receiving end of the call, when the callee answers the video INVITE in Office Communicator, the audio/video RTP media are consumed on Office Communicator and the audio media is streamed to Office Communicator Phone Edition speakerphone through the USB link.

Configuring VoIP

VoIP, or Enterprise Voice, requires additional configuration and the deployment of new server roles to support this functionality. Enterprise Voice can be easily added to an existing Office Communications Server 2007 R2 IM and Web Conferencing deployment. Enabling Enterprise Voice involves the following activities, which are covered in the next section:

- Configuring global Voice settings
- Administrating users to be Enterprise Voice–enabled
- Deploying media gateways to connect to the PSTN or PBX network
- Deploying a Mediation Server for each corresponding media gateway

- Optionally deploying one or more Monitoring Servers to collect, aggregate, and report Call Detail Records (CDRs)
- Optionally deploying the Deployment Validation Tool to monitor voice quality within and outside the organization's network

Configuring Global Enterprise Voice Settings

Now that you have a better understanding of the VoIP design of Office Communications Server 2007 R2, this section jumps into the details of configuring VoIP by using the Admin Tools Microsoft Management Console (MMC). The Office Communications Server 2007 R2 Resource Kit also provides useful tools. In particular, the Resource Kit Tool Enterprise Voice Route Helper has several advantages currently not available in the Admin Tools MMC.

DIRECT FROM THE SOURCE

Enterprise Voice Route Helper

Paul Tidwell
Software Development Engineer

Enterprise Voice Route Helper enables you to test changes made to the global voice settings before making them persistent. You eventually want to make changes persistent; otherwise, you are wasting your time.

Another advantage of Enterprise Voice Route Helper is the ability to simulate the behavior of the system when a particular phone number is dialed. The route taken will be highlighted. Once the administrator is satisfied with her voice configuration, the Route Helper tool can apply the new configuration to Active Directory while maintaining a tracking history of the configurations applied to Active Directory.

The global Enterprise Voice settings can be configured only by administrators who are members of the RTCUniversalGlobalWriteGroup or RTCUniversalServerAdmins groups. Administrator members of RTCUniversalGlobalReadOnlyGroup can view the global settings, but they cannot modify them. The user configures inbound routing rules (simultaneous ringing, call forwarding, and so on).

Configuring Voice Policies

The administrator can create as many Voice policies as desired regardless of whether they are used. To create a Voice policy by using the Admin Tools MMC, select Voice Properties from the forest node and click the Policy tab. The Policy tab enables administrators to manage their Voice policies, as shown in Figure 11-21. Out of the box, a default policy is defined. The administrator can assign all users the same Voice policy or allow users to be assigned a different Voice policy by selecting the Use Per User Policy option from the drop-down list for the Global Policy setting.

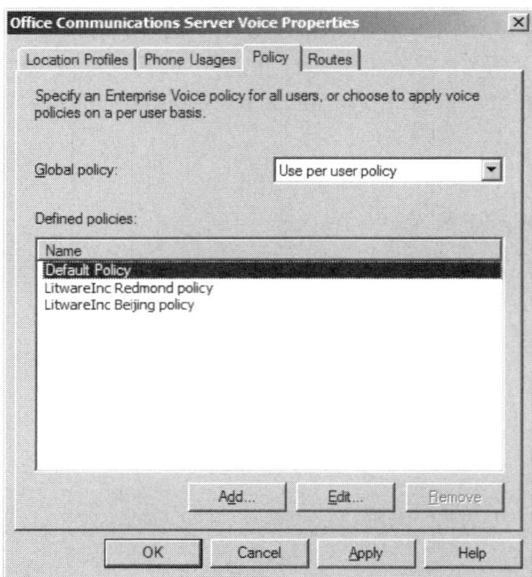

FIGURE 11-21 Voice policy management

Because Voice policies are associated with phone usages, the administrator also needs to create phone usages to represent routing restrictions. To create a phone usage, navigate to the Phone Usages tab, shown in Figure 11-22. A phone usage consists of a keyword and a description that is used purely for the benefit of the administrator to describe what that phone usage is used for. Out of the box, a default phone usage is defined.

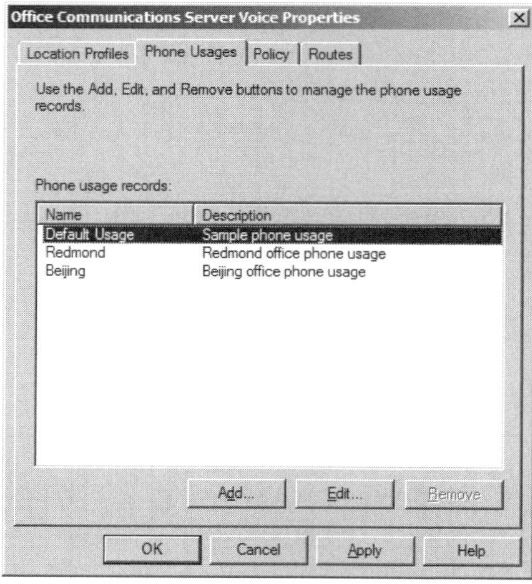

FIGURE 11-22 Phone usage management

Given the two geographic locations with their own egress to the PSTN in our example, the administrator responsible for this Office Communications Server 2007 R2 deployment defined two Voice policies with associated usages for each office.

Configuring Phone Routes

A phone route assigns defined sets of phone numbers to various media gateways. Consequently, a phone route consists of a name for the route, a description that the administrator creates, a target set of phone numbers expressed in the form of a regex, a list of gateways to route phone numbers that match the target regex pattern, and a list of usages, as shown in Figure 11-23.

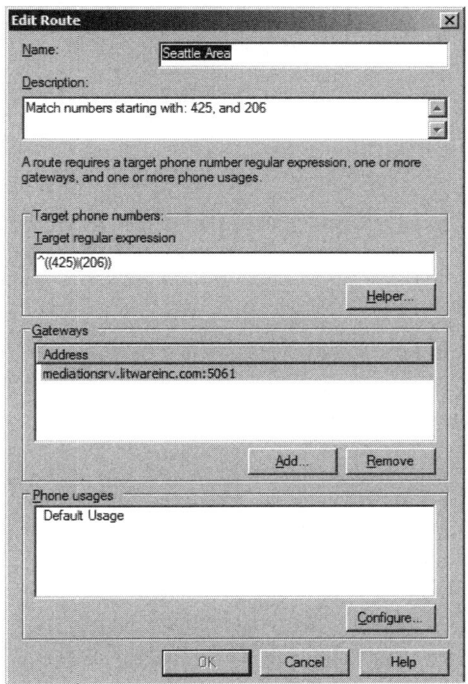

FIGURE 11-23 Phone route management

The phone usage ties the phone route to the Voice policy (shown earlier in Figure 11-21). Therefore, only users assigned a Voice policy that specifies the same phone usage associated with a phone route can use that route. The list of gateways is specified by its FQDN and the port number to connect to. This FQDN can be the fully qualified name of an advanced media gateway or the fully qualified name of a Mediation Server if you are using a basic media gateway.

Specifying a target regex can be a little daunting at first when using the Admin Tools MMC. The Enterprise Voice Route Helper tool provides more assistance in defining phone routes. The user interface simplifies the creation of regular expressions. It automatically translates the regular expressions into plain English in the Description field of the route. This makes it easier to understand the meaning of the regex. In addition, the Enterprise Voice Route Helper tool offers the ability to test the regex before saving it.

Figure 11-24 shows the same route defined in Figure 11-18, this time using the Enterprise Voice Route Helper. To view the syntax of the regular expression, click the Raw tab.

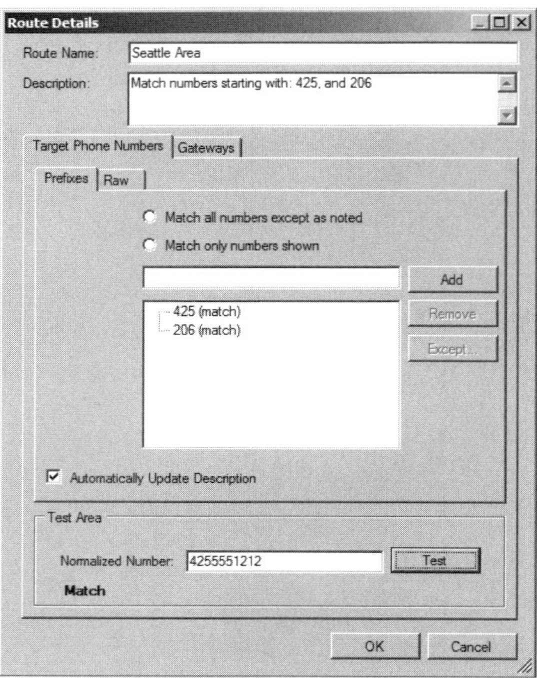

FIGURE 11-24 Phone route management using Enterprise Voice Route Helper

Another valuable feature of this tool is the ability to test which route(s) is triggered for a given phone number. This feature is particularly useful because it enables administrators to quickly test phone routes. Administrators can simulate the scenario of a user dialing a phone number and see how the call gets routed without applying the phone route in production (that is, in Active Directory). The route that matches is highlighted. The tool even simulates the phone number normalization performed by the client when the user's location profile is specified. This feature is available on the Ad-hoc Test tab.

Configuring Location Profiles

A location profile is a container that holds a name, a description, and a list of normalization rules. Future versions of Office Communications Server will extend the location profile to include additional attributes. Each normalization rule consists of two regular expressions. The first regex is the matching pattern; the second regex is the translation expression. To manage your location profiles, open the Voice properties at the Active Directory forest node and select the Location Profiles tab, shown in Figure 11-25. Embedded within this tab is the UI to create/edit normalization rules.

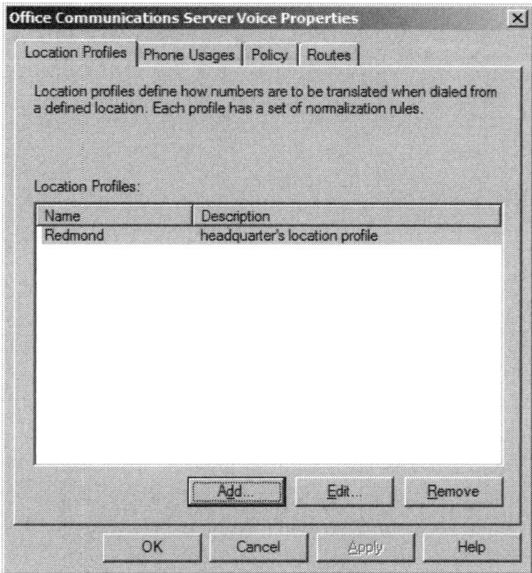

FIGURE 11-25 Location profile management

> ***NOTE*** **In the Add Location Profile option, Office Communications Server 2007 R2 provides an Optimize Device Dialing check box. This check box enables the administrator to add an external access prefix of up to four characters (chosen from #, *, and 0–9) that Office Communicator Phone Edition R2 can use to access the outside line.**

The Enterprise Voice Route Helper provides a slightly different user interface, with additional features such as assistance in creating regular expressions, seeing which normalization rules are matched as the user types a phone number, and automatically creating or updating the description of the normalization rule.

A default location profile can be assigned to pools. (See Figure 11-26.) Users inherit the location profile of their home pool if the administrator hasn't assigned a specific location profile to the user. Office Communicator 2007 R2 and Office Communicator Phone Edition 2007 R2 download the location profile from in-band provisioning.

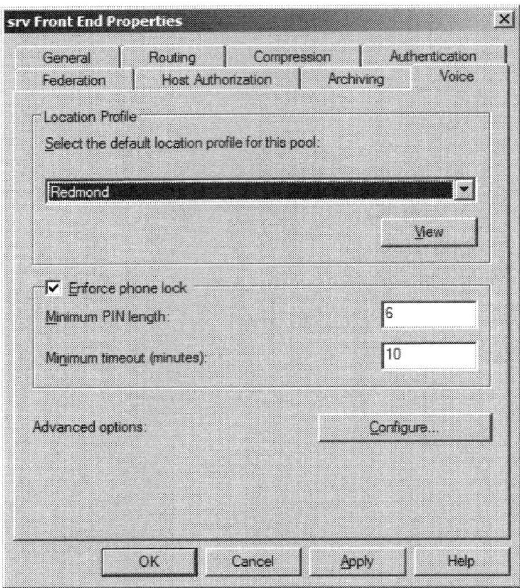

FIGURE 11-26 Assigning Office Communications Server location profiles

In addition, each Mediation Server is assigned a location profile, as shown in Figure 11-27, because an incoming call from the PSTN might list a phone number that is ambiguous to Office Communications Server. The location profile assigned to the Mediation Server is used to help disambiguate the target phone number.

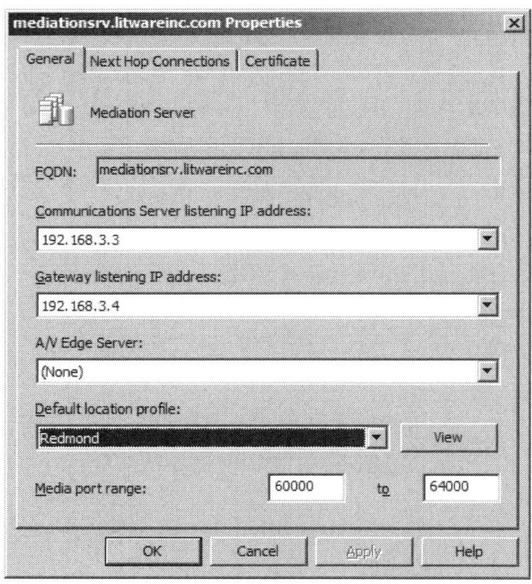

FIGURE 11-27 Assigning Mediation Server location profiles

Configuring Users for Unified Communications

Configuring users for Unified Communications (UC) is quite simple. Before a user or group of users can be configured for Enterprise Voice, they must be enabled for Office Communications Server and assigned a SIP URI and a home pool. A different license agreement than the standard IM or Web Conferencing Client Access license (CAL) is required before enabling users for Enterprise Voice. The CALs should not be confused with the Office Communications Server SKUs, which come in two offerings: Standard Edition and Enterprise Edition.

To configure a single user for Enterprise Voice, select the user's Properties from the right-click menu in DSA.MSC or the Admin Tools MMC. On the Communications tab, select the Configure button to view additional options. In the Telephony section, select the Enable Enterprise Voice Routing option and configure the user's phone number. The option to change the policy selection becomes available so that administrators can specify a different Voice policy. Every Enterprise Voice user must be assigned a Voice policy. This phone number is specified in a valid TEL URI format that is globally unique, meaning no other person has the same phone number extension within the organization. This number is entered in the *Line URI* field by using the format *tel:<phone>*. These settings are shown in Figure 11-28.

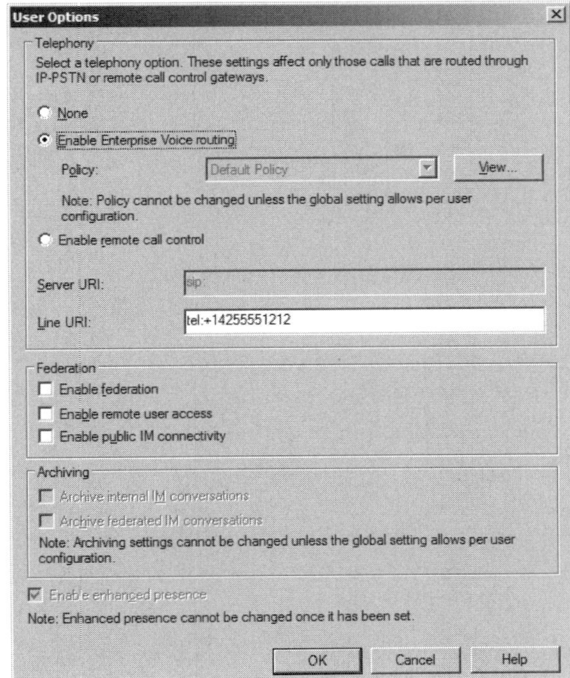

FIGURE 11-28 Enterprise Voice user properties

If an incorrect format is entered, an error warning is displayed. To specify an extension in addition to the phone number, use the following format: *tel:<phone>;ext=<extension>*. The phone number specified in the *Line URI* field uniquely associates the user's SIP URI to this TEL

URI. This association enables Office Communications Servers to translate between the two URI formats.

By default, the Policy drop-down option is disabled. The global Voice policy is set to the out-of-the-box default policy. To be able to modify the policy assigned to the user, the Global Policy setting must be changed. To access this global policy, navigate to the forest-level Voice Properties in the Admin Tools MMC and click the Policy tab. Click the Global Policy drop-down list and choose Use Per User Policy. This is illustrated in Figure 11-29. Once the global Voice policy is modified, the user's Voice policy can be changed and viewed. When the View button is selected, the phone usage associated with the policy is shown.

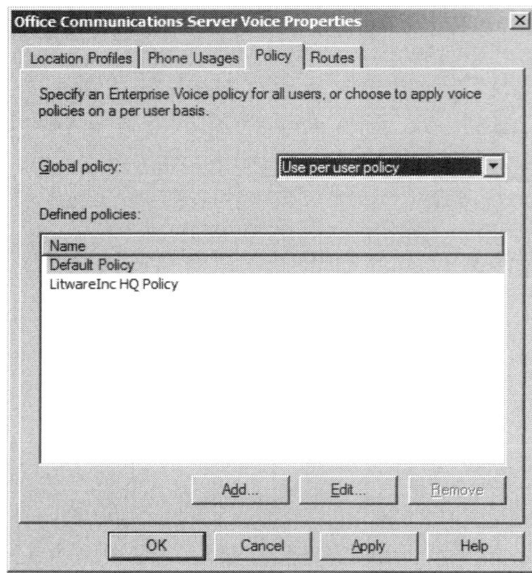

FIGURE 11-29 Global Voice policy

To configure multiple users at once, a better option is to use the Configure Communications Server Users Wizard. To bulk-configure, select all the users to enable for Enterprise Voice from DSA.MSC or Admin Tools MMC and choose this wizard from the right-click menu, as shown in Figure 11-30.

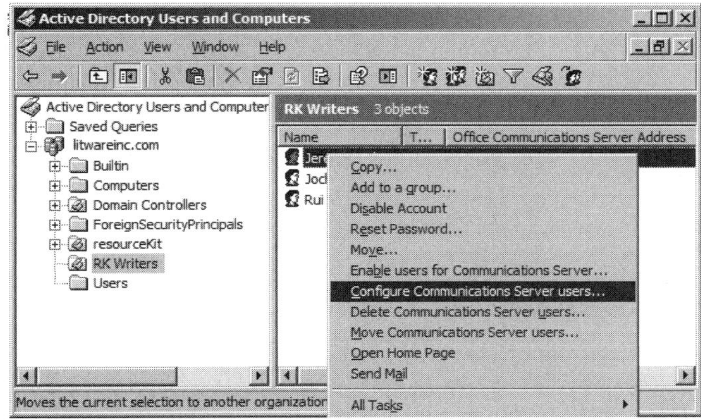

FIGURE 11-30 Selecting the Configure Communications Server Users Wizard

Because this wizard enables the configuring of all user settings, click Next to arrive at the Enterprise Voice settings. The Enterprise Voice settings to configure are shown in Figure 11-31. The top-level check box, Change Enterprise Voice Settings, must be selected to enable users for Enterprise Voice. The top-level check box indicates that you want to configure the embedded settings. To enable users for Enterprise Voice, the Enable Voice check box must be selected. The policy drop-down list becomes available if the global policy permits it. (See Figure 11-29.) To bulk-disable users, select the Change Enterprise Voice Settings check box and leave the Enable Voice check box unselected. This combination of settings effectively prevents users from using Enterprise Voice. Click Next and finally Finish to complete the wizard. The final page of the wizard displays the results of the operation performed. If the wizard indicates that the operation failed for some or all of the users, check whether these users are enabled for Office Communications Server and are assigned a SIP URI and a home pool.

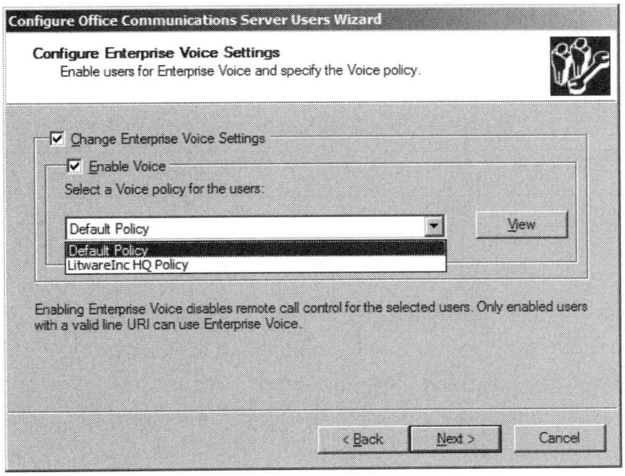

FIGURE 11-31 Configure Enterprise Voice settings

One important point to keep in mind about using the Configure Office Communications Server Users Wizard is although users might be enabled for Enterprise Voice, unless these users were previously provisioned with a TEL URI that remains unique, they will not be reachable via a phone number if the Line URI field remains blank. The Configure Office Communications Server Users Wizard does not configure the Line URI field because each user must have a unique TEL URI. To bulk-configure the Line URI field, you need to resort to using the following Office Communications Server WMI interface: MSFT_SIPESUserSetting.LineURI.

Configuring the Media Gateway

The media gateway is a third-party server role offered by Microsoft's partners that is used to convert the signaling portion, SS7, of the PSTN traffic into SIP and the media portion of the PSTN traffic into RTP. Because each media gateway vendor will likely expose its management settings differently, this book will not cover the step-by-step procedure necessary to configure all the settings of the media gateway. Instead, the administrator should refer to the media gateway vendor's documentation, which is often available online.

Microsoft differentiates media gateway vendors into three categories that it supports. The first category, referred to as *basic media gateways*, requires the deployment of Office Communications Server Mediation Server to work with Office Communications Server 2007 R2. Depending on the vendor, installing its media gateway service on the same physical server colocated with the Mediation Server service might be supported. Nevertheless, from a logical perspective, they are considered separate servers. The second category, referred to as *advanced media gateways*, does not require deploying Mediation Servers to interface with Office Communications Server 2007 R2. The third category, referred to as *hybrid media gateways*, consists of a basic media gateway with the functionality of the Mediation Server coexisting on the same physical server. More details are covered in the section titled "Bridging VoIP to the PSTN Network by Using a Media Gateway" in Chapter 4, "Infrastructure and Security Considerations."

DIRECT FROM THE SOURCE

Finding UC Certified Gateways

Padu Padmanabhan
Senior Test Lead

The list of UC certified gateways can be found at *http://technet.microsoft.com/en-us/office/bb735838.aspx*. This site also contains links to qualified IP PBXs for Office Communications Server 2007. Each certified gateway vendor has a link to its Web site, which will host the user guide and the deployment documents for the gateway model that were qualified independently through Tekvision (the Microsoft UC Open Interoperability Program leverages Tekvision as an independent third-party lab for qualification/certification) or at Microsoft to meet the qualification requirements.

The media gateway must be configured with the Primary Rate Interface/Basic Rate Interface (PRI/BRI) lines allocated by your telecom provider, which connect it to the PSTN network. On the network interface card (NIC) connected to the internal IP network, the gateway should be configured to connect to the Mediation Server if you are using a basic media gateway. To configure the media gateway to send and receive traffic from the Mediation Server, the following settings must be configured:

- **Inbound traffic** A listening port on the media gateway must be configured to listen for incoming traffic from the Mediation Server.
- **Outbound traffic** The media gateway must be configured with the FQDN or IP address of the Mediation Server and the port number it will send outbound traffic to.

This configuration is illustrated in Figure 11-32.

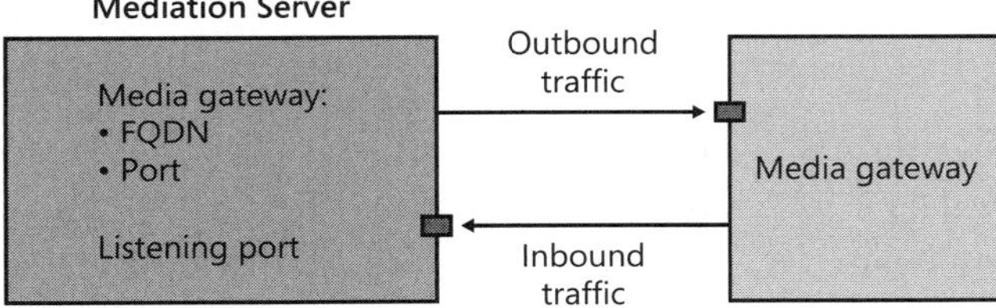

FIGURE 11-32 Media gateway configuration

Configuring the Mediation Server

The Mediation Server is a server role that is required if you are using a basic media gateway to function with Office Communications Server 2007 R2. Because the majority of basic media gateways support only SIP over Transmission Control Protocol (TCP) or UDP, the Mediation Server extends the security of the Office Communications Server system up to the basic media gateways by translating SIP over TCP/UDP to SIP over mutual transport layer security (MTLS). This is why it is recommended that you deploy a Mediation Server within proximity to its associated media gateway. To prevent internal users from eavesdropping on phone conversations, the network connection between the Mediation Server and media gateway should be placed on a separate network inaccessible to the users. Microsoft's objective is to help media gateway third-party vendors integrate as much of the Mediation Server functionality into the media gateway servers, referred to as advanced media gateways. The objective is to remove the Mediation Server role entirely. This will help reduce the added complexity that deploying and managing another server running the Mediation Server role creates, and consequently it will likely reduce total cost of ownership (TCO). Until third-party media gateway vendors are able to integrate this functionality into their offerings, a Mediation Server is required. The Mediation Server provides the following functions:

- Intermediate signaling (SIP) between Office Communications Servers and the media gateway.
- Transcodes RTP media traffic from legacy codecs—such as G.711, G.722.1/SIREN, G.723.1, G.726, and GSM—that are used by media gateways to the Office Communications Server 2007 R2 advanced audio codec, Real-Time Audio (RTAudio). Note that G.729 is not supported by Office Communications Server.
- Acts as an Interactive Connectivity Establishment (ICE) client to enable PSTN-originated media flows to traverse intervening Network Address Translations (NATs) and firewalls.
- Provides management, provisioning, and monitoring for the media gateway to integrate into Office Communications Server's infrastructure of Active Directory, WMI, and MMC.

The Mediation Server installation can be found under the Deploy Other Server Roles option in Office Communications Server 2007 R2 Setup. This is illustrated in Figure 11-33. Office Communications Server 2007 R2 Setup provides a step-by-step set of wizards for installing your Mediation Server.

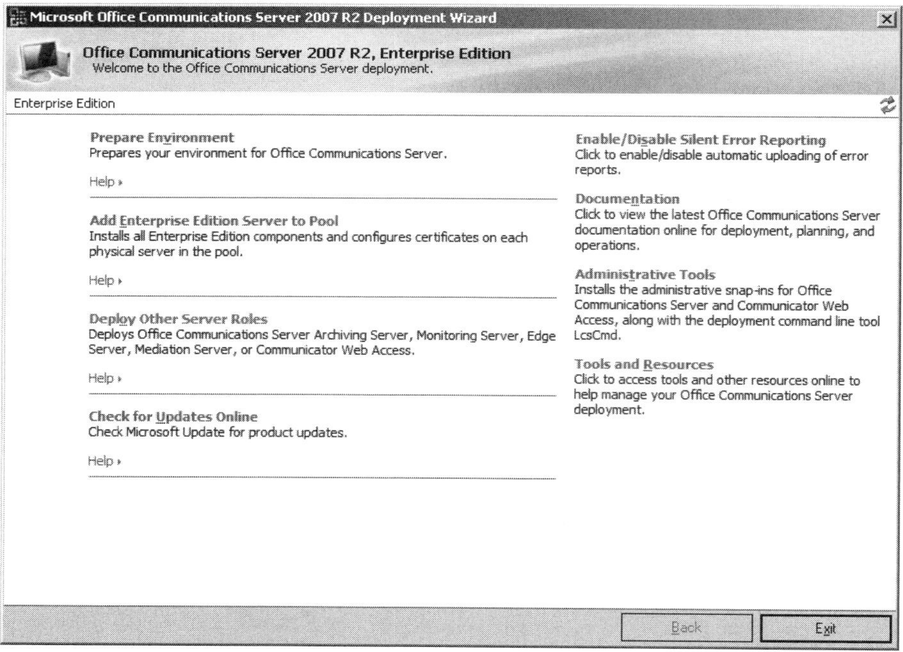

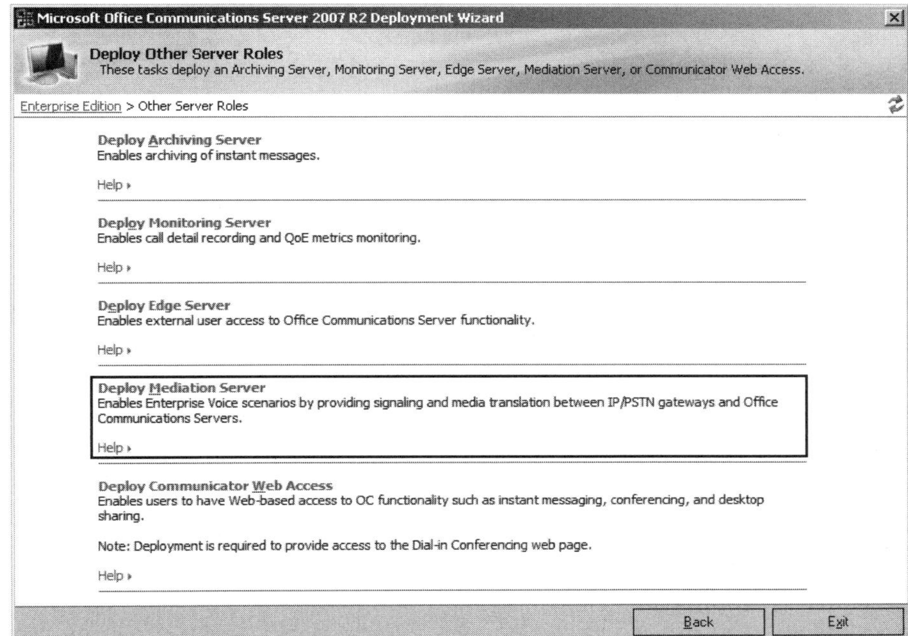

FIGURE 11-33 Mediation Server setup

From a configuration perspective, a one-to-one correspondence between Mediation Server and the media gateway is required. That is, one Mediation Server is required for each media gateway deployed. The Mediation Server role must run on a computer that is domain-joined to the Active Directory forest where the Office Communications Server 2007 R2 infrastructure is deployed. The Mediation Server must be configured to connect to an Office Communications Server. If a Director is deployed, the Mediation Server can be configured to route calls to the Director; otherwise, the Mediation Server should be configured to route traffic to the home pool closest to it.

Because the Mediation Server is the only Office Communications Server role that connects directly to a basic media gateway, it must be configured to send and receive network traffic to and from the media gateway. The Mediation Server must have at least two NICs configured on the physical computer—one NIC is used for sending and receiving signaling (SIP protocol) traffic from Office Communications Servers as well as audio (RTAudio codec) traffic from internal phone clients, and the other NIC is for sending and receiving signaling (SIP protocol) and audio (G.711 codec) traffic from the media gateway. This is illustrated in Figure 11-34.

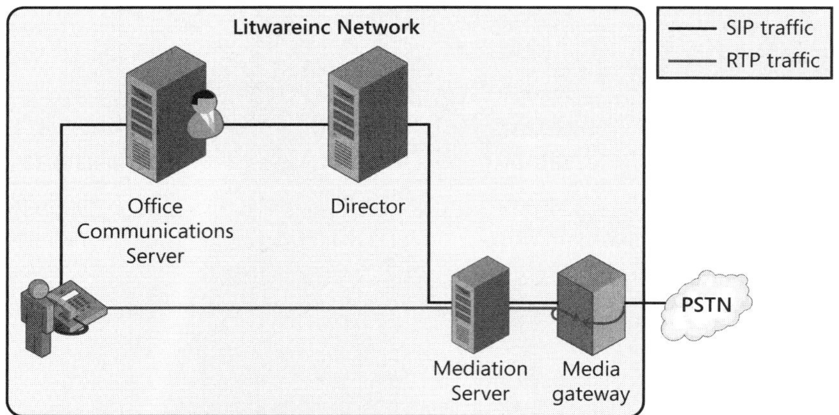

FIGURE 11-34 Internal call routing. Note that the lines connecting the different server roles represent protocol traffic and do not necessarily represent the number of NICs the server must be configured with.

To allow remote users (users connecting from the Internet) who are Enterprise Voice–enabled to dial and receive calls from outside the enterprise's network, the administrator must specify the A/V Edge Server that the Mediation Server should connect to for both inbound and outbound calls. For security reasons, the A/V Edge Server does not initiate connections to servers in the corporate internal network. When a remote user dials a phone number, the signaling (SIP) traffic to initiate the call traverses the Access Edge Server to the Director, which routes the request to the user's home pool. The home pool sends the request to the Mediation Server. The Mediation Server forwards the request out to the PSTN through the media gateway. When the call is answered, the Mediation Server needs to establish a connection with the client to obtain the audio media of the call. Using the ICE protocol, the Mediation Server specifies the address of the A/V Edge Server the client should connect to through the signaling channel, and on its end establishes a connection to the A/V Edge Server. The address of the A/V Edge Server is the one the administrator configured the Mediation Server with. Once the client and the Mediation Server set up a tunnel across the A/V Edge Server, audio can flow through. The Mediation Server forwards this audio to the media gateway. A similar process occurs when the remote user receives a call. This is illustrated in Figure 11-35.

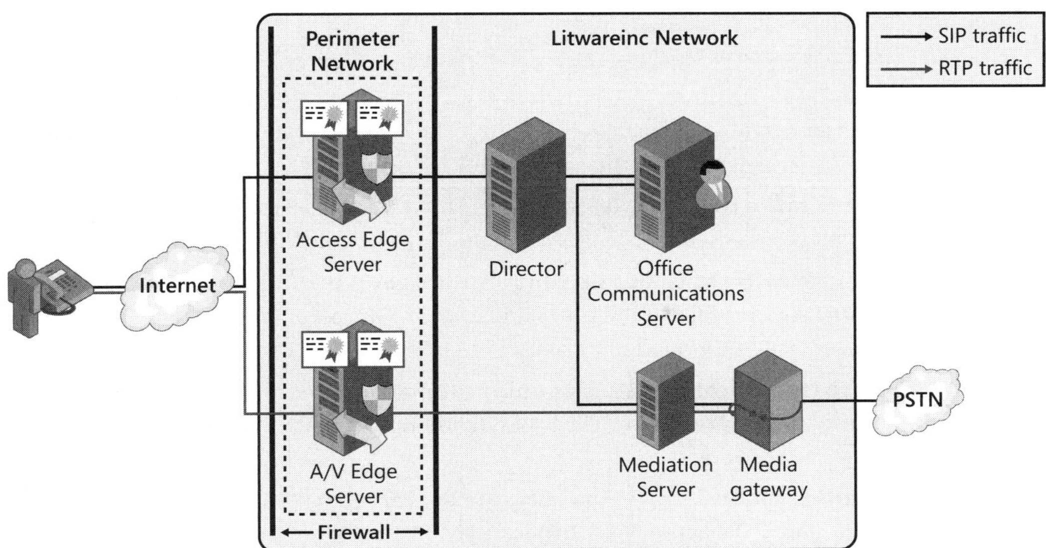

FIGURE 11-35 External call routing. Note that the lines connecting the different server roles represent protocol traffic and do not necessarily represent the number of NICs the server must be configured with.

Figure 11-36 shows, from the perspective of the Mediation Server, what configuration is necessary to make it work with the other server roles.

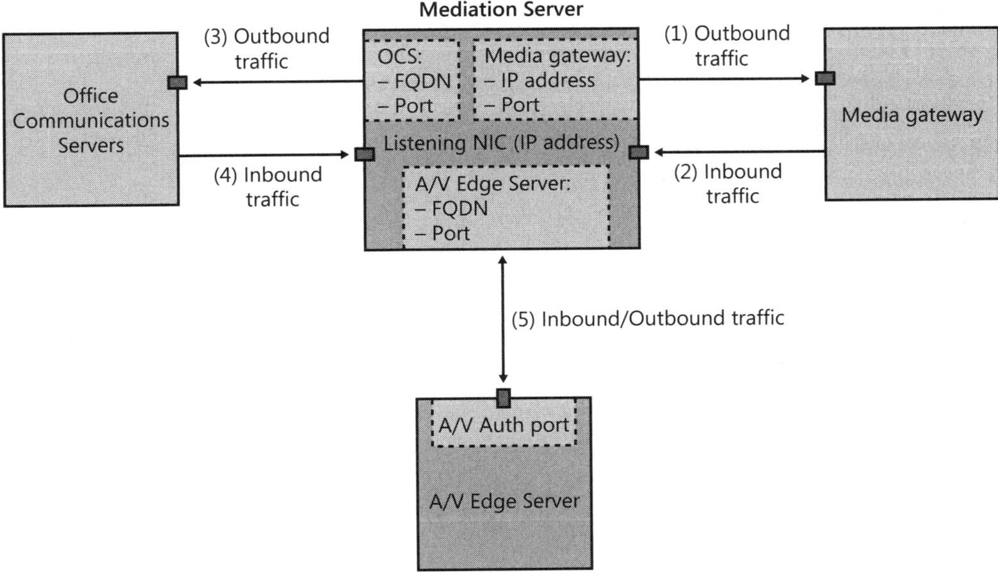

FIGURE 11-36 Mediation Server configuration

The following are descriptions of the numbers keyed to Figure 11-36:

- **Outbound traffic to media gateway** The Mediation Server must be configured with the IP address of the media gateway and port number it will send outbound traffic to. It receives this information from the Office Communications Server or A/V Edge Server.
- **Inbound traffic from media gateway** This is the IP address on the Mediation Server that will be used to listen for inbound traffic from the media gateway.
- **Outbound traffic to Office Communications Server** The Mediation Server is configured with the FQDN and port number of an Office Communications Server to which it will send outbound traffic it receives from the media gateway.
- **Inbound traffic from Office Communications Server** This is the IP address on the Mediation Server that will be used to listen for inbound traffic from the Office Communications Server.
- **Inbound/outbound traffic to A/V Edge Server** The Mediation Server is configured with the FQDN and A/V Authentication port number of the A/V Edge Server. The Mediation Server should be configured with a local A/V Edge Server to enable remote users to dial out to the PSTN as well as receive calls originating from outside the user's organization.

To configure the Mediation Server, the administrator must use the Admin Tools MMC. After installing the Mediation Server, open the Admin Tools MMC and locate your Mediation Server by its FQDN. Right-click your Mediation Server and select Properties, as shown in Figure 11-37.

FIGURE 11-37 Mediation Server properties

The six settings to configure the Mediation Server so that it can route traffic between the Office Communications Server and A/V Edge Server to the media gateway are split between two tabs. These settings are shown in Figure 11-38, and they are numbered to match the logical representation of these settings, which was shown in Figure 11-36. The first tab, the General tab, is used to specify the IP addresses that the Mediation Server listens on for inbound connections (numbered item 4 in Figure 11-38). In addition, the administrator can specify a location profile for the Mediation Server (numbered item 6). The range of media ports used by the Mediation Server is configurable; however, in most cases the default values do not need to be modified. The second tab, Next Hop Connections, is where the administrator specifies the outbound connections to the Office Communications Server (numbered item 3) and media gateway (numbered item 1 in Figure 11-38).

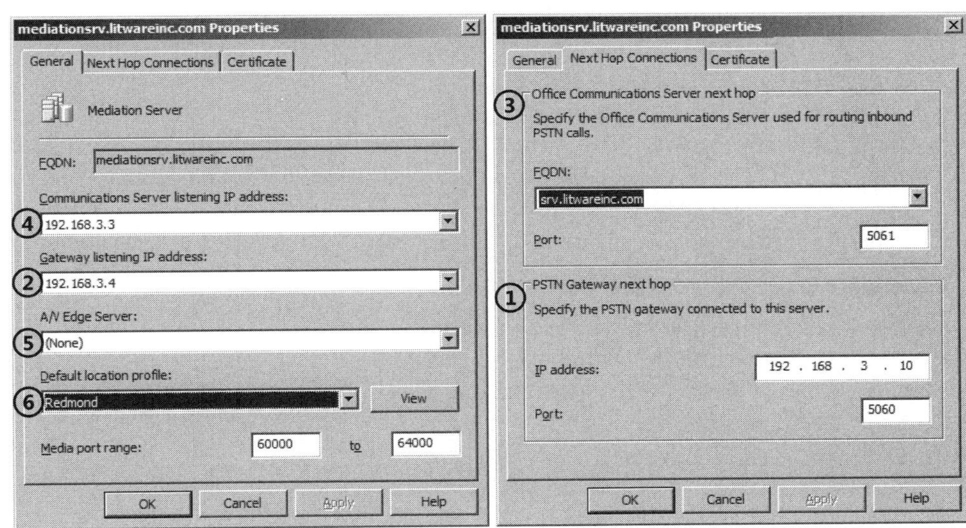

FIGURE 11-38 Mediation Server configuration

Before the Mediation Server can establish network connections with other Office Communications Servers it interacts with, it must be configured with a server certificate issued by a certificate authority (CA) that is trusted by the other Office Communications Servers. This configuration can be completed from the Certificate tab.

Returning to the configuration of an A/V Edge Server connection in the Mediation Server properties, if the A/V Edge Server drop-down option (shown as numbered item 5 in Figure 11-38) is empty, this is because no trusted A/V Edge Servers were configured in the Office Communications Server's global settings at the Active Directory forest level. Once an A/V Edge Server is specified, it becomes visible in the drop-down list of the General tab of the Mediation Server's properties. To configure your A/V Edge Server, navigate to the Global Properties of the forest node in the Admin Tools MMC and select the Edge Servers tab, shown in Figure 11-39. Click the Add button to specify an A/V Edge Server. The dialog box will prompt you for the FQDN and authentication port number of the A/V Edge Server.

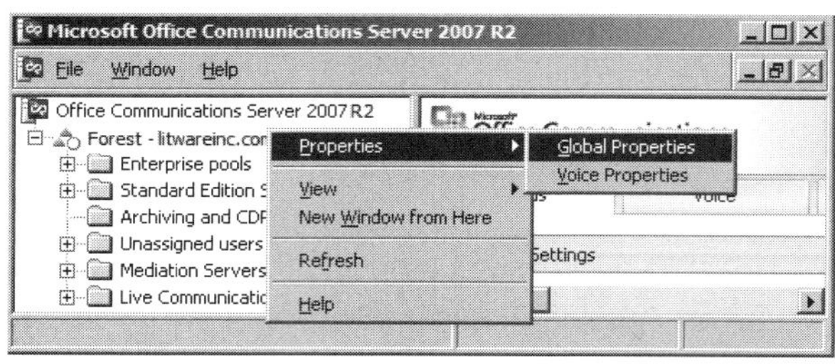

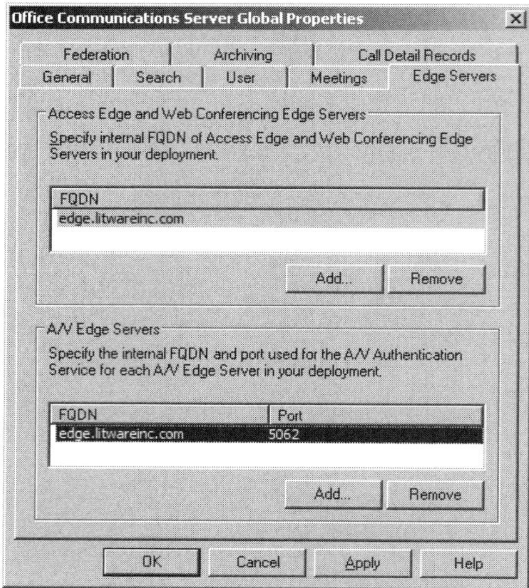

FIGURE 11-39 Global Edge Server settings

To determine the FQDN and A/V authentication port number of the A/V Edge Server, navigate to the Admin Tools MMC of your A/V Edge Server. The way to get to the Admin Tools MMC of Edge Servers is to right-click My Computer and select Manage, as shown in Figure 11-40.

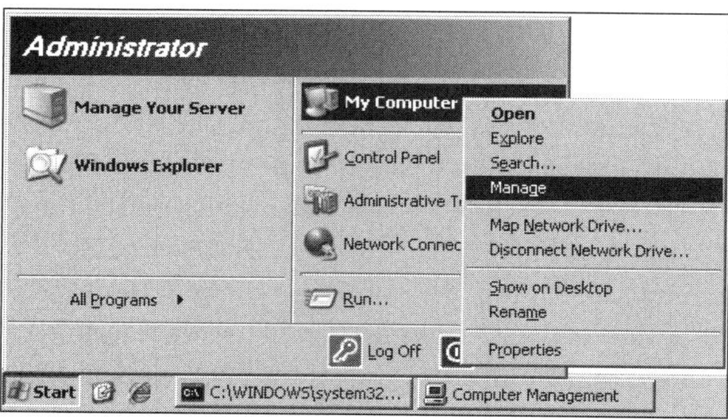

FIGURE 11-40 Administer A/V Edge Server

Expand the Services And Applications node to reach the Microsoft Office Communications Server 2007 R2 node. Click the plus sign (+) next to Internal Interface Settings in the Status pane to expand it. The information to configure the global Edge Server settings is displayed in the Status pane, as shown in Figure 11-41.

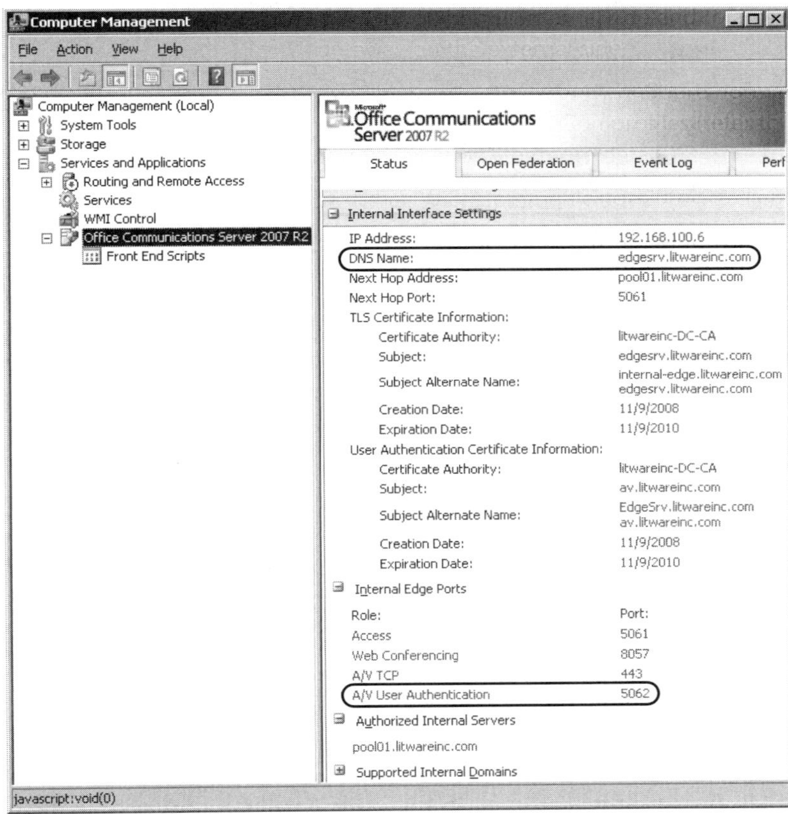

FIGURE 11-41 A/V Edge Server settings

Once the A/V Edge Server is specified in the global settings, the A/V Edge Server's FQDN and authentication port number are visible on the General tab of the Mediation Server, as shown in Figure 11-42.

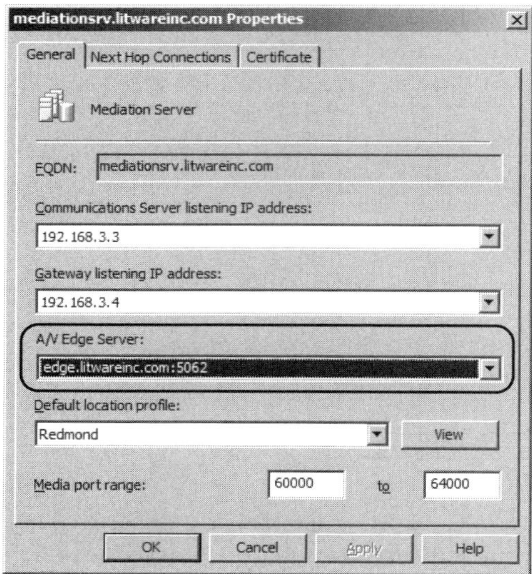

FIGURE 11-42 A/V Edge Server setting on the Mediation Server

Configuring the Mediation Server to connect is nearly complete. The Mediation Server is now configured to connect to the A/V Edge Server; however, the A/V Edge Server is not configured to trust incoming network connections from the Mediation Server. To specify the A/V Edge Server to trust the Mediation Server, the administrator must return to the Admin Tools MMC of the A/V Edge Server, select Properties, and navigate to the Internal tab. To add the Mediation Server as an internal server authorized to connect to the A/V Edge Server, click the Add Server button and specify the FQDN of your Mediation Server, as shown in Figure 11-43.

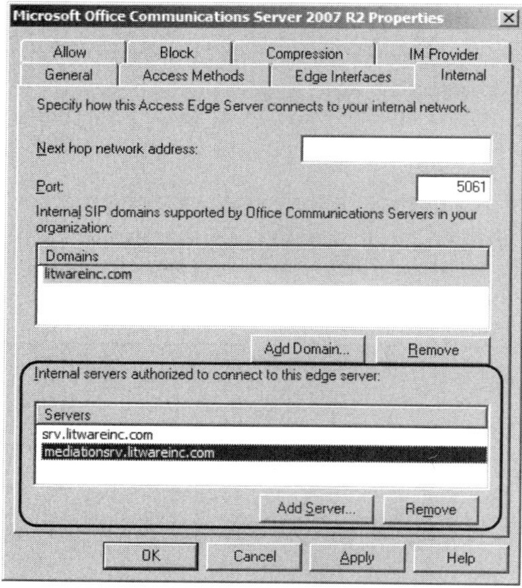

FIGURE 11-43 Mediation Server configured to connect to the A/V Edge Server

Your configuration of the Mediation Server now enables remote users to place and receive calls when signing in from the Internet.

DIRECT FROM THE SOURCE

Supporting + with Gateways and PBXs

Padu Padmanabhan
Senior Test Lead

Office Communications Server uses normalized E.164 numbers (such as +14255551212) for routing outgoing calls as well as for incoming calls. However, not all gateways or PBXs support the plus sign, +, correctly. Office Communications Server 2007 R2 can still interoperate with such gateways.

This problem can surface in two scenarios:

1. Calls going from Office Communications Server to gateway/PBX. If the gateway/IP PBX does not support receiving a phone number with a + in the SIP INVITE, then the Mediation Server needs to be configured to strip the + out for each outgoing call by setting the WMI configuration RemovePlusFromRequestURI to TRUE.
2. Calls going from gateway/PBX to Office Communications Server. If the gateway/IP PBX does not support sending + as part of the phone number, it should present the phone number in the From field as per the RFC 3966 format, except the + is replaced by another symbol. Microsoft strongly recommends using * as this symbol. Please note that replacing + with # as a prefix is not supported. The Mediation Server can be configured with a normalization rule to strip this prefix, say *, and replace it with a + to make the phone conform to RFC 3966.

Note that such a normalization rule should also apply to all outgoing calls routed to this gateway/PBX. For example, if a user dials *14258828080 from Office Communicator, Office Communications Server will convert the number to +14258828080.

Summary

Office Communications Server 2007 introduced support for VoIP for the enterprise. Microsoft changed the way users use telephony by conveniently integrating it into the information worker's computing environment for simpler and seamless communication from anywhere with a network connection. Office Communications Server 2007 R2 offers a paradigm shift from how the application has traditionally been used. Now, a call can be quickly placed within the context of a Microsoft Office application (Word, Outlook, SharePoint, and so on) and third-party applications that integrate with Office Communicator 2007 R2.

With Office Communicator, a softphone can also provide a richer user experience than is possible with the 10-digit dial pad of most phones. Advanced features such as call transfer, placing a call on hold, and so on are more easily done by clicking a mouse than pressing * key sequences. Being able to take your office phone with you on the road is an appealing feature as more and more of the people in today's workforce have the flexibility to decide where they work from—whether it be the office, a home office, a local restaurant, or wherever they need to be.

With Office Communicator Phone Edition 2007 R2, it is now possible to integrate the desk-phone with Office Communicator 2007 R2 and enable the same scenarios possible with a PBX phone using RCC.

Office Communications Server's Enterprise Voice provides a streamlined design so that it is simple to manage while remaining extensible to support future requirements.

Additional Resources

- Microsoft Office Communications Server 2007 Quality of Experience Monitoring Server, found at *http://go.microsoft.com/fwlink/?LinkID=133703*
- Office Communications Server 2007 Document: Enterprise Voice Planning and Deployment Guide, found at *http://go.microsoft.com/fwlink/?LinkID=133698*
- Office Communications Server 2007 Telephony Integration, found at *http://go.microsoft.com/fwlink/?LinkID=133704*
- Office Communications Server 2007 partners, found at *http://go.microsoft.com/fwlink/?LinkID=133699*
- Office Communications Server 2007 Enterprise Voice Route Helper documentation, found at *http://go.microsoft.com/fwlink/?LinkID=133705*
- Office Communications Server 2007 Resource Kit Tools, found on the companion media and also at *http://go.microsoft.com/fwlink/?LinkID=133706*
- Route Target regular expressions, found at *http://go.microsoft.com/fwlink/?LinkID=133700*
- TEL URI RFC 3966, found at *http://go.microsoft.com/fwlink/?LinkID=133700*
- .NET Regular Expression Syntax, found at *http://go.microsoft.com/fwlink/?LinkID=133708*
- Office Communications Server 2007 Document: Microsoft Quality of Experience, found at *http://go.microsoft.com/fwlink/?LinkID=133709*
- Office Communications Server 2007 Resource Kit Tools, in the OCS 2007 Resource Kit Tools folder

CHAPTER 12

Voice Mail Scenarios

Microsoft Office Communications Server 2007 R2 offers the ability to integrate with Microsoft Exchange Unified Messaging (UM) Server for voice mail functionality. Exchange UM Server is the voice mail solution for Office Communications Server. This chapter covers the integration between these two products and not integration between Exchange UM Server and third-party Internet Protocol Private Branch eXchange (IP PBX). Users must be enabled for both an Exchange Server 2007 Service Pack 1 (SP1) (or later) mailbox and UM with a defined extension as well as Office Communications Enterprise Voice.

Overview of Voice Mail Scenarios

Integration of Exchange UM Server with Office Communications Server offers users a rich user experience and access to the following Exchange UM features:

- **Call history** Users can view their call history as well as missed call notifications directly from their mailbox.
- **Voice mail** When the user is unable to answer an incoming call or is not signed in to Office Communications, incoming calls are routed by Office Communications Server to the user's mailbox for later retrieval. The message is recorded by the Exchange UM Server and delivered to the recipient's mailbox.
- **Call answering** Call answering includes answering an incoming call on behalf of a user, playing their personal greeting, recording a message, and submitting it for delivery to their inbox as an e-mail message.

- **Subscriber access** Subscriber access enables dial-in access for internal users. Users (referred to as subscribers in Exchange UM) dialing into the UM system can access their mailbox by using Microsoft Office Outlook Voice Access. Subscribers who use Office Outlook Voice Access can access the UM system by using voice recognition or the telephone keypad using dual-tone multifrequency (DTMF) tones. By dialing into the subscriber access number, a user (that is, a subscriber) can:
  - Access voice mail over a telephone.
  - Listen, forward, or reply to e-mail messages over a telephone.
  - Listen to calendar information over a telephone.
  - Access or dial contacts stored in the global address list or a personal contact list over a telephone.
  - Accept or cancel meeting requests over a telephone.
  - Set a voice mail Out-of-Office message.
  - Set user security preferences and personal options.
- **Auto-Attendant** Auto-Attendant is a set of voice prompts that gives external users access to the Exchange 2007 UM system. Auto-Attendant lets the user use either the telephone keypad or speech inputs to navigate the menu structure, place a call to a user, or locate a user and then place a call to that user. Auto-Attendant gives the administrator the ability to:
  - Create a customizable set of menus for external users.
  - Define informational greetings, business hours greetings, and non–business hours greetings.
  - Define holiday schedules.
  - Describe how to search the organization's directory.
  - Describe how to connect to a user's extension so that external callers can call a user by specifying their extension.
  - Describe how to search the organization's directory so that external callers can search the organization's directory and call a specific user.
  - Enable external users to call the operator.

Redirecting Incoming Calls to Voice Mail

When an incoming call appears, users who cannot immediately answer the call can redirect the call to their voice mail immediately. This avoids having to listen to the call ringing until the default timeout routes it to voice mail. Figure 12-1 shows how to redirect the incoming call to voice mail from the notification alert.

FIGURE 12-1 Redirect call to voice mail

Call Forwarding to Voice Mail

Users have the option to specify their voice mail as one of the options when configuring their call forwarding rules. When configured, calls will be directed to voice mail immediately or after a 20-second notification delay. Figure 12-2 illustrates where to configure this option in Microsoft Office Communicator.

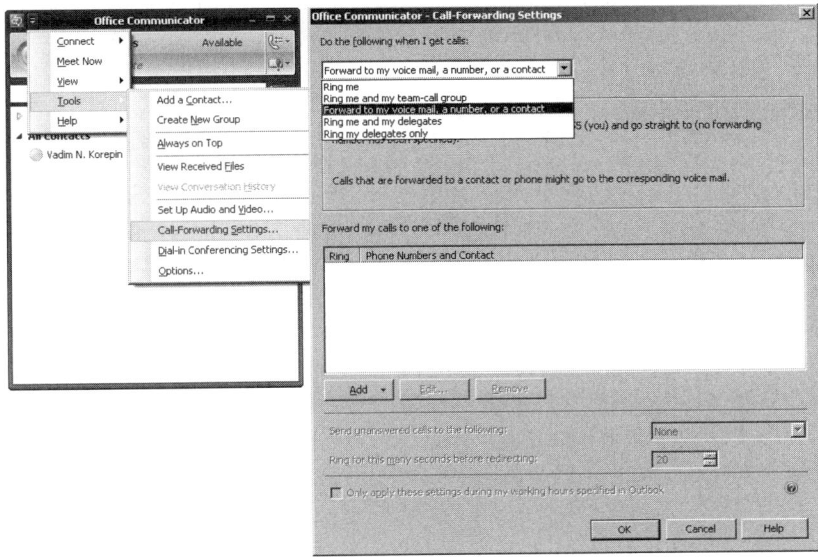

FIGURE 12-2 Call forwarding to voice mail

Calling Your Voice Mail

Instead of requiring a special number to access voice mail, Office Communicator offers an intuitive single-click interface. Figure 12-3 shows how to call your voice mail directly from within Communicator and switches to the Subscriber Access menu (see the section titled "Subscriber Access" later in this chapter).

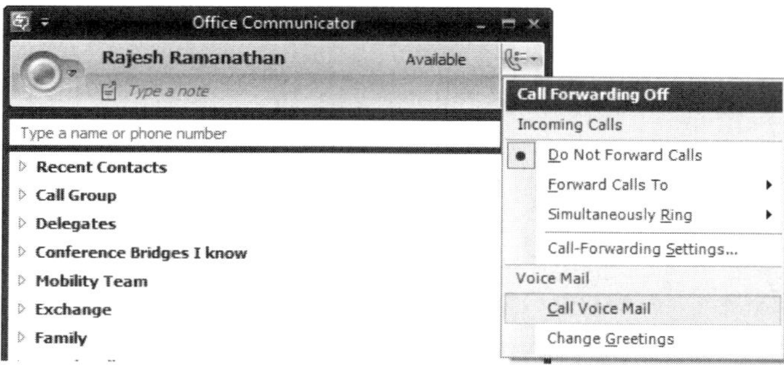

FIGURE 12-3 Calling voice mail from within Communicator

Note that along with the ability to call voice mail, users can change the greetings that they have set in their Exchange voice mailbox directly from Office Communicator 2007 R2 using the Change Greetings options, as shown in Figure 12-3.

Listening to Voice Mail

With Exchange UM Server, users can experience a rich voice mail experience from within Microsoft Office Outlook 2007. Users can get notification of voice mail (in the telecom industry, commonly known as message waiting indicator) from Office Communicator as well as from the system tray. Voice messages can be listened to directly from within Outlook. Users can launch Outlook directly from Office Communicator. Voice mail messages are treated as separate e-mails within Outlook. This makes the experience of listening to voice mails similar to reading e-mail messages within Outlook (see Figure 12-4). Caller ID information is provided in the voice mail message so that users can decide the easiest way to respond, whether to reply by voice message, e-mail, or instant message or to click to initiate a return voice call.

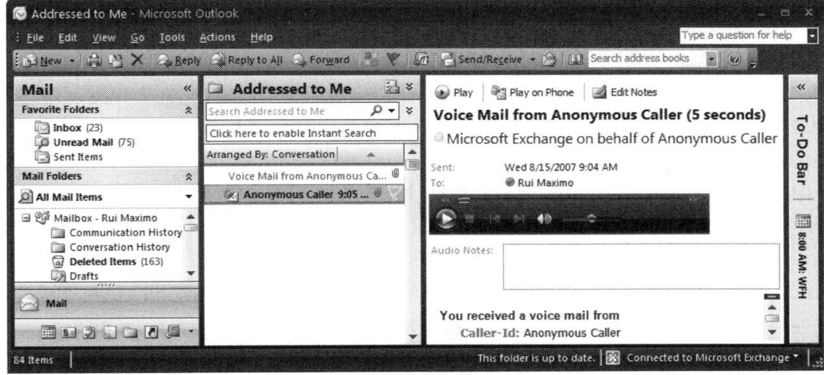

FIGURE 12-4 Listening to voice mail from Outlook 2007

DIRECT FROM THE SOURCE

Resolving Names in Exchange Unified Messaging and Office Communicator

Rajesh Ramanathan

Senior Program Manager Lead, Office Communicator

Exchange Unified Messaging can resolve phone numbers against the numbers stored in Outlook contacts. Whenever a missed call or a voice mail is generated on UM, the contact name and information stored in the callee's address book is resolved from the caller's phone number and put into the e-mail body. The phone number is inserted as clickable links. For example, Figure 12-5 shows what a missed call from John Doe (stored as an Outlook contact) from Phone 4255551212 looks like.

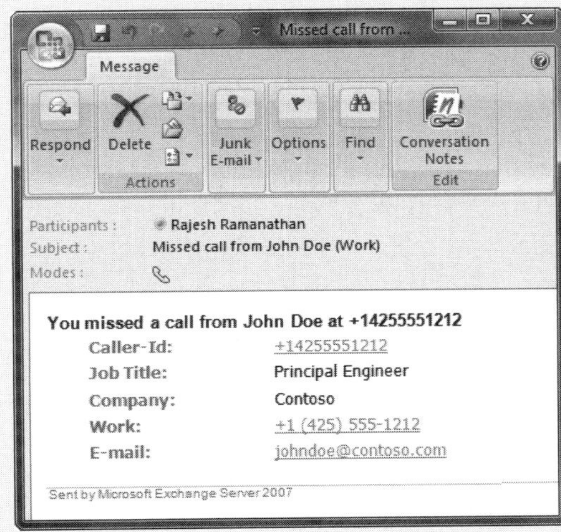

FIGURE 12-5 Missed call notification e-mail

This name resolution from phone to a contact works for most common scenarios. However, Office Communications Server does provide a richer location profile mechanism, as we discussed in Chapter 11, "VoIP Scenarios," that enables incoming numbers to be more accurately resolved to the corresponding E.164 number. This enables Office Communicator to complete and match a wider range of incoming numbers. Additionally, Office Communicator does have access to phone numbers in presence as well. For example, rather than using Outlook contacts, if user John Doe were a federated contact who had shared his mobile phone number (4255551212) in Communicator Phones, then we would see John Doe in the coming call notification alert in Office Communicator 2007 R2. However, if the call is missed or a voice mail is generated, then Exchange UM does not have knowledge of the same contact that was shared through presence and will not be able to map this to John Doe. It would therefore create a call from the phone number 425551212 (instead of John Doe). In this particular example, Office Communicator would show the display name of the caller, but voice mail or missed call generated by Exchange Unified Messaging would not.

Call Logs

Missed calls are shown in the user's inbox as e-mail notifications showing the caller ID and a link to call back the calling party.

The Conversation History folder in Outlook 2007 stores a history of instant messages and conferences as well as a call log of all outgoing and incoming calls made (shown in Figure 12-6). Office Communicator automatically creates this folder upon installation.

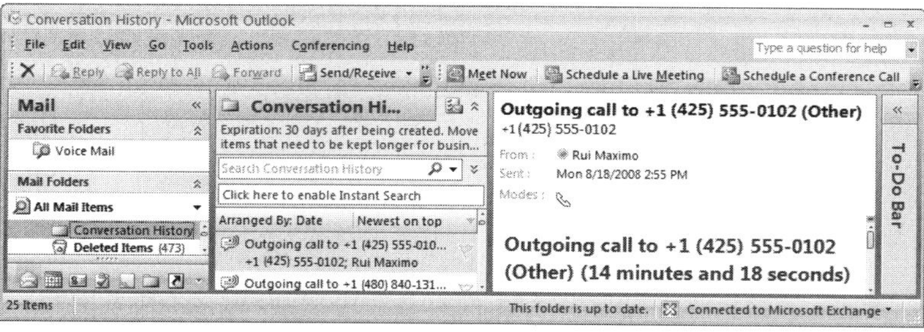

FIGURE 12-6 Conversation history in Outlook 2007

Leaving a Voice Mail

Office Communicator provides callers the ability to leave a voice mail while bypassing any delegate or team member ringing. (See Figure 12-7.)

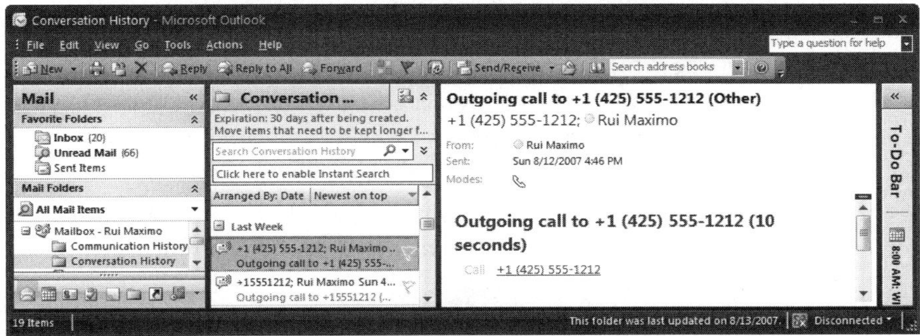

FIGURE 12-7 Calling voice mail directly from Communicator

Subscriber Access

Exchange UM enables users to use Outlook to access their mailboxes from a phone when they are away from their computers. Users dial the subscriber access number and enter their personal identification number (PIN) to authenticate themselves to Exchange UM Server. Once authenticated, users can read their e-mails, check their voice mail, schedule and modify meetings, and so on using speech recognition as if they were using Outlook.

Auto-Attendant

Most organizations have a published company number that outside users can call to get general information about the company and navigate using speech recognition or DTMF tones to the desired department. Outside callers can also reach employees in the organization by using speech recognition. This functionality is called Auto-Attendant in Exchange UM.

Examining the Technical Details Behind the Voice Mail Scenario

To enable the previous scenarios requires deploying Office Communications Server as the Enterprise Voice solution and Exchange Server as the Enterprise Mailbox solution. The additional server role required to enable voice mail when using Exchange Server 2007 SP1 is the Exchange Unified Messaging server role. For details on how to deploy Enterprise Voice, refer to Chapter 11. Information for deploying Exchange Server and UM is beyond the scope of this book.

Exchange UM Server interoperates with several IP gateways as well as Office Communications Server by using SIP over Transmission Control Protocol (TCP) or Mutual Transport Layer Security (MTLS). When interoperating with Office Communications Server, Exchange UM Server uses SIP over MTLS, which offers stronger security. Because most gateways do not integrate with Active Directory, administrators must use the Exchange Server Management Console to create an UM IP gateway object in Active Directory to represent the IP gateway. This object has organization-wide scope. It encapsulates configuration settings related to a single physical IP gateway, including how to connect to the SIP-enabled IP gateway. This enables Exchange UM Server to discover available IP gateways and resolve their addresses by using the Domain Name System (DNS) to route to them. This is a manual process. Every time a new IP gateway is configured, a new UM IP gateway object must be created in Active Directory. When an existing IP gateway is decommissioned, the corresponding UM IP gateway object must be deleted from Active Directory.

In the case of Office Communications Server, the different server roles, with the exception of the Edge Servers, automatically publish themselves in Active Directory during server activation. Unfortunately, Exchange UM Server does not recognize the Active Directory objects that represent the Office Communications Server, which is a trusted server in the Trusted Server list (see Chapter 4, "Infrastructure and Security Considerations," for more details). Therefore, it is necessary to create a corresponding UM IP gateway object in Active Directory for every Standard Edition Server and Enterprise pool front-end server for Exchange UM Server to recognize the Office Communications Server as an IP gateway. This is automated by the tool exchUCutil.ps1, as described in step 4 in the section titled "Configuring Voice Mail" later in this chapter.

Dial rules are used to route incoming calls to the appropriate gateway. In this case, the gateway is an Office Communications Server.

DIRECT FROM THE SOURCE

Multiple Language Support

Geoff Winslow
Principal Technology Specialist, Unified Communications

If you support international users in your company, perhaps you're wondering if Exchange UM can support multiple languages without having to deploy additional servers. For example, Litware, Inc Corporation has a primary datacenter located in Los Angeles that houses its Exchange and Office Communications Server servers. They also have an office in Mexico City, and they want to use their existing infrastructure to support those users.

You can manage languages on Exchange UM Servers by using the Exchange Management Console or the Exchange Management Shell administrative interfaces. However, to make a language available in the list on the Settings tab of a UM Dial Plan, you must first install the appropriate UM language pack on the Exchange UM Server by using the following command:

```
Setup.com /AddUmLanguagePack:<UmLanguagePackName> /s:<LanguagePackFile>
```

<UmLanguagePackName> is the name of the UM Language pack. For example, es-US for Latin American Spanish. For a complete list of Unified Messaging language packs, see the Exchange Server 2007 SP1 help file or the link, http://technet.microsoft.com/en-us/library/aa995964.aspx.

<LanguagePackFile> refers to the location where the language pack is located.

After installing the appropriate UM language pack, view the list of UM language packs by viewing properties on the UM Settings tab for the Exchange UM Server.

Once a new language pack is installed, a Dial Plan can be configured on the Exchange UM Server so that users retrieving their messages from the Mexico City office will hear their prompts in Latin American Spanish, and the US-English users will continue to hear their prompts in English (see Figure 12-8). Another benefit is that now when the Exchange UM Server is reading the user's e-mail to them, the messages will be read back in the correct language, in this case, Latin American Spanish for users in the Mexico City office.

Further details about how to create a UM Dial Plan can be found at *http://go.microsoft.com/fwlink/?LinkID=133710.*

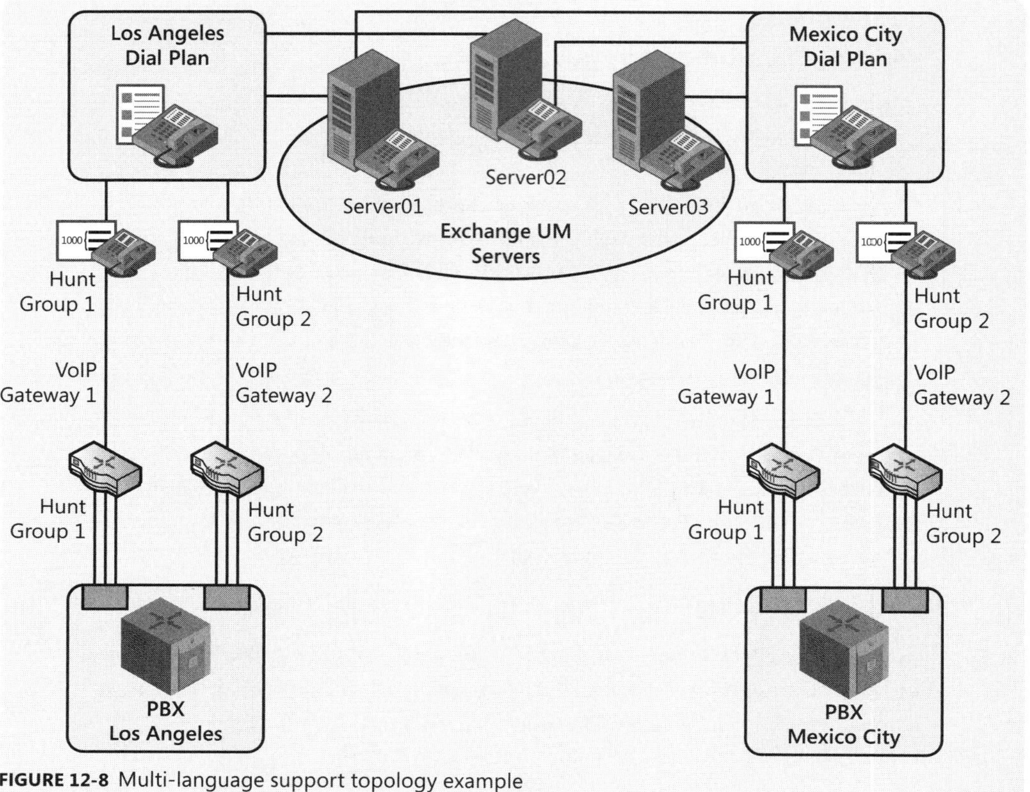

FIGURE 12-8 Multi-language support topology example

To support Exchange UM's subscriber access and Auto-Attendant features, Office Communications Server must be able to route those phone numbers to the correct destination. These features require storing routing information that maps the subscriber access or Auto-Attendant phone number to a SIP URI and then into an unconditional forwarding address so that Office Communications Server knows how to route the call to the correct Exchange UM Server. This mapping information is stored in contact objects in Active Directory that are specially marked based on the *msRTCSIP-SourceObjectType* attribute. The tool, OcsUMutil.exe (described in step 8), automates the process of creating contact objects for each subscriber access and Auto-Attendant associated with a UM Dial Plan that is associated with an IP gateway that corresponds to an Office Communications Server.

The Exchange UM subscriber access feature offers the ability for users to access their mailboxes by using their subscriber access numbers and PINs to dial out from Exchange UM. This dial-out functionality uses Auto-Attendant and Play on Phone features. This functionality requires that Exchange UM Servers be configured with a location profile. When the Exchange UM Server dials out a phone number on behalf of the mailbox user, Office Communications Server must determine which normalization rules to use for normalizing the user-dialed phone number. These normalization rules are defined in a location profile normally assigned to an Office Communications Server. However, the Exchange Active Directory schema does not have any provision to assign a location profile to an Exchange UM Server or preferably a UM Dial Plan, which is more specific to the user calling from Exchange UM. The method for relating a mailbox user to a location profile is matching the name of the location profile and the name of the UM Dial Plan assigned to the user. Therefore, it's strongly recommended that you not rename the UM Dial Plan and corresponding location profile.

Figure 12-9 illustrates the logical relationship between Office Communications Server and Exchange UM Active Directory schema.

Although these two products are loosely coupled, one can expect Microsoft to better integrate Exchange UM Server and Office Communications Server in future releases.

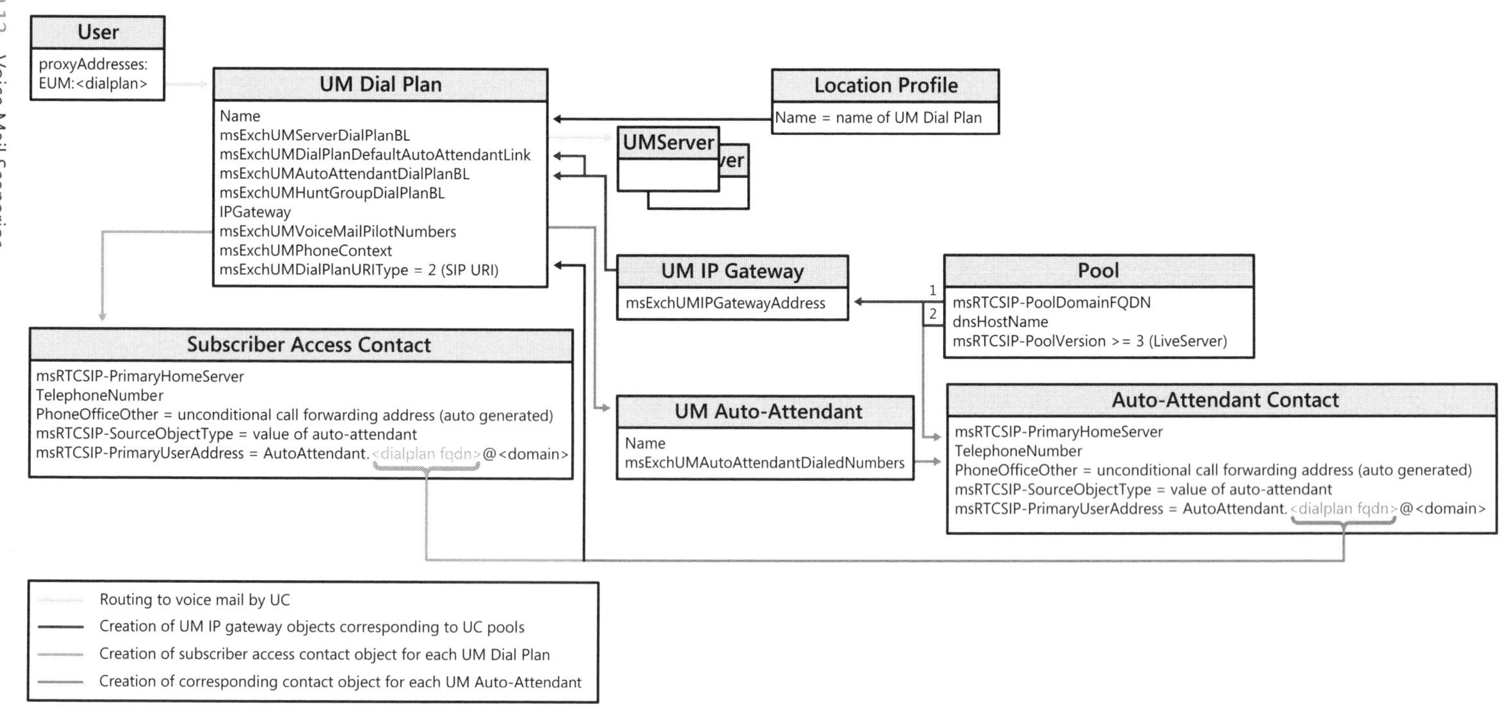

FIGURE 12-9 Active Directory dependency

Configuring Voice Mail

Before configuring Exchange UM Server as the voice mail system for Office Communications Server, Exchange Server and Office Communications Server must already be deployed in the enterprise. Users must be configured with an Exchange mailbox and be enabled for Enterprise Voice. This chapter covers the steps specific to configuring Exchange UM to integrate with Office Communications Server.

This integration requires the following steps.

1. Give Office Communications Server servers read-only permissions to the Exchange UM objects in Active Directory.
2. Create the corresponding Exchange UM IP gateway objects in Active Directory for every Standard Edition Server and Enterprise pool.
3. Assign the UM IP gateways to every Unified Communications (UC)–related UM Dial Plan.
4. Create special contact objects for every UM subscriber access and Auto-Attendant.
5. Map Office Communications Server location profiles with Exchange UM Dial Plans.

Configuring Exchange Unified Messaging

To configure Exchange UM Server as the voice mail system for Office Communications, the following steps must be performed.

1. Configuring the Exchange UM Servers
2. Creating a UM Dial Plan for every location profile
3. Configuring the subscriber access number
4. Running the Microsoft Windows PowerShell tool ExchUCUtil.ps1
5. Creating a UM Auto-Attendant
6. Configuring users for Exchange UM

Step 1: Configuring Exchange UM Servers

Exchange UM Servers must be configured with a server certificate issued by a certificate authority (CA) trusted by the Office Communications Server servers. If the Office Communications Server servers' certificates were issued by an internal Certificate Server, then the Exchange UM Server certificate must be issued by the same CA. The certificate's subject name must match the Exchange UM Server's fully qualified domain name (FQDN). Install this certificate in the Local Computer store. It is recommended to restart the Exchange UM Servers after installing the server certificate.

NOTE **Confirm the UM Server has loaded the correct certificate by examining event 1112 under the system event log.**

Next, the server certificate must be enabled for UM. On the Exchange UM Server, find the thumbprint of the certificate configured in step 1 by calling the Powershell command Get-ExchangeCertificate. This command will return the thumbprint of all server certificates configured on the server. Using the thumbprint returned, call the PowerShell command Enable-ExchangeCertificate to enable the UM service on the certificate:

```
Get-ExchangeCertificate
Enable-ExchangeCertificate -thumbprint <value> -services UM
```

Step 2: Creating a UM Dial Plan for Every Location Profile

For every Office Communications Server location profile defined, create a corresponding UM Dial Plan. The name of the Dial Plan must match the name of the corresponding location profile. A UM Dial Plan is a logical representation of a telephony Dial Plan. In the case of Office Communications Server, this telephony Dial Plan is equivalent to a location profile. Therefore, a UM Dial Plan is equivalent to a location profile. The number of digits specified in the UM Dial Plan is recommended to match the number of digits defined in Office Communications Server as the extension number of users enabled for Enterprise Voice. In large organizations, this extension is often five digits. A UM Dial Plan establishes a link from the telephone extension number of an Exchange 2007 recipient in Active Directory to a UM-enabled mailbox. Each time that you create a UM Dial Plan, a UM Mailbox policy is also created. The UM Mailbox policy is named "<*DialPlanName*> Default Policy".

To create the UM Dial Plan using Exchange Server PowerShell, use the following command:

```
new-umdialplan -name <Dial Plan name> -UriType "SipName" -VoipSecurity SIPSecured
-NumberOfDigitsInExtension <number of digits> [-AccessTelephoneNumbers <access number
in E.164 format>]
```

> ***NOTE*** **The *AccessTelephoneNumbers* field is optional and necessary only if creating a subscriber access number.**

To create the UM Dial Plan by using Exchange Server Management Console, refer to Figure 12-10 and perform the steps that follow it.

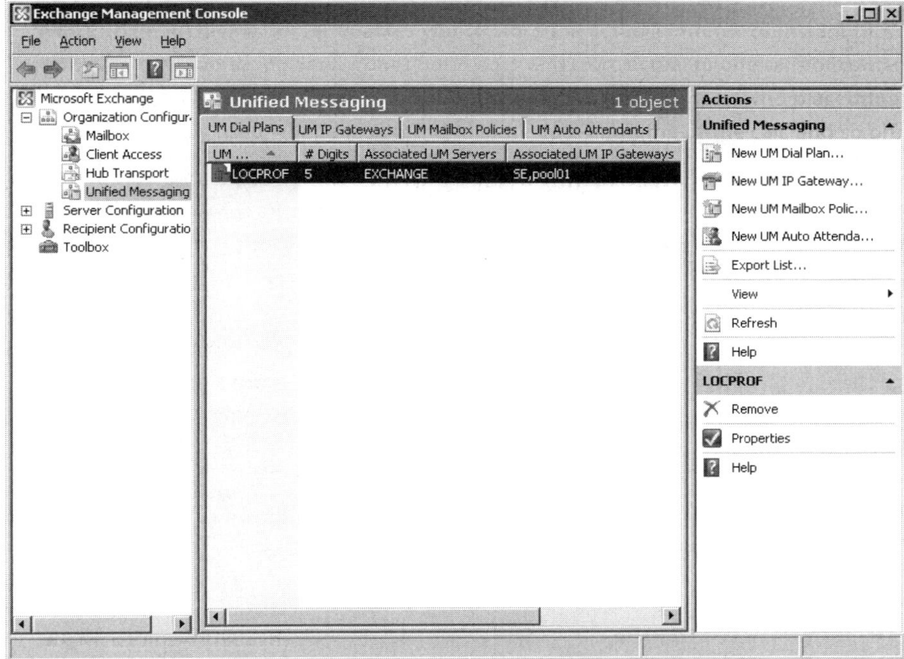

FIGURE 12-10 Creating the UM Dial Plan

1. Navigate to the UM Dial Plans tab in the Unified Messaging node under the Organization Configuration tree.
2. Click New UM Dial Plan in the action pane.
3. Specify a name for the UM Dial Plan that matches the name of a corresponding location profile created in Office Communications Server.
4. Select SIPName as the URI type.
5. Select SIPSecured as the VoIP security setting. If using Office Communicator Phone Edition, select Secured.
6. Complete the New UM Dial Plan Wizard.
7. Associate the Exchange UM Server with the Dial Plan created. To do this, use the following command:

```
$umsrv = get-umserver;
$dp = get-umdialplan -id <name of dial-plan created in step 1>;
$umsrv.DialPlans +=$dp.Identity;
$umsrv | set-umserver
```

To associate the Dial Plan with the UM Server by using the Exchange Server Management Console, refer to Figure 12-11 and perform the steps that follow it.

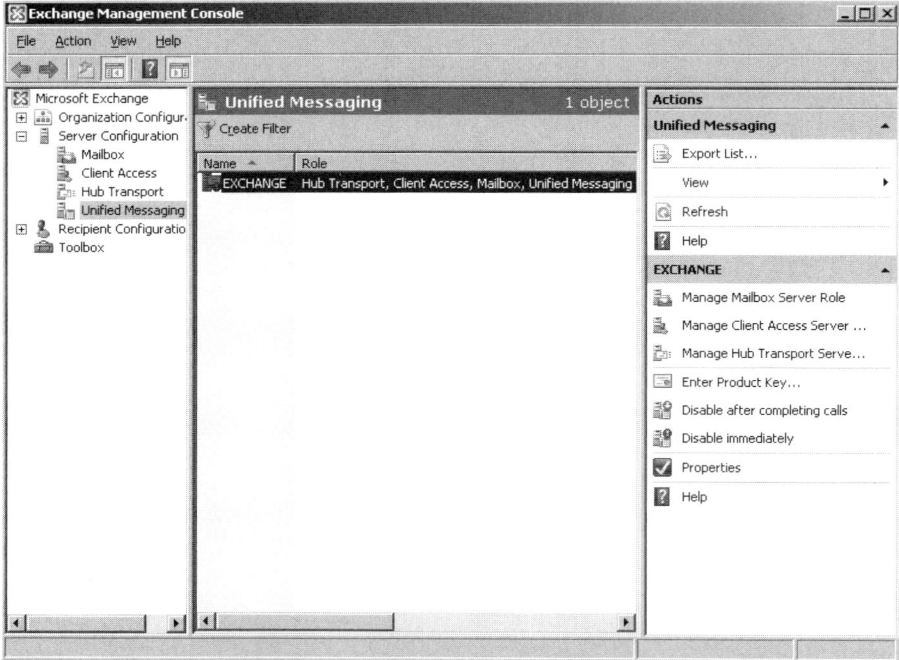

FIGURE 12-11 Associating the Dial Plan with the UM Server

1. Navigate to the Unified Messaging node under the Server Configuration tree.
2. Select the Exchange UM Server to associate.
3. Click Properties in the action pane.
4. Click the UM Settings tab.
5. Click the Add button in the Associated Dial Plans section.
6. Select the Dial Plan created.
7. Click OK.

Step 3: Configuring the Subscriber Access Number

The subscriber access number permits UM-enabled users to call the Exchange UM Server. After authenticating using their PIN, users can access their mailbox, calendar, and address book from any phone. To configure the subscriber access number:

1. Double-click the newly created UM Dial Plan to open the Dial Plan's properties.
2. Navigate to the Subscriber Access tab.
3. Modify the Welcome greeting and Informational announcement if desired.
4. Specify an access telephone number and click Add.
5. Click OK.

Step 4: Running the PowerShell Tool ExchUCUtil.ps1

Run ExchUCUtil.ps1 by using an administrative account with membership in RTCUniversal-ServerReadOnlyGroup and Exchange Organization Administrators. This tool grants the RTCComponentUniversalServices group read-only permissions to the Exchange UM objects in Active Directory. It also creates a corresponding UM IP gateway object in Active Directory that corresponds to every Office Communications Server and Enterprise pool front-end server deployed in the forest. It then associates each of these UM IP gateways with every UM Dial Plan created.

Run this command from Exchange UM Server PowerShell:

```
Cd %ProgramFiles%\Microsoft\Exchange Server\Scripts

exchUCUtil.ps1
exchUCUtil.ps1 -verify (to verify configuration)
```

Step 5: Creating a UM Auto-Attendant

If you plan to provide a company main phone number that external users can call, then you'll want to create a UM Auto-Attendant for the UM Dial Plan created. If you choose not to create a UM Auto-Attendant, skip this step. Make sure to specify the Auto-Attendant's phone number in E.164 format recognized by Office Communications Server; otherwise, Office Communications Server will not be able to properly route it.

To create a UM Auto-Attendant by using Exchange Server PowerShell, use the following command:

```
New-umautoattendant -name <auto attendant name> -umdialplan < Dial Plan name (step 2)>
-PilotIdentifierList <auto attendant phone number in E.164 format> -SpeechEnabled
$true -Status Enabled
```

To create a UM Auto-Attendant by using the Exchange Server Management Console, refer to Figure 12-12 and perform the steps that follow it.

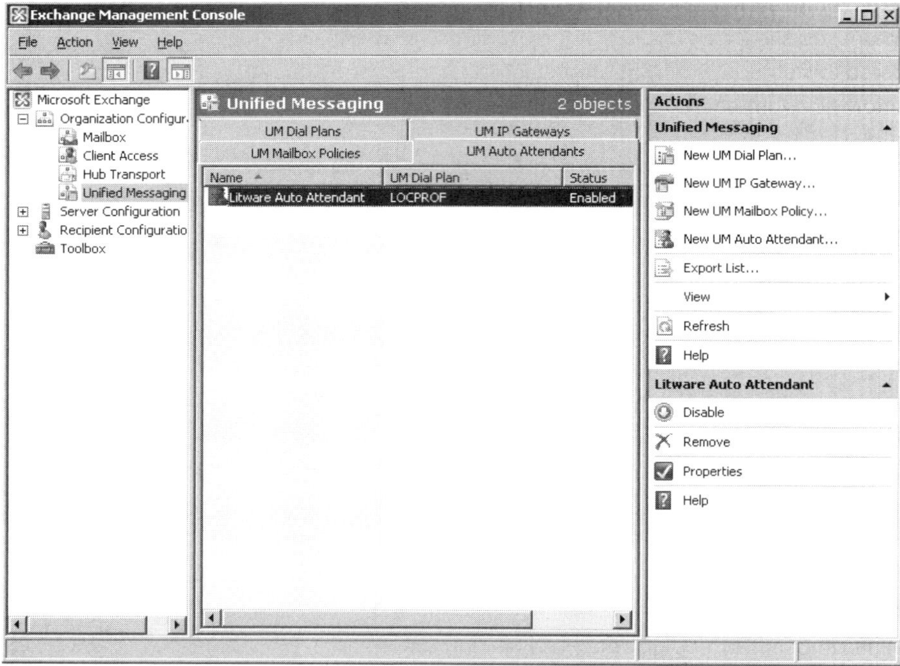

FIGURE 12-12 Creating an Auto-Attendant in the Exchange Server Management Console

1. Navigate to the UM Auto Attendant tab in the Unified Messaging node under the Organization Configuration tree.
2. Click New UM Auto Attendant in the action pane.
3. Specify a name for the Auto-Attendant.
4. Click Browse to select the UM Dial Plan created.
5. Specify an extension number in E-164 format.
6. Check Create Auto Attendant As Enabled.
7. Check Create Auto Attendant As Speech-Enabled.
8. Complete the New UM Auto Attendant Wizard.

Step 6: Configuring Users for Exchange UM

Enable users for UM. By default, users enabled with an Exchange mailbox are not enabled for UM.

To enable a user for UM by using Exchange Server PowerShell, use the following command:

```
enable-ummailbox -identity <user alias> -ummailboxpolicy <name of the mailbox policy
for UM Dial Plan (step 2)> -Extensions <extension> -SIPResourceIdentifier "<user SIP
URI>" -PIN <user pin>
```

To enable a user for UM by using the Exchange Server Management Console, refer to Figure 12-13 and perform the steps that follow it.

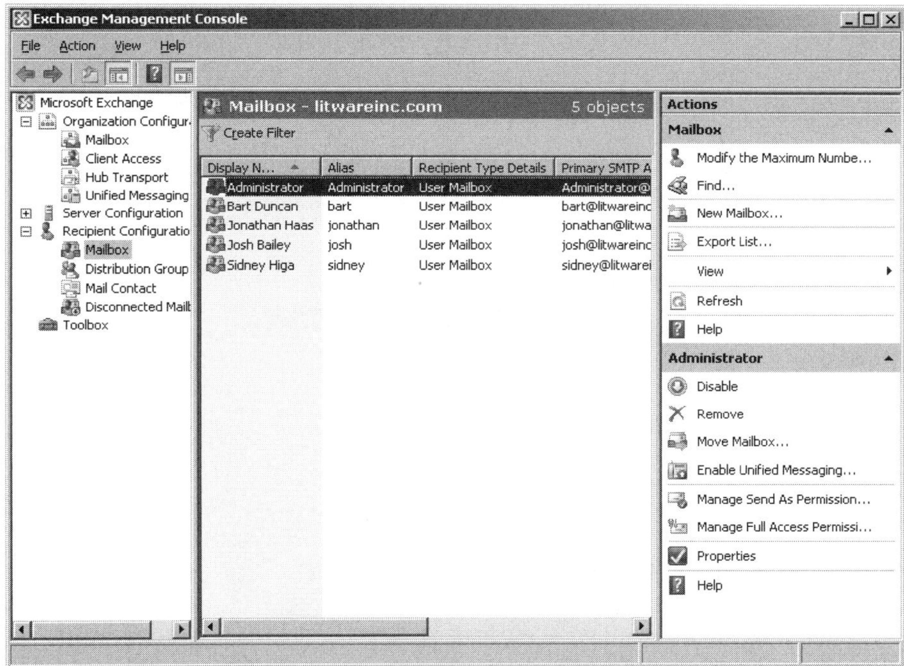

FIGURE 12-13 Enabling a user for UM by using the Exchange Server Management Console

1. Navigate to the Mailbox node under the Recipient Configuration tree.
2. Select the user to enable for UM.
3. Click Enable Unified Messaging in the action pane.
4. Select the UM Mailbox policy associated with the UM Dial Plan created.
5. Verify that the correct SIP URI for the user is specified in the *SIP Resource Identifier* field.
6. Complete the Enable Unified Messaging Wizard.

Configuring Office Communications Server

To configure Office Communications Server as the VoIP gateway for Exchange UM Server, run the tool, OcsUMutil.exe. This Exchange UM Integration Utility as shown in Figure 12-14 provides a graphical user interface (GUI) to create contact objects in Active Directory for every Auto-Attendant and subscriber access associated with the UM Dial Plan created. If the UM Dial Plan defines a pilot number, a subscriber access contact object must be created in Active Directory. The contact object makes it possible for Office Communications Server to route the phone number. This tool also verifies that there is a location profile name that matches the name of the UM Dial plan created.

```
%ProgramFiles%\Common Files\Microsoft Office Communications Server 2007 R2\Support\
ocsumutil.exe
```

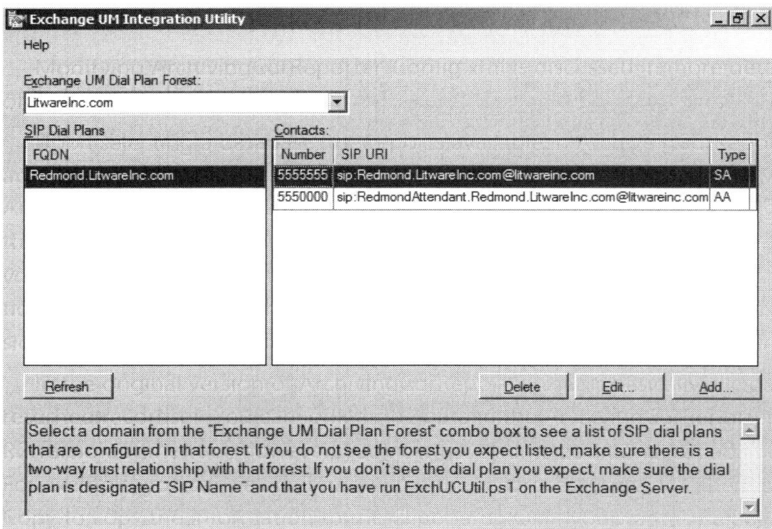

FIGURE 12-14 Exchange UM Integration Utility

1. Click Load Data to find all trusted Active Directory forests.
2. In the SIP Dial Plans list, select the UM Dial Plan created earlier in the chapter, and click Add.
3. Click Browse... to the right of the *Organizational Unit* field and then select an organizational unit (OU), or click Make New OU to create a new OU where the contact object will be created. Click OK when you finish.
4. In the *Name* field, either accept the default Dial Plan name or type a new user-friendly name for the contact object to create. For example, if you are creating a subscriber access contact object, you might simply name it Subscriber Access.

5. In the *SIP Address* field, specify a new SIP address or leave the default. It must begin with SIP.
6. Select the Enterprise pool or Standard Edition Server to home the contact object. Preferably, you should select the same pool where users enabled for Enterprise Voice and Exchange UM are also homed in.
7. In the *Phone Number* field, select the radio option, "use this pilot number from Exchange UM".
8. In the *Contact Type* field, select the contact type (Subscriber Access or Auto-Attendant) to create and click OK.
9. Repeat steps 1–9 for additional contact objects you want to create. You should create at least one contact object for each Auto-Attendant and each subscriber access number.
10. Confirm you can access your voice mail by selecting Call Voice Mail, as shown in the section titled "Overview of Voice Mail Scenarios" earlier in this chapter.

Summary

Users enabled for Enterprise Voice and UM can experience the full measure of Microsoft's UC solution by integrating Office Communications Server and Exchange UM Server. Users can retrieve voice mails and view call logs as well as missed calls directly from Outlook 2007 in the same way they read their e-mails. This gives information workers an integrated and powerful experience.

To integrate the two systems requires deploying the server role Exchange UM, which is available in Exchange Server 2007 SP1. This server role serves as the voice mail solution for Office Communications Server, and Office Communications Server serves as an IP voice gateway to Exchange UM Server. Office Communications Server must also be configured for Enterprise Voice (VoIP). This integration is currently not seamless and requires a number of manual steps, which are detailed in this chapter.

Additional Resources

- TechNet Technical Library for Exchange Server 2007 Unified Messaging, found at *http://go.microsoft.com/fwlink/?LinkID=133711*
- TechNet Technical Library for Exchange UM Integration Utility (ocsumutil.exe), found at *http://go.microsoft.com/fwlink/?LinkID=133712*
- The article "Understanding Unified Messaging Dial Plans," found at *http://go.microsoft.com/fwlink/?LinkID=133713*

- White Paper: Unified Messaging Technical Overview, found at *http://go.microsoft.com/fwlink/?LinkID=133714*
- White Paper: Planning for Exchange 2007 Unified Messaging, Part 1, found at *http://go.microsoft.com/fwlink/?LinkID=133715*
- White Paper: Deploying Exchange 2007 Unified Messaging, Part 2, found at *http://go.microsoft.com/fwlink/?LinkID=133716*
- White Paper: Managing Exchange 2007 Unified Messaging, Part 3, found at *http://go.microsoft.com/fwlink/?LinkID=133717*
- White Paper: Educating Information Workers About Unified Messaging, Part 4, found at *http://go.microsoft.com/fwlink/?LinkID=133718*
- White Paper: Testing and Troubleshooting Unified Messaging, Part 5, found at *http://go.microsoft.com/fwlink/?LinkID=133719*
- White Paper: Unified Messaging Technical Reference, Part 6, found at *http://go.microsoft.com/fwlink/?LinkID=133720*

CHAPTER 13

Enterprise Voice Application Scenarios

What Is Enterprise Voice?

Enterprise Voice is another medium of communication, in addition to instant messaging (IM), e-mail, audio/video (A/V), or application sharing. Voice-based applications can be built using the Microsoft Office Communications Server Enterprise Voice features. Office Communications Server 2007 R2 provides the following Enterprise Voice applications: voice mail, Response Group Service, Conferencing Attendant, Conference Announcement Service, and Outside Voice Control. Each of these applications requires that Enterprise Voice be deployed in the organization.

This chapter covers the following Enterprise Voice applications in detail: Response Group Service and Conferencing Attendant.

Response Group Service provides similar functionality as a call center. Using Response Group Service, callers can be routed via a variety of methods to a group of agents. The routing leverages the presence information of agents to connect callers to the best available agent. Agents can answer calls directly from the familiarity of Office Communicator without requiring training to use a custom call center application although one is available if needed.

Conferencing Attendant enables callers dialing from the Public Switched Telephone Network (PSTN) to join the audio portion of a meeting created using Office Communications Server. Callers can be external users, such as customers and partners, or employees that currently do not have access to Office Communicator and Microsoft Office Live

Meeting client. Conferencing Attendant makes Office Communications Server 2007 R2 Enterprise Voice more accessible to all users, regardless from where they are dialing. Users dialing in from the PSTN can join meetings; however, they cannot schedule new meetings.

ON THE COMPANION MEDIA **Please see the companion CD for information related to topics in this book.**

Overview of Enterprise Voice Scenarios

This section covers the scenarios applicable to the Response Group Service and Conferencing Attendant. Response Group Service uses speech recognition to provide an interactive user experience to callers and Conferencing Attendant uses DMTF inputs from the user.

Response Group Service Scenarios

The Response Group Service uses different methods to locate an agent to answer the call—these are referred to as routing methods. If no agents are available to answer the call, the call is first queued and then directed to a different destination, such as a voice mail. The transfer to voice mail happens after a configurable time—defined by the queue timeout—has elapsed. While the call is in the queue, music-on-hold can be played back to the caller.

Typical usage scenarios for the Response Group Service are:

- Handling the mainline number for an enterprise or any of its offices. In this scenario, the Response Group Service plays a welcome message to the caller and then handles the call differently, depending on whether the call is placed during or outside of business hours.
- Handling of calls similar to a small call center, such as a help desk hotline or a departmental help number. In these situations, the caller wants to reach someone from a given department rather than a specific person.

Interactive Voice Response

The Response Group Service supports an IVR that can be used to play messages back to the caller, as well as accept input from the caller, to determine how the call should be routed.

The caller input can be accepted in Voice format, for which Voice Recognition is used, or in DTMF format. Messages can be played back to the caller in the form of text, which is read to the caller using text-to-speech technologies, or simply a WAV file that is played to the caller.

Call Queuing, Timeout, and Overflow Actions

The Response Group Service allows for queuing of calls until an agent is found who can answer the call. Typically, music-on-hold is played to the caller while the caller is waiting in the queue. To avoid queues filling up endlessly, the following two metrics are put in place, which when reached, result in an action being taken on the next call to be queued or on existing calls in the queue:

- **Queue timeout** This setting measures the amount of time a call has spent in a queue.
- **Queue overflow** This setting measures the number of calls that are allowed to be queued in a given queue.

The action can be to move the call into another queue ("overflow queue") or to route it to another destination, such as voice mail.

Note that the action can be taken on the first call in the queue or on the last call in the queue depending on the result that is desired. If, for example, you want to reduce the amount of time that callers have to wait in the queue and allow them to leave a message and be called back later, the action can be set to route the next call to the queue voice mail after the queue threshold is reached. If, on the other hand, the goal is to add capacity when the call volume is too high, the action can be set to place the first call to the queue (the one that is "oldest" in the queue) into another queue (an overflow queue).

Conferencing Attendant Scenarios

An external user calling from a PSTN phone can join an audio conference on Office Communications Server. The PSTN user dials a phone number associated with the Conferencing Attendant. When prompted, the user enters the conference ID and meeting pass code to get directly connected to the audio portion of the conference.

An organizer (who must be enabled for Office Communications and permitted to schedule meetings) typically schedules a conference using the Microsoft Conferencing Add-in for Microsoft Office Outlook and sends the conference information via email. To enable PSTN callers to attend the audio portion of a meeting, the organizer must allow participants to join the meeting by selecting "Use computer audio or dial in from any phone" option in the Conference Call Audio Options, as shown in Figure 13.1. The "Require a passcode to join the conference" check box, if selected, provides additional security by requiring a pass code to be entered in addition to the conference ID to join the meeting. Because there may be multiple geographic regions in the conference, the region selected needs to be the one to which most of the users in the conference are expected to belong, to give the most optimal experience to users.

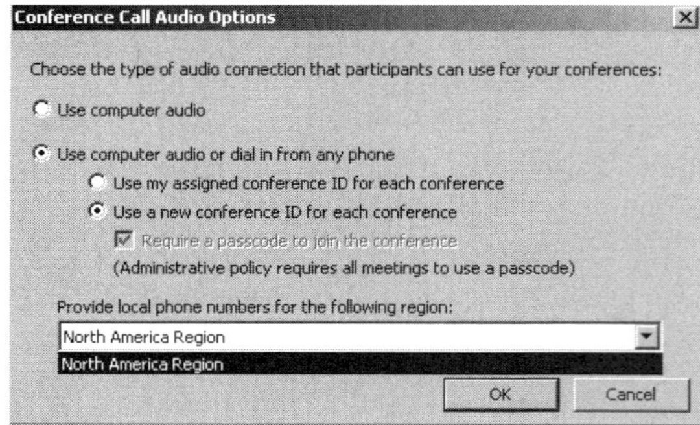

FIGURE 13-1 Conference Call Audio Options dialog box

To allow PSTN dial-in access to external callers, Invite Anyone must be selected as the access permissions level when creating the meeting, as shown in Figure 13-2. Otherwise, external callers will not be able to join the conference.

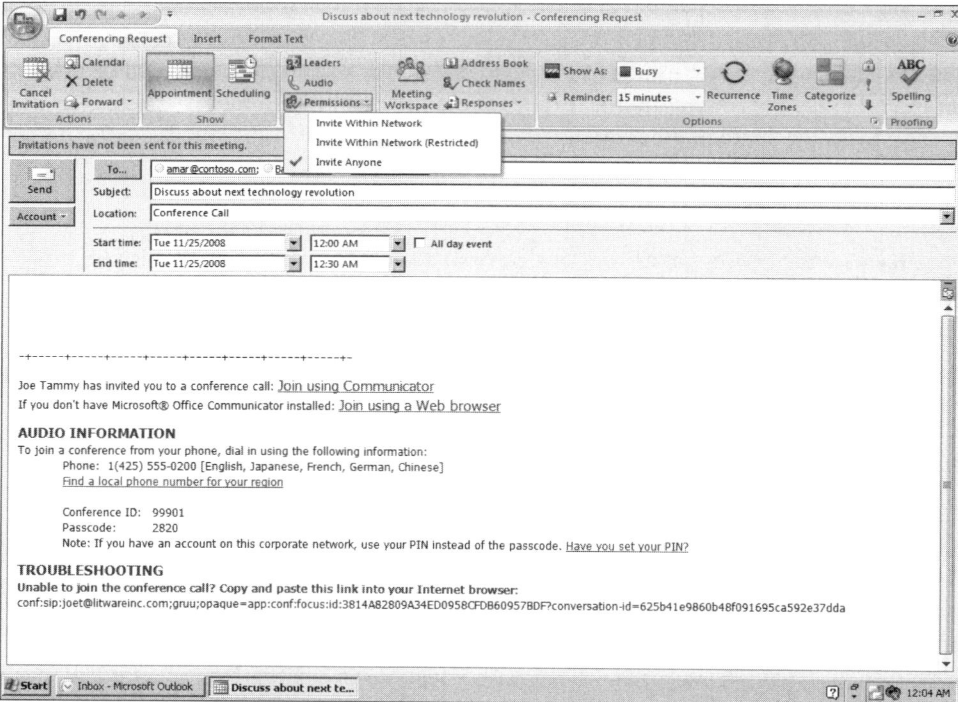

FIGURE 13-2 Creating a conferencing request

In Figure 13-2, the Audio Information section in the body of the conference request shows the details for how to join the conference. The phone numbers listed are associated with the Conferencing Attendant.

Notice the link labeled, Have you set your PIN? shown in Figure 13-2. To configure the Personal Corporate Pin, use the above link. Alternatively, open Office Communicator 2007 R2, and under Tools, select Dial-in Conferencing Settings, as shown in Figure 13-3. This will take the user to the same Web page where they can set their corporate pin number.

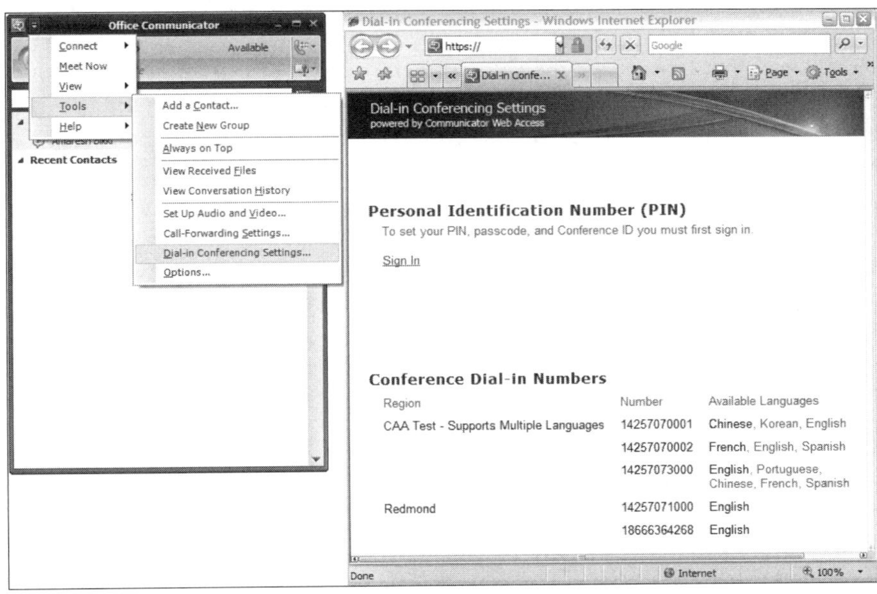

FIGURE 13-3 Configuring corporate pin

Examining the Technical Details Behind Enterprise Voice Scenarios

Common to all Enterprise Voice applications, these applications require the use of a special type of Active Directory contact object called an application contact. These application contact objects serve the purpose of providing routing information so that Office Communications Server knows how to route requests to a specific voice application. Because voice applications, similar to Enterprise Voice–enabled users, are associated with a Session Initiation Protocol (SIP) Uniform Resource Identifier (URI) and a phone number and behave as endpoints in Office Communications Server, they are routable by a phone number, as is a user.

Instead of using a user object, which is an NT principal account, to represent the application, a contact object is safer because a malicious user cannot use a contact object to fraudulently log on to Active Directory. Because contact objects do not have credentials associated with them, there is no need for password management either.

Office Communications Server 2007 R2 extends the contact object with new attributes. Among these new attributes, the attribute *msRTCSIP-ApplicationDestination* contains the distinguished name (DN) of the Enterprise Voice application listed in the Trusted Services list in Active Directory that the contact object represents. Similar to a user being logged on to Office Communications Server from a particular client, such as Office Communicator, this DN represents the endpoint from where the Enterprise Voice application is logged on. Figure 13-4 illustrates the routing logic of an Enterprise Voice application. The user calls the application's phone number, for example, an Auto-Attendant number. Office Communications Server, using the logic defined in Chapter 11, "VoIP Scenarios," normalizes the number and performs a reverse number lookup (RNL) to convert the phone number into its corresponding SIP URI. Office Communications Server determines the contact object's home server and routes the call to the appropriate server. When the request reaches the home server, it routes the call to the appropriate Enterprise Voice application. For Office Communications Server 2007 R2, Enterprise Voice applications must be running on the Standard Edition Server or Enterprise pool where the application's contact object is homed.

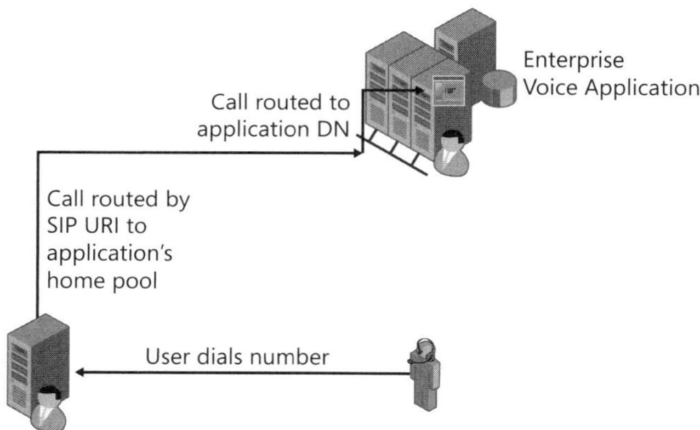

FIGURE 13-4 Enterprise Voice application routing

Response Group Service Architecture

While a Response Group can have agents that are homed on any pool in the enterprise, it is recommended to deploy the Response Group on the Office Communications Server pool that has the highest number of agents.

Overview of the Different Components on which the Response Group Service Is Built

The core Response Group Service is built on top of the following components, all of which run in the main service process, ocsappserverhost. (Note that the name of the process used by the other Office Communications Server applications is the same.)

- **Hosting component** Responsible for accepting incoming calls
- **Workflow Runtime component** Responsible for running the workflow attached to each Response Group and built on the Microsoft Windows workflow foundation
- **Match Making component** Responsible for the following tasks:
  - Keeping track of agents' presence and determining which agents are available to pick up the calls
  - Queuing the calls
  - Monitoring which agents are signed in to the system
- **Call Routing component** Responsible for routing the incoming call to one of the available agents

In addition to these four components, the Response Group Service has a Web Component that is used for:

- Enabling the agents to sign in or sign out of the Response Groups. This functionality is implemented as a tab for the Office Communicator client and also in the Agent Communications Panel for the Dynamics CRM 4.0 client.
- Offering the Response Group Deployment tool functionality and enabling administrators and Response Group managers to administer Response Groups in a Web interface.

The Response Group Service uses a database to store dynamic data used in call routing. This database, called acddyn, is installed on the SQL back-end server in the case of an Enterprise pool or on the local SQL Express in the case of a Standard Edition Server. In Enterprise Edition, this database offers high availability in case a front-end server goes down. Figure 13-5 shows the logical component architecture for the Response Group Service.

In addition, the Response Group Service is using RTCconfig as a database to store all its configuration settings. This is the same database Office Communications Server uses for its settings.

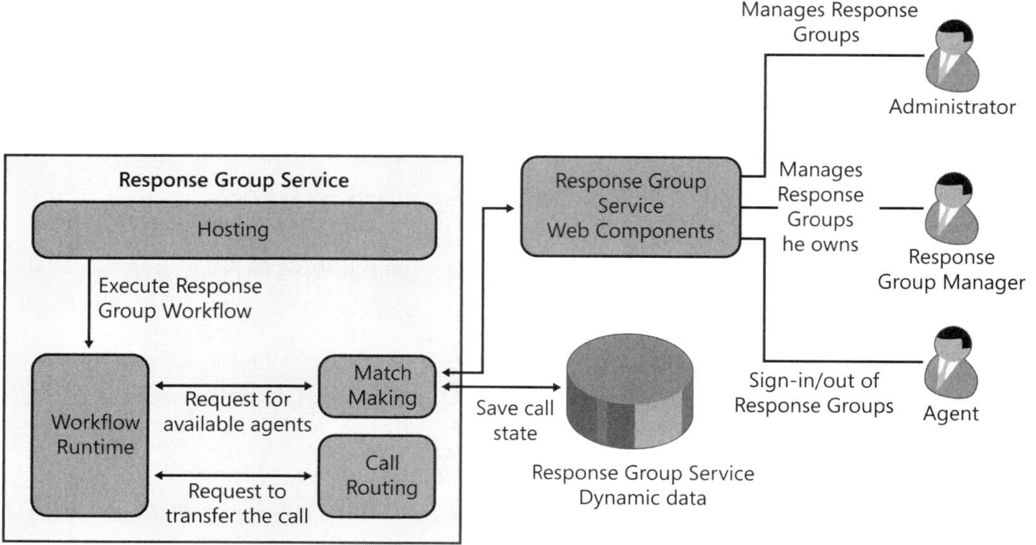

FIGURE 13-5 Summary view of the different elements that constitute a Response Group

Understanding the Hosting Component

The Hosting component is an entity that handles the interaction with the Office Communications Server Hosting Service and is able to receive audio calls from a client application. There is one instance of the Hosting component for each Response Group Service. The Hosting component is implemented as a SIP application agent that is addressable by using any of the Response Group URIs.

The Hosting component is responsible for the following tasks:

- Starting and initializing the Response Group Service components
- Accepting incoming calls
- Validating incoming calls
- Instantiating the specific workflow for each Response Group

When an incoming call is received, the Hosting component validates that the incoming call is an audio-only call. After this is done, the Hosting component fetches the settings for the Response Group associated with the called phone number or SIP URI from the RTCconfig database and instantiates the workflow.

Understanding the Workflow Runtime Component

The Workflow Runtime component provides the environment under which the Response Group's workflows are run. The Response Group Service Workflow Runtime component is built using Microsoft Workflow Runtime. The component creates a new workflow instance for each incoming call and controls its execution.

The workflow component is responsible for asking the caller questions, recording the caller's answers, and playing music-on-hold while the Response Group Service routes the call by using the Call Routing component.

The Response Group Service offers four predefined templates that the administrator can use when configuring a new workflow. Table 13-1 summarizes the capabilities of each of these templates. Two of the Response Group templates are for hunt groups and two others are for interactive templates, such as templates that use questions and answers.

TABLE 13-1 Capabilities Offered in Four Supported Response Group Templates

	TEMPLATE NAME			
CAPABILITIES	**BASIC HUNT GROUP**	**ENHANCED HUNT GROUP**	**ONE-LEVEL INTERACTIVE TEMPLATE**	**TWO-LEVEL INTERACTIVE TEMPLATE**
Activation of the Response Group and contact object selection	Yes	Yes	Yes	Yes
Language selection	Yes*	Yes	Yes	Yes
Welcome message	No	Yes	Yes	Yes
Availability and holiday configuration	No	Yes	Yes	Yes
Question and answers	No	No	Yes	Yes
Assignment of Response Group managers	Yes	Yes	No	No

**This is in the user interface (UI) for consistency reasons, but the language selection has no impact.*

Understanding the Match Making Component

The Match Making component is responsible for keeping track of available agents and calls in the queue and creating a match between them. This means finding an available agent for a call in the queue and finding a call to be handled when an agent becomes available. This component tracks the availability of agents, to which groups they are assigned, and the lists of callers in the different Response Group queues. The Match Making component subscribes to agents' presence to determine if an agent is available to answer a call. Information about calls processed by the Response Group Service—such as call ID, the serving queue, calling URI, and the workflow that should service the incoming call—is stored in the pool's back-end database.

There is a Match Making instance on each front-end server in an Enterprise pool deployment, each of which is connected to the pool back end. In each pool, only one Match Making instance can assume the role of finding the available agents for an incoming call. This instance is called the active instance. All other Match Making instances query the active Match Making instance to get the list of available agents. Figure 13-6 shows the interaction between the active Match Making instance and nonactive Match Making instances.

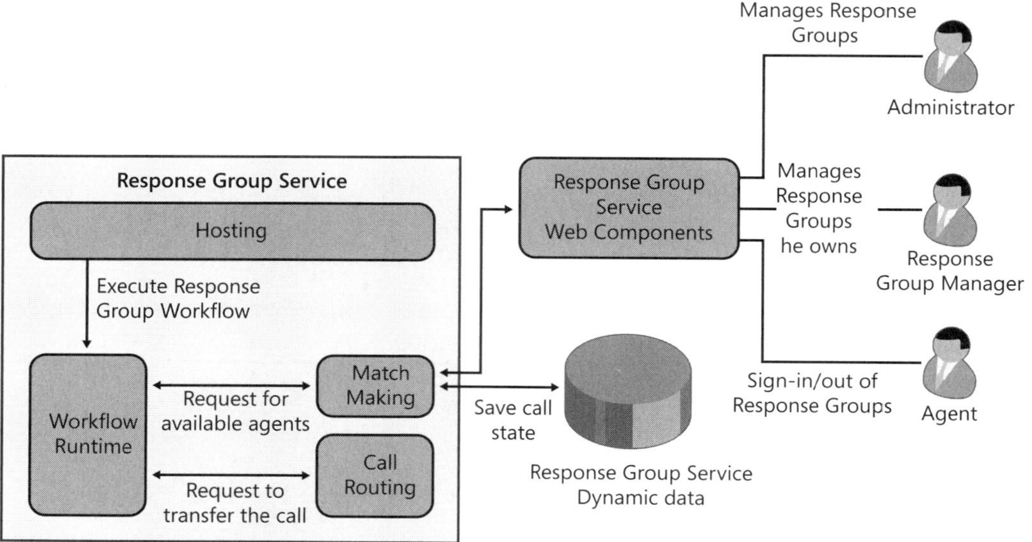

FIGURE 13-6 The Response Group Service components in Enterprise Edition

If the active Match Making instance fails, this active role is assumed by one of the other Match Making instances in the pool. To determine which Match Making instance becomes the new "active" instance, the Response Group Service uses a record in its database, acddyn. Each Match Making instance tries to update that record, writing its own fully qualified domain name (FQDN) and updating a timestamp. The instances first check the timestamp of the record. If the timestamp is not older than 10 seconds, the record specifies the FQDN of the active Match Making instance. If the record is expired, the other instances attempt to update the record with their own FQDN and update the timestamp of the record. The record is considered expired if the timestamp is older than 10 seconds. After an instance becomes active and has successfully published its own FQDN, it must periodically update the record to keep its role as an active instance. As it is being carried out, the workflow issues a request to the Match Making service that returns, based on the Response Group configuration and current user availability, one or more agents to whom the call can be routed.

The main role of the Match Making instance is to service requests coming from the workflow components on the different front ends in a pool. The Workflow component expects Match Making to return a set of one or more agents that are available to answer the incoming call. To build this result set, Match Making fetches first the queue settings from the RTCconfig database, such as:

- The list of groups of agents that serve the given queue
- The list of agents and their presence status

Based on this information, Match Making determines which agents are available to answer the incoming call. This list of available agents is returned to the Workflow component.

Understanding the Call Routing Component

The Call Routing component is the entity that actually performs the routing of calls from the Response Group to one or more agents. This component performs different types of routing, as explained in Table 13-2.

TABLE 13-2 Summary of Response Group Service Routing Methods

ROUTING METHOD	DEFINITION	WHEN TO USE IT
Serial routing	Agents in the group are called one after another in a predefined order determined by the administrator. Each call attempts to ring the first agent in the list if he is available, then the second in the list, and so on. Note that this routing method makes sense only when an administrator-created group used as the admin can define the ordered list. If a distribution list is used, the list is randomly ordered by the system.	When there is a clear list of people who should be receiving a call, starting first with the ideal, next with the second-best choice, and so on.
Parallel routing	All available agents are called at the same time for every incoming call. The first agent who accepts the call from the Response Group Service gets the call routed to her. All other agents get a notification telling them that the call has been accepted by another agent.	When all agents are equally qualified to respond: ■ When the call should be answered in the fastest manner possible. ■ When the call volume is not high.
Longest Idle	The agent who has been idle for the longest time receives the call in this configuration.	When calls should be equally distributed amongst all agents so that all agents receive approximately the same call volume. This method works well in higher-call-volume scenarios.
Round Robin	Calls are routed to all available agents in a round-robin manner.	When calls should be equally distributed amongst all agents such that all agents receive approximately the same call volume. The calls are distributed to the agents in a round-robin manner in the order the administrator defines.

Understanding the Call Flow

This section details a sample call flow in a serial routing example in which the Response Group is configured for serial routing to agent 1 and then agent 2. The following text describes the main steps in the scenario.

Step 1: Call to the Response Group To use the Response Group Service routing features, the caller must establish an audio session with a Response Group. This is done by placing an audio call from a client application to the Response Group SIP URI.

Step 2: Interactive Voice Response portion After the audio call is established between the caller and the Response Group Service, the caller goes through the IVR portion (note that this is only the case if it is not a hunt group; in a hunt group scenario, the logic proceeds directly with the next step).

Step 3: Request match After the caller has finished going through the IVR, the call is placed in a queue and the Workflow Runtime component requests the Match Making component for a target agent—or a set of target agents in a parallel routing scenario—it should route the call to. Note that if no agent is available, the call is placed on music-on-hold until an agent becomes available or until the queue timeout is reached.

Step 4: Alert agent After the Match Making component has returned the agent or set of agents, the Call Routing component calls that agent(s). This is a consultative call. The consultative call results in a system alert being displayed to the agent showing which Response Group Service the call is coming from and who the caller is. At that point, the agent has the choice to accept or not accept the consultative call. If the agent declines the consultative call, a new target agent is requested and the Call Routing component will make a new consultative call to that agent. After an agent accepts the consultative call, the Call Routing component attempts to transfer the call to the agent, as described in the next step.

Step 5: Transfer call from the caller to the agent After an agent accepts the consultative call from call routing, the agent is transferred to the caller. Upon completion of the transfer, the caller drops the connection with the Response Group Service, and the service disconnects the consultative call with the agent. If call routing had consulted several agents in parallel, the remaining consultative calls would be cancelled, and the agents would get information about who accepted the call.

Figure 13-7 shows the call flow for a declined routing attempt to an agent, followed by a successful transfer to another agent.

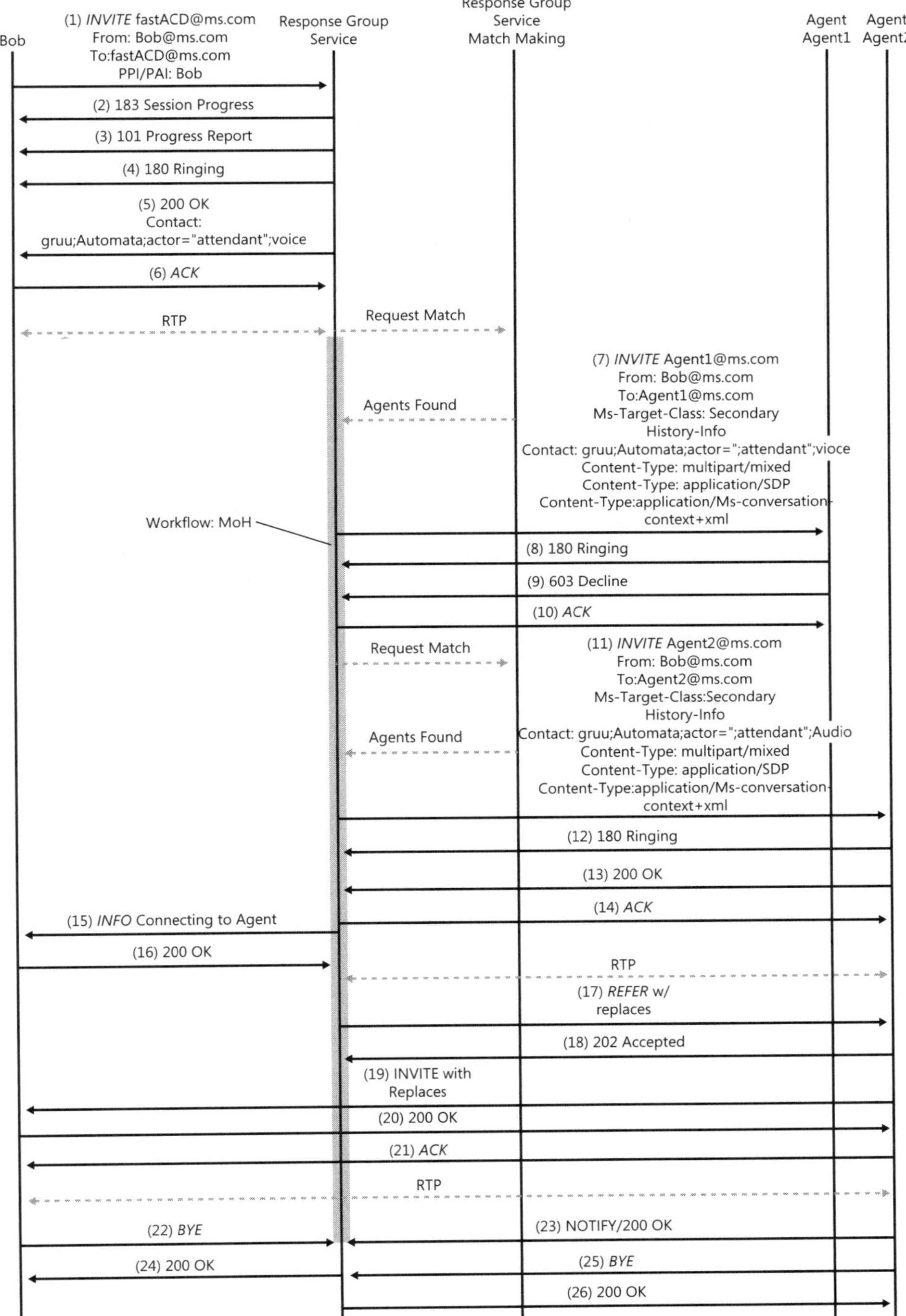

FIGURE 13-7 Sample call flow of a Response Group Service call

Conferencing Attendant Architecture

The Conferencing Attendant provides a simple service. It enables users dialing from the PSTN to join the audio portion of a conference. Consequently, this service is much simpler than the Response Group Service. The Conferencing Attendant distinguishes between two types of callers dialing in. One type of caller is an external user. The second type of caller is an internal user that is authenticated by Conferencing Attendant.

Understanding How External PSTN Callers Join the Conference

When calling the PSTN dial-in number of a conference, the call from the PSTN user is forwarded by the Mediation Server to the enterprise pool on which the Conferencing Attendant is homed. The enterprise pool then routes the call to the Conferencing Attendant that is associated with the phone number dialed. The Conferencing Attendant prompts the user to enter the conference ID provided in the meeting invite. It then sends the conference ID to the front-end server to resolve into the corresponding conference URI. This conference URI is the same URI as used by an Office Communicator user to join the conference by clicking the link in the meeting invite. The Conferencing Attendant joins the conference and monitors the roster for the arrival of other participants and leaders into the conference on behalf of the PSTN user. This call flow is illustrated in Figure 13-8.

The Conferencing Attendant does not allow PSTN participants to join the conference until the leader enters the conference. The leader may use any modality and is not required to use the audio modality. PSTN participants are played music while on hold until the leader enters the meeting. If the leader does not join the meeting within 15 minutes, of this PSTN user being on music-on-hold, the PSTN participant is disconnected from the call by the Conferencing Attendant.

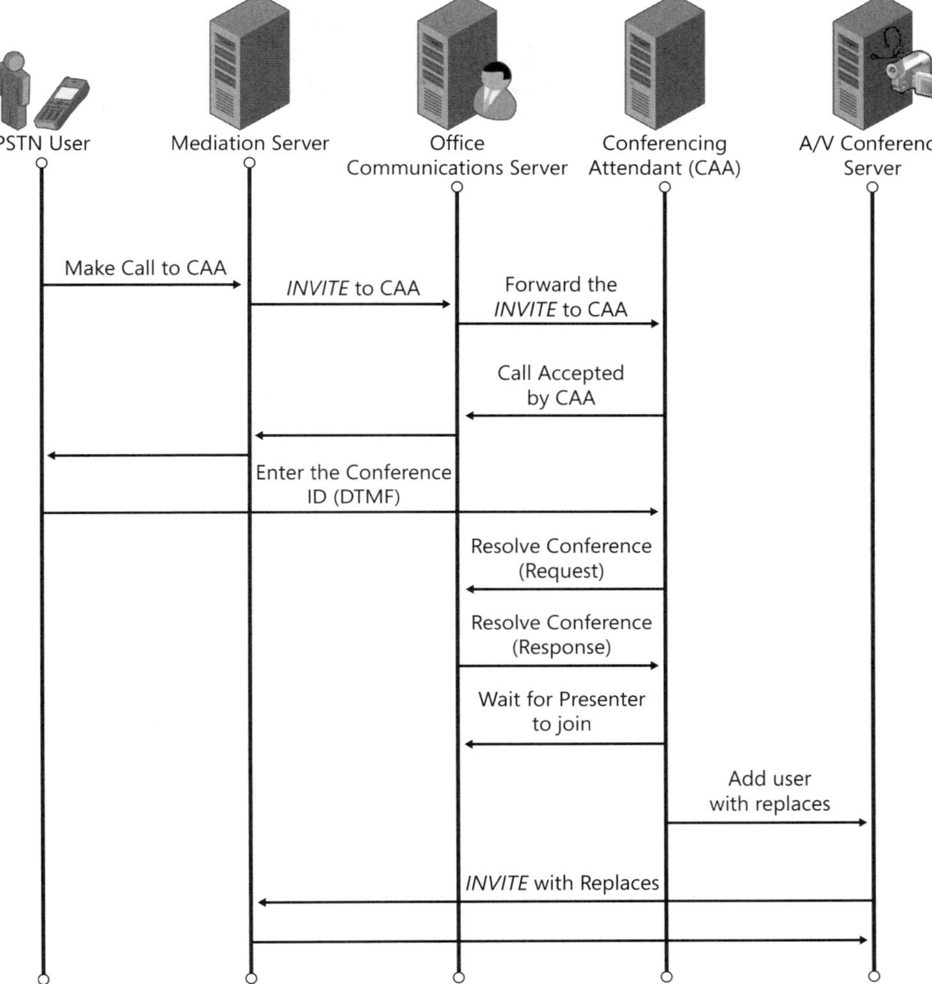

FIGURE 13-8 Conferencing Attendant call flow external callers

Understanding How Authenticated PSTN Callers Join the Conference

When an internal participant joins a conference using the PSTN dial-in number, the Conferencing Attendant can authenticate the user before joining them to the conference. After entering the DTMF tones for the conference ID, the user has the option to be authenticated by entering their work phone number (or extension) and personal identification number (PIN). The Conferencing Attendant verifies the user information and then transfers the user to the conference using their SIP URI identity. This call flow is shown in Figure 13-9.

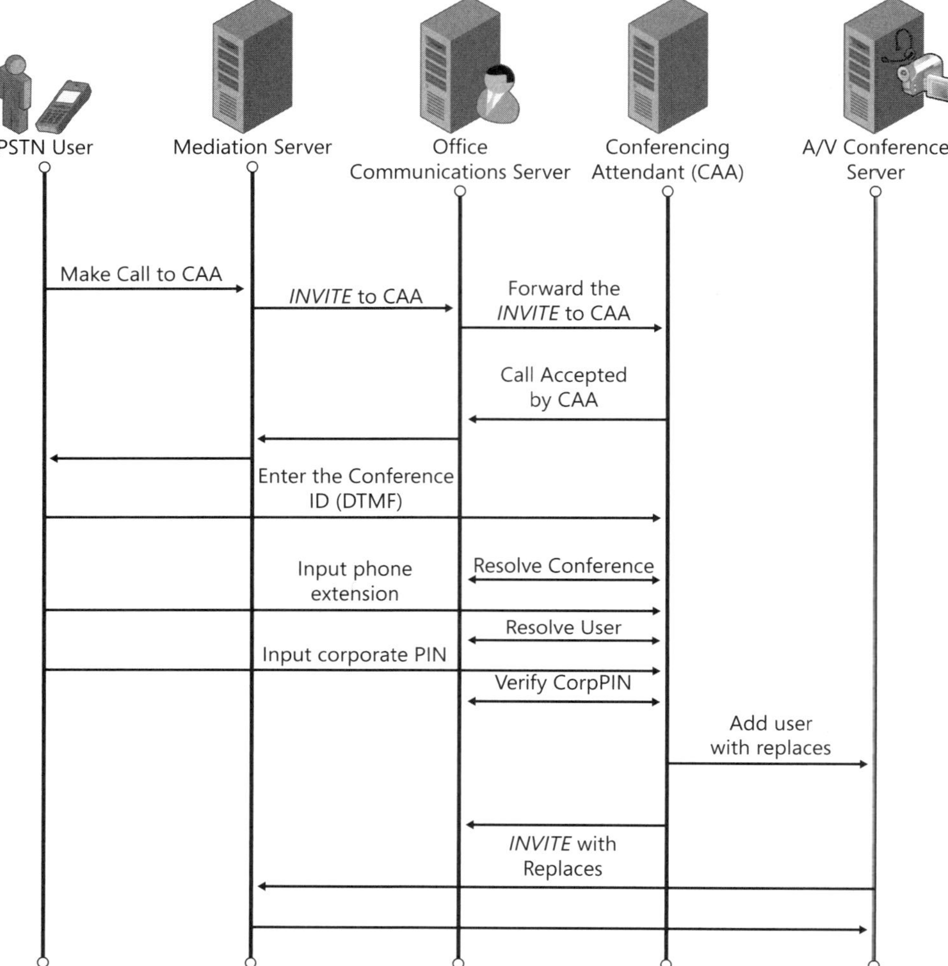

FIGURE 13-9 Conferencing Attendant call flow for internal callers

Configuring Enterprise Voice Applications

The Enterprise Voice applications that come as part of Office Communications Server 2007 R2 (Response Group Service, Conferencing Attendant, Conference Announcement Service, and Outside Voice Control) are by default deactivated. To active one or more of them, run the Application Activation Wizard from the Office Communications Server 2007 R2 Management Console in the Administrative Tools folder, as shown in Figure 13-10. Installing and running Enterprise Voice applications is available only on Standard Edition Servers and Enterprise pool front-end servers.

FIGURE 13-10 Activating Enterprise Voice Applications

It is best not to activate the same Enterprise Voice application on different front-end servers in the same Enterprise pool at the same time. Because of delays in Active Directory replication, allow sufficient time for replication to propagate to all Global Catalog Domain Controllers between installations of the application. Enterprise Voice applications are installed uniformly on all front-end servers in an Enterprise pool, so the application benefits from the high availability that an Enterprise pool provides.

Configuring the Response Group Service

Terminology

This section gives an overview of concepts used in the Response Group Service.

- **Response Group** This term is used for the name of the application, but also to represent a particular instance of a workflow that has been configured by an admin.
- **Workflow** This term is used to represent the interactive part of the Response Group, for instance, where a user may hear music-on-hold or may be prompted for input.
- **Contact objects** Contact objects are Active Directory objects that are used to identify and route to Response Groups. Each Response Group must correspond to one and only one unique contact object (that is, two Response Groups cannot share the same contact object).
- **Hunt group** This is a special case of a Response Group configuration where the system attempts to route calls to a set of defined agents without prior interaction with the caller. Different routing methods (or "hunting" methods) can be defined to control in which order the system rings the agents.

- **Queues** Queues are used to hold the calls in the order they were received until an agent is available to answer the call or until an action is taken on the call because a timeout has been reached. Each Response Group routes to at least one queue. The IVR can be represented as a tree with one starting point that branches out every time a caller is presented an option. Each "end node" of the IVR (that is, a place where the caller has finished selecting the options he wants in the IVR) in which a caller may reach a queue needs to be configured. For a simple hunt group, a single queue needs to be configured. For a Response Group with one question leading to two options, two queues need to be configured. Note that a queue can be referenced by different Response Groups and could even be referenced several times by one Response Group.
- **Agent groups** This defines the set of agents that have the same agent Participation policy and can be routed to by using the same routing method (such as serial routing or parallel routing). At least one agent group must be associated with each queue. An agent group can be used for any number of queues that may be linked to different Response Groups. There are two types of agents:
  - *Formal agents* These are agents who sign in to the Response Groups of which they are a member to receive calls from that Response Group. Note that Office Communicator and Agent Communications Panel for Dynamics CRM 4.0 are the only clients that support signing in to specific Response Groups by using the Agent tab.
  - *Informal agents* These are agents who do not need to sign in to a Response Group to receive a call from the Response Groups to which they are a member. The Response Group effectively considers them to always be signed in to the group and only looks at the presence state of the agent to know whether he is available to take a call.

Overview of the Management Model

The Response Group Service management consists of two parts:

- **Response Group Configuration tool** This is the Web interface used to manage the configuration settings related to the caller experience, such as the description for the Response Group in Office Communicator, the welcome message heard when calling the Response Group, the business hours, and the questions that are asked to the caller in case of an interactive template. The Office Communications Server administrator and the Response Group manager use this tool.
- **Response Group Administration snap-in** This is the Microsoft Management Console (MMC) interface used to manage the way the system handles the routing of calls. This is where various settings can be administered, such as the set of groups that handle a queue and their order, the group membership, the routing methods, the queue timeout, and overflow values. This tool is used only by the Office Communications Server administrator.

Figure 13-11 shows the elements that make up a Response Group.

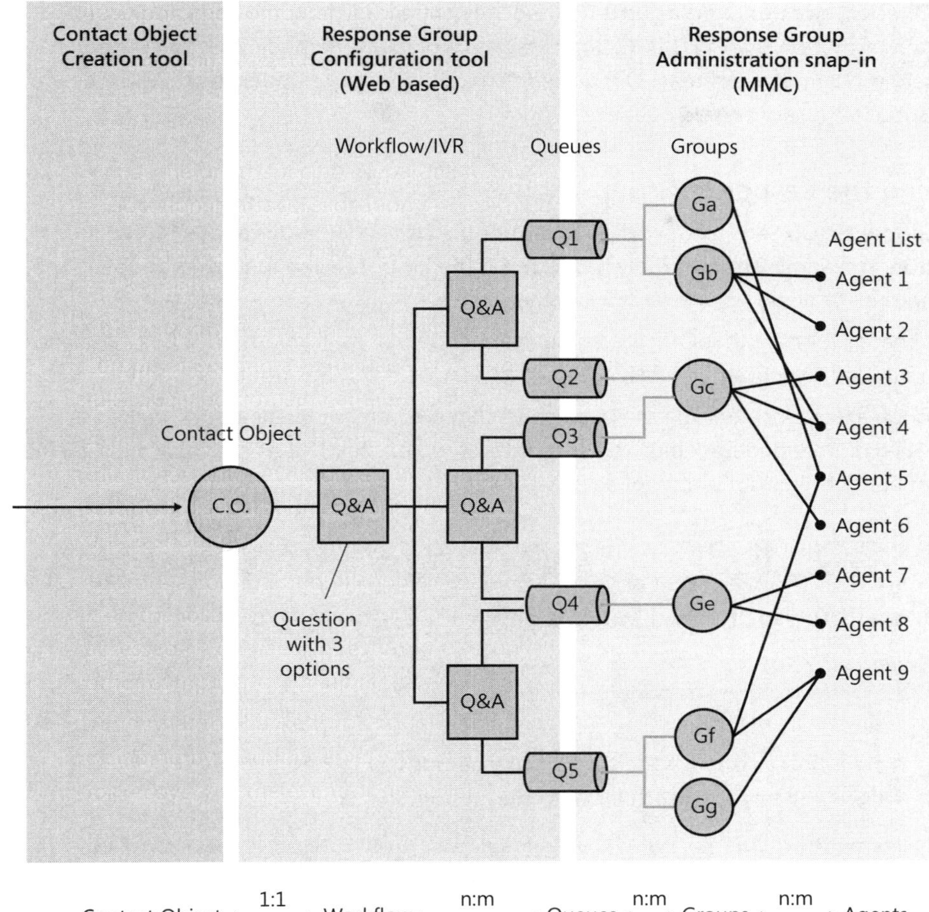

FIGURE 13-11 Summary view of the different elements that constitute a Response Group

Figure 13-11 is an example of a Response Group deployment that shows how the contact object, IVR, queue, agent group, and agents work together. This figure is composed of the following three parts that correspond to the administrative steps and tools required to create and configure a Response Group:

- **Contact object** This is configured using the Contact Object Creation tool.
- **Workflow or IVR** In the diagram, the example depicts a workflow in which the caller is asked a question. The answer must lead to one of three possible options. Each of the options prompts another question that leads to two other possible options. These final options lead the caller to a queue, Q1–Q4. This workflow is configured using the Response Group Configuration tool. Note that queues, as in the case of Q4, can be used for multiple options.

- **Queues, groups, and agents** These are configured using the Response Group Administration snap-in (MMC). In the example diagram, some queues have one group serving them (for example, Q4) and some have two groups (for example, Q1). The Group Gc is serving two queues.

Installing the Response Group Service

The Response Group Service is installed as part of the Office Communications Server 2007 R2 installation. The administrator simply has to select the Response Group Service option in the UI during the installation phase to activate the service.

Note that as for the other Office Communications Server applications, the LCS Command tool can be used to activate the Response Group Service, if this was not done during setup.

Although a Response Group can have agents that are homed on any pool in the enterprise, it is recommended to deploy the Response Group on the Office Communications Server pool that has the highest number of agents.

DIRECT FROM THE SOURCE

Installing Additional Languages for Response Groups

Roger Keller SDE II
Office Communications Server, Microsoft

Here is how to support additional languages for speech recognition in IVR workflows and text-to-speech for welcome messages.

1. **From the product CD, install the language pack on all Enterprise pool front-end servers running the Response Group Service.**
2. **Next, run the RgsLang.exe tool, which is available with the Office Communications Server 2007 R2 Resource Kit (in the \Rgs folder) on one front-end server of the Enterprise pool:**

   ```
   RgsLang.exe sync
   ```

   The tool will check which languages are installed and will update the Response Group Service's list of supported languages in Windows Management Instrumentation (WMI).
3. **Restart the Response Group Service on all front-end servers in the Enterprise pool.**

   At this point, the new language can be used for workflows in the Response Group Configuration tool.

Deploying a Response Group

The Response Group deployment is performed in four simple steps:

STEP 1: CREATE THE CONTACT OBJECTS TO BE USED FOR YOUR RESPONSE GROUPS

Contact objects are Active Directory objects that Office Communications Server uses to represent application endpoints, such as Response Groups. For each Response Group that needs to be created, a corresponding contact object needs to be created. This step can be completed using RGSCOT and requires domain admin privileges to be run.

STEP 2: DEFINE THE SET OF AGENTS, GROUPS, AND QUEUES THAT HANDLE CALLS RECEIVED BY THE RESPONSE GROUPS

In this step, the following actions must be taken:

- The Unified Communications (UC)–enabled Office Communications Server users that are to be considered for an agent role on a given Response Group pool must be added as agents to that pool. This is an operation that must be done once for each agent, regardless of the number of Response Groups for which he ends up acting as an agent.
- The agent groups that define a group of agents need to be created. When the group is defined, the routing method for that group should be selected.
- The queues that are to be used by each Response Group must be created.

STEP 3: SELECT AND CONFIGURE THE RESPONSE GROUP TEMPLATE FOR DEFINITION OF THE CALLER EXPERIENCE

In this step, you must select the template that you want to use for a given Response Group, which then defines what the caller experience is. As part of the template configuration, the administrator can select the queues to be used to handle the calls for the Response Group.

STEP 4: DEPLOY THE OFFICE COMMUNICATOR TAB FOR FORMAL AGENTS

This step is required only for agents who must be able to sign in and sign out of agent groups.

The following sections and Tables 13-3 through 13-5 summarize the deployment steps referenced in the preceding step 4.

STEP 1: CONTACT OBJECT CREATION

- **Tool used** Response Group Service Contact Object Tool (RGSCOT)
- **Permissions required** Domain Administrators

TABLE 13-3 Content Object Creation

TASK	MANDATORY OR OPTIONAL	SETTING	DESCRIPTION
Contact object creation	Mandatory	Contact object URI	This is the address of the Response Group, by which it can be reached.
	Mandatory	Display Name	This is the display name for the Response Group, as seen by the caller in the Office Communicator client.
	Mandatory	Home server or pool FQDN	This is the Office Communications Server server pool on which the Response Group is homed.

STEP 2: AGENTS, GROUPS, AND QUEUE CONFIGURATION

- **Tool used** Response Group Administration MMC snap-in
- **Permissions required** Office Communications Server administrator

TABLE 13-4 Agents, Groups, and Queue Configuration

TASK	MANDATORY OR OPTIONAL	SETTING	DESCRIPTION
Agent selection	Optional*	Agents	Before agents can be added to a group, they need to be defined as agents for the Response Group Service. To be able to be considered as agents, the users must be UC-enabled users.
Group creation and configuration	Mandatory	Group name	The name of the agent group created by the administrator. This name is used only for administrative purposes.
	Mandatory	Members	These are the agents that are members of the group.
	Optional**	Routing method	The method that will be used to route to the agents that are members of the group. Configuration is marked optional because this method has a default value of longest idle.
	Optional**	Agent type selection	This defines whether the agent is required to sign in to the Response Group to receive calls from it.

TABLE 13-4 Agents, Groups, and Queue Configuration

TASK	MANDATORY OR OPTIONAL	SETTING	DESCRIPTION
Queue creation	Mandatory	Name	The name of the queue. This name is used only for administrative purposes.
	Mandatory	Groups	This is the list of groups associated with the queue. At least one group should be associated with each queue. If multiple groups are configured, the first group is considered first for a new call, then the second group, and so on.

**Not necessary if all groups are defined using distribution lists.*

***These fields are marked optional because they have default values that the administrator has to modify only if she wants to use a different value.*

STEP 3: TEMPLATE SELECTION AND CONFIGURATION

- **Tool used** Response Group Configuration tool (Web interface). This page can be launched by right-clicking the Workflow node in the MMC and selecting New.
- **Permissions required** Office Communications Server admin.

TABLE 13-5 Template Selection and Configuration

TASK	MANDATORY OR OPTIONAL	SETTING	DESCRIPTION
Workflow template selection and configuration	Mandatory	Selection of the contact object	This is the contact object that is to be used for the workflow being configured.
Language selection	Mandatory	Language	Selection of the language used for the workflow. Note that the language matters only in cases where text to speech is being used.
Response Group activation	Optional	Active/Inactive	This setting indicates whether the given Response Group is active, that is, it can receive calls.
Description	Optional	Description	The description of the Response Group that is being displayed to the caller.

TABLE 13-5 Template Selection and Configuration

TASK	MANDATORY OR OPTIONAL	SETTING	DESCRIPTION
Business hours definition	Optional	Business hours and holidays	This is where the opening hours can be defined and the holiday sets can be selected. Note that the holiday sets themselves need to be defined in the MMC.
	Optional	Out of business hours message	This is the message that is played to the caller when the call is received outside of business hours
Queue and action	Mandatory	Queue	Selection of the queue to be used for calls made to the given Response Group. In scenarios where an interactive template was selected, one queue needs to be selected for each option that the caller can select.
	Mandatory	Timeout and action	This is the maximum amount of time a call should stay in the queue and the action that should be taken on the call after the timeout has been reached.
Response Group manager definition	Optional	Manager	This is the set of owners who can be assigned to the Response Group. The owners are the users who are enabled to configure certain settings using the Web interface. This is available only on simple and enhanced hunt group templates.

STEP 4: DEPLOYING THE AGENT TAB FOR FORMAL AGENTS

If in the previous steps, you defined some of your agent groups to be configured with an agent Participation policy of formal, you should deploy the Office Communicator Agent tab for these agents so that they can sign in and out of the agent groups to which they are a member.

DIRECT FROM THE SOURCE

Importing and Exporting Response Group Settings

Vassili Kaplan
SDE, Office Communications Server

It is recommended to test and fine-tune configurations for Response Groups in a test environment before applying them to the production environment. The Office Communications Server Resource Kit provides a tool to export settings from one environment to another. This tool must be run from one of the front-end servers on which the Response Group Service is running. This tool can export the application-specific settings of the Response Group Service to an XML file and generate a zip file containing all Response Group Service–related files (workflows, wave audio files, and so on).

To export, run the following command from the Office Communications Server Resource Kit directory:

```
ApplicationSettingsExport.exe /backup /pool:<pool name>  /app:Microsoft.
Rtc.Applications.Acd  /file:<filename of the main output file>  /
tempWorkspace:<local UNC path to temporary file area>
```

To import settings, change the first argument */backup to /restore* and remove the */pool* argument.

The tool does not update existing settings when importing. The only exceptions are the Response Group Service settings (MSFT_SIPRgsGroupOrderData and MSFT_SIPRgsPoolData WMI classes), which will update existing settings during import.

Configuring Conferencing Attendant

Configuring Conferencing Attendant is a simple process. It involves defining an application contact object that associates a phone number, SIP URI, and location profile to the Conferencing Attendant. This process can be summarized with the following steps.

1. Reserve a phone number.
2. Associate the phone number to the Conferencing Attendant.
3. Map the Conferencing Attendant to a location profile.

PSTN users who want to join a conference need to be able to dial in. One or more phone numbers, including toll-free numbers, can be associated with the Conferencing Attendant. Reserve the Direct Inward Dialing (DID) numbers from your service provider.

After the phone number is reserved, it must be associated to the Conferencing Attendant. To perform this action, follow these steps.

1. Run the Office Communications Server 2007 R2 Management Console under the Administrative Tools folder.
2. Right-click the forest node and select Conferencing Attendant properties.
3. Click the Access Phone Numbers tab. This lists all phone numbers associated with all Conferencing Attendant instances in the forest.
4. Click Add to add a new Conferencing Attendant phone number, as shown in Figure 13-12.

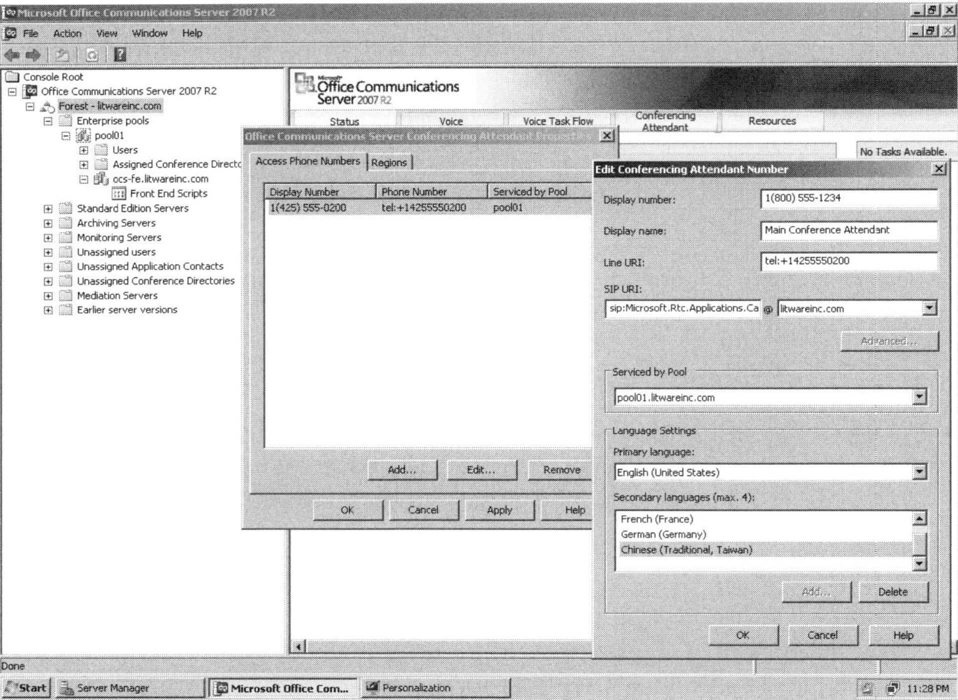

FIGURE 13-12 Adding a Conferencing Attendant number

The following settings for adding a new Conferencing Attendant number are described in detail:

- **Display number** The display number is included in the meeting request the organizer sends to all participants. Participants will dial this number. Make sure this number can be dialed from different countries and is easy to read.
- **Display Name** This name identifies the Conferencing Attendant. It will appear in the caller ID information when dialed by users.
- **LineURI** This represents the Tel URI of the Conferencing Attendant. This is the phone number reserved for the Conferencing Attendant in E164 format, as shown in step 1.

- **SIP URI** Similar to a user, the Conferencing Attendant must be configured with a SIP URI. When calling the Conferencing Attendant from Office Communicator, this SIP URI appears in the conversation history. It is recommended to keep it short and readable because users will see it.
- **Serviced by pool** Select the pool to which the Conferencing Attendant belongs.
- **Languages** A Conferencing Attendant must be associated with a primary language. Secondary languages are optional. The language chosen is used to interact with the caller when the user calls the Conferencing Attendant.

> ***NOTE*** **A Conferencing Attendant can be provisioned with multiple phone numbers.**

After the phone number is associated with the Conferencing Attendant, it must be mapped to a location profile, also referred to as a region.

To create a region, select a location profile and associate the phone number from step 1, as shown in Figure 13-13. Each region may have multiple phone numbers.

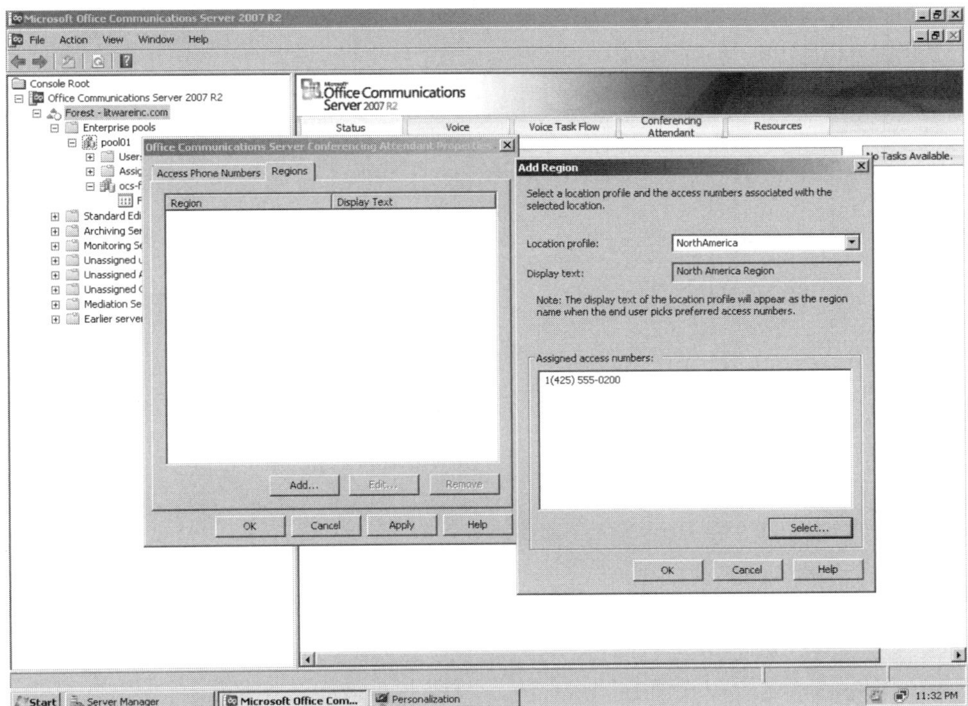

FIGURE 13-13 The Add Region dialog box

Summary

Office Communications Server 2007 R2 offers several Enterprise Voice applications that provide additional important functionality to support the telephony needs of an enterprise. This chapter covered in detail two of these Enterprise Voice applications: Response Group Service and Conferencing Attendant. These applications seamlessly integrate into the Office Communications Server Enterprise Voice infrastructure without additional hardware or software cost because they run on the same servers as the Standard Edition Servers and Enterprise pools.

Additional Resources

- Please see the companion CD for additional resources.

PART III

Planning and Deployment

CHAPTER 14

Planning Example

Planning for Microsoft Office Communications Server 2007 R2 is a necessary step in the life cycle of deploying the product. Planning must be done in advance of deployment to ensure that you meet all of the business requirements, capture all of the technical requirements, and define validation and testing to be performed in a proof-of-concept lab. A well-structured, complete design with the right subject matter experts (SMEs) supported by upper management can mean the difference between success, timely delivery, and being on or under budget versus an out-of-control project that is doomed to failure, cost overruns, and overall dissatisfaction from your customers—the user community.

The outcome of the planning sessions will be a defined set of requirements. These requirements will translate into features in Office Communications Server 2007 R2 that are mapped to your infrastructure.

A final note: Planning is the activity of taking the business requirements and translating them into meaningful technical specifications. The final outcome should convey how technical elements of an application or server will enhance business and user productivity.

Defining a Statement of Work

In our example, Litware, Inc. has requested that we put together a proposal for deploying Office Communications Server 2007 R2 within its organization. The initial task is to deliver a statement of work (SOW) to Litware. A SOW is a vital part of the planning process. A SOW is not the proposal to do the project but is an outcome of the approved proposal itself. The SOW sets the tone and direction for the project. It defines what will happen, puts a time line in place, and communicates what the project intends to accomplish. A SOW also puts into place a proposed team structure and the budgeted dollars for the project, and it usually includes deployment, hardware needs, and the potential for outside services to assist. The outside services might include, but would not be limited to, consultants, contractors, and other vendors to ensure success of the project.

The SOW will include the following items:

- Proposed time line, but not the project plan
- Business needs addressed
- Definition of internal and external people required and team(s) makeup
- What the project outcome will attain
- Estimated cost of the project
- Risk assessment

What should be clear from the preceding list is that most of the items in the SOW are not yet known. These are rough estimates based on findings from the proposal phase. Management needs to understand that until hard numbers can be obtained during the planning session, budgetary and people requirements may change. That being said, all projects have known constraints.

Gathering and Defining Business Requirements

Technical solutions are valuable only when they contribute to reducing expenses or if they contribute to increasing revenue. The cost of implementing such technology must be lower than the expected gain from the solution. Therefore, the SOW must demonstrate the potential gain from implementing a rollout of Office Communications Server 2007 R2 at Litware, Inc.

Terms such as *return on investment (ROI)* and *total cost of ownership* become important in this discussion. The simple fact is that if a business cannot justify the cost of a new installation or an upgrade to an existing solution, there is little to no incentive to spend capital monies to implement the solution.

Return on investment defines what the capital expenditure will be to implement the planned solution and how long it will take to realize the return of the expenditure.

Total cost of ownership defines what—on a recurring basis—the actual year-to-year cost of the solution will be. Few solutions are implemented that have only a one-time cost associated with them. Such things as the monthly cost of additional phone and data lines, Internet access fees, electricity, maintenance of hardware, and licensing costs of software—as well as the people to manage all of it—are recurring costs that affect the total cost of ownership.

The SOW should make budgetary assumptions and define business requirements as determined from upper management proposals. Using these in the initial phases of your planning is vital.

There are a number of ways that you can reconfirm the actual business requirements by talking with the stakeholders. An interview format is the most typical method because the information gathered should be heavily documented to support your ultimate cost and potential for return on investment. Being the business owners, the stakeholders are likely to be directors, general managers, or vice presidents of the departments or divisions that will actually use the technology you are planning. Their input is the most important information you will gather. These are the actual business requirements that will drive your planning process.

Litware, Inc. is a publishing firm. Its products are published materials of all types, from brochures to manuals for technical companies. They employ 145,000 people in three locations:

- Chicago, Illinois (100,000)
- Paris, France (40,000)
- Singapore (5,000)

Upper management has decided that they need to enhance the company's ability to work and collaborate in a more real-time manner. The key reasons for deploying Office Communications Server as defined by the stakeholders are the following:

- Reduce overall long-distance telephone costs, especially international, by providing alternative means for communicating with business partners and other Litware locations
- Reduce human latency, that is, the time it takes to collaborate to develop a product
- Optimize communication workflow with suppliers and provide alternate means of communicating with suppliers to reduce overall time to market
- Provide a means for upper management to hold conferences with employees in Litware's remote sites
- Reduce the overall travel costs of the sales force by providing a means for them to connect and work with customers remotely in an effective and easy way

DIRECT FROM THE SOURCE

Selecting Your Office Communications Server Deployment

Nick Smith
Consultant, U.S. Services

Selecting your Office Communications Server deployment is not as simple as just picking the deployment option that meets your organization's user population from the Office Communications Server Planning Guide. Office Communications Server deployment configurations are not limited to just the 5,000; 30,000; 50,000; or 125,000 increments. It is important to "do the math" for your environment to determine the right option for your needs.

I had a design session with a customer that believed it had to deploy an Enterprise Edition in expanded pool configuration because they were planning to host 50,000 users. As we explored their requirements, we identified that some of their initial user count included employees who did not have access to computers and users who worked different shifts. This decreased the expected user numbers to a maximum of 35,000–40,000 concurrent users. Furthermore, we identified that, although the customer was expecting what they defined as "heavy" conferencing, they did not expect to have more than 5 percent of their users participating in conferences at one time.

The Office Communications Server 2007 Planning Guide stated that a consolidated Enterprise pool with 4 front-end servers has a user capacity of 30,000. Using a rule of thumb that each consolidated front-end server can support 7,500 users, the user capacity can be increased by 15,000 users by adding 2 additional front-end servers. A consolidated pool can also support 5 percent of the user population for conferencing concurrency. Drawing a simple matrix on a whiteboard as shown in Table 14-1 illustrates the options between a consolidated and expanded Enterprise pool deployment.

TABLE 14-1 Consolidated Enterprise Pool vs. Expanded Configuration Comparison of User Capacity

	ENTERPRISE EDITION, CONSOLIDATED	ENTERPRISE EDITION, EXPANDED
Instant message user capacity	45,000	50,000
Simultaneous conferencing capacity	2,250	2,500
Total number of servers	8	12

TABLE 14-1 Consolidated Enterprise Pool vs. Expanded Configuration Comparison of User Capacity

	ENTERPRISE EDITION, CONSOLIDATED	ENTERPRISE EDITION, EXPANDED
SQL Servers	2 (active/passive cluster)	2 (active/passive cluster)
Front-end servers	6	4
Web Conferencing Servers	N/A	2
A/V Conferencing Servers	N/A	2
Web Component Servers	N/A	2

N/A = not applicable.

Given the preceding example, it's important to recall that this customer was designing for Office Communications Server 2007, and the numbers for users and supported connections have changed for Office Communications Server 2007 R2. Always refer to the documentation for what you are deploying because the recommendations and supported configurations can change from version to version as well as from service pack to service pack.

Assigning a Priority to Each Requirement

A list of requirements is interesting and valuable input to the planning process. It becomes much more valuable when the team is able to analyze each requirement and assign a meaningful priority to each. This priority system is driven by two factors:

1. Business urgency and need
2. Technical ability to implement in a timely way

Weighing both of these factors with input from your stakeholders and technical team, Litware will be able to determine which of the requirements are attainable in the first phase and which need to be planned for subsequent phases of the project. This prioritizing enables the team to set reasonable expectations for what will be delivered, when it will be delivered, and what will have to be postponed or eliminated due to time constraints, budgetary limits, or technical gaps.

In Table 14-2, each requirement is explained with mitigating factors and is assigned a priority from P0 to P2. P0 indicates that this is a must-have requirement for the initial release. P1 is a should-have requirement. P2 is a nice-to-have feature that can be dropped if time and funding were to impact its availability.

TABLE 14-2 Requirements and Priority Assignment with Justification

PRIORITY	REQUIREMENT	JUSTIFICATION NOTES
P0	Retire legacy Private Branch eXchanges (PBXs) in all locations	Requires much more planning than the current time line allows for; will roll out pilot in Chicago.
P0	Allow for availability and status of employees visible to others at a glance in often-used applications	Standard feature of integration with servers, client software, and user configuration.
P0	Make use of presence ability to manage communication type with users	Standard feature of server, client, and configuration and features of integration with Exchange/Microsoft Office Outlook.
P1	Presence enable in-house developed line of business applications	Developers must plan for either the dot version upgrade or for the next version. Expectation is 3–12 months for all line of business applications.
P0	Enable use of collaboration tools (whiteboard, desktop sharing, instant messaging [IM])	Feature enabled with conferencing and client software.
P0	Team meetings for small (2–50) to medium (50–100) attendees	As long as scale requirements are considered, this will be a native part of the conferencing features.
P1	Rich media for presentations and desktop sharing for meetings	Audio/video (A/V) conferencing can be installed and is available by default; requires more bandwidth and needs to be studied in test for realistic limits and expectations.
P2	Larger meetings should be an option; no actual number has been set for this requirement, but it would be used for company meetings and shareholder meetings	The solution has a theoretical upper limit of 250 attendees; the online service scales much higher, and this is the expected optional route.
P0	Voice over Internet Protocol (VoIP) inter-site and intra-site	Using voice-enabled devices, interoffice communication is attainable; as defined earlier, voice calls outside will pilot in Chicago due to complexity and costs associated.
P1	Advanced voice mail system allowing for access from many places and many devices	Attainable goal, assuming that the integration with Exchange is done and the Exchange Servers can be scaled to handle additional loads.
P0	Remote access for employees at home and on the road	Using external access controls (Edge Servers), enabled employees will able to access the system remotely.

TABLE 14-2 Requirements and Priority Assignment with Justification

PRIORITY	REQUIREMENT	JUSTIFICATION NOTES
P2	Cell phone access and enhancements	Full feature and functionality is potentially dependent on the PBX retirement. Access, such as IM, is available with proper software on phone.
P0	Administrative assistants able to answer calls for assigned staff and management	Addition of the Attendant Console will allow for this feature.
P1	Administrative assistants able to take messages and forward directly to voice mail	Addition of the Attendant Console from above would allow for this; dependent on the Exchange concerns mentioned.
P0	Employees able to manage own phone forwarding and location options	Options for forwarding out of the environment are limited to the Chicago pilot group; other features will be available inside the infrastructure.
P2	Ability to staff a call center by using in-house technology rather than outsourcing to a third party	The Response Server feature that is available can act as an automatic call distribution system; full function is dependent on PBX goals; would be tested and piloted in Chicago.
P0	IM, desktop sharing, and presentations with federated partners	This ability is attainable with perimeter Access Edge Servers and agreements/configuration with partners who use Microsoft Office Communications Server or Microsoft Office Live Communications Server 2005 Service Pack 1 (SP1).
P1	IM with customers not using Office Communications Server	Goal is attainable using the public IM connectivity feature with Access Edge Servers; the customer would have to use Yahoo!, AOL, or MSN instant messenger software; additional licensing and costs apply to this requirement.
P0	A/V conferences, presentations with partners and customers	This is an attainable goal, with the caveat that A/V is a much higher consumer of bandwidth and will need to be studied; presentations using Web conferencing are available with Edge Servers in perimeter.
P0	Ability to better communicate with suppliers to more easily collaborate and ease workflow bottlenecks	Federation goals cited previously meet most of the pre-existing conditions necessary to enable and use this feature; the supplier would need Office Communications Server to make best use of this requirement.

Mapping Business Requirements to Office Communications Server 2007 R2 Features

When planning to deploy Office Communications Server, the Litware team needs to define the technical elements of the project. This team should be composed of IT members with different expertise in the Litware environment. The planning team should be staffed appropriately to avoid gaps in the input to the planning process. As a team, members should have the following roles represented:

- **Server management and administration** Builds and deploys servers; manages and maintains in production. Responsible for defining the proper hardware to support a given functional requirement. Include Exchange and SQL management in this group, with appropriate representation.
- **Infrastructure and Internet network engineering** Responsible for the day-to-day management and maintenance of all networking and network infrastructure, including perimeter networks, firewall configuration and design, routers, and switches.
- **Desktop deployment** Responsible for the day-to-day maintenance and deployment of desktop machines, operating systems, and applications. Also responsible for the definition of desktop standards, including the computer hardware, peripheral hardware, and software standards.
- **Telephony** Responsible for managing, configuring, and maintaining the PBX, phone trunks, and data-carrying infrastructure provided from the phone company (for example, Integrated Services Digital Network [ISDN] lines). Also responsible for managing and deploying desktop phones and telephony devices for employees.
- **Training** Responsible for internal training of employees for the majority of needs. They develop their own training materials and conduct classes on business and light technical topics.
- **Information security** Responsible for the security of data at rest and in motion in your company. They define and set policies that govern what must be protected and how it must be protected. Areas of influence span from the desktop to servers and software, telephony infrastructure, and the physical security of data centers.

  Also, this team is likely to have input on these recommendations and requirements. Take each of these down and look at them in the same context as you would any other recommendation from a known technical expert. These requirements have been added to their feature mapping because of internal team requirements:

  - Strong authentication and encryption between servers. Strong encryption is required between servers and clients.
  - Internal public key infrastructure (PKI). Required for all certificates in the environment, public certificates must be used on external (public-facing) edges of all infrastructure and servers.

Taking the P0 and P1 requirements mentioned previously, the team can now discuss and decide on reasonable plans of action, potential blockers, cost issues, and upgrades needed. Mapping the requirements to features offered will produce results similar to those shown in Table 14-3.

TABLE 14-3 Mapping Requirements to Features of Office Communications Server 2007 R2

REQUIREMENT	HARDWARE AND COMPONENTS FOR OFFICE COMMUNICATIONS SERVER OR OFFICE COMMUNICATOR
Retire legacy PBXs in all locations	Mediation Server, media gateway (third party), direct Session Initiation Protocol (SIP), and IP-PBX
Allow for availability and status of employees visible to others at a glance in often-used applications	Front-end server, SQL Server (back-end server), Office Communicator client, presence-aware applications (for example, Office Outlook, Microsoft Office SharePoint)
Make use of presence ability to manage communication type with users	Front-end server, SQL Server (back-end server), Office Communicator client, Exchange for calendar features, Outlook client, or other presence-aware applications
Presence enable in-house developed line of business applications	Office Communications Server Software Development Kit (SDK), test environment
Enable use of collaboration tools (desktop sharing, IM)	Front-end server, SQL Server (back-end server), Office Communicator client, conferencing component
Team meetings for small (2–50) to medium (50–100) attendees	Front-end server, SQL Server (back-end server), Office Communicator client, A/V component
Rich media for presentations and desktop sharing for meetings	Front-end server, SQL Server (back-end server), Office Communicator client, conferencing component (potential for Application Sharing Server component)
VoIP inter-site and intra-site	Front-end server, SQL Server (back-end server), Office Communicator client
Advanced voice mail system allowing for access from many places and many devices	Front-end server, SQL Server (back-end server), Office Communicator client, Exchange Unified Messaging (UM), plus dependencies on PBX pilot mentioned for external access
Remote access for employees at home and on the road	Front-end server, SQL Server (back-end server), Office Communicator client, Edge Server(s) in perimeter (potential discussion topic: Communicator Web Access Server(s) in Phase II), reverse proxy

TABLE 14-3 Mapping Requirements to Features of Office Communications Server 2007 R2

REQUIREMENT	HARDWARE AND COMPONENTS FOR OFFICE COMMUNICATIONS SERVER OR OFFICE COMMUNICATOR
Administrative assistants able to answer calls for assigned staff and management	Front-end server, SQL Server (back-end server), Office Communicator client, Attendant Console
Administrative assistants able to take messages and forward directly to voice mail	Front-end server, SQL Server (back-end server), Office Communicator client, Attendant Console, Exchange integration
Employees able to manage own phone forwarding and location options	Front-end server, SQL Server (back-end server), Office Communicator, Communicator Phone Edition, Communicator Web Access, Communicator Mobile, and Communicator Mobile for Java
IM, desktop sharing, and presentations with federated partners	Front-end server, SQL Server (back-end server), Office Communicator client, perimeter-placed Edge Servers, reverse proxy, agreement and configuration for federation, partner must have Office Communications Server
IM with customers not using Office Communications Server	Front-end server, SQL Server (back-end server), Office Communicator client, perimeter-placed Edge Servers, reverse proxy, public IM connectivity enabled and configured, license for public IM connector
A/V conferences, presentations with partners and customers	Front-end server, SQL Server (back-end server), Office Communicator client, perimeter-placed Edge Servers, reverse proxy
Ability to better communicate with suppliers to more easily collaborate and ease workflow bottlenecks	Front-end server, SQL Server (back-end server), Office Communicator client, perimeter-placed Edge Servers, reverse proxy, conferencing components on Edge (potential for Application Sharing Server on front end), federation agreement, partner must have Office Communications Server
Requires strong authentication and encryption between servers; strong encryption is required between servers and clients	Office Communications Server and clients require either Mutual Transport Layer Security (MTLS) or Transport Layer Security (TLS) certificates; this requirement is met
Internal PKI is required for all certificates in the environment; public certificates must be used on external edge of Edge Servers and load balancers	Office Communications Server can use the certificates as required from the security team

Office Communications Server 2007 R2 Planning Tool

In an effort to assist customers, Microsoft has developed a Planning Tool for Office Communications Server 2007 R2 (see the section titled "Additional Resources" at the end of this chapter for the link to the Planning Tool). This tool uses metrics that Microsoft has tested and can support for a given number of criteria, such as the number of users in your environment mapped against features (IM, Web Conferencing, audio, video, telephony) you plan to enable. Litware will use the tool to map out the required number of servers per location to meet the requirements that have been set forth. This tool will estimate the requirements based on the input provided by Litware's administrator.

DIRECT FROM THE SOURCE

The Office Communications Server 2007 R2 Planning Tool

Stephanie Pierce
Sr. Technical Writer, Office Communications Server

The Planning Tool for Office Communications Server 2007 R2 is an application that provides you with prescriptive guidance to facilitate the planning and deployment of Office Communications Server 2007 R2 in your organization, including creation of topology diagrams, identification of hardware requirements for each component, and identification of the appropriate planning and deployment steps for your organization.

The Planning Tool includes a series of questions that are divided into three main sections:

- Features section   On the Welcome page of the wizard when you click Get Started, the wizard starts a series of questions that introduces the features for Office Communications Server 2007 R2 and enables you to specify which of these features your organization requires.
- Central sites section   This section enables you to customize the design of each of your central sites (sites in your organization where you plan to deploy Office Communications Server 2007 R2 locally) by selecting the features in Office Communications Server 2007 R2 that you want. Enter the site name, domain name, and the number of Unified Communications (UC)–enabled users in this section.
- Capacity planning section   The questions in this section focus on capacity planning and ask you a series of questions about how you anticipate the users at each site to use these features.

After you have finished designing each of your sites, the Planning Tool will dynamically draw out your global topology as well as the topology for each of your sites. The Planning Tool uses the Office Communications Server 2007 R2 user model, the number of users at each site, the features that are enabled, as well as the capacity information you provided to calculate the types and number of hardware components needed across all sites. You can easily modify your topologies by adding, editing, or deleting sites.

To access hardware and port requirements for each of the hardware components, double-click any of the hardware components in the topology. You can also access port requirements for the firewall by clicking on the firewall icon. The Planning Tool also provides customized planning and deployment steps that, when clicked, will open the documentation on the TechNet Library. The Planning Tool also provides a way to export your topology to Microsoft Office Visio as well as export all of your hardware and port requirements to Microsoft Office Excel.

Additional resources to blogs, forums, other tools, and documentation can be found in the Additional Resources pane inside the Planning Tool.

When you have finished using the Planning Tool, you can save your topology information in an XML file that you can display later in the Planning Tool.

Using the Office Communications Server 2007 R2 Planning Tool

1. Download the Planning Tool from *http://go.microsoft.com/fwlink/?LinkID=132927&clcid=0x409*.
2. Launch the Planning Tool
3. On the Welcome page, select Get Started.

A series of questions will be presented to record what Litware, Inc.'s requirements will be. The team would answer the questions, which are typically radio buttons or check boxes, until the initial section of the tool is completed.

- **Audio and video conferencing** Within the enterprise for computer-to-computer audio and video using Office Communicator or Microsoft Office Live Meeting. (Litware, Inc. intends to use this feature.)
- **Web Conferencing** Enterprise users inside and outside the firewall can create and join real-time Web conferences or meetings. (Litware, Inc. intends to use this feature.)
- **Communicator Web Access** By using a browser, users can access IM, presence, and conference features. (Litware, Inc. has moved this consideration to Phase II.)
- **Enterprise Voice** A VoIP solution enabling users to place calls from their computers and find contacts through Outlook or Office Communicator (Litware, Inc. plans to use Enterprise Voice internally, but external testing is being deployed to a pilot group in Chicago.)

- **Monitoring** Monitoring Server A role that captures call detail records and quality metrics for A/V sessions. (Litware, Inc. plans to employ monitoring.)
- **Archiving Server** Role that allows for the capture and storage of IM conversations for compliance purposes. (Litware, Inc. plans to install archiving.)
- **Unified Communications Applications Application Server** A platform on which to deploy, host, and manage UC applications. There are four options currently available:
  - Response Group Service Automatically answers and distributes calls to a configured pool of live agents. (Litware, Inc. is considering this for a later phase.)
  - Conference Auto-Attendant Enables callers for the Public Switched Telephone Network (PSTN) to connect to and join conferences. (Litware, Inc. plans to pilot this in Chicago.)
  - Conference Announcement Service Plays announcements in conferences, such as a recorded name. (Litware, Inc. plans to use this feature.)
  - Outside Voice Control Provides Enterprise Voice functionality and call control to mobile phones not enabled for Enterprise Voice. (Litware, Inc. plans to pilot this feature in Chicago.)
- **Group Chat Server** Powerful business and communication tool that enables large numbers of people to communicate in real time in a persistent chat mode. Information from the Group Chat sessions can be persisted as long as necessary, and federated partners can also join in. (Litware, Inc. is not planning on implementing this feature.)
- **Device Update Service** An automated method with which to update all UC devices deployed in your enterprise. (Litware, Inc. plans to implement this feature.)
- **Federation** Provides the enterprise the ability to establish communication between your infrastructure and another partner using Office Communications Server. Public IM connectivity is a form of federation and is included. (Litware, Inc. plans to deploy this feature.)
- **High Availability** Select this feature if your infrastructure should not suffer unplanned downtime. (Litware, Inc. desires this functionality.)

The interview portion of the tool has concluded and it now prompts the team for basic information on sites, domain name(s), and number of UC–enabled users (Figure 14-1). There is also a summary of selections that were made during the interview, and the selections can be fine-tuned here.

Litware, Inc. continues to fill out the tool with the first site name (Chicago), domain name (litwareinc.com), and 70,000 users.

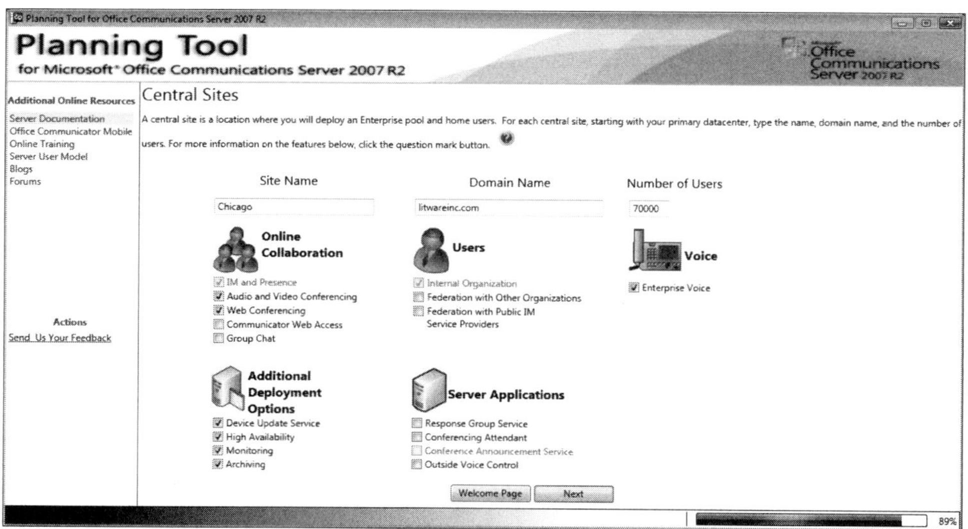

FIGURE 14-1 Output of the Planning Tool after interview and during first site definition

After the initial site screen, the team is presented with selections and questions relating to phone settings (Figure 14-2). Because Litware, Inc. is intending to pilot full voice capabilities at the Chicago site, the planning team decides to pilot 5 percent of the population, or 3,000 users. In the Enabled Users text box, the number 5 is provided. The next selection asks about external phone traffic and how many calls to the PSTN users will make at this site. Litware, Inc. decided to leave this at two calls per hour. Litware, Inc. is asked if there is a T-1 or an E-1 in their facility, and they answer T-1 for the Chicago site. The next question asks whether they have an IP PBX that is compatible with Office Communications Server. Litware does not, so they leave this unchecked. (There has been discussion of an option to upgrade the existing PBX to an IP PBX, but this is in the early phases of discussion.) When asked about a media gateway, they respond that they will use a four-port gateway. When asked about the Mediation Server that they will use, they respond with a dual processor, quad core, 3-gigahertz (GHz) server.

The Planning Tool is now asking about external user access, which Litware, Inc. is interested in, as shown in Figure 14-3. Because this is the first site, they select, Yes, And I Want To Deploy My Edge Servers In My Perimeter Network. They have also selected high availability.

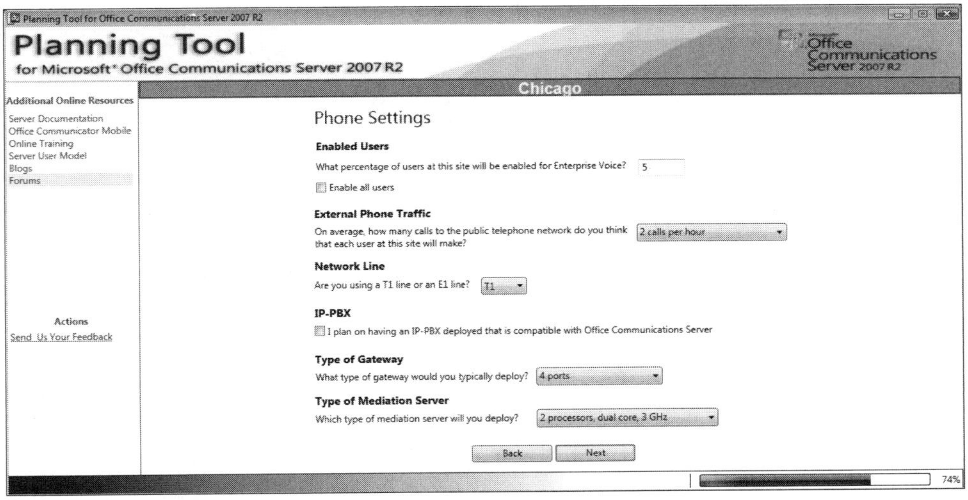

FIGURE 14-2 The Planning Tool asks for details about your phone requirements and equipment.

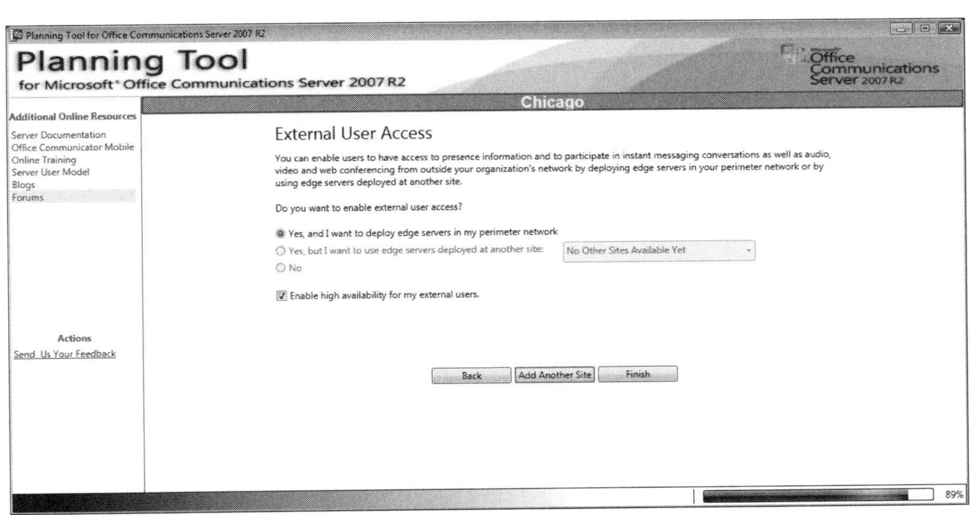

FIGURE 14-3 External User Access enables you to define the location of your perimeter network and high availability option.

The team then defines the site information for Paris and Singapore and removes the check mark for Enterprise Voice because Paris and Singapore will not use Enterprise Voice initially. They indicate that Paris has Edge services, but Singapore will use the Edge located in Chicago. On completing the Planning Tool Wizard, they have the output shown in Figure 14-4.

Figure 14-5 illustrates the Planning Tool output once you have double-clicked the site of interest. In this case, the team selects Chicago to view and to review for any missing elements or other requirements.

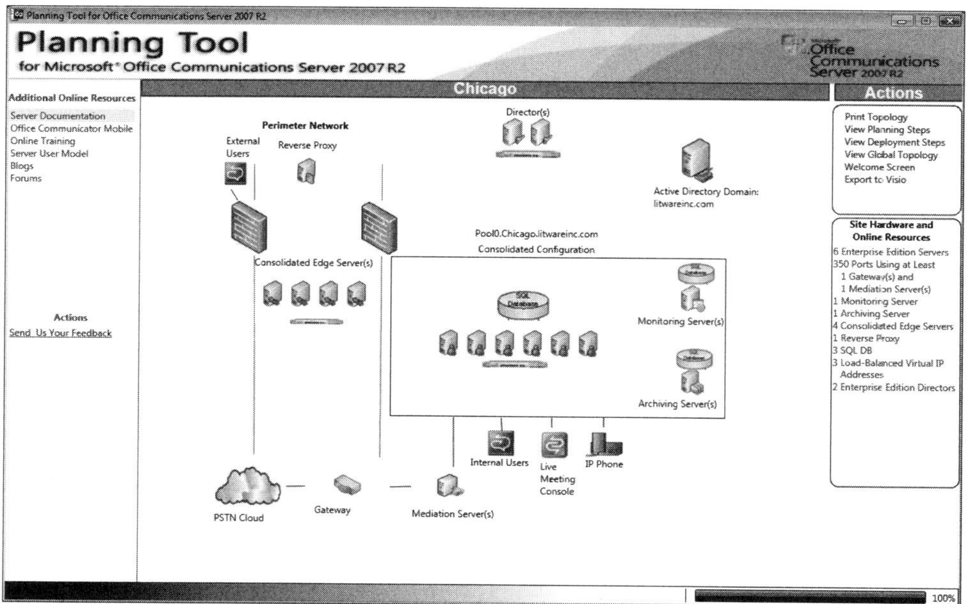

FIGURE 14-4 Global topology view of the Litware, Inc. proposed design output from the Planning Tool

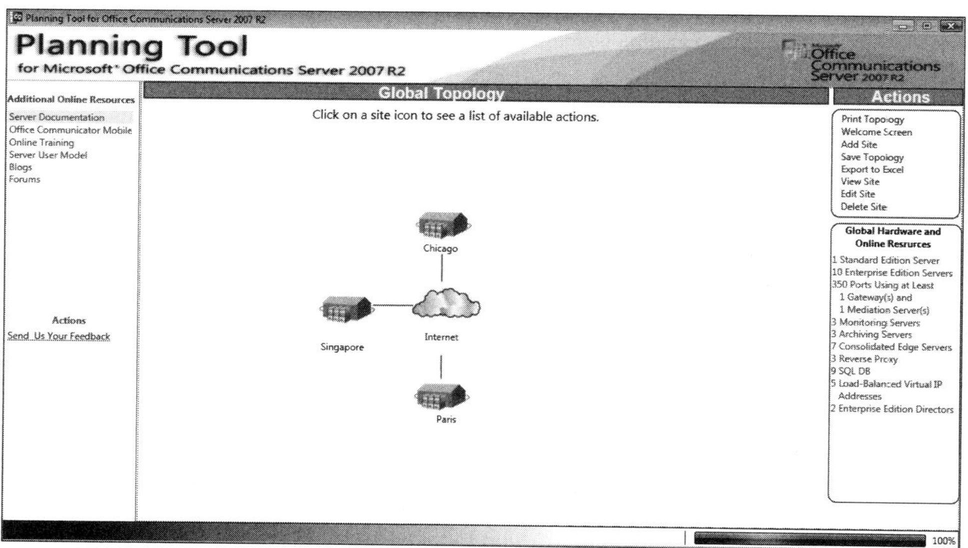

FIGURE 14-5 Chicago site layout and site hardware recommendations

The topology diagram that is output by the Planning Tool shows the suggested number of servers based on the team's input. However, this does not mean that this is the required number; it is just recommended.

The team reviews the output and makes a few recommendations based on their experience with traffic and load on these sites.

1. The Singapore site should have a single Standard Edition Server instead of an Enterprise pool. At present, the need for high availability does not justify the added expense. They adjust this in the Planning Tool by editing the Singapore site and removing the High Availability option.
2. Chicago should have six front-end servers, over the recommended five. Traffic will be heaviest and grow faster in this site than any other.
3. Chicago currently needs only two Edge Servers. More can be added later, but the current external access is not anticipated to grow for another 6–12 months, and the number of servers can be easily scaled because of the load balancers.
4. Paris needs an additional front-end server for the same reasons as Chicago. Internal use will be heavier, especially between Paris and Chicago.

Because of the Planning Tool and gathering detailed environment information, the team now has enough information to put together a reasonable recommended server count, location, and configuration of the topology. Table 14-4 illustrates this configuration, with active/passive SQL Server clusters defied by (A/P) and hardware load balancers defined by (LB).

TABLE 14-4 Recommendations of the Planning Team for Server Equipment and Placement

LITWARE, INC. REQUIREMENTS	CHICAGO	PARIS	SINGAPORE
Total number of employees	100,000	40,000	5,000
Concurrent users	70,000	38,000	4,000
Server roles			
Standard Edition Server			1
Enterprise pool			
Front-end server	6	4	
Back-end server	2 (A/P)	2 (A/P)	
Director			
Role	EE 2 (LB)		
SQL	2 (A/P)		
Mediation Server	1		
Monitor Server			
Role	1	1	1 (Monitor Server and Archiving Server are collocated)
SQL	1	1	

TABLE 14-4 Recommendations of the Planning Team for Server Equipment and Placement

LITWARE, INC. REQUIREMENTS	CHICAGO	PARIS	SINGAPORE
Archiving Server			
Role	1	1	
SQL	1	1	
External server roles			
Reverse proxy	1	1	1
Edge Server	2 (LB)	2 (LB)	1

NOTE **A TechNet article posted at** ***http://go.microsoft.com/fwlink/?LinkID=134841&clcid=0x409*** **specifically discusses server user models.**

Notice that Table 14-4 shows that Litware has chosen to use separate SQL Servers for their deployment in Paris and Chicago for the monitoring and archiving roles. The database administrator and the server administrator brought to the project management's attention that the SQL Servers can host multiple instances (one instance for archiving and another separate instance for monitoring), requiring only one cluster in each location as suggested in the UC blog post, "OCS Support for Shared SQL Server," at *http://communicationsserverteam.com/archive/2008/01/18/73.aspx*. Project management has taken the suggestion under consideration for future deployments.

Determining Interoperational Requirements

There are few environments, especially at an Enterprise scale, that do not have a multitude of vendors supplying solutions. And, quite often, these solutions may not work together, or interoperate, without either vendors working on the issue or the team finding a third-party solution. Figure 14-6 depicts the current telephony infrastructure in the Chicago site at Litware, Inc.

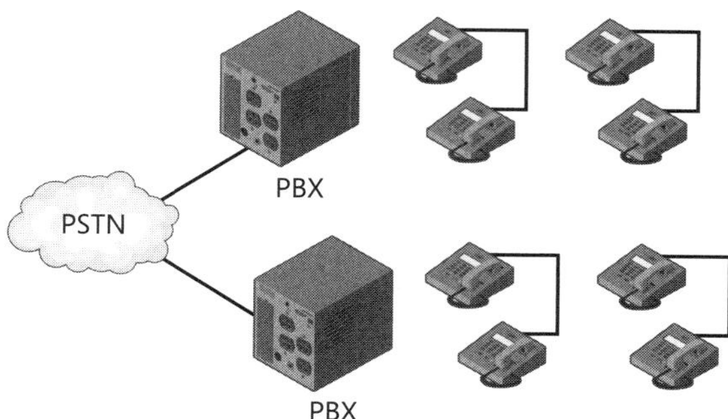

FIGURE 14-6 Current PBX telephony system at Litware, Inc.'s Chicago location

Consultation with the PBX vendor may prove that the Office Communications Server can be configured to communicate directly with the PBX by using direct SIP, but will require an upgrade of the hardware to be IP-enabled as well as configuration changes to the upgraded IP PBX. This leaves Litware with two options for enabling Enterprise Voice at the Chicago site.

1. Retain the current PBX and deploy Office Communications Server in parallel.
2. Upgrade the PBX to an IP PBX and use SIP trunking to the IP PBX.

In the first option, Litware could decide to keep the existing PBX system and enable interoperability with Office Communications Server using Remote Call Control or dual forking. This configuration requires deploying a media gateway that bridges between the PBX and a Mediation Server, as shown in Figure 14-7. This does add additional costs but would introduce the telephony team and the server administration team to the components that they may ultimately be responsible for. Users would also be able to benefit from the new telephony experience that Office Communications Server offers while maintaining the comfort of their existing PBX phone.

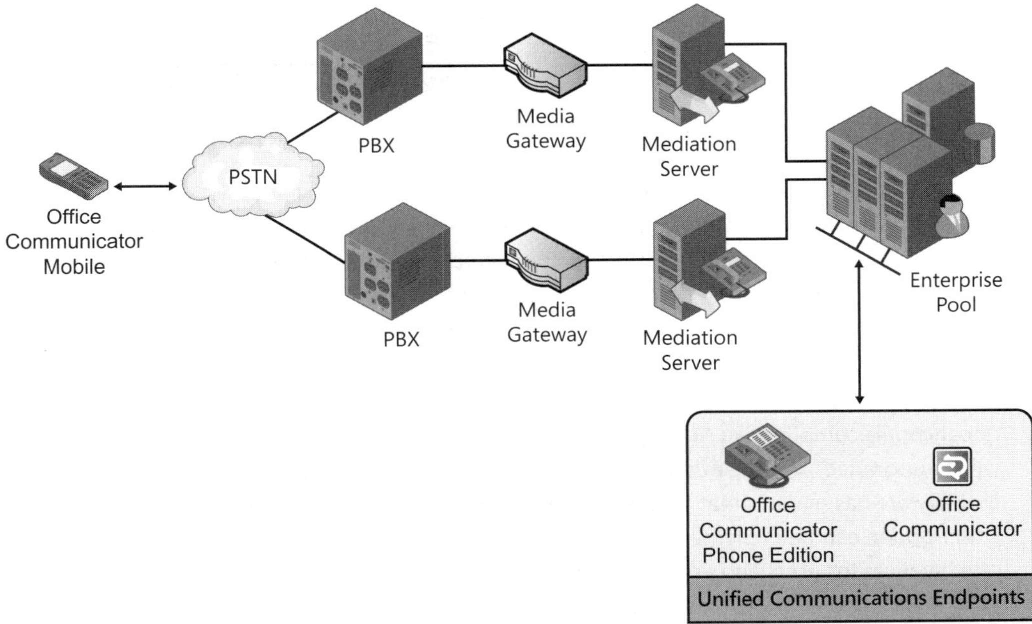

FIGURE 14-7 Integration of Office Communications Server to the existing PBXs using media gateways and Mediation Servers

In the second option, Litware would upgrade the existing PBXs to IP PBXs, allowing the upgraded IP PBXs to connect directly with Office Communications Server. This would eliminate the need for the media gateway. However, the Mediation Server will still be required. Figure 14-8 shows the configuration of the proposed upgrade to IP PBXs, and Office Communications Server would appear logically.

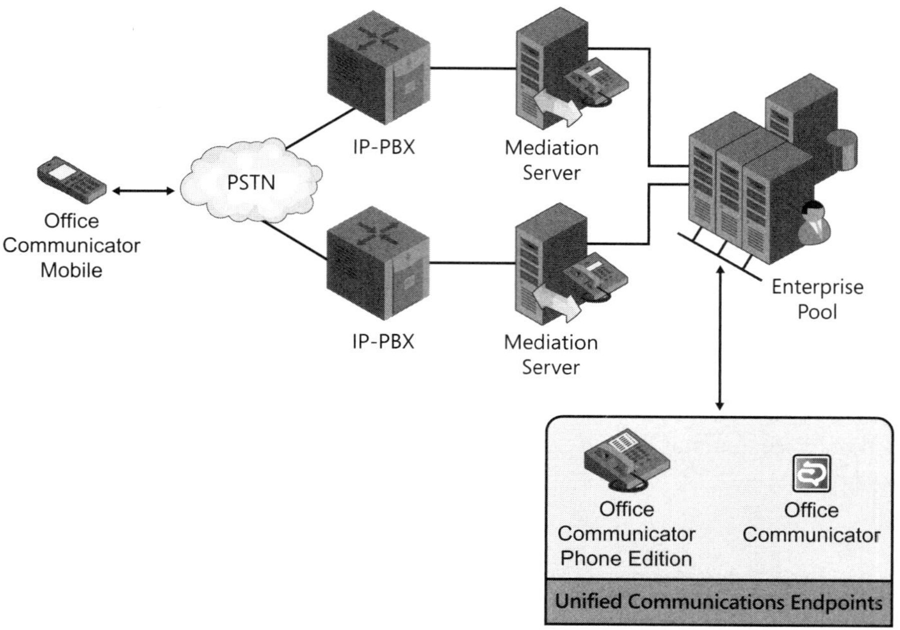

FIGURE 14-8 Conceptual view of the upgraded IP PBXs with Office Communications Server 2007 R2 Mediation Servers and potential clients

After discussions with the stakeholders, project management decided that the existing PBXs should be upgraded to IP PBXs and connected to Office Communications Server using Direct SIP. The PBX vendor is currently not ready to ship the IP PBX solution. Litware, Inc. will continue to use the PBXs as they currently are, implement Option 1, and move to implement the IP PBX upgrade once the product is released.

Both options are actionable and are valid for use in Litware's environment. Once the proof of concept is completed in Chicago with 5 percent of the site population, the rest of the site will be upgraded; and the other locations will be upgraded as well. The important discovery that Litware has made is that they actually have two paths for delivering a comparable service. Either option can be implemented in any of Litware's sites, lowering costs and maximizing effectiveness for users and enhancing the overall experience for all.

Performing a Gap Analysis

A gap analysis is a process that should be performed on all projects, regardless of size. The concept of a gap analysis is to review, in detail, the requirements of what the project is designed to deliver and the current plan of action. For example, in the case of Litware, Inc. and the solution that is being delivered using Office Communications Server, the original primary requirements were:

- Retire the legacy PBXs and replace those with VoIP

- Implement collaboration offered through Web Conferencing with federated business partners (for example, whiteboard use for product discussions, document sharing, and presentations)
- Give workers multiple ways to communicate when travelling or when otherwise away from the office

The planning team has reached conclusions on all three of the primary requirements. Retirement of the PBXs may take more time than originally desired, but the tradeoff is that they were able to still meet the goals of the project by providing a path to migrate users to Office Communicator as a computer client, Office Communicator Phone Edition as a desk phone, and remote access for remote users. For the federated business partners, the ability for workers—regardless of location—to collaborate with suppliers and partners will be realized by Web Conferencing and the tools available within.

The gap is the cost of this effort without a massive amount of work and service disruption. A less costly and less disruptive approach is to upgrade the existing PBX to be IP-enabled (IP PBX) and integrate it directly with Office Communications Server by using Direct SIP. The document, "Direct SIP with IP-PBX," on the companion CD provides step-by-step details on configuring Direct SIP with Cisco Unified Communications Manager 4.2.1.

However, this does not mean that the project is at risk. A pilot is going forward in Chicago that will help to define how large the effort really is and what the actual costs will be to retire the PBXs. This will allow for a much better understanding of the costs associated with such an effort.

Litware also has goals of providing a method for offering better collaboration with business partners. This is a good example of where Litware has a gap to address. What if the partner doesn't have Office Communications Server? In this case, Litware would need to look to suitable alternatives that might integrate with Office Communications Server and provide a consistent experience for the user. Litware could look at using the hosted Live Meeting service and public IM connectivity as a solution to this particular gap.

Architectural Design of the Solution

The planning team needs to perform some final steps before handing off a template deployment plan to the deployment team. They need to do the architectural design and provide guidance to the deployment team as to what servers go where, how servers should be configured (basic server sizing), and what network capabilities need to go where.

They also need to define who from each of the technical groups represented in the planning team is going to act as the subject matter expert in each of the areas represented. Taking the knowledge of the plan first hand into implementation is one of the best ways to ensure that there is a direct transition from planning to deployment.

The Planning Tool helps with the transition process as well. It will output Office Visio diagrams of your completed infrastructure. The Litware team decides to take advantage of this ability.

This diagram provides a framework from which to refine the architecture of Office Communications Server for Litware. The networking and the server teams should drill down into more specifics. The server team will need to communicate real-world data figures for IM traffic, conferencing traffic, and (with input from the telephony team) the Enterprise Voice traffic to the networking team. The networking team will need to determine the expected network bandwidth requirements to support the additional load on the network. These calculations are based on metrics defined in the Office Communications Server 2007 R2 Planning Guide. The results from this network capacity planning should be helpful for the telephony team to plan for additional phone trunks if necessary.

Most companies already have hardware standards in place. Litware is no exception to this, and they are fortunate to have standards beyond what the recommendations call for. The information that was gathered through the Planning Tool provides for a strong basis for determining number and suggested configuration for servers. The server team defines the hardware requirements based on their existing standards but does not change the quantity of recommended servers. They believe that by exceeding the requirements, the servers will remain sufficient for the company's needs up to the three-year cycle that is currently dictated by their policy for server hardware refresh.

Output to the Deployment Team for Development of the Deployment Plan

The deployment team, led by selected members from the planning team, will need to develop their plan for the actual deployment. The deployment plan consists of a set of technical instructions in a specific order of what will be deployed, what the dependencies are, and how it will be deployed. Setting up server hardware, installing operating systems, and installing and configuring the Office Communications Server software is part of the implementation process.

The deployment team will consist of IT members from nearly all technical areas of the company. As mentioned in the introduction to this chapter, a lot of expertise needs to be brought to bear on a project the size that Litware is implementing. Having a good project manager and a detailed schedule is key to making sure the rollout of Office Communications Server is successful. The project manager has developed a master schedule, as shown in Figure 14-9. All other teams will work within this time line for their own planning for the deployment of the project and will likely submit their own time lines to further define subtasks within the overall project.

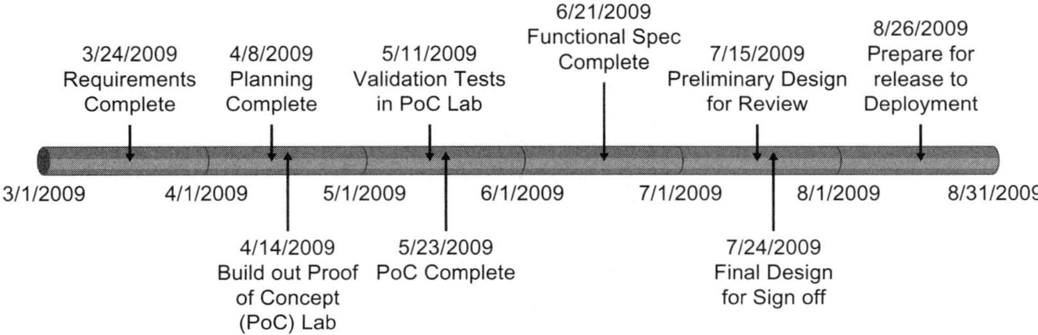

FIGURE 14-9 Time line for the overall Litware, Inc. Office Communications Server rollout

Summary

Planning is defined by setting a series of objectives to be accomplished to attain a goal that is first driven by a set of business requirements. Your planning should be arranged around phases of the overall project. Planning is the first phase of your overall project. Litware has ambitious goals and complex requirements. Good planning with the right people moving toward a common goal of delivering exceptional value for Litware, Inc. is important for success. It is likely that Litware will encounter unforeseen issues in the implementation of their goals. The more flexible the plan is, and the more time that is built into the plan to deal with the unknown, the better.

Remember that, ultimately, planning is about satisfying a set of business requirements. Rarely is a project begun for purely technical reasons. For a project to be successful, there has to be a net financial gain or a prevention of loss. Implementations rarely happen for the sake of "what if."

If you plan properly, your rate of success increases dramatically. There is an old saying that may or may not be global, but it is a perfect fit to end this chapter on planning.

"If you fail to plan, plan to fail."

Additional Resources

- OCS Support for Shared SQL Server, found at *http://communicationsserverteam.com/archive/2008/01/18/73.aspx*
- Cisco and Microsoft Collaboration in Unified Communications, found at *http://www.cisco.com/en/US/prod/collateral/voicesw/ps6788/vcallcon/ps556/prod_white_paper0900aecd805e9000.html?vs_f=Products+Launch+RSS+Feeds&vs_p=Cisco+Unified+Communications+Interoperable+with+Microsoft+Products&vs_k=1*
- Office Communications Server 2007 R2 Planning Guide, found at *http://go.microsoft.com/fwlink/?LinkID=133603*
- Office Communications Server 2007 R2 Planning Tool, found at *http://go.microsoft.com/fwlink/?LinkID=132927&clcid=0x409*

CHAPTER 15

Deployment Example

In Chapter 14, "Planning Example," we presented a detailed planning process of a fictitious globally distributed company named Litware, Inc. The goal of this chapter is to demonstrate a deployment path for Litware, Inc. The focus is to explain the deployment sequence, starting with the preparatory steps. This chapter doesn't provide step-by-step instructions to set up individual server roles. These are covered in various Microsoft Office Communications Server 2007 R2 deployment guides located at: *http://go.microsoft.com/fwlink/?LinkID=133729*.

ON THE COMPANION MEDIA **Links to information related to this book are described in the section titled "Additional Resources" at the end of this chapter. These links are provided on this book's companion CD.**

Understanding Litware, Inc.'s Deployment Process for Office Communications Server 2007 R2

Preparation is the most critical aspect of an Office Communications Server deployment. Certain steps, such as developing a server naming convention, preparing Domain Name System (DNS) entries, creating certificates, and installing and configuring network interface cards (NICs), should be done before proceeding with the actual deployment. This approach saves you from having to come back to the preparation of the environment after each step. The advantage in doing all the server preparation up front is that when you deploy server roles later in your deployment path (for example, when deploying the

Edge Server after you have set up the pool), you do not have to ask DNS administrators to create additional entries for them because you already took care of this a few days earlier. In environments where multiple administrators are involved, the deployment process becomes smoother if adequate preparation is done in advance. This chapter demonstrates an example deployment path for large multisite deployments.

Establishing a Server Naming Convention

At first, it is important to define the naming convention for all servers that Litware, Inc. wants to deploy. It's essential to choose a naming convention that is easily understandable to all organizations involved in the deployment because doing so decreases the possibility of miscommunication. As Table 15-1 shows, Litware, Inc. chooses a naming convention for its servers that easily identifies each of the Office Communications Server 2007 R2 roles and their locations.

Note that some exceptions to this naming convention exist for non–Office Communications Server 2007 R2 roles, such as load balancers.

If you have used Office Communications Server 2007, you will notice that a number of server roles seem to be missing from Table 15-1. The reason for this is that in Office Communications Server 2007 R2, the recommended topology has changed from an expanded Enterprise Edition topology to the collocated Enterprise Edition topology. In the collocated Enterprise Edition topology, all pool services are collocated on every front-end server. This greatly simplifies deployment and management.

Similarly, the recommended Edge Server topology is the collocated Edge Server. In fact, in Office Communications Server 2007 R2, you will not find the setup user interface (UI) to deploy an expanded Enterprise pool or the non-collocated Edge Servers. This option is available only via a command line tool called LcsCmd.exe. For more information, refer to the Office Communications Server 2007 R2 Command Line Reference documentation found at *http://go.microsoft.com/fwlink/?LinkID=133728*.

TABLE 15-1 Litware, Inc.'s Server Naming Convention

ATTRIBUTE	NAMING CONVENTION
Server name	X-Y-Z
Server-FQDN (fully qualified domain name)	x-y-z.litwareinc.com
X	Server locations are abbreviated as follows: CHI = Chicago PAR = Paris SPO = Singapore
Y	Server roles are abbreviated as follows: ■ FE = Front-end server of an Office Communications Server 2007 R2 Enterprise Edition pool ■ BE = Back-end server of an Office Communications Server 2007 R2 Enterprise Edition pool ■ SE = Office Communications Server 2007 R2 Standard Edition ■ DIR = Director (Office Communications Server 2007 R2 Standard Edition) ■ ES = Edge Server ■ WCE = Web Component Edge Service (on Edge Server role) ■ AVE = Audio/Visual (A/V) Edge Service (on Edge Server role) ■ MED = Mediation Server ■ RP = Hypertext Transfer Protocol (HTTP) Reverse Proxy ■ UM = Exchange Unified Messaging Server ■ ARC = Archiving Server ■ MON = Monitoring Server ■ ARCBE = Archiving Server back-end SQL Server ■ MONBE = Monitoring Server back-end SQL Server
Z	Role number (if this is missing, the server is a load balancer)

DIRECT FROM THE SOURCE

Why Consolidated Topology Is the Recommended Option for Office Communications Server 2007 R2

Peter Schmatz
Program Manager II, Office Communications Server

With Office Communications Server 2007 R2, even more features and server roles have been added to an already complex Office Communications Server 2007 topology design. This made it even more important for the designers to simplify the overall deployment, management, and monitoring experience.

The following factors make it possible to collate server roles on a single server system and reduce the overall number of required servers for a full enterprise-scale deployment without compromising on performance too much:

- The fact that Office Communications Server 2007 R2 is supported only on 64-bit operating systems and 64-bit architectures
- The ability to address a larger memory space
- The trend toward multicore central processing units (CPUs) (4-core or dual 4-core CPUs)

Moving to a simpler Enterprise pool in a consolidated configuration with fewer, more powerful server systems will make it easier to plan, deploy, and maintain your deployment. At the same time, you'll be able to reduce the total cost of ownership. A consolidated configuration, running on hardware that meets or exceeds the recommended specifications, will perform much better than the corresponding consolidated Office Communications Server 2007 deployment does.

It is important to note that Office Communications Server 2007 R2 continues to support an Enterprise pool in an expanded topology to accommodate existing deployments via command line installation options only.

Table 15-2 through Table 15-4 show the server names, IP addresses, and FQDNs of the servers for the three Litware, Inc. sites.

TABLE 15-2 Litware, Inc. Server Names for Chicago

SERVER ROLE	SERVER NAME	IP ADDRESS	SERVER FQDN
Consolidated Enterprise Edition (EE) pool name (load balancer Virtual Internet Protocol (VIP) for the pool)	CHI-POOL	10.18.10.1	chi-pool.litwareinc.com
EE front-end server 1	CHI-FE-01	10.18.10.2	chi-fe-01.litwareinc.com
EE front-end server 2	CHI-FE-02	10.18.10.3	chi-fe-02.litwareinc.com
EE front-end server 3	CHI-FE-03	10.18.10.4	chi-fe-03.litwareinc.com
EE front-end server 4	CHI-FE-04	10.18.10.5	chi-fe-04.litwareinc.com
EE front-end server 5	CHI-FE-05	10.18.10.6	chi-fe-05.litwareinc.com
EE front-end server 6	CHI-FE-06	10.18.10.7	chi-fe-06.litwareinc.com
Back-end SQL cluster name	CHI-BE	10.18.10.10	chi-be.litwareinc.com
Back-end Node 1	CHI-BE-01	10.18.10.11	chi-be-01.litwareinc.com
Back-end Node 2	CHI-BE-02	10.18.10.12	chi-be-02.litwareinc.com
Archiving Server	CHI-ARC-01	10.18.10.20	chi-arc-01.litwareinc.com
Archiving Server Back-end SQL	CHI-ARCBE-01	10.18.10.21	chi-arcbe-01.litwareinc.com
Monitoring Server	CHI-MON-01	10.18.10.22	chi-mon-01.litwareinc.com
Monitoring Server Back-end SQL	CHI-MONBE-01	10.18.10.23	chi-monbe-01.litwareinc.com
EE Director pool name (load balancer VIP for EE Director pool)	CHI-DIR	10.18.10.32	chi-dir.litwareinc.com
EE Director front-end server 1	CHI-DIR-01	10.18.10.30	chi-dir-01.litwareinc.com
EE Director front-end server 2	CHI-DIR-02	10.18.10.31	chi-dir-02.litwareinc.com
Back-end SQL cluster name (for Director pool)	CHI-DIRBE	10.18.10.40	chi-dirbe.litwareinc.com
Back-end Node 1 (for Director pool)	CHI-DIRBE-01	10.18.10.41	chi-dirbe-01.litwareinc.com
Back-end Node 2 (for Director pool)	CHI-DIRBE-02	10.18.10.42	chi-dirbe-02.litwareinc.com
Exchange Unified Messaging (UM) Server	CHI-UM-01	10.18.10.70	chi-um-01.contoso.com
Load balancer VIP for collocated Edge Server (internal)	CHI-ES	192.168.10.40	chi-es.litwareinc.com

TABLE 15-2 Litware, Inc. Server Names for Chicago

SERVER ROLE	SERVER NAME	IP ADDRESS	SERVER FQDN
Load balancer VIP for collocated Edge Server (external)	—	64.65.66.1 (Access Edge Service)	sip.litwareinc.com
		64.65.66.2 (Web Conferencing Edge Service)	chi-wcs.litwareinc.com
		64.65.66.3 (A/V Edge Service)	chi-ave.litwareinc.com
Edge Server 1 (internal NIC)	CHI-ES-01	192.168.10.41	chi-es-01.litwareinc.com
Edge Server 1 (external NIC)	—	64.65.66.11 (Access Edge Service)	—
		64.65.66.21 (Web Conferencing Edge Service)	
		64.65.66.31 (A/V Edge Service)	
Edge Server 2 (internal NIC)	CHI-ES-02	192.168.10.42	chi-es-02.litwareinc.com
Edge Server 2 (external NIC)	—	64.65.66.12 (Access Edge Service)	—
		64.65.66.22 (Web Conferencing Edge Service)	
		64.65.66.32 (A/V Edge Service)	

TABLE 15-2 Litware, Inc. Server Names for Chicago

SERVER ROLE	SERVER NAME	IP ADDRESS	SERVER FQDN
Mediation Server (internal NIC)	CHI-MED-01	10.18.10.50	chi-med-01.litwareinc.com
Mediation Server (external NIC)	CHI-MED-01	10.18.10.51	chi-med-01.litwareinc.com
HTTP reverse proxy server (internal NIC)	CHI-RP-01	192.168.10.60	chi-rp-01.litwareinc.com
HTTP reverse proxy server (external NIC)	—	64.65.66.30	chi-rp-01.litwareinc.com

> ***NOTE*** **Because some of the users in the Chicago site are enabled for Voice in addition to the regular server roles, the Mediation Server, Session Initiation Protocol (SIP)/Public Switched Telephone Network (PSTN) gateway, and Exchange UM Server are also deployed in this site. Also note that Litware, Inc. decided to go with an Enterprise Edition pool to serve as a Director for higher availability and better performance.**

TABLE 15-3 Litware, Inc. Server Names for Paris

SERVER ROLE	SERVER NAME	IP ADDRESS	SERVER FQDN
Consolidated EE Pool Name (load balancer VIP for the pool)	PAR-POOL	10.17.10.1	par-pool.litwareinc.com
EE front-end server 1	PAR-FE-01	10.17.10.2	par-fe-01.litwareinc.com
EE front-end server 2	PAR-FE-02	10.17.10.3	par-fe-02.litwareinc.com
EE front-end server 3	PAR-FE-03	10.17.10.4	par-fe-03.litwareinc.com
EE front-end server 4	PAR-FE-04	10.17.10.5	par-fe-04.litwareinc.com
Back-end SQL cluster name	PAR-BE	10.17.10.10	par-be.litwareinc.com
Back-end Node 1	PAR-BE-01	10.17.10.11	par-be-01.litwareinc.com
Back-end Node 2	PAR-BE-02	10.17.10.12	par-be-02.litwareinc.com
Archiving Server	PAR-ARC-01	10.17.10.20	par-arc-01.litwareinc.com
Archiving Server Back-end SQL	PAR-ARCBE-01	10.17.10.21	par-arcbe-01. litwareinc.com
Monitoring Server	PAR-MON-01	10.17.10.22	par-mon-01.litwareinc.com
Monitoring Server Back-end SQL	PAR-MONBE-01	10.17.10.23	par-monbe-01. litwareinc.com
Load balancer VIP for collocated Edge Access Server (internal)	PAR-ES	192.167.10.40	par-es.litwareinc.com

TABLE 15-3 Litware, Inc. Server Names for Paris

SERVER ROLE	SERVER NAME	IP ADDRESS	SERVER FQDN
Load balancer VIP for col-located Edge Access Server (external)	—	64.64.66.1 (Access Edge Service)	par-es-ext.litwareinc.com
		64.64.66.2 (Web Conferencing Edge Service)	par-wcs.litwareinc.com
		64.64.66.3 (A/V Edge Service)	par-ave.litwareinc.com
Edge Server 1 (internal NIC)	PAR-ES-01	192.167.10.41	par-es-01.litwareinc.com
Edge Server 1 (external NIC)	—	64.64.66.11 (Access Edge Service) 64.64.66.21 (Web Conferencing Edge Service) 64.64.66.31 (A/V Edge Service)	—
Edge Server 2 (internal NIC)	PAR-ES-02	192.168.10.42	par-es-02.litwareinc.com
Edge Server 2 (external NIC)	—	64.64.66.12 (Access Edge Service) 64.64.66.22 (Web Conferencing Edge Service) 64.64.66.32 (A/V Edge Service)	—
HTTP reverse proxy server (internal NIC)	PAR-RP-01	192.167.10.60	par-rp-01.litwareinc.com

TABLE 15-3 Litware, Inc. Server Names for Paris

SERVER ROLE	SERVER NAME	IP ADDRESS	SERVER FQDN
HTTP reverse proxy server (external NIC)	—	64.64.66.30	par-rp-01.litwareinc.com

TABLE 15-4 Litware, Inc. Server Names for Singapore

SERVER ROLE	SERVER NAME	IP ADDRESS	SERVER FQDN
SE Server (with archiving and monitoring servers collocated)	SPO-SE-01	10.15.10.1	spo-se-01.litwareinc.com
Archiving and Monitoring Server back-end SQL	SPO-ARCMONBE-01	10.15.10.21	spo-arcmonbe-01.litwareinc.com
Edge Server (internal NIC)	SPO-ES-01	192.165.10.41	spo-ep-01.litwareinc.com
Edge Server (external NIC)	—	64.62.66.11 (Access Edge Service)	spo-es-ext.litwareinc.com
		64.62.66.21 (Web Conferencing Edge Service)	spo-wcs.litwareinc.com
		64.62.66.31 (A/V Edge Service)	spo-ave.litwareinc.com
HTTP reverse proxy server (internal NIC)	SPO-RP-01	192.165.10.60	spo-rp-01.litwareinc.com
HTTP Reverse Proxy Server (external NIC)	—	64.62.66.30	spo-rp-01.litwareinc.com

NOTE **Because the user population at the Singapore site is small, Litware, Inc. decided to go with a Standard Edition server with Archiving and Monitoring Servers collocated on the same physical machine. Also note that for the Singapore site, the external IP addresses for the Edge Server also need an FQDNs assigned. This is because there is no external load balancer in Singapore, and therefore the external IP addresses have to be in the external DNS.**

DIRECT FROM THE SOURCE

Archiving and Monitoring Roles in Office Communications Server 2007 R2

Peter Schmatz
Program Manager II, Office Communications Server

In Office Communications Server 2007 R2, the Archiving and Call Detail Record (CDR) functionality is split into two different server roles. The archiving functionality remains in the Archiving Server role while the CDR functionality merged with Media Quality Metric collection functionality (formally the QMS Server role) and is now available in the Monitoring Server role.

The main driver for creating a dedicated Archiving Server role is to provide flexibility to deployments that don't archive instant messaging (IM) traffic at all (and therefore do not have to deploy this server role). Or, if archiving instant messages is required, deployments need appropriately sized SQL databases due to the large volume of IM data that archiving introduces.

CDR and Quality of Experience (QoE) data contain similarly structured data (per call CDR and per call QoE metrics) that usually generate much smaller quantities of data and can typically be accommodated on a single monitoring SQL Server database. Most deployments need both these functionalities and can now get it by deploying a single server role (the Monitoring Server) instead of two server roles (the QMS and Archiving Servers). Additionally, because both the CDR and QoE data are contained in one SQL Server, correlating and reporting become easier.

Preparing the Server Hardware

Each Litware, Inc. server role requires dedicated server hardware, as described in the Office Communications Server 2007 R2 Planning Guide. When preparing server hardware for an Office Communications Server 2007 R2 deployment, the required number of NICs in each server should be checked. Table 15-5 through Table 15-19, found later in this chapter, show where Litware, Inc. needs multiple NICs as required by the server roles.

Litware, Inc.'s Deployment Path

Litware, Inc. decided to enable several scenarios with a high level of redundancy for its users. This resulted in a high number of individual servers and server roles needing to be deployed. Figure 15-1 through Figure 15-3 provide a graphical view of the target deployment for each of the Litware, Inc. sites.

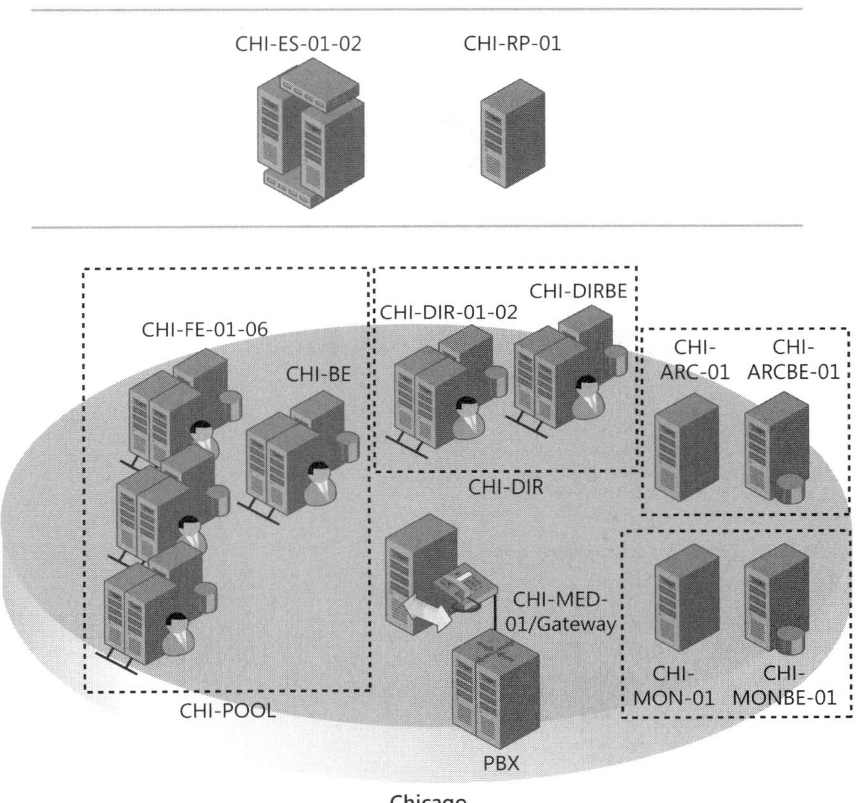

FIGURE 15-1 Litware, Inc.'s target architecture in Chicago

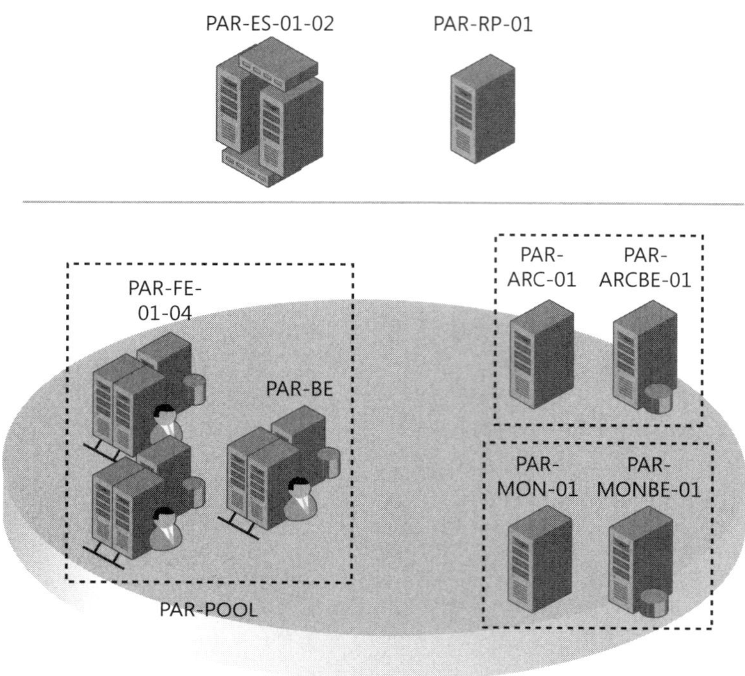

FIGURE 15-2 Litware, Inc.'s target architecture in Paris

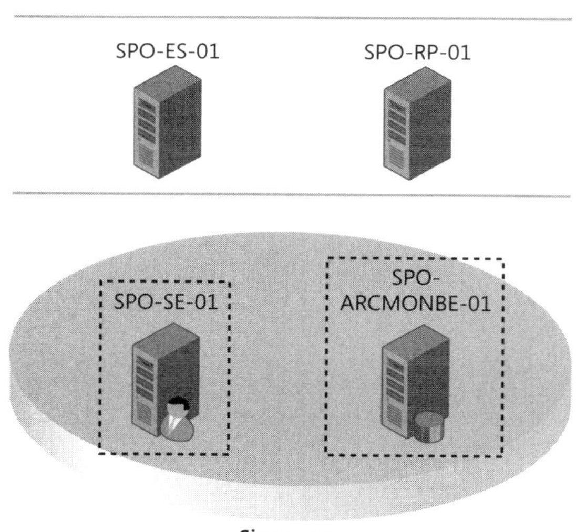

FIGURE 15-3 Litware, Inc.'s target architecture in Singapore

Preparing Active Directory

Litware, Inc. decided to install the entire Office Communications Server 2007 R2 deployment in a single domain (Litware, Inc.com) because domain controllers are available at each of the sites. The Office Communications Server 2007 R2 Active Directory Guide, found at *http://go.microsoft.com/fwlink/?LinkID=133727*, explains in detail the steps that have to be taken to prepare Active Directory for an Office Communications Server 2007 R2 deployment.

In the future, Litware, Inc. would like to add Office Communications Servers in a different Active Directory domain at a new site. Because that site doesn't have good connectivity to the root domain, Litware, Inc. decided to put its global settings in the Configuration Partition rather than in the System container.

IMPORTANT **Active Directory administrators need to have good control over Active Directory schema updates because these events can affect the entire enterprise's directory infrastructure. Therefore, you'll need to coordinate with the Active Directory administrators to prepare Active Directory in an Office Communications Server 2007 R2 deployment. Depending on the enterprise and its business, there can be periods in which an Active Directory schema update is not allowed by company policy and therefore the Office Communications Server 2007 R2 deployment can be delayed. The effects of such policies on the deployment schedule need to be incorporated into the deployment plan.**

Overview of Preparing Firewall Ports, Certificates, NICs, and DNS

In large enterprises, the configurations of DNS, certificates, and firewalls are sometimes, from an organizational perspective, separate from the administrators who install and configure Office Communications Servers. Therefore, the administrators responsible for deploying Office Communications Servers must collaborate with other administrators within the company.

As part of Litware, Inc.'s Office Communications Server 2007 R2 planning process, the number of individual server roles has been identified, as shown in Chapter 14. This enables Litware, Inc. to summarize all DNS and firewall port requirements so that the preparation of the surrounding infrastructure can be done at one time before the actual deployment takes place. Table 15-5 through Table 15-19 summarize all preparations that need to be done for Litware, Inc.'s Office Communications Server 2007 R2 deployment. In addition, a detailed view with all the infrastructure requirements—including certificate requirements for Chicago—will be shown later in the chapter.

Preparing DNS, Firewall Ports, and Certificates for the Chicago Deployment

Table 15-5 provides a summary of Litware, Inc.'s infrastructure requirements for Chicago.

TABLE 15-5 Summary of Chicago Infrastructure Requirements

SERVER ROLE	NAME	EXTERNAL DNS NAME (IP ADDRESS)	INTERNAL DNS NAME (IP ADDRESS)	EXTERNAL FIREWALL PORT (DIRECTION)	INTERNAL FIREWALL PORT (DIRECTION)
Edge Server —Access Edge Service (load balancer)	CHI-ES	sip.litwareinc.com VIP = (64.65.66.1) _sip._tls.*domain* (SRV) 443 sip. litwareinc.com _sipfederation-tls._tcp.*domain* (SRV) 5061 sip. litwareinc.com	chi-es. litwareinc.com VIP = (192.168.10.40)	443 Transmission Control Protocol (TCP) (inbound) (Internet → Access Edge Service for Remote User Access) 5061 TCP (both) (Internet ↔ Access Edge Service for federation)	5061 TCP (both) (Office Communications Server 2007 R2 pool ↔ Access Edge Service)
Edge Server —Web Conferencing Edge Service (load balancer)	CHI-ES	chi-wce.litware-inc.com VIP = (64.65.66.2)	N/A (internal edge of Web Conferencing Service can't be behind a load balancer	443 TCP (inbound) (Internet → Web Conferencing Edge Server)	8057 TCP (outbound) (Office Communications Server 2007 R2 pool → Web Conferencing Edge Service)

TABLE 15-5 Summary of Chicago Infrastructure Requirements

SERVER ROLE	NAME	EXTERNAL DNS NAME (IP ADDRESS)	INTERNAL DNS NAME (IP ADDRESS)	EXTERNAL FIREWALL PORT (DIRECTION)	INTERNAL FIREWALL PORT (DIRECTION)
Edge Server—A/V Edge Service (load balancer)	CHI-ES	chi-ave.litwareinc.com VIP = (64.65.66.3)	chi-es.litwareinc.com VIP = (192.168.10.40)	443 TCP (inbound) (Internet → A/V Edge Service) 3478 User Datagram Protocol (UDP) (inbound) (Internet → A/V Edge Service) 50,000–59,999 TCP & UDP (both) (Internet ↔ A/V Edge Service)	443 TCP (outbound) (Internal Net [all IPs] → A/V Edge Service) 3478 UDP (outbound) (internal Net [all IPs] → A/V Edge Service) 5062 TCP (outbound) (internal Net [all IPs] → A/V Edge Service)
NODES (EDGE SERVER)					
Node1	CHI-ES-01	N/A (64.65.66.11, 64.65.66.21, 64.65.66.31)	chi-es-01.litwareinc.com (192.168.10.41)	N/A	N/A
Node2	CHI-ES-02	N/A (64.65.66.12, 64.65.66.22, 64.65.66.32)	chi-es-02.litwareinc.com (192.168.10.42)	N/A	N/A

TABLE 15-5 Summary of Chicago Infrastructure Requirements

SERVER ROLE	NAME	EXTERNAL DNS NAME (IP ADDRESS)	INTERNAL DNS NAME (IP ADDRESS)	EXTERNAL FIREWALL PORT (DIRECTION)	INTERNAL FIREWALL PORT (DIRECTION)
HTTP reverse proxy server	CHI-RP-01	chi-rp-01.litware-inc.com (64.65.66.30)	chi-rp-01.litwareinc.com (192.168.10.60)	443 TCP (inbound) Internet → HTTP reverse proxy server	443 TCP (inbound) HTTP reverse proxy server → Office Communications Server 2007 R2 pool
EE Director pool (load balancer)	CHI-DIR	N/A	chi-dir.litwareinc.com (10.18.10.32)	N/A	5061 TCP (both) (Access Edge [internal load balancer VIP] ↔ Director)
EE DIRECTOR FRONT-END NODES					
Node1	CHI-DIR-01	N/A	chi-dir-01.litwareinc.com (10.18.10.30)	N/A	N/A
Node2	CHI-DIR-02	N/A	chi-dir-02.litwareinc.com (10.18.10.31)	N/A	N/A
Back-end SQL Server for Director pool (cluster name)	SQL-DIRBE	N/A	chi-dirbe.litwareinc.com VIP = (10.18.10.40)	N/A	N/A
BACK-END SQL NODES (FOR DIRECTOR POOL)					
Node 1	CHI-DIRBE-01	N/A	chi-dirbe-01.litwareinc.com (10.18.10.41)	N/A	N/A
Node 2	CHI-DIRBE-02	N/A	chi-dirbe-02.litwareinc.com (10.18.10.42)	N/A	N/A

TABLE 15-5 Summary of Chicago Infrastructure Requirements

SERVER ROLE	NAME	EXTERNAL DNS NAME (IP ADDRESS)	INTERNAL DNS NAME (IP ADDRESS)	EXTERNAL FIREWALL PORT (DIRECTION)	INTERNAL FIREWALL PORT (DIRECTION)
EE pool (load balancer)	CHI-POOL	N/A	chipool. litwareinc.com VIP = (10.18.10.1) _sipinternal._ tcp.*domain* (SRV) 5061 chi-pool. litwareinc.com _sipinternal-tls._tcp.*domain* (SRV) 5061 chipool. litwareinc.com	N/A	N/A
EE FRONT ENDS					
Node1	CHI-FE-01	N/A	chi-fe-01. litwareinc.com (10.18.10.2)	N/A	N/A
Node2	CHI-FE-02	N/A	chi-fe-02. litwareinc.com (10.18.10.3)	N/A	N/A
Node3	CHI-FE-03	N/A	chi-fe-03. litwareinc.com (10.18.10.4)	N/A	N/A
Node4	CHI-FE-04	N/A	chi-fe-04. litwareinc.com (10.18.10.5)	N/A	N/A
Node5	CHI-FE-05	N/A	chi-fe-05. litwareinc.com (10.18.10.6)	N/A	N/A
Node6	CHI-FE-06	N/A	chi-fe-06. litwareinc.com (10.18.10.7)	N/A	N/A

TABLE 15-5 Summary of Chicago Infrastructure Requirements

SERVER ROLE	NAME	EXTERNAL DNS NAME (IP ADDRESS)	INTERNAL DNS NAME (IP ADDRESS)	EXTERNAL FIREWALL PORT (DIRECTION)	INTERNAL FIREWALL PORT (DIRECTION)
Back-end SQL Server (cluster name)	SQL-BE	N/A	chi-be. litwareinc.com VIP = (10.18.10.10)	N/A	N/A
BACK-END SQL NODES					
Node 1	CHI-BE-01	N/A	chi-be-01. litwareinc.com (10.18.10.11)	N/A	N/A
Node 2	CHI-BE-02	N/A	chi-be-02. litwareinc.com (10.18.10.12)	N/A	N/A
Mediation Server	CHI-MED-01	chi-med-01. litwareinc.com (10.18.10.51)	chi-med-01. litwareinc.com (10.18.10.50)	N/A	N/A
Archiving Server	CHI-ARC-01	N/A	chi-arc-01. litwareinc.com (10.18.10.20)	N/A	N/A
Archiving Server Back-End SQL Server	CHI-ARCBE-01	N/A	chi-arcbe-01. litwareinc.com (10.18.10.21)	N/A	N/A
Monitoring Server	CHI-MON-01	N/A	chi-mon-01. litwareinc.com (10.18.10.22)	N/A	N/A
Monitoring Server Back-End SQL Server	CHI-MONBE-01	N/A	chi-monbe-01.litwareinc.com (10.18.10.23)	N/A	N/A

Note that in Table 15-5, a total of 12 IP addresses are used, which point to the same two physical Edge Servers. Here is a summary to further clarify the addressing scheme for these servers:

- One IP address for the Access Edge VIP (externally) = 64.65.66.1
- One IP address for the Web Conferencing Edge VIP (externally) = 64.65.66.2
- One IP address for the A/V Edge VIP (externally) = 64.65.66.3
- One IP address for the Edge Server VIP (internally) shared by the Access Edge and A/V Edge = 192.168.10.40
- Two IP addresses for the Access Edge (externally) = 64.65.66.11 and 64.65.66.12 (these addresses are the node addresses, and the VIPs point to them)
- Two IP addresses for the Web Conferencing Edge (externally) = 64.65.66.21 and 64.65.66.22 (these addresses are the node addresses, and the VIPs point to them)
- Two IP addresses for the A/V Edge (externally) = 64.65.66.31 and 64.65.66.32 (these addresses are the node addresses, and the VIPs point to them)
- Two IP addresses for the Edge Server shared by Access Edge, Web Conferencing Edge, and A/V Edge (internally) = 192.168.10.41 and 192.168.10.42

Note that the internal edge of the Web Conferencing Service cannot be behind a load balancer. The individual FQDNs of two Web Conferencing Service boxes (chi-es-01.litwareinc.com and chi-es-02.liwareinc.com) must be addressable by all the Web Conferencing Services in the internal network.

Table 15-6 through Table 15-8 provide detailed views of the infrastructure requirements for the Edge Server arrays in the Chicago perimeter network. An *array* is a set of servers running the same server roles.

TABLE 15-6 Details for Chicago External Load Balancer for Co-located Edge Servers

ROLE/FEATURE	QUANTITY/ VALUE(S)	LOCATION/ SETTING	NOTE/EXAMPLE
LOAD BALANCER			
Access Edge	sip.litwareinc.com	Perimeter network	Externally facing hardware load balancer with 3 VIPs
Web Conferencing Edge	chi-wce.litwareinc.com	Perimeter network	Externally facing hardware load balancer with 3 VIPs
A/V Edge	chi-ave.litwareinc.com	Perimeter network	Externally facing hardware load balancer with 3 VIPs

TABLE 15-6 Details for Chicago External Load Balancer for Co-located Edge Servers

ROLE/FEATURE	QUANTITY/ VALUE(S)	LOCATION/ SETTING	NOTE/EXAMPLE
VIPS			
Access Edge VIP (external)	(1) 64.65.66.1	100-megabit Full	VIP address on the external load balancer for array of Access Edge Services
Web Conferencing Edge VIP (external)	(1) 64.65.66.2	100-megabit Full	VIP address on the external load balancer for array of Web Conferencing Edge Services
A/V Edge VIP (external)	(1) 64.65.66.3	100-megabit Full	VIP address on the external load balancer for array of A/V Edge Services
PORTS			
Firewall (external)	443 TCP	Inbound	Traffic from Internet → Access Edge Service, Web Conferencing Edge Service, and A/V Edge Service external load balancer VIPs (sip.litwareinc.com, chi-wce.litware.com, and chi-ave.litware.com, respectively)
	5061 TCP	Bi-directional	Traffic to/from Internet ↔ Access Edge Service external load balancer VIP (sip.litwareinc.com)

TABLE 15-6 Details for Chicago External Load Balancer for Co-located Edge Servers

ROLE/FEATURE	QUANTITY/ VALUE(S)	LOCATION/ SETTING	NOTE/EXAMPLE
	3478 UDP	Inbound	Traffic from Internet → A/V Edge Service external load balancer VIP (chi-ave.litwareinc.com)
	50,000–59,999 TCP and UDP	Bi-directional	Traffic to/from Internet ↔ A/V Edge Service external load balancer VIP (chi-ave.litwareinc.com); if you don't want to open the entire range of ports from 50,000 to 59,999, allow 6 ports for each concurrent external user
Certificates			
Certificate Name (CN)/Subject Name (SN)	N/A	N/A	N/A
DNS (Internal)			
(A)	N/A	N/A	N/A
DNS (External)			
(A)	sip.litwareinc.com	64.65.66.1	
(A)	chi-wce.litwareinc.com	64.65.66.2	
(A)	chi-ave.litware.com	64.65.66.3	

DIRECT FROM THE FIELD

Using Nonpublic Certificate Authorities for Certificates Assigned on the External Edge

R. Lee Mackey, Jr.
Americas Unified Communications Technical Lead, Consulting and Integration, Hewlett Packard Services

Deciding what certificate to use and where can be one of the biggest challenges in deploying Office Communications Server 2007 R2. If your company has an internal public key infrastructure (PKI), you have the ability to use certificates from your internal certificate authority (CA). If you are deploying an Edge Server and allow non–domain joined systems to connect to your Office Communications Servers (for example, an Office Communications client installed on a non–domain joined machine), you'll want to make sure you are using a certificate from a public CA. A public certificate is required for federation, as well as the public IM connectivity (PIC) to connect with AOL, MSN, and Yahoo!. The option of using an internal certificate is available if you are not going to use federation or PIC, but again, this is not a decision to be made lightly.

When using an internal CA to issue your certificates on the external Edge, non–domain joined computers have no way to authenticate the certificate or to check if it was revoked. So, for those clients to connect to your Office Communications Servers, you'll have to download the Certificate Chain from your internal CA. Depending on your support organization, this might be a fairly large task depending on how many users you have to support and the types of operating systems that your end users have at home. It may cause a rise in support costs as well as calls. Computers today have a list of public CAs and a copy of their Certificate Chains. This will enable end users to use non-domain systems to connect without having to download and install a Certificate Chain. So, consider this when trying to determine if you are going to use an external certificate from a public CA.

TABLE 15-7 Details for Chicago—Internal Load Balancer for Co-located Edge Servers

ROLE/FEATURE	QUANTITY/ VALUE(S)	LOCATION/ SETTING	NOTE/EXAMPLE
Load Balancer			
Access Edge and A/V Edge (shared)	chi-es.litwareinc.com	Perimeter network	Internally facing hardware load balancer with 1 VIP. Note that the internal edge of the Web Conferencing Edge Services is not load balanced.
VIPs			
Access Edge and A/V Edge VIP (internal)	(1) 192.168.10.40	100-megabit Full	Virtual IP address on the internal load balancer for an array of Edge Servers (shared by all Edge Services).
Ports			
Firewall (internal)	8057 TCP	Outbound	Traffic from Data Conferencing Servers of the EE pool → Web Conferencing Edge Service Node1 (chi-es-01.litwareinc.com) and Node2 (chi-es-02.litwareinc.com).
	5061 TCP	Bi-directional	Traffic to/from Edge Server internal load balancer VIP (chi-es.litwareinc.com) ↔ Director load balancer VIP (chi-dir.litwareinc.com) and to Web Conferencing Servers and A/V Conferencing Servers in EE pool.
	443 TCP	Outbound	Traffic from Internal Network (all) → A/V Edge Service internal load balancer VIP (chi-es.litwareinc.com).

TABLE 15-7 Details for Chicago—Internal Load Balancer for Co-located Edge Servers

ROLE/FEATURE	QUANTITY/ VALUE(S)	LOCATION/ SETTING	NOTE/EXAMPLE
	3478 UDP	Outbound	Traffic from internal network (all) → A/V Edge Service internal load balancer VIP (chi-es.litwareinc.com).
	5062 TCP	Outbound	Traffic from internal network (all) → A/V Edge Service internal load balancer VIP (chi-es.litwareinc.com). Note that the internal firewall rule must enable traffic from any computer on the internal network that will be involved in A/V calls or A/V conferencing to reach the A/V Edge Service internal load balancer VIP over all three ports.
Certificates			
CN/SN	N/A	N/A	N/A
DNS (Internal)			
(A)	chi-es.litwareinc.com	192.168.10.40	N/A
DNS (External)			
(A)	N/A	N/A	N/A

TABLE 15-8 Details for Chicago Edge Server Nodes

ROLE/FEATURE	QUANTITY/VALUE(S)	LOCATION/ SETTING	NOTE/EXAMPLE
Server			
Edge Server (Access Edge Service, Web Conferencing Edge Service, A/V Edge Service)			
Node1	CHI-ES-01	Perimeter network	Workgroup servers in the perimeter network. Each node is running Access Edge Service, Web Conferencing Edge Service, and A/V Edge Service.
Node2	CHI-ES-02	Perimeter network	
NICs			
Node1 (internal-facing)	(1) 192.168.10.41	100-megabit Full	Shared by all Edge Services
Node2 (internal-facing)	(1) 192.168.10.42	100-megabit Full	Shared by all Edge Services
Node1 (external-facing)	(1/3) 64.65.66.11	100-megabit Full	Used by Access Edge Service. Can be behind a Network Address Translation (NAT) or port-forwarding firewall.
	(2/3) 64.65.66.21	100-megabit Full	Used by Web Conferencing Edge Service. Can be behind a NAT or port-forwarding firewall.

TABLE 15-8 Details for Chicago Edge Server Nodes

ROLE/FEATURE	QUANTITY/VALUE(S)	LOCATION/ SETTING	NOTE/EXAMPLE
	(3/3) 64.65.66.31	100-megabit Full	Used by A/V Edge Service. Must be a publicly addressable IP address. Can be behind a port-forwarding firewall but not translated with NAT. Note that the default gateway should be on the external NIC in each node and point to the Internet, or you might not get audio on remote Microsoft Office Communicator 2007 R2/Office Communicator Phone Edition calls.
Node2 (external-facing)	(1/3) 64.65.66.12	100-megabit Full	Used by Access Edge Service. Can be behind a NAT or port-forwarding firewall.
	(2/3) 64.65.66.22	100-megabit Full	Used by Web Conferencing Edge Service. Can be behind a NAT or port-forwarding firewall.
	(3/3) 64.65.66.32	100-megabit Full	Used by A/V Edge Service. Must be a publicly addressable IP address. Can be behind a port-forwarding firewall but not translated with NAT.
Ports			
Firewall (internal)	N/A	N/A	All Edge Services on the Edge Server array will use ports opened for those services on the internal load balancer VIP (sip-es.litwareinc.com).

TABLE 15-8 Details for Chicago Edge Server Nodes

ROLE/FEATURE	QUANTITY/VALUE(S)	LOCATION/ SETTING	NOTE/EXAMPLE
Firewall (external)	N/A	N/A	All Edge Services on the Edge Server array will use ports opened for those services on the external load balancer VIPs (sip.litwareinc.com, chi-wce.litwareinc.com, chi-ave.litwareinc.com).
Certificates (internal)			
Internal certificate shared by all Edge Services (for both nodes)	CN/SN=chi-es.litwareinc.com	Enhanced Key Usage (EKU): Server/Client	Used for client/server Transport Layer Security (TLS)/ Mutual Transport Layer Security (MTLS).
Certificates (external)			
External certificate assigned to Access Edge Service (for both nodes)	CN/SN=sip.litware-inc.com SAN=sip.litwareinc.com; sip.additional-SIPDomainName.com	EKU: Server/ Client	First entry in Subject Alternative Name (SAN) must match the CN/SN of certificate. If federation is enabled, the certificate must be issued by a public CA. Same physical certificate must be present on both nodes. The SAN must contain additional entries for each SIP domain that federated partners and/or remote users will access.
External certificate assigned to Web Conferencing Edge Service (for both nodes)	CN/SN=chi-wce.litwareinc.com	EKU: Server/ Client	The same certificate can be applied to both nodes. If federation is enabled, the certificate must be issued by a public CA.
Authentication certificate assigned to the A/V Edge Service (for both nodes)	CN/SN=chi-ave.litwareinc.com	EKU: Server	A certificate is used to create Media Relay Access Server (MRAS) access tokens. They are not exposed to the client. The same physical certificate must be present on both nodes.

TABLE 15-8 Details for Chicago Edge Server Nodes

ROLE/FEATURE	QUANTITY/VALUE(S)	LOCATION/ SETTING	NOTE/EXAMPLE
DNS (Internal)			
(A)	chi-es-01.litwareinc.com	192.168.10.41	This is the internal FQDN of the Edge Server (Node1).
(A)	chi-es-02.litwareinc.com	192.168.10.42	This is the internal FQDN of the Edge Server (Node2).
DNS (External)			
(A)	N/A	N/A	External NICs in Node1 and Node2 are externally accessible only via the respective load balancer VIPs; use internal IP addresses for managing each node.
(SRV)	_sip._tls.*litwareinc.com* _sipfederationtls._tcp.*litwareinc.com*	_tls for port 443 _tcp for port 5061	

Table 15-9 provides a detailed view of the infrastructure requirements for the HTTP reverse proxy server in the Chicago perimeter network.

TABLE 15-9 Details for Chicago HTTP Reverse Proxy Server

ROLE/FEATURE	QUANTITY/VALUE(S)	LOCATION/ SETTING	NOTE/EXAMPLE
Server			
HTTP reverse proxy server	CHI-RP-01	Perimeter network	Workgroup server running Internet Security and Acceleration (ISA) Standard Edition in the perimeter network.
NICs			
Internal	(1) 192.168.10.60	100-megabit Full	
External	(1) 64.65.66.30	100-megabit Full	The HTTP Reverse Proxy Server role can be behind a NAT or port-forwarding firewall.

TABLE 15-9 Details for Chicago HTTP Reverse Proxy Server

ROLE/FEATURE	QUANTITY/VALUE(S)	LOCATION/ SETTING	NOTE/EXAMPLE
Ports			
NOTE That if internal and external facing Internet Security and Acceleration (ISA) Server NICs reside in the perimeter network, port 443 needs to be open inbound from the ISA Server to the Office Communications Server 2007 R2 Enterprise Edition Load Balancer VIP.			
Firewall (internal)	443 TCP	Inbound	Traffic from HTTP reverse proxy server (chi-rp-01.litwareinc.com) → Office Communications Server 2007 R2 Enterprise Edition load balancer VIP (chi-pool.litwareinc.com).
Firewall (external)	443 TCP	Inbound	Traffic from Internet HTTP → reverse proxy server (chi-rp-01.litwareinc.com).
Certificates			
Certificate assigned on reverse proxy	CN/SN=chi-rp-01.litwareinc.com	EKU: Server	Exportable Machine certificate: used for client/server TLS/MTLS.
DNS (Internal)			
(A)	chi-rp-01.litwareinc.com	192.168.10.60	This is the internal FQDN of the HTTP reverse proxy server.
DNS (External)			
(A)	chi-rp-01.litwareinc.com	64.65.66.30	This is the external FQDN of the HTTP reverse proxy server.

Table 15-10 and Table 15-11 provide detailed views of the infrastructure requirements for the Director servers in Chicago.

TABLE 15-10 Details for Chicago Load Balancer for Office Communications Server 2007 R2 Enterprise Edition Director Pool

ROLE/FEATURE	QUANTITY/VALUE(S)	LOCATION/ SETTING	NOTE/EXAMPLE
Load Balancer			
Office Communications Server R2 Enterprise Edition pool	chi-dir.litwareinc.com	Internal network	Hardware load balancer with 1 VIP.
VIPs			
EE Director pool VIP (external)	(1) 10.18.10.32	100-megabit Full	VIP Address on the load balancer for EE Director pool.
Ports			
Firewall (internal)	5061 TCP	Bi-directional	Traffic to/from Access Edge Server internal load balancer VIP (chi-es.litwareinc.com) ↔ EE Director pool load balancer VIP (chi-dir.litwareinc.com).
Firewall (external)	N/A	N/A	N/A
Certificates			
N/A	N/A	N/A	N/A
DNS (Internal)			
(A)	N/A	N/A	N/A
DNS (External)			
(A)	chi-dir.litwareinc.com	10.18.10.32	Note that this DNS entry must be made both in the internal corp network as well as the perimeter network so that it is resolvable by internal EE servers as well as the Edge Servers.

TABLE 15-11 Details for Chicago EE Director Pool

ROLE/FEATURE	QUANTITY/VALUE(S)	LOCATION/ SETTING	NOTE/EXAMPLE
Server			
EE Director Pool Front-End Server			
Node1 Node2	CHI-DIR-01 CHI-DIR-02	Internal network Internal network	Domain members on the internal network. Each node is running a copy of Office Communications Server 2007 R2 Enterprise Edition.
NICs			
Node1 Node2	(1) 10.18.10.30 (1) 10.18.10.31	100-megabit Full 100-megabit Full	
Ports			
Firewall (internal)	N/A	N/A	N/A
Certificates			
Certificate assigned to both front-end nodes	CN/SN=chi-dir.litware-inc.com	EKU: Server	
DNS (Internal)			
(A)	chi-dir-01.litwareinc.com	10.18.10.30	This is the internal FQDN of each front-end server in the EE Director pool.
(A)	chi-dir-02.litwareinc.com	10.18.10.31	
DNS (External)			
(A)	N/A	N/A	N/A

Note that the infrastructure requirements for the back-end SQL cluster for the Director pool are not described in detail. These requirements are the same as the back-end SQL cluster for the EE pool described in Table 15-14.

Table 15-12 and Table 15-13 provide detailed views of the infrastructure requirements for the expanded Office Communications Server 2007 R2 Enterprise Edition pool in Chicago.

TABLE 15-12 Details for Chicago Load Balancer for Office Communications Server 2007 R2 Enterprise Edition Pool

ROLE/FEATURE	QUANTITY/VALUE(S)	LOCATION/ SETTING	NOTE/EXAMPLE
Load Balancer			
Office Communications Server 2007 R2 Enterprise Edition pool	chi-pool.litwareinc.com	Internal network	Hardware load balancer with 1 VIP; accessed by way of the Director.
VIPs			
EE pool VIP (internal)	(1) 10.18.10.1	100-megabit Full	Virtual IP address on the load balancer for the Office Communications Server 2007 R2 Enterprise Edition front-end servers.
Ports			
Firewall (internal)	N/A	N/A	N/A
Certificates			
CN/SN	N/A	N/A	N/A
DNS (Internal)			
(A)	chi-pool.litwareinc.com	10.18.10.1	
DNS (External)			
(A)	N/A	N/A	N/A

TABLE 15-13 Details for the Chicago Office Communications Server 2007 R2 Enterprise Edition Front-End Servers

ROLE/FEATURE	QUANTITY/VALUE(S)	LOCATION/ SETTING	NOTE/EXAMPLE
Server			
EE Front-End Server			
Node1	chi-fe-01.litwareinc.com	Internal network	Domain member Office Communications Server 2007 R2 Enterprise Edition expanded pool. Each front-end server in the pool contains all the server roles that belong to an EE pool (for example, Front End role, Web Conferencing Server role, A/V Conferencing Server role, Web Component Server role) and is configured exactly the same way. The pool name is CHI-POOL.
Node2	chi-fe-02.litwareinc.com	Internal network	
Node3	chi-fe-03.litwareinc.com	Internal network	
Node4	chi-fe-04.litwareinc.com	Internal network	
Node5	chi-fe-05.litwareinc.com	Internal network	
Node6	chi-fe-06.litwareinc.com	Internal network	
NICs			
Node1 (internal)	(1) 10.18.10.2	100Mb Full	
Node2 (internal)	(1) 10.18.10.3	100Mb Full	
Node3 (internal)	(1) 10.18.10.4	100Mb Full	
Node4 (internal)	(1) 10.18.10.5	100Mb Full	
Node5 (internal)	(1) 10.18.10.6	100Mb Full	
Node6 (internal)	(1) 10.18.10.7	100Mb Full	
Ports			
Firewall (internal)	N/A	N/A	N/A
Certificates			
Certificate assigned to every front-end node	CN/SN=chi-pool.litwareinc.com	EKU: Server	Used for client/server TLS/MTLS.

TABLE 15-13 Details for the Chicago Office Communications Server 2007 R2 Enterprise Edition Front-End Servers

ROLE/FEATURE	QUANTITY/VALUE(S)	LOCATION/ SETTING	NOTE/EXAMPLE
	SAN=chi-pool.litware-inc.com sip.litwareinc.com	sip.additionalSIP-DomainName.com	The first entry in the SAN must match the CN/SN of the certificate. The SAN must contain additional entries for each SIP domain that federated partners and/or remote users will access.
DNS (Internal)			
(A)	chi-fe-01.litwareinc.com	10.18.10.2	This is the internal FQDN of each EE front-end server in the pool.
(A)	chi-fe-02.litwareinc.com	10.18.10.3	
(A)	chi-fe-03.litwareinc.com	10.18.10.4	
(A)	chi-fe-04.litwareinc.com	10.18.10.5	
(A)	chi-fe-05.litwareinc.com	10.18.10.6	
(A)	chi-fe-06.litwareinc.com	10.18.10.7	
(SRV)	_sipinternal._tcp.*litwareinc.com*	_tcp for port 5061	
	_sipinternaltls._tcp. *litware-inc.com*	_tcp for port 5061	
DNS (External)			
(A)	N/A		The Office Communications Server 2007 R2 EE pool is not addressable externally accept via the Access Edge Service/Director pool.

Table 15-14 provides a detailed view of the infrastructure requirements for the back-end SQL cluster in the Chicago pool.

TABLE 15-14 Details for Chicago Back-End SQL Cluster

ROLE/FEATURE	QUANTITY/VALUE(S)	LOCATION/ SETTING	NOTE/EXAMPLE
Server			
SQL Server cluster	chi-be.litwareinc.com	Internal network	This is the virtual name for the SQL Server cluster.
Node1	CHI-BE-01	Internal network	Domain member SQL Server (EE pool back end).
Node2	CHI-BE-02	Internal network	Domain member SQL Server (EE pool back end).
NICs			
Node1 (internal) Node2 (internal)	(1) 10.18.10.11 (1) 10.18.10.12	100-megabit Full 100-megabit Full	
Ports			
Firewall (internal)	N/A	N/A	N/A
Certificates			
N/A	N/A	N/A	N/A
DNS (Internal)			
(A)	chi-be.litwareinc.com	10.18.10.10	This is the internal FQDN of the SQL Server cluster.
(A)	chi-be-01.litwareinc.com	10.18.10.11	
(A)	chi-be-02.litwareinc.com	10.18.10.12	
DNS (External)			
(A)	N/A		The SQL Server is not addressable externally.

DIRECT FROM THE SOURCE

Windows Server 2008 and the Windows Firewall with Advanced Security

Rick Kingslan
Senior Technical Writer, Office Communications Server Group

Deploying Office Communications Server 2007 R2 is usually a streamlined process once you have done the planning and requirements mapping. The Setup Wizard does a very good job in leading your deployment team along the steps necessary to install the infrastructure. However, if you are installing on Windows Server 2008, there is a potential issue that you will need to plan for.

Windows Server 2008 includes a much more powerful firewall than was included with Windows Server 2003. By default, all ports inbound are closed. As you install roles or features onto the server, the installers are designed to open ports as necessary. For example, if you install file services, you would find port 445 is opened for inbound traffic, among others.

Why is this information important to your deployment efforts? If you deploy your back-end SQL Server on Windows Server 2008 and use either SQL Server 2005 or SQL Server 2008, you will need to manually open ports for SQL Server to communicate with your front-end server. SQL Server 2005 does not automatically open ports or inform you of what ports to open. SQL Server 2008 will warn the administrator with a dialog box stating what ports to open and refers to the appropriate reference material.

To open ports in Windows Server 2008, you can either use the command line tool, "netsh", or you can use the administrative management tool, "Windows Firewall with Advanced Security." However, the first step that you need to do is to plan out what port(s) you need to open and which protocols will be used. In the case of the communication between SQL Server and the front-end server, you will need to open port 1433 on TCP.

Windows Server 2008 also introduces a concept known as network profiles. There are three possible profiles: public, domain, and private. This is important because the firewall enforces rules based on these profiles and you can include one, two, or all three profiles in your rule. If you are not sure which profile your network currently is defined as, check the "Network and Sharing Center." You will find each interface defined, and in the case of the back-end and the front-end servers, both should be automatically defined as 'domain'. Also, all rules require a name to identify them, and a description is optional but suggested to document WHY you created this rule.

A recap of the rule to create on the back-end server:

- Protocol and Port: TCP/1433
- Direction: Inbound
- Profile: Domain
- Name: SQL inbound for port 1433
- Source: Front-End Server IP
- Destination: Back-End Server
- Action: Allow

With Windows Server 2008 Windows Firewall with Advanced Security, a wizard guides you through entering the appropriate information from the rule above. Starting the Windows Firewall with Advanced Security Microsoft Management Console (MMC), right-click the Inbound node, and select 'New Rule...' to add a new rule – then follow the wizard.

The command line is only slightly more difficult to configure this rule. If you are already familiar with 'netsh', then you might find this method much easier than the wizard – especially if there are a number of rules to define. The netsh command that creates the same rule as defined earlier is:

```
netsh advfirewall firewall add rule name="SQL Inbound for Port 1433"
profile=domain protocol=TCP dir=in localport=1433 action=allow
```

For a complete listing of all options with the 'add rule' command, type the following at the command prompt:

```
netsh advfirewall firewall add rule /?
```

Table 15-15 provides detailed views of the infrastructure requirements for the Archiving Server in Chicago.

TABLE 15-15 Details for the Chicago Archiving Server

ROLE/FEATURE	QUANTITY/VALUE(S)	LOCATION/ SETTING	NOTE/EXAMPLE
Server			
Archiving	CHI-ARC-01	Internal network	Domain member.
NICs			
Internal	(1) 10.18.10.20	100-megabit Full	
Ports			
Firewall (internal)	N/A	N/A	N/A

TABLE 15-15 Details for the Chicago Archiving Server

ROLE/FEATURE	QUANTITY/VALUE(S)	LOCATION/ SETTING	NOTE/EXAMPLE
Certificates			
N/A	N/A	N/A	The Archiving Server doesn't require a certificate
DNS (Internal)			
(A)	chi-arc-01.litwareinc.com	10.18.10.20	
DNS (External)			
(A)	N/A	N/A	N/A

Table 15-16 provides a detailed view of the infrastructure requirements for the Archiving Server's back-end SQL Server cluster.

TABLE 15-16 Details for Chicago Back-End SQL Cluster

ROLE/FEATURE	QUANTITY/VALUE(S)	LOCATION/ SETTING	NOTE/EXAMPLE
Server			
SQL	CHI-ARCBE-01	Internal network	Domain member SQL Server.
NICs			
Internal	(1) 10.18.10.21	100-megabit Full	
Ports			
Firewall (internal)	N/A	N/A	N/A
Certificates			
N/A	N/A	N/A	N/A
DNS (Internal)			
(A)	chi-arcbe.litwareinc.com	10.18.10.21	This is the internal FQDN of the SQL Server.
DNS (External)			
(A)	N/A		The SQL Server is not addressable externally.

Note that the infrastructure requirements for the Monitoring Server and the Monitoring Server back-end SQL are exactly the same as those of the Archiving Server and the Archiving Server back-end SQL.

Table 15-17 provides a detailed view of the infrastructure requirements for the Mediation Server in Chicago.

TABLE 15-17 Details for the Chicago Mediation Server

ROLE/FEATURE	QUANTITY/ VALUE(S)	LOCATION/SETTING	NOTE/EXAMPLE
Server			
Mediation	chi-med-01. litwareinc.com	Internal network	Domain member running the Office Communications Server 2007 R2 Mediation Server role.
NICs			
Internal	(1) 10.18.10.50	100-megabit Full	
External	(1) 10.18.10.51	100-megabit Full	Carries unsecured PSTN traffic to/from the IP/PSTN gateway. Enables 64 Kbps per concurrent PSTN call.
Ports			
Firewall (internal)	N/A	N/A	N/A
Firewall (gateway network)	N/A	N/A	N/A
Certificates			
Certificate assigned to the Mediation Server	CN/SN= chi-med-01. litwareinc.com	EKU: Server	Used for Server MTLS/ Secure Real-Time Protocol (SRTP).
DNS (Internal)			
(A)	chi-med-01.litwareinc.com	10.18.10.50	This is the internal FQDN of the Mediation Server. (Ping resolves to this IP address.)

TABLE 15-17 Details for the Chicago Mediation Server

ROLE/FEATURE	QUANTITY/ VALUE(S)	LOCATION/SETTING	NOTE/EXAMPLE
(A)	chi-med-01. litwareinc.com	10.18.10.51	This is the IP address used for the Mediation Server ↔ SIP/PSTN gateway communication. Considered an external interface by the Mediation Server.
DNS (External)			
(A)	N/A		

Preparing DNS and Firewall Ports for the Paris Deployment

Table 15-18 contains the summary view of all infrastructure requirements for the deployment in Paris.

TABLE 15-18 Summary of Paris Infrastructure Requirements

SERVER ROLE	NAME	EXTERNAL DNS NAME (IP ADDRESS)	INTERNAL DNS NAME (IP ADDRESS)	EXTERNAL FIREWALL PORT (DIRECTION)	INTERNAL FIREWALL PORT (DIRECTION)
Edge Server—Access Edge Service (load balancer)	PAR-ES	par-es-ext. litwareinc.com VIP = (64.64.66.1)	par-es. litwareinc.com VIP = (192.167.10.40)	443 TCP (inbound) (Internet → Access Edge Service for remote access) 5061 TCP (both) (Internet ↔ Access Edge Service for federation)	5061 TCP (both) (Office Communications Server 2007 R2 pool ↔ Access Edge Service)

TABLE 15-18 Summary of Paris Infrastructure Requirements

SERVER ROLE	NAME	EXTERNAL DNS NAME (IP ADDRESS)	INTERNAL DNS NAME (IP ADDRESS)	EXTERNAL FIREWALL PORT (DIRECTION)	INTERNAL FIREWALL PORT (DIRECTION)
Edge Server—Web Conferencing Edge Service	PAR-ES	par-wce.litwareinc.com VIP = (64.64.66.2)	N/A	443 TCP (inbound) (Internet → Web Conferencing Edge Server)	8057 TCP (outbound) (Office Communications Server 2007 R2 pool → Web Conferencing Edge Service)
Edge Server—A/V Edge Service (load balancer)	PAR-ES	par-ave.litwareinc.com VIP = (64.64.66.3)	par-es.litwareinc.com VIP = (192.167.10.40)	443 TCP (inbound) (Internet → A/V Edge Service) 3478 UDP (inbound) (Internet → A/V Edge Service) 50,000–59,999 TCP & UDP (both) (Internet ↔ A/V Edge Service)	443 TCP (outbound) (Internal Net [all IPs] → A/V Edge Service) 3478 UDP (outbound) (internal Net [all IPs] → A/V Edge) 5062 TCP (outbound) (internal Net [all IPs] → A/V Edge Service)
NODES (EDGE SERVER)					
Node1	PAR-ES-01	N/A (64.64.66.11, 64.64.66.21, 64.64.66.31)	par-es-01.litwareinc.com (192.167.10.41)	N/A	N/A

TABLE 15-18 Summary of Paris Infrastructure Requirements

SERVER ROLE	NAME	EXTERNAL DNS NAME (IP ADDRESS)	INTERNAL DNS NAME (IP ADDRESS)	EXTERNAL FIREWALL PORT (DIRECTION)	INTERNAL FIREWALL PORT (DIRECTION)
Node2	PAR-ES-02	N/A (64.64.66.12, 64.64.66.22, 64.64.66.32)	par-es-02.litwareinc.com (192.167.10.42)	N/A	N/A
HTTP reverse proxy server	PAR-RP-01	par-rp-01.litwareinc.com (64.64.66.30)	par-rp-01.litwareinc.com (192.167.10.60)	443 TCP (inbound) Internet → HTTP reverse proxy server	443 TCP (inbound) HTTP reverse proxy server → Office Communications Server 2007 R2 pool
EE pool (load balancer)	PAR-POOL	N/A	chipool.litwareinc.com VIP = (10.17.10.1)	N/A	N/A
EE FRONT ENDS					
Node1	PAR-FE-01	N/A	par-fe-01.litwareinc.com (10.17.10.2)	N/A	N/A
Node2	PAR-FE-02	N/A	par-fe-02.litwareinc.com (10.17.10.3)	N/A	N/A
Node3	PAR-FE-03	N/A	par-fe-03.litwareinc.com (10.17.10.4)	N/A	N/A
Node4	PAR-FE-04	N/A	par-fe-04.litwareinc.com (10.17.10.5)	N/A	N/A
Back-end SQL Server (cluster name)	SQL-BE	N/A	par-be.litwareinc.com VIP = (10.17.10.10)	N/A	N/A

TABLE 15-18 Summary of Paris Infrastructure Requirements

SERVER ROLE	NAME	EXTERNAL DNS NAME (IP ADDRESS)	INTERNAL DNS NAME (IP ADDRESS)	EXTERNAL FIREWALL PORT (DIRECTION)	INTERNAL FIREWALL PORT (DIRECTION)
BACK-END SQL NODES					
Node 1	PAR-BE-01	N/A	par-be-01.litwareinc.com (10.17.10.11)	N/A	N/A
Node 2	PAR-BE-02	N/A	par-be-02.litwareinc.com (10.17.10.12)	N/A	N/A
Archiving Server	PAR-ARC-01	N/A	par-arc-01.litwareinc.com (10.17.10.20)	N/A	N/A
Archiving Server back-end SQL Server	PAR-ARCBE-01	N/A	par-arcbe-01.litwareinc.com (10.17.10.21)	N/A	N/A
Monitoring Server	PAR-MON-01	N/A	par-mon-01.litwareinc.com (10.17.10.22)	N/A	N/A
Monitoring Server back-end SQL Server	PAR-MONBE-01	N/A	par-monbe-01.litwareinc.com (10.17.10.23)	N/A	N/A

Preparing DNS and Firewall Ports for the Singapore Deployment

Table 15-19 contains the summary view of all infrastructure requirements for the deployment in Singapore.

TABLE 15-19 Summary of Singapore Infrastructure Requirements

SERVER ROLE	NAME	EXTERNAL DNS NAME (IP ADDRESS)	INTERNAL DNS NAME (IP ADDRESS)	EXTERNAL FIREWALL PORT (DIRECTION)	INTERNAL FIREWALL PORT (DIRECTION)
Edge Server—Access Edge Service	SPO-ES-01	spo-es-ext.litwareinc.com (64.62.66.11)	spo-es.litwareinc.com (192.165.10.41)	443 TCP (inbound) (Internet → Access Edge Service for remote access) 5061 TCP (both) (Internet ↔ Access Edge Service for federation)	5061 TCP (both) (Office Communications Server 2007 R2 pool ↔ Access Edge Service)
Edge Server—Web Conferencing Edge Service	SPO-ES-01	spo-wce.litwareinc.com (64.62.66.21)	spo-es.litwareinc.com (192.165.10.41)	443 TCP (inbound) (Internet → Web Conferencing Edge Server)	8057 TCP (outbound) (Office Communications Server 2007 R2 pool → Web Conferencing Edge Service)

TABLE 15-19 Summary of Singapore Infrastructure Requirements

SERVER ROLE	NAME	EXTERNAL DNS NAME (IP ADDRESS)	INTERNAL DNS NAME (IP ADDRESS)	EXTERNAL FIREWALL PORT (DIRECTION)	INTERNAL FIREWALL PORT (DIRECTION)
Edge Server—A/V Edge Service (load balancer)	SPO-ES-01	spo-ave.litwareinc.com (64.62.66.31)	spo-es.litwareinc.com (192.168.10.41)	443 TCP (inbound) (Internet → A/V Edge Service) 3478 UDP (inbound) (Internet → A/V Edge Service) 50,000–59,999 TCP & UDP (both) (Internet ↔ A/V Edge Service)	443 TCP (outbound) (Internal Net [all IPs] → A/V Edge Service) 3478 UDP (outbound) (Internal Net [all IPs] → A/V Edge) 5062 TCP (outbound) (Internal Net [all IPs] → A/V Edge Service)
HTTP reverse proxy server	SPO-RP-01	spo-rp-01.litwareinc.com (64.62.66.30)	spo-rp-01.litwareinc.com (192.165.10.60)	443 TCP (inbound) Internet → HTTP reverse proxy server	443 TCP (inbound) HTTP reverse proxy server → Office Communications Server 2007 R2 pool
SE Server (with archiving and monitoring servers collocated)	SPO-SE-01	N/A	spo-se-01.litwareinc.com (10.15.10.1)	N/A	N/A

TABLE 15-19 Summary of Singapore Infrastructure Requirements

SERVER ROLE	NAME	EXTERNAL DNS NAME (IP ADDRESS)	INTERNAL DNS NAME (IP ADDRESS)	EXTERNAL FIREWALL PORT (DIRECTION)	INTERNAL FIREWALL PORT (DIRECTION)
Archiving Server and Monitoring Server back-end SQL Server	SPO-ARC-MONBE-01	N/A	spo-arcmonbe-01.litwareinc.com (10.15.10.21)	N/A	N/A

Litware, Inc.'s Deployment Path for Chicago

After preparing the server hardware and surrounding infrastructure—such as DNS and firewall configuration—Litware, Inc. can begin its Office Communications Server 2007 R2 deployment. Litware, Inc. decides to start with the deployment in the Chicago headquarters and follows the deployment path presented in Table 15-20. For each server role deployment, Litware, Inc. reads the information in the corresponding Office Communications Server 2007 R2 Deployment Guides at *http://go.microsoft.com/fwlink/?LinkID=133726.*

TABLE 15-20 Deployment Path for Chicago

STEP	SERVER	ACTION
1	CHI-BE	Install SQL cluster.
2	CHI-BE-01	Install SQL back end.
3	CHI-BE-02	Install SQL back end.
4		Create Enterprise Edition pool by using the Create Pool step from the Office Communications Server 2007 R2 setup program on the installation media (point to CHI-BE when prompted for a SQL Server).
5	CHI-POOL	Install and configure the pool load balancer
6	CHI-FE-01	Install the first front-end server. Install and assign the certificate on the server.
7	CHI-FE-02	Install the second front-end server. Install and assign the certificate on the server.
8	CHI-FE-03	Install the third front-end server. Install and assign the certificate on the server.
9	CHI-FE-04	Install the fourth front-end server. Install and assign the certificate on the server.

TABLE 15-20 Deployment Path for Chicago

STEP	SERVER	ACTION
10	CHI-FE-05	Install the fifth front-end server. Install and assign the certificate on the server.
11	CHI-FE-06	Install the sixth front-end server. Install and assign the certificate on the server.
12		Test basic IM/presence functionality: Create two test user accounts and home them on the new pool. Test Office Communicator 2007 R2 client IM access first with one or more front-end servers offline and then with all of them online. Test the client with both manual and automatic configuration options. Sign in using two clients.
13		Test Web Access: Test Office Communicator 2007 R2 client Group Expansion and Global Address List download first with one IIS (installed on the front-end servers) offline and then with both online.
14		Test Web Conferencing: Install two Microsoft Office Meeting 2007 R2 clients to test Web Conferencing first with one or more Web Conferencing Services (installed on the front-end box) offline and then with all of them online.
15		Test A/V: Test Office Live Meeting 2007 R2 and Office Communicator 2007 R2 A/V Conferencing first with one or more A/V Conferencing Services (installed on the front-end box) offline and then with all of them online.
16	CHI-ARCBE-01	Install SQL Server for the Archiving back end.
17	CHI-ARC-01	Install Archiving Server (point to CHI-ARCBE-01 when prompted to specify a SQL Server).
18		Test IM archiving: Use Office Communicator 2007 R2 clients to send test messages and ensure the messages are being archived in the archiving database on the CHI-ARCBE-01 server.
19	CHI-MONBE-01	Install SQL Server for the Monitoring back end.
20	CHI-MON-01	Install the Monitoring Server (point to CHI-MONBE-01 when prompted to specify a SQL server).
21		Test Call Detail Record: Use Office Communicator 2007 R2 clients to send instant messages and Live Meeting clients to do A/V and Web Conferencing. Ensure these sessions are being recorded in the monitoring database on CHI-MONBE-01 server.
22	CHI-DIRBE	Install the SQL cluster for the Director pool.
23	CHI-DIRBE-01	Install the SQL back end.

TABLE 15-20 Deployment Path for Chicago

STEP	SERVER	ACTION
24	CHI-DIRBE-02	Install the SQL back end.
25		Create Enterprise Edition Director pool by using the Create Pool step from the Office Communications Server 2007 R2 setup program (point to CHI-DIRBE when prompted for a SQL Server).
26	CHI-DIR	Install and configure the Director pool load balancer.
27	CHI-DIR-01	Install the first front-end server for the Director pool. Install and assign the certificate on the server.
28	CHI-DIR-02	Install the second front-end server for the Director pool. Install and assign the certificate on the server.
29		Test Office Communicator 2007 R2 client IM access first with one front-end server of the Director offline and then with both of them online. To ensure that the Office Communicator client hits the Director, manually configure Office Communicator to point to the Director pool.
30	CHI-ES	Install load balancers for the internal and external edges of the Edge Server.
31	CHI-ES-01	Install the first Edge Server. Install and assign the appropriate certificates. Configure the Edge Server to point to the Director pool.
32	CHI-ES-02	Install the second Edge Server. Install and assign the appropriate certificates. Configure the Edge Server to point to the Director pool.
33		Test Office Communicator 2007 R2 client IM external access first with one of the Access Edge Services offline and then with both online.
34		Test Live Meeting 2007 R2 client external Web Conferencing Edge Service access first with one of the Web Conferencing Edge Services offline and then with both online.
35		Test Office Communicator 2007 R2 client A/V Edge Service external access first with one of the A/V Edge Services offline and then with both online.
36		Test Live Meeting 2007 R2 client external A/V Edge Service access first with one or more A/V Edge Services offline and then with all of them online.
37		Install the SIP/PSTN gateway and connect it to the PSTN network.

TABLE 15-20 Deployment Path for Chicago

STEP	SERVER	ACTION
38	CHI-MED-01	Install the Mediation Server. Install and assign certificates. Configure the Mediation Server to point to the Director pool (or EE pool) on the internal side and to an existing SIP/PSTN gateway on the external side.
39		Enable users for Voice and configure normalization rules, phone routes, and location profiles (refer to Chapter 11, "VoIP Scenarios," for more details).
40		Test the Office Communicator 2007 R2 client by placing and receiving PSTN calls.

DIRECT FROM THE SOURCE

Validating Automatic Configuration Entries

Byron Spurlock
Consultant II, Microsoft Consulting Services

To allow users in the organization to sign in automatically requires they use SRV records. There may be times when you as the Office Communications Server administrator do not have access to creating the necessary DNS records in Active Directory and need to validate that the DNS "SRV" and "A" host records are created correctly. The Validation Wizard has a SIP Logon Checker that validates that the users are able to leverage the automatic configuration records that were created. When running the Validation Wizard for this test, omit the Configuration and Connectivity Checker and select only the SIP Logon Checker. Once selected, be sure to enable the option for Automatic Configuration. This allows the test user accounts that you specify during the test to attempt to sign in to Office Communications Server via NT LAN Manager (NTLM) or Kerberos authentication. Once the client signs in, the DNS "SRV" and "A" host records that were created in Active Directory will be leveraged to sign in to Office Communicator. If the DNS records have not been created, the results will show in the validation report.

Litware, Inc.'s Deployment Path for Paris

The next location to be configured after the Chicago deployment in Litware, Inc.'s Office Communications Server 2007 R2 deployment is Paris. Litware, Inc. decides to deploy in the order described in Table 15-21.

TABLE 15-21 Deployment Path for Paris

STEP	SERVER	ACTION
1	PAR-BE	Install the SQL cluster.
2	PAR-BE-01	Install the SQL back end.
3	PAR-BE-02	Install the SQL back end.
4		Create the Enterprise Edition pool by following the "Create Pool" step from the Office Communications Server 2007 R2 setup program (point to PAR-BE when prompted for a SQL server).
5	PAR-POOL	Install and configure the pool load balancer.
6	PAR-FE-01	Install the first front-end server. Install and assign the certificate on the server.
7	PAR-FE-02	Install the second front-end server. Install and assign the certificate on the server.
8	PAR-FE-03	Install the third front-end server. Install and assign the certificate on the server.
9	PAR-FE-04	Install the fourth front-end server. Install and assign the certificate on the server.
10		Test basic IM/presence functionality: Create two test user accounts and home them on the new pool. Test Office Communicator 2007 R2 client IM access first with one or more front-end servers offline and then with all of them online. Test the client with both manual and automatic configuration options. Sign in using two clients.
11		Test Web Access: Test the Office Communicator 2007 R2 client Group Expansion and Global Address List download first with one IIS (installed on the Front End Servers)offline and then with both online.
12		Test Web Conferencing: Install two Live Meeting 2007 R2 clients to test Web Conferencing first with one or more Web Conferencing Services (installed on the front-end box) offline and then with all of them online.

TABLE 15-21 Deployment Path for Paris

STEP	SERVER	ACTION
13		Test A/V: Test Live Meeting 2007 R2 and Office Communicator 2007 R2 A/V Conferencing first with one or more A/V Conferencing Services (installed on the front-end box) offline and then with all of them online.
14	PAR-ARCBE-01	Install the SQL Server for the Archiving back end.
15	PAR-ARC-01	Install the Archiving Server (point to PAR-ARCBE-01 when prompted to specify a SQL Server).
16		Test IM Archiving: Use Office Communicator 2007 R2 clients to send test messages and ensure the messages are being archived in the archiving database on the PAR-ARCBE-01 server.
17	PAR-MONBE-01	Install the SQL Server for the Monitoring back end.
18	PAR-MON-01	Install the Monitoring Server (point to PAR-MONBE-01 when prompted to specify a SQL Server).
19		Test Call Detail Record: Use Office Communicator 2007 R2 Clients to send instant messages and Live Meeting clients to do A/V and Web Conferencing. Ensure these sessions are being recorded in the monitoring database on PAR-MONBE-01 server.
21	PAR-ES	Install internal and external load balancers Edge Server.
22	PAR-ES-01	Install the first Edge Server. Install and assign the appropriate certificates. Configure the Edge Server to point to the Director pool (in Chicago).
23	PAR-ES-02	Install the second Edge Server. Install and assign the appropriate certificates. Configure the Edge Server to point to the Director pool (in Chicago).
24		Test Office Communicator 2007 R2 client IM external access first with one or more Access Edge Services offline and then with all of them online.
25		Test Live Meeting 2007 R2 client external Web Conferencing Edge Service access first with one or more Web Conferencing Edge Services offline and then with all of them online.
26		Test Office Communicator 2007 R2 client A/V Edge Service external access first with one or more A/V Edge Services offline and then with all of them online.
27		Test Live Meeting 2007 R2 client external A/V Edge Service access first with one or more A/V Edge Services offline and then with all of them online.

Litware, Inc.'s Deployment Path for Singapore

The last pool location for Litware, Inc.'s Office Communications Server 2007 R2 deployment is Singapore. Litware, Inc. decides to deploy Office Communications Server 2007 R2 server roles in the order described in Table 15-22.

TABLE 15-22 Deployment Path for Singapore

STEP	SERVER	ACTION
1	SPO-SE-01	Install the Standard Edition Server. Install and set up certificates.
2	SPO-ARCMONBE-01	Install the SQL Server that will be shared by the Archiving and Monitoring back end.
3	SPO-SE-01	Install the Archiving and Monitoring Servers on the Standard Edition Server machine.
4		Test basic IM/presence functionality: Create two test user accounts and home them on the Standard Edition Server. Test Office Communicator 2007 R2 client IM access. Test the client with both manual and automatic configuration options. Sign in using two clients.
5		Test Web Access: Test the Office Communicator 2007 R2 client Group Expansion and Global Address List download.
6		Test Web Conferencing: Install two Live Meeting 2007 R2 clients to test Web Conferencing.
7		Test A/V: Test Live Meeting 2007 R2 and Office Communicator 2007 R2 A/V Conferencing.
8	SPO-ES-01	Install the Edge Server. Install and assign the appropriate certificates. Configure the Edge Server to point to the Director pool (in Chicago).
9		Test Office Communicator 2007 R2 client IM external access.
10		Test Live Meeting 2007 R2 client external Web Conferencing Edge Service access.
11		Test Office Communicator 2007 R2 client A/V Edge Service external access.
12		Test Live Meeting 2007 R2 client external A/V Edge Service access.

Final Litware, Inc. Architecture

The final Litware, Inc. architecture is shown in Figure 15-4.

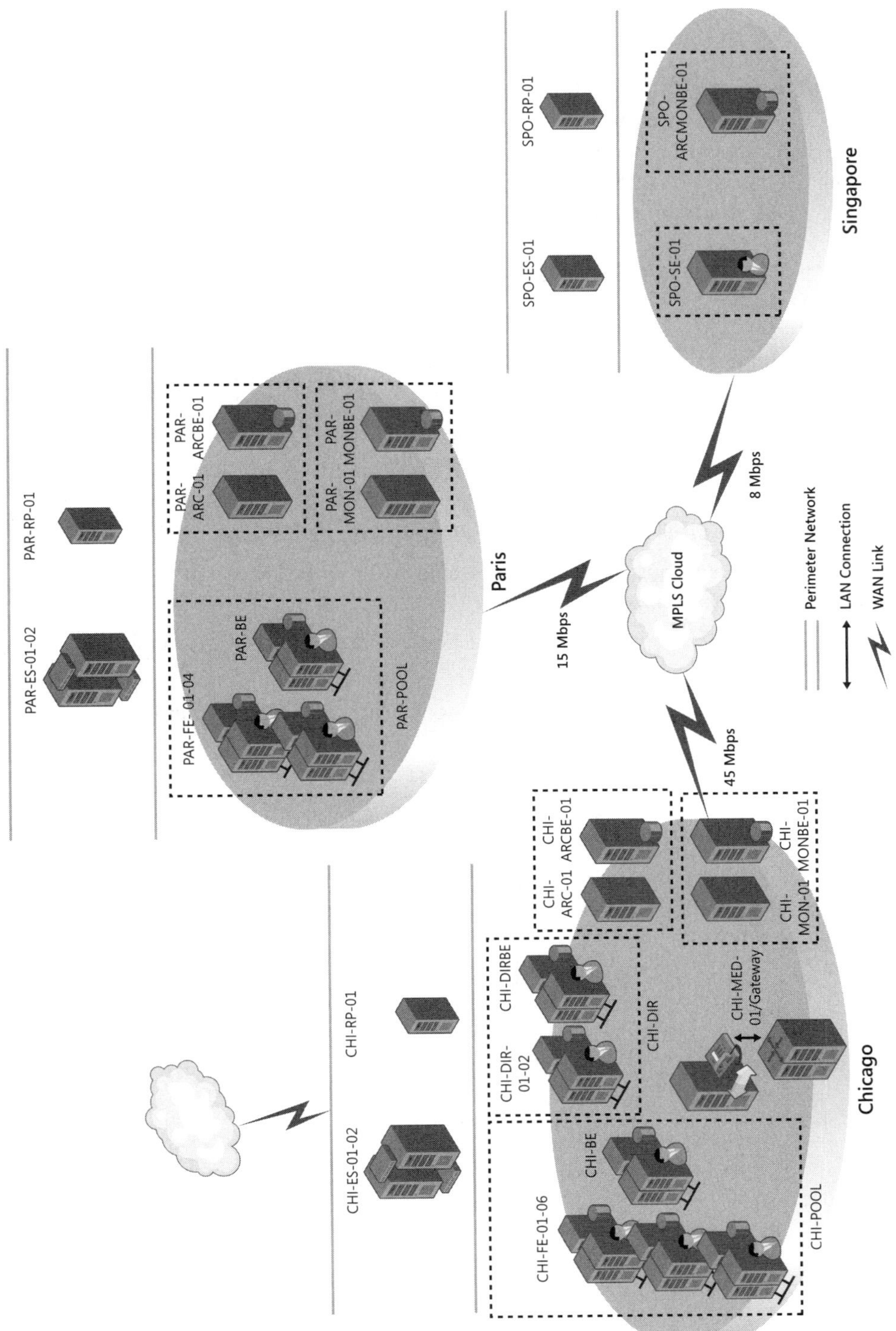

FIGURE 15-4 Litware, Inc.'s global Office Communications Server 2007 R2 architecture

Summary

It is important to develop an architectural diagram that shows the entire Office Communications Server 2007 R2 deployment in an enterprise environment as a record of the topology and to explain the deployment to other departments that are involved with the deployment or to management. It can also be useful during troubleshooting and for any technical discussions that require a high-level system overview.

Additional Resources

- Office Communications Server 2007 R2 downloads, found at *http://go.microsoft.com/fwlink/?LinkID=133654*
- Office Communications Server 2007 R2 Planning Guide, found at *http://go.microsoft.com/fwlink/?LinkID=133725*
- Office Communications Server 2007 R2 Enterprise Voice Planning and Deployment Guide, found at *http://go.microsoft.com/fwlink/?LinkID=133698*
- Office Communications Server 2007 R2 Deployment Guides, found at *http://go.microsoft.com/fwlink/?LinkID=133729*
- Office Communications Server 2007 R2 Command Line Reference, found at *http://technet.microsoft.com/en-us/library/bb894706.aspx*
- Office Communications Server 2007 R2 Active Directory Guide, found at *http://go.microsoft.com/fwlink/?LinkID=133727*

PART IV

Operations and Administration

CHAPTER 16

Monitoring

Getting Microsoft Office Communications Server 2007 properly deployed is important; however, a successful deployment does not ensure administrators can walk away and assume their job is done. After all, even the most perfectly deployed piece of infrastructure can be derailed by unforeseen circumstances. Hardware can fail; network segments can go down; a set of mergers can, overnight, triple the number of people who use the system. Because of this, Office Communications Server administrators need to constantly monitor the system and usage. That way, if anything goes wrong, the problem can be caught and fixed before the organization's communications infrastructure spirals out of control.

Office Communications Server includes tools that administrators can use to monitor their Office Communications Server infrastructure. These tools—all of which are either built into the system or are available as free downloads—include the following:

- Event logs
- Performance Monitor
- Archiving Server and Monitoring Server
- Deployment Validation Tool
- System Center Operations Manager management pack

In this chapter, we'll take a closer look at these tools and explain how they can be used to help monitor the health of and track usage information for Office Communications Server.

Event Logs

Similar to most applications, Office Communications Server records milestone events—successes, failures, and warnings—in the event log. In the case of Office Communications Server, that's an event log named Office Communications Server (%windir%\System32\Config\Office Communications Server.evt). For example, a milestone event would occur if your Archiving Server is unable to connect to its back-end database. Should that happen, the following event will be recorded in the event log:

```
Failed to connect to the back-end database. Office Communications Server Archiving
Service will continuously attempt to reconnect to the back-end. While this condition
persists, incoming messages will not be archived and will remain in the queue.
```

Any plan you develop for monitoring the health of an Office Communications Server installation should include a regular review of the Office Communications Server event log. Because there's nothing special about the Office Communications Server event log, you can perform these reviews by using the Microsoft Windows Event Viewer. However, you might want to take a closer look at the event log capabilities included in the Office Communications Server 2007 R2 Microsoft Management Console (MMC) snap-in (hereafter referred to as the Administrative Tool). Most people find it faster and more efficient to view Office Communications Server events by using the Office Communications Server Administrative Tool rather than Event Viewer.

Using the Administrative Tool to View Office Communications Server Events

Using the Administrative Tool is recommended due to the filtering mechanisms built into it. If you use Event Viewer to open the Office Communications Server event log, you will, by default, see all the events recorded in that event log. However, suppose you were interested in only a subset of events—for example, suppose you wanted to see only events related to the operation of a Mediation Server. To view a subset of events in Event Viewer, you need to go to the View menu, click Filter, and then create an event filter that prevents the display of any events that do not have an event source equal to Mediation Server.

This is not a hard task, but you will likely find yourself creating filters similar to this each and every time you run Event Viewer, which can get tedious. More important, even *this* might not give you the information you're interested in. For example, an Event Viewer filter enables you to select events from only a single event source. Is that a problem? It can be. For example, server applications for Office Communications Server use multiple event sources, including these:

- Applications Module
- Client Version Filter
- Intelligent Instant Messaging (IM) Filter

Therefore, the only way to get a comprehensive look at server application events by using Event Viewer is to create at least three different filters, one for each event source. In addition, you'll have to view the events returned by these filters one at a time: first the *Applications Module* events, then the *Client Version* events, and finally the *Intelligent IM* events. You cannot select multiple event sources when creating an event filter.

In addition, Event Viewer also assumes that you know which three event sources are used for *Mediation Server* events. If you don't have this information at hand, you'll find it difficult to create filters that help you focus on the Mediation Server. And if you have more than one Mediation Server, you'll need to create another instance of the Event Viewer snap-in to be able to switch back and forth between the event logs for the two computers; Event Viewer can show events from only a single computer at any given time.

By contrast, the Administrative Tool has some intelligent filtering built into it. By default, using the Administrative Tool to access the event log will show you the 10 latest events (regardless of event source or category) recorded for that server. But as you will see, you're not limited to that default dataset. Nor do you need to run multiple copies of the tool just to view events from multiple computers. For example, suppose you have more than one Mediation Server. All you have to do is click the node for a different Mediation Server. *All* your servers will appear in the Administrative Tool, and you can easily access the event logs for any of them.

> ***NOTE*** **How exactly do you access an event log in the Administrative Tool? In the Administrative Tool, expand the nodes until you locate the particular server you're looking for. Once you locate the desired server, click the server name and then click the Event Log tab in the right window pane. You'll see the events for that particular server displayed on the screen.**

As mentioned earlier, the Administrative Tool, by default, shows the 10 latest events recorded for a server. To see more than just the last 10 events, that default view can easily be changed by expanding Event Log Filter in the right window pane and then using the filter-setting user interface.

The Administrative Tool offers a considerable amount of flexibility in selecting which events will, or will not, be displayed. For example, you can select any (or all) of the standard event types: Information, Warning, and Error. You can limit the returned events to just those records written after a specified date and time, and you can specify the number of events to view up to a maximum of 999.

Perhaps even more important, you can also filter events by event category. It should be noted that the event categories the Administrative Tool uses are different than the event categories Event Viewer uses. If you look at an event log in Event Viewer, you'll notice that each event source has been assigned a numeric *Category* value—for example, Office Communications Server has a *Category* of 1000, and the Office Communications Server Protocol Stack has a *Category* of 1001. In the Administrative Tool, the Event category typically encompasses multiple event sources and event categories. For example, the Server Applications category found in the Administrative Tool includes such event sources as the Office Communications Server Applications Module (*Category* 1010), the Office Communications Server Client Version Filter (1041), and the Office Communications Server Intelligent IM Filter (1025). In other words, all the events related to a general category—such as Server Applications—can be viewed at the same time using a single filter. Remember when we said that Event Viewer requires you to write multiple event filters to view events from multiple event sources? The Administrative Tool makes it easier to work around that limitation.

> ***NOTE*** **The event categories—and the event sources that are included in each Category—are built into the product and cannot be modified.**

As if that weren't enough, the events and event categories have also been prefiltered for you based on server role. For example, if you click a server in the Standard Edition Servers node, you will see categories similar to the following (the actual categories will vary depending on the different roles that server plays):

- Front-End Components
- Voice Applications
- Server Applications
- IM and Telephony Conferencing
- Quality of Experience (QoE) Agent
- Archiving Agent
- Management
- Deployment
- Web Conferencing
- Audio/Visual (A/V) Conferencing
- Application Sharing
- Web Components
- Conference Auto Attendant
- Conference Announcement Service
- Application Management
- Call Control Service

By contrast, clicking on this same server in the Archiving Server node reveals the following categories:

- Archiving Server
- Management
- Deployment

Why so few categories? Because these three are the categories most relevant to the server's role as an Archiving Server. Other categories (such as IM and Telephony Conferencing) don't apply to the archiving service and thus do not appear in the Event Categories drop-down list. Therefore, the total number of events that can be viewed from the Event Log tab will also vary depending on server role. For example, on one test computer, viewing the Event Log tab under the Standard Edition Server node revealed 999 events (the maximum number of events that can be viewed in the Administrative Tool). By comparison, this same server listed only 169 events under the Archiving Server node and just 151 under the Monitoring Server node. The difference has to do with the number of events relevant to a given role. And that's good; after all, if you're interested in the Monitoring Server, all you really need to see are the 151 events that pertain to the Monitoring Server. The other 848 events in the event log (the ones that the Administrative Tool filters out) just make it harder for you to locate relevant information.

Incidentally, the Administrative Tool has another useful feature: the Expand All Records option. One weakness of the Event Viewer is that events can be displayed only in a spreadsheet-type view; if you want to see the detailed description for an event, you must double-click that event and open the record in a separate window. By contrast, if you select Expand All Records in the Administrative Tool, each event will automatically be expanded to show the event description. This makes it easy to scroll through the list and see the actual reason for each event.

The Administrative Tool provides a quick and easy way to get an overview of the Office Communications Server event log. However, this convenience does come at a small price: Despite its many advantages, the Administrative Tool does have a few limitations when compared to Event Viewer. For one thing, the Administrative Tool *is* limited to 999 events; if you need to see more than 999 events, you must use Event Viewer. Unlike Event Viewer, the Administrative Tool does not enable you to sort events by fields such as *Source* or *Event ID*; instead, you are limited to sorting events chronologically (in either ascending or descending order). In addition, events viewed in the Administrative Tool cannot be saved as a text file or comma-separated values file; that can only be done using Event Viewer.

Accessing the Event Log by Using Scripts

Scripting—using VBScript, Windows PowerShell, or another Windows scripting language—provides another approach to accessing the events in the Office Communications Server event log. Using the Windows Management Instrumentation (WMI) class *Win32_NTLogEvent*, administrators can write sophisticated SQL-like queries that make it easy to search the event log for specific events. This information can then easily be exported to a text file, a database, or a spreadsheet. With WMI eventing, administrators can also receive immediate notification any time a particular event (or type of event) is recorded in the event log. For example, you could write a script that alerts you any time an error event is recorded or any time an event with a specified event source is recorded.

A complete explanation of accessing event logs by using scripts lies outside the scope of this chapter. For additional information and for sample scripts, please see the Office Communications Server Tech Center at *http://go.microsoft.com/fwlink/?LinkID=133618.*

Performance Monitoring

Event logs are good at informing you that a problem has occurred; however, the information recorded in the event logs isn't always sufficient to tell you *why* the problem occurred. In addition, event log notifications tend to happen after the fact, that is, problems are usually recorded in the event log only *after* they occur. Although there are exceptions, event log events generally don't give you advance notice that a problem is likely to occur; instead, the event log simply reports the incident after the problem has occurred.

As a system administrator, this means that, in addition to reviewing the event logs, you will often find it necessary to conduct a more finite analysis of your Office Communications Server infrastructure. This often involves real-time monitoring of the system and its individual components. As a system administrator, you also know that the best way to monitor the performance of any Windows component is to use the Performance Monitor snap-in. And that's good news for Office Communications Server users. Office Communications Server has been instrumented with scores of performance counters—counters that enable you to monitor everything from the total number of users currently connected to the system to the fine-grained details telling you how server components such as Mediation Server are doing.

Monitoring Performance Using the Administrative Tool

Although you can monitor performance using a standalone instance of Performance Monitor, you might find it easier to use the instances of Performance Monitor that are embedded in the Administrative Tool because these instances of Performance Monitor have been prepopulated with the performance counters most relevant to a specific server role (in much the same way the Event Log tab prepopulated the Event Viewers with relevant event categories). For example, click a Standard Edition Server node in the Administrative Tool and then click the Performance tab in the right window pane. When you do that, you'll see an instance of Performance Monitor already up and running and using the following performance counters:

- SIP – 024 –Flow-controlled Connections Dropped
- DATAMCU – 000 – HTTP Stack load
- SIP – 001 – Incoming Messages/sec
- DATAMCU – 001 – HTTP Stack state
- SIP – 000 – Average Holding Time for Incoming Messages

For comparison purposes, click the Performance tab in an Archiving Server node. You'll see an instance of Performance Monitor that, by default, uses these performance counters:

- Arch Service – 000 – Messages successfully parsed

- Arch Service – 002 – Messages that failed validation
- Arch Service – 000 – Messages written to DB
- Arch Service – 002 – Messages failed to be written to DB

Again, this is a quick and easy way to get an overview of your servers and how (or even if) they are carrying out their appointed tasks.

Of course, you aren't limited to the default set of counters provided for you; after all, these are regular—and extensible—instances of Performance Monitor. This means that you can add any performance counter to any of these Performance Monitor instances. For example, suppose you want to add the % Processor Time counter to a Performance Monitor instance. To do that, find the desired instance and then click the Add button to bring up the Add Counter dialog box.

In the Add Counter dialog box, select the Performance object from the drop-down list (for this example, that's the Processor object). After choosing the object, select the desired counter and counter instances, and then click Add. When you are finished adding performance counters, click Close to dismiss the dialog box.

Modifying the Default Counter Sets

If there's a downside to using the Performance Monitors embedded in the Administrative Tool, it's this: Any customizations you make to these Performance Monitors are not saved when you exit the Administrative Tool. For example, suppose you *do* add the % Processor Time counter to a Performance Monitor instance. When you close the Administrative Tool and later restart the application, that additional performance counter will be gone. You'll see only the default set of performance counters for each instance of Performance Monitor. You cannot customize a Performance Monitor instance and then save that customization by using the Administrative Tool.

Fortunately, you can work around that problem by modifying the default set of performance counters for a particular server role. Performance counter information is stored in a file named ServerPerfmon.xml, a file that is read each time the Administrative Tool starts. (Typically, you will find this file in the folder C:\Program Files\Common Files\Microsoft Office Communications Server 2007 R2.) You can change the default set of counters for a server role simply by adding or removing counters from ServerPerfmon.xml.

> ***NOTE*** **Of course, you should make a backup copy of ServerPerfmon.xml before you begin making adjustments to it. Performance Monitor is a fairly resilient application. For example, if you specify a nonexistent counter, Performance Monitor will still run; it just won't display that particular counter. Nevertheless, it's still a good idea to make a backup copy of the XML file. If nothing else, this provides a quick and easy way for you to restore the default values.**

Removing performance counters for a server role is easy. Locate and delete the appropriate line (or lines) in ServerPerfmon.xml. For example, suppose you want to remove one of the default performance counters used by your Archiving Servers. To do that, find the section of the XML file that deals with Archiving Server. That section should look something like this:

```
    <!-- Performance counters for Office Communications Server 2007 R2, Archiving
Service -->
    <counters serverRole="ARCH">
      <counter scaleFactor="0"  path="LC:Arch Service - 01 - READ\Arch Service - 000 -
Messages successfully parsed" />
      <counter scaleFactor="0"  path="LC:Arch Service - 01 - READ\Arch Service - 002 -
Messages that failed validation" />
      <counter scaleFactor="0"  path="LC:Arch Service - 02 - WRITE\Arch Service - 000
- Messages written to DB" />
      <counter scaleFactor="0"  path="LC:Arch Service - 02 - WRITE\Arch Service - 002
- Messages failed to be written to DB" />
    </counters>
```

Now, delete the line of text corresponding to the performance counter you want removed. For example, if you don't want the *Messages failed to be written to DB* counter to appear by default, simply delete this line from the XML file:

```
      <counter scaleFactor="0"  path="LC:Arch Service - 02 - WRITE\Arch Service - 002
- Messages failed to be written to DB" />
```

Once you've deleted the entry corresponding to the counter you want to remove (in our example "LC:Arch Service – 02 – WRITE\Arch Service – 002 – Messages failed to be written to DB") the Archiving Server section will look like this:

```
    <!-- Performance counters for Office Communications Server 2007 R2, Archiving
Service -->
    <counters serverRole="ARCH">
      <counter scaleFactor="0"  path="LC:Arch Service - 01 - READ\Arch Service - 000 -
Messages successfully parsed" />
      <counter scaleFactor="0"  path="LC:Arch Service - 01 - READ\Arch Service - 002 -
Messages that failed validation" />
      <counter scaleFactor="0"  path="LC:Arch Service - 02 - WRITE\Arch Service - 000
- Messages written to DB" />
    </counters>
```

Save ServerPerfmon.xml and then restart the Administrative Tool. Now look at the Performance Monitoring tab for one of your Archiving Servers. You should see just three performance counters; Messages failed to be written to DB will no longer appear by default.

Removing a performance counter from the default counter set is easy. But what if you want to *add* a new performance counter to a default instance of Performance Monitor? You first need to know the exact path of the performance counter. The easiest way to determine the path to a performance counter is to add that counter to an existing instance of Performance Monitor.

To determine the path, right-click the counter name and then click Properties. The counter path will appear on the Data tab of the System Monitor Properties dialog box.

From the counter's properties, the path for the % Processor Time counter is \\server.fabrikam.com\Processor(_Total)\% Processor Time. (If you are monitoring performance on the local machine, you can leave off the \\server.fabrikam.com\.) To add this counter to ServerPerfmon.xml, add the following line to the Archiving Server section:

```
<counter scaleFactor="0" path=" Processor(_Total)\% Processor Time " />
```

NOTE **Setting *scaleFactor* to 0 causes Performance Monitor to use the default scale value for that counter.**

If you are reluctant to modify ServerPerfmon.xml, you can also create a custom monitoring console by dragging a text file of performance counter data onto a running instance of Performance Monitor. (This is most useful when you simply want to add additional performance counters to an instance of Performance Monitor.)

To do so, add additional counters as needed to an existing instance of Performance Monitor. (For example, add the Processor\%Processor Time counter to the Archiving Server's instance of Performance Monitor.) After all the counters have been added, click the Copy Properties button on the Performance Monitor toolbar. This copies information about each performance counter to the Clipboard. From there, paste the information into Notepad and then save the data as a text file. That file will include lines similar to the following lines that define each counter used in the instance:

```
    <PARAM NAME="Counter00001.Path" VALUE="\\server.Vdomain.com\LC:DATAMCU - 02 -
MCU Health And Performance\DATAMCU - 000 - HTTP Stack load"/>
    <PARAM NAME="Counter00001.Color" VALUE="16711680"/>
    <PARAM NAME="Counter00001.Width" VALUE="1"/>
    <PARAM NAME="Counter00001.LineStyle" VALUE="0"/>
    <PARAM NAME="Counter00001.ScaleFactor" VALUE="0"/>
    <PARAM NAME="Counter00001.Minimum" VALUE="0"/>
    <PARAM NAME="Counter00001.Maximum" VALUE="0"/>
    <PARAM NAME="Counter00001.Average" VALUE="0"/>
    <PARAM NAME="Counter00001.StatisticStatus" VALUE="0"/>
```

So what do you do with this text file? The next time you want to use this same set of counters, start up an instance of Performance Monitor (either from within the Administrative Tool or as a standalone instance). As soon as Performance Monitor is up and running, drag the text file onto that instance. When you do that, any counters listed in the text file that are not currently in use will be added to that instance of Performance Monitor.

The Archiving Server and the Monitoring Server

There are many reasons you should monitor the performance of Office Communications Server. For example, on a fundamental level, you need to know whether Office Communications Server is still running and whether the various server components are still functioning. In addition, it is also useful to know if Office Communications Server is running *optimally*. In other words, are you—and your users—getting the best possible service? Do you have enough front-end servers to handle the typical morning rush when users first sign on? Do you have sufficient network bandwidth to allow for high-quality video and audio conferencing? Just how many users *are* using IM? To answer these questions, you don't necessarily need performance data; instead, you need detailed statistical information on how Unified Communications (UC) is used in your organization. How do you get that kind of detailed statistical information? By using the Archiving Server or the Monitoring Server.

The Archiving Server

The Archiving Server was introduced in Office Communications Server 2007 as a way to: (1) archive the actual contents of instant message conversations and group conferences; and (2) capture usage information (in the form of Call Detail Records, or CDRs) related to Office Communications Server activities such as file transfers, A/V conversations, application sharing, remote assistance, and so on. Prior to the R2 release, if you were interested in capturing usage information, you needed to install the Archiving Server.

> ***NOTE*** Is it really necessary to archive the contents of all your users' IM sessions? As it turns out, it might be very important. A number of industries (including banking and financial services) are required, by law, to keep records of all their electronic communications, including IM.

With the R2 release of Office Communications Server, most of the CDR capabilities originally found in the Archiving Server have been moved to the Monitoring Server. The Archiving Server is now used exclusively for monitoring (and archiving) instant message conversations. If that's the only type of communication you're interested in tracking, then the Archiving Server is probably all you need. However, if you need to track usage information for other media—such as conferences, file transfers, or Enterprise Voice calls—you will also need to install the Monitoring Server.

NOTE The Archiving Server enables you to store the actual contents of instant messages. However, the Monitoring Server does not record and store actual phone calls or conferences. Instead, it simply records information about those calls (for example, who placed the call, what device they used when placing the call, the date and time of the call, and so on).

As noted earlier, many of the CDR capabilities originally included in the Archiving Server have been moved to the Monitoring Server. This has resulted in changes being made to the Archiving Server database. That's important if you are upgrading from Office Communications Server 2007 to Office Communications Server 2007 R2. For example, the following tables have been removed from the database:

- MediaList
- Roles
- Gateways
- Multipoint Control Units (MCUs)
- Phones
- FocusJoinsAndLeaves
- McuJoinsAndLeaves
- ConferenceMessageCount
- FileTransfers
- Media
- VoIPDetails

These tables can now be found in the Monitoring Server CDR database (LcsCDR). If you have scripts that access these tables, you will need to modify those scripts so that they connect to the LcsCDR database. If you are upgrading from the original release of Office Communications Server to the R2 release, be aware that your previous Archiving Server data will *not* be migrated when you make the switch. Instead, the old database will be overwritten by the new one.

If you decide to deploy the Archiving Server, keep in mind that simply installing the component does not mean that all your instant message information will be archived. Archiving does not take place by default; instead, you must explicitly configure archiving within the organization. To configure archiving, do the following.

1. Open the Administrative Tool, right-click the forest node, point to Properties, and then click Global Properties. You do this on the forest node because archiving properties are configured at the forest level and then enabled at the pool level.
2. In the Office Communications Server Global Properties dialog box, on the Archiving Tab, select the desired setting for both internal and federated communications. Three mutually exclusive options are available: Archive For All Users, Do Not Archive For Any Users, and Archive According To User Settings.

3. If you selected Archive According To User Settings, you will then need to access the user accounts for each pool (found in the Users node) and specify whether archiving should be enabled for each individual user. If you chose Archive For All Users or Do Not Archive For Any Users, you do not have to modify the archive settings for an individual account. (In fact, this option will be unavailable to you.) In these two cases, the forest-level settings take precedence.
4. Finally, access each pool, right-click the pool name, point to Properties, and then click Front End Properties. In the Properties dialog box, on the Archiving tab, select Activate IM Content Archiving. After that's done, click the Associate button and then select the Archiving Server that should be used for this particular pool.

> ***NOTE*** **You also have the option to have the Archiving Server shut down any time archiving fails. This prevents users from conducting IM sessions that cannot be monitored and archived.**

The Monitoring Server

If you ask people to rate the voice quality of a phone call or A/V conference, you will likely get back answers similar to the following:

- The speakers sounded funny, like they were under water or something.
- I kept hearing an echo over and over.
- Everyone was talking too quietly.

Is that useful information? Well, it might be. On the other hand, answers like these are highly subjective and are difficult to correlate and compare. Because of this, voice quality researchers typically don't ask open-ended questions such as, "How did the voice quality sound to you?" Instead, they employ an absolute categorization rating (ACR) scale. With an ACR scale, users are asked a set of questions about the listening experience and are asked to rate the quality of their experience on a scale of 1–5 (with 1 representing a bad experience and 5 representing an excellent experience). The researchers then average these values to calculate a mean opinion score (MOS). Although MOS scores are not a perfect representation of the listening experience, they do make it possible to compare and contrast listening experiences. If group A reports an MOS of 4.1 and group B reports an MOS of 2.2, it's safe to say that—on average—listeners in group A had a much better experience than listeners in group B.

This same philosophy underlines the quality of experience metrics used by the Monitoring Server, an Office Communications Server 2007 component first introduced as an optional download and now fully integrated into the product. The only difference is that the Monitoring Server does not ask users to rate their listening experiences on a scale of 1–5; instead, the Monitoring Server uses a series of algorithms to predict how users would rate the quality of each listening experience. Based on those algorithms, the Monitoring Server reports the following MOS scores:

- **Listening MOS** A prediction of the wideband quality of an audio stream being played to a user. The MOS score takes into account audio fidelity and distortion as well as speech and noise levels.
- **Sending MOS** A prediction of the wideband quality of an audio stream sent from a user. The MOS score takes into account audio fidelity and distortion as well as speech and noise levels.
- **Network MOS** Another prediction of the wideband quality of an audio stream played to a user. In this case, however, only network factors are considered such as the audio codec used, packet loss, packet errors, and jitter (the variation in the delay time of packets arriving at a destination).
- **Conversational MOS** A prediction of the narrowband conversational quality of the audio stream played to the user. This value is indicative of how a large group of people would rate the quality of the connection for holding a conversation.

> ***NOTE*** **When dealing with the Monitoring Server, *narrowband* refers to audio codecs that use an 8-kHz (kilohertz) sample rate. *Wideband* refers to audio codecs that use a 16-kHz sample rate. Telephone-quality communication is normally categorized as narrowband.**

Like archiving, the Monitoring Server's CDRs must be configured at the forest level and then enabled at the pool level. To configure CDRs, right-click the forest node in the Administrative Tool, point to Properties, and then point to Global Properties. In the Office Communications Server Global Properties dialog box, on the Call Detail Records tab, select the call types you would like to track (you may select as many, or as few, of these call types as you like).

- **Peer-to-Peer call details** Includes IM, A/V, file transfers, and application sharing
- **Conferencing call details** Includes all multiparty sessions, including Group Chat, A/V, file transfers, and any conferencing sessions conducted using the Microsoft Office Live Meeting client
- **Voice call details** Includes all Enterprise Voice calls

Monitoring itself must then be enabled at the pool level. To enable monitoring for a given pool, right-click the pool node, point to Properties, and then click Front End Properties. In the Front End Properties dialog box, on the Monitoring tab, select one (or both) of the following:

- **Enable Call Detail Recording (CDR)** Enables you to record the CDR information specified at the forest level
- **Enable QoE Monitoring** Enables you to track Quality of Experience data

Unlike archiving, you do not have to configure user accounts to work with the Monitoring Server; usage information for all the users in the pool will automatically be monitored and recorded. However, you do have to associate a specific Monitoring Server with each pool. That task can also be performed from the Monitoring tab (click Associate and then select a server).

Monitoring Server Reports

By default, the Monitoring Server stores QoE data in a SQL Server database named QoEMetrics. If you prefer, you can write your own scripts or applications to access the data in this database. Alternatively, you can install Monitoring Server Reports and take advantage of predefined reports that both retrieve and aggregate data from the QoEMetrics database. This is definitely the fastest and easiest way to retrieve information collected by the Monitoring Server.

The Monitoring Server Reports pack contains 12 predefined reports, including 3 CDR Activity Summary Reports and 9 different Media Quality Reports. Each report includes a filtering mechanism that enables you to customize the information that is displayed. For example, the UC-to-UC Summary Trend report enables you to filter on the following:

- **From/To** Allows you to specify a start date and an end date for the report
- **Granularity** Hourly, daily, weekly, monthly
- **Location** You can select all subnets or single out one or two specific subnnets
- **Media Connectivity** Direct, Relay, HTTP Proxy
- **Client Type** Communicator, Internet Protocol (IP) Phone, Samara
- **Capture Device**

INSTALLING MONITORING SERVER REPORTS

Before you can install and use the Monitoring Server Reports, you must first install SQL Server Reporting Services. Reporting Services is not installed by default when you install SQL Server; consequently, it's possible that you are running SQL Server but *not* running SQL Server Reporting Services. If that's the case, simply restart SQL Server setup. When the Setup Wizard reaches the Components To Install page, select Reporting Services and then complete setup.

Likewise, you might have already installed Monitoring Server without installing Monitoring Server Reports. In that case, restart the setup program for Office Communications Server. On the Deployment Wizard Welcome page, click Deploy Other Server Roles and then, on the Deploy Other Server Roles page, click Deploy Monitoring Server. Finally, on the Deploy Monitoring Server page, click Step 4, Deploy Monitoring Server Reports.

After installation is complete, you can access these reports by pointing your Web browser toward the URL specified during setup. If you installed the reports on a computer named reportserver1 in the domain fabrikam.com, the URL will be the following: *https://reports.fabrikam.com/reportserver?%2fOCSReports*.

Accessing the Archiving Server and the Monitoring Server Databases

Monitoring Server Reports are incredibly useful any time you want detailed information about UC usage in your organization. However, there might be times when the information included within these reports is too much. Sometimes, you might want nothing more than a quick overview of UC usage. Likewise, only a handful of predefined reports are included with Monitoring Server Reports; it's possible that the information you want (or, at the least, the format of that information) cannot be found on one of the prebuilt reports.

In addition, Monitoring Server Reports work only with the Monitoring Server database. They cannot be used to retrieve and report data stored in the Archiving Server database. If you want to extract data from the Archiving Server database, or if you want to extract custom data from the Monitoring Server database, then you have two primary approaches at your disposal: you can access this data by using the ArchivingCdrReporter tool, or you can directly access the database in question.

Accessing the Databases by Using the ArchivingCdrReporter Tool

If you are interested in a quick overview of how Office Communications Server is being used in your organization, then the ArchivingCdrReporter Tool is the tool for you. ArchivingCdrReporter is a Resource Kit application that enables you to quickly and easily retrieve basic statistics from the Archiving and Monitoring databases. ArchivingCdrReporter is not a full-fledged, enterprise-ready reporting tool, but it can be extremely useful, especially for administrators with a limited knowledge of SQL Server and/or database programming. (The only real alternatives to ArchivingCdrReporter are to use scripts or a third-party application to directly access one of the databases.)

So how easy is it to use ArchivingCdrReporter? You install the tool by copying two files—ArchivingCdrReporter.exe and ArchivingCdrReporter_Config.xml—from the Resource Kit CD to a folder on your hard drive. From there, you start the program by double-clicking ArchivingCdrReporter.exe.

After ArchivingCdrReporter has started, you need to specify the database that you want to work with. To do this, click the Backend Details menu, which will bring up the Edit Database Details dialog box.

In the dialog box, click the appropriate tab (CDR to access Monitoring Server's CDRs or Archiving to work with the Archiving Server's IM records) and then specify both the server name (as well as the instance of SQL Server, if needed) and the database name. Click OK, and you will be connected to the database.

> **NOTE** Monitoring Server's QoE metrics are not accessible using ArchivingCdrReporter. (Rather, they are not readily accessible.) To work with QoE data, use the Monitoring Server Reports discussed earlier in this chapter.

Incidentally, ArchivingCdrReporter can also retrieve information about Response Group Services. You can easily configure the utility to retrieve information from other SQL Server databases. To do so, you must modify the file ArchivingCdrReporter_Config.xml. For example, suppose you have a database named UserDatabase located on a server named ocs2007. To add this database to ArchivingCdrReporter_Config.xml, you would create a node similar to the following:

```
<Database>
  <Alias>New Database</Alias>
  <Server>ocs2007 </Value>
  <Name>UserDatabase</Name>


</Database>
```

Modifying ArchivingCdrReporter_Config.xml is discussed in more detail in the next section of this chapter.

Upon selecting a database, the reports available in ArchivingCdrReporter will be adjusted accordingly. Some reports are valid only in the CDR database, some are valid only in the Archiving database, and a few are valid in either database. After selecting a database, you can then retrieve information by clicking on the desired report. For example, suppose you would you like to know the total number of IM sessions that have been conducted in your organization. In that case, select the Archiving database and then click the Total Number of IM Sessions report. The total number of IM sessions will then be displayed in ArchivingCdrReporter.

In the original version of ArchivingCdrReporter, that is basically all you can do with the returned recordset. You can look at the data in the ArchivingCdrReporter window. With the R2 version of the tool, however, you now have some additional capabilities at your disposal. For example, you can select items within the recordset, right-click the records, and then click Copy to copy the information to the Clipboard. (Or, if you want to select all the records, right-click anywhere on the recordset and then click Select All.) Alternatively, you can right-click the recordset and then click Export To Excel to save the data to an Excel spreadsheet.

Adding Custom Queries to ArchivingCdrReporter

Ideally, ArchivingCdrReporter would come pre-equipped with every report—and every database query—you would ever need; in that case, retrieving usage information would be as simple as starting up ArchivingCdrReporter and clicking the desired report.

In reality, of course, it would be impossible to anticipate every report every administrator might need (not to mention the logistical nightmare of trying to accommodate all those reports within the ArchivingCdrReporter user interface). This means that it's quite possible that the database query you *really* need won't be found anywhere in ArchivingCdrReporter. This is not a problem because if you believe a particular query is missing from ArchivingCdrReporter, all you have to do is modify an XML file and add that query to the tool.

Each report shown in ArchivingCdrReporter is stored as a node in the file ArchivingCdr-Reporter_Config.xml. For example, the node for the report Total Number of IM Sessions looks like this:

```
<Query>
  <Name>Total Number of IM Sessions</Name>
  <Value>Select Count(*) as 'Number of IM Sessions' From Messages</Value>
  <Database>Archiving</Database>
</Query>
```

As you can see, the report is enclosed in a <Query> node, a node consisting of three child items:

- **<Name>** The name of the report as it appears in ArchivingCdrReporter
- **<Value>** The SQL query used to retrieve data from the database
- **<Database>** The database (CDR or Archiving) that the query should be run against

Any new report you add to ArchivingCdrReporter requires that you supply this same type of information.

> ***NOTE*** **You can also include an option <Description> node where you can type a description of the query; for example <Description>This query returns the number of instant messages sent in the past week.</Description>. This comment will appear as a tool tip any time an ArchivingCdrReporter user hovers his or her mouse over the query title.**

For example, suppose you need a count of all the instant messages sent from a particular user. One way to get this information is to specify the user's ID number (for example, 2) as part of the SQL query. (This can also be done by linking tables and using the user's Uniform Resource Identifier (URI), but using the ID number enables us to keep this example as simple as possible.) In that case, the node for your new report might look something like this:

```
<Query>
  <Name>Total Number of IM Sessions Sent By User 2</Name>
  <Value>Select Count(*) as 'Number of IM Sessions' From Messages Where FromID = 2
</Value>
  <Database>Archiving</Database>
</Query>
```

All we have done here is to create a new <Query> node. Inside that node, we set the *<Name>* to Total Number of IM Sessions Sent By User 2; we set the *<Value>* (that is, our SQL query) to the following:

```
Select Count(*) as 'Number of IM Sessions' From Messages Where FromID = 2
```

This query will retrieve all the records from the Messages table where the *FromID* field is equal to 2. This might not be that useful a report to have hard-coded into ArchivingCdr-Reporter. Again, however, the goal here is to show you how to modify the XML file, not to suggest which queries you should or should not add to that file.

Finally, we assign Archiving as the target *<Database>*. What if this query would be valid in either the Archiving database or the CDR database? In that case, our node would include two *<Database>* elements, one for each database:

```
<Database>Archiving</Database>
<Database>CDR</Database>
```

All that is left now is to decide where you want to place the new report. If you look closely at the ArchivingCdrReporter window, you see that reports have been categorized for you. For example, Total Number of IM Sessions is included in the section labeled Peer to Peer Usage Reports. Each of these sections is contained in a <Queries> node, a node that includes a *<Name>* element followed by all the individual report nodes. For example:

```
<Queries>
  <Name>Peer to Peer Usage Reports>
  <Query>


    <Name>Total Number of IM Sessions</Name>
    <Value>Select Count(*) as 'Number of IM Sessions' From Messages</Value>
    <Database>Archiving</Database>
  </Query>
<Queries>
```

You can either add your new report to an existing section, or you can create a brand new section for your report. For example, to create a new section titled Custom Reports and place your new report within that section, add the following <Queries> nodes:

```
<Queries>
  <Name>Custom Reports>
  <Query>
    <Name>Total Number of IM Sessions Sent By User 2</Name>
    <Value>Select Count(*) as 'Number of IM Sessions' From Messages Where FromID = 2
</Value>
    <Database>Archiving</Database>
  </Query>
<Queries>
```

Save the file ArchivingCdrReporter_Config.xml and then exit ArchivingCdrReporter. When you restart the application, your new section—and your new report—will be available for use.

Accessing the Databases by Using Scripts

As noted earlier, scripts offer an alternate method for accessing the events in event logs. In much the same way, scripts can also be used to access the data stored in the various Office Communications Server databases. For more information and for sample scripts, see the Office Communications Server Tech Center at *http://go.microsoft.com/fwlink/?LinkID=133618*.

Viewing the Database Schemas

Of course, before you can use a script to access a database, you need to know several things about that database, including the names of all the tables in the database, the fields that comprise each of those tables, and the data type of each of those fields. One way to get this information is to use Microsoft SQL Server Management Studio, a tool that is automatically installed when you install SQL Server.

For example, to access the Archiving Server database, start the SQL Server Management Studio. When the Connect To Server dialog box appears, type the name of the SQL Server instance in the Server Name box. For example, if the Archiving database were installed in a SQL Server instance named *archinst* on a server named server1, type the following and then click Connect:

```
server1\archinst
```

If you can't remember the name of the SQL Server instance where the Archiving Server database or the Monitoring Server databases were installed, locate the server in the Administrative Tool, and then look at the Status pane. There you'll find the name of the SQL Server instance and the name of the actual database itself.

After the connection is made, expand the Databases node and then expand the node for the Archiving database (LcsLog). After expanding the database node, expand the Tables node. When you do so, you will see all the tables in the LcsLog database:

- ClientVersions
- Computers
- ConferenceMessage RecipientList
- ConferenceMessages
- Conferences
- ContentTypes
- DbConfigDateTime

- DbConfigInt
- DbErrorMessage
- Dialogs
- Messages
- Pools
- SessionDetails
- Users

At this point, you know the names of all the tables in the database. To determine the fields for a given table, expand the table node and then expand the Columns node. This will show you the fields for that particular table. For example, if you expand the ClientVersions table, you will see the following two items:

- VersionID (PK, int, not null)
- Version (nvarchar[256], not null)

These two items indicate that the ClientVersions table has a field named *VersionID*; this field happens to be a primary key (PK), contains integer data (int), and does not allow for null values (that is, each record in the table must have a *VersionID*). It also means that this table includes a field named *Version*, which uses the *nvarchar* data type, can accept a maximum of 256 characters and does not allow for null values. If you are familiar with databases and database programming, this will be enough information to get you started.

If you aren't familiar with databases and database programming, knowing the structure of the database and its tables is likely to be of little use to you. However, you can still use SQL Server Management Studio to look at the records stored in one of these tables. To do that, right-click the table name and then click Open Table. The table records will appear in the accompanying window pane.

Deployment Validation Tool

A few years ago, a cell phone company began running a series of TV commercials that featured a technician who traveled all across the United States. Each time this technician arrived in a new spot, he would phone his home office and utter the by now ubiquitous phrase, "Can you hear me now?"

Why did the cell phone company run these commercials? To hammer home the point that, no matter where users of this service might find themselves, they would not only be able to get a connection, but they would be able to get a good, high-quality connection. How could users be assured that they really *would* be able to get such a connection? Because the cell phone company was testing and verifying connectivity from any place you could think of.

You knew your cell phone would work because the cell phone company had already been there and made *sure* that it would work.

This same idea—proactively monitoring and validating connectivity—is the reason for the Deployment Validation Tool, which is included with the Office Communications Server 2007 R2 Resource Kit. The Deployment Validation Tool simulates an audio call between two endpoints, enabling administrators (or, depending on the configuration, end users) to not only determine whether a connection can be made between these two endpoints, but to also to determine the quality of that connection.

> ***NOTE*** **Don't let the name of the tool throw you. The Deployment Validation Tool can, and should, be used after an Office Communications Server deployment to help verify that installation succeeded and that your audio/voice connections are working as expected. However, the Deployment Validation Tool shouldn't be run just that one time immediately after deployment. Instead, it should be used on a regular basis.**

Using Answering Agents

Administrators can use the Deployment Validation Tool in two different ways. To begin with, administrators can set up answering agents. Answering agents (found in the single .msi file that makes up the Deployment Validation Tool) provide an easy way for anyone in an organization (not just administrators) to test the audio quality of a connection. For example, suppose a user is on the road and needs to call in from a hotel room to join an online conference. Prior to joining the conference, the user can call an answering agent, using the same process they use to call a real person. When the call goes through, the answering agent (which operates along the lines of a standard answering machine) prompts to user to record a message. After this message has been recorded, the answering agent then plays it back, allowing the user to judge the quality of the audio connection.

Installing an Answering Agent

Answering agents should be set up on specific computers, based on your needs. (Depending on those needs, you can set up multiple agents on multiple computers.) For example, to test audio connections across the Internet, you might want to install an answering agent on a computer that lies outside your organization's firewall. In addition, if users are going to be dialing in using standard telephone lines, you might want to install an agent on a computer equipped with a dial-up modem and a valid phone number.

DIRECT FROM THE SOURCE

Deploying Answering Agents

Byron Spurlock
Microsoft Unified Communications Consultant

When deploying the Deployment Validation Tool (DVT) auto answering agent, it's a good idea to deploy an auto answering agent per pool. By deploying it per pool, you get a good representation of the quality of calls from internal or remote user(s) making a call who are homed on that particular pool. Let's say that you have two pools in your organization, one in Texas and another in Toronto. Because you have two pools with users homed in their respective pool, you should deploy and configure an agent in each pool.

In this scenario, users in Toronto can call the auto answering agent in Toronto to simulate making a call and not have to call an agent homed on a separate pool that they are not a part of.

After calling the auto answering agent, the caller should review the event logs to see if any errors occurred while the call was taking place, such as the call was not able to be made. Normally, you get an error if a call is not successful for any reason. For successful calls, don't expect to see any error logs in the Event Viewer.

Once the user makes the call and leaves a message, it's important to hear the audio quality from the playback. The recording that the end user hears is how other users will hear them while calling with Microsoft Office Communicator. Audio headphones play a vital role in audio quality when using Office Communicator to make Voice over Internet Protocol (VoIP) calls.

To install an agent, log on to the computer where the agent will reside and start the batch file SetupAgent.cmd (a file found on the Resource Kit CD). Follow the prompts, being sure to specify the following:

- When asked to enter a Session Initiation Protocol (SIP) URI, enter a URI for a valid domain user account, which is an account that has been enabled for Office Communications Server. This account should not be tied to an actual user; instead, it should be limited to use as an answering agent. In addition, each agent should be associated with a unique user account. Having more than one agent with the same SIP URI will cause problems.
- When asked to select an agent type, choose Answering Agent and enter the phone number associated with that agent. Phone numbers should be entered using the E.164 format.

By default, agent files are stored in the folder C:\Program Files\Microsoft\DVT\Agent.

NOTE When installing an agent, you might see a message box telling you that an unexpected error occurred while running Netsh.exe. This error occurs if the Windows Firewall Internet Connection Sharing Service is not running and can be safely ignored. Simply click OK and the setup program will continue.

After you install an agent, you must then log on to Office Communicator by using the agent account. If an agent is not logged on to Office Communicator, users will not be able to contact the agent and perform the audio check. (This effectively limits you to one agent per computer.)

You can change the properties of an agent at any time by starting the Agent Configurator application (click Start, click All Programs, point to Deployment Validation Tool, and then click Agent Configurator). In the SIP URI box, type the URI for the agent in question (for example, test@fabrikam.com), make your changes to the agent configuration, and then click OK.

Note that after making a change to an agent, you must restart the Office Communications Server Deployment Validation Tool Agent Service before those changes will take effect.

To make a call to an answering agent, select the desired agent from your list of Office Communicator contacts (or type in the appropriate SIP URI). Once that's done, call the agent the same way you would call any other contact. When prompted, use the Office Communicator Dialpad to press the pound key (#), record your message, and then use the Dialpad to press # a second time. At that point, the agent will replay the recorded message.

Running Formal Tests with the Deployment Validation Tool

In addition to the ad hoc, one-off testing that answering agents provide, administrators can conduct more formal (and fully automated) testing by using the complete Deployment Validation Tool. The Deployment Validation Tool consists of two components: an Organizer and a collection of agents (as many as 16 per Organizer). The Organizer's job is to run a set of tests with each of these agents. By default, each agent will call every other agent in both a peer-to-peer conversation and in a conference session mediated by Office Communications Server. For example, suppose you have three agents: A, B, and C. In that case, the default test suite would consist of the following peer-to-peer tests:

- Agent A calls agent B
- Agent A calls agent C
- Agent B calls agent A
- Agent B calls agent C
- Agent C calls agent B
- Agent C calls agent A

A similar set of tests would then be carried out for conference sessions. Each call is evaluated on multiple QoE criteria and then given a pass/fail score.

Installing the Deployment Validation Tool

To install the Deployment Validation Tool, you must first select a computer where the Organizer will run. (A complete set of tests has the potential to use a considerable amount of system resources and network bandwidth. Therefore, it's recommended that the Organizer be installed on a dedicated computer whenever possible.) The computer that hosts the Organizer must also run the following software:

- Microsoft Visual C++ 2005 Service Pack 1 (SP1) Development System Redistributable
- .NET Framework 2.0
- Microsoft SQL Server 2005, Express Edition

If any of these applications are not currently installed, setup will install them for you. Note that you must install SQL Server Express even if SQL Server is already installed on the computer.

NOTE Unlike the Organizer, agents do not have to be installed on a dedicated computer. You can safely install agents on computers that perform other tasks because the agent service is relatively lightweight and has little impact on system resources.

DIRECT FROM THE SOURCE

Deploying Validation Tool Agents

Byron Spurlock
Microsoft Unified Communications Consultant

When deploying the Deployment Validation Tool (DVT) agents, it is important to strategically place them. Let's take the following example. Our fictitious environment has five geographic locations: Houston, New York, San Francisco, Seattle, and Miami. Each location represents a substantial number of users that make up the organization. Houston is the headquarters. In this scenario, the DVT Organizer should be deployed in Houston where the IT administration is centralized.

To detect call-related issues between users in these locations, deploy an agent in each location. During configuration of the Deployment Validation Tool, leave the default settings. When running the DVT test, each agent will call the other in peer-to-peer and conference calls. So, your test matrix of agents calling each other would look similar to the following:

Houston - > New York
Houston - > San Francisco
Houston - > Seattle
Houston - > Miami

New York - > Houston
New York - > San Francisco
New York - > Seattle
New York - > Miami

San Francisco - > Houston
San Francisco - > New York
San Francisco - > Seattle
San Francisco - > Miami

Seattle - > Houston
Seattle - > New York
Seattle - > San Francisco
Seattle - > Miami

Miami - > Houston
Miami - > New York
Miami - > San Francisco
Miami - > Seattle

Each agent would call the other agents, simulating a user in one location calling another user in the defined location.

If you don't have multiple geographic offices, deployed agents should still be strategically placed around the organization. You might have a single location for your Office Communications Server deployment; however, users are separated throughout the single physical location by residing on different subnets. You could then deploy agents on different subnets within the organization.

Incidentally, when you use the complete Deployment Validation Tool, you have three different agent types at your disposal:

- **Answering Agent** This is the same type of agent that can function in standalone mode. This agent simulates an answering system any time it gets called.
- **Unified Communication** This type of agent simulates an Office Communicator 2007 client.
- **PSTN** This type of agent simulates a Public Switched Telephone Network (PSTN) phone.

After you have installed the Organizer and created all your agents, you must then add these agents to the Organizer. To do this, bring up the Admin Console (click Start, click All Programs, point to Deployment Validation Tool, and then click Admin Console). On the Roster tab, click Add Agent and then, in the URI dialog box, type in the SIP URI of the agent, a nickname to make it easy to identify the agent, and, if you wish, a description of that agent. Click OK, and the agent will be added to the roster. Remember, you can have as many as 16 agents in a single Organizer.

Running Tests and Viewing Reports

By default, the Organizer automatically runs a complete set of tests every 60 minutes. That is, each agent calls every other agent in both a peer-to-peer call and a conference call. The 60-minute interval can be modified within the Admin Console by clicking the Test Suite tab and entering a new value. You can also disable auto-checking by clearing the Auto Run check box. If you clear that check box, the test suite will no longer run at the specified interval. However, you can manually run the complete set of tests at any time by clicking the Run Suite button.

Of course, sometimes you might want to do some testing, but you don't want to run every possible test. (For example, you might only be concerned with connectivity through the Edge Servers and not with connectivity on the internal network.) In such a case, you have at least two options available to you.

First, you can test the connectivity between any two agents by right-clicking the appropriate test in the test suite matrix and then clicking Run Testcase. The Organizer will immediately run a test verifying the connectivity between those two endpoints. If you want to run tests between multiple agents but not *all* the agents, you can remove specified tests from the test suite by right-clicking each of those tests and then clicking Disable Testcase. Disabled test cases will not be run the next time the test suite executes. To restore a case to the test matrix, right-click the case and then click Enable Testcase. Alternatively, click Restore Default to re-enable all the test cases.

Each time a test is conducted, the appropriate cell in the test matrix is updated to reflect the results of that test. Green means that the test case passed, and red means that the test case failed. This provides a simple visual indicator not only of how the tests are turning out, but also of how the test suite itself is proceeding. (Tests that have not yet run will be colored white, and tests currently in process will be colored grey.)

You are not limited to this pass/fail type of reporting. For more detailed information, click the Reports tab. On this tab, you can see the following information for the tests you have conducted:

- Alert status
- Date/time
- Test type
- Connectivity results
- Quality results
- Initiator agent
- Receive agent
- Test description

If you want even *more* detailed information, click Send Reports To File. This will generate a text file report (named Reports.txt) that will automatically be saved to your Documents folder. If a file named Reports.txt already exists in that folder, it will be overwritten.

NOTE **Alternatively, you can write scripts to access the Deployment Validation Tools database, DALDB.**

Summary

This chapter introduced tools and techniques useful for monitoring Microsoft Office Communications Server. These tools—including event logs, performance monitoring, the Archiving Server, the Monitoring Server, the Deployment Validation Tool, and management packs for Microsoft Operations Manager and System Center Operations Manager—enable you to track the health both of your Office Communications Server infrastructure in general and of individual Office Communications Server servers in particular. These tools also enable you to gather data that provides information about how UC is actually used in your organization.

Additional Resources

- Product Documentation: Microsoft Office Communications Server 2007 R2 Planning for Monitoring Server found at *http://go.microsoft.com/fwlink/?LinkID=133730*
- Product Documentation: Microsoft Office Communications Server 2007 R2 Deploying Monitoring Server found at *http://go.microsoft.com/fwlink/?LinkID=133731*
- The following tools mentioned in this chapter are included as part of the Office Communications Server 2007 R2 Resource Kit Tools:
  - ArchivingCdrReporter
  - Deployment Validation Tool
- Microsoft Office Communications Server 2007 R2 Management Pack (can be found at *http://technet.microsoft.com/en-us/opsmgr/cc539535.aspx* in early February next year)

You can install the Office Communications Server 2007 R2 Resource Kit tools from the Office Communications Server 2007 Resource Kit Tools folder on the companion media.

CHAPTER 17

Backup and Restore

As Microsoft Office Communications Server 2007 R2 becomes a critical service for real-time communications within organizations, it is important to devise a backup and restore plan to ensure that communication is restored to the end users as quickly as possible in case of a failure.

This chapter presents step-by-step guidance for planning your backup and restore strategy for Office Communications Server 2007 R2. You can use the recommendations in this chapter for creating a backup and restore plan tailored for your organization. Multiple tools and programs are available for backing up and restoring data, settings, and systems. This chapter focuses on the use of tools and programs provided with Office Communications Server 2007 R2, as well as components available in Microsoft SQL Server 2005 and Microsoft SQL Server 2008.

Planning for Backup and Restore

An essential component of effective backup and restore operations is establishing a comprehensive and concise strategy. Typically, an organization's business priorities affect this strategy. Following is a list of some of these priorities:

- **Business continuity requirements** These requirements are driven by the number of business-critical applications that rely on Office Communications Server 2007 R2. If instant messaging (IM), Web conferencing, or Voice over Internet Protocol (VoIP) is indispensable to conduct your organization's business, you must account for it in your backup and restore plan. For instance, if IM is critical to your organization, but Web conferencing would be less critical at times of disaster, you can devise your backup and restore strategy accordingly by investing in restoring the components required for IM before any other components.

- **Data completeness** Office Communications Server 2007 R2 stores three main types of data:
  - User data
  - Communications data (IM and meeting data, archiving data, and Call Detail Record (singular) [CDR] data)
  - Configuration data

  Depending on the need for completeness of this data, you can decide the frequency of backups. For instance, if you back up the user data every 24 hours, a user's contact list or buddy list will be accurate up to the last backup (which could be a day before the data loss).
- **Data criticality** This typically applies to compliance-specific data. If your organization functions in a regulated industry and is mandated to maintain an up-to-date record of all communications, the data stored by Office Communications Server 2007 R2 is critical for your organization.
- **Cost constraints** In addition to the cost of physical hardware and any backup software costs, you might need to consider implicit costs. These costs typically include, but are not limited to, the cost of lost business (if applicable), the cost of re-creating the deployment, and the administrative cost of backing up data.

DIRECT FROM THE SOURCE

What Functionality Is Most Important to You?

Byron Spurlock
Microsoft Consulting Services (MCS) Consultant

One of the main things to consider when determining a backup and restore plan is to decide what is important to your organization. You should define the order of service availability based on the priority your organization gives to the following Office Communications Server functionality: IM and presence, conferencing, and voice.

The more components that are deployed and used in the environment, the more complex it is to restore them in a short amount of time during disaster recovery. For each major component that you want to restore quickly, you should evaluate the time it will take for the component to become operational again. IM and presence are probably the easiest to get up and running.

Addressing the recovery requirements of Office Communications Server is similar in approach to the recovery requirements for e-mail. With e-mail, we no longer just say, "Get my e-mail up and running." Instead, we might specify that the first priority is for users to be able to send and receive e-mail, and a secondary priority is for users to have access to backups.

You should take this same approach to Office Communications Server 2007 R2 recovery. For example, you might determine that you want users to have IM and presence functionality first and to access to their contacts second. Or, you may want users to be able to access IM first and conferencing second. Or, you might want users to be able to make and receive calls first and then obtain access to IM second. Whatever your organization's priority, plan a process to restore services that are aligned with your organization's priorities.

Backup and Restore Requirements

The organization's business priorities should drive backup and restore requirements. These requirements can be classified as follows:

- **Hardware and software requirements** Specific hardware and software requirements should be determined based on the organization's needs. This includes not only the hardware to be used for backup storage and restoration of specific services, but also any software and network connectivity required to support backup and restoration.
- **Backup and restore tools** The following tools can be used for backing up and restoring Office Communications Server environments:
  - *LCSCmd.exe* The Office Communications Server command-line tool to export and import server settings
  - *SQL Server Management Studio in SQL Server 2005 or SQL Server 2008* Used to back up the Enterprise pool and the Archiving Server and Monitoring Server databases
  - *SQL Server Management Studio Express in SQL Server 2005 Express Edition* Used to back up databases on the Standard Edition Servers
  - *NTBackup* File system backup solution available in Microsoft Windows for backing up meeting content and meeting compliance logs
- **Administrative computer** This is the computer that will perform the regular backups. This operation can be performed on an Office Communications Server or a separate administrative computer joined to Active Directory.

- **Recovery time** Depending on the criticality of the system to the organization, the system must be restored as quickly as possible and according to the organization's service level agreement.
- **Backup location** The backup location can be local or remote depending on security and availability requirements. The backup should be stored securely to prevent tampering and ensure privacy. If storing the backup in a remote server, network bandwidth constraints and the impact on business use should be taken into consideration.
- **Disaster recovery site (if applicable)** In the most extreme cases, loss of a complete site—because of either a total loss of power, a natural disaster, or other issues—can delay or prevent restoration of service at the original site. So, use of a separate, secondary site might be a priority to meet an organization's availability requirements.

Backup of an Office Communications Server 2007 R2 deployment entails backing up settings and data. This section covers the requirements and options for backing up settings and data required for operation.

Backing Up Settings

When determining the settings and data that need to be backed up, first consider the environmental dependencies that are required to support Office Communications Server 2007 R2. These environmental dependencies include components such as Active Directory, Domain Name System (DNS) settings, and reverse proxy settings.

Next, consider the Office Communications Server 2007 R2 settings that need to be backed up. Office Communications Server 2007 R2 has three levels of settings:

- Global-level settings, which apply to all computers in the forest
- Pool-level settings, which apply to a Standard Edition Server or to all servers in an Enterprise pool
- Computer-level settings (also referred to as machine-level settings), which are specific to each computer running Office Communications Server 2007 R2

Table 17-1 describes which of the three levels of settings must be backed up for each server role.

TABLE 17-1 Setting Requirements

SERVER ROLE	SETTINGS REQUIRED
Standard Edition Servers or front-end servers in Enterprise pools Web Conferencing Servers (Enterprise Edition, expanded configuration only) Audio/Video (A/V) Conferencing Servers (Enterprise Edition, expanded configuration only) Application Sharing Conferencing Server	**Global-level, pool-level, and computer-level settings:** Global-level, pool-level, and computer-level settings are backed up from the Standard Edition Server or one front-end server so that only computer-level settings are backed up from other front-end servers, each Web Conferencing Server, each A/V Conferencing Server, and each Application Sharing Conferencing Server. **For restoration:** In the event of loss of the Active Directory Domain Services, restoration of all three levels is generally required. In the event of an Enterprise pool loss (all front-end servers in an Enterprise pool or the back-end server) or the loss of a Standard Edition Server, restoration of pool-level and computer-level settings is generally required. In the event of loss of an individual front-end server, Web Conferencing Server, A/V Conferencing Server, or Application Sharing Conferencing Server, restoration of computer-level settings is generally all that is required.
Web Components Servers (Enterprise Edition expanded configuration only)	**Pool-level and computer-level settings:** Pool-level settings are backed up from the Standard Edition Server or a front-end server so that only computer-level settings are backed up from each Web Components Server. In the event of loss of a Web Components Server, restoration of computer-level settings is generally all that is required.
Application Server	**Pool-level and computer-level settings:** The Application Server role is always installed with the front-end server and cannot be configured as a standalone server. Backing up a front-end server will also back up the Application Server properties.

TABLE 17-1 Setting Requirements

SERVER ROLE	SETTINGS REQUIRED
Mediation Servers Forwarding proxy servers Archiving Server Monitoring Server	**Global-level and computer-level settings:** Global settings are backed up from the Standard Edition Server or front-end server so that only computer-level settings are backed up from each Mediation Server, Archiving Server, Monitoring Server, and forward proxy server. In the event of loss of a Mediation Server, Archiving Server, Monitoring Server, or forward proxy server, restoration of computer-level settings is generally all that is required.
Edge Servers	**Computer-level settings:** Computer-level settings are backed up from each Edge Server. In the event of loss of an Edge Server, restoration of computer-level settings is all that is required.

If an Office Communications Server has multiple server roles installed, each server role setting must be backed up. The administrator should not assume that because the backup has been completed for a front-end server's settings, the settings for the Conferencing Server have also been backed up.

Backing Up Pool, Global, and Computer Settings

The LCSCmd.exe command-line tool can be used to back up global-level settings, pool-level settings, and computer-level settings. The LCSCmd.exe tool is automatically installed when Office Communications Server 2007 R2 is installed. This tool is also available on any computer where Office Communications Server 2007 R2 Admins tools are installed.

Backing up the settings needed to restore Office Communications Server 2007 R2 requires backing up the following:

- Global-level and pool-level settings. This requires the following:
  - For a Standard Edition Server environment, back up these settings on only one Standard Edition Server.
  - For an Enterprise pool, back up these settings on only one front-end server.
- Computer-level (machine-level) settings. Back up these settings on each Office Communications Server 2007 R2 server in your deployment.

Tables 17-2 and 17-3 describe the server roles in each configuration that require backing up of computer-level settings. Table 17-2 also indicates which internal servers require backing up of computer-level settings.

TABLE 17-2 Internal Servers Requiring Backup of Computer-Level Settings

SERVERS	STANDARD EDITION SERVER ENVIRONMENT	ENTERPRISE POOL, CONSOLIDATED CONFIGURATION	ENTERPRISE POOL, EXPANDED CONFIGURATION
Standard Edition servers	√		
Front-end servers		√	√
Directors (optional)		√	√
Web Components Servers			√
Web Conferencing Servers			√
A/V Conferencing Servers			√
Application Sharing Conferencing Servers		√	√
Archiving Servers	√	√	√
Monitoring Servers	√	√	√
Mediation Servers	√	√	√
Forwarding proxy servers	√	√	√

Table 17-3 indicates which servers in the perimeter network require backing up of computer-level settings if your deployment includes Edge Servers.

TABLE 17-3 Perimeter Network Servers Requiring Backup of Computer-Level Settings

SERVERS	CONSOLIDATED EDGE TOPOLOGY	SINGLE-SITE EDGE TOPOLOGY	SCALED SINGLE-SITE EDGE TOPOLOGY	REMOTE SITE EDGE TOPOLOGY IN A MULTIPLE-SITE TOPOLOGY
Access Edge Servers	√	√	√	√
Web Conferencing Edge Servers	√	√	√	√
A/V Edge Servers	√	√	√	√

NOTE **Office Communications Server 2007 R2 is not installed on reverse proxy servers; however, reverse proxy settings should be included in your environmental dependencies backup, along with Active Directory settings, DNS settings, and other component settings that are vital to a working Office Communications Server 2007 R2 environment.**

To export settings, use the LCSCmd.exe command-line tool and the following procedure. Complete this procedure for each server in your deployment if you are exporting machine-level settings.

To back up global, pool, and computer-level settings, do the following:

1. Log on to a Standard Edition Server or a front-end server in an Enterprise pool, or to a separate computer on which Office Communications Server 2007 R2 administrative tools have been installed (such as a management console), with an account that has RTCUniversalReadOnlyAdmins or equivalent user rights, as well as write permissions for the folder to which settings are to be backed up.
2. Open a command prompt. Click Start, click Run, type **cmd**, and then click OK.
3. At the command prompt, change to the directory containing the LCSCmd.exe tool (by default, <*drive*>:\Program Files\Common Files\Microsoft Office Communications Server 2007 R2).
4. To back up both levels of settings (global and pool), do one of the following:
   - To export global-level and pool-level settings in an Enterprise pool to a single configuration file (XML file), type the following command:

     ```
     lcscmd /config /action:export /level:global,pool /configfile:
     <drive>:\<path>\<filename>.xml /poolname:[name of pool for which settings are
     to be exported]
     ```

   - To back up global-level and pool-level settings for a Standard Edition Server to a single configuration file (XML file), type the following command:

     ```
     lcscmd /config /action:export /level:global,pool /configfile:<drive>:\<path>\
     <filename>.xml /poolname: [name of the Standard Edition Server]
     ```

   - For the drive, specify a separate, removable media or mapped drive to a separate location in a secure location. For example, for an Enterprise pool, type the following:

     ```
     lcscmd /config /action:export /level:global,pool /configfile:C:\Backup\
     OCS1Serversettings.xml /poolname:ocspool1
     ```

   - If you prefer to back up each of the two levels of settings to a separate configuration file (XML file), run the command two times, with the following modifications:
     - For the */level* attribute, specify only one of the two setting levels (global or pool) each time you run the command.
     - For the */configfile* attribute, specify a different, unique file name for each level.

5. To export the computer-level settings for a server, type the following command:

```
lcscmd /config /action:export /level:machine /configfile:
<drive>:\<path>\<filename>.xml /fqdn:[FQDN of server from which settings are to be
exported]
```

   - For the drive, specify a separate, removable media or mapped drive to a separate location in a secure location, for example:

   ```
   lcscmd /config /action:export /level:machine /configfile:C:\Backup\
   OCS1Serversettings.xml /fqdn:ocspool1server1.litware.com
   ```

   If running this command from the server being backed up (instead of a separate computer serving as a management console), you can omit the */fqdn* attribute (for the fully qualified domain name [FQDN] of the server).

6. After the command completes, open the configuration file you created and verify that it has both levels of settings (global and pool). If you backed up the two levels of settings to separate files, verify that each of the two files contains the level of settings that it should.
7. To store a configuration file on a separate computer or in a secure location other than the location to which you backed it up (a computer or other location that can be accessed if you need to restore the settings), copy it from the backup location to the other computer or location.
8. Verify that the backed-up configuration file is accessible for restoration purposes, including by standby servers if your organization is deploying separate, secondary sites for recovery in the event of site failure.

Backing Up Office Communications Server Data

Office Communications Server 2007 R2 stores data in databases and file shares. These databases and file shares reside on the following servers:

- Standard Edition Servers
- Front-end servers in an Enterprise pool
- Back-end servers in an Enterprise pool
- Archiving Server

Additionally, domain information is stored in the Active Directory Domain Services. Restoration of service can require recovery and restoration of specific data or entire servers.

Table 17-4 describes the specific databases and file shares used by Office Communications Server 2007 R2.

TABLE 17-4 Data Stored in Databases

TYPE OF DATA	DATABASE	DATABASE LOCATION
Persistent user data (such as access control lists [ACLs], contacts, home server or pool data, and scheduled conferences); this includes user contact lists as well as Allow and Block lists	RTC (Real-Time Communications)	Standard Edition: SQL Server 2005 Express Edition Enterprise Edition: SQL Server 2005 or SQL Server 2008 database on back-end server
Persistent Office Communications Server 2007 R2 global-level, pool-level, and computer-level settings	RTCConfig	Standard Edition: SQL Server 2005 Express Edition Enterprise Edition: SQL Server 2005 or SQL Server 2008 database on back-end server
Transient user data (such as endpoints and subscriptions, active conferencing servers, and transient conferencing states)	RTCDyn	Standard Edition: SQL Server 2005 Express Edition Enterprise Edition: SQL Server 2005 or SQL Server 2008 database on back-end server
Archiving data	LCSLog (default name)	SQL Server database for archiving data, which is typically deployed on a separate computer, the Archiving Server
Monitoring Server Call Detail Records (CDRs) and Quality of Experience (QoE) data	RTCCDR QOEMetrics	SQL Server database for CDRs and QoE data, which is typically deployed on a separate computer, the Monitoring Server

Tables 17-5 and 17-6 describe the file shares used by Office Communications Server 2007 R2 and where they are located.

TABLE 17-5 Data Stored in File Shares for Enterprise Edition

TYPE OF DATA	FILE SHARE	FILE SHARE LOCATION
Meeting content (such as Microsoft Office PowerPoint presentations, Q&A logs, polling data, chat data, and uploaded content)	User-specified (Universal Naming Convention [UNC] path)	Typically created on a separate computer, such as a file server. By default, it is on the front-end server. This file share is often on the same file share as the address book.
Meeting content metadata (XML data that describes the meeting content, such as the date and time that a presentation is uploaded)	User-specified (UNC path)	Typically created on a separate computer, such as a file server. By default, it is on the front-end server. This file share is often on the same file share as the address book.
Meeting content compliance log (XML data that records content upload activities, along with the uploaded meeting content)	User-specified (UNC path)	Typically created on a separate computer, such as a file server. By default, it is on the front-end server. This file share is often on the same file share as the address book.
Address book files	User-specified (UNC path)	Typically created on a separate computer, such as a file server. By default, it is on the front-end server. This file share is often on the same file share as meeting content.

TABLE 17-6 Data Stored in File Shares for Standard Edition

TYPE OF DATA	FILE SHARE	FILE SHARE LOCATION
Meeting content (such as presentations based on the Office PowerPoint presentation graphics program, Q&A logs, polling data, chat data, and uploaded content)	<*drive*>:\Program Files\Microsoft Office Communications Server 2007\Web Components\Data MCU Web\Web (default, created automatically during deployment, but can be changed using Microsoft Windows Management Instrumentation [WMI])	Standard Edition Server

TABLE 17-6 Data Stored in File Shares for Standard Edition

TYPE OF DATA	FILE SHARE	FILE SHARE LOCATION
Meeting content metadata (XML data that describes the meeting content, such as the date and time that a PowerPoint presentation is uploaded)	<*drive*>:\Program Files\Microsoft Office Communications Server 2007\Web Components\Data MCU Web\Non-Web (default, created automatically during deployment, but can be changed using WMI)	Standard Edition Server
Meeting content compliance log (XML data that records content upload activities, along with the uploaded meeting content)	User specified (UNC path)	Standard Edition Server
Address book files	<*drive*>:\Program Files\Microsoft Office Communications Server 2007\Web Components\Address Book Files (default, created automatically during deployment, but can be changed using WMI)	Standard Edition Server

Backing Up Databases

This section describes the tools and mechanisms that can be used to back up databases in Office Communications Server 2007 R2. Table 17-7 describes database backup utilities.

TABLE 17-7 Database Backup Utilities

DATA TO BE BACKED UP	SERVER OR COMPONENT REQUIRING BACKUP	DATABASE BACKUP UTILITY
RTC Database	Standard Edition Server	Microsoft SQL Server Management Studio Express in SQL Server 2005 Express Edition, to back up the database on the Standard Edition Server
	Enterprise Edition back-end database	SQL Server database backup utilities, such as Microsoft SQL Server Management Studio in SQL Server 2005 or SQL Server 2008, to back up the back-end database

TABLE 17-7 Database Backup Utilities

DATA TO BE BACKED UP	SERVER OR COMPONENT REQUIRING BACKUP	DATABASE BACKUP UTILITY
LCSLog database	Archiving Server	SQL Server database backup utilities, as described previously in this table
RTCConfig	Standard Edition and Enterprise Edition Servers	Not applicable; the database does not need to be backed up because restoring settings (using the LCSCmd.exe tool, as covered in the procedures in this chapter) restores the required global-level, pool-level, and computer-level settings
RTCDyn database	Standard Edition and Enterprise Edition Servers	Not applicable; transient information that does not need to be backed up
RTCCDR	Monitoring Server	SQL Server database backup utilities, as described previously in this table
QoEMetrics	Monitoring Server	SQL Server database backup utilities, as described previously in this table

For the Office Communications Servers that use SQL Server 2008, SQL Server 2005, or SQL Server 2005 Express Edition, only full backups are supported. A full backup is optimal because the data that Office Communications Server stores is typically smaller than the transaction log files and is significantly smaller than those created by line of business (LOB) database applications. Follow the best practices recommended by SQL Server to back up the databases that Office Communications Server uses.

Backing Up File Shares

Backing up file shares requires backing up the following content:

- Meeting data
- Meeting metadata
- Meeting compliance logs

Table 17-8 describes file system backup utilities.

TABLE 17-8 File System Backup Utilities

DATA TO BE BACKED UP	SERVER OR COMPONENT REQUIRING BACKUP	BACKUP UTILITY
Meeting content, meeting metadata, and meeting compliance log file shares	Meeting content and compliance logs	File share tools and other backup tools, such as NTBackup
Address book files	None	Not applicable; automatically generated by the User Replicator

For the location of these files, see Table 17-5 (for Enterprise Edition) and Table 17-6 (for Standard Edition), which show the default locations. Verify that the backed-up file shares are accessible for restoration purposes, including by standby servers if your organization is deploying separate, secondary sites for recovery in the event of a site failure.

Best Practices

This section describes some best practices that you can follow when backing up and restoring your database environment.

Guidelines for Backup and Restoration

Use the following guidelines as best practices for establishing your backup and restore requirements:

- Perform regular backups at appropriate intervals. The simplest and most commonly used backup type and rotation schedule is a full nightly backup of the entire SQL database. If restoration is necessary, the restore process requires only one backup tape. In addition, no more than a day's worth of data can be lost.
- Schedule backups when normal Office Communications Server 2007 R2 usage is low. Scheduling backups at times when the server is not under peak load improves server performance and the user experience.

Guidelines for Minimizing the Impact of a Disaster

The best strategy for dealing with disastrous service interruptions (because of unmanageable events such as power outages or sudden hardware failures) is to assume they will happen and plan accordingly.

The disaster management plans you develop as part of your backup and restoration strategy should include the following:

- Keeping your software media and your software and firmware updates readily available.
- Maintaining hardware and software records.
- Monitoring servers proactively.
- Backing up your data regularly and ensuring the integrity of your backups (test the actual restore process to ensure end-to-end integrity).
- Training your staff in disaster recovery, documenting procedures, and implementing disaster-recovery simulation drills.
- Keeping spare hardware available or, if operating under a Service Level Agreement (SLA), contracting with hardware vendors and suppliers for prompt replacements. This can include setting up a separate, secondary site with standby servers that can be brought online quickly.
- Separating the location of your transaction log files (.ldf files) and database files (.mdf files).

> ***NOTE*** **Many organizations are moving to a model of just-in-time inventories for their IT organizations. They contract with hardware vendors and suppliers, and the contract specifies an SLA of a few hours for delivery of certain pieces of hardware in the event of a catastrophe. The advantage of this method is that it eliminates the need to keep multiple spare servers sitting unused.**

Restoring Service

To minimize the impact on users, restoration of service should be done in a way that causes the least disruption while bringing the environment back to an acceptable level of service. An organization's backup and restore plan should contain criteria for deciding when and how to restore service.

If you need to restore multiple servers, you must restore them in the appropriate sequence. Table 17-9 indicates the restoration sequence for each type of deployment. Use the sequence shown, skipping any servers (such as Edge Servers) that are not in your deployment.

TABLE 17-9 Restoration Sequence for Servers

SERVERS	STANDARD EDITION SERVER ENVIRONMENT	ENTERPRISE POOL, CONSOLIDATED CONFIGURATION	ENTERPRISE POOL, EXPANDED CONFIGURATION
Restoring domain information	1	1	1
Back-end servers	Not applicable	2	2
Standard Edition servers	2	Not applicable	Not applicable
Front-end servers	Not applicable	3	3
Directors (optional)	Not applicable	4	4
Web Components Servers	Part of Standard Edition Server restoration	Part of front-end server restoration	5
Web Conferencing Servers	Part of Standard Edition Server restoration	Part of front-end server restoration	6
A/V Conferencing Servers	Part of Standard Edition Server restoration	Part of front-end server restoration	7
Archiving Servers	3	5	8
Mediation Servers	4	6	9
Edge servers	5 (For any A/V Conferencing Server that is not collocated, restore each after restoring other Edge Servers)	7	10
Forwarding proxy servers	6	8	11
Reassigning users	7	9	12

The components (such as a sites, servers, and databases) to be restored determine the sequence in which to restore them. Figure 17-1 summarizes the restoration sequence for restoring the various services.

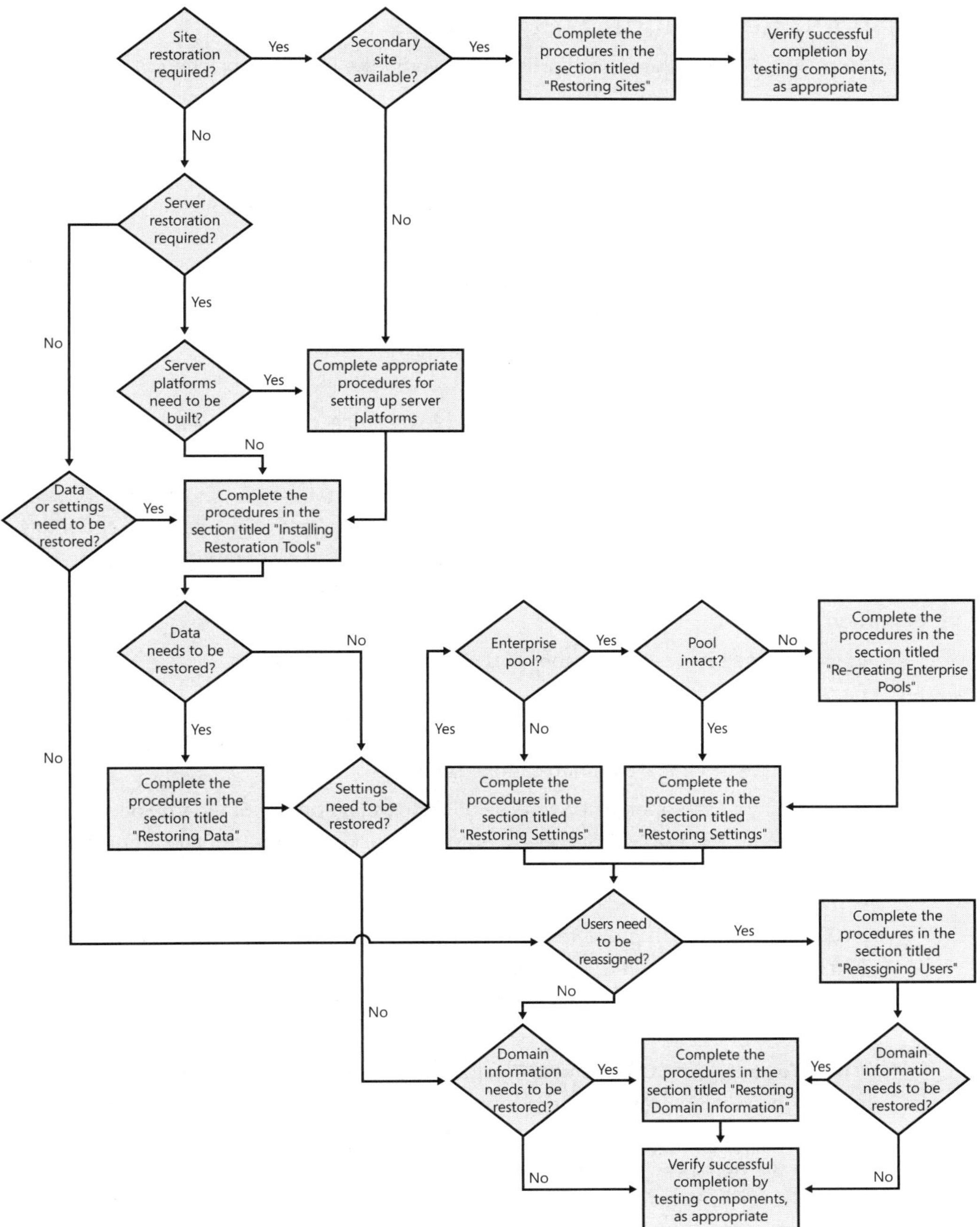

FIGURE 17-1 Restoration process

Verifying Restoration Prerequisites

Before performing any of the restore procedures, verify the following prerequisites:

- All required hardware and software for each procedure is available to restore service.
- The backup and restoration plan for your organization has been determined, and information from the completed worksheets in Appendix D of this book (or other equivalent information provided by your organization) are available.

> **Appendix D and the worksheets are on the companion media in the \Appendixes,Scripts,Resources folder.**

Preparing to Use an Existing Server's Hardware and Software for Database Recovery

On servers using an RTC database or on which an LCSLog database resides, loss of service can be caused by database corruption. Restoring data to the database might be sufficient. If this type of loss occurs, use the following procedure to verify that the operating system and programs installed on the server are operating as they should before proceeding with a database restoration.

1. Log on to the server as a member of the Administrators group.
2. Verify that the required services are running.
3. Check Event Viewer to ensure that no errors exist that would indicate any failures of the database or Office Communications Server.
4. Verify that you can open SQL Server 2005 Express Edition (for Standard Edition Server) or SQL Server 2005 or SQL Server 2008 (for the back-end server of an Enterprise pool and the Archiving Server or Monitoring Server), as appropriate, and that no other software problems are indicated other than the unavailability or corruption of the RTC or LCSLog database. If problems exist that you cannot resolve, refer to the SQL Server 2005 or SQL Server 2008 troubleshooting information. (See the following note.) In the worst case, you can uninstall and reinstall the appropriate SQL Server software.

> ***NOTE*** **To verify that LCSLog and RTC databases exist and that they have valid data, you can open the Management Studio in SQL Server 2005 or SQL Server 2008 and run a simple query (for example, select * from *table_name*). For more information about troubleshooting SQL Server 2005, see *http://support.microsoft.com/ph/2855/en-us/?aid=3&GSA_AC_More3*.**

After you complete these steps, if the server and the software running on it appear to be operable except for the availability of data in the database, proceed with database restoration, using the information in the section titled "Restoring Databases" later in this chapter, as appropriate.

If you determine that the server on which the database resides is not operating correctly (and therefore is not a stable platform for restoring the database), set up the server platform by using one of the other three procedures in this section:

- Recover an existing server by reinstalling and configuring Office Communications Server 2007 R2.
- Reinstall an existing server by reinstalling and configuring the operating system and all other software, including Office Communications Server 2007 R2.
- Rebuild a server on new hardware, including installing and configuring the operating system and all other software.

Recovering an Existing Server

If an Office Communications Server service fails, it might be possible to restore service by uninstalling and reinstalling only Office Communications Server 2007 R2 and then restoring data and settings as necessary. However, keep in mind that there are more components to activate and uninstall in Office Communications Server 2007 R2 than there were in Office Communications Server 2007. Use the following procedure to recover an existing server without reinstalling the operating system.

1. Log on to the server as a member of the Administrators group.
2. Verify that the required services are running.
3. Check Event Viewer to ensure that no errors exist that indicate use of the current operating system and other programs (other than Office Communications Server 2007 R2) is not advisable.
4. Obtain the deployment plan for your organization that specifies how the server was originally set up. That plan should provide information about the configuration of the server, including the initial configuration of Office Communications Server 2007 R2, which you need to complete the reinstallation of the software.
5. Log on to the server to be recovered or a separate computer (such as a management console) as a member of the RTCUniversalServerAdmins group or a group with equivalent user rights.
6. Deactivate Office Communications Server 2007 R2 by opening Office Communications Server 2007 R2 Administrative Tools, right-clicking the name of the server, pointing to Deactivate, and then clicking the server.
7. Open Services and verify that no services with a name beginning with Office Communications Server are running.
8. Uninstall Office Communications Server 2007 R2 on the server to be recovered.
9. Verify that all installation prerequisites have been met.

10. If the server is a Standard Edition Server, a back-end server, an Archiving Server, or a Monitoring Server, verify that you can open SQL Server 2005 Express Edition (for a Standard Edition Server) or SQL Server 2005 or SQL Server 2008 (for the back-end server of an Enterprise pool, the Archiving Server, or the Monitoring Server), as appropriate, and that no other software problems are indicated other than the unavailability or corruption of the RTC or LCSLog database. If problems exist that you cannot resolve, uninstall and reinstall the appropriate SQL Server software as follows:
    - If you are rebuilding a Standard Edition Server, reinstall Office Communications Server 2007 R2, which will reinstall SQL Server 2005 Express Edition.
    - If you are rebuilding a back-end server in an Enterprise pool, install SQL Server 2005 or SQL Server 2008.
    - If you are rebuilding an Archiving Server or Monitoring Server, install SQL Server 2005 or SQL Server 2008.
11. Reinstall Office Communications Server 2007 R2 on the server (as appropriate to the server role to be recovered), completing the setup of all required software, including configuring certificates, starting services, and validating services. You do not need to set up user accounts as part of the basic setup because the restoration of user accounts is covered by the procedures in the section titled "Reassigning Users" later in this chapter.

After you complete these steps, if the restored Office Communications Server is operational but does not contain the original data and settings, proceed with restoring the data by using the appropriate procedures in the following sequence (for detailed information about each procedure, refer to the referenced section):

- Install restoration tools by using the information in the section titled "Installing Restoration Tools" later in this chapter.
- If the server to which service is being restored is a database server, restore the database by using the information in the section titled "Restoring Databases" later in this chapter.
- If required in an Enterprise pool, re-create the Enterprise pool by using the information in the section titled "Re-creating Enterprise Pools" later in this chapter.
- Restore settings by using the information in the section titled "Restoring Settings" later in this chapter.
- If required, reassign users by using the information in the section titled "Reassigning Users" later in this chapter.
- If loss of service included loss of Active Directory, restore Active Directory information by using the information in the section titled "Restoring Domain Information" later in this chapter.

If you determine that the server is not operating correctly (and therefore is not a stable platform), set up the server platform by doing one of the following:

- Reinstall an existing server by using the procedure "Reinstalling an Existing Server" to reinstall and configure the operating system and all other software, including Office Communications Server 2007 R2.
- Rebuild a server on new hardware, including installing and configuring the operating system and all other software.
- Restore service from standby servers.

Reinstalling an Existing Server

If you have determined that a server loss requires reinstallation of the operating system and other software, and you want to use the same hardware for the deployment, use the following procedure to install and configure the operating system and other software:

1. Obtain your organization's deployment plan that specifies how the server was originally set up. This plan should provide information about the configuration of the server—including the configuration of the operating system, Office Communications Server 2007 R2, and other programs—which you need to complete the reinstallation of the software.
2. Verify that all deployment prerequisites have been met.
3. Verify that the environment is set up to support the existing server, including preparing Active Directory, configuring the DNS, configuring certificates, setting up load balancers, and configuring routing and other infrastructure components, as applicable (such as would be required if you use different server names or IP addresses for the new server).
4. Install and configure the operating system and all required software, such as SQL Server 2005 or SQL Server 2008 (only on a back-end server, Archiving Server, or Monitoring Server), by using the information in your organization's backup and restore plan and deployment plans.
5. Install and configure Office Communications Server 2007 R2 (Standard Edition or Enterprise Edition, as appropriate) and all other required software. Configure certificates, start services, and validate services as well. You do not need to set up user accounts as part of the basic setup because the recovery of user accounts is covered by the procedures in the section titled "Reassigning Users" later in this chapter.

After you reinstall the operating system and all required software, including Office Communication Server 2007 R2 and the appropriate version of SQL Server (if applicable), proceed with restoration of the server by using the appropriate procedures described later in this chapter, in the following sequence:

- Install restoration tools by using the information in the section titled "Installing Restoration Tools" of this chapter.

- If the server to which service is being restored is a database server, restore the database by using the information in the section titled "Restoring Databases" later in this chapter.
- In an Enterprise pool, re-create the Enterprise pool by using the information in the section titled "Re-creating Enterprise Pools" later in this chapter.
- Restore settings by using the information in the section titled "Restoring Settings" later in this chapter.
- If required, reassign users by using the information in the section titled "Reassigning Users" later in this chapter.
- If loss of service included loss of Active Directory, restore Active Directory information by using the information in the section titled "Restoring Domain Information" later in this chapter.

If you determine that the server cannot be made to operate correctly (to provide a stable platform) because of hardware problems that cannot be resolved, set up the server on a new platform by doing one of the following:

- Rebuild a server on new hardware, including installing and configuring the operating system and all other software.
- Restore service from standby servers.

Installing Restoration Tools

The tools required to restore service are the same as those used to back up settings and data.

- LCSCmd.exe, which is used to restore settings to the server on which service is being restored. This tool is available on any computer on which you have installed the Office Communications Server 2007 R2 administrative tools (such as a management console). By default, these tools are in the \Program Files\Common Files\Microsoft Office Communications Server 2007 R2 folder on the computer.
- Database tools. To restore databases on Standard Edition Servers, use SQL Server Management Studio Express in SQL Server 2005 Express Edition. To restore databases on Enterprise pool back-end servers, Archiving Servers, or Monitoring Servers, use SQL Server Management Studio in SQL Server 2005 or SQL Server 2008.
- The appropriate SQL Server program should already be installed on each server that hosts a database, either as a result of the original deployment or rebuilding the server.
- File system management tool or tools used by your organization to restore file shares.

If the required tools are not already installed on each server from which you will be restoring service, install the tools before proceeding.

Restoring Data

If data becomes corrupted, use the information in the following sections to restore it. This includes the following:

- RTC (user services), LCSLog (archiving), RTCCDR (monitoring) and QOEMetrics (QoE monitoring) databases
- File shares containing meeting content, meeting content metadata, and meeting compliance logs

Restoring Databases

In the event of the loss of an RTC database, an Archiving Server, or a Monitoring Server, you can restore the database to the point of the last backup. If the server on which the database resides needs to be restored also, restore the server first.

To restore a database, use the appropriate tool:

- For the RTC database on a Standard Edition Server, use SQL Server 2005 Express Edition.
- For the RTC database on a back-end server in an Enterprise pool, use SQL Server 2005 or SQL Server 2008.
- For the LCSLog database on the Archiving Server or the RTCCDR and QOEMetrics databases on the Monitoring Server, use SQL Server 2005 or SQL Server 2008.

It is not necessary to restore the RTCConfig database or RTCDyn database.

Complete the following procedure for each database server that requires restoration:

NOTE **The following restoration procedure assumes that you are using Integrated Windows Authentication to access SQL Server 2005 or SQL Server 2008.**

IMPORTANT **The service account you use to restore the SQL database must be the same one that you used to back up the SQL database.**

1. Log on to the servers on which Office Communication Server is installed as a member of the RTCUniversalServerAdmins group or a group with equivalent user rights and stop all Office Communications Server services that use the database to be restored.
2. Log on to the server on which the database resides as a member of the Administrators group on the local computer or a group with equivalent user rights.
3. To restore the required databases, use the database restoration mechanism and procedures identified in the backup and restoration strategy for your organization.

Restoring File Shares

In the event of the loss of the file shares containing files related to meeting content, you can restore the file shares to the point of the last backup. This includes the following content:

- Meeting content
- Meeting content metadata
- Meeting content compliance log

You do not need to restore the address book because User Replicator automatically creates it.

If the server on which each file share is to reside needs to be restored also, restore it first.

To restore the required file shares, use the file system restoration mechanism and procedures identified in your organization's backup and restore strategy.

Restoring Settings

To restore service for either a Standard Edition Server or an Enterprise pool configuration, use the procedures and guidelines in this section to complete the following steps:

1. Prepare for restoration of settings.
2. Restore settings.
3. Activate servers (re-created Enterprise pool only).
4. Start services.
5. Validate services.

Repeat procedures in the first two steps as appropriate to restore each server that requires restoration of settings. Then complete step 3.

Step 1: Prepare for Restoration of Settings

Before restoring settings, you should ensure that servers are ready for restoration. To prepare for restoration of settings, use the following procedure:

1. Ensure that all environmental dependencies, such as Active Directory and the DNS, are fully functional.
2. Set up hardware and software for each server requiring restoration.
3. For a Standard Edition Server, if required, restore the RTC database by using the information in the section titled "Restoring Databases" earlier in this chapter. If you need to re-create an entire Enterprise pool, use the information in the sections titled "Installing Restoration Tools" and "Re-creating Enterprise Pools" earlier in this chapter to re-create the pool before using the information in the next section, "Step 2: Restore Settings," to restore any server settings.

4. If required, restore files by using the information in the section titled "Restoring File Shares" earlier in this chapter. Restoration of files is always required if you need to restore settings as a result of re-creating a pool.
5. Verify that the configuration file (XML file) containing the most recently backed-up settings is accessible from the computer that you will use to restore settings. This computer can be the server to be restored or a separate computer on which Office Communications Server 2007 R2 administrative tools have been installed (such as a management console). If the configuration file is in a backup location that is not accessible, copy it from the backup location to an accessible location.

Step 2: Restore Settings

To restore settings, you import the required settings to the lost service. In a Standard Edition Server environment, this can include the following settings:

- **Global-level settings** Restoration of global-level settings is required only when Active Directory has been lost or corrupted or if any of its settings have been deleted. If you need to restore global-level settings, you need to do so only once on a single Standard Edition Server (or in the case of an Enterprise pool, on a single front-end server).
- **Pool-level settings** Restoration of pool-level settings is required only if a Standard Edition Server has been lost (or in the case of an Enterprise pool, if all front-end servers or a back-end server have been lost). If you need to restore pool-level settings, you need to do so only once on the Standard Edition Server or on a single front-end server.
- **Computer-level (machine-level) settings** You must restore computer-level settings on each server requiring restoration. This can be a single server or multiple servers, including any of the following:
  - Standard Edition Servers
  - Front-end servers (Enterprise pool configuration), which also restores Application Server settings
  - Directors (Enterprise pool configuration)
  - Web Components Servers (Enterprise pool, expanded configuration only)
  - Application Servers (Enterprise pool, expanded configuration only)
  - Web Conferencing Servers (Enterprise pool, expanded configuration only)
  - A/V Conferencing Servers (Enterprise pool, expanded configuration only)
  - Application Sharing Conferencing Servers (Enterprise pool, expanded configuration only)
  - Archiving Servers
  - Monitoring Servers

- Mediation Servers
- Forwarding proxy servers
- Edge Servers

To import the required settings, use the LCSCmd.exe command-line tool and the following procedures as appropriate. If restoration of both global-level settings and pool-level settings—or only pool-level settings—is required, restore them before restoring any computer-level settings.

To restore global-level and pool-level settings in a Standard Edition Server or Enterprise pool environment, do the following:

1. Log on to the Standard Edition Server (or in an Enterprise pool, the first front-end server) to be restored, or to a computer on which Office Communications Server 2007 R2 administrative tools have been installed, as a member of the RTCUniversalServer-Admins group or a group with equivalent user rights. Stop all Office Communications Server 2007 R2 services (all services that have Office Communications Server at the front of the name).
2. Ensure that the required configuration file (XML file) is accessible.
3. Open a command prompt. Click Start, click Run, type **cmd**, and then click OK.
4. At the command prompt, change to the directory containing the LCSCmd.exe tool (by default, <*drive*>:\Program Files\Common Files\Microsoft Office Communications Server 2007 R2).
5. Restore settings by doing one of the following:
   - To restore both global-level and pool-level settings for a Standard Edition Server (required if both Active Directory and all Standard Edition Servers have been lost) from a configuration file that contains both levels of settings, type the following command:

     ```
     lcscmd /config /action:import /level:global,pool /restore:true /configfile:
     <drive>:\<path>\<filename>.xml /poolname:[name of computer]
     ```

   - To restore only pool-level settings for a Standard Edition Server (required if a Standard Edition Server has been lost but Active Directory has not been lost) from a configuration file containing the pool-level settings, type the following command:

     ```
     lcscmd /config /action:import /level:pool /restore:true /configfile:<drive>:
     \<path>\<filename>.xml /poolname:[name of computer]
     ```

   - To restore both global-level and pool-level settings for an Enterprise pool on one front-end server only (required if Active Directory and all front-end servers have been lost) from a configuration file that contains both levels of settings, type the following command:

     ```
     lcscmd /config /action:import /level:global,pool /configfile:<drive>:\<path>\
     <filename>.xml /poolname:[name of pool to which to restore server] /restore:true
     ```

- To restore only pool-level settings for an Enterprise pool on one front-end server only (required if all front-end servers or a back-end server have been lost, but Active Directory has not) from a configuration file containing the pool-level settings, type the following command:

  ```
  lcscmd /config /action:import /level:pool /configfile:<drive>:\<path>\
  <filename>.xml /poolname:[name of pool to which to restore server] /restore:true
  ```

For any of these commands, for the drive, specify a separate, removable media or mapped drive to a separate location in a secure location, for example:

```
lcscmd /config /action:import /level:global,pool /restore:true /configfile:C:\
Backup\OCS1Serversettings.xml /poolname:ocsstandardedition1
```

If running the command from a Standard Edition Server (instead of a separate computer serving as a management console), you can omit the */poolname* attribute. If you backed up global-level and pool-level settings to separate configuration files (XML files) and need to restore both levels of settings, run the command once for each level of settings (global and pool) to be imported, with the following modifications:

- For the */level* attribute, specify only one setting level (global or pool) each time you run the command.
- For the */configfile* attribute, specify the name of the file to which the single level of settings was backed up.

6. After typing the command, to start importing settings, press Enter.
7. After importing the settings, verify that the settings are appropriately applied. Do this by opening Office Communications Server 2007 R2 Administrative Tools, right-clicking the server name, clicking Properties, and then verifying that both levels of settings are correct.

To restore computer-level settings on a computer in a Standard Edition Server or Enterprise pool environment, do the following:

1. Log on to the server to which computer-level settings are to be restored, or to a computer on which Office Communications Server 2007 R2 administrative tools have been installed, as a member of the RTCUniversalServerAdmins group or a group with equivalent user rights, and stop all Office Communications Server 2007 R2 services (all services that have Office Communications Server at the front of the name).
2. Ensure that the required configuration file that was saved during the initial build-out of the server (XML file) is available.
3. Open a command prompt. Click Start, click Run, type **cmd**, and then click OK.
4. At the command prompt, change to the directory containing the LCSCmd.exe tool (by default, <*drive*>:\Program Files\Common Files\Microsoft Office Communications Server 2007 R2).

5. Import computer-level settings to the server by typing the following command:

```
lcscmd /config /action:import /level:machine /restore:true /configfile:<drive>:\<path>\<filename>.xml /fqdn:[FQDN of Standard Edition or front-end server to which settings are to be imported]
```

   For the drive, specify a separate, removable media or mapped drive to a separate location in a secure location, for example:

```
lcscmd /config /action:import /level:machine /restore:true /configfile:C:\Backup\OCS1Serversettings.xml /fqdn:ocsstandardedition1.litware.com

lcscmd /config /action:import /level:machine /configfile:C:\Backup\OCS1FrontEndServersettings.xml /fqdn:ocspool1frontend.litware.com /restore:true
```

   For a Standard Edition Server, the */fqdn* attribute is required only for restoration of a Standard Edition Server and only if running the command on a separate computer serving as a management console. For an Enterprise pool, the */fqdn* attribute is required only for a front-end server. In an Enterprise pool, expanded configuration, the */fqdn* attribute is required for the following server roles: Web Components Server, Web Conferencing Server, and A/V Conferencing Server.

6. After typing the command, to start importing settings, press Enter.
7. After importing the settings, verify that the computer-level settings are appropriately applied by opening Office Communications Server 2007 R2 Administrative Tools, right-clicking the server name, clicking Properties, and then verifying that the settings are correct.

Repeat this procedure for each server in your deployment to which settings are to be restored, except the server on which you restored multiple levels of settings (as described in the previous procedure).

Step 3: Activate Servers

If you have re-created an Enterprise pool, to complete the restoration of a front-end server, activate the server by using the following command:

```
lcscmd /server:[<server FQDN>] /action:activate /role:ee [/user:<service account name>] /password:<pw> /poolname:<name of Enterprise Edition pool to join> [/archserver:<name of Archiving Server> /nostart /unregspn /queuename:<name of queue on the Archiving service>
```

In this command, *role:ee* is used for the front-end server of an Enterprise pool in the consolidated configuration.

To activate the Web Conferencing Server and the A/V Conferencing Server, use the following command:

```
lcscmd /mcu[:<mcu server FQDN>] /action:activate /role:<datamcu|avmcu> [/user:<service account name>] /password:<pw> /poolname:<name of Enterprise Edition pool to join> /nostart:<true|false>
```

In this command, *role:datamcu* is used to activate a Web Conferencing Server role, and *role:avmcu* is used to activate an A/V Conferencing Server.

Step 4: Start Services

To complete restoration of service in the Standard Edition Server environment, after restoring all required settings, start all applicable services in the following sequence:

1. SQL Server 2005 Express Edition (for a Standard Edition Server) or SQL Server 2005 or SQL Server 2008
2. Office Communications Server Archiving Server service, if required
3. Office Communications Server Front End service
4. Office Communications Server IM Conferencing Server service
5. Office Communications Server Telephony Conferencing Server service
6. Office Communications Server Web Components service (Enterprise pool)
7. Office Communications Server Web Conferencing Server service
8. Office Communications Server A/V Conferencing Server service
9. Office Communications Server Proxy Server service, if required
10. Office Communications Server Access Edge Server service, if required
11. Office Communications Server Web Conferencing Edge Server service, if required
12. Office Communications Server A/V Edge Server service, if required
13. Office Communications Server A/V Authentication Service, if required

Step 5: Validate Services

For a Standard Edition Server, after starting services, use the Validation Wizard to validate the individual server roles by following these steps:

1. Log on to a computer that is running Office Communications Server 2007 R2 Standard Edition, or to a computer on which the Office Communications Server 2007 R2 Administrative Tools are installed, with an account that is a member of the Administrators group.
2. Open the Office Communications Server 2007 R2 Administrative Tools snap-in. Click Start, point to All Programs, point to Administrative Tools, and then click Office Communications Server 2007 R2.
3. In the console tree, expand Standard Edition Servers and expand the pool name and role (such as Front Ends).
4. Right-click the FQDN of the restored server, point to Validation, and then click the server role (such as Front End Server) to start the Validation Wizard.
5. Complete the steps in the Validation Wizard.

Repeat this procedure for each of the four primary services (Front End, Web Conferencing, A/V Conferencing, and Web Components).

If you have re-created the Enterprise pool, run the Validation Wizard from the Office Communications 2007 Server Deployment Wizard to validate the functionality of the pool and servers in the pool. As part of the validation task, you can validate each Enterprise pool server role that you restore, which includes:

- Front-end servers
- Web Conferencing Servers
- A/V Conferencing Servers
- Web Components Servers

Each server role for the topology can also be validated using the Office Communications Server 2007 R2 administrative snap-in.

Next Steps

After you have completed the procedures in this section, do the following:

1. Reassign users, if required, by using the information in the section titled "Reassigning Users" later in this chapter.
2. Restore domain information, if required, by using the information in the section titled "Restoring Domain Information" later in this chapter.

Re-creating Enterprise Pools

To re-create a pool, complete the following procedure before doing any other restoration for the pool, including restoring data, adding servers, and restoring settings in the pool. Repeat the procedures in this section for each pool that needs to be re-created.

To re-create a pool, use the LCSCmd.exe command-line tool and the following procedure:

1. Log on to the server as a member of the RTCUniversalServerAdmin and DomainAdmins groups or a group with equivalent user rights.
2. Open a command prompt. Click Start, click Run, type **cmd**, and then click OK.
3. At the command prompt, change to the directory containing the LCSCmd.exe tool (by default, *<drive>*:\Program Files\Common Files\Microsoft Office Communications Server 2007 R2).
4. At the command prompt, type the following command:

```
lcscmd
/forest:<forest FQDN> /action:<action name>
/poolname:<pool name>
/poolbe:<SQL instance name (computer\instance name)>
/refdomain:<domain FQDN> /dbdatapath:<database data file path>
/dblogpath:<database log file path>
```

```
/dyndatapath:<dynamic database data path>
/dynlogpath:<dynamic database log path>
/meetingcontentpath:<meeting content UNC path>
/meetingmetapath:<meeting metadata UNC path>
/clean
```

> **NOTE** The preceding text should be entered as a single command, with no returns until the final switch is typed.

5. After typing the command, to start re-creating the pool, press Enter.

Repeat this procedure for each Enterprise pool in your organization that needs to be re-created.

After you have completed the procedure in this section to re-create a pool, do the following:

1. Restore all required servers in the Enterprise pool configuration by using the information in the section titled "Restoring Settings" earlier in this chapter.
2. Reassign users, if required, by using the information in the section titled "Reassigning Users" below.
3. Restore domain information, if required, by using the information in the section titled "Restoring Domain Information" below.

Reassigning Users

If restoring users' contact lists and permissions is not a priority, reassigning users to another functioning Office Communications Server is sufficient. This can easily be done through the Move Users Wizard, which is available in the Admins Tools Microsoft Management Console (MMC) and Active Directory Users and Computers MMC (DSA.MSC).

If restoring users' contact lists and permissions is a priority, in addition to using the Move Users Wizard to reassign the users to another functioning Office Communications Server, the administrator must also restore the data from the failed Office Communications Server. Restoring this data must be done on the Office Communications Server to which the users are reassigned. Refer to the section titled "Restoring Databases" earlier in this chapter for more details.

Restoring Domain Information

The user database (RTC) on Office Communications Server 2007 R2 (back-end database) retains a mapping of Active Directory user globally unique identifiers (GUIDs) and security identifiers (SIDs) for every Session Initiation Protocol (SIP)–enabled user. The user's Office Communications settings (SIP Uniform Resource Identifier [URI], remote access, federation, archiving, telephony, Line URI, and so on) are stored in the database. As a result, backups taken of the SQL database contain these mappings and settings.

If Active Directory encounters a problem, and global and user settings in Active Directory specific to Office Communications Server 2007 R2 are not restored as part of the service restoration procedure, you might need to restore the RTC database through the steps described in the section titled "Restoring Databases" earlier in this chapter.

If you need to restore the Active Directory domain, these mappings will change, and you will need to export user data by using the Office Communications Server user database (RTC), restoring your Active Directory domain, and importing user data back into the database. Although this is a rare occurrence, considering the separate processes and procedures for managing the health of Active Directory (as well as the inherent redundancy of Active Directory when more than one domain controller is used per domain), it would be wise to ensure that your processes for recovering Active Directory are up to date.

Restoring Sites

If an entire site fails, which can happen due to a natural disaster, all servers in the internal network and perimeter network must be restored. This can be done using one of the following methods:

- Restoring the servers at the original site or another site after the failure by rebuilding servers. You can do this by using the procedure in the section titled "Reinstalling an Existing Server" earlier in this chapter or by rebuilding a server on new hardware, as appropriate, and restoring servers in the same sequence as in the original deployment.
- Setting up standby servers at a secondary site in advance of a disaster to provide recovery support and using them to provide interim support until the primary site is restored. This approach is recommended for optimal site recovery. To help ensure availability of the secondary site, in the event of a catastrophic loss such as might be caused by a natural disaster, we recommend that the standby servers be located at a separate site at a different geographical location than the primary site. Servers are brought online in the same sequence as in the original deployment.

This section focuses on the second method, setting up a secondary site, which requires deployment of appropriate hardware and software at the secondary site, as well as other preparations and ongoing maintenance of the site. The information in this section is based on using the secondary site as an interim solution until the primary site can be restored. To set up and use a secondary site to support recovery, use the procedures and guidelines in this section.

> ***NOTE*** **The following steps describe site restoration for an Enterprise pool. To restore a site for a Standard Edition Server deployment, you can use the same steps, modifying them as appropriate (such as using the IP address of the Standard Edition Server instead of the virtual IP address of the load balancer). These steps assume that Active Directory is set up with the appropriate configuration to support the secondary site in the same domain as the primary site and that Active Directory remains available and functional if the primary site has been lost.**

Step 1: Determine the Recovery Support to Be Provided by the Secondary Site

Using standby servers at a secondary site for recovery helps ensure minimal disruption if services fail. Your backup and restore strategy should specify what is deployed in the secondary site. If it does not provide full functionality, the plan should specify why recovery support for specific functionality is not implemented. The determination of what is required at the secondary site is generally made based on the following factors:

- Business criticality of specific functionality. At a minimum, setting up a secondary site requires support of core services, which are provided by the Standard Edition Server or, for an Enterprise pool, by the front-end server and back-end database. Other functionality, such as the A/V Conferencing Server, can be deployed in the primary site but might not have the same level of criticality as core services.
- Cost of the hardware, software, and maintenance for the secondary site.
- Service availability requirements. Bringing a secondary site online takes time, during which functionality is not available to users in your organization. If your organization requires immediate recovery, you might want to limit the functionality that is restored to shorten the time required to bring services back online. Or you might want to plan for a staged recovery, with critical functionality brought online at the secondary site first and other functionality introduced on a delayed schedule (such as during off-peak hours).

When using a secondary site for service restoration, all backed-up data and settings must be available at the secondary site. Testing should include restoration of the data and settings from the secondary site.

Step 2: Create a Deployment Plan and Restoration Strategy for the Secondary Site

The deployment plan for the secondary site should match the deployment plan for the primary site, including being in the same domain and having the same network configuration, except for the following:

- The secondary site should have a pool name that is different than the pool name used for the primary site.
- The _sipinternaltls and _sip_tcp DNS records should be modified to the secondary site.

Step 3: Set Up the Secondary Site

Setting up the secondary site requires first doing the following:

1. Setting up the infrastructure. This includes verifying the setup and configuration of Active Directory, the DNS, certificates, load balancers, routing, and other infrastructure components, as specified in the deployment plan.
2. Installing and configuring the required server platforms at the secondary site.

After the infrastructure is in place and the standby server platforms are installed and configured, prepare them for use by doing the following:

1. On the server that will provide the back-end database for the secondary site, install a new SQL Server database.
2. Create a new Enterprise pool (for example, backuppool.boston.corp.litware.com), associate it with the new SQL Server instance, and do not select the option to replace existing databases.
3. Set up the front-end servers at the secondary site and join them to the new Enterprise pool.
4. Set up the other servers required at the secondary site by configuring them to use the new pool.

Step 4: Prepare the Primary Site to Support Recovery at the Secondary Site

The only thing you have to do at the primary site is to ensure that the backups are routinely stored at a location accessible by the servers at the secondary site. It is generally recommended that all backups be routinely copied to the secondary site to ensure availability in the event of failure.

Step 5: Maintain the Secondary Site

On an ongoing basis, verify that each standby server is ready to be put into service.

Step 6: Validate Site Recovery Capabilities by Simulating an Outage

To ensure that the secondary site can effectively be brought online in the event of an outage, you should do at least one test to verify that everything works as it should. To do this, shut down all the Office Communication Server 2007 R2 servers at the primary site. Then use the information in steps 7 and 8 to bring the primary and secondary sites online.

Step 7: Bring the Secondary Site Online

If service fails at the primary site, bring the secondary site online by doing the following.

1. Restore the backup of the primary site's RTC database to the RTC database of the pool in the secondary site.
2. Modify the _sipinternaltls and _sip_tcp DNS records to point to the pool FQDN of the secondary site. (If using a load balancer, modify the DNS records of the pool in the secondary site to use the same virtual IP address configured on the load balancer in the original site.)

3. Configure the front-end servers in the new pool created for the secondary site, as specified in the deployment plan, and verify the setup. This can include verifying specific configurations, such as the following:
   - Front-end servers within a pool behind a load balancer must be capable of routing to each other. There can be no Network Address Translation (NAT) device in this path of communication. Any such device will prevent successful interpool communication over remote procedure call (RPC).
   - Front-end servers behind a load balancer must have access to the Active Directory environment.
   - Front-end servers must have static IP addresses that can be used to configure them for use with the load balancer. In addition, these IP addresses must have DNS registrations (front-end server FQDNs).
   - Administration computers must be able to route through the load balancer to the pool FQDN, as well as the front-end server FQDN of every front-end server in the pool or pools to be managed. In addition, there can be no NAT device in the path of communication to the front-end servers to be managed (a restriction enforced by the usage of the RPC protocol by the Distributed Component Object Model [DCOM]).
4. Use the Office Communications Server 2007 R2 administrative snap-in and the Force User option to force a move of all users to the new pool.
5. Test connectivity by logging on to Office Communicator from a client computer. Depending on the configuration and situation, you might need to modify configurations to do this. For instance, if the virtual IP address and pool FQDN change, it might be necessary to modify the client configuration unless auto-logon is enabled. It might also be necessary to use the ipconfig /flushdns command to flush the DNS cache from the client computers.

Step 8: Restore the Primary Site and Bring It Back Online

When the primary site is ready to return to service, bring it back online.

> ***NOTE*** **The information that follows describes how to bring the primary site back online after server loss at the primary site. Before starting this step, first set up the required server platforms.**
>
> **If the failure of service at the original site was a temporary condition (such as a power outage) that did not damage the servers, you do not need to do anything except turn the servers back on.**

To restore the primary site, after setting up server platforms, do the following:

1. Back up the RTC database from the secondary site and store it at a location accessible from the primary site.

2. Log on to the front-end server in the primary site and then use the Office Communications Server 2007 R2 administrative snap-in to deactivate the server roles (as appropriate to your configuration) in the following sequence:

> ***IMPORTANT*** **Use the log file to verify successful deactivation of each server role (and all deactivation tasks for that server role) before proceeding with deactivation of the next server role.**

   a. Microsoft Office Communications Server 2007 R2, Audio/Video Conferencing Server
   b. Microsoft Office Communications Server 2007 R2, Web Conferencing Server
   c. Microsoft Office Communications Server 2007 R2, Web Components Server
   d. Microsoft Office Communications Server 2007 R2, front-end server
3. Expand the pool, right-click Users, and then click Delete Users to remove SIP-enabled users from the pool (after verifying the availability of the database backup in the secondary site pool).
4. Use the Remove Pool Wizard to remove the original pool and corresponding files of the primary site, using the Force option but clearing the Keep Existing Databases option.

> ***IMPORTANT*** **Use the log file to verify successful removal of the pool and all removal tasks before proceeding to the next step.**

5. Use Add/Remove Programs to uninstall each of the server roles (as appropriate to your configuration) in the following sequence:
   a. Microsoft Office Communications Server 2007 R2, Administrative Tools
   b. Microsoft Office Communications Server 2007 R2, Audio/Video Conferencing Server
   c. Microsoft Office Communications Server 2007 R2, Standard Edition Server or Microsoft Office Communications Server 2007 R2, Enterprise Edition Server
   d. Microsoft Office Communications Server 2007 R2, Web Conferencing Server
   e. Microsoft Office Communications Server 2007 R2, Web Components Server
6. Delete share folders that have been created during pool and server creation for meeting content, meeting metadata, and the address book file store.
7. Use the Office Communications Server 2007 R2 Deployment Wizard to set up all required server roles.
8. Create a new pool with the same pool name as the original primary site, using the default Remove Existing Databases option.

9. Restore the RTC database backup from the secondary site to the same instance of SQL used by the original pool of the primary site (specifying the appropriate instance name if the default was not used originally).
10. With both pools (for the primary site and secondary site) online, use the Office Communications Server 2007 R2 administrative snap-in to move all the users from the secondary site pool to the primary site pool. Do not use the Force option.
11. On the load balancer, disable the front-end servers associated with the pool in the secondary site and configure the front-end servers in the primary site pool as specified in the deployment plan.
12. Modify DNS records to point back to the original primary site pool.
13. Log on to Office Communicator and verify connectivity to the primary site. Also verify the functionality of IM, contact groups, and contact lists. Depending on the configuration and situation, you might need to modify configurations to do this. For instance, if the virtual IP address and pool FQDN change, it might be necessary to modify the client configuration unless auto-logon is enabled. It might also be necessary to use the ipconfig /flushdns command.

Summary

The key to a successful backup and restore plan is setting up a clear process that matches the business requirements of your organization before a failure occurs. Without such a plan, it's likely to be difficult to restore service in an efficient and timely manner under pressure if a failure occurs. Creating a backup and restore plan might involve members from various teams working together in the event of a disaster. It is critical to develop and agree on a well-thought-out plan in advance. The time to restore a service depends directly on the investments made in backing up the data and defining procedures. Getting the sequence of the restoration steps correct is critical to ensure service is returned to proper functionality. Near-real-time failover when a natural disaster occurs can be achieved by maintaining an active site and a standby site. It is important to align your business priorities with the backup and restoration plan.

Additional Resources

- Microsoft Office Communications Server 2007 R2 Administration Guide, found at *http://go.microsoft.com/fwlink/?LinkID=133733*
- Microsoft Office Communications Server 2007 R2 Planning Guide, found at *http://go.microsoft.com/fwlink/?LinkID=133734*
- Backup and Restoration Worksheets, found on Appendix D, "Troubleshooting External Audio/Video Call Failures," in the \Appendixes, Scripts, Resources folder on the companion CD

CHAPTER 18

Administration

Microsoft Office Communications Server 2007 R2 has a simple administration model. After you complete your deployment by using the Setup program, which provides wizards to facilitate the configuration of your servers, ongoing administration of those servers is performed using the Admin Tools Microsoft Management Console (MMC) snap-in called Office Communications Server 2007 R2. This management console automatically discovers all the Office Communications Servers in the deployment by querying Active Directory.

Office Communications Server also provides a Windows Management Instrumentation (WMI) interface that abstracts the underlying provider whether it is Active Directory, Microsoft Server, or the WMI repository. This WMI interface simplifies the effort to write management tools and scripts. The Admin Tools MMC uses this WMI interface. A graphical representation of this logical structure is shown in Figure 18-1.

NOTE **Not all WMI settings are exposed via the Admin Tools MMC. The design philosophy of the Admin Tools MMC is to expose approximately 80 percent of the configurable settings that administrators will most commonly use. For more advanced configuration scenarios or less commonly used settings not exposed in the Admin Tools MMC, administrators must use the WMI interface.**

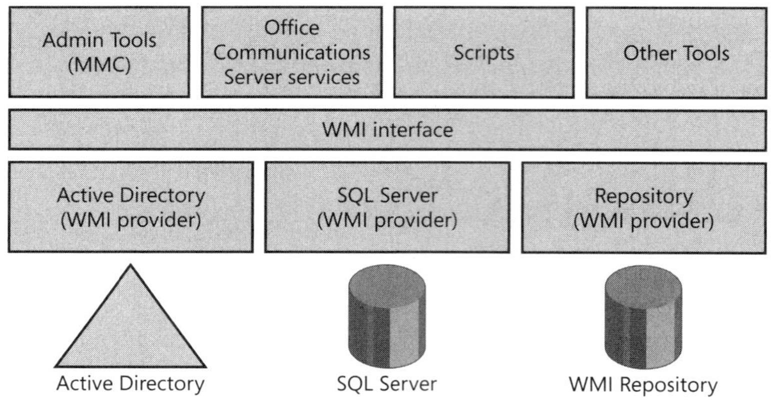

FIGURE 18-1 Office Communications Server 2007 R2 management model

The design philosophy behind the Office Communications Server management infrastructure is to store in Active Directory any information that needs to be available to all servers deployed in the forest, such as global settings and user information. Settings that must be available within the scope of a pool (that is, all servers associated with a pool) are stored in SQL. Server settings (that is, information specific to a server) are stored in the local server's WMI repository. The WMI interface exposes all these settings in an object model representation that provides semantic validation to prevent administrators or developers from creating an invalid state that the system cannot recover from. Office Communications Server exposes more than 100 different WMI classes, and the organizational structure of these WMI classes is described in the following sections.

Configuring Global Settings

Office Communications Server leverages Active Directory to store settings that are used by all Office Communications Servers deployed within a forest. Office Communications Server provides two options for storing global settings:

- Global settings can be stored in the Active Directory Configuration Partition. (This option can be used for new installations only.)
- Global settings can be stored in the Active Directory System Container in the root domain partition. (You must use this option if you are already running Office Communications Server 2007 or Microsoft Office Communications Server 2005 SP1.)

When using the System Container to store global settings, Office Communications Servers connect to root domain Domain Controllers (DCs) to retrieve this data. When using the Configuration container, Office Communications Servers connect to servers DCs in their local domain to obtain global settings.

For distributed topologies, the recommended default is to use Configuration Partition for storing global settings. Note that if Office Communications Server 2007 or Office Live Communications Server 2005 SP1 is already installed in a forest, Office Communications

Server 2007 R2 will not permit you to change the global settings' location from System Container to the Configuration Partition or vice versa. However, Office Communications Server 2007 provides a tool that does a one-time migration of global settings from System Container to Configuration Partition. This tool must be run before the Office Communications Server 2007 R2 schema has been extended in the forest. This tool can be found at *http://go.microsoft.com/fwlink/?LinkID=133735*.

The servers retrieve its global configuration data via WMI. This data is not to be confused with user data, which is retrieved via the user replicator (UR) process. These global settings are created during the Forest Prep step in Setup.

Global Office Communications Server settings are configurable from the Admin Tools MMC by right-clicking the forest node and selecting Properties. Three settings are available: Global Properties, Voice Properties, and Conference Auto Attendant Properties, as shown in Figure 18-2. Voice properties are global settings that are applicable only to Enterprise Voice scenarios. Similarly, the Conference Auto Attendants properties are applicable only for PSTN dial-in scenarios.

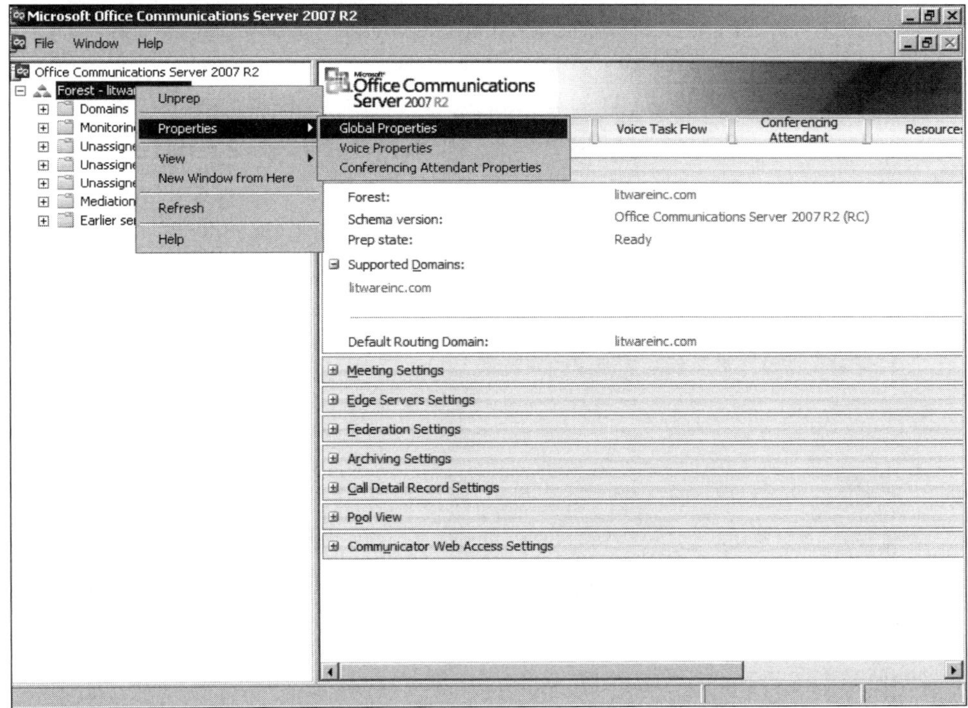

FIGURE 18-2 Configuring global settings

Office Communications Server 2007 R2 exposes these global settings via WMI. Administrators should access these settings from the WMI interface instead of directly modifying them in Active Directory via the Active Directory Services Interface (ADSI) or Lightweight Directory

Access Protocol (LDAP). The WMI interface builds in a safety measure to prevent setting values that are invalid.

The following is a list of the most commonly used WMI classes for global settings configuration. Note that this is not a complete list. The complete list can be found at the Microsoft Developer Network (MSDN) website: *http://msdn.microsoft.com*.

- ***MSFT_SIPDomainData*** This WMI class defines the Session Initiation Protocol (SIP) domains authoritative for the Office Communications Servers deployed within the forest. In our example environment, Litwareinc.com is the SIP domain. Messages to users with SIP Uniform Resource Identifiers (URIs) of *username*@litwareinc.com, will be routed internally to the user's home pool. If a message is addressed to a user with a SIP URI of *username*@fabrikam.com, for example, the request will be routed outside the organization's network through the federated connection as defined by the administrator on the Federation tab. The Admin Tools MMC exposes the settings from this class on the General tab of Office Communications Server Global Properties. One (and only one) of the SIP domains must be marked as the default routing domain. The default domain is used in constructing Globally Routable User Agent URIs (GRUUs) for each Office Communications Server in the deployment. Figure 18-3 shows how to configure SIP domains using the Admin Tools MMC.

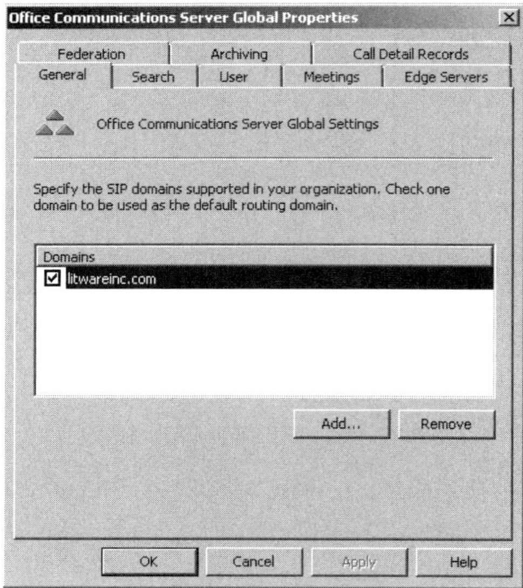

FIGURE 18-3 Configuring SIP domains

- ***MSFT_SIPESGlobalSearchSetting*** As the class name indicates, all global search settings are configurable through this WMI class. This class is exposed in the Admin Tools MMC on the Search tab of the Global Properties page.

- ***MSFT_SIPESGlobalRegistrarSetting*** This WMI class defines the restrictions for searching the registrar (database) to maintain system performance. Part of the class's configuration settings are exposed on the User tab of the Global Properties page.
- ***MSFT_SIPGlobalFederationSetting*** This WMI class exposes the global federation settings. This global configuration setting enables the administrator to centrally disable federation without going to every server to block federation traffic in the case of a virus or worm outburst. Also, this class enables the administrator to configure an outbound route for federation without having to configure this same setting on all Office Communications Servers. Typically, this setting is set to the Director pool so that all other pools funnel their outside traffic via the Director. The Admin Tools MMC displays these settings on the Federation tab of the Global Properties page, as shown in Figure 18-4.

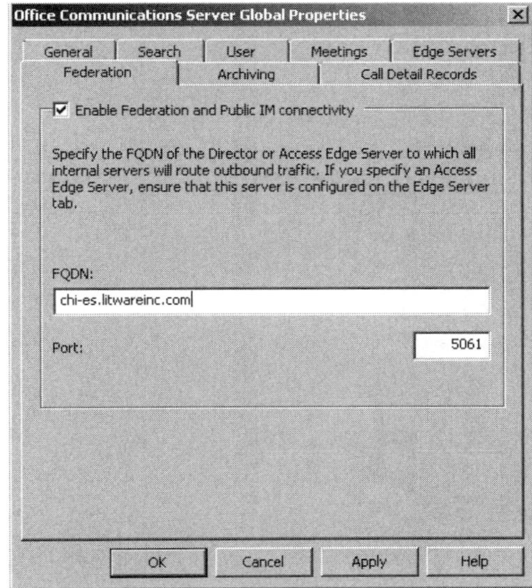

FIGURE 18-4 Configuring global federation settings

- ***MSFT_SIPGlobalArchivingSetting*** This WMI class exposes the global Archiving settings, and it is enforced by every Office Communications Server Standard Edition server and Enterprise Edition pool front-end server deployed in the forest that is configured to archive user communications. Settings from this class are available from the Admin Tools MMC on the Archiving tab of the Global Properties dialog box.
- ***MSFT_SIPGlobalCDRSetting*** This WMI class exposes settings to configure Call Detail Records (CDRs). These settings can be found in the Admin Tools MMC on the Call Detail Records tab of the Global Properties dialog box.
- ***MSFT_SIPEdgeProxySetting*** This WMI class defines the list of trusted Edge Servers. This list includes the Web Edge Servers and Access Edge Servers. (Note that the Audio/Video (A/V) Edge Servers can be found in *the MSFT_SIPTrustedMRASSetting*

class described in the section titled "Configuring Trusted Server Settings" later in this chapter.) This list serves as an added measure of security. Internal Office Communications Servers establish mutual transport layer security (MTLS) connections with Edge Servers in the organization's perimeter network only if they are registered in this class. The Admin Tools MMC exposes this list of trusted Edge Servers on the Edge Servers tab of the Global Properties page, as shown in Figure 18-5.

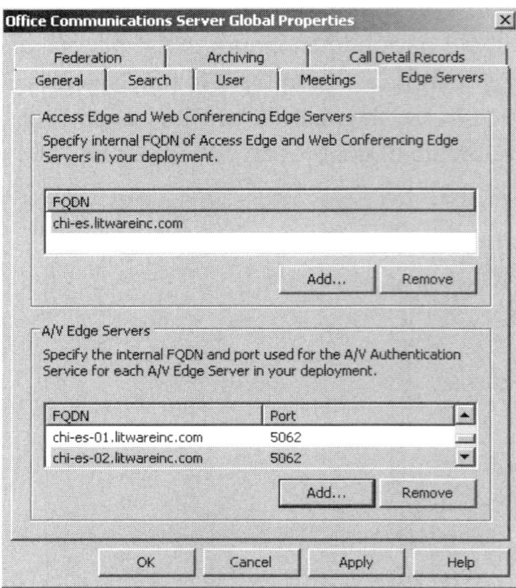

FIGURE 18-5 Configuring global edge settings

Configuring Enterprise Voice Settings

When a user enabled for Enterprise Voice places a call by dialing a phone number, Office Communications Server needs to know how to route the call to the correct destination. The administrator must configure this routing logic, configure who is allowed to use this route, and define the different phone number patterns that can be interpreted to use this route. (For more information about how phone routes are defined, see Chapter 11, "VoIP Scenarios.")

Configuration of Voice over Internet Protocol (VoIP) settings is exposed by the WMI classes listed next. These settings are also exposed in the Admin Tools MMC in the Voice Properties section located under the forest node.

- ***MSFT_SIPPhoneRouteUsageData*** This WMI class defines a list of usage names that the administrator creates. A usage name is a friendly name that is associated with a phone route to indicate its intent or usage. For example, a Litware, Inc. administrator might create the following usages in his organization: local, domestic long distance, and international long distance.

- ***MSFT_SIPPhoneRouteData*** This WMI class defines a phone route. A phone route is composed of a phone pattern that is associated with one or more Mediation Servers (and therefore a media gateway). If a dialed phone number matches the pattern, the route specifies the call to be routed to the associated Mediation Servers.
- ***MSFT_SIPLocalNormalizationRuleData*** This WMI class defines a list of 2-tuples. A 2-tuple, or pair, is composed of a matching regular expression and a transform regular expression. When a user dials a phone number, the number is checked against all the matching regular expressions that are associated with the location profile assigned to the user. If a match is found, the regular expression transforms the phone number. This process is called normalization of the phone number because a phone number can be interpreted in different ways depending on the context (such as country, state, county, and city). These are called local normalization rules. The normalized phone number is then used to match a phone pattern to a phone route, and then it's routed to the correct Mediation Server.
- ***MSFT_SIPLocationProfileData*** This WMI class defines location profiles. A location profile is simply a name that describes a collection of normalization rules to translate a phone number into E.164 format. Location profiles can be assigned to users or pools. If a user object doesn't have a location profile directly assigned to it, it will use the location profile assigned to the pool that it belongs to.

Configuring Policy-Specific Settings

To ease the administrative burden, instead of requiring administrators to configure each user individually, Office Communications Server exposes the concept of policies. A policy is simply a collection of user-specific settings abstracted by the name of the policy. Once the administrator configures the values of the settings to her needs, she can assign users to this policy. If the administrator later modifies settings in the policy, these updates are automatically enforced on all users assigned to this policy without needing to configure each user individually.

Every policy type must have one instance defined as the default instance. Office Communications Server will not permit the deletion of this instance. Policies are stored in Active Directory in XML format. Policies can be assigned to users in one of two ways:

- Any one policy instance can be applied to all users in the organization at the global level. In this case, if the policy instance that is globally assigned to all users is subsequently deleted, all users will automatically be assigned the default policy instance.
- Any policy instance can be assigned to individual users. To do this, the administrator specifies at the global level that policy assignment will be done on a per-user basis. In this case, if the user is not assigned a policy or if the user is assigned a policy that is subsequently deleted, Office Communications Server will automatically assign the default policy instance to that user object.

Office Communications Server has three types of policies:

- **Meeting policy** The WMI class *MSFT_SIPGlobalMeetingPolicyData* enables the administrator to create new Meeting policy instances as well as list, modify, or delete existing instances. The *MSFT_SIPGlobalMeetingSetting* WMI class defines the default global Meeting policy. This class lets the administrator assign one instance of the Meeting policy to all users in the organization or specify that each user will individually be assigned a Meeting policy. The Meetings tab of the Global Properties dialog box is shown in Figure 18-6.

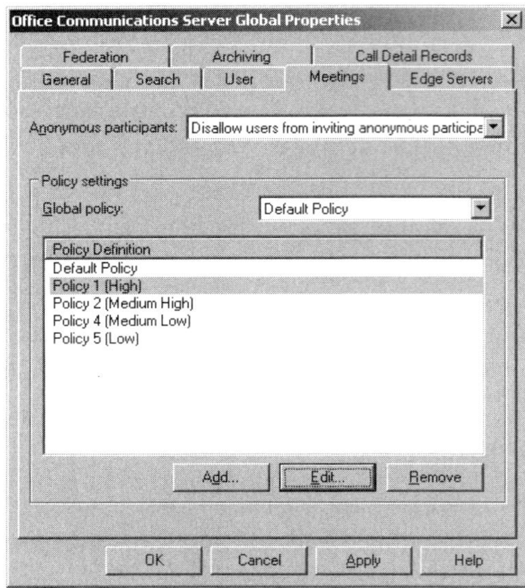

FIGURE 18-6 Configuring Meeting policies

- **Enterprise Voice policy** Similar to the Meeting policy classes, the *MSFT_SIPGlobal-UCPolicyData* WMI class lets the administrator manipulate instances of the Enterprise Voice policy, and the *MSFT_SIPGlobalUCSetting* WMI class lets the administrator assign one instance of the Voice policy to the entire organization. This class is also available in the Admin Tools MMC. The Policy tab of the Voice Properties dialog box is shown in Figure 18-7.
- **Presence policy** The Presence policy has a class called *MSFT_SIPGlobalPresence-PolicyData* that lets the administrator manipulate instances of the Mobility policy and a class called *MSFT_SIPGlobalPresenceSetting* that lets the administrator assign one instance of the Presence policy to the entire organization. This class is not available in the Admin Tools MMC.

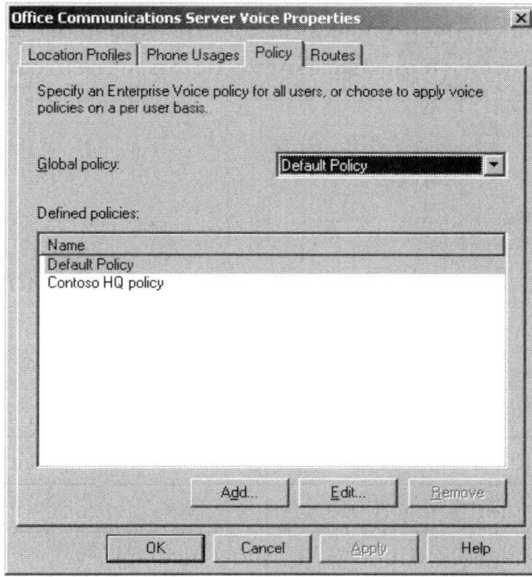

FIGURE 18-7 Configuring Enterprise Voice policies

Configuring Service Connection Point Settings

When installed, each Office Communications Server (with the exception of Edge Server roles) creates a service connection point (SCP) on the corresponding computer object in Active Directory. The SCP marker registers in Active Directory the type of service installed on the computer joined to the Active Directory forest. This makes it possible for administrators and monitoring services (e.g., SMS, HP OpenView, IBM Tivoli) to determine what types of services are running on every computer. When the Office Communications Server is uninstalled, the SCP is removed from the corresponding computer object in Active Directory. This is part of Microsoft's best practice standards for Active Directory.

The following WMI classes are used for configuring SCP settings:

- ***MSFT_SIPESServerSetting*** This WMI class defines the SCP for Office Communications Server 2007 R2 Standard Edition Servers and Enterprise Edition pool front-end servers. The *ES* in the name of the class stands for *Enterprise Services*.
- ***MSFT_SIPMCUSetting*** This WMI class defines the SCP for Conferencing Servers.
- ***MSFT_SIPWebComponentsServerSetting*** This WMI class defines the SCP for Web Components Servers.
- ***MSFT_SIPMediationServerSetting*** This WMI class defines the SCP for Mediation Servers.
- ***MSFT_SIPArchivingServerSetting*** This WMI class defines the SCP for Archiving Servers.
- ***MSFT_SIPMonitoringServerSetting*** This WMI class defines the SCP for Monitoring Servers.

- ***MSFT_SIPApplicationServerSetting*** This WMI class defines the SCP for Application Host service. The Applications property of this class contains a list of all applications hosted on this instance of Application Host. The following applications ship with the Office Communications Server 2007 R2:
  - Conference Auto Attendant
  - Conference Announcement Service
  - Response Group Service
  - Call Control Service

> ***NOTE*** **There is no SCP created for Office Communicator Web Access Servers.**

Configuring Trusted Server Settings

To avoid the scenario of a rogue server inside the organization posing as a legitimate Office Communications Server and therefore gaining access to other users' data, Office Communications Server uses a trusted server list. This list prevents rogue servers from spoofing as Office Communications Servers. If a server's fully qualified domain name (FQDN) is not on the trusted server list, none of the Office Communications Servers will accept MTLS connections from it.

All internal Office Communications Servers create an entry in the appropriate trusted server list during activation. This is one of the reasons administrators must be members of the RTCUniversalServerAdmins group to run activation. Rogue users with insufficient permissions are not able to add their server's FQDN to this trusted server list.

Most trusted server entries contain an FQDN, port, type, and version. The FQDN, port pair uniquely identifies a service installed on the machine. If a port is not present, it is assumed to be 5061. The type is used only on classes that contain entries from multiple trusted server sources. For example, the type on the *MSFT_SIPTrustedMCUSetting* class tells which type of multipoint control unit (MCU) is installed on the *<FQDN:port>* specified in the entry. The version represents the version of the SIP protocol that this server talks.

The following WMI classes are used for configuring trusted server settings.

- ***MSFT_SIPESTrustedServerSetting*** This WMI class defines the list of Office Communications Servers to be trusted. This list contains FQDNs for each Standard Edition Server, Enterprise Edition Server, and Enterprise Edition pool. This is a read-only class. Instances are written to this class during activation and, after that, they can be read via WMI. Office Communications Server doesn't support modifying these instances after the initial activation step.
- ***MSFT_SIPTrustedMCUSetting*** This WMI class lists all the Microsoft trusted conferencing servers (Web Conferencing Server, Instant Messaging (IM)

Conferencing Server, A/V Conferencing Server, Application Sharing Server, and Telephony Conferencing Server). This is a read-only class.

- ***MSFT_SIPTrustedWebComponentsServerSetting*** This WMI class defines the list of trusted Web Components Servers. This is a read-only class.
- ***MSFT_SIPEdgeProxySetting*** This WMI class defines a list of trusted Edge Servers. This is a writable class. Instances of this class can be written to from the Edge Server tab of the Global Properties page.
- ***MSFT_SIPForwardingProxySetting*** This WMI class defines a list of all trusted forwarding proxy servers. This is a read-only class.
- ***MSFT_SIPTrustedServiceSetting*** This WMI class defines the list of services that other Office Communications Servers trust. The following servers and services are represented in this class:
  - Communicator Web Access Servers
  - Mediation Servers
  - A/V Edge Servers, referred to internally as Media Relay Access Servers (MRASs)
  - Monitoring Servers
  - All services hosted by Application Host: Conference Auto Attendant, Conference Announcement Service, Response Group Service, and Call Control Service

  This is a read-only class. However, certain service types represented in this class are writable. Office Communications Server provides two other classes (described in next chapter), which are writable views of this class.
- ***MSFT_SIPTrustedAddInServiceSetting*** Third-party independent software vendors (ISVs) can create SIP servers that Office Communications Server trusts by creating an entry in this trusted service list. In reality, this class is a view on top of the *MSFT_SIPTrustedServiceSetting* class. That is, internal instances of this class are stored at the same location as instances of *MSFT_SIPTrustedServiceSetting*. Office Communications Server doesn't provide a generic user interface (UI) for writing instances of this class. However, instances can be written to by accessing WMI directly.
- ***MSFT_SIPTrustedMRASServer*** This WMI class lists all trusted A/V Edge Servers. This is also a writable view on top of the *MSFT_SIPTrustedServiceSetting* class. Instances of this class can be written to from the Edge Server tab of the Global Properties page.

Configuring User-Specific Settings

Office Communications Server 2007 R2 leverages existing user information available in Active Directory, plus it adds more attributes to the user object that are specific to Office Communications. These additional attributes are made available through the schema extension performed during Schema Prep and hold Office Communications Server–specific information such as SIP URI, home server FQDN, federation setting, Remote User setting, public IM connectivity (PIC) setting, Remote Call Control (RCC) settings, and Enterprise Voice settings.

In addition to the user attributes stored in Active Directory that need to be available to every home server in the forest, the user's home server stores user settings that need to be available only to the user's endpoint (for example, Microsoft Office Communicator, which can be considered an endpoint for communications from user to user across various systems). These settings are often large and change more frequently than the user settings stored in Active Directory. Storing these settings in Active Directory is not the right use of this technology. These settings are stored in the pool's back-end SQL server. Settings stored in SQL Server are contacts, contact groups, permissions, and user options (call-forwarding rules, notes, and so on).

The Office Communications Server–specific user settings are exposed to administrators via the four WMI classes listed next. Unlike the client application programming interfaces (APIs) offered—such as the UC Communicator Web Access (AJAX) APIs and Communicator APIs—the advantage of these WMI APIs is that the administrator can administer a user's contacts, groups, and permissions without needing to sign in with the user's credentials. These WMI APIs do not expose the full functionality that the client's APIs offer, though. For example, an administrator can prepopulate a user's contact list with the peers from her working group or organizational structure.

The following WMI classes are used for configuring user-specific settings.

- ***MSFT_SIPESUserContactGroupData*** This WMI class exposes the user's contact groups.
- ***MSFT_SIPESUserContactData*** This WMI class exposes the user's contact list.
- ***MSFT_SIPESUserACEData*** This WMI class exposes permissions that are applied on the user's contacts. Note that this class is obsolete for users that are enabled for enhanced presence.
- ***MSFT_SIPESUserSetting*** This is the main WMI class that exposes the user's settings stored in Active Directory. Settings in this class can be divided into four main categories:
  - Basic settings Configure these settings to indicate whether the user is enabled for SIP, the user's SIP URI, and the pool that the user is homed on. These are mandatory attributes that must be set before the user can start using Office Communications Server.
  - Meeting settings These settings are related to scheduling and participating in meetings, such as the Meeting policy assigned to the user.
  - Voice settings These settings are related to voice communications. This category contains settings such as whether the user is enabled for Enterprise Voice, the Voice policy and location profile associated with the user, the phone number for the user (also referred to as the line URI), and so on.
  - Miscellaneous entitlement settings This category contains settings that determine whether the user is enabled for various functionality such as archiving, federation, and so on.

Figure 18-8 shows the User Property dialog boxes that can be accessed either from the Admin Tools MMC or from the Active Directory Users and Computers snap-in.

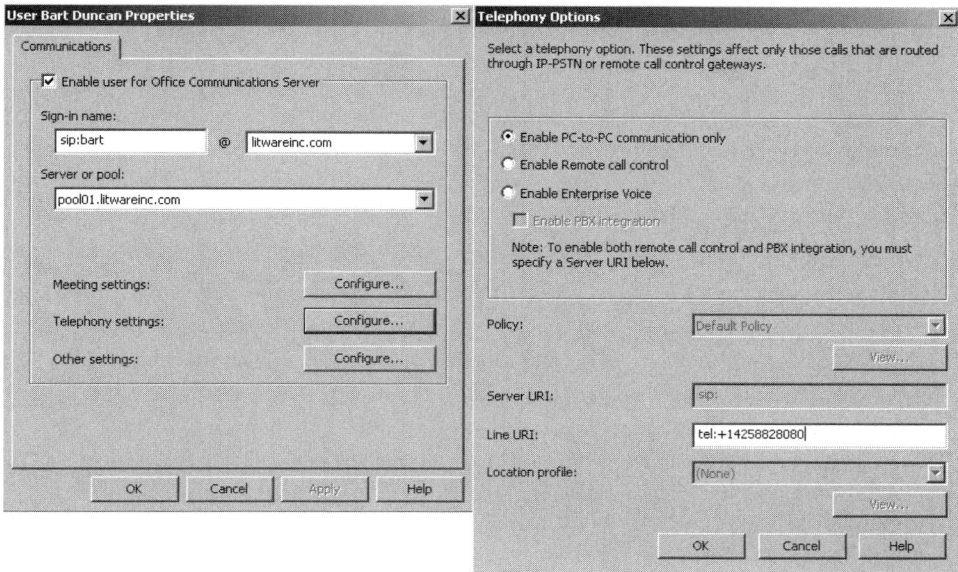

FIGURE 18-8 Configuring user properties

DIRECT FROM THE SOURCE

Enabling Users and Assigning Policies

Salman Khalid
Software Design Engineer in Test, Office Communications Server

WMI data stored in Active Directory is accessed using the distinguished name (DN). All users, pools, and policies are stored in Active Directory and referenced using their corresponding DNs.

To enable a user for Office Communications Server, create an instance of the WMI class *MSFT_SIPESUserSetting*, which requires the following information:

- PrimaryURI   SIP address to be assigned to the user, for example, sip:Office Communications Serveruser@litwareinc.com
- HomeServerDN   DN of the pool the user is assigned to
- UserDN   DN of the user object in Active Directory
- Enabled   Indicates whether the user is enabled for Office Communications Server
- EnabledForEnhancedPresence   Indicates that the user is enabled for enhanced presence; always set to True unless the user is connecting via legacy clients

To look up the value for HomeServerDN, query the WMI class *MSFT_SIPPoolSetting* and retrieve the value for the property, PoolDN. The following script illustrates enabling a user for Office Communications Server:

```
'Lookup value for PoolDN
strComputer = "."
wmiQuery = "SELECT * FROM MSFT_SIPPoolSetting WHERE PoolDisplayName =
'PoolLitwareinc'"
Set poolList = GetObject("winmgmts:\\" & strComputer).ExecQuery(wmiQuery)
For Each poolInstance In poolList
poolDn = poolInstance.PoolDN
Next
'Create instance of MSFT_SIPESUserSetting
wmiUserClassname = "MSFT_SIPESUserSetting"
Set userInstance = GetObject("winmgmts:\\" & strComputer).
Get(wmiUserClassname).SpawnInstance_
userInstance.UserDN = "CN=User1,CN=Users,DC=litwareinc,DC=com"
userInstance.HomeServerDN = poolDn
userInstance.PrimaryURI = "sip:user1@litwareinc.com"
userInstance.Enabled = True
userInstance.EnabledForEnhancedPresence = True
userInstance.Put_ 0
```

Once the user has been enabled, relevant policies can be assigned to the user. To retrieve a DN of the policy to be assigned to the user, query the WMI class for the policy; retrieve the value of property, PolicyDN; and assign it for the user. The following script illustrates this:

```
'Retrieve Meeting Policy DN. This example gets the last policy in the
list.
strComputer = "."
wmiQuery = "SELECT * FROM MSFT_SIPGlobalMeetingPolicyData WHERE Name =
'Default Policy'"
Set policyList = GetObject("winmgmts:\\" & strComputer).
ExecQuery(wmiQuery)
For Each policyInstance In policyList
policyDn = policyInstance.PolicyDN
Next
'Get Instance of User to be assigned a meeting policy
wmiQuery = "SELECT * FROM MSFT_SIPESUserSetting WHERE PrimaryURI =
'sip:user1@litwareinc.com'"
Set userList = GetObject("winmgmts:\\" & strComputer).ExecQuery(wmiQuery)
For Each userInstance In userList
userInstance.MeetingPolicy = policyDn
userInstance.Put_ 0
Next
```

Configuring Conference Directory Settings

Office Communications Server 2007 R2 introduces a new concept, Conference Directories. They are used for generating and resolving personal identification numbers (PINs) used for Public Switched Telephone Network (PSTN) conferencing. When a new pool is set up, exactly one Conference Directory is associated with the pool. The *MSFT_SIPConferencingDirectoryData* WMI class lists all Conference Directories in your deployment. The PoolD property of this class indicates the pool that each directory is associated with. The list of Conference Directories associated with a pool can be found by clicking the Assigned Conference Directories node under the pool node in the Admin Tools MMC.

Each Conference Directory contains a unique number in the *ConferencingID* attribute. This number is used to construct the PSTN dial-in PIN generated when a conference enabled for PSTN dial-in is scheduled. When a dial-in request for an audio conference is received, the Office Communications Server extracts the *ConferencingID* from the PIN that the user supplied and looks up the pool where this conference is hosted. When a pool is decommissioned permanently, the Conferencing Directory associated with that pool must be moved to a different pool. This ensures that meetings that were already scheduled on this pool can be serviced by a different pool in the future. The Conference Directory can be moved to a different pool by right-clicking the Conference Directory object in the Admin Tools MMC and launching the Move Conference Directories Wizard.

Configuring Application Contact Object Settings

New with Office Communications Server 2007 R2, administrators and third-party application writers can create SIP endpoints that represent server applications in an Office Communications Server deployment. For example, if a third-party application writer creates a SIP application, such an application can be provisioned so that Office Communications Servers can both receive and route SIP traffic to these applications.

The following steps describe the process for registering a third-party server application with Office Communications Server.

1. To deploy a server application, the application needs to create an entry in the *MSFT_SIPTrustedAddInServiceSetting* WMI class (described in the section titled "Configuring Trusted Server Settings" earlier in this chapter). This will ensure that Office Communications Servers will trust network traffic that comes from this server application.
2. If the application contains a SIP endpoint that needs to be routed to, the application needs to create an entry in the *MSFT_SIPApplicationContactSetting* WMI class. This class contains all the attributes that the MSFT_SIPESUserSetting WMI class has (SIP URI, telephone number, and so on).
3. The ApplicationDestinationDN property of the *MSFT_SIPApplicationContactSetting* instance has to be set to the instance of the application in the *MSFT_SIPTrustedAddIn-ServiceSetting* class.

Once these three steps are completed, Office Communications Servers can route SIP traffic sent to the application's SIP URI or telephone number to the application instance specified by the FQDN, port pair of the *MSFT_SIPTrustedAddInServiceSetting* class instance.

The Admin Tools MMC doesn't provide a UI for directly manipulating these settings. Therefore, configuring server applications for Office Communications Server 2007 R2 requires using WMI directly. Note that all of the applications hosted by the Application Host use this method to route SIP traffic addressed to them.

Configuring Conference Auto Attendant Settings

The Conference Auto Attendant feature enables meeting participants to dial in to meetings. The following WMI classes are used for configuring these numbers:

- ***MSFT_SIPApplicationContactSetting*** As described in the section titled "Configuring Application Contact Object Settings" earlier in this chapter, this WMI class lists all the SIP-enabled server endpoints. The Conference Auto Attendant access phone numbers are defined by creating instances of this class. The Access Phone Numbers tab of the Conference Auto Attendant dialog box is shown in Figure 18-9.

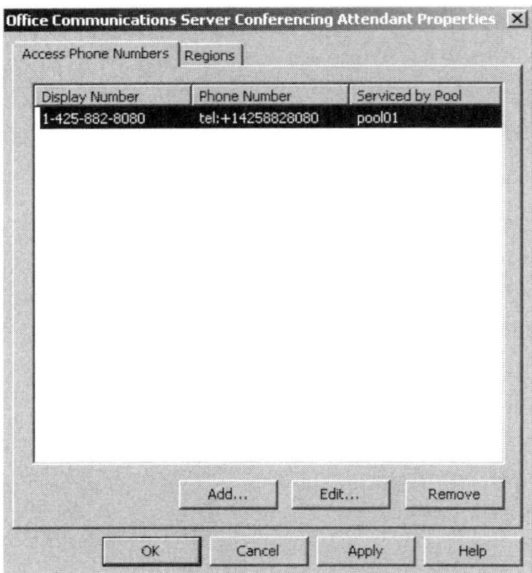

FIGURE 18-9 Configuring Conference Auto Attendant numbers

- ***MSFT_SIPLocationContactsMapping*** This WMI class maps a location profile to one or more Conference Auto Attendant access numbers. When an Office Communications Server conference is scheduled, an email is sent out to the meeting participants that contain instructions on how to join the meeting. If the meeting has PSTN dial-in capability, the mapping defined in this WMI class is used to generate a list of phone numbers to call into the meeting with. The Regions dialog box of the Conference Auto Attendant Properties is shown in Figure 18-10.

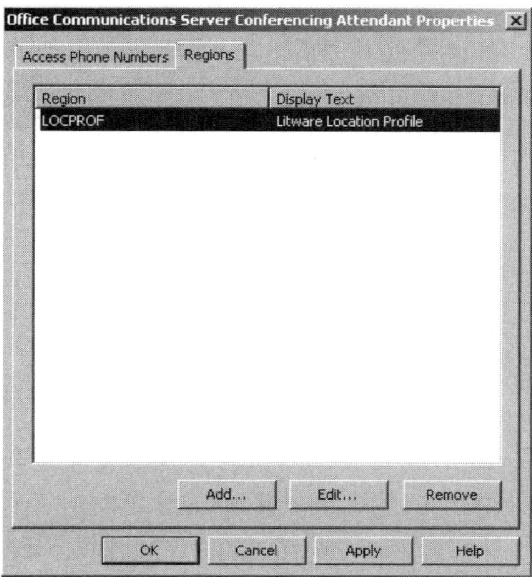

FIGURE 18-10 Configuring Conference Auto Attendant region mapping

DIRECT FROM THE SOURCE

Complete Listing of All WMI Classes

Adam Dudsic
Technical Writer 2, UC Developer Documentation

WMI Classes Roles and Scopes for R2.pdf on the companion CD contains a table listing all of the WMI classes that belong to Office Communications Server 2007 R2. The class listings are organized according to management scope. For each class, the table contains a row that lists the class name, briefly describes the purpose of the class, indicates whether the class is a singleton (meaning it can contain only one instance), and shows the server roles on which the class is installed. The table is a convenient tool for quickly understanding which classes you can leverage when deploying or managing a particular server role.

Configuring Pool Settings

Settings that are specific to the scope of a pool are stored in the SQL Server database. These settings are accessible from the Admin Tools MMC by right-clicking a pool in the tree view pane and selecting Properties, as shown in Figure 18-11. Pool-level settings expose settings that are common to all servers of the same role within the scope of a pool, and they are organized based on roles in the Admin Tools MMC.

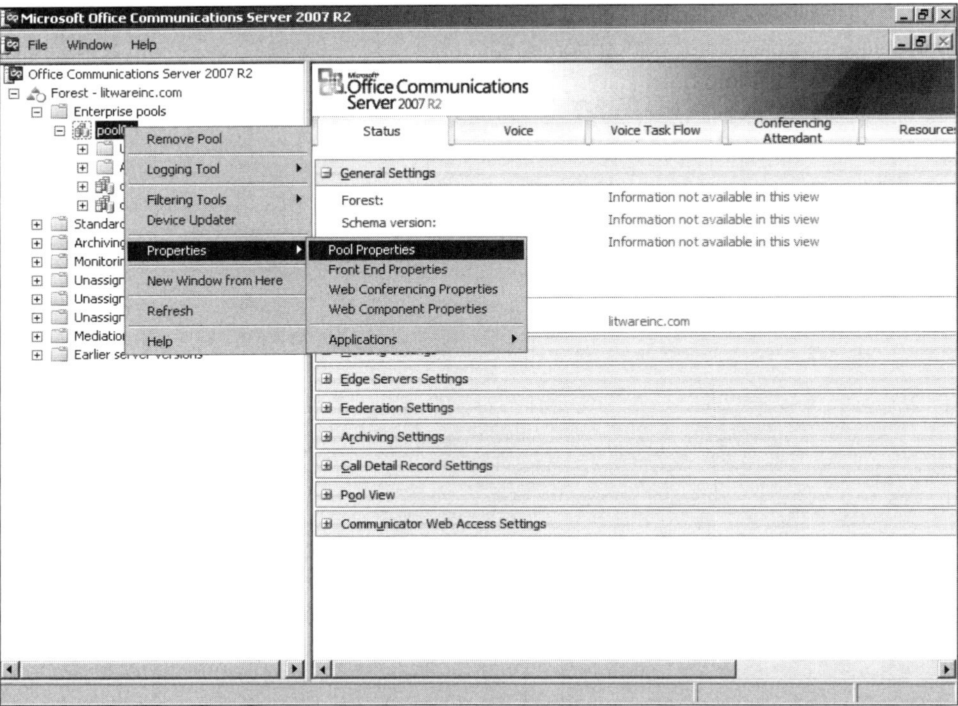

FIGURE 18-11 Configuring pool settings

The set of pool-level WMI classes is listed in the next several sections. A convenient way to discover the properties that each of these WMI classes expose is to use the WMI Common Information Model (CIM) Studio tool. This tool is available for free on the Microsoft Web site as part of the WMI Administrative Tools download at *http://go.microsoft.com/fwlink/?LinkID=133736*. Using the WMI CIM Studio, you can browse all WMI classes exposed by Office Communications Server 2007 R2 on a computer with the Admin Tools installed.

The global class *MSFT_SIPPoolSetting* lists all the pools in the deployment. This class contains references to all the front-end servers, MCUs, Web Component Servers, and Application Host Servers that belong to this pool. The Admin Tools MMC uses this class to discover all the Office Communications Server pools in the enterprise.

Configuring Front-End Pool Properties

The following WMI classes (not inclusive, just selected examples) are used for configuring front-end servers in a pool:

- ***MSFT_SIPProxySetting*** This WMI class lists the various compression and federation settings used by the front-end servers of the pool. The settings from this class are exposed on the Compression and Federation tabs of the Front End Properties dialog box.

- ***MSFT_SIPRoutingTableData*** This WMI class permits the administrator to set up routing rules specific to the pool. For example, the administrator can set up a rule that routes all SIP traffic addressed to a particular URI to a predefined FQDN and port. Note that this class is similar to the *MSFT_SIPApplicationContactSetting* WMI class described in the section titled "Configuring Application Contact Object Settings" earlier in the chapter. The main difference between the two classes is scope. The *MSFT_SIPApplication-ContactSetting* class is used to set up global routing rules that will be honored by all Office Communications Servers in the enterprise. The *MSFT_SIPRoutingTableData* class is used to set up pool-level routing rules that will be honored only by servers in this pool. This WMI class is exposed in the pool-level Front End Properties on the Routing tab, as shown in Figure 18-12.

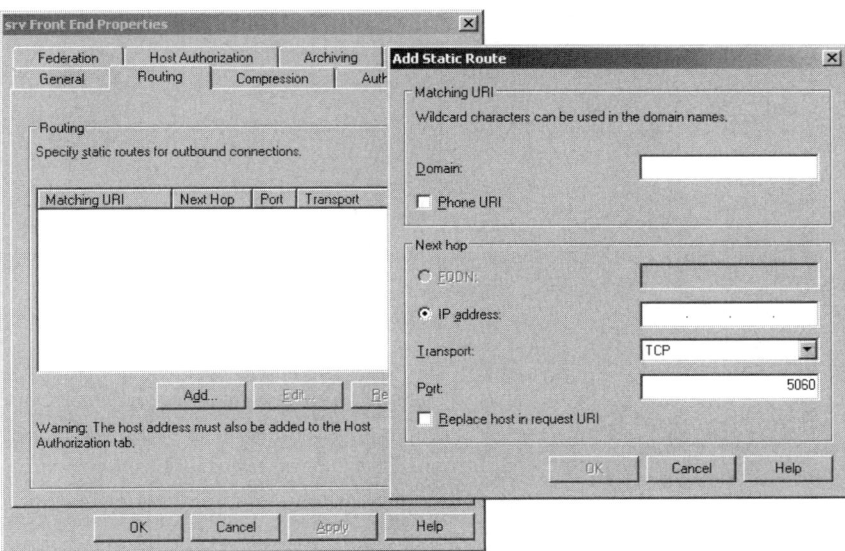

FIGURE 18-12 Configuring static routes

- ***MSFT_SIPRemoteAddressData*** This class defines a list of FQDNs that will be trusted by servers in this pool. In the Admin Tools MMC UI, the Host Authorization tab of the Front End Properties dialog box permits the administrator to modify instances of this class. Again, this class is similar to the *MSFT_SIPTrustedAddInServiceSetting* WMI class described previously, except it is at the pool scope.
- ***MSFT_SIPEsEmSetting*** This WMI class contains general settings used by the Enterprise Services module of the Office Communications Servers. The settings from this class can be found on the General tab of the Front End Properties dialog box.
- ***MSFT_SIPLogSetting*** This WMI class defines various archiving settings and can be accessed from the Archiving tab of the Front End Properties dialog box.
- ***MSFT_SIPPSTNConferencingSetting*** This class defines various settings for enforcing security on the PIN used for PSTN conferencing. This class can be accessed from the PSTN Conferencing tab of the Front End Properties page.

Configuring MCU Pool Properties

The following WMI classes (not inclusive, just selected examples) are used for configuring MCU servers in a pool.

- ***MSFT_SIPDataMCUCapabilitySetting*** This WMI class defines various settings used to configure Web Conferencing Servers in the pool. The settings from this class are not exposed in the Admin Tools MMC UI.
- ***MSFT_SIPDataMCUProxyServerData, MSFT_SIPDataMCUProxyServerPort-Setting*** These WMI classes define the Web Conferencing Edge Servers that the Web Conferencing Servers of this pool connect to. The settings from this class can be found on the Web Conferencing Edge Server tab of the Web Conferencing Properties dialog box, as shown in Figure 18-13.

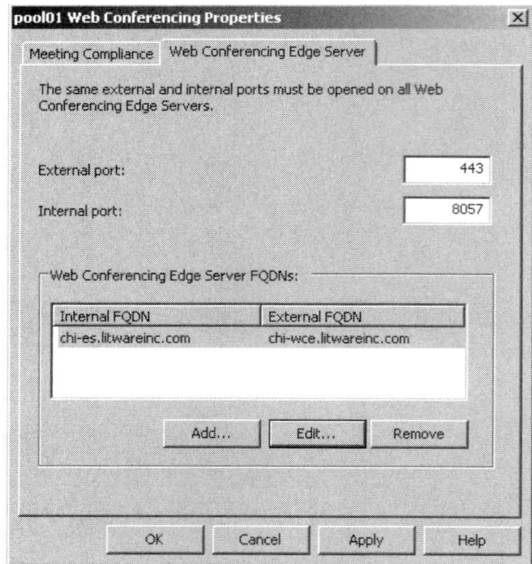

FIGURE 18-13 Configuring Web Conferencing Edge Servers

- ***MSFT_SIPDataComplianceSetting*** This class defines administrative settings for configuring compliance for meeting content. This class is exposed on the Meeting Compliance tab of the Web Conferencing Properties.

Configuring Web Component Pool Properties

The following WMI classes (not inclusive, just selected examples) are used for configuring services installed on the Web Component Servers in a pool.

- ***MSFT_SIPMeetingScheduleSetting*** This class defines Web Conferencing settings such as maximum meeting size, maximum number of meetings a user can schedule, the organization name, and the length of time unauthenticated or anonymous users are allowed to remain in a meeting before the meeting starts and after the meeting ends. Part of these settings is shown on the General tab of the Web Components Properties page.

- ***MSFT_SIPMeetingInviteSetting*** Properties of this class define administrative settings to configure Web Conferencing invitations sent to users, such as the URLs for users to download the Meeting client, where users can obtain help desk assistance, and branding the client. Settings from this class are exposed on the Meeting Invitations tab of the Web Components Properties page.
- ***MSFT_SIPGroupExpansionSetting*** This class exposes the administrative control to enable expansion of distribution lists in the user's contact list. The settings from this class can be found on the Group Expansion tab of the Web Components Properties page.
- ***MSFT_SIPAddressBookSetting*** The properties of this class describe settings used to configure the Address Book service.

Configuring Response Group Service Pool Properties

The following WMI classes (not inclusive, just selected examples) are used for configuring Response Group services installed in a pool.

- ***MSFT_SIPRgsPoolData*** Properties of this class define the settings for the Response Group pool, such as the port used to communicate between Response Group services within a pool and the maximum number of attempts to transfer an incoming call to an agent.
- ***MSFT_SIPRgsAgentData*** This class defines Response Group agent settings, such as user security identifier (SID), SIP URI, and whether the user is enabled for receiving calls. These settings are shown on the Agent page of the Response Group Properties management console.
- ***MSFT_SIPRgsGroupData*** Properties of this class define the settings for groups of agents, such as group display name, call routing method (longest idle, serial, parallel), ring timeout, the list of agents that are part of the group, and whether the members of the group are from a given Exchange distribution list. These settings are shown on the Group page of the Response Group Properties management console.
- ***MSFT_SIPRgsQueueData*** This class exposes administrative control to the settings for Call Waiting queues, such as display name, the list of groups that serve the queue, and actions performed when the threshold is reached (transfer the call to voice mail or park the call into a different Call Waiting queue). These settings are shown on the Queue page of the Response Group Properties management console, as shown in Figure 18-14.

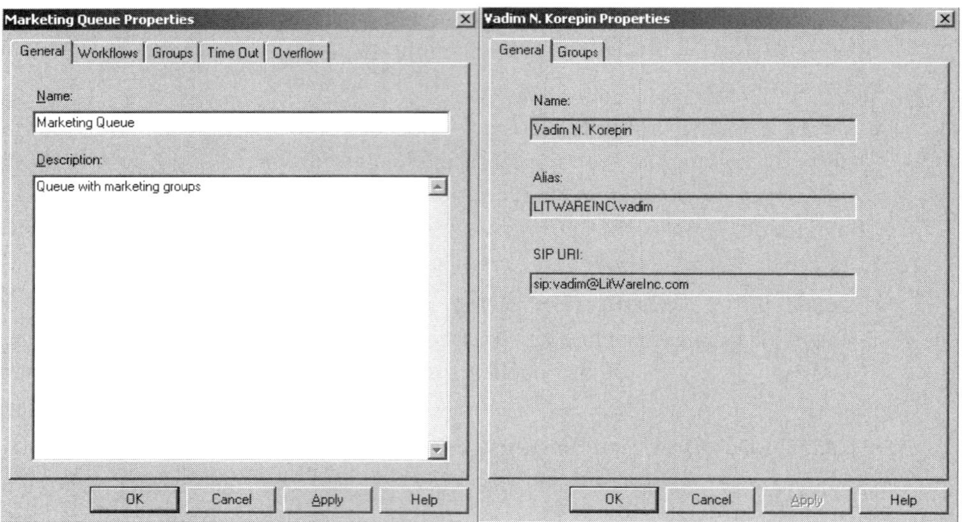

FIGURE 18-14 Configuring Response Group service queues

- ***MSFT_SIPRgsWorkflowData*** This class defines the settings for deployed Response Group, such as display name, the type of response group (basic hunt group, complex hunt group), the list of queues that could serve the call, the language in which the messages are played back to the caller, and the list of owners and the schedule (open/close hours). These settings are shown on the Workflow page of the Response Group Properties management console.

The following WMI classes are used to store preconfigured Response Group settings.

- ***MSFT_SIPRgsWorkflowTemplateData*** This class defines the settings for a predefined set of types of Response Group templates supported by the current version of Response Group service: basic hunt group, complex hunt group, first-level questions (in which your answer to a question directs you to the correct queue or agent), or second-level questions (in which your answer may lead to another set of questions). This class is used in the Response Group service Web solution that enables administrators to deploy and/or configure response groups, as shown in Figure 18-15.
- ***MSFT_SIPRgsBusinessHoursPresetsData*** This class defines the settings for a predefined set of types of schedules (for example, open Monday to Friday, open 24/7). These settings are used in the Response Group service Web solution that enables administrators to deploy and/or configure response groups.
- ***MSFT_SIPRgsHolidayData*** This class exposes administrative control to the settings that define a holiday, such as the start and end of the holiday. These settings are used in the Response Group service Web solution that enables administrators to deploy and/or configure response groups.

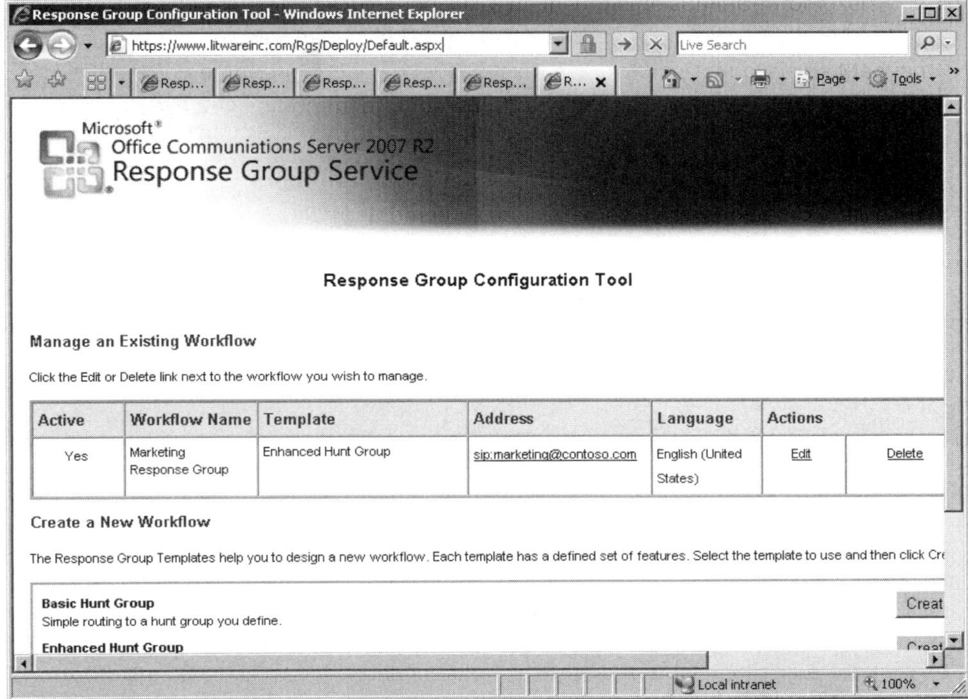

FIGURE 18-15 Configuring Interactive Voice Response (IVR)

Configuring Miscellaneous Pool Properties

In addition to the various settings described previously, a few settings fall into the miscellaneous bucket.

- **Pool properties** These are properties that are used by more than one server type in the pool. For example, almost all the servers in the pool use the *MSFT_SIPPoolConfigSetting* class, which specifies the Network Address Translation (NAT) settings for a pool and the media port ranges. Similarly, the media encryption level for all servers that exchange media can be found in the *MSFT_SIPVoIPEncryptionSetting* class. These settings can be accessed from the Media tab of the Pool Properties page.
- **Intelligent Instant Message (IIM) Filter properties** The *MSFT_SIPIIMFilterUrlFilterSetting* and *MSFT_SIPIIMFilterFileFilterSetting* classes describe the various IIM filter settings that can be set on the pool. These can be accessed from the Instant Messaging Filter submenu of the Filtering Tools menu on the pool node, as shown in Figure 18-16.

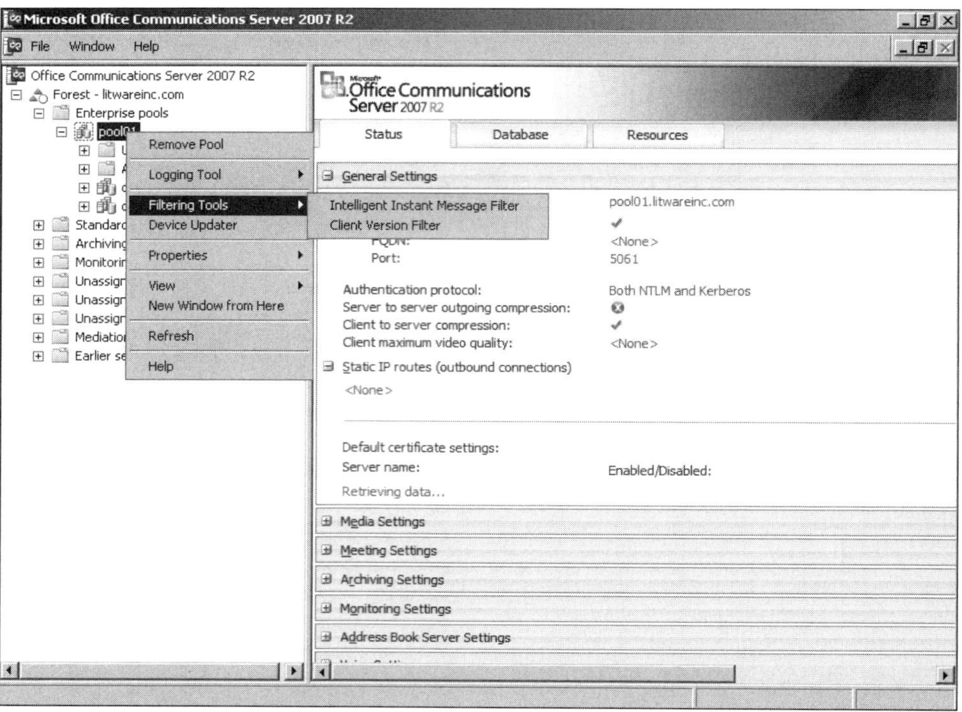

FIGURE 18-16 Configuring Filtering Tools settings

- **Client Version Filter properties** The *MSFT_SIPClientVersionFilterSetting* and *MSFT_SIPClientVersionFilterData* classes can be used to set restrictions on which clients can connect to servers in this pool. Office Communications Server 2007 R2 introduces a Client Auto-Upgrade feature that enables administrators to automatically upgrade older clients. The *MSFT_SIPClientUpdaterSetting* class contains URLs for the auto-update functionality. Note that this feature is available only for the Office Communications client. These can be accessed from the Client Version Filter submenu of the Filtering Tools menu on the pool node.
- **Device Update Filter properties** The *MSFT_SIPDeviceUpdaterRules* and *MSFT_SIPDeviceUpdaterTestDevices* classes can be used to set up rules to automatically update phones and devices with the latest hotfix released by Microsoft. The *MSFT_SIPUpdatesServerSetting* class contains URLs that various devices connect to so that they can get the latest updates the administrator has uploaded. These settings can be accessed from the Device Update submenu of the Filtering Tools menu on the pool node.
- **Logging Tool properties** The *MSFT_SIPLoggingToolSetting* class defines properties of the Logging Tool. The Logging Tool can be accessed by clicking the New Debug Session submenu of the Logging Tool menu on the pool node.

- **Client configuration Settings** The *MSFT_SIPClientPortSettings, MSFT_SIPCommunicatorConfigSetting*, and *MSFT_SIPUCPhoneConfigSetting* classes contain settings that can be used to configure clients. These settings are sent to clients when they register with the server via a mechanism known as *inband provisioning*.

You can connect to the local WMI service to perform the following types of operations on pool-level classes: query, set, and delete. This requires installing OcsCore.msi on the local computer if it's not an Office Communications Server 2007 R2 server. By default, OcsCore.msi is installed on all Office Communications Servers. You can find OcsCore.msi on the Office Communications Server CD in the Setup folder.

Each of these WMI classes requires specifying the back-end server to identify the pool to connect to. The most efficient way to retrieve pool-level settings is to perform an SQL query specifying the back-end server in the following form for an Enterprise Edition pool:

```
'Backend_FQDN\\SQL_Instance_Name'
```

For a Standard Edition Server, use the following form:

```
'(local)\\rtc'
```

The following pseudocode illustrates how to query the attributes from the *MSFT_SIPProxySetting* class.

```
If(srv == "Standard Edition")
{
Backend = '(local)\\rtc';
}
If(srv == "Enterprise Edition")
{
Backend = "backend_FQDN\\SQL_Instance_Name';
}
Query = "SELECT * FROM MSFT_SIPProxySetting WHERE Backend =" + Backend;
```

For set operations, specify the back-end attribute as you would any other attribute, for example:

```
Set DefaultRoutingInstance = GetObject("WinMgmts:MSFT_SIPRoutingTableData")
Set NewRoutingInstance = DefaultRoutingInstance.SpawnInstance_
'Populate the properties for new instance.
NewRoutingInstance.DropRouterHeaders = False;
'No escaping required here.
If(srv == "Standard Edition")
{
NewRoutingInstance.Backend = "(local)\\rtc";
}
If(srv == "Enterprise Edition")
{
NewRoutingInstance.Backend = "Backend_FQDN\SQL_Instance_Name";
}
NewRoutingInstance.Put_ 0
```

DIRECT FROM THE SOURCE

Accessing Pool-Level Classes by Using WMI

Salman Khalid
Software Design Engineer in Test, Office Communications Server

In Office Communications Server 2007 R2, enumerate instance for pool-level classes are not supported. In previous releases, running open-ended queries (that is, enumerating or querying for all instances without the *WHERE* clause) on pool-level classes was not recommended. With the current release, there is a hard requirement of specifying the BackEnd property whenever a pool-level class is queried.

Open-ended queries are not supported because by omitting the *WHERE* clause, you are asking for all instances of the pool-level class from all pools. This request results in the Office Communications Server WMI provider first discovering all pools and then connecting to each of the pools and retrieving data for this WMI class from them. If any of these pools are accessed across slow links, the operation takes longer and might even time out.

The format of querying pool-level classes is as follows:

```
SELECT * FROM <className> WHERE Backend = "<BackendDBPath>"
```

For example, on a Standard Edition Server, you would run the following query to get instances of the *MSFT_SIPProxySetting* class:

```
Select * from MSFT_SIPProxySetting Where Backend = "(local)\\rtc"
```

> **NOTE** In WMI Query Language (WQL), \ (backslash) is the escape character. So, whenever the database path has a single \, two backslashes will have to be used in its place. For example, (local)\rtc becomes (local)\\rtc.

A convenient way of looking up the back-end database path for a pool is to query the WMI class *MSFT_SIPPoolSetting* and look up the value for the property Backend-DBPath.

The following script illustrates how to get the BackEnd property for a pool called PoolLitwareinc.

```
strComputer = "."
wmiQuery = "SELECT * FROM MSFT_SIPPoolSetting WHERE PoolDisplayName =
'PoolLitwareinc'"
Set poolList = GetObject("winmgmts:\\" & strComputer).ExecQuery(wmiQuery)
For Each poolInstance In poolList
poolBackend = poolInstance.BackEndDBPath
```

Configuring Server Settings

Settings specific to a server are stored in the local WMI repository that is created when installing a server role. These settings are accessible from the Admin Tools MMC by right-clicking a server in the tree view pane and selecting Properties, as shown in Figure 18-17.

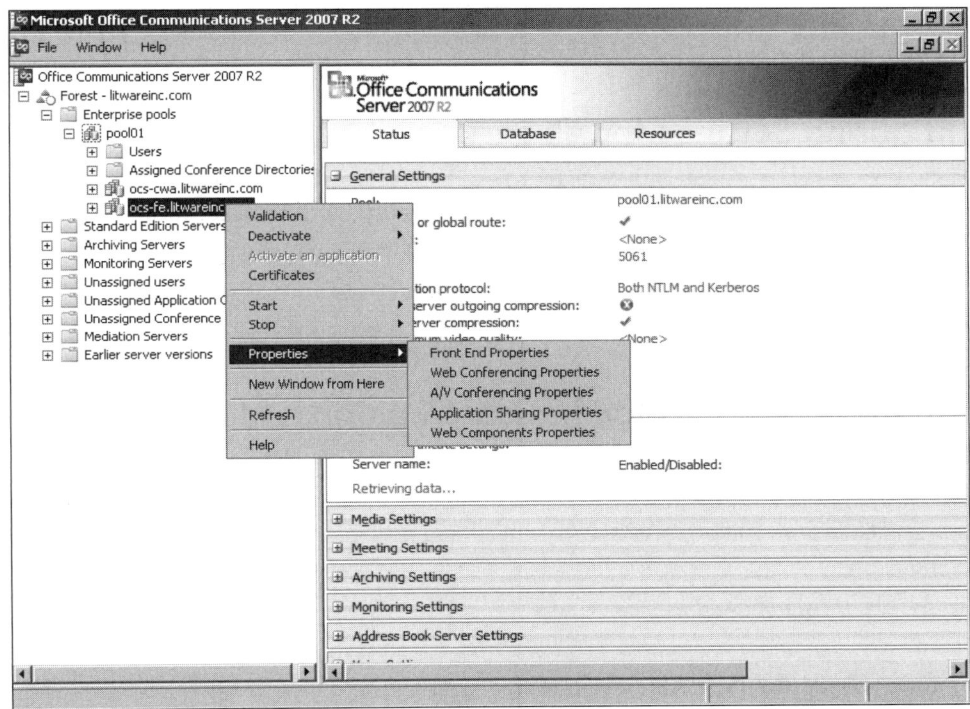

FIGURE 18-17 Configuring server settings

Generally speaking, for servers that belong to the pool, most settings are configured at the pool level. That way, an administrator can configure settings only once and they will be picked up by all servers in the pool. The only settings configured at the server scope are settings that differ from server to server. For example, setting up Internet Protocol (IP) addresses, ports, and certificates fall into this category.

For servers that don't belong to a pool (for example, Edge Servers, Mediation Servers, and Communicator Web Access Servers), all classes are scoped at the server level. Note that some pool-level classes are also accessible on certain server roles. For example, the *MSFT_SIPProxy-Setting* class is available as both a pool-level class on the front-end server and as a machine-level class on Edge Servers. To access such classes on the Edge Server, WMI must be queried with a "*NULL*" specified for the BackEnd property. For example, when querying for the *MSFT_SIPProxySetting* class on an Edge Server, the following query must be used:

```
select * from MSFT_SIPProxySetting where BackEnd="NULL"
```

The following sections present a selective subset of machine-level WMI classes. The complete list can be found at the Microsoft Developer Network (MSDN) website: *http://msdn.microsoft.com*.

Configuring Settings for All Servers

The following WMI classes apply to all server roles. The first lists all the Office Communications Server roles installed on the machine, and the second is used to set the certificate that all Office Communications Server services installed on the machine will use.

- *MSFT_SIPServerInstalledComponentData*:
- *MSFT_SIPRoutingSetting*

Configuring Settings for Standard Edition and Enterprise Edition Servers

The following WMI class applies only to Office Communications Server 2007 R2 Standard Edition and Enterprise Edition servers. It lists the IP and port information for individual servers in the pool.

- *MSFT_SIPListeningAddressData*

Configuring Application Server Settings

The following WMI classes apply only to Standard Edition Servers and Enterprise Edition pool front-end servers. These classes are used to register inbuilt and third-party applications that the servers run.

- *MSFT_SIPApplicationSetting*
- *MSFT_SIPApplicationPriorityList*

Configuring Archiving Settings

The following WMI classes can be used to configure logging settings.

- ***MSFT_SIPLogOptions*** This WMI class exposes the Archiving settings on the Standard Edition Servers and Enterprise Edition pool front-end servers, as shown in Figure 18-18.

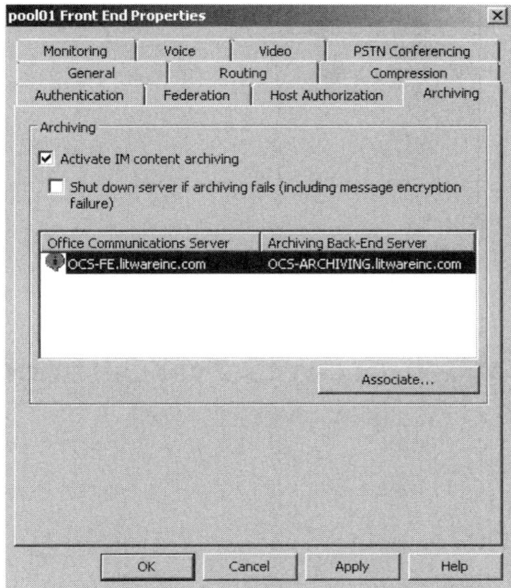

FIGURE 18-18 Configuring archiving settings

- ***MSFT_SIPArchivingServiceSetting*** This WMI class defines logging settings that are exposed on the Archiving Server.

Configuring Monitoring Server Settings

The following WMI classes can be used to configure the CDR and Quality Metric Service (QMS) features on the Monitoring Server.

- *MSFT_SIPCDRServiceSetting*
- *MSFT_SIPQoESetting*
- *MSFT_SIPQMSExternalConsumer*
- *MSFT_SIPQMSAlertingDefaults*
- *MSFT_SIPQMSAlertingOverrides*
- *MSFT_SIPQMSMonitoredMediationServer*
- *MSFT_SIPQMSMonitoredAVMCU*
- *MSFT_SIPQMSStaticSubnet*
- *MSFT_SIPQMSStaticLocation*
- *MSFT_SIPQMSDynamicSubnet*
- *MSFT_SIPQMSSingleMaskSubnet*
- *MSFT_SIPQMSDBConfigSetting*

Configuring Conferencing Server Settings

The following WMI classes apply only to Conferencing Servers.

- *MSFT_SIPAVMCUSetting*
- *MSFT_SIPIMMCUSetting*
- *MSFT_SIPACPMCUSetting*
- *MSFT_SIPASMCUSetting*
- *MSFT_SIPDataMCUSetting*

Configuring Communicator Web Access Server Settings

The following WMI classes apply only to Communicator Web Access Servers.

- *MSFT_CWAServerSetting*
- *MSFT_CWASupportedLanguage*
- *MSFT_CWASiteSetting*

Configuring Mediation Server Settings

The following WMI class applies only to Mediation Servers.

- *MSFT_SIPMediationServerConfigSetting*

Configuring Edge Server Settings

The following WMI classes apply only to Edge Servers.

- *MSFT_SIPEdgeServerListeningAddressSetting*
- *MSFT_SIPMediaRelaySetting*
- *MSFT_SIPMediaRelayNetworkInterfaceData*
- *MSFT_SIPDataProxySetting*

Configuring Federation Settings

The following WMI classes apply only to the Access Edge Servers, with the exception of the class *MSFT_SIPFederationInternalEdgeListeningAddressSetting*. This class applies to all Edge Server roles.

- *MSFT_SIPFederationPartnerTable*
- *MSFT_SIPFederationNetworkProviderTable*
- *MSFT_SIPFederationInternalEdgeListeningAddressSetting*
- *MSFT_SIPFederationInternalEdgeSetting*
- *MSFT_SIPFederationInternalServerData*
- *MSFT_SIPFederationInternalDomainData*

- *MSFT_SIPFederationExternalEdgeListeningAddressSetting*
- *MSFT_SIPFederationExternalEdgeSetting*
- *MSFT_SIPFederationDeniedDomainSetting*
- *MSFT_SIPEnhancedFederationConnectionLimitsData*
- *MSFT_SIPEnhancedFederationDomainData*

Migrating to Office Communications Server 2007 R2

There are two main paths for migrating to Office Communications Server 2007 R2 depending on the version you are currently running in your environment. The majority of existing customers will be running either Live Communications Server 2005 Service Pack 1 (SP1) or Office Communications Server 2007. If you're running an older version such as Microsoft Office Communications Server 2003, then you must first migrate to Microsoft Office Communications Server 2005 SP1 before migrating to Office Communications Server 2007 R2. This section discusses the considerations and strategies for migrating from Office Communications Server 2007 or Live Communications Server 2005 SP1 to Office Communications Server 2007 R2.

One of the factors to consider when upgrading to Office Communications Server 2007 R2 is the requirement for 64-bit hardware. Administrators will need to carefully plan their hardware and operating system (OS) requirements because it's unlikely that you will be able to repurpose your existing servers for Office Communications Server 2007 R2 unless you plan for 64-bit hardware. The only exception is the Enterprise pool back-end SQL Server. The existing SQL Server can be leveraged to run the back-end server for your Office Communications Server 2007 R2 Enterprise pool as long as a separate database instance is used. For more information, see the UC blog article published by Rui Maximo at *http://go.microsoft.com/fwlink/?LinkID=133723*.

Another consideration is whether you want to migrate global settings from the System Container to the Configuration container in Active Directory if your existing deployment is currently using the System Container to store the global settings. Migrating global settings to the Configuration container is highly recommended, particularly if you plan to deploy Enterprise Voice globally.

Keep in mind that the hardware load balancers used to load balance front-end servers for your existing Enterprise pools and Edge Servers can be reused for your Office Communications Server 2007 R2 deployment. This should help reduce your hardware expenditure.

A restriction to be mindful of is that the Administrative Tools (Admin Tools) for Live Communications Server 2005 SP1, Microsoft Office Communications Server 2007, and Office Communications Server 2007 R2 are not mutually compatible. Each Admin Tools can administer servers only for their respective version. Until your migration is complete and your previous deployment is decommissioned, you will need to administer the mixed environment by using different Admin Tools.

Because Office Communications Server 2007 R2 can coexist in the same Active Directory forest as Office Communications Server 2007 and Live Communications Server 2005 SP1, Office Communications Server 2007 R2 can be rolled out alongside your existing infrastructure. This means that an Active Directory forest can have Live Communications Server 2005 SP1 servers and Office Communications Server 2007 servers with Office Communications Server 2007 R2 servers. Users homed on different versions of the product can still communicate with each other at the lowest common level of functionality.

Rolling out Office Communications Server 2007 R2 alongside an existing version of Live Communications Server 2005 SP1 or Office Communications Server 2007 is the recommended option to avoid disruption of service during migrating. The other option is to back up the databases of Standard Edition Servers and Enterprise pools and restore them onto corresponding Office Communications Server 2007 R2 Standard Edition Servers and Enterprise pools. However, this will result in discontinuity of service until the migration is completed. Also, data exported from a Standard Edition Server must be imported into another Standard Edition Server. Similarly, data exported from an Enterprise pool should be imported into another Enterprise pool. In no case is an in-place upgrade supported.

The migration strategy is nearly identical whether migrating from Live Communications Server 2005 SP1 or Office Communications Server 2007 to Office Communications Server 2007 R2. The process is considered an inside-out strategy. This migration strategy is described next.

Migration Process

1. [OPTIONAL] Migrate global settings from the System Container to the Configuration container in Active Directory using the tool provided at *http://go.microsoft.com/fwlink/?LinkID=133735*. If you're using the System Container to store global settings, it's highly recommended to move these settings to the Configuration container, particularly if you're planning to deploy Enterprise Voice in a distributed environment across different geographic locations.
2. Prepare Active Directory by running Schema Prep, Forest Prep, and Domain Prep. Domain Prep must be run in every domain where you have users enabled for Office Communications and every domain where Office Communications Server 2007 R2 servers will be deployed.
3. Deploy Office Communications Server 2007 R2 alongside the Office Communications Server 2007 deployment. The recommended option is to deploy a complete configuration running Office Communications Server 2007 R2, including Standard Edition Servers, Enterprise pools, Directors, and Edge Servers. This Office Communications Server 2007 R2 deployment is independent of your existing Live Communications Server 2005 SP1 or Office Communications Server 2007 deployment.

4. Migrate users to Office Communications Server 2007 R2. This activity can easily be performed using the bulk Move Users Wizard in the Admin Tools for Office Communications Server 2007 R2, as shown in Figure 18-19.

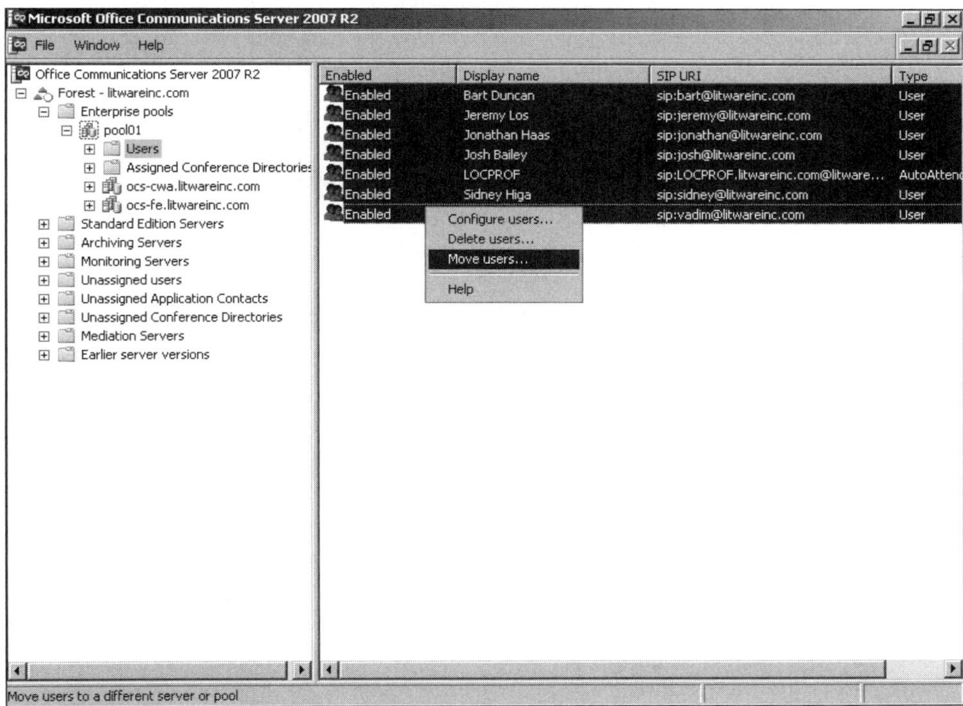

FIGURE 18-19 Selecting the Move Users Wizard

5. Users running Microsoft Office Communicator 2005 or Office Communicator 2007 will continue to use existing functionality they are familiar with. However, to access the advanced features offered by Office Communications Server 2007 R2 and Office Communicator 2007 R2, the following two steps must be performed.

   a. Deploy Office Communicator 2007 R2 to users.

   b. [Live Communications Server 2005 SP1 *only*] Enable users homed on Office Communications Server 2007 R2 for enhanced presence. This action can be performed using the bulk Configure Users Wizard, as shown in Figure 18-20. This step is not necessary if your existing deployment is running Office Communications Server 2007.

FIGURE 18-20 Configure Users Wizard

When your migration to Office Communications Server 2007 R2 is complete, decommission your previous deployment.

Summary

Office Communications Server 2007 R2 provides two management interfaces out of the box. The Admin Tools MMC offers a UI based on the Microsoft Management Console that integrates with the Windows management infrastructure. The WMI layer exposed by Office Communications Server provides a scriptable interface that administrators can use to automate management tasks. This WMI interface provides more flexibility and access to additional settings that might not be exposed at the MMC interface. Office Communications Server settings are stored in three different locations. Global settings are stored in Active Directory. Pool-level settings are stored in the SQL Server database on the back-end server, and settings specific to a server are stored in the local WMI repository on the server. WMI exposes all these settings in a consistent way by abstracting their storage location. Because of the abstraction layer WMI provides, administrators do not need to use a different set of APIs for each storage location—such as LDAP or ADSI to query Active Directory, structured query language to access the SQL database, and WQL to query the local WMI repository.

Additional Resources

- *Office Communications Server WMI Reference,* found at *http://go.microsoft.com/fwlink/?LinkID=133570.*
- For more information about WMI, see Windows Management Instrumentation (WMI), found at *http://go.microsoft.com/fwlink/?LinkID=92569.*
- On the companion media, you will find the WMI Classes Roles and Scopes for R2.pdf, which contains a table listing all of the WMI classes that belong to Office Communications Server 2007 R2.

CHAPTER 19

Client and Device Administration

Depending on the size and complexity of an organization that uses Microsoft Office Communications Server 2007 R2, administrators must configure, maintain, and manage a variety of Unified Communications desktop clients and telephony devices. At times, client computers must be configured for specific purposes that range from limited to full use.

This chapter covers common methods for managing Unified Communications clients and devices. Most organizations that deploy Office Communications Server 2007 R2 also deploy Microsoft Office Communicator 2007 R2 and Microsoft Office Live Meeting 2007 R2 to their organization's client desktops. Depending on the Client Access license (CAL) that an organization has purchased, there are varying degrees of client function available to users. In addition, many organizations are deploying Microsoft RoundTable communications and archival system along with Microsoft Office Communicator Phone Edition devices across their networks. Therefore, this chapter also discusses how to manage the combination of Unified Communications clients and devices in your organization so that you get the most benefit from each.

ON THE COMPANION MEDIA **Links to information related to the topics addressed in this chapter can be found on this book's companion CD.**

Office Communicator 2007 R2

To deploy Office Communicator 2007 R2 across your organization, you can use any method that supports the Microsoft Windows Installer package (.msi file). In addition, you can control key features and settings by using installation scripts or Active Directory Domain Services Group policies.

This section assumes that you have already deployed Office Communications Server 2007 R2 Enterprise Edition or Standard Edition.

Generating a Log File

Log files are important tools for diagnosing and troubleshooting issues with Office Communicator 2007 R2 setup and operation. You can generate a log file during Communicator 2007 R2 setup by adding `/l*v` followed by a file name to the Windows Installer command prompt. For example:

```
msiexec /qn /i Communicator.msi /l*v logfile.txt
```

The asterisk specifies that all possible errors, warnings, and status messages are written to the log file. The v specifies that all messages are verbose.

Other log file flags are also possible. For example, `/lem` generates a log file that contains error messages as well as out-of-memory and fatal exit information. For a complete list of log file options, see the Windows Installer documentation on the MSDN Web site at *http://go.microsoft.com/fwlink/?LinkID=133739*.

You can also configure event trace log (ETL) files to be generated on your computer in the <*username*>/Tracing folder. ETL files enable administrators and Microsoft support technicians to troubleshoot problems. For more information, contact your Microsoft support representative.

> ***NOTE*** **Administrator privileges or administrator credentials (in Windows Vista Standard User mode) are required to install Communicator 2007 R2. Digital signatures protect the files in the installation package from tampering.**

Using Group Policy Settings

Table 19-1 summarizes the Group Policy settings that you can use to control certain features in Communicator 2007 R2. For more information about Meeting policies, see the section titled "Configuring Meeting Policy" in the *Microsoft Office Communications Server 2007 R2 Administration Guide*.

TABLE 19-1 Group Policies for Telephony

LICENSE TYPE	SERVER SETTING	GROUP POLICY SETTING
Standard (basic computer-to-computer calling)	None (TelephonyMode 0)	Not present, or TelephonyMode 0
Voice (also called Standard with Voice)	■ TelephonyMode 1, 2, or 3 ■ Enterprise Voice ■ Remote call control and computer-to-computer calling ■ Enables both remote call control and Enterprise Voice	■ TelephonyMode 1, 2, 3, 4, or 5 ■ Enterprise Voice ■ Remote call control and computer-to-computer calling ■ Enables both remote call control and Enterprise Voice ■ Remote call control, no computer-to-computer calling ■ No audio, only instant messaging (IM) and presence information available
Enterprise	In the Meeting section of Global Policies:* ■ EnableIPAudio = True ■ EnableIPVideo = True ■ EnableDataCollaboration = True	■ DisableAVConferencing = 0 ■ DisableDataConferencing = 0
Enterprise with Voice	See the settings in the Voice and Enterprise rows earlier in this table	See the settings in the Voice and Enterprise rows earlier in this table

**Using the Office Communications Server 2007 Administrative Tools snap-in.*

Table 19-2 summarizes the set of functions that are available for each telephony mode.

TABLE 19-2 Function Based on Group Policy Telephony Mode

FUNCTION	MODE 0	MODE 1	MODE 2	MODE 3	MODE 4	MODE 5
Computer-to-computer	●	●	●	●		
Computer-to-phone		●	●	●		
Remote call control			●	●	●	
Forking				●		
Unified Communications forwarding		●		●*		

TABLE 19-2 Function Based on Group Policy Telephony Mode

FUNCTION	MODE 0	MODE 1	MODE 2	MODE 3	MODE 4	MODE 5
HandSet phone		●	●	●		
Basic Voice over Internet Protocol (VoIP)	●	●	●	●		
Advanced VoIP features		●		●		

**When remote call control is not present.*

Communicator 2007 R2 Call Configurations

Office Communications Server 2007 R2 can operate with the telephony infrastructure that is commonly found on users' desktops. With Office Communications Server 2007 R2, users can send and receive calls by using the Public Switched Telephone Network (PSTN) and also integrate with a company's Private Branch eXchange (PBX) system.

Office Communications Server 2007 R2 also combines VoIP with open standards to provide the platform for the telephone menu–based part of the Unified Communications strategy. This combination enables integration features that bridge the VoIP standards supported by Office Communications Server 2007 R2 with implementations that use older standards.

At the center of this integration is the Mediation Server role in Office Communications Server 2007 R2. This server role provides a single interface and uses open-standard Session Initiation Protocol (SIP) for signaling interoperability. The Mediation Server takes calls from third-party IP PBX systems or SIP/PSTN gateways and moves them through the network by using the adaptive codec, remote user, and security models that are the basis for call setup and media in Office Communications Server 2007 R2.

The following are common configurations for Office Communications Server 2007 R2:

- A standalone configuration that is based on Office Communications Server and that uses Communicator 2007 R2 (TelephonyMode=1)
- A coexistence configuration that uses a mixture of Office Communications Server 2007 R2 and PBX capabilities (TelephonyMode=2)
- A dual forking configuration that enables a user to share a single phone number with Office Communications Server 2007 R2 and the organization's PBX (TelephonyMode=3)

The following sections explain how calls are routed based on the configuration.

Standalone Communicator 2007 R2 (TelephonyMode=1)

In a standalone configuration, users replace their legacy phone systems with Office Communicator 2007 or Office Communications Server 2007 IP phones. This configuration enables Office Communications Server 2007 R2 users to use Office Communicator 2007 to make and receive calls. PBX users can use the PBX to make and receive calls. Each group continues to have a smooth calling experience, including extension-based dialing capability. This configuration works especially well for organizations that have mobile employees. The standalone configuration can be implemented by using either a SIP/PSTN gateway or a direct SIP connection to the PBX.

A peer-to-peer call using Communicator 2007 R2 occurs when one Communicator 2007 R2 client places a call to another Communicator 2007 R2 client. In this case, the call is a direct VoIP call and is handled exclusively by Office Communications Server 2007 R2. The presence status (in a call) is broadcast to other Office Communicator 2007 R2 endpoints. The call is a SIP *INVITE* from one client to another and audio is established.

Notice also that when a PSTN gateway and Mediation Server are present, PSTN calls can be made to Communicator clients, and Communicator clients can place calls to the outside PSTN network.

Figure 19-1 demonstrates how a call is routed in an environment configured for the TelephonyMode=1 server setting when a Communicator 2007 R2 client (Client A) places a peer-to-peer call to another Communicator 2007 R2 client (Client B).

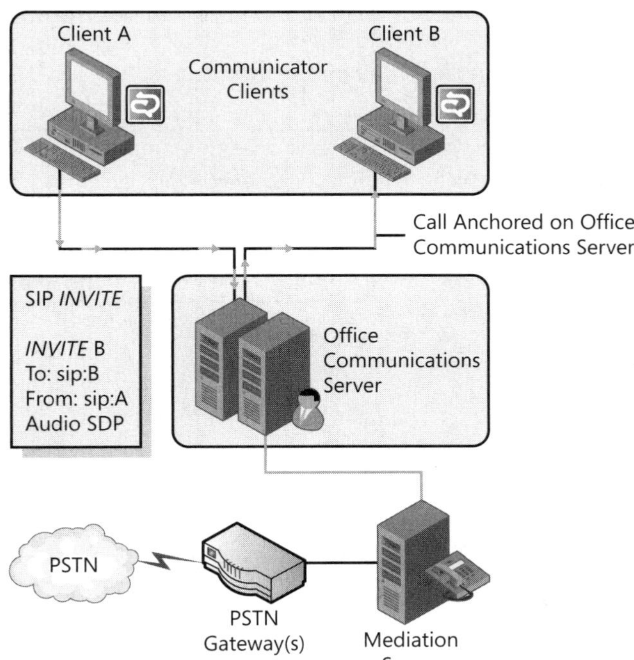

FIGURE 19-1 Office Communications Server–based calling using Communicator 2007 R2 (TelephonyMode=1)

Coexistence of Communicator 2007 R2 and PBX (TelephonyMode=2)

Coexistence occurs when an incoming call is forked between the PBX phone and the Office Communicator 2007 R2 endpoints that the user is logged on to. Both the PBX phone and Office Communicator 2007 coexist for the user. The result is a mix of PBX and Office Communications Server 2007 R2 communication capabilities that are configured for call routing by using IP PBX integration between the user's legacy phone and Office Communicator 2007 R2.

Remote Call Control (RCC) enables Office Communicator 2007 R2 to control a user's PBX phone line and indicate their presence based on the status of their phone. Using Office Communicator 2007, users can answer their PBX phone and update their presence to In A Call.

Figure 19-2 demonstrates the TelephonyMode=2 server setting for a call placed from a PBX phone and received using either the recipient's PBX phone or the recipient's Communicator 2007 R2 client.

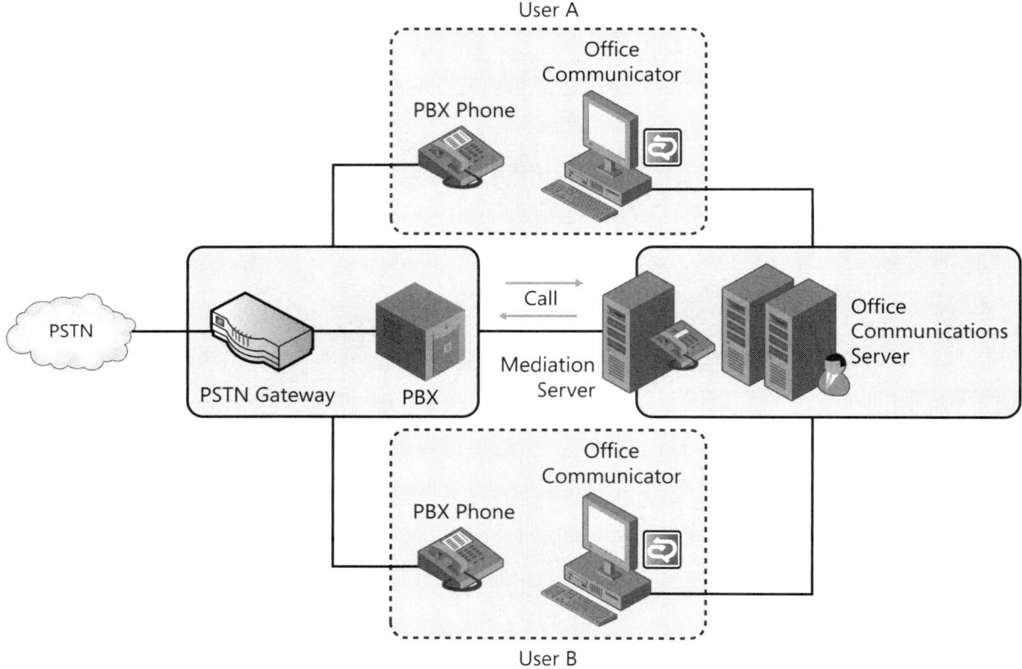

FIGURE 19-2 Coexistence of Office Communications Server and PBX (TelephonyMode=2)

As shown in Figure 19-2, the following occurs.

1. PBX phone User B places a direct call to PBX phone User A. The PBX phone for User A rings. The PBX phone can be answered.
2. At the same time the PBX phone for User A is ringing, User A receives an alert from Communicator 2007 R2 that they can receive the call by using Communicator. The Communicator client can be used to answer the call via RCC.

Dual Forking (TelephonyMode=3)

Most IP PBXs support dual forking. Dual forking enables a user to share a single phone number with Office Communications Server 2007 R2 and the organization's PBX. Additionally, the PBX can support direct SIP for certain numbers that are managed by Office Communications Server 2007 R2, or it can enable users who are not enabled for voice via Office Communications Server 2007 to manage numbers themselves. It is also possible to configure dual forking with RCC. Remote Call Control provides information to Office Communications Server 2007 R2 about the state of PBX-connected lines. This enables presence updates when the user is on the PBX-connected station set.

Figure 19-3 demonstrates how a call is routed in a dual forking configuration (TelephonyMode=3).

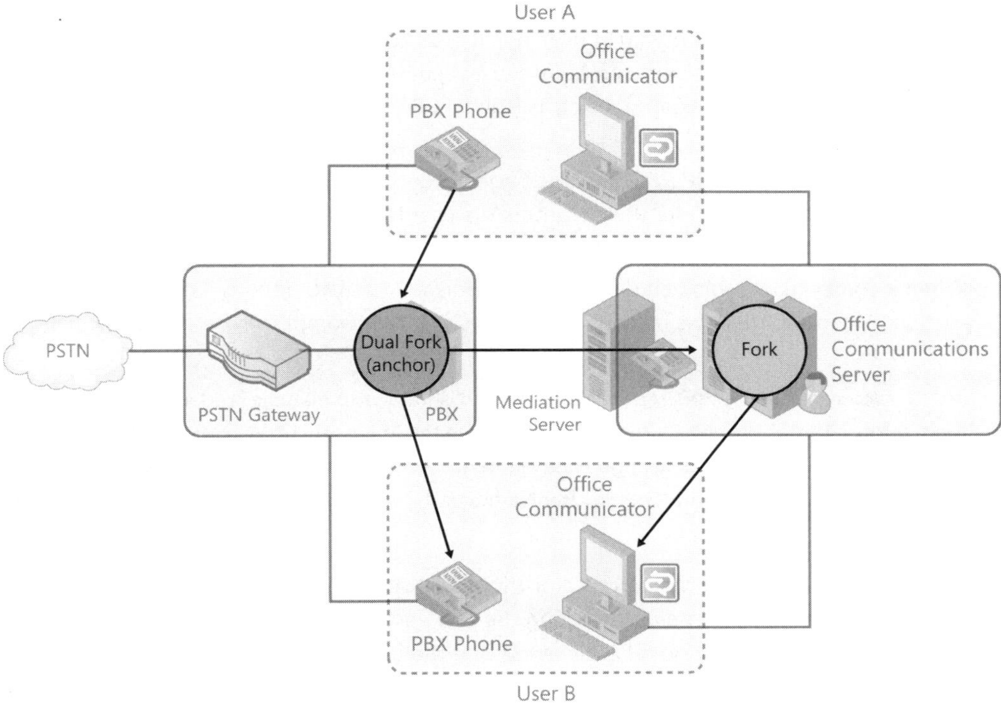

FIGURE 19-3 Dual forking (TelephonyMode=3)

In Figure 19-3, the following scenarios demonstrate dual forking for sending and receiving a phone call:

Scenario 1: User A uses a PBX phone to place a direct call to the PBX phone for User B. The PBX phone for User B rings. User B can answer the PBX phone. However, the call is also forked to a Mediation Server, and the call simultaneously displays an alert on the Communicator client for User B. User B could also choose to use Communicator to answer the call.

Scenario 2: A Communicator call is placed from User A to User B. The Communicator client for User B receives an alert to receive the call from User A. Simultaneously, the PBX phone for User B rings.

What Happens During User Sign-In

When a user initiates the sign-in process, Communicator must determine which server to log on to by using the user's Uniform Resource Identifier (URI; for example, jeremy@litwareinc.com) and any manual settings that are configured on the client. If manual settings were provided, it is clear which server to use. But if the URI is the only indicator provided, some discovery is necessary.

Communicator discovery varies based on configuration. After the client discovers the server to which to connect, it attempts to connect by using Transmission Control Protocol (TCP) or Transport Layer Security (TLS) over TCP. If TLS is used, the server provides a certificate to authenticate itself to the client. The client must validate the certificate before proceeding. The client negotiates compression if using TLS over TCP, and then the client initiates a SIP registration.

Next, the client sends a SIP *REGISTER* message to the server without any credentials. Office Communications Server 2007 R2 then prompts the user for credentials and specifies to the Communicator client the authentication protocols that it accepts.

When it comes to providing credentials, Communicator has two options. Communicator can use the user's current Windows credentials to log in, or it can prompt the user for credentials.

> ***NOTE*** **You can also use the Credential Manager in Windows to manage credentials. For more information about the Credential Manager, see the Microsoft TechNet article "Windows XP Resource Kit: Understanding Logon and Authentication" at *http://go.microsoft.com/fwlink/?LinkID=133674*, in the "Stored User Names and Passwords" section.**

Due to the order in which Communicator tries to satisfy the server's request for credentials, authentication failures can occur during the first part of logon processing. This can happen when credentials are not already saved or if the desktop credentials do not match the account that Communicator is trying to use. This can also happen when the SIP URI, account name, or password is typed incorrectly or when credentials and the SIP URI do not match. An example of this is if Jeremy tries to log in using the URI sip:jeremy@litwareinc.com, but he uses the user account and password for LITWAREINC\vadim instead of the account owner's own credentials, LITWAREINC\jeremy.

Understanding Client Automatic Configuration and DNS Discovery

When the client is set to use automatic configuration, it discovers where it should log on by using the SIP URI that was provided. Communicator does this by using Domain Name System (DNS) Service Record Locator (SRV) records published for the domain portion of the SIP URI.

For example, if sip:jeremy@litwareinc.com is the URI that is provided, Communicator takes litwareinc.com and tries to use DNS to discover a SIP server. Communicator can query for the following SRV records in its search for an appropriate server:

- _sipinternaltls._tcp.litwareinc.com
- _sipinternal._tcp.litwareinc.com
- _sip._tls.litwareinc.com

The first query looks for an internal server in the litwareinc.com domain that has ports that support TLS over TCP for clients. The second query looks for an internal server in the litwareinc .com domain that offers TCP ports for clients. The third query looks for an Internet-reachable server for the litwareinc.com domain that has ports that support TLS over TCP for clients. Communicator never looks for an Internet-reachable server that supports TCP because clear-text SIP on the Internet is not secure. In other words, Communicator is not aware whether the network that is being used is internal or external. Communicator queries for all DNS SRV records; however, it tries TLS over TCP connections first. TLS over TCP is forced through an Edge Server. There is not an option to allow for unsecured TCP connections.

If Communicator fails to find the correct server by using these files, it falls back to host (A) record queries:

- sipinternal.litwareinc.com
- sipexternal.litwareinc.com

If no DNS SRV records exist (not if they fail to be valid; only if they do not exist), the client queries sipinternal.<*URI domain*> and attempts to resolve that host name. If the host name resolves to an IP address, Communicator tries to connect using TLS over TCP, TCP, or both, depending on what the policy allows. If this fails, Communicator will try one last query with sipexternal.<*URI domain*>.

Communicator policies can be put in place to prevent TCP from being used, and this prevents the second query from being issued. You can also specify a policy that requires strict names for the computers that Communicator discovers. In this case, the only server name allowed is sip. If this policy is not imposed, any server name in the form of <*servername*>.<*URI domain*> is allowed. For example, for sip:jeremy@litwareinc.com, the host sip.litwareinc.com is always allowed whether strict policy is implemented or not. Server77.litwareinc.com, sipfed. litwareinc.com, and ap.litwareinc.com are also allowed if a strict naming policy is not enabled. The following server names are never allowed because they do not closely fit the domain that the user's URI specified, and therefore the client does not trust these servers as valid logon points: sip.eng.litwareinc.com, sip.litwareinc.net, sip.com, sip.litwareinc.com.cpandl.com, and so on.

This close validation between the host name and the URI is done because the only configuration with which the client is provided is the SIP URI. Because of this, the client must be careful not to allow DNS attacks that enable the client to connect to any middle point that could thereby intercept Communicator traffic. By having close validation between the

URI and the host names that are allowed for logon, Communicator can be more certain that the certificate the user is validating has authority for the domain to which he is trying to log on.

After the host name is identified, Communicator also resolves the host name to an IP address. This usually happens as the result of the DNS SRV request, but until the IP address is resolved, Communicator cannot connect.

In the latest version of Communicator, you can manually specify an internal and external server to which to log on. Communicator always attempts to connect to the internal server if it is available, but it will connect to the external server as an alternative. Earlier versions of Communicator have only a single manual entry, which makes it difficult to accommodate mobile workers. With the ability to specify an internal and external server, administrators can configure and enable portable computers and other mobile devices to work across internal and external networks. This increased functionality also accommodates companies where the domain in the user's URI is not the same as their SIP enterprise server's domain. Because the administrator can configure Communicator (for example, on a laptop), the user does not need to remember the internal or external servers, and administrators do not have to publish DNS SRV records for all the domains they want to support for remote access users.

REAL WORLD

Role of SRV Records in Office Communicator Log

Indranil Dutta
Premier Field Engineer

The Office Communicator client enables the user to automatically connect to the appropriate Office Communications Server 2007 R2 server without putting in the server name. Whether the client is inside the internal network or is working externally, this feature redirects the client and enables it to authenticate and connect to its own Office Communications Server 2007 R2 server (in the case of Standard Edition) or home pool (in the case of Enterprise Edition). This ability to automatically connect has a significant DNS dependency. For this to work successfully, the appropriate SRV records must be published internally and externally.

When the Office Communicator client first starts and the user tries to connect, Office Communicator always tries to connect to the server or home pool in its same domain or to one that uses the same SIP URI that is in the sign-in address. For example, if the sign-in name used is kim.akers@fabrikam.com, Office Communicator looks for the home pool or Office Communications Server 2007 R2 server that is in the same DNS namespace, which is fabrikam.com. This process is facilitated by using DNS SRV records that point the client to the fully qualified domain name (FQDN) of the home pool or server in the correct domain. The process works the same whether the client is in an internal or external network. Figure 19-4 illustrates the automatic server discovery process.

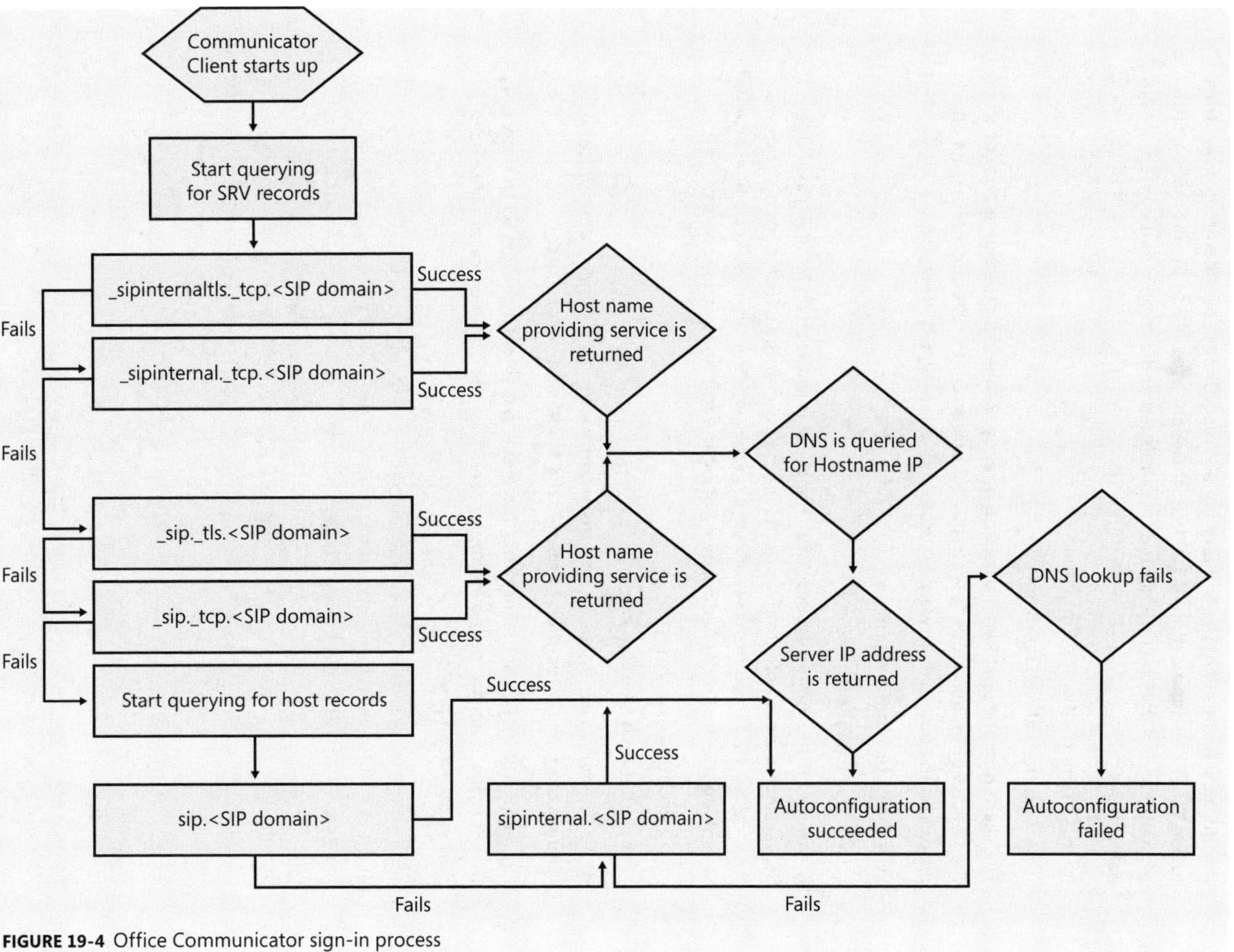

FIGURE 19-4 Office Communicator sign-in process

In Figure 19-4, the client starts querying SRV records and, by default, it always tries to use TLS for authentication. If TLS fails, the client uses TCP as an alternative. Either of the following DNS records should be published and available in the internal DNS namespace:

- _sipinternaltls._tcp.fabrikam.com
- _sipinternal._tcp.fabrikam.com

The client gets the host name back and directly connects to the home pool or to the Office Communications Server 2007 R2 server. Or, the client continues its query process in the external network by using the following DNS records:

- _sip._tls.fabrikam.com
- _sip._tcp.fabrikam.com

If either of these queries is successful, the client is redirected to the Access Edge Server and subsequently to the internal home pool or the Office Communications Server 2007 R2 server. However, if these queries fail, the client makes a final attempt to look up the host records directly by using the following DNS records:

- sip.fabrikam.com
- sipinternal.fabrikam.com

If this attempt to configure its settings automatically fails, Office Communicator requires manual intervention to resolve the failed sign-on process.

Figure 19-5 shows an actual network trace that was filtered on port 53 to show only DNS queries. It illustrates the lookup process that the Communicator client uses during the logon process.

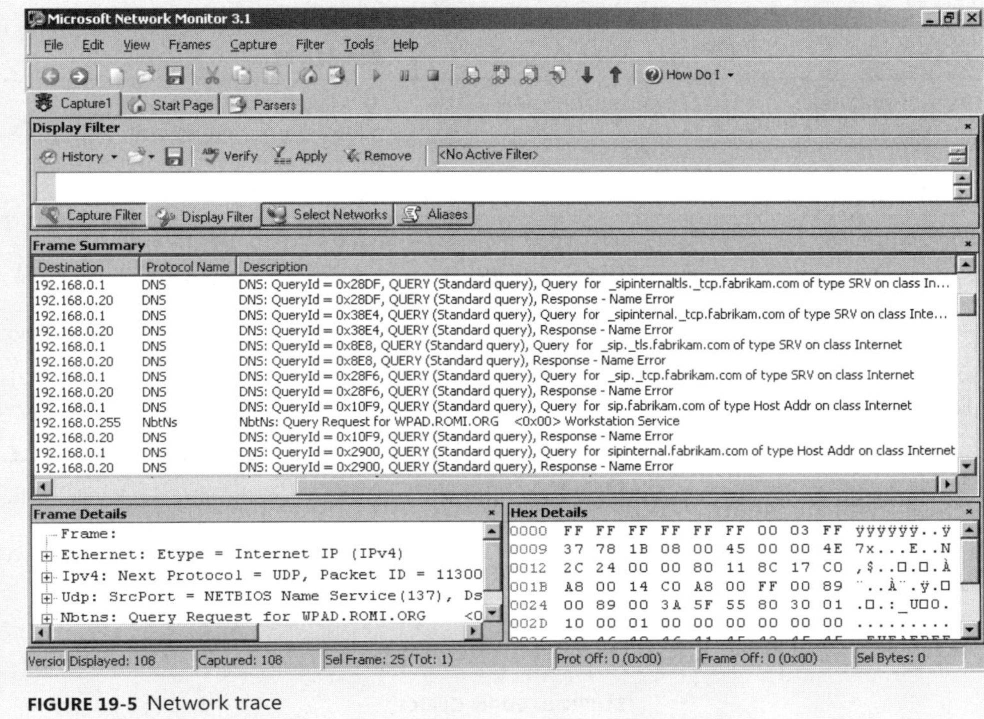

FIGURE 19-5 Network trace

Understanding Office Communicator Compatibility

This section describes the way in which Office Communicator 2007 R2 is compatible with previous versions of Office Communicator, Microsoft Office, Microsoft Exchange Server, and Microsoft Windows. The following topics are discussed:

- Office Communicator 2007 R2 and Office Communicator 2005 compatibility
- Office Communicator 2007 R2 and Microsoft Office compatibility
- Office Communicator 2007 R2 and Exchange Server compatibility
- Office Communicator 2007 R2 and Windows compatibility
- Exchange Server Communication interfaces

Communicator 2005 and Communicator 2007 R2 Compatibility

Table 19-3 describes the features supported in Communicator 2005 and Communicator 2007 R2.

TABLE 19-3 Communicator 2007 R2 and Communicator 2005 Compatibility

FEATURE	COMMUNICATOR 2005	COMMENTS
Instant messages	Supports only plain text in IM	Office Communicator 2007 R2 has an 8-kilobyte (KB) limit on IM message size and supports .rtf and .ink extensions
Multiparty IM	Can receive multiple IM and perform sentGroup IM dial-out	Office Communicator 2007 R2 can receive mesh-based multiple instant messages but can only create IM multipoint control unit (MCU)–based group IM
File transfer	Supported	Supported in Office Communicator 2007 R2

Office Communicator 2007 R2 and Microsoft Office Compatibility

Table 19-4 describes the features supported in various versions of Microsoft Office and Office Communicator 2007 R2.

TABLE 19-4 Communicator 2007 R2 and Microsoft Office Compatibility

MICROSOFT OFFICE VERSION	SUPPORTED IN OFFICE COMMUNICATOR 2007 R2?	COMMENTS
Office 2000	No	Office 2000 does not support Office Communicator 2007 R2
Office XP SP3	Yes	Contacts are supported; however, there is no Persona menu (only INFO line)
Office 2003 SP3	Yes	■ Persona menu ■ Call capability ■ IM reply capability ■ Search of folders and notifications
Office 2007 SP1	Yes	■ Consistent presence icon ■ Ability to reply with IM or Conference ■ Tagging ■ Contextual data

Microsoft Exchange Server and Office Communicator 2007 R2 Compatibility

Table 19-5 describes the features that are supported in various versions of Exchange Server and Office Communicator 2007 R2.

> ***NOTE*** **Office Communicator 2007 depends on Microsoft Office Outlook to install the Extended Messaging Application Programming Interface (MAPI) on the client computer. Thus, all the features in Table 19-5 require Office Outlook.**

TABLE 19-5 Office Communicator 2007 R2 and Microsoft Exchange Server Compatibility

EXCHANGE SERVER VERSION	SUPPORTED IN OFFICE COMMUNICATOR 2007 R2?	COMMENTS
Exchange Server 5.5	No	Not supported
Exchange Server 2000	Yes	MAPI only
Exchange Server 2003	Yes	Extended MAPI only
Exchange Server 2007	Yes	Time-of-the-day forwarding is available only with Exchange Web Services; note that public folders are optional in Exchange Server 2007

Microsoft Windows and Office Communicator 2007 R2 Compatibility

Table 19-6 describes the features that are supported in various versions of Windows and Office Communicator 2007 R2.

TABLE 19-6 Office Communicator 2007 R2 and Microsoft Windows Compatibility

MICROSOFT WINDOWS VERSION	SUPPORTED IN OFFICE COMMUNICATOR 2007 R2?	COMMENTS
Windows 2000 SP4	Yes	Must have Microsoft DirectX 9.0 installed
Windows XP SP2	Yes	—
Windows 2003 Server SP2	Yes	—
Windows Vista SP1	Yes	—

Exchange Server Communication Interfaces

Table 19-7 describes the various versions of Exchange Server–related communication interfaces for Office Communicator 2007 R2.

> ***NOTE*** **Office Communicator 2007 R2 depends on Exchange MAPI or Exchange Web Services to determine an active user's own free/busy status. After the free/busy information is retrieved, it is published into the presence containers to be seen by others.**

TABLE 19-7 Exchange Server Communication Interfaces

COMMUNICATION INTERFACE	EXCHANGE SERVER VERSION	SUPPORTED FEATURES
Outlook object model	N/A	■ Send e-mail ■ Schedule meetings ■ Receive seed information for Exchange Web Services (in Outlook) ■ Open Voice Mail folder ■ Open the Missed Conversation folder ■ Find previous conversations
MAPI	Exchange Server 2000, Exchange Server 2003, and Exchange Server 2007	■ Create a Conversation History folder ■ Write call logs ■ Write missed calls ■ Read Contact information ■ Receive voice mail notifications (new item in the Search folder) ■ Receive missed conversation notifications (new item in the Search folder) ■ Read self free/busy (public folder) ■ Read self Out of Office note

TABLE 19-7 Exchange Server Communication Interfaces

COMMUNICATION INTERFACE	EXCHANGE SERVER VERSION	SUPPORTED FEATURES
Exchange Web Services	Exchange Server 2007	■ Read self free/busy (no public folder) ■ Read Working Hours (related to free/busy) ■ Read self Out of Office note (Out of Office service present)

MUI Pack for Office Communicator 2007 R2

Office Communicator 2007 is available in several languages, each with its own installer package. In addition, a Multilingual User Interface (MUI) package for Office Communicator 2007 is available. The MUI package for Office Communicator 2007 contains the localized resources for the user interface in Office Communicator.

The following issues must be taken into account when installing the Office Communicator 2007 MUI package:

- The MUI package installs 36 languages (Listed in Table 19-8).
- No custom installation option is available.
- The MUI Setup will automatically determine the language used by the computer operating system and display that language during setup.
- You can select any of the 36 languages to be displayed by Office Communicator 2007 independent of the language that is installed for the Office Communicator 2007 client. For example, if the Spanish version of Office Communicator 2007 is installed on your computer, you can select the French language from the MUI pack to display Office Communicator 2007 in French.
- When Office Communicator 2007 is removed from your computer, the MUI package for Office Communicator 2007 remains on the computer and must be removed separately.

To install the MUI package for Office Communicator 2007, visit *http://go.microsoft.com/fwlink/?LinkID=133740.*

Table 19-8 lists the languages and regions installed with the MUI package for Office Communicator 2007 R2 in their locale identifier (LCID) hexadecimal and decimal format.

TABLE 19-8 MUI Package for Office Communicator Languages

LANGUAGE COUNTRY/REGION	LCID HEX	LCID DEC
Arabic, Saudi Arabia	0401	1025
Bulgarian	0402	1026
Chinese, People's Republic of China	0804	2052
Chinese, Taiwan	0404	1028
Chinese, Hong Kong SAR	0c04	3076
Croatian	041a	1050
Czech	0405	1029
Danish	0406	1030
Dutch, Netherlands	0413	1043
English, United States	0409	1033
Estonian	0425	1061
Finnish	040b	1035
French, France	040c	1036
German, Germany	0407	1031
Greek	0408	1032
Hebrew	040d	1037
Hindi	0439	1081
Hungarian	040e	1038
Italian, Italy	0410	1040
Japanese	0411	1041
Korean	0412	1042
Latvian	0426	1062
Lithuanian	0427	1063
Norwegian (Bokmål)	0414	1044
Polish	0415	1045
Portuguese, Brazil	0416	1046
Portuguese, Portugal	0816	2070

TABLE 19-8 MUI Package for Office Communicator Languages

LANGUAGE COUNTRY/REGION	LCID HEX	LCID DEC
Romanian	0418	1048
Russian	0419	1049
Serbian (Latin)	081a	2074
Slovak	041b	1051
Slovenian	0424	1060
Spanish, Spain (Modern)	0c0a	3082
Swedish	041d	1053
Thai	041e	1054
Turkish	041f	1055
Ukrainian	0422	1058

To select a language for MUI for Office Communicator 2007, do the following.

1. In the Office Communicator 2007 title bar, click the down arrow, click Tools, and click Options, as shown in Figure 19-6.

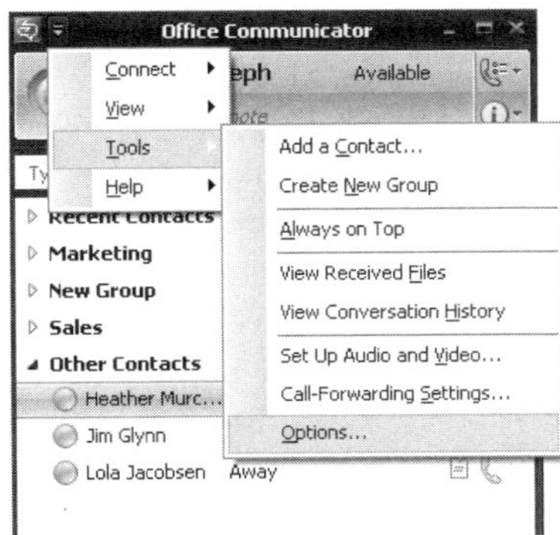

FIGURE 19-6 Opening the Options dialog box in Office Communicator 2007

2. Click the General tab and then, under Language, select a language, as shown in Figure 19-7.

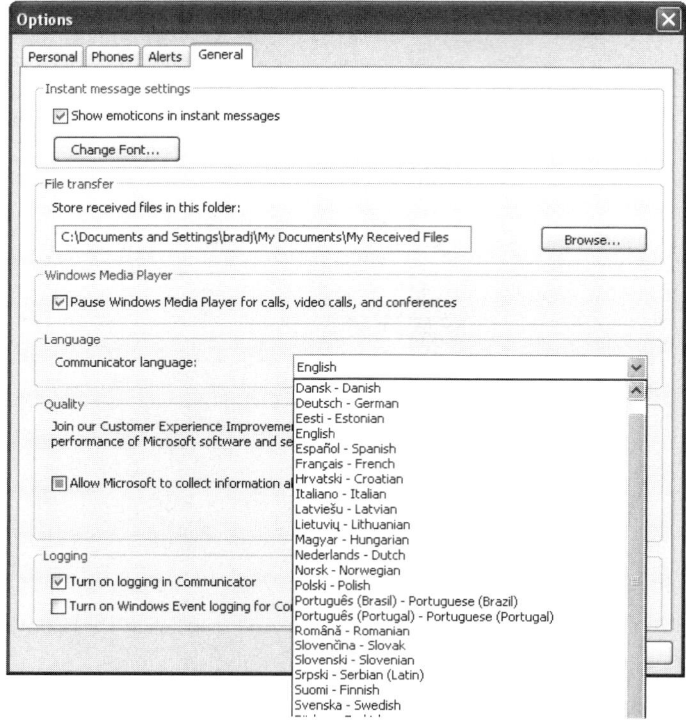

FIGURE 19-7 Selecting languages for the MUI package

You can also use the Microsoft Registry Editor to configure the language for the MUI pack. To use the Registry Editor to select a language, perform the following steps.

1. Click Start, click Run, and type **Regedt32**.
2. Under My Computer, click HKEY_CURRENT_USER.
3. Click Software, click Microsoft, and then click Communicator.
4. Double-click Language and (referring to Table 19-8) type the LCID for the language/region.
5. Click OK and close the Registry Editor.

Office Live Meeting 2007 R2

This section is for people who administer the Live Meeting client for Office Communications Server 2007 R2. Administrators can modify the behavior of the Office Live Meeting 2007 R2 client by setting registry keys that are specific to the Live Meeting client. The Office Live Meeting client also shares a number of registry keys with Office Communicator 2007 R2. When you install one of these clients, the shared registry keys are provisioned for both clients.

Office Live Meeting 2007 R2 Registry Keys

Table 19-9 lists the registry keys that Office Live Meeting uses.

TABLE 19-9 Registry Keys that Live Meeting Uses

REGISTRY KEY	DESCRIPTION
HKEY_LOCAL_MACHINE\Software\Microsoft\Live Meeting\8.0\ProductCode	In the client computer's registry, string value that represents the Live Meeting version.
HKEY_LOCAL_MACHINE\Software\Microsoft\Live Meeting\8.0\Lockdown	Disables upgrade notifications.
HKEY_LOCAL_MACHINE\Software\Policies\Microsoft\LiveMeeting\AllowAnonymousServerJoin	Prevents users from joining Office Communications Server meetings as an anonymous user.
HKEY_LOCAL_MACHINE\Software\Policies\Microsoft\LiveMeeting\AllowServiceJoin	Prevents users from joining meetings that are hosted on the Microsoft Office Live Meeting Service.
HKEY_LOCAL_MACHINE\Software\Policies\Microsoft\Windows\Installer\DisableUserInstalls	Disables per-user installations.
HKEY_LOCAL_MACHINE\Software\Policies\Microsoft\LiveMeeting\MaxAudioVideoBitrate	Specifies the maximum bandwidth for audio and video.[1]
HKEY_CURRENT_USER\Software\Microsoft\Live Meeting\Console\Version 8.0\Attendee\MediaPortRangeMin	Specifies a minimum value for the User Datagram Protocol (UDP)/TCP port range that is used when the client is running in Attendee mode.[2]
HKEY_CURRENT_USER\Software\Microsoft\Live Meeting\Console\Version 8.0\Attendee\MediaPortRangeMax	Specifies a maximum value for the UDP/TCP port range that is used when the client is running in Attendee mode.[2]
HKEY_CURRENT_USER\Software\Microsoft\Live Meeting\Console\Version 8.0\Presenter\MediaPortRangeMin	Specifies a minimum value for the UDP/TCP port range that is used when the client is running in Presenter mode.[2]
HKEY_CURRENT_USER\Software\Microsoft\Live Meeting\Console\Version 8.0\Presenter\MediaPortRangeMax	Specifies a maximum value for the UDP/TCP port range that is used when the client is running in Presenter mode.[2]
HKEY_CURRENT_USER\Software\Microsoft\Live Meeting\Preferences\Server\ServerAudioProviderName	If you are using an Audio Conferencing Provider (ACP) with Office Communications Server 2007, specifies the ACP URL. This key prepopulates the ACP provider name field in the client audio settings.

TABLE 19-9 Registry Keys that Live Meeting Uses

REGISTRY KEY	DESCRIPTION
HKEY_CURRENT_USER\Software\Microsoft\Live Meeting\Preferences\Server\ServerAudioProviderAccount	If you are using an ACP, specifies the ACP URL. This key prepopulates the ACP provider account field in the client audio settings.
HKEY_CURRENT_USER\Software\Microsoft\Live Meeting\Preferences\Server\ServerTollFreeNumber	If you are using an ACP, specifies the ACP toll-free number in the format +1-8665556738. This key prepopulates the ACP toll-free number field in the client audio settings.
HKEY_CURRENT_USER\Software\Microsoft\Live Meeting\Preferences\Server\ServerTollNumber	If you are using an ACP, specifies the ACP toll number in the format +1-2035558000. This key prepopulates the ACP toll number field in the client audio settings.
[HKEY_CURRENT_USER\Software\Microsoft\Tracing\uccp\LiveMeeting] "EnableFileTracing"= DWORD:00000001 "Tracing"= DWORD:00000001	Enables client-side logging, which maintains a detailed log in the %USERPROFILE%\tracing\ directory (filename LiveMeeting-uccp-*.log). Client-side logging supplements the default logging in the %TEMP% directory (filename pwconsole-debug*.txt).
HKEY_CURRENT_USER\Software\Microsoft\Office\12.0\Outlook\Options\ConflictMsgCls "IPM.Appointment.Live Meeting Request"= DWORD:00000004	Minimizes a conflict error that users of the Conferencing add-in for Outlook may see when they are running the 2007 Microsoft Office System and Exchange Server 2007. In some circumstances, when the user creates or modifies a Live Meeting appointment, an erroneous Outlook message appears indicating that the appointment conflicts with another appointment.

1 The selected bitrate should account for transmission of both main and panoramic video. Therefore, the value should be higher than the equivalent setting for Office Communicator. This setting applies to audio and video traffic. It does not apply to data traffic related to application sharing.

2 The default UDP/TCP port range is 1024–65535. By default, none of these registry keys is set. Values in both the Attendee and Presenter modes must be set to make any of these settings become effective.

Live Meeting Registry Keys Shared with Office Communicator 2007 R2

The registry keys in Table 19-10 are shared between the Office Live Meeting client and Office Communicator 2007 R2. When you install one client, these registry keys are created and provisioned for both clients. If a user changes his or her account information manually on one client, the account information will change on the other client.

Instead of requiring users to enter their account settings manually, administrators may want to configure these registry keys during client deployment. Otherwise, administrators will need to provide instructions to users about how to enter account settings.

TABLE 19-10 Registry Keys Shared Between Office Communicator 2007 R2 and the Office Live Meeting 2007 R2 Client

REGISTRY KEY	DESCRIPTION
HKEY_CURRENT_USER\Software\Microsoft\Shared\UcClient\ServerAddressExternal	Specifies the server name or IP address a federated contact uses when connecting from outside the external firewall
HKEY_CURRENT_USER\Software\Microsoft\Shared\UcClient\ServerAddressInternal	Specifies the server name or IP address the client uses when connecting from inside the organization's firewall
HKEY_CURRENT_USER\Software\Microsoft\Shared\UcClient\ServerSipUri	Specifies the SIP URI the client uses when connecting to Office Live Meeting, the Conferencing add-in for Outlook, and Office Communicator sign-in name
HKEY_CURRENT_USER\Software\Microsoft\Shared\UcClient\Transport	Defines the network protocol the client uses: TCP or TLS

Multiple Client Installation Script

Enabling your organization to use the complete set of Office Communications Server 2007 R2 features requires that a combination of client applications are installed on each computer in your organization. For example, you can install Office Communicator 2007 R2 for IM presence and telephony, Office Live Meeting 2007 R2 for enhanced audio/video conferencing, and the Outlook add-in for application integration with Outlook 2007. The task of individually installing these applications for multiple users, locally or remotely, can be challenging.

One method for managing and deploying multiple client applications to individual computers is to use a Windows Script Host (WSH) script. The advantage of using an automated WSH script is that WSH is natively supported on computers running Windows XP and Windows Vista. Another method is to use a third-party tool to install these clients as an image to user's desktop computers, which is a process that is outside the scope of this book.

ON THE COMPANION MEDIA **For a list of Office Live Meeting 2007 R2 Group Policy settings, see Appendix C on the companion CD in the folder \Appendixes,Scripts,Resources\Chapter 19\Scripts.**

REAL WORLD

Using the Multiple Client Installation Script

Rui Maximo

Senior Writer, Unified Communications

Here's how to use the OCinstall.wsf script for silent installation of Office Communicator 2007 R2, Office Live Meeting 2007 R2, and the Outlook add-in for 2007 R2. The script does not require users to run installation wizards or perform manual installations. The script helps to reduce the introduction of user setup errors that result in calls to the technical support help desk. The OCinstall.wsf script detects whether a previous client version is installed and uninstalls Office Communicator 2007 before installing Office Communicator 2007 R2. It also configures Office Communicator 2007 R2 with the user's sign-in address (SIP URI) and certain policy settings.

ON THE COMPANION MEDIA The OCinstall.wsf client installation script is available on the companion CD in the folder \Appendixes,Scripts,Resources\Chapter 19\Scripts. This script is useful for managing and deploying multiple client applications to individual computers.

To set up the configuration for this script to work in your environment and to help the installation on the client computers run smoothly, you must complete following steps.

1. Extract the Installer (.msi) files from the setup (.exe) files for the individual application.
2. Make the MSI files available to users on a read-only network file share.
3. Modify the OCinstall.wsf script to correspond to your environment.
4. Add the OCinstall.wsf script file as a logon script.

The following sections explain each of the previous steps in more detail.

Step 1: Extract the Installer Files

The first step is to extract the Installer files. You must first obtain the following Microsoft Installer (extension .msi) files:

- Office Communicator 2007 R2 installer package (Communicator.msi)
- Office Live Meeting 2007 R2 (LMConsole.msi)
- Office Outlook Add-in 2007 R2 (LMAddinPack.msi)

To perform a silent install, you must use the MSI version of the installation file. For the previously mentioned clients, the Microsoft Installer file (for example, LMConsole.msi) must be extracted from the application setup file (for example, LMConsole.exe).

To obtain the setup file for these applications, please refer to your installation CD.

To extract each application's Microsoft Installer file from the application setup file, use the following command:

```
<application>.exe -out
```

This will extract the following Microsoft Installer application file:

```
<application>.msi
```

Table 19-11 lists each application, its setup file, and its Microsoft Installer file.

TABLE 19-11 Unified Clients Installer Files

APPLICATION	SETUP FILE	MICROSOFT INSTALLER FILE
Office Live Meeting 2007 R2	LMSetup.exe	LMConsole.msi
Office Communicator 2007 R2	Communicator.exe	Communicator.msi
Conferencing add-in for Office Outlook R2	ConfAddins_Setup.exe	LMAddinPack.msi

Step 2: Make the MSI Files Available to Users

The second step is to set up a network file share if you do not already have one. Copy the Installer files to this file share. The security properties on the files and network share must enable your target end-users read-only and execute permissions for the Installer files.

Step 3: Modify the OCinstall.wsf Script

The third step is to configure the default settings in the OCinstall.wsf script. It is necessary to modify the following entries located at the beginning of the script:

- SIP domain name
- Network file share location of the Microsoft Installer files (see step 2)
- A URL that will appear in Office Communicator 2007 R2 and provide help and assistance locations for your organization
- Branding resources

The following example uses the fictitious organization litwareinc.com to illustrate how to specify these entries in the OCinstall.wsf script.

```
' --------------------------------------------------------------------------
-------
' SETTINGS THAT MUST BE CONFIGURED BEFORE RUNNING
'---------------------------------------------------------------------------
-------
# Organization SIP domain name
Const c_strDomainName = "litwareinc.com"

# Network share where the installation files are located
Const c_strRoot = "\\server\share\dir\

# URL that users can click on within Office Communicator to get help
Const c_strHelpURL = "http://help.litwareinc.com"

# Branding resources
Const c_strBranding = "Litwareinc Unified Communications"
Const c_strBrandingXML = http://litwareinc.com/branding.xml
```

Step 4: Add the OCinstall.wsf Script File as a Logon Script

The fourth step is to add OCinstall.wsf as a logon script so that when users log on to their computers, the installation is automatically started. Because OCinstall.wsf detects whether Office Communicator 2007 R2, Office Live Meeting 2007 R2, and the Conferencing add-in are already installed, it will silently terminate without performing a reinstall. So, even if the user logs on multiple times and the script is run each time, it will install these clients only once.

Alternatively, you can use other methods to get the OCinstall.wsf script to run on users' computers. For example, you can notify users by e-mail or the company Web portal to run this script.

If the installation failed or did not implement your configuration changes, you can view the OCinstall.wsf log file that is stored in %WINDIR%\Debug\OfficeCommunications.log to help you troubleshoot the problem.

ON THE COMPANION MEDIA The OCinstall.wsf client installation script is available on the companion CD in the folder \Appendixes,Scripts,Resources\Chapter 19.

Group Policy for Unified Communications Clients

Group Policy is the infrastructure that enables administrators to deliver and apply these and other configurations to targeted users and computers within an Active Directory directory service environment.

How Group Policy Works

Group Policy components are administered by using two primary tools. The first tool is the Group Policy Management Console (GPMC). GPMC lets you create, view, and manage Group Policy objects (GPOs). The second tool is the Group Policy Object Editor, which lets you configure and modify settings within GPOs.

ON THE COMPANION MEDIA **A full collection of client GPOs are on the companion CD in the folder \Appendixes,Scripts,Resources\Chapter 19\Group Policy. These are useful for understanding the object functions and the various settings.**

Administrative template files contain specific information about which Group Policies the application implements, where policies are stored, and how to configure policies. The user interface for registry-based policies is controlled by using Administrative Template (.adm) files. These files describe the user interface that is displayed in the Administrative Templates node of the Group Policy snap-in.

Adding Administrative Templates

The Administrative Template file (.adm) consists of a hierarchy of categories and subcategories that together define how options are organized in the Group Policy user interface.

To add Administrative Template (.adm) files:

1. In the Group Policy console, double-click Active Directory Users And Computers, select the domain or organizational unit (OU) for which you want to set policy, click Properties, and then click Group Policy.
2. On the Group Policy properties page, select the GPO that you want to edit from the Group Policy objects links list, and then click Edit to open the Group Policy snap-in.

3. In the Group Policy console, click the plus sign (+) next to either User Configuration or Computer Configuration. The .adm file defines which of these locations the policy is displayed in, so it does not matter which node you choose.
4. Right-click Administrative Templates and select Add/Remove Templates. This shows a list of the currently active template files for this Active Directory container.
5. Click Add. This shows a list of the available .adm files in the *%systemroot%/inf* directory of the computer where Group Policy is being run. You can choose an .adm file from another location. After you select the .adm file, it is copied into the GPO.

Figure 19-8 is an example of how Communicator 2007 R2 Group Policies are displayed in the GPMC.

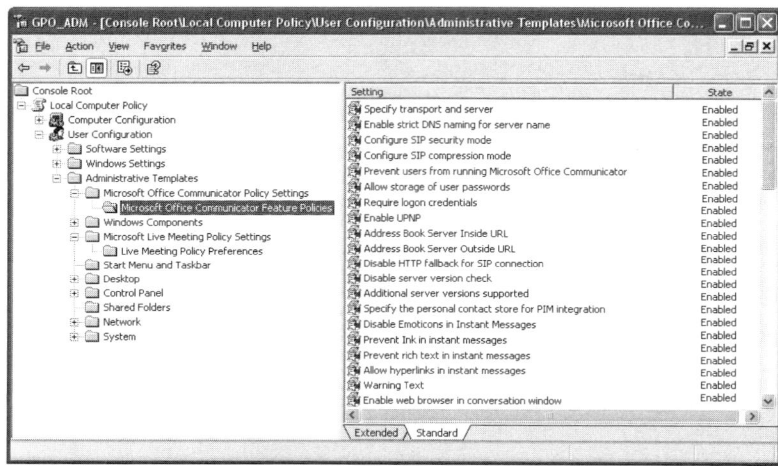

FIGURE 19-8 Group Policy Management Console

Because Live Meeting, Office Communicator 2007 R2 Group Chat, Communicator 2007, and Communicator 2007 R2 Attendant policies are separate, you can deploy Group policies for any one of the clients without affecting current or future deployments for the other clients.

Office Communicator 2007 R2 Group Policy Settings

One way to provide the appropriate registry settings for each user when you deploy Office Communicator 2007 R2 is to define Group policies by using the Communicator.adm Administrative Template.

To download the package that contains the Communicator.adm file and the Communicator Group Policy spreadsheet that lists the Group Policy settings for Office Communicator 2007 R2, visit: *http://go.microsoft.com/fwlink/?LinkID=133746*.

Communicator 2007 R2 Group Policy Precedence

You can configure some features and behaviors in Communicator 2007 R2 by using Office Communications Server 2007 R2 in-band provisioning. The user can also configure some options by using the Communicator 2007 R2 Options dialog box. However, Group policies take precedence over both of these methods.

Table 19-12 summarizes the order in which settings take precedence when a conflict occurs.

TABLE 19-12 Order of Precedence for Group Policies, In-Band Provisioning, and Options Dialog Box Settings

PRECEDENCE	LOCATION OR METHOD OF SETTING
1	HKEY_LOCAL_MACHINE\Software\Policies\Microsoft\Communicator
2	HKEY_CURRENT_USER\Software\Policies\Microsoft\Communicator
3	Office Communications Server 2007 R2 in-band provisioning
4	Communicator 2007 R2 Options dialog box

ON THE COMPANION MEDIA **For a list of Office Communicator 2007 R2 Group Policy settings, see Appendix C on the companion CD in the folder \Appendixes,Scripts,Resources\Chapter 19\Group Policy.**

Office Live Meeting 2007 R2 Group Policy

You can deploy Office Live Meeting 2007 R2 Group policies without affecting users who are currently running Live Meeting 2007 R2. This section introduces the Office Live Meeting 2007 R2 Group policies.

The administrator can configure some Office Live Meeting 2007 R2 features and behaviors by using Office Communications Server 2007 R2 in-band provisioning. Alternatively, the user can configure the same items through the Office Live Meeting 2007 R2 Options dialog box. However, Group policies take precedence over both of these methods.

If no policy is set for the Windows-based Live Meeting 2007 client or for the Conferencing add-in for Outlook, default settings will apply.

Computer policies are observed before user policies. Preferences are observed last. If a preference is set before policies are set, the preferences will not be overwritten. If only one policy is set for a server or for a service, the preference will be used for the unset policies. If policies are removed, the previous preference settings will be used.

ON THE COMPANION MEDIA For a list of Office Live Meeting 2007 R2 Group Policy settings, see the companion CD in the folder \Appendixes,Scripts,Resources\Chapter 19\Group Policy.

Response Group Service Clients

The Response Group Service is an optional Office Communications Server 2007 R2 application that is installed by default. It offers organizations a solution for deploying and administering a voice hunt group and basic Interactive Voice Response (IVR) routing.

The Response Group Service is a server application that routes voice calls to a specific group of agents and that is configured by an administrator. For example, upon receiving a customer call for a particular number, the Response Group Service is responsible for finding an available agent to take the customer call.

The following are the supported Response Group Service clients:

- Caller side:
  - PSTN client
  - Office Communicator 2007
  - Office Communicator 2007 R2
  - Office Communications Server 2007 R2 Attendant Console
  - Office Communicator 2007 R2 Phone Edition
- Agent side:
  - Office Communicator 2007 R2
  - Agent Communications Panel for Dynamics CRM 4.0
  - Office Communicator 2007 R2 Phone Edition

Communicator Phone Edition

Communicator Phone Edition is an intelligent IP phone designed to get the most out of Microsoft's Unified Communications platform. It combines network voice, user-driven design, up-time reliability, quality audio, and the enhanced communication and collaboration of Office Communications Server 2007 R2.

This section describes the elements necessary to manage Communicator Phone Edition within an organization.

DHCP and Communicator Phone Edition

To properly function, all computers on a TCP/IP network must have an IP address for the network. In general, you can configure IP addresses manually at each computer, or you can install a Dynamic Host Configuration Protocol (DHCP) server that automatically assigns IP addresses to each client computer or device on the network. Communicator Phone Edition is no exception. It is a DHCP client that can receive only DHCP-assigned IP addresses and requires no configuration on the device.

DHCP Search Options

You can create a list of DNS suffixes that can be appended to unqualified DNS names for use by clients when they perform DNS queries. For DHCP clients, a suffix can be set by assigning the DNS domain name option (option 015) and providing one DNS suffix for the client to append and use in searches.

DHCP search option 119 is passed from the DHCP server to the DHCP client to specify the domain search list to be used when resolving host names with DNS. DHCP search option 119 applies only to DNS and does not apply to other name resolution mechanisms. Table 19-13 lists DHCP options for domain search lists.

TABLE 19-13 DHCP Options for domain search list

DHCP OPTION	DESCRIPTION
015	Specifies the connection-specific DNS domain suffix to be used by the DHCP client
119	DNS domain search list option that specifies the domain search list to be used when resolving host names with DNS

Figure 19-9 illustrates how support for multiple DNS suffixes is enabled by using DHCP option 15 and DHCP search option 119.

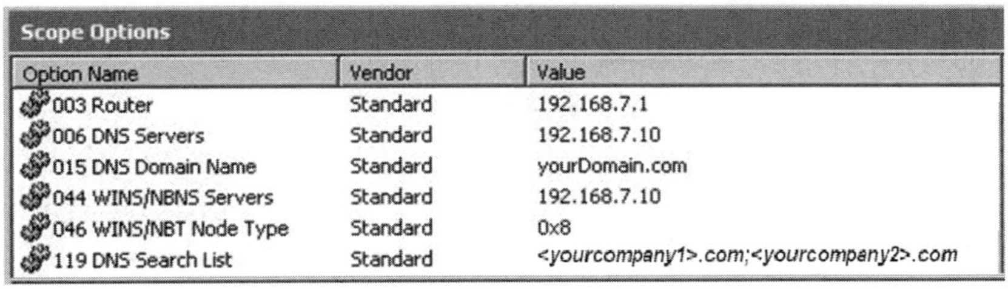

Scope Options

Option Name	Vendor	Value
003 Router	Standard	192.168.7.1
006 DNS Servers	Standard	192.168.7.10
015 DNS Domain Name	Standard	yourDomain.com
044 WINS/NBNS Servers	Standard	192.168.7.10
046 WINS/NBT Node Type	Standard	0x8
119 DNS Search List	Standard	*<yourcompany1>.com;<yourcompany2>.com*

FIGURE 19-9 DHCP options for Communicator Phone Edition

To enable search option 119 for the Microsoft Windows Server 2003 DHCP server, do the following.

1. Open DHCP by clicking Start, pointing to Settings, clicking Control Panel, double-clicking Administrative Tools, and then double-clicking DHCP.

2. In the console tree, click the applicable DHCP server.
3. On the Action menu, click Set Predefined Options.
4. Under Predefined Options And Values, click Add (Option Class Standard), and click OK.
5. In the Name box, type **DNS Search List**.
6. Set Code to 119 and Data Type to string (it is not an array) and then click OK.
7. Right-click Scope Options, select Configure Options, and then select Option 119 DNS Search List.
8. Enter a list of domain suffixes that are in your organization, delimited by semicolons. For example, litwareinc.com;dev.litwareinc.com;corp.microsoft.com.
9. Click OK.

REAL WORLD

Query Order that Communicator Phone Edition Uses to Locate Office Communications Server 2007 R2

Jens Trier Rasmussen
Senior Program Manager, Unified Communications

Communicator Phone Edition uses the following DNS domains when querying information in DNS:

- `SIP domain = Right Hand Side of Sign-in Address`
- `SMTP domain = Right Hand Side of Primary E-mail address`

If the query fails, Communicator Phone Edition tries to look up the same record with DNS suffixes appended as follows:

- `host.<SIP domain>`
- `host.<SIP domain>.<DNS suffix>`

When Communicator Phone Edition connects to Office Communications Server 2007 R2, it queries in the following order:

1. Hosts and ports pointed to by the following SRV records:
   - _sipinternaltls._tcp.<SIP domain>
   - _sip._tls.<SIP domain>
   - _sipinternal. tcp.<SIP domain>
2. sipinternal.<SIP domain>:5061
3. sipinternal.<SIP domain>:443

4. sip.<SIP domain>:5061
5. sip.<SIP domain>:443
6. sipexternal.<SIP domain>:5061
7. sipexternal.<SIP domain>:443

Microsoft Exchange Server 2007 Autodiscover

Exchange Server 2007 includes a new Microsoft Exchange service named the Autodiscover service. The Autodiscover service configures client computers that are running Outlook 2007. The Autodiscover service can also configure supported mobile devices. The Autodiscover service provides access to Exchange features for Outlook 2007 clients that are connected to an Exchange messaging environment. The Autodiscover service must be deployed and configured correctly for Outlook 2007 clients to automatically connect to Exchange features, such as the offline address book, the Availability service, and Unified Messaging (UM).

How Communicator Phone Edition Retrieves Outlook Contacts, Call Logs, and Voice Mail

Communicator Phone Edition retrieves Outlook contacts, call logs, and voice mails and displays them on mobile devices. Communicator Phone Edition does this by accessing the Exchange Server 2007 Client Access server and retrieving the information by using Exchange Web Services (EWS). Communicator Phone Edition locates the Exchange Server 2007 Client Access server through the use of an A record found in the DNS. It uses the Simple Mail Transfer Protocol (SMTP) domain of the primary e-mail address for the user to locate the A record. The primary e-mail address is sent to the device during the sign-in process through in-band provisioning. Communicator Phone edition queries the A records in the following order:

1. https://<*SMTP domain*>/autodiscover/autodiscover.xml
2. https://autodiscover.<*SMTP domain*>/autodiscover/autodiscover.xml
3. http -> https redirect

Outlook 2007 uses Active Directory service connection points (SCPs) and DNS SRV records to locate the Exchange Server 2007 Client Access server. However, the device does not support these additional methods.

The Autodiscover service is responsible for finding and presenting the various URLs that are used to interact with EWS and information about how to connect Outlook 2007 to Exchange Server 2007. The device uses those URLs to retrieve Outlook contacts, call logs, and voice mail messages from Exchange Server 2007.

Communicator Phone Edition Query Order of Microsoft Exchange Server 2007

Communicator Phone Edition must connect to the EWS URL by using HTTP or HTTPS. If HTTPS is enabled, the certificate from the Exchange Server must be trusted.

Communicator Phone Edition attempts to connect to the Exchange Server 2007 Autodiscover service in the following order:

1. https://<*SMTP domain*>/autodiscover/autodiscover.xml
2. https://autodiscover.<*SMTP domain*>/autodiscover/autodiscover.xml
3. http -> https redirect

After Communicator Phone Edition receives a successful response, it connects to the EWS URL in the Autodiscover response XML.

Troubleshooting Contacts, Call Logs, and Voice Mail on Communicator Phone Edition

To troubleshoot missing Outlook contacts, call logs, and voice mail messages on the Communicator Phone Edition device, try some of the following from a computer that is on the same network as the device:

- Use dnslookup to test that you can find an A record in DNS for <*SMTP domain*> or autodiscover.<*SMTP domain*> .
- Try to access the following URLs by using Internet Explorer to see if you get an XML response back with a 600 Invalid request.
  - *https://*<SMTP domain>*/autodiscover/autodiscover.xml*and the http version of this URL
  - *https://autodiscover.*<SMTP domain>*/autodiscover/autodiscover.xml* and the http version of this URL
- Make special note of the certificates used by the Autodiscover service and on the Client Access server. Ensure that the device trusts each certificate. If the certificate is the default self-signed certificate that is used by Exchange 2007, the device does not trust it. Therefore, Exchange 2007 will not communicate with the Autodiscover service.
- Try to use the Outlook 2007 Test E-mail AutoConfiguration feature. To do this, press Ctrl and right-click the Outlook icon in the system tray. Select Use AutoDiscover, type your e-mail address, and then click Test. Click the XML tab to see if XML is returned.
- Try to access the URL ending with */ews/exchange.asmx* that is shown on the XML tab from your browser. If XML is returned, EWS is working.
- If the previous methods have shown that Exchange Server 2007 Autodiscover service and EWS are working, check the Internet Information Services (IIS) log on the Exchange Server 2007 Client Access server for signs that the device is trying to communicate with the Exchange Server 2007 Client Access server.

NTP and Communicator Phone Edition

Network Time Protocol (NTP) is the default time synchronization protocol used by the Windows Time service in Windows Server 2003. NTP is a fault-tolerant, highly scalable time protocol and is the protocol used most often for synchronizing computer clocks by using a designated time reference. Communicator Phone Edition requires NTP to set the correct time and date for Communicator Phone Edition.

NTP Time Provider

The NTP provider is the standard time provider included with Windows Server 2003. The NTP provider in the Windows Time service consists of the following two parts:

- **NtpServer output provider** This is a time server that responds to client time requests on the network.
- **NtpClient input provider** This is a time client that obtains time information from another source, either a hardware device or an NTP server, and can return time samples that are useful for synchronizing the local clock.

Although the actual operations of these two providers are closely related, they appear independent to the time service. By default, when a computer that is running Windows Server 2003 is connected to a network, it is configured as an NTP client.

Communicator Phone Edition searches for a NTP server in DNS by using the following code:

```
NTP SRV record (UDP port 123)

_ntp._udp.<SIP domain> pointing to NTP Server
```

If it cannot find the NTP SRV record, it will attempt to use time.windows.com as an NTP server.

```
NTP A record

time.windows.com
```

To set Group Policy for Windows Time service global configuration settings, perform the following steps.

1. From the Microsoft Management Console (MMC), click Active Directory Users And Computers.
2. Right-click the domain that contains your NTP server, and then select Properties.
3. Click the Group Policy tab, make sure the Default Domain Policy is highlighted, and click Edit.
4. Click Computer Configuration, click Administrative Templates, click System, and then click Windows Time Service.

5. Click Time Providers. In the right pane, double-click Enable Windows NTP Server. Click the Enabled button and then click OK.
6. From the Group Policy Object Editor menu, select File and click Exit.

Server Security Framework Overview

The following section provides an overview of the fundamental elements that form the security framework for Office Communications Server 2007 R2. Understanding how these elements work together is helpful when deploying Communicator Phone Edition in your organization.

Root CA Certificate for Communicator Phone Edition

Office Communications Server 2007 R2 relies on certificates for server authentication and to establish a chain of trust between clients and servers and among the different server roles. The Windows Server 2003 public key infrastructure (PKI) provides the infrastructure for establishing and validating this chain of trust.

Communication between the Communicator Phone Edition and Office Communications Server 2007 R2 is by default encrypted using TLS and Secure Real-Time Transport Protocol (SRTP). Therefore, the device needs to trust certificates that are presented by Office Communications Server 2007 R2 servers. If Office Communications Server 2007 servers use public certificates, they will most likely be automatically trusted by the device because public certificates contain the same list of trusted certification authorities (CAs) as Windows CE. However, because most Office Communications Server 2007 R2 deployments use internal certificates for the internal Office Communications Server server roles, it is necessary to install the root CA certificate from the internal CA to the device. It is not possible to manually install the root CA certificate on the device, so it must be installed through the network. Communicator Phone Edition can download the certificate by using two methods.

In the first method, the device will search for Active Directory objects in the category certificationAuthority. If the search returns any objects, it will use the attribute *caCertificate*. That attribute is assumed to hold the certificate, and the device will install the certificate.

The root CA certificate must be published in the *caCertificate* for Communicator Phone Edition. To have the root CA certificate placed in the *caCertificate* attribute, use the following command:

```
certutil -f -dspublish <Root CA certificate in .cer file> RootCA
```

If the search for Active Directory objects in the category certificationAuthority does not return any objects or if the objects have empty *caCertificate* attributes, the device will search for Active Directory objects in the category pKIEnrollmentService in the configuration naming context. Such objects exist if certificate AutoEnrollment has been enabled in Active Directory. If the search returns any objects, Communicator Phone Edition will use the *dNSHostName* attribute that is returned to reference the CA, and it will then use the Web interface of the

Microsoft Certificates Service to retrieve the root CA certificate by using the following HTTP GET command:

```
http://<dNSHostname>/certsrv/certnew.p7b?ReqID=CACert&Renewal=-1&Enc=b64
```

If neither of these methods succeeds, the device will present the error message "Cannot validate server certificate" and the user will not be able to use the device.

Using Communicator Phone Edition Certificates

The following is a list of considerations for issuing certificates to Communicator Phone Edition:

- By default, Communicator Phone Edition uses TLS and SRTP.
  - Requirement: The Communicator Phone Edition device must trust certificates presented by Office Communications Server 2007 R2 and the Exchange Server 2007 server.
  - Requirement: The root CA chain certificate must reside on the device.
- Manual installation of the certificate on the device is not possible.
- Other options for certificates include the following:
  - Use public certificates.
  - Preload public certificates on the device.
  - Use enterprise certificates.
  - Install the root CA chain from the network.

Enterprise Root CA Chain

Communicator Phone Edition can find the certificate by using the PKI auto-enrollment object in Active Directory or through a well-known distinguished name (DN).

Following are the two ways in which Communicator Phone Edition locates certificates on your network:

- Enable PKI auto-enrollment through the enterprise CA.
  - The device makes a Lightweight Directory Access Protocol (LDAP) request to find the pKIEnrollmentService/CA server address and eventually download the certificate via HTTP to the Windows CA /certsrv site by using the user's credentials.
- Use certutil -f -dspublish ".cer file location" RootCA to upload certificates to the Configuration naming context.
  - Cn=Certificate Authorities, cn=Public Key Services, CN=Services, cn=Configuration, dc=<Active Directory Domain>

NOTE The LDAP request is BaseDN: CN=Configuration, dc= <Domain> Filter: (objectCategory=pKIEnrollmentService). The searched-for attribute is *dNSHostname*. Please be aware that the device downloads the certificate using the HTTP GET command http://<dNSHostname>/certsrv/certnew.p7b?ReqID=CACert&Renewal=-1&Enc=b64.

Trusted Authorities

Table 19-14 lists the public certificates that are trusted by Communicator Phone Edition.

TABLE 19-14 Public Certificates

VENDOR	CERTIFICATE NAME	EXPIRATION DATE	KEY LENGTH
Comodo	AAA Certificate Services	12/31/2020	2,048
Comodo	AddTrust External CA Root	5/30/2020	2,048
Cybertrust	Baltimore CyberTrust Root	5/12/2025	2,048
Cybertrust	GlobalSign Root CA	1/28/2014	2,048
Cybertrust	GTE CyberTrust Global Root	8/13/2018	1,024
VeriSign	Class 2 Public Primary Certification Authority	8/1/2028	1,024
VeriSign	Thawte Premium Server CA	12/31/2020	1,024
VeriSign	Thawte Server CA	12/31/2020	1,024
VeriSign	Comodo	1/7/2010	1,000
VeriSign	Class 3 Public Primary Certification Authority	8/1/2028	1,024
Entrust	Entrust.net Certification Authority (2048)	12/24/2019	2,048
Entrust	Entrust.net Secure Server Certification Authority	5/25/2019	1,024
Equifax	Equifax Secure Certificate Authority	8/22/2018	1,024
GeoTrust	GeoTrust Global CA	5/20/2022	2,048
Go Daddy	Go Daddy Class 2 Certification Authority	6/29/2034	2,048
Go Daddy	*http://www.valicert.com/*	6/25/2019	1,024
Go Daddy	Starfield Class 2 Certification Authority	6/29/2034	2,048

RoundTable Management

This section describes tools and configuration settings for managing Microsoft RoundTable.

Installing the Microsoft RoundTable Management Tool

Before you can configure the RoundTable device, you must install the Microsoft RoundTable Management Tool, RoundTable.msi. You can obtain RoundTable.msi from the Microsoft Download Center (*http://go.microsoft.com/fwlink/?LinkID=133745*).

By default, RoundTable.msi installs the End-User License Agreement (EULA) to the %ProgramFiles%\Microsoft RoundTable\ directory and creates two directories—Device Management and Drivers—under this directory.

RoundTable.msi copies the following files to the Microsoft RoundTable\Device Management\ directory.

- **Rtmanage.exe** The Microsoft RoundTable Management Tool. The current version of this tool is in English only. For more information about how to use this tool, see the section titled "Using Rtmanage.exe" later in this chapter.
- **DeviceConfig.xsn** The Microsoft Office InfoPath template for RoundTable configuration.
- **DefaultConfig.xml** An example XML file for configuring the device.

RoundTable.msi copies the following files to the Microsoft RoundTable\Driver\ directory.

> ***NOTE*** **Windows XP 32-bit edition uses the driver files in the following list. Windows Vista does not require these files.**

- Rtyuv.dll
- RoundTable.inf
- RoundTable.cat

Using Rtmanage.exe

Rtmanage.exe is used with a switch that specifies one of following three modes:

- Image mode
- Diagnostic mode
- Configuration mode

Tables 19-13, 19-14, and 19-15 describe the mode commands and show the syntax for each mode. Image mode commands are used to update the firmware images of the RoundTable device's operating system or boot loader, or to download a new configuration. Diagnostic mode commands are used to send diagnostic logs to the image update server. Configuration mode commands are used for a variety of purposes, including resetting the password, setting the device time, and uploading a device configuration to the image update server.

All but two of the following operations will prompt the user for the RoundTable password. The operations that do not require a password are the following:

- Rtmanage.exe -help
- Rtmanage.exe -m:diag -l:flush

For clarity, Tables 19-15, 19-16, and 19-17 show only the switches that are used with Rtmanage.exe. A complete command must include Rtmanage or Rtmanage.exe with the applicable switch, as in the following example.

```
Rtmanage <switch>
Rtmanage.exe <switch>
```

TABLE 19-15 Image Mode Commands

OPTION	DESCRIPTION
-m:img -help	Shows usage and flags of the image mode
-m:img -i:nk -f:<file path to nk.bin> -s:<file path to nk.cat>	Performs a Universal Serial Bus (USB) image update of Nk.bin, the operating system of the RoundTable device.
-m:img -i:EBOOT -f:<file path to CPUEBOOT.bin> -s:<file path to CPUEBOOT.cat>	Performs a USB image update of Cpueboot.bin, the boot loader of the RoundTable device.
-m:img -i:config -f:<file path to rtconfig.xml>	Downloads a new configuration file to the RoundTable device. The device must be rebooted before the new configuration takes effect.

After you perform any of the image mode commands, you must reboot the Round-Table device. You can do this by using the Rtmanage boot command, as shown in the following example.

```
Rtmanage.exe m:cfg -r
```

TABLE 19-16 Diagnostic Mode Commands

OPTION	DESCRIPTION
-m:diag -help	Shows usage and flags of the diagnostic mode.
-m:diag -l:flush	Flushes diagnostics to the image update server. The exact location will be referenced in future documentation for the Office Communications Server 2007 Update Service. You will not be prompted for a password for this operation.

TABLE 19-17 Configuration Mode Commands

OPTION	DESCRIPTION
-m:cfg -help	Shows usage and flags of the configuration mode.
-m:cfg -t:now	Sets the time of the RoundTable device with the time on the computer.
-m:cfg -r	Reboots the device.
-m:cfg -p	Sets the password for the device. The factory default password is 78491.
-m:cfg -q:cfgparseresult	Queries the parser result after a new configuration is downloaded to the device.
-m:cfg -f:rtconfig.xml	Uploads the RoundTable device configuration file to a server share on the Office Communications Server 2007 Update Service.

Common Configuration Tasks

This section provides information about common tasks that can be performed for configuring RoundTable. For each command, it is assumed that you have the Command Prompt window open and that the current directory is %ProgramFiles%\Microsoft RoundTable\Device Management\.

Set the Time

The following command uses the computer's time to reset the time on the RoundTable device:

```
Rtmanage.exe -m:cfg -t:now
```

Change the Display Language

To change the display language on the RoundTable device, perform the following steps.

1. Double-click DeviceConfig.xsn to launch the InfoPath form.
2. In the LCD Display section of the InfoPath form, change the display language setting to the appropriate value.
3. Save the file (as RTConfig.xml, for example) to the directory that contains Rtmanage.exe.
4. Open a command prompt and run the following command:

```
Rtmanage.exe -m:img -i:config -f:RTConfig.xml
```

5. Check for XML parsing errors by using the following command:

```
Rtmanage.exe -m:cfg -q:cfgparseresult
```

6. If there is no error, proceed to the next step. Otherwise, fix the errors and repeat from step 3.
7. Reboot the device by using the following command:

```
Rtmanage.exe -m:cfg -r
```

Change the Time Zone

To change the time zone on the RoundTable device, perform the following steps.

1. Double-click DeviceConfig.xsn to launch the InfoPath form.
2. In the Time section of the InfoPath form, change the Time Zone setting to the appropriate time zone.
3. Save the file (as RTConfig.xml, for example) to the directory that contains Rtmanage.exe.
4. Open a command prompt and run the following command:

```
Rtmanage.exe -m:img -i:config -f:RTConfig.xml
```

5. Check for XML parsing errors by using the following command:

```
Rtmanage.exe -m:cfg -q:cfgparseresult
```

6. If there are no errors, proceed to the next step. Otherwise, fix the errors and repeat from step 3.
7. Reboot the device by using the following command:

```
Rtmanage.exe -m:cfg -r
```

Get the Device's Current Configuration

To see the RoundTable device's current configuration settings, open a command prompt and run the following command:

```
Rtmanage.exe -m:cfg -f:RTconfig.xml
```

The device configuration file will be uploaded to a server share on the Office Communications Server 2007 Update Service.

Update the Firmware Images

The fastest way to update the RoundTable device is by means of an automatic image update using the image update server. However, if you must update the device in the absence of the update server, you can use the USB image update function.

To update the device by using the USB image update function, perform the following steps.

1. Obtain the latest firmware image files from the Microsoft Download Center. Following is the list of firmware image files:
   - Boot loader package: CPUEBOOT.cat and CPUEBOOT.bin
   - Operating system package: nk.cat and nk.bin
2. To update the boot loader, run the following command at a command prompt:

```
Rtmanage.exe -m:img -i:EBOOT -f:<file path to CPUEBOOT.bin> -s:<file path to
CPUEBOOT.cat>
```

3. To update nk.bin, run the following command at a command prompt:

```
Rtmanage.exe -m:img -i:nk -f:<file path to nk.bin> -s:<file path to nk.cat>
```

Reset the Device to Factory Settings

A RoundTable device stores two copies of its firmware: a read-only copy that is installed at the factory and an updateable working copy. A RoundTable device ordinarily runs the updateable copy. When a device reset is performed, the working copy is erased. The device then uses the read-only factory firmware. The purpose of the factory firmware copy is to enable the user to update the RoundTable device with current firmware revisions without having to return the device to the factory.

If you forget your device password or the firmware images have become corrupted (due to a power outage, for example), you can undertake a factory reset by performing the following steps.

1. Press and hold down the On/Off Hook button.
2. While still holding down the On/Off Hook button, press and then release the Reset button at the back of the device. You will see a screen that prompts you to confirm that you want to continue with the reset or to continue without resetting.
3. Press the Flash/Conference button if you want to proceed with the reset. Alternatively, press the Mute button to continue without resetting. Hold the Flash/Conference button until the device light-emitting diode (LED) lights start to blink. If you do not hold this button long enough, the factory reset will not occur and the device will restart.

After you perform a factory reset, apply the latest RoundTable firmware to the device to ensure the most secure operation and best performance. After a factory reset, you will need to reapply the configuration for your device.

Reset the Device Password

As a security best practice, change the device password from its default setting by running the following command line:

```
Rtmanage.exe -m:cfg -p
```

You will be prompted to enter the existing password, enter the new password, and then re-enter the new password.

The password contains American National Standards Institute (ANSI) characters and must be at least one character, but no more than 15 characters.

> ***NOTE*** **Failure to apply the latest RoundTable firmware after a factory reset can result in the device becoming noncompliant with telephony regulations in your country or region. Any liability resulting from failure to apply the latest firmware upgrade is the responsibility of the end user.**

Upload the Diagnostics Logs

The following command line flushes diagnostic logs on the RoundTable device and sends them to the image update server.

```
rtmanage.exe -m:diag -l:flush
```

Interpreting the Diagnostics Logs

RoundTable writes to the CE log for hardware functional tests and critical system issues. To send the CE log to the Update Service server, open a command prompt and run the following command:

```
rtmanage.exe -m:diag -l:flush
```

This command causes the RoundTable CE log to be uploaded to a server share on the Office Communications Server 2007 Update Service. For the location of the file share, see the Office Communications Server 2007 R2 documentation.

The CE log for the device is written to a directory on the share. The directory name is the device's product ID.

The CE log file name has the form YYYYMMDDHHMMSS-CELOG*n*.clg, where *n* is 0 or 1. An example CE log file name is 20070501170926-CELOG0.clg.

Summary

This chapter covers methods for managing Unified Communications clients and devices. Most organizations that deploy Office Communications Server 2007 R2 also deploy Office Communicator 2007 R2 and Office Live Meeting 2007 R2 clients to their desktops. Depending on the CAL that an organization has purchased, varying degrees of features are available to users. Similarly, many organizations are deploying the RoundTable and Communicator Phone Edition devices across their networks. This chapter discusses how to manage the combination of Unified Communications clients and devices in your organization so that you get the most from each.

Additional Resources

- Office Communicator 2007 R2 Deployment Guide, found at *http://go.microsoft.com/fwlink/?LinkID=133744*
- Communicator 2007 R2 Testing and Troubleshooting Guide, found at *http://go.microsoft.com/fwlink/?LinkID=133741*
- Microsoft RoundTable Users Guide, found at *http://go.microsoft.com/fwlink/?LinkID=133742*
- Microsoft RoundTable Setup Guide, found at *http://go.microsoft.com/fwlink/?LinkID=133743*
- Microsoft Office Live Meeting Service Administrator's Guide, found at *http://go.microsoft.com/fwlink/?LinkID=136752*
- Microsoft Office Live Meeting Service Portal Administrator's Guide, found at *http://go.microsoft.com/fwlink/?LinkID=136753*. A full collection of client Group Policy objects are on the companion CD in the folder \Appendixes,Scripts,Resources\Chapter 19\Group Policy. These are useful for understanding the object functions and the various settings.
- The OCinstall.wsf client installation script is available on the companion CD in the folder \Appendixes,Scripts,Resources\Chapter 19\Scripts. This script is useful for managing and deploying multiple client applications to individual computers.

PART V

Technical Troubleshooting and Diagnostics

CHAPTER 20

Diagnostic Tools and Resources

This chapter introduces diagnostic tools and resources that are available in Microsoft Office Communications Server 2007 R2 and Microsoft Office Communicator 2007 R2. The useful diagnostic tools that are available in the Office Communications Server 2007 R2 Resource Kit are identified and explained to help you understand this toolset and how you can use it to diagnose problems.

Identifying Diagnostic Tools by Scenario

A variety of tools are available to help diagnose problems. Table 20-1 presents a selection of available tools, the scenarios to which they generally apply (whether they are specific to instant messaging [IM], conferencing, or voice applications), and a brief note about what they do and where you can access them.

TABLE 20-1 Diagnostic Tools for Different Scenarios

TOOL NAME	DESCRIPTION	INSTALLATION SOURCE
CORE SCENARIO (BASIC PRESENCE AND IM)		
Validation Wizard	Analyzes and validates current configuration and connectivity to detect errors, validate basic end-to-end scenarios, and provide recommendations	Office Communications Server 2007 R2 (in the Deployment Wizard); can also be launched from the server Microsoft Management Console (MMC) snap-in
Office Communications Server 2007 R2 Logging Tool	Starts and stops server logs as well as filters and displays logs	Office Communications Server 2007 R2; can also be launched from the server MMC snap-in
Event Viewer	MMC snap-in that enables client and/or server event logs to be viewed and examined (the snap-in also has an embedded viewer that shows only errors and warnings)	Part of all Microsoft Windows operating systems
Office Communicator Error Message	Clickable hyperlink that points to the Web page containing an explanation and the cause of an issue as well as the resolution; generated by the Office Communicator client and presented to the user when an issue occurs	Part of Office Communicator client
ClientLogReader	Script that scans client trace log files to highlight errors, provide protocol summaries, or filter out specific protocol messages	Office Communications Server 2007 R2 Resource Kit Tools
Snooper	Graphical user interface (GUI) for summarizing, searching, and viewing client and server protocol and trace logs; also works for Microsoft Office Communications Server 2007 server logs	Office Communications Server 2007 R2 Resource Kit Tools
Archiving-CDR Reporter	GUI for querying, archiving, and calling Call Detail Records (CDRs)	Office Communications Server 2007 R2 Resource Kit Tools

TABLE 20-1 Diagnostic Tools for Different Scenarios

TOOL NAME	DESCRIPTION	INSTALLATION SOURCE
CheckSPN	Validates service principal names (SPNs) to avoid authentication and topology errors	Office Communications Server 2007 R2 Resource Kit Tools
DbAnalyze	Gathers analysis reports from the Office Communications Server 2007 R2 database	Office Communications Server 2007 R2 Resource Kit Tools
LCSDiscover	Discovers settings for previous and current versions of Microsoft Office Live Communications Server 2005 and Office Communications Server 2007 R2	Office Communications Server 2007 R2 Resource Kit Tools
SIPParser	Protocol parser for Session Initiation Protocol (SIP); can be plugged into Network Monitor (Netmon) for viewing unencrypted SIP over Transmission Control Protocol (TCP)	Office Communications Server 2007 R2 Resource Kit Tools
SRVLookup	Queries relevant Domain Name System (DNS) Service Record Locator (SRV) records for the specified domain; useful for federation and logon diagnostics	Office Communications Server 2007 R2 Resource Kit Tools
SQL Server 2005 Performance Dashboard Reports	Microsoft SQL Server 2005 Performance Dashboard Reports are used to monitor and resolve performance problems on your SQL Server 2005 database server	Web download is available at *http://go.microsoft.com/fwlink/?LinkID=133747*
Office Communications Server 2007 Best Practices Analyzer	Designed for administrators who want to determine the overall health of their Office Communications Server 2007 R2 servers and topology	Web download is available at *http://go.microsoft.com/fwlink/?LinkID=133748*
CONFERENCING SCENARIO		
Network Monitor (Netmon)	Network protocol analyzer used to view raw network traffic for media interactions	Web download is available at Microsoft Download Center at *http://go.microsoft.com/fwlink/?LinkID=133750*

TABLE 20-1 Diagnostic Tools for Different Scenarios

TOOL NAME	DESCRIPTION	INSTALLATION SOURCE
Wireshark (formerly Ethereal)	Network protocol analyzer from the open source community	Available on many operating systems; also available for free at *http://go.microsoft.com/fwlink/?LinkID=133749*
Monitoring Server	New server role that enables collection of CDR information by intercepting and parsing certain SIP messages on the Office Communications Server 2007 R2 front-end servers; it also collects quality metrics data sent by participant endpoints at the end of each audio/video (A/V) session	Office Communications Server 2007 R2
ENTERPRISE VOICE SCENARIO		
Enterprise Voice Route Helper	GUI for visualization, testing, modification, archiving, and sharing of voice routing configuration data	Office Communications Server 2007 R2 Resource Kit Tools (the user's guide for this tool is available from the Microsoft Download Center; search for "Microsoft Office Communications Server 2007 R2 Enterprise Voice Route Helper User's Guide" at *http://go.microsoft.com/fwlink/?LinkID=133751*
Deployment Validation Tool (DVT) agents	Enables test endpoints and the ability to schedule tests and report results via System Center Operations Manager 2007 or e-mail	Web download is available at *http://go.microsoft.com/fwlink/?LinkID=133752*
Pre-Call Diagnostics	Tool tests the "last-hop" network conditions and provides guidance about possible quality issues before placing calls	Office Communications Server 2007 R2 Resource Kit Tools

ON THE COMPANION MEDIA All tools that are part of Microsoft Office Communications Server 2007 R2 Resource Kit Tools are provided on the companion media to make them easier to find and use. Please reference the short document included in the toolset for detailed instructions about how to run each tool. More tools exist in the Microsoft Office Communications Server 2007 R2 Resource Kit Tools than those listed in Table 20-1. Only the primary tools of interest to most readers are highlighted here.

Using Server Setup Logs

Installation is one of the first places in which help may be required if an error occurs. When seemingly silent failures occur during installation, activation, or preparation steps during deployment, installation information is the first place to look.

DIRECT FROM THE SOURCE

Diagnosing Setup Failures

Nirav Kamdar
Principal Development Lead, Office Communications Server

Setup logs are located under %TEMP% and have either the .log (for Microsoft Installer [MSI] logs) or .html extension (for activation/prep failures). In MSI logs, look for the phrase *value 3* (MSI errors are cryptic, and this is a quick method to locate them). The HTML logs are self explanatory and can be expanded to the point of the failure. LcsCmd's *CheckXXState* is usually also helpful. For example, to check whether the A/V multipoint control unit (MCU) is activated, you can run LcsCmd /mcu /action:CheckLcServerState /role:AVMCU.

Usage Example

As explained earlier, the setup operation will generate an accompanying HTML file. Occasionally, the following question is asked: What happens during schema prep, forest prep, or similar setup operations? If you have the HTML file that has the respective setup operations, all the information you need is there.

Another frequently asked question is: How do I find the root cause for setup failure? One way to research the problem is to open the HTML logs in Internet Explorer and expand the contents of the file. Scroll to the bottom of the file and start moving up. After you see the first occurrence of the issue, you are at the right starting point. Carefully analyze the action information and execution result for this issue because both can provide valuable troubleshooting information and hints.

Using Event Logs

Office Communications Server has always provided event logs to help identify problems and point out irregularities in the system. In Office Communications Server 2007 R2, there is even a filtered view of server warnings and errors that is presented in the MMC snap-in as a tabbed overview for each server. Office Communicator 2007 R2 can create event logs that you can enable by clicking Tools, clicking Options, and then on the General tab, selecting Turn On Windows Event Logging For Communicator, as shown in Figure 20-1. When issues arise, the event log is the first place to look for high-level guidance on problems that the server or client might already have identified. In general, warnings and errors will be of interest, but informational event logs will not.

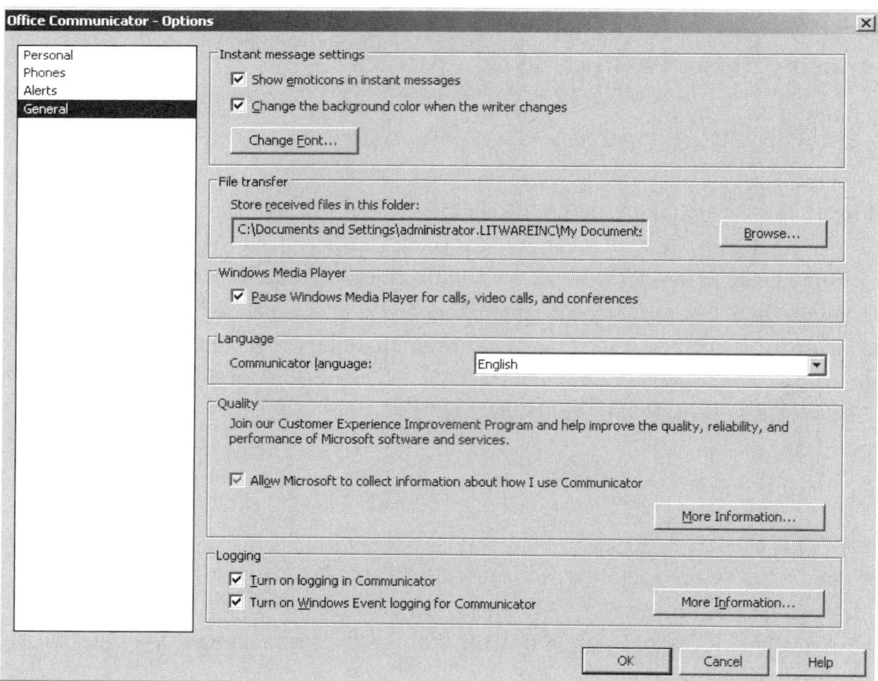

FIGURE 20-1 Enabling Windows Event Logging For Communicator in Office Communicator

Because the event log has the capability to filter and sort itself, it is not necessary to spend time searching the Application Event Log. All events the client logs show up in the Application Event Log, and all events from servers show up in the Office Communications Server Event Log. The View menu enables you to filter by event source; therefore, filtering for Office Communicator events or a particular server role is possible, as is filtering for only warnings and errors.

Usage Example: Using Event Logs

If event logs are enabled in Office Communicator, Office Communicator will create various event log entries, some informational and some that indicate issues. When an issue occurs, these entries are useful for diagnosing the root cause of the problem. The following example explains the problem, identifies data that is related to the problem, and explains the steps involved for solving the problem.

In the following example, event log message 1007 occurs because Office Communicator is configured with an invalid server name, IConfiguredAnInvalidServerName.litwareinc.com. The message explains that Office Communicator cannot find a server with that name when attempting to resolve the host name specified using the DNS. As is typical for most events, the actions to be taken next are explained in the event log Resolution.

```
Type: Error EventID: 1007 Source: Communicator
 Description:
Communicator was unable to resolve the DNS hostname of the login server
IConfiguredAnInvalidServerName.litwareinc.com.

Resolution:
If you are using manual configuration for Communicator, please check that
the server name is typed correctly and in full.  If you are using automatic
configuration, the network administrator will need to double-check the DNS
A record configuration for IConfiguredAnInvalidServerName.litwareinc.com
because it could not be resolved.
```

Using the Validation Wizard

When working through problems in the topology or on specific servers, a good way to minimize the scope or to quickly identify errors is to use the Validation Wizard, which is available as a tool in the Office Communications Server 2007 R2 Administration MMC snap-in. This tool checks configuration against connectivity and does basic validation checks to point out and avoid misconfigurations in Office Communications Server 2007 R2 settings or in network and certificate configurations that relate to the server. The next Direct from the Source sidebar provides a usage example for using the Validation Wizard.

DIRECT FROM THE SOURCE

Using the Validation Wizard

Thomas Laciano
Senior Program Manager, Office Communications Server Customer Experience

I have an Office Communications Server 2007 R2 Standard Edition Server and an Office Communications Server 2007 R2 Edge Server deployed. Most often, I log on internally by using the Office Communicator 2007 R2 client. If this does not work, I check the error message to see whether I can quickly resolve the problem because DNS and certificate issues are the easiest errors to identify. If I still can't identify the problem, I use the Validation Wizard.

After one client has successfully logged on, I know that my Standard Edition Server is running and accounts are able to log on. I then move to the Edge Server; open Computer Management, Services and Applications; and then right-click Microsoft Office Communications Server 2007 R2 to launch Validation for the Access Edge Server role as shown in Figure 20-2.

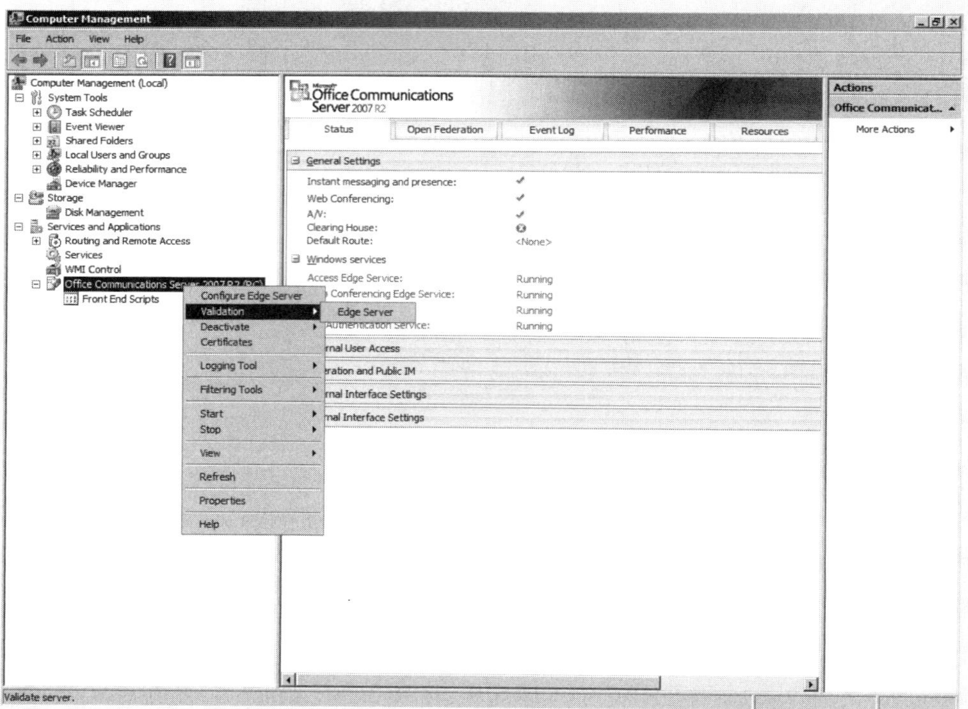

FIGURE 20-2 Launching Validation for the Access Edge Server Role Wizard

I select the Validate Local Server Configuration, Validate Connectivity, and Validate SIP Logon (1-Party) And IM (2-Party) check boxes as shown in Figure 20-3.

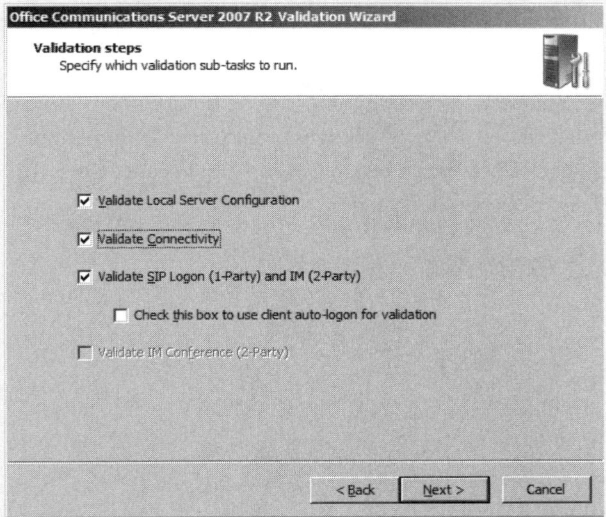

FIGURE 20-3 Selecting Access Edge validation subtasks

Because I am giving an introduction to the Validation Wizard here in this sidebar, I will not explain all the tests; I will not include a federation test in this chapter.

First, I run the Validation Wizard on the Access Edge Server and receive errors. I select the View Logs option because logs are created by default in the user's temporary directory. The resulting log page looks like Figure 20-4 when opened in Internet Explorer.

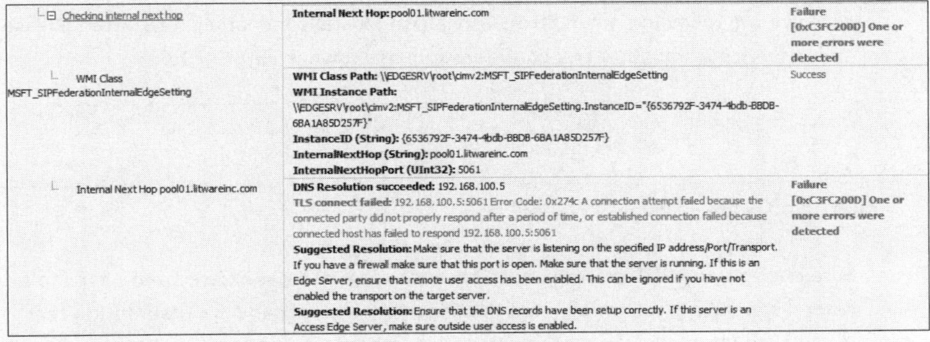

Checking internal next hop	**Internal Next Hop:** pool01.litwareinc.com	**Failure [0xC3FC200D] One or more errors were detected**
WMI Class MSFT_SIPFederationInternalEdgeSetting	**WMI Class Path:** \\EDGESRV\root\cimv2:MSFT_SIPFederationInternalEdgeSetting **WMI Instance Path:** \\EDGESRV\root\cimv2:MSFT_SIPFederationInternalEdgeSetting.InstanceID="{6536792F-3474-4bdb-BBDB-6BA1A85D257F}" **InstanceID (String):** {6536792F-3474-4bdb-BBDB-6BA1A85D257F} **InternalNextHop (String):** pool01.litwareinc.com **InternalNextHopPort (UInt32):** 5061	Success
Internal Next Hop pool01.litwareinc.com	**DNS Resolution succeeded:** 192.168.100.5 **TLS connect failed:** 192.168.100.5:5061 Error Code: 0x274c A connection attempt failed because the connected party did not properly respond after a period of time, or established connection failed because connected host has failed to respond 192.168.100.5:5061 **Suggested Resolution:** Make sure that the server is listening on the specified IP address/Port/Transport. If you have a firewall make sure that this port is open. Make sure that the server is running. If this is an Edge Server, ensure that remote user access has been enabled. This can be ignored if you have not enabled the transport on the target server. **Suggested Resolution:** Ensure that the DNS records have been setup correctly. If this server is an Access Edge Server, make sure outside user access is enabled.	**Failure [0xC3FC200D] One or more errors were detected**

FIGURE 20-4 Access Edge Validation Deployment Log page

The errors point out problems, such as TLS connect failed: 192.168.100.5:5061 Error Code: 0x274c. No connection can be made because the target server actively refused it. Note that the log contains other errors. Experience has taught me to go through all the errors to find the biggest problem, which in this case is that I cannot connect to the Standard Edition Server.

The next step is to run the Validation Wizard on the Office Communications Server 2007 Standard Edition Server. I select only the Validate Local Server Configuration and Validate Connectivity check boxes (as shown in Figure 20-5) because the errors indicate a server problem and not a logon problem.

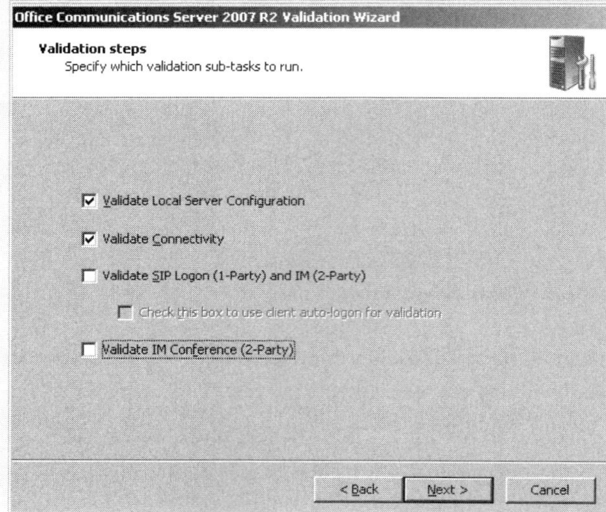

FIGURE 20-5 Selecting Standard Edition Server validation subtasks

I receive the following error: Error: Service isn't installed, enabled, or started. Please check service installation and configuration, as shown in Figure 20-6.

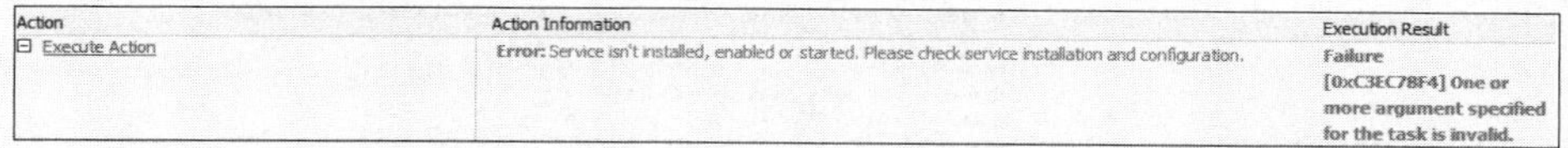

Action	Action Information	Execution Result
⊟ Execute Action	**Error:** Service isn't installed, enabled or started. Please check service installation and configuration.	**Failure [0xC3EC78F4] One or more argument specified for the task is invalid.**

FIGURE 20-6 Standard Edition Server Validation Deployment Log page

Sure enough, the RTCService service account password has expired and needs to be reset. I started my validation from the Edge Server and made the assumption that everything internally was working properly. Because it was not, I took actions to resolve problems for the internal server. So now, I will begin the Validation Wizard testing at the internal server and work my way back to the Access Edge Server to minimize the number of possible problems.

I have configured my deployment so that I will select all the options on the Validation Steps page (as shown in Figure 20-7).

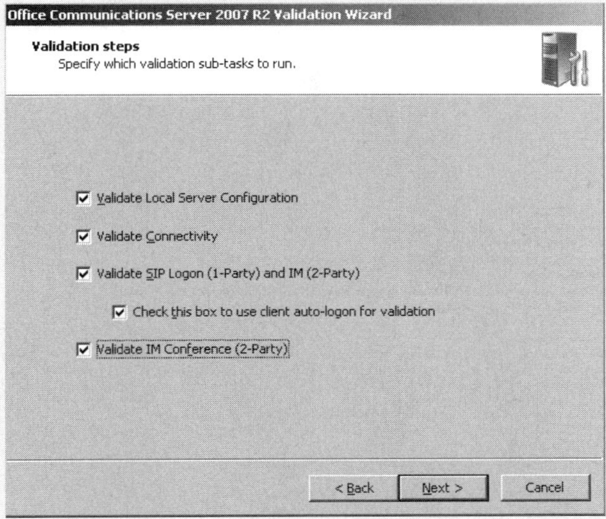

FIGURE 20-7 Selecting Standard Edition Server validation subtasks

I also have another failure to investigate. Now is the time to select Expand All at the top right of the log file page and scroll through the list. Remember that the first red text is not always the error but is typically a rolling up of the error from the steps contained within it. You will almost always scroll all the way to the bottom of the file.

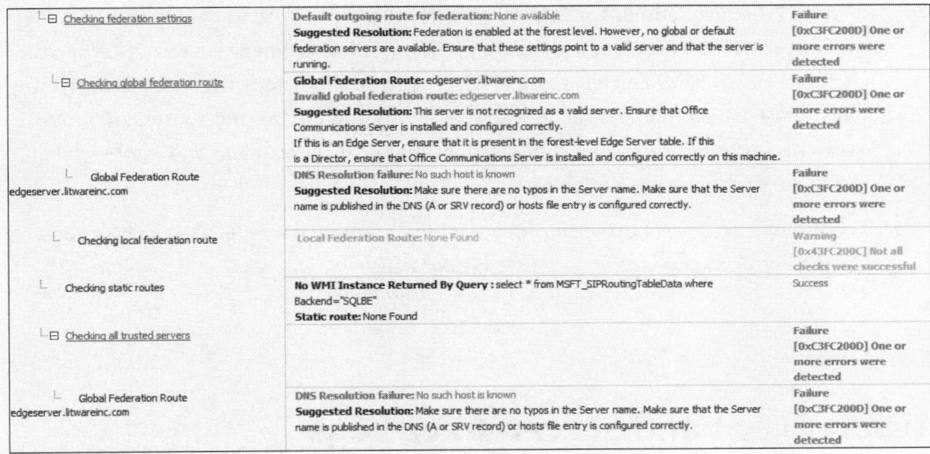

Checking federation settings	**Default outgoing route for federation:** None available **Suggested Resolution:** Federation is enabled at the forest level. However, no global or default federation servers are available. Ensure that these settings point to a valid server and that the server is running.	Failure [0xC3FC200D] One or more errors were detected
Checking global federation route	**Global Federation Route:** edgeserver.litwareinc.com **Invalid global federation route:** edgeserver.litwareinc.com **Suggested Resolution:** This server is not recognized as a valid server. Ensure that Office Communications Server is installed and configured correctly. If this is an Edge Server, ensure that it is present in the forest-level Edge Server table. If this is a Director, ensure that Office Communications Server is installed and configured correctly on this machine.	Failure [0xC3FC200D] One or more errors were detected
Global Federation Route edgeserver.litwareinc.com	**DNS Resolution failure:** No such host is known **Suggested Resolution:** Make sure there are no typos in the Server name. Make sure that the Server name is published in the DNS (A or SRV record) or hosts file entry is configured correctly.	Failure [0xC3FC200D] One or more errors were detected
Checking local federation route	**Local Federation Route:** None Found	Warning [0x43FC200C] Not all checks were successful
Checking static routes	**No WMI Instance Returned By Query :** select * from MSFT_SIPRoutingTableData where Backend="SQLBE" **Static route:** None Found	Success
Checking all trusted servers		Failure [0xC3FC200D] One or more errors were detected
Global Federation Route edgeserver.litwareinc.com	**DNS Resolution failure:** No such host is known **Suggested Resolution:** Make sure there are no typos in the Server name. Make sure that the Server name is published in the DNS (A or SRV record) or hosts file entry is configured correctly.	Failure [0xC3FC200D] One or more errors were detected

FIGURE 20-8 Standard Edition Server Validation Deployment Log page

I have two problems on which to focus, as shown in Figure 20-8: federation settings are failing, which also includes a DNS error for the name I put into the configuration. I can see here that no records exist. I either failed to enter the correct DNS A record, or I do not have the next hop server of edgeserver.litware.com. The second problem is that I was not able to log on one of the two users for whom I provided credentials.

Check user logon		**Failure [0xC3FC200D] One or more errors were detected**
Attempting to login user using Kerberos	**Maximum hops:** 2 **Successfully established security association with the server:** User vadim Domain litwareinc.com Protocol Kerberos Target sip/OCS-FE.litwareinc.com **User registration succeeded:** User sip:vadim@litwareinc.com @ Server pool01.litwareinc.com	Success
Attempting to login user using NTLM	**Maximum hops:** 2 **Successfully established security association with the server:** User vadim Domain litwareinc.com Protocol NTLM Target OCS-FE.litwareinc.com **User registration succeeded:** User sip:vadim@litwareinc.com @ Server pool01.litwareinc.com	Success
Attempting to login user using Kerberos	**Maximum hops:** 2 **Failed to establish security association with the server:** User jeremy Domain litwareinc.com Protocol Kerberos Server sip/OCS-FE.litwareinc.com Target Invalidated **Suggested Resolution:** Check whether the typed password and sign-in name are correct. Check whether the user is present in the AD and enabled for SIP. Check whether the target server is part of the Windows AD domain in which this user account is present. If this is a Kerberos failure check whether the client machine has access to the KDC. In some cases, Kerberos SA negotiation failures may be expected and hence can this error can be ignored. **Failed to register user:** User sip:jeremy@litwareinc.com @ Server pool01.litwareinc.com **Failed to send SIP request:** NegotiateSecurityAssociation failed, error: -2146893044 **Suggested Resolution:** Make sure that the server is listening on the specified IP address/Port/Transport. If you have a firewall make sure that this port is open. Make sure that the server is running. If this is an Edge Server, ensure that remote user access has been enabled. This can be ignored if you have not enabled the transport on the target server.	**Failure [0xC3FC200D] One or more errors were detected**
Attempting to login user using NTLM	**Maximum hops:** 2 **Failed to establish security association with the server:** User jeremy Domain litwareinc.com Protocol NTLM Server OCS-FE.litwareinc.com Target Invalidated **Suggested Resolution:** Check whether the typed password and sign-in name are correct. Check whether the user is present in the AD and enabled for SIP. Check whether the target server is part of the Windows AD domain in which this user account is present. If this is a Kerberos failure check whether the client machine has access to the KDC. In some cases, Kerberos SA negotiation failures may be expected and hence can this error can be ignored.	**Failure [0xC3FC200D] One or more errors were detected**

FIGURE 20-9 Standard Edition Server Validation Deployment Log page

Notice the information contained in the wizard about user logons, as shown in Figure 20-9. Credentials for Jeremy were passed using both Kerberos and NT LAN Manager (NTLM) and failed, whereas credentials for Vadim passed with Kerberos. The failure for both Kerberos and NTLM is a strong indicator that the password was mistyped (which I did on purpose to create this dialog), but the success of Vadim with Kerberos confirms that there is no authentication problem and, more specifically, no problem with Kerberos.

I corrected the next hop server fully qualified domain name (FQDN) to be edgesrv.litwareinc.com and verified my user credentials.

Using Client and Server Trace Logs

Tables 20-2 and 20-3 provide an overview of different components and their respective logging capabilities.

TABLE 20-2 UCCP Logging

COMPONENT	LOCATION OF LOG	HOW TO ENABLE LOGGING
Office Communicator	%USERPROFILE%\tracing	[HKEY_CURRENT_USER\Software\Microsoft\Tracing\uccp\Communicator] "EnableFileTracing"= DWORD:00000001
Microsoft Office Live Meeting Console	%USERPROFILE%\tracing	[HKEY_CURRENT_USER\Software\Microsoft\Tracing\uccp\LiveMeeting] "EnableFileTracing"= DWORD:00000001
Office Communicator Attendant	%USERPROFILE%\tracing	[HKEY_CURRENT_USER\Software\Microsoft\Tracing\uccapi\Attendant] "EnableFileTracing"= DWORD:00000001
Office Communications Server	As configured by Office Communications Server 2007 R2 Logging Tool	Use Office Communications Server 2007 R2 Logging Tool

TABLE 20-3 Media Logging

COMPONENT	LOCATION OF LOG	HOW TO ENABLE LOGGING
Office Communicator	%USERPROFILE%\tracing\WPPMedia	[HKEY_CURRENT_USER\Software\Microsoft\Tracing\WPPMedia\DebugUI] "TraceLevelThreshold" = DWORD:00000101 "WPP_FLAG_S_DEBUGUI_AEC_PCM" = DWORD:00000001
Office Live Meeting Console	%USERPROFILE%\tracing\WPPMedia	[HKEY_CURRENT_USER\Software\Microsoft\Tracing\WPPMedia\DebugUI] "TraceLevelThreshold" = DWORD:00000101 "WPP_FLAG_S_DEBUGUI_AEC_PCM" = DWORD:00000001
Office Communicator Attendant	%USERPROFILE%\tracing\WPPMedia	[HKEY_CURRENT_USER\Software\Microsoft\Tracing\UcClient\Attendant] "EnableTracing" = DWORD:00000001
Office Communications Server	As configured by Office Communications Server 2007 R2 Logging Tool	Use Office Communications Server 2007 R2 Logging Tool

NOTE In Microsoft Windows Vista, the user account that captures media logs must belong to the local Performance Log Users group.

Both Office Communications Server and Office Communicator use the Windows Trace Pre-processor (WPP) utility that is part of the operating system. The client manages this itself and stores logs based on a check box in the user interface (UI). This also drives one of several registry keys. The server stores logs based on the tracing tool provided in the MMC snap-in. Although these logs are extremely useful, they also contain a great deal of detailed information—much of which might not pertain to any problem or issue that is being investigated or analyzed. The following sections introduce tracing and offer some basic insights into looking through logs. Other sections in this chapter about debugging and diagnostics delve into the more technical details that are included in tracing log files.

Understanding Office Communicator Traces

As of the Office Communicator 2007 release, Office Communicator logging can be controlled by using the General menu that is accessed by clicking Tools and then Options. Two check boxes in the General dialog box control logging and event log messages. Refer to Figure 20-1 earlier in this chapter to view this dialog box. All protocol messages that are used in the remainder of this section were captured by enabling logging in Office Communicator and gathering protocol messages from the log.

Configuring Trace Settings

Values under the registry key HKCU\Software\Microsoft\Tracing\Uccp\Communicator are used for Office Communicator log configuration. Table 20-4 provides an overview of important registry keys that enable Office Communicator logging.

TABLE 20-4 Trace Settings

REGISTRY KEY	DESCRIPTION	VALUE
EnableFileTracing	Enables and disables Office Communicator tracing	0 To turn logging off (default) 1 To turn logging on
MaxFiles	Defines the number of log files that Office Communicator will create when tracing is enabled	2 Default
MaxFileSize	Determines how large the log file can get before it is cleared and starts over	0x800000 (~8.3 MB) Default
FileDirectory	Determines the directory where log files will be stored	%USERPROFILE%\Tracing Default

Default settings create the log in %USERPROFILE%\tracing\Communicator-uccapi-0.uccapilog, which is generally located in C:\Documents and Settings\<*username*>\tracing\Communicator-uccapi-0.uccapilog on a computer running the Microsoft Windows XP operating system. As previously mentioned, default settings create two log files with up to approximately 8.3 megabytes (MB) of logs for each. After the first file (mentioned earlier) fills up, the second file, Communicator-uccapi-1.uccapilog, is used. After the second file fills up, its content overwrites the first log file, and the second file will clear itself and add new content until it runs out of space and overwrites the first log file again.

> ***NOTE*** **Be aware of your logging settings. If logging is run for too long, it can be difficult to find the data that you need, and (if there is a lot of network activity) important data might eventually be overwritten. It is important to limit the time when logging is enabled and to avoid logging during actions that create large amounts of traffic (such as an initial logon) unless necessary. For ease of use during an investigative session, increasing the MaxFileSize value (0 x 2000000 allows for ~33.5 MB) and setting MaxFiles to 1 allows larger amounts of data to be analyzed in a single file.**

Looking at Trace Files

Learning to effectively view trace files can be an involved process as you learn what to look for and what can be safely ignored. Trace files contain protocol data as well as internal programmer logs that can make them difficult to decipher at first. Using tools such as findstr.exe, grep.exe, and qgrep.exe makes it easier to scan through trace files if you know what you are looking for. For more information about advanced tools for reviewing log files, see the sections titled "Using ClientLogReader" and "Using Snooper" later in this chapter. In general, few problems require searching the raw logs, and using the Snooper or ClientLogReader tools is a much faster way to gather diagnostic information.

> ***NOTE*** **If you configure logging to allow it, log files can grow to 20 MB or more for an active client. Logs of this size will not load easily in Notepad. Therefore, other editors should be used such as WordPad, Emacs, or Vi. Tools such as ClientLogReader and Snooper are discussed later in this chapter and are specifically built to interpret and quickly display information from these log files.**

The first thing to understand is the structure of the log. The following is an example of one line from the log file.

```
07/13/2007|11:13:51.203 A38:82C TRACE ::
CUccSubscriptionEventInfo::GetOperationInfo - enter [0x04356808]
```

The first 10 characters always contain the date, with a "|" character separating it from the next 12 characters that contain the time. A space separates the time and the next field, which is always seven characters and represents the thread that logged the message (normally a single thread). A space separates the thread ID from the next five characters that identify the type of log (for example, TRACE, INFO, WARN, ERROR). A space, two colons (::), and a space then separate the log type from the content of the log. In the previous example, CUccSubscriptionEventInfo::GetOperationInfo - enter [0x04356808] is the content. Because of this rigid formatting, it is much easier to write scripts and tools to parse the log files.

The TRACE log type is generally only of interest to the product development team and product support. INFO logs are informational and can be of interest, but they can also provide more detail than necessary and create confusion. WARN logs highlight warnings to indicate that a problem might exist or to indicate that an issue might be handled by other components. ERROR logs highlight errors, although some of these errors more closely resemble warnings. Therefore, if the ERROR logs do not make sense, you can probably ignore them. Most problematic errors eventually show up as INFO or ERROR logs that are more meaningful and understandable.

ON THE COMPANION MEDIA **To simplify things, the ClientLogReader script or the Snooper tool (which are included on the companion media in the Office Communicator Server 2007 R2 Resource Kit Tools) can both help with reading Office Communicator 2005 and Office Communicator 2007 R2 trace logs instead of having to manually search the log file. The Snooper tool, which is explained later in this chapter, can be launched from the server MMC and is a viewer for server logs. However, it can also load the client trace file to look at protocol messages in a summary and in full view.**

Using ClientLogReader

When common problems occur, the logs provide useful information. The Practical Extraction and Report Language (PERL) script ClientLogReader from the Office Communications Server 2007 R2 Resource Kit Tools helps diagnose these problems. ClientLogReader has to be run from a computer that has PERL already installed. This tool (also available on the companion media) sifts through the client logs and identifies problem records in a meaningful way. The tool can be used to analyze a log file and point out potential problems as well as to show all protocol messages in full or summary mode. The following examples of using the script (with the resulting data trimmed for brevity) introduce the script's capabilities and the output that can be expected.

```
C:\Documents and Settings\Jeremy\Tracing>perl clientlogreader.pl -help

Version: 1.0, Last Update: 07JUN2006
```

```
USAGE:
perl clientLogReader.pl [-f fileToProcess] [-protocol] [-protocolSummary]
[-tail]

    fileToProcess - if not specified input is taken from standard input
      the file to process - can contain wildcards
    -protocol - SIP protocol messages will all be output along with hints
    -protocolSummary - SIP protocol messages will have start lines displayed
    -tail - log file will be watched if it grows and/or is recreated
EXAMPLE:
  perl clientLogReader.pl -f lcapi*.log -protocolSummary
  perl clientLogReader.pl -f lcapi*.log -protocol
  perl clientLogReader.pl -f lcapi4.log -tail

Look in the README.txt file for this tool for more help and examples

C:\Documents and Settings\Jeremy\Tracing> perl clientlogreader.pl
-f Communicator-uccp-0.uccplog  WARNING: DNS resolution failed for oldserver.
litwareinc.com because the  hostname wasn't found (WSANO_DATA)

C:\Documents and Settings\Jeremy\Tracing> perl clientlogreader.pl
    -f Communicator-uccp-0.uccplog -protocol  INFO: Incoming from 192.168.1.100:443
(via 192.168.1.103:2780)
$$$begin-message$$$
...
$$$end-message$$$
INFO: Outgoing to 192.168.1.100:443 (via 192.168.1.103:2780)
$$$begin-message$$$
...
$$$end-message$$$
...

C:\Documents and Settings\Jeremy\Tracing> perl clientlogreader.pl
    -f Communicator-uccp-0.uccplog -protocolSummary  INFO: Outgoing to
192.168.1.100:443 (via 192.168.1.103:2780)
        SUBSCRIBE sip:sip.litwareinc.com:443;transport=tls;lr;ms-route-sig=hu4T8Jd65_
O8xKIjN1aUGxssauUPBSsbQNNOYHwAAA SIP/2.0
INFO: Incoming from 192.168.1.100:443 (via 192.168.1.103:2780)
        SIP/2.0 200 OK
...
```

The *–tail* option is not shown in the preceding example, but it enables a log file that is being written by Office Communicator to be analyzed and its output data to be shown as Office Communicator runs. This can be especially useful for detecting problems or protocol failures daily in the summary view that might otherwise be hidden or go unnoticed.

Media Logging

Occasionally, you will have to troubleshoot audio or video issues. You will typically do that at the request of Microsoft Product Support. Media components provide logging capabilities in WPP format. The Resulting ETL log file contains all aspects of a component's interaction with the media stack.

Understanding Office Communications Server Traces

Server tracing changed significantly with the release of Office Communications Server 2007, and logging can now be initiated and configured, and files can be viewed directly from the MMC. The logging infrastructure is now using WPP instead of the flat-file logging component used in the past. This update results in all client and server traces being logged with the same mechanism and enables remote and interactive logging of server components across the topology. It is now also possible to filter by server component as well as by user and server when looking for logs to reduce processing time and the volume of logs created when specific debugging is in process.

You can open the Office Communications Server 2007 R2 Logging Tool by right-clicking the node that corresponds to the server's short name, clicking Logging Tool, and then clicking New Debug Session, as shown in Figure 20-10.

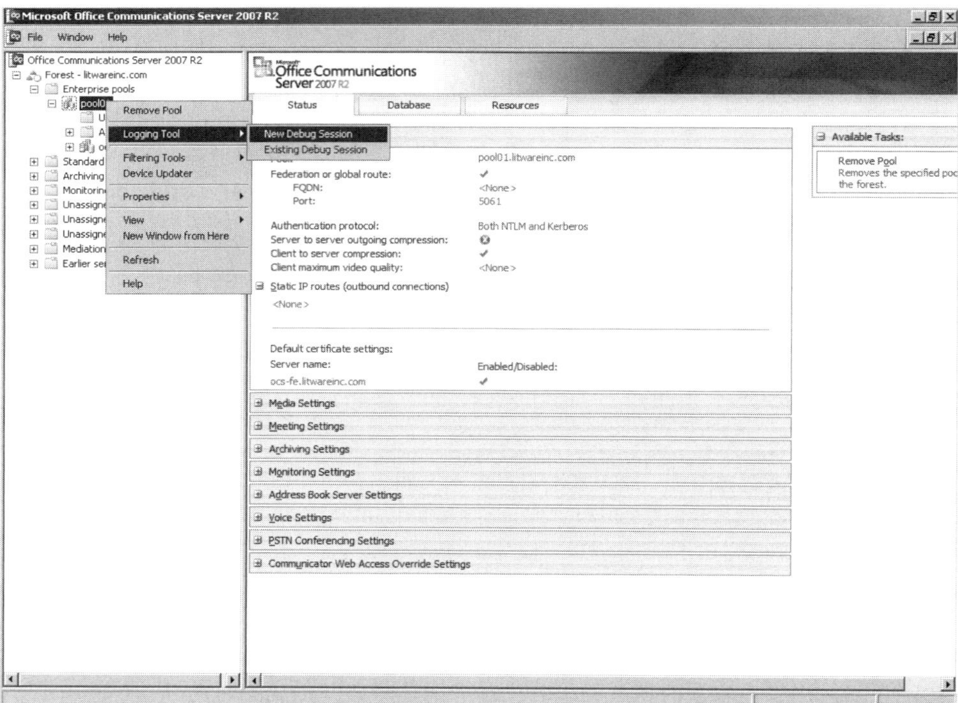

FIGURE 20-10 Opening the Office Communications Server 2007 R2 Logging Tool

The Logging Tool shown in Figure 20-11 contains a large set of features in one tool to make it easy to learn and then apply across topologies and technologies. The features include:

- Starting and stopping logging
- Enabling and disabling logging individually by server component
  - Enabling various logging types (flags) within each server component
  - Enabling various logging levels within each server component
- Controlling logging options
  - Defining specific log file options, such as recycling type and maximum size
  - Formatting information for the log prefix, buffering, and clock resolution
- Enabling real-time monitoring instead of only log-based mechanisms
- Enabling user Uniform Resource Identifier (URI) and server FQDN filtering of protocol logs
- Viewing and analyzing the log directly by using the Snooper tool (if the Office Communications Server 2007 R2 Resource Kit Tools have been installed)

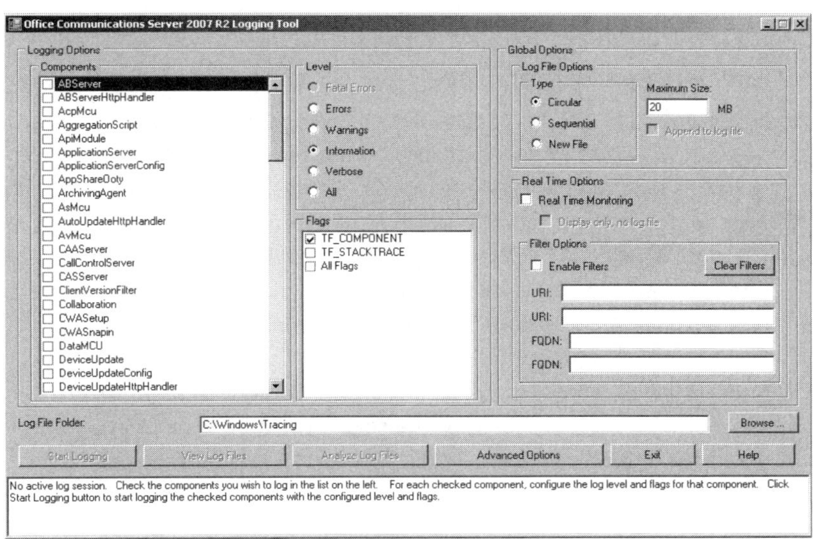

FIGURE 20-11 Office Communications Server 2007 Logging Tool dialog box

Snooper is included in the Office Communications Server 2007 R2 Resource Kit Tools. It can show protocol summaries and enable full-message text to be displayed. It can load all server and client logs and identify errors by looking up user information in the archiving database (if one exists). Snooper can also look up conferencing and presence reports for individual users and conferences and health reports for MCUs, and it can display users who have more than a specified number of contacts or permission settings. An example of Snooper with a client log loaded is shown in Figure 20-12. For more information about the Snooper tool, see the section titled "Using Snooper" later in this chapter.

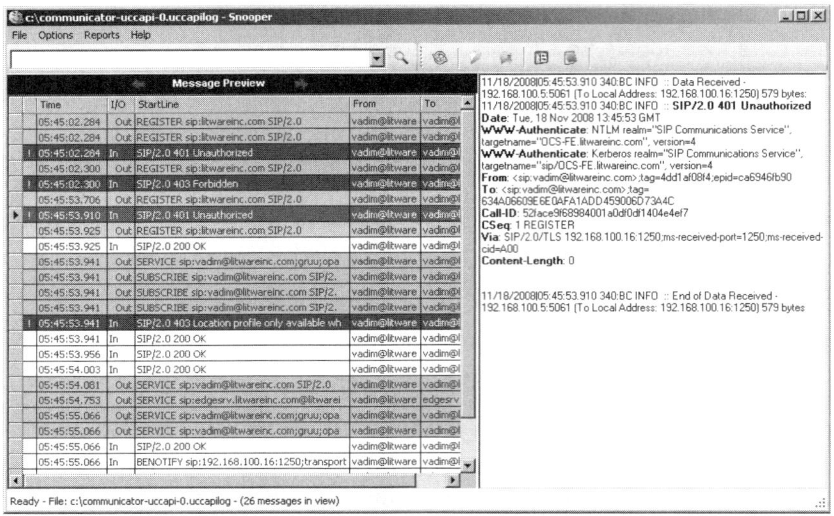

FIGURE 20-12 Snooper log file analysis and diagnostic tool

Example of Gathering a Server Trace

After the Office Communications Server 2007 R2 Logging Tool is launched (refer to Figures 20-10 and 20-11 earlier in this chapter), a few steps must be taken to gather a server trace log. In this example, a SIP stack log is collected into a log file. To do this, only the SIPStack component check box should be selected, all levels and flags should be enabled, logging to C:\Windows\Tracing should be left as the default, and no real-time options should be selected (no active display or filtering of the content). For reference, the Flags section identifies subcomponents that log information if they are enabled, thereby allowing protocol, diagnostic information, connection level, or other details to be logged or ignored (for SIPStack) to prevent the trace logs from being overwhelmed by too much information if a precise area of the server must be investigated. After this configuration is selected, the dialog box should appear, as shown in Figure 20-13.

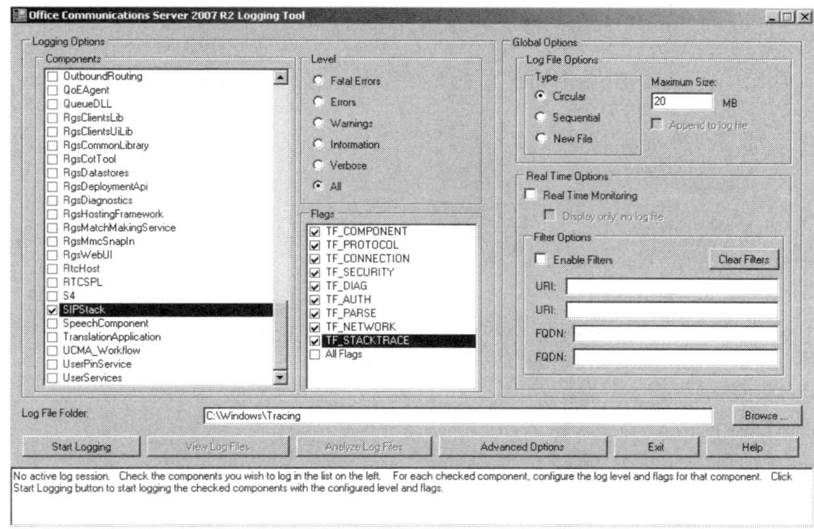

FIGURE 20-13 Gathering a SIPStack trace with the Office Communications Server 2007 R2 Logging Tool

After the tracing configuration is set, select the Start Logging menu item to begin logging for the server. If you want to, you can enable real-time monitoring to show the log output in a console as it occurs or to show the console output and log to the log file as normal. After the network or communication actions of interest are complete, you can select the Stop Logging menu item to finish logging and prepare the text trace log. Finally, you can click the View Log Files menu and view the text files (in Notepad), or you can click Analyze Log Files to see a summary view of the protocol messages in Snooper. This assumes that the Office Communications Server 2007 R2 Resource Kit Tools are already installed. Note that log files can contain errors and other issues that will not show up in protocol logs, so be aware that the way in which you view the log files can make it easy for you to forget that errors might exist.

> ***NOTE*** **Remember that log files larger than 20 MB will not load easily in Notepad and that you will need to use other editors such as WordPad, Emacs, or Vi. Snooper is specifically built to interpret and quickly display information from these log files, but it does not show all of the details that can be seen if the log file is interpreted directly.**

The Real Time Monitoring option can enable a text window that shows the logs as they occur, and filters can be enabled to prevent logs that do not pertain to specific users or servers from showing. This capability is useful when working on a busy server because it can reduce the amount of data that scrolls past on the display.

For more information about the Logging Tool, see the product documentation. Most of the remaining features on the Options menu are of interest only during an engagement with product support.

DIRECT FROM THE SOURCE

Using Trace Filters to Diagnose a Problem on a Busy Server

Conal Walsh
Senior Software Design Engineer

Logs collected by the Office Communications Server 2007 R2 Logging Tool are valuable but can quickly become very large on a busy server. For example, a Standard Edition Server that hosts thousands of users could log 1 MB or more per second of SIP message data. If the problem being investigated requires logging to be enabled for more than a few minutes, the resultant log files might be several gigabytes in size. Such log files are difficult to view and manipulate and might impact server performance because of the disk space that they consume. Fortunately, most problems can be isolated to one or two users or, in the case of an Edge proxy server, one or two peer servers. The filter options that the Office Communications Server 2007 R2 Logging Tool supports can thus be used to greatly reduce the size of log files on a busy server. The following sections discuss problems that have been seen in customers' live deployments of Office Communications Server 2007 and its predecessor, Office Live Communications Server 2005 with Service Pack 1 (SP1).

Scenario: Incorrectly Configured Firewall Causes Intermittent Failure of IMs to Users in a Federated Partner

In this scenario, one or more users in a large company have called the help desk and reported intermittent failures when sending and receiving instant messages from users in another company. Routing between the two companies is achieved by federation between their respective Edge proxy servers. The local Edge proxy routes traffic to many federated partners and public IM connectivity (PIC) providers, so hundreds or thousands of SIP messages per second might pass through the Edge proxy.

Simply running the Office Communications Server 2007 R2 Logging Tool on the local Edge proxy will quickly result in very large log files. Instead, enter the FQDN of the Edge proxy server for the federated partner in the first *FQDN* field under Filter Options and then select the Enable Filters check box, as shown in Figure 20-14.

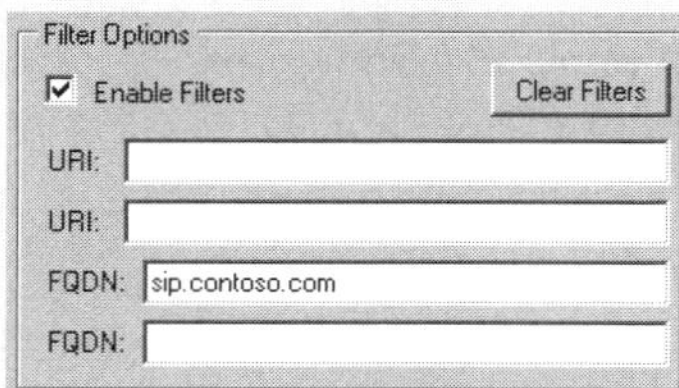

FIGURE 20-14 Enabling a peer server FQDN filter

When logging is started, only SIP messages and related events that originate from, or are destined to, the FQDN of interest appear in the trace log. All other data is ignored, resulting in a small and focused log file. In this particular scenario, the remote Edge proxy server appears to be dropping the Mutual Transport Layer Security (MTLS) connection. This manifests itself as TF_CONNECTION and TF_DIAGNOSTIC messages at the TL_ERROR level in the trace log, as shown in the following example.

```
TL_ERROR(TF_CONNECTION) [0]0B90.07F8::09/05/2007-07:06:29.805.00000088
$$begin_record
LogType: connection
Severity: error
Text: Receive operation on the connection failed
Local-IP: 10.0.0.13:1142
Peer-IP: 10.0.0.10:5061
Peer-FQDN: sip.contoso.com
Peer-Name: sip.contoso.com
Connection-ID: 0x502
Transport: M-TLS
Result-Code: 0x80072746 WSAECONNRESET
$$end_record
TL_ERROR(TF_DIAG) [0]0B90.07F8::09/05/2007-07:06:31.991.0000008d
$$begin_record
LogType: diagnostic
Severity: error
Text: Message was not sent because the connection was closed
SIP-Start-Line: MESSAGE sip:fred@contoso.com;opaque=user:epid:
G-AWNAmf8Vqf8tSG2CexVwAA;gruu SIP/2.0
SIP-Call-ID: a524eda4c75e49e58a3777d0478d49a8
SIP-CSeq: 7 MESSAGE
Peer: sip.contoso.com:5061
$$end_record
```

Furthermore, the MTLS connection is being dropped at a regular interval of every 30 seconds or so.

```
TL_ERROR(TF_DIAG) [0]0B90.07F8::09/05/2007-07:07:01.871.00000094
$$begin_record
LogType: diagnostic
Severity: error
Text: Message was not sent because the connection was closed
SIP-Start-Line: MESSAGE sip:fred@contoso.com;opaque=user:epid:
G-AWNAmf8Vqf8tSG2CexVwAA;gruu SIP/2.0
SIP-Call-ID: 75e49e58a3777d0478d49aa524eda4c8
SIP-CSeq: 9 MESSAGE
Peer: sip.contoso.com:5061
$$end_record
```

The most likely cause of this problem is a firewall that is not correctly configured for SIP traffic, thereby causing it to drop connections when they are idle for 30 seconds. This process is typical of many firewalls and load balancers in which the default configuration assumes a protocol such as HTTP rather than SIP.

Understanding Office Communicator Mobile Traces

Microsoft Office Communicator Mobile devices are based on the Microsoft Windows CE operating system. To collect traces, device logging must first be enabled.

To enable logging on Office Communicator Mobile, click Menu, select Options, and then click General. Select Turn On Logging. You can find the log files in the My Device\Tracing folder.

Understanding Office Communicator Phone Edition Traces

Microsoft Office Communicator Phone Edition devices are based on the Windows CE operating system. To collect traces, device logging must first be enabled and only then can log files be submitted to Office Communications Server 2007 R2 Update Server. Log files cannot be viewed from the device itself, and Office Communications Server 2007 R2 Update Server provides infrastructure for files to be uploaded and then later retrieved for viewing as necessary.

To enable logging on Office Communicator Phone Edition, click the Settings tab and then select the Set Logging option. After logging has been enabled, send log files by selecting Send Logs.

To read the uploaded log files, you must use Readlog.exe, which comes with Windows CE Platform Builder. Log files have a .clg extension, and you can find them in the Office Communications Server 2007 R2 Update Server Logs folder. For more information about Readlog.exe, see *http://go.microsoft.com/fwlink/?LinkID=133753*.

To extract the contents of the .clg file to a text file, use the *-v* (verbose) print option when you run Readlog.exe, as shown in the following example:

```
readlog.exe -v CE_log_file.clg output_file.txt
```

Office Communicator Phone Edition logs contain the results of the hardware functional tests as well as critical system errors.

Understanding Microsoft RoundTable Traces

Microsoft RoundTable devices are based on the Windows CE operating system. To collect traces, device logging must first be enabled and only then can log files be submitted to Office Communications Server 2007 R2 Update Server.

To enable logging on RoundTable, install the RoundTable Device Management Tool on a local computer and then configure logging by using the provided Microsoft Office InfoPath template (Office InfoPath must be installed before you try to perform this operation). Use Rtmanage.exe to upload this InfoPath configuration template to RoundTable. To send log files from RoundTable to Office Communications Server 2007 R2 Update Server, run the following command line:

```
rtmanage.exe -m:diag -l:flush
```

To read uploaded log files, you must use Readlog.exe, which ships with the Windows CE Platform Builder. Log files have a .clg extension, and you can find them on Office Communications Server 2007 R2 Update Server logs share. For more information about Readlog.exe, see *http://msdn2.microsoft.com/en-us/library/ms905162.aspx*.

To extract the contents of the CLG file to a text file, use the *-v* (verbose) print option when you run Readlog.exe, as shown in the following example:

```
readlog.exe -v CE_log_file.clg output_file.txt
```

RoundTable log files contain the results of the hardware functional tests as well as critical system errors.

Using Snooper

The Snooper utility is a tremendous advance for diagnostics when working with the Office Communications Server 2007 R2 product suite and is available as part of Office Communications Server 2007 R2 Resource Kit Tools. Unlike many tools, it has a complete reference manual that is available directly within the tool by clicking Help and then clicking Using Snooper. Snooper is capable of viewing logs from the current client and server components as well as Live Communications Server 2005 flat-file server logs. Snooper summarizes protocol messages, identifies diagnostic and connection-level events, and offers full content for any message that is selected. Snooper is also capable of querying the archiving server and other Structured Query Language (SQL) repositories to gather reports that contain useful overview and detailed information. Snooper can be run remotely for pools, but Standard Edition Servers might have connection errors when logging remotely. If this is the case, Snooper.exe should be run locally on the Standard Edition Server.

Snooper enables searches and complex queries related to specific fields in the message. For example, if the user jeremy@litwareinc.com is of interest but only for messages that were sent to vadim@litwareinc.com, a search such as from:jeremy@litwareinc.com to:vadim@litwareinc.com would get the protocol messages of interest. When each message is viewed in detail, the matching text in the protocol message is highlighted. A useful search method for Director and Access Edge Server logs is to specify a direction—whether the message is incoming (in) or outgoing (out)—to avoid seeing messages twice. Such a specification might be direction:in. Likewise, to see nonprotocol messages, specifying direction:none allows a view of just these messages (connection events, diagnostic notes, and other messages).

DIRECT FROM THE SOURCE

Using Snooper to Jump Into Larger Log Files

CJ Vermette

Software Design Engineer on the Office Communications Server Team

Snooper can be used to quickly find the protocol message that you're interested in. Click Open In Notepad on the Snooper toolbar to open the file in Notepad and quickly go to that part of the file. You can then look at the lower-level trace statements for more details.

Snooper is also capable of building useful reports based on queries against the SQL repositories maintained by Office Communications Server 2007 R2. The Reports menu offers this functionality, and the Error Analysis option enables an Archiving Server to be queried to gather error reports that have been logged. These records can be filtered by user or by attributes of the error messages and provide an insightful way for IT support to identify problems that a user is experiencing without more information or logs from the users themselves. Gathering overview information for all errors or specific types of errors allows administrators to proactively look at the errors that have been occurring to predict and resolve problems before many users encounter them. The Analyze Error Reports dialog box is shown in Figure 20-15.

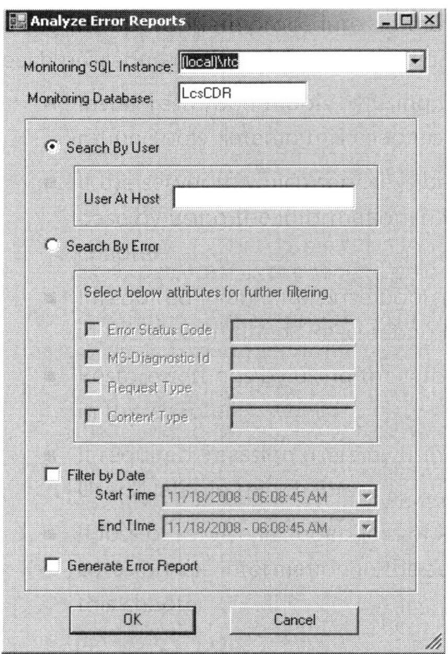

FIGURE 20-15 Snooper Analyze Error Reports dialog box

The Conferencing and Presence Reports option provides a variety of useful reports that were not so easily available in the past. Information can be retrieved about users, conferences, MCUs, and diagnostic overview information for the repository. An example of a user query is shown in Figure 20-16. This report contains detailed information about the user, their rights, their contacts and groups, the rich presence information they are publishing, conferences they organized, and conferences to which they are invited.

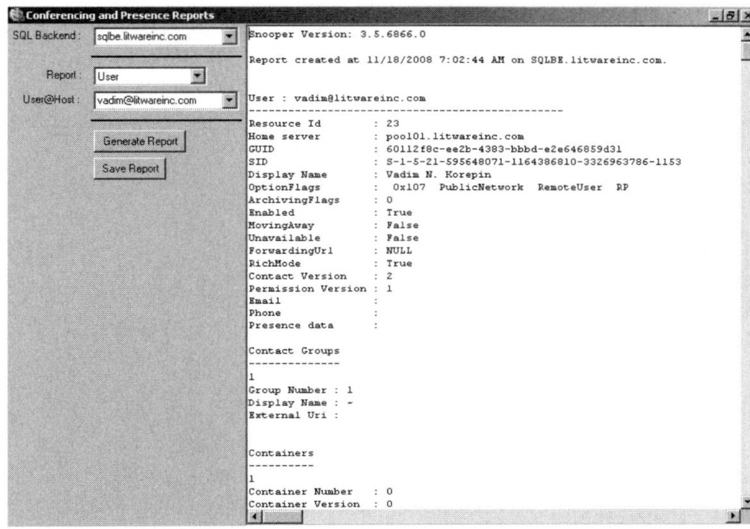

FIGURE 20-16 Snooper Conferencing and Presence Report for a User

The conference report shows the current settings as well as the current state of the conference that was queried. The schedule for the conference, the invitee list, the media types allowed in the conference, the active MCUs, the active participant list, and the state of each participant are all shown. This information can be helpful when monitoring a running conference or when diagnosing problems for users when they are connecting to or interacting in a conference.

The MCU Health report identifies all MCUs that are present on the server and provides detailed information about them. Their ID, media type, URL, heartbeat status, number of assigned conferences, and number of connected participants are all displayed. An example of this report is shown in Figure 20-17. Heartbeats to the MCU Factory should generally occur within 15 seconds, but the heartbeat to the Focus depends on the activity level of the MCU.

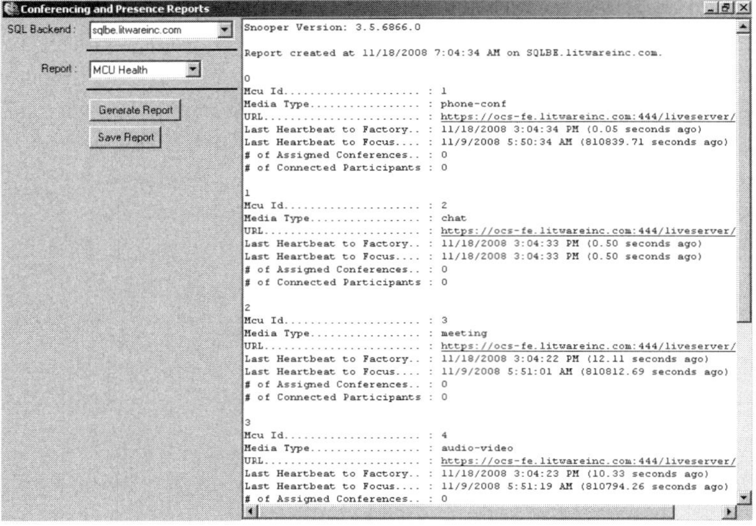

FIGURE 20-17 Snooper Conferencing and Presence Report for MCU Health

The diagnostic report identifies overview information about many aspects of the repository in question, but focuses on statistics for record counts as well as the size of the database on the disk and how this space is allocated across internal records. An example of the report in Snooper is shown in Figure 20-18. The following data is presented in the log, with notes in parentheses to explain the usefulness of the information:

- Database version (can highlight errors during the update process if the database was not updated)
- Database internal statistics along with storage space utilized (helps during maintenance and in understanding what is taking up space if the database grows too large)
  - List of tables in the database along with record count and data, index, and total size counts
  - Database size and dynamic database size
  - Files that make up the database (MDF and LDF files) plus their sizes and growth
- Server statistics (helps determine server load in terms of storage space and network activity)
  - Distribution of contacts across enterprise servers as well as the percentage of contacts that are outside of the enterprise
  - Number of active endpoints (Office Communicator clients or otherwise)
- Maintenance, replication, and expiration tasks and the server on which they are scheduled to run

- Number of users with no contacts or permissions (likely idle or have never logged in)
- Presence statistics, all with min, max, average, and standard deviation (helps to get a feel for usage and how users compare with each other in terms of usage)
  - Contacts per user
  - Container member users per user
  - Container member domains per user
  - Cached container members per user
  - Permissions per user
  - Prompted subscribers per user
  - Static publications per user
  - User-bound publications per user
  - Time-bound publications per user
  - Endpoint-bound publications per user
  - Publication data size per user
  - Subscribers per user
  - Category subscriptions per user
  - Endpoints per user
  - Conferences per user
- Overview of activity (quick view of current usage)
  - Number of unique users with endpoints
  - Number of conferences (total and currently active)

> ***NOTE*** **Generating the Diagnostic Conferencing and Presence Report can create a large amount of load on database servers. Therefore, during high-activity intervals, it should be done infrequently to prevent creating delays for users. This report effectively locks the database to get a snapshot report, which holds up all traffic on the servers that require a database query from this repository.**

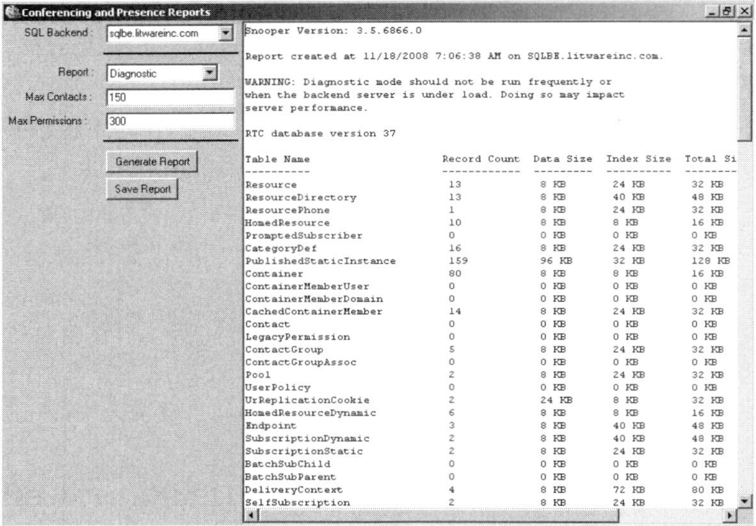

FIGURE 20-18 Snooper Conferencing and Presence Report for Diagnostics

Overall, Snooper is a helpful resource for gathering information about the configuration and state of servers and users and is a useful tool for scanning logs that have been collected to analyze them. However, it is always good to start by reviewing the event logs and looking at the MMC overviews for each server because many times the problems have already been identified or will be mentioned. Forgetting to look for event log messages before starting an investigation can waste a great deal of time when the error has already been identified and highlighted to make things easier.

Using Best Practices Analyzer

The Office Communications Server 2007 Best Practices Analyzer is a diagnostic tool that gathers information from an Office Communications Server environment and determines whether the configuration is set according to Microsoft best practices. Office Communications Server 2007 Best Practices Analyzer was released in September 2007 and is similar in usage to the Best Practices Analyzer for other Microsoft products, such as Exchange Server and SQL Server. A new analyzer will not be released for Office Communications Server 2007 R2. However, a new set of XML files will be released that will update the tool when run against an Office Communications Server 2007 R2 infrastructure.

DIRECT FROM THE SOURCE

Inside Best Practices Analyzer

Sasa Juratovic

Senior Program Manager, Office Communications Server Customer Experience

If you are familiar with Exchange Server, Internet Security and Acceleration (ISA) Server, or SQL Server Best Practices Analyzer, you will quickly become familiar with Office Communications Server 2007 Best Practices Analyzer. All of these tools are based on the same Best Practices Analyzer framework, which offers a similar interface.

Office Communications Server 2007 Best Practices Analyzer checks for the following:

- Readiness of your environment before you begin to deploy Office Communications Server
- Compliance with Microsoft's best practices as you install the different Office Communications Server components
- Ongoing operational compliance with Microsoft's best practices, for example, by highlighting missing updates as well as providing information about how to rectify the problem

After you install the tool, you will find the following files in the installation directory:

- **rtcbpa.exe and accompanying dynamic link libraries (DLLs)** Managed code binaries that implement GUI and core engine
- **XML configuration files** Set of files that implement and drive data collection and rules logic
- **Help file** Provides background information about the tool and articles that go with the rules

> ***NOTE*** Although the Best Practices Analyzer targets Office Communications Server, it can also discover Live Communications Server servers. However, the rules are primarily focused on the latest version.

The first time you run Best Practices Analyzer, the tool will ask you if you want to automatically check for updates every time it starts. Even if you do not select this option, you can always select Updates (located on the left-hand side in Graphical User Interface) and manually check for updates. When Best Practices Analyzer checks for updates, it will do so over Hypertext Transfer Protocol Secure (HTTPS). Downloaded updates can be found in the tools installation directory.

By selecting Select A Best Practices Scan to View (located on the left-hand side in Graphical User Interface), you can view any previously generated or imported report. Reports contain information that is categorized in three main buckets:

Informational For example, the version of the product that the server is running

Warnings For example, data and log files for the Real-Time Communications (RTC) database are located on the same physical hard disk

Errors For example, the server is missing a critical update

One of the tool's best features is its ability to report error or warning information, depending on the severity of the identified issue. Warning and error information can be easily addressed by following guidance on the screen and reading the accompanying Help file. This specific aspect of the tool is implemented through the rules engine. The key value of the Best Practices Analyzer is the rules engine that automates the condensed knowledge from Microsoft engineers and consultants' expertise learned through years of experience. This tool also generates log files that contain runtime information to troubleshoot issues.

There are number of scenarios that Best Practices Analyzer is particularly well suited for, such as:

Auditing Best Practices Analyzer can generate a report that provides extensive information about the Office Communications Servers it was able to detect.

Troubleshooting The Best Practices Analyzer can be used to troubleshoot problems, either internally or with the help of Microsoft Support. The report generated will highlight errors and warnings when the configuration does not follow Microsoft's best practices, and it provides help topics as additional information.

Patch Management As your Office Communications Server environment changes, either through reconfiguration, addition of new server roles, or removal of others, Best Practices Analyzer will identify and highlight updates that are missing.

The following Real World sidebar describes a usage example for using the Best Practices Analyzer.

REAL WORLD

Using the Best Practices Analyzer

Mike Warren
Senior Consultant, Modality Systems Ltd.

As a consultant, I occasionally find myself troubleshooting Office Communications Server 2007 issues while out in the field on customer sites. Prior to the availability of the Best Practices Analyzer tool, it was difficult to track down the root cause of customer issues and very time consuming to generate a report detailing the Office Communications Server infrastructure.

We had a customer that installed Office Communications Server 2007 Standard Edition. The person who did the installation had left the company and the IT staff was not happy about the lack of knowledge transfer and documentation, so I was commissioned to perform a detailed report of the installation.

One of the results of a full Best Practices Analyzer environment scan indicated that an important update, KB945055, was missing from the Office Communications Server 2007 Standard Edition Server in this installation (shown as an error rule in Figure 20-19). Double-clicking the item and selecting Tell Me More About This Issue And How To Resolve It opened a Help file that provided most of the important information about the issue, as well as how to resolve it.

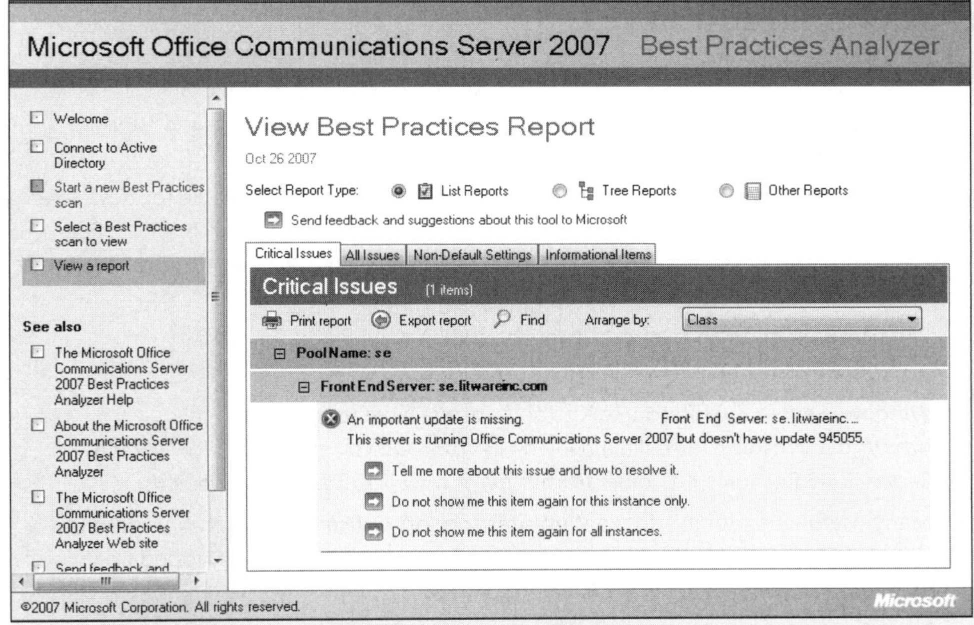

FIGURE 20-19 Best Practices Analyzer report

I consistently tell customers that it is imperative to have a good Patch Management Process in place to ensure all servers are kept up to date with the latest hotfixes and service packs from Microsoft. I resolved this issue by downloading and installing the Office Communications Server 2007 update package and applying it on all Office Communications Server 2007 Severs within the pool.

Summary

A variety of tools and resources are available for diagnosing problems, and the event log, server and client logs, and MMC diagnostic tools, such as the Office Communications Server Logging Tool and Snooper, all make diagnosing problems easier than it was in the past. Note that it is highly recommended that you check the event log before starting a diagnostic session. The problems that the event log identifies often point out exactly what needs to be done without any additional work. For more information about how to put these tools and resources to work, see Chapter 21, "Troubleshooting Problems," which describes generic and specific troubleshooting steps for various scenarios.

Additional Resources

- Official Microsoft Office Communications Server Web site, found at *http://go.microsoft.com/fwlink/?LinkID=133631*. Documents, tools, and support information are always available at this location.
- Office Communications Server 2007 R2 Resource Kit Tools are available for download at *http://go.microsoft.com/fwlink/?LinkID=133686*. Or, you can search for "Office Communications Server 2007 R2 Resource Kit Tools" from *http://www.microsoft.com/downloads*.
- Practical Extraction and Report Language (PERL) downloads, found at http://go.microsoft.com/fwlink/?LinkID=133754.
- Windows Server 2003 Resource Kit Tools are available for download at http://go.microsoft.com/fwlink/?LinkId=134705 . Or, you can search for "Windows Server 2003 Resource Kit Tools" from *http://www.microsoft.com/downloads*.
- Many useful community-driven Web sites support Office Communications Server. One that stands out is the Live Communications Server Guides site, found at *http://go.microsoft.com/fwlink/?LinkID=133680*.
- The companion media contains Office Communications Server 2007 R2 Resource Kit Tools.

CHAPTER 21

Troubleshooting Problems

The Microsoft Office Communications Server 2007 R2 product suite builds on the functionality and features of Microsoft Office Communications Server 2007. However, to enable these new functions and feature sets, the product requires many complex and sophisticated technologies distributed across several machines on a variety of networks with different software components installed on each. Inconsistent local and global settings, network connectivity, and external dependency failures can cause problems that can be difficult to troubleshoot. The goal of this chapter is to provide a systematic troubleshooting process to guide architects and administrators through hurdles that may be encountered during the initial deployment. It is also intended to provide a framework that experts can use to explore more complex issues.

ON THE COMPANION MEDIA **You can find links to additional resources on the topics addressed in this chapter and book on this book's companion CD.**

Troubleshooting Process

This chapter identifies common problems and illustrates effective ways to diagnose a problem's source. This troubleshooting framework is engineered to isolate the component(s) responsible for the problem so that the steps needed to find a resolution may be properly researched. Guidelines for the safe implementation of the changes required for resolution are also included.

The remainder of the chapter focuses on problem scenarios and includes specific ways to gather information to resolve the most common issues. For reference, most of the tools and resources that are used to work through these problems have been described in Chapter 20, "Diagnostic Tools and Resources," which also includes information on where to locate them.

Determining the Root Cause

The purpose of troubleshooting an issue is to determine the root cause, which starts by understanding the issue's symptoms. Often the symptoms reported can mask a deeper issue; an analysis of the symptoms will help isolate the components causing the problem. Once the faulty component is isolated, collect the relevant logs and use them to research the root cause. It is important to isolate the troubled component prior to starting the data collection process—this prevents information overload. If the problem appears complex or involves multiple components, the collection of preliminary data may be necessary to assist with root cause determination.

The next few sections outline the various steps of root cause determination.

Understanding the Symptoms

The first step in the troubleshooting process is to document and understand the symptoms. Common examples of symptoms are not being able to connect to a Web conference, a desktop sharing attempt fails, or less noticeable issues arise such as incorrect presence. This step can lead an architect or administrator to the wrong conclusion if the symptoms first reported were incorrect or inconsistent. In resolving problems in a complex, distributed environment, understanding the full nature of the symptoms is key to reducing the time and effort spent determining the next steps in resolving the problems.

During symptom review, start to look for underlying relationships. Common correlations to look for:

- Determine which users are impacted. Are they in the same Active Directory organizational unit (OU)? Do they belong to the same security group? Are they not enabled for a particular functionality? Are they in the same physical location?
- Determine when the issue occurs. Does it occur the same time every day? Does the issue happen immediately after another process, such as a backup, completes? Does the issue occur during peak hours?
- Determine whether the issue is related to a specific server. Are users experiencing the same problem homed on the same pool? Are call failures routed to the same Mediation Server?

Finding these correlations is often key to determining the problem component(s). Remember to keep track of your findings via documentation to prevent duplication of work and to facilitate the sharing of information with team members.

Collecting Information

Once the symptoms are fully understood, begin collecting relevant data to further isolate the components by using tools such as installation logs, event logs, validation wizards, the Best Practices Analyzer (BPA), Client Logging (UCCAPI logs), and Server Logging (Office Communications Server logger). Detailed information regarding these tools, including their location and how to use them, can be found in Chapter 20.

INSTALLATION LOGS

During installation, the Office Communications Server 2007 R2 setup process generates two sets of logs that can be used to resolve various problems related to setup and installation. These setup logs are located under the %temp% directory and have the .log or .html extension.

EVENT LOGS

Office Communications Server reports a lot of information in the event logs that is extremely helpful when locating and resolving problems. With the addition of the MS-Diagnostic headers introduced in Office Communications Server 2007, the event logs can help pinpoint which component has failed and on which server. If the event logs cannot isolate the exact component that is experiencing the issues, they should at least isolate the server on which the error was generated, reducing the amount of information that needs to be collected.

Following is a list of common event logs used to troubleshoot Office Communications Server 2007 R2 issues and the types of problems they help resolve.

- System logs:
  - Certificate failures
  - Logon failures
  - Distributed Component Object Model (DCOM) (Microsoft Management Console [MMC] administration errors)
- Application logs:
  - Back-end database issues
- Office Communications Server logs:
  - Service failing to start
  - Certificate problems
  - Domain Name System (DNS) issues
  - Server Trust failures

DIRECT FROM THE SOURCE

Event Log Tips

Nirav Kamdar
Senior Development Lead, Office Communications Server

Office Communications Server services usually generate more than one event log. Generally speaking, the first event log contains the most information, but it is beneficial to go through all of the error event logs. I often see people look at the top-most event log and give up because it is a general event log that might not point out enough details on its own to completely identify the problem.

VALIDATION WIZARDS

The validation wizards are built directly into the setup process as well as the Office Communications Server 2007 R2 Management Console (Admin Tools). They are best used for resolving issues with initial installation as well as validating that the current environment is operating correctly.

BEST PRACTICES ANALYZER

The Office Communications Server 2007 BPA is a diagnostic tool that gathers configuration information from an Office Communications Server 2007 and R2 environment and determines whether the configuration abides by Microsoft best practices. Rule updates for this tool are being released with Office Communications Server 2007 R2 to accommodate the new server roles and functionality found in this release. This tool is often one of the default tools used to collect information needed to resolve issues in an established Office Communications Server 2007 R2 environment. Here are some troubleshooting areas in which the BPA can assist:

- Perform health checks proactively, verifying that the configuration is set according to recommended best practices
- Generate a list of issues, such as suboptimal, unsupported, or ill-advised configuration settings
- Judge the general health of a system
- Help troubleshoot specific problems
- Prompt you to download updates if they are available
- Provide online and local documentation about reported issues, including troubleshooting tips
- Generate configuration information that can be captured for later review

DIRECT FROM THE SOURCE

Diagnosing Active Directory Errors

Yong Zhao
Software Developer on the Office Communications Server Team

When collecting data, if you receive an Active Directory error (that has a symbolic name starting with ERROR_DS_*, for example, ERROR_DS_NO_SUCH_OBJECT) during deployment, the first thing to check is which account credentials are being used. You can accomplish this by using the following Windows command-line tool (Whoami.exe is included in Microsoft Windows 2008 and can be found in the Support Tools of earlier versions of Windows):

```
whoami /groups
```

Using the output of the tool, verify that the RTCUniversalServerAdmins group shows up in the list. If it does, use the tools Nltest.exe and NetDiag.exe to rule out problems with domain controllers (DCs) and the local machine network. (These tools are included in Microsoft Windows Vista and Windows Server 2008 and can be found in the Resource Kit of earlier versions.)

Nltest.exe and NetDiag.exe are Windows server tools that allow for testing of basic functionality of the operating system. Nltest provides a large number of command-line functions, such as retrieving the names of servers that provide a given role (global catalog, PDC emulator). NetDiag can test and diagnose network connectivity issues, narrowing down where the problem might be in a given failure state.

Their usage is shown in the following examples:

```
Nltest.exe /DsGetDC:[Root Domain FQDN] /GC - Outputs the GC of the root domain
Nltest.exe /DsGetDC:[Root Domain FQDN] /PDC - Outputs the PDC of the root domain
Nltest.exe /DsGetDC:[Local Domain FQDN] /PDC  - Outputs the PDC of the local domain
NetDiag.exe - runs through all tests that NetDiag can perform on the local system
```

The root and local domain fully qualified domain names (FQDNs; shown in the following example as [Root Domain FQDN] and [Local Domain FQDN]) must be replaced with the root DC FQDN for the top-level domain and DC FQDN for the domain from which you are running the commands. Examples of domain names are litwareinc.com for the root domain and eng.litwareinc.com for the local domain, with the command sequence being:

```
Nltest.exe /DsGetDC:litwareinc.com /GC
Nltest.exe /DsGetDC:litwareinc.com /PDC
Nltest.exe /DsGetDC:eng.litwareinc.com /PDC
NetDiag.exe
```

CLIENT LOGGING (UCCAPI LOGS)

When a server is experiencing a high volume of traffic, it is difficult to collect and analyze server logs pertaining to the failure of a small number of clients. When the issue involves a modest client population, client-side logs available in Microsoft Office Communicator, Office Communicator 2007 R2 Attendant, Group Chat Console, and the Microsoft Office Live Meeting client are a great place to start. For details on how to configure logging, see Chapter 20.

DIRECT FROM THE SOURCE

Enabling Client Logging

Jeff Reed
Software Design Engineer in Test on the Office Communications Server Team

In case of a Session Initiation Protocol (SIP) failure, try searching for the ms-diagnostics header in the log file. If the user is successfully authenticated and is not coming across a federated link, the faulting server often adds information about where the response was generated as well as a reason for the failure. This should aid in the debugging process.

DIRECT FROM THE SOURCE

Extracting Errors from Communicator Logs

Joel Schaeffer
Escalation Engineer, Product Support Services

If you are using Office Communicator logging to troubleshoot issues, you can extract "error" entries quickly by using FINDSTR. The syntax is as follows:

```
findstr /I error %userprofile%\tracing\<log file> <output file>
```

For example, you might use the following command:

```
findstr /I error %userprofile%\tracing\Communicator-uccp-0.uccplog
errors.txt
```

The errors.txt file will contain all log entries tagged as ERROR. You can then find the entry in the source log file and place the error in its proper context. You should then be able to discern what happened before and after the error was thrown.

Server Logging (Office Communications Server Logger) Server Logging is valuable when troubleshooting problems because it provides the most detailed information in a single place. However, due to the fact that servers often process requests for thousands of users at a time, the logs expand quickly and it can be difficult to find the specific information that you are looking for. Depending on the problem and the volume of the server, going straight to Server Logging can be as effective as looking for a needle in a haystack. Some data can be collected only at the server, so if the appropriate information cannot be collected from other easier-to-review sources, you can use Office Communications Server Logger and Snooper.

When reviewing a large server log, remember to also collect the logs from affected client(s) at the same time. Use the smaller client log to find the information specific to the issue, then filter the server log accordingly to obtain the detailed information you need.

For more information on how to install and use the Office Communications Server Logger and Snooper tools, refer to Chapter 20.

DIRECT FROM THE SOURCE

Resolving Mysterious Error Codes

Jason Epperly
Escalation Engineer, Product Support Services

As you are troubleshooting any product, you are inevitably confronted by a mysterious error code. What do you do with this mysterious error code? Microsoft has published a tool named Microsoft Exchange Server Error Code Look-up (err.exe) that is available for download at *http://go.microsoft.com/fwlink/?LinkID=133755.*

First, disregard the fact that the tool states that it is for use with Microsoft Exchange. This message is included only because the Exchange team published the tool. The tool is *not* Exchange-specific. At its most basic level, Err.EXE maps return codes (for example, 0x54F) to symbolic names (such as ERROR_INTERNAL_ERROR).

ERR takes into account that you don't always know whether your input value is hexadecimal or decimal. If there's any ambiguity in how the error code is specified, ERR returns multiple results to show the hexadecimal (base 16) and decimal (base 10) error code symbolic names. For example, if the command err.exe 10 was run, the parameter '10' could represent a decimal value of 10 (ERROR_BAD_ENVIRONMENT) or a hexadecimal value of 0x10 (ERROR_CURRENT_DIRECTORY), so running ERR 10 produces both errors.

Mapping between symbolic names and error codes goes both ways—you can search for an error code by name as well as by ID, which can be useful when you need an error code for a script or cannot remember the exact name of a symbolic constant. To find an error code by its exact name, preface that name with an equal sign on the command line (err =ERROR_BAD_ENVIRONMENT). The search is case insensitive. ERR doesn't call the operating system (such as via FormatMessage) to look up errors in any way because all of its error codes are kept in internal tables within the binary. This keeps ERR from depending on one operating system or another to produce the right results. In most cases, the symbolic name that is relative to Windows error codes represents the errors associated with the winerror.h table.

Reducing Complexity

Often while working through issues in complex deployments of Office Communications Server 2007 R2, it becomes difficult to find the relevant data to be able to troubleshoot the problem due to the number of servers and components involved. In these situations, it is necessary to reduce the complexity of the environment by removing redundant or unnecessary server roles. Examples of reducing complexity are:

- When working on resolving intermittent nondelivery reports for sent instant messages against a pool with two servers behind a load balancer, reducing complexity could mean turning one of the servers off or changing the client to manual configuration and connecting directly to one of the servers.
- For failed external communication or remote access in an environment containing a Director, reducing complexity could be configuring the Edge Server to route directly to the pool, thus reducing the number of servers in the communication path.

The objective of reducing complexity is not to put the scalability or redundancy of your Office Communications Server 2007 R2 infrastructure at risk. Once you have resolved the problem, any modifications made to the infrastructure for the purpose of isolating the problem must be restored to their original state. It is recommended to make modifications in a controlled manner that is recorded in detail to ensure no new problems are introduced into the environment and steps can be retraced.

Isolating the Component

Now that we have collected relevant data concerning the problem, the next step in the process is to use this information to identify the actual Office Communications Server component that is failing. Success in this step requires an understanding of how the individual components interact with each other.

Knowing how the components work when everything is operating optimally makes it easier to identify failing components. One way of building a better understanding of this interaction is to collect detailed logging from the Office Communications Server environment while performing tasks, such as joining a Web conference. Beginning to thoroughly review these logs will help build experience and knowledge on how the different components communicate and interact.

Issues can occur in a variety of components. The following list can help you narrow down the scope of components where the root cause might be occurring. This will help to further simplify your investigation. This list is not comprehensive.

- Client issue
  - Authentication
  - Connectivity
  - Certificate validation

- Server issues
  - Certificates
  - Active Directory
  - Front-end services
  - Address Book services
  - Web Components
  - Data conferencing
  - Enterprise Voice
  - Server applications
- Networking issues
  - Blocked ports
  - Improper network load balancer configuration
  - Missing or incorrect DNS records
- Enterprise Voice
  - Public Switched Telephone Network (PSTN) gateways
  - IP Private Branch eXchange (PBX) interoperability
  - Number normalization
  - Inbound/outbound routing

Researching Your Findings

Based on the information collected, use keywords from the logs to research the common body of knowledge for this problem. This research can take multiple paths such as reading blogs, searching Knowledge Bases (KBs), and leveraging search engines, such as *http://www.live.com*. The objective is to determine the root cause of your issue and possible solutions to resolve it.

Over the years, a large open online community has developed around the Office Communications suite of products and is available to help you identify similar problems and offer solutions that others have used. This support community can save you a considerable amount of time, effort, and money by providing information found in real-world scenarios that goes beyond the technical documentation.

Following is a list of some of the most active and valuable online resources that can be used for research:

- The Microsoft Support Web site, located at *http://go.microsoft.com/fwlink/?LinkId=136417*, is the best resource for finding commonly reported problems and Microsoft-supported resolutions. Microsoft KB articles are a public compilation of known issues, causes, workarounds, patches, and hotfixes known to Microsoft support. Note that some hotfixes require you to contact Microsoft Support before you are can download the files. These additional steps enable Microsoft to track all customers that are using the fix and also ensure that the problem you are experiencing will indeed be resolved by the requested hotfix.

- The TechNet Unified Communications Forum, located at *http://go.microsoft.com/fwlink/?LinkID=133756*, is an excellent resource for getting assistance with Office Communications Server 2007 R2 and Office Communicator 2007 R2. This forum assists in all aspects of Microsoft Unified Communications (UC), including server deployment, client deployment, troubleshooting, telephony, customization, administration, and monitoring.
- The Microsoft Office Communications Server Team Blog, located at *http://go.microsoft.com/fwlink/?LinkID=133634*, is a resource from the product group members for many topics that are being discussed or addressed for the first time. You will find many articles that are posted will eventually become Microsoft KB articles or provide a more through explanation than a KB article allows.
- The Microsoft Office Communicator Team Blog, located at *http://go.microsoft.com/fwlink/?LinkID=133635*, is an excellent resource from the product group members for many topics that are being discussed or addressed for the first time. You will find many of the postings will become Microsoft KB articles or go into much more detail than existing KB *articles*. Additional topics covered are UC devices, sample scripts, and usage best practices.

If you are still not able to isolate the root cause, some external support options are available to you. You can contact one of the Office Communications Server 2007 R2 certified partners (*http://go.microsoft.com/fwlink/?LinkID=133699*) or Microsoft Support Services (*http://go.microsoft.com/fwlink/?Linkld=136417*).

The benefit of taking either of these options is that they enable you to work directly with engineers and architects who have an extensive understanding of Office Communications Server 2007 R2. In some rare situations, based on the criticality of the problem and time needed to resolve the problem, it might be beneficial to immediately engage with an outside support organization, whether that organization is a UC certified partner or Microsoft Support Services.

When working with Microsoft Support Services or a UC certified partner, here are several things to keep in mind to help expedite the process:

- Ensure that you have the necessary permissions to access the resources needed to troubleshoot the environment.
- Provide as much detail as possible concerning the environment (see the section titled "Collecting Information" earlier in this chapter)—infrastructure diagrams, BPA logs, server and client logs, and so on. This will help the certified partner or Microsoft Support to help you quickly resolve the problem.

- Provide the team with your documented symptoms, as well as steps that were previously taken in attempting to resolve the problem.

Our intended goal of this chapter is provide you with information and guidance to avoid the need to rely on external support; however, it is always good to know what to do if the need arises.

Resolving the Issue

Once you have identified the root cause, you must determine how to resolve the problem. Prior to implementing a change, here are a few best practices to keep in mind:

- Perform a backup of the system you'll be modifying or ensure you have a recent backup.
- Implement one change at a time. Often in troubleshooting an issue, you will identify multiple solutions to a problem, and it is only normal to want to implement all of the changes at the same time. However, this is not advisable because it will not be possible to determine which solution resolved the problem or, worse, one of the steps might introduce a new issue that can cause further frustration. By implementing only one change at a time, you can better determine the effects of the change and quickly back out the change if it creates an adverse result.
- Once the change is implemented, test the entire environment to ensure that not only is the problem resolved, but no new problems are created.
- Once you have tested the environment and have verified that the problem is resolved and no new issues have appeared, back up the entire environment. This step helps ensure you have a valid backup.
- As a final step, document the implemented changes and update any necessary recorded baselines. This helps provide documentation for the future in the event that you need to repeat the steps if you encounter a similar situation.

Troubleshooting Common Problems

The best way to illustrate how to troubleshoot problems is by example. This section covers some of the common problems that customers encounter and offers pointers and hints for possible causes as well as how to resolve them.

To facilitate diagnostics, install the Office Communications Server 2007 R2 Resource Kit Tools, which provides additional tools to help diagnose problems. For more information on these tools, see Chapter 20.

Common Communicator Scenarios

This section details login and basic operation troubleshooting when using Office Communicator. Specific examples of failures as well as the data or troubleshooting steps associated with them are presented, and appropriate next steps are identified. Enabling Communicator event logs and using protocol trace logs on the client and server can make most problems readily apparent and even point out helpful next steps.

> ***NOTE*** **In the following log examples, the date, time, and thread columns have been removed to keep the data succinct and easy to read.**

Scenario 1: Resolving Issues That Involve DNS Service Record Locator Queries

DESCRIPTION OF PROBLEM

In this scenario, internal users are unable to log on using Office Communicator 2007 R2. The IT administrator has validated that the Office Communications Server 2007 R2 services are running and the users reporting the problem have been properly enabled for Office Communications. The following is one approach that can be used to troubleshoot the problem.

TROUBLESHOOTING

The IT administrator troubleshoots this issue by requesting that an affected user enable client logging on Office Communicator and attempt the logon process. Doing so will result in the information being recorded in the logs. The following excerpt from the Communicator log file shows the client doing DNS Service Record Locator (SRV) resolutions as part of automatic configuration and shows where errors are reported as indicated by the tag, ERROR, at the beginning of each log entry:

```
INFO  :: QueryDNSSrv - DNS Name[_sipinternaltls._tcp.litwareinc.com]
ERROR :: QueryDNSSrv GetDnsResults query: _sipinternaltls._tcp.litwareinc.com
         failed 0
ERROR :: DNS_RESOLUTION_WORKITEM::ProcessWorkItem ResolveHostName failed
         8007232a
INFO  :: QueryDNSSrv - DNS Name[_sip._tls.litwareinc.com]
INFO  :: CUccDnsQuery::UpdateLookup - error code=80ee0066, index=0
INFO  :: CUccDnsQuery::CompleteLookup - index=0
ERROR :: QueryDNSSrv GetDnsResults query: _sip._tls.litwareinc.com failed 0
ERROR :: DNS_RESOLUTION_WORKITEM::ProcessWorkItem ResolveHostName failed
         8007232a
INFO  :: CUccDnsQuery::UpdateLookup - error code=80ee0066, index=1
INFO  :: CUccDnsQuery::CompleteLookup - index=1
...
```

```
ERROR :: gethostbyname failed for host sipinternal.litwareinc.com, error:
        0x2afc
ERROR :: DNS_RESOLUTION_WORKITEM::ProcessWorkItem ResolveHostName failed
        80072afc
TRACE :: SIP_MSG_PROCESSOR::OnDnsResolutionComplete[012CAC60] Entered host
sipinternal.litwareinc.com
ERROR :: SIP_MSG_PROCESSOR::OnDnsResolutionComplete - error : 80ee0066
...
ERROR :: gethostbyname failed for host sip.litwareinc.com, error: 0x2afc
ERROR :: DNS_RESOLUTION_WORKITEM::ProcessWorkItem ResolveHostName failed
        80072afc
TRACE :: SIP_MSG_PROCESSOR::OnDnsResolutionComplete[01D93130] Entered host sip.
litwareinc.com
ERROR :: SIP_MSG_PROCESSOR::OnDnsResolutionComplete - error : 80ee0066
...
ERROR :: gethostbyname failed for host sipexternal.litwareinc.com, error:
        0x2afc
ERROR :: DNS_RESOLUTION_WORKITEM::ProcessWorkItem ResolveHostName failed
        80072afc
TRACE :: SIP_MSG_PROCESSOR::OnDnsResolutionComplete[01D93130] Entered host
sipexternal.litwareinc.com
ERROR :: SIP_MSG_PROCESSOR::OnDnsResolutionComplete - error : 80ee0066
```

In this case, the DNS resolution for the SRV records failed with error code 0x80ee0066. By using the Resource Kit Tool Err.EXE, the error message means that no record existed. In the absence of the SRV records, Office Communicator attempts to resolve the following host names: sipinternal.litwareinc.com, sip.litwareinc.com, and finally sipexternal.litwareinc.com. Note that these requests also fail. It is likely that the issue is due to the DNS infrastructure not being reachable or that the infrastructure is configured incorrectly.

NEXT STEPS

To further isolate the root cause of this issue, use nslookup.exe to determine what DNS server is being used and change the default server to the publishing point for the domain's DNS SRV records (the server <NewDnsServerName> command changes the default DNS server from the NSLookup command prompt). Failure to resolve the DNS entries directly from the server that should be hosting these service records indicates that either the DNS service is not running on that machine or that the entries are configured incorrectly on the DNS server. Failures to resolve the records from intermediate machines could be related to the machines' inability to see the publishing server as an authority or to existing DNS caches holding invalid entries.

Make sure that all necessary autoconfiguration records exist in the same domain name space as the user's SIP domain. The server's A record that the SRV records point to needs to have a domain name suffix that matches the user's domain. If either of these do not match, Communicator will not accept the returned DNS information. Communicator will not be able to log on.

Scenario 2: Resolving Issues That Arise from Certificate Negotiation Failures

DESCRIPTION OF PROBLEM

This section shows three common scenarios that are encountered when users are unable to connect due to certificate-related issues.

TROUBLESHOOTING

```
Case 1: Certificate Name Does Not Match DNS Name


TRACE :: SIP_MSG_PROCESSOR::OnDnsResolutionComplete[01D87BA0] Entered host sipserver.
litwareinc.com
...
ERROR :: SECURE_SOCKET: negotiation failed: 80090322
```

In case 1, the error shown is recorded in the Communicator log when the client is unable to connect due to the certificate validation process. These types of issues occur when Communicator uses Transport Layer Security (TLS) and isn't able to validate the server's certificate.

Scanning for the keyword ERROR, we can discover that Communicator received the error code 0x80090322 (err.exe translates into SEC_E_WRONG_PRINCIPLE), which means that the FQDN to which the client connected does not match the subject name (SN) of the certificate or an entry on the certificate's Subject Alternate Name (SAN) list. By looking back in the trace log, you can see the FQDN name of the server or pool that the client connected to: sipserver.litwareinc.com. Make sure that this name matches the SN or an entry in the SAN list on the certificate installed on the front-end services. The SN and the SAN list of a certificate can be checked by viewing the certificate in the Communications Server Management Snap-In and checking the Subject and Subject Alternate Names settings on the assigned certificate's Details tab.

This failure can also occur when the client is configured manually to use an IP address to identify the server when using TLS. The host name needs to be used so that it can be matched against the name in the certificate.

```
Case 2: Server Certificate Is Not Issued by a Trusted CA


ERROR :: SECURE_SOCKET: negotiation failed: 80090325
```

In case 2, the client's TLS negotiation failed because the server certificate isn't trusted. The error code 0x80090325 maps to SEC_E_UNTRUSTED_ROOT, which indicates that the root certification authority (CA) isn't trusted. The root CA certificate must be present in the list of

Trusted Root CAs found in the Computer Certificate store. For testing, you can add the root CA certificate to the Trusted Root CA path in the user's store. If doing so resolves the issue, repeat this process for the Computer store so that it will impact all users of the machine.

> ***NOTE*** **Windows servers are configured to hand out the root and intermediate CA certificates along with the server certificate to avoid certificate authentication problems. However, because some public instant messaging (IM) connectivity (PIC) partners do not use Windows-based servers, it is recommended that the intermediate CA certificates be placed in the Computer's Certificate Store list of intermediate CAs.**

```
Case 3: Root CA Certificate Is Missing the Server EKU

ERROR :: SECURE_SOCKET: negotiation failed: 80090349
```

In case 3, Communicator received the SEC_E_CERT_WRONG_USAGE failure message (0x80090349), which means that the certificate is not trusted for the purpose that it is being presented. It does not have rights to be used as a server certificate. Often this is caused due to the root CA certificate not being enabled for Server Authentication and Client Authentication usage; the certificate that Office Communications Server presents has the usage listed in its *Enhanced Key Usage (EKU)* field. This can be verified by using the Certificate MMC snap-in. Figure 21-1 shows the property of an incorrectly configured root CA certificate.

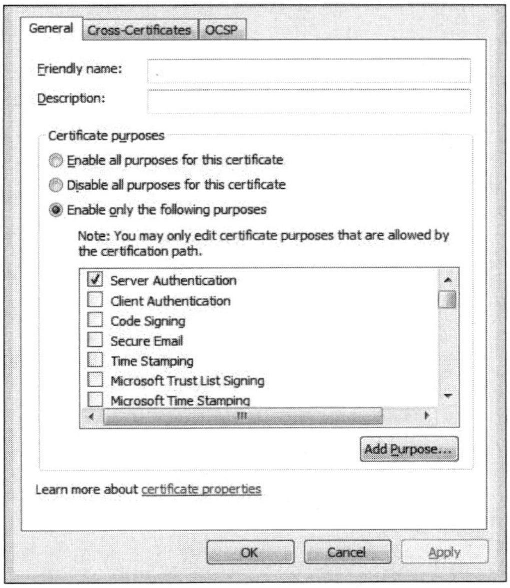

FIGURE 21-1 Root CA certificate properties

To resolve this issue, make sure that the root CA and Intermediate CA certificates stored in the Machine store are enabled for at least Server Authentication and Client Authentication as defined by the *EKU* field of the certificate being used by Office Communications Server.

NEXT STEPS

If problems validating or negotiating certificates arise, use the Certificate MMC snap-in to validate the certificate configuration on the client and server. Using a combination of the Office Communications Server event log and the Certificate MMC, you can also determine if the issue is due to an expired certificate.

Remember to use lcserror.exe from the Office Communications Server Resource Kit or err.exe to interpret any error codes into strings for more information about the failure. Err.exe is included in Windows Server 2008 and Windows Vista operating systems and can be obtained from the Windows Resource Kit for earlier releases. Last, the validation wizards can be used to help verify that the certificates are properly installed on the Office Communications Server.

DIRECT FROM THE SOURCE

Tips for Troubleshooting the Sign-In Process

Jason Epperly
Escalation Engineer, Product Support Services

The following list presents some tips for troubleshooting the sign-in process, ranging from basic tips to strategies for simplifying the discovery of problems by eliminating complexity.

- **Validate that the user is enabled for Communications Server (Active Directory Users and Computers).**
- **Validate that the SIP Uniform Resource Identifier (URI) the customer used to sign in matches the URI configured on the client.**
- **Determine whether the issue affects one user or all users.**
- **Test sign-in with an alternate account. (If no other accounts are available, create and enable a test user.)**
- **Determine whether the issue affects one client machine or all client machines (isolate the machine and the operating system).**
- **Test sign-in from another machine.**
- **Test sign-in from a client on either the same network as the server or on a different network than the current client that is failing (thereby isolating potential network infrastructure issues).**
- **Determine whether the issue also affects a particular version of Office Communicator.**

Simplify

To isolate the component that is failing during the sign-in process, it is a best practice to make the sign-in process as simple as possible. Start with an internal client on the local area network (LAN) before testing with a remote user.

How to Change to a Simple Configuration

- Validate that you can resolve the fully qualified name of the server and/or name of the pool (that is, use ping.exe or nslookup.exe).
- Manually configure the client with the name of the server (Standard Edition) or name of the pool to try and rule out issues with client-side automatic configuration logic.
- If the configuration includes a load balancer, create a host file entry that resolves the fully qualified name of the pool directly to one of the front-end servers, using the actual address (not the virtual IP) to try and rule out problems with the load balancer configuration.
- Try to rule out issues with certificates configured on the server and certificate infrastructure (CA, certificate revocation list [CRL]) by configuring Communicator to use Transmission Control Protocol (TCP) to connect to the server (after making sure that the server is configured to allow this type of connection).

DIRECT FROM THE SOURCE

Tips for Troubleshooting Communicator Sign-In Issues

Josh Jones
Senior Support Escalation Engineer

When troubleshooting Communicator sign-in issues, you can divide the problem in half simply by seeing if you are prompted for credentials. If you are prompted for credentials, SIP is functioning because a Register has been sent to the pool and a 401 error requesting credentials has been sent back.

If you see a prompt but sign-in fails, check to see if the user is properly enabled for remote access and ensure that the user is not attempting something such as providing a SIP URI in the *User Name* field instead of their Active Directory account.

If you do not see a prompt, the problem lies with establishing a SIP conversation. This requires name lookup, TCP/IP connectivity, and certificate verification. You can check name lookup with nslookup or by using a manual server configuration in Communicator. TCP/IP connectivity can be verified by connecting with Telnet to port 5061. Certificate issues are almost always an improper SN or SAN, an untrusted root, or inaccessible CRL.

DIRECT FROM THE SOURCE

Diagnosing Connection Failures (Load Balancers and Firewalls)

James Undery
Software Design Engineer II

When diagnosing connection issues, my first guess is that a load balancer is involved, especially if the connections close at regular intervals (5 minutes is a popular default). When a network device such as a load balancer causes connection problems, both servers see that the other end has closed the connection. The Winsock error code for the remote host closing the connection is WSAECONNRESET (10054 in decimal, 2746 in hexadecimal, or 0x80002746 as a HRESULT in the logs). In a network trace, both sides will see a TCP segment with the RST (TCP reset) flag set. In defense of load balancers, most are optimized for Web traffic that has short-lived connections (unlike connections between Office Communications Server servers); therefore, the default length of time before a load balancer assumes that a connection is "dead" tends to be lower than the value needed by the Office Communications Server.

For firewall issues, the Winsock WSAETIMEDOUT error code (10060 in decimal, 274C in hexadecimal, or 0x8000274C as a HRESULT in the logs) is usually a good indicator. Because firewalls tend to drop the network packets they are blocking, connection attempts that fail will simply time out. If you know that the IP address being tried is correct and that the server at the other end is running, you can be more confident that a firewall is blocking the traffic.

Troubleshooting Web Conferencing

This section details the troubleshooting steps used to resolve a common Web conferencing issue.

NOTE In the following log example, the date, time, and thread columns have been removed to keep the data succinct and easy to read.

Problem Description

In this scenario, participants are unable to download content, such as handouts or a Microsoft Office PowerPoint presentation, that the meeting organizer has successfully uploaded. This problem is reproducible and occurs with all meetings hosted on a single pool. This scenario assumes that the files are successfully uploaded to the Web Component Server.

Troubleshooting

The first step an administrator takes is to reproduce the problem to generate a set of logs to be used for troubleshooting. PWConsole logging, which is used in this scenario, is enabled by default. Start by creating a new meeting by using the Office Live Meeting client. There are two ways to attempt to reproduce the issue:

- Upload an Office PowerPoint file to the meeting (on the Content menu, click Share, select Add File To Meeting, and then choose View). Once the file is uploaded, the main console window displays a gray background with an error message: Content failed to download due to a problem with the Conference Center configuration. Contact your administrator.
- Upload a file by using the Handouts feature (see the Handouts button on the toolbar). Once you have uploaded a file, try to download it. A message box pops up with the following error message: Download failed.

Once the problem has been reproduced, review the console trace file, which can be found in the user's default temp folder (%temp%). This folder is easily accessed by running the following in the command console:

```
cd  %temp%
```

Usually, this folder will contain multiple console trace files for the user. To view these trace files from the command prompt window, run the following command:

```
dir pwconsole-debug*.txt
```

Using your favorite text editor (for example, Notepad), open the most recent trace file. This can be determined by using the modified date/timestamp. Look for the section in which the failure occurs by searching the trace log for Downloader::addRequest(). This will help you review all areas in the log relating to the file download process. The error will look similar to the following:

```
[MC] 21:06:10:064 GMT [THREAD 4888]  [I] Downloader::addRequest()
    - Found previously failed request, will not download https://se.litwareinc.com/
etc/place/null/FileTree/IE6HRFPCBJ3K1CCUC1
    HH75UPN8Q/6a24bb55f381433285cc878baa11ed3a/slidefiles/
    xc75dbd0baa6a.epng
```

This trace line indicates that the console failed to download the content from a specific URL. The URL is printed at the end of the trace line, starting with *HTTPS* (for example, *https://se.litwareinc.com*). When debugging the problem, copy the URL from the actual log for use later in the investigation.

Next, verify that Internet Explorer can browse to the URL. Open Internet Explorer and paste the URL copied from the trace file. Change the URL HTTPS to *http://se.litwareinc.com*. If Internet Explorer is properly configured, the result will be a page that says *Under construction*.

If Internet Explorer returns a result that says *Internet Explorer cannot display the webpage* instead of *Under construction*, verify that Internet Information Services (IIS) is running on the Office Communications Server. To do this check, connect to the Office Communications Server running the Web Conferencing service and open the IIS Management Console.

Use the IIS Management Console and view the SE\Web Sites\Default Web Site icons in the left panel tree. Red circles on the icons indicate that a failure has occurred within IIS. If the service is not running, try to restart IIS by right-clicking the machine icon. From the context menu, select All Tasks and then Restart IIS. If the red circles remain, there are two options to resolve the issue:

- Reinstall IIS.
  a. Deactivate Web Components.
  b. Uninstall IIS.
  c. Reinstall IIS.
  d. Activate Web Components.
- Contact Microsoft Support Services or an Office Communications Server certified partner for assistance with issue resolution.

Upon resolution, retest by opening Internet Explorer and browsing to the base URL listed in the trace log, for example, *http://se.litwareinc.com*. If the Web page still does not display correctly, verify that the DNS is working properly by using NSLookup. In this scenario, Internet Explorer displays the Under Construction page, and the next step is to check if the file was uploaded successfully.

Using the IIS Manager console, expand the nodes in the left panel tree:

- Internet Information Services
- SE
- Web Sites
- Default Web Site
- Etc
- Null
- FileTree
- <organizerguid>
- <consoleguid>
- sidefiles

The following image, Figure 21-2, shows what the expanded IIS Management Console will look like.

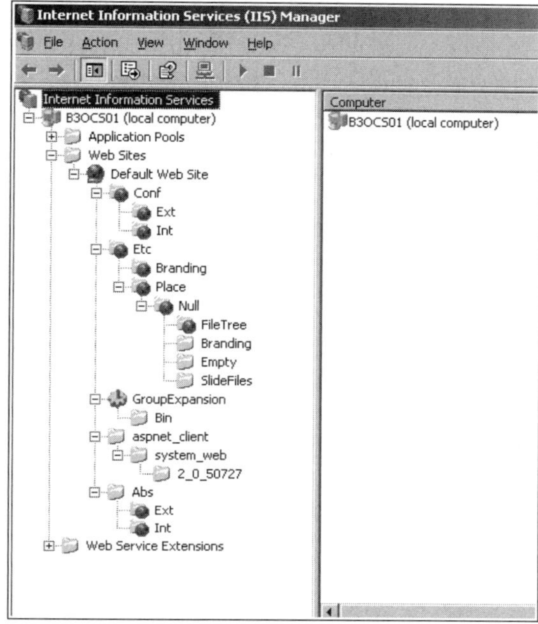

FIGURE 21-2 Expanded IIS Manager View

> ***NOTE*** **The <organizerguid> and <consoleguid> come from the URL copied from the PWConsole log. In this scenario, the <organizeguid> is IE6HRFPCBJ3K1CCUC1HH75UPN8Q and the <conferenceguid> is 6a24bb55f381433285cc878baa11ed3a.**

Click the Sidefiles node, and a list of files should appear in the right panel list. One of these files should be the EPNG file from the end of the URL (xc75dbd0baa6a.epng).

If the file is not located in the directory, there are multiple possible issues: problems with the Web Conferencing Server or connectivity problems between the Web Conferencing Server and meeting participants. Check the Office Communications Server event logs for issues reported on the service running the Web Conferencing Server role. Also verify that the necessary ports are open between the meeting organizer and the Web Conferencing Server (these ports are discussed in detail in Chapter 4, "Infrastructure and Security Considerations"). In the case where the organizer is remotely connected, check port connectivity to the Web Conferencing service on the Edge Server.

The Live Meeting Console downloads the conference content by using Hypertext Transfer Protocol Secure (HTTPS), and therefore the server must be configured to accept such requests. Verify that IIS is properly configured for HTTPS. IIS does not accept such requests by default, and it must be manually activated. There is a chance that this configuration step for IIS was overlooked.

Using the IIS Management Console, right-click Default Web Site. Select Properties, then Directory Security, and then Server Certificate. Follow the steps in the wizard by selecting

Assign An Existing Certificate. (A Web certificate must already be installed on the server machine. See Chapter 4.) Select the certificate and ensure that the port is set to 443. Save the settings by clicking Finish in the wizard and then clicking OK on the Properties page.

IIS should now be configured for HTTPS. Double-check that everything is working by repeating the resolution procedures by using the original HTTPS URL (for example, *https://se.litwareinc.com*). Internet Explorer should be able to display the Under Construction page.

Next Steps

If the issue is still unresolved, run the validation wizard and the Best Practices Analyzer tools. These tools verify the functionality of the underlying components and may identify additional problems that are preventing issue resolution.

DIRECT FROM THE SOURCE

Diagnosing Problems with Group Expansion Failures

Kiran Kulkarni
Software Design Engineer II, Office Communications Server Product Group

To diagnose Group Expansion failures when using Communicator, open Internet Explorer and navigate to *https://*<webfqdn>*/GroupExpansion/Int/service.asmx* (replace <*webfqdn*> with the server FQDN in use, such as srv.litwareinc.com). Using Internet Explorer, select Tools, then Internet Options, then Advanced. Then remove the check from Show Friendly HTTP Error Messages so that any internal failures are displayed in Internet Explorer on the bottom left of the window.

Communicator obtains the Group Expansion URLs (which are a pool-level setting) through in-band provisioning. Internal clients use *https://*<internalwebfqdn>*/GroupExpansion/Int/service.asmx*. External clients use *https://*<externalwebfqdn>*/GroupExpansion/Int/service.asmx*.

Whenever a user expands a directory list, the Group Expansion URLs are connected. Debugging DL expansion failures involves directly accessing these URLs from within Internet Explorer so that errors come up front (IIS errors, access errors, proxy errors, or service failures or crashes).

Fully Qualified Domain Names

When a pool is created during deployment, the administrator must define the Web farm FQDN. There are two FQDNs to be specified: InternalWebFqdn and ExternalWebFqdn.

- **InternalWebFqdn** Used by intranet clients. This FQDN is either the same as the SIP server (for Standard Edition) or the pool load balancer (for Enterprise Edition, case 1). Or, it can be different (for Enterprise Edition, case 2, in which IIS servers are deployed behind a separate load balancer for scalability purposes).

- **ExternalWebFqdn** Used by remote clients. This is the FQDN of the reverse proxy (or farm) in the perimeter network. The reverse proxy, in turn, proxies requests to the internal Web Components Server.

DIRECT FROM THE SOURCE

First Verify Connectivity

Checking for Web Conferencing Connections on Edge Servers

Jeff Reed

Software Design Engineer in Test on the Office Communications Server Team

The Web Conferencing Edge Server relies on incoming connections from Web Conferencing Servers in the enterprise network, so the inability of the internal server to connect to the Edge Server can result in an external meeting participant failing to connect to the meeting. To check that connections have been established, use netstat.exe on the configured internal port that the Web Conferencing Edge Server is listening on by typing:

```
netstat -aon | findstr 8057
```

Troubleshooting External Audio/Video

This section details external audio troubleshooting when using Office Communicator. Specific examples of failures as well as troubleshooting steps associated with them are presented and appropriate next steps are identified. Enabling Communicator event logs and using protocol trace logs on the client and server can make most problems readily apparent and even point out helpful next steps.

NOTE In the following log examples, the date, time, and thread columns have been removed to keep the data succinct and easy to read.

Description of Problem

In this scenario, internal users can call other internal users; however, they are unable to place or receive calls when they are outside the corporate network behind a Network Address Translation (NAT) device, such as a router or firewall. The IT administrator has validated that the Office Communications Server 2007 R2 services are running, and the users reporting the problem have been properly enabled for Office Communications and remote access. The following is one approach that can be used to troubleshoot the problem.

Troubleshooting

The IT administrator begins to troubleshoot this issue by enabling client logging on Office Communicator and attempting to place a call to an external user behind a firewall. The call attempt will be recorded in the log file.

Now that the IT administrator has a set of logs from the customer, he can view the log output by using Snooper, a tool from the Office Communications Server 2007 R2 Resource Kit. For detailed information on Snooper and how to use it, please refer to Chapter 20. To isolate the failed call attempt, the IT administrator uses the following search string:

```
Invite m=audio


The m= field in the message body can be used to determine the specific modality of a
particular INVITE.  The following are some common examples:
      - m=message is used for IM messages
      - m=audio is used for audio calls
```

This will return multiple SIP messages, including INVITE messages and other messages related to the invitation. The next step is to find the correct INVITE message from the failed call attempt. This is accomplished by looking at the TO header in the SIP message, as well as the Time/Date timestamp. Because the log was taken from the person making the call, the *TO* field should be to the SIP URI of the remote user, and the timestamp should match when the call was placed. The following is an example of the INVITE message:

```
10/1/2008|14:31:53.354 2A44:2B98 INFO  :: INVITE sip:janedoe@litwareinc.com
...
From: <sip:johndoe@litwareinc.com>;tag=616870b365;epid=3da06eb148
To: sip:janedoe@litware.com
```

After finding the specific INVITE, the IT administrator looks at the details of the INVITE message, searching for the listed *a=candidate* entries. The following lists *a=candidate* entries returned in this scenario:

```
a=candidate:wL0o20SkJFunhXCMnB6ql+Z/kzBn0FuzWk1XGE28clY 1 GtkmEX1ZUj65wXiQ4YyfhQ UDP
0.870 192.168.0.198 50035


a=candidate:wL0o20SkJFunhXCMnB6ql+Z/kzBn0FuzWk1XGE28clY 2 GtkmEX1ZUj65wXiQ4YyfhQ UDP
0.870 192.168.0.198 50027
```

Note that this list contains only entries with the user's internal IP address, 192.168.0.198, and does not include any *a=candidate* entries that contain the IP address of the Edge Server.

Because the information for the Edge Server is not listed and the internal user's IP address is in a non–publicly routable network, the external user will not be able to establish a point-to-point audio connection. In most situations in which the Edge Server's *a=candidate* entries are missing, there is an issue with the configuration of the A/V Authentication service or a communications issue caused by an improperly configured firewall.

Next Steps

To further verify the root cause of the issue, the IT administrator uses Snooper to search the log for the keyword *MRAS*.

Note that the registration with the Media Relay Authentication Server (MRAS) occurs only at login. If the search turns up no responses, it means one of two things:

- The log does not contain the user logon information. This is common when logging is enabled after the user is logged in. After logging is enabled, have the user log back in and then repeat the test.
- There is not an MRAS Server defined for the pool. Check the pool's A/V Conferencing setting to pick the correct MRAS Server for the environment.

This will show you the original request sent to MRAS, as well as the response returned. A common failure response code in these types of issues is a 504. The MS diagnostic header of the 504 message will provide further information that can be used to understand the cause of the problem and which servers are involved. The following is the MS diagnostics header from a 504 error:

```
ms-diagnostics: 1007;reason="Temporarily cannot route";source="se.litwareinc.com";
ErrorType="Connect Attempt Failure";WinsockFailureDescription="The peer actively
refused the connection attempt";WinsockFailureCode="274D(WSAECONNREFUSED)";Peer="edge.
litwareinc.com"
```

This error shows that the connection attempt to the MRAS, edge.litwareinc.com, was actively refused. These types of errors normally occur due to port configuration on the Edge Server being improperly set in the Global Settings properties. The default port for the Edge Server audio/video (A/V) authentication is 5062; however, when setting the Edge Server configuration in the Global Settings properties, it is commonly set to 5061 or another port. Verify that these port numbers match on the Edge Server, pools, Mediation Servers, and global settings.

Another common issue that shows similar symptoms is caused by specific ports being blocked on either the internal or external firewall. Refer to Chapter 4 for additional information on firewall requirements.

DIRECT FROM THE SOURCE

Tips for Audio and Video Conferencing

Joel Schaeffer
Escalation Engineer, Product Support Services

The following tips are useful for gathering more details related to audio and video conferencing.

Determining Metrics from a Point-to-Point Conferencing Session

In some circumstances, it might be helpful to determine metrics from a point-to-point conferencing session. This may hold true when poor video or audio is observed on either side. To gather basic statistics from a point-to-point conferencing session, you can do the following.

1. Enable Communicator logging.
2. Start the conferencing session, communicate, and then terminate the session.
3. Open the log file (by default, Communicator-uccp-0.uccplog) and search for *VQReportEvent*.
4. Beginning at <VQReportEvent xmlns="ms-rtcp-metrics">, do the following:
   - Copy/paste the text into an editor ending at </VQReportEvent>.
   - Save it as VQReportEvent.xml.
5. Double-click VQReportEvent.xml to view the report.

In the report, you will find items such as SIP URIs, IP configuration, ports used, and the A/V drivers used during the conversation. You will also see statistics such as jitter, packet loss, video resolution, bit rate, and frame rate.

Viewing Session Description Protocol Session Information

To properly set up a video conference session, some parameters must be passed between endpoints to set up the session. The protocol used for this session setup is called the Session Description Protocol (SDP).

To view SDP information for a session, do the following.

1. Enable Communicator logging.
2. Start the conferencing session, communicate, and then terminate the session.
3. Open the log file (by default, Communicator-uccp-0.uccplog) and search for *Content-Type: application/sdp*.

Inside of the SIP packet containing this entry, you will see an SDP session description. Each line is in the format *<type>=<value>*. Types of interest include:

- **originator** Usually includes the IP address of the initiator or receiver of the session.
- **media name and transport address** Either audio or video with various parameters of each media type.
- **attribute line** Used for all other configuration parameters of the session (for example, codecs and bit rate).

See Request for Comment (RFC) 4566 (*http://www.ietf.org*) for details and a full description of each SDP type.

DIRECT FROM THE SOURCE

Troubleshooting Tips for External A/V Call Failures

Radu Constantinescu
Senior Lead Software Development Engineer in Test, Office Communications Server

If users are experiencing connectivity failures while placing calls from outside the corporate firewall, the checklist below can help you troubleshoot problems with the following symptoms:

- Calls between external and internal users (using Office Communicator, Tanjay, and so on) fail to connect.
- External users (using Office Communicator, Tanjay, Live Meeting Console, and so on) cannot join a conference.

NOTE The assumption is that A/V calls between internal users can be made successfully.

Verify A/V Edge Server Configuration

Verify the following settings on every A/V Edge Server in your environment.

1. Ensure the Office Communications Server 2007 R2 Admin Tools are installed on the box.
2. Open Computer Management Console.
3. Expand the Services And Applications node.
4. Right-click Office Communications Server 2007 R2 and click Properties.
5. Navigate to the Internal tab.

6. Verify the following settings:
   - Is the Authorized Internal SIP Domains list populated correctly? Add each SIP domain supported in your Office Communications Server deployment.
   - Is the Authorized Internal Servers list populated correctly? If using a Director, add the FQDN of the Director; otherwise, type the FQDN of each Enterprise pool and Standard Edition Server in your organization.
7. Navigate to the Edge Interfaces tab.
8. Click Configure For Internal Interface.
9. Verify the following settings:
   - Is the proper certificate selected? The SN of the certificate must match the FQDN of the internal interface. If a hardware load balancer is used, the SN must match the FQDN corresponding to the virtual IP (VIP) of the hardware load balancer. Also make sure the EKU for the certificate is present and the intended purpose is Server Authentication.
   - Is the certificate chain of the CA that issued the certificate for the internal interface installed on your Edge Server? Download and install the CA certificate chain for the internal interface.
   - Is the root certificate of the CA that issued the certificate for the internal interface in the list of trusted root CAs? Add the root certificate to the list of trusted root CAs.

   NOTE: For more info about certificates, refer to Chapter 4.

10. Navigate to the Edge Interfaces tab.
11. Click Configure For A/V Edge Server.
12. Verify the following settings:
    - Does the A/V Authentication Certificate have a private key? Use a certificate that has a private key.
    - Are hardware load balancers used on the external and internal edges? Make sure all the A/V Edge Servers use the same TCP and User Datagram Protocol (UDP) port values for the external interface; the same rule applies to the internal edge. Also the same A/V Authentication certificate must be used on all A/V Edge Servers.
    - Did you change the default TCP and UDP port values for the external interface? (The UDP port can be changed via Windows Management Instrumentation [WMI].) To allow federated calls between users in different organizations, you should keep the TCP port as 443 and the UDP port as 3478 for the external interface.
    - Is the external IP address translated by NAT? Verify that the External IP Address Is Translated By NAT check box is checked.

- Is the IP address for the external interface publicly routable? If the External IP Address Is Translated By NAT check box is not checked, then the IP address for the external interface must be publicly routable; otherwise, if the check box is checked, the NAT-ed IP address must be publicly routable.
- If the external IP address is translated by NAT, is the external FQDN resolvable from the A/V Edge Server? Use the ping or nslookup commands to check that. You can either add a DNS entry or modify the local hosts file to map the FQDN to the NAT-ed address.

Verify NAT Settings

- Is a hardware load balancer used and also a NAT? NAT in conjunction with a load balancer is not a supported deployment.
- Is the internal IP address of the A/V Edge Server translated by NAT? NAT on the internal edge is not a supported deployment.
- Are ports mapped straight through by the NAT/firewall? Ensure there is a one-to-one port mapping with the A/V Edge Server ports.

Verify Firewall Settings

Does the internal firewall allow the necessary inbound/outbound traffic? The internal firewall must allow the following A/V Edge Server traffic:

- Outbound only on UDP port 3478 for Traversal Using Relay NAT (TURN)/Simple Traversal of UDP through NAT (STUN)/Real-Time Transport Protocol (RTP)/UDP.
- Outbound only on TCP port 443 for TURN/STUN/RTP/UDP
- Outbound only on TCP port 5062 for SIP/TLS

Does the external firewall allow the necessary inbound/outbound traffic? The external firewall must allow the following A/V Edge Server traffic:

- Inbound/outbound on UDP port 3478 for TURN/STUN/RTP/UDP
- Inbound only on TCP port 443 for TURN/STUN/RTP/TCP

If federated calls are made to users belonging to different organizations and there are A/V Edge Servers in the communication path that are *not* running Office Communications Server 2007 R2, then consider the following:

- Are UDP media ports open in the external firewall for inbound and outbound traffic? The external firewall must allow inbound and outbound traffic on UDP media ports between 50000-59999 for STUN/RTP (see step 11 for where to configure this setting).
- Are TCP media ports open in the external firewall for outbound traffic? The external firewall must allow outbound traffic on TCP media ports between 50000-59999 for STUN/RTP (see step 11 for where to configure this setting).

If federated desktop sharing is used with users belonging to different organizations and all A/V Edge Servers in the communication path are running Office Communications Server 2007 R2:

- Are TCP media ports open in the external firewall for outbound traffic? The external firewall must allow outbound traffic on TCP media ports between 50000-59999 for STUN/RTP (see step 11 for where to configure this setting).
- Are you using Windows Server 2008 Firewall? Make sure the firewall exception rules described earlier in this sidebar are defined for the program *System* as explained here.
    1. Display Properties for the exception rule.
    2. Click the Programs And Services tab.
    3. Type **System** in the appropriate box.

NOTE: For more information about firewall rules, please refer to Chapter 4.

Verify Global and Pool Settings

1. Open Office Communications Server 2007 R2 Management Console.
2. Right-click the forest node and select Global Properties.
3. Navigate to the Edge Servers tab.
    - Is Audio/Video Edge Server in the A/V Edge Servers list? Add the A/V Edge Server to the A/V Edge Servers list.
4. For every Enterprise pool and Standard Edition Server, right-click the pool node and select Pool Properties.
    - Is Audio/Video Edge Server selected in the A/V Authentication Service list? Select the A/V Edge Server in the A/V Authentication Service list.

Summary

This chapter contains many tips and practical guidelines directly from the Office Communications Server 2007 R2 product, support, and consulting teams. When working through a problem, start with the guidance provided at the beginning of the chapter. Attempt to simplify the scenario and gather as much information as possible about what is occurring. Look at event logs and trace logs from the client or server, validate network connectivity, and validate that servers are operational and configured as expected. The validation wizard is helpful in this regard, and many problems can be discovered easily before they are actually encountered.

Additional Resources

- Documents, tools, and support information for Office Communications Server are always available at the official Microsoft Office Communications Server Web site, found at *http://go.microsoft.com/fwlink/?LinkID=133631*.
- Office Communications Server 2007 R2 Resource Kit Tools download, found at *http://go.microsoft.com/fwlink/?LinkID=133686*.
- Windows Server 2003 Resource Kit, found at *http://go.microsoft.com/fwlink/?LinkId=134705*.
- Microsoft Office Communications Server Team blog, found at *http://go.microsoft.com/fwlink/?LinkID=133634*.
- TechNet Unified Communications forums, found at *http://go.microsoft.com/fwlink/?LinkID=133756*.
- Microsoft Office Communicator team blog, found at *http://go.microsoft.com/fwlink/?LinkID=133635*.
- Office Communications Server 2007 VoIP Troubleshooting Guide, found at *http://go.microsoft.com/fwlink/?LinkID=133758*.
- Microsoft Knowledge Base article 200525 provides a detailed explanation on how to use NSLookup and can be found at *http://go.microsoft.com/fwlink/?LinkID=133759*.
- TechNet article providing information on how to create and use the host file, found at *http://go.microsoft.com/fwlink/?LinkID=133760*.

CHAPTER 22

Routing and Authentication

This chapter provides an in-depth discussion of the fundamental technologies that Microsoft Office Communications Server 2007 R2 uses. This chapter covers Session Initiation Protocol (SIP), SIP routing, Globally Routable User Agent Uniform Resource Identifier [URI] (GRUU), and authentication.

SIP is an Internet Engineering Task Force (IETF) standard (Request for Comment [RFC] 3261). *SIP* is an application-layer signaling protocol used for signaling an incoming call, terminating a call, placing a call on hold, joining an audio/video (A/V) conferencing, initiating an instant message conversation, and so on. Just as Signaling System #7 (*SS7*) is the signaling protocol for the Public Switched Telephone Network (PSTN), SIP is the signaling protocol for the Internet Protocol (IP) network. It is used to establish communication sessions between the server and client endpoints.

SIP routing ensures that communication sessions are established with the right people. Office Communications Server uses routing logic to route all requests inside and outside the enterprise.

The *Globally Routable User Agent URI* (GRUU) is an IETF standard that extends the SIP protocol designed to make it possible to route reliably to a specific device belonging to an end user anywhere on the IP network.

Authentication is the process of determining whether someone is in fact who she claims to be. Authentication as it applies to SIP enables users to communicate over the Internet securely. Strong authentication protects users and corporate resources (servers) from malicious users and helps enterprises protect their sensitive data.

Understanding Session Initiation Protocol

SIP is an agile, application-layer control protocol for creating, modifying, and terminating sessions. It works independently of the underlying transport protocols and the type of session that is being established.

Many applications that use the Internet require the creation and management of a session. The implementation of these applications is complicated by the practices of participants. For example, users might move between endpoints, be addressable by multiple names, and communicate using several different media (sometimes simultaneously). Numerous protocols have been authored that carry various forms of real-time multimedia session data, such as voice, video, or text messages. SIP works in concert with these protocols by enabling Internet endpoints to discover one another and to agree on the characterization of a session they want to share.

SIP is a lightweight, text-based protocol, which makes it simpler than many other protocols to debug and troubleshoot. It provides five main functions for establishing and terminating multimedia communications.

- **User location** The determination of the end system to be used for communication
- **User availability** The determination of the called party's willingness to engage in communications
- **User capabilities** The determination of the media and media parameters to be used
- **Session setup** The establishment of session parameters at both called and calling parties (also known as ringing)
- **Session management** The transfer and termination of sessions, modification of session parameters, and invocation of services

Because SIP is a signaling protocol, it is used with other IETF protocols to build a complete multimedia architecture. Typically, these architectures include media protocols such as the Real-Time Transport Protocol (RTP) for transporting real-time data, the Real-Time Control Protocol (RTCP) for providing Quality of Service (QoS) feedback, the Real-Time Streaming Protocol (RTSP) for controlling the delivery of streaming media, the Media Gateway Control (MEGACO) protocol for controlling gateways to the PSTN, and the Session Description Protocol (SDP) for describing multimedia sessions. Although SIP can be used with other IETF protocols to build a complete multimedia architecture, the basic functionality and operation of SIP does not depend on any of these protocols.

Figure 22-1 is an architecture diagram illustrating how SIP fits into the Transmission Control Protocol/Internet Protocol (TCP/IP) networking stack.

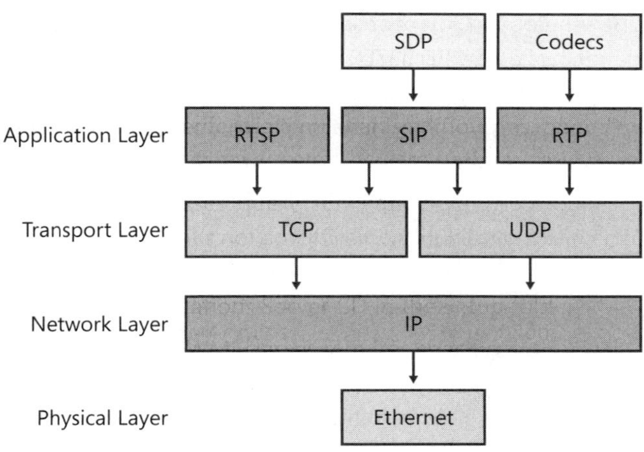

FIGURE 22-1 How SIP fits into the TCP/IP networking stack

Common SIP Requests

In SIP, the server receives requests from client endpoints. Following are the commonly issued SIP requests:

- REGISTER
- SUBSCRIBE and NOTIFY
- SERVICE
- INVITE
- ACK
- CANCEL
- BYE
- MESSAGE

REGISTER is used for endpoint registration. INVITE, ACK, CANCEL, and BYE are used for session establishment. MESSAGE is used for exchanging messages within the session. SUBSCRIBE and NOTIFY are used for watching someone's presence. SERVICE requests are used for changing your information, such as your contact list and presence information. The following sections describe each of the requests in more detail.

REGISTER

Clients use the REGISTER request to register their endpoints with a SIP registrar server. More than one endpoint can be registered simultaneously for a user. For each endpoint that the user is logged in from, the endpoint client sends a REGISTER request to the server.

The data flow diagram in Figure 22-2 shows an example of a client registering with Office Communications Server. The client sends a REGISTER request, and the server challenges the client for authentication credentials by sending a 401 response with the supported authentication technologies. Then the client initiates a new REGISTER request with authentication credentials. In this example, the client has requested to use Kerberos authentication. More details on authentication technologies, including NT LAN Manager (NTLM) and Kerberos, are discussed in the section titled "Understanding Authentication" later in this chapter.

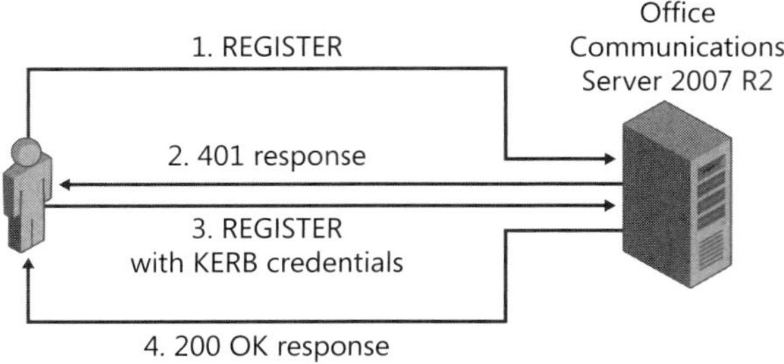

FIGURE 22-2 Data flow diagram for registration

The client first sends a REGISTER request to the server. The following block of code is an example of a REGISTER packet. Notice that the From and To headers are the same, and the Contact header identifies the endpoint where the client is logging in from.

```
REGISTER sip:example.com SIP/2.0
From: Callee <sip:callee@example.com>;tag=calee1111;epid=01010101
To: Callee <sip:callee@example.com>
Call-ID: REG1111@192.0.1.1
CSeq: 1 REGISTER
Supported: gruu-10
Contact: <sip:callee@192.0.1.1:1111;msopaque=1111>; proxy-replace;+sip.
instance="<urn:uuid:4b1682a8-f968-5701-83fc-7c6741dc6697>"
Via: SIP/2.0/TLS 192.0.1.1:1111;branch=z9hG4bK1111


Expires: 0
...
```

After receiving a REGISTER request, Office Communications Server can do one of the following:

- **Query** If a Contact header is *not* present, the request is considered a query for the user's list of registered endpoints.
- **Remove a registration** If an Expires:0 header is present, the request is interpreted to delete any existing registration for the user endpoint. The endpoint is identified in the *+sip.instance* parameter of the Contact header in Microsoft Office Communicator 2007 and the *epid* parameter of the From header in Live Communicator 2005. Office Communicator 2007 also supplies the *epid* parameter for backward compatibility because *+sip.instance* is the currently preferred method.

- **Add or update a registration** If a Contact header is present with a nonempty value other than "*", Office Communications Server updates any existing registration for the user endpoint or adds a new registration if no previous registration is present.

After removing, adding, or updating a registration or querying the server, the server responds with a 200 OK response upon success or with an error response. More details on common error responses can be found in the section titled "Common SIP Responses" later in this chapter.

SUBSCRIBE and NOTIFY

SUBSCRIBE and NOTIFY requests are used to set up event notifications from the server. The client uses SUBSCRIBE to subscribe to information from the server that is dynamic in nature—that is, the information can change as a result of updates that other clients make or as a result of administrative functions. The server uses NOTIFY to notify clients that information they had previously subscribed to has changed and to deliver the updated information.

In Office Communications Server, these requests are used to subscribe to a contact's presence and to the user's own data, such as in-band provisioning information and contact lists. Additionally, these requests are used to specify who the user allows to view his presence. Figure 22-3 shows an example data flow diagram of a client subscribing to get the presence status of his contacts.

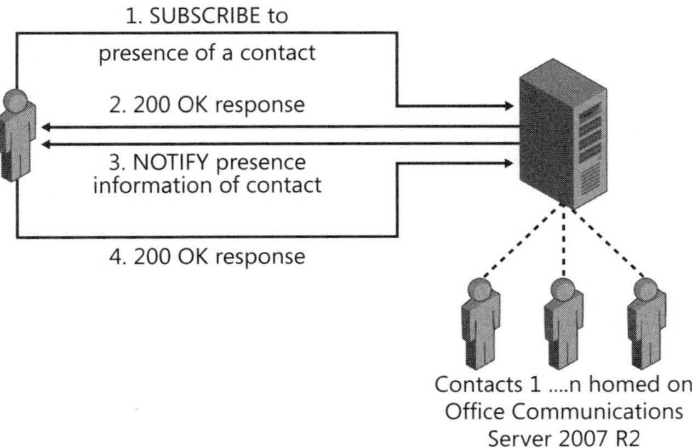

FIGURE 22-3 SUBSCRIBE and NOTIFY data flow diagram

Typically, Office Communicator will respond to the NOTIFY request with a 200 response. However, if Office Communicator responds to the NOTIFY request with a 404, 480, or 481 response, Office Communications Server assumes that the corresponding subscription is invalid and deletes the subscription from its records.

SERVICE

SERVICE requests are used to request a server to perform a particular service or request information, such as changing a user's presence, fetching a user's location profile, and creating or modifying conferences. Additionally, a SERVICE request can be used to control access control entries (ACEs), modify contact lists and groups, set personal presence, and retrieve presence information. For example, if you want to add or change your presence information, the client sends a SERVICE request to the server to perform this operation. Figure 22-4 shows a typical dataflow from the client to the server for the SERVICE requests. The type of service requested is described in the XML payload Simple Object Access Protocol [SOAP] within the SERVICE request.

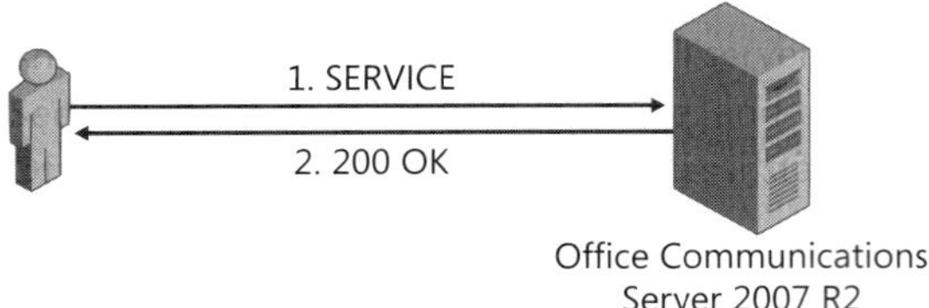

FIGURE 22-4 Sample SERVICE request

After Office Communicator sends a valid SERVICE request, Office Communications Server responds with one of the following responses: 100 Trying, 200 OK, or 4*xx* error. If the initial response is 100 Trying, Office Communications Server responds with a 200 OK or a 4*xx* error response when it completes the processing.

INVITE

The INVITE request helps to establish sessions for client-to-client communication, as well as to establish sessions with servers including the A/V Conferencing Server, the IM Conferencing Server, and the Audio Conferencing Provider (ACP) Conferencing Server. For instance, when user A wants to send an instant message to user B, user A's client sends an INVITE request to user B.

Office Communicator uses the INVITE dialog to establish various types of sessions with other users. The user negotiates what type of session she wants to create in the SDP payload of the INVITE request. Office Communicator 2007 supports the following types of sessions:

- Instant messaging (IM)
- Audio and video
- Application sharing
- Use of the whiteboard feature

With the exception of IM, these media session types are peer-to-peer sessions. Only the SIP signaling messages related to an INVITE dialog traverse the Office Communications Server, and the media itself is based on peer-to-peer communication of the information exchanged between the users in the SDP. The server does not validate or otherwise consume or modify the SDP payload located in the SIP messages. In the case of A/V conferencing, all conferencing participants establish the media session directly with the A/V Conferencing Server. In this case, media flows directly from the client to the A/V Conferencing Server, where the server mixes the media stream with the conferencing stream and broadcasts to all the participants.

Office Communications Server enables its users to create and manage an INVITE dialog (by using INVITE, ACK, CANCEL, and BYE requests). Office Communications Server does not consume any of these requests itself in a normal scenario; however, in some error cases, Office Communications Server intervenes, such as when redirecting an audio call (INVITE) to the recipient's voice mail if the caller doesn't answer the call in a timely fashion.

> ***IMPORTANT*** **An INVITE isn't used when establishing a session with the Web Conferencing Server because it doesn't support SIP—it uses a proprietary protocol named Persistent Shared Object Model (PSOM) to establish a session. The Web conferencing traffic flows from the client to the Web Conferencing Server, which then fans it out to all the participants.**

ACK

The ACK request is used in a three-way handshake, similar to TCP. If user A sends an INVITE to user B, user B accepts the session and sends a 200 OK response back to user A. Then user A's client responds with an ACK. This is the three-way handshake process to establish a session between endpoints.

CANCEL

The CANCEL request is used to cancel a session establishment process. For example, if user A sends an INVITE to user B but then decides not to go through with the call, user A's client sends a CANCEL request to user B.

BYE

The BYE request is used to terminate a session. For example, if user A and user B have established a call session and now user A has decided to hang up, user A's client sends a BYE request to user B.

MESSAGE

The MESSAGE request is used for exchanging IM messages within established sessions. IM sessions are not peer-to-peer communication because the body of a MESSAGE request is proxied through Office Communications Server to the destination user. Office Communications Server does not process the contents of a MESSAGE request (or any other client-specific requests) in any special way compared with other general SIP requests. It tries to proxy the requests as usual to the destination based on the registration information of the target user or the routing information present in the request.

Common SIP Responses

Following a SIP request, the server sends a SIP response back to the client. The SIP responses are almost a one-to-one mapping to Hypertext Transfer Protocol (HTTP) responses. In general, the following SIP responses will be sent back to the client:

- Informational
- Success
- Redirection
- Client error
- Server error
- Global failure

Informational

This response ranges from 100 to 199. This response class indicates that the server is trying to process the client's request. This response is typically followed by another response once the server has finished processing the request.

Success

This response ranges from 200 to 299. This response class indicates that the request was received and processed successfully.

Redirection

This response ranges from 300 to 399. This error class indicates that a response is being redirected to another server.

Client Error

This response ranges from 400 to 499. This error class represents client errors, such as when a server challenges the client with a password and the password fails.

Server Error

This response ranges from 500 to 599. This error class represents an error that occurred on the server, such as when the server is down and does not respond.

Global Failure

This response ranges from 600 to 699. This response represents global errors, such as when the user explicitly declines to accept a call from any endpoint.

How Office Communications Server Uses SIP

Office Communications Server uses SIP to register client endpoints, fetch and publish presence information, and help establish communications sessions between clients, such as IM, multiparty conferencing, and Voice over Internet Protocol (VoIP). Office Communications Server acts as a User Agent Server (UAS) and a SIP proxy. A UAS responds to SIP requests sent by clients, whereas a SIP proxy forwards them from one client to another.

Understanding SIP Routing

When sending SIP requests to Office Communications Server, the server makes a series of routing decisions based on predefined rules to route the requests to the right person or location depending on the types of requests and the given topology. The server uses the information in the headers in each of the requests to determine how to route the request through the network.

SIP Routing Headers

Office Communications Server uses the header information found in the SIP messages to know how to route messages through the network to the right user or location. The headers that are primarily used for routing in SIP are Record-Route, Route, Via, and Contact headers. Routing signatures are placed in the headers to guarantee the integrity of the messages.

Following is a series of requests between two clients, caller and callee, to illustrate the routing headers that are described later in this section. In the following example, the caller sends an initial INVITE request to the callee to establish a session, which the callee accepts by responding with 200 OK. The session is eventually terminated by the caller with a BYE request.

INVITE request:

```
INVITE sip:callee@example.com SIP/2.0
Via: SIP/2.0/TLS 192.168.0.1:49171
From: <sip:caller@example.com>;tag=8ca09007a0;epid=999d248d94
To: <sip:callee@example.com>
Call-ID: 886d6ef69a55472aa89cc34a69f23edc
CSeq: 1 INVITE
Contact: <sip:caller@example.com;opaque=user:epid:caller1111;gruu>
...
```

200 OK response:

```
SIP/2.0 200 OK
Via: SIP/2.0/TLS 192.168.0.1:49171
FROM: caller@example.com;tag=8ca09007a0;epid=999d248d94
TO: <sip:callee@example.com>;epid=5869277E95;tag=3a5f6462bb
```

```
CSEQ: 1 INVITE
CALL-ID: 886d6ef69a55472aa89cc34a69f23edc
Contact: <sip:callee@example.com;opaque=user:epid:callee1111;gruu>
Record-Route: <sip:srv3.example.com:5061;transport=tls>
Record-Route: <sip:srv2.example.com:5061;transport=tls>
Record-Route: <sip:srv1.example.com:443;transport=tls;ms-route-
sig=aafynjdGOoa08ORug09qSeJ6_gK5X8RZbwFpMfiAAA>
...
```

Bye request:

```
BYE sip:callee@example.com SIP/2.0
Via: SIP/2.0/TLS 192.168.0.1:49171
From: <sip:caller@example.com>;tag=8ca09007a0;epid=999d248d94
To: <sip:callee@example.com>;epid=5869277E95;tag=3a5f6462bb
Call-ID: 886d6ef69a55472aa89cc34a69f23edc
CSeq: 3 BYE
Route: <sip:srv1.example.com:443;transport=tls;ms-route-sig=aafynjdGOoa08ORug09qSeJ6_
gK5X8RZbwFpMfiAAA>
Route: <sip:srv2.example.com:5061;transport=tls>
Route: <sip:srv3.example.com:5061;transport=tls>
...
```

The preceding three SIP messages are used as examples in the following sections to demonstrate the four common routing headers. The following sections describe each of these headers and routing signatures in more detail.

Record-Route Headers

Proxy servers use Record-Route headers. A server that proxies a message can add its own fully qualified domain name (FQDN) or IP address to the Record-Route header to indicate that it wants to remain in the signaling path for all subsequent SIP traffic in the current session. For example, for security reasons, an Office Communications Server Access Edge Server inserts its FQDN into all requests. It does this to ensure that all subsequent messages in the established session have to go back through the Access Edge Server before crossing the firewall.

In the previous 200 OK response example, the message has three Record-Route headers, so these three servers—srv1.example.com, srv2.example.com, and srv3.example.com—have requested to be included in the path of all future requests in this session.

Route Headers

Route headers consist of a list of FQDNs or IP addresses of all entities in the path of a request. The client copies the Record-Route headers from the server response and uses those headers to create the Route headers for all new requests within a dialog. Upon receiving a message, each Office Communications Server removes its own FQDN or IP address from the list and forwards the message to the next URI in the Route header list.

In the preceding example, the Route headers in the BYE request demonstrate that the request follows a specific route to the recipient, which in this case is the same path defined by the Record-Route headers in the 200 OK response.

Via Headers

Via headers contain FQDNs or IP addresses of the client and all Office Communications Servers that have handled a request. Via headers are used to direct responses back to a client by using the same path by which it was sent, but in the opposite direction. A server can also inspect the Via header to determine whether it has previously handled a request.

In the preceding example, the Via header is shown in all of the requests and responses. In this snapshot where the SIP messages have been capture on the client, these messages contain only a single Via header because by the time the message reaches the client, all the additional Via headers have already been consumed and stripped off by each of the servers along the route path.

Contact Headers

A user's address, as opposed to the address of the SIP server on which the user is hosted, is stored in the Contact header. A server redirecting a message can write the address of the intended recipient in a Contact header returned in a response to the client. Subsequently, the client can contact the recipient directly without having to go through the server.

The Contact header appears in the first two messages in the preceding example. In the case of the INVITE request, the caller identifies its address. In the case of the 200 OK response, the callee identifies its address.

Route Signatures

Office Communications Server uses route signatures to guarantee the integrity of the messages flowing through the network. Without route signatures, the server would not be able to verify that the routing headers were not compromised by an attacker while traversing the network. Office Communications Server uses a cryptographic signature to verify that the packets did actually come through every hop that was expected.

Office Communications Server signs routing information in the Record-Route, Contact, and Via headers. Access Edge Servers perform the signing on connections to federated domains and untrusted connections. When signing the Record-Route and Contact headers, the signature is placed in the route URI so that it is retained in the dialog state by the clients and echoed back in Route headers in each request in the dialog. When a request is received from an untrusted network boundary (such as client or federated), Office Communications Server uses the route signature contained in the route URI to verify that the route path has not been tampered with.

In the preceding example, the route signature is shown in the *ms-route-sig* parameter of both the 200 OK response's Record-Route header and the BYE request's Route header. The routing signature appears only in the routing header belonging to the server that is directly connected to the client.

How Office Communications Server Uses SIP Routing

To demonstrate how Office Communications Server uses SIP routing, Figure 22-5 shows an example topology with a mixture of federated users, extranet clients, and intranet clients, as well as multiple pools and multiple front-end (FE) servers.

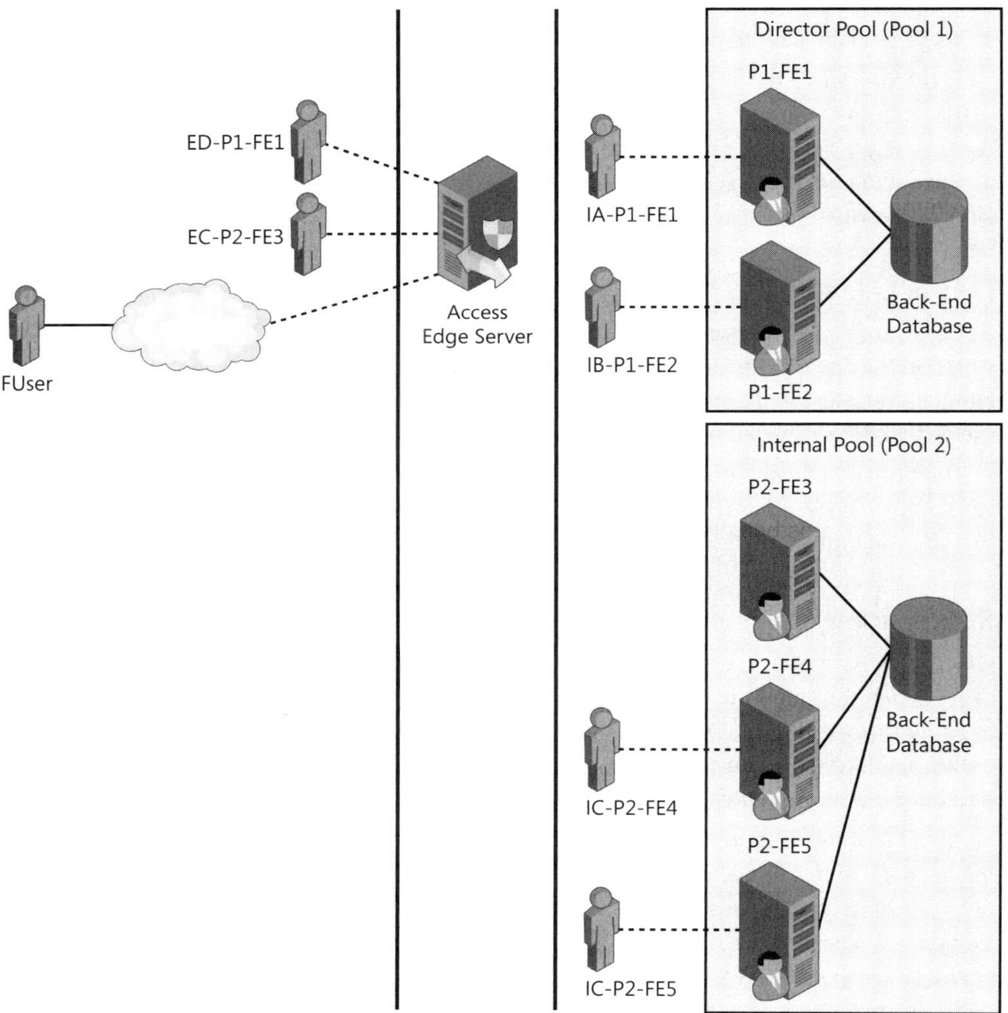

FIGURE 22-5 Sample topology

Figure 22-5 shows a sample topology with intranet users (users A, B, and C), extranet users (users C and D), and a federated user (FUser). Note that user C is both an intranet and an extranet user because the user is logged in from an internal endpoint, such as an Office Communicator Phone Edition device, and an external endpoint, such as Office Communicator running on his laptop. Federated users belong to another organization; however, they can also be users from the public cloud, such as Yahoo!, MSN, or AOL. Federated users do not belong to the enterprise but are able to get presence information and start communications with users within that enterprise. The following list identifies each type of user and how each user accesses the enterprise:

- **Intranet users** Enterprise users connected from within the enterprise
- **Extranet users** Remote enterprise users connected to the enterprise through an Access Edge Server
- **Federated users** Nonenterprise users connected to the enterprise through an Access Edge Server

Each intranet and extranet user belongs to a pool in the enterprise. Users A, B, and D belong to pool 1, and user C belongs to pool 2. In this topology, pool 1 is configured as the Director pool, and pool 2 is an internal pool. For each endpoint, a user is connected to a single FE server within their pool. For instance, user A is connected to FE server 1 in pool 1 in this figure.

The full name of each user in the diagram encapsulates whether the user is internal or external, the user's ID, the pool that the user belongs to, and the FE server that the endpoint is connected to. For example, IC-P2-FE5 indicates that user C ("C") is an internal (I) user belonging to pool 2 (P2) and connected to FE server 5 (FE5).

Routing varies depending on the type of request that comes in, who originated the request, and for whom the request is intended. All requests are first redirected (for internal users) or proxied (for external users) to the home server of the user specified in the From header for logging and registration purposes, and then the routing logic applies according to the destination in the To header. Table 22-1 describes the routing logic in the context of the example topology shown in Figure 22-5.

TABLE 22-1 Routing Logic Example

DESTINATION	ROUTE PATH	DESCRIPTION
REGISTER REQUEST		
Extranet user: Request arrives at the Access Edge Server, where it is deterministically forwarded to one of the front-end servers in the Director pool. Then it is forwarded based on which pool the user belongs to.		
Director pool	ED-P1-FE1 → Access Edge Server → P1-FE1	User ED registers itself. SA would be established on P1-FE1.

TABLE 22-1 Routing Logic Example

DESTINATION	ROUTE PATH	DESCRIPTION
Internal pool	EC-P2-FE3 → Access Edge Server → P1-FE2 → P2-FE3	User EC registers itself. The SA would be established on P1-FE2.
Intranet user: Request arrives at a pool's front-end server and is redirected based on which pool the user belongs to.		
Same pool	IA-P1-FE1 → P1-FE1	User IA registers itself. The SA would be established on P1-FE1.
Different pool	IA-P1-FE1 → P2-FE3 → P1-FE1	User IA registers itself. The SA would be established on P2-FE3.
Federated user: Request arrives at the Access Edge Server, and all requests are blocked. The Access Edge Server returns a 403 Forbidden response because Office Communications Server does not enable federated users to register with its server.		
SUBSCRIBE REQUEST		
Extranet user: Request arrives at the Access Edge Server, where it is deterministically forwarded to one of the front-end servers in the Director pool. Then it is forwarded based on which pool the user belongs to. Most likely, the SA would have been established by a prior REGISTER request.		
Director pool	ED-P1-FE1 → Access Edge Server → P1-FE1	User ED subscribes to user IB.
Internal pool	ED-P1-FE1 → Access Edge Server → P1-FE1 → P2-FE3	User ED subscribes to user IC.
Intranet user: Request arrives at the front-end server where the client is logged in and is redirected based on which pool the destination user belongs to.		
Same pool	IA-P1-FE1 →P1-FE1	User IA subscribes to its roaming contacts.
Different pool	IA-P1-FE1 →P1-FE1 →P2-FE4	User IA subscribes to user IC.
Federated user: Request arrives at the Access Edge Server, where it is deterministically forwarded to one of the front-end servers in the Director pool. Then it is forwarded based on which pool the destination user belongs to.		
Director pool	FUser →Access Edge Server →P1-FE2	FUser subscribes to user IA.
Internal pool	FUser →Access Edge Server →P1-FE2 →P2-FE4	FUser subscribes to user IC.

TABLE 22-1 Routing Logic Example

DESTINATION	ROUTE PATH	DESCRIPTION
SERVICE REQUEST		
Extranet user: Request arrives at the Access Edge Server, where it is deterministically forwarded to one of the front-end servers in the Director pool. Then it is forwarded based on which pool the user belongs to. Most likely, the SA would have been established by a prior REGISTER request.		
Director pool	EC-P2-FE3 →Access Edge Server → P1-FE2 →P2-FE3	User EC adds a new contact.
Internal pool	EC-P2-FE3 →Access Edge Server → P1-FE1 →P2-FE3 →P1-FE1	User EC issues a get presence request for user IA.
Intranet user: Request arrives at the front-end server where the client is logged in and is redirected based on which pool the destination user belongs to.		
Same pool	IB-P1-FE2 →P1-FE2	User IB deletes an existing contact.
Different pool	IB-P1-FE2 → P1-FE2 → P2-FE3	User IB issues a get presence request for user EC.
Federated user: Request comes in from a FUser to the Access Edge Server, and the Access Edge Server blocks the request because Office Communications Server does not support SERVICE requests from federated networks.		
INVITE REQUEST		
Extranet user: Request arrives at the Access Edge Server, where it is deterministically forwarded to one of the front-end servers in the Director pool. Then it is forwarded based on which pool the user belongs to. Most likely, the SA would have been established by a prior REGISTER request. The INVITE request is routed to a destination user's particular endpoint by using the Multiple Points of Presence (MPOP) routing logic.		
Director pool	ED-P1-FE1 → Access Edge Server → P1-FE1 → IB-P1-FE2	User ED sends an INVITE to user IB (user IB has only 1 endpoint, IB-P1-FE2).
Internal pool	ED-P1-FE1 → Access Edge Server → P1-FE1 → P2-FE5 → P2-FE3 → Access Edge Server → EC-P2-FE3	User ED sends an INVITE to user C (user C has three endpoints: IC-P2-FE4, IC-P2-FE5, and EC-P2-FE3. This also assumes that EC-P2-FE3 wins MPOP logic).
Federated domain	EC-P2-FE3 → Access Edge Server → P1-FE2 → P2-FE3 → P1-FE2 → Access Edge Server → FUser's federation server → Fuser	User EC sends an INVITE to FUser.

TABLE 22-1 Routing Logic Example

DESTINATION	ROUTE PATH	DESCRIPTION
Intranet user: Request arrives at the front-end server where the client is logged in and is redirected based on which pool the destination user belongs to.		
Same pool	IA-P1-FE1 → P1-FE1 → P1-FE2 → IB-P1-FE2	User IA invites user IB.
Different pool	IA-P1-FE1 → P1-FE1 → P2-FE3 → Access Edge Server → EC-P2-FE3	User IA invites user EC.
Federated user: Request comes in from a FUser to the Access Edge Server, where it is deterministically forwarded to one of the front-end servers in the Director pool. Then it is forwarded based on which pool destination the user belongs to.		
Director pool	FUser → Access Edge Server → P1-FE2 → P1-FE1 → IA-P1-FE1	FUser sends an INVITE to user IA, and user IA has only one endpoint, IA-P1-FE1.
Internal pool	FUser → Access Edge Server → P1-FE2 → P2-FE3 → Access Edge Server → EC-P2-FE3	FUser sends an INVITE to user C (user C has three endpoints: IC-P2-FE4, IC-P2-FE5, and EC-P2-FE3. This also assumes that EC-P2-FE3 wins the MPOP logic).
NOTIFY REQUEST		
Extranet user: Request is sent to a watcher, who is an extranet user.		
N/A	P2-FE5 → P2-FE3 → P1-FE2 → Access Edge Server → EC-P2-FE3	User IC-P2-FE5 changes its presence and user EC-P2-FE3 is one of its watchers.
Intranet user: request is sent to a watcher, who is an intranet user.		
N/A	P2-FE4 → P2-FE5 → IC-P2-FE5	User C has two endpoints with roaming subscriptions (IC-P2-FE4 and IC-P2-FE5). IC-P2-FE4 adds a new contact, and a roaming delta NOTIFY request is sent to IC-P2-FE5.
Federated user: Request is sent to a watcher, who is a federated user.		
N/A	P1-FE2 → Access Edge Server → FUser's federation server to FUser	User IB changes its presence and FUser is one of its watchers.

Understanding the Globally Routable User Agent URI

The Globally Routable User Agent URI (GRUU) is an extension of SIP that is currently defined in an Internet Draft published by IETF. The GRUU is specifically designed to implement reliable routing to a specific device of an end user. A plain SIP URI, such as sip:janedoe@contoso.com, is a URI that refers specifically to a user, and a GRUU is a URI that refers to a specific device. The Communicator client running on each user's computer will have its own GRUU that enables other applications to route messages specifically to a particular device. A GRUU can be used within multiple separate SIP dialogs to reach the same device. This works not just for client applications but also for server applications (for example, the Mediation Server, which was discussed in Chapter 3, "Server Roles").

The GRUU is widely applied across the server to solve a variety of problems, including but not limited to Enterprise Voice call transfer or conference escalation scenarios, which require the ability to establish a new dialog with a specific endpoint. The GRUU is also used to address scenarios where one endpoint in a dialog is server based and, therefore, the To and From headers in the dialog cannot be resolved to a specific user agent. In the original SIP standard, it is not possible to construct a URI that could be routed to and from anywhere (including the Internet) and reach a specific device or user agent.

The GRUU is a SIP URI that follows the general form shown here:

```
sip:<user>@<domain or FQDN>;opaque=<private>;grid=<optional cookie>;gruu
```

Here is an example:

```
sip:janedoe@contoso.com;opaque=user:epid:qIIWS2j5AVeD_HxnQdxmlwAA;gruu
```

The *opaque* parameter in combination with the address of record (AOR) (as in this example, janedoe@contoso.com) makes this URI unique even though the prefix of the URI is still the standard user address. The *gruu* parameter specifies that this URI has all the properties of a GRUU and can be used with multiple separate SIP dialogs to reach the same endpoint. The *grid* parameter is optional, and a user agent instance inserts it when the user agent uses the GRUU to route to itself. If the *grid* parameter is included in a request, it helps the user agent instance determine the context of the request.

GRUU Creation

The server is responsible for creating a GRUU and returning it to the client through the SIP registration mechanism if the client requests one at registration time. The GRUU returned to the client during the registration process is not managed or exposed to the administrator in any way. This process is handled entirely by the User Services module and can be inspected only by examining the registration database itself. The GRUU can be used anywhere you would normally use a URI.

How Office Communications Server Uses GRUU

Prior to Office Communications Server 2007, the server used a proprietary extension called an End-Point Identifier (EPID) to address a specific endpoint. In Office Communications Server 2007, the GRUU replaces the EPID where possible. Office Communications Server 2007 supports backward compatibility with EPIDs, but as much as possible, all new applications and clients should use the GRUU instead.

Office Communications Server uses the GRUU in the following ways:

- Communicator 2007 clients request and receive a GRUU at registration time that they will use in their Contact header for all subsequent SIP dialogs, such as Enterprise Voice calls, conferencing, and so on.
- Microsoft Live Meeting 2007 uses one aspect of GRUU known as the +sip.instance to create a unique identifier for each meeting client in a conference. This is necessary because the meeting client does not actually register with the server and therefore cannot obtain a genuine GRUU from the server for use in its SIP Contact header.
- Clients use the GRUU of the Media Relay Access Server (MRAS) application (co-located with the A/V Conferencing Server) to send requests to the MRAS without necessarily knowing the FQDN of the server or being able to directly connect to the MRAS. The client learns the MRAS application's GRUU through in-band provisioning. The A/V Conferencing Server uses the MRAS application GRUU that is configured in Windows Management Instrumentation (WMI).
- Enterprise Voice user agents send their QoS metric reports to a GRUU, which identifies the metrics collection point. (The Mediation Server and A/V Conferencing Server use the collection point GRUU that is configured in WMI.
- The voice mail server (Microsoft Exchange Server's Unified Messaging) for a given user will be identified by a GRUU. The user's client learns this GRUU through in-band provisioning (for itself) and through presence (for someone else). An application running on the server, Exchange Unified Messaging (Ex-UM) Routing, resolves the GRUU to a specific Ex-UM server that handles user voice mailboxes. An application can be written that resolves the GRUU for non–Microsoft Exchange voice mail systems.
- Pools use GRUU to address other pools for batched subscriptions.
- The Mediation Server uses GRUU to identify different outbound gateways that are connected to the Mediation Server. This enables Office Communications Server to send messages to a single FQDN/port on the Mediation Server and have the messages routed correctly to the proper outbound IP-PSTN gateway. (This GRUU is not exposed in any way to the client; it is used only for server-to-server communications.)
- During conference creation, the client addresses the Focus Factory by using a GRUU that is composed in part by the meeting organizer's SIP URI. This Focus Factory GRUU is sent to the client via in-band provisioning. The Focus Factory is the central policy and state manager for a conference and acts as the coordinator for all aspects of the conference. For details about the Focus Factory, see Chapter 6, "Conferencing Scenarios."

- Conferences are identified using a GRUU that is constructed from the organizer's SIP URI. This GRUU is routable within the SIP network and enables conference requests to be routed to the appropriate conference Focus. The Focus is the central policy and state manager for a conference and acts as the coordinator for all aspects of the conference. For details about the Focus, see Chapter 6.

Understanding Authentication

Authentication is a method of associating an identity with an entity. The process of authentication is to collect some form of authentication information from an entity, analyze it, and determine whether an identity can be associated with the entity. In computer technology, four forms of information are used to confirm an entity's identity:

- What the entity knows (such as passwords or secrets)
- What the entity is (such as biometrics)
- What the entity can do (such as typing analysis)
- What the entity has (such as a security badge)

The following sections discuss the authentication technologies—NTLM and Kerberos—that Office Communications Server uses. Digest authentication is used by anonymous conference participants, which is discussed in Chapter 4, "Infrastructure and Security Considerations."

NTLM Overview

NT LAN Manager (NTLM) is a Microsoft authentication protocol that is the successor of Microsoft LAN Manager (LANMAN). NTLM was later followed by NTLMv2, which is the strongest authentication protocol of these three. NTLM is a challenge/response authentication protocol, which means the server sends a challenge to the client that the client then encrypts with a hash of its password and responds back to the server for validation.

Kerberos Overview

Kerberos is a considerably more secure authentication protocol than NTLMv2. Kerberos provides server authentication in addition to client authentication. Unlike NTLM, Kerberos makes use of a trusted third party, called a Key Distribution Center (KDC), which maintains a database of secret keys. These secret keys are known only by the KDC and the entity requesting authentication. Knowledge of these keys proves the identity of the entity.

Where possible, the client should always try to use the most secure authentication mechanism. However, when the client is accessing the server via an external network, the server will offer only NTLMv2 authentication because the client will be unable to access the internal KDC, which runs on an Active Directory domain controller.

Security Association Establishment

At the time a client issues its first request, no security associations (SA) are between the client and any entities in the network. An SA is an establishment of shared security information between two user agents to enable them to communicate securely. Typically, the first request a client issues is a REGISTER request when it registers its presence in the network. This registration process requires the establishment of SAs between the client and any proxies in the path that have proxy-level authentication enabled. In addition, the registrar might require authentication, establishing an SA between the client and the registrar.

The establishment of an SA is based on authentication using NTLM or Kerberos. Once an SA has been established, subsequent messages are signed using this SA. Multiple SAs might be established at this time, potentially one for each proxy along the signaling path and one for the registrar itself. Each of these SAs falls under the same security domain or realm.

Refreshing a Security Association

To avoid resource denial because of an abundance of inactive SAs, SAs that are inactive are dropped by Office Communications Server. *Inactive* means no properly signed message has been received or sent within the time-to-live (TTL) interval. The TTL interval is determined based on the registration refresh interval or any other session timers in the dialogs that traverse the server. A client can avoid resource denial by issuing another request in the defined time period and signing with the SA. Any properly signed request refreshes the SA. The server resets the TTL interval of the SA every time it authenticates a request with that SA. An SA lives a maximum of 8 hours on the server, after which time the client must establish a new SA. The SA is valid for the maximum of either the lifetime of the Kerberos ticket (if Kerberos is used to establish the SA) or 8 hours.

Pre-Authentication of a Message

Once an SA has been established between a client and server, the client might want to *pre-authenticate* future requests by inserting a Proxy-Authorization header with credentials matching the SAs for proxies that are likely to be on the signaling path for that request. Pre-authenticating requests avoids one round trip from having the client's first hop server challenge a request, which it would do for a request without any Proxy-Authorization header.

Within a SIP dialog established by an INVITE, SUBSCRIBE, or REGISTER request, the client pre-authenticates the request by inserting the same set of Proxy-Authorization headers for all requests based on the proxies that challenged the first request of that session.

Additionally, the client keeps track of the SA that it established with the first authenticating proxy for REGISTER requests the client sends for registration. When the client receives a 401 or 407 challenge to a REGISTER request that is not signed by any other proxy (that is, there are no Proxy-Authentication-Info headers), the client remembers the SA established with this proxy. In all subsequent requests, the client pre-authenticates those requests by inserting a signature for the request using the SA established at registration time.

Note that in the case where a re-registration traverses a different path (and therefore has a different authenticating proxy), the new SA established with the new authenticating proxy replaces the old SA, and the client from that point onward pre-authenticates with the new SA.

How Office Communication Server Uses NTLM

During an NTLM SA establishment phase, a three-way handshake occurs between the client and the server, as detailed in the following steps.

1. The client sends a request with no credentials or authentication information. The server responds to that request with a 401 or 407 response, indicating that it supports NTLM and Kerberos and requires authentication.
2. The client re-issues the request, indicating its preference for NTLM authentication. The server responds with an appropriate challenge in a 401 or 407 response.
3. The client re-issues the request with a response to the server's challenge. The server processes the request and responds, including its signature in the response.
4. The SA is now established on both the client and server, and subsequent messages between the client and server are signed.

The call flow shown in Figure 22-6 outlines how the NTLM authentication mechanism works for a local area network (LAN) user. At this point in time, the client discovers its outbound proxy and initializes a security context with it. The outbound proxy is determined by a Domain Name System (DNS) query and differs depending on whether the user is an extranet or intranet user. For extranet users, the Access Edge Server is the outbound proxy. For intranet users, the Director generally is the outbound proxy (however, the administrator can configure it differently).

The process is detailed in the following steps.

1. Ned's client selects an Office Communications Server at random from a list of servers obtained from a DNS Service Record Locator (SRV) query. This server will be referred to as the outbound server.
2. Ned's client sends a REGISTER request with no credentials (that is, no Proxy-Authorization header) to the outbound server it selected. In the following example, the FQDN of the server selected by Ned's client is registrar.litwareinc.com.

```
REGISTER sip:registrar.litwareinc.com SIP/2.0
Via: SIP/2.0/TLS ned1.litwareinc.com;branch=z9hG4bK7
From: "Ned" <sip:ned@litwareinc.com>;tag=354354535;epid=6534555
To: "Ned" <sip:ned@litwareinc.com>
Call-ID: 123213@ned1.litwareinc.com
CSeq: 12345 REGISTER
Max-Forwards: 70
User-Agent: Windows RTC/1.1.2600
Contact: "Ned" <sip:ned@ned1.litwareinc.com>
Content-Length: 0
```

The *epid* parameter on the From header uniquely identifies this particular endpoint of the user. The server uses this *epid* value in subsequent messages to determine the SA with which to sign the message. The server establishes a different SA for each endpoint (client) the user signs in from.

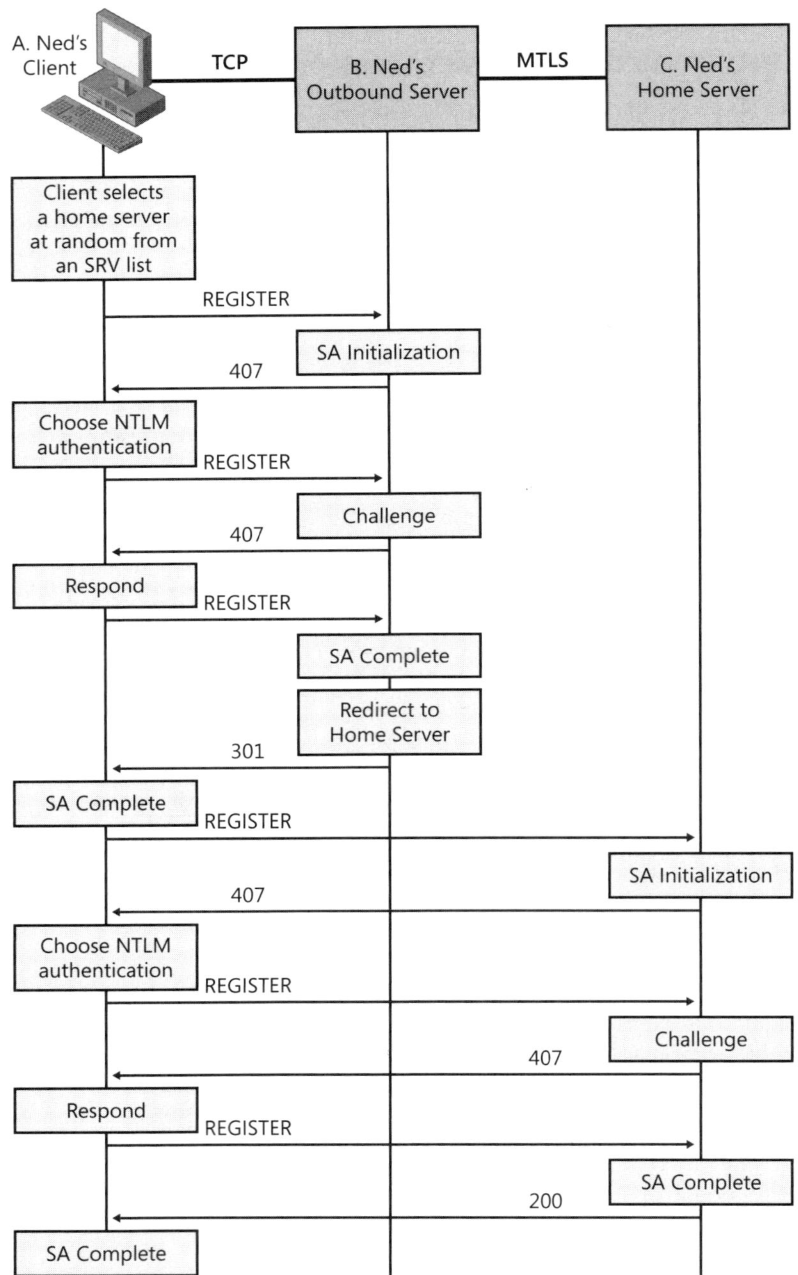

FIGURE 22-6 NTLM call flow example

3. Authentication is enabled at the outbound server, and it challenges Ned's client. The server indicates support for NTLM and Kerberos in the challenge.

```
SIP/2.0 407 Proxy Authentication Required
Via: SIP/2.0/TLS ned1.litwareinc.com;branch=z9hG4bK7
From: "Ned" <sip:ned@litwareinc.com>;tag=354354535;epid=6534555
To: "Ned" <sip:ned@litwareinc.com>;tag=5564566
Call-ID: 123213@ned1.litwareinc.com
CSeq: 12345 REGISTER
Date: Sat, 13 Nov 2010 23:29:00 GMT
Proxy-Authenticate: Kerberos realm="SIP Communications Service",
   targetname="sip/hs1.litwareinc.com", qop="auth"
Proxy-Authenticate: NTLM realm="SIP Communications Service", targetname="hs1.
litwareinc.com", qop="auth"
Content-Length: 0
```

The *targetname* parameter carries the FQDN of the outbound server for NTLM and the service principal name (SPN) of the outbound server for Kerberos. The actual contents of this parameter must be meaningful for this outbound server, but they are opaque to other proxies and the client. It is merely a unique string for correlation of the message header to an SA. Two Proxy-Authenticate headers are present, indicating the server's ability to do either Kerberos or NTLM authentication.

The outbound server inserts a Date header in the 407 challenge to enable the client to detect clock skew between the client and server. Both NTLMv2 and Kerberos V5 require synchronization of the client and server clocks. Clock skew can cause authentication to fail even with valid credentials. The presence of the Date header enables the client to log this condition and the administrator to correct the deviation.

4. The client re-issues the REGISTER request, indicating support for NTLM authentication.

```
REGISTER sip:registrar.litwareinc.com SIP/2.0
Via: SIP/2.0/TLS ned1.litwareinc.com;branch=z9hG4bK8
From: "Ned" <sip:ned@litwareinc.com>;tag=354354535;epid=6534555
To: "Ned" <sip:ned@litwareinc.com>
Call-ID: 123213@ned1.litwareinc.com
CSeq: 12346 REGISTER
Max-Forwards: 70
User-Agent: Windows RTC/1.1.2600
Proxy-Authorization: NTLM realm="SIP Communications Service",
   targetname="hs1.litwareinc.com",qop="auth",gssapi-data=""
Contact: "Ned" <sip:ned@ned1.litwareinc.com>
Content-Length: 0
```

The *Cseq* header value has been incremented. The *Cseq* header value is a command sequence number and is incremented by the client. The *Call-ID* and *epid* remain the same. The Call-ID header is used to uniquely identify a session between two clients.

The *targetname* parameter echoes the value of the *targetname* parameter in the previous Proxy-Authenticate header. The empty *gssapi-data* parameter indicates that no credentials (password) are being sent in this header. The choice of NTLM authentication is indicated by the scheme (*NTLM*) shown as the first token in the Proxy-Authorization header.

5. The outbound server responds with a 407 response containing a Proxy-Authenticate header, which includes the NTLM challenge.

```
SIP/2.0 407 Proxy Authentication Required
Via: SIP/2.0/TLS ned1.litwareinc.com;branch=z9hG4bK8
From: "Ned" <sip:ned@litwareinc.com>;tag=354354535;epid=6534555
To: "Ned" <sip:ned@litwareinc.com>;tag=5564566
Call-ID: 123213@ned1.litwareinc.com
CSeq: 12346 REGISTER
Date: Sat, 13 Nov 2010 23:29:00 GMT
Proxy-Authenticate: NTLM realm="SIP Communications Service",
   targetname="hs1.litwareinc.com", qop="auth", gssapi-data
="345435acdecbba",opaque="ACDC123"
Content-Length: 0
```

The *gssapi-data* parameter carries the challenge. The *opaque* parameter serves as an index to the incomplete SA state on the outbound server.

6. Ned's client re-issues the REGISTER request with a response to the outbound server's challenge.

```
REGISTER sip:registrar.litwareinc.com SIP/2.0
Via: SIP/2.0/TLS ned1.litwareinc.com;branch=z9hG4bK9
From: "Ned" <sip:ned@litwareinc.com>;tag=354354535;epid=6534555
To: "Ned" <sip:ned@litwareinc.com>
Call-ID: 123213@ned1.litwareinc.com
CSeq: 12347 REGISTER
Max-Forwards: 70
User-Agent: Windows RTC/1.1.2600
Proxy-Authorization: NTLM realm="SIP Communications Service",
   targetname="hs1.litwareinc.com",qop="auth",
gssapi-data="34fcdf9345345",opaque="ACDC123"
Contact: "Ned" <sip:ned@ned1.litwareinc.com>
Content-Length: 0
```

The *Cseq* header value has been incremented. The *Call-ID* and *epid* remain the same. The *gssapi-data* parameter carries the client's response to the challenge. The *opaque* parameter is echoed from the previous challenge.

Upon receipt of the REGISTER request, the outbound server authenticates the user with the information in the Proxy-Authorization header. Authentication succeeds, and an SA is created in the outbound server for Ned's client.

7. The outbound server then redirects the REGISTER request to point the client at the appropriate home server for this user. The redirect response is signed using the newly established SA between the client and this proxy.

```
SIP/2.0 301 Moved Permanently
Via: SIP/2.0/TLS ned1.litwareinc.com;branch=z9hG4bK9
From: "Ned" <sip:ned@litwareinc.com>;tag=354354535;epid=6534555
To: "Ned" <sip:ned@litwareinc.com>
Call-ID: 123213@ned1.litwareinc.com
CSeq: 12347 REGISTER
Proxy-Authenticate-Info: NTLM realm="SIP Communications Service",
   targetname="hs1.litwareinc.com", qop="auth", opaque="ACDC123",
srand="3453453", snum=1, rspauth="23423acfdee2"
Contact: <sip:hs2.litwareinc.com>
Content-Length: 0
```

The Proxy-Authenticate-Info header carries the signature for this SIP message. The *snum* parameter is set to 1 because this is the first message signed with the newly established SA. The *srand* parameter contains the random *SALT* value used by the server to generate the signature.

8. The client receives the redirect response, verifies the signature by using the now complete SA for the outbound server, and re-issues the REGISTER request to its proper home server, hs2.litwareinc.com, as specified in the Contact header.

```
REGISTER sip:hs2.litwareinc.com SIP/2.0
Via: SIP/2.0/TLS ned1.litwareinc.com;branch=z9hG4bKa
From: "Ned" <sip:ned@litwareinc.com>;tag=354354535;epid=6534555
To: "Ned" <sip:ned@litwareinc.com>
Call-ID: 123213@ned1.litwareinc.com
CSeq: 12348 REGISTER
Max-Forwards: 70
User-Agent: Windows RTC/1.1.2600
Contact: "Ned" <sip:ned@ned1.litwareinc.com>
Content-Length: 0
```

The client replaces its current outbound server with the proxy indicated in the Contact header of the 301 response. The REGISTER request is sent to this new proxy, hs2.litwareinc.com (the user's true home server). Because no SA exists yet with this new proxy, no Proxy-Authenticate header is present in the request.

9. Ned's home server receives the REGISTER request and issues a challenge indicating support for NTLM and Kerberos authentication.

```
SIP/2.0 407 Proxy Authentication Required
Via: SIP/2.0/TLS ned1.litwareinc.com;branch=z9hG4bKa
From: "Ned" <sip:ned@litwareinc.com>;tag=354354535;epid=6534555
To: "Ned" <sip:ned@litwareinc.com>;tag=8823488
Call-ID: 123213@ned1.litwareinc.com
CSeq: 12348 REGISTER
Date: Sat, 13 Nov 2010 23:29:00 GMT
Proxy-Authenticate: Kerberos realm="Litwareinc RTC Service
   Provider", targetname="hs2.litwareinc.com", qop="auth"
Proxy-Authenticate: NTLM realm="SIP Communications Service",
   targetname="hs2.litwareinc.com", qop="auth"
Content-Length: 0
```

The *targetname* parameter contains the FQDN for Ned's home server. The two Proxy-Authenticate headers indicate support for Kerberos and NTLM, respectively. The *realm* is the same as for HS1 because they fall under the same protection space. This means the client will use the same credentials in responding to HS2's challenge.

10. Ned's client receives the challenge, selects NTLM authentication, and re-issues the REGISTER request to his home server.

```
REGISTER sip:hs2.litwareinc.com SIP/2.0
Via: SIP/2.0/TLS ned1.litwareinc.com;branch=z9hG4bKb
From: "Ned" <sip:ned@litwareinc.com>;tag=354354535;epid=6534555
To: "Ned" <sip:ned@litwareinc.com>
Call-ID: 123213@ned1.litwareinc.com
CSeq: 12349 REGISTER
Max-Forwards: 70
User-Agent: Windows RTC/1.1.2600
Proxy-Authorization: NTLM realm="SIP Communications Service",
   targetname="hs2.litwareinc.com",qop="auth",gssapi-data=""
Contact: "Ned" <sip:ned@ned1.litwareinc.com>
Content-Length: 0
```

The *Cseq* header value is incremented. The *Call-ID* and *epid* remain the same. The Proxy-Authorization header indicates support for NTLM authentication.

11. Ned's home server receives the REGISTER request and issues an appropriate NTLM challenge.

```
SIP/2.0 407 Proxy Authentication Required
Via: SIP/2.0/TLS ned1.litwareinc.com;branch=z9hG4bKb
From: "Ned" <sip:ned@litwareinc.com>;tag=354354535;epid=6534555
To: "Ned" <sip:ned@litwareinc.com>;tag=8823488
```

```
Call-ID: 123213@ned1.litwareinc.com
CSeq: 12349 REGISTER
Date: Sat, 13 Nov 2010 23:29:00 GMT
Proxy-Authenticate: NTLM realm="SIP Communications Service",
   targetname="hs2.litwareinc.com", qop="auth", opaque="CDEF1245",
gssapi-data="dfd345435d"
Content-Length: 0
```

The *gssapi-data* parameter contains the NTLM challenge. The *opaque* parameter identifies the incomplete SA on Ned's home server.

12. Ned's client responds to the challenge from Ned's home server by re-issuing the REGISTER request.

```
REGISTER sip:hs2.litwareinc.com SIP/2.0
Via: SIP/2.0/TLS ned1.litwareinc.com;branch=z9hG4bKc
From: "Ned" <sip:ned@litwareinc.com>;tag=354354535;epid=6534555
To: "Ned" <sip:ned@litwareinc.com>
Call-ID: 123213@ned1.litwareinc.com
CSeq: 12350 REGISTER
Max-Forwards: 70
User-Agent: Windows RTC/1.1.2600
Proxy-Authorization: NTLM realm="SIP Communications Service",
   targetname="hs2.litwareinc.com",qop="auth",
gssapi-data="8234934234", opaque="CDEF1245"
Contact: "Ned" <sip:ned@ned1.litwareinc.com>
Content-Length: 0
```

The *CSeq* header value is incremented. The *Call-ID* remains the same. The *opaque* parameter is echoed from the server's challenge. The *gssapi-data* parameter carries the response to the server's challenge.

13. Ned's home server receives the REGISTER request, verifies the response to its challenge, and processes the REGISTER request. The SA between Ned's home server and Ned's client is now complete. The server responds to the REGISTER request and signs the response by using the newly completed SA. The *epid* parameter from the From header is saved as part of the registration information for Ned. This value will be inserted in the To header of subsequent requests that are forwarded to Ned via his home server (registrar).

```
SIP/2.0 200 OK
Via: SIP/2.0/TLS ned1.litwareinc.com;branch=z9hG4bKc
From: "Ned" <sip:ned@litwareinc.com>;tag=354354535;epid=6534555
To: "Ned" <sip:ned@litwareinc.com>;tag=8823488
Call-ID: 123213@ned1.litwareinc.com
CSeq: 12350 REGISTER
```

```
Expires: 3600
Proxy-Authentication-Info: NTLM realm="SIP Communications Service",
   targetname="hs2.litwareinc.com", qop="auth", opaque="CDEF1245",
   rspauth="fefeacdd", srand=98984345, snum=1
Contact: "Ned" <sip:ned@ned1.litwareinc.com>
Content-Length: 0
```

The server uses the *epid* parameter on the From header to determine how to sign this response (find the SA). The signature for this response is carried in the *rspauth* parameter of the Proxy-Authentication-Info header.

How Office Communication Server Uses Kerberos

During a Kerberos SA establishment phase, a two-way handshake occurs between the client and the server, as detailed in the following steps.

1. The client sends a request with no credential or authentication information. The server responds to that request with a 401 or 407 response, indicating that it supports NTLM and Kerberos and requires authentication.
2. The client requests a Kerberos ticket for the server from a KDC and re-issues the request with this encoded Kerberos ticket information.
3. The server processes the request and responds, including its signature in the response.
4. The SA is now established on both the client and server, and subsequent messages between the client and server are signed.

With Kerberos, the client first acquires a Kerberos ticket from the KDC (on an Active Directory domain controller) for the specific server that is issuing the challenge. The server is identified by an SPN containing a FQDN.

If the client is configured to talk to its local outbound proxy via Transport Layer Security (TLS), the client enables any SPN for the very first challenge it receives. Otherwise, the client requires that the SPN for the very first challenge it receives match *sip:<FQDN of local outbound proxy>*. The intention is to require either TLS connectivity to the service provider or the local outbound proxy to authenticate to the client. The SPN for a challenge is carried in the *targetname* parameter in the Proxy-Authenticate header of the challenge.

In the event the client receives a challenge with an SPN of any other form, particularly one that has a service other than "sip", the client ignores the challenge (response) and, as necessary, fails the request if no other final response is received. This action is taken to prevent an attacker from obtaining Kerberos tickets from the client for any other service besides Office Communications Server.

The SPN of the server is associated with the service account under which the Office Communications Server runs. This association is managed in Active Directory and initialized at the time of installation of the server. Any changes in either the FQDN or the service account of the server require the administrator to re-establish this association of SPN to server.

NOTE The lifetime of the SA established using Kerberos is set to 8 hours (the same as for NTLM) regardless of the lifetime of the Kerberos ticket. If the Kerberos ticket expires before 8 hours, the underlying Security Support Provider Interface (SSPI) calls to verify or create a signature for a message will fail and, if possible, the server will challenge the request to establish a new SA.

The call flow shown in Figure 22-7 outlines how the Kerberos authentication mechanism works.

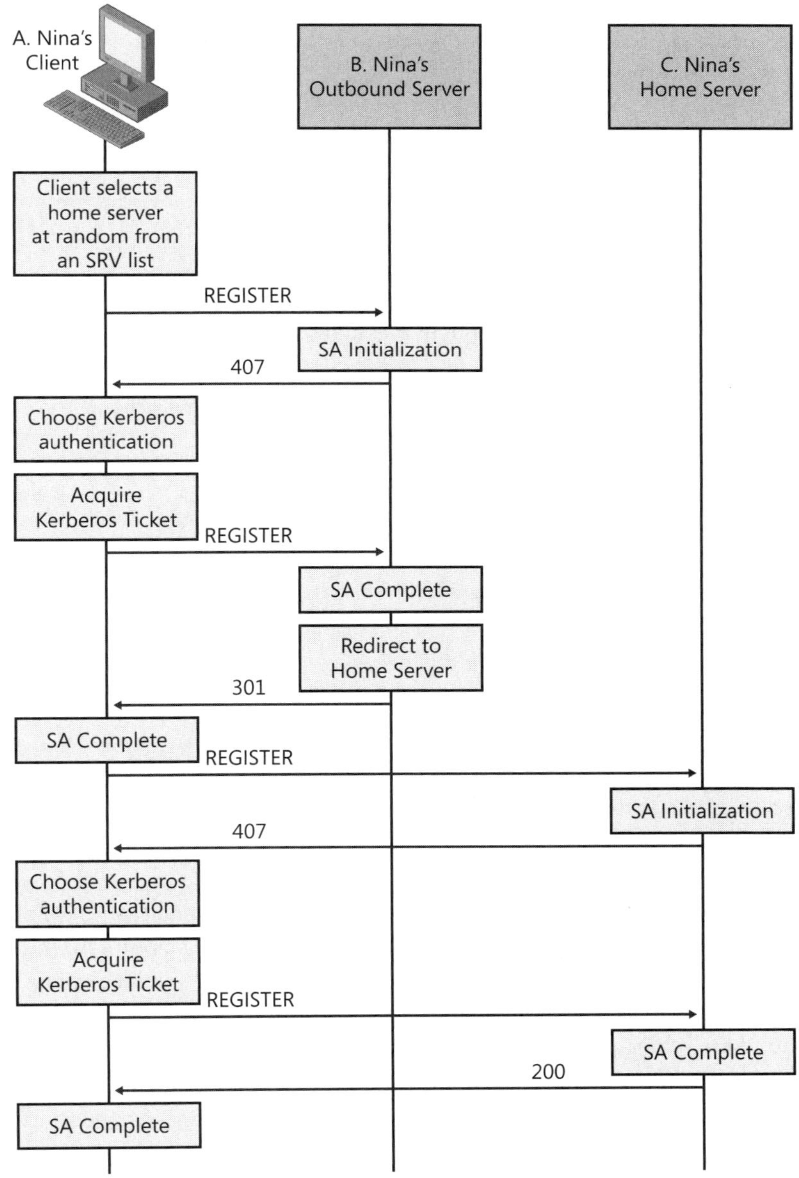

FIGURE 22-7 Kerberos call flow example

The process is detailed in the following steps.

1. Nina's client selects a home server at random from a list of servers attained from a DNS SRV query.
2. Nina's client sends a REGISTER request with no credentials (that is, no Proxy-Authorization header) to the outbound server it selected.

```
REGISTER sip:registrar.litwareinc.com SIP/2.0
Via: SIP/2.0/TLS ned1.litwareinc.com;branch=z9hG4bK7
From: "Nina" <sip:nina@litwareinc.com>;tag=354354535;epid=6534555
To: "Nina" <sip:nina@litwareinc.com>
Call-ID: 123213@nina1.litwareinc.com
CSeq: 12345 REGISTER
Max-Forwards: 70
User-Agent: Windows RTC/1.1.2600
Contact: "Nina" <sip:nina@nina1.litwareinc.com>
Content-Length: 0
```

   The *epid* parameter on the From header uniquely identifies this particular endpoint for the user. The server uses this value in subsequent messages to determine the SA with which to sign the message.
3. Authentication is enabled at the outbound server, and it challenges Nina's client. The server indicates support for NTLM and Kerberos in the challenge.

```
SIP/2.0 407 Proxy Authentication Required
Via: SIP/2.0/TLS nina1.litwareinc.com;branch=z9hG4bK7
From: "Nina" <sip:nina@litwareinc.com>;tag=354354535;epid=6534555
To: "Nina" <sip:nina@litwareinc.com>;tag=5564566
Call-ID: 123213@nina1.litwareinc.com
CSeq: 12345 REGISTER
Date: Sat, 13 Nov 2010 23:29:00 GMT
Proxy-Authenticate: Kerberos realm="SIP Communications Service",
   targetname="sip/hs1.litwareinc.com", qop="auth"
Proxy-Authenticate: NTLM realm="Litwareinc RTC Service Provider",
   targetname="hs1.litwareinc.com", qop="auth"
Content-Length: 0
```

   The *targetname* parameter carries the SPN for this proxy for Kerberos and the FQDN of the proxy for NTLM. The actual contents of this parameter must be meaningful for this proxy, but they are opaque to other proxies and the client. It is merely a unique string for correlation of the message header to an SA. Two Proxy-Authenticate headers are present, indicating the server's ability to do either Kerberos or NTLM authentication.

   The proxy inserts a Date header in the 407 challenge to enable the client to detect clock skew between the client and server. Both NTLMv2 and Kerberos V5 require synchronization of the client and server clocks. Clock skew can cause authentication to fail even with valid credentials. The presence of the Date header enables the client to log this condition and the administrator to correct the deviation.

4. The client acquires a Kerberos ticket for the outbound server indicated in the *target-name* of the Kerberos Proxy-Authenticate header. The client re-issues the request with a Proxy-Authorization header containing the encoded Kerberos ticket.

```
REGISTER sip:registrar.litwareinc.com SIP/2.0
Via: SIP/2.0/TLS nina1.litwareinc.com;branch=z9hG4bK9
From: "Nina" <sip:nina@litwareinc.com>;tag=354354535;epid=6534555
To: "Nina" <sip:nina@litwareinc.com>
Call-ID: 123213@nina1.litwareinc.com
CSeq: 12346 REGISTER
Max-Forwards: 70
User-Agent: Windows RTC/1.1.2600
Proxy-Authorization: Kerberos realm="SIP Communications Service",
   targetname="sip/hs1.litwareinc.com",qop="auth",
gssapi-data="34fcdf9345345"
Contact: "Ned" <sip:ned@ned1.litwareinc.com>
Content-Length: 0
```

The *Cseq* header value has been incremented. The *Call-ID* and *epid* remain the same.

The *targetname* parameter echoes the value of the *targetname* parameter in the previous Proxy-Authenticate header. The *gssapi-data* parameter contains the Kerberos ticket information. The choice of Kerberos authentication is indicated by the scheme (*Kerberos*) as the first token in the header.

5. Upon reception of the REGISTER request, the outbound server authenticates the user with the information in the Proxy-Authorization header. Authentication succeeds, and an SA is created in the outbound server for Nina's client.

   The outbound server then redirects the REGISTER request to point the client at the appropriate home server for this user. The redirect response is signed using the newly established SA between the client and this proxy.

```
SIP/2.0 301 Moved Permanently
Via: SIP/2.0/TLS nina1.litwareinc.com;branch=z9hG4bK9
From: "Nina" <sip:nina@litwareinc.com>;tag=354354535;epid=6534555
To: "Nina" <sip:nina@litwareinc.com>
Call-ID: 123213@nina1.litwareinc.com
CSeq: 12346 REGISTER
Proxy-Authenticate-Info: Kerberos realm="SIP Communications Service",
   targetname="sip/hs1.litwareinc.com", qop="auth", opaque="ACDC123",
   srand="3453453", snum=1, rspauth="23423acfdee2"
Contact: <sip:hs2.litwareinc.com>
Content-Length: 0
```

The Proxy-Authenticate-Info header carries the signature for this SIP message. The *snum* parameter is set to 1 because this is the first message signed with the newly established SA. The *srand* parameter contains the random *SALT* value the server uses to generate the signature. The *opaque* parameter contains a unique token for this newly established SA.

6. The client receives the redirect response, verifies the signature using the now complete SA for the outbound proxy, and re-issues the REGISTER request to its proper home server.

```
REGISTER sip:hs2.litwareinc.com SIP/2.0
Via: SIP/2.0/TLS nina1.litwareinc.com;branch=z9hG4bKa
From: "Nina" <sip:nina@litwareinc.com>;tag=354354535;epid=6534555
To: "Nina" <sip:nina@litwareinc.com>
Call-ID: 123213@nina1.litwareinc.com
CSeq: 12347 REGISTER
Max-Forwards: 70
User-Agent: Windows RTC/1.1.2600
Contact: "Nina" <sip:nina@nina1.litwareinc.com>
Content-Length: 0
```

The client replaces its current outbound proxy with the proxy indicated in the Contact header of the 301 response. The REGISTER request is sent to this new outbound proxy (the user's true home server). Because no SA exists yet with this new outbound proxy, no Proxy-Authorization header is present in the request.

7. Nina's home server receives the REGISTER request and issues a challenge indicating support for NTLM and Kerberos.

```
SIP/2.0 407 Proxy Authentication Required
Via: SIP/2.0/TLS nina1.litwareinc.com;branch=z9hG4bKa
From: "Nina" <sip:nina@litwareinc.com>;tag=354354535;epid=6534555
To: "Nina" <sip:nina@litwareinc.com>;tag=8823488
Call-ID: 123213@nina1.litwareinc.com
CSeq: 12347 REGISTER
Date: Sat, 13 Nov 2010 23:29:00 GMT
Proxy-Authenticate: Kerberos realm="SIP Communications Service",
   targetname="sip/hs2.litwareinc.com", qop="auth"
Proxy-Authenticate: NTLM realm="Litwareinc RTC Service Provider",
   targetname="hs2.litwareinc.com", qop="auth"
Content-Length: 0
```

The *targetname* parameter for Kerberos contains the SPN for Nina's home server. The two Proxy-Authenticate headers indicate support for Kerberos and NTLM, respectively. The *realm* is the same as for HS1 because they fall under the same protection space. This means the client will use the same credentials in responding to HS2's challenge.

8. Nina's client receives the challenge, selects Kerberos authentication, and re-issues the REGISTER request to her home server. The client acquires a Kerberos ticket for HS2 and includes this information in the *gssapi-data* parameter of the Proxy-Authorization header.

```
REGISTER sip:hs2.litwareinc.com SIP/2.0
Via: SIP/2.0/TLS nina1.litwareinc.com;branch=z9hG4bKc
From: "Nina" <sip:nina@litwareinc.com>;tag=354354535;epid=6534555
To: "Nina" <sip:nina@litwareinc.com>
Call-ID: 123213@nina1.litwareinc.com
CSeq: 12348 REGISTER
Max-Forwards: 70
User-Agent: Windows RTC/1.1.2600
Proxy-Authorization: Kerberos realm="SIP Communications Service",
   targetname="sip/hs2.litwareinc.com",qop="auth",
gssapi-data="8234934234", opaque="CDEF1245"
Contact: "Ned" <sip:ned@ned1.litwareinc.com>
Content-Length: 0
```

The *Cseq* header value is incremented. The *Call-ID* and *epid* remain the same. The Proxy-Authorization header indicates support for Kerberos authentication.

9. Nina's home server receives the REGISTER request, verifies the Kerberos ticket, and processes the REGISTER request. The SA between Nina's home server and Nina's client is now complete. The server responds to the REGISTER request and signs the response by using the newly completed SA. The *epid* parameter from the From header is saved as part of the registration information for Nina. This value will be inserted in the To header of subsequent requests that are forwarded to Nina via her home server (registrar).

```
SIP/2.0 200 OK
Via: SIP/2.0/TLS nina1.litwareinc.com;branch=z9hG4bKc
From: "Nina" <sip:nina@litwareinc.com>;tag=354354535;epid=6534555
To: "Nina" <sip:nina@litwareinc.com>;tag=8823488
Call-ID: 123213@nina1.litwareinc.com
CSeq: 12348 REGISTER
Expires: 3600
Proxy-Authentication-Info: Kerberos realm="SIP Communications
   Service", targetname="sip/hs2.litwareinc.com", qop="auth",
opaque="CDEF1245", rspauth="fefeacdd", srand=98984345, snum=1
Contact: "Nina" <sip:nina@nina1.litwareinc.com>
Content-Length: 0
```

The server uses the *epid* parameter on the From header to determine how to sign this response (that is, to find the SA). The signature for this response is carried in the *rspauth* parameter of the Proxy-Authentication-Info header. The *opaque* parameter indicates the newly established SA. Because this is the first signed message from HS2 to the client, the *snum* parameter is set to 1.

The server generally challenges with a 407 response. The headers associated with proxy authentication are Proxy-Authenticate, Proxy-Authentication-Info, and Proxy-Authorization. The format and content of these headers correspond to the WWW-Authenticate, Authentication-Info, and Authorization headers, respectively, which are used in conjunction with a 401 response. Either a 401 or a 407 response achieves the goals of this document.

The server inserts a Date header into all 407 responses to the client so that the client can detect clock skew, which can cause NTLMv2 and Kerberos V5 authentication to fail.

The Proxy-Authenticate header is used to signal that a proxy requires authentication and to carry a challenge (from a proxy) during the SA initialization phase. The server initially inserts one Proxy-Authenticate header for every authentication method it supports (for example, NTLM, Kerberos, and so on). In the event the request has been forked, it is also possible to receive a 407 response containing a list of Proxy-Authenticate headers—one for each proxy that requested authentication.

The Proxy-Authorization header is used to carry the client's response to a challenge from an Office Communications Server (proxy). A client also uses it in signing a request or response. There might be more than one *Proxy-Authorization* header in a given request/response—one for each proxy with which the client has an SA established on this signaling path.

The Proxy-Authentication-Info header is used to carry the signature created by the Office Communications Server for a request or response once an SA has been established with the client.

The protocol information used during the SA establishment phase differs from the information used once an SA has been established. During the establishment phase, the *gssapi-data* parameter carries the bulk of the credentials information. The *realm* parameter provides additional context information. Once an SA has been established, the *srand*, *crand*, *cnum*, *snum*, and *opaque* parameters are used in the signing of requests and responses. Those signatures are carried in the *response* and *rspauth* parameters.

Troubleshooting Authentication

In the event that problems occur while signing in to Office Communications Server, a 401 response might be sent back to the client even though users have provided valid sign-in credentials. This can occur if you have configured Office Communications Server to use Kerberos authentication and one of the following is true:

- NetBIOS is disabled on the computer
- The computer is running Microsoft Windows XP Home Edition
- The computer is configured to run behind an Internet Connection Sharing device or behind another Universal Plug and Play (UPnP) Network Address Translation (NAT) device

- The computer is not joined to the same domain as the Office Communications Server computer
- The account is disabled, or time-based restrictions apply to the account login

In certain Office Communications Server topologies, you cannot successfully sign in by entering your credentials in the user principal name (UPN) format (username@example.com). You might have to specify the FQDN together with your user name when you enter it in Universal Naming Convention (UNC) format to successfully sign in. For example, when you type your user name information in a dialog box, you might have to use the following format to successfully sign in:

```
domain.example.com\username
```

Where *domain.example.com* is the FQDN of your domain, and *username* is your user name. If entering the FQDN of your domain does not work, try enabling NTLM instead of Kerberos.

Summary

This chapter provided a technical overview of four major areas of Office Communications Server technologies: SIP, SIP routing, GRUU, and authentication. These fundamental areas are necessary for establishing secure communications in your deployment. Now that you have read this chapter, you should have a better understanding of the main SIP requests that are used to establish communication sessions and what SIP call flows look like. You should also be familiar with routing logic that Office Communications Server uses to route these main SIP requests inside and outside the enterprise. Finally, you should have an understanding of authentication technologies used when signing in to Office Communications Server and the different call flows for these technologies. There are additional resources you can leverage to gain a deeper understanding of each of these areas, and this information is provided in the next section.

Additional Resources

For product documentation, community tools, frequently asked questions (FAQs), discussion groups, and pointers to up-to-date information on product and community events, see the Office Communications Server home page at *http://go.microsoft.com/fwlink/?LinkID=133631*. The following resources contain additional information and tools related to this chapter:

- Additional information about NTLM and Kerberos requirements, also know as Integrated Windows Authentication (IIS 6.0) found at *http://go.microsoft.com/fwlink/?LinkID=133761*.
- For more Information about TLS, found at *http://go.microsoft.com/fwlink/?LinkID=133762*.
- For information about SIP, see "Session Initiation Protocol [RFC 3261]," *http://go.microsoft.com/fwlink/?LinkID=133679*.

- For more information about event notifications, see "Session Initiation Protocol (SIP) Specific Event Notification [RFC 3265]," *http://go.microsoft.com/fwlink/?LinkID=133763*.
- For information about TLS, see "The TLS Protocol [RFC 2246]," *http://go.microsoft.com/fwlink/?LinkID=134678*.
- For more information about GRUU, see the current GRUU Mechanism Internet Draft, found at *http://go.microsoft.com/fwlink/?LinkID=133764*.
- For more information about NTLM, Kerberos, and TLS/SSL, see the Windows Security Collection of the Windows 2003 Technical Reference, found at *http://go.microsoft.com/fwlink/?LinkID=133678*.
- Additional information about how to enable NTLM version 2, found at *http://support.microsoft.com/kb/239869*.
- For more information about SOAP, see *http://go.microsoft.com/fwlink/?LinkID=133766*.
- Additional information about NTLM and Kerberos requirements, found at *http://go.microsoft.com/fwlink/?LinkID=133761*.
- Additional customizations enable application developers to create custom clients for publishing and subscribing to other publications from different clients. For more information about creating custom clients for publishing and subscribing to other publications from different clients, see the Unified Communications Managed API documentation at *http://go.microsoft.com/fwlink/?LinkID=133767*.
- For more information about problems signing in to Live Communications Server, see the Microsoft Knowledge Base article about NTLM and Kerberos at *http://go.microsoft.com/fwlink/?LinkID=133768*.
- For more information about enabling diagnostic logging for Office Communicator and Windows Messenger, see the Microsoft Knowledge Base article about NTLM and Kerberos at *http://go.microsoft.com/fwlink/?LinkID=133769*.
- For more information about enabling NTLM 2 authentication, see the Microsoft Knowledge Base article about Integrated Windows Authentication (IIS 6.0) (formerly NTLM) at *http://go.microsoft.com/fwlink/?LinkID=133765*.

Index

Symbols and Numbers

A

B

C

D

E

F

G

H

N

O

Q

R

S

T

U

V

W

X

Y

Z

About the Authors

Rui Maximo is a Senior Technical Writer in the Office Communications Group. He has worked on different aspects of the product (management, migration, topology, Voice over Internet Protocol [VoIP], Communicator Web Access), and shipped Live Communications Server 2003, 2005, Service Pack 1 (SP1), and Office Communications Server 2007 as a lead program manager and program manager. With 12 years of experience at Microsoft, Rui has been fortunate to work in diverse roles (program manager, software design engineer, software design engineer in test) and various products (including Windows NT 4.0 Option Pack, Windows 2000, Windows XP, Smartphone 2002, Pocket PC 2002, and Microsoft Information Server 2002), primarily focused on security. Rui holds a master's degree in mathematics, specializing in abstract algebra and cryptography. Prior to Microsoft, Rui worked at IBM as a software tester and at Brigham Young University as a UNIX administrator.

Rick Kingslan is a Senior Technical Writer in the Office Communications Group. Rick worked as both contributing author and technical reviewer for the *Office Communications Server 2007 Resource Kit* book. Prior to joining the Office Communications Server product group, he worked as a Consultant in U.S. Services, Microsoft Consulting Services (MCS) delivering solutions to enterprise customers by assisting them with the process and project management of implementing infrastructure services in their environment. Specifically, Rick worked with Windows Server, Exchange Server, Internet Security and Acceleration Server, desktop deployment and maintenance, and Office Communications Server /Live Communications Server. Rick is also versed in security practices, holds the Certified Information Security Systems Professional (CISSP) credential, and has helped enterprises attain higher levels of security with smarter implementations of security processes. In the year prior to leaving MCS (June 2007 to July 2008), Rick worked with the Windows Server 2008 and Vista SWAT Team as a subject matter expert on solving application compatibility issues with both operating systems and customer applications. He also delivered 20+ workshops in 12 countries to independent software vendors (ISVs) and enterprise customers on how to adapt their software to work with Windows Server 2008 and Vista. Rick has been with Microsoft since 2005 and has worked in various areas of information technology for nearly 25 years.

Rajesh Ramanathan is a Lead Program Manager on the Microsoft Office Communicator product team. His team shipped VoIP, instant messaging (IM), and Conferencing for Communicator 2007, and currently owns the Communicator

2007 Remote Call Control/Computer Supported Telephony Applications (CSTA) protocol, Microsoft Office Communicator Phone Edition Remote Call Control, existing VoIP/video and conferencing features, as well as new features, such as Boss/Admin, Team Call, and Microsoft Office Communications Server 2007 R2 Response Group service support. Previously, Rajesh worked in the telecommunications arena for several years, designing protocols in the satellite communication/ Global System for Mobile (GSM)/Integrated Services Distributed Network (ISDN) areas, before joining Microsoft in 2001 as a program manager for the release of Microsoft Office Outlook 2003 and Outlook 2007. He has 15 years experience in technology communications, protocols, and applications.

Nirav Kamdar is a Development Lead on the Microsoft Office Communications Server team. Nirav Kamdar joined Microsoft in 1999. Since then, he has worked on various Microsoft products, including Microsoft Exchange, Office, and Windows as a software design engineer and development lead. Nirav has worked on Office Communications Server since the Live Communications Server 2003 release. Currently, Nirav is working on the manageability aspects of Office Communications Server.

Amaresh Bikki has worked for the Microsoft Unified Communications Media team since joining Microsoft in 2005. During this time, he worked for specific product components, such as Audio/Video Conferencing Server and Conferencing Attendant. He holds a masters degree in computer science from the University of Texas at Dallas and previously wrote a book chapter, "Mobile Adhoc Networking," which was based on his master's thesis.

Brad Joseph is a Content Publishing Manager on the Microsoft Unified Communications team. Brad has worked in the software industry for more than 16 years as a software test engineer, network engineer, and technical writer. Brad joined Microsoft in 1995 as a technical writer working on the first version of Microsoft Exchange Server and remained with the Exchange Server group for more than 8 years. Additionally, he has worked with Windows CE, Microsoft Systems Management Server (SMS), Windows Media Server, and most recently with Microsoft Office Communicator, Microsoft Office Live Meeting, Microsoft RoundTable, and a variety of hardware telephony devices designed for Microsoft Office Communications Server 2007.

Byron Spurlock works in the U.S. Services division as a Unified Communications Consultant within Microsoft Consulting Services (MCS) and has been with Microsoft for four years. Byron's primary function for the past several years has been working with customers and partners designing and deploying Office Communication Server 2007 and Office Communication Server 2007 R2 within the TAP/RDP group. Byron also contributed in the previous edition of the *Office Communications Server 2007 Resource Kit* and has delivered training to partners around the globe with Voice Ignite, which is a specialized training on the voice aspects of Office Communications Server.

Francois Doremieux is Director for Engineering Strategic Customers Engagements in the Office Communications Product Group at Microsoft. Since joining Microsoft five years ago, Francois has been part of the Office Communications Group and instrumental in driving strategy and implementation for Microsoft's voice and telephony capabilities. Francois has been involved with VoIP and connected technologies for many years, working with companies such as Comcast, AT&T, and Level(3) Communications, where he was responsible for the VoIP offerings. He is a frequent speaker at international events on VoIP and Unified Communications. Francois' current role involves working closely alongside Microsoft's leading customers during their deployment of Microsoft Unified Communications solutions, formulating technical strategy, and supporting execution. His role also involves working collaboratively with the product teams, helping frame specifications on the basis of customer experience. In addition, his primary technical domain of expertise is interoperability with IP PBX. Francois holds advanced engineering and business degrees from the Ecole Centrale in Paris, the University of Paris, the University of Tokyo, and Stanford University.

James O'Neill was born in 1965 and started using Microsoft products in 1979. Being something of a slow developer, it took him until 2000 to join Microsoft. His career has been spent working on operating system and messaging technologies, and passing on his knowledge of them to others, first in support, then as a trainer. He became an IT Pro Evangelist in March 2006 after six years working for Microsoft Consulting Services on a variety of projects for several well-known, large organizations. He has been a Microsoft Certified Professional since 1993, holding MCSE from NT 3.1 to Windows 2003.

Jay Carnley is the Unified Communications Technology Specialist for the Heartland District. Jay covers the states of Michigan, Ohio, Kentucky, and Tennessee and is responsible for delivering technical expertise for the Microsoft Communication and Collaboration Platform. Jay has worked at Microsoft in the collaboration space since 1999, in both Microsoft Consulting Services (MCS) and Technical Sales. He started with Exchange IM, then worked on Live Communications Server 2003, Live Communications Server 2005, Office Communications Server 2007, and now Office Communications Server 2007 R2. Prior to working at Microsoft, Jay worked as a fiber optic engineer and technical consultant.

Jérôme Bernière is a Senior Program Manager in the Microsoft Office Communications Group. He works on large Office Communications Server topologies and deployments, with particular expertise in Voice over IP technologies. Prior to working in Redmond, Washington, Jérôme worked for Microsoft France, where he was in charge of developing the adoption of Microsoft Unified

Communications. Prior to working for Microsoft, which he joined 3 years ago, Jérôme worked for Newbridge Networks, Cisco Systems, and Alcatel Reseaux d'Entreprise (Nextiraone). He has 10 years experience in telecommunications, including Unified Communications, unified messaging, contacts centers, interoperability, and data networking. He holds a master's degree in telecommunication and computer sciences.

Michael Trommsdorff is a Principal Group Manager in the Microsoft Zurich Development Center in charge of the development projects in that center. Since moving to Zurich in January 2007, he has focused on the delivery of the Response Group Service functionality as part of Office Communications Server 2007 R2. Prior to moving to Zurich, Michael worked in the Office Communications Server team as Lead Program Manager in charge of federation, outside user access, and presence. He joined the team in November 2000 as a Program Manager and was responsible for a number of different features, such as Windows Management Instrumentation (WMI), Microsoft Management Console (MMC), Active Directory, and setup and content archiving in the first releases of Office Communications Server. Before joining the Office Communications Group, Michael worked on an in-car computing project with Microsoft and also spent time at Hewlett-Packard working on Intelligent Networks in their telecom division. Michael Trommsdorff holds a master's degree in theoretical physics and in telecommunications.

Michele Martin is a Senior Technical Writer with the Unified Communications team. Michele has worked in the technical communications field since 1992, developing and managing documentation within the medical device, Web development, and computer software industries. She joined Microsoft in 2000 with the Exchange team, where she created documentation and tools for Microsoft Exchange 2000 planning and deployment. For the past three years, Michele has worked with Office Communications Server clients, including Communicator, Live Meeting, and Communicator Web Access.

Radu Constantinescu is a Senior Lead Software Development Engineer in Test on the Audio/Video Edge Server team. He has been a software engineer for more than 15 years, working on radio-telecommunication applications, Geographic Information Systems, smart card applications, online games, legal practice management software, Application Service Provider software, grid computing, and VoIP systems. He joined Microsoft in 2006 and became a Subject Matter Expert in Office Communications Server protocols MS-TURN and MS-AVEDGEA used in conjunction with Audio/Video Edge Server.

Rajmohan Rajagopalan is a Lead SDET in the Microsoft Office Communications Group. Rajmohan joined Microsoft in 2004 and has been working on various Live Communications Server/Office Communications Server projects, responsible for quality aspects of Office Communications Server deployment, Archiving and

Call Detail Record (CDR), IIMF-CVC for Office Communications Server 2007 and R2 release, and the Archiving/Monitoring Server roles for R2 release.

Sasa Juratovic is a Senior Program Manager in the Unified Communications Group. He is part of a globally dispersed team ensuring that customers have the best possible experience when deploying and working with Microsoft Unified Communications technologies. Sasa is also principal author of *Office Communications Server 2007 Best Practices Analyzer*. Previously, Sasa worked as a consultant and trainer for a number of Microsoft Partner companies before joining Microsoft in 2001 as a consultant in Microsoft Consulting Services in the United Kingdom. He has more than 15 years experience in program management, consultancy, technical training, user support, and system administration.

Shahzaib Younis, Software Development Engineer, joined Microsoft three years ago upon completing a B.S in computer science from Iowa State University. He has worked on Microsoft Office Communication products since joining. In his latest endeavors, he has been working on designing and implementing protocols to enable rich voice experiences on mobile platforms. Prior to that, he worked on delivering VoIP functionality for Microsoft Office Live Meeting 2007.

Shawn Mahan, Program Manager, joined Microsoft in 2005 as a Support Escalation Engineer supporting Live Communications Server and Office Communications Server. In June 2008, Shawn joined the Office Communications Group's Technology Adoption Program team, as a Project Manager, working to help enterprises deploy and validate future versions of Office Communication Server products. Prior to joining Microsoft, Shawn spent 10 years in various roles and endeavors supporting enterprises across the United States.

Stephanie Pierce is a Senior Technical Writer on the Microsoft Office Communications Server User Assistance team. Stephanie has been with Microsoft for 8 years. She worked as a program manager in the Unified Communications Group for five years and was responsible for various aspects of Office Communications Server and Live Communications Server, including MMC, Windows Messenger, Real-time Collaboration 1.3 APIs, as well as integrating presence and real-time collaboration into Office 2003 SP2 and Office 2007. Stephanie transitioned to the User Assistance group as a Senior Technical writer 2 years ago, and is the principal developer of the Office Communications Server 2007 R2 Planning Tool.

Tina Fan is a Test Lead on the Microsoft Office Communications Server team. Tina joined Microsoft in 2000. Since then, she has worked on various Microsoft products, including Microsoft Exchange, Office, and Windows as a software design engineer in test and test lead. Tina has worked on Office Communications Server since the Live Communications Server 2003 release. Currently, Tina is working on the manageability aspects of Office Communications Server.

Vlad Eminovici is a Senior Development Lead in the Microsoft Zurich Development Center. Since moving to Zurich in November 2007, he has focused on leading the development team that delivered the Response Group Service as part of Office Communications Server 2007 R2. Prior to moving to Zurich, Vlad worked on the Office Communications Server team, joining the team in 2000. In the first releases of Office Communications Server, he contributed to the implementation of a number of features, such as federation, outside user access, Session Initiation Protocol (SIP) authentication, and Web conferencing. Vlad Eminovici holds a bachelor's degree in mathematics and computer science.

System Requirements

As described in the following sections, these are the specific requirements necessary to view and use the tools and documents that are included on the companion CD.

For OCS-All.ps1 PowerShell Script

The PowerShell script provides access to the Windows Management Instrumentation (WMI) functions of Office Communications Server from PowerShell. The same functionality available in Office Communications Server WMI can now be easily scripted in PowerShell to create tools to automate administrative tasks with Office Communications Server, Exchange Server, Windows Server and other Microsoft server products that offer a PowerShell interface.

- Supported operating systems: Windows Server 2003 R2, Windows XP Service Pack 2 (SP2), Windows Vista SP1, and Windows Server 2008
- Supported processor architecture: x86, x64, IA64
- Installation of .Net Framework 3.5 SP1 or greater
    - .Net Framework 3.5 SP1 Web bootstrap loader: *http://www.microsoft.com/downloads/details.aspx?FamilyID=AB99342F-5D1A-413D-8319-81DA479AB0D7&displaylang=en*
    - .Net Framework 3.5 SP1 full download: *http://download.microsoft.com/download/2/0/e/20e90413-712f-438c-988e-fdaa79a8ac3d/dotnetfx35.exe*
    - .Net Framework 3.5 SP1 readme: *http://download.microsoft.com/download/A/2/8/A2807F78-C861-4B66-9B31-9205C3F22252/dotNet35SP1Readme.htm*
- Installation of PowerShell 1.0 or greater For Windows Server 2008; PowerShell is added as a feature in the Server Manager program but is not installed by default
- For all other versions of Windows, PowerShell is available at *http://www.microsoft.com/windowsserver2003/technologies/management/powershell/default.mspx*

- After installation of .Net Framework and PowerShell, refer to Appendix A, "Using the Windows PowerShell Functions," in the \Appendixes,Scripts,Resources folder on the companion CD, for detailed information about how to configure the environment and PowerShell to properly run the PowerShell functions contained in the OCS-All.ps1 script. Failure to follow the directions in Appendix A might result in unexpected behavior of the script, up to and including loss of data.

For Resource Kit Tools and Reference Material

The Resource Kit Tools provide an additional toolbox to help troubleshoot and manage Office Communications Server. Because the tools manipulate system and server level objects, the user is expected to be a local administrator on the system on which the tool is run and possibly a domain administrator. Many tools will not function properly, if at all, unless the user is an Administrator or a member of the Administrators group.

These tools will run on the following operating systems: Windows Server 2003 R2 x64 or Windows Server 2008 x64 with Office Communications Server 2007 R2.

Note that as of this writing, there is not a set of Resource Kit Tools available for 32-bit clients or servers. This is not to say that they will not be available later. Please periodically check Microsoft Downloads for a 32-bit version, if and when it becomes available.

A prerequisite for installing and running the Resource Kit Tools is the .Net Framework 3.5 SP1, and the Microsoft Visual C++ 2008 (x64) redistributable, which can be downloaded from here:

- .Net Framework 3.5 SP1 Web bootstrap loader: *http://www.microsoft.com/downloads/details.aspx?FamilyID=AB99342F-5D1A-413D-8319-81DA479AB0D7&displaylang=en*
- .Net Framework 3.5 SP1 full download: *http://download.microsoft.com/download/2/0/e/20e90413-712f-438c-988e-fdaa79a8ac3d/dotnetfx35.exe*
- .NET Framework 3.5 SP1 readme: *http://download.microsoft.com/download/A/2/8/A2807F78-C861-4B66-9B31-9205C3F22252/dotNet35SP1Readme.htm*
- Microsoft Visual C++ 2008 SP1 Redistributable Package (x64): *http://www.microsoft.com/downloads/details.aspx?familyid=BA9257CA-337F-4B40-8C14-157CFDFFEE4E&displaylang=en*

Documents provided on the companion CD can be viewed with Microsoft Office Word and Excel as delivered in Microsoft Office 2000 and later. Additionally, some files are delivered in PDF format and can be viewed with Adobe Reader. Viewers are available at the following locations from the Microsoft Download Center and from Adobe Corporation:

- Word viewer: *http://www.microsoft.com/downloads/details.aspx?FamilyId=95E24C87-8732-48D5-8689-AB826E7B8FDF&displaylang=en*
- Excel viewer: *http://www.microsoft.com/downloads/details.aspx?familyid=1CD6ACF9-CE06-4E1C-8DCF-F33F669DBC3A&displaylang=en*
- Adobe Reader: *http://www.adobe.com*

What do you think of this book?

We want to hear from you!

Your feedback will help us continually improve our books and learning resources for you. To participate in a brief online survey, please visit:

microsoft.com/learning/booksurvey

...and enter this book's ISBN-10 or ISBN-13 number (appears above barcode on back cover). As a thank-you to survey participants in the U.S. and Canada, each month we'll randomly select five respondents to win one of five $100 gift certificates from a leading online merchant. At the conclusion of the survey, you can enter the drawing by providing your e-mail address, which will be used for prize notification only.*

Thank you in advance for your input!

Where to find the ISBN on back cover

Example only. Each book has unique ISBN.

* No purchase necessary. Void where prohibited. Open only to residents of the 50 United States (includes District of Columbia) and Canada (void in Quebec). For official rules and entry dates see: **microsoft.com/learning/booksurvey**

Stay in touch!

To subscribe to the *Microsoft Press® Book Connection Newsletter*—for news on upcoming books, events, and special offers—please visit:

microsoft.com/learning/books/newsletter